Africa 68-69

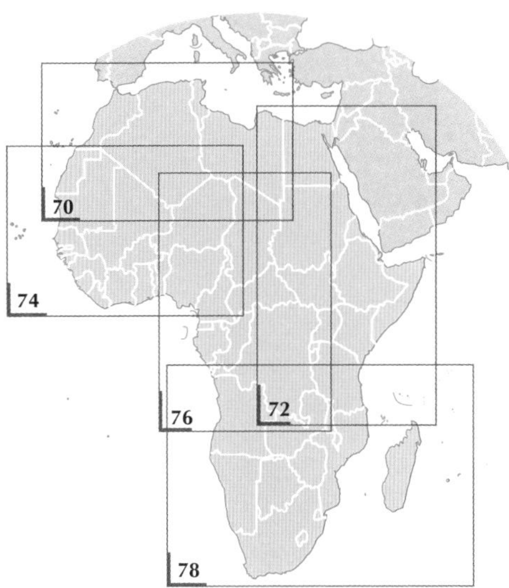

Europe 80-81

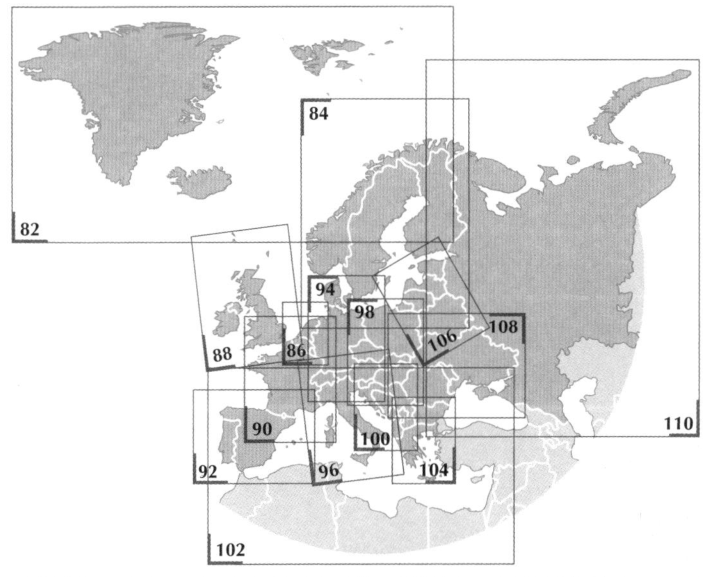

ESSENTIAL WORLD ATLAS

FOR THE NINTH EDITION

SENIOR CARTOGRAPHIC EDITOR Simon Mumford
PRODUCTION CONTROLLER Vivienne Yong PRODUCER, PRE-PRODUCTION Luca Frassinetti
JACKET DESIGN DEVELOPMENT Sophia MTT
PUBLISHER Jonathan Metcalf ASSOCIATE PUBLISHER Liz Wheeler
ART DIRECTOR Karen Self

FOR PREVIOUS EDITIONS

DORLING KINDERSLEY CARTOGRAPHY

PROJECT CARTOGRAPHY AND DESIGN
Julia Lunn, Julie Turner

CARTOGRAPHERS
James Anderson, Roger Bullen, Martin Darlison, Simon Mumford, John Plumer, Peter Winfield

DESIGN
Katy Wall

INDEX-GAZETTEER
Natalie Clarkson, Ruth Duxbury, Margaret Hynes, Margaret Stevenson

EDITORIAL DIRECTION
Andrew Heritage

ART DIRECTION
Chez Picthall

First published in Great Britain in 1997 by
Dorling Kindersley Limited,
80 Strand, London WC2R 0RL
A Penguin Random House Company

2 4 6 8 10 9 7 5 3 1

001 - 265172 - May/2016

Second edition 1998, Third edition 2001, Fourth edition 2003, Fifth edition 2005,
Sixth edition 2008, Seventh edition 2011, Eighth edition 2013, Ninth edition 2016.

A CIP catalogue record for this book is available from the British Library.

ISBN: 978-0-2412-2635-3

Printed and bound in Hong Kong.

A WORLD OF IDEAS:
SEE ALL THERE IS TO KNOW

www.dk.com

Key to map symbols

Physical features

Elevation

6000m/19,686ft
4000m/13,124ft
3000m/9843ft
2000m/6562ft
1000m/3281ft
500m/1640ft
250m/820ft
0
Below sea level

Mountain
Depression
Volcano
Pass/tunnel
Sandy desert

Drainage features

Major perennial river
Minor perennial river
Seasonal river
Canal
Waterfall
Perennial lake
Seasonal lake
Wetland

Ice features

Permanent ice cap/ice shelf
Winter limit of pack ice
Summer limit of pack ice

Borders

Full international border
Disputed de facto border
Territorial claim border
Cease-fire line
Undefined boundary
Internal administrative boundary

Communications

Major road
Minor road
Railway
International airport

Settlements

Above 500,000
100,000 to 500,000
50,000 to 100,000
Below 50,000
National capital
Internal administrative capital

Miscellaneous features

Site of interest
Ancient wall

Graticule features

Line of latitude/longitude/ Equator
Tropic/Polar circle
25° Degrees of latitude/ longitude

Names

Physical features

Andes / *Sahara* / *Ardennes*	Landscape features
Land's End	Headland
Mont Blanc 4,807m	Elevation/volcano/pass
Blue Nile	River/canal/waterfall
Ross Ice Shelf	Ice feature
PACIFIC OCEAN / *Sulu Sea* / *Palk Strait*	Sea features
Chile Rise	Undersea feature

Regions

FRANCE	Country
JERSEY (to UK)	Dependent territory
KANSAS	Administrative region
Dordogne	Cultural region

Settlements

PARIS	Capital city
SAN JUAN	Dependent territory capital city
Chicago / Kettering / Burke	Other settlements

Inset map symbols

Urban area
City
Park
Place of interest
Suburb/district

Contents

The World Today

Flags of the World 6-7
The Political World 8-9
The Physical World 10-11
Standard Time Zones 12-13
Geology & Structure 14-15
World Climate 16-17
Ocean Currents 18-19
Life Zones 20-21
Population 22-23
Languages 24-25
Religion 26-27
The Global Economy 28-29
Politics and Conflict 30-31

The World's Regions

North & Central America

North & Central America 34-35
Western Canada & Alaska 36-37
Eastern Canada 38-39
USA: The Northeast 40-41
USA: The Southeast 42-43
Bermuda
USA: Central States 44-45
USA: The West 46-47
Los Angeles & Hawaii
USA: The Southwest 48-49
Mexico 50-51
Central America 52-53
The Caribbean 54-55
Jamaica, St. Lucia, & Barbados

South America

South America 56-57
Northern South America 58-59
Western South America 60-61
Galápagos Islands
Brazil 62-63
Southern South America 64-65
The Atlantic Ocean 66-67

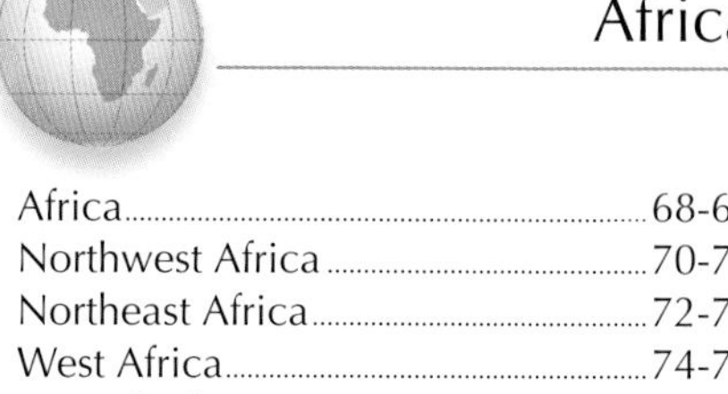

Africa

Africa 68-69
Northwest Africa 70-71
Northeast Africa 72-73
West Africa 74-75
Central Africa 76-77
Sao Tome & Principe
Southern Africa 78-79

Europe

Europe 80-81
The North Atlantic 82-83
Scandinavia & Finland 84-85
The Low Countries 86-87
The British Isles 88-89
London

continued....

Europe *continued*

France, Andorra, & Monaco 90-91
Paris, Andorra, & Monaco
Spain & Portugal 92-93
Azores & Gibraltar
Germany & the Alpine States 94-95
Liechtenstein
Italy 96-97
San Marino & Vatican City
Central Europe 98-99
Southeast Europe 100-101
Bosnia & Herzegovina
The Mediterranean 102-103
Malta & Cyprus
Bulgaria & Greece 104-105
The Baltic States & Belarus 106-107
Ukraine, Moldova, & Romania 108-109
European Russia 110-111

North & West Asia

North & West Asia 112-113
Russia & Kazakhstan 114-115
Turkey & the Caucasus 116-117
The Near East 118-119
West Bank
The Middle East 120-121
Central Asia 122-123

South & East Asia

South & East Asia 124-125
Western China & Mongolia 126-127
Eastern China & Korea 128-129
Hong Kong
Japan 130-131
Tokyo & Nansei-Shoto
South India & Sri Lanka 132-133
North India, Pakistan, & Bangladesh 134-135
Mainland Southeast Asia 136-137
Maritime Southeast Asia 138-139
Singapore
The Indian Ocean 140-141

Australasia & Oceania

Australasia & Oceania 142-143
The Southwest Pacific 144-145
Western Australia 146-147
Eastern Australia 148-149
Sydney
New Zealand 150-151
The Pacific Ocean 152-153
Antarctica 154
The Arctic Ocean 155

Index–Gazetteer

Overseas Territories & Dependencies 156-159
Glossary of Geographical Terms 160-161
Continental Factfiles 162-163
Geographical Comparisons 164-166
Index-Gazetteer of Places & Countries 167-256

Flags of the World

NORTH & CENTRAL AMERICA

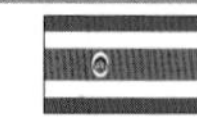

CANADA PAGES 36-39

UNITED STATES OF AMERICA PAGES 40-49

MEXICO PAGES 50-51

BELIZE PAGES 52-53

COSTA RICA PAGES 52-53

EL SALVADOR PAGES 52-53

GUATEMALA PAGES 52-53

HONDURAS PAGES 52-53

GRENADA PAGES 54-55

HAITI PAGES 54-55

JAMAICA PAGES 54-55

ST KITTS & NEVIS PAGES 54-55

ST LUCIA PAGES 54-55

ST VINCENT & THE GRENADINES PAGES 54-55

TRINIDAD & TOBAGO PAGES 54-55

SOUTH AME

COLOMBIA PAGES 58-59

URUGUAY PAGES 64-65

CHILE PAGES 64-65

PARAGUAY PAGES 64-65

AFRICA

ALGERIA PAGES 70-71

LIBYA PAGES 70-71

MOROCCO PAGES 70-71

TUNISIA PAGES 70-71

BURUNDI PAGES 72-73

SUDAN PAGES 72-73

TANZANIA PAGES 72-73

UGANDA PAGES 72-73

BENIN PAGES 74-75

BURKINA FASO PAGES 74-75

CAPE VERDE PAGES 74-75

CÔTE D'IVOIRE (IVORY COAST) PAGES 74-75

GAMBIA PAGES 74-75

GHANA PAGES 74-75

SIERRA LEONE PAGES 74-75

TOGO PAGES 74-75

CAMEROON PAGES 76-77

CENTRAL AFRICAN REPUBLIC PAGES 76-77

CHAD PAGES 76-77

CONGO PAGES 76-77

DEM. REP. CONGO PAGES 76-77

EQUATORIAL GUINEA PAGES 76-77

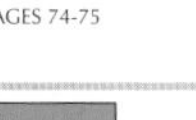

MAURITIUS PAGES 78-79

MOZAMBIQUE PAGES 78-79

NAMIBIA PAGES 78-79

SEYCHELLES PAGES 78-79

SOUTH AFRICA PAGES 78-79

SWAZILAND PAGES 78-79

ZAMBIA PAGES 78-79

ZIMBABWE PAGES 78-79

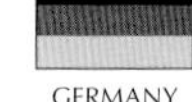

UNITED KINGDOM PAGES 88-89

FRANCE PAGES 90-91

MONACO PAGES 90-91

ANDORRA PAGES 90-91

PORTUGAL PAGES 92-93

SPAIN PAGES 92-93

AUSTRIA PAGES 94-95

GERMANY PAGES 94-95

POLAND PAGES 98-99

SLOVAKIA PAGES 98-99

ALBANIA PAGES 100-101

BOSNIA & HERZEGOVINA PAGES 100-101

CROATIA PAGES 100-101

KOSOVO PAGES 100-101

MACEDONIA PAGES 100-101

MONTENEGRO PAGES 100-101

MOLDOVA PAGES 108-109

ROMANIA PAGES 108-109

UKRAINE PAGES 108-109

RUSSIAN FEDERATION PAGES 110-115

ASIA

KAZAKHSTAN PAGES 114-115

ARMENIA PAGES 116-117

AZERBAIJAN PAGES 116-117

GEORGIA PAGES 116-117

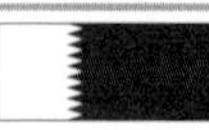

KUWAIT PAGES 120-121

OMAN PAGES 120-121

QATAR PAGES 120-121

SAUDI ARABIA PAGES 120-121

UNITED ARAB EMIRATES PAGES 120-121

YEMEN PAGES 120-121

AFGHANISTAN PAGES 122-123

KYRGYZSTAN PAGES 122-123

JAPAN PAGES 130-131

INDIA PAGES 132-135

SRI LANKA PAGES 132-133

MALDIVES PAGES 132-133

PAKISTAN PAGES 134-135

BANGLADESH PAGES 134-135

BHUTAN PAGES 134-135

NEPAL PAGES 134-135

CAMBODIA PAGES 136-137

PHILIPPINES PAGES 138-139

SINGAPORE PAGES 138-139

AUSTRALASIA & OCEANIA

FIJI PAGES 144-145

KIRIBATI PAGES 144-145

MARSHALL ISLANDS PAGES 144-145

MICRONESIA PAGES 144-145

NAURU PAGES 144-145

PALAU PAGES 144-145

NICARAGUA PAGES 52-53
PANAMA PAGES 52-53
ANTIGUA & BARBUDA PAGES 54-55
BAHAMAS PAGES 54-55
BARBADOS PAGES 54-55
CUBA PAGES 54-55
DOMINICA PAGES 54-55
DOMINICAN REPUBLIC PAGES 54–55

GUYANA PAGES 58-59
SURINAME PAGES 58-59
VENEZUELA PAGES 58-59
BOLIVIA PAGES 60-61
ECUADOR PAGES 60-61
PERU PAGES 60-61
BRAZIL PAGES 62-63
ARGENTINA PAGES 64-65

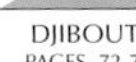

DJIBOUTI PAGES 72-73
EGYPT PAGES 72-73
ERITREA PAGES 72-73
ETHIOPIA PAGES 72-73
KENYA PAGES 72-73
RWANDA PAGES 72-73
SOMALIA PAGES 72-73
SOUTH SUDAN PAGES 72-73

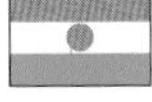

GUINEA PAGES 74-75
GUINEA–BISSAU PAGES 74-75
LIBERIA PAGES 74-75
MALI PAGES 74-75
MAURITANIA PAGES 74-75
NIGER PAGES 74-75
NIGERIA PAGES 74-75
SENEGAL PAGES 74-75

GABON PAGES 76-77
SAO TOME & PRINCIPE PAGES 76-77
ANGOLA PAGES 78-79
BOTSWANA PAGES 78-79
COMOROS PAGES 78-79
LESOTHO PAGES 78-79
MADAGASCAR PAGES 78-79
MALAWI PAGES 78-79

EUROPE

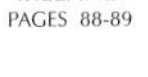

ICELAND PAGES 82-83
DENMARK PAGES 84-85
FINLAND PAGES 84-85
NORWAY PAGES 84-85
SWEDEN PAGES 84-85
BELGIUM PAGES 86-87
LUXEMBOURG PAGES 86-87
NETHERLANDS PAGES 86-87
IRELAND PAGES 88-89

LIECHTENSTEIN PAGES 94-95
SLOVENIA PAGES 94-95
SWITZERLAND PAGES 94-95
ITALY PAGES 96-97
MALTA PAGES 96-97
SAN MARINO PAGES 96-97
VATICAN CITY PAGES 96-97
CZECH REPUBLIC PAGES 98-99
HUNGARY PAGES 98-99

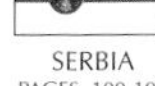

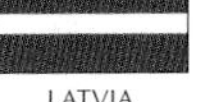

SERBIA PAGES 100-101
CYPRUS PAGES 102-103
BULGARIA PAGES 104-105
GREECE PAGES 104-105
BELARUS PAGES 106-107
ESTONIA PAGES 106-107
LATVIA PAGES 106-107
LITHUANIA PAGES 106-107

TURKEY PAGES 116-117
ISRAEL PAGES 118-119
JORDAN PAGES 118-119
LEBANON PAGES 118-119
SYRIA PAGES 118-119
BAHRAIN PAGES 120-121
IRAN PAGES 120-121
IRAQ PAGES 120-121

TAJIKISTAN PAGES 122-123
TURKMENISTAN PAGES 122-123
UZBEKISTAN PAGES 122-123
CHINA PAGES 126-129
MONGOLIA PAGES 126-127
NORTH KOREA PAGES 128-129
SOUTH KOREA PAGES 128-129
TAIWAN PAGES 128-129

LAOS PAGES 136-137
MYANMAR (BURMA) PAGES 136-137
THAILAND PAGES 136-137
VIETNAM PAGES 136-137
BRUNEI PAGES 138-139
EAST TIMOR PAGES 138-139
INDONESIA PAGES 138-139
MALAYSIA PAGES 138-139

PAPUA NEW GUINEA PAGES 144-145
SAMOA PAGES 144-145
SOLOMON ISLANDS PAGES 144-145
TONGA PAGES 144-145
TUVALU PAGES 144-145
VANUATU PAGES 144-145
AUSTRALIA PAGES 146-149
NEW ZEALAND PAGES 150-151

The Political World

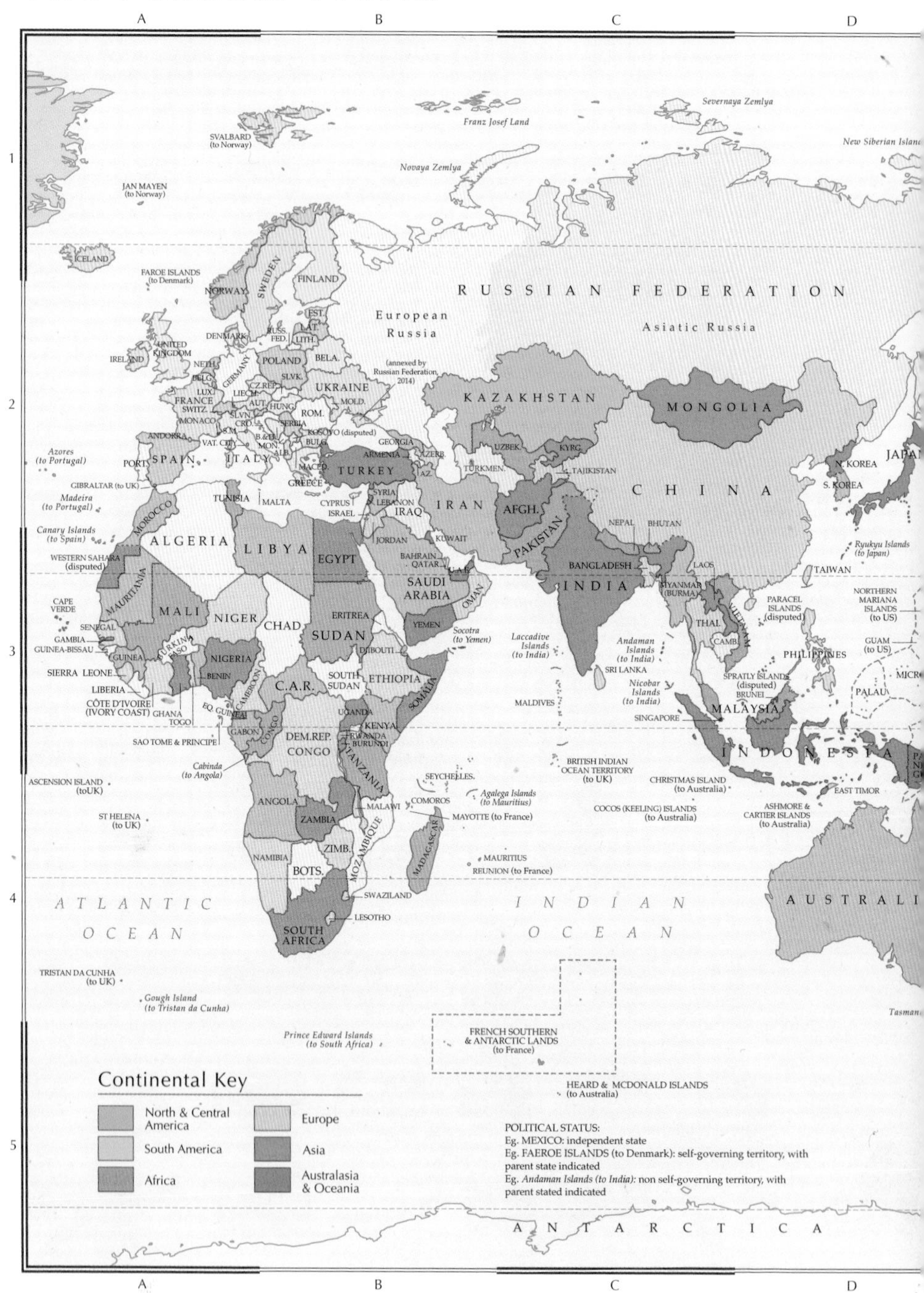

E
F
G
H
1
2
3
4
5
ARCTIC OCEAN
Queen Elizabeth Islands
GREENLAND (to Denmark)
Baffin Island
Arctic Circle
Alaska (to US)
CANADA
Aleutian Islands (to US)
l Islands
uss. Fed.)
ST PIERRE & MIQUELON (to France)
PACIFIC OCEAN
UNITED STATES OF AMERICA
ATLANTIC OCEAN
BERMUDA (to UK)
PUERTO RICO (to US)
DOM. REP.
BRITISH VIRGIN ISLANDS (to UK)
MIDWAY ISLANDS (to US)
Guadelupe (to Mexico)
MEXICO
TURKS & CAICOS ISLANDS (to UK)
VIRGIN ISLANDS (to US)
ANGUILLA (to UK)
CAYMAN ISLANDS (to UK)
THE BAHAMAS
ST KITTS & NEVIS
Tropic of Cancer
HONDURAS
ANTIGUA & BARBUDA
MONTSERRAT (to UK)
WAKE ISLAND (to US)
Hawaii (to US)
Revillagigedo Islands (to Mexico)
BELIZE
CUBA
JAMAICA
GUADELOUPE (to France)
NAVASSA I. (to US)
HAITI
DOMINICA
CURAÇAO (to Neth.)
MARTINIQUE (to France)
JOHNSTON ATOLL (to US)
GUATEMALA
ST LUCIA
EL SALVADOR
ARUBA (to Neth.)
BARBADOS
MARSHALL ISLANDS
NICARAGUA
ST VINCENT & THE GRENADINES
CLIPPERTON ISLAND (to French Polynesia)
COSTA RICA
GRENADA
WALLIS & FUTUNA (to France)
KINGMAN REEF (to US)
VENEZUELA
TRINIDAD & TOBAGO
PALMYRA ATOLL (to US)
PANAMA
BAKER & HOWLAND ISLANDS (to US)
COLOMBIA
FRENCH GUIANA (to France)
JARVIS ISLAND (to US)
Galápagos Islands (to Ecuador)
Equator
URU
GUYANA
KIRIBATI
ECUADOR
SURINAME
LOMON
LANDS
TUVALU
TOKELAU (to NZ)
BRAZIL
PERU
COOK ISLANDS (to NZ)
BOLIVIA
VANUATU
EW
DONIA
rance)
FIJI
FRENCH POLYNESIA (to France)
PARAGUAY
Tropic of Capricorn
San Felix Island (to Chile)
SEA ISLANDS
ralia)
TONGA
SAMOA
NIUE (to NZ)
AMERICAN SAMOA (to US)
Easter Island (to Chile)
Sala y Gomez (to Chile)
San Ambrosio Island (to Chile)
CHILE
NORFOLK ISLAND (to Australia)
Kermadec Island (to NZ)
PITCAIRN, HENDERSON, DUCIE & OENO ISLANDS (to UK)
ARGENTINA
URUGUAY
Lord Howe Island (to Australia)
Juan Fernandez Island (to Chile)
NEW ZEALAND
Chatham Island (to NZ)
PACIFIC OCEAN
Bounty Island (to NZ)
FALKLAND ISLANDS (to UK)
Campbell Island (to NZ)
CHILE
Macquarie Island (to Australia)
SOUTH GEORGIA & SOUTH SANDWICH ISLANDS (to UK)
BBREVIATIONS: AFGH. Afghanistan, ALB. Albania, AUT. Austria,
Z. or AZERB. Azerbaijan, BELG. Belgium, BELA. Belarus,
&H. Bosnia & Herzegovina, BOTS. Botswana, BULG. Bulgaria,
AMB. Cambodia, C.A.R. Central African Republic, CRO. Croatia,
Z. REP. Czech Republic, DOM. REP. Dominican Republic, EST. Estonia,
UNG. Hungary, KYRG. Kyrgyzstan, LAT. Latvia, LIECH. Liechtenstein,
TH. Lithuania, LUX. Luxembourg, MACED. Macedonia,
MOLD. Moldova, MON. Montenegro, NETH. Netherlands,
NETH. ANT. Netherlands Antilles, PORT. Portugal, ROM. Romania,
RUSS. FED. Russian Federation, S.M. San Marino, SLVK. Slovakia,
SLVN. Slovenia, SWITZ. Switzerland, THAI. Thailand,
TURKMEN. Turkmenistan, U.A.E. United Arab Emirates,
UZBEK. Uzbekistan, VAT. CITY Vatican City, ZIMB. Zimbabwe.
Antarctic Circle
ANTARCTICA
E
F
G
H

The Physical World

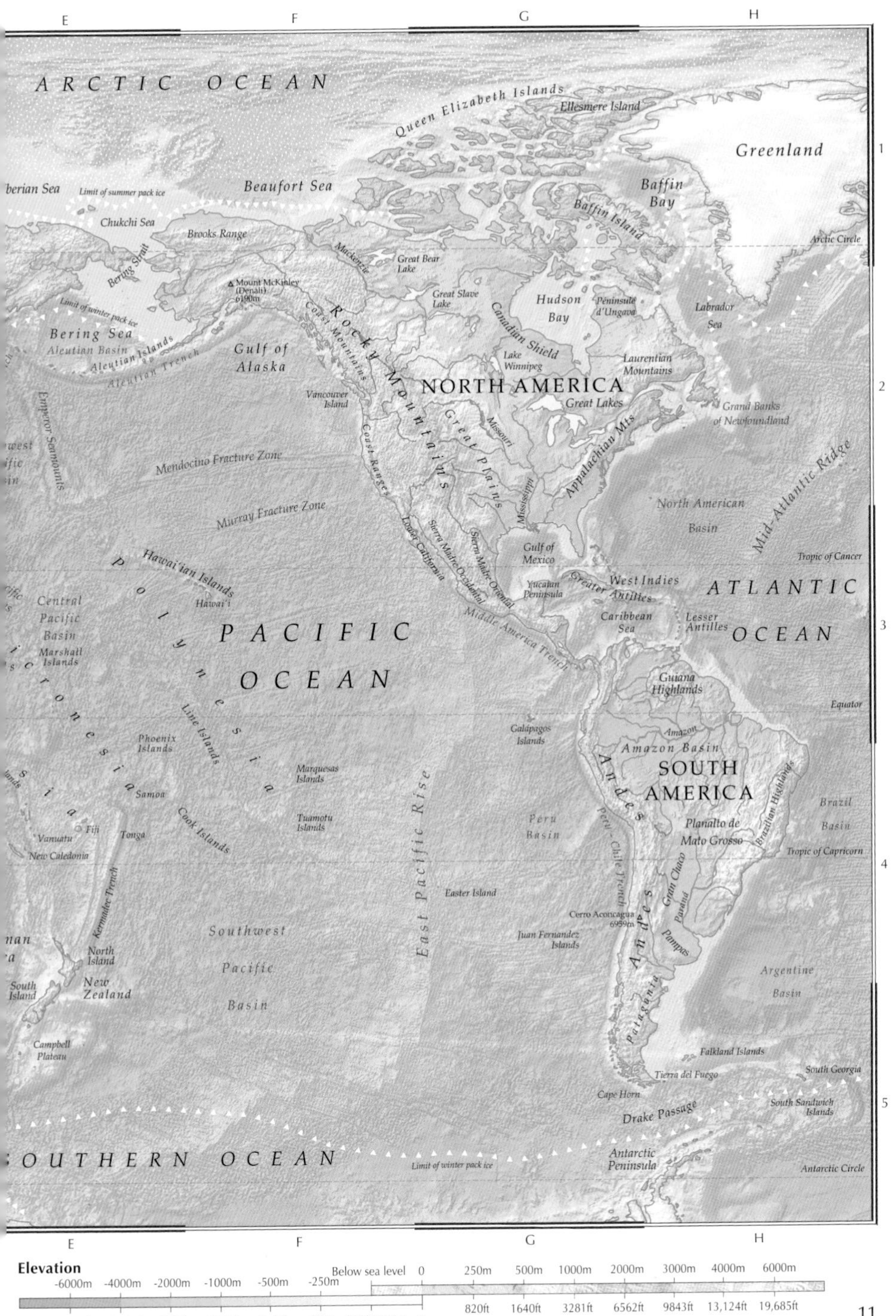

Elevation

Below sea level								Above sea level						
-6000m	-4000m	-2000m	-1000m	-500m	-250m		0	250m	500m	1000m	2000m	3000m	4000m	6000m
-19,658ft	-13,124ft	-6562ft	-3281ft	-1640ft	-820ft	-328ft/-100m	0	820ft	1640ft	3281ft	6562ft	9843ft	13,124ft	19,685ft

Standard Time Zones

The numbers represented thus; +2/-2, indicate the number of hours each time zone is ahead or behind UCT (Coordinated Universal Time)

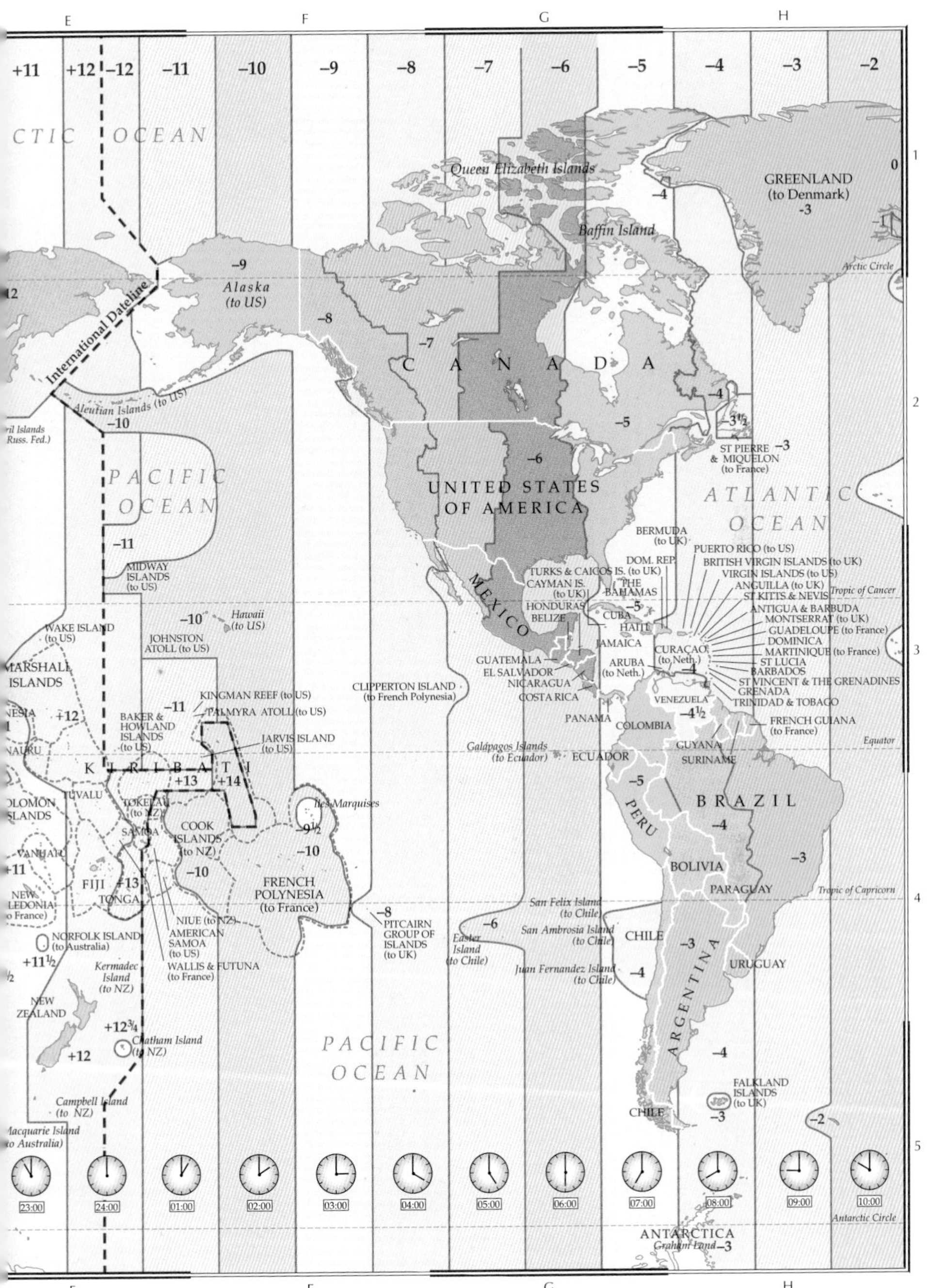

The clocks and 24-hour times given at the bottom of the map show time in each time zone when it is 12.00 hours noon UCT

Geology & Structure

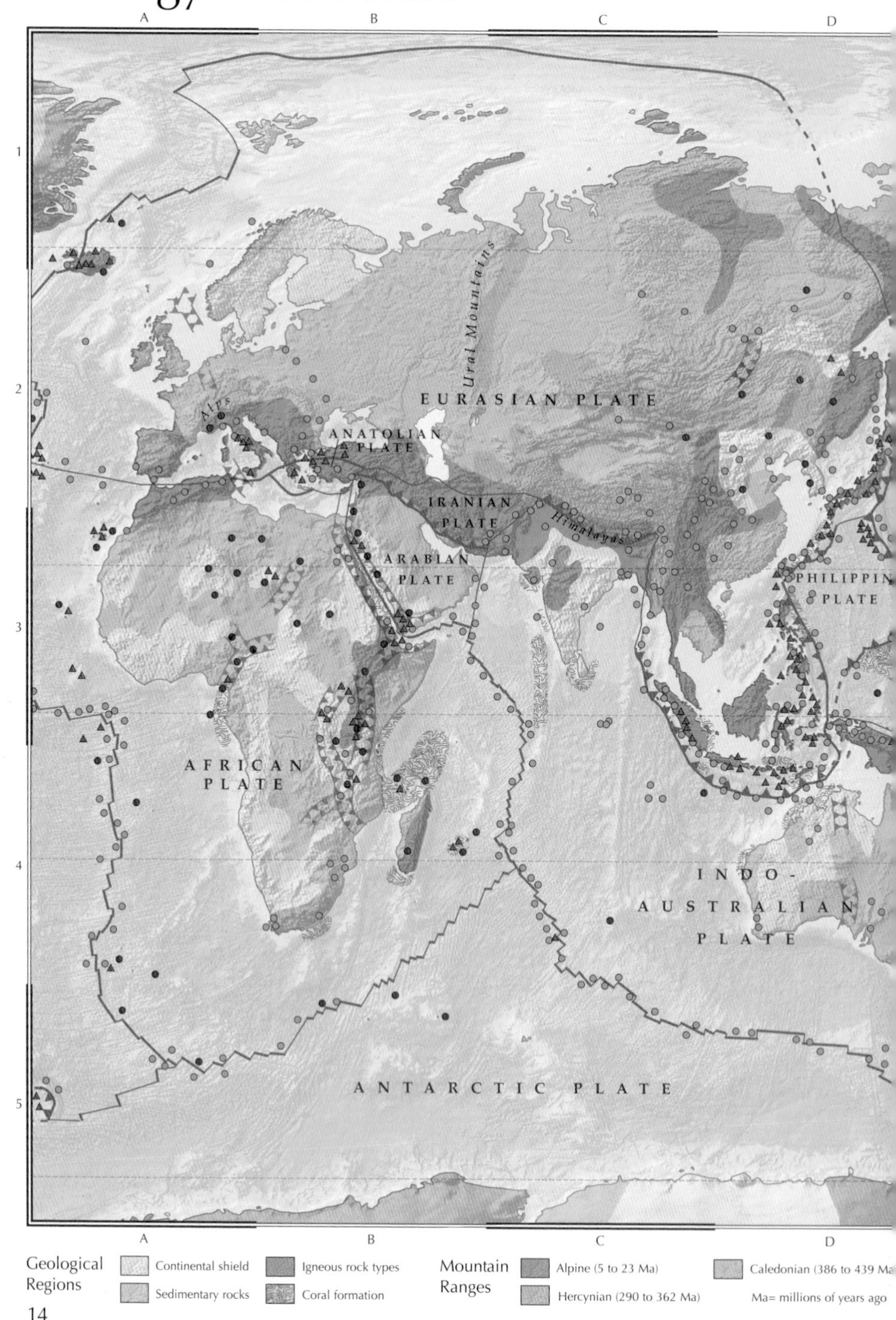

Geological Regions

- Continental shield
- Sedimentary rocks
- Igneous rock types
- Coral formation

Mountain Ranges

- Alpine (5 to 23 Ma)
- Hercynian (290 to 362 Ma)
- Caledonian (386 to 439 Ma

Ma= millions of years ago

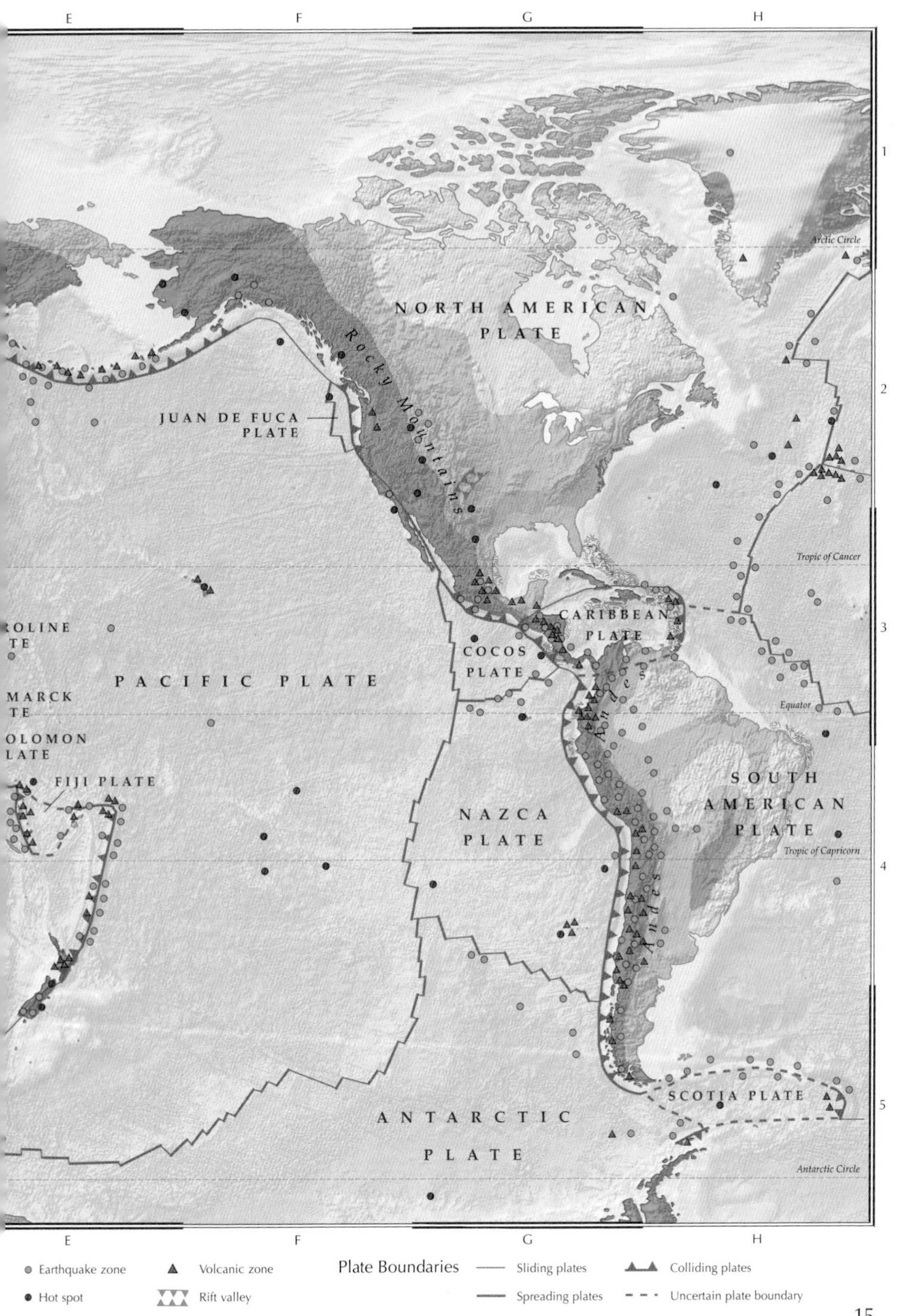

Earthquake zone
Hot spot
Volcanic zone
Rift valley

Plate Boundaries
Sliding plates
Spreading plates
Colliding plates
Uncertain plate boundary

World Climate

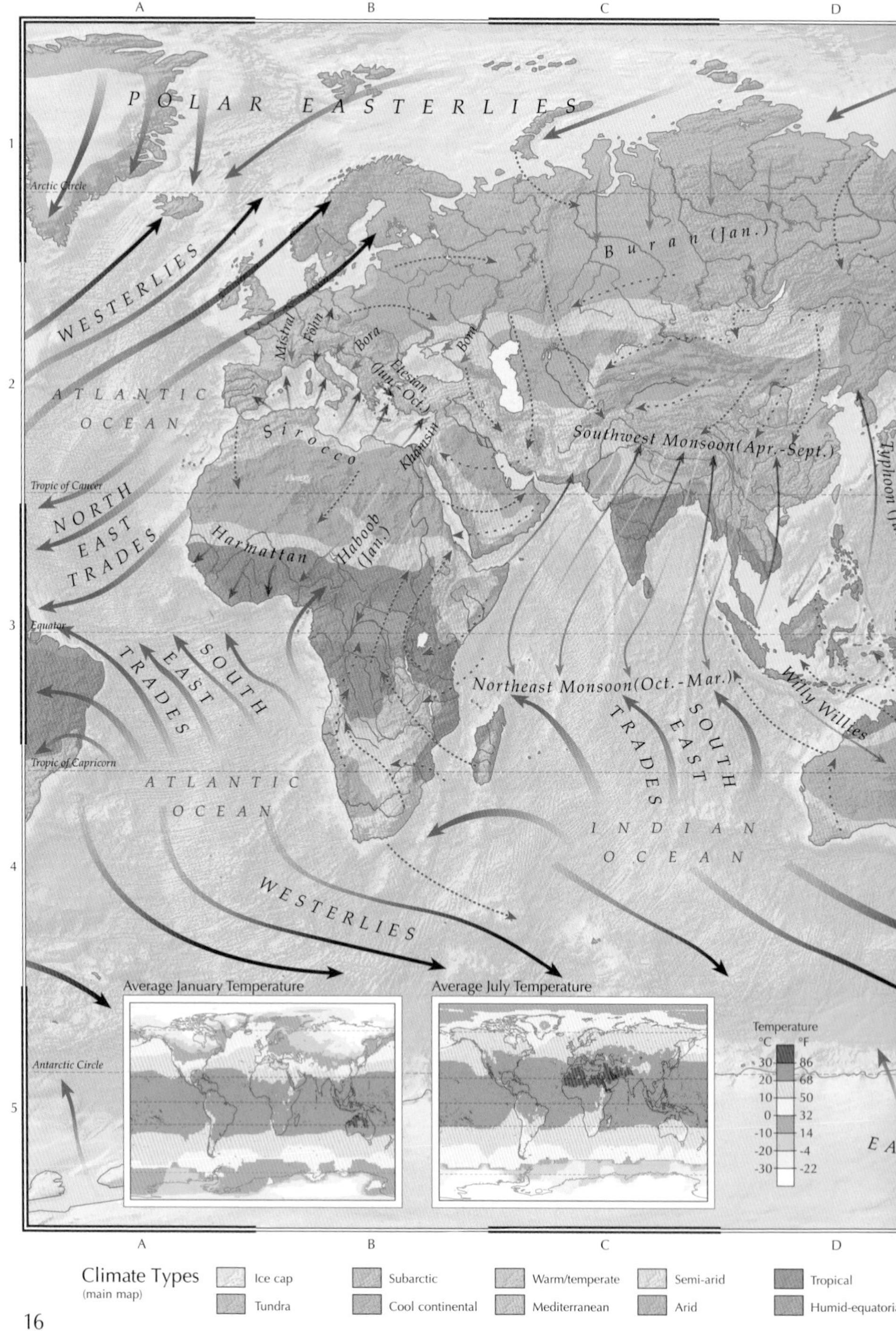

Climate Types (main map)

- Ice cap
- Tundra
- Subarctic
- Cool continental
- Warm/temperate
- Mediterranean
- Semi-arid
- Arid
- Tropical
- Humid-equatoria

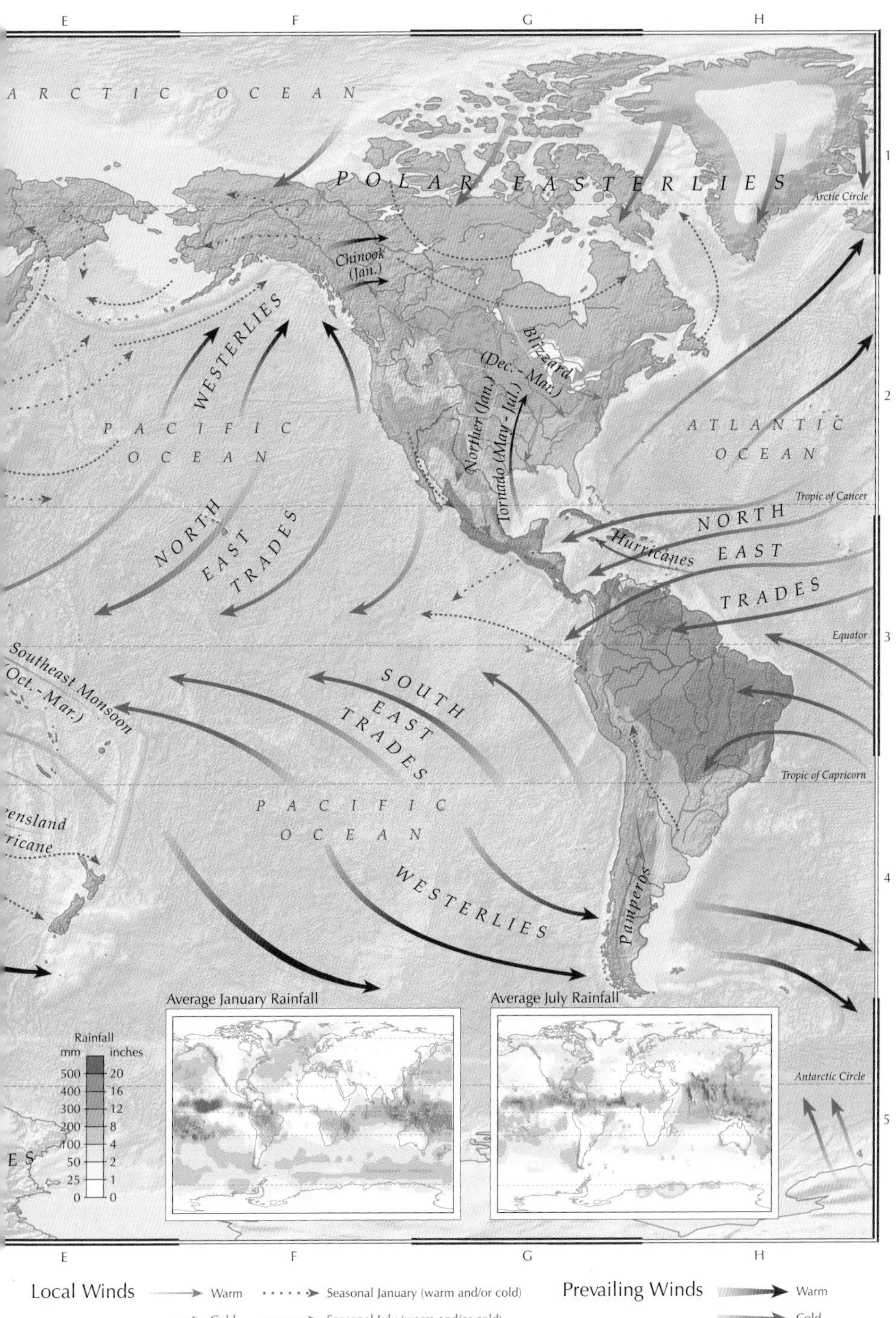

Local Winds — Warm — Cold — Seasonal January (warm and/or cold) — Seasonal July (warm and/or cold)

Prevailing Winds — Warm — Cold

Ocean Currents

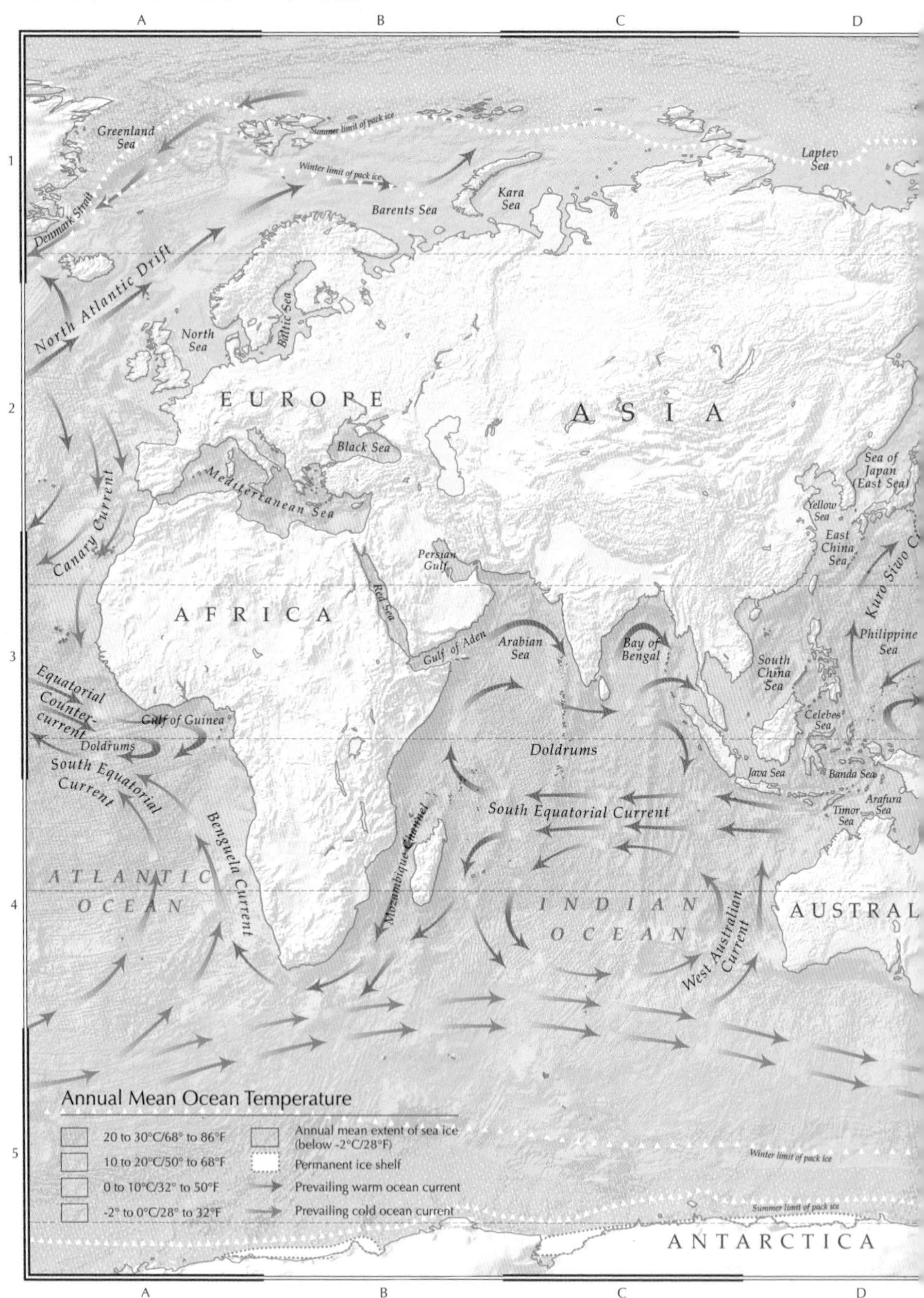

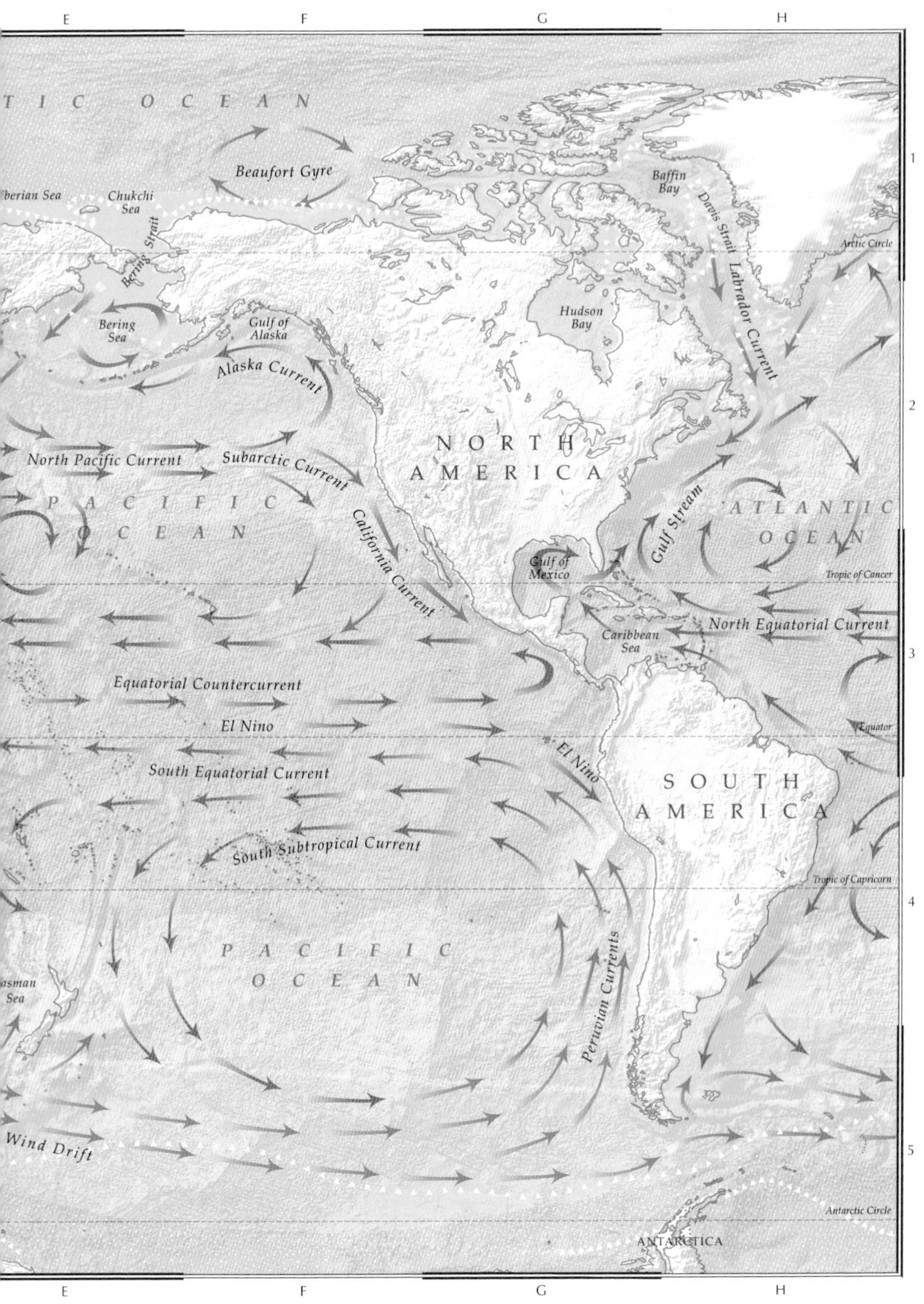
E
F
G
H
1
2
3
4
5
TIC OCEAN
Beaufort Gyre
berian Sea
Chukchi Sea
Bering Strait
Bering Sea
Gulf of Alaska
Alaska Current
Baffin Bay
Davis Strait
Labrador Current
Hudson Bay
Arctic Circle
NORTH AMERICA
North Pacific Current
Subarctic Current
PACIFIC OCEAN
California Current
Gulf Stream
ATLANTIC OCEAN
Gulf of Mexico
Tropic of Cancer
North Equatorial Current
Caribbean Sea
Equatorial Countercurrent
El Nino
Equator
South Equatorial Current
El Nino
SOUTH AMERICA
South Subtropical Current
Tropic of Capricorn
PACIFIC OCEAN
Peruvian Currents
asman Sea
Wind Drift
Antarctic Circle
ANTARCTICA

Life Zones

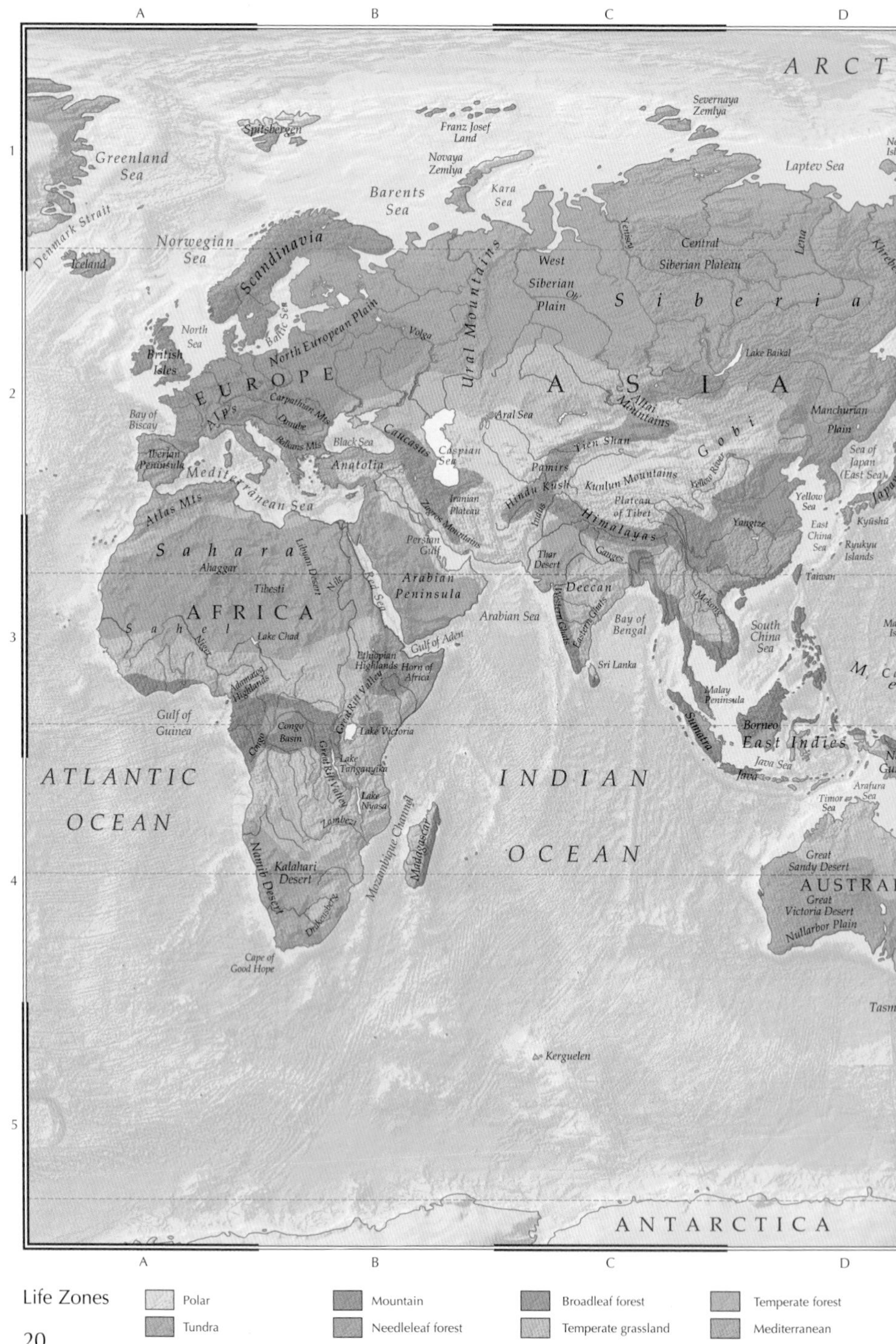

Life Zones

- Polar
- Tundra
- Mountain
- Needleleaf forest
- Broadleaf forest
- Temperate grassland
- Temperate forest
- Mediterranean

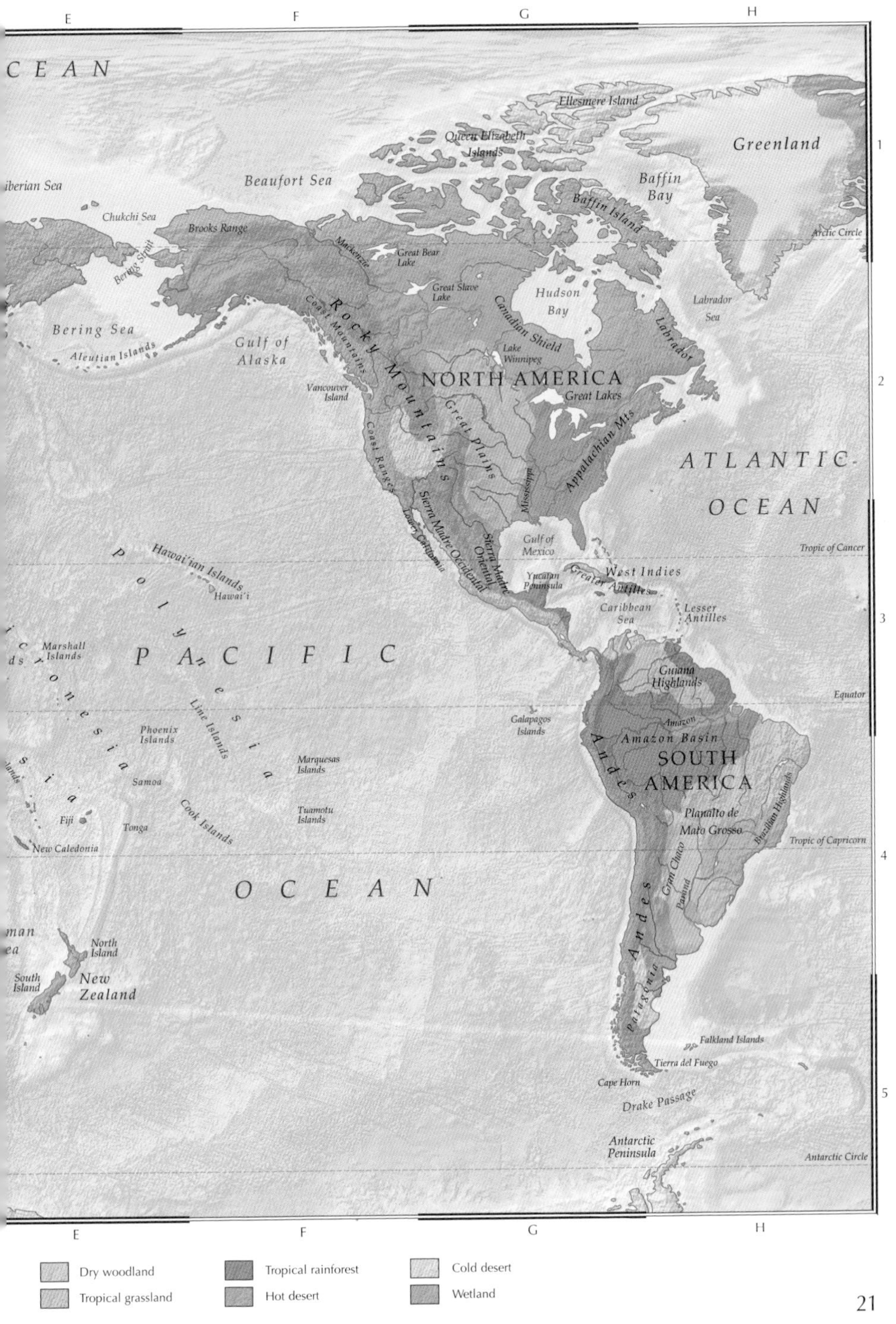
E
F
G
H
CEAN
Ellesmere Island
Queen Elizabeth Islands
Greenland
Beaufort Sea
Baffin Bay
Baffin Island
iberian Sea
Chukchi Sea
Brooks Range
Arctic Circle
Mackenzie
Great Bear Lake
Bering Strait
Great Slave Lake
Hudson Bay
Labrador Sea
Bering Sea
Aleutian Islands
Gulf of Alaska
Coast Mountains
Rocky Mountains
Canadian Shield
Lake Winnipeg
Labrador
NORTH AMERICA
Vancouver Island
Great Lakes
Great Plains
Coast Ranges
Appalachian Mts
ATLANTIC
OCEAN
Mississippi
Sierra Madre Occidental
Lower California
Sierra Madre Oriental
Gulf of Mexico
Tropic of Cancer
Hawai'ian Islands
Hawai'i
Yucatan Peninsula
Greater Antilles
West Indies
Caribbean Sea
Lesser Antilles
Marshall Islands
PACIFIC
Polynesia
Micronesia
Guiana Highlands
Equator
Line Islands
Galapagos Islands
Amazon
Phoenix Islands
Amazon Basin
Andes
SOUTH AMERICA
Marquesas Islands
Samoa
Tuamotu Islands
Planalto de Mato Grosso
Brazilian Highlands
Fiji
Tonga
Cook Islands
Tropic of Capricorn
New Caledonia
Gran Chaco
Paraná
OCEAN
North Island
South Island
New Zealand
Patagonia
Falkland Islands
Tierra del Fuego
Cape Horn
Drake Passage
Antarctic Peninsula
Antarctic Circle
1
2
3
4
5
Dry woodland
Tropical grassland
Tropical rainforest
Hot desert
Cold desert
Wetland

Population

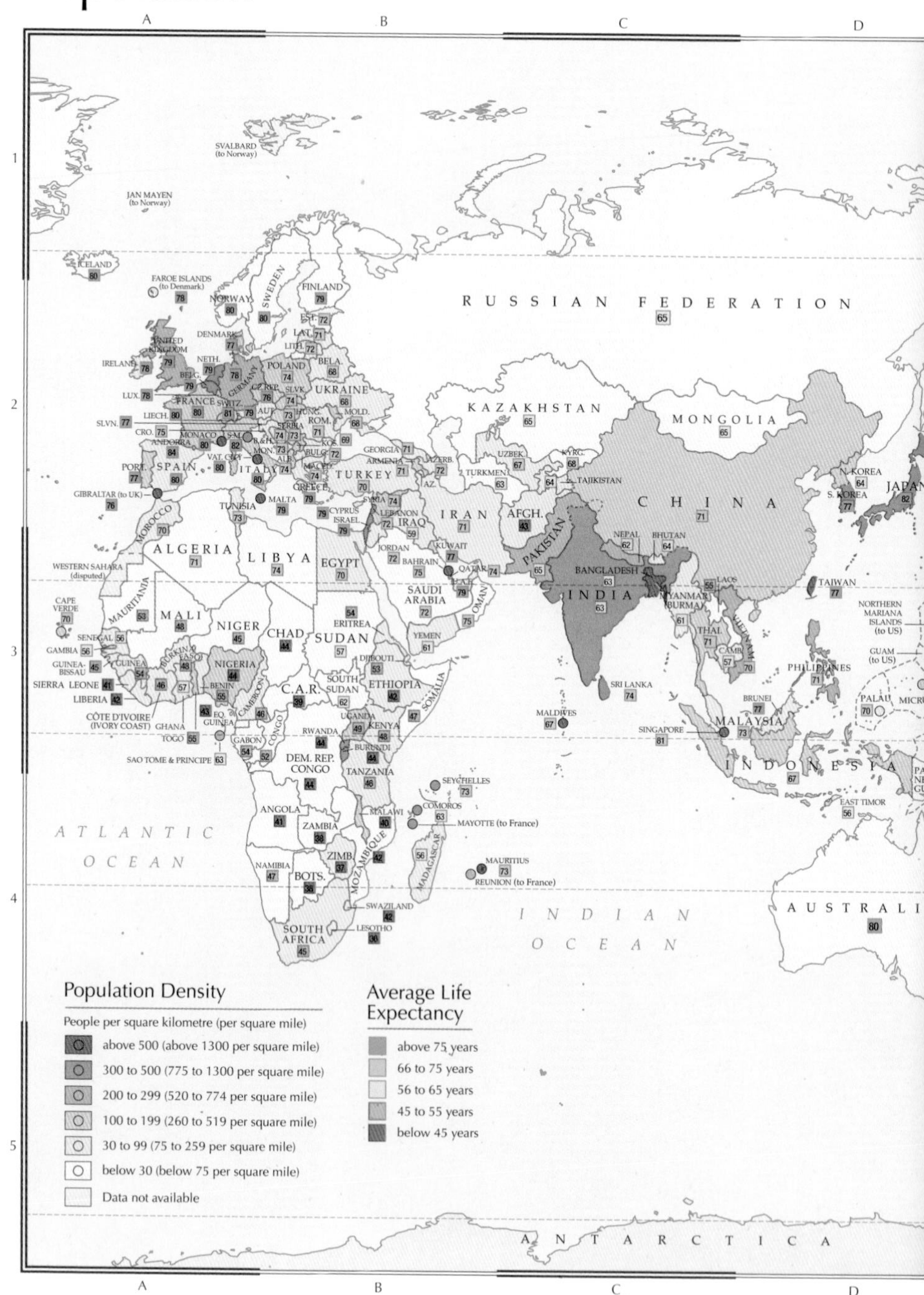
A
B
C
D
1
2
3
4
5
SVALBARD (to Norway)
JAN MAYEN (to Norway)
ICELAND 80
FAROE ISLANDS (to Denmark) 78
NORWAY 80
SWEDEN 80
FINLAND 79
EST. 72
LAT. 71
LITH. 72
DENMARK 77
UNITED KINGDOM 79
IRELAND 78
NETH. 79
BELG. 79
GERMANY 78
LUX. 78
FRANCE 80
LIECH. 80
SWITZ. 81
AUT. 79
SLVN. 77
CZ. REP. 76
SLVK. 74
POLAND 74
BELA. 68
UKRAINE 68
MOLD. 68
HUNG. 73
ROM. 71
CRO. 75
MONACO 80
ANDORRA 84
S.M.
B.&H. 74
SERBIA 73
MON. 73
ALB.
KOS. 69
BULG. 72
MACE. 74
GREECE 79
VAT. CITY 80
ITALY 80
PORT. 77
SPAIN 80
GIBRALTAR (to UK) 76
MALTA 79
TUNISIA 73
MOROCCO 70
ALGERIA 71
LIBYA 74
EGYPT 70
WESTERN SAHARA (disputed)
CAPE VERDE 70
MAURITANIA 53
MALI 48
NIGER 45
CHAD 44
SUDAN 57
ERITREA 54
SENEGAL 56
GAMBIA 56
GUINEA-BISSAU 45
GUINEA 54
SIERRA LEONE 41
LIBERIA 42
BURKINA FASO 48
CÔTE D'IVOIRE (IVORY COAST) 46
GHANA 57
TOGO 55
BENIN 55
NIGERIA 44
CAMEROON 46
EQ. GUINEA 43
SAO TOME & PRINCIPE 63
GABON 54
CONGO 52
C.A.R. 39
SOUTH SUDAN 62
ETHIOPIA 42
DJIBOUTI 53
SOMALIA 47
UGANDA 49
KENYA 48
RWANDA 44
BURUNDI 44
DEM. REP. CONGO 44
TANZANIA 46
ANGOLA 41
ZAMBIA 38
MALAWI 40
MOZAMBIQUE 42
ZIMB. 37
NAMIBIA 47
BOTS. 38
SOUTH AFRICA 45
SWAZILAND 42
LESOTHO 36
MADAGASCAR 56
SEYCHELLES 73
COMOROS 63
MAYOTTE (to France)
MAURITIUS 73
REUNION (to France)
TURKEY 70
CYPRUS 79
SYRIA 74
LEBANON 72
ISRAEL 79
GEORGIA 71
ARMENIA 71
AZERB. 72
AZ.
IRAQ 59
JORDAN 72
KUWAIT 77
BAHRAIN 75
QATAR 74
U.A.E. 79
SAUDI ARABIA 72
OMAN 75
YEMEN 61
IRAN 71
RUSSIAN FEDERATION 65
KAZAKHSTAN 65
UZBEK. 67
TURKMEN. 63
KYRG. 68
TAJIKISTAN 64
AFGH. 43
PAKISTAN 65
INDIA 63
NEPAL 62
BHUTAN 64
BANGLADESH 63
SRI LANKA 74
MALDIVES 67
MONGOLIA 65
CHINA 71
N. KOREA 64
S. KOREA 77
JAPAN 82
TAIWAN 77
MYANMAR (BURMA) 61
LAOS 55
THAI. 71
CAMB. 57
VIETNAM 70
MALAYSIA 73
SINGAPORE 81
BRUNEI 77
PHILIPPINES 71
INDONESIA 67
EAST TIMOR 56
NORTHERN MARIANA ISLANDS (to US)
GUAM (to US)
PALAU 70
AUSTRALI 80
ATLANTIC OCEAN
INDIAN OCEAN
ANTARCTICA
Population Density
People per square kilometre (per square mile)
above 500 (above 1300 per square mile)
300 to 500 (775 to 1300 per square mile)
200 to 299 (520 to 774 per square mile)
100 to 199 (260 to 519 per square mile)
30 to 99 (75 to 259 per square mile)
below 30 (below 75 per square mile)
Data not available
Average Life Expectancy
above 75 years
66 to 75 years
56 to 65 years
45 to 55 years
below 45 years

E
F
G
H
1
2
3
4
5
ARCTIC OCEAN
GREENLAND (to Denmark)
67
Arctic Circle
Alaska (to US)
CANADA
80
PACIFIC OCEAN
UNITED STATES OF AMERICA
77
ATLANTIC OCEAN
75 BERMUDA (to UK)
PUERTO RICO (to US)
74
CAYMAN ISLANDS (to UK)
77
DOM. REP.
68
THE BAHAMAS
70
72 ST KITTS & NEVIS
75 ANTIGUA & BARBUDA
75 GUADELOUPE (to France)
77 DOMINICA
76 MARTINIQUE (to France)
73 ST LUCIA
75 BARBADOS
71 ST VINCENT & THE GRENADINES
73 GRENADA
70 TRINIDAD & TOBAGO
FRENCH GUIANA (to France)
75
Tropic of Cancer
MEXICO
75
HONDURAS
CUBA
77
BELIZE
72
68
JAMAICA
71
HAITI
52
CURAÇAO (to Neth.)
ARUBA (to Neth.)
76
73
Hawai'i (to US)
GUATEMALA 68
EL SALVADOR 71
NICARAGUA 70
COSTA RICA 79
PANAMA 75
VENEZUELA
74
COLOMBIA
73
64
69
GUYANA
SURINAME
Equator
ECUADOR 75
MARSHALL ISLANDS
70
WALLIS & FUTUNA (to France)
63
KIRIBATI
63
TUVALU
68
TOKELAU (to NZ)
COOK ISLANDS (to NZ)
70
VANUATU
69
FIJI
68
72
FRENCH POLYNESIA (to France)
70
TONGA
SAMOA
NIUE (to NZ)
AMERICAN SAMOA (to US)
PITCAIRN, HENDERSON, DUCIE & OENO ISLANDS (to UK)
PERU
70
BRAZIL
71
BOLIVIA
65
PARAGUAY
71
Tropic of Capricorn
CHILE
78
ARGENTINA
75
75 URUGUAY
NEW ZEALAND
79
PACIFIC OCEAN
FALKLAND ISLANDS (to UK)
76
CHILE
SOUTH GEORGIA & SOUTH SANDWICH ISLANDS (to UK)
Antarctic Circle
ANTARCTICA
E
F
G
H

Languages

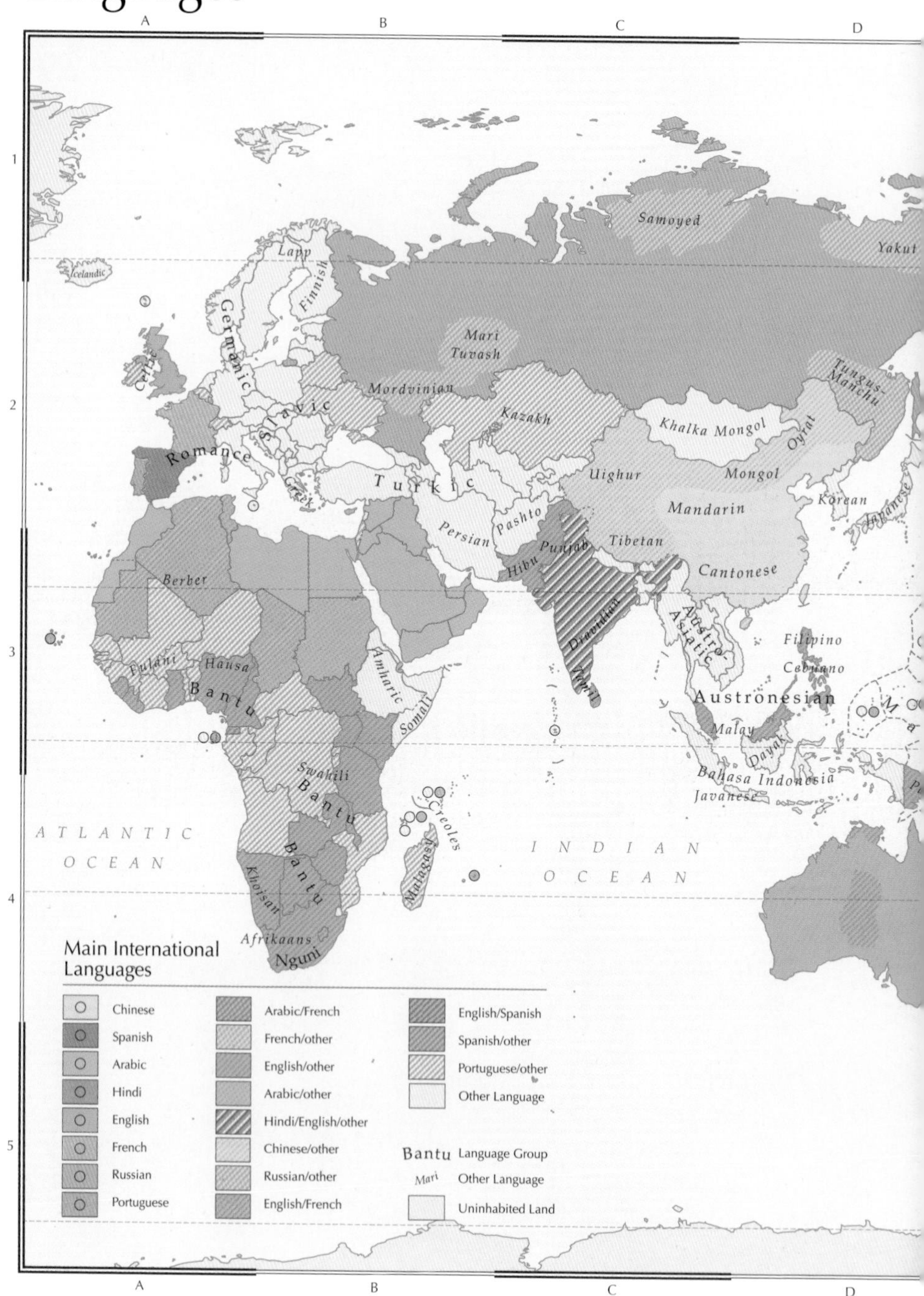
A
B
C
D
1
2
3
4
5
Icelandic
Lapp
Finnish
Germanic
Celtic
Slavic
Romance
Greek
Samoyed
Yakut
Mari
Tuvash
Mordvinian
Kazakh
Tungus-Manchu
Khalka Mongol
Oyrat
Turkic
Uighur
Mongol
Korean
Japanese
Mandarin
Persian
Pashto
Punjab
Tibetan
Hibu
Cantonese
Berber
Dravidian
Tamil
Austro-Asiatic
Filipino
Cebuano
Fulani
Hausa
Bantu
Amharic
Somali
Austronesian
Malay
Dayak
Bahasa Indonesia
Javanese
Swahili
Creoles
Malagasy
Khoisan
Afrikaans
Nguni
ATLANTIC OCEAN
INDIAN OCEAN
Main International Languages
Chinese
Spanish
Arabic
Hindi
English
French
Russian
Portuguese
Arabic/French
French/other
English/other
Arabic/other
Hindi/English/other
Chinese/other
Russian/other
English/French
English/Spanish
Spanish/other
Portuguese/other
Other Language
Bantu Language Group
Mari Other Language
Uninhabited Land

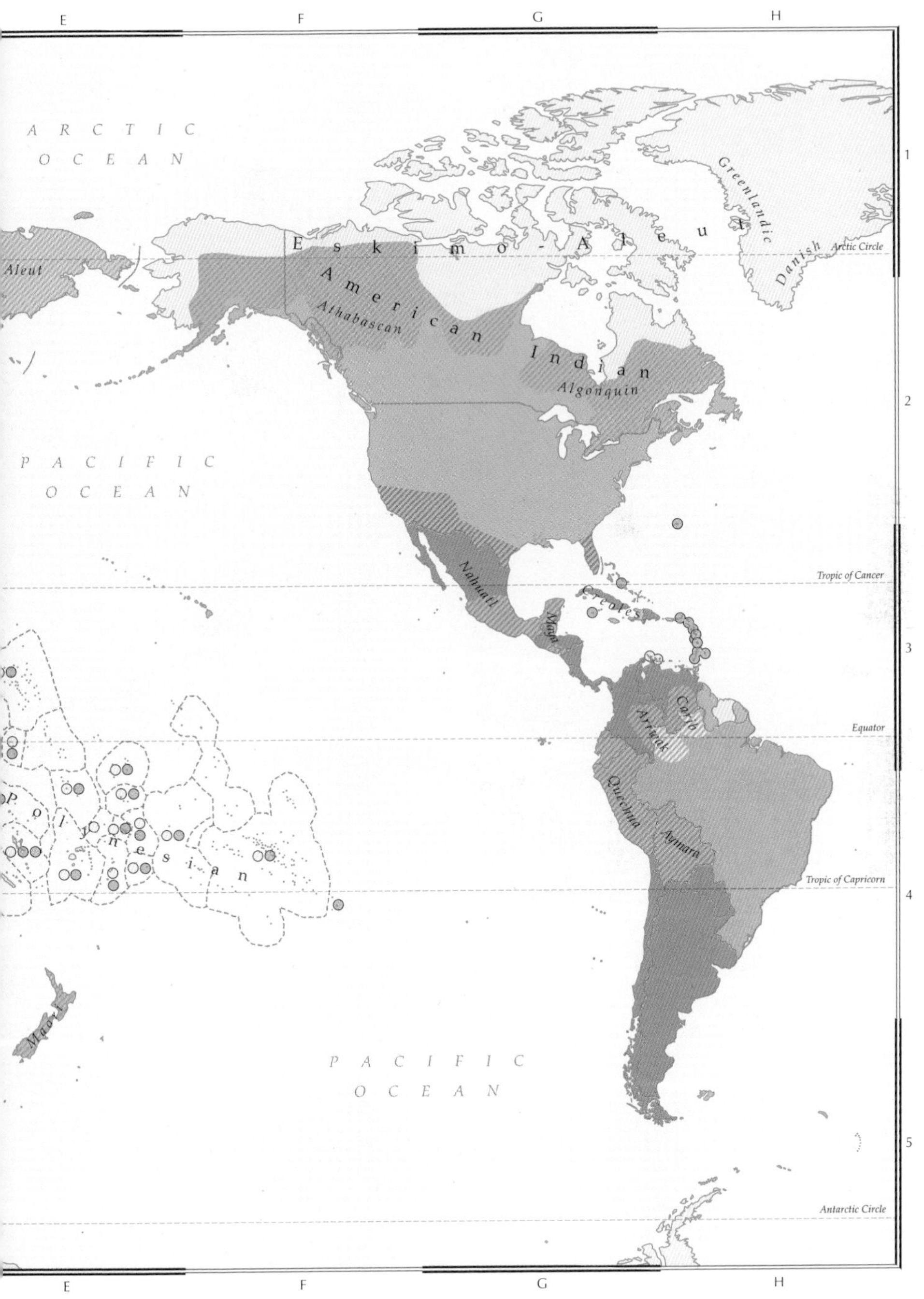
E
F
G
H
ARCTIC OCEAN
Greenlandic
Danish
Arctic Circle
Aleut
Eskimo-Aleut
American Indian
Athabascan
Algonquin
PACIFIC OCEAN
Tropic of Cancer
Nahuatl
Creoles
Maya
Carib
Arawak
Equator
Quechua
Aymara
Tropic of Capricorn
Polynesian
Maori
PACIFIC OCEAN
Antarctic Circle
1
2
3
4
5

Religion

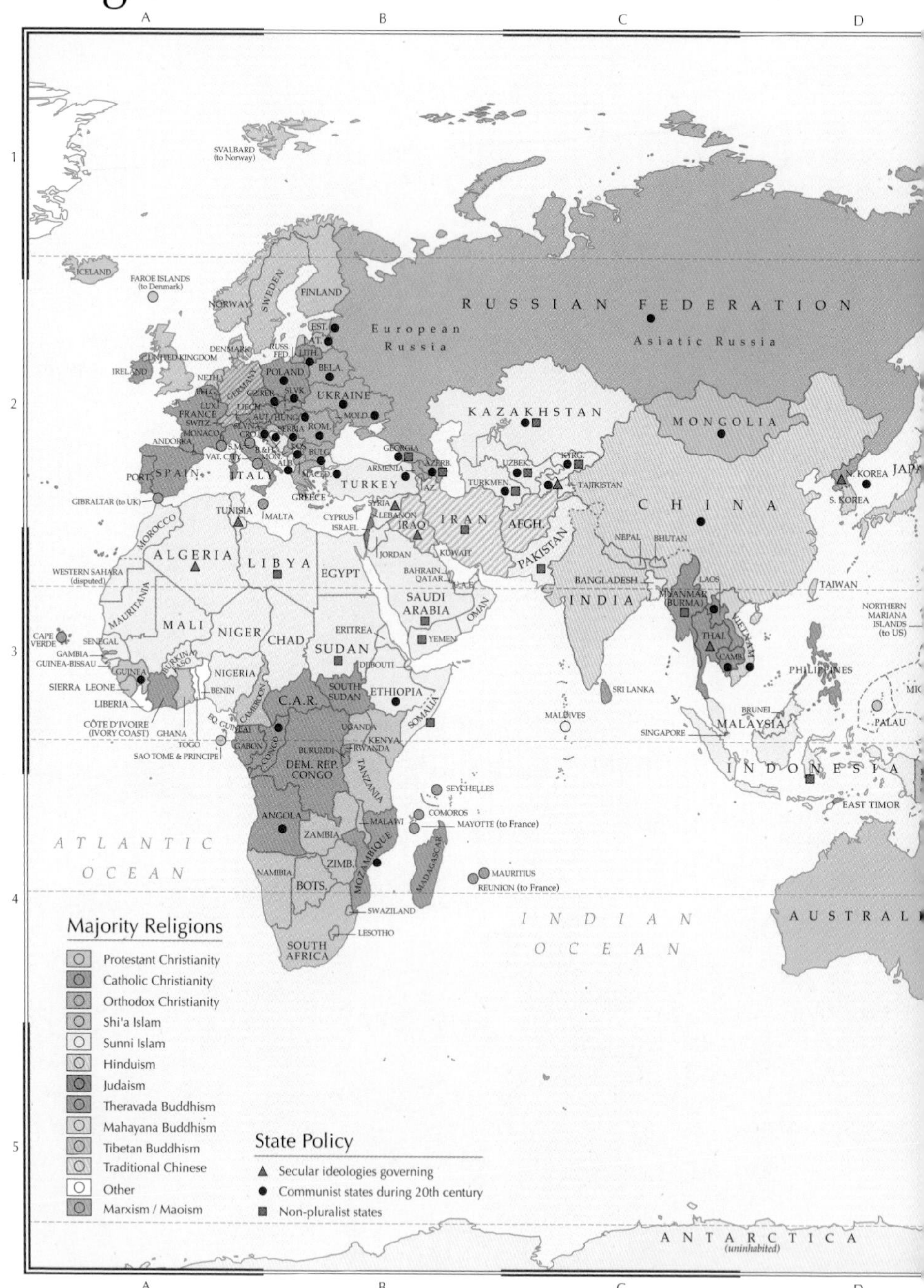
A
B
C
D
1
2
3
4
5
SVALBARD (to Norway)
ICELAND
FAROE ISLANDS (to Denmark)
NORWAY
SWEDEN
FINLAND
EST.
LAT.
LITH.
RUSS. FED.
DENMARK
UNITED KINGDOM
IRELAND
NETH.
GERMANY
POLAND
BELA.
BELG.
LUX.
CZ.REP.
SLVK.
UKRAINE
FRANCE
SWITZ.
LIECH.
AUT.
HUNG.
MOLD.
SLVN.
CRO.
ROM.
MONACO
SERBIA
ANDORRA
S.M.
B.&H.
KOS.
BULG.
VAT. CITY
MON.
ALB.
MACED.
PORT.
SPAIN
ITALY
GREECE
TURKEY
GIBRALTAR (to UK)
MALTA
CYPRUS
SYRIA
LEBANON
ISRAEL
GEORGIA
ARMENIA
AZERB.
AZ.
RUSSIAN FEDERATION
European Russia
Asiatic Russia
KAZAKHSTAN
MONGOLIA
UZBEK.
KYRG.
TURKMEN.
TAJIKISTAN
N. KOREA
S. KOREA
JAPAN
CHINA
IRAQ
IRAN
AFGH.
PAKISTAN
KUWAIT
JORDAN
NEPAL
BHUTAN
TUNISIA
MOROCCO
ALGERIA
LIBYA
EGYPT
WESTERN SAHARA (disputed)
BAHRAIN
QATAR
U.A.E.
BANGLADESH
LAOS
TAIWAN
SAUDI ARABIA
OMAN
INDIA
MYANMAR (BURMA)
MAURITANIA
MALI
NIGER
CHAD
ERITREA
YEMEN
SUDAN
THAI.
VIETNAM
NORTHERN MARIANA ISLANDS (to US)
CAPE VERDE
SENEGAL
GAMBIA
GUINEA-BISSAU
GUINEA
BURKINA FASO
NIGERIA
DJIBOUTI
CAMB.
PHILIPPINES
SIERRA LEONE
LIBERIA
BENIN
CAMEROON
SOUTH SUDAN
C.A.R.
ETHIOPIA
SRI LANKA
CÔTE D'IVOIRE (IVORY COAST)
GHANA
TOGO
EQ. GUINEA
GABON
CONGO
UGANDA
SOMALIA
MALDIVES
BRUNEI
MALAYSIA
PALAU
SAO TOME & PRINCIPE
KENYA
RWANDA
BURUNDI
DEM. REP. CONGO
SINGAPORE
INDONESIA
TANZANIA
SEYCHELLES
EAST TIMOR
ANGOLA
COMOROS
MAYOTTE (to France)
MALAWI
ZAMBIA
ATLANTIC OCEAN
ZIMB.
MADAGASCAR
NAMIBIA
MOZAMBIQUE
MAURITIUS
BOTS.
REUNION (to France)
SWAZILAND
LESOTHO
SOUTH AFRICA
INDIAN OCEAN
AUSTRALIA
Majority Religions
Protestant Christianity
Catholic Christianity
Orthodox Christianity
Shi'a Islam
Sunni Islam
Hinduism
Judaism
Theravada Buddhism
Mahayana Buddhism
Tibetan Buddhism
Traditional Chinese
Other
Marxism / Maoism
State Policy
Secular ideologies governing
Communist states during 20th century
Non-pluralist states
ANTARCTICA (uninhabited)

E
F
G
H
1
2
3
4
5
ARCTIC OCEAN
GREENLAND (to Denmark)
Arctic Circle
Alaska (to US)
CANADA
PACIFIC OCEAN
UNITED STATES OF AMERICA
ATLANTIC OCEAN
BERMUDA (to UK)
PUERTO RICO (to US)
BRITISH VIRGIN ISLANDS (to UK)
VIRGIN ISLANDS (to US)
DOM. REP.
TURKS & CAICOS ISLANDS (to UK)
ANGUILLA (to UK)
CAYMAN ISLANDS (to UK)
ST KITTS & NEVIS
Tropic of Cancer
THE BAHAMAS
ANTIGUA & BARBUDA
MONTSERRAT (to UK)
HONDURAS
CUBA
BELIZE
GUADELOUPE (to France)
MEXICO
Hawai'i (to US)
JAMAICA
HAITI
DOMINICA
MARTINIQUE (to France)
CURAÇAO (to Neth.)
GUATEMALA
ST LUCIA
ARUBA (to Neth.)
EL SALVADOR
BARBADOS
NICARAGUA
ST VINCENT & THE GRENADINES
COSTA RICA
GRENADA
VENEZUELA
TRINIDAD & TOBAGO
PANAMA
FRENCH GUIANA (to France)
COLOMBIA
Equator
KIRIBATI
ECUADOR
GUYANA
SURINAME
TUVALU
TOKELAU (to NZ)
BRAZIL
COOK ISLANDS (to NZ)
PERU
BOLIVIA
FRENCH POLYNESIA (to France)
FIJI
PARAGUAY
Tropic of Capricorn
TONGA
SAMOA
AMERICAN SAMOA (to US)
PITCAIRN, HENDERSON, DUCIE & OENO ISLANDS (to UK)
CHILE
URUGUAY
ARGENTINA
NEW ZEALAND
PACIFIC OCEAN
FALKLAND ISLANDS (to UK)
CHILE
Antarctic Circle
ANTARCTICA

The Global Economy

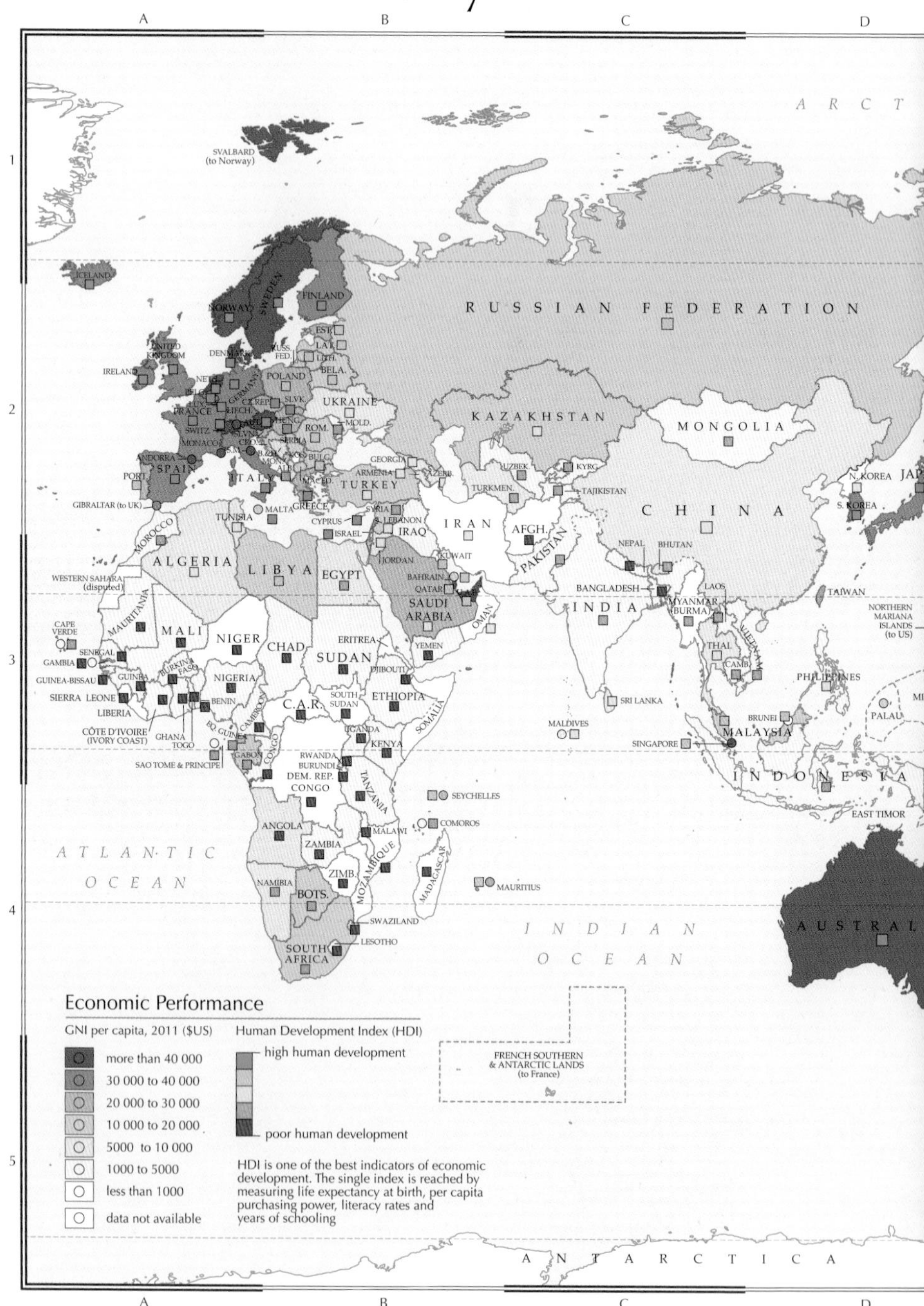

E
F
G
H
1
2
3
4
5
GREENLAND
(to Denmark)
Arctic Circle
Alaska
(to US)
CANADA
PACIFIC
OCEAN
UNITED STATES
OF AMERICA
ATLANTIC
OCEAN
BERMUDA
(to UK)
PUERTO RICO
(to US)
DOM. REP.
TURKS & CAICOS ISLANDS (to UK)
CAYMAN ISLANDS
(to UK)
THE
BAHAMAS
ST KITTS & NEVIS
ANTIGUA & BAR.
Tropic of Cancer
GUADELOUPE (to France)
DOMINICA
MARTINIQUE (to France)
ST LUCIA
BARBADOS
ST VINCENT &
THE GRENADINES
GRENADA
TRINIDAD & TOBAGO
FRENCH GUIANA
(to France)
MEXICO
HONDURAS
BELIZE
CUBA
JAMAICA
HAITI
CURAÇAO
(to Neth.)
ARUBA
(to Neth.)
GUATEMALA
EL SALVADOR
NICARAGUA
COSTA RICA
PANAMA
VENEZUELA
COLOMBIA
Equator
ECUADOR
GUYANA
SURINAME
BRAZIL
PERU
BOLIVIA
PARAGUAY
Tropic of Capricorn
CHILE
ARGENTINA
URUGUAY
FALKLAND ISLANDS
(to UK)
CHILE
Hawai'i
(to US)
MARSHALL
ISLANDS
NAURU
KIRIBATI
TUVALU
TOKELAU
(to NZ)
SAMOA
COOK
ISLANDS
(to NZ)
TONGA
FIJI
FRENCH POLYNESIA
(to France)
PITCAIRN, HENDERSON,
DUCIE & OENO ISLANDS
(to UK)
NEW
ZEALAND
PACIFIC
OCEAN
Antarctic Circle
ANTARCTICA

Politics and Conflict

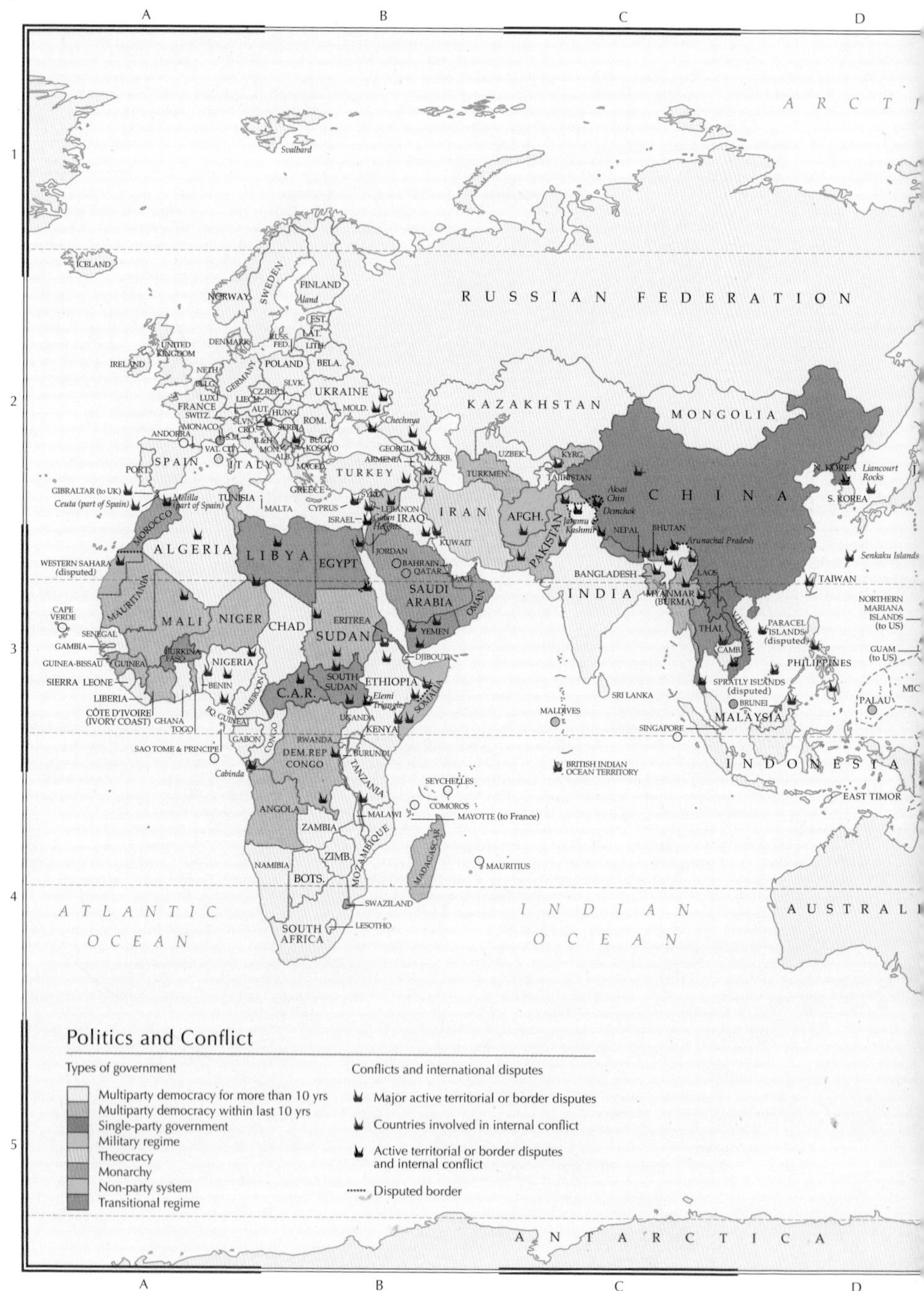

E
F
G
H
1
2
3
4
5
GREENLAND
(to Denmark)
Arctic Circle
Alaska
(to US)
CANADA
ST PIERRE
& MIQUELON
(to France)
PACIFIC
OCEAN
UNITED STATES
OF AMERICA
ATLANTIC
OCEAN
MEXICO
THE
BAHAMAS
Tropic of Cancer
CUBA
GUANTANAMO BAY
(to US)
DOM. REP.
ST KITTS & NEVIS
ANTIGUA & BARBUDA
Hawai'i
(to US)
BELIZE
JAMAICA
HAITI
DOMINICA
GUATEMALA
HONDURAS
ST LUCIA
EL SALVADOR
BARBADOS
NICARAGUA
ST VINCENT & THE GRENADINES
COSTA RICA
GRENADA
PANAMA
VENEZUELA
TRINIDAD & TOBAGO
FRENCH GUIANA
(to France)
COLOMBIA
Equator
ECUADOR
GUYANA
SURINAME
KIRIBATI
TUVALU
COOK
ISLANDS
(to NZ)
BRAZIL
PERU
SAMOA
BOLIVIA
FIJI
TONGA
FRENCH POLYNESIA
(to France)
PARAGUAY
Tropic of Capricorn
PITCAIRN, HENDERSON,
DUCIE & OENO
ISLANDS
(to UK)
CHILE
URUGUAY
ARGENTINA
PACIFIC
OCEAN
FALKLAND ISLANDS
(to UK)
CHILE
Antarctic Circle
ANTARCTICA

The WORLD'S REGIONS

North & Central America

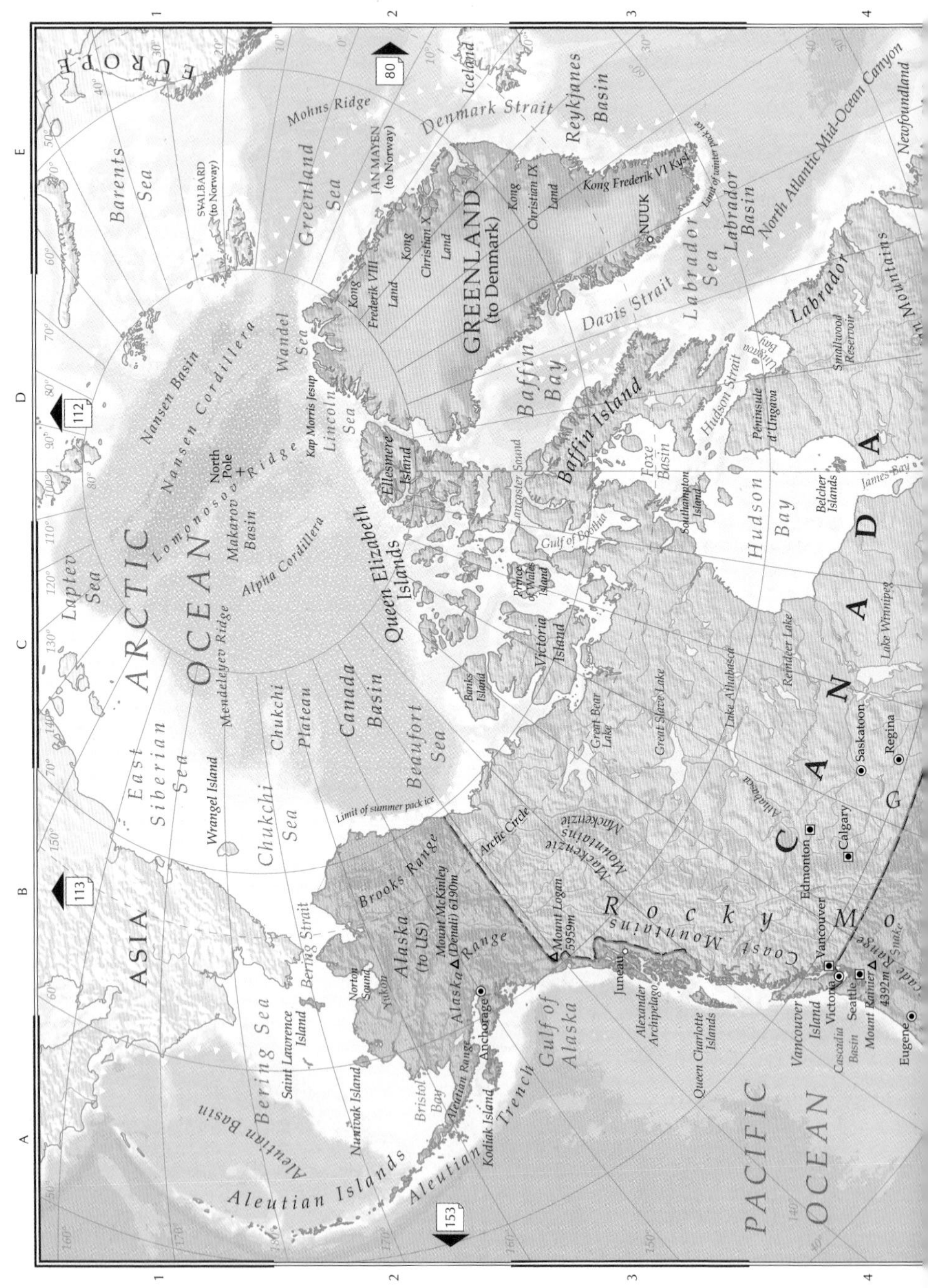

0 km 1000

0 miles 1000

Population

● National capital

○ below 50,000 ○ 50,000 to 100,000 ◉ 100,000 to 500,000 ▣ above 500,000

UNITED STATES OF AMERICA
MEXICO
ATLANTIC OCEAN
PACIFIC OCEAN
SOUTH AMERICA
Gulf of Mexico
Caribbean Sea
Sargasso Sea
Gulf of California
Lower California
THE BAHAMAS
CUBA
HAITI
DOMINICAN REPUBLIC
JAMAICA
BELIZE
GUATEMALA
HONDURAS
EL SALVADOR
NICARAGUA
COSTA RICA
PANAMA
TRINIDAD & TOBAGO
BARBADOS
GRENADA
DOMINICA
ST LUCIA
ST VINCENT & THE GRENADINES
ST KITTS & NEVIS
ANTIGUA & BARBUDA
BERMUDA (to UK)
TURKS & CAICOS ISLANDS (to UK)
CAYMAN ISLANDS (to UK)
VIRGIN ISLANDS (to US)
BRITISH VIRGIN ISLANDS (to UK)
ANGUILLA (to UK)
PUERTO RICO (to US)
GUADELOUPE (to France)
MONTSERRAT (to UK)
MARTINIQUE (to France)
ARUBA (Neth.)
CURAÇAO (Neth.)
BONAIRE (to Neth.)
CLIPPERTON ISLAND (to French Polynesia)
Revillagigedo Islands (to Mexico)
Galapagos Islands (to Ecuador)
WASHINGTON D.C.
MEXICO CITY
HAVANA
NASSAU
KINGSTON
PORT-AU-PRINCE
SANTO DOMINGO
BELMOPAN
GUATEMALA CITY
SAN SALVADOR
TEGUCIGALPA
MANAGUA
SAN JOSÉ
PANAMA CITY
PORT-OF-SPAIN
Appalachian Mountains
Sierra Madre Oriental
Sierra Madre Occidental
Andes
Greater Antilles
Lesser Antilles
Hatteras Plain
Nares Plain
Bermuda Rise
Blake Plateau
Straits of Florida
Yucatan Peninsula
Mississippi Delta
Middle America Trench
Guatemala Basin
Panama Basin
Colombian Basin
Cocos Ridge
Colón Ridge
East Pacific Rise
Clarion Fracture Zone
Gallego Rise
Tropic of Cancer
Equator
Mount Whitney 4418m
Death Valley -86m
Volcán Pico de Orizaba 5700m
Grand Canyon
Guantanamo Bay (to US)
Georges Bank
Cape Cod
Lake Ontario
Lake Erie
Niagara Falls
Lake Nicaragua
Rio Grande
Red River
Mississippi
Missouri
Arkansas
Ohio
Colorado
Los Angeles
San Diego
Phoenix
El Paso
Denver
Lincoln
Des Moines
Kansas City
Oklahoma City
Dallas
Austin
San Antonio
Houston
Little Rock
Springfield
Madison
Milwaukee
Chicago
Indianapolis
Lansing
Detroit
Toronto
Cleveland
Columbus
Nashville
Memphis
Jackson
Baton Rouge
New Orleans
Atlanta
Montgomery
Columbia
Raleigh
Richmond
Baltimore
Philadelphia
New York
Albany
Boston
Jacksonville
Tampa
Miami
Monterrey
Guadalajara
Acapulco
153
56
66

Western Canada & Alaska

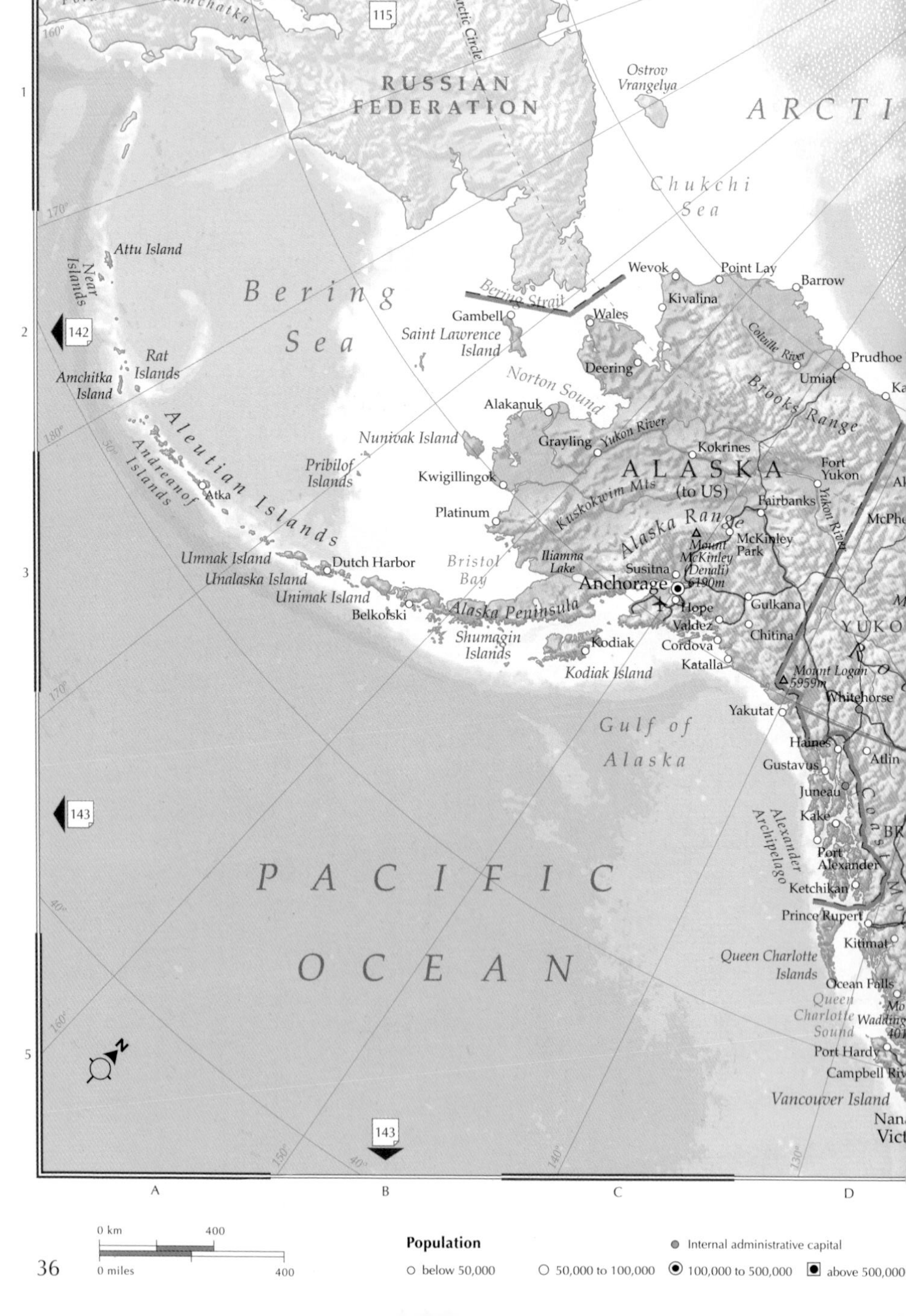

Elevation

Below sea level	0	250m	500m	1000m	2000m	3000m	4000m	6000m
		820ft	1640ft	3281ft	6562ft	9843ft	13,124ft	19,685ft

-6000m	-4000m	-2000m	-1000m	-500m	-250m	
-19,658ft	-13,124ft	-6562ft	-3281ft	-1640ft	-820ft	-328ft/-100m 0

Eastern Canada

0 km 300
0 miles 300

Population
● National capital
● Internal administrative capital
○ below 50,000
○ 50,000 to 100,000
⊙ 100,000 to 500,000
▣ above 500,000

82
66
66
66

Elevation

Below sea level								0	250m	500m	1000m	2000m	3000m	4000m	6000m
-6000m	-4000m	-2000m	-1000m	-500m	-250m										
-19,658ft	-13,124ft	-6562ft	-3281ft	-1640ft	-820ft	-328ft/-100m		0	820ft	1640ft	3281ft	6562ft	9843ft	13,124ft	19,685ft

USA: The Northeast

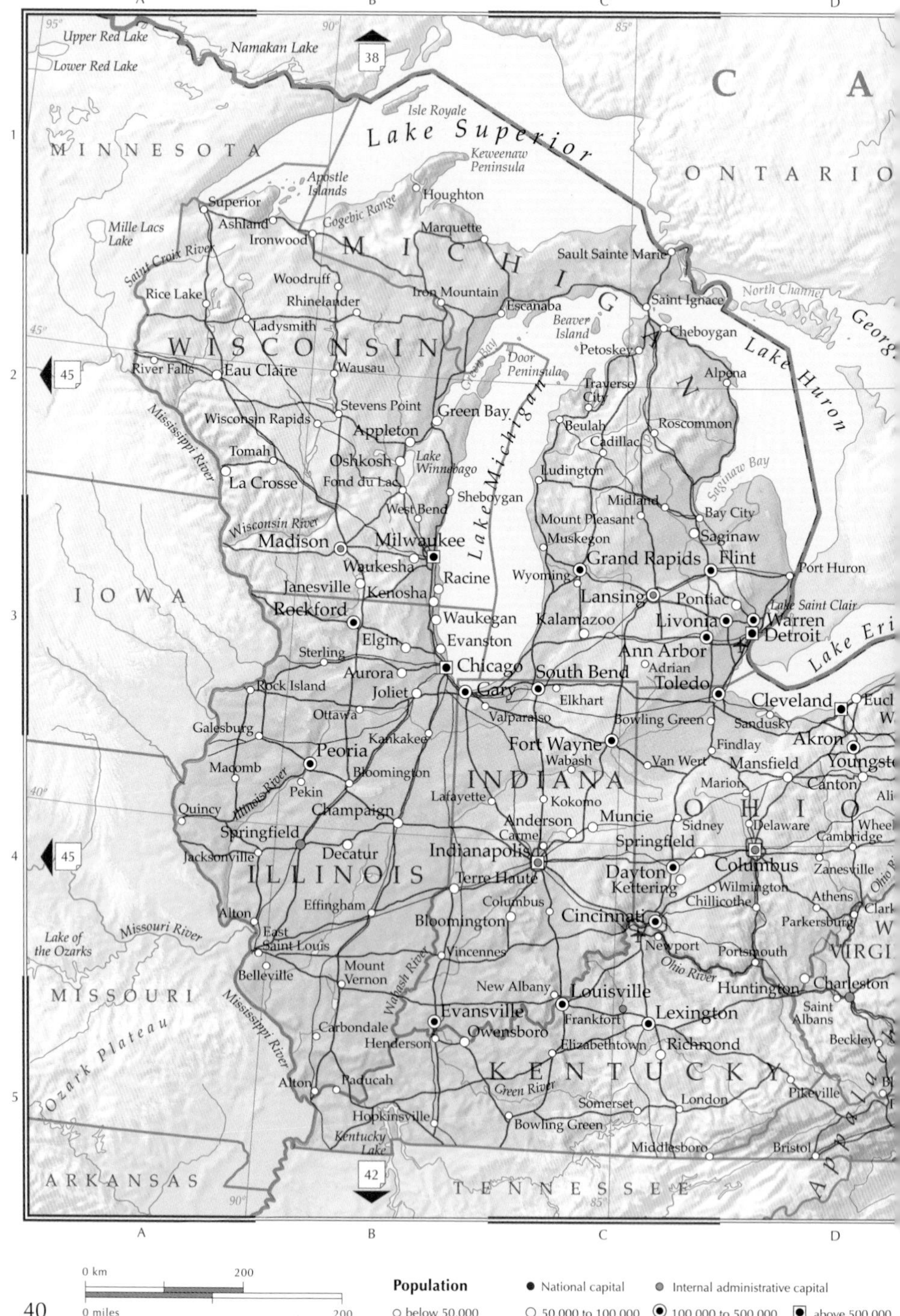

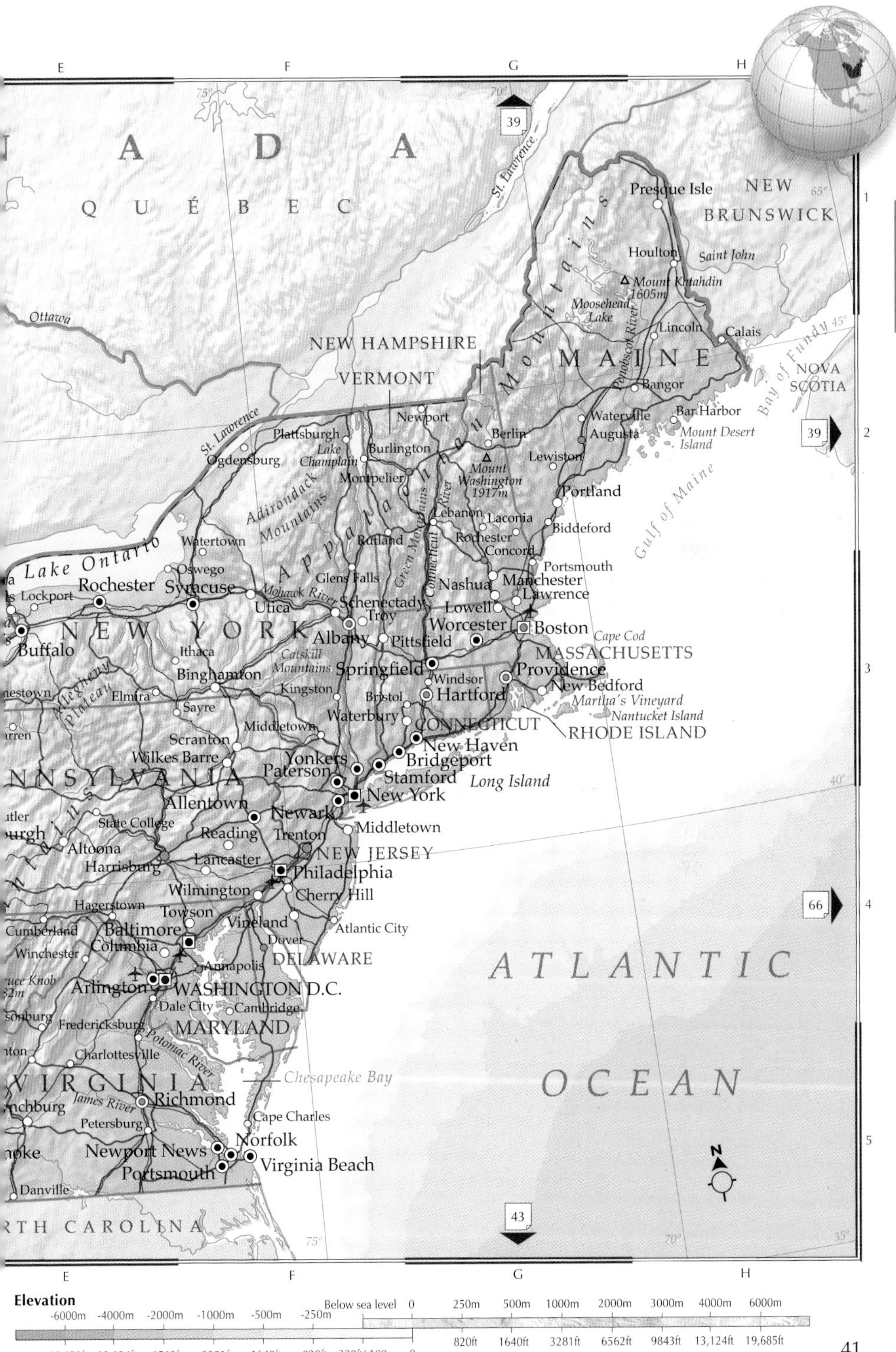

CANADA
QUÉBEC
NEW BRUNSWICK
NOVA SCOTIA
NEW HAMPSHIRE
VERMONT
MAINE
NEW YORK
MASSACHUSETTS
CONNECTICUT
RHODE ISLAND
NEW JERSEY
DELAWARE
MARYLAND
WASHINGTON D.C.
VIRGINIA
NORTH CAROLINA
ATLANTIC OCEAN
Appalachian Mountains
Adirondack Mountains
Green Mountains
Catskill Mountains
Allegheny Plateau
Lake Ontario
St. Lawrence
Ottawa
Lake Champlain
Mohawk River
Connecticut River
Penobscot River
Moosehead Lake
Mount Katahdin 1605m
Mount Washington 1917m
Saint John
Bay of Fundy
Gulf of Maine
Mount Desert Island
Cape Cod
Martha's Vineyard
Nantucket Island
Long Island
Chesapeake Bay
Potomac River
James River
Presque Isle
Houlton
Lincoln
Calais
Bangor
Bar Harbor
Waterville
Augusta
Lewiston
Portland
Biddeford
Portsmouth
Berlin
Newport
Burlington
Plattsburgh
Montpelier
Rutland
Lebanon
Laconia
Rochester
Concord
Manchester
Nashua
Lawrence
Lowell
Boston
Worcester
Springfield
Pittsfield
Providence
New Bedford
Windsor
Hartford
Bristol
Waterbury
New Haven
Bridgeport
Stamford
New York
Yonkers
Paterson
Newark
Middletown
Trenton
Philadelphia
Cherry Hill
Atlantic City
Vineland
Dover
Wilmington
Ogdensburg
Watertown
Oswego
Rochester
Syracuse
Utica
Lockport
Buffalo
Schenectady
Troy
Albany
Glens Falls
Ithaca
Binghamton
Elmira
Sayre
Kingston
Middletown
Scranton
Wilkes Barre
Allentown
Reading
Lancaster
Harrisburg
State College
Altoona
Hagerstown
Cumberland
Towson
Baltimore
Columbia
Annapolis
Winchester
Arlington
Dale City
Cambridge
Fredericksburg
Charlottesville
Richmond
Petersburg
Cape Charles
Norfolk
Newport News
Portsmouth
Virginia Beach
Danville
75°
70°
65°
45°
40°
35°
E
F
G
H
1
2
3
4
5
39
66
43
Elevation
Below sea level
0
250m
500m
1000m
2000m
3000m
4000m
6000m
820ft
1640ft
3281ft
6562ft
9843ft
13,124ft
19,685ft
-6000m
-4000m
-2000m
-1000m
-500m
-250m
-19,658ft
-13,124ft
-6562ft
-3281ft
-1640ft
-820ft
-328ft/-100m

USA: The Southeast

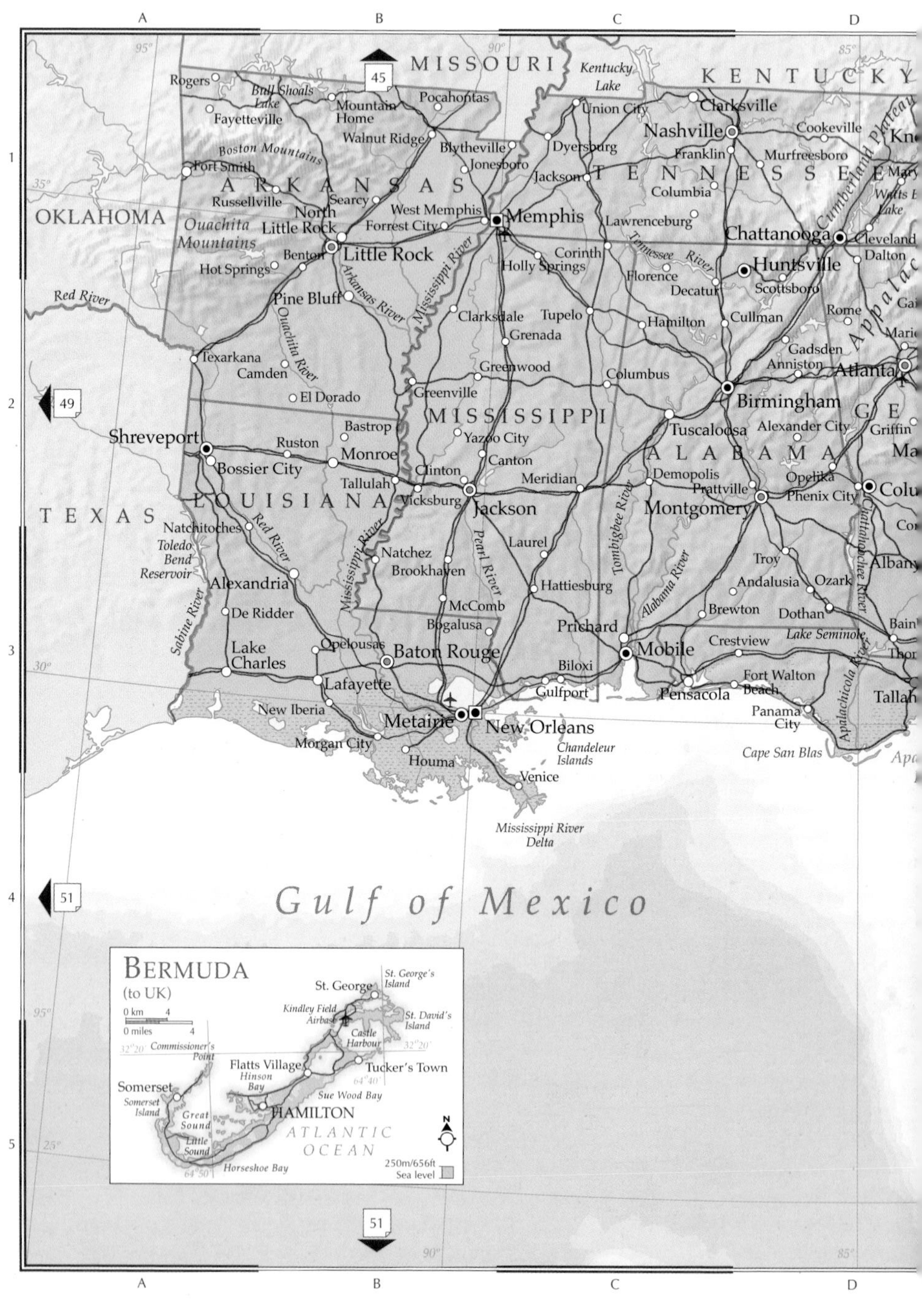

45
49
51
51

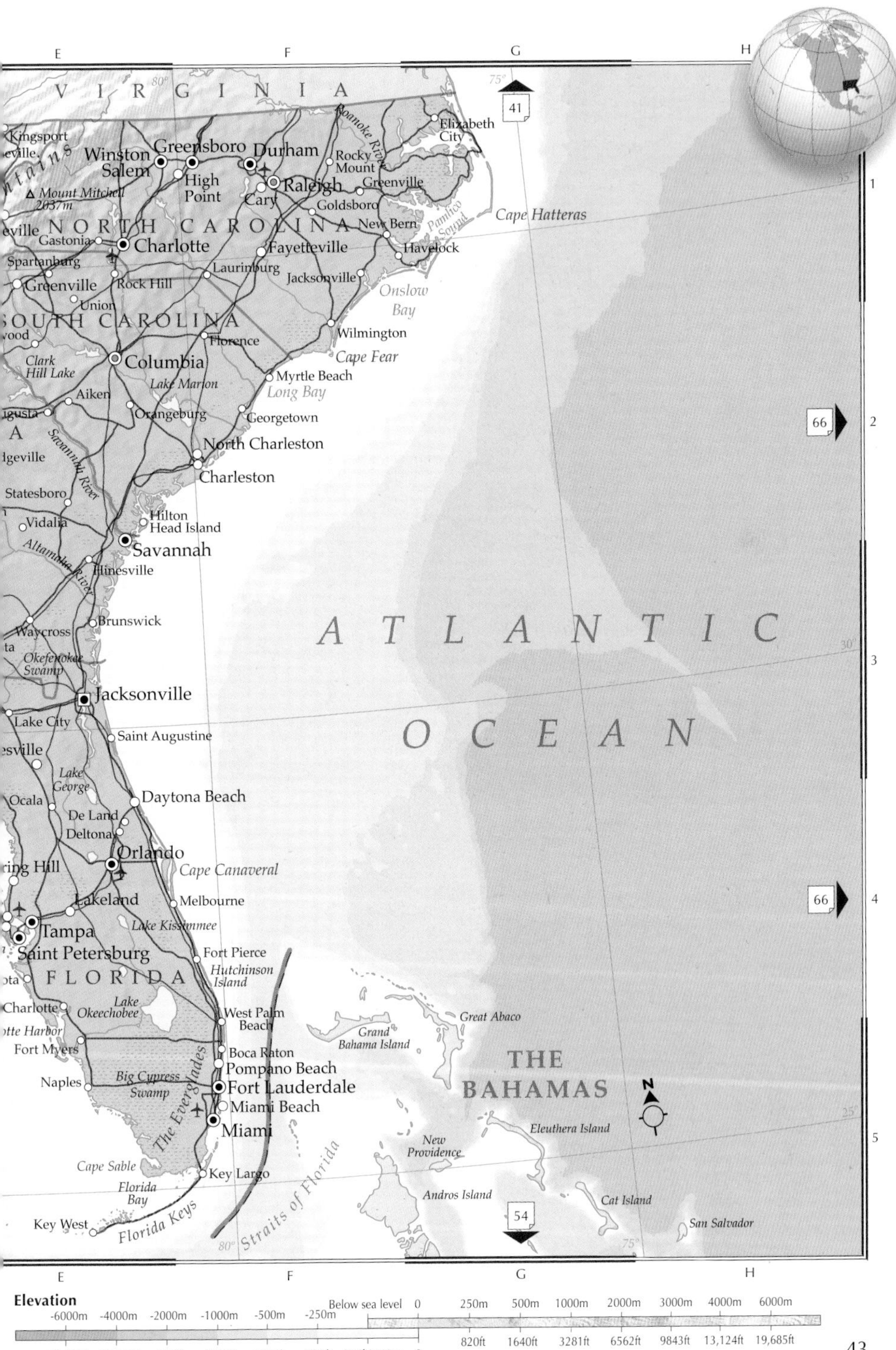

E
F
G
H
1
2
3
4
5
41
66
66
54
VIRGINIA
Kingsport
Winston Salem
Greensboro
Durham
Rocky Mount
Roanoke River
Elizabeth City
High Point
Raleigh
Cary
Greenville
Mount Mitchell 2037m
Goldsboro
NORTH CAROLINA
New Bern
Pamlico Sound
Cape Hatteras
Gastonia
Charlotte
Fayetteville
Havelock
Spartanburg
Laurinburg
Greenville
Rock Hill
Jacksonville
Onslow Bay
Union
SOUTH CAROLINA
Florence
Wilmington
Clark Hill Lake
Columbia
Cape Fear
Aiken
Lake Marion
Myrtle Beach
Long Bay
Orangeburg
Georgetown
Savannah River
North Charleston
Charleston
Statesboro
Hilton Head Island
Vidalia
Savannah
Altamaha River
Hinesville
Brunswick
Waycross
Okefenokee Swamp
ATLANTIC
OCEAN
Jacksonville
Lake City
Saint Augustine
Lake George
Ocala
Daytona Beach
De Land
Deltona
Orlando
Cape Canaveral
Lakeland
Melbourne
Tampa
Lake Kissimmee
Saint Petersburg
Fort Pierce
FLORIDA
Hutchinson Island
Charlotte
Lake Okeechobee
West Palm Beach
Fort Myers
Boca Raton
Pompano Beach
Naples
Big Cypress Swamp
Fort Lauderdale
Miami Beach
The Everglades
Miami
Cape Sable
Key Largo
Florida Bay
Key West
Florida Keys
Straits of Florida
Great Abaco
Grand Bahama Island
THE BAHAMAS
Eleuthera Island
New Providence
Andros Island
Cat Island
San Salvador
Elevation
Below sea level
-6000m -4000m -2000m -1000m -500m -250m
-19,658ft -13,124ft -6562ft -3281ft -1640ft -820ft -328ft/-100m 0
0 250m 500m 1000m 2000m 3000m 4000m 6000m
820ft 1640ft 3281ft 6562ft 9843ft 13,124ft 19,685ft

USA: Central States

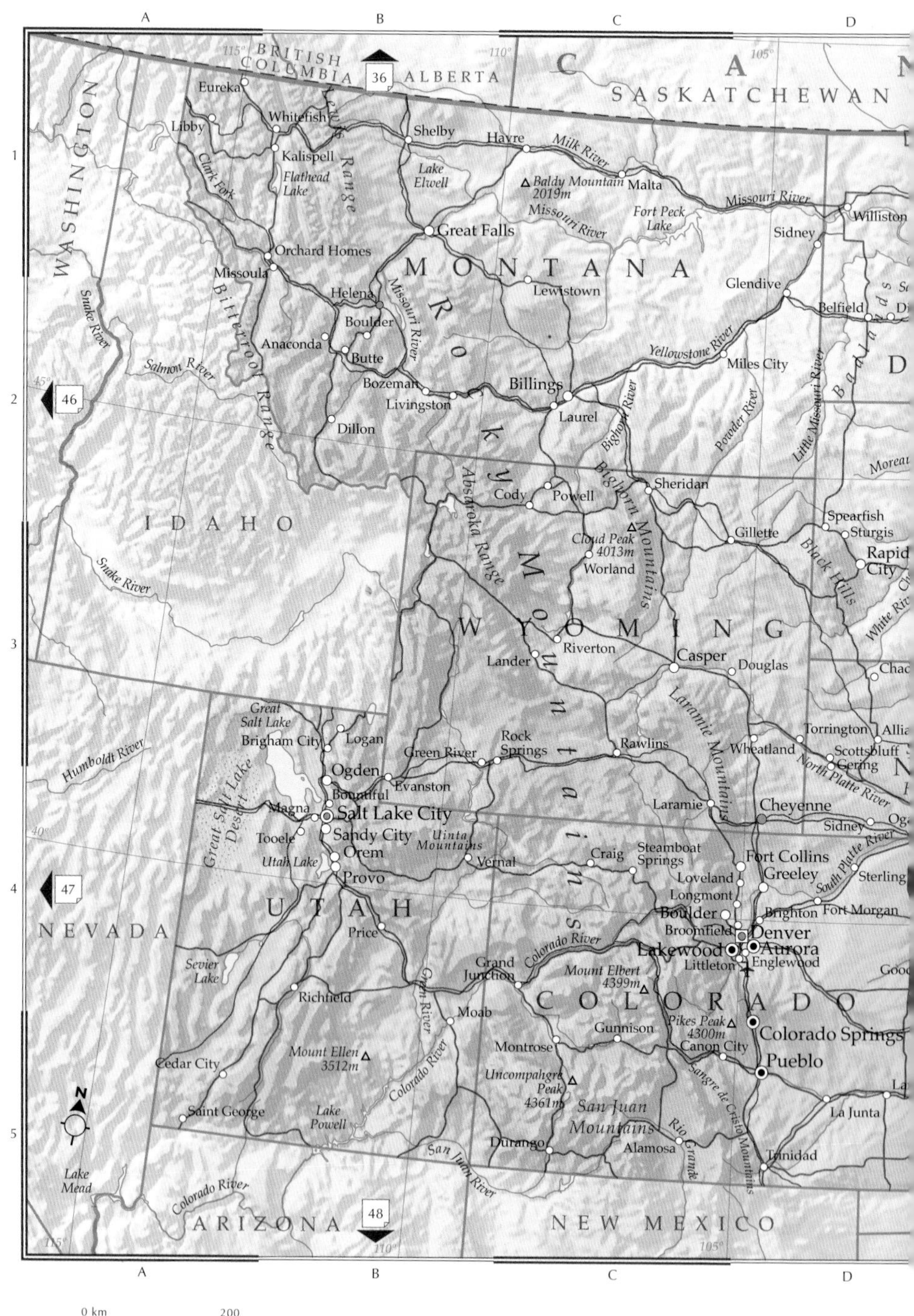

0 km 200
0 miles 200

Population
○ below 50,000
○ 50,000 to 100,000
◉ 100,000 to 500,000
■ above 500,000
● Internal administrative capital

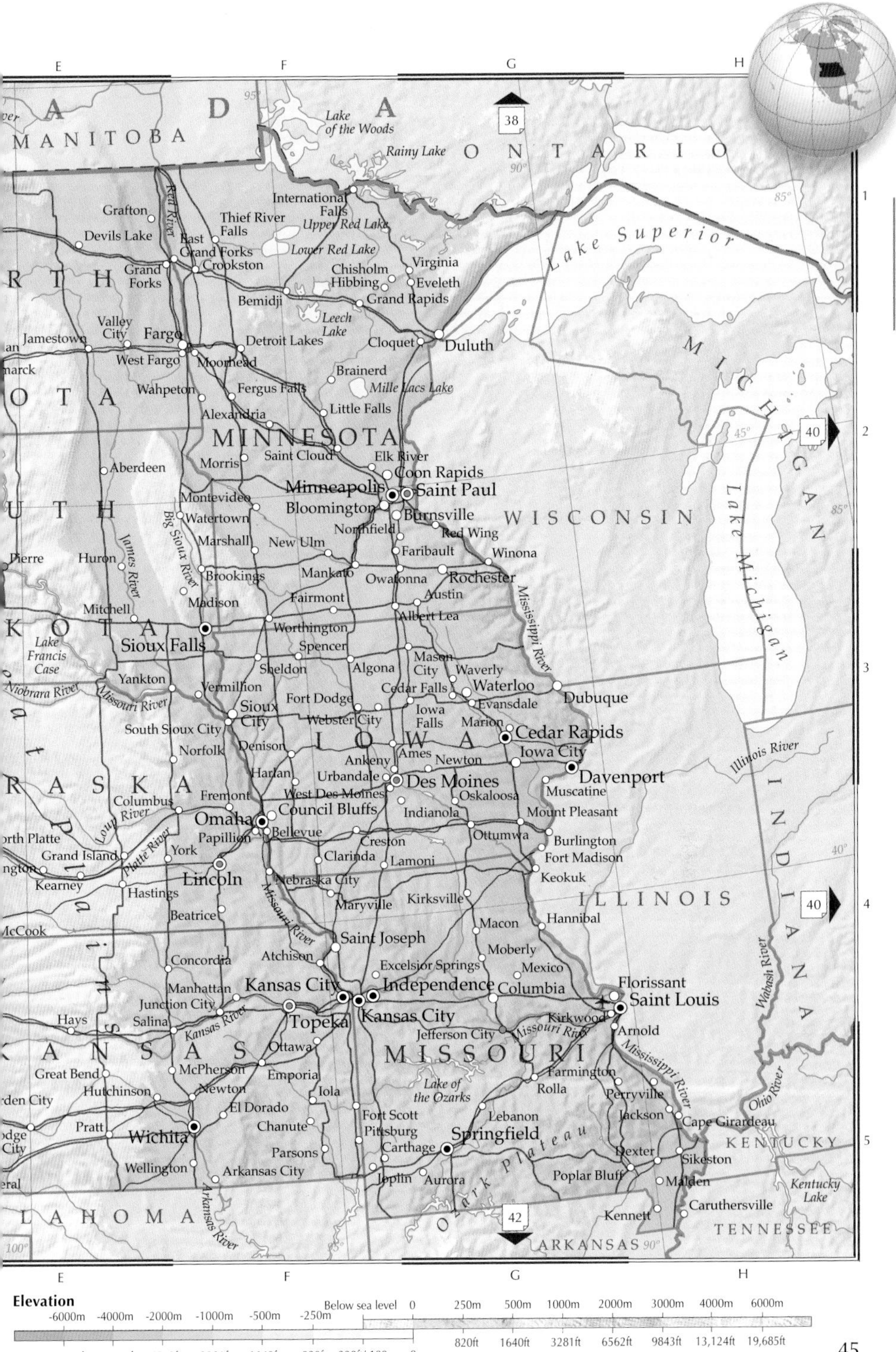

E
F
G
H
1
2
3
4
5
38
40
40
42
CANADA
MANITOBA
ONTARIO
NORTH DAKOTA
SOUTH DAKOTA
NEBRASKA
KANSAS
OKLAHOMA
MINNESOTA
IOWA
MISSOURI
WISCONSIN
MICHIGAN
ILLINOIS
INDIANA
KENTUCKY
TENNESSEE
ARKANSAS
Lake of the Woods
Rainy Lake
Lake Superior
Lake Michigan
Upper Red Lake
Lower Red Lake
Leech Lake
Mille Lacs Lake
Lake Francis Case
Lake of the Ozarks
Kentucky Lake
Red River
Big Sioux River
James River
Missouri River
Niobrara River
Loup River
Platte River
Kansas River
Arkansas River
Mississippi River
Illinois River
Wabash River
Ohio River
Ozark Plateau
Great Plains
95°
90°
85°
45°
40°
100°
Grafton
Devils Lake
Grand Forks
East Grand Forks
Crookston
Thief River Falls
International Falls
Bemidji
Chisholm
Hibbing
Virginia
Eveleth
Grand Rapids
Valley City
Jamestown
Fargo
West Fargo
Moorhead
Detroit Lakes
Cloquet
Duluth
Brainerd
Wahpeton
Fergus Falls
Little Falls
Alexandria
Bismarck
Aberdeen
Morris
Saint Cloud
Elk River
Coon Rapids
Minneapolis
Saint Paul
Bloomington
Burnsville
Montevideo
Watertown
Northfield
Red Wing
Marshall
New Ulm
Faribault
Winona
Pierre
Huron
Brookings
Mankato
Owatonna
Rochester
Madison
Fairmont
Austin
Mitchell
Albert Lea
Worthington
Sioux Falls
Spencer
Sheldon
Algona
Mason City
Waverly
Yankton
Vermillion
Fort Dodge
Cedar Falls
Waterloo
Evansdale
Dubuque
Sioux City
South Sioux City
Webster City
Iowa Falls
Marion
Cedar Rapids
Norfolk
Denison
Ames
Iowa City
Ankeny
Newton
Davenport
Harlan
Urbandale
Des Moines
Muscatine
Columbus
Fremont
West Des Moines
Oskaloosa
Omaha
Council Bluffs
Indianola
Mount Pleasant
North Platte
Papillion
Bellevue
Creston
Ottumwa
Burlington
Grand Island
York
Clarinda
Fort Madison
Lamoni
Lexington
Kearney
Lincoln
Nebraska City
Keokuk
Hastings
Maryville
Kirksville
Beatrice
Macon
Hannibal
McCook
Saint Joseph
Moberly
Concordia
Atchison
Excelsior Springs
Mexico
Manhattan
Kansas City
Independence
Columbia
Florissant
Saint Louis
Junction City
Topeka
Kirkwood
Hays
Salina
Jefferson City
Arnold
Ottawa
Great Bend
McPherson
Emporia
Farmington
Rolla
Perryville
Hutchinson
Newton
Iola
Garden City
El Dorado
Fort Scott
Lebanon
Jackson
Pratt
Chanute
Pittsburg
Springfield
Cape Girardeau
Dodge City
Wichita
Carthage
Parsons
Dexter
Sikeston
Wellington
Arkansas City
Joplin
Aurora
Poplar Bluff
Malden
Liberal
Kennett
Caruthersville
Elevation
Below sea level
0
250m
500m
1000m
2000m
3000m
4000m
6000m
820ft
1640ft
3281ft
6562ft
9843ft
13,124ft
19,685ft
-6000m
-4000m
-2000m
-1000m
-500m
-250m
-19,658ft
-13,124ft
-6562ft
-3281ft
-1640ft
-820ft
-328ft/-100m
0

USA: The West

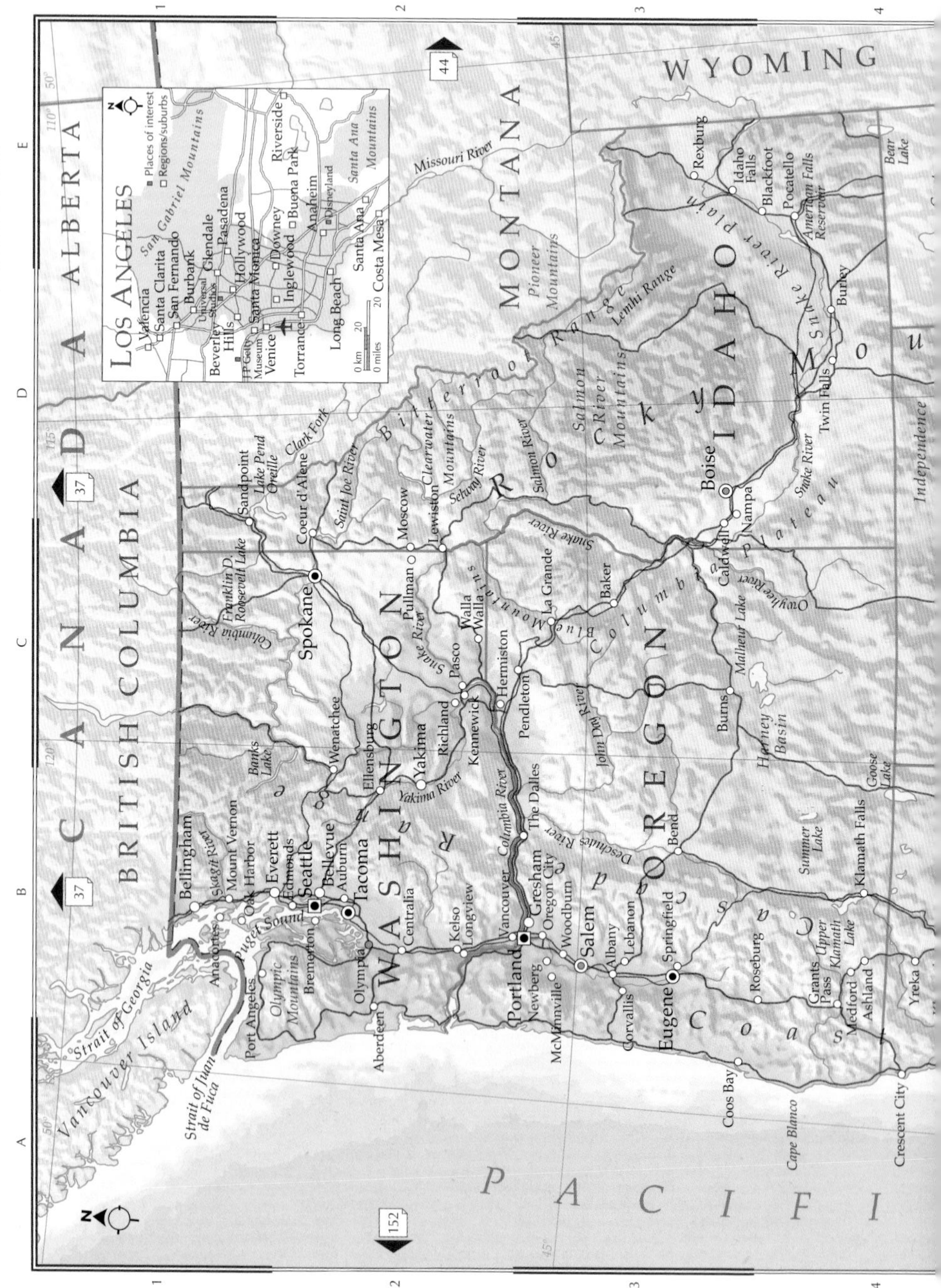

0 km 200
0 miles 200

Population
○ below 50,000
○ 50,000 to 100,000
◉ 100,000 to 500,000
▣ above 500,000
● Internal administrative capital

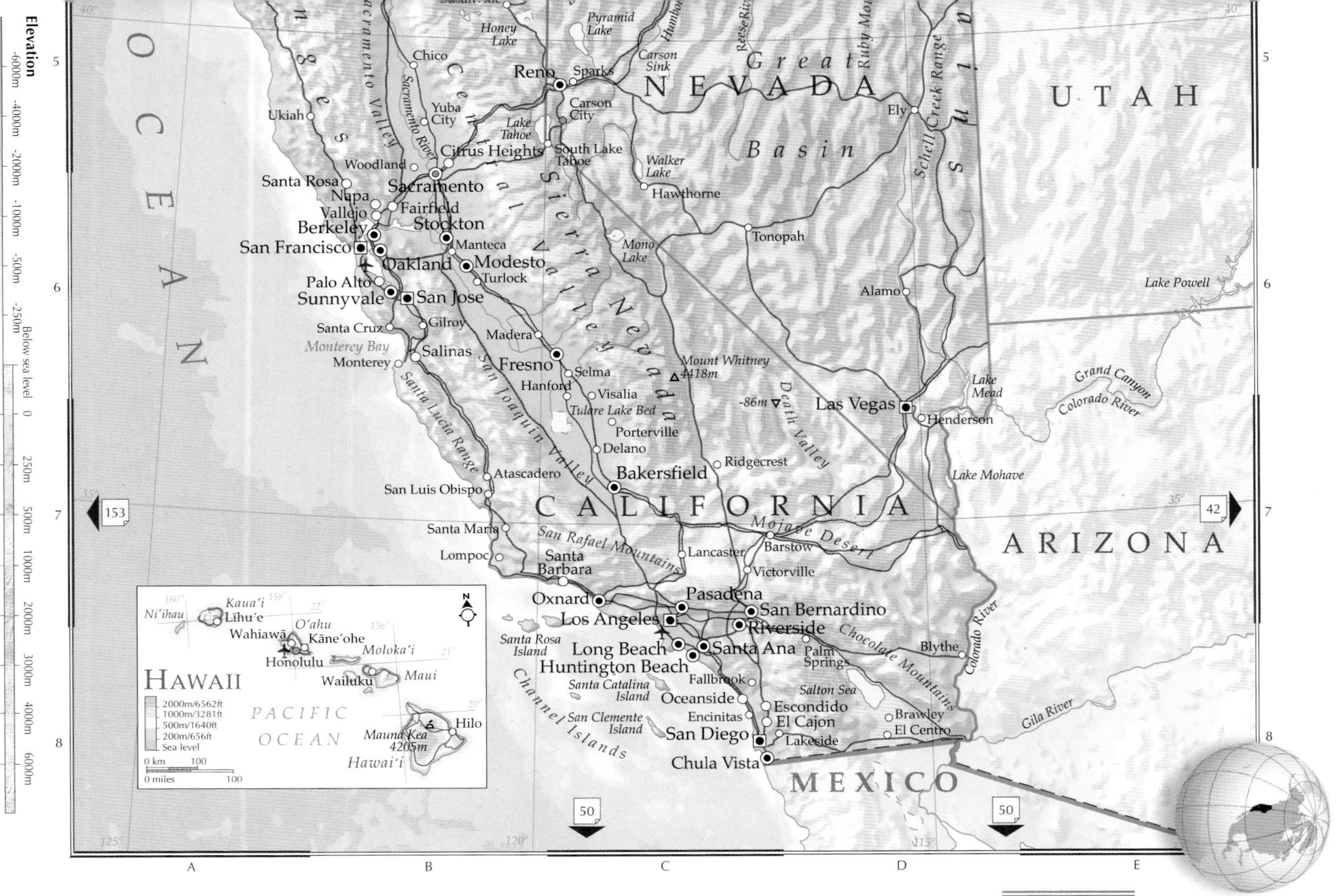

Elevation

Below sea level: -6000m (-19,658ft), -4000m (-13,124ft), -2000m (-6562ft), -1000m (-3281ft), -500m (-1640ft), -250m (-820ft), -328ft/-100m, 0

Above sea level: 0, 250m (820ft), 500m (1640ft), 1000m (3281ft), 2000m (6562ft), 3000m (9843ft), 4000m (13,124ft), 6000m (19,685ft)

USA: The Southwest

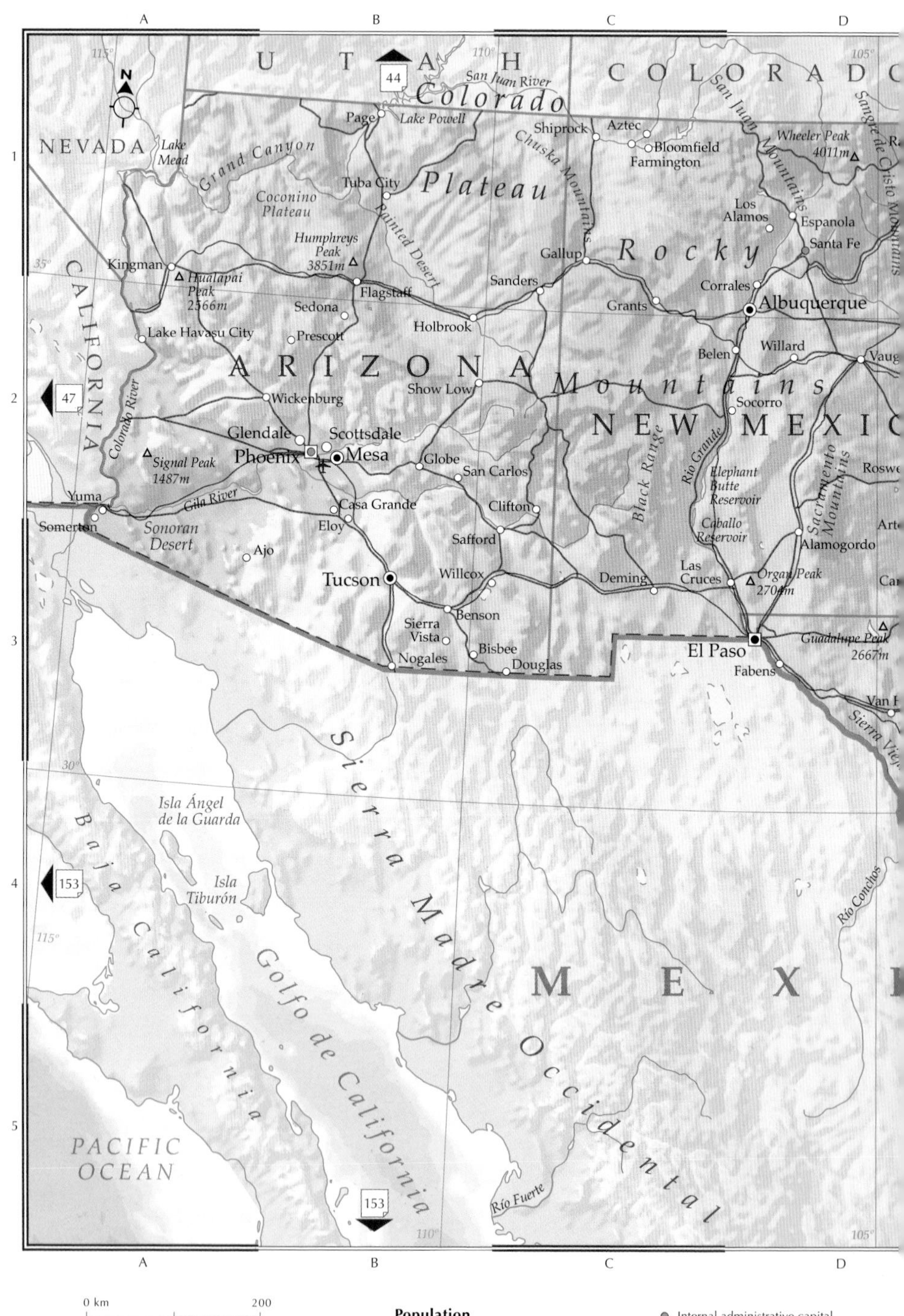

0 km 200
0 miles 200

Population
○ below 50,000
○ 50,000 to 100,000
◉ 100,000 to 500,000
■ above 500,000
● Internal administrative capital

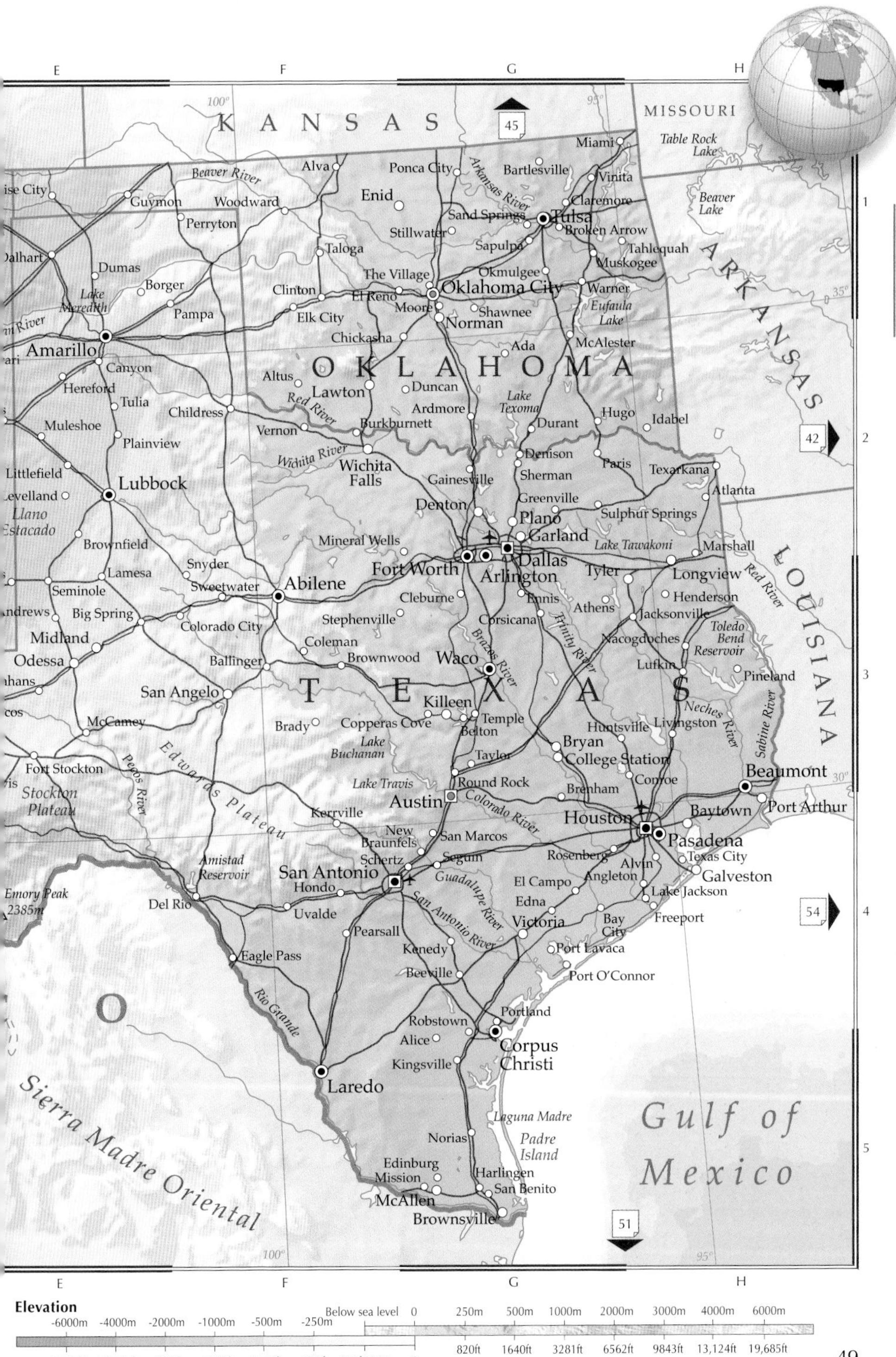
E
F
G
H
1
2
3
4
5
100°
95°
30°
35°
KANSAS
MISSOURI
45
42
54
51
Table Rock Lake
Beaver Lake
ARKANSAS
LOUISIANA
OKLAHOMA
TEXAS
O
Gulf of Mexico
Sierra Madre Oriental
Miami
Vinita
Bartlesville
Ponca City
Alva
Arkansas River
Claremore
Enid
Tulsa
Sand Springs
Broken Arrow
Stillwater
Sapulpa
Tahlequah
Muskogee
Taloga
Okmulgee
The Village
Clinton
El Reno
Oklahoma City
Warner
Eufaula Lake
Moore
Shawnee
Elk City
Norman
Chickasha
Ada
McAlester
Altus
Lawton
Duncan
Lake Texoma
Ardmore
Hugo
Idabel
Red River
Durant
Burkburnett
Vernon
Wichita River
Denison
Paris
Texarkana
Wichita Falls
Gainesville
Sherman
Atlanta
Greenville
Denton
Plano
Sulphur Springs
Garland
Mineral Wells
Lake Tawakoni
Marshall
Dallas
Fort Worth
Arlington
Tyler
Longview
Cleburne
Ennis
Henderson
Athens
Stephenville
Corsicana
Jacksonville
Toledo Bend Reservoir
Nacogdoches
Coleman
Brownwood
Lufkin
Waco
Brazos River
Trinity River
Pineland
Killeen
Neches River
Temple
Belton
Huntsville
Livingston
Sabine River
Bryan
College Station
Taylor
Conroe
Beaumont
Round Rock
Brenham
Port Arthur
Baytown
Houston
Pasadena
Texas City
Galveston
Rosenberg
Alvin
Angleton
Lake Jackson
Freeport
El Campo
Edna
Bay City
Victoria
Port Lavaca
Port O'Connor
Beavre River
Beaver River
Guymon
Woodward
Perryton
Dalhart
Dumas
Borger
Lake Meredith
Pampa
Amarillo
Canyon
Hereford
Tulia
Childress
Muleshoe
Plainview
Littlefield
Lubbock
Levelland
Llano Estacado
Brownfield
Snyder
Lamesa
Sweetwater
Abilene
Seminole
Big Spring
Andrews
Colorado City
Midland
Odessa
Ballinger
San Angelo
McCamey
Brady
Copperas Cove
Lake Buchanan
Fort Stockton
Pecos River
Edwards Plateau
Stockton Plateau
Lake Travis
Austin
Colorado River
Kerrville
New Braunfels
San Marcos
Schertz
Seguin
Amistad Reservoir
San Antonio
Guadalupe River
Emory Peak 2385m
Hondo
Del Rio
Uvalde
San Antonio River
Pearsall
Kenedy
Eagle Pass
Beeville
Rio Grande
Portland
Robstown
Alice
Corpus Christi
Kingsville
Laredo
Laguna Madre
Padre Island
Norias
Edinburg
Mission
Harlingen
San Benito
McAllen
Brownsville
Elevation
Below sea level
-6000m -4000m -2000m -1000m -500m -250m
0 250m 500m 1000m 2000m 3000m 4000m 6000m
-19,658ft -13,124ft -6562ft -3281ft -1640ft -820ft -328ft/-100m 0
820ft 1640ft 3281ft 6562ft 9843ft 13,124ft 19,685ft

Mexico

0 km 300

0 miles 300

Population

● National capital

○ below 50,000 ○ 50,000 to 100,000 ◉ 100,000 to 500,000 ■ above 500,000

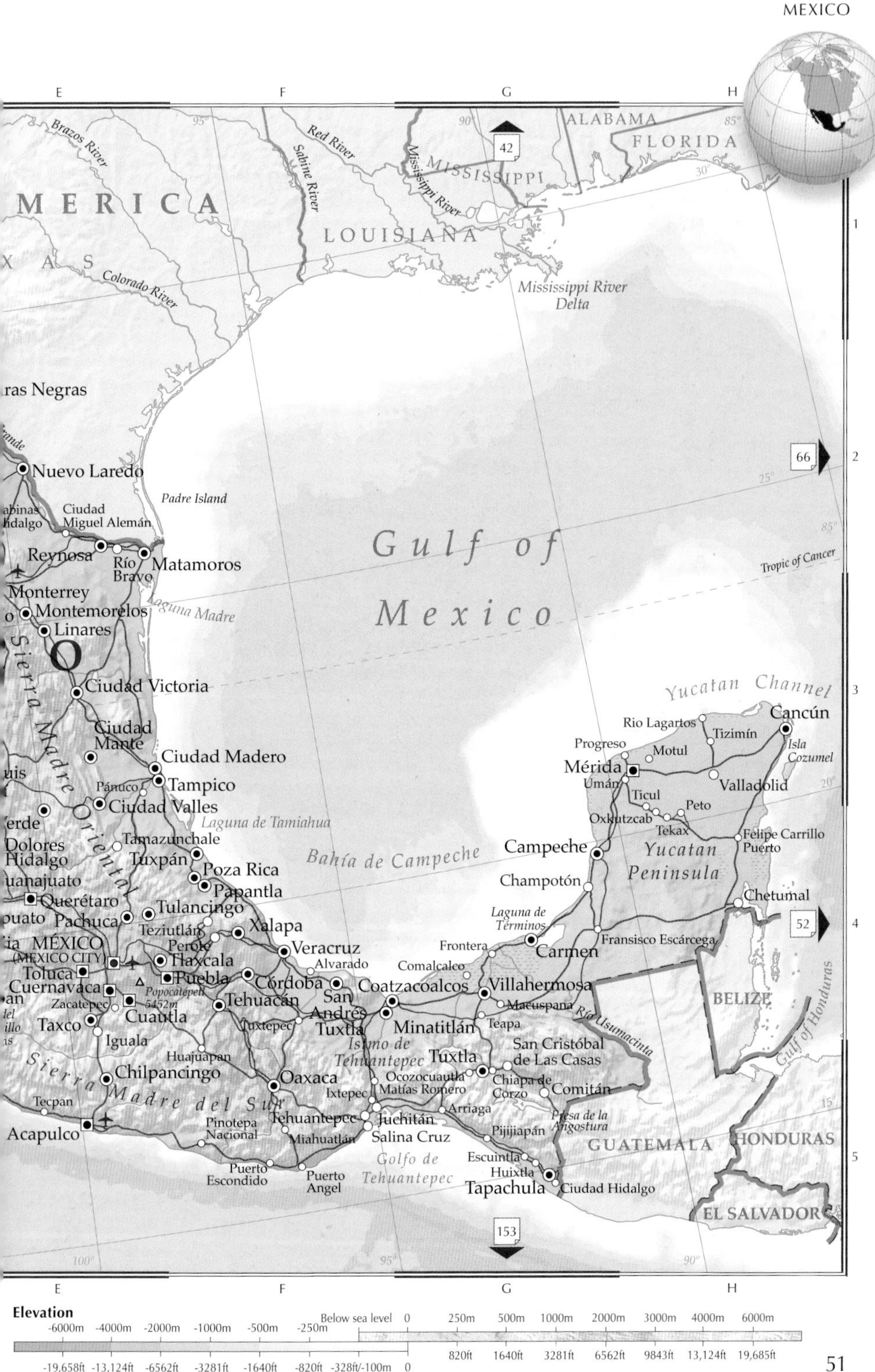

E
F
G
H
1
2
3
4
5
42
66
52
153
ALABAMA
FLORIDA
MISSISSIPPI
LOUISIANA
MERICA
XAS
Brazos River
Red River
Sabine River
Mississippi River
Colorado River
Mississippi River Delta
ras Negras
Nuevo Laredo
Padre Island
Ciudad Miguel Alemán
Reynosa
Río Bravo
Matamoros
Monterrey
Montemorelos
Laguna Madre
Linares
Gulf of Mexico
Tropic of Cancer
Ciudad Victoria
Sierra Madre Oriental
Ciudad Mante
Ciudad Madero
Tampico
Pánuco
Ciudad Valles
Laguna de Tamiahua
Tamazunchale
Tuxpán
Poza Rica
Papantla
Bahía de Campeche
Querétaro
Pachuca
Tulancingo
Teziutlán
Xalapa
Perote
MÉXICO (MEXICO CITY)
Tlaxcala
Veracruz
Alvarado
Toluca
Puebla
Córdoba
Cuernavaca
Popocatépetl 5452m
Zacatepec
Cuautla
Tehuacán
Taxco
Iguala
Tuxtepec
San Andrés Tuxtla
Coatzacoalcos
Minatitlán
Istmo de Tehuantepec
Huajuapan
Oaxaca
Chilpancingo
Sierra Madre del Sur
Tecpan
Acapulco
Pinotepa Nacional
Tehuantepec
Juchitán
Salina Cruz
Miahuatlán
Puerto Escondido
Puerto Angel
Golfo de Tehuantepec
Ixtepec
Matías Romero
Ocozocuautla
Tuxtla
Arriaga
Pijijiapán
Escuintla
Huixtla
Tapachula
Ciudad Hidalgo
Chiapa de Corzo
San Cristóbal de Las Casas
Comitán
Presa de la Angostura
Teapa
Macuspana
Villahermosa
Comalcalco
Frontera
Carmen
Laguna de Términos
Río Usumacinta
Fransisco Escárcega
Champotón
Campeche
Yucatan Peninsula
Oxkutzcab
Tekax
Ticul
Peto
Umán
Mérida
Progreso
Motul
Rio Lagartos
Tizimín
Valladolid
Cancún
Isla Cozumel
Yucatan Channel
Felipe Carrillo Puerto
Chetumal
BELIZE
Gulf of Honduras
GUATEMALA
HONDURAS
EL SALVADOR
Elevation
Below sea level
-6000m -4000m -2000m -1000m -500m -250m 0 250m 500m 1000m 2000m 3000m 4000m 6000m
-19,658ft -13,124ft -6562ft -3281ft -1640ft -820ft -328ft/-100m 0 820ft 1640ft 3281ft 6562ft 9843ft 13,124ft 19,685ft

Central America

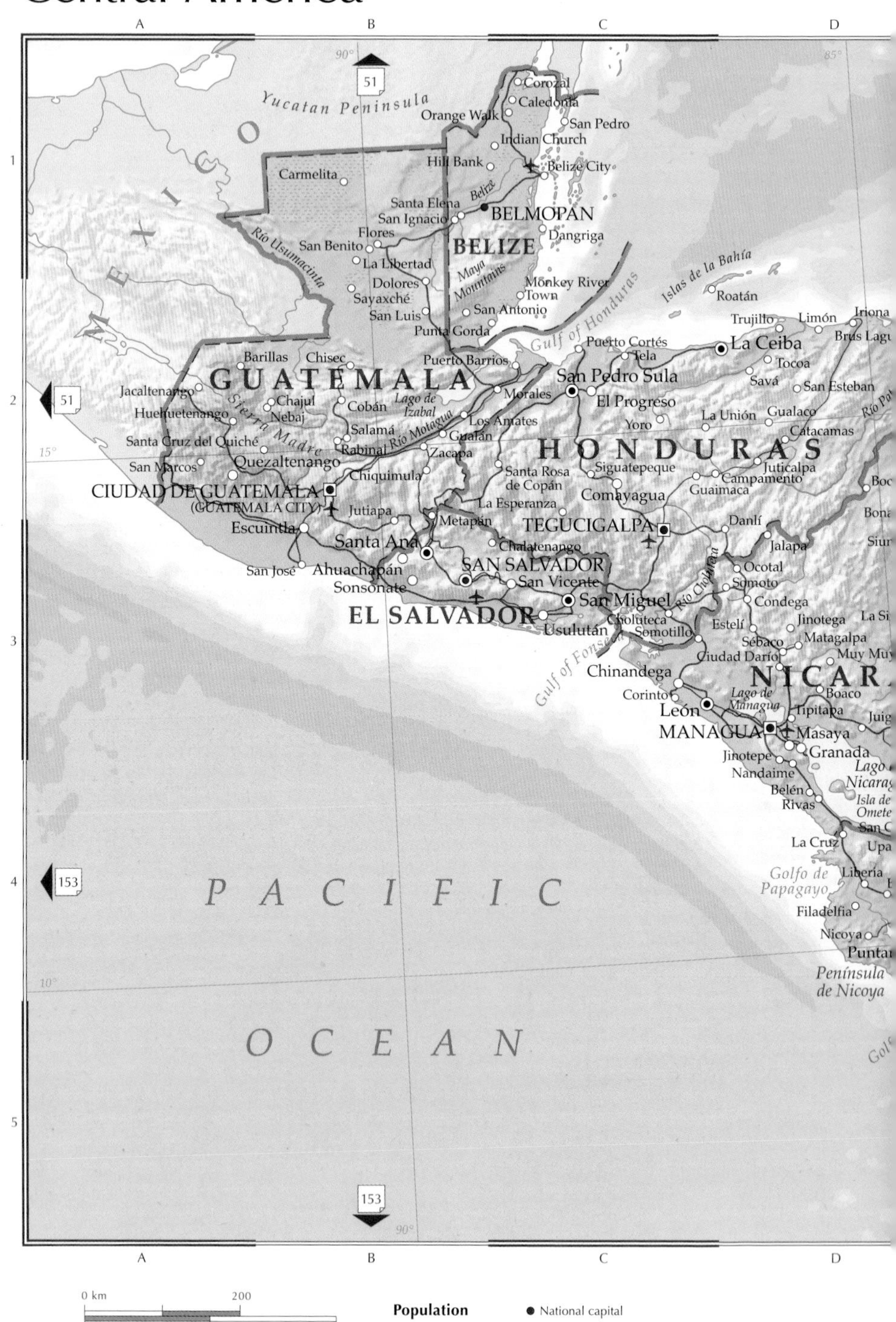

0 km 200
0 miles 200

Population

● National capital
○ below 50,000
○ 50,000 to 100,000
◉ 100,000 to 500,000
▣ above 500,000

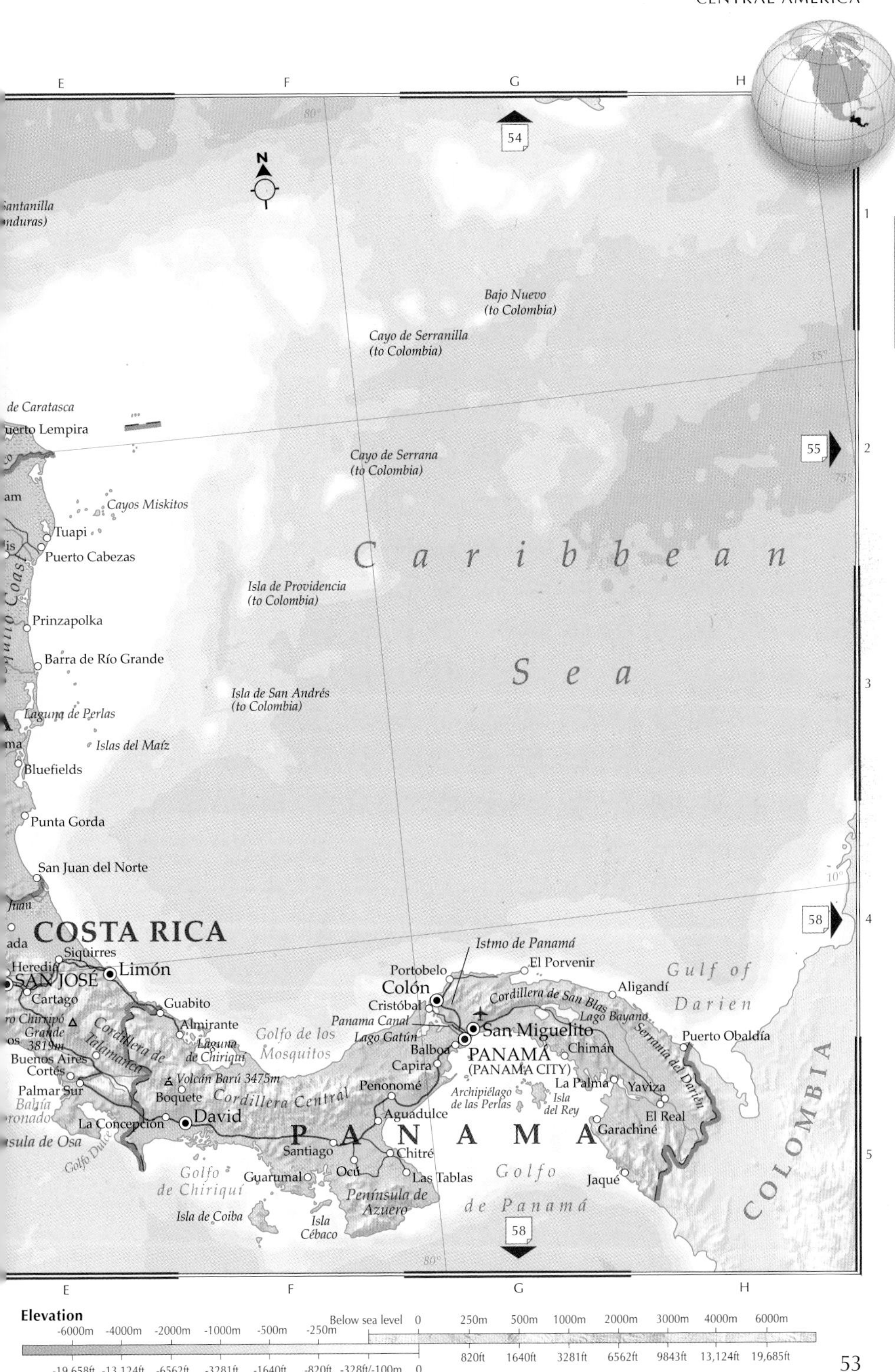

Caribbean Sea
Bajo Nuevo (to Colombia)
Cayo de Serranilla (to Colombia)
Cayo de Serrana (to Colombia)
Isla de Providencia (to Colombia)
Isla de San Andrés (to Colombia)
Cayos Miskitos
Tuapi
Puerto Cabezas
Prinzapolka
Barra de Río Grande
Laguna de Perlas
Islas del Maíz
Bluefields
Punta Gorda
San Juan del Norte
Puerto Lempira
de Caratasca
COSTA RICA
Siquirres
Heredia
SAN JOSÉ
Limón
Cartago
Guabito
Almirante
Laguna de Chiriquí
Cordillera de Talamanca
Grande 3819m
Buenos Aires
Cortés
Palmar Sur
La Concepción
David
Boquete
Volcán Barú 3475m
Cordillera Central
Golfo de los Mosquitos
Golfo de Chiriquí
Guarumal
Isla de Coiba
Golfo Dulce
PANAMA
Santiago
Ocú
Chitré
Las Tablas
Península de Azuero
Isla Cébaco
Aguadulce
Penonomé
Capira
Balboa
Lago Gatún
Panama Canal
Cristóbal
Colón
Portobelo
Istmo de Panamá
El Porvenir
Cordillera de San Blas
San Miguelito
PANAMÁ (PANAMA CITY)
Chimán
Lago Bayano
Serranía del Darién
Aligandí
Gulf of Darien
Puerto Obaldía
La Palma
Yaviza
El Real
Garachiné
Archipiélago de las Perlas
Isla del Rey
Golfo de Panamá
Jaqué
COLOMBIA
54
55
58
58
E F G H
1 2 3 4 5
Elevation
Below sea level 0 250m 500m 1000m 2000m 3000m 4000m 6000m
-6000m -4000m -2000m -1000m -500m -250m
820ft 1640ft 3281ft 6562ft 9843ft 13,124ft 19,685ft
-19,658ft -13,124ft -6562ft -3281ft -1640ft -820ft -328ft/-100m 0

The Caribbean

0 km 200
0 miles 200

Population
● National capital
○ below 50,000
○ 50,000 to 100,000
◉ 100,000 to 500,000
▣ above 500,000

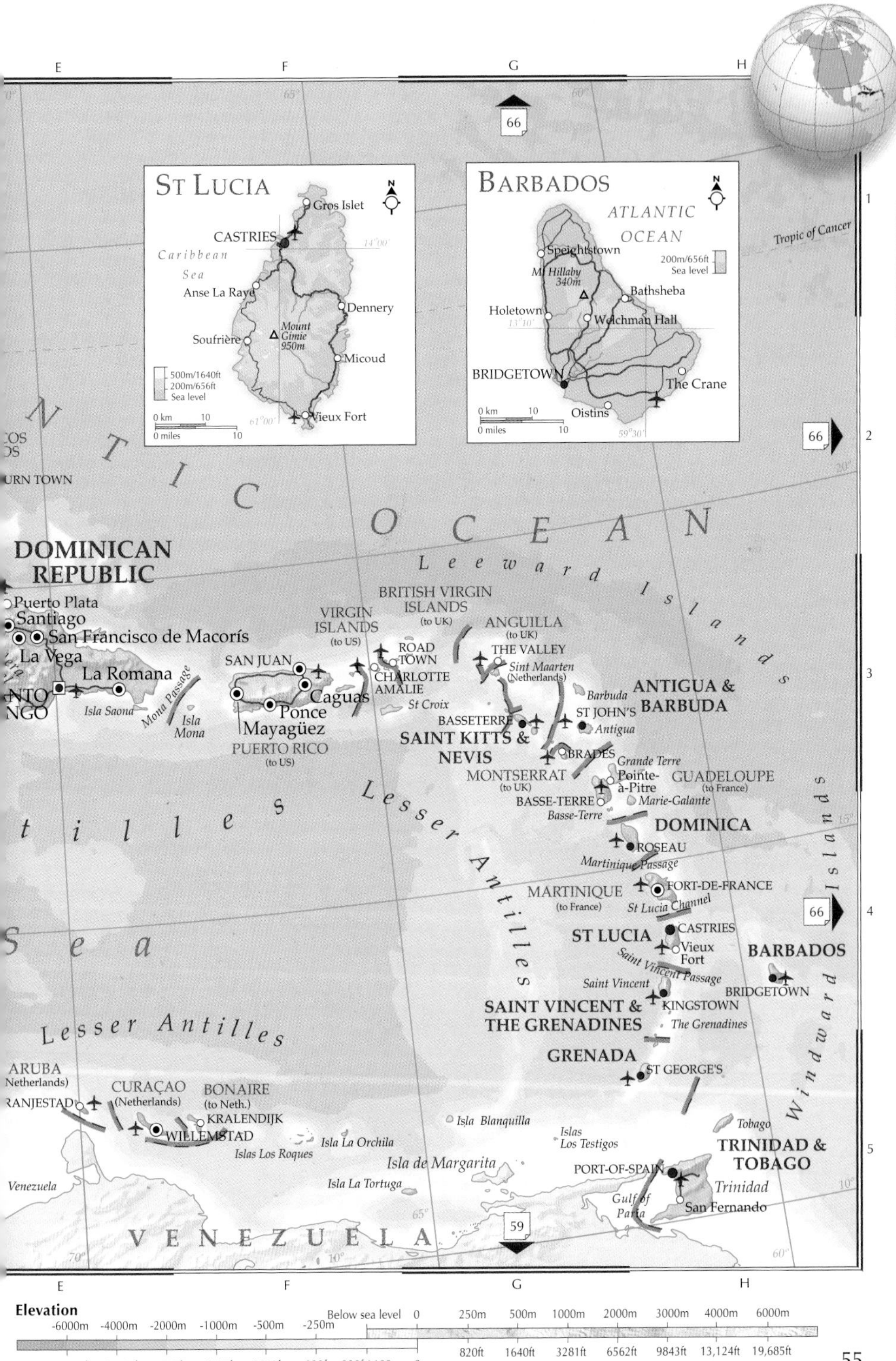

E
F
G
H
66
ST LUCIA
Gros Islet
CASTRIES
Caribbean Sea
14°00'
Anse La Raye
Dennery
Mount Gimie 950m
Soufrière
Micoud
500m/1640ft
200m/656ft
Sea level
0 km 10
0 miles 10
61°00'
Vieux Fort
BARBADOS
ATLANTIC OCEAN
Speightstown
Mt Hillaby 340m
200m/656ft
Sea level
Bathsheba
Holetown
13°10'
Welchman Hall
BRIDGETOWN
The Crane
0 km 10
0 miles 10
Oistins
59°30'
Tropic of Cancer
1
2
3
4
5
66
66
ATLANTIC OCEAN
DOMINICAN REPUBLIC
Puerto Plata
Santiago
San Francisco de Macorís
La Vega
La Romana
Isla Saona
Mona Passage
Isla Mona
SAN JUAN
Caguas
Ponce
Mayagüez
PUERTO RICO (to US)
VIRGIN ISLANDS (to US)
BRITISH VIRGIN ISLANDS (to UK)
ROAD TOWN
CHARLOTTE AMALIE
St Croix
ANGUILLA (to UK)
THE VALLEY
Sint Maarten (Netherlands)
Leeward Islands
Barbuda
ANTIGUA & BARBUDA
BASSETERRE
ST JOHN'S
Antigua
SAINT KITTS & NEVIS
BRADES
MONTSERRAT (to UK)
Grande Terre
Pointe-à-Pitre
GUADELOUPE (to France)
BASSE-TERRE
Basse-Terre
Marie-Galante
Lesser Antilles
DOMINICA
ROSEAU
Martinique Passage
MARTINIQUE (to France)
FORT-DE-FRANCE
St Lucia Channel
ST LUCIA
CASTRIES
Vieux Fort
Saint Vincent Passage
BARBADOS
BRIDGETOWN
Saint Vincent
KINGSTOWN
SAINT VINCENT & THE GRENADINES
The Grenadines
GRENADA
ST GEORGE'S
Windward Islands
Caribbean Sea
Lesser Antilles
ARUBA (Netherlands)
ORANJESTAD
CURAÇAO (Netherlands)
WILLEMSTAD
BONAIRE (to Neth.)
KRALENDIJK
Islas Los Roques
Isla La Orchila
Isla Blanquilla
Islas Los Testigos
Tobago
TRINIDAD & TOBAGO
Isla de Margarita
Isla La Tortuga
PORT-OF-SPAIN
Trinidad
Gulf of Paria
San Fernando
Venezuela
VENEZUELA
59
15°
10°
20°
65°
60°
70°
E
F
G
H
Elevation
Below sea level 0
-6000m -4000m -2000m -1000m -500m -250m
-19,658ft -13,124ft -6562ft -3281ft -1640ft -820ft -328ft/-100m 0
250m 500m 1000m 2000m 3000m 4000m 6000m
820ft 1640ft 3281ft 6562ft 9843ft 13,124ft 19,685ft

South America

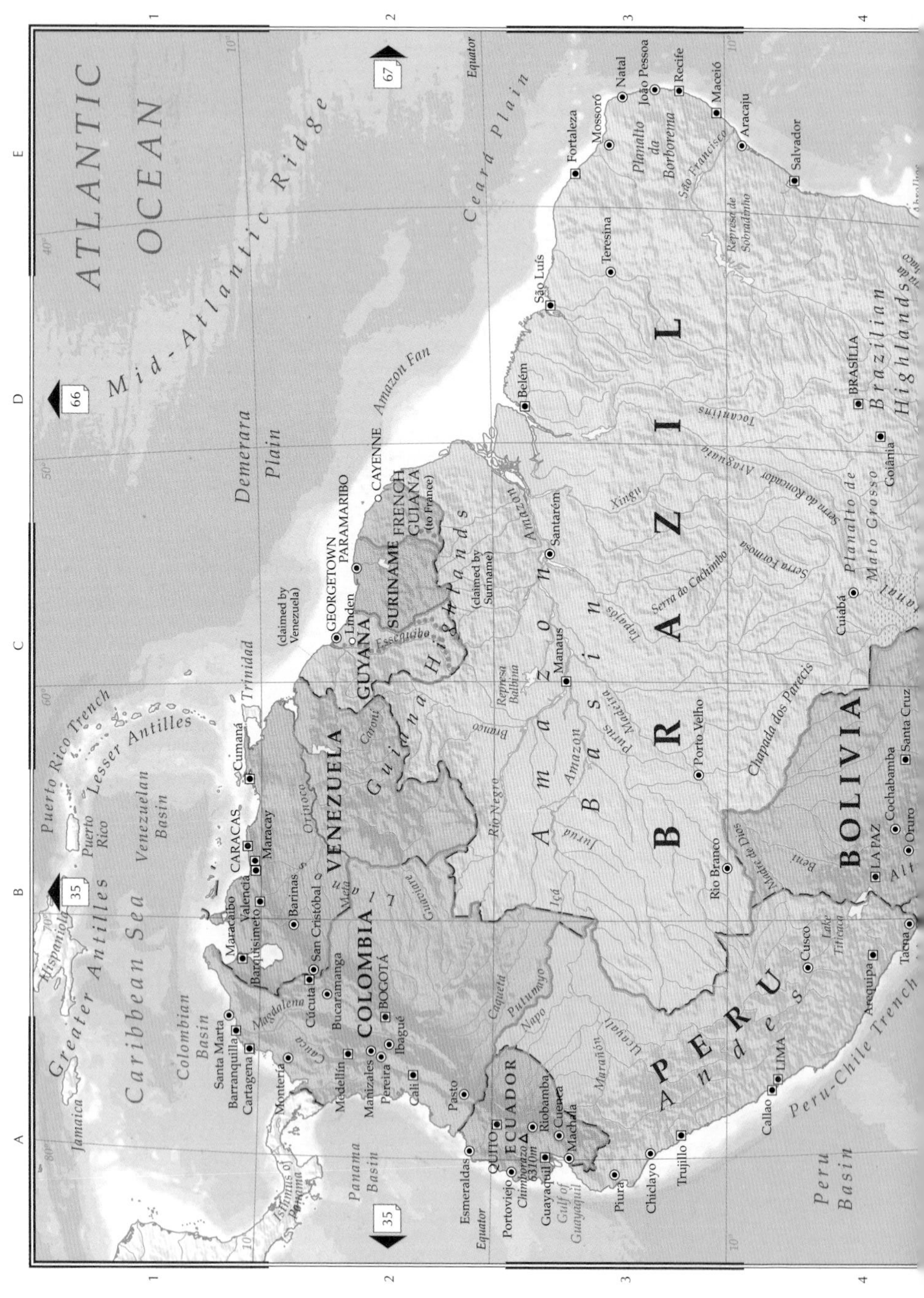

0 km 500
0 miles 500

Population

● National capital

○ below 50,000 ○ 50,000 to 100,000 ◉ 100,000 to 500,000 ▣ above 500,000

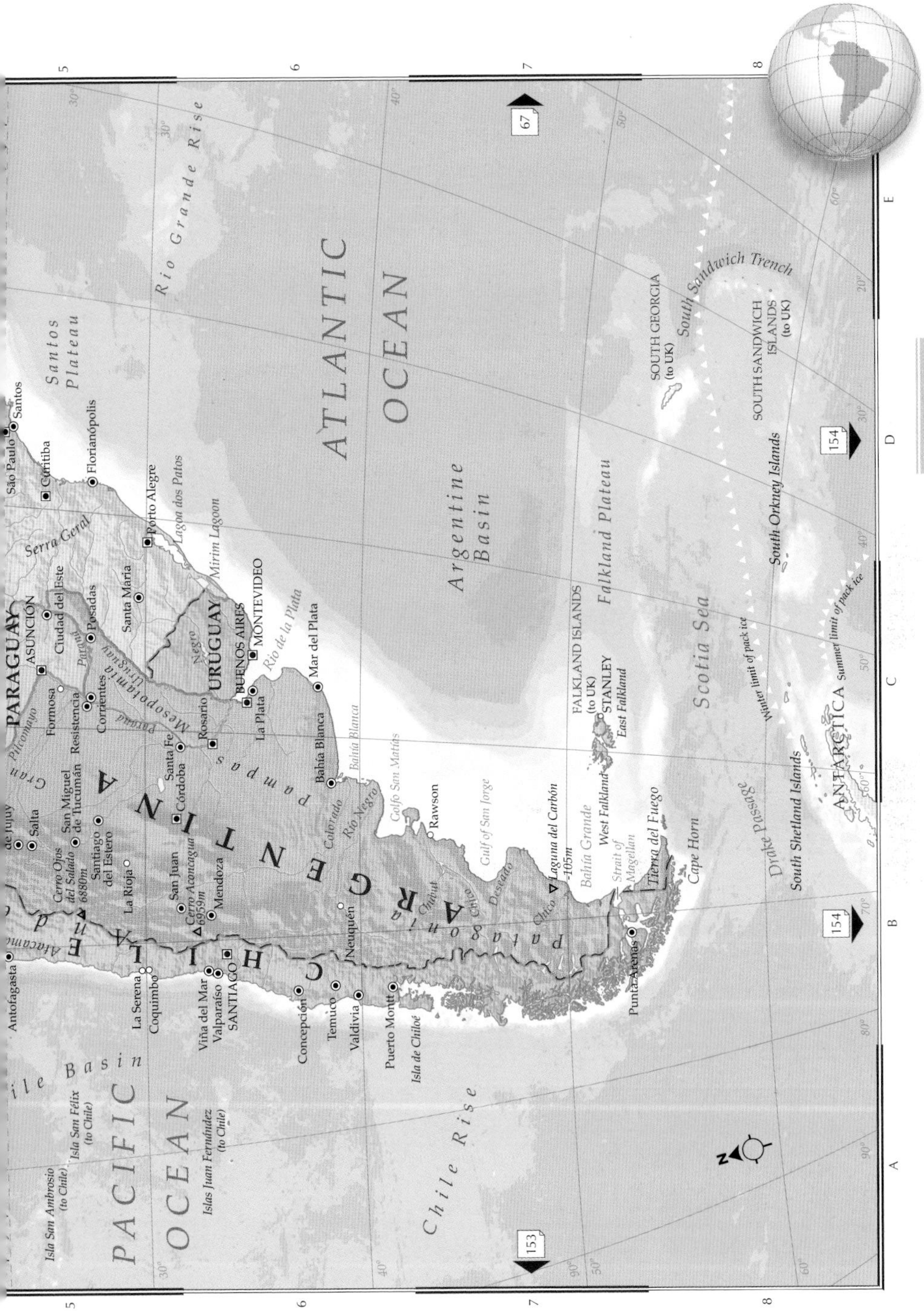

PACIFIC OCEAN
Chile Basin
Chile Rise
Isla San Ambrosio (to Chile)
Isla San Félix (to Chile)
Islas Juan Fernández (to Chile)
Antofagasta
La Serena
Coquimbo
Viña del Mar
Valparaíso
SANTIAGO
Concepción
Temuco
Valdivia
Puerto Montt
Isla de Chiloé
Punta Arenas
CHILE
Atacama
Cerro Ojos del Salado 6880m
Cerro Aconcagua 6959m
San Juan
Mendoza
La Rioja
Santiago del Estero
San Miguel de Tucumán
Salta
de Jujuy
Gran Chaco
Pilcomayo
ARGENTINA
Córdoba
Santa Fe
Rosario
Pampas
Neuquén
Colorado
Río Negro
Chubut
Chico
Deseado
Chico
Patagonia
Laguna del Carbón -105m
Bahía Blanca
Bahía Blanca
Golfo San Matías
Rawson
Gulf of San Jorge
Bahía Grande
Strait of Magellan
Tierra del Fuego
Cape Horn
PARAGUAY
ASUNCIÓN
Formosa
Resistencia
Corrientes
Ciudad del Este
Posadas
Paraná
Mesopotamia
Uruguay
Santa Maria
URUGUAY
Negro
BUENOS AIRES
MONTEVIDEO
La Plata
Río de la Plata
Mar del Plata
Serra Geral
Porto Alegre
Lagoa dos Patos
Mirim Lagoon
São Paulo
Santos
Curitiba
Florianópolis
Santos Plateau
Rio Grande Rise
ATLANTIC OCEAN
Argentine Basin
Falkland Plateau
FALKLAND ISLANDS (to UK)
STANLEY
East Falkland
West Falkland
SOUTH GEORGIA (to UK)
South Sandwich Trench
SOUTH SANDWICH ISLANDS (to UK)
South Orkney Islands
Scotia Sea
Winter limit of pack ice
Summer limit of pack ice
Drake Passage
South Shetland Islands
ANTARCTICA

67
153
154
154

Northern South America

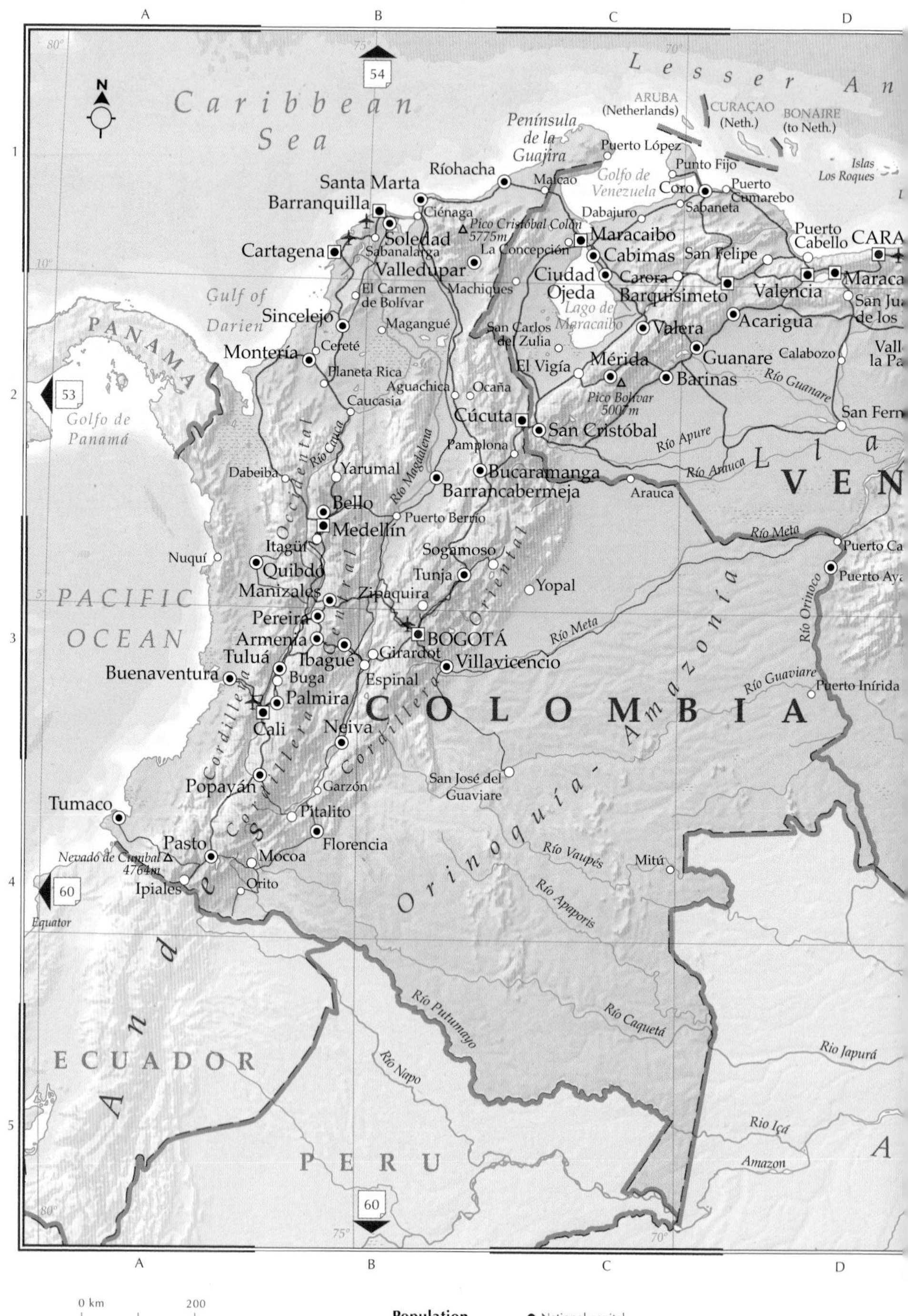

0 km 200

0 miles 200

Population

● National capital

○ below 50,000

○ 50,000 to 100,000

⊙ 100,000 to 500,000

◘ above 500,000

SAINT VINCENT & THE GRENADINES
BARBADOS
GRENADA
Isla Blanquilla
Isla de Margarita
Islas Los Testigos
Tobago
La Asunción
Carúpano
Güiria
Cariaco
Gulf of Paria
TRINIDAD & TOBAGO
Trinidad
Puerto La Cruz
Barcelona
The Serpent's Mouth
San Mateo
Maturín
Anaco
Cantaura
Tucupita
El Tigre
Río Orinoco
Ciudad Guayana
Ciudad Bolívar
Upata
Embalse de Guri
El Callao
Matthews Ridge
Charity
Spring Garden
Parika
GEORGETOWN
El Dorado
Cuyuni River
Aurora
New Amsterdam
Peters Mine
Bartica
Rockstone
Linden
Salto Angel
Kamarang
Río Paragua
Río Caura
Río Caroní
Mount Roraima 2810m
GUYANA
Orealla
Apoera
Totness
PARAMARIBO
Nieuw Amsterdam
Nieuw Nickerie
Kaaimanston
W. J. van Blommesteinmeer
Maroni River
St-Laurent-du-Maroni
Sinnamary
Kourou
CAYENNE
Montagnes de la Trinité
Montagne Tortue
Grand-Santi
Ouanary
Kurupukari
Pakaraima Mountains
SURINAME
Juliana Top 1230m
FRENCH GUIANA (to France)
St-Georges
Camopi
Lethem
(Venezuela claims all of Guyana west of Essequibo River)
Essequibo River
Courantyne River
Tumuc-Humac Mountains
(claimed by Suriname)
Acarai Mountains
Guiana Highlands
(claimed by Suriname)
ATLANTIC OCEAN
Equator
Negro
Amazon
BRAZIL
Amazon Basin
Rio Purus
Rio Tapajós
55
67
62
62
Elevation
Below sea level
-6000m -4000m -2000m -1000m -500m -250m 0
-19,658ft -13,124ft -6562ft -3281ft -1640ft -820ft -328ft/-100m 0
250m 500m 1000m 2000m 3000m 4000m 6000m
820ft 1640ft 3281ft 6562ft 9843ft 13,124ft 19,685ft

Western South America

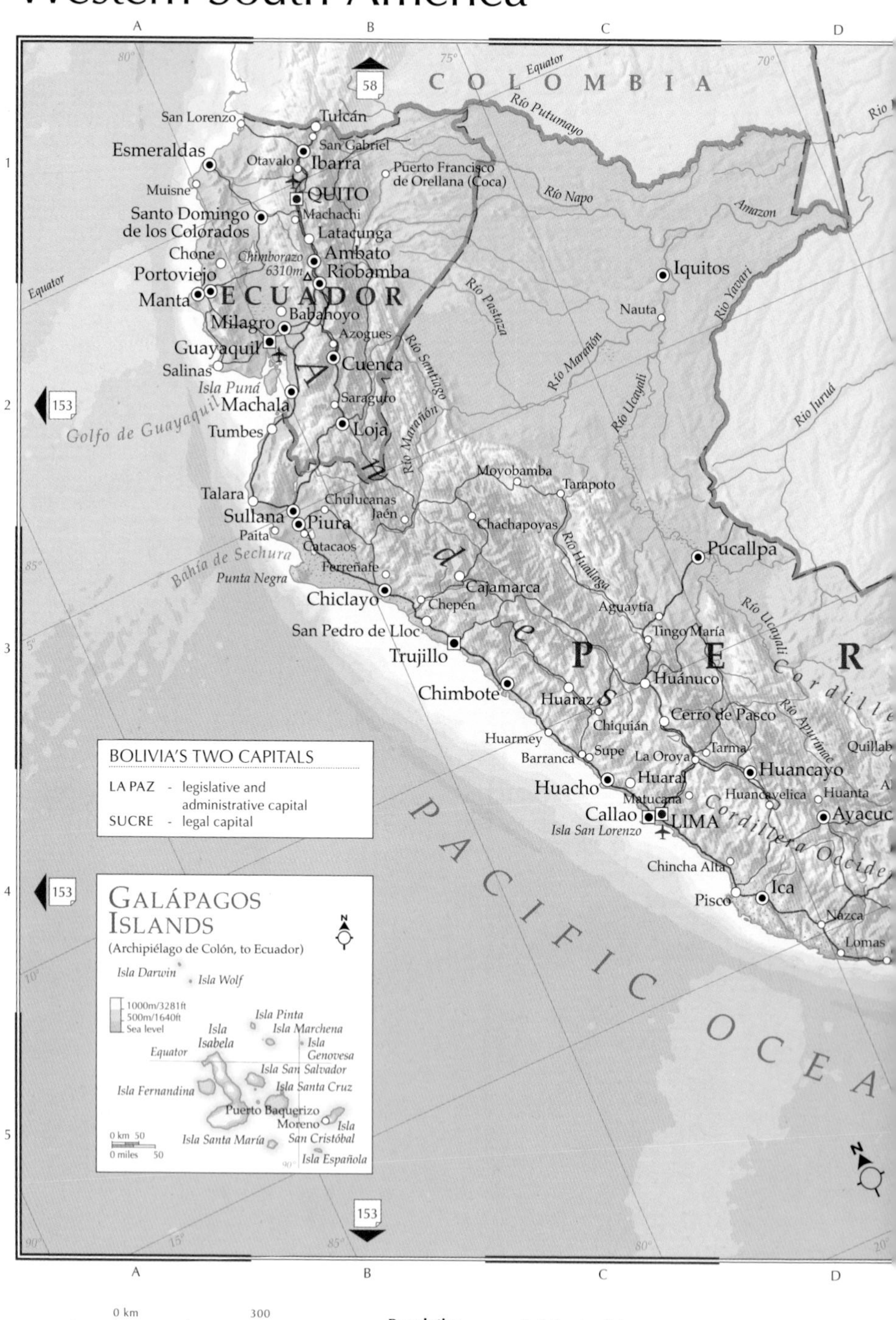

0 km 300

0 miles 300

Population

● National capital

○ below 50,000 ○ 50,000 to 100,000 ⊙ 100,000 to 500,000 ▣ above 500,000

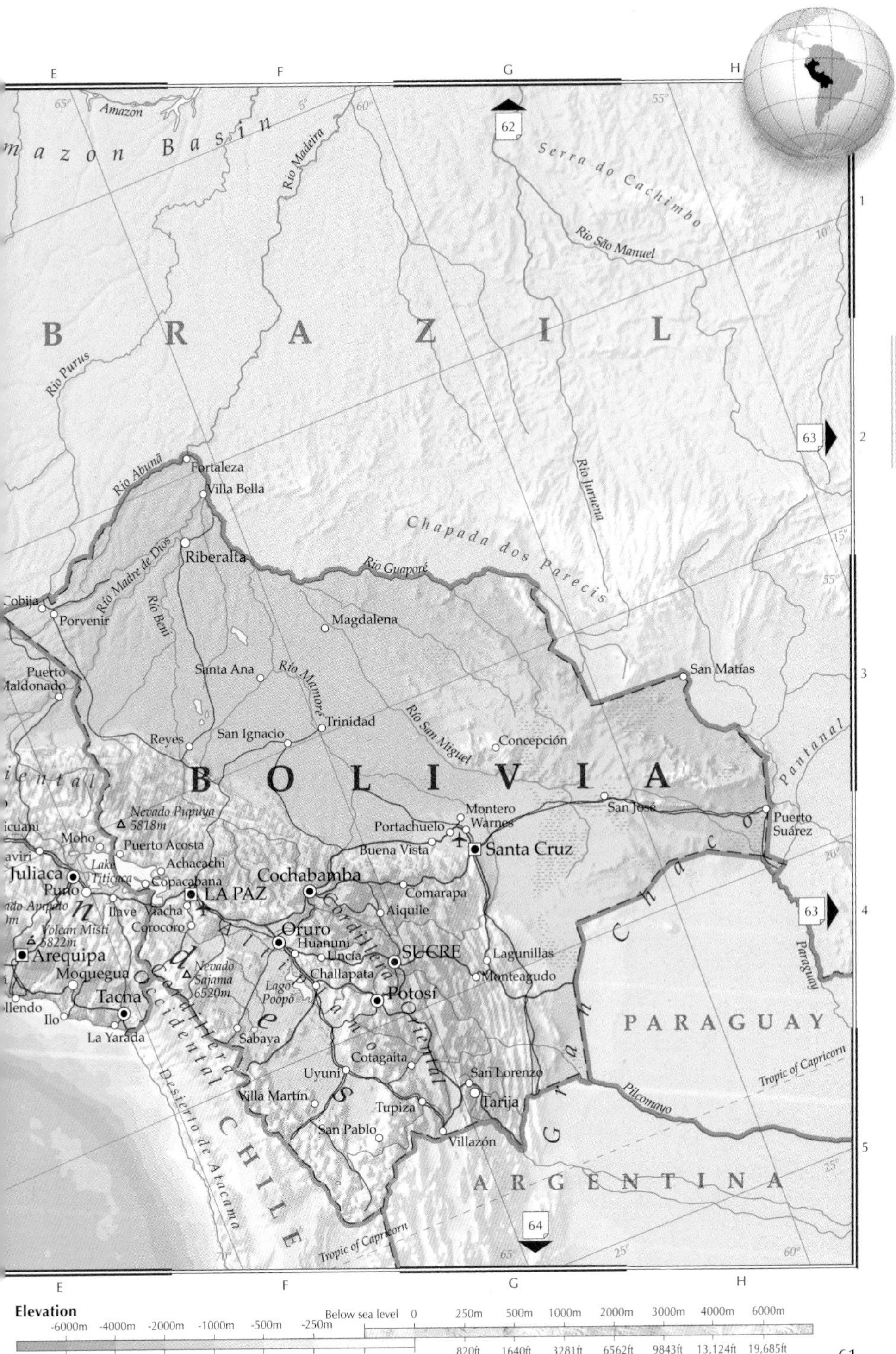

BRAZIL
BOLIVIA
PARAGUAY
ARGENTINA
CHILE
Amazon Basin
Serra do Cachimbo
Chapada dos Parecis
Gran Chaco
Pantanal
Cordillera Occidental
Cordillera Oriental
Desierto de Atacama
Río Madeira
Río São Manuel
Río Purus
Río Abunã
Río Madre de Dios
Río Beni
Río Mamoré
Río Guaporé
Río Juruena
Río San Miguel
Paraguay
Pilcomayo
Amazon
Fortaleza
Villa Bella
Riberalta
Cobija
Porvenir
Puerto Maldonado
Magdalena
Santa Ana
Trinidad
San Ignacio
Reyes
Concepción
San Matías
Montero
Warnes
Portachuelo
Buena Vista
Santa Cruz
San José
Puerto Suárez
Nevado Pupuya 5818m
Moho
Puerto Acosta
Achacachi
Lake Titicaca
Copacabana
LA PAZ
Juliaca
Puno
Ilave
Viacha
Corocoro
Cochabamba
Comarapa
Aiquile
Oruro
Huanuni
Uncía
SUCRE
Lagunillas
Monteagudo
Challapata
Potosí
Lago Poopó
Nevado Sajama 6520m
Volcán Misti 5822m
Arequipa
Moquegua
Tacna
Ilo
La Yarada
Sabaya
Cotagaita
Uyuni
Villa Martín
Tupiza
San Pablo
Villazón
San Lorenzo
Tarija
Tropic of Capricorn
62
63
64
E
F
G
H
1
2
3
4
5
Elevation
-6000m -4000m -2000m -1000m -500m -250m Below sea level 0 250m 500m 1000m 2000m 3000m 4000m 6000m
-19,658ft -13,124ft -6562ft -3281ft -1640ft -820ft -328ft/-100m 0 820ft 1640ft 3281ft 6562ft 9843ft 13,124ft 19,685ft

Brazil

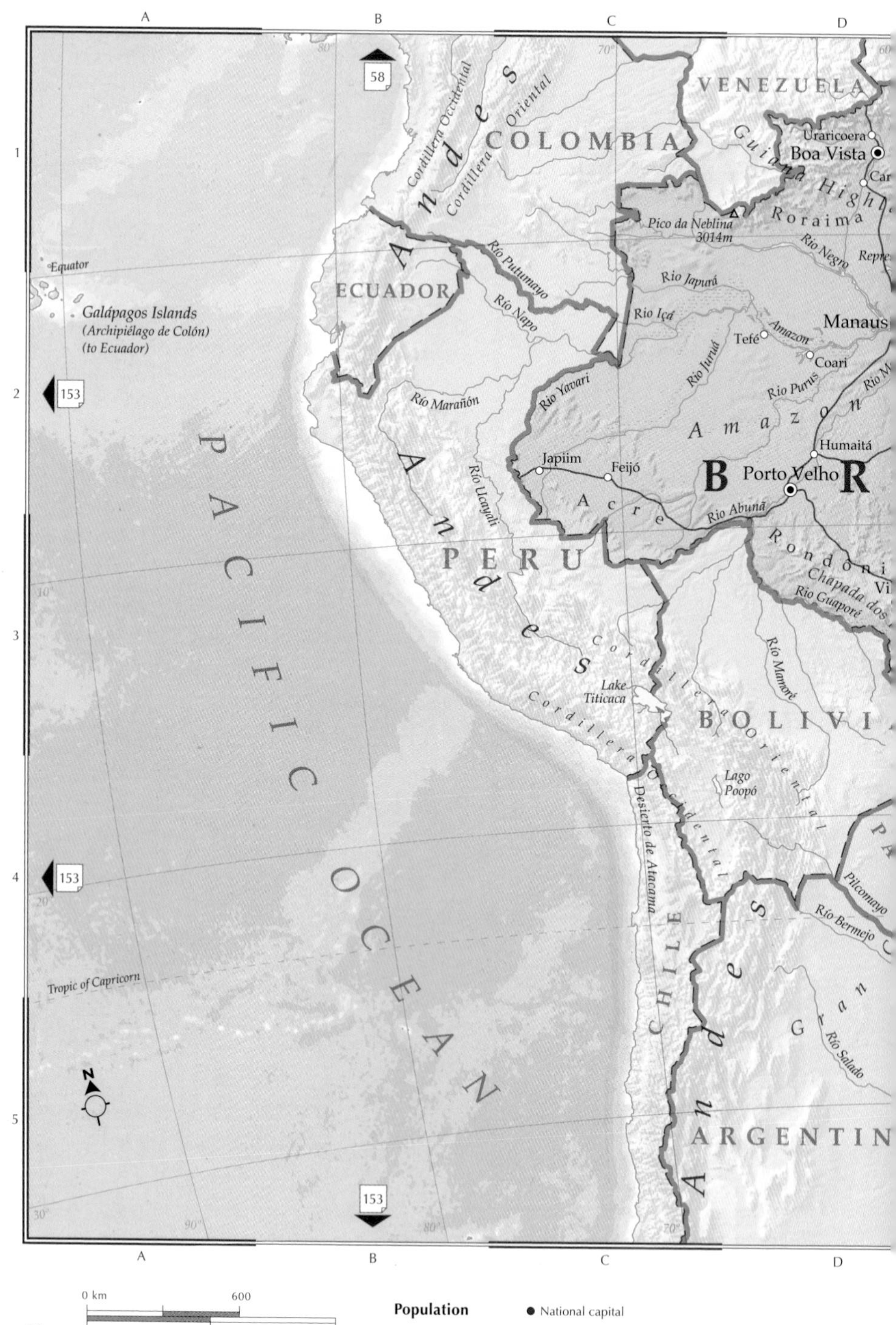

0 km 600

0 miles 600

Population

● National capital

○ below 50,000

○ 50,000 to 100,000

⊙ 100,000 to 500,000

▣ above 500,000

E
F
G
H
66
67
67
67
1
2
3
4
5
FRENCH GUIANA (to France)
Tumuc-Humac Mountains
Amapá
Macapá
Mouths of the Amazon
Ilha Caviana de Fora
Ilha de Marajó
Baía de Marajó
Belém
Baía de São Marcos
Amazon
ATLANTIC OCEAN
Equator
São Luís
Parnaíba
Camocim
Altamira
Bacabal
Piripiri
Fortaleza
Atol das Rocas
San Fernando de Noronha (to Brazil)
Represa de Tucuruí
Teresina
Imperatriz
Marabá
Rio Xingu
Pará
Maranhão
Ceará
Mossoró
Assu
Cabo de São Roque
Natal
Rio Grande do Norte
Floriano
Juazeiro do Norte
Carolina
Balsas
Picos
Paraíba
João Pessoa
Campina Grande
Piauí
Pernambuco
Recife
Alagoas
Represa de Sobradinho
Juazeiro
Maceió
Rio Tocantins
Serra dos Gradaús
Serra Formosa
Palmas do Tocantins
Tocantins
Rio São Francisco
Chapada Diamantina
Aracaju
Estância
Taguatinga
Rio São Francisco
Feira de Santana
Salvador
Baía de Todos os Santos
Bahia
Rio Araguaia
Goiás
Planalto Central
Cuiabá
BRASÍLIA
Itabuna
Janaúba
Vitória da Conquista
Anápolis
Goiânia
Canavieiras
Montes Claros
Jataí
Araçuaí
Minas Gerais
Araguari
Mato Grosso do Sul
Governador Valadares
Espírito Santo
Uberlândia
Uberaba
Campo Grande
Belo Horizonte
Divinópolis
Vitória
Ribeirão Preto
Juiz de Fora
Campos dos Goytacazes
Marília
São Paulo
Campinas
Londrina
Maringá
Nova Iguaçu
Rio de Janeiro
São Paulo
Santos
Paraná
Represa de Itaipú
Ponta Grossa
Curitiba
Saltos do Iguaçu
Rio Iguaçu
Tropic of Capricorn
Joinville
Blumenau
Santa Catarina
Florianópolis
Passo Fundo
Rio Grande do Sul
Canoas
Porto Alegre
Bagé
Lagoa dos Patos
Rio Grande
Mirim Lagoon
Elevation
Below sea level
0
250m
500m
1000m
2000m
3000m
4000m
6000m
-6000m
-4000m
-2000m
-1000m
-500m
-250m
820ft
1640ft
3281ft
6562ft
9843ft
13,124ft
19,685ft
-19,658ft
-13,124ft
-6562ft
-3281ft
-1640ft
-820ft
-328ft/-100m

Southern South America

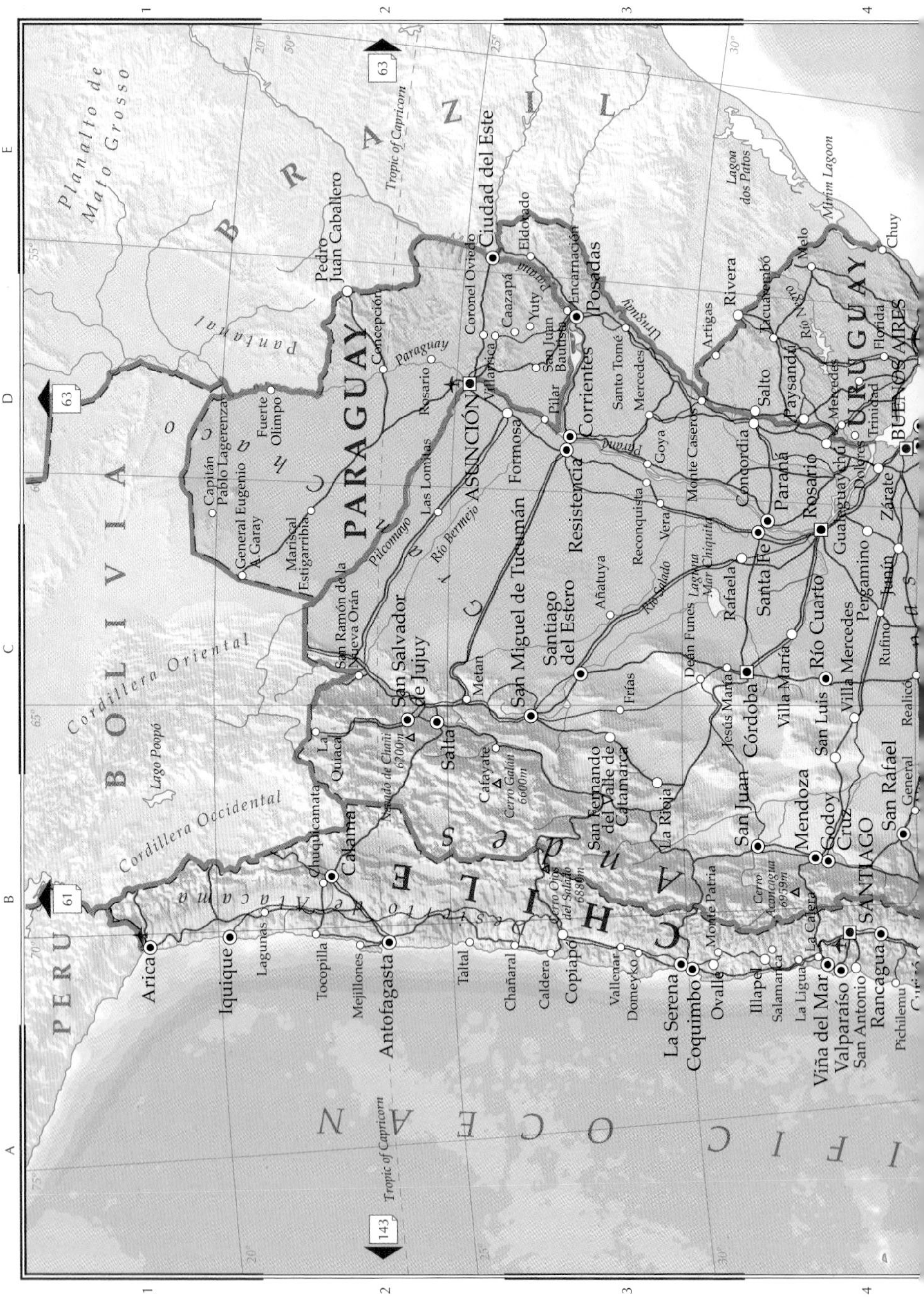

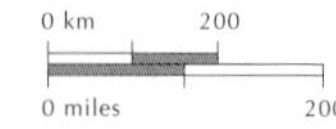

Population

● National capital

○ below 50,000 ○ 50,000 to 100,000 ⦿ 100,000 to 500,000  above 500,000

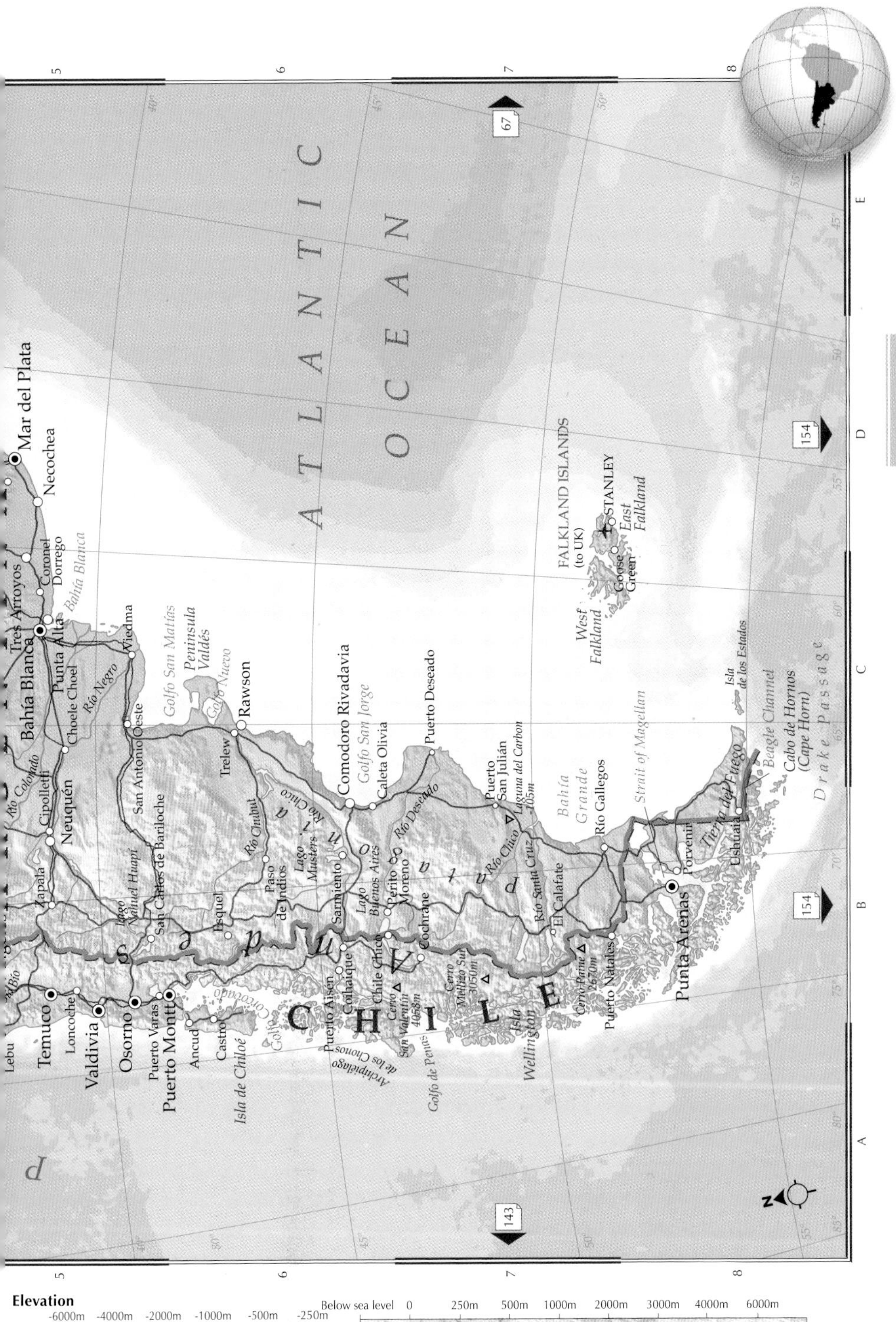

Elevation

Below sea level: -6000m (-19,658ft), -4000m (-13,124ft), -2000m (-6562ft), -1000m (-3281ft), -500m (-1640ft), -250m (-820ft), -328ft/-100m, 0

Above sea level: 0, 250m (820ft), 500m (1640ft), 1000m (3281ft), 2000m (6562ft), 3000m (9843ft), 4000m (13,124ft), 6000m (19,685ft)

The Atlantic Ocean

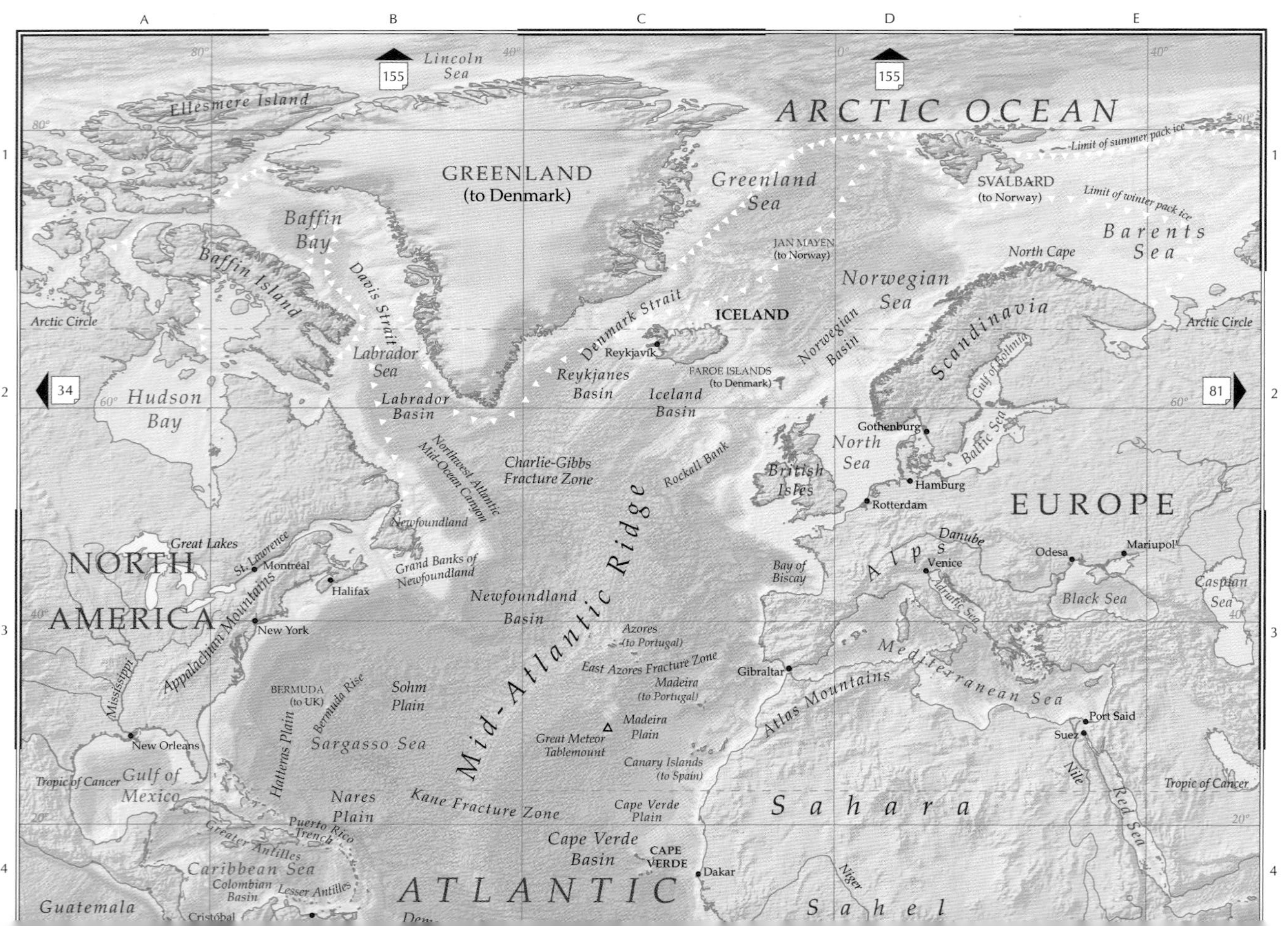

SOUTH AMERICA
Andes
Recife
Fernando de Noronha (to Brazil)
Rio de Janeiro
Buenos Aires
Paraná
Peru-Chile Trench
Peru Basin
Chile Basin
PACIFIC OCEAN
Tropic of Capricorn
Chile Rise
Mornington Abyssal Plain
Bellingshausen Plain
Bellingshausen Sea
Antarctic Circle
Brazil Basin
Ilha da Trindade (to Brazil)
Vitória Seamount
Santos Plateau
Rio Grande Rise
Argentine Basin
Gulf of San Matías
Gulf of San Jorge
Zapiola Ridge
FALKLAND ISLANDS (to UK)
Falkland Plateau
Yaghan Basin
Cape Horn
Drake Passage
South Shetland Islands
Scotia Sea
South Orkney Islands
SOUTH GEORGIA (to UK)
East Scotia Basin
South Sandwich Trench
SOUTH SANDWICH ISLANDS (to UK)
America-Antarctica Ridge
Weddell Plain
Weddell Sea
SOUTHERN OCEAN
ANTARCTICA
Mid - Atlantic Ridge
Gough Fracture Zone
Ascension Fracture
ASCENSION ISLAND (to UK)
ST HELENA (to UK)
TRISTAN DA CUNHA (to UK)
Gough Island (to Tristan da Cunha)
Spiess Seamount
BOUVET ISLAND (to Norway)
Atlantic-Indian Ridge
Atlantic-Indian Basin
Lazarev Sea
Angola Basin
Lobito
Zuboz Seamount
Walvis Ridge
Cape Basin
Orange Fan
Cape Town
Cape of Good Hope
Agulhas Plateau
Agulhas Basin
Southwest Indian Ridge
Enderby Plain
Limit of winter pack ice
Limit of summer pack ice
Lake Tanganyika
Lake Nyasa
Zambezi
Mozambique Channel
Madagascar
Mozambique Plateau
INDIAN OCEAN

141
153
154
154

Elevation

-6000m	-4000m	-2000m	-1000m	-250m	0
-19,658ft	-13,124ft	-6562ft	-3281ft	-820ft	0

Africa

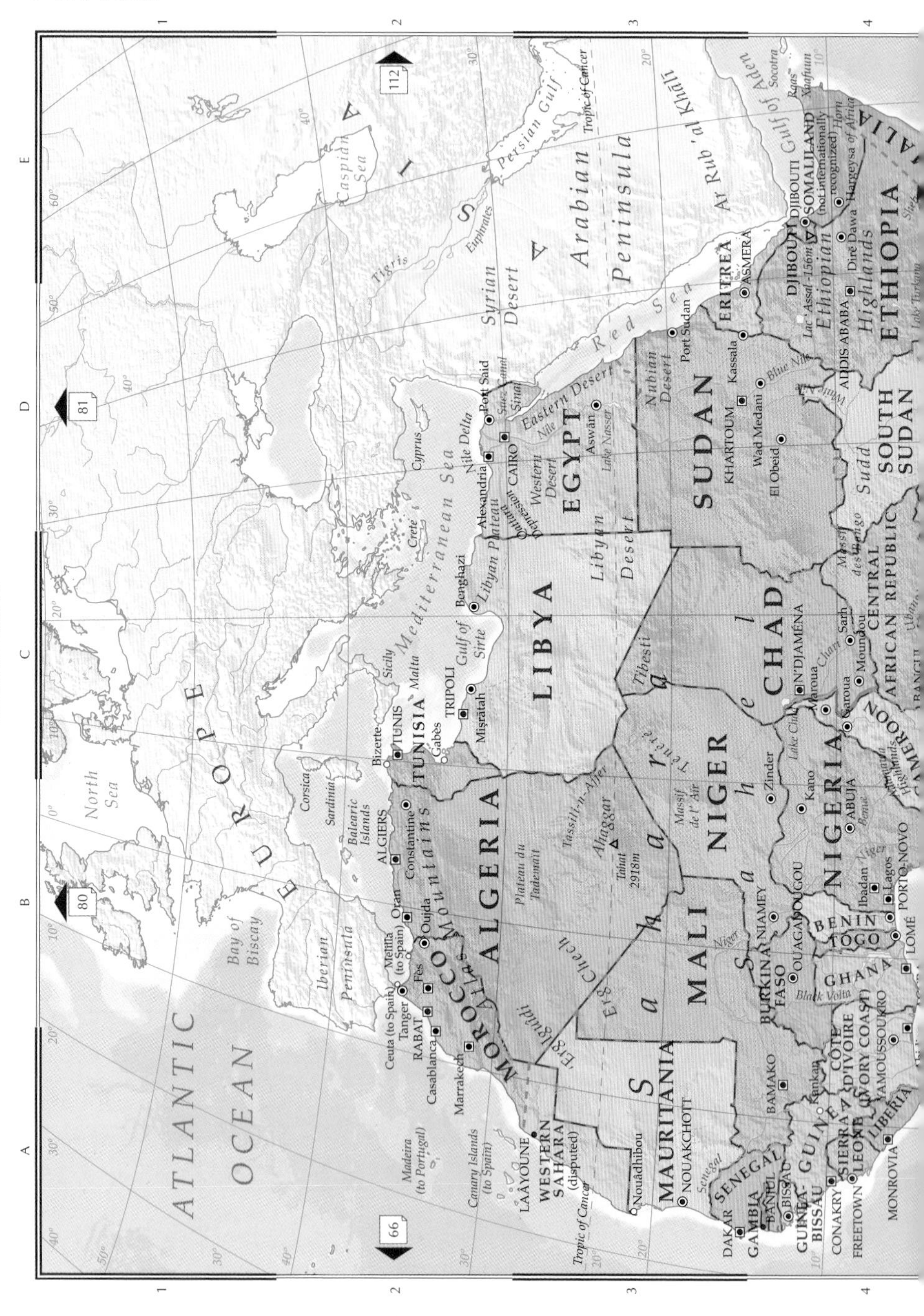

0 km 1000
0 miles 1000

Population
● National capital
○ below 50,000
○ 50,000 to 100,000
◉ 100,000 to 500,000
◼ above 500,000

Mid-Atlantic Ridge
Ascension Fracture Zone
ASCENSION ISLAND (to UK)
SAINT HELENA (to UK)
ATLANTIC OCEAN
Angola Basin
Tropic of Capricorn
Walvis Ridge
Orange Fan
Cape Basin
TRISTAN DA CUNHA (to UK)
Gough Island (to Tristan da Cunha)
Atlantic-Indian Ridge
Winter limit of pack ice
CONGO
BRAZZAVILLE
KINSHASA
Cabinda (to Angola)
Matadi
Ilebo
Kananga
Kasai
Lualaba
Cuango
Cuanza
LUANDA
ANGOLA
Bié Plateau
Môco 2619m
Huambo
Lubango
Namibe
Cunene
Cubango
Cuando
Etosha Pan
NAMIBIA
WINDHOEK
Namib Desert
Nossob
Orange River
Okavango Delta
Francistown
BOTSWANA
Kalahari Desert
GABORONE
PRETORIA
Johannesburg
Vaal
SOUTH AFRICA
LESOTHO
MASERU
BLOEMFONTEIN
Great Karoo
Drakensberg
CAPE TOWN
Cape of Good Hope
Port Elizabeth
East London
Durban
MAPUTO
MBABANE
SWAZILAND
Limpopo
ZIMBABWE
HARARE
Bulawayo
Lake Kariba
Victoria Falls
ZAMBIA
LUSAKA
Zambezi
Lubumbashi
Kitwe
Ndola
Lake Mweru
Luvua
Kalemie
Great Rift Valley
BUJUMBURA
BURUNDI
Lake Tanganyika
DODOMA
TANZANIA
Lake Rukwa
Masai Steppe
5895m
Mombasa
Tanga
Pemba
Zanzibar
Dar es Salaam
MALAWI
LILONGWE
Lake Nyasa
Ruvuma
Blantyre
Lurio
MOZAMBIQUE
Beira
Nampula
Nacala
Mozambique Channel
Mozambique Plateau
COMOROS
MORONI
MAYOTTE (to France)
Aldabra Group
Somali Basin
MADAGASCAR
Mahajanga
ANTANANARIVO
Fianarantsoa
Toliara
Madagascar Plateau
Madagascar Basin
INDIAN OCEAN
Agulhas Plateau
Agulhas Basin
Southwest Indian Ridge
Crozet Plateau
Prince Edward Islands (to South Africa)
67
141
154
154

Northwest Africa

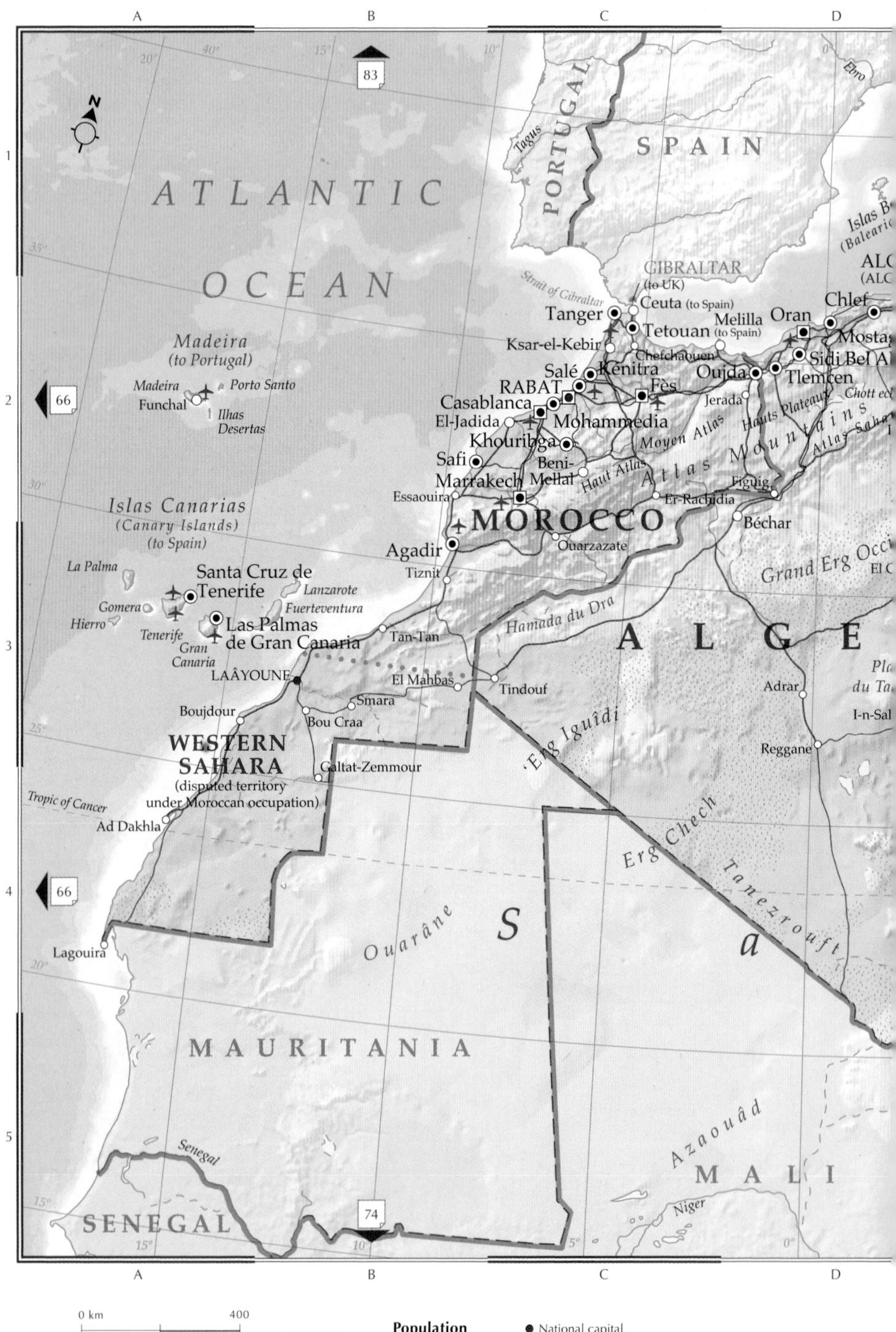

0 km 400

0 miles 400

Population

● National capital

○ below 50,000 ○ 50,000 to 100,000 ◉ 100,000 to 500,000 ▣ above 500,000

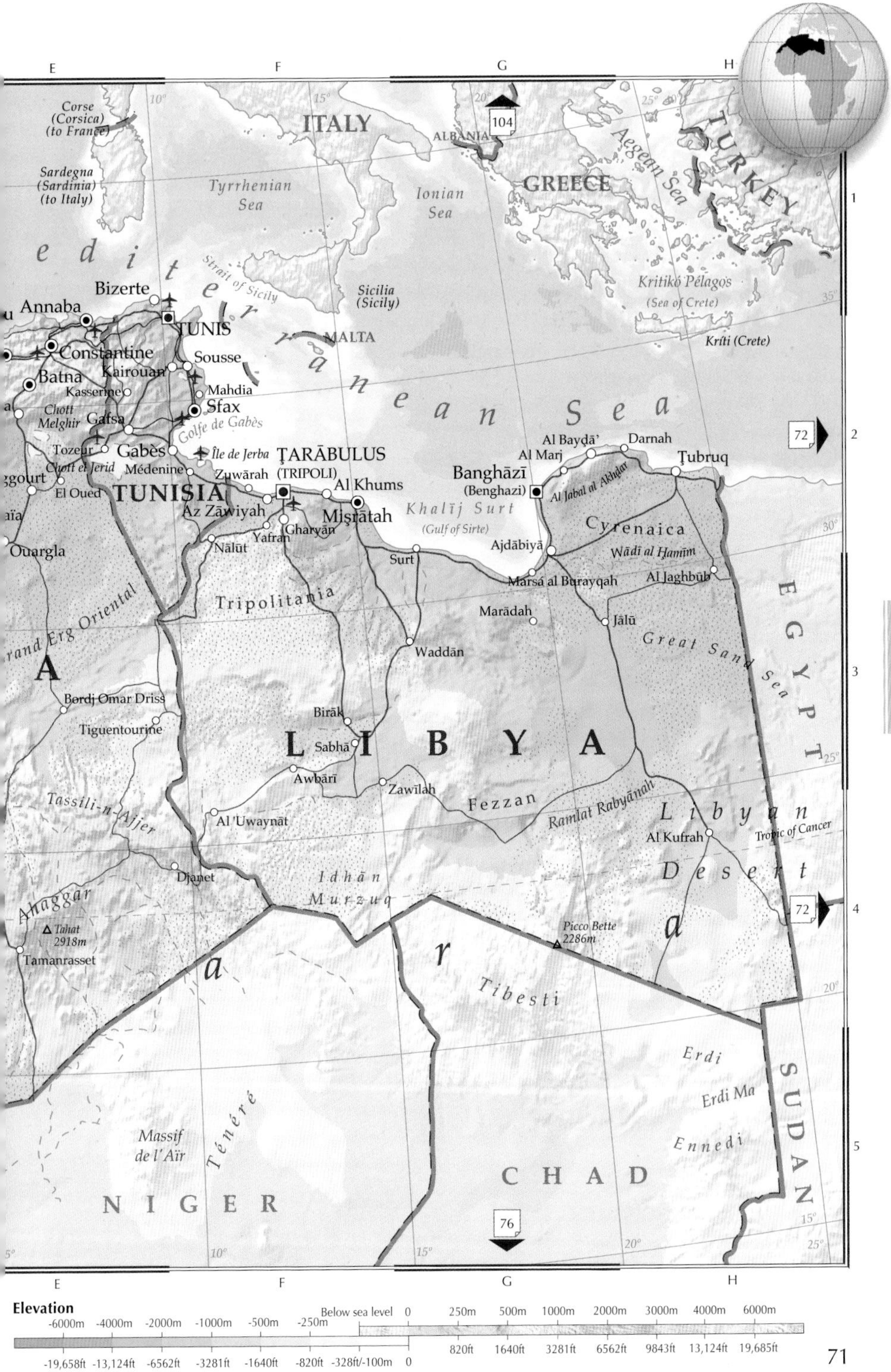

E F G H

Corse (Corsica) (to France)
ITALY
104
ALBANIA
Sardegna (Sardinia) (to Italy)
Tyrrhenian Sea
Ionian Sea
GREECE
Aegean Sea
TURKEY
Mediterranean Sea
Strait of Sicily
Sicilia (Sicily)
Kritikó Pélagos (Sea of Crete)
Kríti (Crete)
MALTA
Bizerte
Annaba
TUNIS
Constantine
Sousse
Kairouan
Batna
Kasserine
Mahdia
Sfax
Chott Melghir
Gafsa
Golfe de Gabès
Tozeur
Gabès
Île de Jerba
ṬARĀBULUS (TRIPOLI)
Al Bayḍā'
Darnah
Al Marj
Ṭubruq
72
Chott el Jerid
Médenine
Zuwārah
Al Khums
Banghāzī (Benghazi)
Al Jabal al Akhḍar
El Oued
TUNISIA
Az Zāwiyah
Miṣrātah
Khalīj Surt (Gulf of Sirte)
Yafran
Gharyān
Cyrenaica
Nālūt
Ouargla
Surt
Ajdābiyā
Wādī al Ḥamīm
Marsá al Burayqah
Al Jaghbūb
EGYPT
Tripolitania
Marādah
Jālū
Grand Erg Oriental
Waddān
Great Sand Sea
Bordj Omar Driss
Tiguentourine
Birāk
LIBYA
Sabhā
Awbārī
Zawīlah
Fezzan
Ramlat Rabyānah
Libyan Desert
Tassili-n-Ajjer
Al 'Uwaynāt
Al Kufrah
Tropic of Cancer
Djanet
Idhān Murzuq
Ahaggar
72
Tahat 2918m
Picco Bette 2286m
Tamanrasset
Sahara
Tibesti
Erdi
Erdi Ma
SUDAN
Ennedi
Massif de l'Aïr
Ténéré
CHAD
NIGER
76

E F G H

1 2 3 4 5

Elevation

Below sea level	-6000m	-4000m	-2000m	-1000m	-500m	-250m	0	250m	500m	1000m	2000m	3000m	4000m	6000m
	-19,658ft	-13,124ft	-6562ft	-3281ft	-1640ft	-820ft	-328ft/-100m 0	820ft	1640ft	3281ft	6562ft	9843ft	13,124ft	19,685ft

Northeast Africa

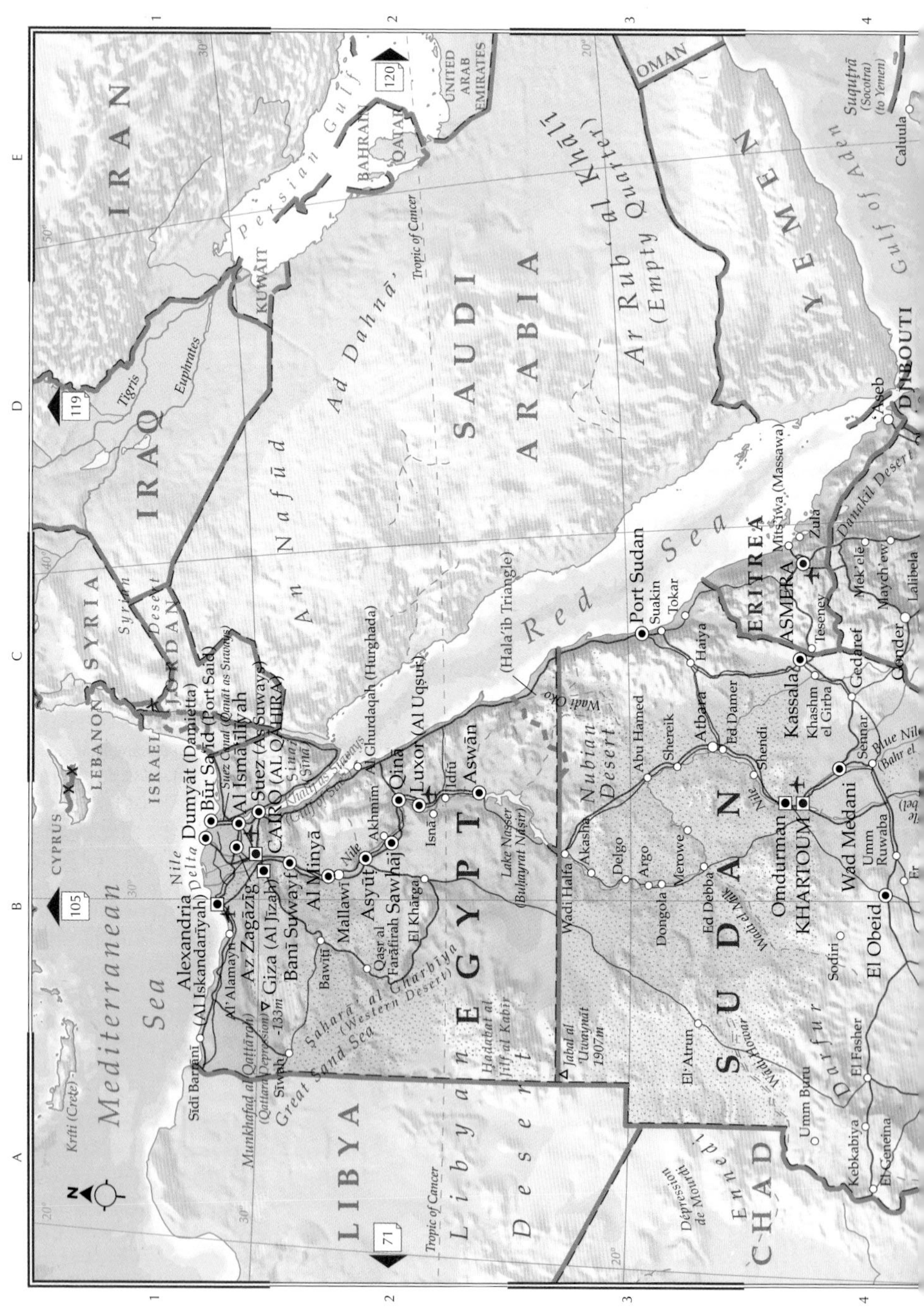

0 km 400
0 miles 400

Population

● National capital

○ below 50,000 ○ 50,000 to 100,000 ◉ 100,000 to 500,000 ▣ above 500,000

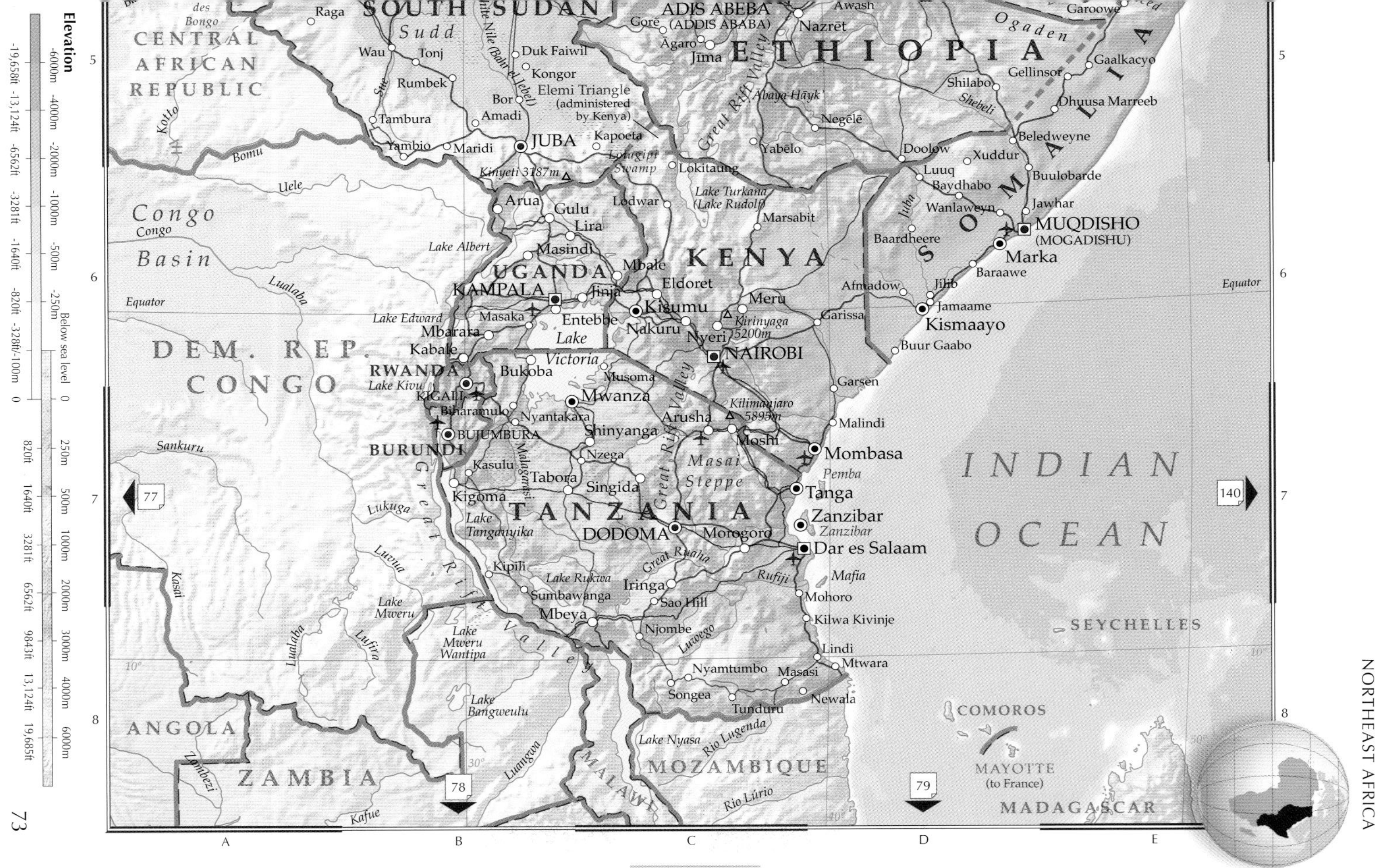
SOUTH SUDAN
CENTRAL AFRICAN REPUBLIC
ETHIOPIA
SOMALIA
KENYA
UGANDA
RWANDA
BURUNDI
TANZANIA
DEM. REP. CONGO
ANGOLA
ZAMBIA
MALAWI
MOZAMBIQUE
INDIAN OCEAN
SEYCHELLES
COMOROS
MAYOTTE (to France)
MADAGASCAR
ADIS ABEBA (ADDIS ABABA)
MUQDISHO (MOGADISHU)
JUBA
KAMPALA
NAIROBI
KIGALI
BUJUMBURA
DODOMA
Dar es Salaam
Zanzibar
Tanga
Mombasa
Malindi
Kismaayo
Marka
Baraawe
Jamaame
Jilib
Buur Gaabo
Baardheere
Wanlaweyn
Jawhar
Buulobarde
Beledweyne
Xuddur
Luuq
Baydhabo
Doolow
Gellinsor
Gaalkacyo
Dhuusa Marreeb
Garoowe
Shilabo
Negēlē
Yabēlo
Nazrēt
Awash
Jīma
Agaro
Gorē
Raga
Wau
Tonj
Rumbek
Tambura
Yambio
Maridi
Amadi
Bor
Duk Faiwil
Kongor
Elemi Triangle (administered by Kenya)
Kapoeta
Lokitaung
Lodwar
Marsabit
Arua
Gulu
Lira
Masindi
Mbale
Jinja
Entebbe
Masaka
Mbarara
Kabale
Eldoret
Kisumu
Nakuru
Nyeri
Meru
Garissa
Afmadow
Garsen
Bukoba
Musoma
Mwanza
Biharamulo
Nyantakara
Shinyanga
Arusha
Moshi
Nzega
Kasulu
Tabora
Singida
Kigoma
Morogoro
Kipili
Sumbawanga
Iringa
Sao Hill
Mbeya
Njombe
Mohoro
Kilwa Kivinje
Lindi
Mtwara
Masasi
Newala
Nyamtumbo
Songea
Tunduru
Kinyeti 3187m
Kirinyaga 5200m
Kilimanjaro 5895m
Lake Albert
Lake Edward
Lake Kivu
Lake Victoria
Lake Turkana (Lake Rudolf)
Lake Tanganyika
Lake Rukwa
Lake Mweru
Lake Mweru Wantipa
Lake Bangweulu
Lake Nyasa
Abaya Hāyk'
Lotagipi Swamp
Sudd
Ogaden
Great Rift Valley
Masai Steppe
Congo Basin
Congo
Lualaba
Uele
Bomu
Kotto
Sankuru
Kasai
Lukuga
Luvua
Lufira
Zambezi
Kafue
Luangwa
Rio Lugenda
Rio Lúrio
Ruvuma
Luwego
Rufiji
Great Ruaha
Malagarasi
Juba
Shebeli
White Nile (Bahr el Jebel)
Pemba
Mafia
Equator
Elevation
-6000m
-4000m
-2000m
-1000m
-500m
-250m
Below sea level
0
250m
500m
1000m
2000m
3000m
4000m
6000m
-19,658ft
-13,124ft
-6562ft
-3281ft
-1640ft
-820ft
-328ft/-100m
0
820ft
1640ft
3281ft
6562ft
9843ft
13,124ft
19,685ft

West Africa

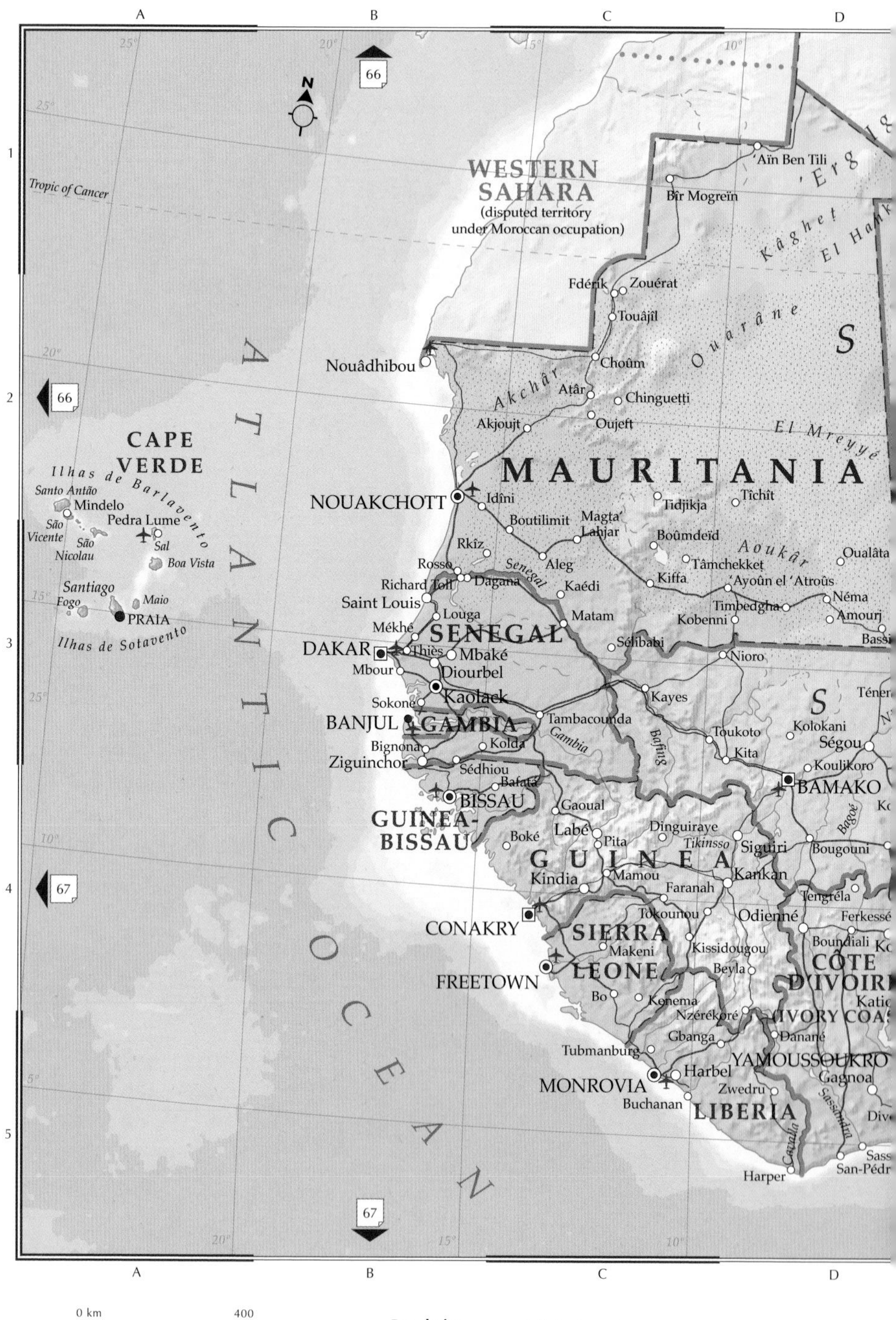

0 km 400
0 miles 400

Population
● National capital
○ below 50,000
○ 50,000 to 100,000
◉ 100,000 to 500,000
◼ above 500,000

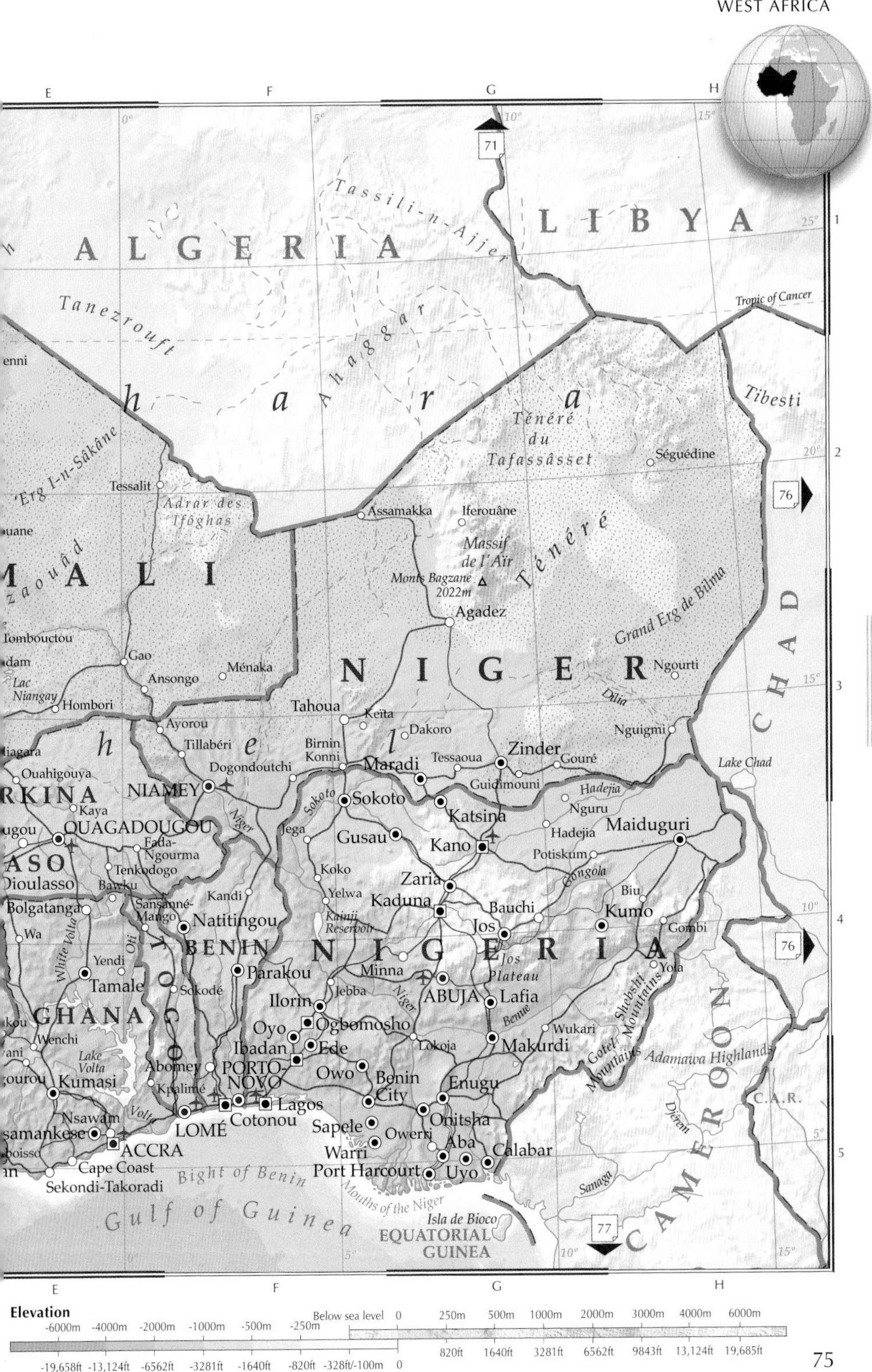
E
F
G
H
71
76
77
1
2
3
4
5
0°
5°
10°
15°
25°
20°
15°
10°
5°
ALGERIA
LIBYA
MALI
NIGER
NIGERIA
CHAD
CAMEROON
BENIN
TOGO
GHANA
BURKINA FASO
EQUATORIAL GUINEA
C.A.R.
Tassili-n-Ajjer
Tanezrouft
Ahaggar
Sahara
Sahel
Tropic of Cancer
Tibesti
Ténéré du Tafassâsset
Séguédine
Erg I-n-Sâkâne
Tessalit
Adrar des Ifôghas
Assamakka
Iferouâne
Massif de l'Aïr
Ténéré
Monts Bagzane 2022m
Agadez
Grand Erg de Bilma
Azaouâd
Tombouctou
Gao
Ménaka
Ansongo
Lac Niangay
Hombori
Ngourti
Dilia
Tahoua
Keïta
Dakoro
Ayorou
Tillabéri
Birnin Konni
Maradi
Tessaoua
Zinder
Gouré
Nguigmi
Lake Chad
Dogondoutchi
Guidimouni
Ouahigouya
NIAMEY
Kaya
Niger
OUAGADOUGOU
Fada-Ngourma
Tenkodogo
Bobo-Dioulasso
Bawku
Sokoto
Jega
Gusau
Katsina
Kano
Hadejia
Nguru
Maiduguri
Potiskum
Gongola
Koko
Zaria
Yelwa
Kaduna
Kainji Reservoir
Bauchi
Biu
Kumo
Gombi
Jos
Jos Plateau
Bolgatanga
Sansanné-Mango
Kandi
Natitingou
Wa
White Volta
Oti
Yendi
Tamale
Parakou
Minna
ABUJA
Jebba
Lafia
Yola
Sokodé
Ilorin
Ogbomosho
Oyo
Ede
Ibadan
Benue
Wukari
Shebshi Mountains
Lokoja
Makurdi
Gotel Mountains
Adamawa Highlands
Wenchi
Lake Volta
Abomey
PORTO-NOVO
Owo
Benin City
Enugu
Kumasi
Kpalimé
Volta
Lagos
Onitsha
Cotonou
LOMÉ
Nsawam
Sapele
Owerri
Aba
Calabar
Warri
Djérem
ACCRA
Cape Coast
Port Harcourt
Uyo
Sekondi-Takoradi
Bight of Benin
Mouths of the Niger
Sanaga
Gulf of Guinea
Isla de Bioco
Elevation
Below sea level
0
250m
500m
1000m
2000m
3000m
4000m
6000m
820ft
1640ft
3281ft
6562ft
9843ft
13,124ft
19,685ft
-6000m
-4000m
-2000m
-1000m
-500m
-250m
-19,658ft
-13,124ft
-6562ft
-3281ft
-1640ft
-820ft
-328ft/-100m

Central Africa

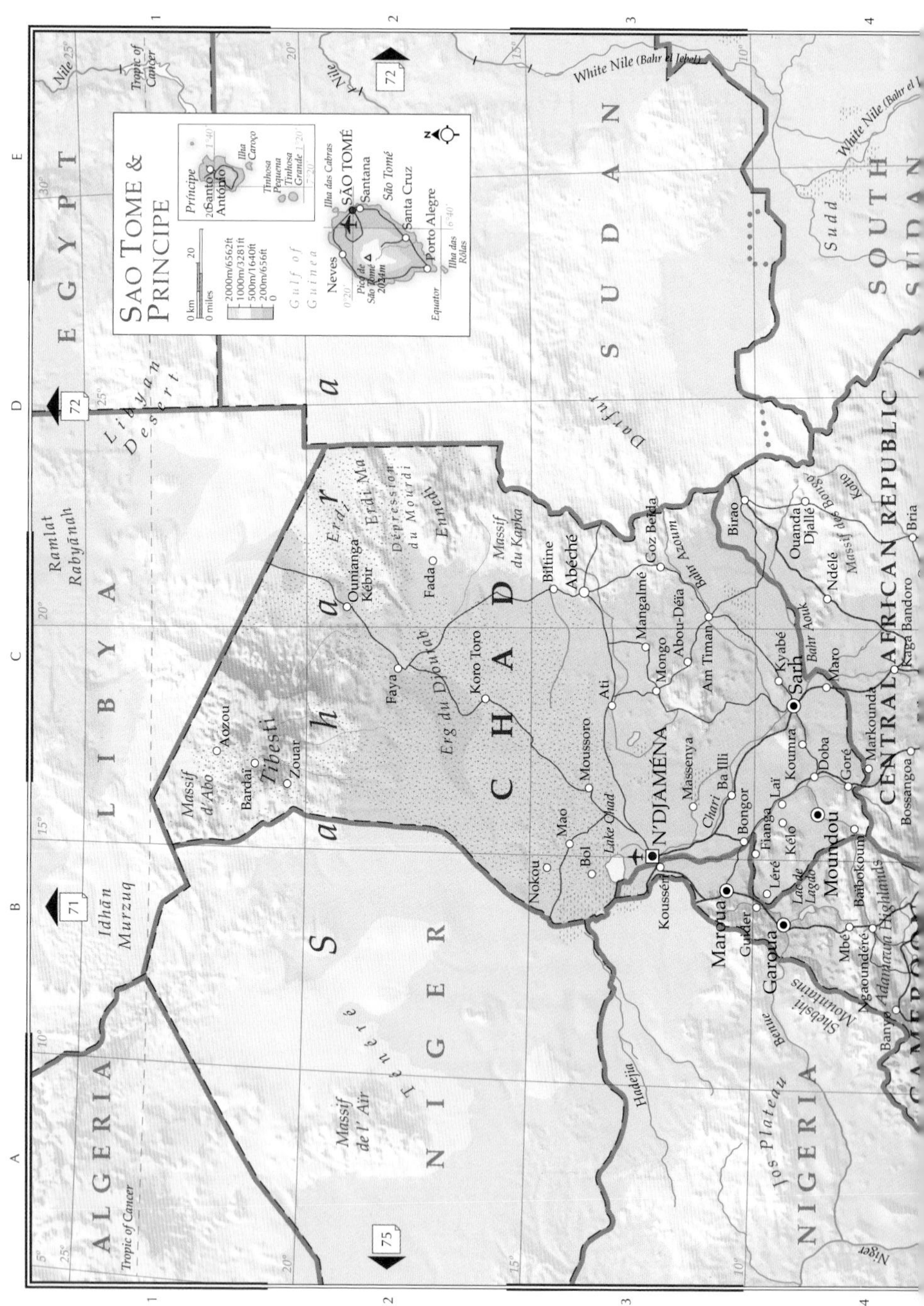

0 km 400
0 miles 400

Population

● National capital
○ below 50,000
○ 50,000 to 100,000
◉ 100,000 to 500,000
▣ above 500,000

Elevation

-6000m	-4000m	-2000m	-1000m	-500m	-250m	Below sea level	0	250m	500m	1000m	2000m	3000m	4000m	6000m
-19,658ft	-13,124ft	-6562ft	-3281ft	-1640ft	-820ft	-328ft/-100m	0	820ft	1640ft	3281ft	6562ft	9843ft	13,124ft	19,685ft

Southern Africa

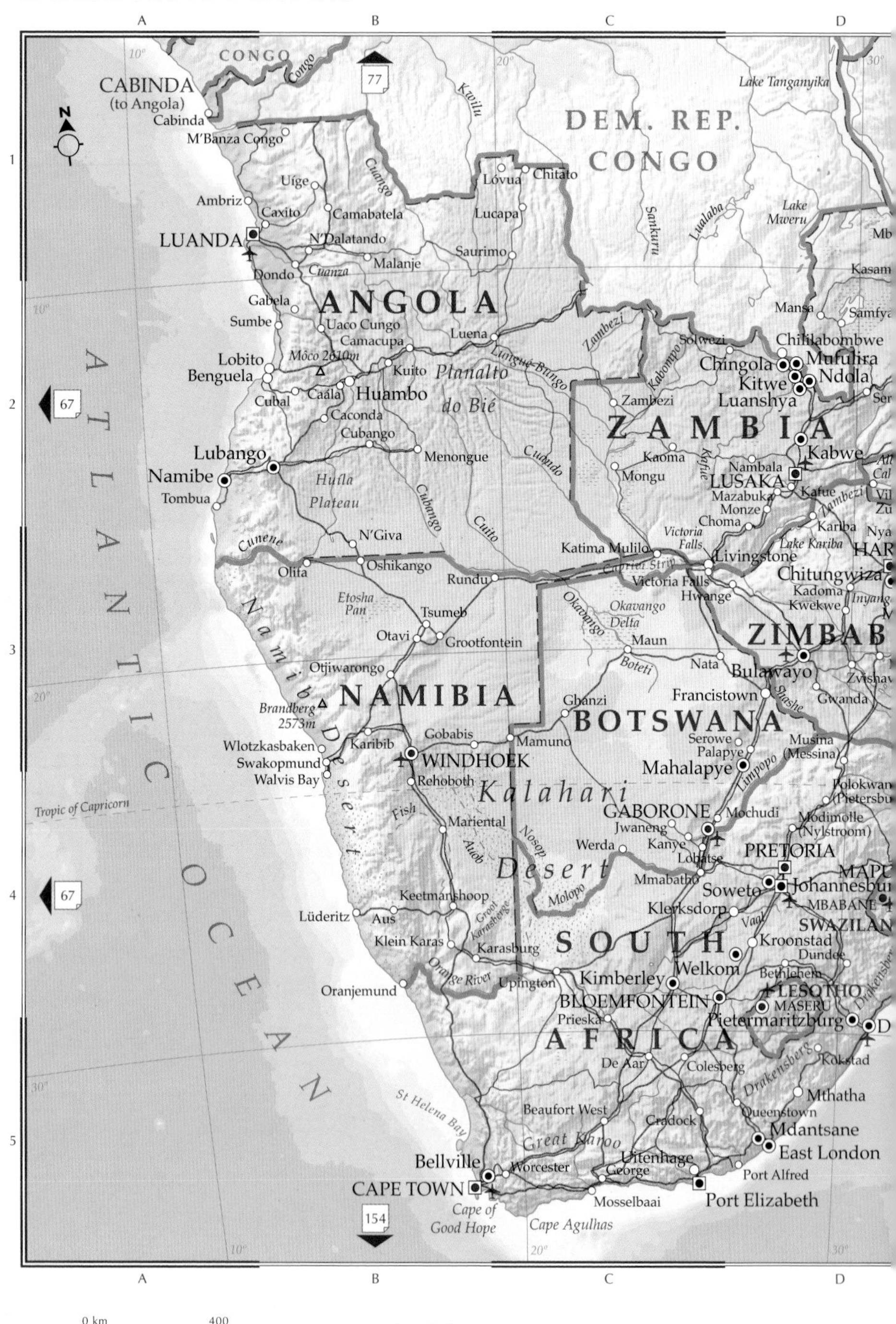

0 km 400

0 miles 400

Population ● National capital ○ below 50,000 ○ 50,000 to 100,000 ⦿ 100,000 to 500,000 ▣ above 500,000

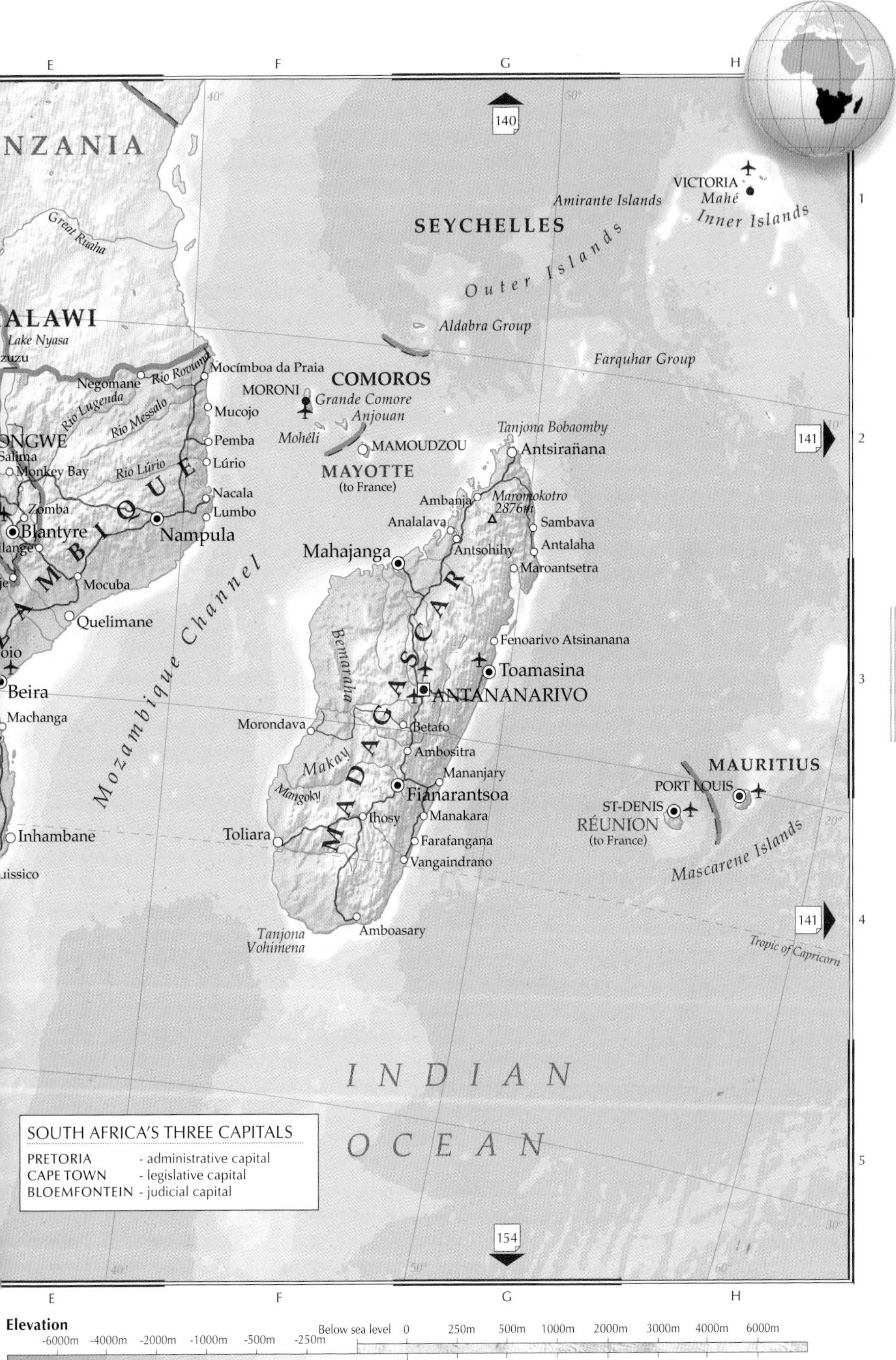

SOUTH AFRICA'S THREE CAPITALS

PRETORIA - administrative capital
CAPE TOWN - legislative capital
BLOEMFONTEIN - judicial capital

Elevation

Below sea level								0	250m	500m	1000m	2000m	3000m	4000m	6000m
-6000m	-4000m	-2000m	-1000m	-500m	-250m										
-19,658ft	-13,124ft	-6562ft	-3281ft	-1640ft	-820ft	-328ft/-100m		0	820ft	1640ft	3281ft	6562ft	9843ft	13,124ft	19,685ft

Europe

0 km 500
0 miles 500

Population
● National capital
○ below 50,000
○ 50,000 to 100,000
◉ 100,000 to 500,000
▣ above 500,000

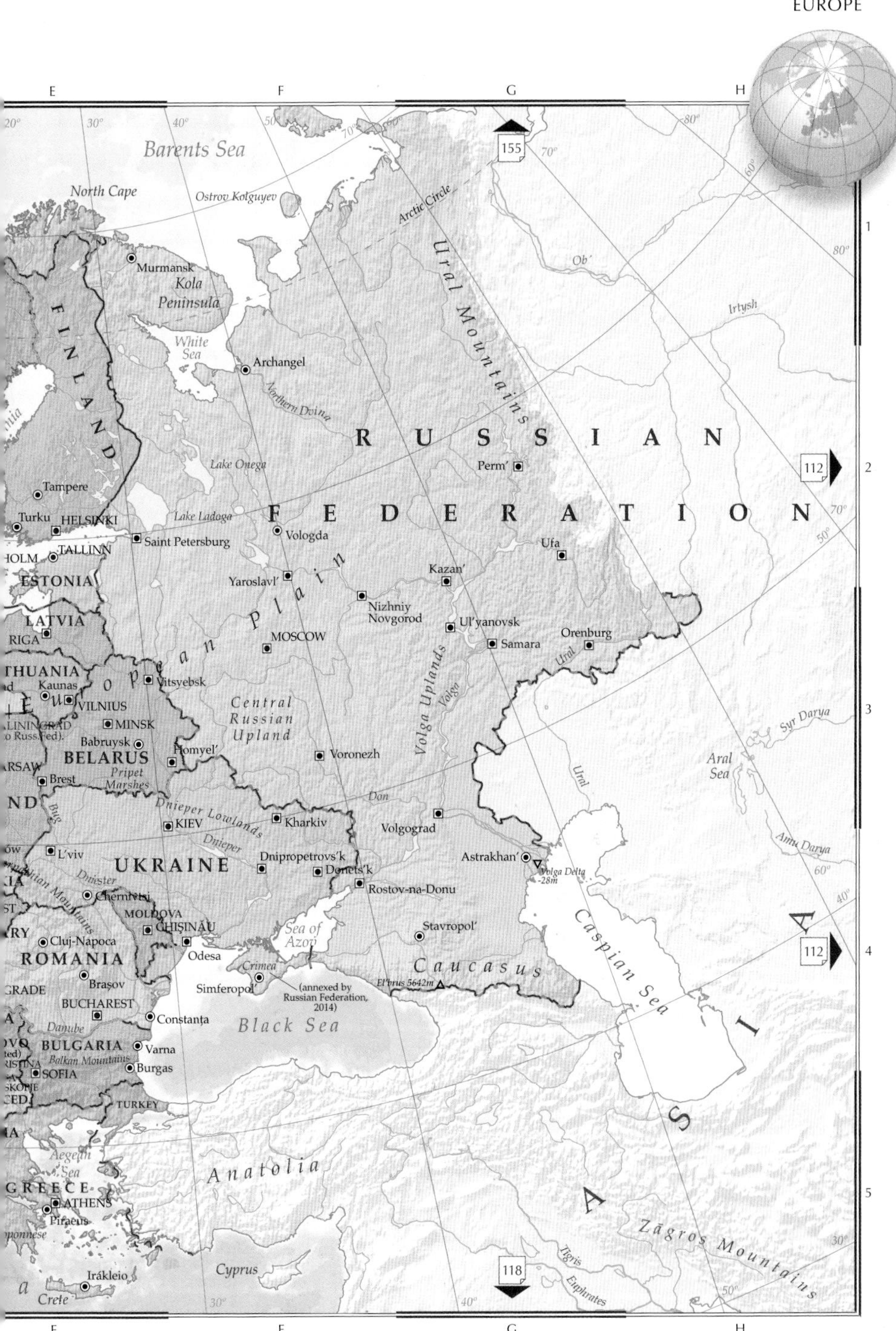
Barents Sea
North Cape
Ostrov Kolguyev
Arctic Circle
Murmansk
Kola Peninsula
White Sea
Archangel
Northern Dvina
Ural Mountains
Ob'
Irtysh
FINLAND
RUSSIAN FEDERATION
Lake Onega
Perm'
Tampere
Turku
HELSINKI
Lake Ladoga
Saint Petersburg
Vologda
TALLINN
ESTONIA
Yaroslavl'
Kazan'
Ufa
Nizhniy Novgorod
Ul'yanovsk
Samara
Orenburg
Ural
LATVIA
RIGA
MOSCOW
European Plain
Vitsyebsk
Kaunas
VILNIUS
MINSK
Central Russian Upland
Volga Uplands
Volga
Syr Darya
Babruysk
BELARUS
Homyel'
Voronezh
Aral Sea
Brest
Pripet Marshes
Don
Dnieper Lowlands
Kharkiv
KIEV
Volgograd
Amu Darya
L'viv
Dnieper
UKRAINE
Dnipropetrovs'k
Donets'k
Astrakhan'
Volga Delta -28m
Dniester
Rostov-na-Donu
Chernivtsi
MOLDOVA
CHIŞINĂU
Stavropol'
Caspian Sea
Cluj-Napoca
Sea of Azov
ROMANIA
Odesa
Crimea
Caucasus
El'brus 5642m
Braşov
Simferopol'
(annexed by Russian Federation, 2014)
BUCHAREST
Constanţa
Black Sea
Danube
BULGARIA
Varna
Balkan Mountains
SOFIA
Burgas
TURKEY
ASIA
Aegean Sea
GREECE
ATHENS
Piraeus
Anatolia
Zagros Mountains
Tigris
Euphrates
Cyprus
Irákleio
Crete
155
112
118

The North Atlantic

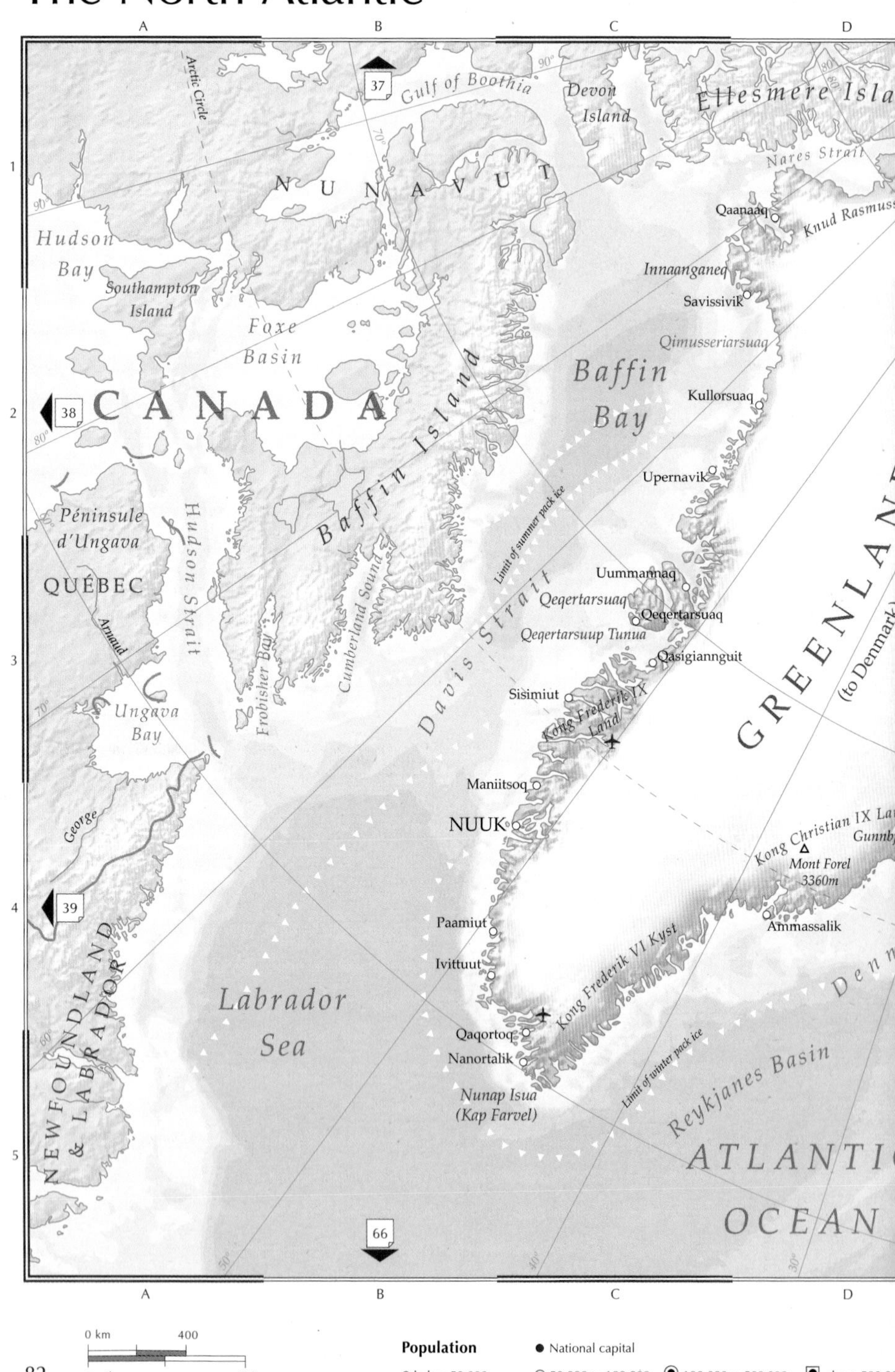

Population

● National capital

○ below 50,000 ○ 50,000 to 100,000 ◉ 100,000 to 500,000 ▣ above 500,000

ARCTIC OCEAN
Kap Morris Jesup
Wandel Sea
Independence Fjord
Nord
SVALBARD
(to Norway)
Zemlya Frantsa-Iosifa
Kvitøya
Nordaustlandet
Kong Karls Land
Spitsbergen
Barentsøya
Edgeøya
LONGYEARBYEN
Barentsburg
Storfjorden
Limit of winter pack ice
Barents Sea
Novaya Zemlya
Kong Frederik VIII Land
Greenland Sea
Limit of summer pack ice
Bjørnøya
(to Norway)
Nordkapp
(North Cape)
Daneborg
Petermann Bjerg
2940m
Mohns Ridge
Kong Oscar Fjord
Ittoqqortoormiit
Kangikajik
JAN MAYEN
(to Norway)
FINLAND
Arctic Circle
Norwegian Sea
Norwegian Basin
Vestfjorden
ICELAND
Siglufjörður
Raufarhöfn
Húsavík
Akureyri
Seyðisfjörður
Neskaupstaður
REYKJAVÍK
Selfoss
Vatnajökull
Djúpivogur
Hvannadalshnúkur
2119m
Vestmannaeyjar
SWEDEN
Gulf of Bothnia
FAROE ISLANDS
(to Denmark)
TÓRSHAVN
NORWAY
Shetland Islands
155
110
84
85
E
F
G
H
1
2
3
4
5
Elevation
Below sea level
-6000m -4000m -2000m -1000m -500m -250m
0 250m 500m 1000m 2000m 3000m 4000m 6000m
-19,658ft -13,124ft -6562ft -3281ft -1640ft -820ft -328ft/-100m 0
820ft 1640ft 3281ft 6562ft 9843ft 13,124ft 19,685ft

Scandinavia & Finland

0 km 200

0 miles 200

Population

● National capital

○ below 50,000

○ 50,000 to 100,000

◉ 100,000 to 500,000

▣ above 500,00

NORWAY
SWEDEN
DENMARK
ESTONIA
LATVIA
LITHUANIA
RUSS. FED.
BELARUS
POLAND
GERMANY
KALININGRAD (to Russian Federation)
North Sea
Baltic Sea
Skagerrak
Kattegat
Gulf of Finland
Gulf of Riga
Gulf of Danzig
Courland Lagoon
Lake Peipus
Ladozhskoye Ozero
Jotunheimen
Glittertind 2472m
OSLO
STOCKHOLM
HELSINKI
KØBENHAVN (Copenhagen)
Bergen
Stavanger
Kristiansand
Göteborg (Gothenburg)
Malmö
Uppsala
Västerås
Örebro
Linköping
Norrköping
Jönköping
Tampere
Turku (Åbo)
Espoo
Vantaa
Jyväskylä
Lahti
Lappeenranta
Kotka
Porvoo
Pori
Aalborg
Århus
Odense
Esbjerg
Gotland
Öland
Åland
Bornholm
Sjælland
Fyn
Jylland
Visby
Kalmar
Karlskrona
Helsingborg
Lund
Halmstad
Borås
Gävle
Sundsvall
Falun
Lillehammer
Drammen
Elbe
Oder
Wisła
Neman
Western Dvina
89
94
98
111
A
B
C
D
E
5
6
7
8
Elevation
-6000m
-4000m
-2000m
-1000m
-500m
-250m
-19,658ft
-13,124ft
-6562ft
-3281ft
-1640ft
-820ft
-328ft/-100m
Below sea level
0
250m
500m
1000m
2000m
3000m
4000m
6000m
820ft
1640ft
3281ft
6562ft
9843ft
13,124ft
19,685ft

The Low Countries

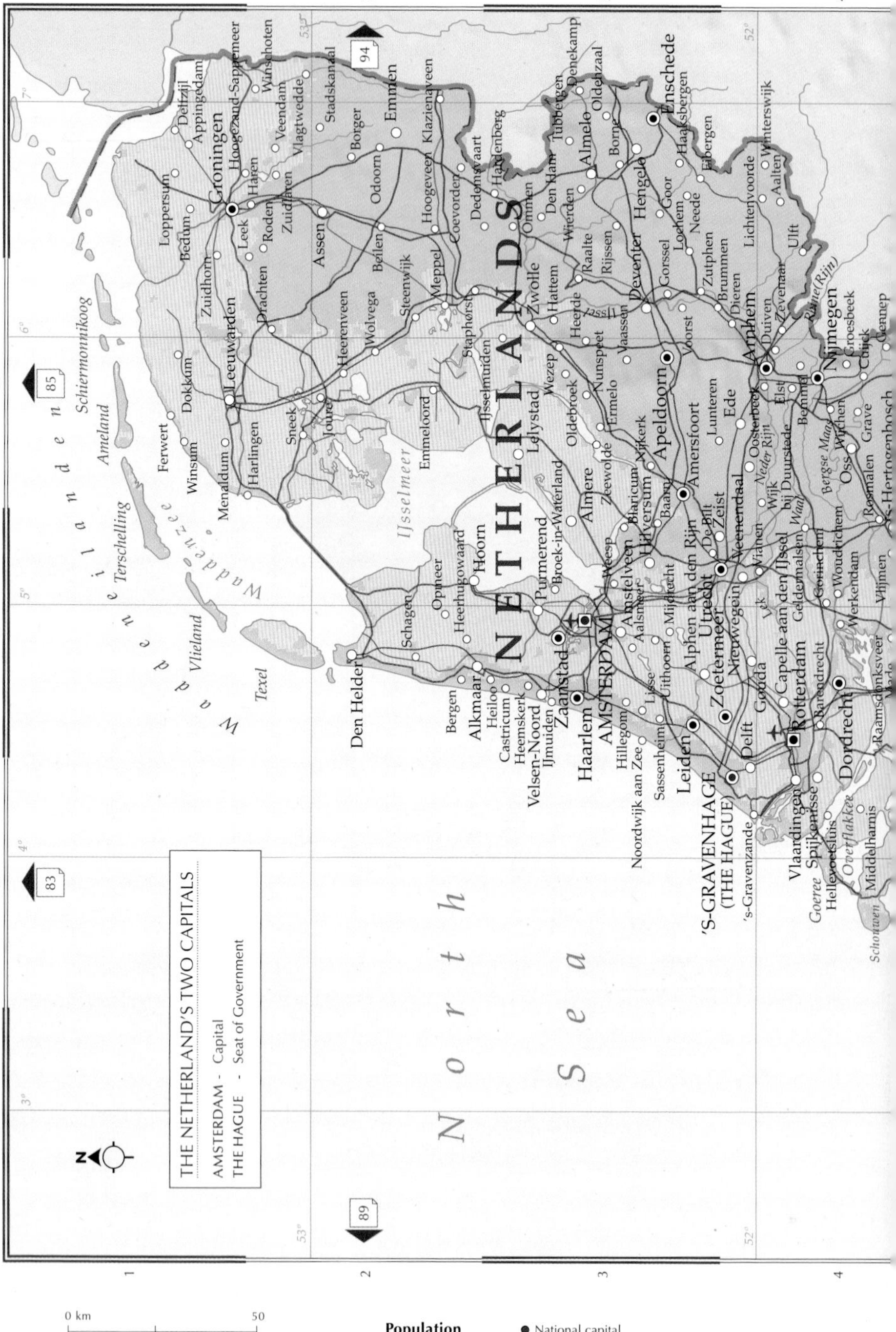

THE NETHERLAND'S TWO CAPITALS

AMSTERDAM - Capital
THE HAGUE - Seat of Government

0 km 50
0 miles 50

Population

● National capital

○ below 50,000 ○ 50,000 to 100,000 ◉ 100,000 to 500,000 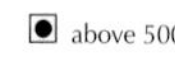

GERMANY
BELGIUM
LUXEMBOURG
FRANCE
Flanders
Fagne
Famenne
Ardennes
Lorraine
Hautes Fagnes
Botrange 694m
Rhine (Rhein)
Mosel
Moselle
Schelde
Scheldt
Rupel
Dender
Leie
IJzer
Meuse
Sambre
Ourthe
Vesdre
Semois
Oise
Somme
Sûre
Our
Alzette
Zeebrugge
Blankenberge
Oostende (Ostend)
Middelkerke
Koksijde
Veurne
Brugge (Bruges)
Torhout
Roeselare
Ieper
Poperinge
Kortrijk
Izegem
Harelbeke
Mouscron
Tournai
Péruwelz
Gent (Ghent)
Deinze
Zwevegem
Aalter
Eeklo
Beernem
Assenede
Oostburg
Terneuzen
Axel
Hulst
Zelzate
Sint-Niklaas
Oostakker
Laarne
Melle
Gavere
Zele
Aalst
Wemmel
Willebroek
Mechelen
Zemst
Vilvoorde
BRUSSEL/BRUXELLES (BRUSSELS)
Sint-Pieters-Leeuw
Halle
Tubize
Enghien
Ath
Leuze-en-Hainaut
Mons
Jemappes
Binche
Anderlues
Erquelinnes
La Louvière
Braine-le-Comte
Ottignies
Charleroi
Thuin
Châtelet
Gerpinnes
Walcourt
Couvin
Schaerbeek
Tervuren
Overijse
Wavre
Louvain-la Neuve
Gembloux
Éghezèe
Namur
Andenne
Dinant
Ciney
Rochefort
Leuven
Haacht
Tremelo
Duffel
Nijlen
Antwerpen (Antwerp)
Kapellen
Brecht
Schoten
Turnhout
Beveren
Wilrijk
Stabroek
Tessenderlo
Herselt
Geel
Mol
Balen
Lommel
Herk-de-Stad
Tienen
Landen
Waremme
Diepenbeek
Zonhoven
Beringen
Hasselt
Genk
Bilzen
Tongeren
Riemst
Peer
Bree
Kinrooi
Maaseik
Neerpelt
Bergeyk
Eersel
Valkenswaard
Someren
Weert
Nederweert
Tegelen
Reuver
Beesel
Roermond
Posterholt
Echt
Susteren
Sittard
Geleen
Heerlen
Kerkrade
Simpelveld
Meerssen
Maastricht
Eijsden
Vaals
Visé
Oupeye
Herstal
Liège
Seraing
Amay
Huy
Eupen
Verviers
Malmédy
Marche-en-Famenne
Bastogne
Weiswampach
Hosingen
Diekirch
Ettelbrück
Grevenmacher
LUXEMBOURG
Dudelange
Differdange
Pétange
Esch-sur-Alzette
Arlon
Aubange
Étalle
Virton
Neufchâteau
Recogne
94
90
A
B
C
D
E
5
6
7
8
3°
4°
5°
6°
7°
50°
51°
Elevation
Below sea level
-6000m
-4000m
-2000m
-1000m
-500m
-250m
0
250m
500m
1000m
2000m
3000m
4000m
6000m
-19,658ft
-13,124ft
-6562ft
-3281ft
-1640ft
-820ft
-328ft/-100m
0
820ft
1640ft
3281ft
6562ft
9843ft
13,124ft
19,685ft

The British Isles

0 km 100
0 miles 100

Population
○ below 50,000
● National capital
○ 50,000 to 100,000
● Internal administrative capital
⊙ 100,000 to 500,000
■ above 500,000

Elevation

-6000m	-4000m	-2000m	-1000m	-500m	-250m	Below sea level 0	250m	500m	1000m	2000m	3000m	4000m	6000m
-19,658ft	-13,124ft	-6562ft	-3281ft	-1640ft	-820ft	-328ft/-100m 0	820ft	1640ft	3281ft	6562ft	9843ft	13,124ft	19,685ft

France, Andorra & Monaco

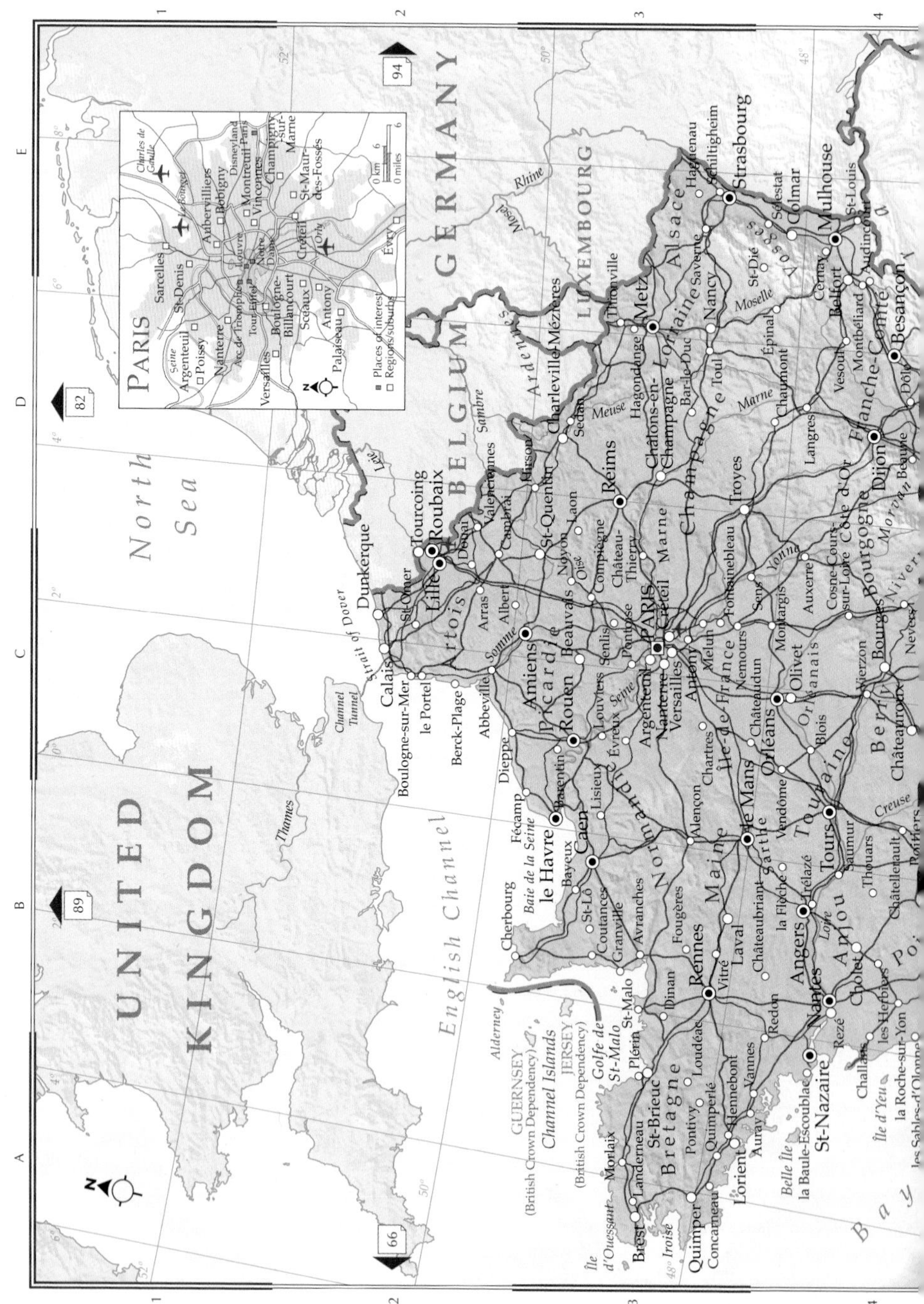

0 km 100
0 miles 100

Population
● National capital
○ below 50,000
○ 50,000 to 100,000
⊙ 100,000 to 500,000
▣ above 500,000

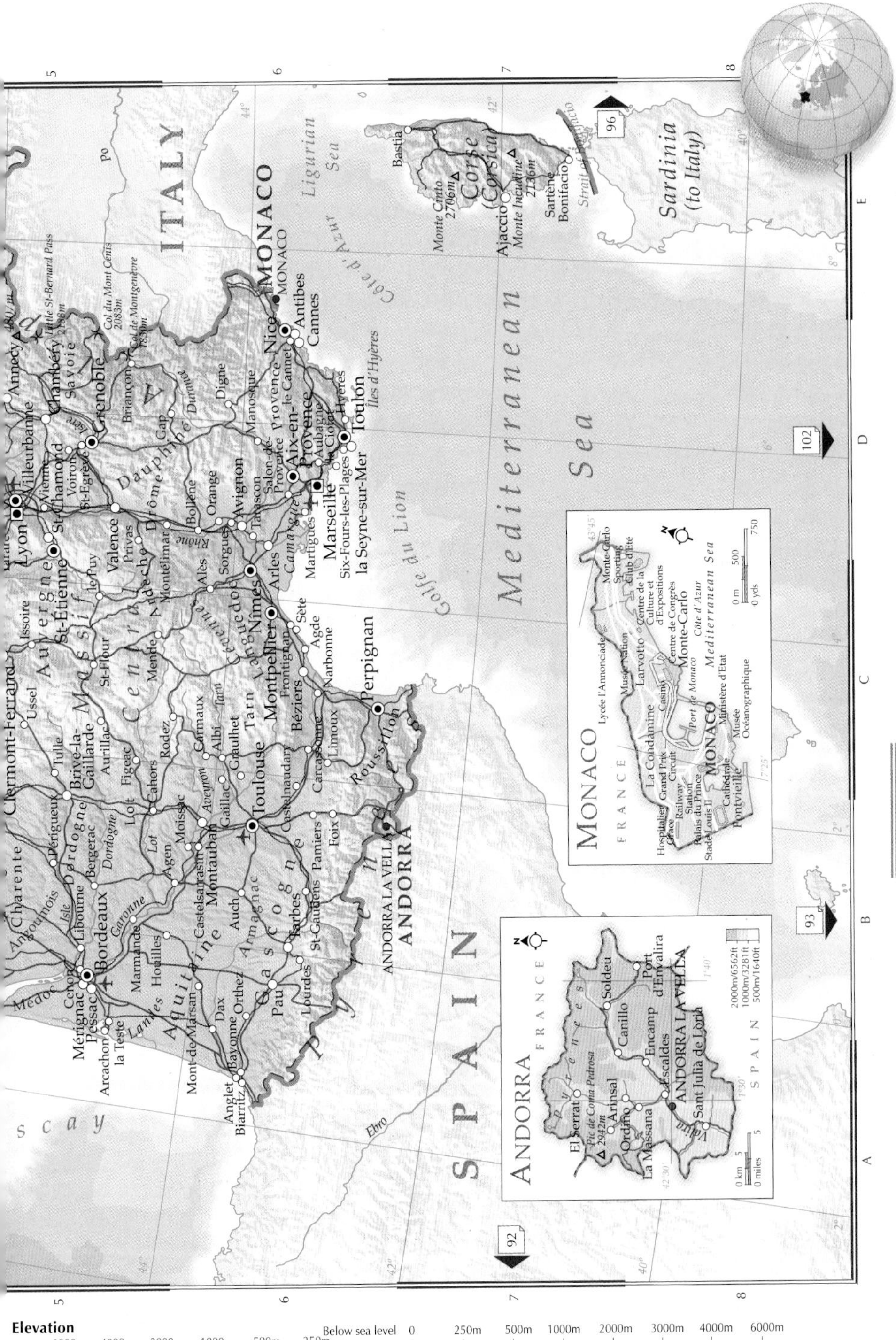

Elevation

-6000m	-4000m	-2000m	-1000m	-500m	-250m	Below sea level	0	250m	500m	1000m	2000m	3000m	4000m	6000m
-19,658ft	-13,124ft	-6562ft	-3281ft	-1640ft	-820ft	-328ft/-100m	0	820ft	1640ft	3281ft	6562ft	9843ft	13,124ft	19,685ft

Spain & Portugal

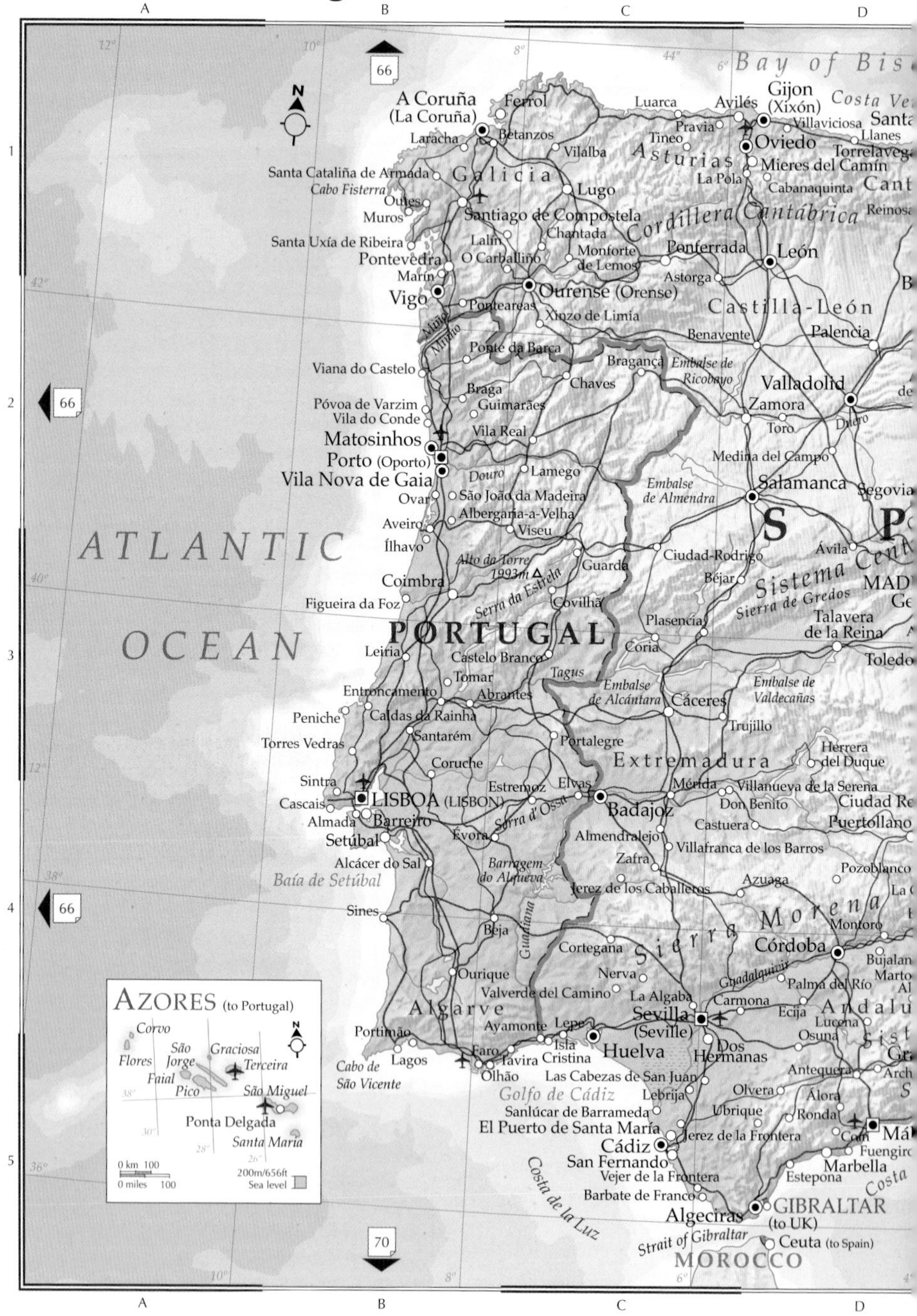

0 km 100
0 miles 100

Population

● National capital
○ below 50,000
○ 50,000 to 100,000
◉ 100,000 to 500,000
▣ above 500,00

FRANCE
Pyrenees
ANDORRA
Golfe du Lion
Donostia/San Sebastián
Irun
Bermeo
Zarautz
Eibar
Tolosa
Bergara
Pamplona
(Iruña)
Estella
Navarra
Jaca
Monte Perdido
3348m
La Seu d'Urgell
Ripoll
Figueres
Girona
(Gerona)
Berga
Manlleu
Banyoles
Palafrugell
Palamós
Vic
Blanes
Arenys de Mar
Mataró
Costa Brava
Cataluña
Huesca
Ejea de los Caballeros
Barbastro
Monzón
Balaguer
Cervera
Lleida
(Lérida)
Tàrrega
Terrassa
Sabadell
Barcelona
L'Hospitalet de Llobregat
Fraga
Vilafranca del Penedès
Valls
Reus
Sitges
El Vendrell
Tarragona
Zaragoza
Ebro
Calahorra
Arnedo
La Rioja
Tudela
Tarazona
Soria
Calatayud
Aragón
Daroca
Medinaceli
Alcañiz
Tortosa
Amposta
Sant Carles de la Ràpita
Vinaròs
Teruel
Javalambre
2020m
Cuenca
País Valenciano
Onda
Castellón de la Plana
Borriana
Vall d'Uxó
Sagunto
(Sagunt)
Burjassot
Valencia
Torrent
Catarroja
Sueca
Cullera
Gandia
Oliva
Dénia
Algemesí
Xàtiva
Júcar
Costa del Azahar
Golfo de Valencia
Castilla-La Mancha
Mota del Cuervo
Socuéllamos
La Roda
Albacete
Almansa
Ontinyent
Alcoy
Villena
Villanueva de los Infantes
Hellín
Segura
Jumilla
Elda
Benidorm
Villajoyosa (La Vila Joíosa)
Monóvar
Sant Joan d'Alacant
Elche
(Elx)
Alicante (Alacant)
Beas de Segura
Moratalla
Cieza
Callosa de Segura
Mula
Orihuela
Murcia
Costa Blanca
Huéscar
Totana
Lorca
La Unión
Cartagena
Baza
Aguilas
Mojácar
Berja
Almería
Mediterranean Sea
Ciutadella
Menorca
(Minorca)
Maó
Pollença
Sa Pobla
Palma
Manacor
Llucmajor
Felanitx
Mallorca
(Majorca)
Illa de Cabrera
Islas Baleares
(Balearic Islands)
Ibiza
Eivissa (Ibiza)
Formentera
ALGERIA
GIBRALTAR (to UK)
SPAIN
Gibraltar Airport
North Mole
Gibraltar Harbour
Catalan Bay
The Rock
Bay of Gibraltar
Sandy Bay
Summit 426m
Rosia
Rosia Bay
Buena Vista
Little Bay
Europa Point
Strait of Gibraltar
200m/656ft
Sea level
0 km 1
0 mile 1
90
96
97
71
E
F
G
H
1
2
3
4
5
Elevation
Below sea level
-6000m -4000m -2000m -1000m -500m -250m
-19,658ft -13,124ft -6562ft -3281ft -1640ft -820ft -328ft/-100m 0
0 250m 500m 1000m 2000m 3000m 4000m 6000m
820ft 1640ft 3281ft 6562ft 9843ft 13,124ft 19,685ft

Germany & the Alpine States

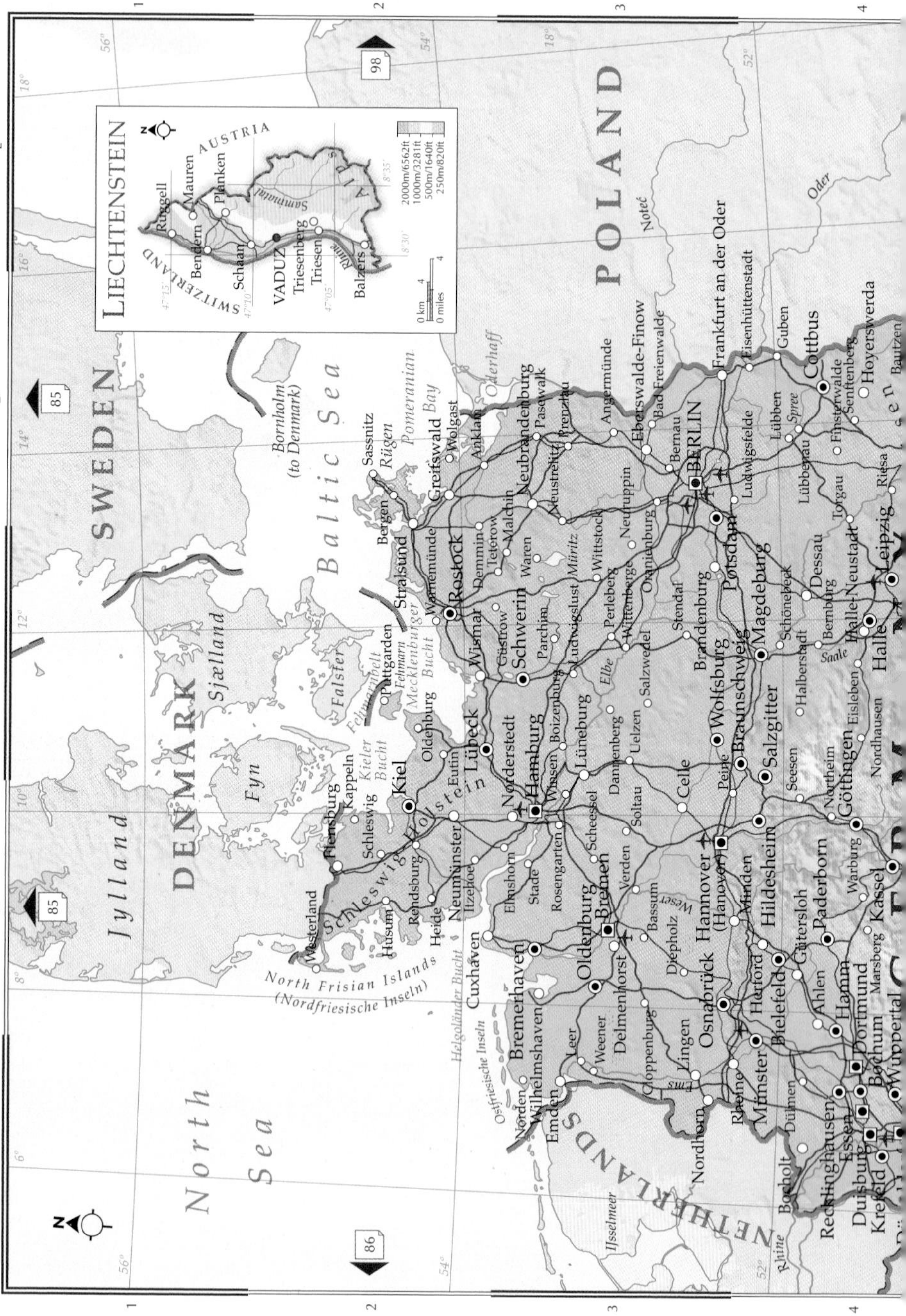

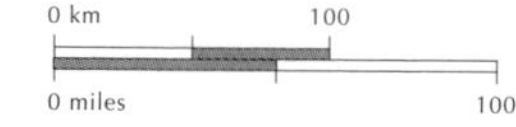

Population

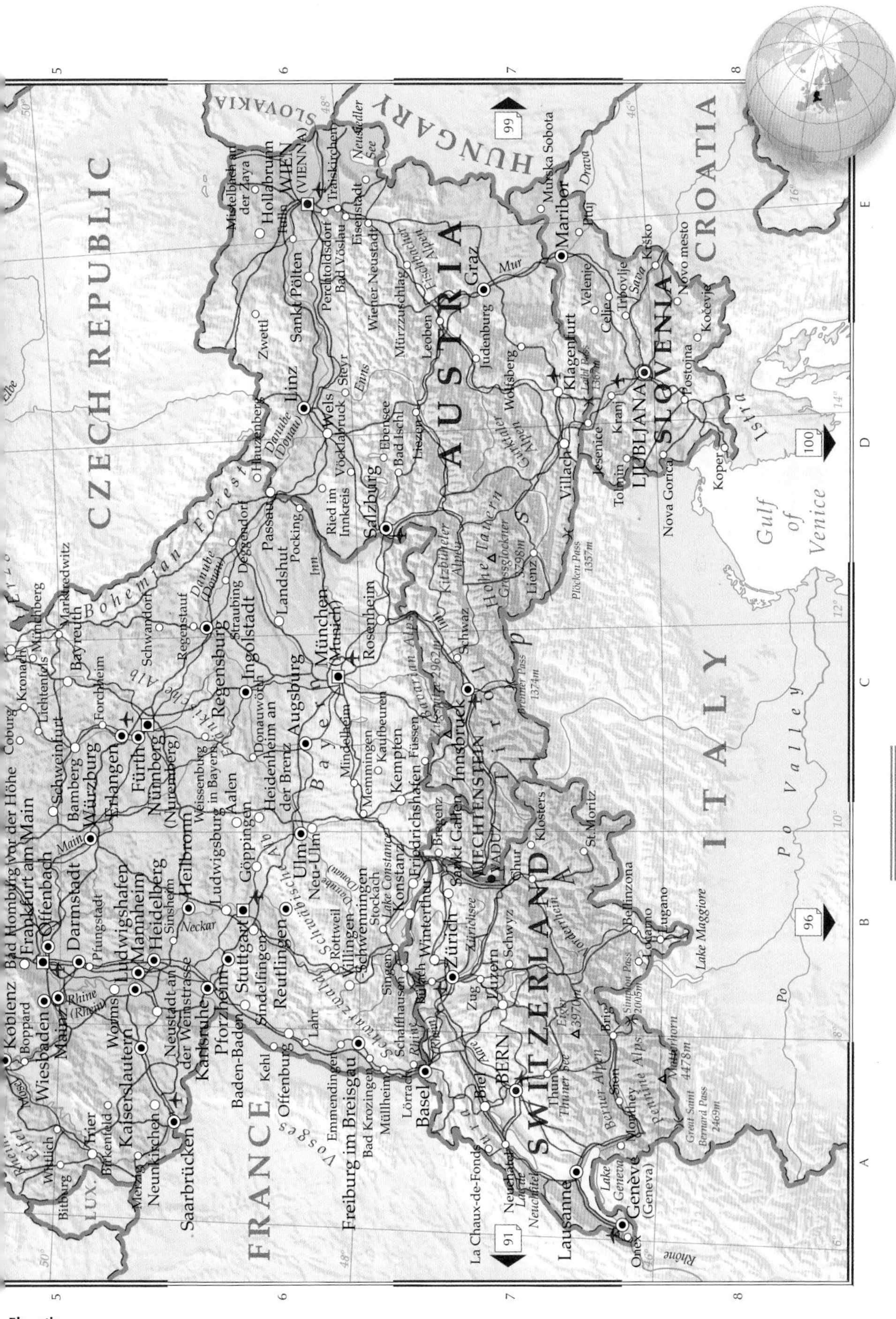

Elevation

Below sea level								0	250m	500m	1000m	2000m	3000m	4000m	6000m
-6000m	-4000m	-2000m	-1000m	-500m	-250m										
-19,658ft	-13,124ft	-6562ft	-3281ft	-1640ft	-820ft	-328ft/-100m	0		820ft	1640ft	3281ft	6562ft	9843ft	13,124ft	19,685ft

Italy

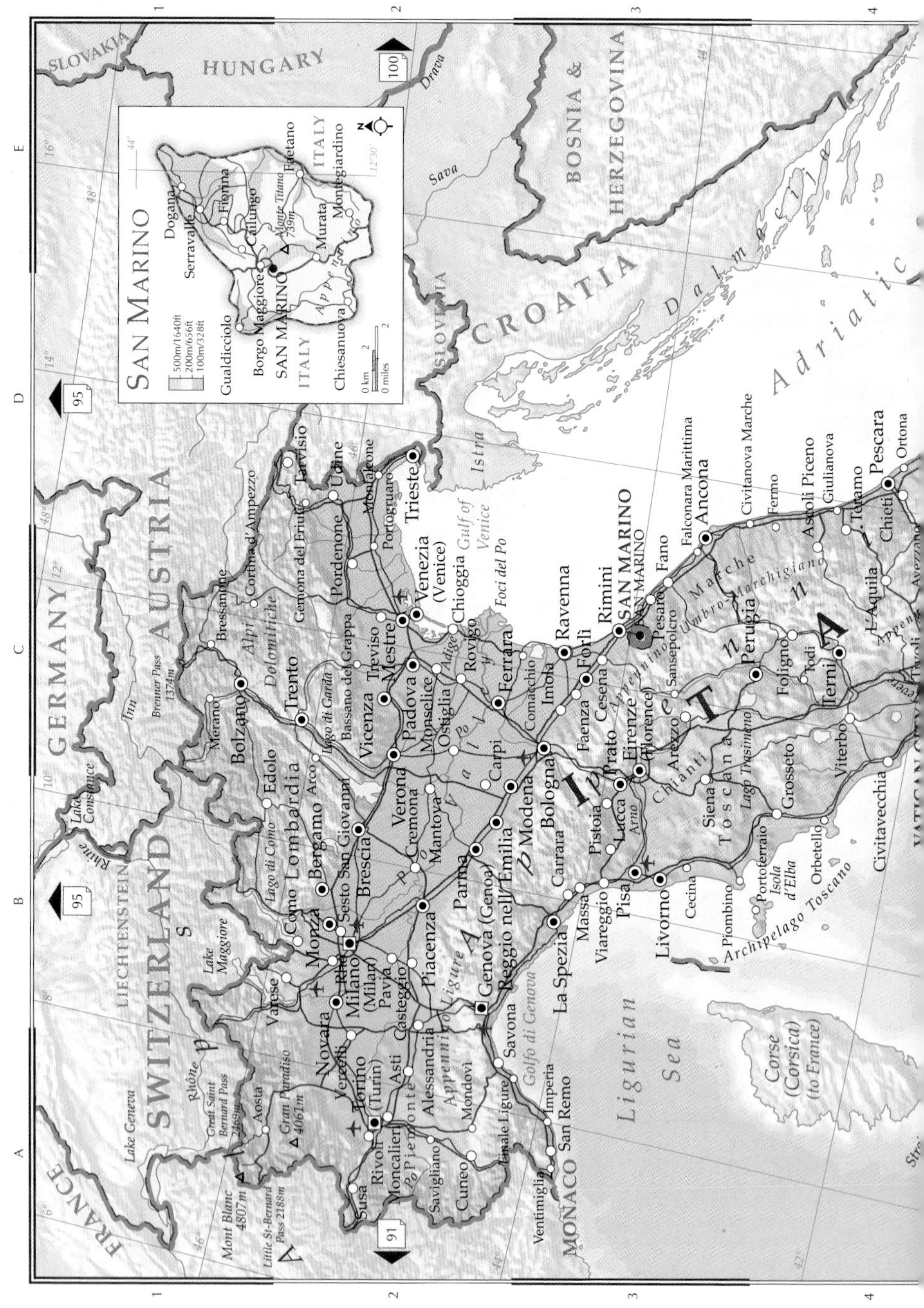

0 km 100
0 miles 100

Population

● National capital

○ below 50,000

○ 50,000 to 100,000

◉ 100,000 to 500,000

◼ above 500,000

Elevation

-6000m	-4000m	-2000m	-1000m	-500m	-250m	Below sea level 0	250m	500m	1000m	2000m	3000m	4000m	6000m
-19,658ft	-13,124ft	-6562ft	-3281ft	-1640ft	-820ft	-328ft/-100m 0	820ft	1640ft	3281ft	6562ft	9843ft	13,124ft	19,685ft

Central Europe

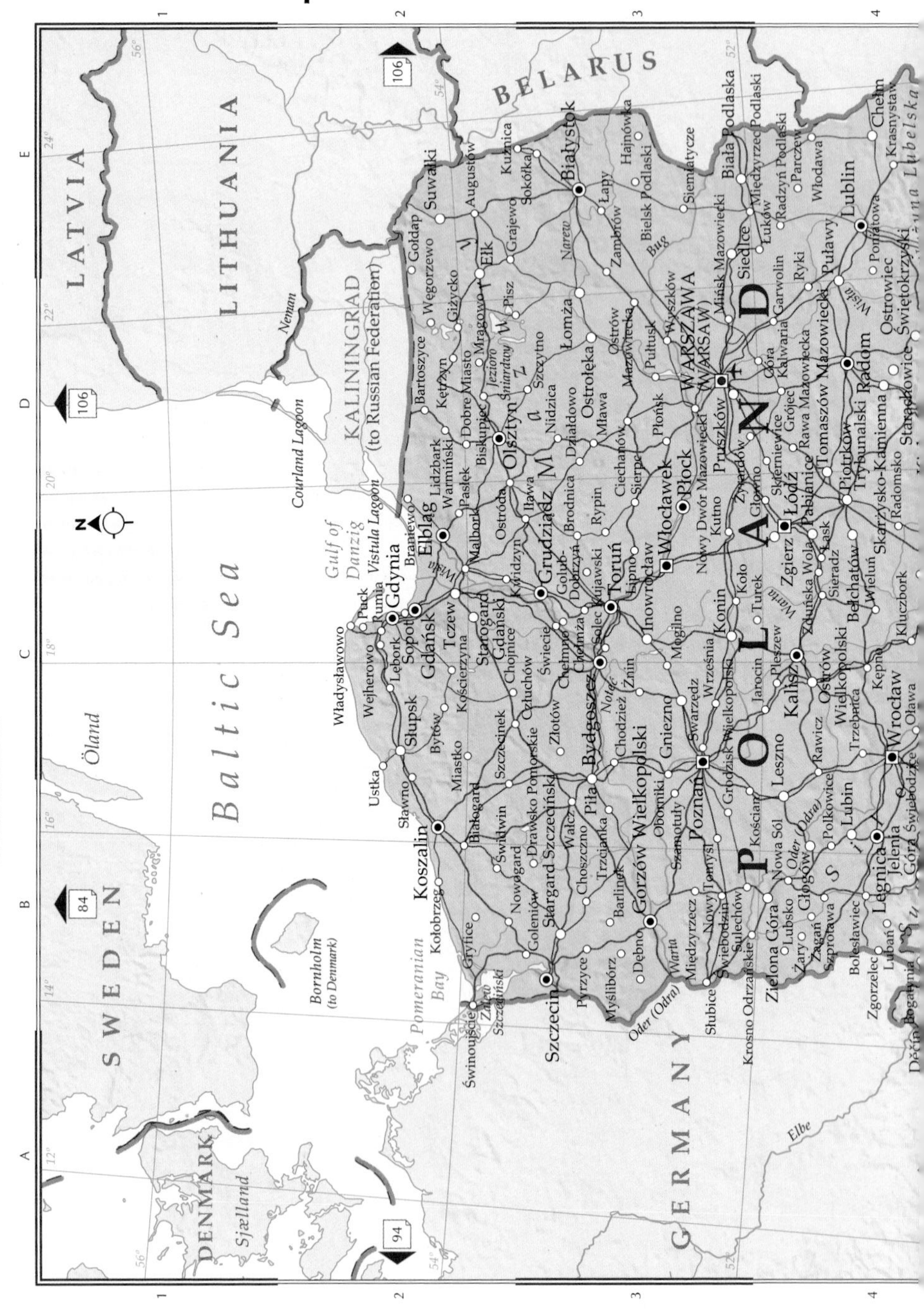

Population
● National capital
○ below 50,000
○ 50,000 to 100,000
◉ 100,000 to 500,000
▣ above 500,00

0 km 100
0 miles 100

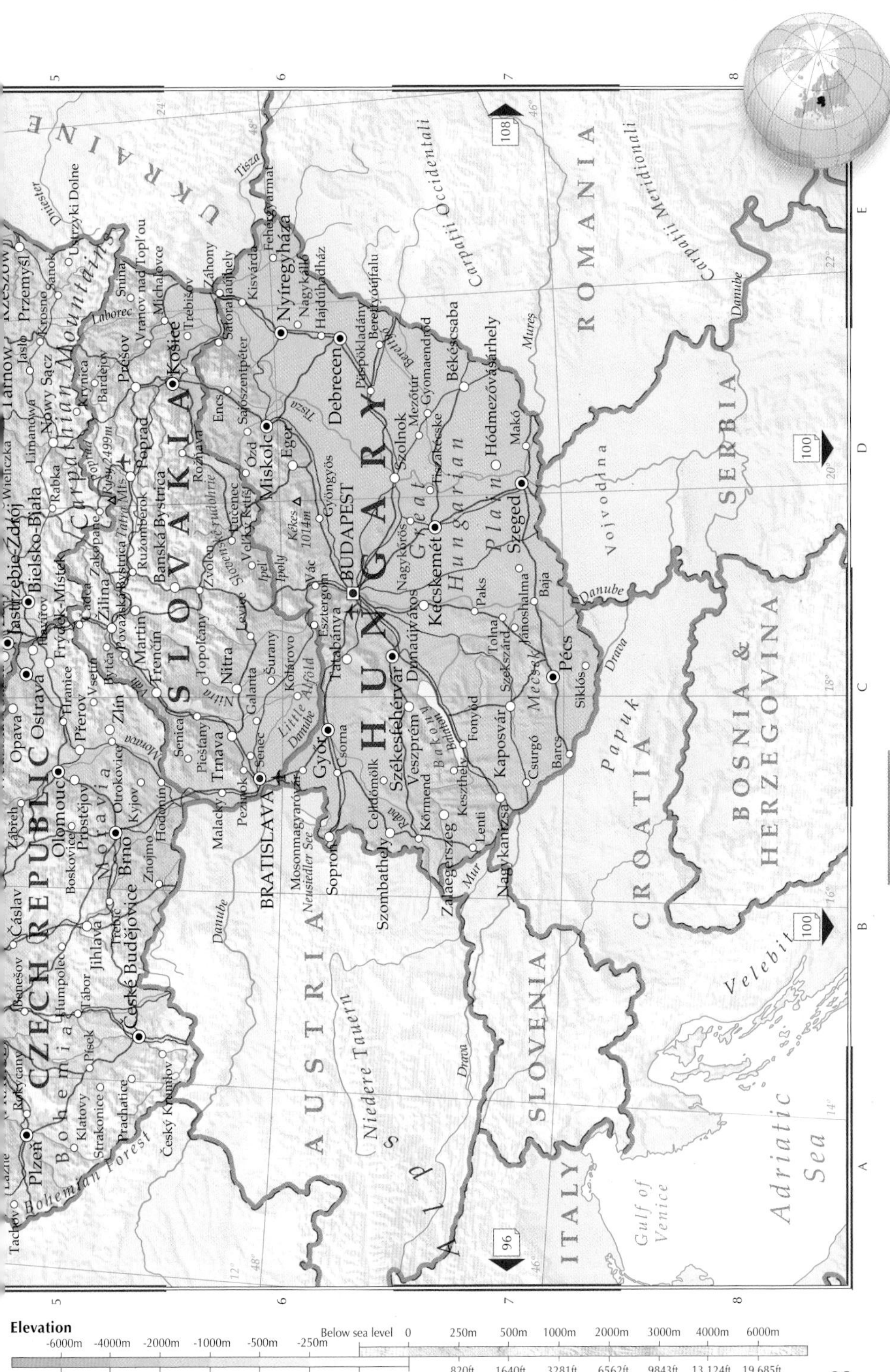

Elevation

Below sea level	-6000m	-4000m	-2000m	-1000m	-500m	-250m	0	250m	500m	1000m	2000m	3000m	4000m	6000m
	-19,658ft	-13,124ft	-6562ft	-3281ft	-1640ft	-820ft	-328ft/-100m 0	820ft	1640ft	3281ft	6562ft	9843ft	13,124ft	19,685ft

Southeast Europe

Population

● National capital ◉ Internal administrative capital

○ below 50,000 ○ 50,000 to 100,000 ◉ 100,000 to 500,000 ■ above 500,000

0 km 100

0 miles 100

Elevation

Below sea level							0	250m	500m	1000m	2000m	3000m	4000m	6000m
-6000m	-4000m	-2000m	-1000m	-500m	-250m									
-19,658ft	-13,124ft	-6562ft	-3281ft	-1640ft	-820ft	-328ft/-100m	0	820ft	1640ft	3281ft	6562ft	9843ft	13,124ft	19,685ft

The Mediterranean

0 km 400
0 miles 400

Population

- National capital
- ○ below 50,000
- ○ 50,000 to 100,000
- ⊙ 100,000 to 500,000
- ▣ above 500,000

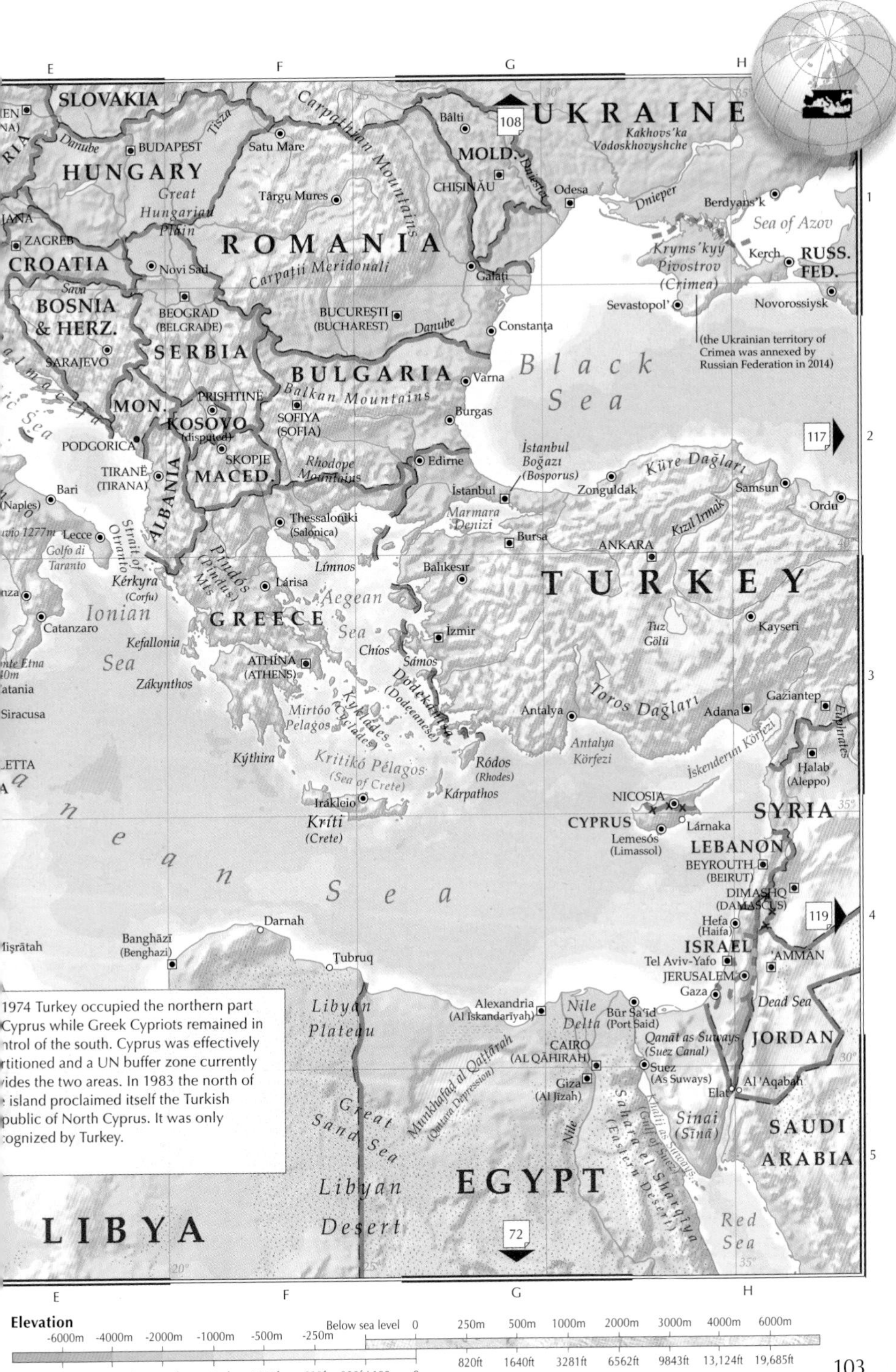
E
F
G
H
1
2
3
4
5
SLOVAKIA
Danube
BUDAPEST
HUNGARY
Great
Hungarian
Plain
Tisza
ZAGREB
CROATIA
Sava
BOSNIA
& HERZ.
SARAJEVO
Novi Sad
BEOGRAD
(BELGRADE)
SERBIA
MON.
PODGORICA
PRISHTINË
KOSOVO
(disputed)
SKOPJE
MACED.
TIRANË
(TIRANA)
ALBANIA
Satu Mare
Carpathian Mountains
Târgu Mureș
ROMANIA
Carpații Meridonali
BUCUREȘTI
(BUCHAREST)
Danube
Bălți
MOLD.
CHIȘINĂU
Dniester
Galați
Constanța
108
UKRAINE
Kakhovs'ka
Vodoskhovyshche
Odesa
Dnieper
Berdyans'k
Sea of Azov
Krymś'kyy
Pivostrov
(Crimea)
Kerch
RUSS.
FED.
Sevastopol'
Novorossiysk
(the Ukrainian territory of
Crimea was annexed by
Russian Federation in 2014)
BULGARIA
Balkan Mountains
Varna
Burgas
SOFIYA
(SOFIA)
Black
Sea
117
Rhodope
Mountains
Edirne
İstanbul
Boğazı
(Bosporus)
İstanbul
Marmara
Denizi
Bursa
Zonguldak
Küre Dağları
Samsun
Ordu
Kızıl Irmak
ANKARA
Bari
(Naples)
Lecce
Golfo di
Taranto
Strait of
Otranto
Kérkyra
(Corfu)
Catanzaro
Ionian
Sea
Kefallonia
Zákynthos
Siracusa
Thessaloníki
(Salonica)
Pindos
(Pindus)
Mts
Lárisa
Límnos
GREECE
Aegean
Sea
ATHÍNA
(ATHENS)
Chíos
Sámos
Balıkesir
İzmir
TURKEY
Tuz
Gölü
Kayseri
Mirtóo
Pelagos
Kykládes
(Cyclades)
Dodekánisa
(Dodecanese)
Toros Dağları
Antalya
Antalya
Körfezi
Adana
Gaziantep
Euphrates
Kýthira
Kritikó Pélagos
(Sea of Crete)
Ródos
(Rhodes)
Kárpathos
İskenderun Körfezi
Halab
(Aleppo)
Irákleio
Kríti
(Crete)
NICOSIA
CYPRUS
Lárnaka
Lemesós
(Limassol)
SYRIA
LEBANON
BEYROUTH
(BEIRUT)
DIMASHQ
(DAMASCUS)
119
Hefa
(Haifa)
ISRAEL
Tel Aviv-Yafo
'AMMAN
JERUSALEM
Gaza
Dead Sea
JORDAN
Sea
Darnah
Banghāzī
(Benghazi)
Tubruq
Libyan
Plateau
Alexandria
(Al Iskandarīyah)
Nile
Delta
Būr Sa'īd
(Port Said)
Qanāt as Suways
(Suez Canal)
CAIRO
(AL QĀHIRAH)
Suez
(As Suways)
Giza
(Al Jīzah)
Munkhafad al Qaţţārah
(Qattara Depression)
Al 'Aqabah
Elat
Sinai
(Sīnā)
SAUDI
ARABIA
Great
Sand Sea
Nile
Libyan
Desert
EGYPT
Red
Sea
72
LIBYA
1974 Turkey occupied the northern part
Cyprus while Greek Cypriots remained in
ntrol of the south. Cyprus was effectively
rtitioned and a UN buffer zone currently
vides the two areas. In 1983 the north of
island proclaimed itself the Turkish
public of North Cyprus. It was only
cognized by Turkey.
Elevation
Below sea level
-6000m -4000m -2000m -1000m -500m -250m
-19,658ft -13,124ft -6562ft -3281ft -1640ft -820ft -328ft/-100m 0
0 250m 500m 1000m 2000m 3000m 4000m 6000m
820ft 1640ft 3281ft 6562ft 9843ft 13,124ft 19,685ft

Bulgaria & Greece

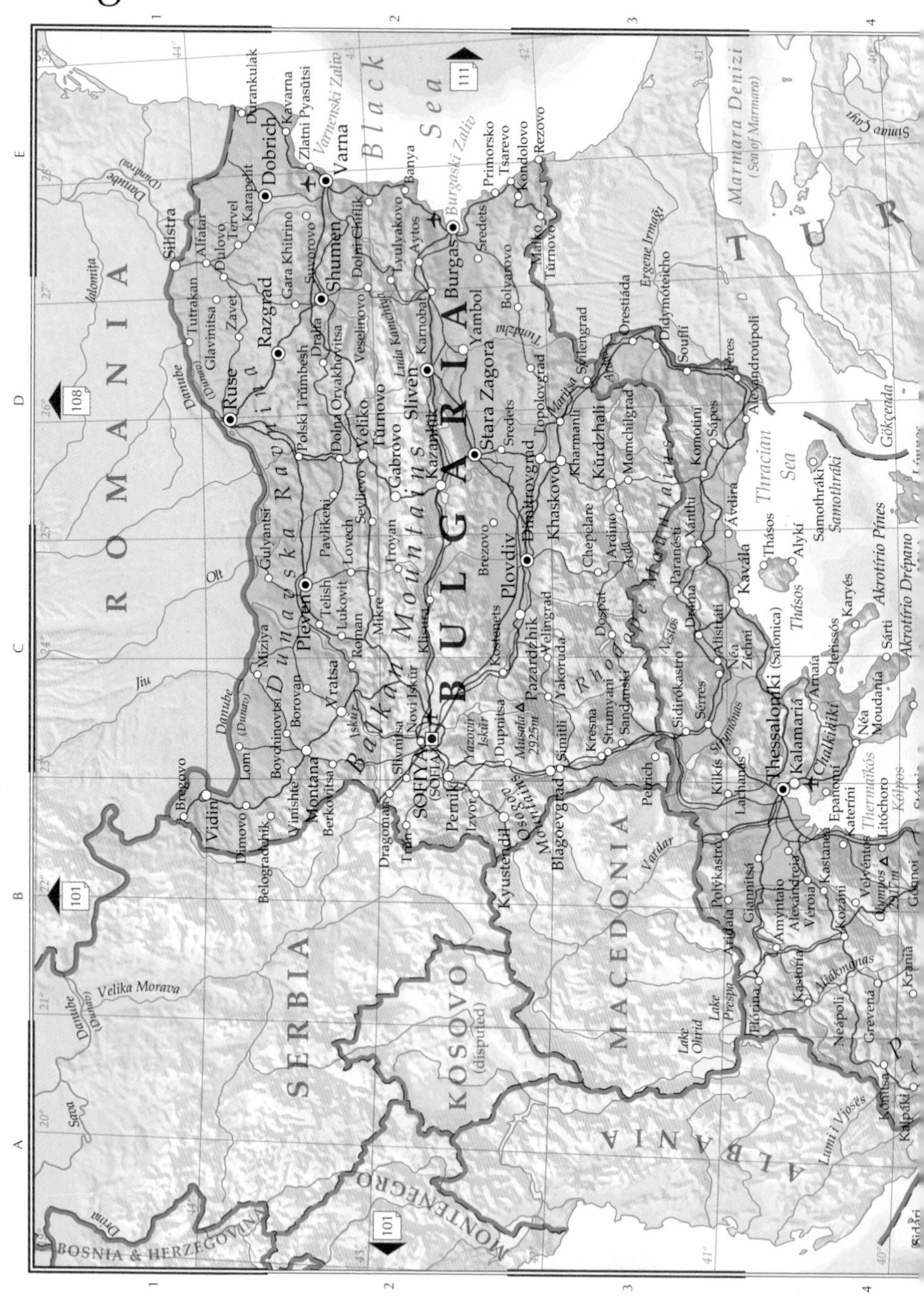

0 km		100
0 miles		100

Population

- ● National capital
- ○ below 50,000
- ○ 50,000 to 100,000
- ⊙ 100,000 to 500,000
- ◘ above 500,000

Elevation

-6000m	-4000m	-2000m	-1000m	-500m	-250m	Below sea level 0	250m	500m	1000m	2000m	3000m	4000m	6000m
-19,658ft	-13,124ft	-6562ft	-3281ft	-1640ft	-820ft	-328ft/-100m 0	820ft	1640ft	3281ft	6562ft	9843ft	13,124ft	19,685ft

The Baltic States & Belarus

0 km 100

0 miles 100

Population

○ below 50,000

● National capital

○ 50,000 to 100,000

⊙ 100,000 to 500,000

▣ above 500,000

Elevation

-6000m	-4000m	-2000m	-1000m	-500m	-250m	Below sea level	0	250m	500m	1000m	2000m	3000m	4000m	6000m
-19,658ft	-13,124ft	-6562ft	-3281ft	-1640ft	-820ft	-328ft/-100m	0	820ft	1640ft	3281ft	6562ft	9843ft	13,124ft	19,685ft

Ukraine, Moldova & Romania

0 km 100

0 miles 100

Population

○ below 50,000

● National capital

○ 50,000 to 100,000

⊙ 100,000 to 500,000

◘ above 500,000

E
F
G
H
110
Srednerusskaya Vozvyshennost'
RUSSIAN FEDERATION
Dnieper (Dnipro)
Desna
Horodnya
Shchors
Shostka
Hlukhiv
Chernihiv
Krolevets'
Konotop
Bakhmach
Nizhyn
Nosivka
Romny
Sumy
Brovary
Pryluky
Psel
Lebedyn
Dnieper Lowland
Yahotyn
Pyryatyn
Okhtyrka
Zolochiv
Derhachi
Don
Hrebinka
Lubny
Myrhorod
Lyubotyn
Kharkiv
Kaniv
Kanivs'ke Vodoskhovyshche
Tserkva
Zolotonosha
Merefa
Oskol
Kup"yans'k
Poltava
Cherkasy
Hlobyne
Kremenchuts'ke Vodoskhovyshche
Donets
Starobil's'k
Smila
Izyum
Kreminna
Rubizhne
Shpola
Chyhyryn
Kremenchuk
Syeverodonets'k
Tal'ne
Oleksandrivka
Svitlovods'k
Dniprodzerzhyns'ke Vodoskhovyshche
Slov"yans'k
Lysychans'k
Kramators'k
Mala Vyska
Znam"yanka
Oleksandriya
Novomoskovs'k
Kostyantynivka
Zolote
Luhans'k
Dniprodzerzhyns'k
Pavlohrad
Kirovohrad
Dnipropetrovs'k
Horlivka
Stakhanov
Zhovti Vody
P"yatykhatky
Synel'nykove
Yenakiyeve
Krasnodon
Vil'shanka
Makiyivka
Krasnyy Luch
Dolyns'ka
Pervomays'k
Bobrynets'
Pokrovs'ke
Torez
Kryvyy Rih
Donets'k
Arbuzynka
Inhulets'
Zaporizhzhya
Amvrosiyivka
Pivdennyy Buh
Novyy Buh
Ordzhonikidze
Nikopol'
Orikhiv
Volnovakha
Dokuchayevs'k
Voznesens'k
Marhanets'
Polohy
Kam"yanka-Dniprovs'ka
Dniprorudne
Kakhovs'ka Vodoskhovyshche
Tokmak
Mariupol'
Novoazovs'k
Molochans'k
Mykolayiv
Black Sea Lowland
Dnieper (Dnipro)
Gulf of Taganrog
Kakhovka
Melitopol'
Yeya
Zhovtneve
Berdyans'k
Ochakiv
Kherson
Prymors'k
Yakymivka
Tsyurupyns'k
Odesa
Hola Prystan'
Novotroyits'ke
Chaplynka
Kalanchak
Heniches'k
Armyans'k
Sea of Azov
RUSSIAN FEDERATION
Krasnoperekops'k
Karkinits'ka Zatoka
Rozdol'ne
Dzhankoy
Kerch Strait
Nyzhn'ohirs'kyy
Krasnohvardiys'ke
Zatoka Syvash
Kerch
Chornomors'ke
Krymskyy Pivostriv (Crimea)
Kuban'
Yevpatoriya
Lenine
Saky
Simferopol'
Feodosiya
Krymski Hory
Bakhchysaray
(the Ukrainian territory of Crimea was annexed by Russian Federation in 2014)
Sevastopol'
Alushta
Yalta
Alupka
Black Sea
116
Elevation
Below sea level
0
250m
500m
1000m
2000m
3000m
4000m
6000m
-6000m -4000m -2000m -1000m -500m -250m
820ft 1640ft 3281ft 6562ft 9843ft 13,124ft 19,685ft
-19,658ft -13,124ft -6562ft -3281ft -1640ft -820ft -328ft/-100m 0

European Russia

0 km 300
0 miles 300

Population

● National capital
○ below 50,000
○ 50,000 to 100,000
⊙ 100,000 to 500,000
▣ above 500,000

Elevation

Below sea level	-6000m	-4000m	-2000m	-1000m	-500m	-250m	0	250m	500m	1000m	2000m	3000m	4000m	6000m
	-19,658ft	-13,124ft	-6562ft	-3281ft	-1640ft	-820ft	-328ft/-100m 0	820ft	1640ft	3281ft	6562ft	9843ft	13,124ft	19,685ft

North & West Asia

155
81
103
69

0 km 800
0 miles 800

Population
- ● National capital
- ○ below 50,000
- ○ 50,000 to 100,000
- ◉ 100,000 to 500,000
- ▣ above 500,000

C E A N
New Siberian Islands
Ostrov Kotel'nyy
Laptev Sea
Yanskiy Zaliv
East Siberian Sea
Chukchi Plain
Chukchi Plateau
Summer limit of pack ice
Wrangel Island
Chukchi Sea
Long Strait
Ekiatapskiy Khrebet
Bering Strait
Arctic Circle
Olenëk
Lena
Verkhoyanskiy Khrebet
Yana
Indigirka
Kolyma
Khrebet Cherskogo
E R A T I O N
Vilyuy
Aldan
Yakutsk
Amga
Kolyma Range
Koryak Range
Anadyr
Gulf of Anadyr
Bering Sea
Winter limit of pack ice
Shelekhov Gulf
Magadan
Khrebet Dzhugdzhur
Stanovoy Khrebet
Sea of Okhotsk
Kamchatka
Aleutian Basin
Aleutian Islands
Aleutian Trench
Petropavlovsk-Kamchatskiy
Sakhalin
Amur
Zeya
Argun
Khabarovsk
Khrebet Sikhote-Alin'
Yuzhno-Sakhalinsk
La Pérouse Strait
Kuril Islands
Kuril Trench
(administered by Russian Federation, claimed by Japan.)
Northwest Pacific Basin
Emperor Seamounts
Chinook Trough
Vladivostok
Sea of Japan (East Sea)
Japan Trench
Yellow Sea
PACIFIC OCEAN
East China Sea
Shikoku Basin
Ryukyu Trench
Hawai'ian Ridge
Tropic of Cancer
Philippine Sea
Mid - Pacific Mountains
Philippine Basin
Mariana Trench
South China Basin
155
34
34
143
E
F
G
H
1
2
3
4
5

Russia & Kazakhstan

0 km 600
0 miles 600

Population
● National capital
○ below 50,000
○ 50,000 to 100,000
◉ 100,000 to 500,000
▣ above 500,000

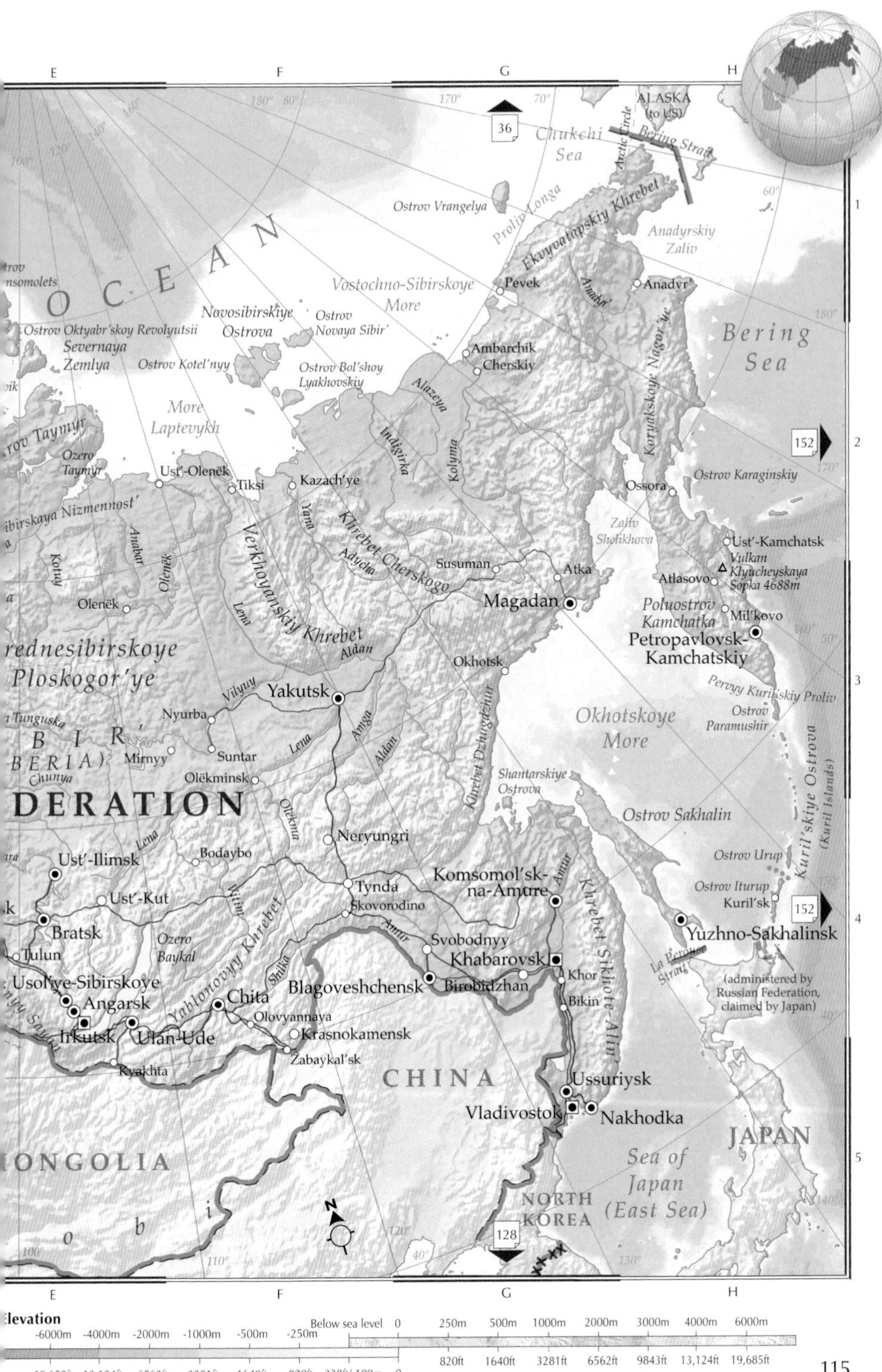
Chukchi Sea
ALASKA (to US)
Bering Strait
Arctic Circle
Ostrov Vrangelya
Proliv Longa
Ekvyvatapskiy Khrebet
Anadyrskiy Zaliv
OCEAN
Vostochno-Sibirskoye More
Pevek
Anadyr'
Novosibirskiye Ostrova
Ostrov Novaya Sibir'
Ostrov Oktyabr'skoy Revolyutsii
Severnaya Zemlya
Ostrov Kotel'nyy
Ostrov Bol'shoy Lyakhovskiy
Ambarchik
Cherskiy
Koryakskoye Nagor'ye
Bering Sea
More Laptevykh
Alazeya
Indigirka
Kolyma
Ozero Taymyr
Ust'-Olenëk
Tiksi
Kazach'ye
Ossora
Ostrov Karaginskiy
Verkhoyanskiy Khrebet
Khrebet Cherskogo
Yana
Adycha
Zaliv Shelikhova
Ust'-Kamchatsk
Vulkan Klyucheyskaya Sopka 4688m
Atlasovo
Susuman
Atka
Anabar
Olenëk
Kotuy
Magadan
Poluostrov Kamchatka
Mil'kovo
Petropavlovsk-Kamchatskiy
Lena
Aldan
Srednesibirskoye Ploskogor'ye
Okhotsk
Pervyy Kuril'skiy Proliv
Yakutsk
Vilyuy
Nyurba
Suntar
Mirnyy
Amga
Okhotskoye More
Ostrov Paramushir
Olëkminsk
Khrebet Dzhugdzhur
Shantarskiye Ostrova
FEDERATION
Olëkma
Ostrov Sakhalin
Kuril'skiye Ostrova (Kuril Islands)
Neryungri
Ust'-Ilimsk
Bodaybo
Ostrov Urup
Tynda
Komsomol'sk-na-Amure
Amur
Khrebet Sikhote-Alin
Ostrov Iturup
Kuril'sk
Ust'-Kut
Skovorodino
Bratsk
Vitim
Ozero Baykal
Svobodnyy
Khabarovsk
Yuzhno-Sakhalinsk
La Perouse Strait
Tulun
Yablonovyy Khrebet
Shilka
Blagoveshchensk
Birobidzhan
Khor
(administered by Russian Federation, claimed by Japan)
Usol'ye-Sibirskoye
Angarsk
Chita
Bikin
Olovyannaya
Irkutsk
Ulan-Ude
Krasnokamensk
Zabaykal'sk
Kyakhta
CHINA
Ussuriysk
Vladivostok
Nakhodka
JAPAN
MONGOLIA
Sea of Japan (East Sea)
NORTH KOREA
Gobi
36
152
128
Elevation
Below sea level
-6000m -4000m -2000m -1000m -500m -250m
-19,658ft -13,124ft -6562ft -3281ft -1640ft -820ft -328ft/-100m 0
0 250m 500m 1000m 2000m 3000m 4000m 6000m
820ft 1640ft 3281ft 6562ft 9843ft 13,124ft 19,685ft

Turkey & the Caucasus

0 km 200

0 miles 200

Population

● National capital

○ below 50,000 ○ 50,000 to 100,000 ◉ 100,000 to 500,000 ▣ above 500,000

E
F
G
H
111
RUSSIAN FEDERATION
Caucasus
Caspian Sea
Ap'khazet'i
Gagra
Gudauta
Sokhumi
Ochamchire
Enguri
Mestia
Kazbek 5047m
South Ossetia
Kutaisi
GEORGIA
Samtredia
Poti
Gori
Tsalka
TBILISI
Rustavi
Kobuleti
Batumi
Achara
Lesser Caucasus
Akhaltsikhe
Hopa
Zaqatala
Greater Caucasus
Xaçmaz
Quba
Siyäzän
122
Şäki
Kura
Sumqayıt
Pazar
Artvin
Rize
Of
Doğu Karadeniz Dağları
Çoruh Nehri
Gyumri
Vanadzor
Gäncä
Mingäçevir
Yevlax
Märäzä
BAKI (BAKU)
Kars
Artik
Sevan
ARMENIA
AZERBAIJAN
Qazimämmäd
Ali-Bayramı
Sarıkamış
YEREVAN
Sevana Lich
Nagorno-Karabakh
İmişli
İspir
Horasan
Aras
Artashat
Xankändi
Pasinler
Aşkale
Erzurum
Büyükağrı Dağı (Mount Ararat) 5137m
Ağri
Goris
AZERBAIJAN
Biläsuvar
Erzincan
Tercan
Doğubayazıt
Kemah
Patnos
Naxçıvan
Länkäran
Erciş
Muradiye
Keban Barajı
Bingöl
Muş
Elazığ
Tatvan
Van Gölü
Van
Bitlis
Toroslar
Gevaş
Daryācheh-ye Orūmīyeh
Reshteh-ye Kūhhā-ye Alborz (Elburz Mountains)
Silvan
Siirt
Batman
Diyarbakır
Silverek
Şırnak
Kurdistan
Mardin
Viranşehir
IRAN
120
Nusaybin
Şanlıurfa
Ceylanpınar
Tigris
Al Jazīrah
Euphrates
IRAQ
Jabal Bishrī
Kūhhā-ye Zāgros (Zagros Mountains)
Buḩayrat ath Tharthār
120
1
2
3
4
5
Elevation
-6000m -4000m -2000m -1000m -500m -250m
Below sea level 0
250m 500m 1000m 2000m 3000m 4000m 6000m
820ft 1640ft 3281ft 6562ft 9843ft 13,124ft 19,685ft
-19,658ft -13,124ft -6562ft -3281ft -1640ft -820ft -328ft/-100m 0

The Near East

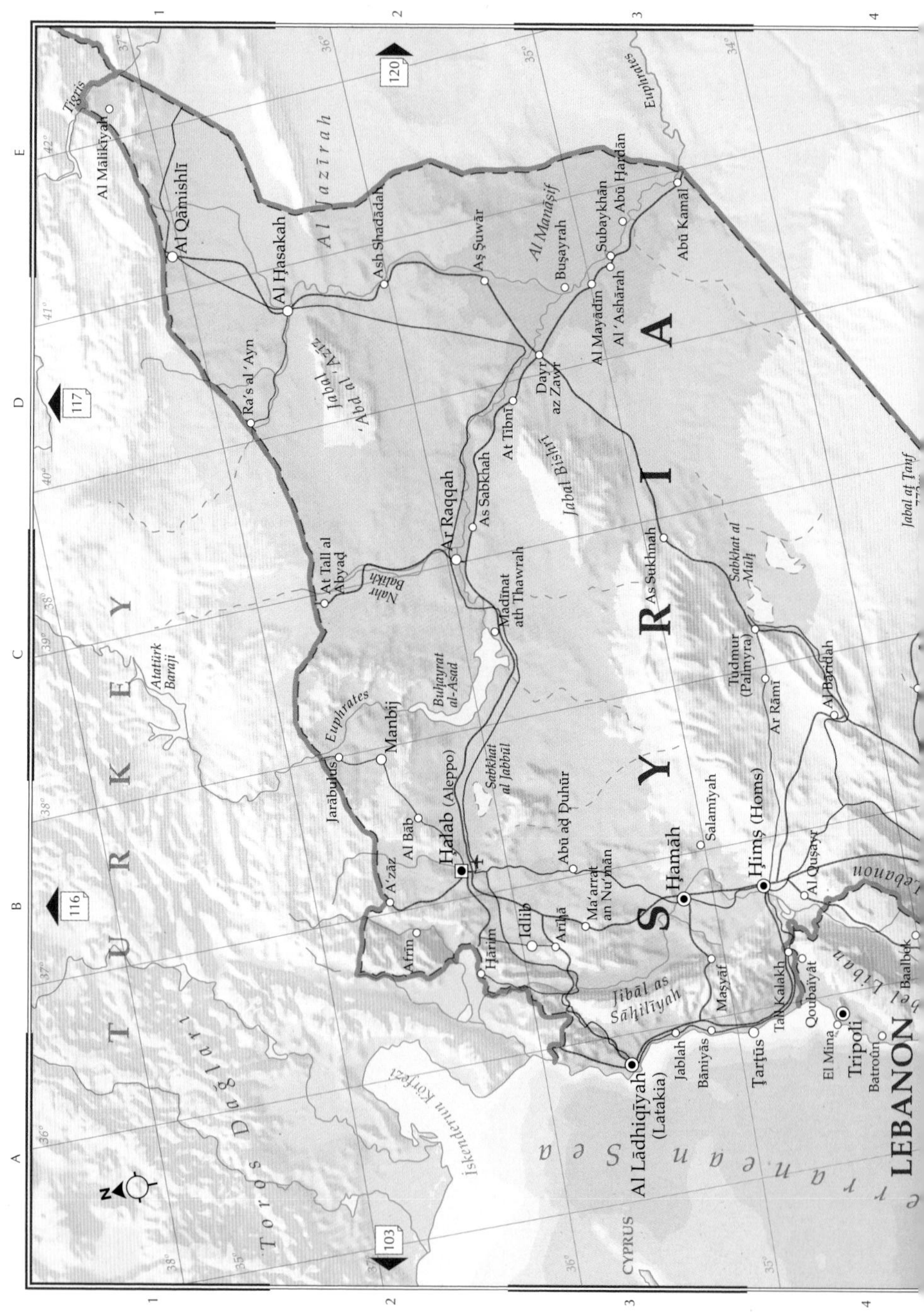

0 km 100
0 miles 100

Population

● National capital
○ below 50,000
○ 50,000 to 100,000
◉ 100,000 to 500,000
▣ above 500,000

Elevation

Below sea level	0	250m	500m	1000m	2000m	3000m	4000m	6000m
		820ft	1640ft	3281ft	6562ft	9843ft	13,124ft	19,685ft

-6000m	-4000m	-2000m	-1000m	-500m	-250m	0
-19,658ft	-13,124ft	-6562ft	-3281ft	-1640ft	-820ft	-328ft/-100m 0

The Middle East

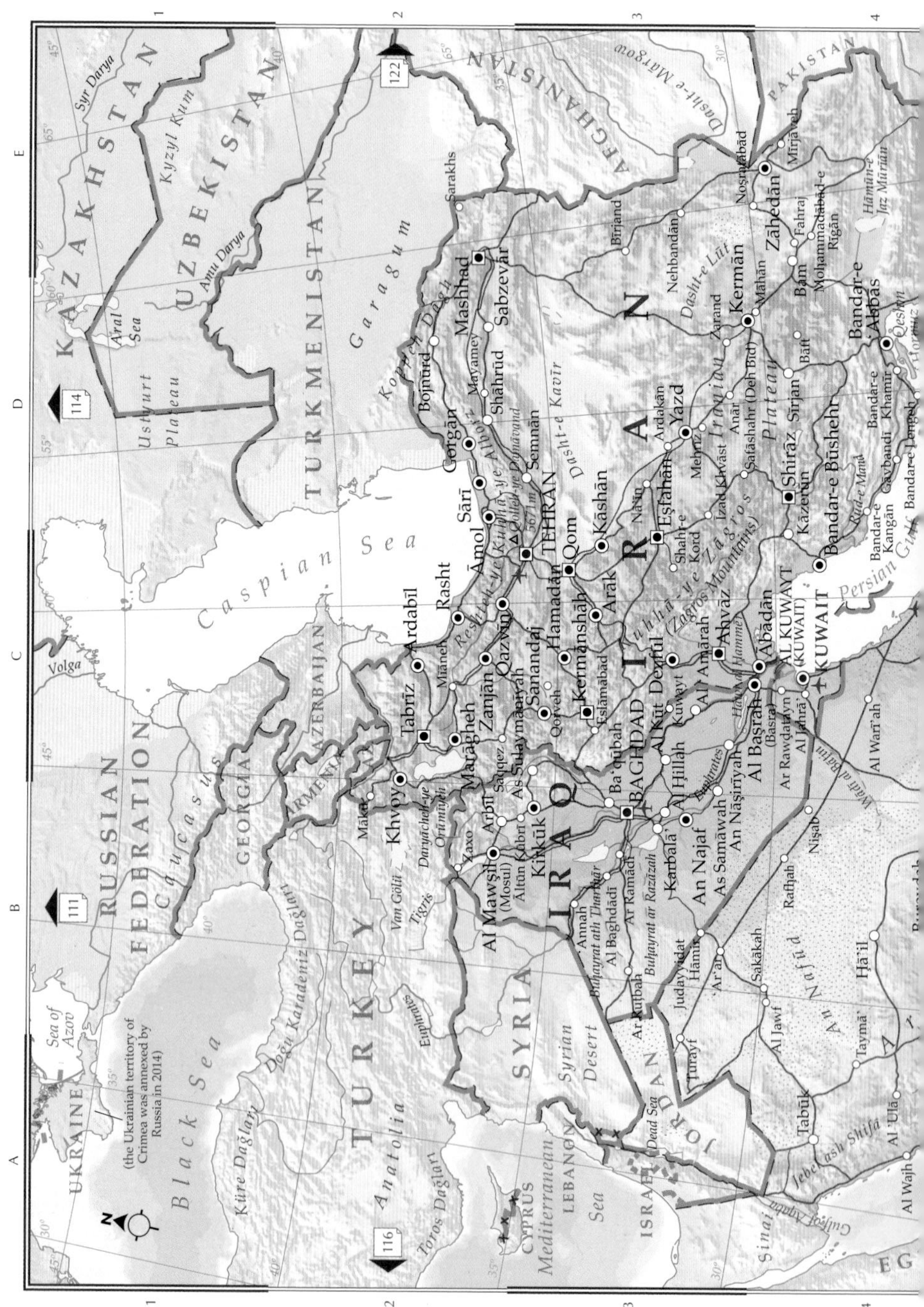

114
111
116
122

0 km 400

0 miles 400

Population

● National capital

○ below 50,000 ○ 50,000 to 100,000 ◉ 100,000 to 500,000 ▣ above 500,000

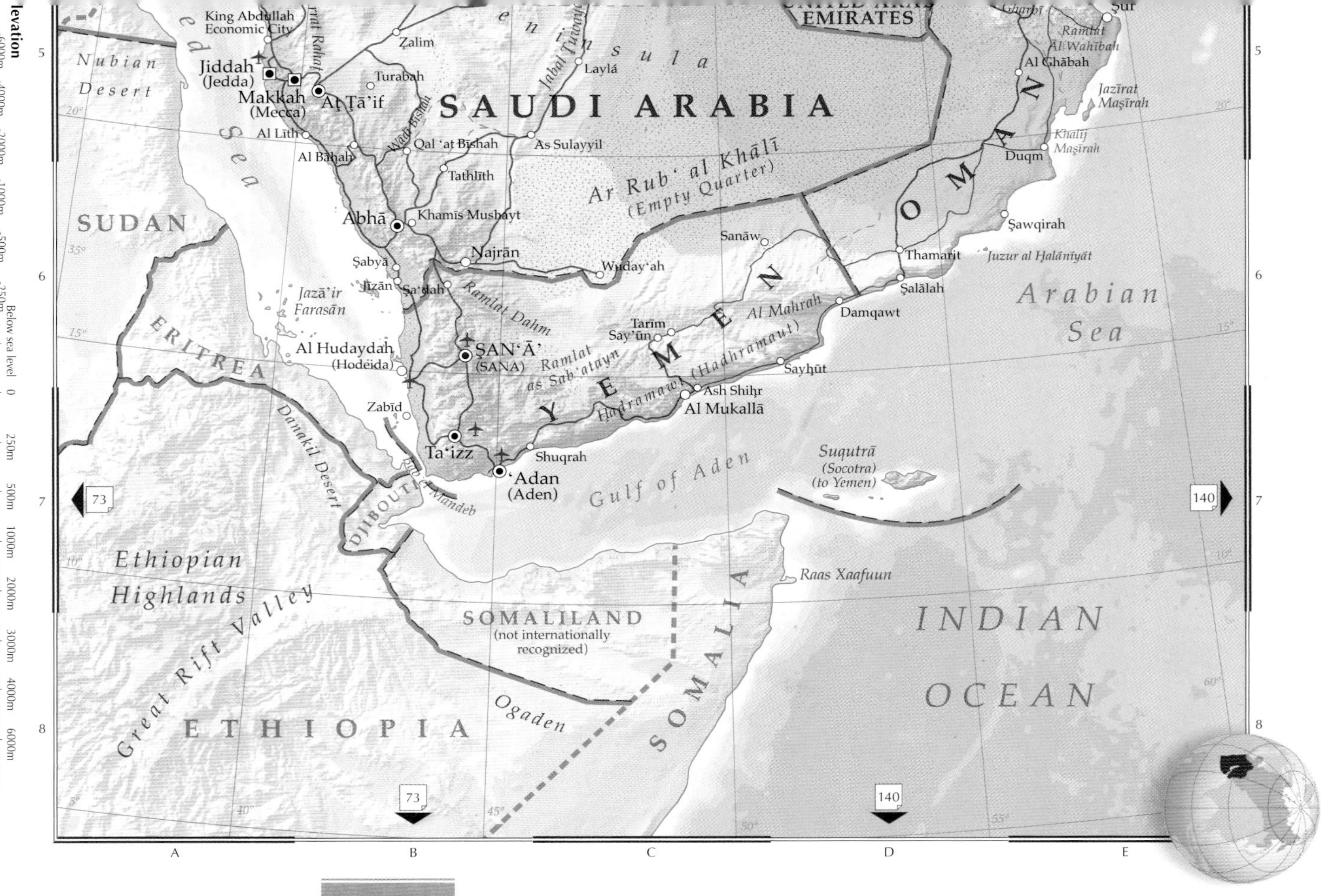
SAUDI ARABIA
Ar Rub' al Khālī
(Empty Quarter)
OMAN
YEMEN
EMIRATES
Arabian Sea
INDIAN OCEAN
Gulf of Aden
SOMALIA
SOMALILAND
(not internationally recognized)
ETHIOPIA
ERITREA
SUDAN
DJIBOUTI
Red Sea
Nubian Desert
Danakil Desert
Ethiopian Highlands
Great Rift Valley
Ogaden
Şan'ā'
(SANA)
'Adan
(Aden)
Ta'izz
Al Hudaydah
(Hodeida)
Makkah
(Mecca)
Jiddah
(Jedda)
Aţ Ţā'if
Abhā
Najrān
Al Mukallā
Ash Shiḩr
Şalālah
Thamarīt
Duqm
Şawqirah
Damqawt
Sayḩūt
Sanāw
Tarīm
Say'ūn
Shuqrah
Zabīd
Şabyā
Jīzān
Şa'dah
Khamīs Mushayt
Tathlīth
As Sulayyil
Laylá
Wuday'ah
Al Bāḩah
Al Līth
King Abdullah Economic City
Turabah
Zalim
Qal 'at Bīshah
Al Ghābah
Şūr
Suquţrā
(Socotra)
(to Yemen)
Raas Xaafuun
Jazā'ir Farasān
Jazīrat Maşīrah
Khalīj Maşīrah
Ramlat Al Wahībah
Ramlat Dahm
Ramlat as Sab'atayn
Ḩaḑramawt
Al Mahrah
(Hadhramaut)
Jabal Tuwayq
Juzur al Ḩalānīyāt
73
140
Elevation
Below sea level
-6000m -4000m -2000m -1000m -500m -250m
-19,658ft -13,124ft -6562ft -3281ft -1640ft -820ft -328ft/-100m
0 250m 500m 1000m 2000m 3000m 4000m 6000m
820ft 1640ft 3281ft 6562ft 9843ft 13,124ft 19,685ft

Central Asia

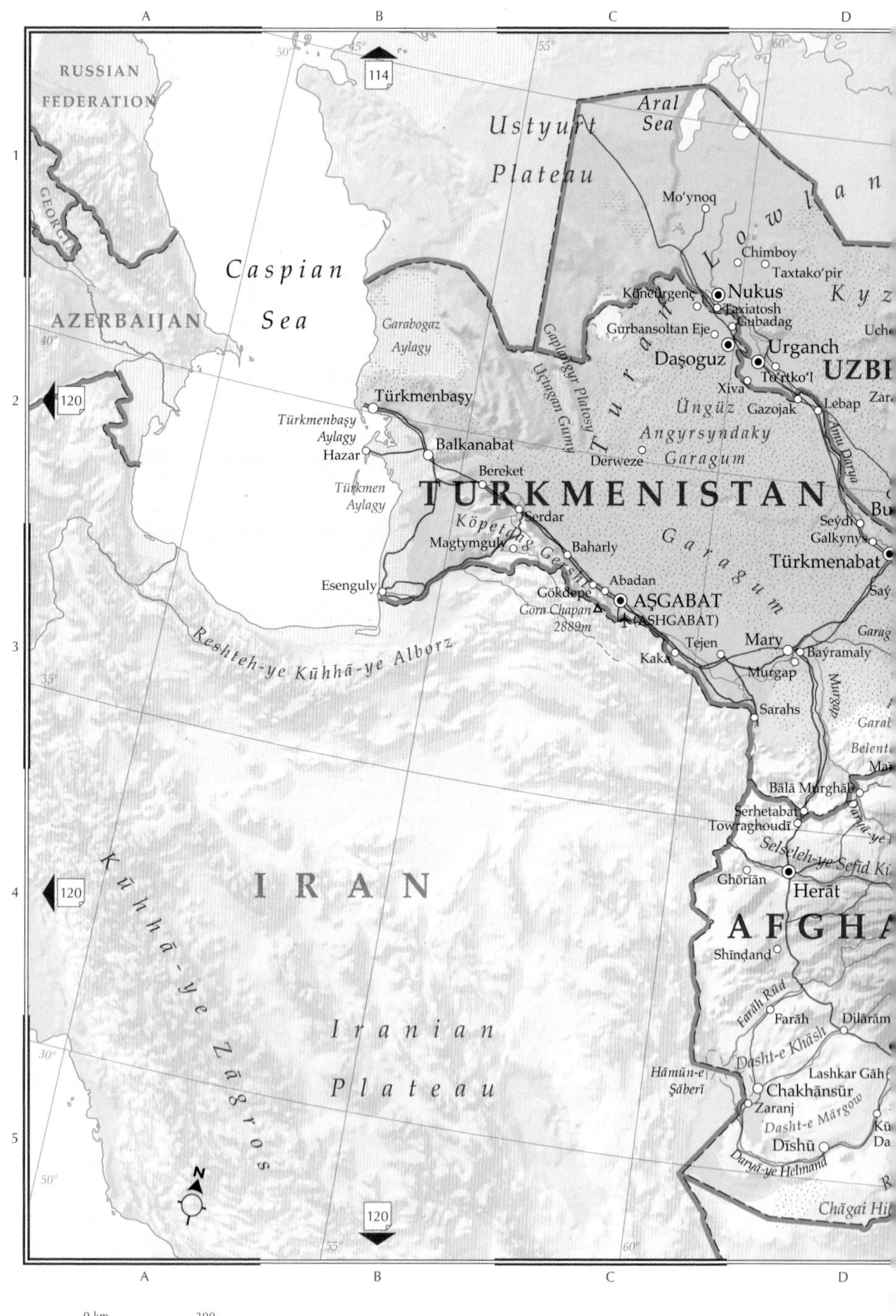

0 km 200
0 miles 200

Population

● National capital
○ below 50,000
○ 50,000 to 100,000
◉ 100,000 to 500,000
▣ above 500,000

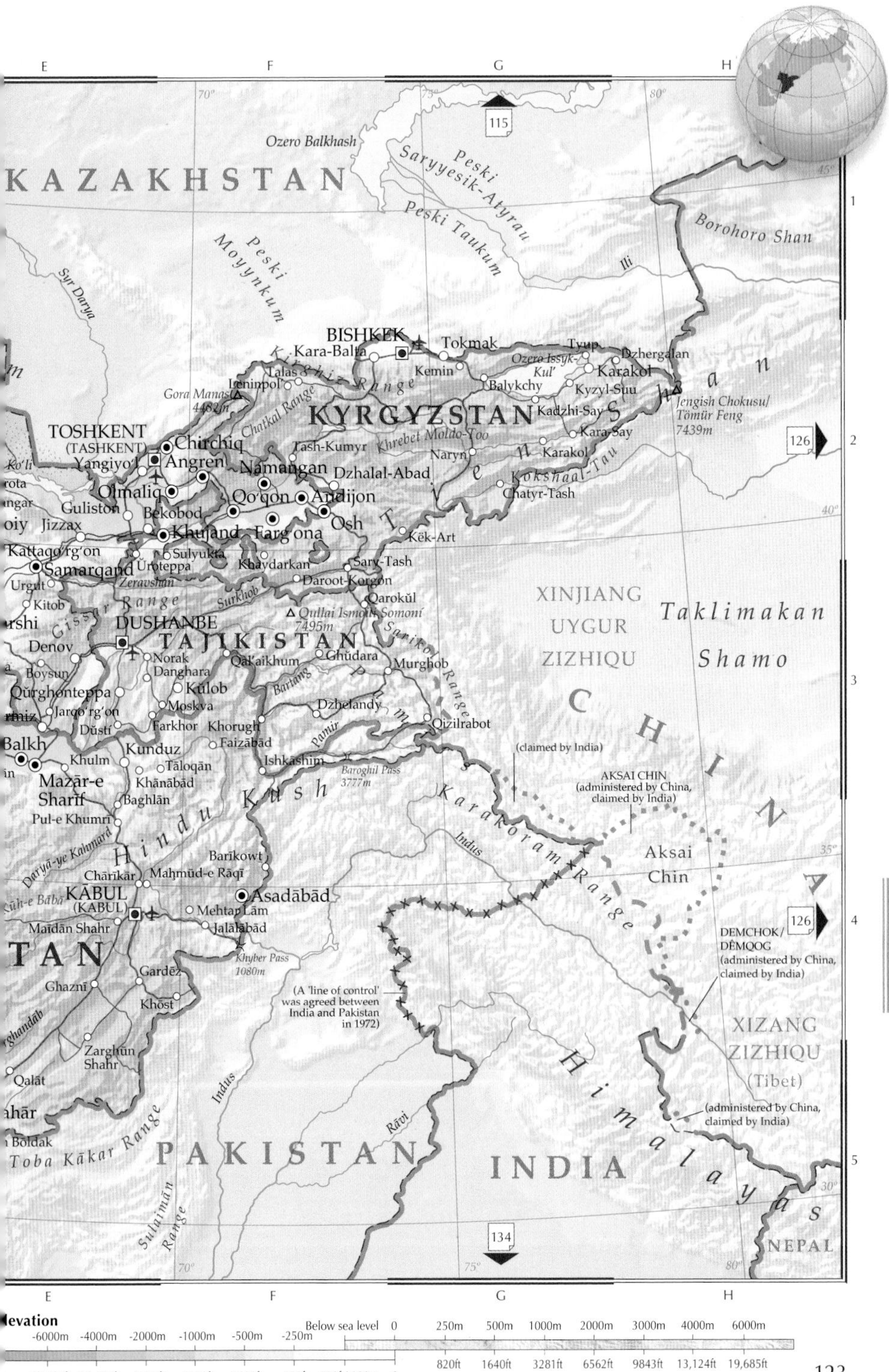

E
F
G
H
1
2
3
4
5
115
126
134
KAZAKHSTAN
Ozero Balkhash
Peski Saryyesik-Atyrau
Peski Taukum
Peski Moyynkum
Borohoro Shan
Ili
Sur Darya
BISHKEK
Kara-Balta
Tokmak
Tyup
Dzhergalan
Ozero Issyk-Kul'
Karakol
Kemin
Balykchy
Kyzyl-Suu
Talas
Leninpol'
Kirghiz Range
Gora Manas 4482m
Chatkal Range
KYRGYZSTAN
Kadzhi-Say
Jengish Chokusu/ Tömür Feng 7439m
Khrebet Moldo-Too
Kara-Say
TOSHKENT (TASHKENT)
Chirchiq
Angren
Yangiyo'l
Tash-Kumyr
Naryn
Karakol
Namangan
Dzhalal-Abad
Kokshaal-Tau
Olmaliq
Qo'qon
Andijon
Chatyr-Tash
Guliston
Bekobod
Osh
Jizzax
Khujand
Farg'ona
Këk-Art
Kattaqo'rg'on
Sulyukta
Samarqand
Ŭroteppa
Khaydarkan
Sary-Tash
Zeravshan
Urgut
Daroot-Korgon
Qarokŭl
Kitob
Gissar Range
Surkhob
Qullai Ismoili Somoní 7495m
XINJIANG UYGUR ZIZHIQU
Taklimakan Shamo
DUSHANBE
TAJIKISTAN
Sarikol Range
Denov
Norak
Qal'aikhum
Ghŭdara
Murghob
Boysun
Danghara
Qŭrghonteppa
Kŭlob
Bartang
Moskva
Dzhelandy
Pamir
Jarqo'rg'on
Dŭstí
Farkhor
Khorugh
Qizilrabot
CHINA
Balkh
Kunduz
Faizābād
Khulm
Tāloqān
Ishkāshim
(claimed by India)
Mazār-e Sharīf
Khānābād
Baroghil Pass 3777m
AKSAI CHIN (administered by China, claimed by India)
Baghlān
Hindu Kush
Karakoram Range
Pul-e Khumrī
Indus
Daryā-ye Kahmard
Barīkowt
Aksai Chin
Chārīkār
Maḥmūd-e Rāqī
KĀBUL (KABUL)
Asadābād
Mehtar Lām
Maīdān Shahr
Jalālābād
DEMCHOK/ DÊMQOG (administered by China, claimed by India)
Khyber Pass 1080m
Gardēz
Ghaznī
(A 'line of control' was agreed between India and Pakistan in 1972)
Khōst
XIZANG ZIZHIQU (Tibet)
Zarghūn Shahr
Himalayas
Qalāt
(administered by China, claimed by India)
Toba Kākar Range
PAKISTAN
Rāvi
INDIA
Sulaimān Range
NEPAL
Elevation
Below sea level
0
250m
500m
1000m
2000m
3000m
4000m
6000m
-6000m
-4000m
-2000m
-1000m
-500m
-250m
820ft
1640ft
3281ft
6562ft
9843ft
13,124ft
19,685ft
-19,658ft
-13,124ft
-6562ft
-3281ft
-1640ft
-820ft
-328ft/-100m

South & East Asia

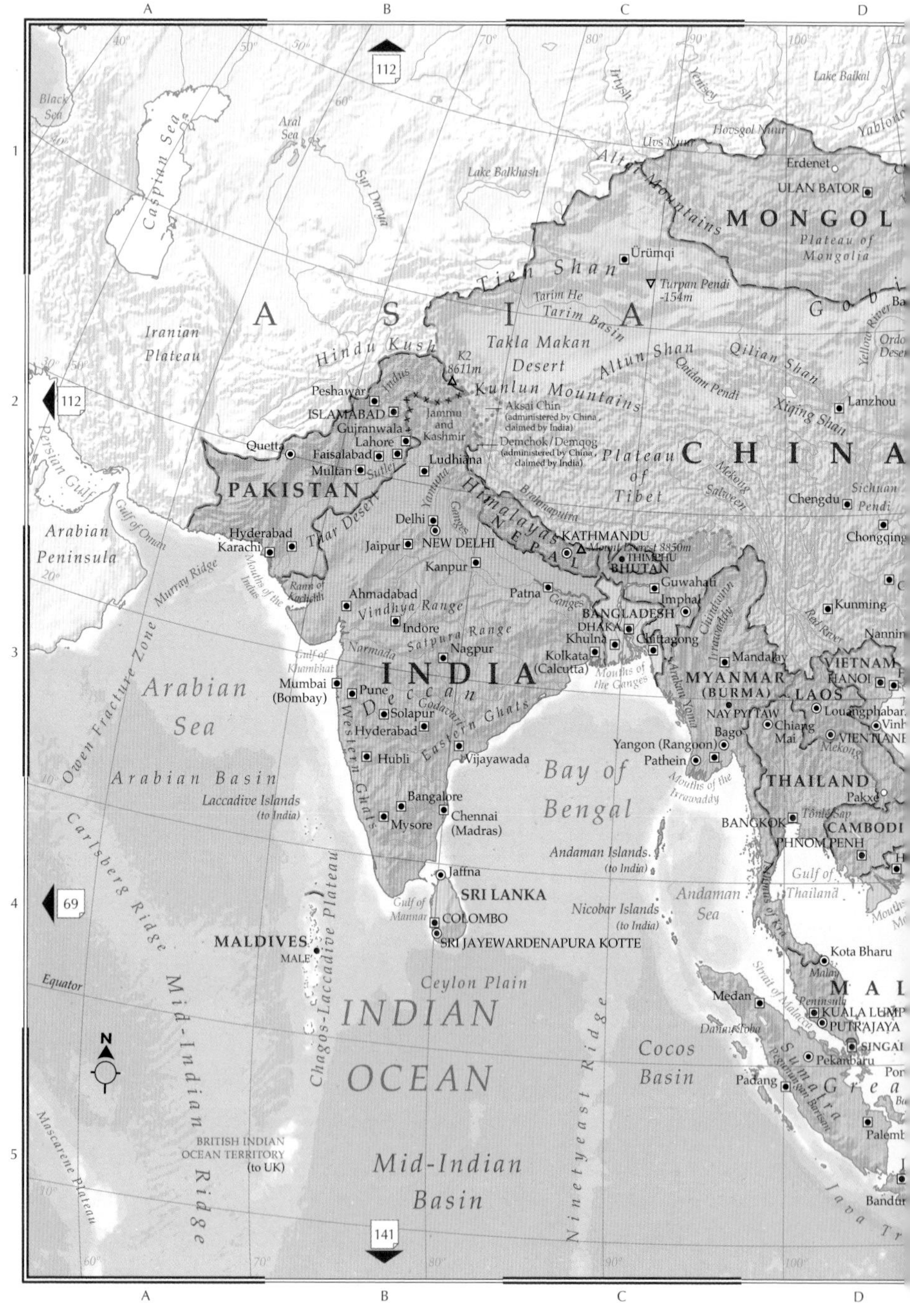

0 km 1000

0 miles 1000

Population

• National capital

○ below 50,000 ○ 50,000 to 100,000 ⦿ 100,000 to 500,000 ◼ above 500,000

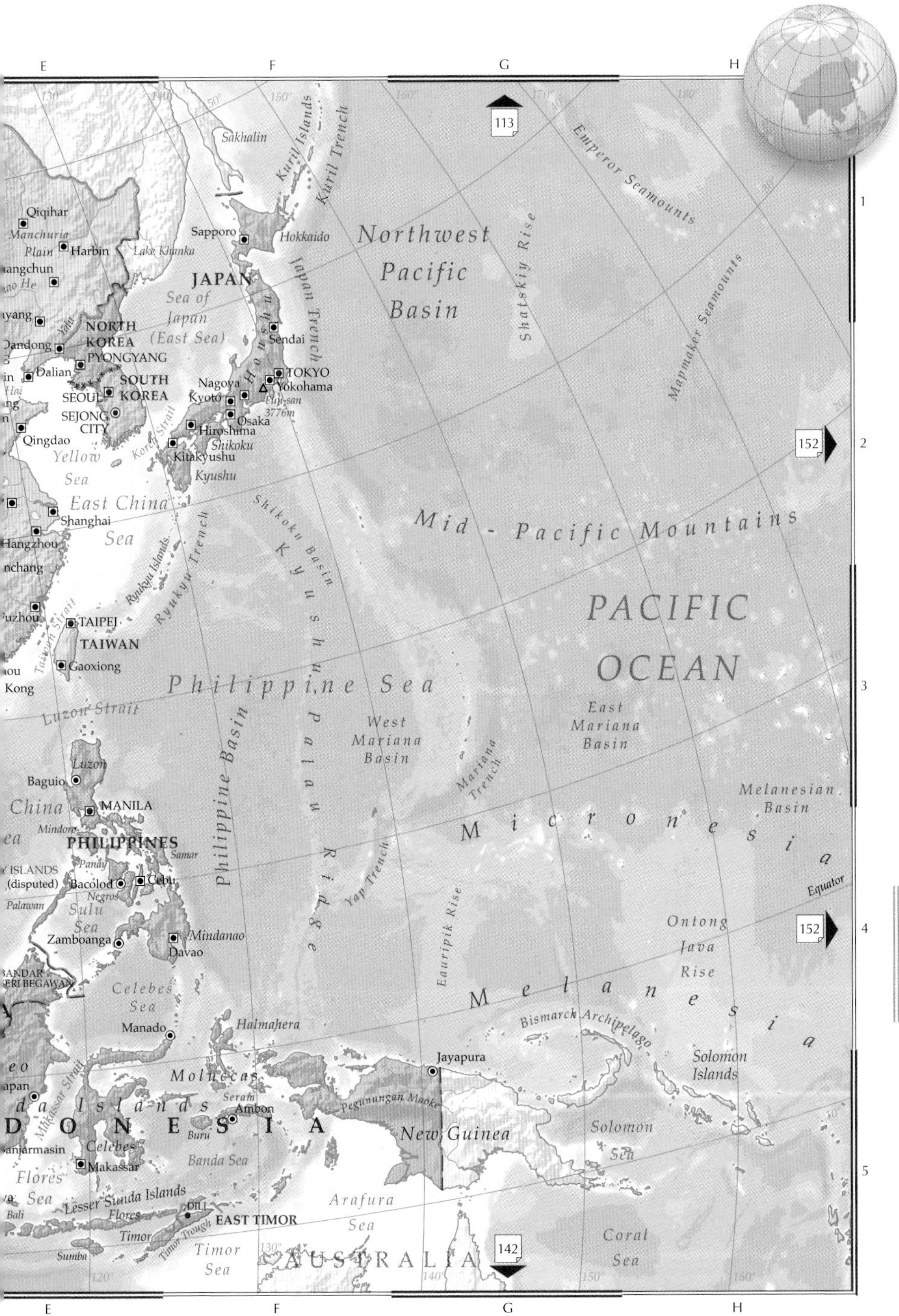

113
152
152
142

Western China & Mongolia

0 km 400
0 miles 400

Population

○ below 50,000

● National capital
○ 50,000 to 100,000

● Internal administrative capital
◉ 100,000 to 500,000

■ above 500,00

RUSS. FED.
HEILONGJIANG
JILIN
LIAONING
NORTH KOREA
SOUTH KOREA
JAPAN
TAIWAN
HEBEI
SHANDONG
SHANXI
HENAN
JIANGSU
ANHUI
SHANGHAI SHI
HUBEI
ZHEJIANG
JIANGXI
HUNAN
FUJIAN
GUIZHOU
CHONGQING
SHAANXI
GANSU
NINGXIA
YUNNAN
BEIJING
TIANJIN
NEI MONGOL ZIZHIQU (Inner Mongolia)
ULAANBAATAR (ULAN BATOR)
Sühbaatar
Darhan
Choybalsan
Dzuunmod
Öndörhaan
Baruun-Urt
Saynshand
Erenhot
Dalandzadgad
Manzhouli
Hulun Buir (Hailar)
Ergun
Jagdaqi
Holin Gol
Tongliao
Xilinhot
Chifeng (Ulanhad)
Ulan Qab (Jining)
Hohhot
Baotou
Wuhai (Haibowan)
Hulun Nur
Menengiyn Tal
Mu Us Shadi
Great Wall of China
Da Hinggan Ling
Lang Shan
Amur (Heilong Jiang)
Argun (Ergun He)
Shilka
Onon
Onon Gol
Kerulen
Liao He
Huang He (Yellow River)
Han Shui
Chang Jiang (Yangtze)
Lake Khanka
Sea of Japan (East Sea)
Korea Bay
Liaodong Wan
Bo Hai
Yellow Sea
East China Sea
Nansei-shotō (to Japan)
Tropic of Cancer
115
128
129
Elevation
Below sea level
0
250m 500m 1000m 2000m 3000m 4000m 6000m
820ft 1640ft 3281ft 6562ft 9843ft 13,124ft 19,685ft
-6000m -4000m -2000m -1000m -500m -250m
-19,658ft -13,124ft -6562ft -3281ft -1640ft -820ft -328ft/-100m

Eastern China & Korea

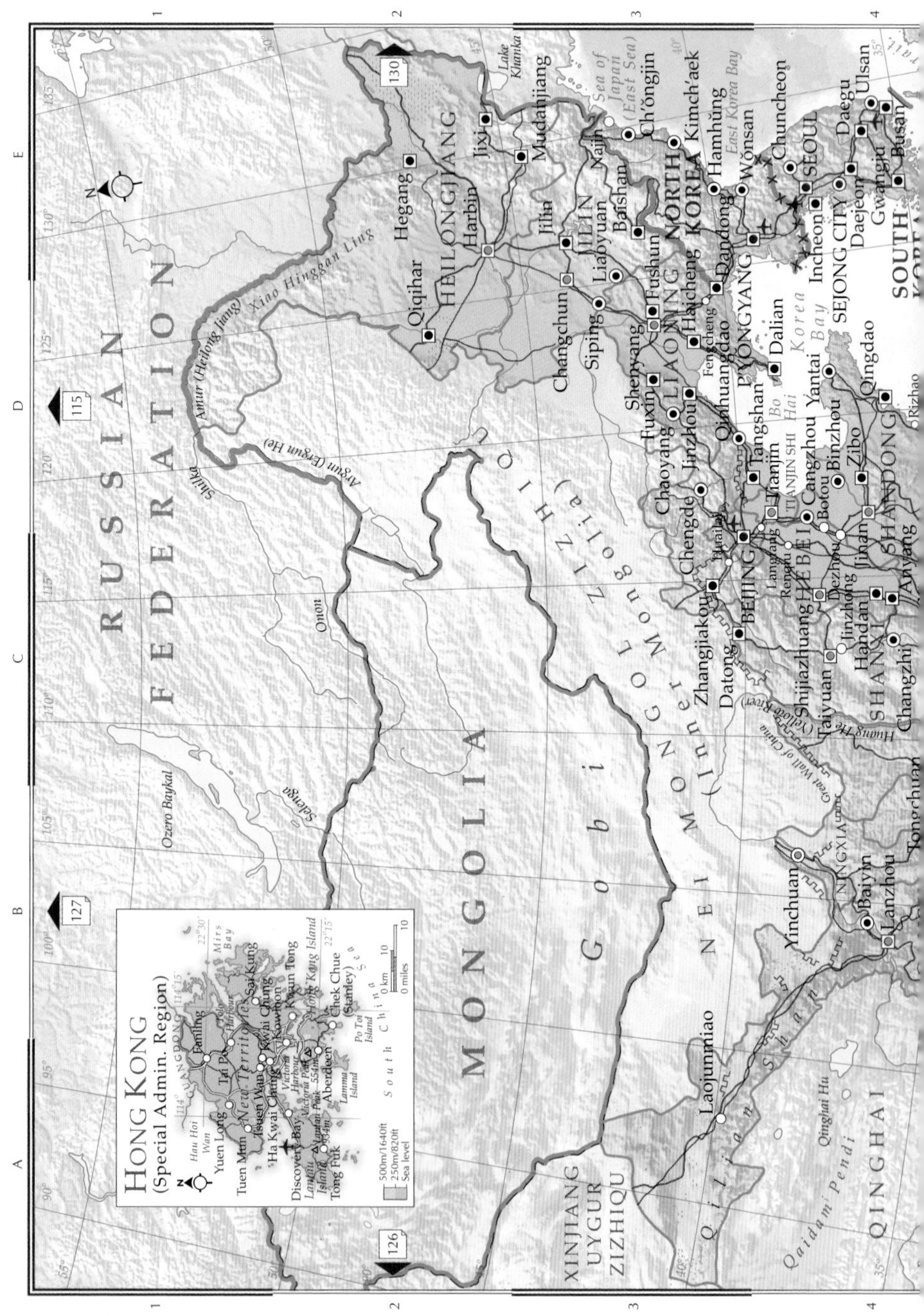

0 km 400
0 miles 400

Population

● National capital ● Internal administrative capital

○ below 50,000 ○ 50,000 to 100,000 ◉ 100,000 to 500,000 ▣ above 500,000

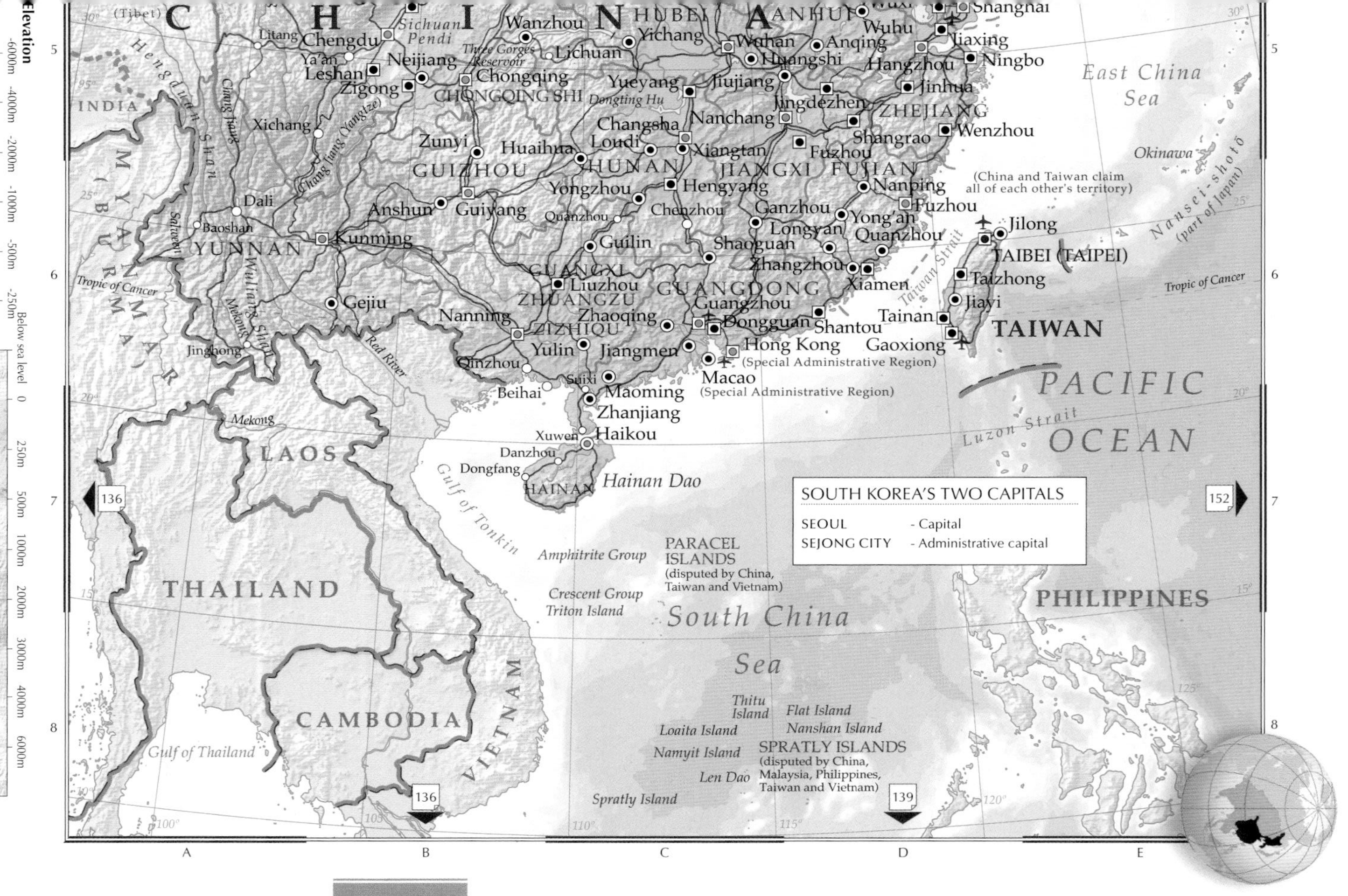

Elevation

-6000m	-4000m	-2000m	-1000m	-500m	-250m	Below sea level	0	250m	500m	1000m	2000m	3000m	4000m	6000m
-19,658ft	-13,124ft	-6562ft	-3281ft	-1640ft	-820ft	-328ft/-100m	0	820ft	1640ft	3281ft	6562ft	9843ft	13,124ft	19,685ft

Japan

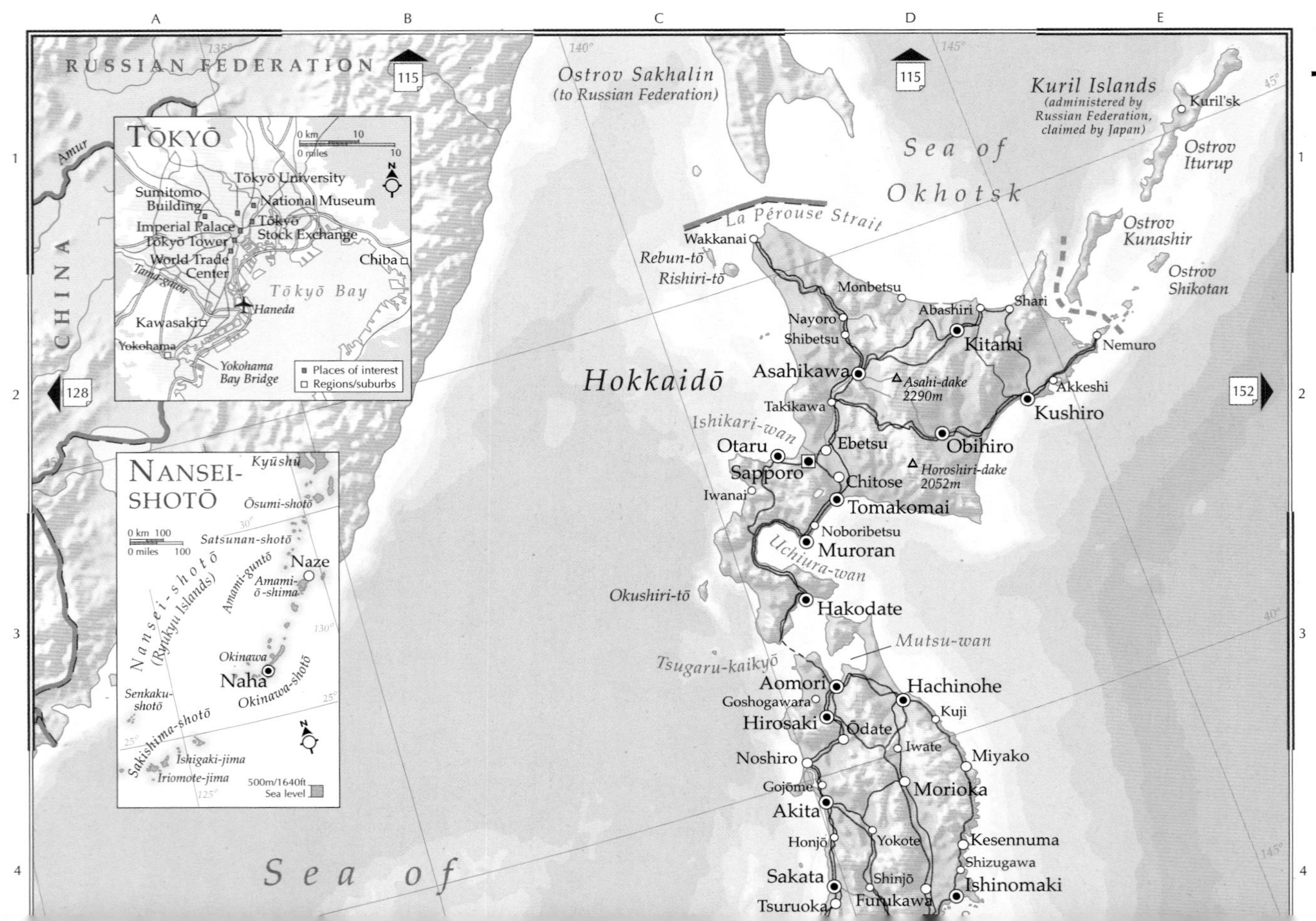

0 km 200

0 miles 200

Population

● National capital

○ below 50,000 ○ 50,000 to 100,000 ⊙ 100,000 to 500,000 ■ above 500,0

PACIFIC OCEAN
East China Sea
SOUTH KOREA
Shikoku
Kyūshū
Korea Strait
Tsushima
Iki
Kō-saki
Gotō-rettō
Koshikijima-rettō
Amakusa-nada
Kagoshima-wan
Ōsumi-shotō
Yaku-shima
Tanega-shima
Shibushi-wan
Bungo-suidō
Iyo-nada
Tosa-wan
Kii-suidō
Harima-nada
Awaji-shima
Biwa-ko
Wakasa-wan
Ise-wan
Suruga-wan
Sagami-nada
Izu-hantō
Bōsō-hantō
Izu-shotō
Ō-shima
Nii-jima
Kōzu-shima
Miyake-jima
Mikura-jima
Hachijō-jima
Oki-shotō
Dōgo
Dōzen
Liancourt Rocks (under South Korean control)
Toyama-wan
Hida-sammyaku
Chūgoku-sanchi
Kasumiga-ura
Fuji-san 3776m
Hitachi
Utsunomiya
Mito
Chōshi
Oyama
Chiba
Kawagoe
TŌKYŌ
Yokohama
Kawasaki
Maebashi
Kōfu
Fuji
Hamamatsu
Shizuoka
Toyota
Okazaki
Nagoya
Gifu
Ōgaki
Ise
Tsu
Ōtsu
Owase
Shingū
Tanabe
Wakayama
Gobō
Ōsaka
Kyōto
Kobe
Himeji
Nagano
Matsumoto
Jōetsu
Itoigawa
Toyama
Takaoka
Kanazawa
Komatsu
Fukui
Tsuruga
Nakatsugawa
Tottori
Okayama
Kurashiki
Tokushima
Niihama
Matsuyama
Kōchi
Nakamura
Sukumo
Yonago
Matsue
Kure
Hiroshima
Iwakuni
Hōfu
Ube
Gōtsu
Hamada
Masuda
Yamaguchi
Nagato
Shimonoseki
Kitakyūshū
Fukuoka
Kurume
Ōmuta
Kumamoto
Sasebo
Nagasaki
Ōita
Nobeoka
Miyazaki
Miyakonojō
Yatsushiro
Satsuma-Sendai
Kagoshima
Elevation
-6000m -4000m -2000m -1000m -500m -250m
Below sea level 0
250m 500m 1000m 2000m 3000m 4000m 6000m
-19,658ft -13,124ft -6562ft -3281ft -1640ft -820ft -328ft/-100m 0
820ft 1640ft 3281ft 6562ft 9843ft 13,124ft 19,685ft

Southern India & Sri Lanka

SRI LANKA'S TWO CAPITALS	
COLOMBO	- Capital
SRI JAYEWARDENAPURA KOTTE	- Administrative capital

0 km 300

0 miles 300

Population

● National capital

○ below 50,000 ○ 50,000 to 100,000 ◉ 100,000 to 500,000 ▣ above 500,000

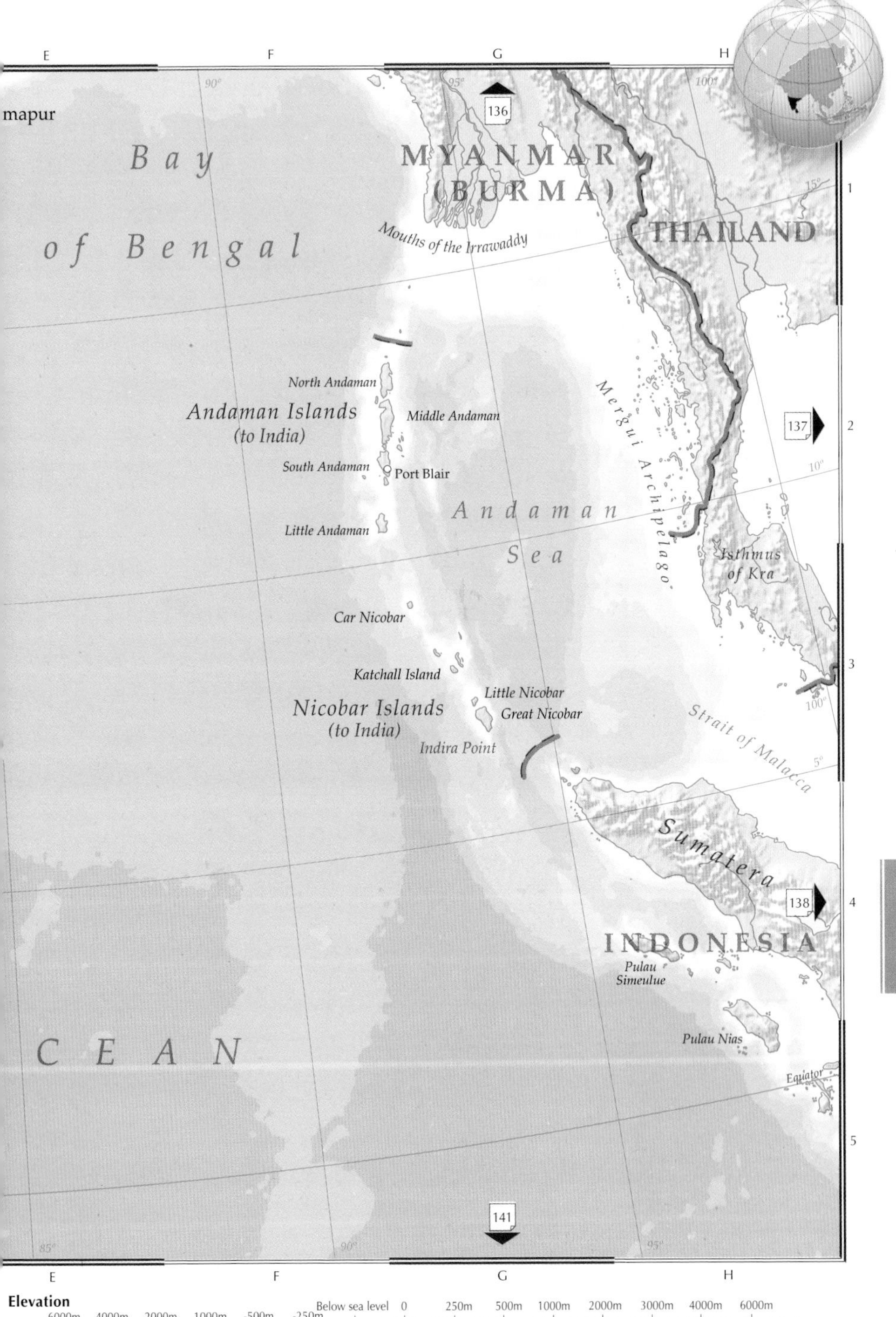
E
F
G
H
136
137
138
141
1
2
3
4
5
mapur
Bay of Bengal
MYANMAR (BURMA)
THAILAND
Mouths of the Irrawaddy
North Andaman
Andaman Islands (to India)
Middle Andaman
South Andaman
Port Blair
Mergui Archipelago
Andaman Sea
Little Andaman
Isthmus of Kra
Car Nicobar
Katchall Island
Little Nicobar
Nicobar Islands (to India)
Great Nicobar
Indira Point
Strait of Malacca
Sumatera
INDONESIA
Pulau Simeulue
Pulau Nias
Equator
CEAN
90°
95°
100°
15°
10°
5°
85°
Elevation
Below sea level
-6000m -4000m -2000m -1000m -500m -250m
0 250m 500m 1000m 2000m 3000m 4000m 6000m
-19,658ft -13,124ft -6562ft -3281ft -1640ft -820ft -328ft/-100m 0
820ft 1640ft 3281ft 6562ft 9843ft 13,124ft 19,685ft

Northern India, Pakistan & Bangladesh

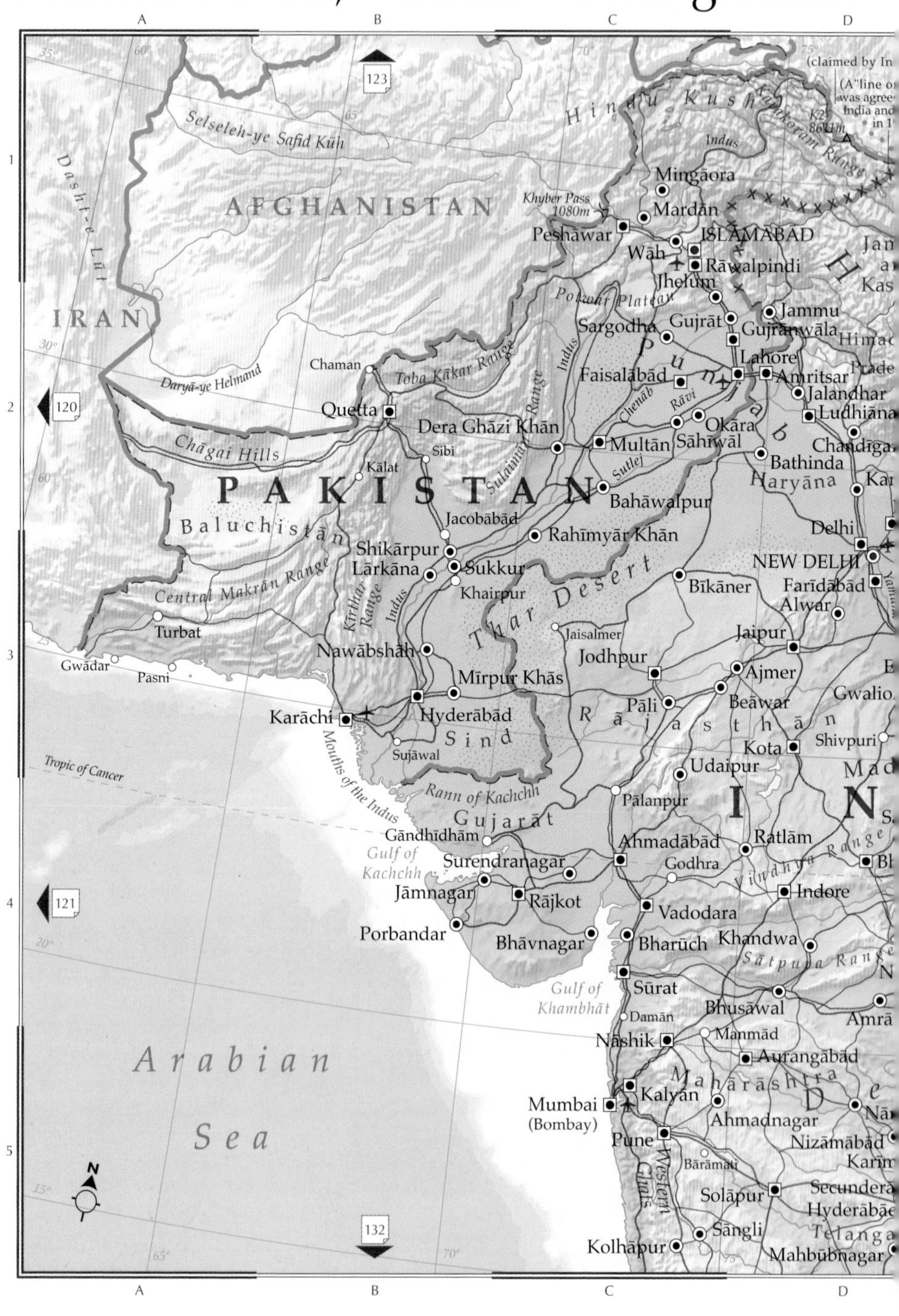

0 km 300
0 miles 300

Population

● National capital

○ below 50,000 ○ 50,000 to 100,000 ◉ 100,000 to 500,000 ◘ above 500,00

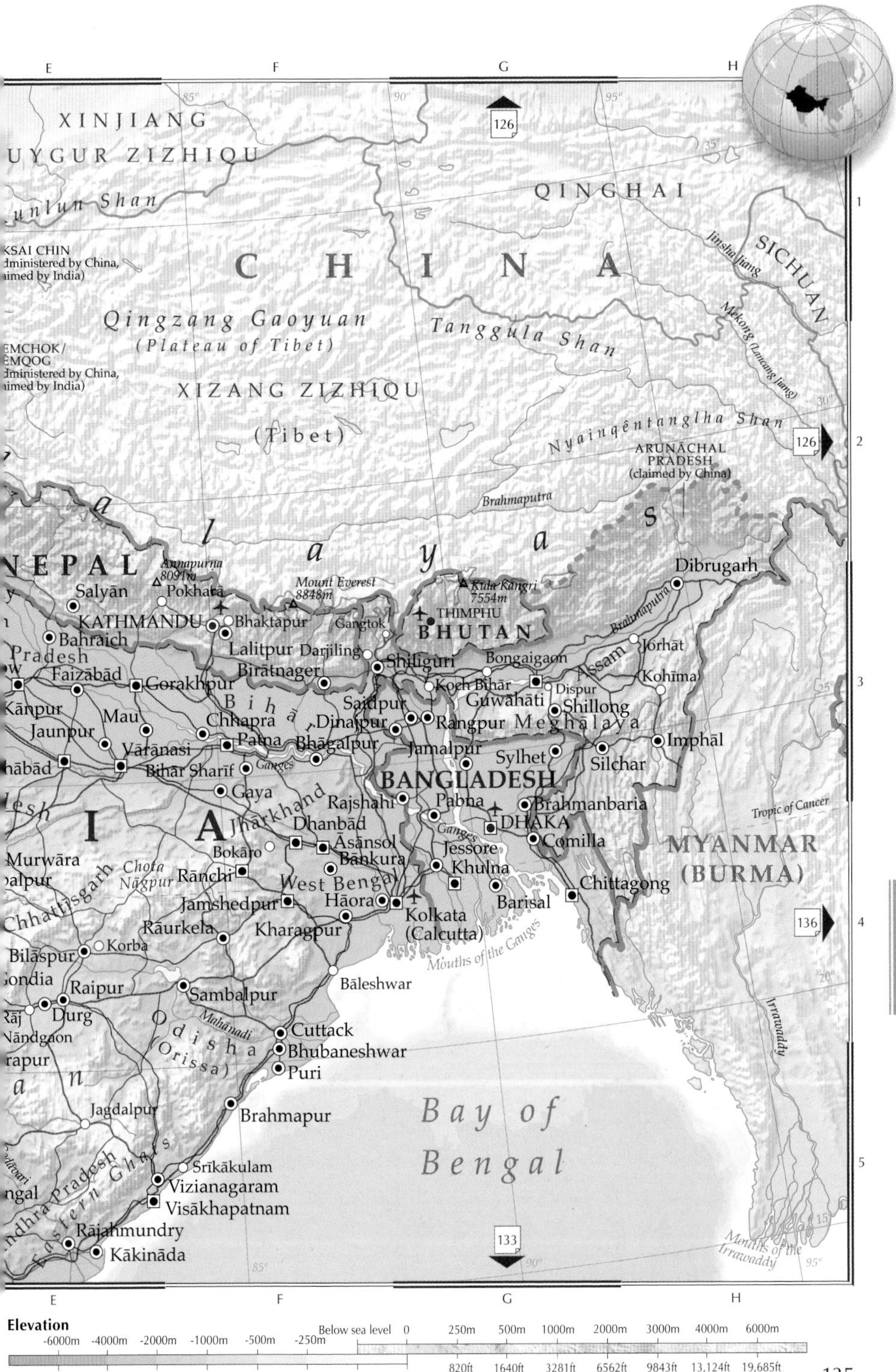
E
F
G
H
126
XINJIANG
UYGUR ZIZHIQU
Kunlun Shan
QINGHAI
1
SICHUAN
Jinsha Jiang
AKSAI CHIN
(administered by China, claimed by India)
CHINA
Qingzang Gaoyuan
(Plateau of Tibet)
Tanggula Shan
Mekong (Lancang Jiang)
DEMCHOK/
DÊMQOG
(administered by China, claimed by India)
XIZANG ZIZHIQU
(Tibet)
Nyainqêntanglha Shan
126
2
ARUNĀCHAL
PRADESH
(claimed by China)
Brahmaputra
Himalayas
NEPAL
Annapurna 8091m
Mount Everest 8848m
Kula Kangri 7554m
Dibrugarh
Salyān
Pokhara
THIMPHU
KATHMANDU
Bhaktapur
Gangtok
BHUTAN
Brahmaputra
Bahraich
Lalitpur
Darjiling
Jorhāt
Pradesh
Shiliguri
Bongaigaon
Assam
Faizābād
Gorakhpur
Birātnager
Koch Bihār
Dispur
Kohīma
3
Kānpur
Bihār
Saidpur
Guwāhāti
Shillong
Jaunpur
Mau
Chhapra
Dinajpur
Rangpur
Meghālaya
Vārānasi
Patna
Bhāgalpur
Jamalpur
Sylhet
Silchar
Imphāl
Allahābād
Bihār Sharīf
Ganges
BANGLADESH
Gaya
Rajshahi
Pabna
Brahmanbaria
Tropic of Cancer
INDIA
Jhārkhand
Dhanbād
DHAKA
Bokāro
Āsānsol
Ganges
Jessore
Comilla
MYANMAR
(BURMA)
Murwāra
Chota Nāgpur
Bānkura
Khulna
Jabalpur
Rānchi
West Bengal
Chittagong
Chhattīsgarh
Jamshedpur
Hāora
Kolkata
(Calcutta)
Barisal
Rāurkela
Kharagpur
136
4
Bilāspur
Korba
Mouths of the Ganges
Gondia
Raipur
Sambalpur
Bāleshwar
Rāj Nāndgaon
Durg
Mahānadi
Irrawaddy
Odisha
(Orissa)
Cuttack
Bhubaneshwar
Puri
Jagdalpur
Brahmapur
Bay of
Bengal
Eastern Ghats
Srīkākulam
5
Vizianagaram
Visākhapatnam
Andhra Pradesh
Rājahmundry
Kākināda
133
Mouths of the Irrawaddy
85°
90°
95°
35°
30°
25°
20°
15°
Elevation
-6000m -4000m -2000m -1000m -500m -250m
Below sea level 0
250m 500m 1000m 2000m 3000m 4000m 6000m
-19,658ft -13,124ft -6562ft -3281ft -1640ft -820ft -328ft/-100m 0
820ft 1640ft 3281ft 6562ft 9843ft 13,124ft 19,685ft

Mainland Southeast Asia

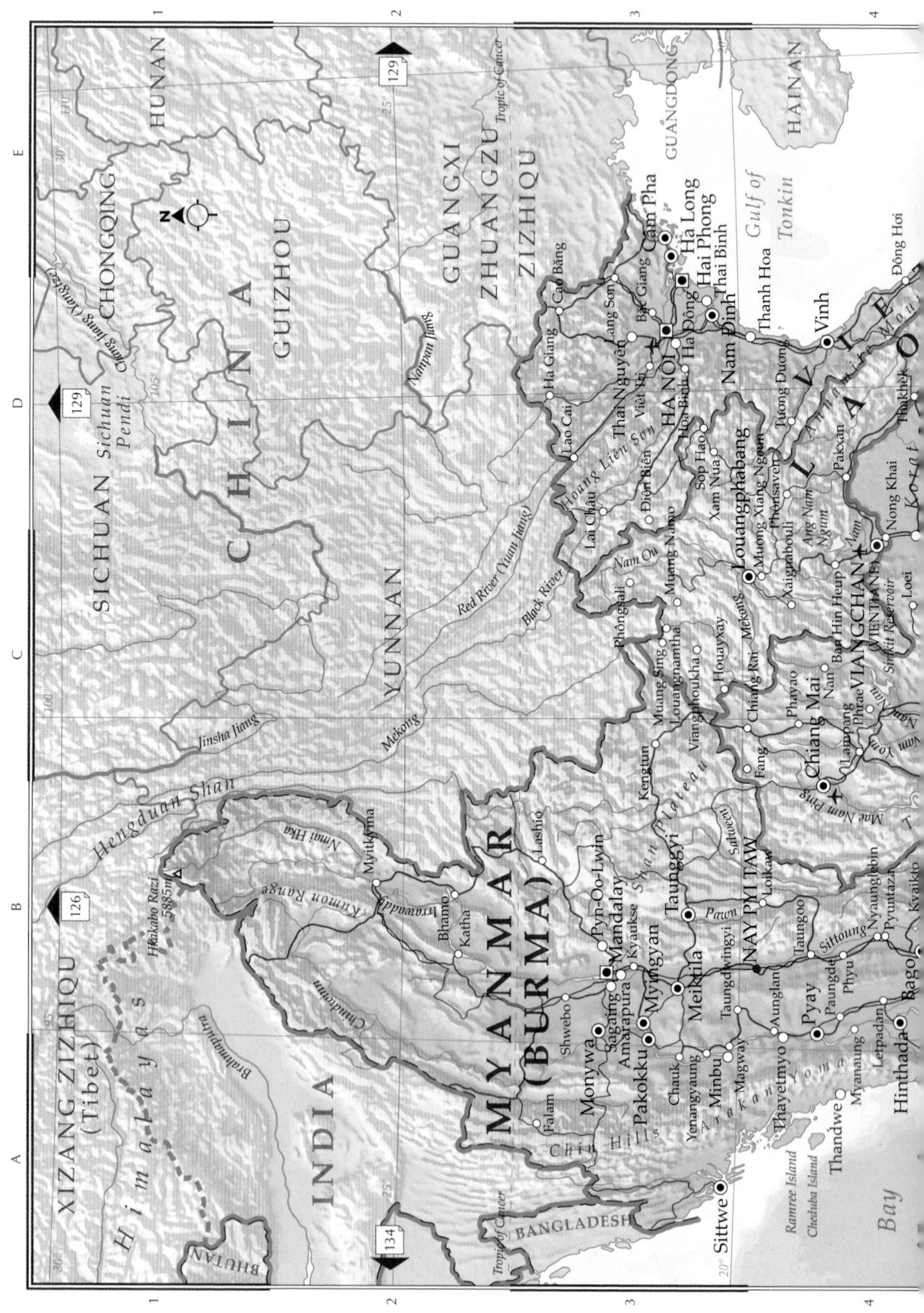

0 km 200
0 miles 200

Population
● National capital
○ below 50,000
○ 50,000 to 100,000
◉ 100,000 to 500,000
▣ above 500,00

Elevation

-6000m	-4000m	-2000m	-1000m	-500m	-250m	Below sea level	0	250m	500m	1000m	2000m	3000m	4000m	6000m
-19,658ft	-13,124ft	-6562ft	-3281ft	-1640ft	-820ft	-328ft/-100m	0	820ft	1640ft	3281ft	6562ft	9843ft	13,124ft	19,685ft

Maritime Southeast Asia

Elevation

Below sea level	-6000m	-4000m	-2000m	-1000m	-500m	-250m	0	250m	500m	1000m	2000m	3000m	4000m	6000m
	-19,658ft	-13,124ft	-6562ft	-3281ft	-1640ft	-820ft	-328ft/-100m 0	820ft	1640ft	3281ft	6562ft	9843ft	13,124ft	19,685ft

The Indian Ocean

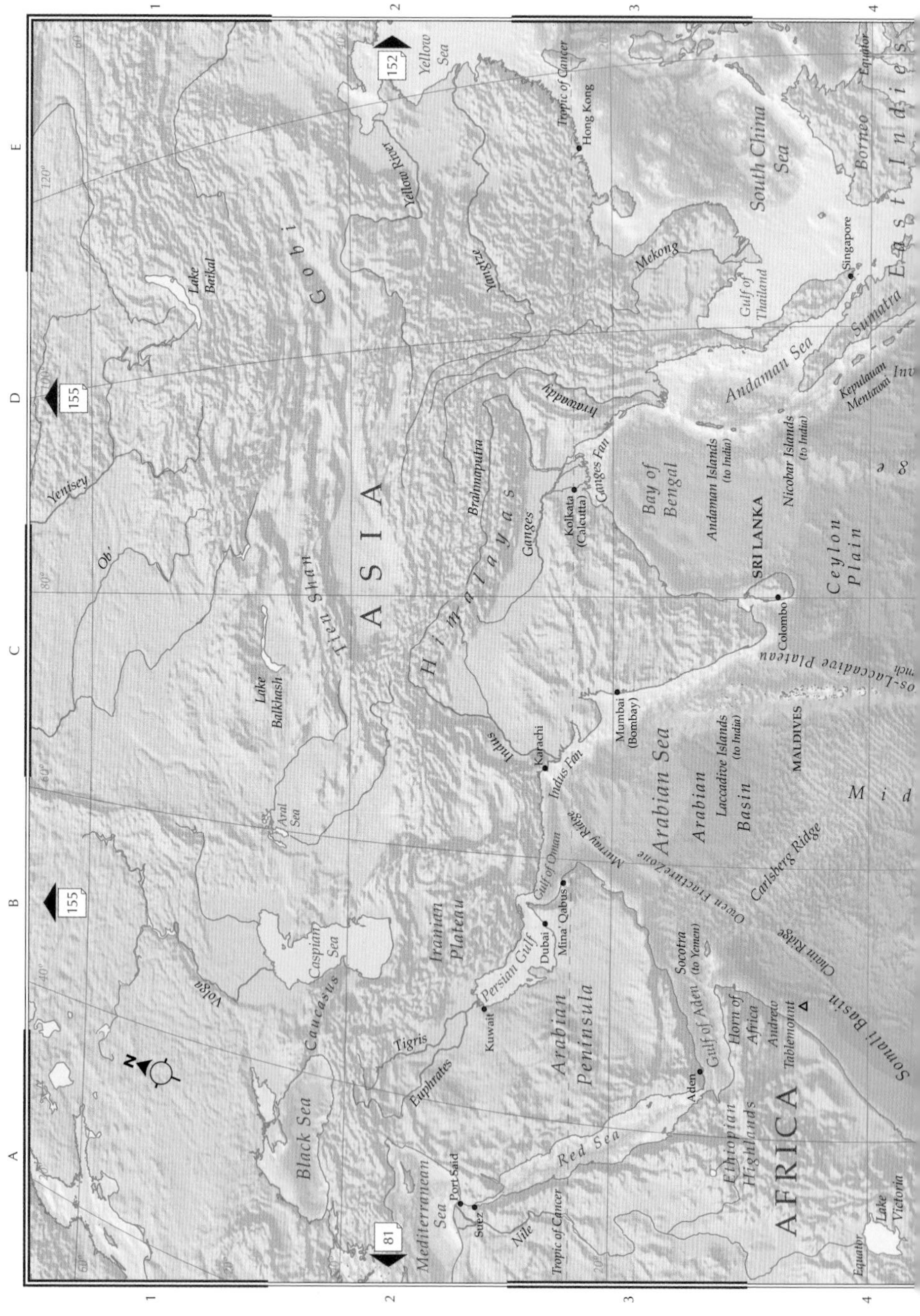

0 km 1500
0 miles 1500

• Major port

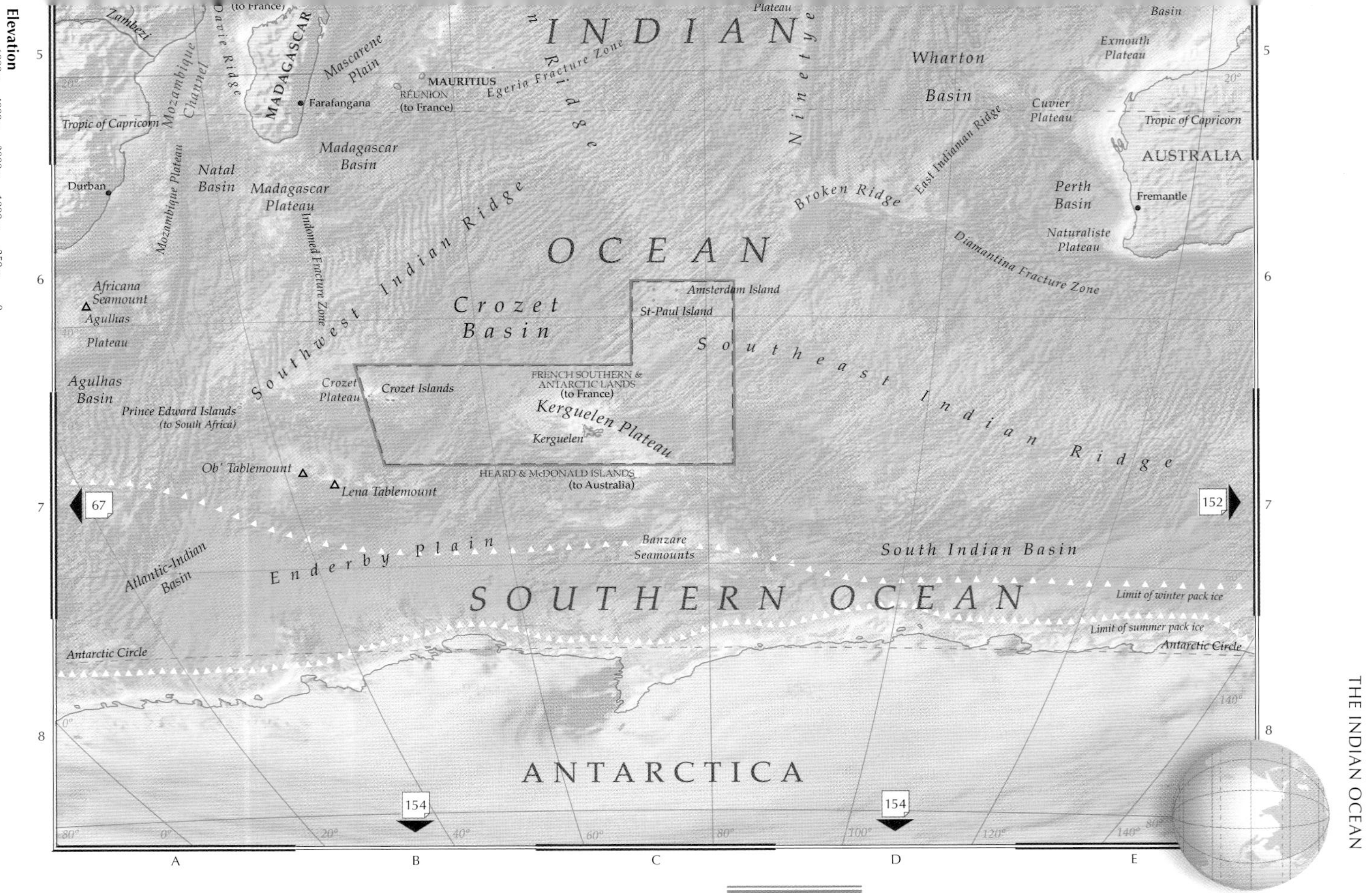

Elevation

-6000m	-4000m	-2000m	-1000m	-250m	0
-19,658ft	-13,124ft	-6562ft	-3281ft	-820ft	0

Australasia & Oceania

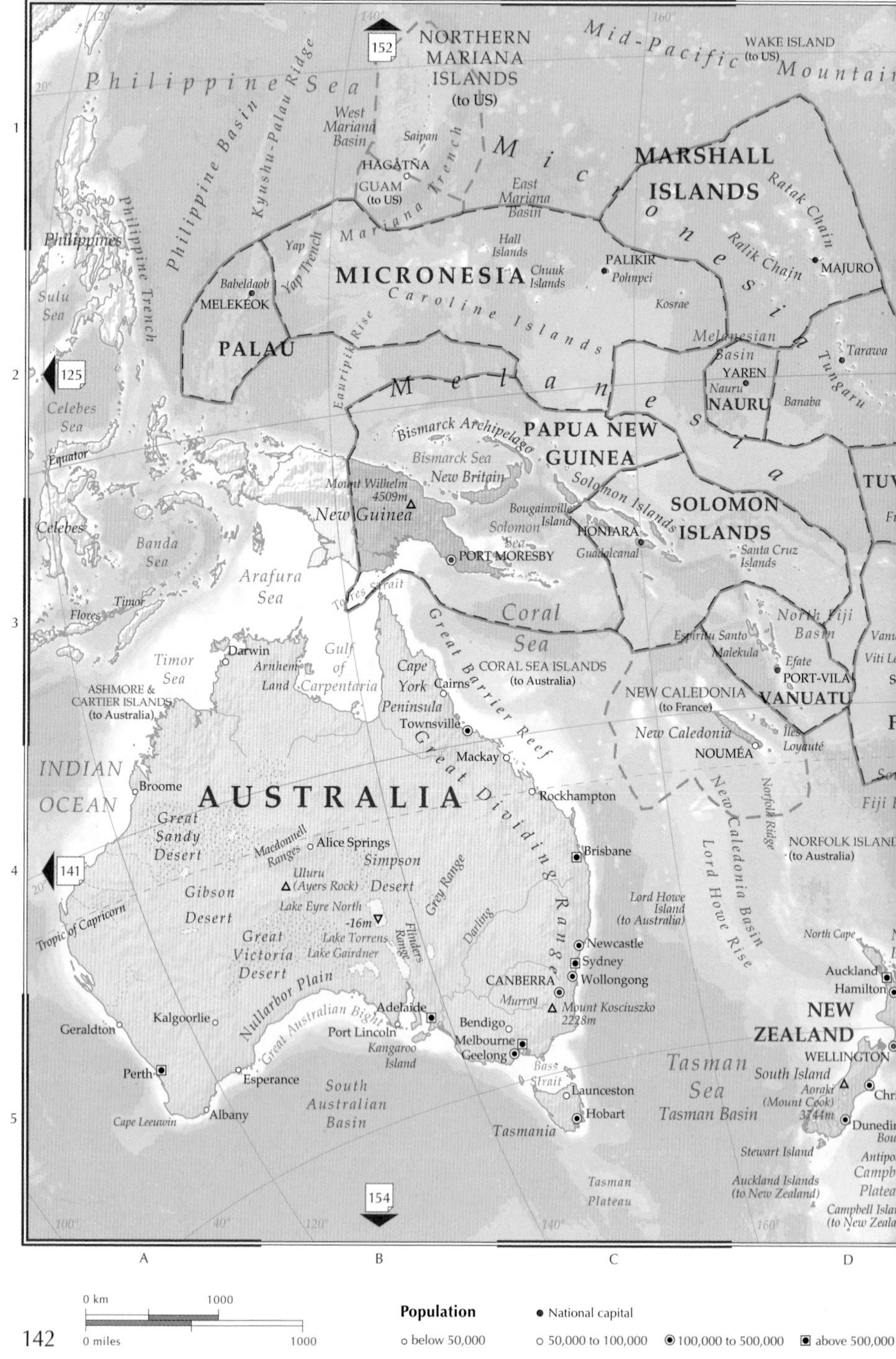

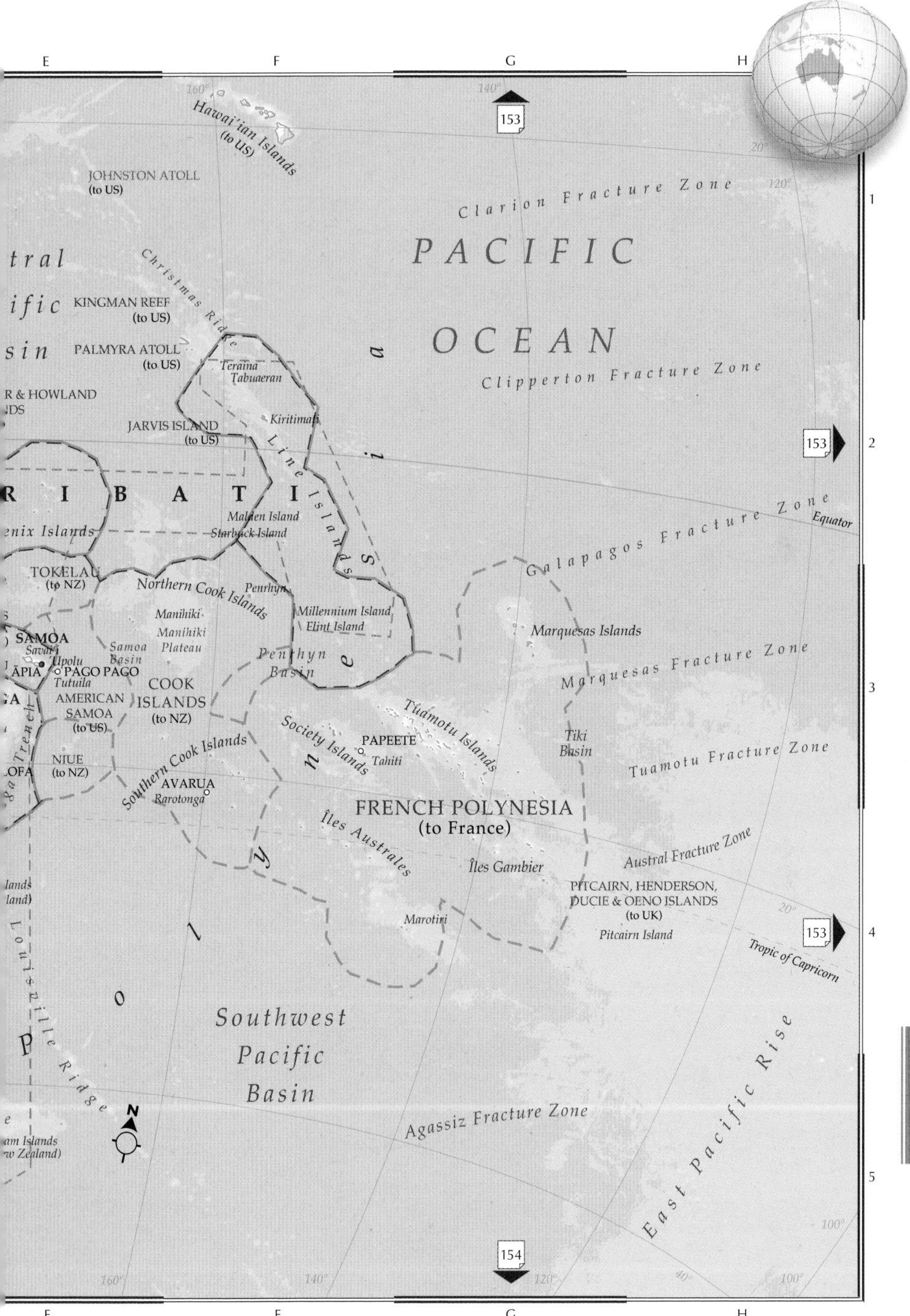
E
F
G
H
Hawai'ian Islands (to US)
JOHNSTON ATOLL (to US)
Clarion Fracture Zone
PACIFIC
OCEAN
Christmas Ridge
KINGMAN REEF (to US)
PALMYRA ATOLL (to US)
Teraina
Tabuaeran
Clipperton Fracture Zone
JARVIS ISLAND (to US)
Kiritimati
Line Islands
Malden Island
Starbuck Island
TOKELAU (to NZ)
Northern Cook Islands
Penrhyn
Manihiki
Manihiki Plateau
SAMOA
Savai'i
'Upolu
APIA
PAGO PAGO
Tutuila
AMERICAN SAMOA (to US)
Samoa Basin
Penrhyn Basin
COOK ISLANDS (to NZ)
Millennium Island
Flint Island
Galapagos Fracture Zone
Equator
Marquesas Islands
Marquesas Fracture Zone
Tuamotu Islands
Society Islands
PAPEETE
Tahiti
Tiki Basin
Tuamotu Fracture Zone
NIUE (to NZ)
Southern Cook Islands
AVARUA
Rarotonga
FRENCH POLYNESIA (to France)
Îles Australes
Îles Gambier
Austral Fracture Zone
PITCAIRN, HENDERSON, DUCIE & OENO ISLANDS (to UK)
Pitcairn Island
Marotiri
Tropic of Capricorn
Southwest Pacific Basin
Louisville Ridge
Agassiz Fracture Zone
East Pacific Rise
153
154
1
2
3
4
5

The Southwest Pacific

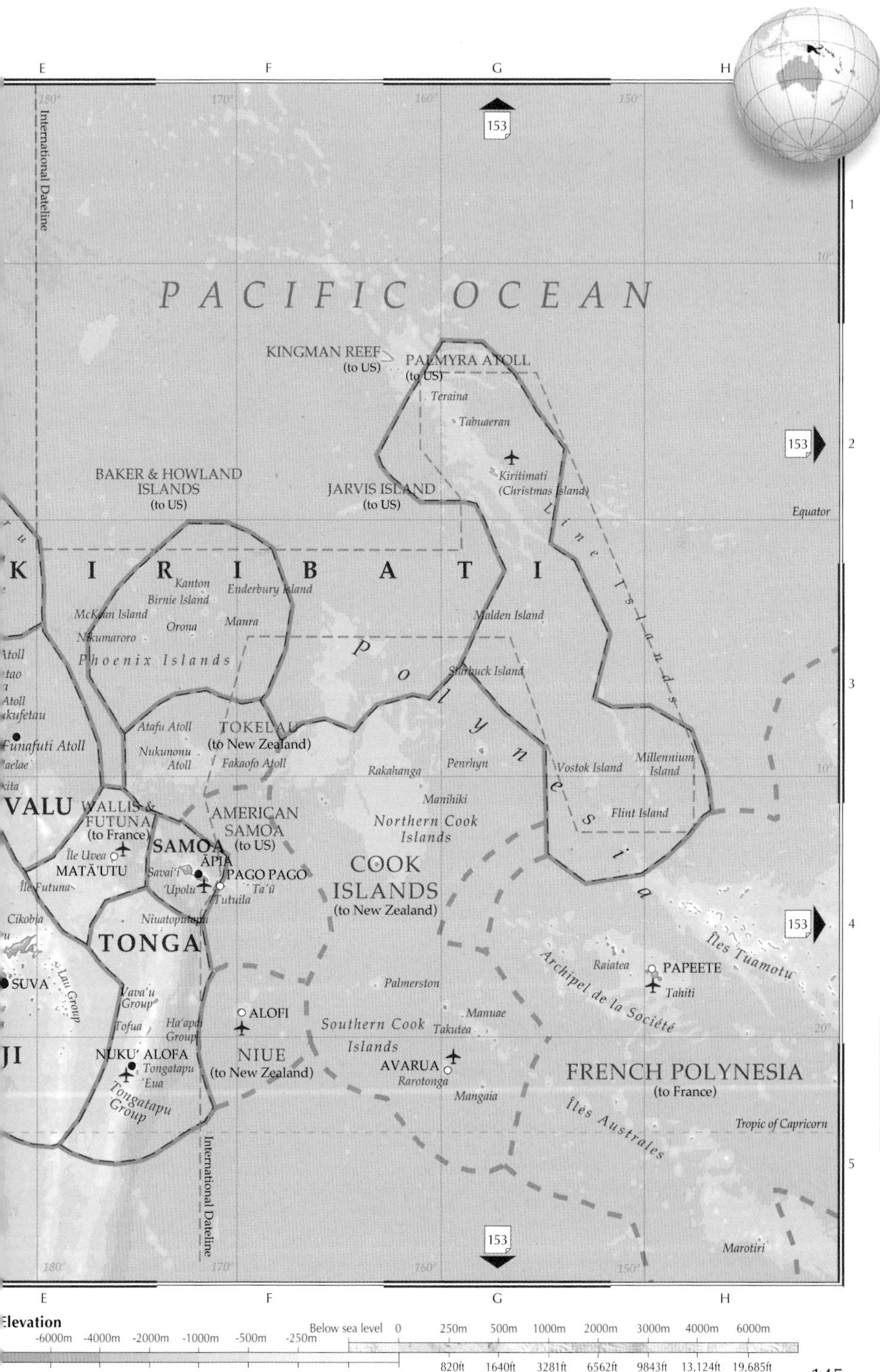
PACIFIC OCEAN
KINGMAN REEF
(to US)
PALMYRA ATOLL
(to US)
Teraina
Tabuaeran
Kiritimati
(Christmas Island)
BAKER & HOWLAND ISLANDS
(to US)
JARVIS ISLAND
(to US)
Equator
KIRIBATI
Kanton
Enderbury Island
Birnie Island
McKean Island
Orona
Manra
Nikumaroro
Phoenix Islands
Malden Island
Line Islands
Polynesia
Starbuck Island
Funafuti Atoll
Atafu Atoll
TOKELAU
(to New Zealand)
Nukunonu Atoll
Fakaofo Atoll
Rakahanga
Penrhyn
Vostok Island
Millennium Island
Flint Island
Manihiki
Northern Cook Islands
TUVALU
WALLIS & FUTUNA
(to France)
AMERICAN SAMOA
(to US)
SAMOA
ĀPIA
Île Uvea
MATĀ'UTU
Savai'i
'Upolu
PAGO PAGO
Ta'ū
Tutuila
Île Futuna
COOK ISLANDS
(to New Zealand)
Cikobia
Niuatoputapu
TONGA
SUVA
Lau Group
Vava'u Group
Palmerston
Raiatea
PAPEETE
Tahiti
Îles Tuamotu
Archipel de la Société
ALOFI
Manuae
Tofua
Ha'apai Group
Southern Cook Islands
Takutea
FIJI
NUKU'ALOFA
Tongatapu
'Eua
Tongatapu Group
NIUE
(to New Zealand)
AVARUA
Rarotonga
Mangaia
FRENCH POLYNESIA
(to France)
Îles Australes
Tropic of Capricorn
Marotiri
International Dateline
153
Elevation
Below sea level
-6000m -4000m -2000m -1000m -500m -250m
-19,658ft -13,124ft -6562ft -3281ft -1640ft -820ft -328ft/-100m 0
0 250m 500m 1000m 2000m 3000m 4000m 6000m
820ft 1640ft 3281ft 6562ft 9843ft 13,124ft 19,685ft

Western Australia

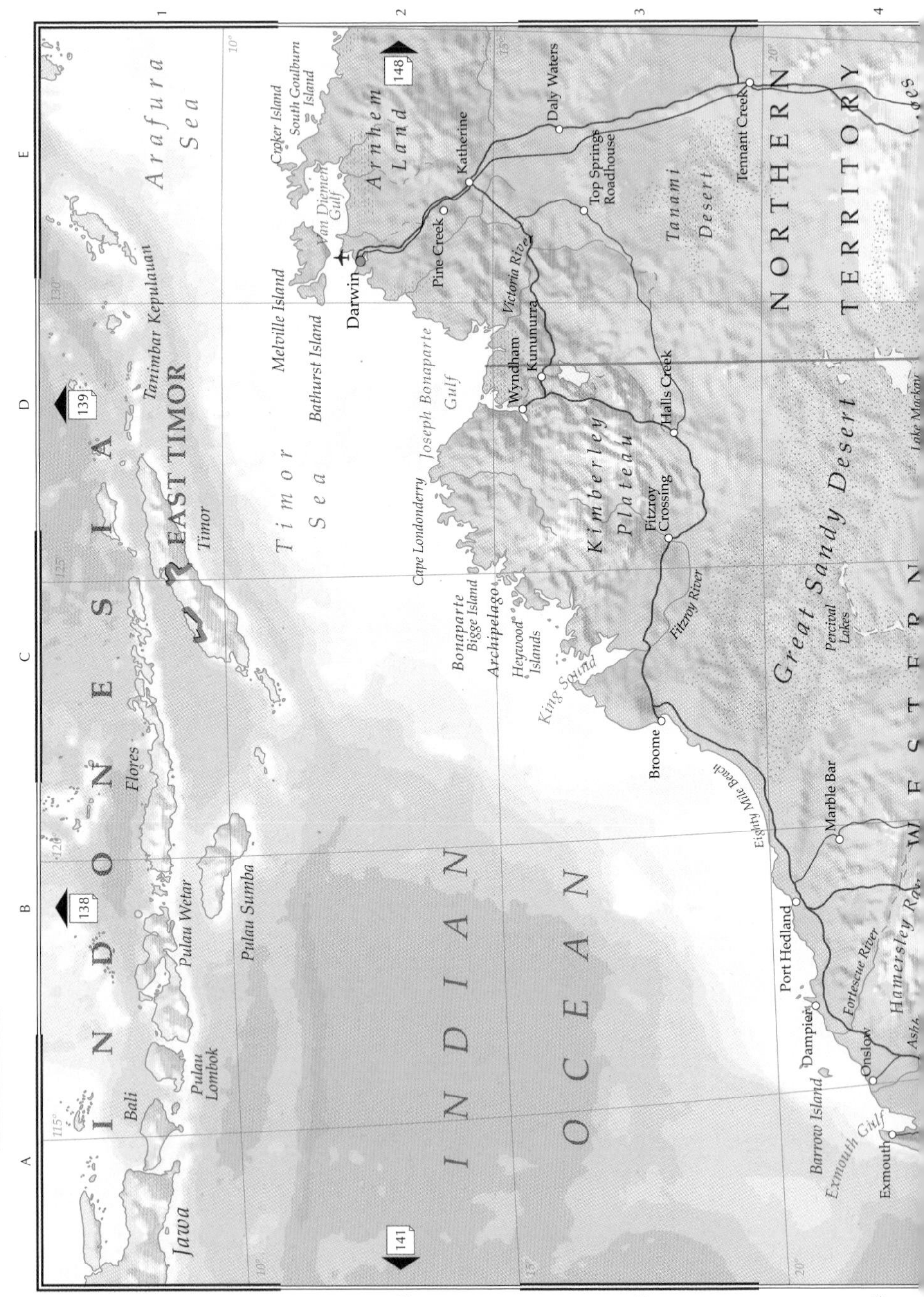

Population

○ below 50,000 ○ 50,000 to 100,000 ◉ 100,000 to 500,000 ▣ above 500,000

● Internal administrative capital

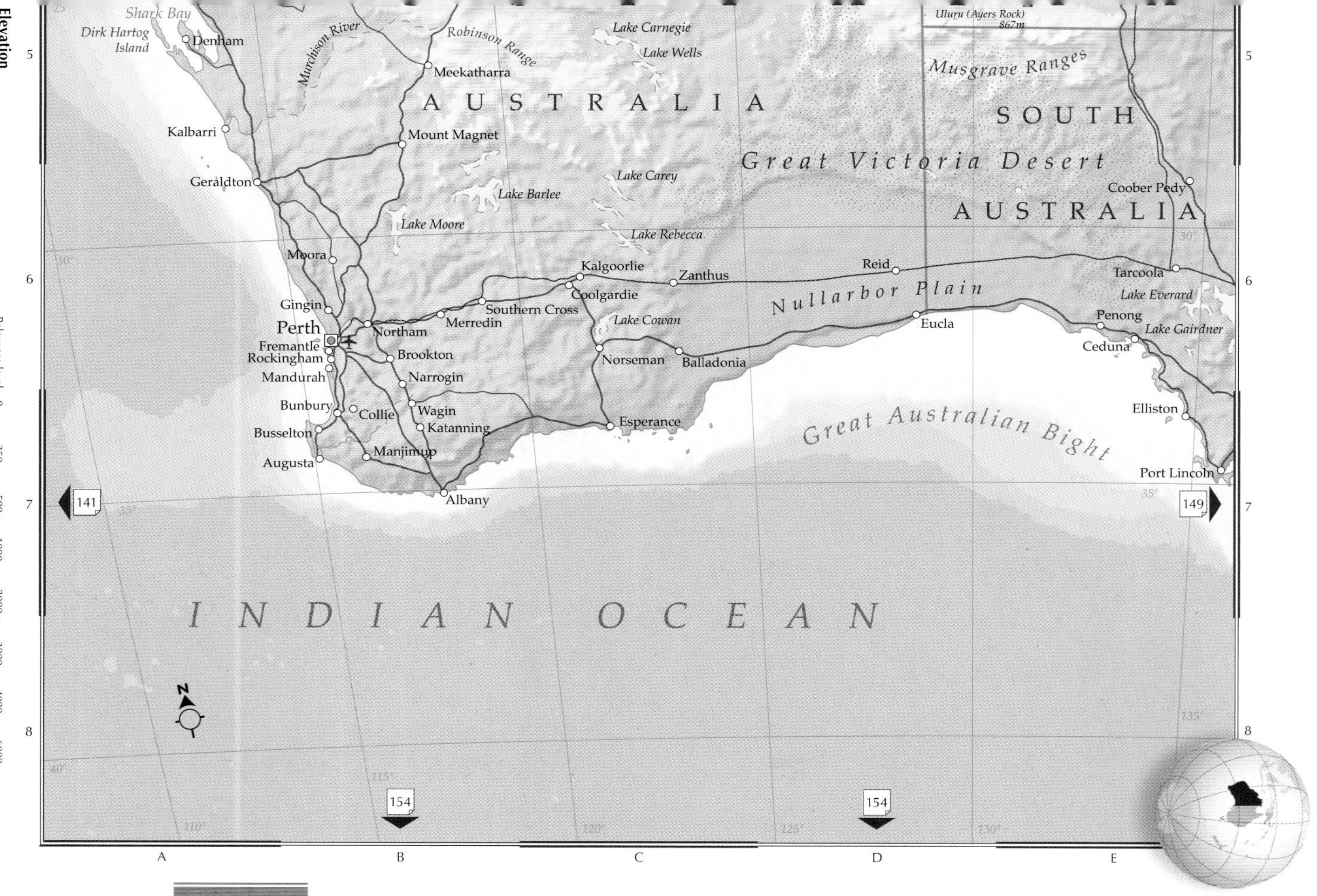
Shark Bay
Dirk Hartog Island
Denham
Murchison River
Robinson Range
Meekatharra
Lake Carnegie
Lake Wells
Uluru (Ayers Rock) 867m
Musgrave Ranges
AUSTRALIA
SOUTH
AUSTRALIA
Kalbarri
Mount Magnet
Great Victoria Desert
Geraldton
Lake Carey
Lake Barlee
Coober Pedy
Lake Moore
Lake Rebecca
Moora
Kalgoorlie
Zanthus
Reid
Tarcoola
Coolgardie
Nullarbor Plain
Lake Everard
Gingin
Southern Cross
Merredin
Penong
Perth
Northam
Lake Cowan
Eucla
Lake Gairdner
Fremantle
Rockingham
Brookton
Norseman
Balladonia
Ceduna
Mandurah
Narrogin
Bunbury
Collie
Wagin
Katanning
Esperance
Elliston
Busselton
Great Australian Bight
Manjimup
Augusta
Port Lincoln
Albany
141
149
INDIAN OCEAN
N
154
154
25°
30°
35°
40°
110°
115°
120°
125°
130°
135°
A
B
C
D
E
5
6
7
8
Elevation
-6000m -4000m -2000m -1000m -500m -250m
Below sea level 0
250m 500m 1000m 2000m 3000m 4000m 6000m
-19,658ft -13,124ft -6562ft -3281ft -1640ft -820ft -328ft/-100m 0
820ft 1640ft 3281ft 6562ft 9843ft 13,124ft 19,685ft

Eastern Australia

Population

● National capital ◉ Internal administrative capital
○ below 50,000 ○ 50,000 to 100,000 ⦿ 100,000 to 500,000 ▣ above 500,000

0 km 300
0 miles 300

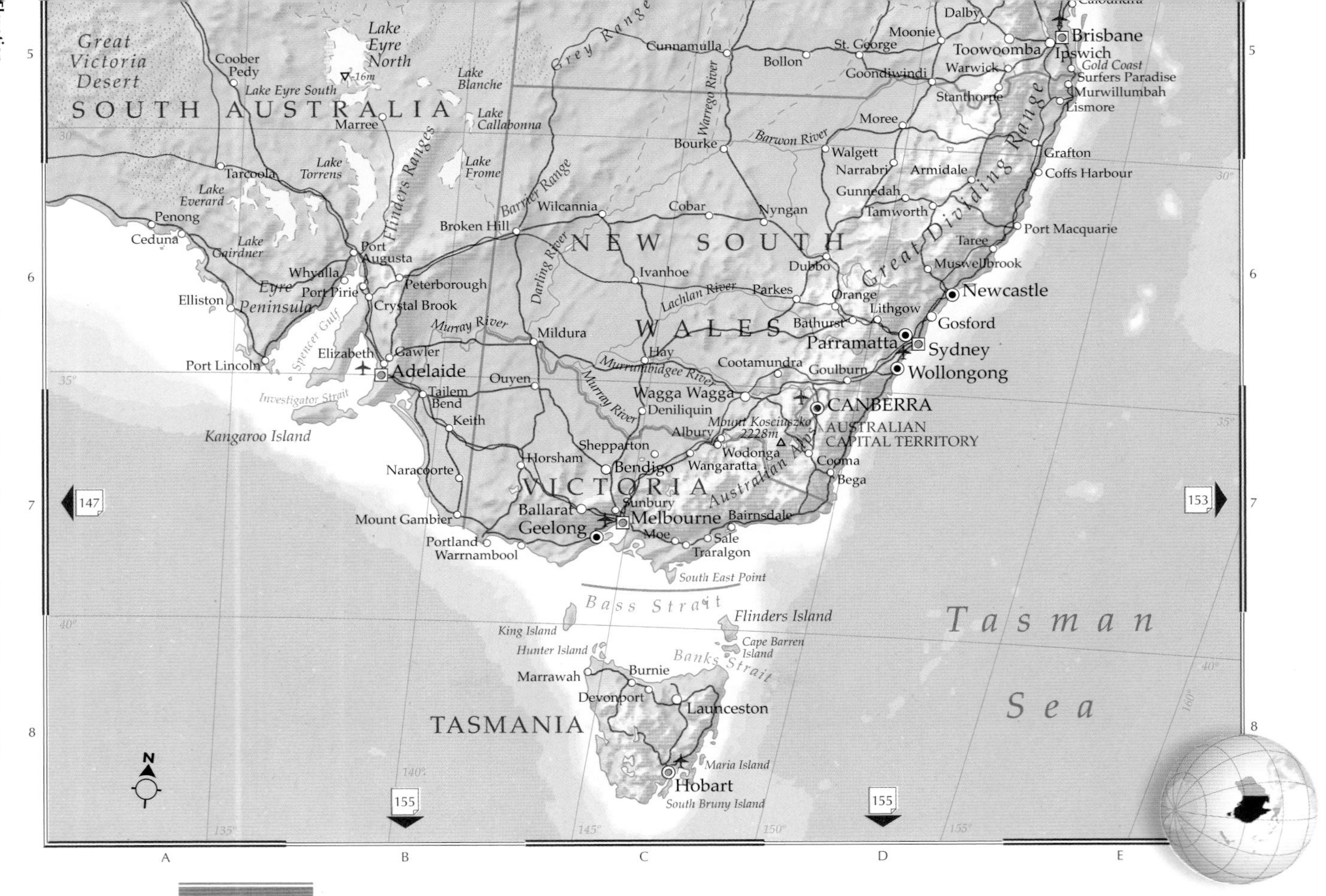

Elevation

Below sea level	-6000m	-4000m	-2000m	-1000m	-500m	-250m	0
	-19,658ft	-13,124ft	-6562ft	-3281ft	-1640ft	-820ft	-328ft/-100m 0

0	250m	500m	1000m	2000m	3000m	4000m	6000m
	820ft	1640ft	3281ft	6562ft	9843ft	13,124ft	19,685ft

New Zealand

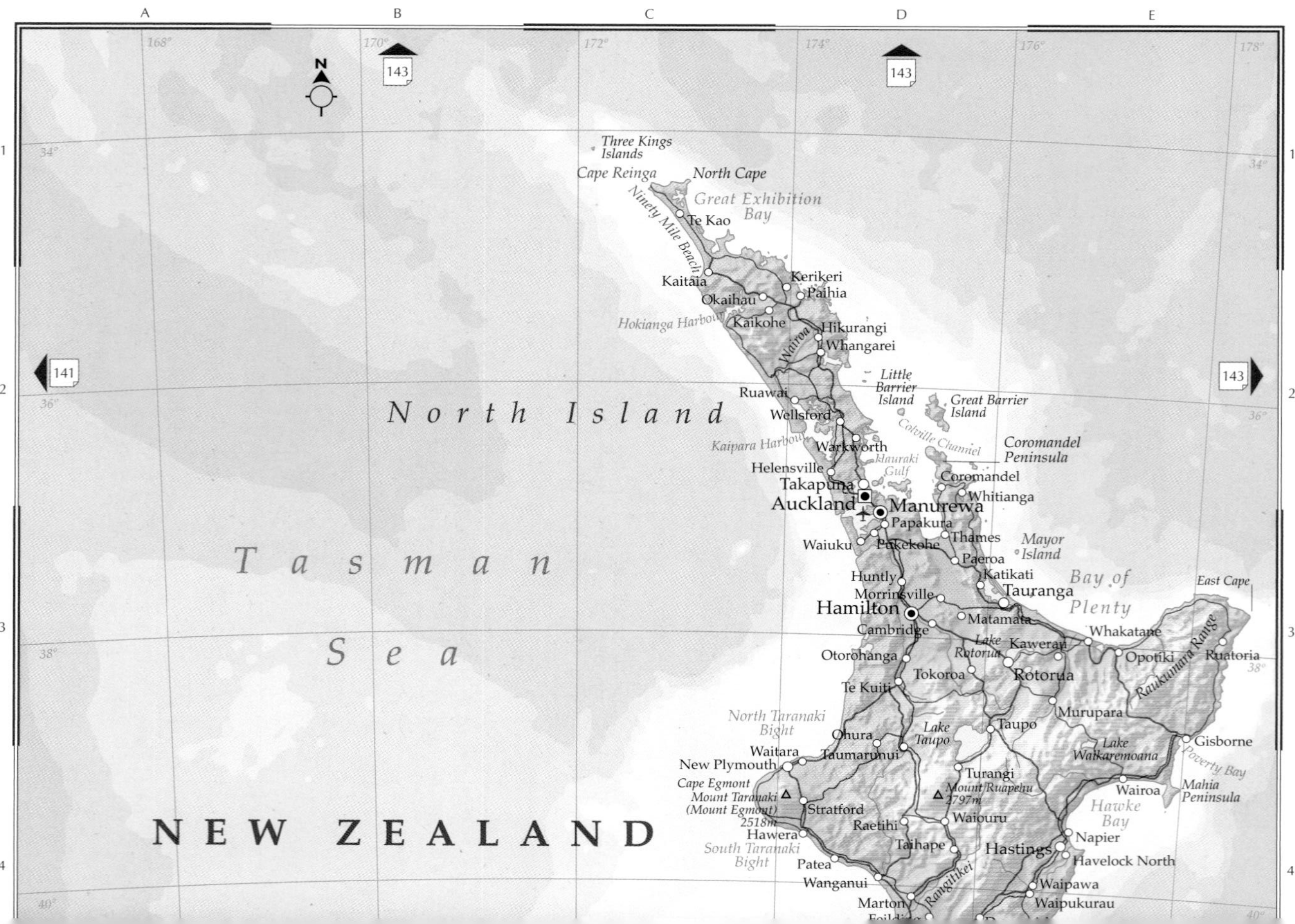

0 km 100
0 miles 100

Population

● National capital
○ below 50,000
○ 50,000 to 100,000
◉ 100,000 to 500,000
▣ above 500,000

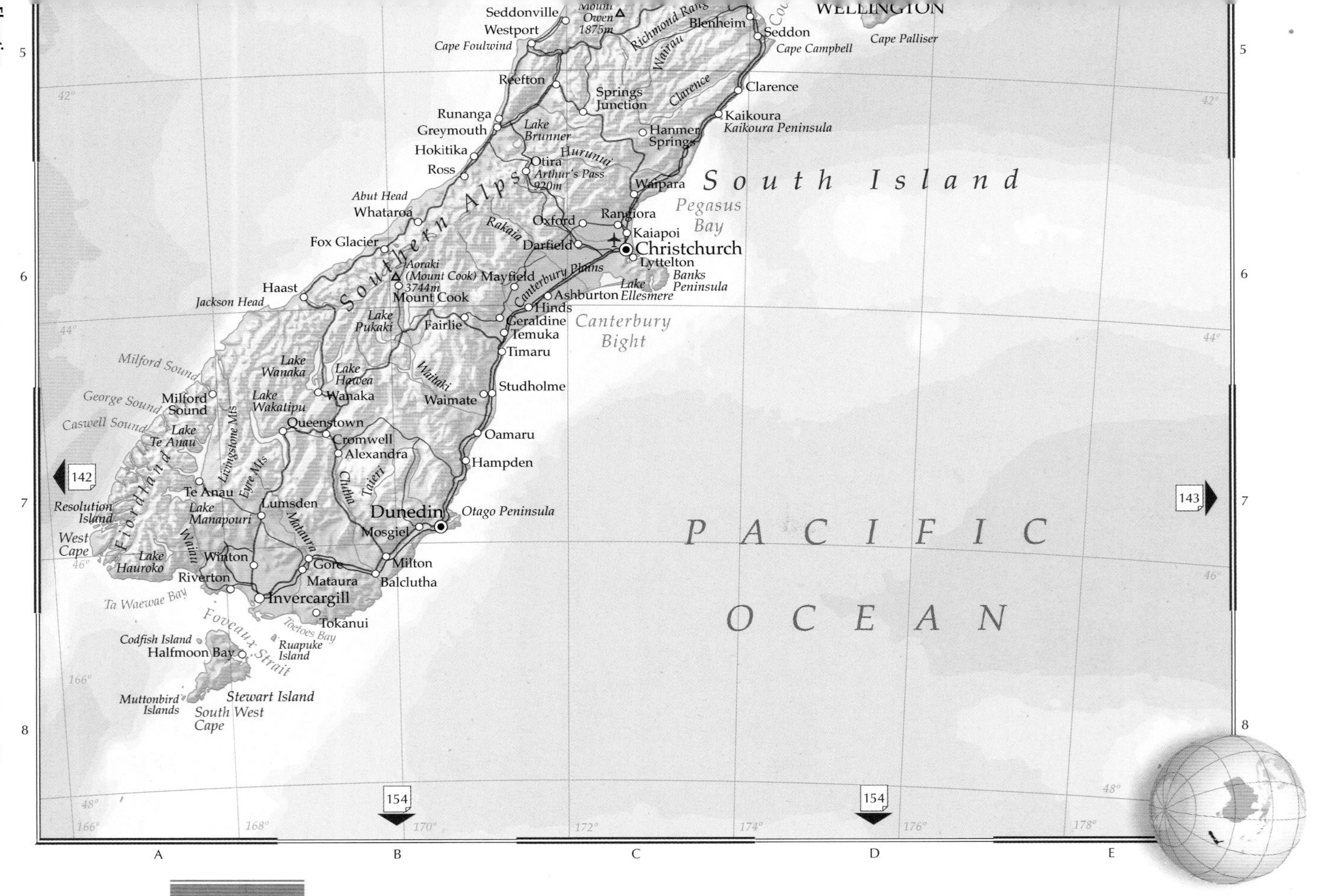

Elevation

Below sea level: -6000m / -19,658ft; -4000m / -13,124ft; -2000m / -6562ft; -1000m / -3281ft; -500m / -1640ft; -250m / -820ft; -328ft/-100m; 0

0; 250m / 820ft; 500m / 1640ft; 1000m / 3281ft; 2000m / 6562ft; 3000m / 9843ft; 4000m / 13,124ft; 6000m / 19,685ft

The Pacific Ocean

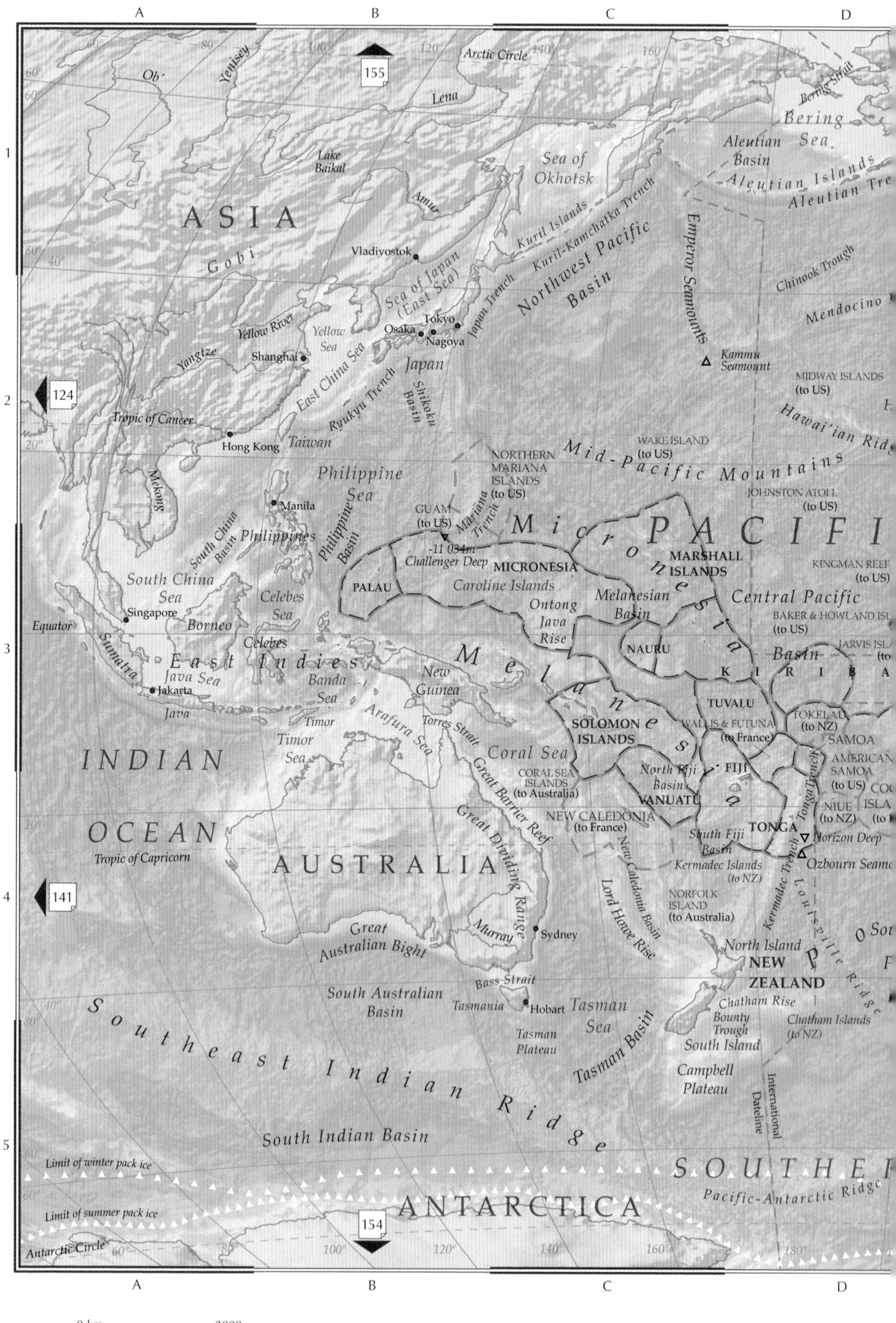

0 km 2000

0 miles 2000

• Major port

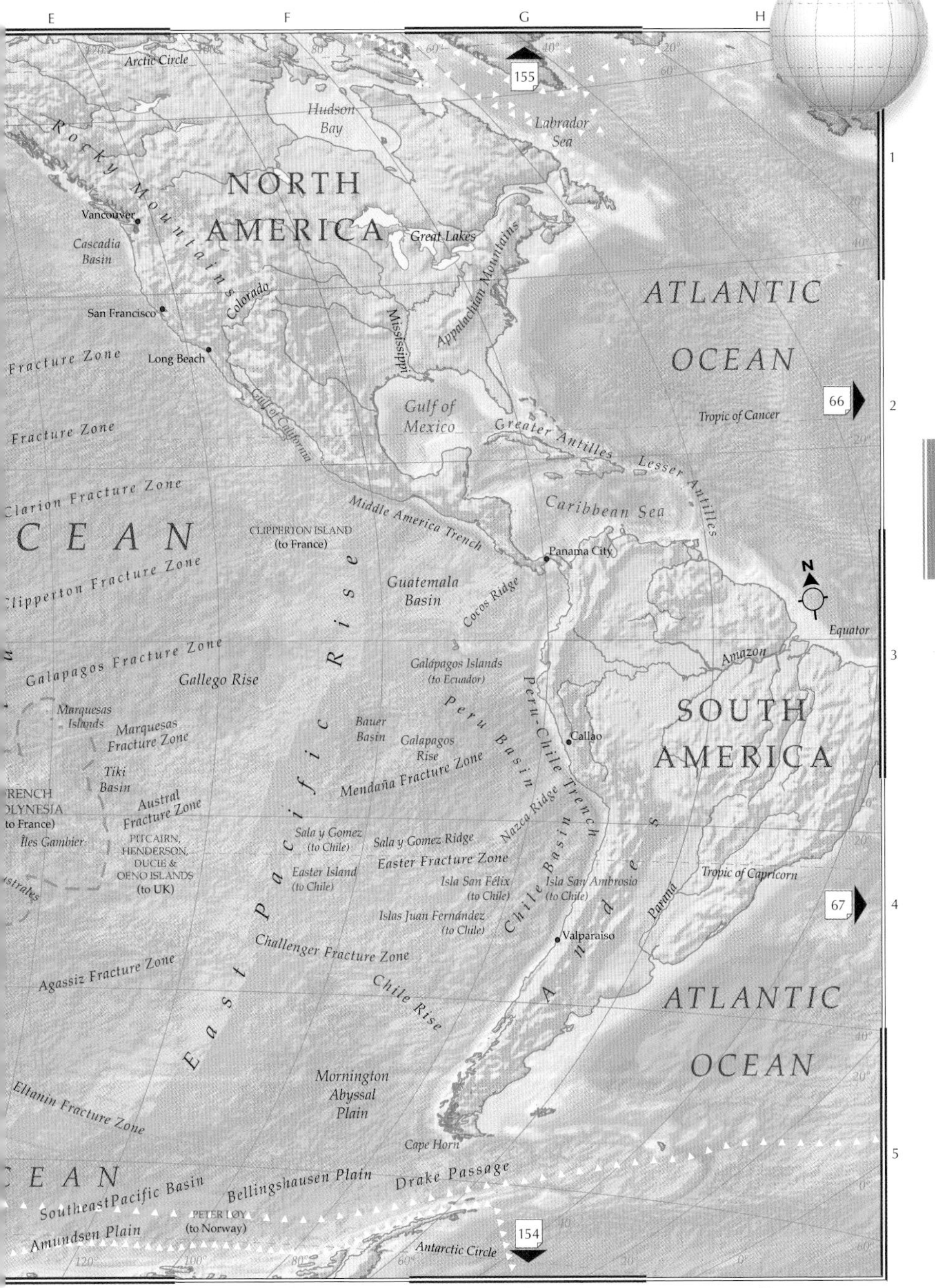

E F G H

Arctic Circle
155
Hudson Bay
Labrador Sea
Rocky Mountains
NORTH AMERICA
Vancouver
Cascadia Basin
Great Lakes
Appalachian Mountains
ATLANTIC OCEAN
San Francisco
Colorado
Mississippi
Fracture Zone
Long Beach
Gulf of California
Gulf of Mexico
66
Tropic of Cancer
Fracture Zone
Greater Antilles
Lesser Antilles
Clarion Fracture Zone
Middle America Trench
Caribbean Sea
OCEAN
CLIPPERTON ISLAND (to France)
Panama City
Clipperton Fracture Zone
Guatemala Basin
Cocos Ridge
Equator
Galapagos Fracture Zone
Gallego Rise
Galápagos Islands (to Ecuador)
Amazon
Marquesas Islands
Marquesas Fracture Zone
Peru Basin
Bauer Basin
Galapagos Rise
Peru-Chile Trench
SOUTH AMERICA
Callao
Tiki Basin
Mendaña Fracture Zone
FRENCH POLYNESIA (to France)
Austral Fracture Zone
Nazca Ridge
Îles Gambier
PITCAIRN, HENDERSON, DUCIE & OENO ISLANDS (to UK)
Sala y Gomez (to Chile)
Sala y Gomez Ridge
Easter Fracture Zone
Easter Island (to Chile)
Isla San Félix (to Chile)
Isla San Ambrosio (to Chile)
Chile Basin
Tropic of Capricorn
Paraná
Andes
67
Islas Juan Fernández (to Chile)
Valparaiso
Challenger Fracture Zone
East Pacific Rise
Agassiz Fracture Zone
Chile Rise
ATLANTIC OCEAN
Mornington Abyssal Plain
Eltanin Fracture Zone
Cape Horn
OCEAN
Southeast Pacific Basin
Bellingshausen Plain
Drake Passage
Amundsen Plain
PETER I ØY (to Norway)
154
Antarctic Circle

1 2 3 4 5

E F G H

Elevation

-6000m	-4000m	-2000m	-1000m	-250m	0
-19,658ft	-13,124ft	-6562ft	-3281ft	-820ft	0

Antarctica

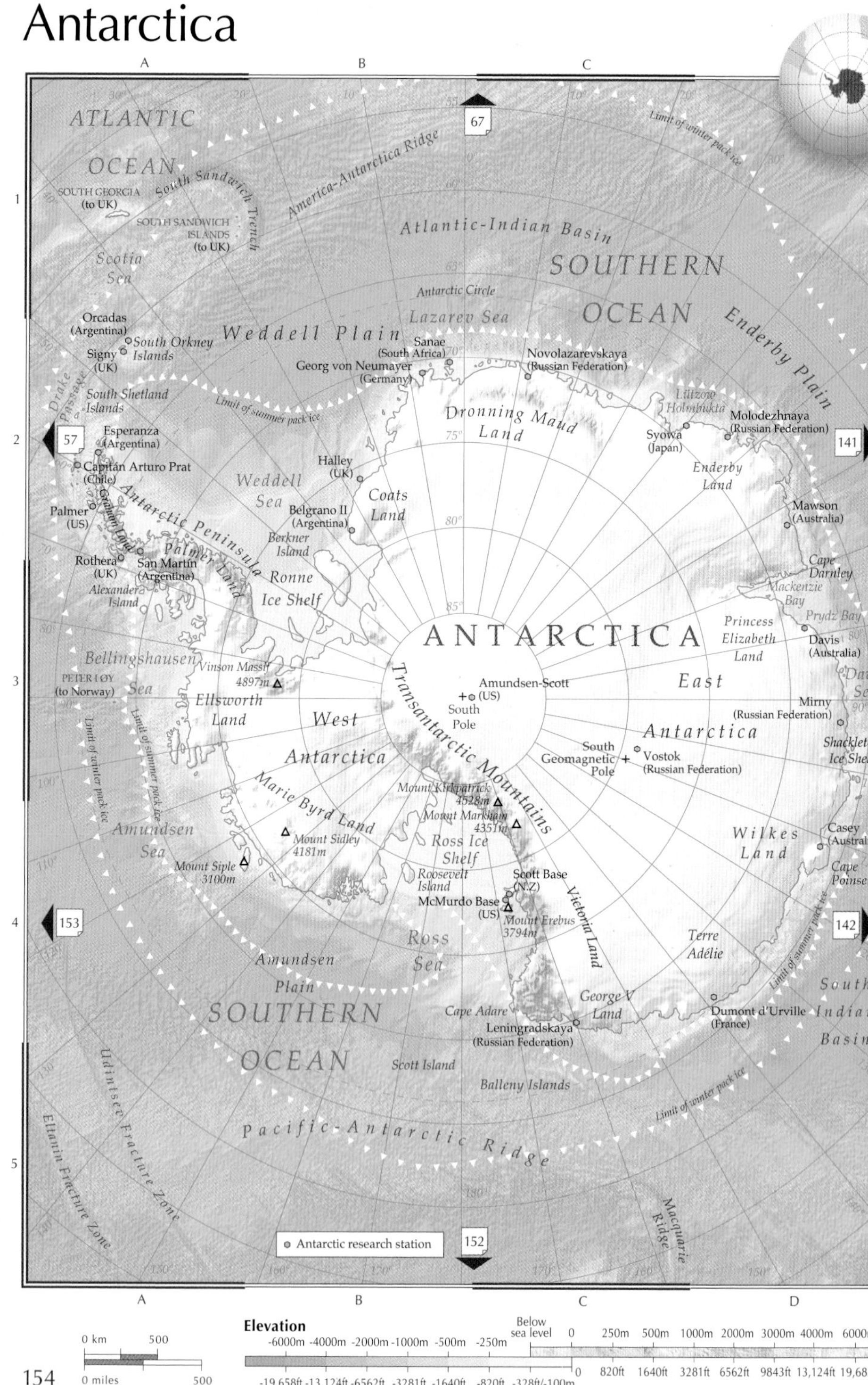

67
57
141
153
142
152

rctic Ocean

A
B
C
D
Saint Lawrence Island
Provideniya
Norton Sound
Bering Sea
152
Bering Strait
Arctic Circle
RUSSIAN FEDERATION
ASIA
ALASKA (to US)
NORTH AMERICA
Chukchi Sea
Ostrov Vrangelya
East Siberian Sea
Limit of summer pack ice
Tuktoyaktuk
Northwind Plain
Chukchi Plain
Beaufort Sea
36
Amundsen Gulf
Chukchi Plateau
Mendeleyev Ridge
Novosibirskiye Ostrova
113
Canada Basin
Wrangel Plain
Limit of permanent ice cap
Laptev Sea
Victoria Island
ARCTIC OCEAN
CANADA
Queen Elizabeth Islands
North Geomagnetic Pole
Makarov Basin
Alpha Cordillera
Lomonosov Ridge
Amundsen Basin
Severnaya Zemlya
North Pole
Gakkel Ridge
Nansen Basin
Dikson
Ellesmere Island
Lancaster Sound
Nares Strait
Lincoln Sea
Svyataya Anna Trough
Kara Sea
Kap Morris Jesup
Knud Rasmussen Land
Franz Josef Land
Ostrov Belyy
Baffin Bay
Wandel Sea
East Novaya Zemlya Trough
Novaya Zemlya
38
112
SVALBARD (to Norway)
Spitsbergen
Longyearbyen
Kong Frederik VIII Land
Limit of winter pack ice
Greenland Sea
GREENLAND (to Denmark)
Bjørnøya (to Norway)
Barents Sea
Ostrov Kotel'nyy
Chëshskaya Guba
North Cape
Murmansk
Kola Peninsula
JAN MAYEN (to Norway)
Mohns Ridge
NORWAY
FINLAND
SWEDEN
Archangel
White Sea
Denmark Strait
Iceland Plateau
Norwegian Sea
66
EUROPE
1
2
3
4
5
Elevation
-6000m -4000m -2000m -1000m -250m 0
-19,658ft -13,124ft -6562ft -3281ft -820ft 0
0 km 500
0 miles 500
Major port

Overseas territories & dependencies

Despite the rapid process of global decolonization since the Second World War, around 8 million people in more than 50 territories around the world continue to live under the protection of France, Australia, the Netherlands, Denmark, Norway, New Zealand, the UK, or the USA. These remnants of former colonial empires may have persisted for economic, strategic or political reasons and are administered in a variety of ways.

AUSTRALIA

Australia's overseas territories have not been an issue since Papua New Guinea became independent in 1975. Consequently there is no overriding policy toward them. Norfolk Island is inhabited by descendants of the H.M.S Bounty mutineers and more recent Australian migrants.

Ashmore & Cartier Islands
Indian Ocean
Status: External territory
Claimed: 1931
Capital: Not applicable
Population: None
Area: 2 sq miles (5.2 sq km)

Christmas Island
Indian Ocean
Status: External territory
Claimed: 1958
Capital: The Settlement
Population: 1530
Area: 52 sq miles (135 sq km)

Cocos Islands
Indian Ocean
Status: External territory
Claimed: 1955
Capital: West Island
Population: 596
Area: 5.5 sq miles (14 sq km)

Coral Sea Islands
South Pacific
Status: External territory
Claimed: 1969
Capital: None
Population: 8 (meteorologists)
Area: Less than 1.2 sq miles (3 sq km)

Heard & McDonald Is.
Indian Ocean
Status: External territory
Claimed: 1947
Capital: Not applicable
Population: None
Area: 161 sq miles (417 sq km)

Norfolk Island
South Pacific
Status: External territory
Claimed: 1774
Capital: Kingston
Population: 2210
Area: 13 sq miles (34 sq km)

DENMARK

The Faroe Islands have been under Danish administration since Queen Margreth I of Denmark inherited Norway in 1380. The Home Rule Act of 1948 gave the Faroese control over all their internal affairs. Greenland first came under Danish rule in 1380. Today, Denmark is responsible for the island's foreign affairs and defense.

Faroe Islands
North Atlantic
Status: External territory
Claimed: 1380
Capital: Tórshavn
Population: 49,469
Area: 540 sq miles (1399 sq km)

Greenland
North Atlantic
Status: External territory
Claimed: 1380
Capital: Nuuk
Population: 56,483
Area: 836,109 sq miles (2,166,086 sq km)

FRANCE

France has developed economic ties with its *Territoires d'Outre-Mer,* thereby stressing interdependence over independence. Overseas *départements,* officially part of France, have their own governments. Territorial *collectivités* and overseas *territoires* have varying degrees of autonomy.

Clipperton Island
East Pacific
Status: Dependency of French Polynesia
Claimed: 1935
Capital: Not applicable
Population: None
Area: 2.7 sq miles (7 sq km)

French Guiana
South America
Status: Overseas department
Claimed: 1817
Capital: Cayenne
Population: 250,109
Area: 35,135 sq miles (91,000 sq km)

French Polynesia
South Pacific
Status: Overseas collectivity
Claimed: 1843
Capital: Papeete
Population: 276,831
Area: 1608 sq miles (4165 sq km)

Guadeloupe
West Indies
Status: Overseas department
Claimed: 1635
Capital: Basse-Terre
Population: 405,739
Area: 629 sq miles (1628 sq km)

Martinique
West Indies
Status: Overseas department
Claimed: 1635
Capital: Fort-de-France
Population: 386,486
Area: 425 sq miles (1100 sq km)

Mayotte
Indian Ocean
Status: Overseas department
Claimed: 1843
Capital: Mamoudzou
Population: 212,645
Area: 144 sq miles (374 sq km)

New Caledonia
South Pacific
Status: Special collectivity
Claimed: 1853
Capital: Nouméa
Population: 262,000
Area: 7347 sq miles (19,100 sq km)

Réunion
Indian Ocean
Status: Overseas department
Claimed: 1638
Capital: Saint-Denis
Population: 840,974
Area: 970 sq miles (2500 sq km)

St. Pierre & Miquelon
North America
Status: Overseas collectivity
Claimed: 1604
Capital: Saint-Pierre
Population: 5716
Area: 93 sq miles (242 sq km)

Wallis & Futuna
South Pacific
Status: Overseas collectivity
Claimed: 1842
Capital: Matá'Utu
Population: 15,561
Area: 106 sq miles (274 sq km)

NETHERLANDS

The country's remaining overseas territories were formerly part of the Dutch West Indies. The Netherlands Antilles dissolved in 2010 leaving the constituent islands with varying degrees of autonomy, but the Netherlands remains responsible for their security.

Aruba
West Indies
Status: Autonomous part of the Netherlands
Claimed: 1643
Capital: Oranjestad
Population: 102,911
Area: 75 sq miles (194 sq km)

Bonaire
West Indies
Status: Special municipality of the Netherlands
Claimed: 1816
Capital: Kralendijk
Population: 18,413
Area: 113 sq miles (294 sq km)

Curaçao
West Indies
Status: Autonomous part of the Netherlands
Claimed: 1816
Capital: Willemstad
Population: 153,500
Area: 171 sq miles (444 sq km)

Sint Maarten
West Indies
Status: Autonomous part of the Netherlands
Claimed: 1648
Capital: Philipsburg
Population: 39,689
Area: 13 sq miles (34 sq km)

NEW ZEALAND

New Zealand's government has no desire to retain any overseas territories. However, the economic weakness of its dependent territory Tokelau and its freely associated states, Niue and the Cook Islands, has forced New Zealand to remain responsible for their foreign policy and defense.

Cook Islands
South Pacific
Status: Associated territory
Claimed: 1901
Capital: Avarua
Population: 13,700
Area: 91 sq miles (235 sq km)

Niue
South Pacific
Status: Associated territory
Claimed: 1901
Capital: Alofi
Population: 1190
Area: 102 sq miles (264 sq km)

Tokelau
South Pacific
Status: Dependent territory
Claimed: 1926
Capital: Not applicable
Population: 1337
Area: 4 sq miles (10 sq km)

NORWAY

In 1920, 41 nations signed the Spits-bergen Treaty recognizing Norwegian sovereignty over Svalbard. There is a NATO base on Jan Mayen. Bouvet Island is a nature reserve.

Bouvet Island
South Atlantic
Status: Dependency
Claimed: 1928
Capital: Not applicable
Population: None
Area: 22 sq miles (58 sq km)

Jan Mayen
North Atlantic
Status: Dependency
Claimed: 1929
Capital: Not applicable
Population: 18 (meteorologists)
Area: 147 sq miles (381 sq km)

Continued on page158

Overseas territories & dependencies

Peter I. Island
Southern Ocean
Status: Dependency
Claimed: 1931
Capital: Not applicable
Population: None
Area: 69 sq miles (180 sq km)

Svalbard
Arctic Ocean
Status: Dependency
Claimed: 1920
Capital: Longyearbyen
Population: 1872
Area: 24,289 sq miles (62,906 sq km)

UNITED KINGDOM

The UK still has the largest number of overseas territories. These are locally-governed by a mixture of elected representatives and appointed officials, and they all enjoy a large measure of internal self-government, but certain powers, such as foreign affairs and defense, are reserved for Governors of the British Crown.

Anguilla
West Indies
Status: Overseas territory
Claimed: 1650
Capital: The Valley
Population: 16,086
Area: 37 sq miles (96 sq km)

Ascension Island
South Atlantic
Status: Overseas territory
Claimed: 1673
Capital: Georgetown
Population: 880
Area: 34 sq miles (88 sq km)

Bermuda
North Atlantic
Status: Overseas territory
Claimed: 1612
Capital: Hamilton
Population: 65,024
Area: 20 sq miles (53 sq km)

British Indian Ocean Territory
Status: Overseas territory
Claimed: 1814
Capital: Diego Garcia
Population: 4000
Area: 23 sq miles (60 sq km)

British Virgin Islands
West Indies
Status: Overseas territory
Claimed: 1672
Capital: Road Town
Population: 32,680
Area: 59 sq miles (153 sq km)

Cayman Islands
West Indies
Status: Overseas territory
Claimed: 1670
Capital: George Town
Population: 58,435
Area: 100 sq miles (259 sq km)

Falkland Islands
South Atlantic
Status: Overseas territory
Claimed: 1832
Capital: Stanley
Population: 2840
Area: 4699 sq miles (12,173 sq km)

Gibraltar
Southwest Europe
Status: Overseas territory
Claimed: 1713
Capital: Gibraltar
Population: 29,185
Area: 2.5 sq miles (6.5 sq km)

Guernsey
Channel Islands
Status: Crown Dependency
Claimed: 1066
Capital: St. Peter Port
Population: 65,849
Area: 25 sq miles (65 sq km)

Isle of Man
British Isles
Status: Crown Dependency
Claimed: 1765
Capital: Douglas
Population: 85,888
Area: 221 sq miles (572 sq km)

Jersey
Channel Islands
Status: Crown Dependency
Claimed: 1066
Capital: St. Helier
Population: 96,513
Area: 45 sq miles (116 sq km)

Montserrat
West Indies
Status: Overseas territory
Claimed: 1632
Capital: Plymouth *(de jure)*, Brades *(de facto)*
Population: 5215
Area: 40 sq miles (102 sq km)

Pitcairn Group of Islands
South Pacific
Status: Dependent territory
Claimed: 1887
Capital: Adamstown
Population: 48
Area: 18 sq miles (47 sq km)

St. Helena
South Atlantic
Status: Overseas territory
Claimed: 1673
Capital: Jamestown
Population: 7776
Area: 47 sq miles (122 sq km)

South Georgia & The South Sandwich Islands
South Atlantic
Status: Overseas territory
Claimed: 1775
Capital: Not applicable
Population: No permanent residents
Area: 1387 sq miles (3592 sq km)

Tristan da Cunha
South Atlantic
Status: Overseas territory
Claimed: 1612
Capital: Edinburgh
Population: 264
Area: 38 sq miles (98 sq km)

Turks & Caicos Islands
West Indies
Status: Overseas territory
Claimed: 1766
Capital: Cockburn Town
Population: 33,098
Area: 166 sq miles (430 sq km)

UNITED STATES OF AMERICA

America's overseas territories have been seen as strategically useful, if expensive, links with its "backyards." The US has, in most cases, given the local population a say in deciding their own status. A US Commonwealth territory, such as Puerto Rico, has a greater level of independence than that of a US unincorporated territory.

American Samoa
South Pacific
Status: Unincorporated territory
Claimed: 1900
Capital: Pago Pago
Population: 55,165
Area: 75 sq miles (195 sq km)

Baker & Howland Islands
South Pacific
Status: Unincorporated territory
Claimed: 1856
Capital: Not applicable
Population: None
Area: 0.5 sq miles (1.4 sq km)

Guam
West Pacific
Status: Unincorporated territory
Claimed: 1898
Capital: Hagåtña
Population: 165,124
Area: 212 sq miles (549 sq km)

Jarvis Island
South Pacific
Status: Unincorporated territory
Claimed: 1856
Capital: Not applicable
Population: None
Area: 1.7 sq miles (4.5 sq km)

Johnston Atoll
Central Pacific
Status: Unincorporated territory
Claimed: 1858
Capital: Not applicable
Population: Not applicable
Area: 1 sq mile (2.8 sq km)

Kingman Reef
Central Pacific
Status: Unincorporated territory
Claimed: 1856
Capital: Not applicable
Population: None
Area: 0.4 sq mile (1 sq km)

Midway Islands
Central Pacific
Status: Unincorporated territory
Claimed: 1867
Capital: Not applicable
Population: 40
Area: 2 sq miles (5.2 sq km)

Navassa Island
West Indies
Status: Unincorporated territory
Claimed: 1856
Capital: Not applicable
Population: None
Area: 2 sq miles (5.2 sq km)

Northern Mariana Islands
West Pacific
Status: Commonwealth territory
Claimed: 1947
Capital: Saipan
Population: 53,855
Area: 177 sq miles (457 sq km)

Palmyra Atoll
Central Pacific
Status: Incorporated territory
Claimed: 1898
Capital: Not applicable
Population: None
Area: 5 sq miles (12 sq km)

Puerto Rico
West Indies
Status: Commonwealth territory
Claimed: 1898
Capital: San Juan
Population: 3.62 million
Area: 3515 sq miles (9104 sq km)

Virgin Islands
West Indies
Status: Unincorporated territory
Claimed: 1917
Capital: Charlotte Amalie
Population: 104,737
Area: 137 sq miles (355 sq km)

Wake Island
Central Pacific
Status: Unincorporated territory
Claimed: 1898
Capital: Not applicable
Population: 150 (US air base)
Area: 2.5 sq miles (6.5 sq km)

Glossary of geographical terms

The following glossary lists all geographical terms occuring on the maps and in the main-entry names in the Index–Gazetteer. These terms may precede, follow or be run together with the proper elements of the name; where they precede it the term is reversed for indexing purposes – thus Poluostov Yamal is indexed as Yamal, Poluostrov.

A

Å *Danish, Norwegian,* River
Alpen *German,* Alps
Altiplanicie *Spanish,* Plateau
Älv(en) *Swedish,* River
Anse *French,* Bay
Archipiélago *Spanish,* Archipelago
Arcipelago *Italian,* Archipelago
Arquipélago *Portuguese,* Archipelago
Aukštuma *Lithuanian,* Upland

B

Bahía *Spanish,* Bay
Baía *Portuguese,* Bay
Baḩr *Arabic,* River
Baie *French,* Bay
Bandao *Chinese,* Peninsula
Banjaran *Malay,* Mountain range
Batang *Malay,* Stream
-berg *Afrikaans, Norwegian,* Mountain
Birket *Arabic,* Lake
Boğazı *Turkish,* Strait
Bucht *German,* Bay
Bugten *Danish,* Bay
Buḩayrat *Arabic,* Lake, reservoir
Buḩeiret *Arabic,* Lake
Bukit *Malay,* Mountain
-bukta *Norwegian,* Bay
bukten *Swedish,* Bay
Burnu *Turkish,* Cape, point
Buuraha *Somali,* Mountains

C

Cabo *Portuguese,* Cape
Cap *French,* Cape
Cascada *Portuguese,* Waterfall
Cerro *Spanish,* Hill
Chaîne *French,* Mountain range
Chau *Cantonese,* Island
Cháy *Turkish,* Stream
Chhâk *Cambodian,* Bay
Chhu *Tibetan,* River
-chôsuji *Korean,* Reservoir
Chott *Arabic,* Salt lake, depression
Ch'ün-tao *Chinese,* Island group *Cambodian,* Mountains
Cordillera *Spanish,* Mountain range
Costa *Spanish,* Coast
Côte *French,* Coast
Cuchilla *Spanish,* Mountains

D

Dağı *Azerbaijani, Turkish,* Mountain
Dağları *Azerbaijani, Turkish,* Mountains
-dake *Japanese,* Peak
Danau *Indonesian,* Lake
Đao *Vietnamese,* Island
Daryá *Persian,* River
Daryácheh *Persian,* Lake
Dasht *Persian,* Plain, desert
Dawḩat *Arabic,* Bay
Dere *Turkish,* Stream
Dili *Azerbaijani,* Spit
-do *Korean,* Island
Dooxo *Somali,* Valley
Düzü *Azerbaijani,* Steppe
-dwíp *Bengali,* Island

E

Embalse *Spanish,* Reservoir
Erg *Arabic,* Dunes
Estany *Catalan,* Lake
Estrecho *Spanish,* Strait
-ey *Icelandic,* Island
Ezero *Bulgarian, Macedonian,* Lake

F

Fjord *Danish,* Fjord
-fjorden *Norwegian,* Fjord
-fjørdhur *Faeroese,* Fjord
Fleuve *French,* River
Fliegu *Maltese,* Channel
-fljór *Icelandic,* River

G

-gang *Korean,* River
Ganga *Nepali, Sinhala,* River
Gaoyuan *Chinese,* Plateau
-gawa *Japanese,* River
Gebel *Arabic,* Mountain
-gebirge *German,* Mountains
Ghubbat *Arabic,* Bay
Gjiri *Albanian,* Bay
Gol *Mongolian,* River
Golfe *French,* Gulf
Golfo *Italian, Spanish,* Gulf
Gora *Russian, Serbian,* Mountain
Gory *Russian,* Mountains
Guba *Russian,* Bay
Gunung *Malay,* Mountain

H

Ḩadd *Arabic,* Spit
-haehyôp *Korean,* Strait
Haff *German,* Lagoon
Hai *Chinese,* Sea, bay
Ḩammádat *Arabic,* Plateau
Hámún *Persian,* Lake
Hawr *Arabic,* Lake
Háyk' *Amharic,* Lake
He *Chinese,* River
Helodrano *Malagasy,* Bay
-hegység *Hungarian,* Mountain range
Hka *Burmese,* River
-ho *Korean,* Lake
Hô *Korean,* Reservoir
/olot *Hebrew,* Dunes
Hora *Belorussian,* Mountain
Hrada *Belorussian,* Mountains, ridge
Hsi *Chinese,* River
Hu *Chinese,* Lake

I

Île(s) *French,* Island(s)
Ilha(s) *Portuguese,* Island(s)
Ilhéu(s) *Portuguese,* Islet(s)
Irmak *Turkish,* River
Isla(s) *Spanish,* Island(s)
Isola (Isole) *Italian,* Island(s)

J

Jabal *Arabic,* Mountain
Jál *Arabic,* Ridge
-järvi *Finnish,* Lake
Jazírat *Arabic,* Island
Jazíreh *Persian,* Island
Jebel *Arabic,* Mountain
Jezero *Serbian/Croatian,* Lake
Jiang *Chinese,* River
-joki *Finnish,* River
-jökull *Icelandic,* Glacier
Juzur *Arabic,* Islands

K

Kaikyó *Japanese,* Strait
-kaise *Lappish,* Mountain
Kali *Nepali,* River
Kalnas *Lithuanian,* Mountain
Kalns *Latvian,* Mountain
Kang *Chinese,* Harbor
Kangri *Tibetan,* Mountain(s)
Kaôh *Cambodian,* Island
Kapp *Norwegian,* Cape
Kavír *Persian,* Desert
K'edi *Georgian,* Mountain range
Kediet *Arabic,* Mountain
Kepulauan *Indonesian, Malay,* Island group
Khalîg, Khalíj *Arabic,* Gulf
Khawr *Arabic,* Inlet
Khola *Nepali,* River
Khrebet *Russian,* Mountain range
Ko *Thai,* Island
Kolpos *Greek,* Bay
-kopf *German,* Peak
Körfäzi *Azerbaijani,* Bay
Körfezi *Turkish,* Bay
Kõrgustik *Estonian,* Upland
Koshi *Nepali,* River
Kowtal *Persian,* Pass
Kúh(há) *Persian,* Mountain(s)
-kundo *Korean,* Island group
-kysten *Norwegian,* Coast
Kyun *Burmese,* Island

L

Laaq *Somali,* Watercourse
Lac *French,* Lake
Lacul *Romanian,* Lake
Lago *Italian, Portuguese, Spanish,* Lake
Laguna *Spanish,*

Lagoon, Lake
Laht *Estonian,* Bay
Laut *Indonesian,* Sea
Lembalemba *Malagasy,* Plateau
Lerr *Armenian,* Mountain
Lerrnashght'a *Armenian,* Mountain range
Les *Czech,* Forest
Lich *Armenian,* Lake
Liqeni *Albanian,* Lake
Lumi *Albanian,* River
Lyman *Ukrainian,* Estuary

M

Mae Nam *Thai,* River
-mägi *Estonian,* Hill
Maja *Albanian,* Mountain
-man *Korean,* Bay
Marios *Lithuanian,* Lake
-meer *Dutch,* Lake
Melkosopochnik *Russian,* Plain
-meri *Estonian,* Sea
Mifraz *Hebrew,* Bay
Monkhafad *Arabic,* Depression
Mont(s) *French,* Mountain(s)
Monte *Italian, Portuguese,* Mountain
More *Russian,* Sea
Mörön *Mongolian,* River

N

Nagor'ye *Russian,* Upland
Naḥal *Hebrew,* River
Nahr *Arabic,* River
Nam *Laotian,* River
Nehri *Turkish,* River
Nevado *Spanish,* Mountain (snow-capped)
Nisoi *Greek,* Islands
Nizmennost' *Russian,* Lowland, plain
Nosy *Malagasy,* Island
Nur *Mongolian,* Lake
Nuruu *Mongolian,* Mountains
Nuur *Mongolian,* Lake
Nyzovyna *Ukrainian,* Lowland, plain

O

Ostrov(a) *Russian,* Island(s)
Oued *Arabic,* Watercourse
-oy *Faeroese,* Island
-øy(a) *Norwegian,* Island
Oya *Sinhala,* River
Ozero *Russian, Ukrainian,* Lake

P

Passo *Italian,* Pass
Pegunungan *Indonesian, Malay,* Mountain range
Pelagos *Greek,* Sea
Penisola *Italian,* Peninsula
Peski *Russian,* Sands
Phanom *Thai,* Mountain
Phou *Laotian,* Mountain
Pic *Catalan,* Peak
Pico *Portuguese, Spanish,* Peak
Pik *Russian,* Peak
Planalto *Portuguese,* Plateau
Planina, Planini *Bulgarian, Macedonian, Serbian, Croatian,* Mountain range
Ploskogor'ye *Russian,* Upland
Poluostrov *Russian,* Peninsula
Potamos *Greek,* River
Proliv *Russian,* Strait
Pulau *Indonesian, Malay,* Island
Pulu *Malay,* Island
Punta *Portuguese, Spanish,* Point

Q

Qá' *Arabic,* Depression
Qolleh *Persian,* Mountain

R

Raas *Somali,* Cape
-rags *Latvian,* Cape
Ramlat *Arabic,* Sands
Ra's *Arabic,* Cape, point, headland
Ravnina *Bulgarian, Russian,* Plain
Récif *French,* Reef
Represa (Rep.) *Spanish, Portuguese,* Reservoir
-rettó *Japanese,* Island chain
Riacho *Spanish,* Stream
Riban' *Malagasy,* Mountains
Rio *Portuguese,* River
Río *Spanish,* River
Riu *Catalan,* River
Rivier *Dutch,* River
Rivière *French,* River
Rowd *Pashtu,* River
Rúd *Persian,* River
Rudohorie *Slovak,* Mountains
Ruisseau *French,* Stream

S

Sabkhat *Arabic,* Salt marsh
Şaḩrā' *Arabic,* Desert
Samudra *Sinhala,* Reservoir
-san *Japanese, Korean,* Mountain
-sanchi *Japanese,* Mountains
-sanmaek *Korean,* Mountain range
Sarír *Arabic,* Desert
Sebkha, Sebkhet *Arabic,* Salt marsh, depression
See *German,* Lake
Selat *Indonesian,* Strait
-selkä *Finnish,* Ridge
Selseleh *Persian,* Mountain range
Serra *Portuguese,* Mountain
Serranía *Spanish,* Mountain
Sha'íb *Arabic,* Watercourse
Shamo *Chinese,* Desert
Shan *Chinese,* Mountain(s)
Shan-mo *Chinese,* Mountain range
Shaţţ *Arabic,* Distributary
-shima *Japanese,* Island
Shui-tao *Chinese,* Channel
Sierra *Spanish,* Mountains
Sòn *Vietnamese,* Mountain
Sông *Vietnamese,* River
-spitze *German,* Peak
Štít *Slovak,* Peak
Stoeng *Cambodian,* River
Stretto *Italian,* Strait
Su Anbarı *Azerbaijani,* Reservoir
Sungai *Indonesian, Malay,* River
Suu *Turkish,* River

T

Tal *Mongolian,* Plain
Tandavan' *Malagasy,* Mountain range
Tangorombohitr' *Malagasy,* Mountain massif
Tao *Chinese,* Island
Tassili *Berber,* Plateau, mountain
Tau *Russian,* Mountain(s)
Taungdan *Burmese,* Mountain range
Teluk *Indonesian, Malay,* Bay
Terara *Amharic,* Mountain
Tog *Somali,* Valley
Tônlé *Cambodian,* Lake
Top *Dutch,* Peak
-tunturi *Finnish,* Mountain
Tur'at *Arabic,* Channel

V

Väin *Estonian,* Strait
-vatn *Icelandic,* Lake
-vesi *Finnish,* Lake
Vinh *Vietnamese,* Bay
Vodokhranilishche (Vdkhr.) *Russian,* Reservoir
Vodoskhovyshche (Vdskh.) *Ukrainian,* Reservoir
Volcán *Spanish,* Volcano
Vozvyshennost' *Russian,* Upland, plateau
Vrh *Macedonian,* Peak
Vysochyna *Ukrainian,* Upland
Vysočina *Czech,* Upland

W

Waadi *Somali,* Watercourse
Wádí *Arabic,* Watercourse
Wāḩat, Wâhat *Arabic,* Oasis
Wald *German,* Forest
Wan *Chinese,* Bay
Wyżyna *Polish,* Upland

X

Xé *Laotian,* River

Y

Yarımadası *Azerbaijani,* Peninsula
Yazovir *Bulgarian,* Reservoir
Yoma *Burmese,* Mountains
Yu *Chinese,* Islet

Z

Zaliv *Bulgarian, Russian,* Bay
Zatoka *Ukrainian,* Bay
Zemlya *Russian,* Land

Continental factfile

North & Central America

Total area: 9,400,000 sq miles (24,346,000 sq km)

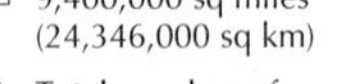
Total number of countries: 23

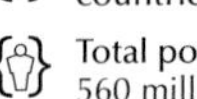
Total population: 560 million

Largest city with population: Mexico City, Mexico 22.2 million

Country with highest population density: Barbados 1807 people per sq mile (698 people per sq km)

Largest country: Canada 3,855,171 sq miles (9,984,670 sq km)

Smallest country: St. Kitts & Nevis 101 sq miles (261 sq km)

Largest lake: Lake Superior, Canada/ USA 32,151 sq miles (83,270 sq km)

Longest river: Mississippi-Missouri, USA 3710 miles (5969 km)

Highest point: Mt. McKinley (Denali), Alaska, USA 20,310 ft (6190 m)

lowest point: Death Valley, California, USA 282 ft (86 m) below sea level

South America

Total area: 6,880,000 sq miles (17,819,000 sq km)

Total number of countries: 12

Total population: 406 million

Largest city with population: São Paulo, Brazil 21.7 million

Country with highest population density: Ecuador 147 people per sq mile (57 people per sq km)

Largest country: Brazil 3,286,470 sq miles (8,511,965 sq km)

Smallest country: Suriname 63,039 sq miles (163,270 sq km)

Largest lake: Lake Titicaca, Bolivia/Peru 3220 sq miles (8340 sq km)

Longest river: Amazon, Brazil 4049 miles (6516 km)

Highest point: Cerro Aconcagua, Argentina 22,831 ft (6959 m)

Lowest point: Laguna del Carbón, Argentina 344 ft (105 m) below sea level

Africa

Total area: 11,677,250 sq miles (30,244,050 sq km)

Total number of countries: 54

Total population: 1109 million

Largest city with population: Cairo, Egypt 16.4 million

Country with highest population density: Mauritius 1671 people per sq mile (645 people per sq km)

Largest country: Algeria 919,590 sq miles (2,381,740 sq km)

Smallest country: Seychelles 176 sq miles (455 sq km)

Largest lake: Lake Victoria, Uganda, Kenya, Tanzania 26,828 sq miles (69,484 sq km)

Longest river: Nile, Uganda/Sudan/Egypt 4160 miles (6695 km)

Highest point: Kilimanjaro, Tanzania 19,340 ft (5895 m)

Lowest point: Lac', Assal, Djibouti 512 ft (156 m) below sea level

Europe

Total area: 4,809,200 sq miles (12,456,000 sq km)

Total number of countries: 44

Total population: 721 million

Largest city with population: Moscow, Euro Russia 16.7 million

Country with highest population density: Monaco 48,181 people per sq mile (18,531 people per sq km)

Largest country: European Russia 1,527,341 sq miles (3,955,818 sq km)

Smallest country: Vatican City, Italy 0.17 sq miles (0.44 sq km)

Largest lake: Ladoga, European Russia 7100 sq miles (18,390 sq km)

Longest river: Volga, European Russia 2290 miles (3688 km)

Highest point: El'brus, Caucasus Mts, European Russia 18,510 ft (5642 m)

Lowest point: Volga Delta, Caspian Sea, European Russia 92 ft (28 m) below sea level

North & West Asia

Total area:
9,585,500 sq miles
(24,826,600 sq km)

Total number of countries: 25

Total population:
446 million

Largest city with population: Tehran, Iran
13.4 million

Country with highest population density: Bahrain
4762 people per sq mile
(1841 people per sq km)

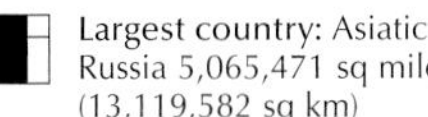

Largest country: Asiatic Russia 5,065,471 sq miles
(13,119,582 sq km)

Smallest country:
Bahrain 239 sq miles
(620 sq km)

Largest lake:
Caspian Sea 142,243 sq miles
(371,000 sq km)

Longest river: Ob'-Irtysh, Asiatic Russia 3461 miles
(5570 km)

Highest point: Pik Pobedy, Kyrgyzstan/China 24,408 ft
(7439 m)

Lowest point: Dead Sea, Israel/Jordan 1401 ft
(427 m) below sea level

South & East Asia

Total area:
7,936,200 sq miles
(20,554,700 sq km)

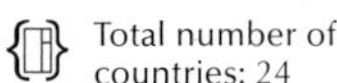

Total number of countries: 24

Total population:
3775 million

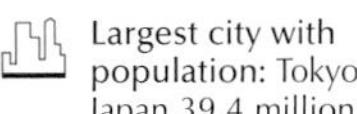

Largest city with population: Tokyo, Japan 39.4 million

Country with highest population density: Singapore
22,881 people per sq mile
(8852 people per sq km)

Largest country:
China 3,705,386 sq miles
(9,596,960 sq km)

Smallest country:
Maldives 116 sq miles
(300 sq km)

Largest lake: Tonle Sap, Cambodia 1000 sq miles
(2850 sq km)

Longest river: Chang Jiang (Yangtze) 3965 miles
(6380 km)

Highest point:
Mount Everest, Nepal
29,029 ft (8848 m)

Lowest point: Turpan Hami, (Turfan basin), China 505 ft
(154 m) below sea level

Australasia & Oceania

Total area:
3,376,700 sq miles
(8,745,750 sq km)

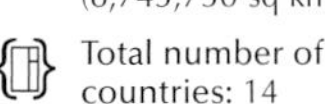

Total number of countries: 14

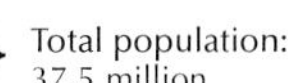

Total population:
37.5 million

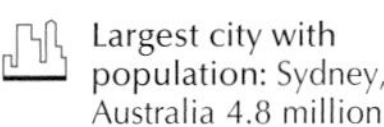

Largest city with population: Sydney, Australia 4.8 million

Country with highest population density: Nauru
1165 people per sq mile
(449 people per sq km)

Largest country:
Australia 2,967,893 sq miles
(7,686,850 sq km)

Smallest country:
Nauru 8 sq miles
(21 sq km)

Largest lake: Lake Eyre, Australia 3700 sq miles
(9583 sq km)

Longest river: Murray-Darling, Australia
2330 miles (3750 km)

Highest point: Mt. Wilhelm, Papua New Guinea 14,795 ft
(4509 m)

Lowest point: Lake Eyre, Australia 52 ft
(16 m) below sea level

Antarctica

Total area: 5,450,500 sq miles (14,000,000 sq km) of which approx. 324,300 sq miles (840,000 sq km) is ice-free.

Total number of countries: The Antarctic Treaty has 30 participating nations and 14 with observer status. Claims by Australia, France, New Zealand, Norway, Argentina, Chile, and the UK are not recognized by other member states.

Total Population: No indigenous population. 74 research stations, (42 are staffed all year-round). Population varies between about 1000 (winter) and 4000 (summer).

Total volume of ice:
7,200,000 cu miles (30,000,000 cu km): contains 90% of Earth's fresh water

Sea ice: 1,158,300 sq miles (3,000,000 sq km) in February. 7,722,000 sq miles (20,000,000 sq km) in October

Lowest temperature: Vostok station -89.5°C (-129°F)

Highest point: Vinson Massif
16,072 ft (4897 m)

Lowest Point: Coastline 0ft/m

Geographical comparisons

Largest countries

Russian Fed.	6,592,735 sq miles	(17,075,200 sq km)
Canada	3,855,171 sq miles	(9,984,670 sq km)
USA	3,717,792 sq miles	(9,626,091 sq km)
China	3,705,386 sq miles	(9,596,960 sq km)
Brazil	3,286,470 sq miles	(8,511,965 sq km)
Australia	2,967,893 sq miles	(7,686,850 sq km)
India	1,269,338 sq miles	(3,287,590 sq km)
Argentina	1,068,296 sq miles	(2,766,890 sq km)
Kazakhstan	1,049,150 sq miles	(2,717,300 sq km)
Algeria	919,590 sq miles	(2,381,740 sq km)

Smallest countries

Vatican City	0.17 sq miles	(0.44 sq km)
Monaco	0.75 sq miles	(1.95 sq km)
Nauru	8 sq miles	(21 sq km)
Tuvalu	10 sq miles	(26 sq km)
San Marino	24 sq miles	(61 sq km)
Liechtenstein	62 sq miles	(160 sq km)
Marshall Islands	70 sq miles	(181 sq km)
St. Kitts & Nevis	101 sq miles	(261 sq km)
Maldives	116 sq miles	(300 sq km)
Malta	122 sq miles	(316 sq km)

Largest islands

Greenland	840,000 sq miles	(2,175,600 sq km)
New Guinea	312,000 sq miles	(808,000 sq km)
Borneo	292,222 sq miles	(757,050 sq km)
Madagascar	226,656 sq miles	(587,040 sq km)
Sumatra	202,300 sq miles	(524,000 sq km)
Baffin Island	183,800 sq miles	(476,000 sq km)
Honshu	88,800 sq miles	(230,000 sq km)
Britain	88,700 sq miles	(229,800 sq km)
Victoria Island	81,900 sq miles	(212,000 sq km)
Ellesmere Island	75,700 sq miles	(196,000 sq km)

Richest countries (GNI per capita, in US$)

Monaco	186,950
Liechtenstein	136,770
Norway	102,610
Switzerland	86,600
Qatar	85,550
Luxembourg	71,810
Australia	65,520
Denmark	61,160
Sweden	59,240
Singapore	54,040

Poorest countries (GNI per capita, in US$)

Malawi	270
Burundi	280
Somalia	288
Central African Republic	320
Congo, Democratic Republic	400
Niger	410
Liberia	410
Madagascar	440
Guinea	460
Ethiopia	470

Most populous countries

China	1.386 billion
India	1.252 billion
USA	320 million
Indonesia	250 million
Brazil	200 million
Pakistan	182 million
Nigeria	174 million
Bangladesh	157 million
Russian Federation	143 million
Japan	127 million

Least populous countries

Vatican City	839
Nauru	9434
Tuvalu	10,698
Palau	21,108
San Marino	32,448
Monaco	36,136
Liechtenstein	37,000
St. Kitts & Nevis	51,134
Marshall Islands	69,747
Dominica	73,286

Most densely populated countries

Monaco	48,181 people per sq mile	(18,531 per sq km)
Singapore	22,881 people per sq mile	(8852 per sq km)
Vatican City	4935 people per sq mile	(1907 per sq km)
Bahrain	4762 people per sq mile	(1841 per sq km)
Malta	3226 people per sq mile	(1250 per sq km)
Bangladesh	3029 people per sq mile	(1169 per sq km)
Maldives	2586 people per sq mile	(1000 per sq km)
Taiwan	1871 people per sq mile	(722 per sq km)
Barbados	1807 people per sq mile	(698 per sq km)
Mauritius	1671 people per sq mile	(645 per sq km)

Most sparsely populated countries

Mongolia......... 5 people per sq mile......... (2 per sq km)
Namibia .... 7 people per sq mile......... (3 per sq km)
Iceland .... 8 people per sq mile......... (3 per sq km)
Suriname......... 8 people per sq mile......... (3 per sq km)
Australia .... 8 people per sq mile......... (3 per sq km)
Botswana......... 9 people per sq mile......... (4 per sq km)
Libya .... 9 people per sq mile......... (4 per sq km)
Mauritania..... 10 people per sq mile......... (4 per sq km)
Canada.......... 10 people per sq mile......... (4 per sq km)
Guyana .... 11 people per sq mile......... (4 per sq km)

Most widely spoken languages

1. Chinese (Mandarin)
2. Spanish
3. English
4. Hindi
5. Arabic
6. Portuguese
7. Bengali
8. Russian
9. Japanese
10. Javanese

Largest conurbations

Tokyo (Japan) 39,400,000
Guangzhou (China)................................. 32,600,000
Shanghai (China)...................................... 29,600,000
Jakarta (Indonesia)................................... 27,000,000
Delhi (India) 25,300,000
Seoul (South Korea)................................. 24,200,000
Karachi (Pakistan).................................... 23,200,000
Mumbai (India) 22,600,000
Manila (Philippines) 22,500,000
Mexico City (Mexico)............................... 22,200,000
New York (USA) 21,800,000
São Paulo (Brazil)..................................... 21,700,000
Beijing (China)... 19,900,000
Osaka (Japan)... 17,8 00,000
Los Angeles (USA).................................... 17,300,000
Dhaka (Bangladesh) 16,700,000
Moscow (Russian Federation) 16,700,000
Cairo (Egypt) 16,400,000
Kolkata (India).. 15,800,000
Buenos Aires (Argentina) 15,700,000
Bangkok (Thailand) 14,900,000
Istanbul (Turkey) 14,000,000
London (UK) 14,000,000
Lagos (Nigeria)... 13,500,000
Tehran (Iran) 13,400,000

Longest rivers

Nile (Northeast Africa) .... 4160 miles ...... (6695 km)
Amazon (South America)........... 4049 miles ...... (6516 km)
Yangtze (China).......................... 3915 miles ...... (6299 km)
Mississippi/Missouri (USA).......... 3710 miles........ (5969 km)
Ob'-Irtysh (Russian Federation) 3461 miles ...... (5570 km)
Yellow River (China) .... 3395 miles ...... (5464 km)
Congo (Central Africa) .... 2900 miles ...... (4667 km)
Mekong (Southeast Asia) .... 2749 miles ...... (4425 km)
Lena (Russian Federation)........ 2734 miles ...... (4400 km)
Mackenzie (Canada) .... 2640 miles ...... (4250 km)
Yenisey (Russian Federation)... 2541 miles ...... (4090 km)

Highest mountains (Height above sea level)

Everest.................................... 29,029 ft....... (8848 m)
K2 .... 28,253 ft....... (8611 m)
Kanchenjunga I........................ 28,210 ft....... (8598 m)
Makalu I .... 27,767 ft....... (8463 m)
Cho Oyu .... 26,907 ft....... (8201 m)
Dhaulagiri I............................. 26,796 ft....... (8167 m)
Manaslu I .... 26,783 ft....... (8163 m)
Nanga Parbat I......................... 26,661 ft....... (8126 m)
Annapurna I .... 26,547 ft....... (8091 m)
Gasherbrum I........................... 26,471 ft....... (8068 m)

Largest bodies of inland water (Area & depth)

Caspian Sea
143,243 sq miles (371,000 sq km).......3215 ft (980 m)
Lake Superior
32,151 sq miles (83,270 sq km).......1289 ft (393 m)
Lake Victoria
26,560 sq miles (68,880 sq km).........328 ft (100 m)
Lake Huron
23,436 sq miles (60,700 sq km).........751 ft (229 m)
Lake Michigan
22,402 sq miles (58,020 sq km).........922 ft (281 m)
Lake Tanganyika
12,703 sq miles (32,900 sq km).... 4700 ft (1435 m)
Great Bear Lake
12,274 sq miles (31,790 sq km)...... 1047 ft (319 m)
Lake Baikal
11,776 sq miles (30,500 sq km).... 5712 ft (1741 m)
Great Slave Lake
10,981 sq miles (28,440 sq km).........459 ft (140 m)
Lake Erie
9915 sq miles (25,680 sq km)...........197 ft (60 m)

......*continued on page 166*

Geographical comparisons continued

Deepest ocean features

Challenger Deep, Mariana Trench (Pacific)	36,201 ft	(11,034 m)
Vityaz III Depth, Tonga Trench (Pacific)	35,704 ft	(10,882 m)
Vityaz Depth, Kurile-Kamchatka Trench (Pacific)	34,588 ft	(10,542 m)
Cape Johnson Deep, Philippine Trench (Pacific)	34,441 ft	(10,497 m)
Kermadec Trench (Pacific)	32,964 ft	(10,047 m)
Ramapo Deep, Japan Trench (Pacific)	32,758 ft	(9984 m)
Milwaukee Deep, Puerto Rico Trench (Atlantic)	30,185 ft	(9200 m)
Argo Deep, Torres Trench (Pacific)	30,070 ft	(9165 m)
Meteor Depth, South Sandwich Trench (Atlantic)	30,000 ft	(9144 m)
Planet Deep, New Britain Trench (Pacific)	29,988 ft	(9140 m)

Greatest waterfalls (Mean flow of water)

Boyoma (D.R. Congo)	600,400 cu. ft/sec	(17,000 cu.m/sec)
Khône (Laos/Cambodia)	410,000 cu. ft/sec	(11,600 cu.m/sec)
Niagara (USA/Canada)	195,000 cu. ft/sec	(5500 cu.m/sec)
Grande, Salto (Uruguay)	160,000 cu. ft/sec	(4500 cu.m/sec)
Paulo Afonso (Brazil)	100,000 cu. ft/sec	(2800 cu.m/sec)
Urubupungá (Brazil)	97,000 cu. ft/sec	(2750 cu.m/sec)
Iguaçu (Argentina/Brazil)	62,000 cu. ft/sec	(1700 cu.m/sec)
Maribondo (Brazil)	53,000 cu. ft/sec	(1500 cu.m/sec)
Victoria (Zimbabwe)	39,000 cu. ft/sec	(1100 cu.m/sec)
Murchison Falls (Uganda)	42,000 cu. ft/sec	(1200 cu.m/sec)
Churchill (Canada)	35,000 cu. ft/sec	(1000 cu.m/sec)
Kaveri Falls (India)	33,000 cu. ft/sec	(900 cu.m/sec)

Highest waterfalls

Angel (Venezuela)	3212 ft	(979 m)
Tugela (South Africa)	3110 ft	(948 m)
Utigard (Norway)	2625 ft	(800 m)
Mongefossen (Norway)	2539 ft	(774 m)
Mtarazi (Zimbabwe)	2500 ft	(762 m)
Yosemite (USA)	2425 ft	(739 m)
Ostre Mardola Foss (Norway)	2156 ft	(657 m)
Tyssestrengane (Norway)	2119 ft	(646 m)
*Cuquenan (Venezuela)	2001 ft	(610 m)
Sutherland (New Zealand)	1903 ft	(580 m)
*Kjellfossen (Norway)	1841 ft	(561 m)

** indicates that the total height is a single leap*

Largest deserts

Sahara	3,450,000 sq miles	(9,065,000 sq km)
Gobi	500,000 sq miles	(1,295,000 sq km)
Ar Rub al Khali	289,600 sq miles	(750,000 sq km)
Great Victorian	249,800 sq miles	(647,000 sq km)
Sonoran	120,000 sq miles	(311,000 sq km)
Kalahari	120,000 sq miles	(310,800 sq km)
Kara Kum	115,800 sq miles	(300,000 sq km)
Takla Makan	100,400 sq miles	(260,000 sq km)
Namib	52,100 sq miles	(135,000 sq km)
Thar	33,670 sq miles	(130,000 sq km)

NB – Most of Antarctica is a polar desert, with only 2 inches (50 mm) of precipitation annually

Hottest inhabited places

Djibouti (Djibouti)	86.0°F	(30.0°C)
Tombouctou (Mali)	84.7°F	(29.3°C)
Tirunelveli (India)	84.7°F	(29.3°C)
Tuticorin (India)	84.7°F	(29.3°C)
Nellore (India)	84.5°F	(29.2°C)
Santa Marta (Colombia)	84.5°F	(29.2°C)
Aden (Yemen)	84.0°F	(29.0°C)
Madurai (India)	84.0°F	(29.0°C)
Niamey (Niger)	84.0°F	(29.0°C)

Driest inhabited places

Aswân (Egypt)	0.02 in	(0.5 mm)
Luxor (Egypt)	0.03 in	(0.7 mm)
Arica (Chile)	0.04 in	(1.1 mm)
Ica (Peru)	0.10 in	(2.3 mm)
Antofagasta (Chile)	0.20 in	(4.9 mm)
El Minya (Egypt)	0.20 in	(5.1 mm)
Asyut (Egypt)	0.20 in	(5.2 mm)
Callao (Peru)	0.50 in	(12.0 mm)
Trujillo (Peru)	0.55 in	(14.0 mm)
Al Fayyum (Egypt)	0.80 in	(19.0 mm)

Wettest inhabited places

Mawsynram (India)	467 in	(11,862 mm)
Mt Waialeale (Hawaii, USA)	460 in	(11,684 mm)
Cherrapunji (India)	450 in	(11,430 mm)
Cape Debundsha (Cameroon)	405 in	(10,290 mm)
Quibdo (Colombia)	354 in	(8892 mm)
Buenaventura (Colombia)	265 in	(6743 mm)
Monrovia (Liberia)	202 in	(5131 mm)
Pago Pago (American Samoa)	196 in	(4990 mm)
Moulmein (Myanmar)	191 in	(4852 mm)
Lae (Papua New Guinea)	183 in	(4645 mm)

GLOSSARY OF ABBREVIATIONS

This Glossary provides a comprehensive guide to the abbreviations used in this Atlas, and in the Index.

A
abbrev. abbreviated
Afr. Afrikaans
Alb. Albanian
Amh. Amharic
anc. ancient
Ar. Arabic
Arm. Armenian
Az. Azerbaijani

B
Basq. Basque
Bel. Belorussian
Ben. Bengali
Bibl. Biblical
Bret. Breton
Bul. Bulgarian
Bur. Burmese

C
Cam. Cambodian
Cant. Cantonese
Cast. Castilian
Cat. Catalan
Chin. Chinese
Cro. Croat
Cz. Czech

D
Dan. Danish
Dut. Dutch

E
Eng. English
Est. Estonian
est. estimated

F
Faer. Faeroese
Fij. Fijian
Fin. Finnish
Flem. Flemish
Fr. French
Fris. Frisian

G
Geor. Georgian
Ger. German
Gk. Greek
Guj. Gujarati

H
Haw. Hawaiian
Heb. Hebrew
Hind. Hindi
hist. historical
Hung. Hungarian

I
Icel. Icelandic
Ind. Indonesian
In. Inuit
Ir. Irish
It. Italian

J
Jap. Japanese

K
Kaz. Kazakh
Kir. Kirghiz
Kor. Korean
Kurd. Kurdish

L
Lao. Laotian
Lapp. Lappish
Lat. Latin
Latv. Latvian
Lith. Lithanian
Lus. Lusatian

M
Mac. Macedonian
Mal. Malay
Malg. Malagasy
Malt. Maltese
Mon. Montenegro
Mong. Mongolian

N
Nepali. Nepali
Nor. Norwegian

O
off. officially

P
Pash. Pashtu
Per. Persian
Pol. Polish
Port. Portuguese
prev. previously

R
Rmsch. Romansch
Roman. Romanian
Rus. Russian

S
SCr. Serbo - Croatian
Serb. Serbian
Slvk. Slovak
Slvn. Slovene
Som. Somali
Sp. Spanish
Swa. Swahili
Swe. Swedish

T
Taj. Tajik
Th. Thai
Tib. Tibetan
Turk. Turkish
Turkm. Turkmenistan

U
Uigh. Uighur
Ukr. Ukrainian
Uzb. Uzbek

V
var. variant
Vtn. Vietnamese

W
Wel. Welsh

X
Xh. Xhosa

Key to country factboxes within the Index:

Formation
Date of independence

Population
Total population / population density - based on total land area .

Calorie consumption
Average number of calories consumed daily per person.

A

Aa *see* Gauja
Aachen *94 A4 Dut.* Aken, *Fr.* Aix-la-Chapelle; *anc.* Aquae Grani, Aquisgranum. Nordrhein-Westfalen, W Germany
Aaiún *see* Laâyoune
Aalborg *85 B7 var.* Ålborg, Ålborg-Nørresundby; *anc.* Alburgum. Nordjylland, N Denmark
Aalen *95 B6* Baden-Württemberg, S Germany
Aalsmeer *86 C3* Noord-Holland, C Netherlands
Aalst *87 B6* Oost-Vlaanderen, C Belgium
Aalten *86 E4* Gelderland, E Netherlands
Aalter *87 B5* Oost-Vlaanderen, NW Belgium
Aanaarjävri *see* Inarijärvi
Äänekoski *85 D5* Länsi-Suomi, W Finland
Aar *see* Aare
Aare *95 A7 var.* Aar. *river* W Switzerland
Aarhus *see* Århus
Aarlen *see* Arlon
Aat *see* Ath
Aba *77 E5* Orientale, NE Dem. Rep. Congo
Aba *75 G5* Abia, S Nigeria
Abā as Su'ūd *see* Najrān
Abaco Island *see* Great Abaco, N Bahamas
Ābādān *120 C4* Khūzestān, SW Iran
Abadan *122 C3 prev.* Bezmein, Büzmeýin, *Rus.* Byuzmeyin. Ahal Welaýaty, C Turkmenistan
Abai *see* Blue Nile
Abakan *114 D4* Respublika Khakasiya, S Russian Federation
Abancay *60 D4* Apurímac, SE Peru
Abariringa *see* Kanton
Abashiri *130 D2 var.* Abasiri. Hokkaidō, NE Japan
Abasiri *see* Abashiri
Ābay Wenz *see* Blue Nile
Abbaia *see* Ābaya Hāyk'
Abbatis Villa *see* Abbeville
Abbazia *see* Opatija
Abbeville *90 C2 anc.* Abbatis Villa. Somme, N France
'Abd al 'Azīz, Jabal *118 D2 mountain range* NE Syria
Abéché *76 C3 var.* Abécher, Abeshr. Ouaddaï, SE Chad
Abécher *see* Abéché
Abela *see* Ávila
Abellinum *see* Avellino
Abemama *144 D2 var.* Apamama; *prev.* Roger Simpson Island. *atoll* Tungaru, W Kiribati
Abengourou *75 E5* E Côte d'Ivoire
Aberbrothock *see* Arbroath
Abercorn *see* Mbala
Aberdeen *88 D3 anc.* Devana. NE Scotland, United Kingdom
Aberdeen *45 E2* South Dakota, N USA
Aberdeen *46 B2* Washington, NW USA
Abergwaun *see* Fishguard
Abertawe *see* Swansea
Aberystwyth *89 C6* W Wales, United Kingdom
Abeshr *see* Abéché
Abhā *121 B6* 'Asīr, SW Saudi Arabia
Abidavichy *107 D7 Rus.* Obidovichi. Mahilyowskaya Voblasts', E Belarus
Abidjan *75 E5* S Côte d'Ivoire
Abilene *49 F3* Texas, SW USA
Abingdon *see* Pinta, Isla
Abkhazia *see* Apkhazeti
Åbo *see* Turku
Aboisso *75 E5* SE Côte d'Ivoire
Abo, Massif d' *76 B1 mountain range* NW Chad
Abomey *75 F5* S Benin
Abou-Déïa *76 C3* Salamat, SE Chad
Aboudouhour *see* Abū aḍ Ḍuhūr
Abou Kémal *see* Abū Kamāl
Abrantes *92 B3 var.* Abrántes. Santarém, C Portugal
Abrashlare *see* Brezovo
Abrolhos Bank *56 E4 undersea bank* W Atlantic Ocean
Abrova *107 B6 Rus.* Obrovo. Brestskaya Voblasts', SW Belarus
Abrud *108 B4 Ger.* Gross-Schlatten, *Hung.* Abrudbánya. Alba, SW Romania
Abrudbánya *see* Abrud
Abruzzese, Appennino *96 C4 mountain range* C Italy
Absaroka Range *44 B2 mountain range* Montana/Wyoming, NW USA
Abū aḍ Ḍuhūr *118 B3 Fr.* Aboudouhour. Idlib, NW Syria
Abu Dhabi *see* Abū Ẓabī
Abu Hamed *72 C3* River Nile, N Sudan
Abū Ḥardān *118 E3 var.* Hajîne. Dayr az Zawr, E Syria
Abuja *75 G4 country capital* (Nigeria) Federal Capital District, C Nigeria
Abū Kamāl *118 E3 Fr.* Abou Kémal. Dayr az Zawr, E Syria
Abula *see* Ávila
Abunã, Rio *62 C2 var.* Río Abuná. *river* Bolivia/Brazil
Abut Head *151 B6 headland* South Island, New Zealand
Abuye Meda *72 D4 mountain* C Ethiopia
Abū Ẓabī *121 C5 var.* Abū Ẓabī, *Eng.* Abu Dhabi. *country capital* (United Arab Emirates) Abū Ẓaby, C United Arab Emirates
Abū Ẓabī *see* Abū Ẓabī
Abyaḍ, Al Baḥr al *see* White Nile
Abyei Area *73 B5 disputed region* Southern Kordofan, S Sudan
Abyla *see* Ávila
Abyssinia *see* Ethiopia
Acalayong *77 A5* SW Equatorial Guinea
Acaponeta *50 D4* Nayarit, C Mexico
Acapulco *51 E5 var.* Acapulco de Juárez. Guerrero, S Mexico
Acapulco de Juárez *see* Acapulco
Acarai Mountains *59 F4 Sp.* Serra Acaraí. *mountain range* Brazil/Guyana
Acaraí, Serra *see* Acarai Mountains
Acarigua *58 D2* Portuguesa, N Venezuela
Accra *75 E5 country capital* (Ghana) SE Ghana
Achacachi *61 E4* La Paz, W Bolivia
Ach'ara *117 F2 prev.* Achara, *var.* Ajaria. *autonomous republic* SW Georgia
Achara *see* Ach'ara
Acklins Island *54 C2 island* SE Bahamas
Aconcagua, Cerro *64 B4 mountain* W Argentina
Açores/Açores, Arquipélago dos/ Açores, Ilhas dos *see* Azores
A Coruña *92 B1 Cast.* La Coruña, *Eng.* Corunna; *anc.* Caronium. Galicia, NW Spain
Acre *62 C2 off.* Estado do Acre. *state* W Brazil
Acre *62 C2 off.* Estado do Acre. *region* W Brazil
Açu *see* Assu
Acunum Acusio *see* Montélimar
Ada *100 D3* Vojvodina, N Serbia
Ada *49 G2* Oklahoma, C USA
Ada Bazar *see* Adapazarı
Adalia *see* Antalya
Adalia, Gulf of *see* Antalya Körfezi
Adama *see* Nazrēt
'Adan *121 B7 Eng.* Aden. SW Yemen
Adana *116 D4 var.* Seyhan. Adana, S Turkey
Adâncata *see* Horlivka
Adapazarı *116 B2 prev.* Ada Bazar. Sakarya, NW Turkey
Adare, Cape *154 B4 cape* Antarctica
Ad Dahna *120 C4 desert* E Saudi Arabia
Ad Dakhla *70 A4 var.* Dakhla. SW Western Sahara
Ad Dalanj *see* Dilling
Ad Damar *see* Ed Damer
Ad Damazīn *see* Ed Damazin
Ad Dāmir *see* Ed Damer
Ad Dammān *120 C4 var.* Dammām. Ash Sharqīyah, NE Saudi Arabia
Ad Dāmūr *see* Damoûr
Ad Dawḥah *120 C4 Eng.* Doha. *country capital* (Qatar) C Qatar
Aḍ Ḍiffah *see* Libyan Plateau
Addis Ababa *see* Ādīs Ābeba
Addoo Atoll *see* Addu Atoll
Addu Atoll *132 A5 var.* Addoo Atoll, Seenu Atoll. *atoll* S Maldives
Adelaide *149 B6 state capital* South Australia
Adelsberg *see* Postojna
Aden *see* 'Adan
Aden, Gulf of *121 C7 gulf* SW Arabian Sea
Adige *96 C2 Ger.* Etsch. *river* N Italy
Adirondack Mountains *41 F2 mountain range* New York, NE USA

Ādīs Ābeba *73 C5 Eng.* Addis Ababa. *country capital* (Ethiopia) Ādīs Ābeba, C Ethiopia
Adıyaman *117 E4* Adıyaman, SE Turkey
Adjud *108 C4* Vrancea, E Romania
Admiralty Islands *144 B3 island group* N Papua New Guinea
Adra *93 E5* Andalucía, S Spain
Adrar *70 D3* C Algeria
Adrian *40 C3* Michigan, N USA
Adrianople/Adrianopolis *see* Edirne
Adriatico, Mare *see* Adriatic Sea
Adriatic Sea *103 E2 Alb.* Deti Adriatik, *It.* Mare Adriatico, *SCr.* Jadransko More, *Slvn.* Jadransko Morje. *sea* N Mediterranean Sea
Adriatik, Deti *see* Adriatic Sea
Adycha *115 F2 river* NE Russian Federation
Aegean Sea *105 C5 Gk.* Aigaíon Pelagos, Aigaío Pélagos, *Turk.* Ege Denizi. *sea* NE Mediterranean Sea
Aegviidu *106 D2 Ger.* Charlottenhof. Harjumaa, NW Estonia
Aegyptus *see* Egypt
Aelana *see* Al 'Aqabah
Aelok *see* Ailuk Atoll
Aelōnlaplap *see* Ailinglaplap Atoll
Aemona *see* Ljubljana
Aeolian Islands *97 C6 var.* Isole Lipari, *Eng.* Aeolian Islands, Lipari Islands. *island group* S Italy
Aeolian Islands *see* Eolie, Isole
Æsernia *see* Isernia
Afar Depression *see* Danakil Desert
Afars et des Issas, Territoire Français des *see* Djibouti
Afghānestān, Dowlat-e Eslāmī-ye *see* Afghanistan
Afghanistan *122 C4 off.* Islamic Republic of Afghanistan, *Per.* Dowlat-e Eslāmī-ye Afghānestān; *prev.* Republic of Afghanistan. *country* C Asia

AFGHANISTAN
Central Asia

Official name The Islamic Republic of Afghanistan
Formation 1919 / 1919
Capital Kabul
Population 30.6 million / 122 people per sq mile (47 people per sq km)
Total area 250,000 sq. miles (647,500 sq. km)
Languages Pashtu*, Tajik, Dari*, Farsi, Uzbek, Turkmen
Religions Sunni Muslim 80%, Shi'a Muslim 19%, Other 1%
Ethnic mix Pashtun 38%, Tajik 25%, Hazara 19%, Uzbek and Turkmen 15%, Other 3%
Government Nonparty system
Currency Afghani = 100 puls
Literacy rate 32%
Calorie consumption 2107 kilocalories

Afmadow *73 D6* Jubbada Hoose, S Somalia
Africa *68 continent*
Africa, Horn of *68 E4 physical region* Ethiopia/Somalia
Africana Seamount *141 A6 seamount* SW Indian Ocean
'Afrīn *118 B2* Ḩalab, N Syria
Afyon *116 B3 prev.* Afyonkarahisar. Afyon, W Turkey
Agadès *see* Agadez
Agadez *75 G3 prev.* Agadès. Agadez, C Niger
Agadir *70 B3* SW Morocco
Agana/Agaña *see* Hagåtña
Āgaro *73 C5* Oromīya, C Ethiopia
Agassiz Fracture Zone *143 G5 fracture zone* S Pacific Ocean
Agatha *see* Agde
Agathónisi *105 D6 island* Dodekánisa, Greece, Aegean Sea
Agde *91 C6 anc.* Agatha. Hérault, S France
Agedabia *see* Ajdābiyā
Agen *91 B5 anc.* Aginnum. Lot-et-Garonne, SW France
Agendicum *see* Sens
Aghri Dagh *see* Büyükağrı Dağı
Agiá *104 B4 var.* Ayiá. Thessalía, C Greece
Agialoúsa *see* Yenierenköy
Agía Marína *105 E6* Léros, Dodekánisa, Greece, Aegean Sea
Aginnum *see* Agen
Ágios Efstrátios *104 D4 var.* Áyios Evstrátios, Hagios Evstrátios. *island* E Greece
Ágios Nikólaos *105 D8 var.* Áyios Nikólaos. Kríti, Greece, E Mediterranean Sea
Āgra *134 D3* Uttar Pradesh, N India
Agra and Oudh, United Provinces of *see* Uttar Pradesh
Agram *see* Zagreb
Ağrı *117 F3 var.* Karaköse; *prev.* Karakılısse. Ağrı, NE Turkey
Agri Dagi *see* Büyükağrı Dağı
Agrigento *97 C7 Gk.* Akragas; *prev.* Girgenti. Sicilia, Italy, C Mediterranean Sea
Agriovótano *105 C5* Évvoia, C Greece
Agropoli *97 D5* Campania, S Italy
Aguachica *58 B2* Cesar, N Colombia
Aguadulce *53 F5* Coclé, S Panama
Agua Prieta *50 B1* Sonora, NW Mexico
Aguascalientes *50 D4* Aguascalientes, C Mexico
Aguaytía *60 C3* Ucayali, C Peru
Aguilas *93 E4* Murcia, SE Spain
Aguililla *50 D4* Michoacán, SW Mexico
Agulhas Basin *69 D8 undersea basin* SW Indian Ocean
Agulhas, Cape *78 C5 headland* SW South Africa
Agulhas Plateau *67 D6 undersea plateau* SW Indian Ocean
Ahaggar *75 F2 high plateau region* SE Algeria
Ahlen *94 B4* Nordrhein-Westfalen, W Germany
Ahmadābād *134 C4 var.* Ahmedabad. Gujarāt, W India
Ahmadnagar *134 C5 var.* Ahmednagar. Mahārāshtra, W India
Ahmedabad *see* Ahmadābād
Ahmednagar *see* Ahmadnagar
Ahuachapán *52 B3* Ahuachapán, W El Salvador
Ahvāz *120 C3 var.* Ahwāz; *prev.* Nāsiri. Khūzestān, SW Iran
Ahvenanmaa *see* Åland
Ahwāz *see* Ahvāz
Aigaíon Pelagos/Aigaío Pélagos *see* Aegean Sea
Aígina *105 C6 var.* Aíyina, Egina. Aígina, C Greece
Aígio *105 B5 var.* Egio; *prev.* Aíyion. Dytikí Ellάda, S Greece
Aiken *43 E2* South Carolina, SE USA
Ailinglaplap Atoll *144 D2 var.* Aelōnlaplap. *atoll* Ralik Chain, S Marshall Islands
Ailuk Atoll *144 D1 var.* Aelok. *atoll* Ratak Chain, NE Marshall Islands
Ainaži *106 D3 Est.* Heinaste, *Ger.* Hainasch. N Latvia
'Aïn Ben Tili *74 D1* Tiris Zemmour, N Mauritania
Aintab *see* Gaziantep
Aïoun el Atrous/Aïoun el Atroûss *see* 'Ayoûn el 'Atroûs
Aiquile *61 F4* Cochabamba, C Bolivia
Aïr *see* Aïr, Massif de l'
Air du Azbine *see* Aïr, Massif de l'
Aïr, Massif de l' *75 G2 var.* Aïr, Air du Azbine, Asben. *mountain range* NC Niger
Aiud *108 B4 Ger.* Strassburg, *Hung.* Nagyenyed; *prev.* Engeten. Alba, SW Romania
Aix *see* Aix-en-Provence
Aix-en-Provence *91 D6 var.* Aix; *anc.* Aquae Sextiae. Bouches-du-Rhône, SE France
Aix-la-Chapelle *see* Aachen
Aíyina *see* Aígina
Aíyion *see* Aígio
Aizkraukle *106 C4* S Latvia
Ajaccio *91 E7* Corse, France, C Mediterranean Sea
Ajaria *see* Ach'ara
Ajastan *see* Armenia
Aj Bogd Uul *126 D2 mountain* SW Mongolia
Ajdābiyā *71 G2 var.* Agedabia, Ajdābiyah. NE Libya
Ajdābiyah *see* Ajdābiyā
Ajjinena *see* El Geneina
Ajmer *134 D3 var.* Ajmere. Rājasthān, N India
Ajo *48 A3* Arizona, SW USA
Akaba *see* Al 'Aqabah
Akamagaseki *see* Shimonoseki
Akasha *72 B3* Northern, N Sudan
Akchâr *74 C2 desert* W Mauritania
Aken *see* Aachen
Akermanceaster *see* Bath
Akhaltsikhe *117 F2 prev.* Akhalts'ikhe. SW Georgia
Akhalts'ikhe *see* Akhaltsikhe
Akhisar *116 A3* Manisa, W Turkey
Akhmīm *72 B2 var.* Akhmîm; *anc.* Panopolis. C Egypt
Akhtubinsk *111 C7* Astrakhanskaya Oblast', SW Russian Federation
Akhtyrka *see* Okhtyrka
Akimiski Island *38 C3 island* Nunavut, C Canada
Akinovka *109 F4* Zaporiz'ka Oblast', S Ukraine
Akita *130 D4* Akita, Honshū, C Japan
Akjoujt *74 C2 prev.* Fort-Repoux. Inchiri, W Mauritania
Akkeshi *130 E2* Hokkaidō, NE Japan
Aklavik *36 D3* Northwest Territories, NW Canada
Akmola *see* Astana
Akmolinsk *see* Astana
Aknavásár *see* Târgu Ocna
Akpatok Island *39 E1 island* Nunavut, E Canada
Akragas *see* Agrigento
Akron *40 D4* Ohio, N USA
Akrotiri *see* Akrotírion
Akrotírion *102 C5 var.* Akrotiri. *UK air base* S Cyprus
Aksai Chin *124 B2 Chin.* Aksayqin. *disputed region* China/India
Aksaray *116 C4* Aksaray, C Turkey
Aksayqin *see* Aksai Chin
Akşehir *116 B4* Konya, W Turkey
Aktash *see* Oqtosh
Aktau *114 A4 Kaz.* Aqtaū; *prev.* Shevchenko. Mangistau, W Kazakhstan
Aktjubinsk/Aktyubinsk *see* Aktobe
Aktobe *114 B4 Kaz.* Aqtöbe; *prev.* Aktjubinsk, Aktyubinsk. Aktyubinsk, NW Kazakhstan
Aktsyabrski *107 C7 Rus.* Oktyabr'skiy; *prev.* Karpilovka. Homyel'skaya Voblasts', SE Belarus
Aktyubinsk *see* Aktobe
Akula *77 C5* Equateur, NW Dem. Rep. Congo
Akureyri *83 E4* Nordhurland Eystra, N Iceland
Akyab *see* Sittwe
Alabama *42 C2 off.* State of Alabama, *also known as* Camellia State, Heart of Dixie, The Cotton State, Yellowhammer State. *state* S USA
Alabama River *42 C3 river* Alabama, S USA
Alaca *116 C3* Çorum, N Turkey
Alacant *see* Alicante
Alagoas *63 G2 off.* Estado de Alagoas. *region* E Brazil
Alagoas *63 G2 off.* Estado de Alagoas. *state* E Brazil
Alais *see* Alès
Alajuela *53 E4* Alajuela, C Costa Rica
Alakanuk *36 C2* Alaska, USA
Al 'Alamayn *72 B1 var.* El 'Alamein. N Egypt
Al 'Amārah *120 C3 var.* Amara. Maysān, E Iraq
Alamo *47 D6* Nevada, W USA
Alamogordo *48 D3* New Mexico, SW USA
Alamosa *44 C5* Colorado, C USA
Aland Islands *85 C6 var.* Aland Islands, *Fin.* Ahvenanmaa. *island group* SW Finland
Aland Islands *see* Åland
Aland Sea *85 C6 var.* Aland Sea. *strait* Baltic Sea/Gulf of Bothnia
Aland Sea *see* Ålands Hav
Alanya *116 C4* Antalya, S Turkey
Alappuzha *132 C3 var.* Alleppey. Kerala, SW India
Al 'Aqabah *119 B8 var.* Akaba, Aqaba, 'Aqaba; *anc.* Aelana, Elath. Al 'Aqabah, SW Jordan
Al 'Arabīyah as Su'ūdīyah *see* Saudi Arabia
Alasca, Golfo de *see* Alaska, Gulf of
Alaşehir *116 A4* Manisa, W Turkey
Al 'Ashārah *118 E3 var.* Ashara. Dayr Zawr, E Syria
Alaska *36 C3 off.* State of Alaska, *also known as* Land of the Midnight Sun, The Last Frontier, Seward's Folly; *pre* Russian America. *state* NW USA
Alaska, Gulf of *36 C4 var.* Golfo de Alasca. *gulf* Canada/USA
Alaska Peninsula *36 C3 peninsula* Alaska, USA
Alaska Range *34 B2 mountain range* Alaska, USA
Al-Asnam *see* Chlef
Alattio *see* Alta
Al Awaynāt *see* Al 'Uwaynāt
Alaykel'/Alay-Kuu *see* Këk-Art
Al 'Aynā *119 B7* Al Karak, W Jordan
Alazeya *115 G2 river* NE Russian Federation
Al Bāb *118 B2* Ḩalab, N Syria
Albacete *93 E3* Castilla-La Mancha, C Spain
Al Baghdādī *120 B3 var.* Khān al Baghdādī. Al Anbār, SW Iraq
Al Bāha *see* Al Bāḩah
Al Bāḩah *121 B5 var.* Al Bāha. Al BāḨa SW Saudi Arabia
Al Baḩrayn *see* Bahrain
Alba Iulia *108 B4 Ger.* Weissenburg, *Hung.* Gyulafehérvár; *prev.* Bălgrad, Karlsburg, Károly-Fehérvár. Alba, W Romania
Albania *101 C7 off.* Republic of Albania, *Alb.* Republika e Shqipqërisë Shqipëria; *prev.* People's Socialist Republic of Albania. *country* SE Euro

ALBANIA
Southeast Europe

Official name Republic of Albania
Formation 1912 / 1921
Capital Tirana
Population 3.2 million / 302 people per sq mile (117 people per sq km)
Total area 11,100 sq. miles (28,748 sq. km)
Languages Albanian*, Greek
Religions Sunni Muslim 70%, Albanian Orthodox 20%, Roman Catholic 10%
Ethnic mix Albanian 98%, Greek 1%, Other 1%
Government Parliamentary system
Currency Lek = 100 qindarka (qintars)
Literacy rate 97%
Calorie consumption 3023 kilocalories

Albania *see* Aubagne
Albany *147 B7* Western Australia
Albany *42 D3* Georgia, SE USA
Albany *41 F3 state capital* New York, NE USA
Albany *46 B3* Oregon, NW USA
Albany *38 C3 river* Ontario, S Canada
Alba Regia *see* Székesfehérvár
Al Bāridah *118 C4 var.* Bāridah. Ḩimş, C Syria
Al Başrah *120 C3 Eng.* Basra, *hist.* Busra Bussora. Al Başrah, SE Iraq
Al Batrūn *see* Batroûn
Al Bayḑā' *71 G2 var.* Beida. NE Libya
Albemarle Island *see* Isabela, Isla
Albemarle Sound *43 G1 inlet* W Atlant Ocean
Albergaria-a-Velha *92 B2* Aveiro, N Portugal
Albert *90 C3* Somme, N France
Alberta *37 E4 province* SW Canada
Albert Edward Nyanza *see* Edward, Lake
Albert, Lake *73 B6 var.* Albert Nyanza, Lac Mobutu Sese Seko. *lake* Uganda/ Dem. Rep. Congo
Albert Lea *45 F3* Minnesota, N USA
Albert Nyanza *see* Albert, Lake
Albertville *see* Kalemie
Albi *91 C6 anc.* Albiga. Tarn, S France
Albiga *see* Albi
Ålborg *see* Aalborg
Ålborg-Nørresundby *see* Aalborg
Albuquerque *48 D2* New Mexico, SW USA
Al Burayqah *see* Marsá al Burayqah
Alburgum *see* Aalborg
Albury *149 C7* New South Wales, SE Australia
Alcácer do Sal *92 B4* Setúbal, W Portug
Alcalá de Henares *93 E3 Ar.* Alkal'a; *an* Complutum. Madrid, C Spain

:amo *97 C7* Sicilia, Italy, C Mediterranean Sea
:añiz *93 F2* Aragón, NE Spain
:ántara, Embalse de *92 C3 reservoir* W Spain
:audete *92 D4* Andalucía, S Spain
:ázar *see* Ksar-el-Kebir
:azarquivir *see* Ksar-el-Kebir
:oi *see* Alcoy
:oy *93 F4 Cat.* Alcoi. Valenciana, E Spain
labra Group *79 G2 island group* SW Seychelles
dan *115 F3 river* NE Russian Federation
Dar al Baida *see* Rabat
derney *90 A2 island* Channel Islands
eg *74 C3* Brakna, SW Mauritania
eksandriya *see* Oleksandriya
eksandropol' *see* Gyumri
eksandrovka *see* Oleksandrivka
eksandrovsk *see* Zaporizhzhya
eksin *111 B5* Tul'skaya Oblast', W Russian Federation
eksinac *100 E4* Serbia, SE Serbia
ençon *90 B3* Orne, N France
enquer *63 E2* Pará, NE Brazil
ep/Aleppo *see* Ḥalab
ert *37 F1* Ellesmere Island, Nunavut, N Canada
ès *91 C6 prev.* Alais. Gard, S France
eșd *108 B3 Hung.* Élesd. Bihor, SW Romania
essandria *96 B2 Fr.* Alexandrie. Piemonte, N Italy
esund *85 A5* Møre og Romsdal, S Norway
eutian Basin *113 G3 undersea basin* Bering Sea
eutian Islands *36 A3 island group* Alaska, USA
eutian Range *34 A2 mountain range* Alaska, USA
eutian Trench *113 H3 trench* S Bering Sea
exander Archipelago *36 D4 island group* Alaska, USA
exander City *42 D2* Alabama, S USA
exander Island *154 A3 island* Antarctica
exander Range *see* Kirghiz Range
exandra *151 B7* Otago, South Island, New Zealand
exándreia *104 B4 var.* Alexándria. Kentrikí Makedonía, N Greece
exandretta *see* İskenderun
exandretta, Gulf of *see* İskenderun Körfezi
exandria *72 B1 Ar.* Al Iskandarīyah. N Egypt
exandria *108 C5* Teleorman, S Romania
exandria *42 B3* Louisiana, S USA
exandria *45 F2* Minnesota, N USA
exándria *see* Alexándreia
lexandrie *see* Alessandria
lexandroúpoli *104 D3 var.* Alexandroúpolis, *Turk.* Dedeagaç, Dedeagach. Anatolikí Makedonía kai Thráki, NE Greece
exandroúpolis *see* Alexandroúpoli
Fāshir *see* El Fasher
fatar *104 E1* Silistra, NE Bulgaria
feiós *105 B6 prev.* Alfiós; *anc.* Alpheius, Alpheus. *river* S Greece
fiós *see* Alfeiós
lföld *see* Great Hungarian Plain
l-Furāt *see* Euphrates
lga *114 B4 Kaz.* Algha. Aktyubinsk, NW Kazakhstan
garve *92 B4 cultural region* S Portugal
geciras *92 C5* Andalucía, SW Spain
gemesí *93 F3* Valenciana, E Spain
l-Genain *see* El Geneina
ger *71 E1 var.* Algiers, El Djazaïr, Al Jazair. *country capital* (Algeria) N Algeria
geria *70 C3 off.* Democratic and Popular Republic of Algeria. *country* N Africa

ALGERIA
North Africa

Official name People's Democratic Republic of Algeria
Formation 1962 / 1962
Capital Algiers

ALGERIA
(continued)

Population 39.2 million / 43 people per sq mile (16 people per sq km)
Total area 919,590 sq. miles (2,381,740 sq. km)
Languages Arabic*, Tamazight (Kabyle, Shawia, Tamashek), French
Religions Sunni Muslim 99%, Christian and Jewish 1%
Ethnic mix Arab 75%, Berber 24%, European and Jewish 1%
Government Presidential system
Currency Algerian dinar = 100 centimes
Literacy rate 73%
Calorie consumption 3220 kilocalories

Algeria, Democratic and Popular Republic of *see* Algeria
Algerian Basin *80 C5 var.* Balearic Plain. *undersea basin* W Mediterranean Sea
Algha *see* Alga
Al Ghābah *121 E5 var.* Ghaba. C Oman
Alghero *97 A5* Sardegna, Italy, C Mediterranean Sea
Al Ghurdaqah *72 C2 var.* Hurghada, Ghurdaqah. E Egypt
Algiers *see* Alger
Al Golea *see* El Goléa
Algona *45 F3* Iowa, C USA
Al Hajar al Gharbi *121 D5 mountain range* N Oman
Al Hamad *see* Syrian Desert
Al Ḥasakah *118 D2 var.* Al Hasijah, El Haseke, *Fr.* Hassetché. Al Ḥasakah, NE Syria
Al Hasijah *see* Al Ḥasakah
Al Ḥillah *120 B3 var.* Hilla. Bābil, C Iraq
Al Ḥisā *119 B7* Aṭ Ṭafīlah, W Jordan
Al Ḥudaydah *121 B6 Eng.* Hodeida. W Yemen
Al Hufūf *120 C4 var.* Hofuf. Ash Sharqīyah, NE Saudi Arabia
Aliákmon *see* Aliákmonas
Aliákmonas *104 B4 prev.* Aliákmon; *anc.* Haliacmon. *river* N Greece
Alíartos *105 C5* Stereá Elláda, C Greece
Alicante *93 F4 Cat.* Alacant, *Lat.* Lucentum. Valenciana, SE Spain
Alice *49 G5* Texas, SW USA
Alice Springs *148 A4* Northern Territory, C Australia
Alifu Atoll *see* Ari Atoll
Aligandí *53 G4* Kuna Yala, NE Panama
Aliki *see* Alykí
Alima *77 B6 river* C Congo
Al Imārāt al 'Arabīyahal Muttaḥidah *see* United Arab Emirates
Alindao *76 C4* Basse-Kotto, S Central African Republic
Aliquippa *40 D4* Pennsylvania, NE USA
Al Iskandarīyah *see* Alexandria
Al Ismā'īlīya *72 B1 var.* Ismailia, Ismâ'ilîya. N Egypt
Alistráti *104 C3* Kentrikí Makedonía, NE Greece
Alivéri *105 C5 var.* Alivérion. Évvoia, C Greece
Alivérion *see* Alivéri
Al Jabal al Akhḍar *71 G2 mountain range* NE Libya
Al Jafr *119 B7* Ma'ān, S Jordan
Al Jaghbūb *71 H3* NE Libya
Al Jahrā' *120 C4 var.* Al Jahrah, Jahra. C Kuwait
Al Jahrah *see* Al Jahrā'
Al Jamāhīrīyah al 'Arabīyah al Lībīyah ash Sha'bīyah al Ishtirākīy *see* Libya
Al Jawf *120 B4 off.* Jauf. Al Jawf, NW Saudi Arabia
Al Jawlān *see* Golan Heights
Al Jazair *see* Alger
Al Jazirah *118 E2 physical region* Iraq/Syria
Al Jīzah *see* Giza
Al Junaynah *see* El Geneina
Alkal'a *see* Alcalá de Henares
Al Karak *119 B7 var.* El Kerak, Karak, Kerak; *anc.* Kir Moab, Kir of Moab. Al Karak, W Jordan
Al-Kasr al-Kebir *see* Ksar-el-Kebir
Al Khalīl *see* Hebron
Al Khārijah *72 B2 var.* El Khârga. C Egypt
Al Khums *71 F2 var.* Homs, Khoms, Khums. NW Libya
Alkmaar *86 C2* Noord-Holland, NW Netherlands
Al Kufrah *71 H4* SE Libya
Al Kūt *120 C3 var.* Kūt al 'Amārah, Kut al Imara. Wāsiṭ, E Iraq
Al-Kuwait *see* Al Kuwayt
Al Kuwayt *120 C4 var.* Al-Kuwait, *Eng.* Kuwait, Kuwait City; *prev.* Qurein. *country capital* (Kuwait) E Kuwait
Al Lādhiqīyah *118 A3 Eng.* Latakia, *Fr.* Lattaquié; *anc.* Laodicea, Laodicea ad Mare. Al Lādhiqīyah, W Syria
Allahābād *135 E3* Uttar Pradesh, N India
Allanmyo *see* Aunglan
Allegheny Plateau *41 E3 mountain range* New York/Pennsylvania, NE USA
Allenstein *see* Olsztyn
Allentown *41 F4* Pennsylvania, NE USA
Alleppey *see* Alappuzha
Alliance *44 D3* Nebraska, C USA
Al Līth *121 B5* Makkah, SW Saudi Arabia
Al Lubnān *see* Lebanon
Alma-Ata *see* Almaty
Almada *92 B4* Setúbal, W Portugal
Al Madīnah *121 A5 Eng.* Medina. Al Madīnah, W Saudi Arabia
Al Mafraq *119 B6 var.* Mafraq. Al Mafraq, N Jordan
Al Mahdīyah *see* Mahdia
Al Mahrah *121 C6 mountain range* E Yemen
Al Majma'ah *120 B4* Ar Riyāḍ, C Saudi Arabia
Al Mālikīyah *118 E1 var.* Malkiye. Al Ḥasakah, N Syria
Almalyk *see* Olmaliq
Al Mamlakah *see* Morocco
Al Mamlaka al Urdunīya al Hashemīyah *see* Jordan
Al Manāmah *120 C4 Eng.* Manama. *country capital* (Bahrain) N Bahrain
Al Manāṣif *118 E3 mountain range* E Syria
Almansa *93 F4* Castilla-La Mancha, C Spain
Al-Mariyya *see* Almería
Al Marj *71 G2 var.* Barka, *It.* Barce. NE Libya
Almaty *114 C5 var.* Alma-Ata. Almaty, SE Kazakhstan
Al Mawṣil *120 B2 Eng.* Mosul. Nīnawá, N Iraq
Al Mayādīn *118 D3 var.* Mayadin, *Fr.* Meyadine. Dayr az Zawr, E Syria
Al Mazra' *see* Al Mazra'ah
Al Mazra'ah *119 B6 var.* Al Mazra', Mazra'a. Al Karak, W Jordan
Almelo *86 E3* Overijssel, E Netherlands
Almendra, Embalse de *92 C2 reservoir* Castilla y León, NW Spain
Almendralejo *92 C4* Extremadura, W Spain
Almere *86 C3 var.* Almere-stad. Flevoland, C Netherlands
Almere-stad *see* Almere
Almería *93 E5 Ar.* Al-Mariyya; *anc.* Unci, *Lat.* Portus Magnus. Andalucía, S Spain
Al'met'yevsk *111 D5* Respublika Tatarstan, W Russian Federation
Al Mīnā' *see* El Mina
Al Minyā *72 B2 var.* El Minya, Minya. C Egypt
Almirante *53 E4* Bocas del Toro, NW Panama
Al Mudawwarah *119 B8* Ma'ān, SW Jordan
Al Mukallā *121 C6 var.* Mukalla. SE Yemen
Al Obayyid *see* El Obeid
Alofi *145 F4 dependent territory capital* (Niue) W Niue
Aloha State *see* Hawaii
Aloja *106 D3* N Latvia
Alónnisos *105 C5 island* Vóreies Sporádes, Greece, Aegean Sea
Álora *92 D5* Andalucía, S Spain
Alor, Kepulauan *139 E5 island group* E Indonesia
Al Oued *see* El Oued
Alpen *see* Alps
Alpena *40 D2* Michigan, N USA
Alpes *see* Alps
Alpha Cordillera *155 B3 var.* Alpha Ridge. *seamount range* Arctic Ocean
Alpha Ridge *see* Alpha Cordillera
Alpheius *see* Alfeiós
Alphen *see* Alphen aan den Rijn
Alphen aan den Rijn *86 C3 var.* Alphen. Zuid-Holland, C Netherlands
Alpheus *see* Alfeiós
Alpi *see* Alps
Alpine *49 E4* Texas, SW USA
Alps *102 C1 Fr.* Alpes, *Ger.* Alpen, *It.* Alpi. *mountain range* C Europe
Al Qaḍārif *see* Gedaref
Al Qāhirah *see* Cairo
Al Qāmishlī *118 E1 var.* Kamishli, Qamishly. Al Ḥasakah, NE Syria
Al Qaṣrayn *see* Kasserine
Al Qayrawān *see* Kairouan
Al-Qsar al-Kbir *see* Ksar-el-Kebir
Al Qubayyāt *see* Qoubaïyât
Al Quds/Al Quds ash Sharīf *see* Jerusalem
Alqueva, Barragem do *92 C4 reservoir* Portugal/Spain
Al Qunayṭirah *119 B5 var.* El Kuneitra, El Quneitra, Kuneitra, Qunaytra. Al Qunayṭirah, SW Syria
Al Quṣayr *118 B4 var.* El Quseir, Quṣayr, *Fr.* Kousseir. Ḥimṣ, W Syria
Al Quwayrah *119 B8 var.* El Quweira. Al 'Aqabah, SW Jordan
Alsace *90 E3 Ger.* Elsass; *anc.* Alsatia. *cultural region* NE France
Alsatia *see* Alsace
Alsdorf *94 A4* Nordrhein-Westfalen, W Germany
Alt *see* Olt
Alta *84 D2 Fin.* Alattio. Finnmark, N Norway
Altai *see* Altai Mountains
Altai Mountains *126 C2 var.* Altai, *Chin.* Altay Shan, *Rus.* Altay. *mountain range* Asia/Europe
Altamaha River *43 E3 river* Georgia, SE USA
Altamira *63 E2* Pará, NE Brazil
Altamura *97 E5 anc.* Lupatia. Puglia, SE Italy
Altar, Desierto de *50 A1 var.* Sonoran Desert. *desert* Mexico/USA
Altar, Desierto de *see* Sonoran Desert
Altay *126 C2* Xinjiang Uygur Zizhiqu, NW China
Altay *126 D2 prev.* Yösönbulag. Govĭ-Altay, W Mongolia
Altay Altai Mountains, Asia/Europe
Altay Shan *see* Altai Mountains
Altbetsche *see* Bečej
Altenburg *see* București, Romania
Altin Köprü *see* Āltūn Kūbrī
Altiplano *61 F4 physical region* W South America
Altkanischa *see* Kanjiža
Alton *40 B5* Illinois, N USA
Alton *40 B4* Missouri, C USA
Altoona *41 E4* Pennsylvania, NE USA
Alto Paraná *see* Paraná
Altpasua *see* Stara Pazova
Alt-Schwanenburg *see* Gulbene
Altsohl *see* Zvolen
Āltūn Kūbrī *120 B3 var.* Altin Köprü. At Ta'mím, N Iraq
Altun Shan *126 C3 var.* Altyn Tagh. *mountain range* NW China
Altus *49 F2* Oklahoma, C USA
Altyn Tagh *see* Altun Shan
Al Ubayyiḍ *see* El Obeid
Alūksne *106 D3 Ger.* Marienburg. NE Latvia
Al 'Ulā *120 A4* Al Madīnah, NW Saudi Arabia
Al 'Umarī *119 C6* 'Ammān, E Jordan
Alupka *109 F5* Avtonomna Respublika Krym, S Ukraine
Al Uqṣur *see* Luxor
Al Urdunn *see* Jordan
Alushta *109 F5* Avtonomna Respublika Krym, S Ukraine
Al 'Uwaynāt *71 F4 var.* Al Awaynāt. SW Libya
Alva *49 F1* Oklahoma, C USA
Alvarado *51 F4* Veracruz-Llave, E Mexico
Alvin *49 H4* Texas, SW USA
Al Wajh *120 A4* Tabūk, NW Saudi Arabia
Alwar *134 D3* Rājasthān, N India
Al Warī'ah *120 C4* Ash Sharqīyah, N Saudi Arabia
Al Yaman *see* Yemen
Alykí *104 C4 var.* Aliki. Thásos, N Greece
Alytus *107 B5 Pol.* Olita. Alytus, S Lithuania

Alzette *87 D8 river* S Luxembourg
Amadeus, Lake *147 D5 seasonal lake* Northern Territory, C Australia
Amadi *73 B5* Western Equatoria, SW South Sudan
Amadjuak Lake *37 G3 lake* Baffin Island, Nunavut, N Canada
Amakusa-nada *131 A7 gulf* SW Japan
Åmål *85 B6* Västra Götaland, S Sweden
Amami-gunto *130 A3 island group* SW Japan
Amami-o-shim *130 A3 island* S Japan
Amantea *97 D6* Calabria, SW Italy
Amapá *63 E1 off.* Estado de Amapá; *prev.* Território de Amapá. *region* NE Brazil
Amapá *63 E1 off.* Estado de Amapá; *prev.* Território de Amapá. *state* NE Brazil
Amapá, Estado de *see* Amapá
Amapá, Território de *see* Amapá
Amara *see* Al 'Amārah
Amarapura *136 B3* Mandalay, C Myanmar (Burma)
Amarillo *49 E2* Texas, SW USA
Amay *87 C6* Liège, E Belgium
Amazon *63 E1 Sp.* Amazonas. *river* Brazil/Peru
Amazonas *see* Amazon
Amazon Basin *62 D2 basin* N South America
Amazon, Mouths of the *63 F1 delta* NE Brazil
Ambam *77 B5* Sud, S Cameroon
Ambanja *79 G2* Antsirañana, N Madagascar
Ambarchik *115 G2* Respublika Sakha (Yakutiya), NE Russian Federation
Ambato *60 B1* Tungurahua, C Ecuador
Ambérieu-en-Bugey *91 D5* Ain, E France
Ambianum *see* Amiens
Amboasary *79 F4* Toliara, S Madagascar
Amboina *see* Ambon
Ambon *139 F4 prev.* Amboina, Amboyna. Pulau Ambon, E Indonesia
Ambositra *79 G3* Fianarantsoa, SE Madagascar
Amboyna *see* Ambon
Ambracia *see* Árta
Ambre, Cap d' *see* Bobaomby, Tanjona
Ambrim *see* Ambrym
Ambriz *78 A1* Bengo, NW Angola
Ambrym *144 D4 var.* Ambrim. *island* C Vanuatu
Amchitka Island *36 A2 island* Aleutian Islands, Alaska, USA
Amdo *126 C5* Xizang Zizhiqu, W China
Ameland *86 D1 Fris.* It Amelân. *island* Waddeneilanden, N Netherlands
Amelân, It *see* Ameland
America *see* United States of America
America-Antarctica Ridge *67 C7 undersea ridge* S Atlantic Ocean
America in Miniature *see* Maryland
American Falls Reservoir *46 E4 reservoir* Idaho, NW USA
American Samoa *145 E4 US unincorporated territory* W Polynesia
Amersfoort *86 D3* Utrecht, C Netherlands
Ames *45 F3* Iowa, C USA
Amfilochía *105 A5 var.* Amfilokhía. Dytikí Elláda, C Greece
Amfilokhía *see* Amfilochía
Amga *115 F3 river* NE Russian Federation
Amherst *39 F4* Nova Scotia, SE Canada
Amherst *see* Kyaikkami
Amida *see* Diyarbakır
Amiens *90 C3 anc.* Ambianum, Samarobriva. Somme, N France
Amíndaion/Amindeo *see* Amýntaio
Amindivi Islands *132 A2 island group* Lakshadweep, India, N Indian Ocean
Amirante Islands *79 G1 var.* Amirantes Group. *island group* C Seychelles
Amirantes Group *see* Amirante Islands
Amistad, Presa de la *see* Amistad Reservoir
Amistad Reservoir *49 F4 var.* Presa de la Amistad. *reservoir* Mexico/USA
Amisus *see* Samsun
Ammaia *see* Portalegre
'Ammān *119 B6 anc.* Philadelphia, *Bibl.* Rabbah Ammon, Rabbath Ammon. *country capital* (Jordan) 'Ammān, NW Jordan
Ammassalik *82 D4 var.* Angmagssalik. Tunu, S Greenland
Ammóchostos *see* Gazimağusa
Ammóchostos, Kólpos *see* Gazimağusa Körfezi
Amnok-kang *see* Yalu
Amoea *see* Portalegre
Amoentai *see* Amuntai
Āmol *120 D2 var.* Amul. Māzandarān, N Iran
Amorgós *105 D6* Amorgós, Kykládes, Greece, Aegean Sea
Amorgós *105 D6 island* Kykládes, Greece, Aegean Sea
Amos *38 D4* Québec, SE Canada
Amourj *74 D3* Hodh ech Chargui, SE Mauritania
Amoy *see* Xiamen
Ampato, Nevado *61 E4 mountain* S Peru
Amposta *93 F2* Cataluña, NE Spain
Amraoti *see* Amrāvati
Amrāvati *134 D4 prev.* Amraoti. Mahārāshtra, C India
Amritsar *134 D2* Punjab, N India
Amstelveen *86 C3* Noord-Holland, C Netherlands
Amsterdam *86 C3 country capital* (Netherlands) Noord-Holland, C Netherlands
Amsterdam Island *141 C6 island* NE French Southern and Antarctic Lands
Am Timan *76 C3* Salamat, SE Chad
Amu Darya *122 D2 Rus.* Amudar'ya, *Taj.* Dar"yoi Amu, *Turkm.* Amyderya, *Uzb.* Amudaryo; *anc.* Oxus. *river* C Asia
Amu-Dar'ya *see* Amyderýa
Amudar'ya/Amudaryo/Amu, Dar"yoi *see* Amu Darya
Amul *see* Āmol
Amund Ringnes Island *37 F2 Island* Nunavut, N Canada
Amundsen Basin *155 C3 prev.* Fram Basin. *undersea basin* Arctic Ocean
Amundsen Plain *154 A4 abyssal plain* S Pacific Ocean
Amundsen-Scott *154 B3 US research station* Antarctica
Amundsen Sea *154 A4 sea* S Pacific Ocean
Amuntai *138 D4 prev.* Amoentai. Borneo, C Indonesia
Amur *115 G4 Chin.* Heilong Jiang. *river* China/Russian Federation
Amvrosiyevka *see* Amvrosiyivka
Amvrosiyivka *109 H3 Rus.* Amvrosiyevka. Donets'ka Oblast', SE Ukraine
Amyderýa *123 E3 Rus.* Amu-Dar'ya. Lebap Welaýaty, NE Turkmenistan
Amyderya *see* Amu Darya
Amýntaio *104 B4 var.* Amindeo; *prev.* Amíndaion. Dytikí Makedonía, N Greece
Anabar *115 E2 river* NE Russian Federation
An Abhainn Mhór *see* Blackwater
Anaco *59 E2* Anzoátegui, NE Venezuela
Anaconda *44 B2* Montana, NW USA
Anacortes *46 B1* Washington, NW USA
Anadolu Dağları *see* Doğu Karadeniz Dağları
Anadyr' *115 H1* Chukotskiy Avtonomnyy Okrug, NE Russian Federation
Anadyr' *115 G1 river* NE Russian Federation
Anadyr, Gulf of *115 H1 Eng.* Gulf of Anadyr. *gulf* NE Russian Federation
Anadyr, Gulf of *see* Anadyrskiy Zaliv
Anáfi *105 D7 anc.* Anaphe. *island* Kykládes, Greece, Aegean Sea
'Ānah *see* 'Annah
Anaheim *46 E2* California, W USA
Anaiza *see* 'Unayzah
Analalava *79 G2* Mahajanga, NW Madagascar
Anamur *116 C5* İçel, S Turkey
Anantapur *132 C2* Andhra Pradesh, S India
Anaphe *see* Anáfi
Anápolis *63 F3* Goiás, C Brazil
Anār *120 D3* Kermān, C Iran
Anatolia *116 C4 plateau* C Turkey
Anatom *see* Aneityum
Añatuya *64 C3* Santiago del Estero, N Argentina
An Bhearú *see* Barrow
Anchorage *36 C3* Alaska, USA
Ancona *96 C3* Marche, C Italy
Ancud *65 B6 prev.* San Carlos de Ancud. Los Lagos, S Chile
Ancyra *see* Ankara
Åndalsnes *85 A5* Møre og Romsdal, S Norway
Andalucía *92 D4 cultural region* S Spain
Andalusia *42 C3* Alabama, S USA
Andaman Islands *124 B4 island group* India, NE Indian Ocean
Andaman Sea *124 C4 sea* NE Indian Ocean
Andenne *87 C6* Namur, SE Belgium
Anderlues *87 B7* Hainaut, S Belgium
Anderson *40 C4* Indiana, N USA
Andes *64 B3 mountain range* W South America
Andhra Pradesh *135 E5 cultural region* E India
Andijon *123 F2 Rus.* Andizhan. Andijon Viloyati, E Uzbekistan
Andikíthira *see* Antikýthira
Andipaxi *see* Antípaxoi
Andípsara *see* Antípsara
Ándissa *see* Ántissa
Andizhan *see* Andijon
Andkhvōy *122 D3 prev.* Andkhvoy. Fāryāb, N Afghanistan
Andorra *91 A7 off.* Principality of Andorra, *Cat.* Valls d'Andorra, *Fr.* Vallée d'Andorre. *country* SW Europe

ANDORRA
Southwest Europe

Official name Principality of Andorra
Formation 1278 / 1278
Capital Andorra la Vella
Population 85,293 / 474 people per sq mile (183 people per sq km)
Total area 181 sq. miles (468 sq. km)
Languages Spanish, Catalan*, French, Portuguese
Religions Roman Catholic 94%, Other 6%
Ethnic mix Spanish 46%, Andorran 28%, Other 18%, French 8%
Government Parliamentary system
Currency Euro = 100 cents
Literacy rate 99%
Calorie consumption Not available

Andorra *see* Andorra la Vella
Andorra la Vella *91 A8 var.* Andorra, *Fr.* Andorre la Vielle, *Sp.* Andorra la Vieja. *country capital* (Andorra) C Andorra
Andorra la Vieja *see* Andorra la Vella
Andorra, Principality of *see* Andorra
Andorra, Valls d'/Andorra, Vallée d' *see* Andorra
Andorre la Vielle *see* Andorra la Vella
Andover *89 D7* S England, United Kingdom
Andøya *84 C2 island* C Norway
Andreanof Islands *36 A3 island group* Aleutian Islands, Alaska, USA
Andrews *49 E3* Texas, SW USA
Andrew Tablemount *140 A4 var.* Gora Andryu. *seamount* W Indian Ocean
Andria *97 D5* Puglia, SE Italy
An Droichead Nua *see* Newbridge
Andropov *see* Rybinsk
Ándros *105 D6* Ándros, Kykládes, Greece, Aegean Sea
Ándros *105 C6 island* Kykládes, Greece, Aegean Sea
Andros Island *54 B2 island* NW Bahamas
Andros Town *54 C1* Andros Island, NW Bahamas
Andryu, Gora *see* Andrew Tablemount
Aneityum *144 D5 var.* Anatom; *prev.* Kéamu. *island* S Vanuatu
Ānewetak *see* Enewetak Atoll
Angara *115 E4 river* C Russian Federation
Angarsk *115 E4* Irkutskaya Oblast', S Russian Federation
Ånge *85 C5* Västernorrland, C Sweden
Ángel de la Guarda, Isla *50 B2 island* NW Mexico
Angeles *139 E1 off.* Angeles City. Luzon, N Philippines
Angeles City *see* Angeles
Angel Falls *59 E3 Eng.* Angel Falls. *waterfall* E Venezuela
Angel Falls *see* Ángel, Salto
Angerburg *see* Węgorzewo
Ångermanälven *84 C4 river* N Swede
Angermünde *94 D3* Brandenburg, NE Germany
Angers *90 B4 anc.* Juliomagus. Maine-Loire, NW France
Anglesey *89 C5 island* NW Wales, United Kingdom
Anglet *91 A6* Pyrénées-Atlantiques, SW France
Angleton *49 H4* Texas, SW USA
Anglia *see* England
Anglo-Egyptian Sudan *see* Sudan
Angmagssalik *see* Ammassalik
Ang Nam Ngum *136 C4 lake* C Laos
Angola *78 B2 off.* Republic of Angola; *prev.* People's Republic of Angola, Portuguese West Africa. *country* SW Africa

ANGOLA
Southern Africa

Official name Republic of Angola
Formation 1975 / 1975
Capital Luanda
Population 21.5 million / 45 people per sq mile (17 people per sq km)
Total area 481,351 sq. miles (1,246,700 sq. km)
Languages Portuguese*, Umbundu, Kimbundu, Kikongo
Religions Roman Catholic 68%, Protestant 20%, Indigenous beliefs 12%
Ethnic mix Ovimbundu 37%, Other 25
Kimbundu 25%, Bakongo 13%
Government Presidential system
Currency Readjusted kwanza = 100 lwe
Literacy rate 71%
Calorie consumption 2400 kilocalories

Angola Basin *69 B5 undersea basin* E Atlantic Ocean
Angola, People's Republic of *see* Angola
Angola, Republic of *see* Angola
Angora *see* Ankara
Angostura *see* Ciudad Bolívar
Angostura, Presa de la *51 G5 reservoi* SE Mexico
Angoulême *91 B5 anc.* Iculisma. Charente, W France
Angoumois *91 B5 cultural region* W France
Angra Pequena *see* Lüderitz
Angren *123 F2* Toshkent Viloyati, E Uzbekistan
Anguilla *55 G3 UK dependent territory* E West Indies
Anguilla Cays *54 B2 islets* SW Bahama
Anhui *128 C5 var.* Anhui Sheng, Anhwei, Wan. *province* E China
AnhuiSheng/Anhwei Wan *see* Anhui
Anicium *see* le Puy
Anina *108 A4 Ger.* Steierdorf, *Hung.* Stájerlakanina; *prev.* Ştaierdorf-Anina, Steierdorf-Anina, Steyerlak-Anina. Caraş-Severin, SW Romania
Anjou *90 B4 cultural region* NW France
Anjouan *see* Nzwani
Ankara *116 C3 prev.* Angora; *anc.* Ancyra. *country capital* (Turkey) Ankara, C Turkey
Ankeny *45 F3* Iowa, C USA
Anklam *94 D2* Mecklenburg-Vorpommern, NE Germany
An Mhuir Cheilteach *see* Celtic Sea
Annaba *71 E1 prev.* Bône. NE Algeria
An Nafud *120 B4 desert* NW Saudi Arabia
'Annah *120 B3 var.* 'Ānah. Al Anbār, NW Iraq
An Najaf *120 B3 var.* Najaf. An Najaf, S Iraq
Annamite Mountains *136 D4 Fr.* Annamitique, Chaîne. *mountain range* C Laos
Annamitique, Chaîne *see* Annamite Mountains
Annamses Cordillera *see* Annamite Mountains
Annapolis *41 F4 state capital* Maryland NE USA
Annapurna *135 E3 mountain* C Nepal
An Nāqūrah *see* En Nâqoûra
Ann Arbor *40 C3* Michigan, N USA
An Nāşirīyah *120 C3 var.* Nasiriya. Dh Qār, SE Iraq

eciacum *see* Annecy
ecy *91 D5 anc.* Anneciacum.
aute-Savoie, E France
Nîl al Abyaḍ *see* White Nile
Nîl al Azraq *see* Blue Nile
iston *42 D2* Alabama, S USA
otto Bay *54 B4* C Jamaica
Omaigh *see* Omagh
ing *128 D5* Anhui, E China
e La Raye *55 F1* NW Saint Lucia
hun *128 B6* Guizhou, S China
ongo *75 E3* Gao, E Mali
Srath Bán *see* Strabane
akya *116 D4 anc.* Antioch,
ntiochia. Hatay, S Turkey
alaha *79 G2* Antsirañana,
E Madagascar
alya *116 B4 prev.* Adalia; *anc.*
ttaleia, *Bibl.* Attalia. Antalya,
W Turkey
alya, Gulf of *116 B4 var.* Gulf of
dalia, *Eng.* Gulf of Antalya. *gulf*
W Turkey
alya, Gulf of *see* Antalya Körfezi
ananarivo *79 G3 prev.* Tananarive.
ountry capital (Madagascar)
ntananarivo, C Madagascar
arctica *154 B3 continent*
arctic Peninsula *154 A2 peninsula*
ntarctica
ep *see* Gaziantep
equera *92 D5 anc.* Anticaria,
ntiquaria. Andalucía, S Spain
equera *see* Oaxaca
ibes *91 D6 anc.* Antipolis. Alpes-
Maritimes, SE France
icaria *see* Antequera
icosti, Île d' *39 F3 Eng.* Anticosti
sland. *island* Québec, E Canada
icosti Island *see* Anticosti, Île d'
igua *55 G3 island* S Antigua and
arbuda, Leeward Islands
igua and Barbuda *55 G3 country*
West Indies

NTIGUA & BARBUDA
West Indies

fficial name Antigua and Barbuda
rmation 1981 / 1981
pital St. John's
pulation 90,156 / 530 people
r sq mile (205 people per sq km)
tal area 170 sq. miles (442 sq. km)
nguages English*, English patois
ligions Anglican 45%, Other Protestant
%, Roman Catholic 10%, Other 2%,
stafarian 1%
nnic mix Black African 95%, Other 5%
overnment Parliamentary system
urrency Eastern Caribbean dollar
00 cents
eracy rate 99%
alorie consumption 2396 kilocalories

tikythira *105 B7 var.* Andikíthira.
sland S Greece
ti-Lebanon *118 B4 var.* Jebel esh
Sharqi, *Ar.* Al Jabal ash Sharqī, *Fr.* Anti-
Liban. *mountain range* Lebanon/Syria
ti-Liban *see* Anti-Lebanon
tioch *see* Antakya
tiochia *see* Antakya
típaxoi *105 A5 var.* Andipaxi.
sland Iónia Nísiá, Greece,
C Mediterranean Sea
tipodes Islands *142 D5 island group*
S New Zealand
tipolis *see* Antibes
típsara *105 D5 var.* Andípsara.
island E Greece
tiquaria *see* Antequera
tissa *105 D5 var.* Ándissa. Lésvos,
E Greece
tIúr *see* Newry
tivari *see* Bar
tofagasta *64 B2* Antofagasta, N Chile
tony *90 E2* Hauts-de-Seine,
N France
tSionainn *see* Shannon
tsirañana *79 G2 province*
N Madagascar
tsohihy *79 G2* Mahajanga,
NW Madagascar
-tung *see* Dandong
twerpen *87 C5 Eng.* Antwerp, *Fr.*
Anvers. Antwerpen, N Belgium
uradhapura *132 D3* North Central
Province, C Sri Lanka
Anvers *see* Antwerpen
Anyang *128 C4* Henan, C China
A'nyêmaqên Shan *126 D4 mountain range* C China
Anykščiai *106 C4* Utena, E Lithuania
Anzio *97 C5* Lazio, C Italy
Ao Krung Thep *137 C5 var.* Krung Thep Mahanakhon, *Eng.* Bangkok. *country capital* (Thailand) Bangkok, C Thailand
Aomori *130 D3* Aomori, Honshū, C Japan
Aóos *see* Vjosës, Lumi i
Aoraki *151 B6 prev.* Aorangi, Mount Cook. *mountain* South Island, New Zealand
Aorangi *see* Aoraki
Aosta *96 A1 anc.* Augusta Praetoria. Valle d'Aosta, NW Italy
Aoukâr *74 D3 var.* Aouker. *plateau* C Mauritania
Aouk, Bahr *76 C4 river* Central African Republic/Chad
Aouker *see* Aoukâr
Aozou *76 C1* Borkou-Ennedi-Tibesti, N Chad
Apalachee Bay *42 D3 bay* Florida, SE USA
Apalachicola River *42 D3 river* Florida, SE USA
Apamama *see* Abemama
Apaporis, Río *58 C4 river* Brazil/ Colombia
Apatity *110 C2* Murmanskaya Oblast', NW Russian Federation
Ape *106 D3* NE Latvia
Apeldoorn *86 D3* Gelderland, E Netherlands
Apennines *96 E2 Eng.* Apennines. *mountain range* Italy/San Marino
Apennines *see* Appennino
Āpia *145 F4 country capital* (Samoa) Upolu, SE Samoa
Apkhazeti *117 E1 var.* Abkhazia; *prev.* Ap'khazet'i. *autonomous republic* NW Georgia
Ap'khazet'i *see* Apkhazeti
Apoera *59 G3* Sipaliwini, NW Suriname
Apostle Islands *40 B1 island group* Wisconsin, N USA
Appalachian Mountains *35 D5 mountain range* E USA
Appingedam *86 E1* Groningen, NE Netherlands
Appleton *40 B2* Wisconsin, N USA
Apulia *see* Puglia
Apure, Río *58 C2 river* W Venezuela
Apurímac, Río *60 D3 river* S Peru
Apuseni, Munții *108 A4 mountain range* W Romania
Aqaba/'Aqaba *see* Al 'Aqabah
Aqaba, Gulf of *120 A4 var.* Gulf of Elat, *Ar.* Khalīj al 'Aqabah; *anc.* Sinus Aelaniticus. *gulf* NE Red Sea
'Aqabah, Khalīj al *see* Aqaba, Gulf of
Āqchah *123 E3 var.* Āqcheh. Jowzjān, N Afghanistan
Āqcheh *see* Āqchah
Aqmola *see* Astana
Aqtöbe *see* Aktobe
Aquae Augustae *see* Dax
Aquae Calidae *see* Bath
Aquae Flaviae *see* Chaves
Aquae Grani *see* Aachen
Aquae Sextiae *see* Aix-en-Provence
Aquae Solis *see* Bath
Aquae Tarbelicae *see* Dax
Aquidauana *63 E4* Mato Grosso do Sul, S Brazil
Aquila/Aquila degli Abruzzi *see* L'Aquila
Aquisgranum *see* Aachen
Aquitaine *91 B6 cultural region* SW France
'Arabah, Wadi al *119 B7 Heb.* Ha'Arava. *dry watercourse* Israel/Jordan
Arabian Basin *124 A4 undersea basin* N Arabian Sea
Arabian Desert *see* Sahara el Sharqiya
Arabian Peninsula *121 B5 peninsula* SW Asia
Arabian Sea *124 A3 sea* NW Indian Ocean
Arabicus, Sinus *see* Red Sea
'Arabī, Khalīj al *see* Persian Gulf
'Arabīyah as Su'ūdīyah, Al Mamlakah al *see* Saudi Arabia
'Arabīyah Jumhūrīyah, Miṣr al *see* Egypt
Arab Republic of Egypt *see* Egypt
Aracaju *63 G3 state capital* Sergipe, E Brazil
Araçuai *63 F3* Minas Gerais, SE Brazil
Arad *119 B7* Southern, S Israel
Arad *108 A4* Arad, W Romania
Arafura Sea *142 A3 Ind.* Laut Arafuru. *sea* W Pacific Ocean
Arafuru, Laut *see* Arafura Sea
Aragón *93 E2 autonomous community* E Spain
Araguaia, Río *63 E3 var.* Araguaya. *river* C Brazil
Araguari *63 F3* Minas Gerais, SE Brazil
Araguaya *see* Araguaia, Río
Ara Jovis *see* Aranjuez
Arāk *120 C3 prev.* Sultānābād. Markazī, W Iran
Arakan Yoma *136 A3 mountain range* W Myanmar (Burma)
Araks/Arak's *see* Aras
Aral *see* Aralsk, Kazakhstan
Aral Sea *122 C1 Kaz.* Aral Tengizi, *Rus.* Aral'skoye More, *Uzb.* Orol Dengizi. *inland sea* Kazakhstan/Uzbekistan
Aral'sk *114 B4 Kaz.* Aral. Kzylorda, SW Kazakhstan
Aral'skoye More/Aral Tengizi *see* Aral Sea
Aranda de Duero *92 D2* Castilla y León, N Spain
Aranđelovac *100 D4 prev.* Arandjelovac. Serbia, C Serbia
Arandjelovac *see* Aranđelovac
Aranjuez *92 D3 anc.* Ara Jovis. Madrid, C Spain
Araouane *75 E2* Tombouctou, N Mali
'Ar'ar *120 B3* Al Ḥudūd ash Shamālīyah, NW Saudi Arabia
Mount Ararat *117 F3 var.* Aghri Dagh, Agri Dagi, Koh I Noh, Masis, *Eng.* Great Ararat, Mount Ararat. *mountain* E Turkey
Ararat, Mount *see* Büyükağrı Dağı
Aras *117 G3 Arm.* Arak's, *Az.* Araz Nehri, *Per.* Rūd-e Aras, *Rus.* Araks; *prev.* Araxes. *river* SW Asia
Aras, Rūd-e *see* Aras
Arauca *58 C2* Arauca, NE Colombia
Arauca, Río *58 C2 river* Colombia/ Venezuela
Arausio *see* Orange
Araxes *see* Aras
Araz Nehri *see* Aras
Arbela *see* Arbīl
Arbīl *120 B2 var.* Erbil, Irbīl, *Kurd.* Hawlēr; *anc.* Arbela. Arbīl, N Iraq
Arbroath *88 D3 anc.* Aberbrothock. E Scotland, United Kingdom
Arbuzinka *see* Arbuzynka
Arbuzynka *109 E3 Rus.* Arbuzinka. Mykolayivs'ka Oblast', S Ukraine
Arcachon *91 B5* Gironde, SW France
Arcae Remorum *see* Châlons-en-Champagne
Arcata *46 A4* California, W USA
Archangel *see* Arkhangel'sk
Archangel Bay *see* Chëshskaya Guba
Archidona *92 D5* Andalucía, S Spain
Arco *96 C2* Trentino-Alto Adige, N Italy
Arctic Mid Oceanic Ridge *see* Gakkel Ridge
Arctic Ocean *155 B3 ocean*
Arda *104 C3 var.* Ardhas, *Gk.* Ardas. *river* Bulgaria/Greece
Ardabīl *120 C2 var.* Ardebil. Ardabīl, NW Iran
Ardakān *120 D3* Yazd, C Iran
Ardas *104 D3 var.* Ardhas, *Bul.* Arda. *river* Bulgaria/Greece
Arḍ aş Şawwān *119 C7 var.* Ardh es Suwwān. *plain* S Jordan
Ardeal *see* Transylvania
Ardebil *see* Ardabīl
Ardèche *91 C5 cultural region* E France
Ardennes *87 C8 physical region* Belgium/France
Ardhas *see* Arda/Ardas
Ardh es Suwwān *see* Arḍ aş Şawwān
Ardino *104 D3* Kŭrdzhali, S Bulgaria
Ard Mhacha *see* Armagh
Ardmore *49 G2* Oklahoma, C USA
Arel *see* Arlon
Arelas/Arelate *see* Arles
Arendal *85 A6* Aust-Agder, S Norway
Arensburg *see* Kuressaare
Arenys de Mar *93 G2* Cataluña, NE Spain
Areópoli *105 B7 prev.* Areópolis. Pelopónnisos, S Greece
Areópolis *see* Areópoli
Arequipa *61 E4* Arequipa, SE Peru
Arezzo *96 C3 anc.* Arretium. Toscana, C Italy
Argalastí *105 C5* Thessalía, C Greece
Argenteuil *90 D1* Val-d'Oise, N France
Argentina *65 B5 off.* Argentine Republic. *country* S South America

ARGENTINA
South America

Official name The Argentine Republic
Formation 1816 / 1816
Capital Buenos Aires
Population 41.4 million / 39 people per sq mile (15 people per sq km)
Total area 1,068,296 sq. miles (2,766,890 sq. km)
Languages Spanish*, Italian, Amerindian languages
Religions Roman Catholic 70%, Other 18%, Protestant 9%, Muslim 2%, Jewish 2%
Ethnic mix Indo-European 97%, Mestizo 2%, Amerindian 1%
Government Presidential system
Currency Argentine peso = 100 centavos
Literacy rate 98%
Calorie consumption 3155 kilocalories

Argentina Basin *see* Argentine Basin
Argentine Basin *57 C7 var.* Argentina Basin. *undersea basin* SW Atlantic Ocean
Argentine Republic *see* Argentina
Argentine Rise *see* Falkland Plateau
Argentoratum *see* Strasbourg
Darya-ye Arghandab *123 E5 river* SE Afghanistan
Argirocastro *see* Gjirokastër
Argo *72 B3* Northern, N Sudan
Argo Fracture Zone *141 C5 tectonic Feature* C Indian Ocean
Árgos *105 B6* Pelopónnisos, S Greece
Argostóli *105 A5 var.* Argostólion. Kefallonía, Iónia Nísiá, Greece, C Mediterranean Sea
Argostólion *see* Argostóli
Argun *125 E1 Chin.* Ergun He, *Rus.* Argun'. *river* China/Russian Federation
Argyrokastron *see* Gjirokastër
Århus *85 B7 var.* Aarhus. Midtjylland, C Denmark
Aria *see* Herāt
Ari Atoll *132 A4 var.* Alifu Atoll. *atoll* C Maldives
Arica *64 B1 hist.* San Marcos de Arica. Arica y Parinacota, N Chile
Aridaía *104 B3 var.* Aridea, Aridhaía. Dytikí Makedonía, N Greece
Aridea *see* Aridaía
Aridhaía *see* Aridaía
Arīḥā *118 B3* Al Karak, W Jordan
Arīḥā *see* Jericho
Ariminum *see* Rimini
Arinsal *91 A7* NW Andorra Europe
Arizona *48 A2 off.* State of Arizona, *also known as* Copper State, Grand Canyon State. *state* SW USA
Arkansas *42 A1 off.* State of Arkansas, *also known as* The Land of Opportunity. *state* S USA
Arkansas City *45 F5* Kansas, C USA
Arkansas River *49 G1 river* C USA
Arkhangel'sk *114 B2 Eng.* Archangel. Arkhangel'skaya Oblast', NW Russian Federation
Arkoí *105 E6 island* Dodekánisa, Greece, Aegean Sea
Arles *91 D6 var.* Arles-sur-Rhône; *anc.* Arelas, Arelate. Bouches-du-Rhône, SE France
Arles-sur-Rhône *see* Arles
Arlington *49 G2* Texas, SW USA
Arlington *41 E4* Virginia, NE USA
Arlon *87 D8 Dut.* Aarlen, *Ger.* Arel, *Lat.* Orolaunum. Luxembourg, SE Belgium
Armagh *89 B5 Ir.* Ard Mhacha. S Northern Ireland, United Kingdom
Armagnac *91 B6 cultural region* S France
Armenia *58 B3* Quindío, W Colombia

Armenia *117 F3 off.* Republic of Armenia, *var.* Ajastan, *Arm.* Hayastani Hanrapetut'yun; *prev.* Armenian Soviet Socialist Republic. *country* SW Asia

ARMENIA
Southwest Asia

Official name Republic of Armenia
Formation 1991 / 1991
Capital Yerevan
Population 3 million / 261 people per sq mile (101 people per sq km)
Total area 11,506 sq. miles (29,800 sq. km)
Languages Armenian*, Azeri, Russian
Religions Armenian Apostolic Church (Orthodox) 88%, Other 6%, Armenian Catholic Church 6%, Other 6%
Ethnic mix Armenian 98%, Other 1%, Yezidi 1%
Government Parliamentary system
Currency Dram = 100 luma
Literacy rate 99%
Calorie consumption 2809 kilocalories

Armenian Soviet Socialist Republic *see* Armenia
Armenia, Republic of *see* Armenia
Armidale *149 D6* New South Wales, SE Australia
Armstrong *38 B3* Ontario, S Canada
Armyans'k *109 F4 Rus.* Armyansk. Avtonomna Respublika Krym, S Ukraine
Arnaía *104 C4 Cont.* Arnea. Kentrikí Makedonía, N Greece
Arnaud *82 A3 river* Québec, E Canada
Arnea *see* Arnaía
Arnedo *93 E2* La Rioja, N Spain
Arnhem *86 D4* Gelderland, SE Netherlands
Arnhem Land *148 A2 physical region* Northern Territory, N Australia
Arno *96 B3 river* C Italy
Arnold *45 G4* Missouri, C USA
Arnswalde *see* Choszczno
Aroe Islands *see* Aru, Kepulauan
Arorae *145 E3 atoll* Tungaru, W Kiribati
Arrabona *see* Győr
Ar Rahad *see* Er Rahad
Ar Ramādī *120 B3 var.* Ramadi, Rumadiya. Al Anbār, SW Iraq
Ar Rāmī *118 C4* Ḥimṣ, C Syria
Ar Ramthā *119 B5 var.* Ramtha. Irbid, N Jordan
Arran, Isle of *88 C4 island* SW Scotland, United Kingdom
Ar Raqqah *118 C2 var.* Rakka; *anc.* Nicephorium. Ar Raqqah, N Syria
Arras *90 C2 anc.* Nemetocenna. Pas-de-Calais, N France
Ar Rawḍatayn *120 C4 var.* Raudhatain. N Kuwait
Arretium *see* Arezzo
Arriaca *see* Guadalajara
Arriaga *51 G5* Chiapas, SE Mexico
Ar Riyāḍ *121 C5 Eng.* Riyadh. *country capital* (Saudi Arabia) Ar Riyāḍ, C Saudi Arabia
Ar Rub 'al Khali *121 C6 Eng.* Empty Quarter, Great Sandy Desert. *desert* SW Asia
Ar Rustāq *121 E5 var.* Rostak, Rustaq. N Oman
Ar Ruṭbah *120 B3 var.* Rutba. Al Anbār, SW Iraq
Árta *105 A5 anc.* Ambracia. Ípeiros, W Greece
Artashat *117 F3* S Armenia
Artemisa *54 B2* La Habana, W Cuba
Artesia *48 D3* New Mexico, SW USA
Arthur's Pass *151 C6 pass* South Island, New Zealand
Artigas *64 D3 prev.* San Eugenio, San Eugenio del Cuareim. Artigas, N Uruguay
Art'ik *117 F2* W Armenia
Artois *90 C2 cultural region* N France
Artsiz *see* Artsyz
Artsyz *108 D4 Rus.* Artsiz. Odes'ka Oblast', SW Ukraine
Artvin *117 F2* Artvin, NE Turkey
Arua *73 B6* NW Uganda
Aruba *58 C1 var.* Oruba. *Dutch autonomous region* S West Indies
Aru Islands *see* Aru, Kepulauan
Aru, Kepulauan *139 G4 Eng.* Aru Islands; *prev.* Aroe Islands. *island group* E Indonesia
Arunāchal Pradesh *135 G3 prev.* North East Frontier Agency, North East Frontier Agency of Assam. *cultural region* NE India
Arusha *73 C7* Arusha, N Tanzania
Arviat *37 G4 prev.* Eskimo Point. Nunavut, C Canada
Arvidsjaur *84 C4* Norrbotten, N Sweden
'Arys' *114 B5 prev.* Arys'. Yuzhnyy Kazakhstan, S Kazakhstan
Arys' *see* 'Arys'
Asadābād *123 F4 var.* Asaḏābād; *prev.* Chaghasarāy. Kunar, E Afghanistan
Asaḏābād *see* Asadābād
Asahi-dake *130 D2 mountain* Hokkaidō, N Japan
Asahikawa *130 D2* Hokkaidō, N Japan
Asamankese *75 E5* SE Ghana
Āsānsol *135 F4* West Bengal, NE India
Asben *see* Aïr, Massif de l'
Ascension Fracture Zone *69 A5 tectonic Feature* C Atlantic Ocean
Ascension Island *67 C5 UK dependent territory* C Atlantic Ocean
Ascoli Piceno *96 C4 anc.* Asculum Picenum. Marche, C Italy
Asculum Picenum *see* Ascoli Piceno
'Aseb *72 D4 var.* Assab, *Amh.* Āseb. SE Eritrea
Assen *86 E2* Drenthe, NE Netherlands
A Serra de Outes *92 B1* Galicia, NW Spain
Aşgabat *122 C3 prev.* Ashgabat, Ashkhabad, Poltoratsk. *country capital* (Turkmenistan) Ahal Welaýaty, C Turkmenistan
Ashara *see* Al 'Ashārah
Ashburton *151 C6* Canterbury, South Island, New Zealand
Ashburton River *146 A4 river* Western Australia
Ashdod *119 A6 anc.* Azotos, *Lat.* Azotus. Central, W Israel
Asheville *43 E1* North Carolina, SE USA
Ashgabat *see* Aşgabat
Ashkelon *119 A6 prev.* Ashqelon. Southern, C Israel
Ashkhabad *see* Aşgabat
Ashland *46 B4* Oregon, NW USA
Ashland *40 B1* Wisconsin, N USA
Ashmore and Cartier Islands *142 A3 Australian external territory* E Indian Ocean
Ashmyany *107 C5 Rus.* Oshmyany. Hrodzyenskaya Voblasts', W Belarus
Ashqelon *see* Ashkelon
Ash Shadādah *118 D2 var.* Ash Shaddādah, Jisr ash Shadadi, Shaddādī, Shedadi, Tell Shedadi. Al Ḥasakah, NE Syria
Ash Shaddādah *see* Ash Shadādah
Ash Sharah *119 B7 var.* Esh Sharā. *mountain range* W Jordan
Ash Shāriqah *120 D4 Eng.* Sharjah. Ash Shāriqah, NE United Arab Emirates
Ash Shawbak *119 B7* Ma'ān, W Jordan
Ash Shiḥr *121 C6* SE Yemen
Asia *112 continent*
Asinara *96 A4 island* W Italy
Asipovichy *107 D6 Rus.* Osipovichi. Mahilyowskaya Voblasts', C Belarus
Aşkale *117 E3* Erzurum, NE Turkey
Askersund *85 C6* Örebro, C Sweden
Asmara *see* Asmera
Asmera *72 C4 var.* Asmara. *country capital* (Eritrea) C Eritrea
Aspadana *see* Eşfahān
Asphaltites, Lacus *see* Dead Sea
Aspinwall *see* Colón
Assab *see* 'Aseb
As Sabkhah *118 D2 var.* Sabkha. Ar Raqqah, NE Syria
Assad, Lake *118 C2 Eng.* Lake Assad. *lake* N Syria
Assad, Lake *see* Asad, Buḩayrat al
Aş Şafāwī *119 C6* Al Mafraq, N Jordan
Aş Şaḩrā' ash Sharqīyah *see* Sahara el Sharqîya
As Salamīyah *see* Salamīyah
'Assal, Lac *68 E4 lake* C Djibouti
As Salṭ *119 B6 var.* Salt. Al Balqā', NW Jordan
Assamaka *see* Assamakka
Assamakka *75 F2 var.* Assamaka. Agadez, NW Niger
As Samāwah *120 B3 var.* Samawa. Al Muthannā, S Iraq
Assenede *87 B5* Oost-Vlaanderen, NW Belgium
Assiout *see* Asyūţ
Assiut *see* Asyūţ
Assling *see* Jesenice
Assouan *see* Aswān
Assu *63 G2 var.* Açu. Rio Grande do Norte, E Brazil
Assuan *see* Aswān
As Sukhnah *118 C3 var.* Sukhne, *Fr.* Soukhné. Ḥimş, C Syria
As Sulaymānīyah *120 C3 var.* Sulaimaniya, *Kurd.* Slēmānī. As Sulaymānīyah, NE Iraq
As Sulayyil *121 B5* Ar Riyāḍ, S Saudi Arabia
Aş Şuwār *118 D2 var.* Şuwār. Dayr az Zawr, E Syria
As Suwaydā' *119 B5 var.* El Suweida, Es Suweida, Suweida, *Fr.* Soueida. As Suwaydā', SW Syria
As Suways *see* Suez
Asta Colonia *see* Asti
Astacus *see* İzmit
Astana *114 C4 prev.* Akmola, Akmolinsk, Tselinograd, Aqmola. *country capital* (Kazakhstan) Akmola, N Kazakhstan
Asta Pompeia *see* Asti
Astarabad *see* Gorgān
Asterābād *see* Gorgān
Asti *96 A2 anc.* Asta Colonia, Asta Pompeia, Hasta Colonia, Hasta Pompeia. Piemonte, NW Italy
Astigi *see* Ecija
Astipálaia *see* Astypálaia
Astorga *92 C1 anc.* Asturica Augusta. Castilla y León, N Spain
Astrabad *see* Gorgān
Astrakhan' *111 C7* Astrakhanskaya Oblast', SW Russian Federation
Asturias *92 C1 autonomous community* NW Spain
Asturias *see* Oviedo
Asturica Augusta *see* Astorga
Astypálaia *105 D7 var.* Astipálaia, *It.* Stampalia. *island* Kykládes, Greece, Aegean Sea
Asunción *64 D2 country capital* (Paraguay) Central, S Paraguay
Aswān *72 B2 var.* Assouan, Assuan, Aswân; *anc.* Syene. SE Egypt
Aswân *see* Aswān
Asyūţ *72 B2 var.* Assiout, Assiut, Asyût, Siut; *anc.* Lycopolis. C Egypt
Asyût *see* Asyūţ
Atacama Desert *64 B2 Eng.* Atacama Desert. *desert* N Chile
Atacama Desert *see* Atacama, Desierto de
Atafu Atoll *145 E3 island* NW Tokelau
Atamyrat *122 D3 prev.* Kerki. Lebap Welaýaty, E Turkmenistan
Aṭâr *74 C2* Adrar, W Mauritania
Atas Bogd *126 D3 mountain* SW Mongolia
Atascadero *47 B7* California, W USA
Atatürk Baraji *117 E4 reservoir* S Turkey
Atbara *72 C3 var.* 'Aṭbārah. River Nile, NE Sudan
'Aṭbārah/'Aṭbarah, Nahr *see* Atbara
Atbasar *114 C4* Akmola, N Kazakhstan
Atchison *45 F4* Kansas, C USA
Aternum *see* Pescara
Ath *87 B6 var.* Aat. Hainaut, SW Belgium
Athabasca *37 E5* Alberta, SW Canada
Athabasca *37 E5 var.* Athabaska. *river* Alberta, SW Canada
Athabasca, Lake *37 F4 lake* Alberta/ Saskatchewan, SW Canada
Athabaska *see* Athabasca
Athenae *see* Athína
Athens *43 E2* Georgia, SE USA
Athens *40 D4* Ohio, N USA
Athens *49 G3* Texas, SW USA
Athens *see* Athína
Atherton *148 D3* Queensland, NE Australia
Athína *105 C6 Eng.* Athens, *prev.* Athínai; *anc.* Athenae. *country capital* (Greece) Attikí, C Greece
Athínai *see* Athína
Athlone *89 B5 Ir.* Baile Átha Luain. C Ireland
Ath Thawrah *see* Madīnat ath Thawrah
Ati *76 C3* Batha, C Chad
Atikokan *38 B4* Ontario, S Canada
Atka *115 G3* Magadanskaya Oblast', E Russian Federation
Atka *36 A3* Atka Island, Alaska, USA
Atlanta *42 D2 state capital* Georgia, SE USA
Atlanta *49 H2* Texas, SW USA
Atlantic City *41 F4* New Jersey, NE
Atlantic-Indian Basin *67 D7 under basin* SW Indian Ocean
Atlantic-Indian Ridge *69 B8 under ridge* SW Indian Ocean
Atlantic Ocean *66 B4 ocean*
Atlas Mountains *70 C2 mountain r* NW Africa
Atlasovo *115 H3* Kamchatskiy Kray E Russian Federation
Atlas, Tell *102 C3 Eng.* Tell Atlas. *mountain range* N Algeria
Atlas, Tell *see* Atlas Tellien
Atlin *36 D4* British Columbia, W Ca
Aṭ Ṭafīlah *119 B7 var.* Et Tafila, Taf Aṭ Ṭafīlah, W Jordan
Aṭ Ṭā'if *121 B5* Makkah, W Saudi A
Attaleia/Attalia *see* Antalya
At Tall al Abyaḍ *118 C2 var.* Tall al Abyaḍ, Tell Abyad, *Fr.* Tell Abiad. Raqqah, N Syria
Aṭ Ṭanf *118 D4* Ḥimş, S Syria
Attapu *137 E5 var.* Samakhixai, Att Attapu, S Laos
Attawapiskat *38 C3* Ontario, C Can
Attawapiskat *38 C3 river* Ontario, S Canada
At Tibnī *118 D2 var.* Tibnī. Dayr az Zawr, NE Syria
Attopeu *see* Attapu
Attu Island *36 A2 island* Aleutian Islands, Alaska, USA
Atyrau *114 B4 prev.* Gur'yev. Atyrau W Kazakhstan
Aubagne *91 D6 anc.* Albania. Bouch du-Rhône, SE France
Aubange *87 D8* Luxembourg, SE Belgium
Aubervilliers *90 E1* Seine-St-Denis, Île-de-France, N France Europe
Auburn *46 B2* Washington, NW US
Auch *91 B6 Lat.* Augusta Auscorum, Elimberrum. Gers, S France
Auckland *150 D2* Auckland, North Island, New Zealand
Auckland Islands *142 C5 island gro* S New Zealand
Audern *see* Audru
Audincourt *90 E4* Doubs, E France
Audru *106 D2 Ger.* Audern. Pärnum SW Estonia
Augathella *149 D5* Queensland, E Australia
Augsbourg *see* Augsburg
Augsburg *95 C6 Fr.* Augsbourg; *anc.* Augusta Vindelicorum. Bayern, S Germany
Augusta *147 A7* Western Australia
Augusta *43 E2* Georgia, SE USA
Augusta *41 G2 state capital* Maine, NE USA
Augusta *see* London
Augusta Auscorum *see* Auch
Augusta Emerita *see* Mérida
Augusta Praetoria *see* Aosta
Augusta Trajana *see* Stara Zagora
Augusta Treverorum *see* Trier
Augusta Vangionum *see* Worms
Augusta Vindelicorum *see* Augsburg
Augustobona Tricassium *see* Troyes
Augustodurum *see* Bayeux
Augustoritum Lemovicensium *see* Limoges
Augustów *98 E2 Rus.* Avgustov. Podlaskie, NE Poland
Aulie Ata/Auliye-Ata *see* Taraz
Aunglan *136 B4 var.* Allanmyo, Mya Magway, C Myanmar (Burma)
Auob *78 B4 var.* Oup. *river* Namibia South Africa
Aurangābād *134 D5* Mahārāshtra, C India
Auray *90 A3* Morbihan, NW France
Aurelia Aquensis *see* Baden-Baden
Aurelianum *see* Orléans
Aurès, Massif de l' *102 C4 mountain range* NE Algeria
Aurillac *91 C5* Cantal, C France
Aurium *see* Ourense
Aurora *59 F2* NW Guyana
Aurora *44 D4* Colorado, C USA
Aurora *40 B3* Illinois, N USA
Aurora *45 G5* Missouri, C USA
Aurora *see* Maéwo, Vanuatu
Aus *78 B4* Karas, SW Namibia
Ausa *see* Vic

sig *see* Ústí nad Labem
stin *45 G3* Minnesota, N USA
stin *49 G3 state capital* Texas, SW USA
strales, Archipel des *see* Australes, Îles
strales et Antarctiques Françaises, Terres *see* French Southern and Antarctic Lands
strales, Îles *143 F4 var.* Archipel des Australes, Îles Tubuai, Tubuai Islands, *Eng.* Austral Islands. *island group* SW French Polynesia
stral Fracture Zone *143 H4 tectonic feature* S Pacific Ocean
stralia *142 A4 off.* Commonwealth of Australia. *country*

USTRALIA
Australasia & Oceania

fficial name Commonwealth of Australia
rmation 1901 / 1901
apital Canberra
pulation 23.3 million / 8 people per sq mile (3 people per sq km)
tal area 2,967,893 sq. miles ,686,850 sq. km)
nguages English*, Italian, Cantonese, reek, Arabic, Vietnamese, boriginal languages
eligions Roman Catholic 26%, onreligious 19%, Anglican 19%, ther 23%, Other Christian 13%, nited Church 6%
hnic mix European 90%, Asian 7%, original 2%, Other 1%
overnment Parliamentary system
urrency Australian dollar = 100 cents
teracy rate 99%
alorie consumption 3265 kilocalories

stralia, Commonwealth of *see* Australia
stralian Alps *149 C7 mountain range* SE Australia
stralian Capital Territory *149 D7 prev.* Federal Capital Territory. *territory* SE Australia
stralie, Bassin Nord de l' *see* North Australian Basin
stral Islands *see* Australes, Îles
strava *see* Ostrov
stria *95 D7 off.* Republic of Austria, *Ger.* Österreich. *country* C Europe

USTRIA
Central Europe

fficial name Republic of Austria
ormation 1918 / 1919
apital Vienna
opulation 8.5 million / 266 people per sq mile (103 people per sq km)
otal area 32,378 sq. miles (83,858 sq. km)
anguages German*, Croatian, Slovenian, ungarian (Magyar)
eligions Roman Catholic 78%, onreligious 9%, Other (including Jewish nd Muslim) 8%, Protestant 5%
thnic mix Austrian 93%, Croat, Slovene, nd Hungarian 6%, Other 1%
overnment Parliamentary system
urrency Euro = 100 cents
teracy rate 99%
alorie consumption 3784 kilocalories

stria, Republic of *see* Austria
tesiodorum *see* Auxerre
tissiodorum *see* Auxerre
tricum *see* Chartres
vergne *91 C5 cultural region* C France
xerre *90 C4 anc.* Autesiodorum, Autissiodorum. Yonne, C France
aricum *see* Bourges
arua *145 G5 dependent territory capital* (Cook Islands) Rarotonga, S Cook Islands
asfelsőfalu *see* Negrești-Oaș
dira *104 C3* Anatolikí Makedonía kai Thráki, NE Greece
eiro *92 B2 anc.* Talabriga. Aveiro, W Portugal
ela *see* Ávila
ellino *97 D5 anc.* Abellinum. Campania, S Italy
enio *see* Avignon
esta *85 C6* Dalarna, C Sweden
eyron *91 C6 river* S France
Avezzano *96 C4* Abruzzo, C Italy
Avgustov *see* Augustów
Aviemore *88 C3* N Scotland, United Kingdom
Avignon *91 D6 anc.* Avenio. Vaucluse, SE France
Ávila *92 D3 var.* Avila; *anc.* Abela, Abula, Abyla, Avela. Castilla y León, C Spain
Avilés *92 C1* Asturias, NW Spain
Avranches *90 B3* Manche, N France
Avveel *see* Ivalo, Finland
Avvil *see* Ivalo
Awaji-shima *131 C6 island* SW Japan
Āwash *73 D5* Āfar, NE Ethiopia
Awbārī *71 F3* SW Libya
Ax *see* Dax
Axel *87 B5* Zeeland, SW Netherlands
Axel Heiberg Island *37 E1 var.* Axel Heiburg. *island* Nunavut, N Canada
Axel Heiburg *see* Axel Heiberg Island
Axiós *see* Vardar
Ayacucho *60 D4* Ayacucho, S Peru
Ayagoz *114 C5 var.* Ayaguz, *Kaz.* Ayakoz. *river* E Kazakhstan
Ayamonte *92 C4* Andalucía, S Spain
Ayaviri *61 E4* Puno, S Peru
Aydarko'l Ko'li *123 E2 Rus.* Ozero Aydarkul'. *lake* C Uzbekistan
Aydarkul', Ozero *see* Aydarko'l Ko'li
Aydın *116 A4 var.* Aïdin; *anc.* Tralles Aydin. Aydın, SW Turkey
Ayers Rock *see* Uluṟu
Ayeyarwady *see* Irrawaddy
Ayiá *see* Agiá
Áyios Evstrátios *see* Ágios Efstrátios
Áyios Nikólaos *see* Ágios Nikólaos
Ayorou *75 E3* Tillabéri, W Niger
'Ayoûn el 'Atroûs *74 D3 var.* Aïoun el Atrous, Aïoun el Atroûss. Hodh el Gharbi, SE Mauritania
Ayr *88 C4* W Scotland, United Kingdom
Ayteke Bi *114 B4 Kaz.* Zhangaqazaly; *prev.* Novokazalinsk. Kzylorda, SW Kazakhstan
Aytos *104 E2* Burgas, E Bulgaria
Ayutthaya *137 C5 var.* Phra Nakhon Si Ayutthaya. Phra Nakhon Si Ayutthaya, C Thailand
Ayvalık *116 A3* Balıkesir, W Turkey
Azahar, Costa del *93 F3 coastal region* E Spain
Azaouâd *75 E3 desert* C Mali
Azärbaycan/Azärbaycan Respublikasī *see* Azerbaijan
A'zāz *118 B2* Ḥalab, NW Syria
Azerbaijan *117 G2 off.* Azerbaijani Republic, *Az.* Azärbaycan, Azärbaycan Respublikası; *prev.* Azerbaijan SSR. *country* SE Asia

AZERBAIJAN
Southwest Asia

Official name Republic of Azerbaijan
Formation 1991 / 1991
Capital Baku
Population 9.4 million / 281 people per sq mile (109 people per sq km)
Total area 33,436 sq. miles (86,600 sq. km)
Languages Azeri*, Russian
Religions Shi'a Muslim 68%, Sunni Muslim 26%, Russian Orthodox 3%, Armenian Apostolic Church (Orthodox) 2%, Other 1%
Ethnic mix Azeri 91%, Other 3%, Lazs 2%, Armenian 2%, Russian 2%
Government Presidential system
Currency New manat = 100 gopik
Literacy rate 99%
Calorie consumption 2952 kilocalories

Azerbaijani Republic *see* Azerbaijan
Azerbaijan SSR *see* Azerbaijan
Azimabad *see* Patna
Azizie *see* Telish
Azogues *60 B2* Cañar, S Ecuador
Azores *92 A4 var.* Açores, Ilhas dos Açores, *Port.* Arquipélago dos Açores. *island group* Portugal, NE Atlantic Ocean
Azores-Biscay Rise *80 A3 undersea rise* E Atlantic Ocean
Azotos/Azotus *see* Ashdod
Azoum, Bahr *76 C3 seasonal river* SE Chad
Azov, Sea of *103 H1 Rus.* Azovskoye More, *Ukr.* Azovs'ke More. *sea* NE Black Sea
Azovs'ke More/Azovskoye More *see* Azov, Sea of
Azraq, Wāḥat al *119 C6 oasis* N Jordan
Aztec *48 C1* New Mexico, SW USA
Azuaga *92 C4* Extremadura, W Spain
Azuero, Península de *53 F5 peninsula* S Panama
Azul *65 D5* Buenos Aires, E Argentina
Azur, Côte d' *91 E6 coastal region* SE France
'Azza *see* Gaza
Az Zaqāzīq *72 B1 var.* Zagazig. N Egypt
Az Zarqā' *119 B6 var.* Zarqa. Az Zarqā', NW Jordan
Az Zāwiyah *71 F2 var.* Zawia. NW Libya
Az Zilfī *120 B4* Ar Riyāḍ, N Saudi Arabia

B

Baalbek *118 B4 var.* Ba'labakk; *anc.* Heliopolis. E Lebanon
Baardheere *73 D6 var.* Bardere, *It.* Bardera. Gedo, SW Somalia
Baarle-Hertog *87 C5* Antwerpen, N Belgium
Baarn *86 C3* Utrecht, C Netherlands
Babadag *108 D5* Tulcea, SE Romania
Babahoyo *60 B2 prev.* Bodegas. Los Ríos, C Ecuador
Bābā, Kūh-e *123 E4 mountain range* C Afghanistan
Babayevo *110 B4* Vologodskaya Oblast', NW Russian Federation
Babeldaob *144 A1 var.* Babeldaop, Babelthuap. *island* N Palau
Babeldaop *see* Babeldaob
Bab el Mandeb *121 B7 strait* Gulf of Aden/Red Sea
Babelthuap *see* Babeldaob
Babian Jiang *see* Black River
Babruysk *107 D7 Rus.* Bobruysk. Mahilyowskaya Voblasts', E Belarus
Babuyan Channel *139 E1 channel* N Philippines
Babuyan Islands *139 E1 island group* N Philippines
Bacabal *63 F2* Maranhão, E Brazil
Bacău *108 C4 Hung.* Bákó. Bacău, NE Romania
Băc Bô, Vinh *see* Tonkin, Gulf of
Băc Giang *136 D3* Ha Băc, N Vietnam
Bacheykava *107 D5 Rus.* Bocheykovo. Vitsyebskaya Voblasts', N Belarus
Back *37 F3 river* Nunavut, N Canada
Bačka Palanka *100 D3 prev.* Palanka. Serbia, NW Serbia
Bačka Topola *100 D3 Hung.* Topolya; *prev. Hung.* Bácstopolya. Vojvodina, N Serbia
Bac Liêu *137 D6 var.* Vinh Loi. Minh Hai, S Vietnam
Bacolod *125 E4 off.* Bacolod City. Negros, C Philippines
Bacolod City *see* Bacolod
Bácsszenttamás *see* Srbobran
Bácstopolya *see* Bačka Topola
Bactra *see* Balkh
Badajoz *92 C4 anc.* Pax Augusta. Extremadura, W Spain
Baden-Baden *95 B6 anc.* Aurelia Aquensis. Baden-Württemberg, SW Germany
Bad Freienwalde *94 D3* Brandenburg, NE Germany
Badger State *see* Wisconsin
Bad Hersfeld *94 B4* Hessen, C Germany
Bad Homburg *see* Bad Homburg vor der Höhe
Bad Homburg vor der Höhe *95 B5 var.* Bad Homburg. Hessen, W Germany
Bad Ischl *95 D7* Oberösterreich, N Austria
Bad Krozingen *95 A6* Baden-Württemberg, SW Germany
Badlands *44 D2 physical region* North Dakota/South Dakota, N USA
Badu Island *148 C1 island* Queensland, NE Australia
Bad Vöslau *95 E6* Niederösterreich, NE Austria
Baeterrae/Baeterrae Septimanorum *see* Béziers
Baetic Cordillera/Baetic Mountains *see* Béticos, Sistemas
Bafatá *74 C4* C Guinea-Bissau
Baffin Bay *37 G2 bay* Canada/Greenland
Baffin Island *37 G2 island* Nunavut, NE Canada
Bafing *74 C3 river* W Africa
Bafoussam *76 A4* Ouest, W Cameroon
Bafra *116 D2* Samsun, N Turkey
Bāft *120 D4* Kermān, S Iran
Bagaces *52 D4* Guanacaste, NW Costa Rica
Bagdad *see* Baghdad
Bagé *63 E5* Rio Grande do Sul, S Brazil
Baghdad *120 B3 var.* Bagdad, *country capital* (Iraq) Baghdad, C Iraq
Baghlān *123 E3* Baghlān, NE Afghanistan
Bago *136 B4 var.* Pegu. Bago, SW Myanmar (Burma)
Bagoé *74 D4 river* Côte d'Ivoire/Mali
Bagrationovsk *106 A4 Ger.* Preussisch Eylau. Kaliningradskaya Oblast', W Russian Federation
Bagrax Hu *see* Bosten Hu
Baguio *139 E1 off.* Baguio City. Luzon, N Philippines
Baguio City *see* Baguio
Bagzane, Monts *75 F3 mountain* N Niger
Bahama Islands *see* Bahamas
Bahamas, The *54 C2 off.* Commonwealth of the Bahamas. *country* N West Indies

BAHAMAS, THE
West Indies

Official name Commonwealth of the Bahamas
Formation 1973 / 1973
Capital Nassau
Population 400,000 / 103 people per sq mile (40 people per sq km)
Total area 5382 sq. miles (13,940 sq. km)
Languages English*, English Creole, French Creole
Religions Baptist 32%, Anglican 20%, Roman Catholic 19%, Other 17%, Methodist 6%, Church of God 6%
Ethnic mix Black African 85%, Other 15%
Government Parliamentary system
Currency Bahamian dollar = 100 cents
Literacy rate 96%
Calorie consumption 2575 kilocalories

Bahamas *35 D6 var.* Bahama Islands. *island group* N West Indies
Bahamas, Commonwealth of the *see* Bahamas, The
Baharly *122 C3 var.* Bäherden, *Rus.* Bakharden; *prev.* Bakherden. Ahal Welaýaty, C Turkmenistan
Bahāwalpur *134 C2* Punjab, E Pakistan
Bäherden *see* Baharly
Bahia *63 F3 off.* Estado da Bahia. *state* E Brazil
Bahia *63 F3 off.* Estado da Bahia. *region* E Brazil
Bahía Blanca *65 C5* Buenos Aires, E Argentina
Bahia, Estado da *see* Bahia
Bahir Dar *72 C4 var.* Bahr Dar, Bahrdar Giyorgis. Āmara, N Ethiopia
Bahraich *135 E3* Uttar Pradesh, N India
Bahrain *120 C4 off.* State of Bahrain, Dawlat al Bahrayn, *Ar.* Al Baḥrayn, *prev.* Bahrein; *anc.* Tylos, Tyros. *country* SW Asia

BAHRAIN
Southwest Asia

Official name Kingdom of Bahrain
Formation 1971 / 1971
Capital Manama
Population 1.3 million / 4762 people per sq mile (1841 people per sq km)
Total area 239 sq. miles (620 sq. km)
Languages Arabic
Religions Muslim (mainly Shi'a) 99%, Other 1%
Ethnic mix Bahraini 63%, Asian 19%, Other Arab 10%, Iranian 8%
Government Monarchical / parliamentary system
Currency Bahraini dinar = 1000 fils
Literacy rate 95%
Calorie consumption Not available

Bahrain, State of *see* Bahrain
Bahrayn, Dawlat al *see* Bahrain
Bahr Dar/Bahrdar Giyorgis *see* Bahir Dar
Bahrein *see* Bahrain

Bahr el, Azraq *see* Blue Nile
Bahr Tabariya, Sea of *see* Tiberias, Lake
Bahushewsk *107 E6 Rus.* Bogushëvsk. Vitsyebskaya Voblasts', NE Belarus
Baia Mare *108 B3 Ger.* Frauenbach, *Hung.* Nagybánya; *prev.* Neustadt. Maramureş, NW Romania
Baia Sprie *108 B3 Ger.* Mittelstadt, *Hung.* Felsőbánya. Maramureş, NW Romania
Baïbokoum *76 B4* Logone-Oriental, SW Chad
Baidoa *see* Baydhabo
Baie-Comeau *39 E3* Québec, SE Canada
Baikal, Lake *115 E4 Eng.* Lake Baikal. *lake* S Russian Federation
Baikal, Lake *see* Baykal, Ozero
Baile Átha Cliath *see* Dublin
Baile Átha Luain *see* Athlone
Bailén *92 D4* Andalucía, S Spain
Baile na Mainistreach *see* Newtownabbey
Băileşti *108 B5* Dolj, SW Romania
Ba Illi *76 B3* Chari-Baguirmi, SW Chad
Bainbridge *42 D3* Georgia, SE USA
Bā'ir *see* Bāyir
Baireuth *see* Bayreuth
Bairiki *144 D2* Tarawa, NW Kiribati
Bairnsdale *149 C7* Victoria, SE Australia
Baishan *129 E3 prev.* Hunjiang. Jilin, NE China
Baiyin *128 B4* Gansu, C China
Baja *99 C7* Bács-Kiskun, S Hungary
Baja California Norte *50 B2 state* NW Mexico
Bajo Boquete *see* Boquete
Bajram Curri *101 D5* Kukës, N Albania
Bakala *76 C4* Ouaka, C Central African Republic
Bakan *see* Shimonoseki
Baker *46 C3* Oregon, NW USA
Baker and Howland Islands *145 E2 US unincorporated territory* W Polynesia
Baker Lake *37 F3 var.* Qamanittuaq. Nunavut, N Canada
Bakersfield *47 C7* California, W USA
Bakharden *see* Baharly
Bakhchisaray *see* Bakhchysaray
Bakhchysaray *109 F5 Rus.* Bakhchisaray. Avtonomna Respublika Krym, S Ukraine
Bakherden *see* Baharly
Bakhmach *109 F1* Chernihivs'ka Oblast', N Ukraine
Bākhtarān *see* Kermānshāh
Bakı *117 H2 Eng.* Baku. *country capital* (Azerbaijan) E Azerbaijan
Bákó *see* Bacău
Bakony *99 C7 Eng.* Bakony Mountains, *Ger.* Bakonywald. *mountain range* W Hungary
Bakony Mountains/Bakonywald *see* Bakony
Baku *see* Bakı
Bakwanga *see* Mbuji-Mayi
Balabac Island *129 C8 island* W Philippines
Balabac, Selat *see* Balabac Strait
Balabac Strait *138 D2 var.* Selat Balabac. *strait* Malaysia/Philippines
Ba'labakk *see* Baalbek
Balaguer *93 F2* Cataluña, NE Spain
Balakovo *111 C6* Saratovskaya Oblast', W Russian Federation
Bālā Morghāb *see* Bālā Murghāb
Bālā Murghāb *122 D4 prev.* Bālā Morghāb. Laghmān, NW Afghanistan
Balashov *111 B6* Saratovskaya Oblast', W Russian Federation
Balasore *see* Bāleshwar
Balaton, Lake *99 C7 var.* Lake Balaton, *Ger.* Plattensee. *lake* W Hungary
Balaton, Lake *see* Balaton
Balbina, Represa *62 D1 reservoir* NW Brazil
Balboa *53 G4* Panamá, C Panama
Balcarce *65 D5* Buenos Aires, E Argentina
Balclutha *151 B7* Otago, South Island, New Zealand
Baldy Mountain *44 C1 mountain* Montana, NW USA
Bâle *see* Basel
Balearic Plain *see* Algerian Basin
Baleares Major *see* Mallorca
Balearic Islands *93 G3 Eng.* Balearic Islands. *island group* Spain, W Mediterranean Sea
Balearic Islands *see* Baleares, Islas
Balearis Minor *see* Menorca
Baleine, Rivière à la *39 E2 river* Québec, E Canada
Balen *87 C5* Antwerpen, N Belgium
Bāleshwar *135 F4 prev.* Balasore. Odisha, E India
Bălgrad *see* Alba Iulia
Bali *138 D5 island* C Indonesia
Balıkesir *116 A3* Balıkesir, W Turkey
Balīkh, Nahr *118 C2 river* N Syria
Balikpapan *138 D4* Borneo, C Indonesia
Balkanabat *122 B2 Rus.* Nebitdag. Balkan Welaýaty, W Turkmenistan
Balkan Mountains *104 C2 Bul./SCr.* Stara Planina. *mountain range* Bulgaria/Serbia
Balkash *see* Balkhash
Balkash, Ozero *see* Balkhash, Ozero
Balkh *123 E3 anc.* Bactra. Balkh, N Afghanistan
Balkhash *114 C5 Kaz.* Balqash; *var.* Balkash. Karagandy, SE Kazakhstan
Balkhash, Lake *see* Balkhash, Ozero
Balkhash, Ozero *114 C5 Eng.* Lake Balkhash, *Kaz.* Balqash; *var.* Ozero Balkash. *lake* SE Kazakhstan
Balladonia *147 C6* Western Australia
Ballarat *149 C7* Victoria, SE Australia
Balleny Islands *154 B5 island group* Antarctica
Ballinger *49 F3* Texas, SW USA
Balochistan *134 B3 prev.* Baluchistan, Beluchistan. *province* SW Pakistan
Balqash *see* Balkhash/Balkhash, Ozero
Balş *108 B5* Olt, S Romania
Balsas *63 F2* Maranhão, E Brazil
Balsas, Río *51 E5 var.* Río Mexcala. *river* S Mexico
Bal'shavik *107 D7 Rus.* Bol'shevik. Homyel'skaya Voblasts', SE Belarus
Balta *108 D3* Odes'ka Oblast', SW Ukraine
Bălţi *108 D3 Rus.* Bel'tsy. N Moldova
Baltic Port *see* Paldiski
Baltic Sea *85 C7 Ger.* Ostee, *Rus.* Baltiskoye More. *sea* N Europe
Baltimore *41 F4* Maryland, NE USA
Baltischport/Baltiski *see* Paldiski
Baltiskoye More *see* Baltic Sea
Baltkrievija *see* Belarus
Baluchistan *see* Balochistan
Balvi *106 D4* NE Latvia
Balykchy *123 G2 Kir.* Ysyk-Köl; *prev.* Issyk-Kul', Rybach'ye. Issyk-Kul'skaya Oblast', NE Kyrgyzstan
Balzers *94 E2* S Liechtenstein
Bam *120 E4* Kermān, SE Iran
Bamako *74 D4 country capital* (Mali) Capital District, SW Mali
Bambari *76 C4* Ouaka, C Central African Republic
Bamberg *95 C5* Bayern, SE Germany
Bamenda *76 A4* Nord-Ouest, W Cameroon
Banaba *144 D2 var.* Ocean Island. *island* Tungaru, W Kiribati
Banaras *see* Vārānasi
Banda Aceh *138 A3 var.* Banda Atjeh; *prev.* Koetaradja, Kutaradja, Kutaraja. Sumatera, W Indonesia
Banda Atjeh *see* Banda Aceh
Banda, Laut *see* Banda Sea
Bandama *74 D5 var.* Bandama Fleuve. *river* S Côte d'Ivoire
Bandama Fleuve *see* Bandama
Bandar 'Abbās *see* Bandar-e 'Abbās
Bandarbeyla *73 E5 var.* Bender Beila, Bender Beyla. Bari, NE Somalia
Bandar-e 'Abbās *120 D4 var.* Bandar 'Abbās; *prev.* Gombroon. Hormozgān, S Iran
Bandar-e Būshehr *120 C4 var.* Būshehr, *Eng.* Bushire. Būshehr, S Iran
Bandar-e Kangān *120 D4 var.* Kangān. Būshehr, S Iran
Bandar-e Khamīr *120 D4* Hormozgān, S Iran
Bandar-e Langeh *see* Bandar-e Lengeh
Bandar-e Lengeh *120 D4 var.* Bandar-e Langeh, Lingeh. Hormozgān, S Iran
Bandar Kassim *see* Boosaaso
Bandar Lampung *138 C4 var.* Bandarlampung, Tanjungkarang-Telukbetung; *prev.* Tandjoengkarang, Tanjungkarang, Teloekbetoeng, Telukbetung. Sumatera, W Indonesia
Bandarlampung *see* Bandar Lampung
Bandar Maharani *see* Muar
Bandar Masulipatnam *see* Machilīpatnam
Bandar Penggaram *see* Batu Pahat
Bandar Seri Begawan *138 D3 prev.* Brunei Town. *country capital* (Brunei) N Brunei
Banda Sea *139 F5 var.* Laut Banda. *sea* E Indonesia
Bandiagara *75 E3* Mopti, C Mali
Bandırma *116 A3 var.* Penderma. Balıkesir, NW Turkey
Bandjarmasin *see* Banjarmasin
Bandoeng *see* Bandung
Bandundu *77 C6 prev.* Banningville. Bandundu, W Dem. Rep. Congo
Bandung *138 C5 prev.* Bandoeng. Jawa, C Indonesia
Bangalore *132 C2 var.* Bengalooru. *state capital* Karnātaka, S India
Bangassou *76 D4* Mbomou, SE Central African Republic
Banggai, Kepulauan *139 E4 island group* C Indonesia
Banghāzī *71 G2 Eng.* Bengazi, Benghazi, *It.* Bengasi. NE Libya
Bangka, Pulau *138 C4 island* W Indonesia
Bangkok *see* Ao Krung Thep
Bangkok, Bight of *see* Krung Thep, Ao
Bangladesh *135 G3 off.* People's Republic of Bangladesh; *prev.* East Pakistan. *country* S Asia

BANGLADESH
South Asia

Official name People's Republic of Bangladesh
Formation 1971 / 1971
Capital Dhaka
Population 157 million / 3029 people per sq mile (1169 people per sq km)
Total area 55,598 sq. miles (144,000 sq. km)
Languages Bengali*, Urdu, Chakma, Marma (Magh), Garo, Khasi, Santhali, Tripuri, Mro
Religions Muslim (mainly Sunni) 88%, Hindu 11%, Other 1%
Ethnic mix Bengali 98%, Other 2%
Government Parliamentary system
Currency Taka = 100 poisha
Literacy rate 59%
Calorie consumption 2430 kilocalories

Bangladesh, People's Republic of *see* Bangladesh
Ba Ngoi *see* Cam Ranh
Bangor *89 C6* NW Wales, United Kingdom
Bangor *89 B5 Ir.* Beannchar. E Northern Ireland, United Kingdom
Bangor *41 G2* Maine, NE USA
Bang Pla Soi *see* Chon Buri
Bangui *77 B5 country capital* (Central African Republic) Ombella-Mpoko, SW Central African Republic
Bangweulu, Lake *73 B8 var.* Lake Bengweulu. *lake* N Zambia
Ban Hat Yai *see* Hat Yai
Ban Hin Heup *136 C4* Viangchan, C Laos
Ban Houayxay/Ban Houei Sai *see* Houayxay
Ban Hua Hin *137 C6 var.* Hua Hin. Prachuap Khiri Khan, SW Thailand
Bani *74 D3 river* S Mali
Banias *see* Bāniyās
Banijska Palanka *see* Glina
Banī Suwayf *72 B2 var.* Beni Suef. N Egypt
Bāniyās *118 B3 var.* Banias, Baniyas, Paneas. Ţarţūs, W Syria
Banjak, Kepulauan *see* Banyak, Kepulauan
Banja Luka *100 B3* Republika Srpska, NW Bosnia and Herzegovina
Banjarmasin *138 D4 prev.* Bandjarmasin. Borneo, C Indonesia
Banjul *74 B3 prev.* Bathurst. *country capital* (Gambia) W Gambia
Banks, Îles *see* Banks Islands
Banks Island *37 E2 island* Northwest Territories, NW Canada
Banks Islands *144 D4 Fr.* Îles Banks. *island group* N Vanuatu
Banks Lake *46 B1 reservoir* Washington, NW USA
Banks Peninsula *151 C6 peninsula* South Island, New Zealand
Banks Strait *149 C8 strait* SW Tasman Sea
Bānkura *135 F4* West Bengal, NE Inc
Ban Mak Khaeng *see* Udon Thani
Banmo *see* Bhamo
Banningville *see* Bandundu
Bañolas *see* Banyoles
Ban Pak Phanang *see* Pak Phanang
Ban Sichon *see* Sichon
Banská Bystrica *99 C6 Ger.* Neusohl, *Hung.* Besztercebánya. Banskobystrický Kraj, C Slovakia
Bantry Bay *89 A7 Ir.* Bá Bheanntraí. *bay* SW Ireland
Banya *104 E2* Burgas, E Bulgaria
Banyak, Kepulauan *138 A3 prev.* Kepulauan Banjak. *island group* NW Indonesia
Banyo *76 B4* Adamaoua, NW Camer
Banyoles *93 G2 var.* Bañolas. Catalu NE Spain
Banzare Seamounts *141 C7 seamount range* S Indian Ocean
Banzart *see* Bizerte
Baoji *128 B4 var.* Pao-chi, Paoki. Shaanxi, C China
Baoro *76 B4* Nana-Mambéré, W Central African Republic
Baoshan *128 A6 var.* Pao-shan. Yunn SW China
Baotou *127 F3 var.* Pao-t'ou, Paotow Nei Mongol Zizhiqu, N China
Ba'qūbah *120 B3 var.* Qubba. Diyālá, C Iraq
Baquerizo Moreno *see* Puerto Baquerizo Moreno
Bar *101 C5 It.* Antivari. S Montenegr
Baraawe *73 D6 It.* Brava. Shabeellaha Hoose, S Somalia
Bārāmati *134 C5* Mahārāshtra, W Inc
Baranavichy *107 B6 Pol.* Baranowicz *Rus.* Baranovichi. Brestskaya Vobla SW Belarus
Baranovichi/Baranowicze *see* Baranavichy
Barbados *55 G1 country* SE West Inc

BARBADOS
West Indies

Official name Barbados
Formation 1966 / 1966
Capital Bridgetown
Population 300,000 / 1807 people per sq mile (698 people per sq km)
Total area 166 sq. miles (430 sq. km)
Languages Bajan (Barbadian English), English*
Religions Anglican 40%, Other 24%, Nonreligious 17%, Pentecostal 8%, Methodist 7%, Roman Catholic 4%
Ethnic mix Black African 92%, White 3 Other 3%, Mixed race 2%
Government Parliamentary system
Currency Barbados dollar = 100 cents
Literacy rate 99%
Calorie consumption 3047 kilocalories

Barbastro *93 F2* Aragón, NE Spain
Barbate de Franco *92 C5* Andalucía, S Spain
Barbuda *55 G3 island* N Antigua and Barbuda
Barcaldine *148 C4* Queensland, Austr
Barcarozsnyó *see* Râşnov
Barcău *see* Berettyó
Barce *see* Al Marj
Barcelona *93 G2 anc.* Barcino, Barcinona. Cataluña, E Spain
Barcelona *59 E2* Anzoátegui, NE Venezuela
Barcino/Barcinona *see* Barcelona
Barcoo *see* Cooper Creek
Barcs *99 C7* Somogy, SW Hungary
Bardaï *76 C1* Borkou-Ennedi-Tibesti, N Chad
Bardejov *99 D5 Ger.* Bartfeld, *Hung.* Bártfa. Presovský Kraj, E Slovakia
Bardera/Bardere *see* Baardheere
Barduli *see* Barletta
Bareilly *135 E3 var.* Bareli. Uttar Pradesh, N India
Bareli *see* Bareilly
Barendrecht *86 C4* Zuid-Holland, SW Netherlands
Barentin *90 C3* Seine-Maritime, N France

rentsburg *83 G2* Spitsbergen, W Svalbard
rentsevo More/Barents Havet *see* Barents Sea
rentsøya *83 G2 island* E Svalbard
rents Sea *110 C2 Nor.* Barents Havet, *Rus.* Barentsevo More. *sea* Arctic Ocean
r Harbor *41 H2* Mount Desert Island, Maine, NE USA
ri *97 E5 var.* Bari delle Puglie; *anc.* Barium. Puglia, SE Italy
ridah *see* Al Bāridah
ri delle Puglie *see* Bari
rikot *see* Barīkowṭ
rīkowṭ *123 F4 var.* Barikot. Kunar, NE Afghanistan
rillas *52 A2 var.* Santa Cruz Barillas. Huehuetenango, NW Guatemala
rinas *58 C2* Barinas, W Venezuela
risal *135 G4* Barisal, S Bangladesh
risan, Pegunungan *138 B4 mountain range* Sumatera, W Indonesia
rito, Sungai *138 D4 river* Borneo, C Indonesia
rium *see* Bari
rka *see* Al Marj
rkly Tableland *148 B3 plateau* Northern Territory/Queensland, N Australia
rlad *108 D4 prev.* Bîrlad. Vaslui, E Romania
rlavento, Ilhas de *74 A2 var.* Windward Islands. *island group* N Cape Verde
r-le-Duc *90 D3 var.* Bar-sur-Ornain. Meuse, NE France
rlee, Lake *147 B6 lake* Western Australia
rlee Range *146 A4 mountain range* Western Australia
rletta *97 D5 anc.* Barduli. Puglia, SE Italy
rlinek *98 B3 Ger.* Berlinchen. Zachodnio-pomorskie, NW Poland
rmen-Elberfeld *see* Wuppertal
rmouth *89 C6* NW Wales, United Kingdom
rnaul *114 D4* Altayskiy Kray, C Russian Federation
rnet *89 A7* United Kingdom
rnstaple *89 C7* SW England, United Kingdom
roda *see* Vadodara
roghil Pass *123 F3 var.* Kowtal-e Barowghīl. *pass* Afghanistan/Pakistan
ron'ki *107 E7 Rus.* Boron'ki. Mahilyowskaya Voblasts', E Belarus
rowghīl, Kowtal-e *see* Baroghil Pass
rquisimeto *58 C2* Lara, NW Venezuela
rra *88 B3 island* NW Scotland, United Kingdom
rra de Río Grande *53 E3* Región Autónoma Atlántico Sur, E Nicaragua
rranca *60 C3* Lima, W Peru
rrancabermeja *58 B2* Santander, N Colombia
rranquilla *58 B1* Atlántico, N Colombia
rreiro *92 B4* Setúbal, W Portugal
rrier Range *149 C6 hill range* New South Wales, SE Australia
rrow *36 D2* Alaska, USA
rrow *89 B6 Ir.* An Bhearú. *river* SE Ireland
rrow-in-Furness *89 C5* NW England, United Kingdom
rrow Island *146 A4 island* Western Australia
rstow *47 C7* California, W USA
r-sur-Ornain *see* Bar-le-Duc
rtang *123 F3 river* SE Tajikistan
rtenstein *see* Bartoszyce
rtfa/Bartfeld *see* Bardejov
rtica *59 F3* N Guyana
rtın *116 C2* Bartın, NW Turkey
rtlesville *49 G1* Oklahoma, C USA
rtoszyce *98 D2 Ger.* Bartenstein. Warmińsko-mazurskie, NE Poland
ruun-Urt *127 F2* Sühbaatar, E Mongolia
rú, Volcán *53 E5 var.* Volcán de Chiriquí. *volcano* W Panama
rwon River *149 D5 river* New South Wales, SE Australia
rysaw *107 D6 Rus.* Borisov. Minskaya Voblasts', NE Belarus
Basarabeasca *108 D4 Rus.* Bessarabka. SE Moldova
Basel *95 A7 Eng.* Basle, *Fr.* Bâle. Basel Stadt, NW Switzerland
Basilan *139 E3 island* Sulu Archipelago, SW Philippines
Basle *see* Basel
Basra *see* Al Baṣrah
Bassano del Grappa *96 C2* Veneto, NE Italy
Bassein *see* Pathein
Basseterre *55 G4 country capital* (Saint Kitts and Nevis) Saint Kitts, Saint Kitts and Nevis
Basse-Terre *55 G3 dependent territory capital* (Guadeloupe) Basse Terre, SW Guadeloupe
Basse Terre *55 G4 island* W Guadeloupe
Bassikounou *74 D3* Hodh ech Chargui, SE Mauritania
Bass, Îlots de *see* Marotiri
Bass Strait *149 C7 strait* SE Australia
Bassum *94 B3* Niedersachsen, NW Germany
Bastia *91 E7* Corse, France, C Mediterranean Sea
Bastogne *87 D7* Luxembourg, SE Belgium
Bastrop *42 B2* Louisiana, S USA
Bastyn' *107 B7 Rus.* Bostyn'. Brestskaya Voblasts', SW Belarus
Basuo *see* Dongfang
Basutoland *see* Lesotho
Bata *77 A5* NW Equatorial Guinea
Batae Coritanorum *see* Leicester
Batajnica *100 D3* Vojvodina, N Serbia
Batangas *139 E2 off.* Batangas City. Luzon, N Philippines
Batangas City *see* Batangas
Batavia *see* Jakarta
Bătdâmbâng *137 C5 prev.* Battambang. Bătdâmbâng, NW Cambodia
Batéké, Plateaux *77 B6 plateau* S Congo
Bath *89 D7 hist.* Akermanceaster; *anc.* Aquae Calidae, Aquae Solis. SW England, United Kingdom
Bathinda *134 D2* Punjab, NW India
Bathsheba *55 G1* E Barbados
Bathurst *149 D6* New South Wales, SE Australia
Bathurst *39 F4* New Brunswick, SE Canada
Bathurst *see* Banjul
Bathurst Island *146 D2 island* Northern Territory, N Australia
Bathurst Island *37 F2 island* Parry Islands, Nunavut, N Canada
Wadi al Batin *120 C4 dry watercourse* SW Asia
Batman *117 E4 var.* İluh. Batman, SE Turkey
Batna *71 E2* NE Algeria
Baton Rouge *42 B3 state capital* Louisiana, S USA
Batroûn *118 A4 var.* Al Batrūn. N Lebanon
Battambang *see* Bătdâmbâng
Batticaloa *132 D3* Eastern Province, E Sri Lanka
Battipaglia *97 D5* Campania, S Italy
Battle Born State *see* Nevada
Batumi *117 F2 prev.* Bat'umi. W Georgia
Bat'umi *see* Batumi
Batu Pahat *138 B3 prev.* Bandar Penggaram. Johor, Peninsular Malaysia
Bauchi *75 G4* Bauchi, NE Nigeria
Bauer Basin *153 F3 undersea basin* E Pacific Ocean
Bauska *106 C3 Ger.* Bauske. S Latvia
Bauske *see* Bauska
Bautzen *94 D4 Lus.* Budyšin. Sachsen, E Germany
Bauzanum *see* Bolzano
Bavaria *see* Bayern
Bavarian Alps *95 C7 Ger.* Bayrische Alpen. *mountain range* Austria/Germany
Bavière *see* Bayern
Bavispe, Río *50 C2 river* NW Mexico
Bawīṭī *72 B2 var.* Bawīṭi. N Egypt
Bawīṭi *see* Bawīṭī
Bawku *75 E4* N Ghana
Bayamo *54 C3* Granma, E Cuba
Bayan Har Shan *126 D4 var.* Bayan Khar. *mountain range* C China
Bayanhongor *126 D2* Bayanhongor, C Mongolia
Bayan Khar *see* Bayan Har Shan
Bayano, Lago *53 G4 lake* E Panama
Bay City *40 C3* Michigan, N USA
Bay City *49 G4* Texas, SW USA
Baydhabo *73 D6 var.* Baydhowa, Isha Baydhabo, *It.* Baidoa. Bay, SW Somalia
Baydhowa *see* Baydhabo
Bayern *95 C6 Eng.* Bavaria, *Fr.* Bavière. *state* SE Germany
Bayeux *90 B3 anc.* Augustodurum. Calvados, N France
Bāyir *119 C7 var.* Bā'ir. Ma'ān, S Jordan
Bay Islands *52 C1 Eng.* Bay Islands. *island group* N Honduras
Bay Islands *see* Bahía, Islas de la
Baymak *111 D6* Respublika Bashkortostan, W Russian Federation
Bayonne *91 A6 anc.* Lapurdum. Pyrénées-Atlantiques, SW France
Bayou State *see* Mississippi
Bayram-Ali *see* Baýramaly
Baýramaly *122 D3 var.* Bayramaly; *prev.* Bayram-Ali. Mary Welaýaty, S Turkmenistan
Bayreuth *95 C5 var.* Baireuth. Bayern, SE Germany
Bayrische Alpen *see* Bavarian Alps
Bayrūt *see* Beyrouth
Bay State *see* Massachusetts
Baysun *see* Boysun
Bayt Laḩm *see* Bethlehem
Baytown *49 H4* Texas, SW USA
Baza *93 E4* Andalucía, S Spain
Bazargic *see* Dobrich
Bazin *see* Pezinok
Beagle Channel *65 C8 channel* Argentina/Chile
Béal Feirste *see* Belfast
Beannchar *see* Bangor, Northern Ireland, UK
Bear Island *see* Bjørnøya
Bear Lake *46 E4 lake* Idaho/Utah, NW USA
Beas de Segura *93 E4* Andalucía, S Spain
Beata, Isla *55 E3 island* SW Dominican Republic
Beatrice *45 F4* Nebraska, C USA
Beaufort Sea *36 D2 sea* Arctic Ocean
Beaufort-Wes *see* Beaufort West
Beaufort West *78 C5 Afr.* Beaufort-Wes. Western Cape, SW South Africa
Beaumont *49 H3* Texas, SW USA
Beaune *90 D4* Côte d'Or, C France
Beauvais *90 C3 anc.* Bellovacum, Caesaromagus. Oise, N France
Beaver Island *40 C2 island* Michigan, N USA
Beaver Lake *49 H1 reservoir* Arkansas, C USA
Beaver River *49 F1 river* Oklahoma, C USA
Beaver State *see* Oregon
Beāwar *134 C3* Rājasthān, N India
Bečej *100 D3 Ger.* Altbetsche, *Hung.* Óbecse, Rácz-Becse; *prev.* Magyar-Becse, Stari Bečej. Vojvodina, N Serbia
Béchar *70 D2 prev.* Colomb-Béchar. W Algeria
Beckley *40 D5* West Virginia, NE USA
Bécs *see* Wien
Bedford *89 D6* E England, United Kingdom
Bedum *86 E1* Groningen, NE Netherlands
Beehive State *see* Utah
Be'er Menuha *119 B7 prev.* Be'ér Menuḩa. Southern, S Israel
Be'ér Menuḩa *see* Be'er Menuha
Beernem *87 A5* West-Vlaanderen, NW Belgium
Beersheba *see* Be'er Sheva
Be'er Sheva *119 A7 var.* Beersheba, *Ar.* Bir es Saba; *prev.* Be'ér Sheva'. Southern, S Israel
Be'ér Sheva' *see* Be'er Sheva
Beesel *87 D5* Limburg, SE Netherlands
Beeville *49 G4* Texas, SW USA
Bega *149 D7* New South Wales, SE Australia
Begoml' *see* Byahoml'
Begovat *see* Bekobod
Behagle *see* Laï
Behar *see* Bihār
Beibu Wan *see* Tonkin, Gulf of
Beida *see* Al Bayḑā'
Beihai *128 B6* Guangxi Zhuangzu Zizhiqu, S China
Beijing *128 C3 var.* Pei-ching, Peking; *prev.* Pei-p'ing. *country capital* (China) Beijing Shi, E China
Beilen *86 E2* Drenthe, NE Netherlands
Beira *79 E3* Sofala, C Mozambique
Beirut *see* Beyrouth
Beit Lekhem *see* Bethlehem
Beiuş *108 B3 Hung.* Belényes. Bihor, NW Romania
Beja *92 B4 anc.* Pax Julia. Beja, SE Portugal
Béjar *92 C3* Castilla y León, N Spain
Bejraburi *see* Phetchaburi
Bekabad *see* Bekobod
Békás *see* Bicaz
Bek-Budi *see* Qarshi
Békéscsaba *99 D7 Rom.* Bichiş-Ciaba. Békés, SE Hungary
Bekobod *123 E2 Rus.* Bekabad; *prev.* Begovat. Toshkent Viloyati, E Uzbekistan
Bela Crkva *100 E3 Ger.* Weisskirchen, *Hung.* Fehértemplom. Vojvodina, W Serbia
Belarus *107 B6 off.* Republic of Belarus, *var.* Belorussia, *Latv.* Baltkrievija; *prev.* Belorussian SSR, *Rus.* Belorusskaya SSR. *country* E Europe

BELARUS
Eastern Europe

Official name Republic of Belarus
Formation 1991 / 1991
Capital Minsk
Population 9.4 million / 117 people per sq mile (45 people per sq km)
Total area 80,154 sq. miles (207,600 sq. km)
Languages Belarussian*, Russian*
Religions Orthodox Christian 80%, Roman Catholic 14%, Other 6%
Ethnic mix Belorussian 81%, Russian 11%, Polish 4%, Ukrainian 2%, Other 2%
Government Presidential system
Currency Belarussian rouble = 100 kopeks
Literacy rate 99%
Calorie consumption 3253 kilocalories

Belarus, Republic of *see* Belarus
Belau *see* Palau
Belaya Tserkov' *see* Bila Tserkva
Bełchatów *98 C4 var.* Belchatow. Łódzski, C Poland
Belchatow *see* Bełchatów
Belcher, Îles *see* Belcher Islands
Belcher Islands *38 C2 Fr.* Îles Belcher. *island group* Nunavut, SE Canada
Beledweyne *73 D5 var.* Belet Huen, *It.* Belet Uen. Hiiraan, C Somalia
Belém *63 F1 var.* Pará. *state capital* Pará, N Brazil
Belén *52 D4* Rivas, SW Nicaragua
Belen *48 D2* New Mexico, SW USA
Belényes *see* Beiuş
Belet Huen/Belet Uen *see* Beledweyne
Belfast *89 B5 Ir.* Béal Feirste. *national capital* E Northern Ireland, United Kingdom
Belfield *44 D2* North Dakota, N USA
Belfort *90 E4* Territoire-de-Belfort, E France
Belgard *see* Białogard
Belgaum *132 B1* Karnātaka, W India
Belgian Congo *see* Congo (Democratic Republic of)
België/Belgique *see* Belgium
Belgium *87 B6 off.* Kingdom of Belgium, *Dut.* België, *Fr.* Belgique. *country* NW Europe

BELGIUM
Northwest Europe

Official name Kingdom of Belgium
Formation 1830 / 1919
Capital Brussels
Population 11.1 million / 876 people per sq mile (338 people per sq km)
Total area 11,780 sq. miles (30,510 sq. km)
Languages Dutch*, French*, German*
Religions Roman Catholic 88%, Other 10%, Muslim 2%
Ethnic mix Fleming 58%, Walloon 33%, Other 6%, Italian 2%, Moroccan 1%
Government Parliamentary system
Currency Euro = 100 cents
Literacy rate 99%
Calorie consumption 3793 kilocalories

Belgium, Kingdom of *see* Belgium

Belgorod *111 A6* Belgorodskaya Oblast', W Russian Federation
Belgrano II *154 A2 Argentinian research station* Antarctica
Belice *see* Belize/Belize City
Beligrad *see* Berat
Beli Manastir *100 C3 Hung.* Pélmonostor; *prev.* Monostor. Osijek-Baranja, NE Croatia
Bélinga *77 B5* Ogooué-Ivindo, NE Gabon
Belitung, Pulau *138 C4 island* W Indonesia
Belize *52 B1 Sp.* Belice; *prev.* British Honduras, Colony of Belize. *country* Central America

BELIZE
Central America

Official name Belize
Formation 1981 / 1981
Capital Belmopan
Population 294,385 / 33 people per sq mile (13 people per sq km) / 48%
Total area 8867 sq. miles (22,966 sq. km)
Languages English*, English Creole, Spanish, Mayan, Garifuna (Carib)
Religions Roman Catholic 62%, Other 13%, Anglican 12%, Methodist 6%, Mennonite 4%, Seventh-day Adventist 3%
Ethnic mix Mestizo 49%, Creole 25%, Maya 11%, Other 6%, Garifuna 6%, Asian Indian 3%
Government Parliamentary system
Currency Belizean dollar = 100 cents
Literacy rate 75%
Calorie consumption 2757 kilocalories

Belize *52 B1 river* Belize/Guatemala
Belize *see* Belize City
Belize City *52 C1 var.* Belize, *Sp.* Belice. Belize, NE Belize
Belize, Colony of *see* Belize
Beljak *see* Villach
Belkofski *36 B3* Alaska, USA
Belle Île *90 A4 island* NW France
Belle Isle, Strait of *39 G3 strait* Newfoundland and Labrador, E Canada
Bellenz *see* Bellinzona
Belleville *40 B4* Illinois, N USA
Bellevue *45 F4* Iowa, C USA
Bellevue *46 B2* Washington, NW USA
Bellingham *46 B1* Washington, NW USA
Belling Hausen Mulde *see* Southeast Pacific Basin
Bellingshausen Abyssal Plain *see* Bellingshausen Plain
Bellingshausen Plain *153 F5 var.* Bellingshausen Abyssal Plain. *abyssal plain* SE Pacific Ocean
Bellingshausen Sea *154 A3 sea* Antarctica
Bellinzona *95 B8 Ger.* Bellenz. Ticino, S Switzerland
Bello *58 B2* Antioquia, W Colombia
Bello Horizonte *see* Belo Horizonte
Bellovacum *see* Beauvais
Bellville *78 B5* Western Cape, SW South Africa
Belmopan *52 C1 country capital* (Belize) Cayo, C Belize
Belogradchik *104 B1* Vidin, NW Bulgaria
Belo Horizonte *63 F4 prev.* Bello Horizonte. *state capital* Minas Gerais, SE Brazil
Belomorsk *110 B3* Respublika Kareliya, NW Russian Federation
Beloretsk *111 D6* Respublika Bashkortostan, W Russian Federation
Belorussia/Belorussian SSR *see* Belarus
Belorusskaya Gryada *see* Byelaruskaya Hrada
Belorusskaya SSR *see* Belarus
Beloshchel'ye *see* Nar'yan-Mar
Belostok *see* Białystok
Belovár *see* Bjelovar
Belozërsk *110 B4* Vologodskaya Oblast', NW Russian Federation
Belton *49 G3* Texas, SW USA
Bel'tsy *see* Bălți
Beluchistan *see* Balochistan
Belukha, Gora *114 D5 mountain* Kazakhstan/Russian Federation
Belynichi *see* Byalynichy
Belyy, Ostrov *114 D2 island* N Russian Federation
Bemaraha *79 F3 var.* Plateau du Bemaraha. *mountain range* W Madagascar
Bemaraha, Plateau du *see* Bemaraha
Bemidji *45 F1* Minnesota, N USA
Bemmel *86 D4* Gelderland, SE Netherlands
Benaco *see* Garda, Lago di
Benares *see* Vārānasi
Benavente *92 D2* Castilla y León, N Spain
Bend *46 B3* Oregon, NW USA
Bender *see* Tighina
Bender Beila/Bender Beyla *see* Bandarbeyla
Bender Cassim/Bender Qaasim *see* Boosaaso
Bendern *94 E1* NW Liechtenstein Europe
Bendery *see* Tighina
Bendigo *149 C7* Victoria, SE Australia
Beneschau *see* Benešov
Beneški Zaliv *see* Venice, Gulf of
Benešov *99 B5 Ger.* Beneschau. Středočeský Kraj, W Czech Republic
Benevento *97 D5 anc.* Beneventum, Malventum. Campania, S Italy
Beneventum *see* Benevento
Bengal, Bay of *124 C4 bay* N Indian Ocean
Bengalooru *see* Bangalore
Bengasi *see* Banghāzī
Bengazi *see* Banghāzī
Bengbu *128 D5 var.* Peng-pu. Anhui, E China
Benghazi *see* Banghāzī
Bengkulu *138 B4 prev.* Bengkoeloe, Benkoelen, Benkulen. Sumatera, W Indonesia
Benguela *78 A2 var.* Benguella. Benguela, W Angola
Benguella *see* Benguela
Bengweulu, Lake *see* Bangweulu, Lake
Ben Hope *88 B2 mountain* N Scotland, United Kingdom
Beni *77 E5* Nord-Kivu, NE Dem. Rep. Congo
Benidorm *93 F4* Valenciana, SE Spain
Beni-Mellal *70 C2* C Morocco
Benin *75 F4 off.* Republic of Benin; *prev.* Dahomey. *country* W Africa

BENIN
West Africa

Official name Republic of Benin
Formation 1960 / 1960
Capital Porto-Novo
Population 10.3 million / 241 people per sq mile (93 people per sq km)
Total area 43,483 sq. miles (112,620 sq. km)
Languages Fon, Bariba, Yoruba, Adja, Houeda, Somba, French*
Religions Indigenous beliefs and Voodoo 50%, Christian 30%, Muslim 20%
Ethnic mix Fon 41%, Other 21%, Adja 16%, Yoruba 12%, Bariba 10%
Government Presidential system
Currency CFA franc = 100 centimes
Literacy rate 29%
Calorie consumption 2594 kilocalories

Benin, Bight of *75 F5 gulf* W Africa
Benin City *75 F5* Edo, SW Nigeria
Benin, Republic of *see* Benin
Beni, Río *61 E3 river* N Bolivia
Beni Suef *see* Banī Suwayf
Ben Nevis *88 C3 mountain* N Scotland, United Kingdom
Bénoué *see* Benue
Benson *48 B3* Arizona, SW USA
Bent Jbaïl *119 A5 var.* Bint Jubayl. S Lebanon
Benton *42 B1* Arkansas, C USA
Benue *76 B4 Fr.* Bénoué. *river* Cameroon/Nigeria
Beograd *100 D3 Eng.* Belgrade. Serbia, N Serbia
Berane *101 D5 prev.* Ivangrad. E Montenegro
Berat *101 C6 var.* Berati, *SCr.* Beligrad. Berat, C Albania
Berătău *see* Berettyó
Berati *see* Berat
Berau, Teluk *139 G4 var.* MacCluer Gulf. *bay* Papua, E Indonesia
Berbera *72 D4* Woqooyi Galbeed, NW Somalia
Berbérati *77 B5* Mambéré-Kadéï, SW Central African Republic
Berck-Plage *90 C2* Pas-de-Calais, N France
Berdichev *see* Berdychiv
Berdyans'k *109 G4 Rus.* Berdyansk; *prev.* Osipenko. Zaporiz'ka Oblast', SE Ukraine
Berdychiv *108 D2 Rus.* Berdichev. Zhytomyrs'ka Oblast', N Ukraine
Beregovo/Beregszász *see* Berehove
Berehove *108 B3 Cz.* Berehovo, *Hung.* Beregszász, *Rus.* Beregovo. Zakarpats'ka Oblast', W Ukraine
Berehovo *see* Berehove
Bereket *122 B2 prev. Rus.* Gazandzhyk, Kazandzhik, *Turkm.* Gazanjyk. Balkan Welaýaty, W Turkmenistan
Beretău *see* Berettyó
Berettyó *99 D7 Rom.* Barcău; *prev.* Berătău, Beretău. *river* Hungary/Romania
Berettyóújfalu *99 D6* Hajdú-Bihar, E Hungary
Berezhany *108 C2 Pol.* Brzeżany. Ternopil's'ka Oblast', W Ukraine
Berezina *see* Byarezina
Berezniki *111 D5* Permskiy Kray, NW Russian Federation
Berga *93 G2* Cataluña, NE Spain
Bergamo *96 B2 anc.* Bergomum. Lombardia, N Italy
Bergara *93 E1* País Vasco, N Spain
Bergen *94 D2* Mecklenburg-Vorpommern, NE Germany
Bergen *86 C2* Noord-Holland, NW Netherlands
Bergen *85 A5* Hordaland, S Norway
Bergen *see* Mons
Bergerac *91 B5* Dordogne, SW France
Bergeyk *87 C5* Noord-Brabant, S Netherlands
Bergomum *see* Bergamo
Bergse Maas *86 D4 river* S Netherlands
Beringen *87 C5* Limburg, NE Belgium
Beringov Proliv *see* Bering Strait
Bering Sea *36 A2 sea* N Pacific Ocean
Bering Strait *36 C2 Rus.* Beringov Proliv. *strait* Bering Sea/Chukchi Sea
Berja *93 E5* Andalucía, S Spain
Berkeley *47 B6* California, W USA
Berkner Island *154 A2 island* Antarctica
Berkovitsa *104 C2* Montana, NW Bulgaria
Berlin *94 D3 country capital* (Germany) Berlin, NE Germany
Berlin *41 G2* New Hampshire, NE USA
Berlinchen *see* Barlinek
Bermejo, Río *64 C2 river* N Argentina
Bermeo *93 E1* País Vasco, N Spain
Bermuda *35 D6 var.* Bermuda Islands, Bermudas; *prev.* Somers Islands. *UK crown colony* NW Atlantic Ocean
Bermuda Islands *see* Bermuda
Bermuda Rise *35 E6 undersea rise* C Sargasso Sea
Bermudas *see* Bermuda
Bern *95 A7 Fr.* Berne. *country capital* (Switzerland) Bern, W Switzerland
Bernau *94 D3* Brandenburg, NE Germany
Bernburg *94 C4* Sachsen-Anhalt, C Germany
Berne *see* Bern
Berner Alpen *95 A7 var.* Berner Oberland, *Eng.* Bernese Oberland. *mountain range* SW Switzerland
Berner Oberland/Bernese Oberland *see* Berner Alpen
Bernier Island *147 A5 island* Western Australia
Beroea *see* Ḥalab
Berry *90 C4 cultural region* C France
Berry Islands *54 C1 island group* N Bahamas
Bertoua *77 B5* Est, E Cameroon
Beru *145 E2 var.* Peru. *atoll* Tungaru, W Kiribati
Berwick-upon-Tweed *88 D4* N England, United Kingdom
Berytus *see* Beyrouth
Besançon *90 D4 anc.* Besontium, Vesontio. Doubs, E France
Beskra *see* Biskra
Besontium *see* Besançon
Bessarabka *see* Basarabeasca
Beszterce *see* Bistrița
Besztercebánya *see* Banská Bystrica
Betafo *79 G3* Antananarivo, C Madagascar
Betanzos *92 B1* Galicia, NW Spain
Bethlehem *78 D4* Free State, C South Africa
Bethlehem *119 B6 var.* Beit Lekhem, *Ar.* Bayt Laḥm, *Heb.* Bet Leḥem. C West Bank
Béticos, Sistemas *92 D4 var.* Sistema Penibético, *Eng.* Baetic Cordillera, Baetic Mountains. *mountain range* S Spain
Bet Leḥem *see* Bethlehem
Bétou *77 C5* Likouala, N Congo
Bette, Pic *see* Bette, Picco
Bette, Picco *71 G4 var.* Bikkū Bittī, Pi Bette. *mountain* S Libya
Beulah *40 C2* Michigan, N USA
Beuthen *see* Bytom
Beveren *87 B5* Oost-Vlaanderen, N Belgium
Beverley *89 D5* E England, United Kingdom
Bexley *89 B8* Bexley, SE England, Unit Kingdom
Beyla *74 D4* SE Guinea
Beyrouth *118 A4 var.* Bayrūt, *Eng.* Beirut; *anc.* Berytus. *country capital* (Lebanon) W Lebanon
Beyşehir *116 B4* Konya, SW Turkey
Beyşehir Gölü *116 B4 lake* C Turkey
Béziers *91 C6 anc.* Baeterrae, Baeterra Septimanorum, Julia Beterrae. Héra S France
Bezmein *see* Abadan
Bezwada *see* Vijayawāda
Bhadrāvati *132 C2* Karnātaka, SW In
Bhāgalpur *135 F3* Bihār, NE India
Bhaktapur *135 F3* Central, C Nepal
Bhamo *136 B2 var.* Banmo. Kachin State, N Myanmar (Burma)
Bhārat *see* India
Bharūch *134 C4* Gujarāt, W India
Bhaunagar *see* Bhāvnagar
Bhāvnagar *134 C4 prev.* Bhaunagar. Gujarāt, W India
Bheanntraí, Bá *see* Bantry Bay
Bhopāl *134 D4 state capital* Madhya Pradesh, C India
Bhubaneshwar *135 F5 prev.* Bhubaneswar, Bhuvaneshwar. *state capital* Odisha, E India
Bhubaneswar *see* Bhubaneshwar
Bhuket *see* Phuket
Bhusaval *see* Bhusāwal
Bhusāwal *134 D4 prev.* Bhusaval. Mahārāshtra, C India
Bhutan *135 G3 off.* Kingdom of Bhuta *var.* Druk-yul. *country* S Asia

BHUTAN
South Asia

Official name Kingdom of Bhutan
Formation 1656 / 1865
Capital Thimphu
Population 800,000 / 44 people per sq mile (17 people per sq km)
Total area 18,147 sq. miles (47,000 sq. km
Languages Dzongkha*, Nepali, Assame
Religions Mahayana Buddhist 75%, Hindu 25%
Ethnic mix Bhutanese 50%, Nepalese 35%, Other 15%
Government Monarchical / parliamentary system
Currency Ngultrum = 100 chetrum
Literacy rate 53%
Calorie consumption Not available

Bhutan, Kingdom of *see* Bhutan
Bhuvaneshwar *see* Bhubaneshwar
Biak, Pulau *139 G4 island* E Indonesia
Biała Podlaska *98 E3* Lubelskie, E Poland
Białogard *98 B2 Ger.* Belgard. Zachodnio-pomorskie, NW Poland
Białystok *98 E3 Rus.* Belostok, Bielost Podlaskie, NE Poland
Bianco, Monte *see* Blanc, Mont
Biarritz *91 A6* Pyrénées-Atlantiques, SW France
Bicaz *108 C3 Hung.* Békás. Neamț, NE Romania
Bichiș-Ciaba *see* Békéscsaba
Biddeford *41 G2* Maine, NE USA
Bideford *89 C7* SW England, United Kingdom
Biel *95 A7 Fr.* Bienne. Bern, W Switzerland
Bielefeld *94 B4* Nordrhein-Westfalen, NW Germany

elitz/Bielitz-Biala *see* Bielsko-Biała
elostok *see* Białystok
elsko-Biała *99 C5 Ger.* Bielitz, Bielitz-Biala. Śląskie, S Poland
elsk Podlaski *98 E3* Białystok, E Poland
en Bien *see* Điên Biên Phu
ên Đông *see* South China Sea
ên Hoa *137 E6* Đông Nai, S Vietnam
enne *see* Biel
enville, Lac *38 D2 lake* Québec, C Canada
é Plateau *78 B2 var.* Bié Plateau. *plateau* C Angola
é Plateau *see* Bié, Planalto do
g Cypress Swamp *43 E5 wetland* Florida, SE USA
gge Island *146 C2 island* Western Australia
ghorn Mountains *44 C2 mountain range* Wyoming, C USA
ghorn River *44 C2 river* Montana/Wyoming, NW USA
gnona *74 B3* SW Senegal
gorra *see* Tarbes
gosovo *see* Bihosava
g Sioux River *45 E2 river* Iowa/South Dakota, N USA
g Spring *49 E3* Texas, SW USA
hać *100 B3* Federacija Bosne I Hercegovine, NW Bosnia and Herzegovina
hār *135 F3 prev.* Behar. *cultural region* N India
hār *see* Bihār Sharīf
haramulo *73 B7* Kagera, NW Tanzania
hār Sharīf *135 F3 var.* Bihār. Bihār, N India
hosava *107 D5 Rus.* Bigosovo. Vitsyebskaya Voblasts', NW Belarus
jeljina *100 C3* Republika Srpska, NE Bosnia and Herzegovina
jelo Polje *101 D5* E Montenegro
kāner *134 C3* Rājasthān, NW India
kin *115 G4* Khabarovskiy Kray, SE Russian Federation
kini Atoll *144 C1 var.* Pikinni. *atoll* Ralik Chain, NW Marshall Islands
kkū Bittī *see* Bette, Picco
lāspur *135 E4* Chhattīsgarh, C India
läsuvar *117 H3 Rus.* Bilyasuvar; *prev.* Pushkino. SE Azerbaijan
la Tserkva *109 E2 Rus.* Belaya Tserkov'. Kyyivs'ka Oblast', N Ukraine
lauktaung Range *137 C6 var.* Thanintari Taungdan. *mountain range* Myanmar (Burma)/Thailand
lbao *93 E1 Basq.* Bilbo. País Vasco, N Spain
lbo *see* Bilbao
lecik *116 B3* Bilecik, NW Turkey
llings *44 C2* Montana, NW USA
lma, Grand Erg de *75 H3 desert* NE Niger
loela *148 D4* Queensland, E Australia
loxi *42 C3* Mississippi, S USA
ltine *76 C3* Biltine, E Chad
lwi *see* Puerto Cabezas
lyasuvar *see* Biläsuvar
lzen *87 D6* Limburg, NE Belgium
mini Islands *54 C1 island group* W Bahamas
nche *87 B7* Hainaut, S Belgium
ndloe Island *see* Marchena, Isla
n Ghalfān, Jazā'ir *see* Ḥalāniyāt, Juzur al
nghamton *41 F3* New York, NE USA
ngöl *117 E3* Bingöl, E Turkey
nt Jubayl *see* Bent Jbaïl
ntulu *138 D3* Sarawak, East Malaysia
nzhou *128 D4* Shandong, E China
o Bío, Río *65 B5 river* C Chile
oco, Isla de *77 A5 var.* Bioko, *Eng.* Fernando Po, *Sp.* Fernando Póo; *prev.* Macías Nguema Biyogo. *island* NW Equatorial Guinea
oko *see* Bioco, Isla de
rāk *71 F3 var.* Brak. C Libya
rao *76 D3* Vakaga, NE Central African Republic
rātnagar *135 F3* Eastern, SE Nepal
r es Saba *see* Be'er Sheva
rjand *120 E3* Khorāsān-e Janūbī, E Iran
rkenfeld *95 A5* Rheinland-Pfalz, SW Germany
rkenhead *89 C5* NW England, United Kingdom
rlad *see* Bârlad
Birmingham *89 C6* C England, United Kingdom
Birmingham *42 C2* Alabama, S USA
Bir Moghrein *see* Bîr Mogreïn
Bîr Mogreïn *74 C1 var.* Bir Moghrein; *prev.* Fort-Trinquet. Tiris Zemmour, N Mauritania
Birnie Island *145 E3 atoll* Phoenix Islands, C Kiribati
Birnin Konni *75 F3 var.* Birni-Nkonni. Tahoua, SW Niger
Birni-Nkonni *see* Birnin Konni
Birobidzhan *115 G4* Yevreyskaya Avtonomnaya Oblast', SE Russian Federation
Birsen *see* Biržai
Birsk *111 D5* Respublika Bashkortostan, W Russian Federation
Biržai *106 C4 Ger.* Birsen. Panevėžys, NE Lithuania
Birżebbuġa *102 B5* SE Malta
Bisanthe *see* Tekirdağ
Bisbee *48 B3* Arizona, SW USA
Biscaia, Baía de *see* Biscay, Bay of
Biscay, Bay of *80 B4 Sp.* Golfo de Vizcaya, *Port.* Baía de Biscaia. *bay* France/Spain
Biscay Plain *80 B3 abyssal plain* SE Bay of Biscay
Bischofsburg *see* Biskupiec
Bishah, Wadi *121 B5 dry watercourse* C Saudi Arabia
Bishkek *123 G2 var.* Pishpek; *prev.* Frunze. *country capital* (Kyrgyzstan) Chuyskaya Oblast', N Kyrgyzstan
Bishop's Lynn *see* King's Lynn
Bishrī, Jabal *118 D3 mountain range* E Syria
Biskara *see* Biskra
Biskra *71 E2 var.* Beskra, Biskara. NE Algeria
Biskupiec *98 D2 Ger.* Bischofsburg. Warmińsko-Mazurskie, NE Poland
Bislig *139 F2* Mindanao, S Philippines
Bismarck *45 E2 state capital* North Dakota, N USA
Bismarck Archipelago *144 B3 island group* NE Papua New Guinea
Bismarck Sea *144 B3 sea* W Pacific Ocean
Bisnulok *see* Phitsanulok
Bissau *74 B4 country capital* (Guinea-Bissau) W Guinea-Bissau
Bistriṭa *108 B3 Ger.* Bistritz, *Hung.* Beszterce; *prev.* Nösen. Bistriṭa-Năsăud, N Romania
Bistritz *see* Bistriṭa
Bitam *77 B5* Woleu-Ntem, N Gabon
Bitburg *95 A5* Rheinland-Pfalz, SW Germany
Bitlis *117 F3* Bitlis, SE Turkey
Bitoeng *see* Bitung
Bitola *101 D6 Turk.* Monastir; *prev.* Bitolj. S FYR Macedonia
Bitolj *see* Bitola
Bitonto *97 D5 anc.* Butuntum. Puglia, SE Italy
Bitterroot Range *46 D2 mountain range* Idaho/Montana, NW USA
Bitung *139 F3 prev.* Bitoeng. Sulawesi, C Indonesia
Biu *75 H4* Borno, E Nigeria
Biwa-ko *131 C6 lake* Honshū, SW Japan
Bizerta *see* Bizerte
Bizerte *71 E1 Ar.* Banzart, *Eng.* Bizerta. N Tunisia
Bjelovar *100 B2 Hung.* Belovár. Bjelovar-Bilogora, N Croatia
Bjeshkët e Namuna *see* North Albanian Alps
Björneborg *see* Pori
Bjørnøya *83 F3 Eng.* Bear Island. *island* N Norway
Blackall *148 C4* Queensland, E Australia
Black Drin *101 D6 Alb.* Lumi i Drinit të Zi, *SCr.* Crni Drim. *river* Albania/FYR Macedonia
Blackfoot *46 E4* Idaho, NW USA
Black Forest *95 B6 Eng.* Black Forest. *mountain range* SW Germany
Black Forest *see* Schwarzwald
Black Hills *44 D3 mountain range* South Dakota/Wyoming, N USA
Blackpool *89 C5* NW England, United Kingdom
Black Range *48 C2 mountain range* New Mexico, SW USA
Black River *54 A5* W Jamaica
Black River *136 C3 Chin.* Babian Jiang, Lixian Jiang, *Fr.* Rivière Noire, *Vtn.* Sông Đa. *river* China/Vietnam
Black Rock Desert *47 C5 desert* Nevada, W USA
Black Sand Desert *see* Garagum
Black Sea *116 B1 var.* Euxine Sea, *Bul.* Cherno More, *Rom.* Marea Neagră, *Rus.* Chernoye More, *Turk.* Karadeniz, *Ukr.* Chorne More. *sea* Asia/Europe
Black Sea Lowland *109 E4 Ukr.* Prychornomor'ska Nyzovyna. *depression* SE Europe
Black Volta *75 E4 var.* Borongo, Mouhoun, Moun Hou, *Fr.* Volta Noire. *river* W Africa
Blackwater *89 A6 Ir.* An Abhainn Mhór. *river* S Ireland
Blackwater State *see* Nebraska
Blagoevgrad *104 C3 prev.* Gorna Dzhumaya. Blagoevgrad, W Bulgaria
Blagoveshchensk *115 G4* Amurskaya Oblast', SE Russian Federation
Blake Plateau *35 D6 var.* Blake Terrace. *undersea plateau* W Atlantic Ocean
Blake Terrace *see* Blake Plateau
Blanca, Bahía *65 C5 bay* E Argentina
Blanca, Costa *93 F4 physical region* SE Spain
Blanche, Lake *149 B5 lake* South Australia
Blanc, Mont *91 D5 It.* Monte Bianco. *mountain* France/Italy
Blanco, Cape *46 A4 headland* Oregon, NW USA
Blanes *93 G2* Cataluña, NE Spain
Blankenberge *87 A5* West-Vlaanderen, NW Belgium
Blankenheim *95 A5* Nordrhein-Westfalen, W Germany
Blanquilla, Isla *59 E1 var.* La Blanquilla. *island* N Venezuela
Blanquilla, La *see* Blanquilla, Isla
Blantyre *79 E2 var.* Blantyre-Limbe. Southern, S Malawi
Blantyre-Limbe *see* Blantyre
Blaricum *86 C3* Noord-Holland, C Netherlands
Blatnitsa *see* Durankulak
Blenheim *151 C5* Marlborough, South Island, New Zealand
Blesae *see* Blois
Blida *70 D2 var.* El Boulaida, El Boulaïda. N Algeria
Bloemfontein *78 C4 var.* Mangaung. *country capital* (South Africa-judicial capital) Free State, C South Africa
Blois *90 C4 anc.* Blesae. Loir-et-Cher, C France
Bloomfield *48 C1* New Mexico, SW USA
Bloomington *40 B4* Illinois, N USA
Bloomington *40 C4* Indiana, N USA
Bloomington *45 F2* Minnesota, N USA
Bloomsbury *148 D3* Queensland, NE Australia
Bluefield *40 D5* West Virginia, NE USA
Bluefields *53 E3* Región Autónoma Atlántico Sur, SE Nicaragua
Bluegrass State *see* Kentucky
Blue Hen State *see* Delaware
Blue Law State *see* Connecticut
Blue Mountain Peak *54 B5 mountain* E Jamaica
Blue Mountains *46 C3 mountain range* Oregon/Washington, NW USA
Blue Nile *72 C4 var.* Abai, Bahr el, Azraq, *Amh.* Ābay Wenz, *Ar.* An Nīl al Azraq. *river* Ethiopia/Sudan
Blumenau *63 E5* Santa Catarina, S Brazil
Blythe *47 D8* California, W USA
Blytheville *42 C1* Arkansas, C USA
Bo *74 C4* S Sierra Leone
Boaco *52 D3* Boaco, S Nicaragua
Boa Vista *62 D1 state capital* Roraima, NW Brazil
Boa Vista *74 A3 island* Ilhas de Barlavento, E Cape Verde
Bobaomby, Tanjona *79 G2 Fr.* Cap d'Ambre. *headland* N Madagascar
Bobigny *90 E1* Seine-St-Denis, N France
Bobo-Dioulasso *74 D4* SW Burkina Faso
Bobrinets *see* Bobrynets'
Bobruysk *see* Babruysk
Bobrynets' *109 E3 Rus.* Bobrinets. Kirovohrads'ka Oblast', C Ukraine
Boca Raton *43 F5* Florida, SE USA
Bocay *52 D2* Jinotega, N Nicaragua
Bocheykovo *see* Bacheykava
Bocholt *94 A4* Nordrhein-Westfalen, W Germany
Bochum *94 A4* Nordrhein-Westfalen, W Germany
Bocşa *108 A4 Ger.* Bokschen, *Hung.* Boksánbánya. Caraş-Severin, SW Romania
Bodaybo *115 F4* Irkutskaya Oblast', E Russian Federation
Bodegas *see* Babahoyo
Boden *84 D4* Norrbotten, N Sweden
Bodensee *see* Constance, Lake, C Europe
Bodmin *89 C7* SW England, United Kingdom
Bodø *84 C3* Nordland, C Norway
Bodrum *116 A4* Muğla, SW Turkey
Boeloekoemba *see* Bulukumba
Boende *77 C5* Equateur, C Dem. Rep. Congo
Boeroe *see* Buru, Pulau
Boetoeng *see* Buton, Pulau
Bogale *136 B4* Ayeyarwady, SW Myanmar (Burma)
Bogalusa *42 B3* Louisiana, S USA
Bogatynia *98 B4 Ger.* Reichenau. Dolnośląskie, SW Poland
Boğazlıyan *116 D3* Yozgat, C Turkey
Bogendorf *see* Łuków
Bogor *138 C5 Dut.* Buitenzorg. Jawa, C Indonesia
Bogotá *58 B3 prev.* Santa Fe, Santa Fe de Bogotá. *country capital* (Colombia) Cundinamarca, C Colombia
Bogushëvsk *see* Bahushewsk
Boguslav *see* Bohuslav
Bo Hai *128 D4 var.* Gulf of Chihli. *gulf* NE China
Bohemia *99 A5 Cz.* Čechy, *Ger.* Böhmen. W Czech Republic
Bohemian Forest *95 C5 Cz.* Český Les, Šumava, *Ger.* Böhmerwald. *mountain range* C Europe
Böhmen *see* Bohemia
Böhmerwald *see* Bohemian Forest
Böhmisch-Krumau *see* Český Krumlov
Bohol Sea *139 E2 var.* Mindanao Sea. *sea* S Philippines
Bohuslav *109 E2 Rus.* Boguslav. Kyyivs'ka Oblast', N Ukraine
Boise *46 D3 var.* Boise City. *state capital* Idaho, NW USA
Boise City *49 E1* Oklahoma, C USA
Boise City *see* Boise
Bois, Lac des *see* Woods, Lake of the
Bois-le-Duc *see* 's-Hertogenbosch
Boizenburg *94 C3* Mecklenburg-Vorpommern, N Germany
Bojador *see* Boujdour
Bojnūrd *120 D2 var.* Bujnurd. Khorāsān-e Shemālī, N Iran
Bokāro *135 F4* Jhārkhand, N India
Boké *74 C4* W Guinea
Bokhara *see* Buxoro
Boksánbánya/Bokschen *see* Bocşa
Bol *76 B3* Lac, W Chad
Bolgatanga *75 E4* N Ghana
Bolgrad *see* Bolhrad
Bolhrad *108 D4 Rus.* Bolgrad. Odes'ka Oblast', SW Ukraine
Bolívar, Pico *58 C2 mountain* W Venezuela
Bolivia *61 F3 off.* Republic of Bolivia. *country* W South America

BOLIVIA
South America

Official name Plurinational State of Bolivia
Formation 1825 / 1938
Capital La Paz (administrative); Sucre (judicial)
Population 10.7 million / 26 people per sq mile (10 people per sq km)
Total area 424,162 sq. miles (1,098,580 sq. km)
Languages Aymara*, Quechua*, Spanish*
Religions Roman Catholic 93%, Other 7%
Ethnic mix Quechua 37%, Aymara 32%, Mixed race 13%, European 10%, Other 8%
Government Presidential system
Currency Boliviano = 100 centavos
Literacy rate 94%
Calorie consumption 2254 kilocalories

Bolivia, Republic of *see* Bolivia
Bollène *91 D6* Vaucluse, SE France
Bollnäs *85 C5* Gävleborg, C Sweden

Bollon *149 D5* Queensland, C Australia
Bologna *96 C3* Emilia-Romagna, N Italy
Bol'shevik *see* Bal'shavik
Bol'shevik, Ostrov *115 E2 island* Severnaya Zemlya, Russian Federation
Bol'shezemel'skaya Tundra *110 E3 physical region* NW Russian Federation
Bol'shoy Lyakhovskiy, Ostrov *115 F2 island* NE Russian Federation
Bolton *89 D5 prev.* Bolton-le-Moors. NW England, United Kingdom
Bolton-le-Moors *see* Bolton
Bolu *116 B3* Bolu, NW Turkey
Bolungarvík *83 E4* Vestfirdhir, NW Iceland
Bolyarovo *104 D3 prev.* Pashkeni. Yambol, E Bulgaria
Bolzano *96 C1 Ger.* Bozen; *anc.* Bauzanum. Trentino-Alto Adige, N Italy
Boma *77 B6* Bas-Congo, W Dem. Rep. Congo
Bombay *see* Mumbai
Bomu *76 D4 var.* Mbomou, Mbomu, M'Bomu. *river* Central African Republic/Dem. Rep. Congo
Bonaire *55 F5 Dutch special municipality* S West Indies
Bonanza *52 D2* Región Autónoma Atlántico Norte, NE Nicaragua
Bonaparte Archipelago *146 C2 island group* Western Australia
Bon, Cap *102 D3 headland* N Tunisia
Bonda *77 B6* Ogooué-Lolo, C Gabon
Bondoukou *75 E4* E Côte d'Ivoire
Bône *see* Annaba, Algeria
Bone *see* Watampone, Indonesia
Bone, Teluk *139 E4 bay* Sulawesi, C Indonesia
Bongaigaon *135 G3* Assam, NE India
Bongo, Massif des *76 D4 var.* Chaîne des Mongos. *mountain range* NE Central African Republic
Bongor *76 B3* Mayo-Kébbi, SW Chad
Bonifacio *91 E7* Corse, France, C Mediterranean Sea
Bonifacio, Bocche de/Bonifacio, Bouches de *see* Bonifacio, Strait of
Bonifacio, Strait of *96 A4 Fr.* Bouches de Bonifacio, *It.* Bocche di Bonifacio. *strait* C Mediterranean Sea
Bonn *95 A5* Nordrhein-Westfalen, W Germany
Bononia *see* Vidin, Bulgaria
Bononia *see* Boulogne-sur-Mer, France
Boosaaso *72 E4 var.* Bandar Kassim, Bender Qaasim, Bosaso, *It.* Bender Cassim. Bari, N Somalia
Boothia Felix *see* Boothia Peninsula
Boothia, Gulf of *37 F2 gulf* Nunavut, NE Canada
Boothia Peninsula *37 F2 prev.* Boothia Felix. *peninsula* Nunavut, NE Canada
Boppard *95 A5* Rheinland-Pfalz, W Germany
Boquete *53 E5 var.* Bajo Boquete. Chiriquí, W Panama
Boquillas *50 D2 var.* Boquillas del Carmen. Coahuila, NE Mexico
Boquillas del Carmen *see* Boquillas
Bor *100 E4* Serbia, E Serbia
Bor *73 B5* Jonglei, E South Sudan
Borås *85 B7* Västra Götaland, S Sweden
Borbetomagus *see* Worms
Borborema, Planalto da *56 E3 plateau* NE Brazil
Bordeaux *91 B5 anc.* Burdigala. Gironde, SW France
Bordj Omar Driss *71 E3* E Algeria
Borgå *see* Porvoo
Børgefjell *84 C4 mountain range* C Norway
Borger *86 E2* Drenthe, NE Netherlands
Borger *49 E1* Texas, SW USA
Borgholm *85 C7* Kalmar, S Sweden
Borgo Maggiore *96 E1* NW San Marino
Borislav *see* Boryslav
Borisoglebsk *111 B6* Voronezhskaya Oblast', W Russian Federation
Borisov *see* Barysaw
Borlänge *85 C6* Dalarna, C Sweden
Borne *86 E3* Overijssel, E Netherlands
Borneo *138 C4 island* Brunei/Indonesia/Malaysia
Bornholm *85 B8 island* E Denmark
Borohoro Shan *126 B2 mountain range* NW China
Borongo *see* Black Volta
Boron'ki *see* Baron'ki
Borosjenő *see* Ineu
Borovan *104 C2* Vratsa, NW Bulgaria
Borovichi *110 B4* Novgorodskaya Oblast', W Russian Federation
Borovo *100 C3* Vukovar-Srijem, NE Croatia
Borriana *93 F3 var.* Burriana. País Valenciano, E Spain
Borşa *108 C3 Hung.* Borsa. Maramureş, N Romania
Boryslav *108 B2 Pol.* Borysław, *Rus.* Borislav. L'vivs'ka Oblast', NW Ukraine
Borysław *see* Boryslav
Bosanska Dubica *100 B3 var.* Kozarska Dubica. Republika Srpska, NW Bosnia and Herzegovina
Bosanska Gradiška *100 B3 var.* Gradiška. Republika Srpska, N Bosnia and Herzegovina
Bosanski Novi *100 B3 var.* Novi Grad. Republika Srpska, NW Bosnia and Herzegovina
Bosanski Šamac *100 C3 var.* Šamac. Republika Srpska, N Bosnia and Herzegovina
Bosaso *see* Boosaaso
Bösing *see* Pezinok
Boskovice *99 B5 Ger.* Boskowitz. Jihomoravský Kraj, SE Czech Republic
Boskowitz *see* Boskovice
Bosna *100 C4 river* N Bosnia and Herzegovina
Bosne I Hercegovine, Federacija *100 B3 republic* Bosnia and Herzegovina
Bosnia and Herzegovina *100 B3 off.* Republic of Bosnia and Herzegovina. *country* SE Europe

BOSNIA & HERZEGOVINA
Southeast Europe

Official name Bosnia and Herzegovina
Formation 1992 / 1992
Capital Sarajevo
Population 3.8 million / 192 people per sq mile (74 people per sq km)
Total area 19,741 sq. miles (51,129 sq. km)
Languages Bosnian*, Serbian*, Croatian*
Religions Muslim (mainly Sunni) 40%, Orthodox Christian 31%, Roman Catholic 15%, Other 10%, Protestant 4%
Ethnic mix Bosniak 48%, Serb 34%, Croat 16%, Other 2%
Government Parliamentary system
Currency Marka = 100 pfeninga
Literacy rate 98%
Calorie consumption 3130 kilocalories

Bosnia and Herzegovina, Republic of *see* Bosnia and Herzegovina
Boso-hanto *131 D6 peninsula* Honshū, S Japan
Bosphorus/Bosporus *see* İstanbul Boğazı
Bosporus Cimmerius *see* Kerch Strait
Bosporus Thracius *see* İstanbul Boğazı
Bossangoa *76 C4* Ouham, C Central African Republic
Bossembélé *76 C4* Ombella-Mpoko, C Central African Republic
Bossier City *42 A2* Louisiana, S USA
Bosten Hu *126 C3 var.* Bagrax Hu. *lake* NW China
Boston *89 E6 prev.* St.Botolph's Town. E England, United Kingdom
Boston *41 G3 state capital* Massachusetts, NE USA
Boston Mountains *42 B1 mountain range* Arkansas, C USA
Bostyn' *see* Bastyn'
Botany *148 E2* New South Wales, E Australia
Botany Bay *148 E2 inlet* New South Wales, SE Australia
Boteti *78 C3 var.* Botletle. *river* N Botswana
Bothnia, Gulf of *85 D5 Fin.* Pohjanlahti, *Swe.* Bottniska Viken. *gulf* N Baltic Sea
Botletle *see* Boteti
Botoşani *108 C3 Hung.* Botosány. Botoşani, NE Romania
Botosány *see* Botoşani
Botou *128 C4 prev.* Bozhen. Hebei, E China
Botrange *87 D6 mountain* E Belgium
Botswana *78 C3 off.* Republic of Botswana. *country* S Africa

BOTSWANA
Southern Africa

Official name Republic of Botswana

BOTSWANA
(continued)

Formation 1966 / 1966
Capital Gaborone
Population 2 million / 9 people per sq mile (4 people per sq km)
Total area 231,803 sq. miles (600,370 sq. km)
Languages Setswana, English*, Shona, San, Khoikhoi, isiNdebele
Religions Christian 70%, Nonreligious 20%, Traditional beliefs 6%, Other 4%
Ethnic mix Tswana 79%, Kalanga 11%, Other 10%
Government Presidential system
Currency Pula = 100 thebe
Literacy rate 87%
Calorie consumption 2285 kilocalories

Botswana, Republic of *see* Botswana
Bottniska Viken *see* Bothnia, Gulf of
Bouar *76 B4* Nana-Mambéré, W Central African Republic
Bou Craa *70 B3 var.* Bu Craa. NW Western Sahara
Bougainville Island *142 B3 island* NE Papua New Guinea
Bougaroun, Cap *102 C3 headland* NE Algeria
Bougouni *74 D4* Sikasso, SW Mali
Boujdour *70 A3 var.* Bojador. W Western Sahara
Boulder *44 C4* Colorado, C USA
Boulder *44 B2* Montana, NW USA
Boulogne *see* Boulogne-sur-Mer
Boulogne-Billancourt *90 D1* Île-de-France, N France Europe
Boulogne-sur-Mer *90 C2 var.* Boulogne; *anc.* Bononia, Gesoriacum, Gessoriacum. Pas-de-Calais, N France
Boûmdeïd *74 C3 var.* Boumdeït. Assaba, S Mauritania
Boumdeït *see* Boûmdeïd
Boundiali *74 D4* N Côte d'Ivoire
Bountiful *44 B4* Utah, W USA
Bounty Basin *see* Bounty Trough
Bounty Islands *142 D5 island group* S New Zealand
Bounty Trough *152 C5 var.* Bounty Basin. *trough* S Pacific Ocean
Bourbonnais *90 C4 cultural region* C France
Bourbon Vendée *see* la Roche-sur-Yon
Bourg *see* Bourg-en-Bresse
Bourgas *see* Burgas
Bourge-en-Bresse *see* Bourg-en-Bresse
Bourg-en-Bresse *91 D5 var.* Bourg, Bourge-en-Bresse. Ain, E France
Bourges *90 C4 anc.* Avaricum. Cher, C France
Bourgogne *90 C4 Eng.* Burgundy. *cultural region* E France
Bourke *149 C5* New South Wales, SE Australia
Bournemouth *89 D7* S England, United Kingdom
Boutilimit *74 C3* Trarza, SW Mauritania
Bouvet Island *67 D7 Norwegian dependency* S Atlantic Ocean
Bowen *148 D3* Queensland, NE Australia
Bowling Green *40 B5* Kentucky, S USA
Bowling Green *40 C3* Ohio, N USA
Boxmeer *86 D4* Noord-Brabant, SE Netherlands
Boyarka *109 E2* Kyyivs'ka Oblast', N Ukraine
Boychinovtsi *104 C2 prev.* Lekhchevo. Montana, NW Bulgaria
Boysun *123 E3 Rus.* Baysun. Surkhondaryo Viloyati, S Uzbekistan
Bozeman *44 B2* Montana, NW USA
Bozen *see* Bolzano
Bozhen *see* Botou
Bozüyük *116 B3* Bilecik, NW Turkey
Brač *100 B4 var.* Brach, *It.* Brazza; *anc.* Brattia. *island* S Croatia
Bracara Augusta *see* Braga
Brach *see* Brač
Brades *55 G3 de facto dependent territory capital, de jure capital, Plymouth, destroyed by volcano in 1995* (Montserrat) SW Montserrat
Bradford *89 D5* N England, United Kingdom
Brady *49 F3* Texas, SW USA
Braga *92 B2 anc.* Bracara Augusta. Braga, NW Portugal
Bragança *92 C2 Eng.* Braganza; *anc.* Ju Briga. Bragança, NE Portugal
Braganza *see* Bragança
Brahestad *see* Raahe
Brahmanbaria *135 G4* Chittagong, E Bangladesh
Brahmapur *135 F5* Odisha, E India
Brahmaputra *135 H3 var.* Padma, Tsangpo, *Ben.* Jamuna, *Chin.* Yarlun Zangbo Jiang, *Ind.* Bramaputra, Dihang, Siang. *river* S Asia
Brăila *108 D4* Brăila, E Romania
Braine-le-Comte *87 B6* Hainaut, SW Belgium
Brainerd *45 F2* Minnesota, N USA
Brak *see* Birāk
Bramaputra *see* Brahmaputra
Brampton *38 D5* Ontario, S Canada
Branco, Rio *56 C3 river* N Brazil
Brandberg *78 A3 mountain* NW Namibia
Brandenburg *94 C3 var.* Brandenburg an der Havel. Brandenburg, NE Germany
Brandenburg an der Havel *see* Brandenburg
Brandon *37 F5* Manitoba, S Canada
Braniewo *98 D2 Ger.* Braunsberg. Warmińsko-mazurskie, N Poland
Brasil *see* Brazil
Brasília *63 F3 country capital* (Brazil) Distrito Federal, C Brazil
Brasil, Repùblica Federativa do *see* Brazil
Braşov *108 C4 Ger.* Kronstadt, *Hung.* Brassó; *prev.* Oraşul Stalin. Braşov, C Romania
Brassó *see* Braşov
Bratislava *99 C6 Ger.* Pressburg, *Hung* Pozsony. *country capital* (Slovakia) Bratislavský Kraj, W Slovakia
Bratsk *115 E4* Irkutskaya Oblast', C Russian Federation
Brattia *see* Brač
Braunsberg *see* Braniewo
Braunschweig *94 C4 Eng./Fr.* Brunswick. Niedersachsen, N Germa
Brava *see* Baraawe
Brava, Costa *93 H2 coastal region* NE Spain
Bravo del Norte, Río/Bravo, Río *see* Grande, Rio
Bravo, Río *50 C1 river* Mexico/USA North America
Brawley *47 D8* California, W USA
Brazil *62 C2 off.* Federative Republic of Brazil, *Port.* Repùblica Federativa do Brasil, *Sp.* Brasil; *prev.* United States c Brazil. *country* South America

BRAZIL
South America

Official name Federative Republic of Brazil
Formation 1822 / 1828
Capital Brasília
Population 200 million / 61 people per sq mile (24 people per sq km)
Total area 3,286,470 sq. miles (8,511,965 sq. km)
Languages Portuguese*, German, Italian, Spanish, Polish, Japanese, Amerindian languages
Religions Roman Catholic 74%, Protestant 15%, Atheist 7%, Other 4%
Ethnic mix White 54%, Mixed race 38% Black 6%, Other 2%
Government Presidential system
Currency Real = 100 centavos
Literacy rate 91%
Calorie consumption 3287 kilocalories

Brazil Basin *67 C5 var.* Brazilian Basin Brazil'skaya Kotlovina. *undersea bas* W Atlantic Ocean
Brazil, Federative Republic of *see* Bra
Brazilian Basin *see* Brazil Basin
Brazilian Highlands *63 F3 var.* Brazili Highlands. *mountain range* E Brazil
Brazilian Highlands *see* Central, Plana
Brazil'skaya Kotlovina *see* Brazil Basin
Brazil, United States of *see* Brazil
Brazos River *49 G3 river* Texas, SW U
Brazza *see* Brač
Brazzaville *77 B6 country capital* (Congo) Capital District, S Congo
Brčko *100 C3* Brčko Distrikt, NE Bosn and Herzegovina

čko Distrikt *100 B3 autonomous district* Bosnia and Herzegovina
recht *87 C5* Antwerpen, N Belgium
recon Beacons *89 C6 mountain range* S Wales, United Kingdom
reda *86 C4* Noord-Brabant, S Netherlands
ree *87 D5* Limburg, NE Belgium
regalnica *101 E6 river* E FYR Macedonia
regenz *57 B7 anc.* Brigantium. Vorarlberg, W Austria
regovo *104 B1* Vidin, NW Bulgaria
remen *94 B3 Fr.* Brême. Bremen, NW Germany
remerhaven *94 B3* Bremen, NW Germany
remerton *46 B2* Washington, NW USA
renham *49 G3* Texas, SW USA
renner, Col du/Brennero, Passo del *see* Brenner Pass
renner Pass *96 C1 var.* Brenner Sattel, *Fr.* Col du Brenner, *Ger.* Brennerpass, *It.* Passo del Brennero. *pass* Austria/Italy
rennerpass *see* Brenner Pass
renner Sattel *see* Brenner Pass
rescia *96 B2 anc.* Brixia. Lombardia, N Italy
reslau *see* Wrocław
ressanone *96 C1 Ger.* Brixen. Trentino-Alto Adige, N Italy
rest *107 A6 Pol.* Brześć nad Bugiem, *Rus.* Brest-Litovsk; *prev.* Brześć Litewski. Brestskaya Voblasts', SW Belarus
rest *90 A3* Finistère, NW France
rest-Litovsk *see* Brest
retagne *90 A3 Eng.* Brittany, *Lat.* Britannia Minor. *cultural region* NW France
rewster, Kap *see* Kangikajik
rewton *42 C3* Alabama, S USA
rezhnev *see* Naberezhnyye Chelny
rezovo *104 D2 prev.* Abrashlare. Plovdiv, C Bulgaria
ria *76 D4* Haute-Kotto, C Central African Republic
riançon *91 D5 anc.* Brigantio. Hautes-Alpes, SE France
ricgstow *see* Bristol
ridgeport *41 F3* Connecticut, NE USA
ridgetown *55 G2 country capital* (Barbados) SW Barbados
ridlington *89 D5* E England, United Kingdom
ridport *89 D7* S England, United Kingdom
rieg *see* Brzeg
rig *95 A7 Fr.* Brigue, *It.* Briga. Valais, SW Switzerland
riga *see* Brig
rigantio *see* Briançon
rigantium *see* Bregenz
righam City *44 B3* Utah, W USA
righton *89 E7* SE England, United Kingdom
righton *44 D4* Colorado, C USA
rigue *see* Brig
rindisi *97 E5 anc.* Brundisium, Brundusium. Puglia, SE Italy
riovera *see* St-Lô
risbane *149 E5 state capital* Queensland, E Australia
ristol *89 D7 anc.* Bricgstow. SW England, United Kingdom
ristol *41 F3* Connecticut, NE USA
ristol *40 D5* Tennessee, S USA
ristol Bay *36 B3 bay* Alaska, USA
ristol Channel *89 C7 inlet* England/Wales, United Kingdom
ritain *80 C3 var.* Great Britain. *island* United Kingdom
ritannia Minor *see* Bretagne
ritish Columbia *36 D4 Fr.* Colombie-Britannique. *province* SW Canada
ritish Guiana *see* Guyana
ritish Honduras *see* Belize
ritish Indian Ocean Territory *141 B5 UK dependent territory* C Indian Ocean
ritish Isles *89 island group* NW Europe
ritish North Borneo *see* Sabah
ritish Solomon Islands Protectorate *see* Solomon Islands
ritish Virgin Islands *55 F3 var.* Virgin Islands. *UK dependent territory* E West Indies
rittany *see* Bretagne
riva Curretia *see* Brive-la-Gaillarde
Briva Isarae *see* Pontoise
Brive *see* Brive-la-Gaillarde
Brive-la-Gaillarde *91 C5 prev.* Brive; *anc.* Briva Curretia. Corrèze, C France
Brixen *see* Bressanone
Brixia *see* Brescia
Brno *99 B5 Ger.* Brünn. Jihomoravský Kraj, SE Czech Republic
Brocēni *106 B3* SW Latvia
Brod/Bród *see* Slavonski Brod
Brodeur Peninsula *37 F2 peninsula* Baffin Island, Nunavut, NE Canada
Brod na Savi *see* Slavonski Brod
Brodnica *98 C3 Ger.* Buddenbrock. Kujawski-pomorskie, C Poland
Broek-in-Waterland *86 C3* Noord-Holland, C Netherlands
Broken Arrow *49 G1* Oklahoma, C USA
Broken Bay *148 E1 bay* New South Wales, SE Australia
Broken Hill *149 B6* New South Wales, SE Australia
Broken Ridge *141 D6 undersea plateau* S Indian Ocean
Bromberg *see* Bydgoszcz
Bromley *89 B8* United Kingdom
Brookhaven *42 B3* Mississippi, S USA
Brookings *45 F3* South Dakota, N USA
Brooks Range *36 D2 mountain range* Alaska, USA
Brookton *147 B6* Western Australia
Broome *146 B3* Western Australia
Broomfield *44 D4* Colorado, C USA
Broucsella *see* Brussel/Bruxelles
Brovary *109 E2* Kyyivs'ka Oblast', N Ukraine
Brownfield *49 E2* Texas, SW USA
Brownsville *49 G5* Texas, SW USA
Brownwood *49 F3* Texas, SW USA
Brozha *107 D7* Mahilyowskaya Voblasts', E Belarus
Bruges *see* Brugge
Brugge *87 A5 Fr.* Bruges. West-Vlaanderen, NW Belgium
Brummen *86 D3* Gelderland, E Netherlands
Brundisium/Brundusium *see* Brindisi
Brunei *138 D3 off.* Brunei Darussalam, *Mal.* Negara Brunei Darussalam. *country* SE Asia

BRUNEI
Southeast Asia

Official name Brunei Darussalam
Formation 1984 / 1984
Capital Bandar Seri Begawan
Population 400,000 / 197 people per sq mile (76 people per sq km)
Total area 2228 sq. miles (5770 sq. km)
Languages Malay*, English, Chinese
Religions Muslim (mainly Sunni) 66%, Buddhist 14%, Christian 10%, Other 10%
Ethnic mix Malay 67%, Chinese 16%, Other 11%, Indigenous 6%
Government Monarchy
Currency Brunei dollar = 100 cents
Literacy rate 95%
Calorie consumption 2949 kilocalories

Brunei Darussalam *see* Brunei
Brunei Town *see* Bandar Seri Begawan
Brünn *see* Brno
Brunner, Lake *151 C5 lake* South Island, New Zealand
Brunswick *43 E3* Georgia, SE USA
Brunswick *see* Braunschweig
Brusa *see* Bursa
Brus Laguna *52 D2* Gracias a Dios, E Honduras
Brussa *see* Bursa
Brussel *87 C6 var.* Brussels, *Fr.* Bruxelles, *Ger.* Brüssel; *anc.* Broucsella. *country capital* (Belgium) Brussels, C Belgium
Brüssel/Brussels *see* Brussel/Bruxelles
Brüx *see* Most
Bruxelles *see* Brussel
Bryan *49 G3* Texas, SW USA
Bryansk *111 A5* Bryanskaya Oblast', W Russian Federation
Brzeg *98 C4 Ger.* Brieg; *anc.* Civitas Altae Ripae. Opolskie, S Poland
Brześć Litewski/Brześć nad Bugiem *see* Brest
Brzeżany *see* Berezhany
Bucaramanga *58 B2* Santander, N Colombia
Buchanan *74 C5 prev.* Grand Bassa. SW Liberia
Buchanan, Lake *49 F3 reservoir* Texas, SW USA
Bucharest *see* București
Buckeye State *see* Ohio
Bu Craa *see* Bou Craa
București *108 C5 Eng.* Bucharest, *Ger.* Bukarest, *prev.* Altenburg; *anc.* Cetatea Damboviţei. *country capital* (Romania) București, S Romania
Buda-Kashalyova *107 D7 Rus.* Buda-Koshelëvo. Homyel'skaya Voblasts', SE Belarus
Buda-Koshelëvo *see* Buda-Kashalyova
Budapest *99 C6 off.* Budapest Főváros, *SCr.* Budimpešta. *country capital* (Hungary) Pest, N Hungary
Budapest Főváros *see* Budapest
Budaun *134 D3* Uttar Pradesh, N India
Buddenbrock *see* Brodnica
Budimpešta *see* Budapest
Budweis *see* České Budějovice
Budyšin *see* Bautzen
Buena Park *46 E2* California, W USA North America
Buenaventura *58 A3* Valle del Cauca, W Colombia
Buena Vista *61 G4* Santa Cruz, C Bolivia
Buena Vista *93 H5* S Gibraltar Europe
Buena Vista *93 H5* S Gibraltar Europe
Buenavista *93 H5* Baja California Sur, NW Mexico
Buenavista *93 H5* Sonora, NW Mexico
Buena Vista *93 H5* Cerro Largo, Uruguay
Buena Vista *93 H5* Colorado, C USA
Buena Vista *93 H5* Georgia, SE USA
Buena Vista *93 H5* Virginia, NE USA
Buenos Aires *64 D4 hist.* Santa Maria del Buen Aire. *country capital* (Argentina) Buenos Aires, E Argentina
Buenos Aires *53 E5* Puntarenas, SE Costa Rica
Buenos Aires, Lago *65 B6 var.* Lago General Carrera. *lake* Argentina/Chile
Buffalo *41 E3* New York, NE USA
Buffalo Narrows *37 F4* Saskatchewan, C Canada
Buff Bay *54 B5* E Jamaica
Buftea *108 C5* Ilfov, S Romania
Bug *81 E3 Bel.* Zakhodni Buh, *Eng.* Western Bug, *Rus.* Zapadnyy Bug, *Ukr.* Zakhidnyy Buh. *river* E Europe
Buga *58 B3* Valle del Cauca, W Colombia
Bughotu *see* Santa Isabel
Buguruslan *111 D6* Orenburgskaya Oblast', W Russian Federation
Buitenzorg *see* Bogor
Bujalance *92 D4* Andalucía, S Spain
Bujanovac *101 E5* SE Serbia
Bujnurd *see* Bojnūrd
Bujumbura *73 B7 prev.* Usumbura. *country capital* (Burundi) W Burundi
Bukarest *see* București
Bukavu *77 E6 prev.* Costermansville. Sud-Kivu, E Dem. Rep. Congo
Bukhara *see* Buxoro
Bukoba *73 B6* Kagera, NW Tanzania
Bülach *95 B7* Zürich, NW Switzerland
Bulawayo *78 D3* Matabeleland North, SW Zimbabwe
Bulgan *127 E2* Bulgan, N Mongolia
Bulgaria *104 C2 off.* Republic of Bulgaria, *Bul.* Bŭlgariya; *prev.* People's Republic of Bulgaria. *country* SE Europe

BULGARIA
Southeast Europe

Official name Republic of Bulgaria
Formation 1908 / 1947
Capital Sofia
Population 7.2 million / 169 people per sq mile (65 people per sq km)
Total area 42,822 sq. miles (110,910 sq. km)
Languages Bulgarian*, Turkish, Romani
Religions Bulgarian Orthodox 83%, Muslim 12%, Other 4%, Roman Catholic 1%
Ethnic mix Bulgarian 84%, Turkish 9%, Roma 5%, Other 2%
Government Parliamentary system
Currency Lev = 100 stotinki
Literacy rate 98%
Calorie consumption 2877 kilocalories

Bulgaria, People's Republic of *see* Bulgaria
Bulgaria, Republic of *see* Bulgaria
Bŭlgariya *see* Bulgaria
Bullion State *see* Missouri
Bull Shoals Lake *42 B1 reservoir* Arkansas/Missouri, C USA
Bulukumba *139 E4 prev.* Boeloekoemba. Sulawesi, C Indonesia
Bumba *77 D5* Equateur, N Dem. Rep. Congo
Bunbury *147 A7* Western Australia
Bundaberg *148 E4* Queensland, E Australia
Bungo-suido *131 B7 strait* SW Japan
Bunia *77 E5* Orientale, NE Dem. Rep. Congo
Bünyan *116 D3* Kayseri, C Turkey
Buraida *see* Buraydah
Buraydah *120 B4 var.* Buraida. Al Qaṣīm, N Saudi Arabia
Burdigala *see* Bordeaux
Burdur *116 B4 var.* Buldur. Burdur, SW Turkey
Burdur Gölü *116 B4 salt lake* SW Turkey
Burē *72 C4* Āmara, N Ethiopia
Burgas *104 E2 var.* Bourgas. Burgas, E Bulgaria
Burgaski Zaliv *104 E2 gulf* E Bulgaria
Burgos *92 D2* Castilla y León, N Spain
Burgundy *see* Bourgogne
Burhan Budai Shan *126 D4 mountain range* C China
Buriram *137 D5 var.* Buri Ram, Puriramya. Buri Ram, E Thailand
Buri Ram *see* Buriram
Burjassot *93 F3* Valenciana, E Spain
Burkburnett *49 F2* Texas, SW USA
Burketown *148 B3* Queensland, NE Australia
Burkina *see* Burkina Faso
Burkina Faso *75 E4 off.* Burkina Faso; *var.* Burkina, *prev.* Upper Volta. *country* W Africa

BURKINA FASO
West Africa

Official name Burkina Faso
Formation 1960 / 1960
Capital Ouagadougou
Population 16.9 million / 160 people per sq mile (62 people per sq km)
Total area 105,869 sq. miles (274,200 sq. km)
Languages Mossi, Fulani, French*, Tuareg, Dyula, Songhai
Religions Muslim 55%, Christian 25%, Traditional beliefs 20%
Ethnic mix Mossi 48%, Other 21%, Peul 10%, Lobi 7%, Bobo 7%, Mandé 7%
Government Transitional regime
Currency CFA franc = 100 centimes
Literacy rate 29%
Calorie consumption 2655 kilocalories

Burley *46 D4* Idaho, NW USA
Burlington *45 G4* Iowa, C USA
Burlington *41 F2* Vermont, NE USA
Burma *136 A3 off.* Union of Myanmar. *country* SE Asia. *See also* Myanmar
Burnie *149 C8* Tasmania, SE Australia
Burns *46 C3* Oregon, NW USA
Burnside *37 F3 river* Nunavut, NW Canada
Burnsville *45 F2* Minnesota, N USA
Burrel *101 D6 var.* Burreli. Dibër, C Albania
Burreli *see* Burrel
Burriana *see* Borriana
Bursa *116 B3 var.* Brussa, *prev.* Brusa; *anc.* Prusa. Bursa, NW Turkey
Būr Sa'īd *72 B1 var.* Port Said. N Egypt
Burtnieks *106 C3 var.* Burtnieks Ezers. *lake* N Latvia
Burtnieks Ezers *see* Burtnieks
Burundi *73 B7 off.* Republic of Burundi; *prev.* Kingdom of Burundi, Urundi. *country* C Africa

BURUNDI
Central Africa

Official name Republic of Burundi
Formation 1962 / 1962
Capital Bujumbura
Population 10.2 million / 1030 people per sq mile (398 people per sq km)
Total area 10,745 sq. miles (27,830 sq. km)
Languages Kirundi*, French*, Kiswahili

BURUNDI
(continued)

Religions Roman Catholic 62%, Traditional beliefs 23%, Muslim 10%, Protestant 5%
Ethnic mix Hutu 85%, Tutsi 14%, Twa 1%
Government Presidential system
Currency Burundian franc = 100 centimes
Literacy rate 87%
Calorie consumption 1604 kilocalories

Burundi, Kingdom of *see* Burundi
Burundi, Republic of *see* Burundi
Buru, Pulau *139 F4 prev.* Boeroe. *island* E Indonesia
Busan *129 E4 off.* Busan Gwang-yeoksi, *prev.* Pusan, *Jap.* Fusan. SE South Korea
Busan Gwang-yeoksi *see* Busan
Buşayrah *118 D3* Dayr az Zawr, E Syria
Būshehr/Bushire *see* Bandar-e Būshehr
Busra *see* Al Başrah, Iraq
Busselton *147 A7* Western Australia
Bussora *see* Al Başrah
Buta *77 D5* Orientale, N Dem. Rep. Congo
Butembo *77 E5* Nord-Kivu, NE Dem. Rep. Congo
Butler *41 E4* Pennsylvania, NE USA
Buton, Pulau *139 E4 var.* Pulau Butung; *prev.* Boetoeng. *island* C Indonesia
Bütow *see* Bytów
Butte *44 B2* Montana, NW USA
Butterworth *138 B3* Pinang, Peninsular Malaysia
Button Islands *39 E1 island group* Nunavut, NE Canada
Butuan *139 F2 off.* Butuan City. Mindanao, S Philippines
Butuan City *see* Butuan
Butung, Pulau *see* Buton, Pulau
Butuntum *see* Bitonto
Buulobarde *73 D5 var.* Buulo Berde. Hiiraan, C Somalia
Buulo Berde *see* Buulobarde
Buur Gaabo *73 D6* Jubbada Hoose, S Somalia
Buxoro *122 D2 var.* Bokhara, *Rus.* Bukhara. Buxoro Viloyati, C Uzbekistan
Buynaksk *111 B8* Respublika Dagestan, SW Russian Federation
Büyükmenderes Nehri *116 A4 river* SW Turkey
Buzău *108 C4* Buzău, SE Romania
Būzmeyīn *see* Abadan
Buzuluk *111 D6* Orenburgskaya Oblast', W Russian Federation
Byahoml' *107 D5 Rus.* Begoml'. Vitsyebskaya Voblasts', N Belarus
Byalynichy *107 D6 Rus.* Belynichi. Mahilyowskaya Voblasts', E Belarus
Byan Tumen *see* Choybalsan
Byarezina *107 D6 prev.* Byerezino, *Rus.* Berezina. *river* C Belarus
Bydgoszcz *98 C3 Ger.* Bromberg. Kujawski-pomorskie, C Poland
Byelaruskaya Hrada *107 B6 Rus.* Belorusskaya Gryada. *ridge* N Belarus
Byerezino *see* Byarezina
Byron Island *see* Nikunau
Bystrovka *see* Kemin
Bytča *99 C5* Zílinský Kraj, N Slovakia
Bytom *99 C5 Ger.* Beuthen. Śląskie, S Poland
Bytów *98 C2 Ger.* Bütow. Pomorskie, N Poland
Byuzmeyin *see* Abadan
Byval'ki *107 D8* Homyel'skaya Voblasts', SE Belarus
Byzantium *see* İstanbul

C

Caála *78 B2 var.* Kaala, Robert Williams, *Port.* Vila Robert Williams. Huambo, C Angola
Caazapá *64 D3* Caazapá, S Paraguay
Caballo Reservoir *48 C3 reservoir* New Mexico, SW USA
Cabanaquinta *92 D1 var.* Cabañaquinta. Asturias, N Spain
Cabañaquinta *see* Cabanaquinta
Cabanatuan *139 E1 off.* Cabanatuan City. Luzon, N Philippines
Cabanatuan City *see* Cabanatuan
Cabillonum *see* Chalon-sur-Saône
Cabimas *58 C1* Zulia, NW Venezuela
Cabinda *78 A1 var.* Kabinda. Cabinda, NW Angola
Cabinda *78 A1 var.* Kabinda. *province* NW Angola
Lake Cabora Bassa *78 D2 var.* Lake Cabora Bassa. *reservoir* NW Mozambique
Cabora Bassa, Lake *see* Cahora Bassa, Albufeira de
Caborca *50 B1* Sonora, NW Mexico
Cabot Strait *39 G4 strait* E Canada
Cabo Verde, Ilhas do *see* Cape Verde
Cabras, Ilha das *76 E2 island* S Sao Tome and Principe, Africa, E Atlantic Ocean
Cabrera, Illa de *93 G3 island* E Spain
Cáceres *92 C3 Ar.* Qazris. Extremadura, W Spain
Cachimbo, Serra do *63 E2 mountain range* C Brazil
Caconda *78 B2* Huíla, C Angola
Čadca *99 C5 Hung.* Csaca. Zílinský Kraj, N Slovakia
Cadillac *40 C2* Michigan, N USA
Cadiz *139 E2 off.* Cadiz City. Negros, C Philippines
Cádiz *92 C5 anc.* Gades, Gadier, Gadir, Gadire. Andalucía, SW Spain
Cadiz City *see* Cadiz
Gulf of Cadiz *92 B5 Eng.* Gulf of Cadiz. *gulf* Portugal/Spain
Cadiz, Gulf of *see* Cádiz, Golfo de
Cadurcum *see* Cahors
Caen *90 B3* Calvados, N France
Caene/Caenepolis *see* Qinā
Caerdydd *see* Cardiff
Caer Glou *see* Gloucester
Caer Gybi *see* Holyhead
Caerleon *see* Chester
Caer Luel *see* Carlisle
Caesaraugusta *see* Zaragoza
Caesarea Mazaca *see* Kayseri
Caesarobriga *see* Talavera de la Reina
Caesarodunum *see* Tours
Caesaromagus *see* Beauvais
Caesena *see* Cesena
Cafayate *64 C2* Salta, N Argentina
Cagayan de Oro *139 E2 off.* Cagayan de Oro City. Mindanao, S Philippines
Cagayan de Oro City *see* Cagayan de Oro
Cagliari *97 A6 anc.* Caralis. Sardegna, Italy, C Mediterranean Sea
Caguas *55 F3* E Puerto Rico
Cahors *91 C5 anc.* Cadurcum. Lot, S France
Cahul *108 D4 Rus.* Kagul. S Moldova
Caicos Passage *54 D2 strait* Bahamas/ Turks and Caicos Islands
Caiffa *see* Hefa
Cailungo *96 E1* N San Marino
Caiphas *see* Hefa
Cairns *148 D3* Queensland, NE Australia
Cairo *72 B2 var.* El Qâhira, *Ar.* Al Qāhirah. *country capital* (Egypt) N Egypt
Caisleán an Bharraigh *see* Castlebar
Cajamarca *60 B3 prev.* Caxamarca. Cajamarca, NW Peru
Čakovec *100 B2 Ger.* Csakathurn, *Hung.* Csáktornya; *prev. Ger.* Tschakathurn. Medimurje, N Croatia
Calabar *75 G5* Cross River, S Nigeria
Calabozo *58 D2* Guárico, C Venezuela
Calafat *108 B5* Dolj, SW Romania
Calafate *see* El Calafate
Calahorra *93 E2* La Rioja, N Spain
Calais *90 C2* Pas-de-Calais, N France
Calais *41 H2* Maine, NE USA
Calais, Pas de *see* Dover, Strait of
Calama *64 B2* Antofagasta, N Chile
Călăras *see* Călăraşi
Călăraşi *108 D3 var.* Călăras, *Rus.* Kalarash. C Moldova
Călăraşi *108 C5* Călăraşi, SE Romania
Calatayud *93 E2* Aragón, NE Spain
Calbayog *139 E2 off.* Calbayog City. Samar, C Philippines
Calbayog City *see* Calbayog
Calcutta *see* Kolkata
Caldas da Rainha *92 B3* Leiria, W Portugal
Caldera *64 B3* Atacama, N Chile
Caldwell *46 C3* Idaho, NW USA
Caledonia *52 C1* Corozal, N Belize
Caleta Olivia *65 B6* Santa Cruz, SE Argentina
Calgary *37 E5* Alberta, SW Canada
Cali *58 B3* Valle del Cauca, W Colombia
Calicut *see* Kozhikode
California *47 B7 off.* State of California, *also known as* El Dorado, The Golden State. *state* W USA
Gulf of California *50 B2 Eng.* Gulf of California; *prev.* Sea of Cortez. *gulf* W Mexico
California, Gulf of *see* California, Golfo de
Călimăneşti *108 B4* Vâlcea, SW Romania
Calisia *see* Kalisz
Callabonna, Lake *149 B5 lake* South Australia
Callao *60 C4* Callao, W Peru
Callatis *see* Mangalia
Callosa de Segura *93 F4* Valenciana, E Spain
Calmar *see* Kalmar
Caloundra *149 E5* Queensland, E Australia
Caltanissetta *97 C7* Sicilia, Italy, C Mediterranean Sea
Caluula *72 E4* Bari, NE Somalia
Camabatela *78 B1* Cuanza Norte, NW Angola
Camacupa *78 B2 var.* General Machado, *Port.* Vila General Machado. Bié, C Angola
Camagüey *54 C2 prev.* Puerto Príncipe. Camagüey, C Cuba
Camagüey, Archipiélago de *54 C2 island group* C Cuba
Camana *61 E4 var.* Camaná. Arequipa, SW Peru
Camargue *91 D6 physical region* SE France
Ca Mau *137 D6 var.* Quan Long. Minh Hai, S Vietnam
Cambay, Gulf of *see* Khambhāt, Gulf of
Camberia *see* Chambéry
Cambodia *137 D5 off.* Kingdom of Cambodia, *var.* Democratic Kampuchea, Roat Kampuchea, *Cam.* Kampuchea; *prev.* People's Democratic Republic of Kampuchea. *country* SE Asia

CAMBODIA
Southeast Asia

Official name Kingdom of Cambodia
Formation 1953 / 1953
Capital Phnom Penh
Population 14.3 million / 210 people per sq mile (81 people per sq km)
Total area 69,900 sq. miles (181,040 sq. km)
Languages Khmer*, French, Chinese, Vietnamese, Cham
Religions Buddhist 93%, Muslim 6%, Christian 1%
Ethnic mix Khmer 90%, Other 5%, Vietnamese 4%, Chinese 1%
Government Parliamentary system
Currency Riel = 100 sen
Literacy rate 74%
Calorie consumption 2411 kilocalories

Cambodia, Kingdom of *see* Cambodia
Cambrai *90 C2 Flem.* Kambryk, *prev.* Cambray; *anc.* Cameracum. Nord, N France
Cambray *see* Cambrai
Cambrian Mountains *89 C6 mountain range* C Wales, United Kingdom
Cambridge *54 A4* W Jamaica
Cambridge *150 D3* Waikato, North Island, New Zealand
Cambridge *89 E6 Lat.* Cantabrigia. E England, United Kingdom
Cambridge *41 F4* Maryland, NE USA
Cambridge *40 D4* Ohio, NE USA
Cambridge Bay *37 F3 var.* Ikaluktutiak. Victoria Island, Nunavut, NW Canada
Camden *42 B2* Arkansas, C USA
Camellia State *see* Alabama
Cameracum *see* Cambrai
Cameroon *76 A4 off.* Republic of Cameroon, *Fr.* Cameroun. *country* W Africa

CAMEROON
Central Africa

Official name Republic of Cameroon
Formation 1960 / 1961
Capital Yaoundé
Population 22.3 million / 124 people per sq mile (48 people per sq km)

CAMEROON
(continued)

Total area 183,567 sq. miles (475,400 sq. km)
Languages Bamileke, Fang, Fulani, French*, English*
Religions Roman Catholic 35%, Traditional beliefs 25%, Muslim 22%, Protestant 18%
Ethnic mix Cameroon highlanders 31%, Other 21%, Equatorial Bantu 19%, Kirdi 11%, Fulani 10%, Northwestern Bantu 8%
Government Presidential system
Currency CFA franc = 100 centimes
Literacy rate 71%
Calorie consumption 2586 kilocalories

Cameroon, Republic of *see* Cameroon
Cameroun *see* Cameroon
Camocim *63 F2* Ceará, E Brazil
Camopi *59 H3* E French Guiana
Campamento *52 C2* Olancho, C Honduras
Campania *97 D5 Eng.* Champagne. *region* S Italy
Campbell, Cape *151 D5 headland* South Island, New Zealand
Campbell Island *142 D5 island* S New Zealand
Campbell Plateau *142 D5 undersea plateau* SW Pacific Ocean
Campbell River *36 D5* Vancouver Island, British Columbia, SW Canada
Campeche *51 G4* Campeche, SE Mexico
Bay of Campeche *51 F4 Eng.* Bay of Campeche. *bay* E Mexico
Campeche, Bay of *see* Campeche, Bahía de
Cẩm Pha *136 E3* Quang Ninh, N Vietnam
Câmpina *108 C4 prev.* Cîmpina. Prahova, SE Romania
Campina Grande *63 G2* Paraíba, E Braz
Campinas *63 F4* São Paulo, S Brazil
Campobasso *97 D5* Molise, C Italy
Campo Criptana *see* Campo de Criptana
Campo de Criptana *93 E3 var.* Campo Criptana. Castilla-La Mancha, C Spain
Campo Grande *63 E4 state capital* Mato Grosso do Sul, SW Brazil
Campos dos Goytacazes *63 F4* Rio de Janeiro, SE Brazil
Câmpulung *108 B4 prev.* Câmpulung-Muşcel, Cîmpulung. Argeş, S Romani
Câmpulung-Muşcel *see* Câmpulung
Campus Stellae *see* Santiago de Compostela
Cam Ranh *137 E6 prev.* Ba Ngoi. Khanh Hoa, S Vietnam
Canada *34 B4 country* N North America

CANADA
North America

Official name Canada
Formation 1867 / 1949
Capital Ottawa
Population 35.2 million / 10 people per sq mile (4 people per sq km)
Total area 3,854,085 sq. miles (9,984,670 sq. km)
Languages English*, French*, Chinese, Italian, German, Ukrainian, Portuguese, Inuktitut, Cree
Religions Roman Catholic 44%, Protestant 29%, Other and nonreligious 27%
Ethnic mix British, French, and other European 87%, Asian 9%, Amerindian, Métis, and Inuit 4%
Government Parliamentary system
Currency Canadian dollar = 100 cents
Literacy rate 99%
Calorie consumption 3419 kilocalories

Canada Basin *34 C2 undersea basin* Arctic Ocean
Canadian River *49 E2 river* SW USA
Çanakkale *116 A3 var.* Dardanelli; *prev.* Chanak, Kale Sultanie. Çanakkale, W Turkey
Cananea *50 B1* Sonora, NW Mexico
Canarreos, Archipiélago de los *54 B2 island group* W Cuba
Canary Islands *70 A2 Eng.* Canary Islands. *island group* Spain, NE Atlantic Ocean

anary Islands *see* Canarias, Islas
añas *52 D4* Guanacaste, NW Costa Rica
anaveral, Cape *43 E4 headland* Florida, SE USA
anavieiras *63 G3* Bahia, E Brazil
anberra *142 C4 country capital* (Australia) Australian Capital Territory, SE Australia
ancún *51 H3* Quintana Roo, SE Mexico
andia *see* Irákleio
anea *see* Chaniá
angzhou *128 D4* Hebei, E China
aniapiscau *39 E2 river* Québec, E Canada
aniapiscau, Réservoir de *38 D3 reservoir* Québec, C Canada
anik Dağları *116 D2 mountain range* N Turkey
anillo *91 A7* Canillo, C Andorra Europe
ankırı *116 C3 var.* Chankiri; *anc.* Gangra, Germanicopolis. Çankın, N Turkey
annanore *see* Kannur
annes *91 D6* Alpes-Maritimes, SE France
anoas *63 E5* Rio Grande do Sul, S Brazil
anon City *44 C5* Colorado, C USA
antabria *92 D1 autonomous community* N Spain
antábrica, Cordillera *92 C1 mountain range* N Spain
antabrigia *see* Cambridge
antaura *59 E2* Anzoátegui, NE Venezuela
anterbury *89 E7 hist.* Cantwaraburh; *anc.* Durovernum, *Lat.* Cantuaria. SE England, United Kingdom
anterbury Bight *151 C6 bight* South Island, New Zealand
anterbury Plains *151 C6 plain* South Island, New Zealand
ân Thơ *137 E6* Cân Thơ, S Vietnam
anton *42 B2* Mississippi, S USA
anton *40 D4* Ohio, N USA
anton *see* Guangzhou
anton Island *see* Kanton
antuaria/Cantwaraburh *see* Canterbury
anyon *49 E2* Texas, SW USA
ao Băng *136 D3 var.* Caobang. Cao Băng, N Vietnam
aobang *see* Cao Băng
ap-Breton, Île du *see* Cape Breton Island
ape Barren Island *149 C8 island* Furneaux Group, Tasmania, SE Australia
ape Basin *69 B7 undersea basin* S Atlantic Ocean
ape Breton Island *39 G4 Fr.* Île du Cap-Breton. *island* Nova Scotia, SE Canada
ape Charles *41 F5* Virginia, NE USA
ape Coast *75 E5 prev.* Cape Coast Castle. S Ghana
ape Coast Castle *see* Cape Coast
ape Girardeau *45 H5* Missouri, C USA
apelle aan den IJssel *86 C4* Zuid-Holland, SW Netherlands
ape Palmas *see* Harper
ape Saint Jacques *see* Vung Tau
ape Town *78 B5 var.* Ekapa, *Afr.* Kaapstad, Kapstad. *country capital* (South Africa-legislative capital) Western Cape, SW South Africa
ape Verde *74 A2 off.* Republic of Cape Verde, *Port.* Cabo Verde, Ilhas do Cabo Verde. *country* E Atlantic Ocean

CAPE VERDE
Atlantic Ocean

Official name Republic of Cape Verde
Formation 1975 / 1975
Capital Praia
Population 500,000 / 321 people per sq mile (124 people per sq km)
Total area 1557 sq. miles (4033 sq. km)
Languages Portuguese Creole, Portuguese*
Religions Roman Catholic 97%, Other 2%, Protestant (Church of the Nazarene) 1%
Ethnic mix Mestiço 71%, African 28%, European 1%
Government Presidential / parliamentary system
Currency Cape Verde escudo = 100 centavos

CAPE VERDE
(continued)

Literacy rate 85%
Calorie consumption 2716 kilocalories

Cape Verde Basin *66 C4 undersea basin* E Atlantic Ocean
Cape Verde Plain *66 C4 abyssal plain* E Atlantic Ocean
Cape Verde, Republic of *see* Cape Verde
Cape York Peninsula *148 C2 peninsula* Queensland, N Australia
Cap-Haïtien *54 D3 var.* Le Cap. N Haiti
Capira *53 G5* Panamá, C Panama
Capitán Arturo Prat *154 A2 Chilean research station* South Shetland Islands, Antarctica
Capitán Pablo Lagerenza *64 D1 var.* Mayor Pablo Lagerenza. Chaco, N Paraguay
Capodistria *see* Koper
Capri *97 C5 island* S Italy
Caprivi Concession *see* Caprivi Strip
Caprivi Strip *78 C3 Ger.* Caprivizipfel; *prev.* Caprivi Concession. *cultural region* NE Namibia
Caprivizipfel *see* Caprivi Strip
Cap Saint-Jacques *see* Vung Tau
Caquetá, Río *58 C5 var.* Rio Japurá, Yapurá. *river* Brazil/Colombia
Caquetá, Río *see* Japurá, Rio
CAR *see* Central African Republic
Caracal *108 B5* Olt, S Romania
Caracaraí *62 D1* Rondônia, W Brazil
Caracas *58 D1 country capital* (Venezuela) Distrito Federal, N Venezuela
Caralis *see* Cagliari
Caratasca, Laguna de *53 E2 lagoon* NE Honduras
Carballiño *see* O Carballiño
Carbón, Laguna del *64 B7 physical feature* SE Argentina
Carbondale *40 B5* Illinois, N USA
Carbonia *97 A6 var.* Carbonia Centro. Sardegna, Italy, C Mediterranean Sea
Carbonia Centro *see* Carbonia
Carcaso *see* Carcassonne
Carcassonne *91 C6 anc.* Carcaso. Aude, S France
Cardamomes, Chaîne des *see* Krâvanh, Chuŏr Phnum
Cardamom Mountains *see* Krâvanh, Chuŏr Phnum
Cárdenas *54 B2* Matanzas, W Cuba
Cardiff *89 C7 Wel.* Caerdydd. *national capital* S Wales, United Kingdom
Cardigan Bay *89 C6 bay* W Wales, United Kingdom
Carei *108 B3 Ger.* Gross-Karol, Karol, *Hung.* Nagykároly; *prev.* Careii-Mari. Satu Mare, NW Romania
Careii-Mari *see* Carei
Carey, Lake *147 B6 lake* Western Australia
Cariaco *59 E1* Sucre, NE Venezuela
Caribbean Sea *54 C4 sea* W Atlantic Ocean
Caribrod *see* Dimitrovgrad
Carlisle *88 C4 anc.* Caer Luel, Luguvallium, Luguvallum. NW England, United Kingdom
Carlow *89 B6 Ir.* Ceatharlach. SE Ireland
Carlsbad *48 D3* New Mexico, SW USA
Carlsbad *see* Karlovy Vary
Carlsberg Ridge *140 B4 undersea ridge* S Arabian Sea
Carlsruhe *see* Karlsruhe
Carmana/Carmania *see* Kermān
Carmarthen *89 C6* SW Wales, United Kingdom
Carmaux *91 C6* Tarn, S France
Carmel *40 C4* Indiana, N USA
Carmelita *52 B1* Petén, N Guatemala
Carmen *51 G4 var.* Ciudad del Carmen. Campeche, SE Mexico
Carmona *92 C4* Andalucía, S Spain
Carmona *see* Uíge
Carnaro *see* Kvarner
Carnarvon *147 A5* Western Australia
Carnegie, Lake *147 B5 salt lake* Western Australia
Car Nicobar *133 F3 island* Nicobar Islands, India, NE Indian Ocean
Caroạo, Ilha *76 E1 island* N Sao Tome and Principe, Africa, E Atlantic Ocean
Carolina *63 F2* Maranhão, E Brazil
Caroline Island *see* Millennium Island
Caroline Islands *144 B2 island group* C Micronesia
Carolopois *see* Châlons-en-Champagne
Caroní, Río *59 E3 river* E Venezuela
Caronium *see* A Coruña
Carora *58 C1* Lara, N Venezuela
Carpathian Mountains *81 E4 var.* Carpathians, *Cz./Pol.* Karpaty, *Ger.* Karpaten. *mountain range* E Europe
Carpathians *see* Carpathian Mountains
Carpathos/Carpathus *see* Kárpathos
Carpații Sudici *see* Carpații Meridionalii
Carpentaria, Gulf of *148 B2 gulf* N Australia
Carpi *96 C2* Emilia-Romagna, N Italy
Carrara *96 B3* Toscana, C Italy
Carson City *47 C5 state capital* Nevada, W USA
Carson Sink *47 C5 salt flat* Nevada, W USA
Carstensz, Puntjak *see* Jaya, Puncak
Cartagena *58 B1 var.* Cartagena de los Indes. Bolívar, NW Colombia
Cartagena *93 F4 anc.* Carthago Nova. Murcia, SE Spain
Cartagena de los Indes *see* Cartagena
Cartago *53 E4* Cartago, C Costa Rica
Carthage *45 F5* Missouri, C USA
Carthago Nova *see* Cartagena
Cartwright *39 F2* Newfoundland and Labrador, E Canada
Carúpano *59 E1* Sucre, NE Venezuela
Carusbur *see* Cherbourg
Caruthersville *45 H5* Missouri, C USA
Cary *43 F1* North Carolina, SE USA
Casablanca *70 C2 Ar.* Dar-el-Beida. NW Morocco
Casa Grande *48 B2* Arizona, SW USA
Cascade Range *46 B3 mountain range* Oregon/Washington, NW USA
Cascadia Basin *34 A4 undersea basin* NE Pacific Ocean
Cascais *92 B4* Lisboa, C Portugal
Caserta *97 D5* Campania, S Italy
Casey *154 D4 Australian research station* Antarctica
Čáslav *99 B5 Ger.* Tschaslau. Střední Čechy, C Czech Republic
Casper *44 C3* Wyoming, C USA
Caspian Depression *111 B7 Kaz.* Kaspiy Mangy Oypaty, *Rus.* Prikaspiyskaya Nizmennost'. *depression* Kazakhstan/Russian Federation
Caspian Sea *114 A4 Az.* Xăzăr Dănizi, *Kaz.* Kaspiy Tengizi, *Per.* Baḥr-e Khazar, Daryā-ye Khazar, *Rus.* Kaspiyskoye More. *inland sea* Asia/Europe
Cassai *see* Kasai
Cassel *see* Kassel
Castamoni *see* Kastamonu
Casteggio *96 B2* Lombardia, N Italy
Castelló de la Plana *see* Castellón de la Plana
Castellón *see* Castellón de la Plana
Castellón de la Plana *93 F3 var.* Castellón, *Cat.* Castelló de la Plana. Valenciana, E Spain
Castelnaudary *91 C6* Aude, S France
Castelo Branco *92 C3* Castelo Branco, C Portugal
Castelsarrasin *91 B6* Tarn-et-Garonne, S France
Castelvetrano *97 C7* Sicilia, Italy, C Mediterranean Sea
Castilla-La Mancha *93 E3 autonomous community* NE Spain
Castilla y León *92 C2 var.* Castillia Leon. *autonomous community* NW Spain
Castillia Leon *see* Castilla y León
Castlebar *89 A5 Ir.* Caisleán an Bharraigh. W Ireland
Castleford *89 D5* N England, United Kingdom
Castle Harbour *42 B5 inlet* Bermuda, NW Atlantic Ocean
Castra Regina *see* Regensburg
Castricum *86 C3* Noord-Holland, W Netherlands
Castries *55 F1 country capital* (Saint Lucia) N Saint Lucia
Castro *65 B6* Los Lagos, W Chile
Castrovillari *97 D6* Calabria, SW Italy
Castuera *92 D4* Extremadura, W Spain
Caswell Sound *151 A7 sound* South Island, New Zealand
Catacamas *52 D2* Olancho, C Honduras
Catacaos *60 B3* Piura, NW Peru
Catalan Bay *93 H4 bay* E Gibraltar, Mediterranean Sea
Cataluña *93 G2* N Spain
Catamarca *see* San Fernando del Valle de Catamarca
Catania *97 D7* Sicilia, Italy, C Mediterranean Sea
Catanzaro *97 D6* Calabria, SW Italy
Catarroja *93 F3* Valenciana, E Spain
Cat Island *54 C1 island* C Bahamas
Catskill Mountains *41 F3 mountain range* New York, NE USA
Cattaro *see* Kotor
Cauca, Río *58 B2 river* N Colombia
Caucasia *58 B2* Antioquia, NW Colombia
Caucasus *81 G4 Rus.* Kavkaz. *mountain range* Georgia/Russian Federation
Caura, Río *59 E3 river* C Venezuela
Cavaia *see* Kavajë
Cavalla *74 D5 var.* Cavally, Cavally Fleuve. *river* Côte d'Ivoire/Liberia
Cavally/Cavally Fleuve *see* Cavalla
Caviana de Fora, Ilha *63 E1 var.* Ilha Caviana. *island* N Brazil
Caviana, Ilha *see* Caviana de Fora, Ilha
Cawnpore *see* Kānpur
Caxamarca *see* Cajamarca
Caxito *78 B1* Bengo, NW Angola
Cayenne *59 H3 dependent territory/ arrondissement capital* (French Guiana) NE French Guiana
Cayes *54 D3 var.* Les Cayes. SW Haiti
Cayman Brac *54 B3 island* E Cayman Islands
Cayman Islands *54 B3 UK dependent territory* W West Indies
Cayo *see* San Ignacio
Cay Sal *54 B2 islet* SW Bahamas
Cazin *100 B3* Federacija Bosne I Hercegovine, NW Bosnia and Herzegovina
Cazorla *93 E4* Andalucía, S Spain
Ceadâr-Lunga *see* Ciadîr-Lunga
Ceará *63 F2 off.* Estado do Ceará. *region* C Brazil
Ceará *63 F2 off.* Estado do Ceará. *state* C Brazil
Ceará *see* Fortaleza
Ceara Abyssal Plain *see* Ceará Plain
Ceará, Estado do *see* Ceará
Ceará Plain *56 E3 var.* Ceara Abyssal Plain. *abyssal plain* W Atlantic Ocean
Ceatharlach *see* Carlow
Cébaco, Isla *53 F5 island* SW Panama
Cebu *139 E2 off.* Cebu City. Cebu, C Philippines
Cebu City *see* Cebu
Čechy *see* Bohemia
Cecina *96 B3* Toscana, C Italy
Cedar City *44 A5* Utah, W USA
Cedar Falls *45 G3* Iowa, C USA
Cedar Lake *38 A2 lake* Manitoba, C Canada
Cedar Rapids *45 G3* Iowa, C USA
Cedros, Isla *50 A2 island* W Mexico
Ceduna *149 A6* South Australia
Cefalù *97 C7 anc.* Cephaloedium. Sicilia, Italy, C Mediterranean Sea
Celebes *139 E4 Eng.* Celebes. *island* C Indonesia
Celebes *see* Sulawesi
Celebes Sea *139 E3 Ind.* Laut Sulawesi. *sea* Indonesia/Philippines
Celje *95 E7 Ger.* Cilli. C Slovenia
Celldömölk *99 C6* Vas, W Hungary
Celle *94 B3 var.* Zelle. Niedersachsen, N Germany
Celovec *see* Klagenfurt
Celtic Sea *89 B7 Ir.* An Mhuir Cheilteach. *sea* SW British Isles
Celtic Shelf *80 B3 continental shelf* E Atlantic Ocean
Cenderawasih, Teluk *139 G4 var.* Teluk Irian, Teluk Sarera. *bay* W Pacific Ocean
Cenon *91 B5* Gironde, SW France
Centennial State *see* Colorado
Centrafricaine, République *see* Central African Republic

Central African Republic *76 C4 var.* République Centrafricaine, *abbrev.* CAR; *prev.* Ubangi-Shari, Oubangui-Chari, Territoire de l'Oubangui-Chari. *country* C Africa

CENTRAL AFRICAN REPUBLIC
Central Africa

Official name Central African Republic
Formation 1960 / 1960
Capital Bangui
Population 4.6 million / 19 people per sq mile (7 people per sq km)
Total area 240,534 sq. miles (622,984 sq. km)
Languages Sango, Banda, Gbaya, French*
Religions Traditional beliefs 35%, Roman Catholic 25%, Protestant 25%, Muslim 15%
Ethnic mix Baya 33%, Banda 27%, Other 17%, Mandjia 13%, Sara 10%,
Government Presidential system
Currency CFA franc = 100 centimes
Literacy rate 37%
Calorie consumption 2154 kilocalories

Central, Cordillera *58 B3 mountain range* W Colombia
Cordillera Central *55 E3 mountain range* C Dominican Republic
Cordillera Central *53 F5 mountain range* C Panama
Central, Cordillera *139 E1 mountain range* Luzon, N Philippines
Central Group *see* Inner Islands
Centralia *46 B2* Washington, NW USA
Central Indian Ridge *see* Mid-Indian Ridge
Central Makran Range *134 A3 mountain range* W Pakistan
Central Pacific Basin *142 D1 undersea basin* C Pacific Ocean
Central Provinces and Berar *see* Madhya Pradesh
Central Range *144 B3 mountain range* NW Papua New Guinea
Central Russian Upland *109 G1 Eng.* Central Russian Upland. *mountain range* W Russian Federation
Central Russian Upland *see* Srednerusskaya Vozvyshennost'
Central Siberian Plateau *114 D3 var.* Central Siberian Uplands, *Eng.* Central Siberian Plateau. *mountain range* N Russian Federation
Central Siberian Plateau/Central Siberian Uplands *see* Srednesibirskoye Ploskogor'ye
Central, Sistema *92 D3 mountain range* C Spain
Central Valley *47 B6 valley* California, W USA
Centum Cellae *see* Civitavecchia
Ceos *see* Tziá
Cephaloedium *see* Cefalù
Ceram *see* Seram, Pulau
Ceram Sea *see* Laut Seram
Cerasus *see* Giresun
Cereté *58 B2* Córdoba, NW Colombia
Cergy-Pontoise *see* Pontoise
Cerignola *97 D5* Puglia, SE Italy
Çerkeş *116 C2* Çankin, N Turkey
Cernăuţi *see* Chernivtsi
Cernay *90 E4* Haut-Rhin, NE France
Cerro de Pasco *60 C3* Pasco, C Peru
Cervera *93 F2* Cataluña, NE Spain
Cervino, Monte *see* Matterhorn
Cesena *96 C3 anc.* Caesena. Emilia-Romagna, N Italy
Cēsis *106 D3 Ger.* Wenden. C Latvia
Česká Republika *see* Czech Republic
České Budějovice *99 B5 Ger.* Budweis. Jihočeský Kraj, S Czech Republic
Český Krumlov *99 A5 var.* Böhmisch-Krumau, *Ger.* Krummau. Jihočeský Kraj, S Czech Republic
Ceský Les *see* Bohemian Forest
Cetatea Damboviţei *see* Bucureşti
Cetinje *101 C5 It.* Cettigne. S Montenegro
Cette *see* Sète
Cettigne *see* Cetinje
Ceuta *70 C2 enclave* Spain, N Africa
Cévennes *91 C6 mountain range* S France
Ceyhan *116 D4* Adana, S Turkey
Ceylanpınar *117 E4* Şanlıurfa, SE Turkey
Ceylon *see* Sri Lanka
Ceylon Plain *124 B4 abyssal plain* N Indian Ocean
Ceyre to the Caribs *see* Marie-Galante
Chachapoyas *60 B2* Amazonas, NW Peru
Chachevichy *107 D6 Rus.* Chechevichi. Mahilyowskaya Voblasts', E Belarus
Chaco *see* Gran Chaco
Chad *76 C3 off.* Republic of Chad, *Fr.* Tchad. *country* C Africa

CHAD
Central Africa

Official name Republic of Chad
Formation 1960 / 1960
Capital N'Djaména
Population 12.8 million / 26 people per sq mile (10 people per sq km)
Total area 495,752 sq. miles (1,284,000 sq. km)
Languages French*, Sara, Arabic*, Maba
Religions Muslim 51%, Christian 35%, Animist 7%, Traditional beliefs 7%
Ethnic mix Other 30%, Sara 28%, Mayo-Kebbi 12%, Arab 12%, Ouaddai 9%, Kanem-Bornou 9%
Government Presidential system
Currency CFA franc = 100 centimes
Literacy rate 37%
Calorie consumption 2061 kilocalories

Chad, Lake *76 B3 Fr.* Lac Tchad. *lake* C Africa
Chad, Republic of *see* Chad
Chadron *44 D3* Nebraska, C USA
Chadyr-Lunga *see* Ciadîr-Lunga
Chagai Hills *134 A2 var.* Chāh Gay. *mountain range* Afghanistan/Pakistan
Chaghasarāy *see* Asadābād
Chagos-Laccadive Plateau *124 B4 undersea plateau* N Indian Ocean
Chagos Trench *141 C5 trench* N Indian Ocean
Chāh Gay *see* Chāgai Hills
Chaillu, Massif du *77 B6 mountain range* C Gabon
Chain Ridge *140 B4 undersea ridge* W Indian Ocean
Chajul *52 B2* Quiché, W Guatemala
Chakhānsūr *122 D5* Nīmrōz, SW Afghanistan
Chala *60 D4* Arequipa, SW Peru
Chalatenango *52 C3* Chalatenango, N El Salvador
Chalcidice *see* Chalkidikí
Chalcis *see* Chalkída
Chalki *105 E7 island* Dodekánisa, Greece, Aegean Sea
Chalkída *105 C5 var.* Halkida, *prev.* Khalkís; *anc.* Chalcis. Evvoia, E Greece
Chalkidikí *104 C4 var.* Khalkidhikí; *anc.* Chalcidice. *peninsula* NE Greece
Challans *90 B4* Vendée, NW France
Challapata *61 F4* Oruro, SW Bolivia
Challenger Deep *152 B3 trench* W Pacific Ocean
Challenger Deep *see* Mariana Trench
Challenger Fracture Zone *153 F4 tectonic feature* SE Pacific Ocean
Châlons-en-Champagne *90 D3 prev.* Châlons-sur-Marne, *hist.* Arcae Remorum; *anc.* Carolopois. Marne, NE France
Châlons-sur-Marne *see* Châlons-en-Champagne
Chalon-sur-Saône *90 D4 anc.* Cabillonum. Saône-et-Loire, C France
Cha Mai *see* Thung Song
Chaman *134 B2* Baluchistān, SW Pakistan
Chambéry *91 D5 anc.* Camberia. Savoie, E France
Champagne *90 D3 cultural region* N France
Champagne *see* Campania
Champaign *40 B4* Illinois, N USA
Champasak *137 D5* Champasak, S Laos
Champlain, Lake *41 F2 lake* Canada/USA
Champotón *51 G4* Campeche, SE Mexico
Chanak *see* Çanakkale
Chañaral *64 B3* Atacama, N Chile
Chan-chiang/Chanchiang *see* Zhanjiang
Chandeleur Islands *42 C3 island group* Louisiana, S USA
Chandīgarh *134 D2 state capital* Punjab, N India
Chandrapur *135 E5* Mahārāshtra, C India
Changan *see* Xi'an, Shaanxi, C China
Changane *79 E3 river* S Mozambique
Changchun *128 D3 var.* Ch'angch'un, Ch'ang-ch'un; *prev.* Hsinking. *province capital* Jilin, NE China
Ch'angch'un/Ch'ang-ch'un *see* Changchun
Chang Jiang *128 A5 Eng.* Yangtze; *var.* Yangtze Kiang. *river* SW China
Changkiakow *see* Zhangjiakou
Chang, Ko *137 C6 island* S Thailand
Changsha *128 C5 var.* Ch'angsha, Ch'ang-sha. *province capital* Hunan, S China
Ch'angsha/Ch'ang-sha *see* Changsha
Changzhi *128 C4* Shanxi, C China
Chaniá *105 C7 var.* Hania, Khaniá, *Eng.* Canea; *anc.* Cydonia. Kríti, Greece, E Mediterranean Sea
Chañi, Nevado de *64 B2 mountain* NW Argentina
Chankiri *see* Çankırı
Channel Islands *89 C8 Fr.* Iles Normandes. *island group* S English Channel
Channel Islands *47 B8 island group* California, W USA
Channel-Port aux Basques *39 G4* Newfoundland and Labrador, SE Canada
Channel, The *see* English Channel
Channel Tunnel *90 C2 tunnel* France/United Kingdom
Chantabun/Chantaburi *see* Chanthaburi
Chantada *92 C1* Galicia, NW Spain
Chanthaburi *137 C6 var.* Chantabun, Chantaburi. Chantaburi, S Thailand
Chanute *45 F5* Kansas, C USA
Chaouèn *see* Chefchaouen
Chaoyang *128 D3* Liaoning, NE China
Chapala, Lago de *50 D4 lake* C Mexico
Chapan, Gora *122 B3 mountain* C Turkmenistan
Chapayevsk *111 C6* Samarskaya Oblast', W Russian Federation
Chaplynka *109 F4* Khersons'ka Oblast', S Ukraine
Chapra *see* Chhapra
Charcot Seamounts *80 B3 seamount range* E Atlantic Ocean
Chardzhev *see* Türkmenabat
Chardzhou/Chardzhui *see* Türkmenabat
Charente *91 B5 cultural region* W France
Charente *91 B5 river* W France
Chari *76 B3 var.* Shari. *river* Central African Republic/Chad
Chārīkār *123 E4* Parwān, NE Afghanistan
Charity *59 F2* NW Guyana
Chärjew *see* Türkmenabat
Charkhlik/Charkhliq *see* Ruoqiang
Charleroi *87 C7* Hainaut, S Belgium
Charlesbourg *39 E4* Québec, SE Canada
Charles de Gaulle *90 E1* (Paris) Seine-et-Marne, N France
Charles Island *38 D1 island* Nunavut, NE Canada
Charles Island *see* Santa María, Isla
Charleston *43 F2* South Carolina, SE USA
Charleston *40 D5 state capital* West Virginia, NE USA
Charleville *149 D5* Queensland, E Australia
Charleville-Mézières *90 D3* Ardennes, N France
Charlie-Gibbs Fracture Zone *66 C2 tectonic feature* N Atlantic Ocean
Charlotte *43 E1* North Carolina, SE USA
Charlotte Amalie *55 F3 prev.* Saint Thomas. *dependent territory capital* (Virgin Islands (US)) Saint Thomas, N Virgin Islands (US)
Charlotte Harbor *43 E5 inlet* Florida, SE USA
Charlottenhof *see* Aegviidu
Charlottesville *41 E5* Virginia, NE USA
Charlottetown *39 F4 province capital* Prince Edward Island, Prince Edward Island, SE Canada
Charlotte Town *see* Roseau, Dominica
Charsk *see* Shar
Charters Towers *148 D3* Queensland, NE Australia
Chartres *90 C3 anc.* Autricum, Civitas Carnutum. Eure-et-Loir, C France
Chashniki *107 D5* Vitsyebskaya Voblasts', N Belarus
Châteaubriant *90 B4* Loire-Atlantique, NW France
Châteaudun *90 C3* Eure-et-Loir, C France
Châteauroux *90 C4 prev.* Indreville. Indre, C France
Château-Thierry *90 C3* Aisne, N France
Châtelet *87 C7* Hainaut, S Belgium
Châtelherault *see* Châtellerault
Châtellerault *90 B4 var.* Châtelherault. Vienne, W France
Chatham Island *see* San Cristóbal, Isla
Chatham Island Rise *see* Chatham Rise
Chatham Islands *143 E5 island group* New Zealand, SW Pacific Ocean
Chatham Rise *142 D5 var.* Chatham Island Rise. *undersea rise* S Pacific Ocean
Chatkal Range *123 F2 Rus.* Chatkal'skiy Khrebet. *mountain range* Kyrgyzstan/Uzbekistan
Chatkal'skiy Khrebet *see* Chatkal Range
Chāttagām *see* Chittagong
Chattahoochee River *42 D3 river* SE USA
Chattanooga *42 D1* Tennessee, S USA
Chatyr-Tash *123 G2* Narynskaya Oblast', C Kyrgyzstan
Châu Đốc *137 D6 var.* Chauphu, Chau Phu. An Giang, S Vietnam
Chauk *136 A3* Magway, W Myanmar (Burma)
Chaumont *90 D4 prev.* Chaumont-en-Bassigny. Haute-Marne, N France
Chaumont-en-Bassigny *see* Chaumont
Chau Phu *see* Châu Đốc
Chausy *see* Chavusy
Chaves *92 C2 anc.* Aquae Flaviae. Vila Real, N Portugal
Chávez, Isla *see* Santa Cruz, Isla
Chavusy *107 E6 Rus.* Chausy. Mahilyowskaya Voblasts', E Belarus
Chaykovskiy *111 D5* Permskiy Kray, NW Russian Federation
Cheb *99 A5 Ger.* Eger. Karlovarský Kraj, W Czech Republic
Cheboksary *111 C5* Chuvashskaya Respublika, W Russian Federation
Cheboygan *40 C2* Michigan, N USA
Chechaouèn *see* Chefchaouen
Chech, Erg *74 D1 desert* Algeria/Mali
Chechevichi *see* Chachevichy
Che-chiang *see* Zhejiang
Cheduba Island *136 A4 island* W Myanmar (Burma)
Chefchaouen *70 C2 var.* Chaouèn, Chechaouèn, *Sp.* Xauen. N Morocco
Chefoo *see* Yantai
Cheju-do *see* Jeju-do
Cheju Strait *see* Jeju Strait
Chekiang *see* Zhejiang
Cheleken *see* Hazar
Chelkar *see* Shalkar
Chełm *98 E4 Rus.* Kholm. Lubelskie, SE Poland
Chełmno *98 C3 Ger.* Culm, Kulm. Kujawski-pomorskie, C Poland
Chełmża *98 C3 Ger.* Culmsee, Kulmsee. Kujawski-pomorskie, C Poland
Cheltenham *89 D6* C England, United Kingdom
Chelyabinsk *114 C3* Chelyabinskaya Oblast', C Russian Federation
Chemnitz *94 D4 prev.* Karl-Marx-Stadt. Sachsen, E Germany
Chemulpo *see* Incheon
Chenāb *134 C2 river* India/Pakistan
Chengchiatun *see* Liaoyuan
Ch'eng-chou/Chengchow *see* Zhengzhou
Chengde *128 D3 var.* Jehol. Hebei, E China
Chengdu *128 B5 var.* Chengtu, Ch'eng-tu. *province capital* Sichuan, C China
Chenghsien *see* Zhengzhou
Chengtu/Ch'eng-tu *see* Chengdu
Chennai *132 D2 prev.* Madras. *state capital* Tamil Nādu, S India
Chenstokhov *see* Częstochowa
Chen Xian/Chenxian/Chen Xiang *see* Chenzhou
Chenzhou *128 C6 var.* Chenxian, Chen Xian, Chen Xiang. Hunan, S China
Chepelare *104 C3* Smolyan, S Bulgaria
Chepén *60 B3* La Libertad, C Peru
Cher *90 C4 river* C France
Cherbourg *90 B3 anc.* Carusbur. Manche, N France

herepovets *110 B4* Vologodskaya Oblast', NW Russian Federation
hergui, Chott ech *70 D2 salt lake* NW Algeria
herikov *see* Cherykaw
Cherkassy *see* Cherkasy
Cherkasy *109 E2 Rus.* Cherkassy. Cherkas'ka Oblast', C Ukraine
herkessk *111 B7* Karachayevo-Cherkesskaya Respublika, SW Russian Federation
hernigov *see* Chernihiv
hernihiv *109 E1 Rus.* Chernigov. Chernihivs'ka Oblast', NE Ukraine
hernivtsi *108 C3 Ger.* Czernowitz, *Rom.* Cernăuţi, *Rus.* Chernovtsy. Chernivets'ka Oblast', W Ukraine
Cherno More *see* Black Sea
Chernomorskoye *see* Chornomors'ke
Chernovtsy *see* Chernivtsi
Chernoye More *see* Black Sea
Chernyakhovsk *106 A4 Ger.* Insterburg. Kaliningradskaya Oblast', W Russian Federation
Cherry Hill *41 F4* New Jersey, NE USA
Cherski Range *see* Cherskogo, Khrebet
herskiy *115 G2* Respublika Sakha (Yakutiya), NE Russian Federation
herskogo, Khrebet *115 F2 var.* Cherski Range. *mountain range* NE Russian Federation
Cherso *see* Cres
Cherven' *see* Chervyen'
Chervonograd *see* Chervonohrad
Chervonohrad *108 C2 Rus.* Chervonograd. L'vivs'ka Oblast', NW Ukraine
Chervyen' *107 D6 Rus.* Cherven'. Minskaya Voblasts', C Belarus
Cherykaw *107 E7 Rus.* Cherikov. Mahilyowskaya Voblasts', E Belarus
Chesapeake Bay *41 F5 inlet* NE USA
hesha Bay *see* Chëshskaya Guba
Chëshskaya Guba *155 D5 var.* Archangel Bay, Chesha Bay, Dvina Bay. *bay* NW Russian Federation
Chester *89 C6 Wel.* Caerleon, *hist.* Legaceaster, *Lat.* Deva, Devana Castra. C England, United Kingdom
Chetumal *51 H4 var.* Payo Obispo. Quintana Roo, SE Mexico
Cheviot Hills *88 D4 hill range* England/ Scotland, United Kingdom
Cheyenne *44 D4 state capital* Wyoming, C USA
Cheyenne River *44 D3 river* South Dakota/Wyoming, N USA
Chezdi-Oşorheiu *see* Târgu Secuiesc
Chhapra *135 F3 prev.* Chapra. Bihār, N India
Chhattīsgarh *135 E4 cultural region* E India
Chia-i *see* Jiayi
Chiai *see* Jiayi
Chiang-hsi *see* Jiangxi
Chiang Mai *136 B4 var.* Chiangmai, Chiengmai, Kiangmai. Chiang Mai, NW Thailand
Chiangmai *see* Chiang Mai
Chiang Rai *136 C3 var.* Chianpai, Chienrai, Muang Chiang Rai. Chiang Rai, NW Thailand
Chiang-su *see* Jiangsu
Chianning/Chian-ning *see* Nanjing
Chianpai *see* Chiang Rai
Chianti *96 C3 cultural region* C Italy
Chiapa *see* Chiapa de Corzo
Chiapa de Corzo *51 G5 var.* Chiapa. Chiapas, SE Mexico
Chiayi *see* Jiayi
Chiba *130 B1 var.* Tiba. Chiba, Honshū, S Japan
Chibougamau *38 D3* Québec, SE Canada
Chicago *40 B3* Illinois, N USA
Ch'i-ch'i-ha-erh *see* Qiqihar
Chickasha *49 G2* Oklahoma, C USA
Chiclayo *60 B3* Lambayeque, NW Peru
Chico *47 B5* California, W USA
Chico, Río *65 B7 river* SE Argentina
Chico, Río *65 B6 river* S Argentina
Chicoutimi *39 E4* Québec, SE Canada
Chiengmai *see* Chiang Mai
Chienrai *see* Chiang Rai
Chiesanuova *96 D2* SW San Marino
Chieti *96 D4 var.* Teate. Abruzzo, C Italy
Chifeng *127 G2 var.* Ulanhad. Nei Mongol Zizhiqu, N China
Chigirin *see* Chyhyryn
Chih-fu *see* Yantai
Chihli *see* Hebei
Chihli, Gulf of *see* Bo Hai
Chihuahua *50 C2* Chihuahua, NW Mexico
Childress *49 F2* Texas, SW USA
Chile *64 B3 off.* Republic of Chile. *country* SW South America

CHILE
South America

Official name Republic of Chile
Formation 1818 / 1883
Capital Santiago
Population 17.6 million / 61 people per sq mile (24 people per sq km)
Total area 292,258 sq. miles (756,950 sq. km)
Languages Spanish*, Amerindian languages
Religions Roman Catholic 89%, Other and nonreligious 11%
Ethnic mix Mestizo and European 90%, Other Amerindian 9%, Mapuche 1%
Government Presidential system
Currency Chilean peso = 100 centavos
Literacy rate 99%
Calorie consumption 2989 kilocalories

Chile Basin *57 A5 undersea basin* E Pacific Ocean
Chile Chico *65 B6* Aisén, W Chile
Chile, Republic of *see* Chile
Chile Rise *57 A7 undersea rise* SE Pacific Ocean
Chilia-Nouă *see* Kiliya
Chililabombwe *78 D2* Copperbelt, C Zambia
Chi-lin *see* Jilin
Chillán *65 B5* Bío Bío, C Chile
Chillicothe *40 D4* Ohio, N USA
Chill Mhantáin, Sléibhte *see* Wicklow Mountains
Chiloé, Isla de *65 A6 var.* Isla Grande de Chiloé. *island* W Chile
Chilpancingo *51 E5 var.* Chilpancingo de los Bravos. Guerrero, S Mexico
Chilpancingo de los Bravos *see* Chilpancingo
Chilung *see* Jilong
Chimán *53 G5* Panamá, E Panama
Chimbay *see* Chimboy
Chimborazo *60 A1 volcano* C Ecuador
Chimbote *60 C3* Ancash, W Peru
Chimboy *122 D1 Rus.* Chimbay. Qoraqalpog'iston Respublikasi, NW Uzbekistan
Chimkent *see* Shymkent
Chimoio *79 E3* Manica, C Mozambique
China *124 C2 off.* People's Republic of China, *Chin.* Chung-hua Jen-min Kung-ho-kuo, Zhonghua Renmin Gongheguo; *prev.* Chinese Empire. . *country* E Asia

CHINA
East Asia

Official name People's Republic of China
Formation 960 / 1999
Capital Beijing
Population 1.39 billion / 385 people per sq mile (149 people per sq km)
Total area 3,705,386 sq. miles (9,596,960 sq. km)
Languages Mandarin*, Wu, Cantonese, Hsiang, Min, Hakka, Kan
Religions Nonreligious 59%, Traditional beliefs 20%, Other 13%, Buddhist 6%, Muslim 2%
Ethnic mix Han 92%, Other 4%, Hui 1%, Miao 1%, Manchu 1%, Zhuang 1%
Government One-party state
Currency Renminbi (known as yuan) = 10 jiao = 100 fen
Literacy rate 95%
Calorie consumption 3074 kilocalories

Chi-nan/Chinan *see* Jinan
Chinandega *52 C3* Chinandega, NW Nicaragua
China, People's Republic of *see* China
China, Republic of *see* Taiwan
Chincha Alta *60 D4* Ica, SW Peru
Chin-chiang *see* Quanzhou
Chin-chou/Chinchow *see* Jinzhou
Chindwin *see* Chindwinn
Chindwinn *136 B2 var.* Chindwin. *river* N Myanmar (Burma)
Chinese Empire *see* China
Chinghai *see* Qinghai
Ch'ing Hai *see* Qinghai Hu, China
Chingola *78 D2* Copperbelt, C Zambia
Ching-Tao/Ch'ing-tao *see* Qingdao
Chinguetti *74 C2 var.* Chinguetti. Adrar, C Mauritania
Chin Hills *136 A3 mountain range* W Myanmar (Burma)
Chinhsien *see* Jinzhou
Chinnereth *see* Tiberias, Lake
Chinook Trough *113 H4 trough* N Pacific Ocean
Chioggia *96 C2 anc.* Fossa Claudia. Veneto, NE Italy
Chíos *105 D5 var.* Hios, Khíos, *It.* Scio, *Turk.* Sakiz-Adasi. Chíos, E Greece
Chíos *105 D5 var.* Khíos. *island* E Greece
Chipata *78 D2 prev.* Fort Jameson. Eastern, E Zambia
Chiquián *60 C3* Ancash, W Peru
Chiquimula *52 B2* Chiquimula, SE Guatemala
Chīrāla *132 D1* Andhra Pradesh, E India
Chirchik *see* Chirchiq
Chirchiq *123 E2 Rus.* Chirchik. Toshkent Viloyati, E Uzbekistan
Chiriqui Gulf *53 E5 Eng.* Chiriqui Gulf. *gulf* SW Panama
Chiriqui Gulf *see* Chiriquí, Golfo de
Chiriquí, Laguna de *53 E5 lagoon* NW Panama
Chiriquí, Volcán de *see* Barú, Volcán
Chirripó, Cerro *see* Chirripó Grande, Cerro
Chirripó Grande, Cerro *52 D4 var.* Cerro Chirripó. *mountain* SE Costa Rica
Chisec *52 B2* Alta Verapaz, C Guatemala
Chisholm *45 F1* Minnesota, N USA
Chisimaio/Chisimayu *see* Kismaayo
Chişinău *108 D4 Rus.* Kishinev. *country capital* (Moldova) C Moldova
Chita *115 F4* Zabaykal'skiy Kray, S Russian Federation
Chitangwiza *see* Chitungwiza
Chitato *78 C1* Lunda Norte, NE Angola
Chitina *36 D3* Alaska, USA
Chitose *130 D2 var.* Titose. Hokkaidō, NE Japan
Chitré *53 F5* Herrera, S Panama
Chittagong *135 G4 Ben.* Chāttagām. Chittagong, SE Bangladesh
Chitungwiza *78 D3 prev.* Chitangwiza. Mashonaland East, NE Zimbabwe
Chkalov *see* Orenburg
Chlef *70 D2 var.* Ech Cheliff, Ech Chleff; *prev.* Al-Asnam, El Asnam, Orléansville. NW Algeria
Chocolate Mountains *47 D8 mountain range* California, W USA
Chodorów *see* Khodoriv
Chodzież *98 C3* Wielkopolskie, C Poland
Choele Choel *65 C5* Río Negro, C Argentina
Choiseul *144 C3 var.* Lauru. *island* NW Solomon Islands
Chojnice *98 C2 Ger.* Konitz. Pomorskie, N Poland
Ch'ok'ē *72 C4 var.* Choke Mountains. *mountain range* NW Ethiopia
Choke Mountains *see* Ch'ok'ē
Cholet *90 B4* Maine-et-Loire, NW France
Choluteca *52 C3* Choluteca, S Honduras
Choluteca, Río *52 C3 river* SW Honduras
Choma *78 D2* Southern, S Zambia
Chomutov *98 A4 Ger.* Komotau. Ústecký Kraj, NW Czech Republic
Chona *113 E2 river* C Russian Federation
Chon Buri *137 C5 prev.* Bang Pla Soi. Chon Buri, S Thailand
Chone *60 A1* Manabí, W Ecuador
Ch'ŏngjin *129 E3* NE North Korea
Chongqing *129 B5 var.* Ch'ung-ching, Ch'ung-ch'ing, Chungking, Pahsien, Tchongking, Yuzhou. Chongqing Shi, C China
Chongqing Shi *129 B5 province* C China
Chonnacht *see* Connaught
Chonos, Archipiélago de los *65 A6 island group* S Chile
Chóra *105 D7* Kykládes, Greece, Aegean Sea
Chóra Sfakíon *105 C8 var.* Sfákia. Kríti, Greece, E Mediterranean Sea
Chorne More *see* Black Sea
Chornomors'ke *109 E4 Rus.* Chernomorskoye. Avtonomna Respublika Krym, S Ukraine
Chorokh/Chorokhi *see* Çoruh Nehri
Chortkiv *108 C2 Rus.* Chortkov. Ternopil's'ka Oblast', W Ukraine
Chortkov *see* Chortkiv
Chorzów *99 C5 Ger.* Königshütte; *prev.* Królewska Huta. Śląskie, S Poland
Chośebuz *see* Cottbus
Chōsen-kaikyō *see* Korea Strait
Chōshi *131 D5 var.* Tyôsi. Chiba, Honshū, S Japan
Chosŏn-minjujuŭi-inmin-kanghwaguk *see* North Korea
Choszczno *98 B3 Ger.* Arnswalde. Zachodnio-pomorskie, NW Poland
Chota Nagpur *135 E4 plateau* N India
Choûm *74 C2* Adrar, C Mauritania
Choybalsan *127 F2 prev.* Byan Tumen. Dornod, E Mongolia
Christchurch *151 C6* Canterbury, South Island, New Zealand
Christiana *54 B5* C Jamaica
Christiania *see* Oslo
Christiansand *see* Kristiansand
Christianshåb *see* Qasigiannguit
Christiansund *see* Kristiansund
Christmas Island *141 D5 Australian external territory* E Indian Ocean
Christmas Island *see* Kiritimati
Christmas Ridge *143 E1 undersea ridge* C Pacific Ocean
Chuan *see* Sichuan
Ch'uan-chou *see* Quanzhou
Chubek *see* Moskva
Chubut, Río *65 B6 river* SE Argentina
Ch'u-chiang *see* Shaoguan
Chudskoye Ozero *see* Peipus, Lake
Chugoku-sanchi *131 B6 mountain range* Honshū, SW Japan
Chuí *see* Chuy
Chukai *see* Cukai
Chukchi Plain *155 B2 abyssal plain* Arctic Ocean
Chukchi Plateau *34 C2 undersea plateau* Arctic Ocean
Chukchi Sea *34 B2 Rus.* Chukotskoye More. *sea* Arctic Ocean
Chukotskoye More *see* Chukchi Sea
Chula Vista *47 C8* California, W USA
Chulucanas *60 B2* Piura, NW Peru
Chulym *114 D4 river* C Russian Federation
Chumphon *137 C6 var.* Jumporn. Chumphon, SW Thailand
Chuncheon *129 E4 prev.* Ch'unch'ŏn, *Jap.* Shunsen. N South Korea
Ch'unch'ŏn *see* Chuncheon
Ch'ung-ch'ing/Ch'ung-ching *see* Chongqing
Chung-hua Jen-min Kung-ho-kuo *see* China
Chungking *see* Chongqing
Chunya *115 E3 river* C Russian Federation
Chuquicamata *64 B2* Antofagasta, N Chile
Chuquisaca *see* Sucre
Chur *95 B7 Fr.* Coire, *It.* Coira, *Rmsch.* Cuera, Quera; *anc.* Curia Rhaetorum. Graubünden, E Switzerland
Churchill *37 G4* Manitoba, C Canada
Churchill *38 B2 river* Manitoba/ Saskatchewan, C Canada
Churchill *39 F2 river* Newfoundland and Labrador, E Canada
Chuska Mountains *48 C1 mountain range* Arizona/New Mexico, SW USA
Chusovoy *111 D5* Permskiy Kray, NW Russian Federation
Chust *see* Khust
Chuuk Islands *144 B2 var.* Hogoley Islands; *prev.* Truk Islands. *island group* Caroline Islands, C Micronesia
Chuy *64 E4 var.* Chuí. Rocha, E Uruguay
Chyhyryn *109 E2 Rus.* Chigirin. Cherkas'ka Oblast', N Ukraine
Ciadîr-Lunga *108 D4 var.* Ceadâr-Lunga, *Rus.* Chadyr-Lunga. S Moldova
Cide *116 C2* Kastamonu, N Turkey
Ciechanów *98 D3 prev.* Zichenau. Mazowieckie, C Poland
Ciego de Ávila *54 C2* Ciego de Ávila, C Cuba
Ciénaga *58 B1* Magdalena, N Colombia
Cienfuegos *54 B2* Cienfuegos, C Cuba
Cieza *93 E4* Murcia, SE Spain
Cihanbeyli *116 C3* Konya, C Turkey

Cikobia *145 E4 prev.* Thikombia. *island* N Fiji
Cilacap *138 C5 prev.* Tjilatjap. Jawa, C Indonesia
Cill Airne *see* Killarney
Cill Chainnigh *see* Kilkenny
Cilli *see* Celje
Cill Mhantáin *see* Wicklow
Cîmpina *see* Câmpina
Cîmpulung *see* Câmpulung
Cina Selatan, Laut *see* South China Sea
Cincinnati *40 C4* Ohio, N USA
Ciney *87 C7* Namur, SE Belgium
Cinto, Monte *91 E7 mountain* Corse, France, C Mediterranean Sea
Cintra *see* Sintra
Cipolletti *65 B5* Río Negro, C Argentina
Cirebon *138 C4 prev.* Tjirebon. Jawa, S Indonesia
Cirkvenica *see* Crikvenica
Cirò Marina *97 E6* Calabria, S Italy
Cirquenizza *see* Crikvenica
Cisnădie *108 B4 Ger.* Heltau, *Hung.* Nagydisznód. Sibiu, SW Romania
Citharista *see* la Ciotat
Citlaltépetl *see* Orizaba, Volcán Pico de
Citrus Heights *47 B5* California, W USA
Ciudad Acuña *see* Villa Acuña
Ciudad Bolívar *59 E2 prev.* Angostura. Bolívar, E Venezuela
Ciudad Camargo *50 D2* Chihuahua, N Mexico
Ciudad Cortés *see* Cortés
Ciudad Darío *52 D3 var.* Dario. Matagalpa, W Nicaragua
Ciudad de Dolores Hidalgo *see* Dolores Hidalgo
Ciudad de Guatemala *52 B2 Eng.* Guatemala City; *prev.* Santiago de los Caballeros. *country capital* (Guatemala) Guatemala, C Guatemala
Ciudad del Carmen *see* Carmen
Ciudad del Este *64 E2 prev.* Ciudad Presidente Stroessner, Presidente Stroessner, Puerto Presidente Stroessner. Alto Paraná, SE Paraguay
Ciudad Delicias *see* Delicias
Ciudad de México *see* México
Ciudad de Panama *see* Panamá
Ciudad Guayana *59 E2 prev.* San Tomé de Guayana, Santo Tomé de Guayana. Bolívar, NE Venezuela
Ciudad Guzmán *50 D4* Jalisco, SW Mexico
Ciudad Hidalgo *51 G5* Chiapas, SE Mexico
Ciudad Juárez *50 C1* Chihuahua, N Mexico
Ciudad Lerdo *50 D3* Durango, C Mexico
Ciudad Madero *51 E3 var.* Villa Cecilia. Tamaulipas, C Mexico
Ciudad Mante *51 E3* Tamaulipas, C Mexico
Ciudad Miguel Alemán *51 E2* Tamaulipas, C Mexico
Ciudad Obregón *50 B2* Sonora, NW Mexico
Ciudad Ojeda *58 C1* Zulia, NW Venezuela
Ciudad Porfirio Díaz *see* Piedras Negras
Ciudad Presidente Stroessner *see* Ciudad del Este
Ciudad Quesada *see* Quesada
Ciudad Real *92 D3* Castilla-La Mancha, C Spain
Ciudad-Rodrigo *92 C3* Castilla y León, N Spain
Ciudad Trujillo *see* Santo Domingo
Ciudad Valles *51 E3* San Luis Potosí, C Mexico
Ciudad Victoria *51 E3* Tamaulipas, C Mexico
Ciutadella *93 H3 var.* Ciutadella de Menorca. Menorca, Spain, W Mediterranean Sea
Ciutadella Ciutadella de Menorca *see* Ciutadella
Civitanova Marche *96 D3* Marche, C Italy
Civitas Altae Ripae *see* Brzeg
Civitas Carnutum *see* Chartres
Civitas Eburovicum *see* Évreux
Civitavecchia *96 C4 anc.* Centum Cellae, Trajani Portus. Lazio, C Italy
Claremore *49 G1* Oklahoma, C USA
Clarence *151 C5* Canterbury, South Island, New Zealand
Clarence *151 C5 river* South Island, New Zealand
Clarence Town *54 D2* Long Island, C Bahamas
Clarinda *45 F4* Iowa, C USA
Clarion Fracture Zone *153 E2 tectonic feature* NE Pacific Ocean
Clarión, Isla *50 A5 island* W Mexico
Clark Fork *44 A1 river* Idaho/Montana, NW USA
Clark Hill Lake *43 E2 var.* J.Storm Thurmond Reservoir. *reservoir* Georgia/South Carolina, SE USA
Clarksburg *40 D4* West Virginia, NE USA
Clarksdale *42 B2* Mississippi, S USA
Clarksville *42 C1* Tennessee, S USA
Clausentum *see* Southampton
Clayton *49 E1* New Mexico, SW USA
Clearwater *43 E4* Florida, SE USA
Clearwater Mountains *46 D2 mountain range* Idaho, NW USA
Cleburne *49 G3* Texas, SW USA
Clermont *148 D4* Queensland, E Australia
Clermont-Ferrand *91 C5* Puy-de-Dôme, C France
Cleveland *40 D3* Ohio, N USA
Cleveland *42 D1* Tennessee, S USA
Clifton *48 C2* Arizona, SW USA
Clinton *42 B2* Mississippi, S USA
Clinton *49 F1* Oklahoma, C USA
Clipperton Fracture Zone *153 E3 tectonic feature* E Pacific Ocean
Clipperton Island *35 A7 French dependency of French Polynesia* E Pacific Ocean
Cloncurry *148 B3* Queensland, C Australia
Clonmel *89 B6 Ir.* Cluain Meala. S Ireland
Cloppenburg *94 B3* Niedersachsen, NW Germany
Cloquet *45 G2* Minnesota, N USA
Cloud Peak *44 C3 mountain* Wyoming, C USA
Clovis *49 E2* New Mexico, SW USA
Cluain Meala *see* Clonmel
Cluj *see* Cluj-Napoca
Cluj-Napoca *108 B3 Ger.* Klausenburg, *Hung.* Kolozsvár; *prev.* Cluj. Cluj, NW Romania
Clutha *151 B7 river* South Island, New Zealand
Clyde *88 C4 river* W Scotland, United Kingdom
Coari *62 D2* Amazonas, N Brazil
Coast Mountains *36 D4 Fr.* Chaîne Côtière. *mountain range* Canada/USA
Coast Ranges *46 A4 mountain range* W USA
Coats Island *37 G3 island* Nunavut, NE Canada
Coats Land *154 B2 physical region* Antarctica
Coatzacoalcos *51 G4 var.* Quetzalcoalco; *prev.* Puerto México. Veracruz-Llave, E Mexico
Cobán *52 B2* Alta Verapaz, C Guatemala
Cobar *149 C6* New South Wales, SE Australia
Cobija *61 E3* Pando, NW Bolivia
Coblence/Coblenz *see* Koblenz
Coburg *95 C5* Bayern, SE Germany
Coca *see* Puerto Francisco de Orellana
Cocanada *see* Kākināda
Cochabamba *61 F4 hist.* Oropeza. Cochabamba, C Bolivia
Cochin *see* Kochi
Cochrane *38 C4* Ontario, S Canada
Cochrane *65 B7* Aisén, S Chile
Cocibolca *see* Nicaragua, Lago de
Cockade State *see* Maryland
Cockburn Town *55 E2* San Salvador, E Bahamas
Cockpit Country, The *54 A4 physical region* W Jamaica
Cocobeach *77 A5* Estuaire, NW Gabon
Coconino Plateau *48 B1 plain* Arizona, SW USA
Coco, Río *53 E2 var.* Río Wanki, Segoviao Wangkí. *river* Honduras/Nicaragua
Cocos Basin *124 C5 undersea basin* E Indian Ocean
Cocos Island Ridge *see* Cocos Ridge
Cocos Islands *141 D5 island group* E Indian Ocean
Cocos Ridge *35 C8 var.* Cocos Island Ridge. *undersea ridge* E Pacific Ocean
Cod, Cape *41 G3 headland* Massachusetts, NE USA
Codfish Island *151 A8 island* SW New Zealand
Codlea *108 C4 Ger.* Zeiden, *Hung.* Feketehalom. Brașov, C Romania
Cody *44 C2* Wyoming, C USA
Coeur d'Alene *46 C2* Idaho, NW USA
Coevorden *86 E2* Drenthe, NE Netherlands
Coffs Harbour *149 E6* New South Wales, SE Australia
Cognac *91 B5 anc.* Compniacum. Charente, W France
Cohalm *see* Rupea
Coiba, Isla de *53 E5 island* SW Panama
Coihaique *65 B6 var.* Coyhaique. Aisén, S Chile
Coimbatore *132 C3* Tamil Nādu, S India
Coimbra *92 B3 anc.* Conimbria, Conimbriga. Coimbra, W Portugal
Coín *92 D5* Andalucía, S Spain
Coira/Coire *see* Chur
Coirib, Loch *see* Corrib, Lough
Colby *45 E4* Kansas, C USA
Colchester *89 E6* Connecticut, NE USA
Coleman *49 F3* Texas, SW USA
Coleraine *88 B4 Ir.* Cúil Raithin. N Northern Ireland, United Kingdom
Colesberg *78 C5* Northern Cape, C South Africa
Colima *50 D4* Colima, S Mexico
Coll *88 B3 island* W Scotland, United Kingdom
College Station *49 G3* Texas, SW USA
Collie *147 A7* Western Australia
Collipo *see* Leiria
Colmar *90 E4 Ger.* Kolmar. Haut-Rhin, NE France
Cöln *see* Köln
Cologne *see* Köln
Colomb-Béchar *see* Béchar
Colombia *58 B3 off.* Republic of Colombia. *country* N South America

COLOMBIA
South America

Official name Republic of Colombia
Formation 1819 / 1903
Capital Bogotá
Population 48.3 million / 120 people per sq mile (47 people per sq km) / 77%
Total area 439,733 sq. miles (1,138,910 sq. km)
Languages Spanish*, Wayuu, Páez, and other Amerindian languages
Religions Roman Catholic 95%, Other 5%
Ethnic mix Mestizo 58%, White 20%, European–African 14%, African 4%, African–Amerindian 3%, Amerindian 1%
Government Presidential system
Currency Colombian peso = 100 centavos
Literacy rate 94%
Calorie consumption 2593 kilocalories

Colombian Basin *56 A1 undersea basin* SW Caribbean Sea
Colombia, Republic of *see* Colombia
Colombie-Britannique *see* British Columbia
Colombo *132 C4 country capital* (Sri Lanka) Western Province, W Sri Lanka
Colón *53 G4 prev.* Aspinwall. Colón, C Panama
Colón, Archipiélago de *see* Galápagos Islands
Colonia Agrippina *see* Köln
Colón Ridge *35 B8 undersea ridge* E Pacific Ocean
Colorado *44 C4 off.* State of Colorado, *also known as* Centennial State, Silver State. *state* C USA
Colorado City *49 F3* Texas, SW USA
Colorado Plateau *48 B1 plateau* W USA
Colorado, Río *65 C5 river* E Argentina
Colorado, Río *see* Colorado River
Colorado River *35 B5 var.* Río Colorado. *river* Mexico/USA
Colorado River *49 G4 river* Texas, SW USA
Colorado Springs *44 D5* Colorado, C USA
Columbia *41 E4* Maryland, NE USA
Columbia *45 G4* Missouri, C USA
Columbia *43 E2 state capital* South Carolina, SE USA
Columbia *42 C1* Tennessee, S USA
Columbia River *46 B3 river* Canada/USA
Columbia Plateau *46 C3 plateau* Idaho/Oregon, NW USA
Columbus *42 D2* Georgia, SE USA
Columbus *40 C4* Indiana, N USA
Columbus *42 C2* Mississippi, S USA
Columbus *45 F4* Nebraska, C USA
Columbus *40 D4 state capital* Ohio, N USA
Colville Channel *150 D2 channel* North Island, New Zealand
Colville River *36 D2 river* Alaska, USA
Comacchio *96 C3 var.* Commachio; *anc.* Comactium. Emilia-Romagna, N Italy
Comactium *see* Comacchio
Comalcalco *51 G4* Tabasco, SE Mexico
Coma Pedrosa, Pic de *91 A7 mountain* NW Andorra
Comarapa *61 F4* Santa Cruz, C Bolivia
Comayagua *52 C2* Comayagua, W Honduras
Comer See *see* Como, Lago di
Comilla *135 G4 Ben.* Kumillā. Chittagong, E Bangladesh
Comino *see* Kemmuna
Comitán *51 G5 var.* Comitán de Domínguez. Chiapas, SE Mexico
Comitán de Domínguez *see* Comitán
Commachio *see* Comacchio
Commissioner's Point *42 A5 headland* W Bermuda
Communism Peak *123 F3 prev.* Qullai Kommunizm. *mountain* E Tajikistan
Como *96 B2 anc.* Comum. Lombardia, N Italy
Comodoro Rivadavia *65 B6* Chubut, SE Argentina
Como, Lake *96 B2 var.* Lario, *Eng.* Lake Como, *Ger.* Comer See. *lake* N Italy
Como, Lake *see* Como, Lago di
Comores, République Fédérale Islamique des *see* Comoros
Comoros *79 F2 off.* Federal Islamic Republic of the Comoros, *Fr.* République Fédérale Islamique des Comores. *country* W Indian Ocean

COMOROS
Indian Ocean

Official name Union of the Comoros
Formation 1975 / 1975
Capital Moroni
Population 800,000 / 929 people per sq mile (359 people per sq km)
Total area 838 sq. miles (2170 sq. km)
Languages Arabic*, Comoran*, French*
Religions Muslim (mainly Sunni) 98%, Other 1%, Roman Catholic 1%
Ethnic mix Comoran 97%, Other 3%
Government Presidential system
Currency Comoros franc = 100 centimes
Literacy rate 76%
Calorie consumption 2139 kilocalories

Comoros, Federal Islamic Republic of the *see* Comoros
Compiègne *90 C3* Oise, N France
Complutum *see* Alcalá de Henares
Compniacum *see* Cognac
Compostella *see* Santiago de Compostela
Comrat *108 D4 Rus.* Komrat. S Moldova
Comum *see* Como
Conakry *74 C4 country capital* (Guinea) SW Guinea
Conca *see* Cuenca
Concarneau *90 A3* Finistère, NW France
Concepción *61 G3* Santa Cruz, E Bolivia
Concepción *65 B5* Bío Bío, C Chile
Concepción *64 D2 var.* Villa Concepción. Concepción, C Paraguay
Concepción *see* La Concepción
Concepción de la Vega *see* La Vega
Conchos, Río *48 D4 river* NW Mexico
Conchos, Río *50 D2 river* C Mexico
Concord *41 G3 state capital* New Hampshire, NE USA
Concordia *64 D4* Entre Ríos, E Argentina
Concordia *45 E4* Kansas, C USA
Côn Đao Sơn *137 E7 var.* Con Son. *island* S Vietnam
Condate *see* Rennes, Ille-et-Vilaine, France
Condate *see* St-Claude, Jura, France
Condega *52 D3* Estelí, NW Nicaragua
Condivincum *see* Nantes
Confluentes *see* Koblenz

ng Hoa Xa Hôi Chu Nghia Viêt Nam *ee* Vietnam
ngo *77 D5 off.* Republic of the Congo, *r.* Moyen-Congo; *prev.* Middle Congo. *ountry* C Africa

ONGO
Central Africa

ficial name Republic of the Congo
rmation 1960 / 1960
pital Brazzaville
pulation 4.4 million / 33 people
r sq mile (13 people per sq km)
tal area 132,046 sq. miles
2,000 sq. km)
nguages Kongo, Teke, Lingala, French*
ligions Traditional beliefs 50%, Roman
tholic 35%, Protestant 13%, Muslim 2%
hnic mix Bakongo 51%, Teke 17%,
her 16%, Mbochi 11%, Mbédé 5%
overnment Presidential system
rrency CFA franc = 100 centimes
eracy rate 79%
lorie consumption 2195 kilocalories

ngo, Dem. Rep. *77 C6 off.* Democratic Republic of Congo; *prev.* Zaire, Belgian Congo, Congo (Kinshasa). *country* Africa

ONGO, DEM. REP.
Central Africa

fficial name Democratic Republic of
e Congo
rmation 1960 / 1960
pital Kinshasa
pulation 67.5 million / 77 people
r sq mile (30 people per sq km)
tal area 905,563 sq. miles
345,410 sq. km)
nguages Kiswahili, Tshiluba, Kikongo,
ngala, French*
ligions Roman Catholic 50%,
otestant 20%, Traditional beliefs and
her 10%, Muslim 10%, Kimbanguist 10%
hnic mix Other 55%, Mongo, Luba,
ngo, and Mangbetu-Azande 45%
overnment Presidential system
rrency Congolese franc = 100 centimes
eracy rate 61%
lorie consumption 1585 kilocalories

ngo *77 C6 var.* Kongo, *Fr.* Zaïre. *iver* C Africa
ngo Basin *77 C6 drainage basin* W Dem. Rep. Congo
ngo/Congo (Kinshasa) *see* Congo (Democratic Republic of)
ni *see* Cuneo
nimbria/Conimbriga *see* Coimbra
njeeveram *see* Kānchīpuram
nnacht *see* Connaught
nnaught *89 A5 var.* Connacht, *Ir.* Chonnacht, Cúige. *province* W Ireland
nnecticut *41 F3 off.* State of Connecticut, *also known as* Blue Law State, Constitution State, Land of Steady Habits, Nutmeg State. *state* NE USA
nnecticut *41 G3 river* Canada/USA
nroe *49 G3* Texas, SW USA
nsentia *see* Cosenza
nsolación del Sur *54 A2* Pinar del Río, W Cuba
n Son *see* Côn Đao Son
nstance *see* Konstanz
nstance, Lake *95 B7 Ger.* Bodensee. *ake* C Europe
nstanța *108 D5 var.* Küstendje, *Eng.* Constanza, *Ger.* Konstanza, *Turk.* Küstence. Constanța, SE Romania
nstantia *see* Coutances
nstantia *see* Konstanz
nstantine *71 E2 var.* Qacentina, *Ar.* Qoussantîna. NE Algeria
nstantinople *see* İstanbul
nstantiola *see* Oltenița
nstanz *see* Konstanz
nstanza *see* Constanța
nstitution State *see* Connecticut
o *see* Kos
ober Pedy *149 A5* South Australia
okeville *42 D1* Tennessee, S USA
ok Islands *145 F4 territory in free association with New Zealand* S Pacific Ocean
Cook, Mount *see* Aoraki
Cook Strait *151 D5 var.* Raukawa. *strait* New Zealand
Cooktown *148 D2* Queensland, NE Australia
Coolgardie *147 B6* Western Australia
Cooma *149 D7* New South Wales, SE Australia
Coomassie *see* Kumasi
Coon Rapids *45 F2* Minnesota, N USA
Cooper Creek *148 C4 var.* Barcoo, Cooper's Creek. *seasonal river* Queensland/South Australia
Cooper's Creek *see* Cooper Creek
Coos Bay *46 A3* Oregon, NW USA
Cootamundra *149 D6* New South Wales, SE Australia
Copacabana *61 E4* La Paz, W Bolivia
Copenhagen *see* København
Copiapó *64 B3* Atacama, N Chile
Copperas Cove *49 G3* Texas, SW USA
Coppermine *see* Kugluktuk
Copper State *see* Arizona
Coquilhatville *see* Mbandaka
Coquimbo *64 B3* Coquimbo, N Chile
Corabia *108 B5* Olt, S Romania
Coral Harbour *37 G3 var.* Salliq. Southampton Island, Nunavut, NE Canada
Coral Sea *142 B3 sea* SW Pacific Ocean
Coral Sea Islands *144 B4 Australian external territory* SW Pacific Ocean
Corantijn Rivier *see* Courantyne River
Corcovado, Golfo *65 B6 gulf* S Chile
Corcyra Nigra *see* Korčula
Cordele *42 D3* Georgia, SE USA
Córdoba *64 C3* Córdoba, C Argentina
Córdoba *51 F4* Veracruz-Llave, E Mexico
Córdoba *92 D4 var.* Cordoba, *Eng.* Cordova; *anc.* Corduba. Andalucía, SW Spain
Cordova *36 C3* Alaska, USA
Cordova/Cordoba *see* Córdoba
Corduba *see* Córdoba
Corentyne River *see* Courantyne River
Corfu *104 A4 var.* Kérkira, *Eng.* Corfu. *island* Iónia Nisiá, Greece, C Mediterranean Sea
Corfu *see* Kérkyra
Coria *92 C3* Extremadura, W Spain
Corinth *42 C1* Mississippi, S USA
Corinth *see* Kórinthos
Corinth, Gulf of *105 B5 Eng.* Gulf of Corinth; *anc.* Corinthiacus Sinus. *gulf* C Greece
Corinth, Gulf of/Corinthiacus Sinus *see* Korinthiakós Kólpos
Corinthus *see* Kórinthos
Corinto *52 C3* Chinandega, NW Nicaragua
Cork *89 A6 Ir.* Corcaigh. S Ireland
Çorlu *116 A2* Tekirdağ, NW Turkey
Corner Brook *39 G3* Newfoundland, Newfoundland and Labrador, E Canada
Cornhusker State *see* Nebraska
Corn Islands *53 E3 var.* Corn Islands. *island group* SE Nicaragua
Corn Islands *see* Maíz, Islas del
Cornwallis Island *37 F2 Island* Nunavut, N Canada
Coro *58 C1 prev.* Santa Ana de Coro. Falcón, NW Venezuela
Corocoro *61 F4* La Paz, W Bolivia
Coromandel *150 D2* Waikato, North Island, New Zealand
Coromandel Coast *132 D2 coast* E India
Coromandel Peninsula *150 D2 peninsula* North Island, New Zealand
Coronado, Bahía de *52 D5 bay* S Costa Rica
Coronel Dorrego *65 C5* Buenos Aires, E Argentina
Coronel Oviedo *64 D2* Caaguazú, SE Paraguay
Corozal *52 C1* Corozal, N Belize
Corpus Christi *49 G4* Texas, SW USA
Corrales *48 D2* New Mexico, SW USA
Corrib, Lough *89 A5 Ir.* Loch Coirib. *lake* W Ireland
Corrientes *64 D3* Corrientes, NE Argentina
Corriza *see* Korçë
Corsica *91 E7 Eng.* Corsica. *island* France, C Mediterranean Sea
Corsica *see* Corse
Corsicana *49 G3* Texas, SW USA
Cortegana *92 C4* Andalucía, S Spain
Cortés *53 E5 var.* Ciudad Cortés. Puntarenas, SE Costa Rica
Cortez, Sea of *see* California, Golfo de
Cortina d'Ampezzo *96 C1* Veneto, NE Italy
Coruche *92 B3* Santarém, C Portugal
Çoruh Nehri *117 E3 Geor.* Chorokh, *Rus.* Chorokhi. *river* Georgia/Turkey
Çorum *116 D3 var.* Chorum. Çorum, N Turkey
Corunna *see* A Coruña
Corvallis *46 B3* Oregon, NW USA
Corvo *92 A5 var.* Ilha do Corvo. *island* Azores, Portugal, NE Atlantic Ocean
Corvo, Ilha do *see* Corvo
Cos *see* Kos
Cosenza *97 D6 anc.* Consentia. Calabria, SW Italy
Cosne-Cours-sur-Loire *90 C4* Nièvre, Bourgogne, C France Europe
Costa Mesa *46 D2* California, W USA North America
Costa Rica *53 E4 off.* Republic of Costa Rica. *country* Central America

COSTA RICA
Central America

Official name Republic of Costa Rica
Formation 1838 / 1838
Capital San José
Population 4.9 million / 249 people per sq mile (96 people per sq km)
Total area 19,730 sq. miles (51,100 sq. km)
Languages Spanish*, English Creole, Bribri, Cabecar
Religions Roman Catholic 71%, Evangelical 14%, Nonreligious 11%, Other 4%
Ethnic mix Mestizo and European 94%, Black 3%, Other 1%, Chinese 1%, Amerindian 1%
Government Presidential system
Currency Costa Rican colón = 100 céntimos
Literacy rate 97%
Calorie consumption 2898 kilocalories

Costa Rica, Republic of *see* Costa Rica
Costermansville *see* Bukavu
Cotagaita *61 F5* Potosí, S Bolivia
Côte d'Ivoire *74 D4 off.* Republic of Côte d'Ivoire; *Fr.* République de la Côte d'Ivoire, *Eng* Ivory Coast. *country* W Africa

CÔTE D'IVOIRE (IVORY COAST)
West Africa

Official name Republic of Côte d'Ivoire
Formation 1960 / 1960
Capital Yamoussoukro
Population 20.3 million / 165 people per sq mile (64 people per sq km)
Total area 124,502 sq. miles (322,460 sq. km)
Languages Akan, French*, Krou, Voltaïque
Religions Muslim 38%, Traditional beliefs 25%, Roman Catholic 25%, Other 6%, Protestant 6%
Ethnic mix Akan 42%, Voltaïque 18%, Mandé du Nord 17%, Krou 11%, Mandé du Sud 10%, Other 2%
Government Presidential system
Currency CFA franc = 100 centimes
Literacy rate 41%
Calorie consumption 2781 calories

Côte d'Ivoire, République de la *see* Côte d'Ivoire
Côte d'Or *90 D4 cultural region* C France
Côte Française des Somalis *see* Djibouti
Côtière, Chaîne *see* Coast Mountains
Cotonou *75 F5 var.* Kotonu. S Benin
Cotrone *see* Crotone
Cotswold Hills *89 D6 var.* Cotswolds. *hill range* S England, United Kingdom
Cotswolds *see* Cotswold Hills
Cottbus *94 D4 Lus.* Chośebuz; *prev.* Kottbus. Brandenburg, E Germany
Cotton State, The *see* Alabama
Cotyora *see* Ordu
Couentrey *see* Coventry
Council Bluffs *45 F4* Iowa, C USA
Courantyne River *59 G4 var.* Corantijn Rivier, Corentyne River. *river* Guyana/Suriname
Courland Lagoon *106 A4 Ger.* Kurisches Haff, *Rus.* Kurskiy Zaliv. *lagoon* Lithuania/Russian Federation
Courtrai *see* Kortrijk
Coutances *90 B3 anc.* Constantia. Manche, N France
Couvin *87 C7* Namur, S Belgium
Coventry *89 D6 anc.* Couentrey. C England, United Kingdom
Covilhã *92 C3* Castelo Branco, E Portugal
Cowan, Lake *147 B6 lake* Western Australia
Coxen Hole *see* Roatán
Coxin Hole *see* Roatán
Coyhaique *see* Coihaique
Coyote State, The *see* South Dakota
Cozhê *126 C5* Xizang Zizhiqu, W China
Cozumel, Isla *51 H3 island* SE Mexico
Cracovia/Cracow *see* Kraków
Cradock *78 C5* Eastern Cape, S South Africa
Craig *44 C4* Colorado, C USA
Craiova *108 B5* Dolj, SW Romania
Cranbrook *37 E5* British Columbia, SW Canada
Crane *see* The Crane
Cranz *see* Zelenogradsk
Crawley *89 E7* SE England, United Kingdom
Cremona *96 B2* Lombardia, N Italy
Creole State *see* Louisiana
Cres *100 A3 It.* Cherso; *anc.* Crexa. *island* W Croatia
Crescent City *46 A4* California, W USA
Crescent Group *128 C7 island group* C Paracel Islands
Creston *45 F4* Iowa, C USA
Crestview *42 D3* Florida, SE USA
Crete *105 C7 Eng.* Crete. *island* Greece, Aegean Sea
Créteil *90 E2* Val-de-Marne, N France
Sea of Crete *105 D7 var.* Kretikon Delagos, *Eng.* Sea of Crete; *anc.* Mare Creticum. *sea* Greece, Aegean Sea
Crete, Sea of/Creticum, Mare *see* Kritikó Pélagos
Creuse *90 B4 river* C France
Crewe *89 D6* C England, United Kingdom
Crexa *see* Cres
Crikvenica *100 A3 It.* Cirquenizza; *prev.* Cirkvenica, Crjkvenica. Primorje-Gorski Kotar, NW Croatia
Crimea *see* Kryms'kyy Pivostriv
Cristóbal *53 G4* Colón, C Panama
Cristóbal Colón, Pico *58 B1 mountain* N Colombia
Cristur/Cristuru Săcuiesc *see* Cristuru Secuiesc
Cristuru Secuiesc *108 C4 prev.* Cristur, Cristuru Săcuiesc, Sitaș Cristuru, *Ger.* Kreutz, *Hung.* Székelykeresztúr, Szitás-Keresztúr. Harghita, C Romania
Crjkvenica *see* Crikvenica
Crna Gora *see* Montenegro
Crna Reka *101 D6 river* S FYR Macedonia
Crni Drim *see* Black Drin
Croatia *100 B3 off.* Republic of Croatia, *Ger.* Kroatien, *SCr.* Hrvatska. *country* SE Europe

CROATIA
Southeast Europe

Official name Republic of Croatia
Formation 1991 / 1991
Capital Zagreb
Population 4.3 million / 197 people per sq mile (76 people per sq km)
Total area 21,831 sq. miles (56,542 sq. km)
Languages Croatian*
Religions Roman Catholic 88%, Other 7%, Orthodox Christian 4%, Muslim 1%
Ethnic mix Croat 90%, Other 5%, Serb 5%
Government Parliamentary system
Currency Kuna = 100 lipa
Literacy rate 99%
Calorie consumption 3052 kilocalories

Croatia, Republic of *see* Croatia
Crocodile *see* Limpopo
Croia *see* Krujë
Croker Island *146 E2 island* Northern Territory, N Australia
Cromwell *151 B7* Otago, South Island, New Zealand
Crooked Island *54 D2 island* SE Bahamas
Crooked Island Passage *54 D2 channel* SE Bahamas

Crookston *45 F1* Minnesota, N USA
Crossen *see* Krosno Odrzańskie
Croton/Crotona *see* Crotone
Crotone *97 E6 var.* Cotrone; *anc.* Croton, Crotona. Calabria, SW Italy
Croydon *89 A8* SE England, United Kingdom
Crozet Basin *141 B6 undersea basin* S Indian Ocean
Crozet Islands *141 B7 island group* French Southern and Antarctic Lands
Crozet Plateau *141 B7 var.* Crozet Plateaus. *undersea plateau* SW Indian Ocean
Crozet Plateaus *see* Crozet Plateau
Crystal Brook *149 B6* South Australia
Csaca *see* Čadca
Csakathurn/Csáktornya *see* Čakovec
Csíkszereda *see* Miercurea-Ciuc
Csorna *99 C6* Győr-Moson-Sopron, NW Hungary
Csurgó *99 C7* Somogy, SW Hungary
Cuando *78 C2 var.* Kwando. *river* S Africa
Cuango *78 B1 var.* Kwango. *river* Angola/Dem. Rep. Congo
Cuango *see* Kwango
Cuanza *78 B1 var.* Kwanza. *river* C Angola
Cuauhtémoc *50 C2* Chihuahua, N Mexico
Cuautla *51 E4* Morelos, S Mexico
Cuba *54 B2 off.* Republic of Cuba. *country* W West Indies

CUBA
West Indies

Official name Republic of Cuba
Formation 1902 / 1902
Capital Havana
Population 11.3 million / 264 people per sq mile (102 people per sq km) / 76%
Total area 42,803 sq. miles (110,860 sq. km)
Languages Spanish
Religions Nonreligious 49%, Roman Catholic 40%, Atheist 6%, Other 4%, Protestant 1%
Ethnic mix Mulatto (mixed race) 51%, White 37%, Black 11%, Chinese 1%
Government One-party state
Currency Cuban peso = 100 centavos
Literacy rate 99%
Calorie consumption 3277 kilocalories

Cubal *78 B2* Benguela, W Angola
Cubango *78 B2 var.* Kuvango, *Port.* Vila Artur de Paiva, Vila da Ponte. Huíla, SW Angola
Cubango *78 B2 var.* Kavango, Kavengo, Kubango, Okavango, Okavanggo. *river* S Africa
Cuba, Republic of *see* Cuba
Cúcuta *58 C2 var.* San José de Cúcuta. Norte de Santander, N Colombia
Cuddapah *132 C2* Andhra Pradesh, S India
Cuenca *60 B2* Azuay, S Ecuador
Cuenca *93 E3 anc.* Conca. Castilla-La Mancha, C Spain
Cuera *see* Chur
Cuernavaca *51 E4* Morelos, S Mexico
Cuiabá *63 E3 prev.* Cuyabá. *state capital* Mato Grosso, SW Brazil
Cúige *see* Connaught
Cúige Laighean *see* Leinster
Cúige Mumhan *see* Munster
Cuijck *86 D4* Noord-Brabant, SE Netherlands
Cúil Raithin *see* Coleraine
Cuito *78 B2 var.* Kwito. *river* SE Angola
Cukai *138 B3 var.* Chukai, Kemaman. Terengganu, Peninsular Malaysia
Cularo *see* Grenoble
Culiacán *50 C3 var.* Culiacán Rosales, Culiacán-Rosales. Sinaloa, C Mexico
Culiacán-Rosales/Culiacán Rosales *see* Culiacán
Cullera *93 F3* Valenciana, E Spain
Cullman *42 C2* Alabama, S USA
Culm *see* Chełmno
Culmsee *see* Chełmża
Cumaná *59 E1* Sucre, NE Venezuela
Cumbal, Nevado de *58 A4 elevation* S Colombia
Cumberland *41 E4* Maryland, NE USA
Cumberland Plateau *42 D1 plateau* E USA
Cumberland Sound *37 H3 inlet* Baffin Island, Nunavut, NE Canada
Cumpas *50 B2* Sonora, NW Mexico
Cuneo *96 A2 Fr.* Coni. Piemonte, NW Italy
Cunnamulla *149 C5* Queensland, E Australia
Ćuprija *100 E4* Serbia, E Serbia
Curaçao *55 E5 Dutch island territory* S West Indies
Curaçao *55 E5 island* Lesser Antilles
Curia Rhaetorum *see* Chur
Curicó *64 B4* Maule, C Chile
Curieta *see* Krk
Curitiba *63 E4 prev.* Curytiba. *state capital* Paraná, S Brazil
Curtbunar *see* Tervel
Curtea de Argeş *108 C4 var.* Curtea-de-Arges. Argeş, S Romania
Curtea-de-Arges *see* Curtea de Argeş
Curtici *108 A4 Ger.* Kurtitsch, *Hung.* Kürtös. Arad, W Romania
Curtis Island *148 E4 island* Queensland, SE Australia
Curytiba *see* Curitiba
Curzola *see* Korčula
Cusco *61 E4 var.* Cuzco. Cusco, C Peru
Cusset *91 C5* Allier, C France
Cutch, Gulf of *see* Kachchh, Gulf of
Cuttack *135 F4* Odisha, E India
Cuvier Plateau *141 E6 undersea plateau* E Indian Ocean
Cuxhaven *94 B2* Niedersachsen, NW Germany
Cuyabá *see* Cuiabá
Cuyuni, Río *see* Cuyuni River
Cuyuni River *59 F3 var.* Río Cuyuni. *river* Guyana/Venezuela
Cuzco *see* Cusco
Cyclades *105 D6 var.* Kikládhes, *Eng.* Cyclades. *island group* SE Greece
Cyclades *see* Kykládes
Cydonia *see* Chaniá
Cymru *see* Wales
Cyprus *102 C4 off.* Republic of Cyprus, *Gk.* Kypros, *Turk.* Kıbrıs, Kıbrıs Cumhuriyeti. *country* E Mediterranean Sea

CYPRUS
Southeast Europe

Official name Republic of Cyprus
Formation 1960 / 1960
Capital Nicosia
Population 1.1 million / 308 people per sq mile (119 people per sq km)
Total area 3571 sq. miles (9250 sq. km)
Languages Greek*, Turkish*
Religions Orthodox Christian 78%, Muslim 18%, Other 4%
Ethnic mix Greek 81%, Turkish 11%, Other 8%
Government Presidential system
Currency Euro = 100 cents (In TRNC, new Turkish lira = 100 kurus)
Literacy rate 99%
Calorie consumption 2661 kilocalories

Cyprus, Republic of *see* Cyprus
Cythnos *see* Kýthnos
Czech Republic *99 A5 Cz.* Česká Republika. *country* C Europe

CZECH REPUBLIC
Central Europe

Official name Czech Republic
Formation 1993 / 1993
Capital Prague
Population 10.7 million / 351 people per sq mile (136 people per sq km)
Total area 30,450 sq. miles (78,866 sq. km)
Languages Czech*, Slovak, Hungarian (Magyar)
Religions Roman Catholic 39%, Atheist 38%, Other 18%, Protestant 3%, Hussite 2%
Ethnic mix Czech 90%, Other 4%, Moravian 4%, Slovak 2%
Government Parliamentary system
Currency Czech koruna = 100 haleru
Literacy rate 99%
Calorie consumption 3292 kilocalories

Czenstochau *see* Częstochowa
Czernowitz *see* Chernivtsi
Częstochowa *98 C4 Ger.* Czenstochau, Tschenstochau, *Rus.* Chenstokhov. Śląskie, S Poland
Człuchów *98 C3 Ger.* Schlochau. Pomorskie, NW Poland

Dabajuro *58 C1* Falcón, NW Venezuela
Dabeiba *58 B2* Antioquia, NW Colombia
Dąbrowa Tarnowska *99 D5* Małopolskie, S Poland
Dabryn' *107 C8 Rus.* Dobryn'. Homyel'skaya Voblasts', SE Belarus
Dacca *see* Dhaka
Daegu *107 E4 off.* Daegu Gwang-yeoksi, *prev.* Taegu, *Jap.* Taikyū. SE South Korea
Daegu Gwang-yeoksi *see* Daegu
Daejeon *107 E4 off.* Daejeon Gwang-yeoksi, *prev.* Taejŏn, *Jap.* Taiden. C South Korea
Daejeon Gwang-yeoksi *see* Daejeon
Dagana *74 B3* N Senegal
Dagda *106 D4* SE Latvia
Dagden *see* Hiiumaa
Dagenham *89 B8* United Kingdom
Dağliq Quarabağ *see* Nagorno-Karabakh
Dagö *see* Hiiumaa
Dagupan *139 E1 off.* Dagupan City. Luzon, N Philippines
Dagupan City *see* Dagupan
Dahm, Ramlat *121 B6 desert* NW Yemen
Dahomey *see* Benin
Daihoku *see* Taipei
Daimiel *92 D3* Castilla-La Mancha, C Spain
Daimoniá *105 B7* Pelopónnisos, S Greece
Dainan *see* Tainan
Daingin, Bá an *see* Dingle Bay
Dairen *see* Dalian
Dakar *74 B3 country capital* (Senegal) W Senegal
Dakhla *see* Ad Dakhla
Dakoro *75 G3* Maradi, S Niger
Đakovica *see* Gjakovë
Đakovo *100 C3 var.* Djakovo, *Hung.* Diakovár. Osijek-Baranja, E Croatia
Dakshin *see* Deccan
Dalain Hob *126 D3 var.* Ejin Qi. Nei Mongol Zizhiqu, N China
Dalai Nor *see* Hulun Nur
Dalaman *116 A4* Muğla, SW Turkey
Dalandzadgad *127 E3* Ömnögovĭ, S Mongolia
Đa Lat *137 E6* Lâm Đông, S Vietnam
Dalby *149 D5* Queensland, E Australia
Dale City *41 E4* Virginia, NE USA
Dalhart *49 E1* Texas, SW USA
Dali *128 A6 var.* Xiaguan. Yunnan, SW China
Dalian *128 D4 var.* Dairen, Dalien, Jay Dairen, Lüda, Ta-lien, *Rus.* Dalny. Liaoning, NE China
Dalien *see* Dalian
Dallas *49 G2* Texas, SW USA
Dalmacija *100 B4 Eng.* Dalmatia, *Ger.* Dalmatien, *It.* Dalmazia. *cultural region* S Croatia
Dalmatia/Dalmatien/Dalmazia *see* Dalmacija
Dalny *see* Dalian
Dalton *42 D1* Georgia, SE USA
Dálvvadis *see* Jokkmokk
Daly Waters *148 A2* Northern Territory, N Australia
Damachava *107 A6 var.* Damachova, *Pol.* Domaczewo, *Rus.* Domachëvo. Brestskaya Voblasts', SW Belarus
Damachova *see* Damachava
Damān *134 C4* Damān and Diu, W India
Damara *76 C4* Ombella-Mpoko, S Central African Republic
Damas *see* Dimashq
Damasco *see* Dimashq
Damascus *see* Dimashq
Qolleh-ye Damavand *120 D3 mountain* N Iran
Damietta *see* Dumyāt
Dammām *see* Ad Dammān
Damoûr *119 A5 var.* Ad Dāmūr. W Lebanon
Dampier *146 A4* Western Australia
Dampier, Selat *139 F4 strait* Papua, E Indonesia
Damqawt *121 D6 var.* Damqut. E Yemen
Damqut *see* Damqawt
Damxung *126 C5 var.* Gongtang. Xiz Zizhiqu, W China
Danakil Desert *72 D4 var.* Afar Depression, Danakil Plain. *desert* E Africa
Danakil Plain *see* Danakil Desert
Danané *74 D5* W Côte d'Ivoire
Đa Nāng *137 E5 prev.* Tourane. Quan Nam-Đa Nāng, C Vietnam
Danborg *see* Daneborg
Dandong *128 D3 var.* Tan-tung; *prev.* An-tung. Liaoning, NE China
Daneborg *83 E3 var.* Danborg. Tunu N Greenland
Dänew *see* Galkynyş
Dangara *see* Danghara
Dangerous Archipelago *see* Tuamotu, Îles
Danghara *123 E3 Rus.* Dangara. SW Tajikistan
Danghe Nanshan *126 D3 mountain range* W China
Dang Raek, Phanom/Dangrek, Chaîr des *see* Dângrêk, Chuŏr Phnum
Chuor Phnum Dangrek *137 D5 var.* Phanom Dang Raek, Phanom Dong Rak, *Fr.* Chaîne des Dangrek. *mount range* Cambodia/Thailand
Dangriga *52 C1 prev.* Stann Creek. Stann Creek, E Belize
Danish West Indies *see* Virgin Islands (US)
Danlí *52 D2* El Paraíso, S Honduras
Danmark *see* Denmark
Danmarksstraedet *see* Denmark Strait
Dannenberg *94 C3* Niedersachsen, N Germany
Dannevirke *150 D4* Manawatu-Wanganui, North Island, New Zealan
Dantzig *see* Gdańsk
Danube *81 E4 Bul.* Dunav, *Cz.* Dunaj, *Ger.* Donau, *Hung.* Duna, *Rom.* Dunărea. *river* C Europe
Danubian Plain *104 C2 Eng.* Danubia Plain. *lowlands* N Bulgaria
Danubian Plain *see* Dunavska Ravnina
Danum *see* Doncaster
Danville *41 E5* Virginia, NE USA
Danxian/Dan Xian *see* Danzhou
Danzhou *128 C7 prev.* Danxian, Dan Xian. Hainan, S China
Danzig *see* Gdańsk
Danziger Bucht *see* Danzig, Gulf of
Danzig, Gulf of *98 C2 var.* Gulf of Gdańsk, *Ger.* Danziger Bucht, *Pol.* Zakota Gdańska, *Rus.* Gdan'skaya Bukhta. *gulf* N Poland
Daqm *see* Duqm
Dar'ā *119 B5 var.* Der'a, *Fr.* Déraa. Dar'ā, SW Syria
Darabani *108 C3* Botoşani, NW Romania
Daraut-Kurgan *see* Daroot-Korgon
Dardanelles *116 A2 Eng.* Dardanelles. *strait* NW Turkey
Dardanelles *see* Çanakkale Boğazı
Dardanelli *see* Çanakkale
Dar-el-Beida *see* Casablanca
Dar es Salaam *73 C7* Dar es Salaam, E Tanzania
Darfield *151 C6* Canterbury, South Island, New Zealand
Darfur *72 A4 var.* Darfur Massif. *cultural region* W Sudan
Darfur Massif *see* Darfur
Darhan *127 E2* Darhan Uul, N Mongol
Darién, Golfo del *see* Darien, Gulf of
Darien, Gulf of *58 A2 Sp.* Golfo del Darién. *gulf* S Caribbean Sea
Darien, Isthmus of *see* Panama, Istmo
Darién, Serranía del *53 H5 mountain range* Colombia/Panama
Dario *see* Ciudad Darío
Dariorigum *see* Vannes
Darjeeling *see* Dārjiling
Dārjiling *135 F3 prev.* Darjeeling. Wes Bengal, NE India
Darling River *149 C6 river* New South Wales, SE Australia
Darlington *89 D5* N England, United Kingdom
Darmstadt *95 B5* Hessen, SW German
Darnah *71 G2 var.* Dérna. NE Libya
Darnley, Cape *154 D2 cape* Antarctica
Daroca *93 E2* Aragón, NE Spain
Daroot-Korgon *123 F3 var.* Daraut-Kurgan. Oshskaya Oblast', SW Kyrgyzstan

rtford *89 B8* SE England, United Kingdom
rtmoor *89 C7 moorland* SW England, United Kingdom
rtmouth *39 F4* Nova Scotia, SE Canada
rvaza *see* Derweze, Turkmenistan
rwin *146 D2 prev.* Palmerston, Port Darwin. *territory capital* Northern Territory, N Australia
rwin, Isla *60 A4 island* Galápagos Islands, W Ecuador
shhowuz *see* Daşoguz
shkawka *107 D6 Rus.* Dashkovka. Mahilyowskaya Voblasts', E Belarus
shkovka *see* Dashkawka
şoguz *122 C2 Rus.* Dashkhovuz, *Turkm.* Dashhowuz; *prev.* Tashauz. Daşoguz Welaýaty, N Turkmenistan
, Sông *see* Black River
tong *128 C3 var.* Tatung, Ta-t'ung. Shanxi, C China
ugava *see* Western Dvina
ugavpils *106 D4 Ger.* Dünaburg; *prev. Rus.* Dvinsk. SE Latvia
ung Kyun *137 B6 island* S Myanmar (Burma)
uphiné *91 D5 cultural region* E France
vangere *132 C2* Karnātaka, W India
vao *139 F3 off.* Davao City. Mindanao, S Philippines
vao City *see* Davao
vao Gulf *139 F3 gulf* Mindanao, S Philippines
venport *45 G3* Iowa, C USA
vid *53 E5* Chiriquí, W Panama
vie Ridge *141 A5 undersea ridge* W Indian Ocean
vis *154 D3 Australian research station* Antarctica
vis Sea *154 D3 sea* Antarctica
vis Strait *82 B3 strait* Baffin Bay/ Labrador Sea
wei *137 B5 var.* Tavoy, Htawei. Tanintharyi, S Myanmar (Burma)
wlat Qaṭar *see* Qatar
x *91 B6 var.* Ax; *anc.* Aquae Augustae, Aquae Tarbelicae. Landes, SW France
yr az Zawr *118 D3 var.* Deir ez Zor. Dayr az Zawr, E Syria
yton *40 C4* Ohio, N USA
ytona Beach *43 E4* Florida, SE USA
Aar *78 C5* Northern Cape, C South Africa
ad Sea *119 B6 var.* Bahret Lut, Lacus Asphaltites, *Ar.* Al Baḥr al Mayyit, Baḥrat Lūt, *Heb.* Yam HaMelaḥ. *salt lake* Israel/Jordan
án Funes *64 C3* Córdoba, C Argentina
ath Valley *47 C7 valley* California, W USA
atnu *84 D2 Fin.* Tenojoki, *Nor.* Tana. *river* Finland/Norway
ebar *101 D6 Ger.* Dibra, *Turk.* Debre. W FYR Macedonia
e Behagle *see* Laï
ębica *99 D5* Podkarpackie, SE Poland
e Bildt *see* De Bilt
e Bilt *86 C3 var.* De Bildt. Utrecht, C Netherlands
ębno *98 B3* Zachodnio-pomorskie, NW Poland
ebre *see* Debar
ebrecen *99 D6 Ger.* Debreczin, *Rom.* Debreţin; *prev.* Debreczen. Hajdú-Bihar, E Hungary
ebreczen/Debreczin *see* Debrecen
ebreţin *see* Debrecen
ecatur *42 C1* Alabama, S USA
ecatur *40 B4* Illinois, N USA
eccan *134 D5 Hind.* Dakshin. *plateau* C India
ěčín *98 B4 Ger.* Tetschen. Ústecký Kraj, NW Czech Republic
edeagaç/Dedeagach *see* Alexandroúpoli
edemsvaart *86 E3* Overijssel, E Netherlands
ee *88 C3 river* NE Scotland, United Kingdom
eering *36 C2* Alaska, USA
eés *see* Dej
eggendorf *95 D6* Bayern, SE Germany
eğirmenlik *102 C5 Gk.* Kythréa. N Cyprus
eh Bīd *see* Şafāshahr
ehli *see* Delhi
eh Shū *see* Dīshū
einze *87 B5* Oost-Vlaanderen, NW Belgium
Deir ez Zor *see* Dayr az Zawr
Deirgeirt, Loch *see* Derg, Lough
Dej *108 B3 Hung.* Dés; *prev.* Deés. Cluj, NW Romania
De Jouwer *see* Joure
Dekéleia *see* Dhekélia
Dékoa *76 C4* Kémo, C Central African Republic
De Land *43 E4* Florida, SE USA
Delano *47 C7* California, W USA
Delārām *see* Dilārām
Delaware *40 D4* Ohio, N USA
Delaware *41 F4 off.* State of Delaware, *also known as* Blue Hen State, Diamond State, First State. *state* NE USA
Delft *86 B4* Zuid-Holland, W Netherlands
Delfzijl *86 E1* Groningen, NE Netherlands
Delgo *72 B3* Northern, N Sudan
Delhi *134 D3 var.* Dehli, *Hind.* Dilli, *hist.* Shahjahanabad. *union territory capital* Delhi, N India
Delicias *50 D2 var.* Ciudad Delicias. Chihuahua, N Mexico
Déli-Kárpátok *see* Carpaţii Meridionalii
Delmenhorst *94 B3* Niedersachsen, NW Germany
Del Rio *49 F4* Texas, SW USA
Deltona *43 E4* Florida, SE USA
Demba *77 D6* Kasai-Occidental, C Dem. Rep. Congo
Dembia *76 D4* Mbomou, SE Central African Republic
Demchok *126 A5 var.* Dêmqog. *disputed region* China/India
Demerara Plain *56 C2 abyssal plain* W Atlantic Ocean
Deming *48 C3* New Mexico, SW USA
Demmin *94 C2* Mecklenburg-Vorpommern, NE Germany
Demopolis *42 C2* Alabama, S USA
Dêmqog *126 A5 var.* Demchok. China/ India
Denali *see* McKinley, Mount
Denau *see* Denov
Dender *87 B6 Fr.* Dendre. *river* W Belgium
Dendre *see* Dender
Denekamp *86 E3* Overijssel, E Netherlands
Den Haag *see* 's-Gravenhage
Denham *147 A5* Western Australia
Den Ham *86 E3* Overijssel, E Netherlands
Den Helder *86 C2* Noord-Holland, NW Netherlands
Dénia *93 F4* Valenciana, E Spain
Deniliquin *149 C7* New South Wales, SE Australia
Denison *45 F3* Iowa, C USA
Denison *49 G2* Texas, SW USA
Denizli *116 B4* Denizli, SW Turkey
Denmark *85 A7 off.* Kingdom of Denmark, *Dan.* Danmark; *anc.* Hafnia. *country* N Europe

DENMARK
Northern Europe

Official name Kingdom of Denmark
Formation 950 / 1944
Capital Copenhagen
Population 5.6 million / 342 people per sq mile (132 people per sq km)
Total area 16,639 sq. miles (43,094 sq. km)
Languages Danish*
Religions Evangelical Lutheran 95%, Roman Catholic 3%, Muslim 2%
Ethnic mix Danish 96%, Other (including Scandinavian and Turkish) 3%, Faroese and Inuit 1%
Government Parliamentary system
Currency Danish krone = 100 øre
Literacy rate 99%
Calorie consumption 3363 kilocalories

Denmark, Kingdom of *see* Denmark
Denmark Strait *82 D4 var.* Danmarksstraedet. *strait* Greenland/ Iceland
Dennery *55 F1* E Saint Lucia
Denov *123 E3 Rus.* Denau. Surkhondaryo Viloyati, S Uzbekistan
Denpasar *138 D5 prev.* Paloe. Bali, C Indonesia
Denton *49 G2* Texas, SW USA
D'Entrecasteaux Islands *144 B3 island group* SE Papua New Guinea
Denver *44 D4 state capital* Colorado, C USA
Der'a/Derá/Déraa *see* Dar'ā
Dera Ghāzi Khān *134 C2 var.* Dera Ghāzikhān. Punjab, C Pakistan
Dera Ghāzikhān *see* Dera Ghāzi Khān
Đeravica *see* Gjeravicë
Derbent *111 B8* Respublika Dagestan, SW Russian Federation
Derby *89 D6* C England, United Kingdom
Derelí *see* Gónnoi
Dergachi *see* Derhachi
Derg, Lough *89 A6 Ir.* Loch Deirgeirt. *lake* W Ireland
Derhachi *109 G2 Rus.* Dergachi. Kharkivs'ka Oblast', E Ukraine
De Ridder *42 A3* Louisiana, S USA
Dérna *see* Darnah
Derry *see* Londonderry
Dertosa *see* Tortosa
Derventa *100 B3* Republika Srpska, N Bosnia and Herzegovina
Derweze *122 C2 Rus.* Darvaza. Ahal Welaýaty, C Turkmenistan
Dés *see* Dej
Deschutes River *46 B3 river* Oregon, NW USA
Desē *72 C4 var.* Desse, *It.* Dessie. Āmara, N Ethiopia
Deseado, Río *65 B7 river* S Argentina
Desertas, Ilhas *70 A2 island group* Madeira, Portugal, NE Atlantic Ocean
Deshu *see* Dīshū
Des Moines *45 F3 state capital* Iowa, C USA
Desna *109 E2 river* Russian Federation/ Ukraine
Dessau *94 C4* Sachsen-Anhalt, E Germany
Desse *see* Desē
Dessie *see* Desē
Destêrro *see* Florianópolis
Detroit *40 D3* Michigan, N USA
Detroit Lakes *45 F2* Minnesota, N USA
Deurne *87 D5* Noord-Brabant, SE Netherlands
Deutschendorf *see* Poprad
Deutsch-Eylau *see* Iława
Deutsch Krone *see* Wałcz
Deutschland/Deutschland, Bundesrepublik *see* Germany
Deutsch-Südwestafrika *see* Namibia
Deva *108 B4 Ger.* Diemrich, *Hung.* Déva. Hunedoara, W Romania
Déva *see* Deva
Deva *see* Chester
Devana *see* Aberdeen
Devana Castra *see* Chester
Đevđelija *see* Gevgelija
Deventer *86 D3* Overijssel, E Netherlands
Devils Lake *45 E1* North Dakota, N USA
Devoll *see* Devollit, Lumi i
Devollit, Lumi i *101 D6 var.* Devoll. *river* SE Albania
Devon Island *37 F2 prev.* North Devon Island. *island* Parry Islands, Nunavut, NE Canada
Devonport *149 C8* Tasmania, SE Australia
Devrek *116 C2* Zonguldak, N Turkey
Dexter *45 H5* Missouri, C USA
Deynau *see* Galkynyş
Dezfūl *120 C3 var.* Dizful. Khūzestān, SW Iran
Dezhou *128 D4* Shandong, E China
Dhaka *135 G4 prev.* Dacca. *country capital* (Bangladesh) Dhaka, C Bangladesh
Dhanbād *135 F4* Jhārkhand, NE India
Dhekélia *102 C5 Eng.* Dhekelia, *Gk.* Dekéleia. *UK air base* SE Cyprus *see* Dhekélia
Dhidhimótikhon *see* Didymóteicho
Dhíkti Ori *see* Díkti
Dhodhekánisos *see* Dodekánisa
Dhomokós *see* Domokós
Dhráma *see* Dráma
Dhrepanon, Akrotírio *see* Drépano, Akrotírio
Dhún na nGall, Bá *see* Donegal Bay
Dhuusa Marreeb *73 E5 var.* Dusa Marreb, *It.* Dusa Mareb. Galguduud, C Somalia
Diakovár *see* Đakovo
Diamantina, Chapada *63 F3 mountain range* E Brazil
Diamantina Fracture Zone *141 E6 tectonic feature* E Indian Ocean
Diamond State *see* Delaware
Diarbekr *see* Diyarbakır
Dibio *see* Dijon
Dibra *see* Debar
Dibrugarh *135 H3* Assam, NE India
Dickinson *44 D2* North Dakota, N USA
Dicle *see* Tigris
Didimotiho *see* Didymóteicho
Didymóteicho *104 D3 var.* Dhidhimótikhon, Didimotiho. Anatolikí Makedonía kai Thráki, NE Greece
Diedenhofen *see* Thionville
Diekirch *87 D7* Diekirch, C Luxembourg
Diemrich *see* Deva
Điên Biên *see* Điên Biên Phu
Điên Biên Phu *136 D3 var.* Bien Bien, Điên Biên. Lai Châu, N Vietnam
Diepenbeek *87 D6* Limburg, NE Belgium
Diepholz *94 B3* Niedersachsen, NW Germany
Dieppe *90 C2* Seine-Maritime, N France
Dieren *86 D4* Gelderland, E Netherlands
Differdange *87 D8* Luxembourg, SW Luxembourg
Digne *91 D6 var.* Digne-les-Bains. Alpes-de-Haute-Provence, SE France
Digne-les-Bains *see* Digne
Digoel *see* Digul, Sungai
Digoin *90 C4* Saône-et-Loire, C France
Digul, Sungai *139 H5 prev.* Digoel. *river* Papua, E Indonesia
Dihang *see* Brahmaputra
Dijlah *see* Tigris
Dijon *90 D4 anc.* Dibio. Côte d'Or, C France
Dikhil *72 D4* SW Djibouti
Dikson *114 D2* Krasnoyarskiy Kray, N Russian Federation
Dikti *105 D8 var.* Dhíkti Ori. *mountain range* Kríti, Greece, E Mediterranean Sea
Dilārām *122 D5 prev.* Delārām. Nīmrūz, SW Afghanistan
Dili *139 F5 var.* Dilli, Dilly. *country capital* (East Timor) N East Timor
Dilia *75 G3 var.* Dillia. *river* SE Niger
Di Linh *137 E6* Lâm Đông, S Vietnam
Dilli *see* Dili, East Timor
Dilli *see* Delhi, India
Dillia *see* Dilia
Dilling *72 B4 var.* Ad Dalanj. Southern Kordofan, C Sudan
Dillon *44 B2* Montana, NW USA
Dilly *see* Dili
Dilolo *77 D7* Katanga, S Dem. Rep. Congo
Dimashq *119 B5 var.* Ash Shām, Esh Sham, *Eng.* Damascus, *Fr.* Damas, *It.* Damasco. *country capital* (Syria) Rīf Dimashq, SW Syria
Dimitrovgrad *104 D3* Khaskovo, S Bulgaria
Dimitrovgrad *111 C6 prev.* Caribrod. Serbia, SE Serbia
Dimitrovo *see* Pernik
Dimovo *104 B1* Vidin, NW Bulgaria
Dinajpur *135 F3* Rajshahi, NW Bangladesh
Dinan *90 B3* Côtes d'Armor, NW France
Dinant *87 C7* Namur, S Belgium
Dinar *116 B4* Afyon, SW Turkey
Dinara *see* Dinaric Alps
Dinaric Alps *100 C4 var.* Dinara. *mountain range* Bosnia and Herzegovina/Croatia
Dindigul *132 C3* Tamil Nādu, SE India
Dingle Bay *89 A6 Ir.* Bá an Daingin. *bay* SW Ireland
Dinguiraye *74 C4* N Guinea
Diourbel *74 B3* W Senegal
Dirē Dawa *73 D5* Dirē Dawa, E Ethiopia
Dirk Hartog Island *147 A5 island* Western Australia
Dirschau *see* Tczew
Disappointment, Lake *146 C4 salt lake* Western Australia
Discovery Bay *54 B4* Middlesex, Jamaica, Greater Antilles, C Jamaica Caribbean Sea
Dīshū *122 D5 prev.* Deh Shū, *var.* Deshu. Helmand, S Afghanistan
Disko Bugt *see* Qeqertarsuup Tunua
Dispur *135 G3 state capital* Assam, NE India
Divinópolis *63 F4* Minas Gerais, SE Brazil
Divo *74 D5* S Côte d'Ivoire

Divodurum Mediomatricum *see* Metz
Diyarbakır *117 E4 var.* Diarbekr; *anc.* Amida. Diyarbakır, SE Turkey
Dizful *see* Dezfūl
Djailolo *see* Halmahera, Pulau
Djajapura *see* Jayapura
Djakarta *see* Jakarta
Djakovo *see* Đakovo
Djambala *77 B6* Plateaux, C Congo
Djambi *see* Hari, Batang
Djambi *see* Jambi
Djanet *71 E4 prev.* Fort Charlet. SE Algeria
Djéblé *see* Jablah
Djelfa *70 D2 var.* El Djelfa. N Algeria
Djéma *76 D4* Haut-Mbomou, E Central African Republic
Djember *see* Jember
Djérablous *see* Jarābulus
Djerba *71 F2 var.* Djerba, Jazīrat Jarbah. *island* E Tunisia
Djerba *see* Jerba, Île de
Djérem *76 B4 river* C Cameroon
Djevdjelija *see* Gevgelija
Djibouti *72 D4 var.* Jibuti. *country capital* (Djibouti) E Djibouti
Djibouti *72 D4 off.* Republic of Djibouti, *var.* Jibuti; *prev.* French Somaliland, French Territory of the Afars and Issas, *Fr.* Côte Française des Somalis, Territoire Français des Afars et des Issas. *country* E Africa

DJIBOUTI
East Africa

Official name Republic of Djibouti
Formation 1977 / 1977
Capital Djibouti
Population 900,000 / 101 people per sq mile (39 people per sq km)
Total area 8494 sq. miles (22,000 sq. km)
Languages Somali, Afar, French*, Arabic*
Religions Muslim (mainly Sunni) 94%, Christian 6%
Ethnic mix Issa 60%, Afar 35%, Other 5%
Government Presidential system
Currency Djibouti franc = 100 centimes
Literacy rate 70%
Calorie consumption 2526 kilocalories

Djibouti, Republic of *see* Djibouti
Djokjakarta *see* Yogyakarta
Djourab, Erg du *76 C2 desert* N Chad
Djúpivogur *83 E5* Austurland, SE Iceland
Dmitriyevsk *see* Makiyivka
Dnepr *see* Dnieper
Dneprodzerzhinsk *see* Romaniv
Dneprodzerzhinskoye Vodokhranilishche *see* Dniprodzerzhyns'ke Vodoskhovyshche
Dnepropetrovsk *see* Dnipropetrovs'k
Dneprorudnoye *see* Dniprorudne
Dnestr *see* Dniester
Dnieper *81 F4 Bel.* Dnyapro, *Rus.* Dnepr, *Ukr.* Dnipro. *river* E Europe
Dnieper Lowland *109 E2 Bel.* Prydnyaprowskaya Nizina, *Ukr.* Prydniprovs'ka Nyzovyna. *lowlands* Belarus/Ukraine
Dniester *81 E4 Rom.* Nistru, *Rus.* Dnestr, *Ukr.* Dnister; *anc.* Tyras. *river* Moldova/Ukraine
Dnipro *see* Dnieper
Dniprodzerzhyns'k *see* Romaniv
Dniprodzerzhyns'ke Vodoskhovyshche *109 F3 Rus.* Dneprodzerzhinskoye Vodokhranilishche. *reservoir* C Ukraine
Dnipropetrovs'k *109 F3 Rus.* Dnepropetrovsk; *prev.* Yekaterinoslav. Dnipropetrovs'ka Oblast', E Ukraine
Dniprorudne *109 F3 Rus.* Dneprorudnoye. Zaporiz'ka Oblast', SE Ukraine
Dnister *see* Dniester
Dnyapro *see* Dnieper
Doba *76 C4* Logone-Oriental, S Chad
Döbeln *94 D4* Sachsen, E Germany
Doberai Peninsula *139 G4 Dut.* Vogelkop. *peninsula* Papua, E Indonesia
Doboj *100 C3* Republiks Srpska, N Bosnia and Herzegovina
Dobre Miasto *98 D2 Ger.* Guttstadt. Warmińsko-mazurskie, NE Poland
Dobrich *104 E1 Rom.* Bazargic; *prev.* Tolbukhin. Dobrich, NE Bulgaria
Dobrush *107 D7* Homyel'skaya Voblasts', SE Belarus
Dobryn' *see* Dabryn'
Dodecanese *105 D6 var.* Nóties Sporádes, *Eng.* Dodecanese; *prev.* Dhodhekánisos, Dodekanisos. *island group* SE Greece
Dodecanese *see* Dodekánisa
Dodekanisos *see* Dodekánisa
Dodge City *45 E5* Kansas, C USA
Dodoma *69 D5 country capital* (Tanzania) Dodoma, C Tanzania
Dogana *96 E1* NE San Marino Europe
Dogo *131 B6 island* Oki-shotō, SW Japan
Dogondoutchi *75 F3* Dosso, SW Niger
Dogrular *see* Pravda
Doğubayazıt *117 F3* Ağrı, E Turkey
Doğu Karadeniz Dağları *117 E3 var.* Anadolu Dağları. *mountain range* NE Turkey
Doha *see* Ad Dawḩah
Doire *see* Londonderry
Dokdo *see* Liancourt Rocks
Dokkum *86 D1* Fryslân, N Netherlands
Dokuchayevs'k *109 G3 var.* Dokuchayevsk. Donets'ka Oblast', SE Ukraine
Dokuchayevsk *see* Dokuchayevs'k
Doldrums Fracture Zone *66 C4 fracture zone* W Atlantic Ocean
Dôle *90 D4* Jura, E France
Dolina *see* Dolyna
Dolinskaya *see* Dolyns'ka
Dolisie *77 B6 prev.* Loubomo. Niari, S Congo
Dolna Oryakhovitsa *104 D2 prev.* Polikrayshte. Veliko Tŭrnovo, N Bulgaria
Dolni Chiflik *104 E2 prev.* Rudnik. Varna, E Bulgaria
Dolomites *96 C1 var.* Dolomiti, *Eng.* Dolomites. *mountain range* NE Italy
Dolomites/Dolomiti *see* Dolomitiche, Alpi
Dolores *64 D4* Buenos Aires, E Argentina
Dolores *52 B1* Petén, N Guatemala
Dolores *64 D4* Soriano, SW Uruguay
Dolores Hidalgo *51 E4 var.* Ciudad de Dolores Hidalgo. Guanajuato, C Mexico
Dolyna *108 B2 Rus.* Dolina. Ivano-Frankivs'ka Oblast', W Ukraine
Dolyns'ka *109 F3 Rus.* Dolinskaya. Kirovohrads'ka Oblast', S Ukraine
Domachëvo/Domaczewo *see* Damachava
Dombås *85 B5* Oppland, S Norway
Domel Island *see* Letsôk-aw Kyun
Domesnes, Cape *see* Kolkasrags
Domeyko *64 B3* Atacama, N Chile
Dominica *55 H4 off.* Commonwealth of Dominica. *country* E West Indies

DOMINICA
West Indies

Official name Commonwealth of Dominica
Formation 1978 / 1978
Capital Roseau
Population 73,286 / 253 people per sq mile (98 people per sq km)
Total area 291 sq. miles (754 sq. km)
Languages French Creole, English*
Religions Roman Catholic 77%, Protestant 15%, Other 8%
Ethnic mix Black 87%, Mixed race 9%, Carib 3%, Other 1%
Government Parliamentary system
Currency East Caribbean dollar = 100 cents
Literacy rate 88%
Calorie consumption 3047 kilocalories

Dominica Channel *see* Martinique Passage
Dominica, Commonwealth of *see* Dominica
Dominican Republic *55 E2 country* C West Indies

DOMINICAN REPUBLIC
West Indies

Official name Dominican Republic
Formation 1865 / 1865
Capital Santo Domingo
Population 10.4 million / 557 people per sq mile (215 people per sq km)

DOMINICAN REPUBLIC
(continued)

Total area 18,679 sq. miles (48,380 sq. km)
Languages Spanish*, French Creole
Religions Roman Catholic 95%, Other and nonreligious 5%
Ethnic mix Mixed race 73%, European 16%, African 11%
Government Presidential system
Currency Dominican Republic peso = 100 centavos
Literacy rate 91%
Calorie consumption 2597 kilocalories

Domokós *105 B5 var.* Dhomokós. Stereá Elláda, C Greece
Don *111 B6 var.* Duna, Tanais. *river* SW Russian Federation
Donau *see* Danube
Donauwörth *95 C6* Bayern, S Germany
Don Benito *92 C3* Extremadura, W Spain
Doncaster *89 D5 anc.* Danum. N England, United Kingdom
Dondo *78 B1* Cuanza Norte, NW Angola
Donegal *89 B5 Ir.* Dún na nGall. Donegal, NW Ireland
Donegal Bay *89 A5 Ir.* Bá Dhún na nGall. *bay* NW Ireland
Donets *109 G2 river* Russian Federation/Ukraine
Donets'k *109 G3 Rus.* Donetsk; *prev.* Stalino. Donets'ka Oblast', E Ukraine
Dongfang *128 B7 var.* Basuo. Hainan, S China
Dongguan *128 C6* Guangdong, S China
Đông Ha *136 E4* Quang Tri, C Vietnam
Dong Hai *see* East China Sea
Đông Hơi *136 D4* Quang Binh, C Vietnam
Dongliao *see* Liaoyuan
Dongola *72 B3 var.* Donqola, Dunqulah. Northern, N Sudan
Dongou *77 C5* Likouala, NE Congo
Dong Rak, Phanom *see* Dângrêk, Chuŏr Phnum
Dongting Hu *128 C5 var.* Tung-t'ing Hu. *lake* S China
Donostia *93 E1* País Vasco, N Spain *see also* San Sebastián
Donqola *see* Dongola
Doolow *73 D5* Sumalē, E Ethiopia
Doornik *see* Tournai
Door Peninsula *40 C2 peninsula* Wisconsin, N USA
Dooxo Nugaaleed *73 E5 var.* Nogal Valley. *valley* E Somalia
Dordogne *91 B5 cultural region* SW France
Dordogne *91 B5 river* W France
Dordrecht *86 C4 var.* Dordt, Dort. Zuid-Holland, SW Netherlands
Dordt *see* Dordrecht
Dorohoi *108 C3* Botoşani, NE Romania
Dorotea *84 C4* Västerbotten, N Sweden
Dorpat *see* Tartu
Dorre Island *147 A5 island* Western Australia
Dort *see* Dordrecht
Dortmund *94 A4* Nordrhein-Westfalen, W Germany
Dos Hermanas *92 C4* Andalucía, S Spain
Dospad Dagh *see* Rhodope Mountains
Dospat *104 C3* Smolyan, S Bulgaria
Dothan *42 D3* Alabama, S USA
Dotnuva *106 B4* Kaunas, C Lithuania
Douai *90 C2 prev.* Douay; *anc.* Duacum. Nord, N France
Douala *77 A5 var.* Duala. Littoral, W Cameroon
Douay *see* Douai
Douglas *89 C5 dependent territory capital* (Isle of Man) E Isle of Man
Douglas *48 C3* Arizona, SW USA
Douglas *44 D3* Wyoming, C USA
Douma *see* Dūmā
Douro *see* Duero
Douvres *see* Dover
Dover *89 E7 Fr.* Douvres, *Lat.* Dubris Portus. SE England, United Kingdom
Dover *41 F4 state capital* Delaware, NE USA
Dover, Strait of *90 C2 var.* Straits of Dover, *Fr.* Pas de Calais. *strait* England, United Kingdom/France
Dover, Straits of *see* Dover, Strait of
Dovrefjell *85 B5 plateau* S Norway
Downpatrick *89 B5 Ir.* Dún Pádraig. SE Northern Ireland, United Kingdom
Dozen *131 B6 island* Oki-shotō, SW Japan
Drâa, Hammada du *see* Dra, Hamada
Drač/Draç *see* Durrës
Drachten *86 D2* Fryslân, N Netherlan
Drăgăşani *108 B5* Vâlcea, SW Roman
Dragoman *104 B2* Sofiya, W Bulgaria
Dra, Hamada du *70 C3 var.* Hammad du Drâa, Haut Plateau du Dra. *plate* W Algeria
Dra, Haut Plateau du *see* Dra, Hamada du
Drahichyn *107 B6 Pol.* Drohiczyn Poleski, *Rus.* Drogichin. Brestskaya Voblasts', SW Belarus
Drakensberg *78 D5 mountain range* Lesotho/South Africa
Drake Passage *57 B8 passage* Atlantic Ocean/Pacific Ocean
Dralfa *104 D2* Tŭrgovishte, N Bulgari
Dráma *104 C3 var.* Dhráma. Anatolik Makedonía kai Thráki, NE Greece
Dramburg *see* Drawsko Pomorskie
Drammen *85 B6* Buskerud, S Norway
Drau *see* Drava
Drava *100 C3 var.* Drau, *Eng.* Drave, *Hung.* Dráva. *river* C Europe
Dráva/Drave *see* Drau/Drava
Drawsko Pomorskie *98 B3 Ger.* Dramburg. Zachodnio-pomorskie, NW Poland
Drépano, Akrotírio *104 C4 var.* Akrotírio Dhrepanon. *headland* N Greece
Drepanum *see* Trapani
Dresden *94 D4* Sachsen, E Germany
Drin *see* Drinit, Lumi i
Drina *100 C3 river* Bosnia and Herzegovina/Serbia
Drinit, Lumi i *101 D5 var.* Drin. *river* NW Albania
Drinit të Zi, Lumi i *see* Black Drin
Drissa *see* Drysa
Drobeta-Turnu Severin *108 B5 prev.* Turnu Severin. Mehedinţi, SW Romania
Drogheda *89 B5 Ir.* Droichead Átha. NE Ireland
Drogichin *see* Drahichyn
Drogobych *see* Drohobych
Drohiczyn Poleski *see* Drahichyn
Drohobych *108 B2 Pol.* Drohobycz, *Rus.* Drogobych. L'vivs'ka Oblast', NW Ukraine
Drohobycz *see* Drohobych
Droichead Átha *see* Drogheda
Drôme *91 D5 cultural region* E France
Dronning Maud Land *154 B2 physica region* Antarctica
Drontheim *see* Trondheim
Drug *see* Durg
Druk-yul *see* Bhutan
Drummondville *39 E4* Québec, SE Canada
Druskienniki *see* Druskininkai
Druskininkai *107 B5 Pol.* Druskiennil Alytus, S Lithuania
Dryden *38 B3* Ontario, C Canada
Drysa *107 D5 Rus.* Drissa. *river* N Belarus
Duacum *see* Douai
Duala *see* Douala
Dubai *see* Dubayy
Dubăsari *108 D3 Rus.* Dubossary. NE Moldova
Dubawnt *37 F4 river* Nunavut, NW Canada
Dubayy *120 D4 Eng.* Dubai. Dubayy, NE United Arab Emirates
Dubbo *149 D6* New South Wales, SE Australia
Dublin *89 B5 Ir.* Baile Átha Cliath; *anc* Eblana. *country capital* (Ireland) Dublin, E Ireland
Dublin *43 E2* Georgia, SE USA
Dubno *108 C2* Rivnens'ka Oblast', NW Ukraine
Dubossary *see* Dubăsari
Dubris Portus *see* Dover
Dubrovnik *101 B5 It.* Ragusa. Dubrovnik-Neretva, SE Croatia
Dubuque *45 G3* Iowa, C USA
Dudelange *87 D8 var.* Forge du Sud, *Ger.* Dudelingen. Luxembourg, S Luxembourg
Dudelingen *see* Dudelange

ero *92 D2 Port.* Douro. *river* Portugal/Spain
sseldorf *see* Düsseldorf
ffel *87 C5* Antwerpen, C Belgium
gi Otok *100 A4 var.* Isola Grossa, *It.* sola Lunga. *island* W Croatia
inekerke *see* Dunkerque
isburg *94 A4 prev.* Duisburg-Hamborn. Nordrhein-Westfalen, W Germany
isburg-Hamborn *see* Duisburg
iven *86 D4* Gelderland, E Netherlands
k Faiwil *73 B5* Jonglei, E South Sudan
lan *126 D4 var.* Qagan Us. Qinghai, C China
lce, Golfo *53 E5 gulf* S Costa Rica
lce, Golfo *see* Izabal, Lago de
lmen *94 A4* Nordrhein-Westfalen, W Germany
lovo *104 E1* Silistra, NE Bulgaria
luth *45 G2* Minnesota, N USA
mā *119 B5 Fr.* Douma. Rīf Dimashq, SW Syria
mas *49 E1* Texas, SW USA
mfries *88 C4* S Scotland, United Kingdom
mont d'Urville *154 C4 French research station* Antarctica
myāt *72 B1 var.* Dumyât, *Eng.* Damietta. N Egypt
na *see* Danube, C Europe
na *see* Western Dvina
na *see* Don, Russian Federation
naburg *see* Daugavpils
naj *see* Wien, Austria
naj *see* Danube, C Europe
napentele *see* Dunaújváros
nărea *see* Danube
naújváros *99 C7 prev.* Dunapentele, Sztálinváros. Fejér, C Hungary
nav *see* Danube
ncan *49 G2* Oklahoma, C USA
ndalk *89 B5 Ir.* Dún Dealgan. Louth, NE Ireland
n Dealgan *see* Dundalk
ndee *78 D4* KwaZulu/Natal, E South Africa
ndee *88 C4* E Scotland, United Kingdom
nedin *151 B7* Otago, South Island, New Zealand
nfermline *88 C4* C Scotland, United Kingdom
ngu *77 E5* Orientale, NE Dem. Rep. Congo
ngun *138 B3 var.* Kuala Dungun. Terengganu, Peninsular Malaysia
nholme *see* Durham
nkerque *90 C2 Eng.* Dunkirk, *Flem.* Duinekerke; *prev.* Dunquerque. Nord, N France
nkirk *see* Dunkerque
ín Laoghaire *89 B6 Eng.* Dunleary; *prev.* Kingstown. E Ireland
unleary *see* Dún Laoghaire
ín Pádraig *see* Downpatrick
unquerque *see* Dunkerque
nqulah *see* Dongola
pnitsa *104 C2 prev.* Marek, Stanke Dimitrov. Kyustendil, W Bulgaria
qm *121 E5 var.* Daqm. E Oman
rance *91 D6 river* SE France
rango *50 D3 var.* Victoria de Durango. Durango, W Mexico
rango *44 C5* Colorado, C USA
urankulak *104 E1 Rom.* Răcari; *prev.* Blatnitsa, Duranulac. Dobrich, NE Bulgaria
urant *49 G2* Oklahoma, C USA
uranulac *see* Durankulak
urazzo *see* Durrës
urban *78 D4 var.* Port Natal. KwaZulu/Natal, E South Africa
urbe *106 B3 Ger.* Durben. W Latvia
urben *see* Durbe
urg *135 E4 prev.* Drug. Chhattīsgarh, C India
urham *89 D5 hist.* Dunholme. N England, United Kingdom
urham *43 F1* North Carolina, SE USA
urocortorum *see* Reims
urostorum *see* Silistra
urovernum *see* Canterbury
urrës *101 C6 var.* Durrësi, Dursi, *It.* Durazzo, *SCr.* Drač, *Turk.* Draç. Durrës, W Albania
urrësi *see* Durrës
ursi *see* Durrës
Durūz, Jabal ad *119 C5 mountain* SW Syria
D'Urville Island *150 C4 island* C New Zealand
Dusa Mareb/Dusa Marreb *see* Dhuusa Marreeb
Dushanbe *123 E3 var.* Dyushambe; *prev.* Stalinabad, *Taj.* Stalinobod. *country capital* (Tajikistan) W Tajikistan
Düsseldorf *94 A4 var.* Duesseldorf. Nordrhein-Westfalen, W Germany
Dŭstí *123 E3 Rus.* Dusti. SW Tajikistan
Dutch East Indies *see* Indonesia
Dutch Guiana *see* Suriname
Dutch Harbor *36 B3* Unalaska Island, Alaska, USA
Dutch New Guinea *see* Papua
Duzdab *see* Zāhedān
Dvina Bay *see* Chëshskaya Guba
Dvinsk *see* Daugavpils
Dyanev *see* Galkynyş
Dyersburg *42 C1* Tennessee, S USA
Dyushambe *see* Dushanbe
Dza Chu *see* Mekong
Dzaudzhikau *see* Vladikavkaz
Dzerzhinsk *111 C5* Nizhegorodskaya Oblast', W Russian Federation
Dzerzhinskiy *see* Nar'yan-Mar
Dzhalal-Abad *123 F2 Kir.* Jalal-Abad. Dzhalal-Abadskaya Oblast', W Kyrgyzstan
Dzhambul *see* Taraz
Dzhankoy *109 F4* Avtonomna Respublika Krym, S Ukraine
Dzharkurgan *see* Jarqo'rg'on
Dzhelandy *123 F3* SE Tajikistan
Dzhergalan *123 G2 Kir.* Jyrgalan. Issyk-Kul'skaya Oblast', NE Kyrgyzstan
Dzhezkazgan *see* Zhezkazgan
Dzhizak *see* Jizzax
Dzhugdzhur, Khrebet *115 G3 mountain range* E Russian Federation
Dzhusaly *see* Zhosaly
Działdowo *98 D3* Warmińsko-Mazurskie, C Poland
Dzuunmod *127 E2* Töv, C Mongolia
Dzüün Soyonī Nuruu *see* Vostochnyy Sayan
Dzvina *see* Western Dvina

E

Eagle Pass *49 F4* Texas, SW USA
East Açores Fracture Zone *see* East Azores Fracture Zone
East Antarctica *154 C3 prev.* Greater Antarctica. *physical region* Antarctica
East Australian Basin *see* Tasman Basin
East Azores Fracture Zone *66 C3 var.* East Açores Fracture Zone. *tectonic feature* E Atlantic Ocean
Eastbourne *89 E7* SE England, United Kingdom
East Cape *150 E3 headland* North Island, New Zealand
East China Sea *125 E2 Chin.* Dong Hai. *sea* W Pacific Ocean
Easter Fracture Zone *153 G4 tectonic feature* E Pacific Ocean
Easter Island *153 F4 var.* Rapa Nui, Easter Island. *island* E Pacific Ocean
Easter Island *see* Pascua, Isla de
Eastern Desert *68 D3 var.* Aş Şaḩrā' ash Sharqīyah, *Eng.* Arabian Desert, Eastern Desert. *desert* E Egypt
Eastern Desert *see* Sahara el Sharqiya
Eastern Ghats *124 B3 mountain range* SE India
Eastern Sayans *see* Vostochnyy Sayan
Eastern Sierra Madre *see* Madre Oriental, Sierra
East Falkland *65 D8 var.* Isla Soledad. *island* E Falkland Islands
East Frisian Islands *94 A3 Eng.* East Frisian Islands. *island group* NW Germany
East Frisian Islands *see* Ostfriesische Inseln
East Grand Forks *45 E1* Minnesota, N USA
East Indiaman Ridge *141 D6 undersea ridge* E Indian Ocean
East Indies *152 A3 island group* SE Asia
East Kilbride *88 C4* S Scotland, United Kingdom
East Korea Bay *129 E3 bay* E North Korea
Eastleigh *89 D7* S England, United Kingdom
East London *78 D5 Afr.* Oos-Londen; *prev.* Emonti, Port Rex. Eastern Cape, S South Africa
Eastmain *38 D3 river* Québec, C Canada
East Mariana Basin *142 B1 undersea basin* W Pacific Ocean
East Novaya Zemlya Trough *112 C1 var.* Novaya Zemlya Trough. *trough* W Kara Sea
East Pacific Rise *153 F4 undersea rise* E Pacific Ocean
East Pakistan *see* Bangladesh
East Saint Louis *40 B4* Illinois, N USA
East Scotia Basin *67 C7 undersea basin* SE Scotia Sea
East Sea *130 A4 var.* Sea of Japan, *Rus.* Yapanskoye More. *Sea* NW Pacific Ocean
East Siberian Sea *115 F1 Eng.* East Siberian Sea. *sea* Arctic Ocean
East Siberian Sea *see* Vostochno-Sibirskoye More
East Timor *139 F5 var.* Loro Sae; *prev.* Portuguese Timor, Timor Timur. *country* S Indonesia

EAST TIMOR
Southeast Asia

Official name Democratic Republic of Timor-Leste
Formation 2002 / 2002
Capital Dili
Population 1.1 million / 195 people per sq mile (75 people per sq km)
Total area 5756 sq. miles (14,874 sq. km)
Languages Tetum* (Portuguese/Austronesian), Bahasa Indonesia, Portuguese*
Religions Roman Catholic 95%, Other 5%
Ethnic mix Papuan groups approx. 85%, Indonesian groups approx. 13%, Chinese 2%
Government Parliamentary system
Currency US dollar = 100 cents
Literacy rate 58%
Calorie consumption 2083 kilocalories

Eau Claire *40 A2* Wisconsin, N USA
Eau Claire, Lac à L' *see* St. Clair, Lake
Eauripik Rise *142 B2 undersea rise* W Pacific Ocean
Ebensee *95 D6* Oberösterreich, N Austria
Eberswalde-Finow *94 D3* Brandenburg, E Germany
Ebetsu *130 D2 var.* Ebetu. Hokkaidō, NE Japan
Ebetu *see* Ebetsu
Eblana *see* Dublin
Ebolowa *77 A5* Sud, S Cameroon
Ebon Atoll *144 D2 var.* Epoon. *atoll* Ralik Chain, S Marshall Islands
Ebora *see* Évora
Eboracum *see* York
Ebro *93 E2 river* NE Spain
Eburacum *see* York
Ebusus *see* Eivissa
Ebusus *see* Eivissa
Ebusus *see* Eivissa
Ecbatana *see* Hamadān
Ech Cheliff/Ech Chleff *see* Chlef
Echo Bay *37 E3* Northwest Territories, NW Canada
Echt *87 D5* Limburg, SE Netherlands
Ecija *92 D4 anc.* Astigi. Andalucía, SW Spain
Eckengraf *see* Viesīte
Ecuador *60 B1 off.* Republic of Ecuador. *country* NW South America

ECUADOR
South America

Official name Republic of Ecuador
Formation 1830 / 1942
Capital Quito
Population 15.7 million / 147 people per sq mile (57 people per sq km)
Total area 109,483 sq. miles (283,560 sq. km)
Languages Spanish*, Quechua, other Amerindian languages
Religions Roman Catholic 95%, Protestant, Jewish, and other 5%
Ethnic mix Mestizo 77%, White 11%, Amerindian 7%, Black 5%

ECUADOR
(continued)

Government Presidential system
Currency US dollar = 100 cents
Literacy rate 93%
Calorie consumption 2477 kilocalories

Ecuador, Republic of *see* Ecuador
Ed Da'ein *72 A4* Southern Darfur, W Sudan
Ed Damazin *72 C4 var.* Ad Damazīn. Blue Nile, E Sudan
Ed Damer *72 C3 var.* Ad Dāmir, Ad Damar. River Nile, NE Sudan
Ed Debba *72 B3* Northern, N Sudan
Ede *86 D4* Gelderland, C Netherlands
Ede *75 F5* Osun, SW Nigeria
Edéa *77 A5* Littoral, SW Cameroon
Edessa *see* Şanlıurfa
Edfu *see* Idfū
Edgeøya *83 G2 island* S Svalbard
Edgware *89 A7* Harrow, SE England, United Kingdom
Edinburg *49 G5* Texas, SW USA
Edinburgh *88 C4 national capital* S Scotland, United Kingdom
Edingen *see* Enghien
Edirne *116 A2 Eng.* Adrianople; *anc.* Adrianopolis, Hadrianopolis. Edirne, NW Turkey
Edmonds *46 B2* Washington, NW USA
Edmonton *37 E5 province capital* Alberta, SW Canada
Edmundston *39 E4* New Brunswick, SE Canada
Edna *49 G4* Texas, SW USA
Edolo *96 B1* Lombardia, N Italy
Edremit *116 A3* Balıkesir, NW Turkey
Edward, Lake *77 E5 var.* Albert Edward Nyanza, Edward Nyanza, Lac Idi Amin, Lake Rutanzige. *lake* Uganda/Dem. Rep. Congo
Edward Nyanza *see* Edward, Lake
Edwards Plateau *49 F3 plain* Texas, SW USA
Edzo *53 E4 prev.* Rae-Edzo. Northwest Territories, NW Canada
Eeklo *87 B5 var.* Eekloo. Oost-Vlaanderen, NW Belgium
Eekloo *see* Eeklo
Eems *see* Ems
Eersel *87 C5* Noord-Brabant, S Netherlands
Eesti Vabariik *see* Estonia
Efate *144 D4 var.* Efate, *Fr.* Vaté; *prev.* Sandwich Island. *island* C Vanuatu
Efate *see* Efate
Effingham *40 B4* Illinois, N USA
Eforie-Sud *108 D5* Constanța, E Romania
Egadi Is. *97 B7 island group* S Italy
Ege Denizi *see* Aegean Sea
Eger *99 D6 Ger.* Erlau. Heves, NE Hungary
Eger *see* Cheb, Czech Republic
Egeria Fracture Zone *141 C5 tectonic feature* W Indian Ocean
Éghezèe *87 C6* Namur, C Belgium
Egina *see* Aígina
Egio *see* Aígio
Egmont *see* Taranaki, Mount
Egmont, Cape *150 C4 headland* North Island, New Zealand
Egoli *see* Johannesburg
Egypt *72 B2 off.* Arab Republic of Egypt, *Ar.* Jumhūrīyah Mişr al 'Arabīyah, *prev.* United Arab Republic; *anc.* Aegyptus. *country* NE Africa

EGYPT
North Africa

Official name Arab Republic of Egypt
Formation 1936 / 1982
Capital Cairo
Population 82.1 million / 214 people per sq mile (82 people per sq km)
Total area 386,660 sq. miles (1,001,450 sq. km)
Languages Arabic*, French, English, Berber
Religions Muslim (mainly Sunni) 90%, Coptic Christian and other 10%
Ethnic mix Egyptian 99%, Nubian, Armenian, Greek, and Berber 1%
Government Transitional regime

EGYPT
(continued)

Currency Egyptian pound = 100 piastres
Literacy rate 74%
Calorie consumption 3557 kilocalories

EL SALVADOR
Central America

Official name Republic of El Salvador
Formation 1841 / 1841
Capital San Salvador
Population 6.3 million / 788 people per sq mile (304 people per sq km)
Total area 8124 sq. miles (21,040 sq. km)
Languages Spanish*
Religions Roman Catholic 80%, Evangelical 18%, Other 2%
Ethnic mix Mestizo 90%, White 9%, Amerindian 1%
Government Presidential system
Currency Salvadorean colón = 100 centavos; US dollar = 100 cents
Literacy rate 86%
Calorie consumption 2513 kilocalories

EQUATORIAL GUINEA
Central Africa

Official name Republic of Equatorial Guinea
Formation 1968 / 1968
Capital Malabo
Population 800,000 / 74 people per sq mile (29 people per sq km)
Total area 10,830 sq. miles (28,051 sq. kr
Languages Spanish*, Fang, Bubi, French
Religions Roman Catholic 90%, Other 10%
Ethnic mix Fang 85%, Other 11%, Bubi 4
Government Presidential system
Currency CFA franc = 100 centimes
Literacy rate 94%
Calorie consumption Not available

ERITREA
East Africa

Official name State of Eritrea
Formation 1993 / 2002
Capital Asmara

ɿITREA
(continued)

ɔpulation 6.3 million / 139 people
er sq mile (54 people per sq km)
ɔtal area 46,842 sq. miles (121,320 sq. km)
anguages Tigrinya*, English*, Tigre,
far, Arabic*, Saho, Bilen, Kunama,
ara, Hadareb
eligions Christian 50%, Muslim 48%,
ther 2%
thnic mix Tigray 50%, Tigre 31%, Other
%, Afar 5%, Saho 5%
overnment Presidential /
arliamentary system
urrency Nakfa = 100 cents
teracy rate 70%
alorie consumption 1640 kilocalories

trea, State of *see* Eritrea
van *see* Yerevan
angen *95 C5* Bayern, S Germany
au *see* Eger
ian *see* Erenhot
melo *86 D3* Gelderland, C Netherlands
mióni *105 C6* Pelopónnisos, S Greece
moúpoli *105 D6 var.* Hermoupolis; *prev.* Ermoúpolis. Sýyros, Kykládes, Greece, Aegean Sea
moúpolis *see* Ermoúpoli
nākulam *132 C3* Kerala, SW India
ode *132 C2* Tamil Nādu, SE India
quelinnes *87 B7* Hainaut, S Belgium
-Rachidia *70 C2 var.* Ksar al Soule. E Morocco
Rahad *72 B4 var.* Ar Rahad. Northern Kordofan, C Sudan
romango *144 D4 island* S Vanuatu
tis *see* Irtysh, C Asia
tra *see* Eritrea
zerum *see* Erzurum
zincan *117 E3 var.* Erzinjan. Erzincan, E Turkey
zinjan *see* Erzincan
zurum *117 E3 prev.* Erzerum. Erzurum, NE Turkey
bjerg *85 A7* Syddtjylland, W Denmark
bo *see* Espoo
caldes *91 A8* Escaldes Engordany, C Andorra Europe
canaba *40 C2* Michigan, N USA
caut *see* Scheldt
ch-sur-Alzette *87 D8* Luxembourg, S Luxembourg
claves, Grand Lac des *see* Great Slave Lake
condido *47 C8* California, W USA
cuinapa *50 D3 var.* Escuinapa de Hidalgo. Sinaloa, C Mexico
cuinapa de Hidalgo *see* Escuinapa
cuintla *52 B2* Escuintla, S Guatemala
cuintla *51 G5* Chiapas, SE Mexico
enguly *122 B3 Rus.* Gasan-Kuli. Balkan Welaýaty, W Turkmenistan
fahān *120 C3 Eng.* Isfahan; *anc.* Aspadana. Eşfahān, C Iran
h Sharā *see* Ash Sharāh
il *see* Ishim, Kazakhstan/Russian Federation
kimo Point *see* Arviat
kişehir *116 B3 var.* Eskishehr. Eskişehir, W Turkey
kishehr *see* Eskişehir
lāmābād *see* Eslāmābād-e Gharb
lāmābād-e Gharb *120 C3 var.* Eslāmābād; *prev.* Harunabad, Shāhābād. Kermānshāhān, W Iran
meraldas *60 A1* Esmeraldas, N Ecuador
na *see* Isnā
paña *see* Spain
panola *48 D1* New Mexico, SW USA
perance *147 B7* Western Australia
peranza *50 B2* Sonora, NW Mexico
peranza *154 A2 Argentinian research station* Antarctica
pinal *58 B3* Tolima, C Colombia
pinhaço, Serra do *56 D4 mountain range* SE Brazil
pírito Santo *63 F4 off.* Estado do Espírito Santo. *state* E Brazil
pírito Santo *63 F4 off.* Estado do Espírito Santo. *region* E Brazil
pírito Santo, Estado do *see* Espírito Santo
piritu Santo *144 C4 var.* Santo. *island* W Vanuatu
Espoo *85 D6 Swe.* Esbo. Etelä-Suomi, S Finland
Esquel *65 B6* Chubut, SW Argentina
Essaouira *70 B2 prev.* Mogador. W Morocco
Esseg *see* Osijek
Es Semara *see* Smara
Essen *87 C5* Antwerpen, N Belgium
Essen *94 A4 var.* Essen an der Ruhr. Nordrhein-Westfalen, W Germany
Essen an der Ruhr *see* Essen
Essequibo River *59 F3 river* C Guyana
Es Suweida *see* As Suwaydā'
Estacado, Llano *49 E2 plain* New Mexico/Texas, SW USA
Estados, Isla de los *65 C8 prev. Eng.* Staten Island. *island* S Argentina
Estância *63 G3* Sergipe, E Brazil
Estelí *52 D3* Estelí, NW Nicaragua
Estella *93 E1 Bas.* Lizarra. Navarra, N Spain
Estepona *92 D5* Andalucía, S Spain
Estevan *37 F5* Saskatchewan, S Canada
Estland *see* Estonia
Estonia *106 D2 off.* Republic of Estonia, *Est.* Eesti Vabariik, *Ger.* Estland, *Latv.* Igaunija; *prev.* Estonian SSR, *Rus.* Estonskaya SSR. *country* NE Europe

ESTONIA
Northeast Europe

Official name Republic of Estonia
Formation 1991 / 1991
Capital Tallinn
Population 1.3 million / 75 people per sq mile (29 people per sq km)
Total area 17,462 sq. miles (45,226 sq. km)
Languages Estonian*, Russian
Religions Evangelical Lutheran 56%, Orthodox Christian 25%, Other 19%
Ethnic mix Estonian 69%, Russian 25%, Other 4%, Ukrainian 2%
Government Parliamentary system
Currency Euro = 100 cents
Literacy rate 99%
Calorie consumption 3214 kilocalories

Estonian SSR *see* Estonia
Estonia, Republic of *see* Estonia
Estonskaya SSR *see* Estonia
Estrela, Serra da *92 C3 mountain range* C Portugal
Estremadura *see* Extremadura
Estremoz *92 C4* Évora, S Portugal
Eszék *see* Osijek
Esztergom *99 C6 Ger.* Gran; *anc.* Strigonium. Komárom-Esztergom, N Hungary
Étalle *87 D8* Luxembourg, SE Belgium
Etāwah *134 D3* Uttar Pradesh, N India
Ethiopia *73 C5 off.* Federal Democratic Republic of Ethiopia; *prev.* Abyssinia, People's Democratic Republic of Ethiopia. *country* E Africa

ETHIOPIA
East Africa

Official name Federal Democratic Republic of Ethiopia
Formation 1896 / 2002
Capital Addis Ababa
Population 94.1 million / 220 people per sq mile (85 people per sq km)
Total area 435,184 sq. miles (1,127,127 sq. km)
Languages Amharic*, Tigrinya, Galla, Sidamo, Somali, English, Arabic
Religions Orthodox Christian 40%, Muslim 40%, Traditional beliefs 15%, Other 5%
Ethnic mix Oromo 40%, Amhara 25%, Other 13%, Sidama 9%, Tigray 7%, Somali 6%
Government Parliamentary system
Currency Ethiopian birr = 100 cents
Literacy rate 39%
Calorie consumption 2105 kilocalories

Ethiopia, Federal Democratic Republic of *see* Ethiopia
Ethiopian Highlands *73 C5 var.* Ethiopian Plateau. *plateau* N Ethiopia
Ethiopian Plateau *see* Ethiopian Highlands
Ethiopia, People's Democratic Republic of *see* Ethiopia
Mount Etna *97 C7 Eng.* Mount Etna. *volcano* Sicilia, Italy, C Mediterranean Sea
Etna, Mount *see* Etna, Monte
Etosha Pan *78 B3 salt lake* N Namibia
Etoumbi *77 B5* Cuvette Ouest, NW Congo
Etsch *see* Adige
Et Tafila *see* Aṭ Ṭafīlah
Ettelbrück *87 D8* Diekirch, C Luxembourg
'Eua *145 E5 prev.* Middleburg Island. *island* Tongatapu Group, SE Tonga
Euboea *105 C5 Lat.* Euboea. *island* C Greece
Euboea *see* Évvoia
Eucla *147 D6* Western Australia
Euclid *40 D3* Ohio, N USA
Eufaula Lake *49 G1 var.* Eufaula Reservoir. *reservoir* Oklahoma, C USA
Eufaula Reservoir *see* Eufaula Lake
Eugene *46 B3* Oregon, NW USA
Eumolpias *see* Plovdiv
Eupen *87 D6* Liège, E Belgium
Euphrates *112 B4 Ar.* Al-Furāt, *Turk.* Firat Nehri. *river* SW Asia
Eureka *47 A5* California, W USA
Eureka *44 A1* Montana, NW USA
Europa Point *93 H5 headland* S Gibraltar
Europe *80 continent*
Eutin *94 C2* Schleswig-Holstein, N Germany
Euxine Sea *see* Black Sea
Evansdale *45 G3* Iowa, C USA
Evanston *40 B3* Illinois, N USA
Evanston *44 B4* Wyoming, C USA
Evansville *40 B5* Indiana, N USA
Eveleth *45 G1* Minnesota, N USA
Everard, Lake *149 A6 salt lake* South Australia
Everest, Mount *126 B5 Chin.* Qomolangma Feng, *Nep.* Sagarmāthā. *mountain* China/Nepal
Everett *46 B2* Washington, NW USA
Everglades, The *43 F5 wetland* Florida, SE USA
Evje *85 A6* Aust-Agder, S Norway
Evmolpia *see* Plovdiv
Évora *92 B4 anc.* Ebora, *Lat.* Liberalitas Julia. Évora, C Portugal
Évreux *90 C3 anc.* Civitas Eburovicum. Eure, N France
Évros *see* Maritsa
Évry *90 E2* Essonne, N France
Ewarton *54 B5* C Jamaica
Excelsior Springs *45 F4* Missouri, C USA
Exe *89 C7 river* SW England, United Kingdom
Exeter *89 C7 anc.* Isca Damnoniorum. SW England, United Kingdom
Exmoor *89 C7 moorland* SW England, United Kingdom
Exmouth *146 A4* Western Australia
Exmouth *89 C7* SW England, United Kingdom
Exmouth Gulf *146 A4 gulf* Western Australia
Exmouth Plateau *141 E5 undersea plateau* E Indian Ocean
Extremadura *92 C3 var.* Estremadura. *autonomous community* W Spain
Exuma Cays *54 C1 islets* C Bahamas
Exuma Sound *54 C1 sound* C Bahamas
Eyre Mountains *151 A7 mountain range* South Island, New Zealand
Eyre North, Lake *149 A5 salt lake* South Australia
Eyre Peninsula *149 A6 peninsula* South Australia
Eyre South, Lake *149 A5 salt lake* South Australia
Ezo *see* Hokkaidō

F

Faadhippolhu Atoll *132 B4 var.* Fadiffolu, Lhaviyani Atoll. *atoll* N Maldives
Fabens *48 D3* Texas, SW USA
Fada *76 C2* Borkou-Ennedi-Tibesti, E Chad
Fada-Ngourma *75 E4* E Burkina Faso
Fadiffolu *see* Faadhippolhu Atoll
Faenza *96 C3 anc.* Faventia. Emilia-Romagna, N Italy
Faeroe Islands *see* Faroe Islands
Færøerne *see* Faroe Islands
Faetano *96 E2* E San Marino
Făgăraş *108 C4 Ger.* Fogarasch, *Hung.* Fogaras. Braşov, C Romania
Fagibina, Lake *see* Faguibine, Lac
Fagne *87 C7 hill range* S Belgium
Faguibine, Lac *75 E3 var.* Lake Fagibina. *lake* NW Mali
Fahlun *see* Falun
Fahraj *120 E4* Kermān, SE Iran
Faial *92 A5 var.* Ilha do Faial. *island* Azores, Portugal, NE Atlantic Ocean
Faial, Ilha do *see* Faial
Faifo *see* Hôi An
Fairbanks *36 D3* Alaska, USA
Fairfield *47 B6* California, W USA
Fair Isle *88 D2 island* NE Scotland, United Kingdom
Fairlie *151 B6* Canterbury, South Island, New Zealand
Fairmont *45 F3* Minnesota, N USA
Faisalābād *134 C2 prev.* Lyallpur. Punjab, NE Pakistan
Faizābād *135 E3* Uttar Pradesh, N India
Faiẕābād *123 F3 var.* Feizābād, Feyzābād, Fyzabad; *prev.* Feyẕābād. Badakhshān, NE Afghanistan
Fakaofo Atoll *145 F3 island* SE Tokelau
Falam *136 A3* Chin State, W Myanmar (Burma)
Falconara Marittima *96 C3* Marche, C Italy
Falkenau an der Eger *see* Sokolov
Falkland Islands *65 D7 var.* Falklands, Islas Malvinas. *UK dependent territory* SW Atlantic Ocean
Falkland Plateau *57 D7 var.* Argentine Rise. *undersea feature* SW Atlantic Ocean
Falklands *see* Falkland Islands
Falknov nad Ohří *see* Sokolov
Fallbrook *47 C8* California, W USA
Falmouth *54 A4* W Jamaica
Falmouth *89 C7* SW England, United Kingdom
Falster *85 B8 island* SE Denmark
Fălticeni *108 C3 Hung.* Falticsén. Suceava, NE Romania
Falticsén *see* Fălticeni
Falun *85 C6 var.* Fahlun. Kopparberg, C Sweden
Famagusta *see* Gazimağusa
Famagusta Bay *102 C5 var.* Famagusta Bay, *Gk.* Kólpos Ammóchostos. *bay* E Cyprus
Famagusta Bay *see* Gazimağusa Körfezi
Famenne *87 C7 physical region* SE Belgium
Fang *136 C3* Chiang Mai, NW Thailand
Fanning Island *see* Tabuaeran
Fanø *96 C3 island* W Denmark
Farafangana *79 G4* Fianarantsoa, SE Madagascar
Farāh *122 D4 var.* Farah, Fararud. Farāh, W Afghanistan
Farah Rud *122 D4 river* W Afghanistan
Faranah *74 C4* Haute-Guinée, S Guinea
Fararud *see* Farāh
Farasan, Jaza'ir *121 A6 island group* SW Saudi Arabia
Farewell, Cape *150 C4 headland* South Island, New Zealand
Farewell, Cape *see* Nunap Isua
Fargo *45 F2* North Dakota, N USA
Farg'ona *123 F2 Rus.* Fergana; *prev.* Novyy Margilan. Farg'ona Viloyati, E Uzbekistan
Faribault *45 F2* Minnesota, N USA
Farīdābād *134 D3* Haryāna, N India
Farkhor *123 E3 Rus.* Parkhar. SW Tajikistan
Farmington *45 G5* Missouri, C USA
Farmington *48 C1* New Mexico, SW USA
Faro *92 B5* Faro, S Portugal
Faroe-Iceland Ridge *80 C1 undersea ridge* NW Norwegian Sea
Faroe Islands *83 E5 var.* Faeroe Islands, *Dan.* Færøerne, *Faer.* Føroyar. *Danish external territory* N Atlantic Ocean
Faroe-Shetland Trough *80 C2 trough* NE Atlantic Ocean
Farquhar Group *79 G2 island group* S Seychelles
Fars, Khalīj-e *see* Persian Gulf
Farvel, Kap *see* Nunap Isua
Fastiv *109 E2 Rus.* Fastov. Kyyivs'ka Oblast', NW Ukraine
Fastov *see* Fastiv

Fauske *84 C3* Nordland, C Norway
Faventia *see* Faenza
Faxa Bay *see* Faxaflói
Faxaflói *82 D5 Eng.* Faxa Bay. *bay* W Iceland
Faya *76 C2 prev.* Faya-Largeau, Largeau. Borkou-Ennedi-Tibesti, N Chad
Faya-Largeau *see* Faya
Fayetteville *42 A1* Arkansas, C USA
Fayetteville *43 F1* North Carolina, SE USA
Fdérick *see* Fdérik
Fdérik *74 C2 var.* Fdérick, *Fr.* Fort Gouraud. Tiris Zemmour, NW Mauritania
Fear, Cape *43 F2 headland* Bald Head Island, North Carolina, SE USA
Fécamp *90 B3* Seine-Maritime, N France
Fédala *see* Mohammedia
Federal Capital Territory *see* Australian Capital Territory
Fehérgyarmat *99 E6* Szabolcs-Szatmár-Bereg, E Hungary
Fehértemplom *see* Bela Crkva
Fehmarn *94 C2 island* N Germany
Fehmarn Belt *94 C2 Dan.* Femern Bælt, *Ger.* Fehmarnbelt. *strait* Denmark / Germany
Fehmarnbelt Fehmarn Belt/Femer Bælt
Feijó *62 C2* Acre, W Brazil
Feilding *150 D4* Manawatu-Wanganui, North Island, New Zealand
Feira *see* Feira de Santana
Feira de Santana *63 G3 var.* Feira. Bahia, E Brazil
Feizābād *see* Faizābād
Feketehalom *see* Codlea
Felanitx *93 G3* Mallorca, Spain, W Mediterranean Sea
Felicitas Julia *see* Lisboa
Felidhu Atoll *132 B4 atoll* C Maldives
Felipe Carrillo Puerto *51 H4* Quintana Roo, SE Mexico
Felixstowe *89 E6* E England, United Kingdom
Fellin *see* Viljandi
Felsőbánya *see* Baia Sprie
Felsőmuzslya *see* Mužlja
Femunden *85 B5 lake* S Norway
Fénérive *see* Fenoarivo Atsinanana
Fengcheng *128 D3 var.* Feng-cheng, Fenghwangcheng. Liaoning, NE China
Feng-cheng *see* Fengcheng
Fenghwangcheng *see* Fengcheng
Fengtien *see* Liaoning, China
Fengtien *see* Shenyang, China
Fenoarivo Atsinanana *79 G3 prev./Fr.* Fénérive. Toamasina, E Madagascar
Fens, The *89 E6 wetland* E England, United Kingdom
Feodosiya *109 F5 var.* Kefe, *It.* Kaffa; *anc.* Theodosia. Avtonomna Respublika Krym, S Ukraine
Ferdinand *see* Montana, Bulgaria
Ferdinandsberg *see* Oţelu Roşu
Féres *104 D3* Anatolikí Makedonía kai Thráki, NE Greece
Fergana *see* Farg'ona
Fergus Falls *45 F2* Minnesota, N USA
Ferizaj *101 D5 Serb.* Uroševac. C Kosovo
Ferkessédougou *74 D4* N Côte d'Ivoire
Fermo *96 C4 anc.* Firmum Picenum. Marche, C Italy
Fernandina, Isla *60 A5 var.* Narborough Island. *island* Galápagos Islands, Ecuador, E Pacific Ocean
Fernando de Noronha *63 H2 island* E Brazil
Fernando Po/Fernando Póo *see* Bioco, Isla de
Ferrara *96 C2 anc.* Forum Alieni. Emilia-Romagna, N Italy
Ferreñafe *60 B3* Lambayeque, W Peru
Ferro *see* Hierro
Ferrol *92 B1 var.* El Ferrol; *prev.* El Ferrol del Caudillo. Galicia, NW Spain
Fertő *see* Neusiedler See
Ferwerd *see* Ferwert
Ferwert *86 D1 Dutch.* Ferwerd. Friesland, N Netherlands
Fès *70 C2 Eng.* Fez. N Morocco
Feteşti *108 D5* Ialomiţa, SE Romania
Fethiye *116 B4* Muğla, SW Turkey
Fetlar *88 D1 island* NE Scotland, United Kingdom
Feuilles, Rivière aux *16 D2 river* Québec, E Canada
Feyzābād *see* Feizābād
Feyzābād *see* Feizābād
Fez *see* Fès
Fianarantsoa *79 F3* Fianarantsoa, C Madagascar
Fianga *76 B4* Mayo-Kébbi, SW Chad
Fier *101 C6 var.* Fieri. Fier, SW Albania
Fieri *see* Fier
Figeac *91 C5* Lot, S France
Figig *see* Figuig
Figueira da Foz *92 B3* Coimbra, W Portugal
Figueres *93 G2* Cataluña, E Spain
Figuig *70 D2 var.* Figig. E Morocco
Fiji *145 E5 off.* Sovereign Democratic Republic of Fiji, *Fij.* Viti. *country* SW Pacific Ocean

FIJI
Australasia & Oceania

Official name Republic of the Fiji Islands
Formation 1970 / 1970
Capital Suva
Population 900,000 / 128 people per sq mile (49 people per sq km)
Total area 7054 sq. miles (18,270 sq. km)
Languages Fijian, English*, Hindi, Urdu, Tamil, Telugu
Religions Hindu 38%, Methodist 37%, Roman Catholic 9%, Muslim 8%, Other 8%
Ethnic mix Melanesian 51%, Indian 44%, Other 5%
Government Parliamentary system
Currency Fiji dollar = 100 cents
Literacy rate 94%
Calorie consumption 2930 kilocalories

Fiji, Sovereign Democratic Republic of *see* Fiji
Filadelfia *52 D4* Guanacaste, W Costa Rica
Filiaşi *108 B5* Dolj, SW Romania
Filipstad *85 B6* Värmland, C Sweden
Finale Ligure *96 A3* Liguria, NW Italy
Finchley *89 A7* United Kingdom
Findlay *40 C4* Ohio, N USA
Finike *116 B4* Antalya, SW Turkey
Finland *84 D4 off.* Republic of Finland, *Fin.* Suomen Tasavalta, Suomi. *country* N Europe

FINLAND
Northern Europe

Official name Republic of Finland
Formation 1917 / 1947
Capital Helsinki
Population 5.4 million / 46 people per sq mile (18 people per sq km)
Total area 130,127 sq. miles (337,030 sq. km)
Languages Finnish*, Swedish*, Sámi
Religions Evangelical Lutheran 83%, Other 15%, Orthodox Christian 1%, Roman Catholic 1%
Ethnic mix Finnish 93%, Other (including Sámi) 7%
Government Parliamentary system
Currency Euro = 100 cents
Literacy rate 99%
Calorie consumption 3285 kilocalories

Finland, Gulf of *85 D6 Est.* Soome Laht, *Fin.* Suomenlahti, *Ger.* Finnischer Meerbusen, *Rus.* Finskiy Zaliv, *Swe.* Finska Viken. *gulf* E Baltic Sea
Finland, Republic of *see* Finland
Finnischer Meerbusen *see* Finland, Gulf of
Finnmarksvidda *84 D2 physical region* N Norway
Finska Viken/Finskiy Zaliv *see* Finland, Gulf of
Finsterwalde *94 D4* Brandenburg, E Germany
Fiordland *151 A7 physical region* South Island, New Zealand
Fiorina *96 E1* NE San Marino
Firat Nehri *see* Euphrates
Firenze *96 C3 Eng.* Florence; *anc.* Florentia. Toscana, C Italy
Firmum Picenum *see* Fermo
First State *see* Delaware
Fischbacher Alpen *95 E7 mountain range* E Austria
Fischhausen *see* Primorsk
Fish *78 B4 var.* Vis. *river* S Namibia
Fishguard *89 C6 Wel.* Abergwaun. SW Wales, United Kingdom
Fisterra, Cabo *92 B1 headland* NW Spain
Fitzroy Crossing *146 C3* Western Australia
Fitzroy River *146 C3 river* Western Australia
Fiume *see* Rijeka
Flagstaff *48 B2* Arizona, SW USA
Flanders *see* Vlaanderen
Flandre *see* Vlaanderen
Flathead Lake *44 B1 lake* Montana, NW USA
Flat Island *128 C8 island* NE Spratly Islands
Flatts Village *42 B5 var.* The Flatts Village. C Bermuda
Flensburg *94 B2* Schleswig-Holstein, N Germany
Flessingue *see* Vlissingen
Flickertail State *see* North Dakota
Flinders Island *149 C8 island* Furneaux Group, Tasmania, SE Australia
Flinders Ranges *149 B6 mountain range* South Australia
Flinders River *148 C3 river* Queensland, NE Australia
Flin Flon *37 F5* Manitoba, C Canada
Flint *40 C3* Michigan, N USA
Flint Island *145 G4 island* Line Islands, E Kiribati
Floreana, Isla *see* Santa María, Isla
Florence *42 C1* Alabama, S USA
Florence *43 F2* South Carolina, SE USA
Florence *see* Firenze
Florencia *58 B4* Caquetá, S Colombia
Florentia *see* Firenze
Flores *52 B1* Petén, N Guatemala
Flores *139 E5 island* Nusa Tenggara, C Indonesia
Flores *92 A5 island* Azores, Portugal, NE Atlantic Ocean
Flores, Laut *see* Flores Sea
Flores Sea *138 D5 Ind.* Laut Flores. *sea* C Indonesia
Floriano *63 F2* Piauí, E Brazil
Florianópolis *63 F5 prev.* Destêrro. *state capital* Santa Catarina, S Brazil
Florida *64 D4* Florida, S Uruguay
Florida *43 E4 off.* State of Florida, *also known as* Peninsular State, Sunshine State. *state* SE USA
Florida Bay *43 E5 bay* Florida, SE USA
Florida Keys *43 E5 island group* Florida, SE USA
Florida, Straits of *54 B1 strait* Atlantic Ocean/Gulf of Mexico
Flórina *104 B4 var.* Phlórina. Dytikí Makedonía, N Greece
Florissant *45 G4* Missouri, C USA
Floúda, Akrotírio *105 D7 headland* Astypálaia, Kykládes, Greece, Aegean Sea
Flushing *see* Vlissingen
Flylân *see* Vlieland
Foča *100 C4 var.* Srbinje. SE Bosnia and Herzegovina
Focşani *108 C4* Vrancea, E Romania
Fogaras/Fogarasch *see* Făgăraş
Foggia *97 D5* Puglia, SE Italy
Fogo *74 A3 island* Ilhas de Sotavento, SW Cape Verde
Foix *91 B6* Ariège, S France
Folégandros *105 C7 island* Kykládes, Greece, Aegean Sea
Foleyet *38 C4* Ontario, S Canada
Foligno *96 C4* Umbria, C Italy
Folkestone *89 E7* SE England, United Kingdom
Fond du Lac *40 B2* Wisconsin, N USA
Fongafale *145 E3 var.* Funafuti. Funafuti Atoll, SE Tuvalu
Fonseca, Golfo de *see* Fonseca, Gulf of
Fonseca, Gulf of *52 C3 Sp.* Golfo de Fonseca. *gulf* C Central America
Fontainebleau *90 C3* Seine-et-Marne, N France
Fontenay-le-Comte *90 B4* Vendée, NW France
Fontvieille *91 B8* SW Monaco Europe
Fonyód *99 C7* Somogy, W Hungary
Foochow *see* Fuzhou
Foochow *see* Fuzhou
Forchheim *95 C5* Bayern, SE Germany
Forel, Mont *82 D4 mountain* SE Greenland
Forfar *88 C3* E Scotland, United Kingdom
Forge du Sud *see* Dudelange
Forlì *96 C3 anc.* Forum Livii. Emilia-Romagna, N Italy
Formentera *93 G4 anc.* Ophiusa, *Lat.* Frumentum. *island* Islas Baleares, Spain, W Mediterranean Sea
Formosa *64 D2* Formosa, NE Argenti
Formosa/Formo'sa *see* Taiwan
Formosa, Serra *63 E3 mountain rang* C Brazil
Formosa Strait *see* Taiwan Strait
Føroyar *see* Faroe Islands
Forrest City *42 B1* Arkansas, C USA
Fort Albany *38 C3* Ontario, C Canada
Fortaleza *61 F2* Pando, N Bolivia
Fortaleza *63 G2 prev.* Ceará. *state capi* Ceará, NE Brazil
Fort-Archambault *see* Sarh
Fort-Bayard *see* Zhanjiang
Fort-Cappolani *see* Tidjikja
Fort Charlet *see* Djanet
Fort-Chimo *see* Kuujjuaq
Fort Collins *44 D4* Colorado, C USA
Fort-Crampel *see* Kaga Bandoro
Fort Davis *49 E3* Texas, SW USA
Fort-de-France *55 H4 prev.* Fort-Roy *dependent territory capital* (Martiniq W Martinique
Fort Dodge *45 F3* Iowa, C USA
Fortescue River *146 A4 river* Western Australia
Fort-Foureau *see* Kousséri
Fort Frances *38 B4* Ontario, S Canada
Fort Good Hope *37 E3 var.* Rádeyilikc Northwest Territories, NW Canada
Fort Gouraud *see* Fdérik
Forth *88 C4 river* C Scotland, United Kingdom
Forth, Firth of *88 C4 estuary* E Scotlar United Kingdom
Fortín General Eugenio Garay *see* General Eugenio A. Garay
Fort Jameson *see* Chipata
Fort-Lamy *see* Ndjamena
Fort Lauderdale *43 F5* Florida, SE US
Fort Liard *37 E4 var.* Liard. Northwes Territories, W Canada
Fort Madison *45 G4* Iowa, C USA
Fort McMurray *37 E4* Alberta, C Cana
Fort McPherson *36 D3 var.* McPherso Northwest Territories, NW Canada
Fort Morgan *44 D4* Colorado, C USA
Fort Myers *43 E5* Florida, SE USA
Fort Nelson *37 E4* British Columbia, W Canada
Fort Peck Lake *44 C1 reservoir* Montai NW USA
Fort Pierce *43 F4* Florida, SE USA
Fort Providence *37 E4 var.* Providence Northwest Territories, W Canada
Fort-Repoux *see* Akjoujt
Fort Rosebery *see* Mansa
Fort Rousset *see* Owando
Fort-Royal *see* Fort-de-France
Fort St. John *37 E4* British Columbia, W Canada
Fort Scott *45 F5* Kansas, C USA
Fort Severn *38 C2* Ontario, C Canada
Fort-Shevchenko *114 A4* Mangistau, W Kazakhstan
Fort-Sibut *see* Sibut
Fort Simpson *37 E4 var.* Simpson. Northwest Territories, W Canada
Fort Smith *37 E4* Northwest Territorie W Canada
Fort Smith *42 B1* Arkansas, C USA
Fort Stockton *49 E3* Texas, SW USA
Fort-Trinquet *see* Bir Mogreïn
Fort Vermilion *37 E4* Alberta, W Canada
Fort Victoria *see* Masvingo
Fort Walton Beach *42 C3* Florida, SE USA
Fort Wayne *40 C4* Indiana, N USA
Fort William *88 C3* N Scotland, Unitec Kingdom
Fort Worth *49 G2* Texas, SW USA
Fort Yukon *36 D3* Alaska, USA
Forum Alieni *see* Ferrara
Forum Livii *see* Forlì
Fossa Claudia *see* Chioggia
Fougamou *77 A6* Ngounié, C Gabon
Fougères *90 B3* Ille-et-Vilaine, NW France
Fou-hsin *see* Fuxin
Foulwind, Cape *151 B5 headland* Sout Island, New Zealand
Foumban *76 A4* Ouest, NW Cameroon
Fou-shan *see* Fushun

veaux Strait *151 A8 strait* S New Zealand
xe Basin *37 G3 sea* Nunavut, N Canada
x Glacier *151 B6* West Coast, South Island, New Zealand
aga *93 F2* Aragón, NE Spain
am Basin *see* Amundsen Basin
ance *90 B4 off.* French Republic, *It./Sp.* Francia; *prev.* Gaul, Gaule, *Lat.* Gallia. *country* W Europe

RANCE
Western Europe

)fficial name French Republic
ormation 987 / 1919
'apital Paris
opulation 64.3 million / 303 people
er sq mile (117 people per sq km)
otal area 211,208 sq. miles
547,030 sq. km)
anguages French*, Provençal, German,
reton, Catalan, Basque
eligions Roman Catholic 88%,
Iuslim 8%, Protestant 2%,
uddhist 1%, Jewish 1%
thnic mix French 90%, North African
mainly Algerian) 6%, German (Alsace) 2%,
reton 1%, Other (including Corsicans) 1%
overnment Presidential /
arliamentary system
'urrency Euro = 100 cents
iteracy rate 99%
'alorie consumption 3524 kilocalories

anceville *77 B6 var.* Massoukou, Masuku. Haut-Ogooué, E Gabon
ancfort *see* Frankfurt am Main
anche-Comté *90 D4 cultural region* E France
ancia *see* France
ancis Case, Lake *45 E3 reservoir* South Dakota, N USA
ancisco Escárcega *51 G4* Campeche, SE Mexico
ancistown *78 D3* North East, NE Botswana
anconian Jura *see* Fränkische Alb
ankenalb *see* Fränkische Alb
ankenstein/Frankenstein in Schlesien *see* Ząbkowice Śląskie
ankfort *40 C5 state capital* Kentucky, S USA
ankfort on the Main *see* Frankfurt am Main
ankfurt *see* Frankfurt am Main, Germany
ankfurt *see* Słubice, Poland
ankfurt am Main *95 B5 var.* Frankfurt, *Fr.* Francfort; *prev. Eng.* Frankfort on the Main. Hessen, SW Germany
ankfurt an der Oder *94 D3* Brandenburg, E Germany
änkische Alb *95 C6 var.* Frankenalb, *Eng.* Franconian Jura. *mountain range* S Germany
anklin *42 C1* Tennessee, S USA
anklin D. Roosevelt Lake *46 C1 reservoir* Washington, NW USA
anz Josef Land *114 D1 Eng.* Franz Josef Land. *island group* N Russian Federation
anz Josef Land *see* Frantsa-Iosifa, Zemlya
aserburgh *88 D3* NE Scotland, United Kingdom
aser Island *148 E4 var.* Great Sandy Island. *island* Queensland, E Australia
auenbach *see* Baia Mare
auenburg *see* Saldus, Latvia
edericksburg *41 E5* Virginia, NE USA
edericton *39 F4 province capital* New Brunswick, SE Canada
ederikshåb *see* Paamiut
edrikshald *see* Halden
edrikstad *85 B6* Østfold, S Norway
eeport *54 C1* Grand Bahama Island, N Bahamas
eeport *49 H4* Texas, SW USA
ee State *see* Maryland
eetown *74 C4 country capital* (Sierra Leone) W Sierra Leone
eiburg *see* Freiburg im Breisgau, Germany
Freiburg im Breisgau *95 A6 var.* Freiburg, *Fr.* Fribourg-en-Brisgau. Baden-Württemberg, SW Germany
Freiburg in Schlesien *see* Świebodzice
Fremantle *147 A6* Western Australia
Fremont *45 F4* Nebraska, C USA
French Guiana *59 H3 var.* Guiana, Guyane. *French overseas department* N South America
French Guinea *see* Guinea
French Polynesia *143 F4 French overseas territory* S Pacific Ocean
French Republic *see* France
French Somaliland *see* Djibouti
French Southern and Antarctic Lands *141 B7 Fr.* Terres Australes et Antarctiques Françaises. *French overseas territory* S Indian Ocean
French Sudan *see* Mali
French Territory of the Afars and Issas *see* Djibouti
French Togoland *see* Togo
Fresnillo *50 D3 var.* Fresnillo de González Echeverría. Zacatecas, C Mexico
Fresnillo de González Echeverría *see* Fresnillo
Fresno *47 C6* California, W USA
Frías *64 C3* Catamarca, N Argentina
Fribourg-en-Brisgau *see* Freiburg im Breisgau
Friedek-Mistek *see* Frýdek-Místek
Friedrichshafen *95 B7* Baden-Württemberg, S Germany
Friendly Islands *see* Tonga
Frisches Haff *see* Vistula Lagoon
Frobisher Bay *82 B3 inlet* Baffin Island, Nunavut, NE Canada
Frobisher Bay *see* Iqaluit
Frohavet *84 B4 sound* C Norway
Frome, Lake *149 B6 salt lake* South Australia
Frontera *51 G4* Tabasco, SE Mexico
Frontignan *91 C6* Hérault, S France
Frostviken *see* Kvarnbergsvattnet
Frøya *84 A4 island* W Norway
Frumentum *see* Formentera
Frunze *see* Bishkek
Frýdek-Místek *99 C5 Ger.* Friedek-Mistek. Moravskoslezský Kraj, E Czech Republic
Fu-chien *see* Fujian
Fu-chou *see* Fuzhou
Fu-chou *see* Fuzhou
Fuengirola *92 D5* Andalucía, S Spain
Fuerte Olimpo *64 D2 var.* Olimpo. Alto Paraguay, NE Paraguay
Fuerte, Río *48 C5 river* C Mexico
Fuerteventura *70 B3 island* Islas Canarias, Spain, NE Atlantic Ocean
Fuhkien *see* Fujian
Fu-hsin *see* Fuxin
Fuji *131 D6 var.* Huzi. Shizuoka, Honshū, S Japan
Fujian *128 D6 var.* Fu-chien, Fuhkien, Fukien, Min, Fujian Sheng. *province* SE China
Fujian Sheng *see* Fujian
Mount Fuji *131 C6 var.* Fujiyama, *Eng.* Mount Fuji. *mountain* Honshū, SE Japan
Fuji, Mount/Fujiyama *see* Fuji-san
Fukang *126 C2* Xinjiang Uygur Zizhiqu, W China
Fukien *see* Fujian
Fukui *131 C6 var.* Hukui. Fukui, Honshū, SW Japan
Fukuoka *131 A7 var.* Hukuoka, *hist.* Najima. Fukuoka, Kyūshū, SW Japan
Fukushima *130 D4 var.* Hukusima. Fukushima, Honshū, C Japan
Fulda *95 B5* Hessen, C Germany
Funafuti *see* Fongafale
Funafuti Atoll *145 E3 atoll* C Tuvalu
Funchal *70 A2* Madeira, Portugal, NE Atlantic Ocean
Fundy, Bay of *39 F5 bay* Canada/USA
Fünen *see* Fyn
Fünfkirchen *see* Pécs
Furnes *see* Veurne
Fürth *95 C5* Bayern, S Germany
Furukawa *130 D4 var.* Hurukawa, Ōsaki. Miyagi, Honshū, C Japan
Fusan *see* Busan
Fushë Kosovë *101 D5 Serb.* Kosovo Polje. C Kosovo
Fushun *128 D3 var.* Fou-shan, Fu-shun. Liaoning, NE China
Fu-shun *see* Fushun
Fusin *see* Fuxin
Füssen *95 C7* Bayern, S Germany
Futog *100 D3* Vojvodina, NW Serbia
Futuna, Île *145 E4 island* S Wallis and Futuna
Fuxin *128 D3 var.* Fou-hsin, Fu-hsin, Fusin. Liaoning, NE China
Fuzhou *128 D5 var.* Foochow, Fu-chou. *province capital* Fujian, SE China
Fuzhou *128 D6 var.* Foochow, Fu-chou. *province capital* Fujian, SE China
Fyn *85 B8 Ger.* Fünen. *island* C Denmark
FYR Macedonia/FYROM *see* Macedonia, FYR
Fyzabad *see* Feizābād

G

Gaafu Alifu Atoll *see* North Huvadhu Atoll
Gaalkacyo *73 E5 var.* Galka'yo, *It.* Galcaio. Mudug, C Somalia
Gabela *78 B2* Cuanza Sul, W Angola
Gaberones *see* Gaborone
Gabès *71 E2 var.* Qābis. E Tunisia
Gabès, Golfe de *71 F2 Ar.* Khalīj Qābis. *gulf* E Tunisia
Gabon *77 B6 off.* Gabonese Republic. *country* C Africa

GABON
Central Africa

Official name Gabonese Republic
Formation 1960 / 1960
Capital Libreville
Population 1.7 million / 17 people per sq mile (7 people per sq km)
Total area 103,346 sq. miles (267,667 sq. km)
Languages Fang, French*, Punu, Sira, Nzebi, Mpongwe
Religions Christian (mainly Roman Catholic) 55%, Traditional beliefs 40%, Other 4%, Muslim 1%
Ethnic mix Fang 26%, Shira-punu 24%, Other 16%, Foreign residents 15%, Nzabi-duma 11%, Mbédé-Teke 8%
Government Presidential system
Currency CFA franc = 100 centimes
Literacy rate 82%
Calorie consumption 2781 kilocalories

Gabonese Republic *see* Gabon
Gaborone *78 C4 prev.* Gaberones. *country capital* (Botswana) South East, SE Botswana
Gabrovo *104 D2* Gabrovo, N Bulgaria
Gadag *132 C1* Karnātaka, W India
Gades/Gadier/Gadir/Gadire *see* Cádiz
Gadsden *42 D2* Alabama, S USA
Gaeta *97 C5* Lazio, C Italy
Gaeta, Gulf of *97 C5 var.* Gulf of Gaeta. *gulf* C Italy
Gaeta, Gulf of *see* Gaeta, Golfo di
Gäfle *see* Gävle
Gafsa *71 E2 var.* Qafşah. W Tunisia
Gagnoa *74 D5* C Côte d'Ivoire
Gagra *117 E1* NW Georgia
Gaillac *91 C6 var.* Gaillac-sur-Tarn. Tarn, S France
Gaillac-sur-Tarn *see* Gaillac
Gaillimh *see* Galway
Gaillimhe, Cuan na *see* Galway Bay
Gainesville *43 E3* Florida, SE USA
Gainesville *42 D2* Georgia, SE USA
Gainesville *49 G2* Texas, SW USA
Lake Gairdner *149 A6 salt lake* South Australia
Gaizina Kalns *see* Gaiziņkalns
Gaiziņkalns *106 C3 var.* Gaizina Kalns. *mountain* E Latvia
Gakkel Ridge *155 B3 var.* Arctic Mid Oceanic Ridge, Nansen Cordillera. *seamount range* Arctic Ocean
Galán, Cerro *64 B3 mountain* NW Argentina
Galanta *99 C6 Hung.* Galánta. Trnavský Kraj, W Slovakia
Galapagos Fracture Zone *153 E3 tectonic feature* E Pacific Ocean
Galápagos Islands *153 F3 var.* Islas de los Galápagos, *Sp.* Archipiélago de Colón, *Eng.* Galapagos Islands, Tortoise Islands. *island group* Ecuador, E Pacific Ocean
Galapagos Islands *see* Galápagos Islands
Galápagos, Islas de los *see* Galápagos Islands
Galapagos Rise *153 F3 undersea rise* E Pacific Ocean
Galashiels *88 C4* SE Scotland, United Kingdom
Galați *108 D4 Ger.* Galatz. Galați, E Romania
Galatz *see* Galați
Galcaio *see* Gaalkacyo
Galesburg *40 B3* Illinois, N USA
Galicia *92 B1 anc.* Gallaecia. *autonomous community* NW Spain
Galicia Bank *80 B4 undersea bank* E Atlantic Ocean
Galilee, Sea of *see* Tiberias, Lake
Galka'yo *see* Gaalkacyo
Galkynyş *122 D3 prev. Rus.* Deynau, Dyanev, *Turkm.* Dänew. Lebap Welaýaty, NE Turkmenistan
Gallaecia *see* Galicia
Galle *132 D4 prev.* Point de Galle. Southern Province, SW Sri Lanka
Gallego Rise *153 F3 undersea rise* E Pacific Ocean
Gallegos *see* Río Gallegos
Gallia *see* France
Gallipoli *97 E6* Puglia, SE Italy
Gällivare *84 C3 Lapp.* Váhtjer. Norrbotten, N Sweden
Gallup *48 C1* New Mexico, SW USA
Galtat-Zemmour *70 B3* C Western Sahara
Galveston *49 H4* Texas, SW USA
Galway *89 A5 Ir.* Gaillimh. W Ireland
Galway Bay *89 A6 Ir.* Cuan na Gaillimhe. *bay* W Ireland
Gámas *see* Kaamanen
Gambell *36 C2* Saint Lawrence Island, Alaska, USA
Gambia *74 B3 off.* Republic of The Gambia, The Gambia. *country* W Africa

GAMBIA
West Africa

Official name Republic of the Gambia
Formation 1965 / 1965
Capital Banjul
Population 1.8 million / 466 people per sq mile (180 people per sq km)
Total area 4363 sq. miles (11,300 sq. km)
Languages Mandinka, Fulani, Wolof, Jola, Soninke, English*
Religions Sunni Muslim 90%, Christian 8%, Traditional beliefs 2%
Ethnic mix Mandinka 42%, Fulani 18%,Wolof 16%, Jola 10%, Serahuli 9%, Other 5%
Government Presidential system
Currency Dalasi = 100 butut
Literacy rate 52%
Calorie consumption 2849 kilocalories

Gambia *74 C3 Fr.* Gambie. *river* W Africa
Gambia, Republic of The *see* Gambia
Gambia, The *see* Gambia
Gambie *see* Gambia
Gambier, Îles *143 G4 island group* E French Polynesia
Gamboma *77 B6* Plateaux, E Congo
Gamlakarleby *see* Kokkola
Gan *132 B5* Addu Atoll, C Maldives
Gan *see* Gansu, China
Gan *see* Jiangxi, China
Ganaane *see* Juba
Gäncä *117 G2 Rus.* Gyandzha; *prev.* Kirovabad, Yelisavetpol. W Azerbaijan
Gand *see* Gent
Gandajika *77 D7* Kasai-Oriental, S Dem. Rep. Congo
Gander *39 G3* Newfoundland and Labrador, SE Canada
Gāndhīdhām *134 C4* Gujarāt, W India
Gandia *93 F3 prev.* Gandía. País Valenciano, E Spain
Gandía *see* Gandia
Ganges *135 F3 Ben.* Padma. *river* Bangladesh/India
Ganges Cone *see* Ganges Fan
Ganges Fan *140 D3 var.* Ganges Cone. *undersea fan* N Bay of Bengal
Ganges, Mouths of the *135 G4 delta* Bangladesh/India
Gangra *see* Çankırı
Gangtok *135 F3 state capital* Sikkim, N India
Gansos, Lago dos *see* Goose Lake
Gansu *128 B4 var.* Gan, Gansu Sheng, Kansu. *province* N China
Gansu Sheng *see* Gansu

Gantsevichi *see* Hantsavichy
Ganzhou *128 D6* Jiangxi, S China
Gao *75 E3* Gao, E Mali
Gaocheng *see* Litang
Gaoual *74 C4* N Guinea
Gaoxiong *128 D6 var.* Kaohsiung, *Jap.* Takao, Takow. S Taiwan
Gap *91 D5 anc.* Vapincum. Hautes-Alpes, SE France
Gaplaňgyr Platosy *122 C2 Rus.* Plato Kaplangky. *ridge* Turkmenistan/ Uzbekistan
Gar *see* Gar Xincun
Garabil Belentligi *122 D3 Rus.* Vozvyshennost' Karabil'. *mountain range* S Turkmenistan
Garabogaz Aylagy *122 B2 Rus.* Zaliv Kara-Bogaz-Gol. *bay* NW Turkmenistan
Garachiné *53 G5* Darién, SE Panama
Garagum *122 C3 var.* Garagumy, Qara Qum, *Eng.* Black Sand Desert, Kara Kum; *prev.* Peski Karakumy. *desert* C Turkmenistan
Garagum Canal *122 D3 var.* Kara Kum Canal, *Rus.* Karagumskiy Kanal, Karakumskiy Kanal. *canal* C Turkmenistan
Garagumy *see* Garagum
Gara Khitrino *104 D2* Shumen, NE Bulgaria
Gárassavon *see* Kaaresuvanto
Garda, Lake *96 C2 var.* Benaco, *Eng.* Lake Garda, *Ger.* Gardasee. *lake* NE Italy
Garda, Lake *see* Garda, Lago di
Gardasee *see* Garda, Lago di
Garden City *45 E5* Kansas, C USA
Garden State, The *see* New Jersey
Gardēz *123 E4 prev.* Gardīz. E Afghanistan
Gardīz *see* Gardēz
Gardner Island *see* Nikumaroro
Garegegasnjárga *see* Karigasniemi
Gargždai *106 B3* Klaipėda, W Lithuania
Garissa *73 D6* Coast, E Kenya
Garland *49 G2* Texas, SW USA
Garoe *see* Garoowe
Garonne *91 B5 anc.* Garumna. *river* S France
Garoowe *73 E5 var.* Garoe. Nugaal, N Somalia
Garoua *76 B4 var.* Garua. Nord, N Cameroon
Garrygala *see* Magtymguly
Garry Lake *37 F3 lake* Nunavut, N Canada
Garsen *73 D6* Coast, S Kenya
Garua *see* Garoua
Garumna *see* Garonne
Garwolin *98 D4* Mazowieckie, E Poland
Gar Xincun *126 A4 prev.* Gar. Xizang Zizhiqu, W China
Gary *40 B3* Indiana, N USA
Garzón *58 B4* Huila, S Colombia
Gasan-Kuli *see* Esenguly
Gascogne *91 B6 Eng.* Gascony. *cultural region* S France
Gascony *see* Gascogne
Gascoyne River *147 A5 river* Western Australia
Gaspé *39 F3* Québec, SE Canada
Gaspé, Péninsule de *39 E4 var.* Péninsule de la Gaspésie. *peninsula* Québec, SE Canada
Gaspésie, Péninsule de la *see* Gaspé, Péninsule de
Gastonia *43 E1* North Carolina, SE USA
Gastoúni *105 B6* Dytikí Elláda, S Greece
Gatchina *110 B4* Leningradskaya Oblast', NW Russian Federation
Gatineau *38 D4* Québec, SE Canada
Gatooma *see* Kadoma
Gatún, Lake *53 F4 reservoir* C Panama
Gauhāti *see* Guwāhāti
Gauja *106 D3 Ger.* Aa. *river* Estonia/ Latvia
Gaul/Gaule *see* France
Gauteng *see* Johannesburg, South Africa
Gāvbandī *120 D4* Hormozgān, S Iran
Gávdos *105 C8 island* SE Greece
Gavere *87 B6* Oost-Vlaanderen, NW Belgium
Gävle *85 C6 var.* Gäfle; *prev.* Gefle. Gävleborg, C Sweden
Gawler *149 B6* South Australia
Gaya *135 F3* Bihār, N India
Gaya *see* Kyjov
Gayndah *149 E5* Queensland, E Australia
Gaysin *see* Haysyn
Gaza *119 A6 Ar.* Ghazzah, *Heb.* 'Azza. NE Gaza Strip
Gaz-Achak *see* Gazojak
Gazandzhyk/Gazanjyk *see* Bereket
Gaza Strip *119 A7 Ar.* Qita Ghazzah. *disputed region* SW Asia
Gaziantep *116 D4 var.* Gazi Antep; *prev.* Aintab, Antep. Gaziantep, S Turkey
Gazi Antep *see* Gaziantep
Gazimağusa *102 D5 var.* Famagusta, *Gk.* Ammóchostos. E Cyprus
Gazli *122 D2* Buxoro Viloyati, C Uzbekistan
Gazojak *122 D2 Rus.* Gaz-Achak. Lebap Welaýaty, NE Turkmenistan
Gbanga *74 D5 var.* Gbarnga. N Liberia
Gbarnga *see* Gbanga
Gdańsk *98 C2 Fr.* Dantzig, *Ger.* Danzig. Pomorskie, N Poland
Gdan'skaya Bukhta/Gdańsk, Gulf of *see* Danzig, Gulf of
Gdańska, Zakota *see* Danzig, Gulf of
Gdingen *see* Gdynia
Gdynia *98 C2 Ger.* Gdingen. Pomorskie, N Poland
Gedaref *72 C4 var.* Al Qaḍārif, El Gedaref. Gedaref, E Sudan
Gediz *116 B3* Kütahya, W Turkey
Gediz Nehri *116 A3 river* W Turkey
Geel *87 C5 var.* Gheel. Antwerpen, N Belgium
Geelong *149 C7* Victoria, SE Australia
Ge'e'mu *see* Golmud
Gefle *see* Gävle
Geilo *85 A5* Buskerud, S Norway
Gejiu *128 B6 var.* Kochiu. Yunnan, S China
Gëkdepe *see* Gökdepe
Gela *97 C7 prev.* Terranova di Sicilia. Sicilia, Italy, C Mediterranean Sea
Geldermalsen *86 C4* Gelderland, C Netherlands
Geleen *87 D6* Limburg, SE Netherlands
Gelib *see* Jilib
Gellinsor *73 E5* Galguduud, C Somalia
Gembloux *87 C6* Namur, Belgium
Gemena *77 C5* Equateur, NW Dem. Rep. Congo
Gem of the Mountains *see* Idaho
Gemona del Friuli *96 D2* Friuli-Venezia Giulia, NE Italy
Gem State *see* Idaho
Genalē Wenz *see* Juba
Genck *see* Genk
General Alvear *64 B4* Mendoza, W Argentina
General Carrera, Lago *see* Buenos Aires, Lago
General Eugenio A. Garay *64 C1 var.* Fortín General Eugenio Garay; *prev.* Yrendagüé. Nueva Asunción, NW Paraguay
General José F.Uriburu *see* Zárate
General Machado *see* Camacupa
General Santos *139 F3 off.* General Santos City. Mindanao, S Philippines
General Santos City *see* General Santos
Gênes *see* Genova
Geneva *see* Genève
Geneva, Lake *95 A7 Fr.* Lac de Genève, Lac Léman, le Léman, *Ger.* Genfer See. *lake* France/Switzerland
Genève *95 A7 Eng.* Geneva, *Ger.* Genf, *It.* Ginevra. Genève, SW Switzerland
Genève, Lac de *see* Geneva, Lake
Genf *see* Genève
Genfer See *see* Geneva, Lake
Genichesk *see* Heniches'k
Genk *87 D6 var.* Genck. Limburg, NE Belgium
Gennep *86 D4* Limburg, SE Netherlands
Genoa *see* Genova
Genoa, Gulf of *96 A3 Eng.* Gulf of Genoa. *gulf* NW Italy
Genoa, Gulf of *see* Genova, Golfo di
Genova *102 D1 Eng.* Genoa; *anc.* Genua, *Fr.* Gênes. Liguria, NW Italy
Genovesa, Isla *60 B5 var.* Tower Island. *island* Galápagos Islands, Ecuador, E Pacific Ocean
Gent *87 B5 Eng.* Ghent, *Fr.* Gand. Oost-Vlaanderen, NW Belgium
Genua *see* Genova
Geok-Tepe *see* Gökdepe
George *78 C5* Western Cape, S South Africa
George *82 A4 river* Newfoundland and Labrador/Québec, E Canada
George, Lake *43 E3 lake* Florida, SE USA
Georgenburg *see* Jurbarkas
Georges Bank *35 D5 undersea bank* W Atlantic Ocean
George Sound *151 A7 sound* South Island, New Zealand
Georges River *148 D2 river* New South Wales, E Australia
Georgetown *59 F2 country capital* (Guyana) (Guyana) N Guyana
George Town *54 C2* Great Exuma Island, C Bahamas
George Town *54 B3 var.* Georgetown. *dependent territory capital* (Cayman Islands) Grand Cayman, SW Cayman Islands
George Town *138 B3 var.* Penang, Pinang. Pinang, Peninsular Malaysia
Georgetown *43 F2* South Carolina, SE USA
Georgetown *see* George Town
George V Land *154 C4 physical region* Antarctica
Georgia *117 F2 off.* Republic of Georgia, *Geor.* Sak'art'velo, *Rus.* Gruzinskaya SSR, Gruziya. *country* SW Asia

GEORGIA
Southwest Asia

Official name Georgia
Formation 1991 / 1991
Capital Tbilisi
Population 4.3 million / 160 people per sq mile (62 people per sq km)
Total area 26,911 sq. miles (69,700 sq. km)
Languages Georgian*, Russian, Azeri, Armenian, Mingrelian, Ossetian, Abkhazian* *(in Abkhazia)*
Religions Georgian Orthodox 74%, Muslim 10%, Russian Orthodox 10%, Armenian Apostolic Church (Orthodox) 4%, Other 2%
Ethnic mix Georgian 84%, Armenian 6%, Azeri 6%, Russian 2%, Ossetian 1%, Other 1%
Government Presidential system
Currency Lari = 100 tetri
Literacy rate 99%
Calorie consumption 2731 kilocalories

Georgia *42 D2 off.* State of Georgia, *also known as* Empire State of the South, Peach State. *state* SE USA
Georgian Bay *40 D2 lake bay* Ontario, S Canada
Georgia, Republic of *see* Georgia
Georgia, Strait of *46 A1 strait* British Columbia, W Canada
Georgi Dimitrov *see* Kostenets
Georgiu-Dezh *see* Liski
Georg von Neumayer *154 A2 German research station* Antarctica
Gera *94 C4* Thüringen, E Germany
Geráki *105 B6* Pelopónnisos, S Greece
Geraldine *151 B6* Canterbury, South Island, New Zealand
Geraldton *147 A6* Western Australia
Geral, Serra *57 D5 mountain range* S Brazil
Gerede *116 C2* Bolu, N Turkey
Gereshk *122 D5* Helmand, SW Afghanistan
Gering *44 D3* Nebraska, C USA
German East Africa *see* Tanzania
Germanicopolis *see* Çankırı
Germanicum, Mare/German Ocean *see* North Sea
German Southwest Africa *see* Namibia
Germany *94 B4 off.* Federal Republic of Germany, Bundesrepublik Deutschland, *Ger.* Deutschland. *country* N Europe

GERMANY
Northern Europe

Official name Federal Republic of Germany
Formation 1871 / 1990
Capital Berlin
Population 82.7 million / 613 people per sq mile (237 people per sq km)
Total area 137,846 sq. miles (357,021 sq. km)
Languages German*, Turkish
Religions Protestant 34%, Roman Catholic 33%, Other 30%, Muslim 3%
European 3%, Other 3%, Turkish 2%

GERMANY
(continued)

Government Parliamentary system
Currency Euro = 100 cents
Literacy rate 99%
Calorie consumption 3539 kilocalories

Germany, Federal Republic of *see* Germany
Geroliménas *105 B7* Pelopónnisos, S Greece
Gerona *see* Girona
Gerpinnes *87 C7* Hainaut, S Belgium
Gerunda *see* Girona
Gerze *116 D2* Sinop, N Turkey
Gesoriacum *see* Boulogne-sur-Mer
Gessoriacum *see* Boulogne-sur-Mer
Getafe *92 D3* Madrid, C Spain
Gevaş *117 F3* Van, SE Turkey
Gevgeli *see* Gevgelija
Gevgelija *101 E6 var.* Đevđelija, Djevdjelija, *Turk.* Gevgeli. SE Macedonia
Ghaba *see* Al Ghābah
Ghana *75 E5 off.* Republic of Ghana. *country* W Africa

GHANA
West Africa

Official name Republic of Ghana
Formation 1957 / 1957
Capital Accra
Population 25.9 million / 292 people per sq mile (113 people per sq km)
Total area 92,100 sq. miles (238,540 sq. k
Languages Twi, Fanti, Ewe, Ga, Adangbe Gurma, Dagomba (Dagbani), English*
Religions Christian 69%, Muslim 16%, Traditional beliefs 9%, Other 6%
Ethnic mix Akan 49%, Mole-Dagbani 17%, Ewe 13%, Other 9%, Ga and Ga-Adangbe 8%, Guan 4%
Government Presidential system
Currency Cedi = 100 pesewas
Literacy rate 72%
Calorie consumption 3003 kilocalories

Ghanzi *78 C3 var.* Khanzi. Ghanzi, W Botswana
Gharandal *119 B7* Al'Aqabah, SW Jordan
Gharbt, Jabal al *see* Liban, Jebel
Ghardaïa *70 D2* N Algeria
Gharvān *see* Gharyān
Gharyān *71 F2 var.* Gharvān. NW Libya
Ghawdex *see* Gozo
Ghaznī *123 E4 var.* Ghazni. Ghaznī, E Afghanistan
Ghazzah *see* Gaza
Gheel *see* Geel
Ghent *see* Gent
Gheorgheni *108 C4 prev.* Gheorghieni Sîn-Miclăuş, *Ger.* Niklasmarkt, *Hung* Gyergyószentmiklós. Harghita, C Romania
Gheorghieni *see* Gheorgheni
Ghōrīān *122 D4 prev.* Ghūrīān. Herāt, W Afghanistan
Ghŭdara *123 F3 var.* Gudara, *Rus.* Kudara. SE Tajikistan
Ghurdaqah *see* Al Ghurdaqah
Ghūrīān *see* Ghōrīān
Giamame *see* Jamaame
Giannitsá *104 B4 var.* Yiannitsá. Kentrikí Makedonía, N Greece
Gibraltar *93 G4 UK dependent territor* SW Europe
Gibraltar, Bay of *93 G5 bay* Gibraltar/ SpainMediterranean Sea Atlantic Oce
Gibraltar, Détroit de/Gibraltar, Estrecho de *see* Gibraltar, Strait of
Gibraltar, Strait of *92 C5 Fr.* Détroit d Gibraltar, *Sp.* Estrecho de Gibraltar. *strait* Atlantic Ocean/Mediterranean S
Gibson Desert *147 B5 desert* Western Australia
Giebnegáisi *see* Kebnekaise
Giedraičiai *107 C5* Utena, E Lithuania
Giessen *95 B5* Hessen, W Germany
Gifu *131 C6 var.* Gihu. Gifu, Honshū, SW Japan
Giganta, Sierra de la *50 B3 mountain range* NW Mexico
Gihu *see* Gifu
G'ijduvon *122 D2 Rus.* Gizhduvon. Buxoro Viloyati, C Uzbekistan

jón *92 D1 var.* Xixón. Asturias, NW Spain
la River *48 A2 river* Arizona, SW USA
lbert Islands *see* Tungaru
lbert River *148 C3 river* Queensland, NE Australia
lf Kebir Plateau *see* Haḍabat al Jilf al Kabīr
llette *44 D3* Wyoming, C USA
lolo *see* Halmahera, Pulau
lroy *47 B6* California, W USA
mie, Mount *55 F1 mountain* C Saint Lucia
mma *see* Jīma
nevra *see* Genève
ngin *147 A6* Western Australia
ohar *see* Jawhar
peswic *see* Ipswich
rardot *58 B3* Cundinamarca, C Colombia
resun *117 E2 var.* Kerasunt; *anc.* Cerasus, Pharnacia. Giresun, NE Turkey
rgenti *see* Agrigento
rin *see* Jilin
rne *102 C5 Gk.* Kerýneia, Kyrenia. N Cyprus
ron *see* Kiruna
rona *93 G2 var.* Gerona; *anc.* Gerunda. Cataluña, NE Spain
isborne *150 E3* Gisborne, North Island, New Zealand
issar Range *123 E3 Rus.* Gissarskiy Khrebet. *mountain range* Tajikistan/ Uzbekistan
issarskiy Khrebet *see* Gissar Range
ithio *see* Gýtheio
iulianova *96 D4* Abruzzi, C Italy
iumri *see* Gyumri
iurgiu *108 C5* Giurgiu, S Romania
iza *72 B1 var.* Al Jīzah, El Gîza, Gizeh. N Egypt
izhduvon *see* G'ijduvon
iżycko *98 D2 Ger.* Lötzen. Warmińsko-Mazurskie, NE Poland
jakovë *101 D5 Serb.* Đakovica. W Kosovo
jeravicë *101 D5 Serb.* Đeravica. *mountain* S Serbia
jilan *101 D5 Serb.* Gnjilane. E Kosovo
jinokastër *see* Gjirokastër
jirokastër *101 C7 var.* Gjirokastra; *prev.* Gjinokastër, *Gk.* Argyrokastron, *It.* Argirocastro. Gjirokastër, S Albania
jirokastra *see* Gjirokastër
joa Haven *37 F3 var.* Uqsuqtuuq. King William Island, Nunavut, NW Canada
jøvik *85 B5* Oppland, S Norway
lace Bay *39 G4* Cape Breton Island, Nova Scotia, SE Canada
ladstone *148 E4* Queensland, E Australia
láma *85 B5 var.* Glommen. *river* S Norway
lavinitsa *104 D1 prev.* Pravda, Dogrular. Silistra, NE Bulgaria
lasgow *88 C4* S Scotland, United Kingdom
lavn'a Morava *see* Velika Morava
lazov *111 D5* Udmurtskaya Respublika, NW Russian Federation
leiwitz *see* Gliwice
lendale *48 B2* Arizona, SW USA
lendive *44 D2* Montana, NW USA
lens Falls *41 F3* New York, NE USA
levum *see* Gloucester
lina *100 B3 var.* Banijska Palanka. Sisak-Moslavina, NE Croatia
littertind *85 A5 mountain* S Norway
liwice *99 C5 Ger.* Gleiwitz. Śląskie, S Poland
lobe *48 B2* Arizona, SW USA
lobino *see* Hlobyne
logau *see* Głogów
łogów *98 B4 Ger.* Glogau, Glogow. Dolnośląskie, SW Poland
logow *see* Głogów
lomma *see* Gláma
lommen *see* Gláma
'loucester *89 D6 hist.* Caer Glou, *Lat.* Glevum. C England, United Kingdom
łowno *98 D4* Łódź, C Poland
lubokoye *see* Hlybokaye
lukhov *see* Hlukhiv
nesen *see* Gniezno
niezno *98 C3 Ger.* Gnesen. Weilkopolskie, C Poland
njilane *see* Gjilan
Gobabis *78 B3* Omaheke, E Namibia
Gobi *126 D3 desert* China/Mongolia
Gobō *131 C6* Wakayama, Honshū, SW Japan
Godavari *124 B3 var.* Godavari. *river* C India
Godavari *see* Godāvari
Godhavn *see* Qeqertarsuaq
Godhra *134 C4* Gujarāt, W India
Göding *see* Hodonín
Godoy Cruz *64 B4* Mendoza, W Argentina
Godthaab/Godthåb *see* Nuuk
Godwin Austen, Mount *see* K2
Goede Hoop, Kaap de *see* Good Hope, Cape of
Goeie Hoop, Kaap die *see* Good Hope, Cape of
Goeree *86 B4 island* SW Netherlands
Goes *87 B5* Zeeland, SW Netherlands
Goettingen *see* Göttingen
Gogebic Range *40 B1 hill range* Michigan/Wisconsin, N USA
Goiânia *63 E3 prev.* Goyania. *state capital* Goiás, C Brazil
Goiás *63 E3 off.* Estado de Goiás; *prev.* Goiaz, Goyaz. *region* C Brazil
Goiás *63 E3 off.* Estado de Goiás; *prev.* Goiaz, Goyaz. *state* C Brazil
Goiás, Estado de *see* Goiás
Goiaz *see* Goiás
Goidhoo Atoll *see* Horsburgh Atoll
Gojōme *130 D4* Akita, Honshū, NW Japan
Gökçeada *104 D4 var.* Imroz Adasī, *Gk.* Imbros. *island* NW Turkey
Gökdepe *122 C3 Rus.* Gëkdepe, Geok-Tepe. Ahal Welaýaty, C Turkmenistan
Göksun *116 D4* Kahramanmaraş, C Turkey
Gol *85 A5* Buskerud, S Norway
Golan Heights *119 B5 Ar.* Al Jawlān, *Heb.* HaGolan. *mountain range* SW Syria
Golaya Pristan *see* Hola Prystan'
Gołdap *98 E2 Ger.* Goldap. Warmińsko-Mazurskie, NE Poland
Gold Coast *149 E5 cultural region* Queensland, E Australia
Golden Bay *150 C4 bay* South Island, New Zealand
Golden State, The *see* California
Goldingen *see* Kuldiga
Goldsboro *43 F1* North Carolina, SE USA
Goleniów *98 B3 Ger.* Gollnow. Zachodnio-pomorskie, NW Poland
Gollnow *see* Goleniów
Golmo *see* Golmud
Golmud *126 D4 var.* Ge'e'mu, Golmo, *Chin.* Ko-erh-mu. Qinghai, C China
Golovanevsk *see* Holovanivs'k
Golub-Dobrzyń *98 C3* Kujawski-pomorskie, C Poland
Goma *77 E6* Nord-Kivu, NE Dem. Rep. Congo
Gombi *75 H4* Adamawa, E Nigeria
Gombroon *see* Bandar-e 'Abbās
Gomel' *see* Homyel'
Gomera *70 A3 island* Islas Canarias, Spain, NE Atlantic Ocean
Gómez Palacio *50 D3* Durango, C Mexico
Gonaïves *54 D3 var.* Les Gonaïves. N Haiti
Gonâve, Île de la *54 D3 island* C Haiti
Gondar *see* Gonder
Gonder *72 C4 var.* Gondar. Āmara, NW Ethiopia
Gondia *135 E4* Mahārāshtra, C India
Gonggar *126 C5 var.* Gyixong. Xizang Zizhiqu, W China
Gongola *75 G4 river* E Nigeria
Gongtang *see* Damxung
Gonni/Gónnos *see* Gónnoi
Gónnoi *104 B4 var.* Gonni, Gónnos; *prev.* Derelí. Thessalía, C Greece
Good Hope, Cape of *78 B5 Afr.* Kaap de Goede Hoop, Kaap die Goeie Hoop. *headland* SW South Africa
Goodland *44 D4* Kansas, C USA
Goondiwindi *149 D5* Queensland, E Australia
Goor *86 E3* Overijssel, E Netherlands
Goose Green *65 D7 var.* Prado del Ganso. East Falkland, Falkland Islands
Goose Lake *46 B4 var.* Lago dos Gansos. *lake* California/Oregon, W USA
Gopher State *see* Minnesota
Göppingen *95 B6* Baden-Württemberg, SW Germany
Góra Kalwaria *114 D4* Mazowieckie, C Poland
Gorakhpur *135 E3* Uttar Pradesh, N India
Gorany *see* Harany
Goražde *100 C4* Federacija Bosne I Hercegovine, SE Bosnia and Herzegovina
Gorbovichi *see* Harbavichy
Goré *76 C4* Logone-Oriental, S Chad
Gorē *73 C5* Oromīya, C Ethiopia
Gore *151 B7* Southland, South Island, New Zealand
Gorgān *120 D2 var.* Astarabad, Astrabad, Gurgan, *prev.* Asterābād; *anc.* Hyrcania. Golestān, N Iran
Gori *117 F2* C Georgia
Gorinchem *86 C4 var.* Gorkum. Zuid-Holland, C Netherlands
Goris *117 G3* SE Armenia
Gorki *see* Horki
Gor'kiy *see* Nizhniy Novgorod
Gorkum *see* Gorinchem
Görlitz *94 D4* Sachsen, E Germany
Görlitz *see* Zgorzelec
Gorlovka *see* Horlivka
Gorna Dzhumaya *see* Blagoevgrad
Gornja Mužlja *see* Mužlja
Gornji Milanovac *100 C4* Serbia, C Serbia
Gorodets *see* Haradzyets
Gorodishche *see* Horodyshche
Gorodnya *see* Horodnya
Gorodok *see* Haradok
Gorodok/Gorodok Yagellonski *see* Horodok
Gorontalo *139 E4* Sulawesi, C Indonesia
Gorontalo, Teluk *see* Tomini, Teluk
Gorssel *86 D3* Gelderland, E Netherlands
Goryn *see* Horyn'
Gorzów Wielkopolski *98 B3 Ger.* Landsberg, Landsberg an der Warthe. Lubuskie, W Poland
Gosford *149 D6* New South Wales, SE Australia
Goshogawara *130 D3 var.* Gosyogawara. Aomori, Honshū, C Japan
Gospić *100 A3* Lika-Senj, C Croatia
Gostivar *101 D6* W FYR Macedonia
Gosyogawara *see* Goshogawara
Göteborg *85 B7 Eng.* Gothenburg. Västra Götaland, S Sweden
Gotel Mountains *75 G5 mountain range* E Nigeria
Gotha *94 C4* Thüringen, C Germany
Gothenburg *see* Göteborg
Gotland *85 C7 island* SE Sweden
Goto-retto *131 A7 island group* SW Japan
Gotska Sandön *106 B1 island* SE Sweden
Gōtsu *131 B6 var.* Gôtu. Shimane, Honshū, SW Japan
Göttingen *94 B4 var.* Goettingen. Niedersachsen, C Germany
Gottschee *see* Kočevje
Gottwaldov *see* Zlín
Gôtu *see* Gōtsu
Gouda *86 C4* Zuid-Holland, C Netherlands
Gough Fracture Zone *67 C6 tectonic feature* S Atlantic Ocean
Gough Island *69 B8 island* Tristan da Cunha, S Atlantic Ocean
Gouin, Réservoir *38 D4 reservoir* Québec, SE Canada
Goulburn *149 D6* New South Wales, SE Australia
Goundam *75 E3* Tombouctou, NW Mali
Gouré *75 G3* Zinder, SE Niger
Goverla, Gora *see* Hoverla, Hora
Governador Valadares *63 F4* Minas Gerais, SE Brazil
Govi Altayn Nuruu *127 E3 mountain range* S Mongolia
Goya *64 D3* Corrientes, NE Argentina
Goyania *see* Goiânia
Goyaz *see* Goiás
Goz Beïda *76 C3* Ouaddaï, SE Chad
Gozo *97 C8 var.* Ghawdex. *island* N Malta
Graciosa *92 A5 var.* Ilha Graciosa. *island* Azores, Portugal, NE Atlantic Ocean
Graciosa, Ilha *see* Graciosa
Gradačac *100 C3* Federacija Bosne I Hercegovine, N Bosnia and Herzegovina
Gradaús, Serra dos *63 E3 mountain range* C Brazil
Gradiška *see* Bosanska Gradiška
Grafton *149 E5* New South Wales, SE Australia
Grafton *45 E1* North Dakota, N USA
Graham Land *154 A2 physical region* Antarctica
Grajewo *98 E3* Podlaskie, NE Poland
Grampian Mountains *88 C3 mountain range* C Scotland, United Kingdom
Gran *see* Esztergom, Hungary
Granada *52 D3* Granada, SW Nicaragua
Granada *92 D5* Andalucía, S Spain
Gran Canaria *70 A3 var.* Grand Canary. *island* Islas Canarias, Spain, NE Atlantic Ocean
Gran Chaco *64 D2 var.* Chaco. *lowland plain* South America
Grand Bahama Island *54 B1 island* N Bahamas
Grand Banks of Newfoundland *34 E4 undersea basin* NW Atlantic Ocean
Grand Bassa *see* Buchanan
Grand Canary *see* Gran Canaria
Grand Canyon *48 A1 canyon* Arizona, SW USA
Grand Canyon State *see* Arizona
Grand Cayman *54 B3 island* SW Cayman Islands
Grand Duchy of Luxembourg *see* Luxembourg
Grande, Bahía *65 B7 bay* S Argentina
Grande Comore *see* Ngazidja
Grande de Chiloé, Isla *see* Chiloé, Isla de
Grande Prairie *37 E4* Alberta, W Canada
Grand Erg Occidental *70 D3 desert* W Algeria
Grand Erg Oriental *71 E3 desert* Algeria/Tunisia
Rio Grande *51 E2 var.* Río Bravo, *Sp.* Río Bravo del Norte, Bravo del Norte. *river* Mexico/USA
Grande Terre *55 G3 island* E West Indies
Grand Falls *39 G3* Newfoundland, Newfoundland and Labrador, SE Canada
Grand Forks *45 E1* North Dakota, N USA
Grandichi *see* Hrandzichy
Grand Island *45 E4* Nebraska, C USA
Grand Junction *44 C4* Colorado, C USA
Grand Paradis *see* Gran Paradiso
Grand Rapids *40 C3* Michigan, N USA
Grand Rapids *45 F1* Minnesota, N USA
Grand-Saint-Bernard, Col du *see* Great Saint Bernard Pass
Grand-Santi *59 G3* W French Guiana
Granite State *see* New Hampshire
Gran Lago *see* Nicaragua, Lago de
Gran Malvina *see* West Falkland
Gran Paradiso *96 A2 Fr.* Grand Paradis. *mountain* NW Italy
Gran San Bernardo, Passo di *see* Great Saint Bernard Pass
Gran Santiago *see* Santiago
Grants *48 C2* New Mexico, SW USA
Grants Pass *46 B4* Oregon, NW USA
Granville *90 B3* Manche, N France
Gratianopolis *see* Grenoble
Gratz *see* Graz
Graudenz *see* Grudziądz
Graulhet *91 C6* Tarn, S France
Grave *86 D4* Noord-Brabant, SE Netherlands
Grayling *36 C2* Alaska, USA
Graz *95 E7 prev.* Gratz. Steiermark, SE Austria
Great Abaco *54 C1 var.* Abaco Island. *island* N Bahamas
Great Alfold *see* Great Hungarian Plain
Great Ararat *see* Büyükağrı Dağı
Great Australian Bight *147 D7 bight* S Australia
Great Barrier Island *150 D2 island* N New Zealand
Great Barrier Reef *148 D2 reef* Queensland, NE Australia
Great Basin *47 C5 basin* W USA
Great Bear Lake *37 E3 Fr.* Grand Lac de l'Ours. *lake* Northwest Territories, NW Canada
Great Belt *85 B8 var.* Store Bælt, *Eng.* Great Belt, Storebelt. *channel* Baltic Sea/Kattegat
Great Belt *see* Storebælt
Great Bend *45 E5* Kansas, C USA
Great Britain *see* Britain

Great Dividing Range *148 D4 mountain range* NE Australia
Greater Antilles *54 D3 island group* West Indies
Greater Caucasus *117 G2 mountain range* Azerbaijan/Georgia/Russian Federation Asia/Europe
Greater Sunda Islands *124 D5 var.* Sunda Islands. *island group* Indonesia
Great Exhibition Bay *150 C1 inlet* North Island, New Zealand
Great Exuma Island *54 C2 island* C Bahamas
Great Falls *44 B1* Montana, NW USA
Great Grimsby *see* Grimsby
Great Hungarian Plain *99 C7 var.* Great Alfold, Plain of Hungary, *Hung.* Alföld. *plain* SE Europe
Great Inagua *54 D2 var.* Inagua Islands. *island* S Bahamas
Great Indian Desert *see* Thar Desert
Great Khingan Range *127 G1 Eng.* Great Khingan Range. *mountain range* NE China
Great Khingan Range *see* Da Hinggan Ling
Great Lake *see* Tônlé Sap
Great Lakes *35 C5 lakes* Ontario, Canada/USA
Great Lakes State *see* Michigan
Great Meteor Seamount *see* Great Meteor Tablemount
Great Meteor Tablemount *66 B3 var.* Great Meteor Seamount. *seamount* E Atlantic Ocean
Great Nicobar *133 G3 island* Nicobar Islands, India, NE Indian Ocean
Great Plain of China *125 E2 plain* E China
Great Plains *45 E3 var.* High Plains. *plains* Canada/USA
Great Rift Valley *73 C5 var.* Rift Valley. *depression* Asia/Africa
Great Ruaha *73 C7 river* S Tanzania
Great Saint Bernard Pass *96 A1 Fr.* Col du Grand-Saint-Bernard, *It.* Passo del Gran San Bernardo. *pass* Italy/Switzerland
Great Salt Desert *see* Kavīr, Dasht-e
Great Salt Lake *44 A3 salt lake* Utah, W USA
Great Salt Lake Desert *44 A4 plain* Utah, W USA
Great Sand Sea *71 H3 desert* Egypt/Libya
Great Sandy Desert *146 C4 desert* Western Australia
Great Sandy Desert *see* Ar Rub' al Khālī
Great Sandy Island *see* Fraser Island
Great Slave Lake *37 E4 Fr.* Grand Lac des Esclaves. *lake* Northwest Territories, NW Canada
Great Socialist People's Libyan Arab Jamahiriya *see* Libya
Great Sound *42 A5 sound* Bermuda, NW Atlantic Ocean
Great Victoria Desert *147 C5 desert* South Australia/Western Australia
Great Wall of China *128 C4 ancient monument* N China Asia
Great Yarmouth *89 E6 var.* Yarmouth. E England, United Kingdom
Grebenka *see* Hrebinka
Gredos, Sierra de *92 D3 mountain range* W Spain
Greece *105 A5 off.* Hellenic Republic, *Gk.* Ellás; *anc.* Hellas. *country* SE Europe

GREECE
Southeast Europe

Official name Hellenic Republic
Formation 1829 / 1947
Capital Athens
Population 11.1 million / 220 people per sq mile (85 people per sq km)
Total area 50,942 sq. miles (131,940 sq. km)
Languages Greek*, Turkish, Macedonian, Albanian
Religions Orthodox Christian 98%, Muslim 1%, Other 1%
Ethnic mix Greek 98%, Other 2%
Government Parliamentary system
Currency Euro = 100 cents
Literacy rate 97%
Calorie consumption 3433 kilocalories

Greeley *44 D4* Colorado, C USA
Green Bay *40 B2* Wisconsin, N USA
Green Bay *40 B2 lake bay* Michigan/Wisconsin, N USA
Greeneville *43 E1* Tennessee, S USA
Greenland *82 D3 Dan.* Grønland, *Inuit* Kalaallit Nunaat. *Danish external territory* NE North America
Greenland Sea *83 F2 sea* Arctic Ocean
Green Mountains *41 G2 mountain range* Vermont, NE USA
Green Mountain State *see* Vermont
Greenock *88 C4* W Scotland, United Kingdom
Green River *44 B3* Wyoming, C USA
Green River *40 C5 river* Kentucky, C USA
Green River *44 B4 river* Utah, W USA
Greensboro *43 F1* North Carolina, SE USA
Greenville *42 B2* Mississippi, S USA
Greenville *43 F1* North Carolina, SE USA
Greenville *43 E1* South Carolina, SE USA
Greenville *49 G2* Texas, SW USA
Greenwich *89 B8* United Kingdom
Greenwood *42 B2* Mississippi, S USA
Greenwood *43 E2* South Carolina, SE USA
Gregory Range *148 C3 mountain range* Queensland, E Australia
Greifenberg/Greifenberg in Pommern *see* Gryfice
Greifswald *94 D2* Mecklenburg-Vorpommern, NE Germany
Grenada *42 C2* Mississippi, S USA
Grenada *55 G5 country* SE West Indies

GRENADA
West Indies

Official name Grenada
Formation 1974 / 1974
Capital St. George's
Population 109,590 / 837 people per sq mile (322 people per sq km)
Total area 131 sq. miles (340 sq. km)
Languages English*, English Creole
Religions Roman Catholic 68%, Anglican 17%, Other 15%
Ethnic mix Black African 82%, Mulatto (mixed race) 13%, East Indian 3%, Other 2%
Government Parliamentary system
Currency East Caribbean dollar = 100 cents
Literacy rate 96%
Calorie consumption 2453 kilocalories

Grenadines, The *55 H4 island group* Grenada/St Vincent and the Grenadines
Grenoble *91 D5 anc.* Cularo, Gratianopolis. Isère, E France
Gresham *46 B3* Oregon, NW USA
Grevená *104 B4* Dytikí Makedonía, N Greece
Grevenmacher *87 E8* Grevenmacher, E Luxembourg
Greymouth *151 B5* West Coast, South Island, New Zealand
Grey Range *149 C5 mountain range* New South Wales/Queensland, E Australia
Greytown *see* San Juan del Norte
Griffin *42 D2* Georgia, SE USA
Grimari *76 C4* Ouaka, C Central African Republic
Grimsby *89 E5 prev.* Great Grimsby. E England, United Kingdom
Grobin *see* Grobiņa
Grobiņa *106 B3 Ger.* Grobin. W Latvia
Gródek Jagielloński *see* Horodok
Grodno *see* Hrodna
Grodzisk Wielkopolski *98 B3* Wielkopolskie, C Poland
Groesbeek *86 D4* Gelderland, SE Netherlands
Grójec *98 D4* Mazowieckie, C Poland
Groningen *86 E1* Groningen, NE Netherlands
Grønland *see* Greenland
Groote Eylandt *148 B2 island* Northern Territory, N Australia
Grootfontein *78 B3* Otjozondjupa, N Namibia
Groot Karasberge *78 B4 mountain range* S Namibia
Gros Islet *55 F1* N Saint Lucia
Grossa, Isola *see* Dugi Otok
Grossbetschkerek *see* Zrenjanin
Grosse Morava *see* Velika Morava
Grosser Sund *see* Suur Väin
Grosseto *96 B4* Toscana, C Italy
Grossglockner *95 C7 mountain* W Austria
Grosskanizsa *see* Nagykanizsa
Gross-Karol *see* Carei
Grosskikinda *see* Kikinda
Grossmichel *see* Michalovce
Gross-Schlatten *see* Abrud
Grosswardein *see* Oradea
Groznyy *111 B8* Chechenskaya Respublika, SW Russian Federation
Grudovo *see* Sredets
Grudziądz *98 C3 Ger.* Graudenz. Kujawsko-pomorskie, C Poland
Grums *85 B6* Värmland, C Sweden
Grünberg/Grünberg in Schlesien *see* Zielona Góra
Grüneberg *see* Zielona Góra
Gruzinskaya SSR/Gruziya *see* Georgia
Gryazi *111 B6* Lipetskaya Oblast', W Russian Federation
Gryfice *98 B2 Ger.* Greifenberg, Greifenberg in Pommern. Zachodnio-pomorskie, NW Poland
Guabito *53 E4* Bocas del Toro, NW Panama
Guadalajara *50 D4* Jalisco, C Mexico
Guadalajara *93 E3 Ar.* Wad Al-Hajarah; *anc.* Arriaca. Castilla-La Mancha, C Spain
Guadalcanal *144 C3 island* C Solomon Islands
Guadalquivir *92 D4 river* W Spain
Guadalupe *50 D3* Zacatecas, C Mexico
Guadalupe Peak *48 D3 mountain* Texas, SW USA
Guadalupe River *49 G4 river* SW USA
Guadarrama, Sierra de *93 E2 mountain range* C Spain
Guadeloupe *55 H3 French overseas department* E West Indies
Guadiana *92 C4 river* Portugal/Spain
Guadix *93 E4* Andalucía, S Spain
Guaimaca *52 C2* Francisco Morazán, C Honduras
Guajira, Península de la *58 B1 peninsula* N Colombia
Gualaco *52 D2* Olancho, C Honduras
Gualán *52 B2* Zacapa, C Guatemala
Gualdicciolo *96 D1* NW San Marino
Gualeguaychú *64 D4* Entre Ríos, E Argentina
Guam *144 B1 US unincorporated territory* W Pacific Ocean
Guamúchil *50 C3* Sinaloa, C Mexico
Guanabacoa *54 B2* La Habana, W Cuba
Guanajuato *51 E4* Guanajuato, C Mexico
Guanare *58 C2* Portuguesa, N Venezuela
Guanare, Río *58 D2 river* W Venezuela
Guangdong *128 C6 var.* Guangdong Sheng, Kuang-tung, Kwangtung, Yue. *province* S China
Guangdong Sheng *see* Guangdong
Guangju *see* Gwangju
Guangxi *see* Guangxi Zhuangzu Zizhiqu
Guangxi Zhuangzu Zizhiqu *128 C6 var.* Guangxi, Gui, Kuang-hsi, Kwangsi, *Eng.* Kwangsi Chuang Autonomous Region. *autonomous region* S China
Guangyuan *128 B5 var.* Kuang-yuan, Kwangyuan. Sichuan, C China
Guangzhou *128 C6 var.* Kuang-chou, Kwangchow, *Eng.* Canton. *province capital* Guangdong, S China
Guantánamo *54 D3* Guantánamo, SE Cuba
Guantánamo, Bahia de *54 D3 Eng.* Guantanamo Bay. *US military base* SE Cuba
Guantanamo Bay *see* Guantánamo, Bahia de
Guaporé, Rio *62 D3 var.* Río Iténez. *river* Bolivia/Brazil
Guarda *92 C3* Guarda, N Portugal
Guarumal *53 F5* Veraguas, S Panama
Guasave *50 C3* Sinaloa, C Mexico
Guatemala *52 A2 off.* Republic of Guatemala. *country* Central America

GUATEMALA
Central America

Official name Republic of Guatemala
Formation 1838 / 1838
Capital Guatemala City
Population 15.5 million / 370 people per sq mile (143 people per sq km)

GUATEMALA
(continued)

Total area 42,042 sq. miles (108,890 sq. km)
Languages Quiché, Mam, Cakchiquel, Kekchí, Spanish*
Religions Roman Catholic 65%, Protestant 33%, Other and nonreligious 2%
Ethnic mix Amerindian 60%, Mestizo 30%, Other 10%
Government Presidential system
Currency Quetzal = 100 centavos
Literacy rate 78%
Calorie consumption 2502 kilocalories

Guatemala Basin *35 B7 undersea basi[n]* E Pacific Ocean
Guatemala City *see* Ciudad de Guatem[ala]
Guatemala, Republic of *see* Guatemal[a]
Guaviare *56 B2 off.* Comisaría Guavia[re]. *province* S Colombia
Guaviare, Comisaría *see* Guaviare
Guaviare, Río *58 D3 river* E Colombia
Guayanas, Macizo de las *see* Guiana Highlands
Guayaquil *60 A2 var.* Santiago de Guayaquil. Guayas, SW Ecuador
Guayaquil, Gulf of *60 A2 var.* Gulf of Guayaquil. *gulf* SW Ecuador
Guayaquil, Gulf of *see* Guayaquil, Golfo de
Guaymas *50 B2* Sonora, NW Mexico
Gubadag *122 C2 Turkm.* Tel'man; *prev.* Tel'mansk. Daşoguz Welaýaty, N Turkmenistan
Guben *94 D4 var.* Wilhelm-Pieck-Stad[t]. Brandenburg, E Germany
Gudara *see* Ghŭdara
Gudauta *117 E1 prev.* Gudaut'a. NW Georgia
Gudaut'a *see* Gudauta
Guéret *90 C4* Creuse, C France
Guernsey *89 D8 British Crown Dependency* Channel Islands, NW Europe
Guerrero Negro *50 A2* Baja California Sur, NW Mexico
Gui *see* Guangxi Zhuangzu Zizhiqu
Guiana *see* French Guiana
Guiana Highlands *62 D1 var.* Macizo [de] las Guayanas. *mountain range* N Sou[th] America
Guiba *see* Juba
Guidder *see* Guider
Guider *76 B4 var.* Guidder. Nord, N Cameroon
Guidimouni *75 G3* Zinder, S Niger
Guildford *89 D7* SE England, United Kingdom
Guilin *128 C6 var.* Kuei-lin, Kweilin. Guangxi Zhuangzu Zizhiqu, S China
Guimarães *92 B2 var.* Guimaráes. Bra[ga], N Portugal
Guimaráes *see* Guimarães
Guinea *74 C4 off.* Republic of Guinea, *var.* Guinée; *prev.* French Guinea, People's Revolutionary Republic of Guinea. *country* W Africa

GUINEA
West Africa

Official name Republic of Guinea
Formation 1958 / 1958
Capital Conakry
Population 11.7 million / 123 people per sq mile (48 people per sq km)
Total area 94,925 sq. miles (245,857 sq. km)
Languages Pulaar, Malinké, Soussou, French
Religions Muslim 85%, Christian 8%, Traditional beliefs 7%
Ethnic mix Peul 40%, Malinké 30%, Soussou 20%, Other 10%
Government Transitional regime
Currency Guinea franc = 100 centimes
Literacy rate 25%
Calorie consumption 2553 kilocalories

Guinea Basin *69 A5 undersea basin* E Atlantic Ocean
Guinea-Bissau *74 B4 off.* Republic of Guinea-Bissau, *Fr.* Guinée-Bissau, *Po[rt.]* Guiné-Bissau; *prev.* Portuguese Guine[a]. *country* W Africa

GUINEA-BISSAU
West Africa

Official name Republic of Guinea-Bissau
Formation 1974 / 1974
Capital Bissau
Population 1.7 million / 157 people per sq mile (60 people per sq km)
Total area 13,946 sq. miles (36,120 sq. km)
Languages Portuguese Creole, Balante, Fulani, Malinké, Portuguese*
Religions Traditional beliefs 50%, Muslim 40%, Christian 10%
Ethnic mix Balante 30%, Fulani 20%, Other 16%, Mandyako 14%, Mandinka 13%, Papel 7%
Government Transitional regime
Currency CFA franc = 100 centimes
Literacy rate 57%
Calorie consumption 2304 kilocalories

Guinea-Bissau, Republic of *see* Guinea-Bissau
Guinea, Gulf of *68 B4 Fr.* Golfe de Guinée. *gulf* E Atlantic Ocean
Guinea, People's Revolutionary Republic of *see* Guinea
Guinea, Republic of *see* Guinea
Guiné-Bissau *see* Guinea-Bissau
Guinée *see* Guinea
Guinée-Bissau *see* Guinea-Bissau
Guinée, Golfe de *see* Guinea, Gulf of
Güiria *59 E1* Sucre, NE Venezuela
Guiyang *128 B6 var.* Kuei-Yang, Kuei-yang, Kueyang, Kweiyang; *prev.* Kweichu. *province capital* Guizhou, S China
Guizhou *128 B6* Guangdong, SE China
Gujarāt *134 C4 var.* Gujerat. *cultural region* W India
Gujerat *see* Gujarāt
Gujrānwāla *134 D2* Punjab, NE Pakistan
Gujrāt *134 D2* Punjab, E Pakistan
Gulbarga *132 C1* Karnātaka, C India
Gulbene *106 D3 Ger.* Alt-Schwanenburg. NE Latvia
Gulf of Liaotung *see* Liaodong Wan
Gulfport *42 C3* Mississippi, S USA
Gulf, The *see* Persian Gulf
Gulistan *see* Guliston
Guliston *123 E2 Rus.* Gulistan. Sirdaryo Viloyati, E Uzbekistan
Gulja *see* Yining
Gulkana *36 D3* Alaska, USA
Gulu *73 B6* N Uganda
Gulyantsi *104 C1* Pleven, N Bulgaria
Guma *see* Pishan
Gumbinnen *see* Gusev
Gumpolds *see* Humpolec
Gümülcine/Gümüljina *see* Komotiní
Gümüşane *see* Gümüşhane
Gümüşhane *117 E3 var.* Gümüşane, Gumushkhane. Gümüşhane, NE Turkey
Gumushkhane *see* Gümüşhane
Güney Doğu Toroslar *117 E4 mountain range* SE Turkey
Gunnbjørn Fjeld *82 D4 var.* Gunnbjörns Bjerge. *mountain* C Greenland
Gunnbjörns Bjerge *see* Gunnbjørn Fjeld
Gunnedah *149 D6* New South Wales, SE Australia
Gunnison *44 C5* Colorado, C USA
Gurbansoltan Eje *122 C2 prev.* Ýylanly, *Rus.* Il'yaly. Daşoguz Welaýaty, N Turkmenistan
Gurbantünggüt Shamo *126 B2 desert* W China
Gurgan *see* Gorgān
Guri, Embalse de *59 E2 reservoir* E Venezuela
Gurkfeld *see* Krško
Gurktaler Alpen *95 D7 mountain range* S Austria
Gürün *116 D3* Sivas, C Turkey
Gur'yev/Gur'yevskaya Oblast' *see* Atyrau
Gusau *75 G4* Zamfara, NW Nigeria
Gusev *106 B4 Ger.* Gumbinnen. Kaliningradskaya Oblast', W Russian Federation
Gustavus *36 D4* Alaska, USA
Güstrow *94 C3* Mecklenburg-Vorpommern, NE Germany
Guta/Gúta *see* Kolárovo
Gütersloh *94 B4* Nordrhein-Westfalen, W Germany
Gutta *see* Kolárovo
Guttstadt *see* Dobre Miasto
Guwāhāti *135 G3 prev.* Gauhāti. Assam, NE India
Guyana *59 F3 off.* Co-operative Republic of Guyana; *prev.* British Guiana. *country* N South America

GUYANA
South America

Official name Cooperative Republic of Guyana
Formation 1966 / 1966
Capital Georgetown
Population 800,000 / 11 people per sq mile (4 people per sq km)
Total area 83,000 sq. miles (214,970 sq. km)
Languages English Creole, Hindi, Tamil, Amerindian languages, English*
Religions Christian 57%, Hindu 28%, Muslim 10%, Other 5%
Ethnic mix East Indian 43%, Black African 30%, Mixed race 17%, Amerindian 9%, Other 1%
Government Presidential system
Currency Guyanese dollar = 100 cents
Literacy rate 85%
Calorie consumption 2648 kilocalories

Guyana, Co-operative Republic of *see* Guyana
Guyane *see* French Guiana
Guymon *49 E1* Oklahoma, C USA
Güzelyurt Körfezi *102 C5 Gk.* Kólpos Mórfu, Morphou. W Cyprus
Gvardeysk *106 A4 Ger.* Tapaiu. Kaliningradskaya Oblast', W Russian Federation
Gwādar *134 A3 var.* Gwadur. Baluchistān, SW Pakistan
Gwadur *see* Gwādar
Gwalior *134 D3* Madhya Pradesh, C India
Gwanda *78 D3* Matabeleland South, SW Zimbabwe
Gwangju *129 E4 off.* Gwangju Gwang-yeoksi, *prev.* Kwangju, *var.* Guangju, Kwangchu, *Jap.* Kōshū. SW South Korea
Gwangju Gwang-yeoksi *see* Gwangju
Gwy *see* Wye
Gyandzha *see* Gäncä
Gyangzê *126 C5* Xizang Zizhiqu, W China
Gyaring Co *126 C5 lake* W China
Gyêgu *see* Yushu
Gyergyószentmiklós *see* Gheorgheni
Gyixong *see* Gonggar
Gympie *149 E5* Queensland, E Australia
Gyomaendrőd *99 D7* Békés, SE Hungary
Gyöngyös *99 D6* Heves, NE Hungary
Győr *99 C6 Ger.* Raab, *Lat.* Arrabona. Győr-Moson-Sopron, NW Hungary
Gýtheio *105 B6 var.* Githio; *prev.* Yíthion. Pelopónnisos, S Greece
Gyulafehérvár *see* Alba Iulia
Gyumri *117 F2 var.* Giumri, *Rus.* Kumayri; *prev.* Aleksandropol', Leninakan. W Armenia
Gyzyrlabat *see* Serdar

H

Haabai *see* Ha'apai Group
Haacht *87 C6* Vlaams Brabant, C Belgium
Haaksbergen *86 E3* Overijssel, E Netherlands
Ha'apai Group *145 F4 var.* Haabai. *island group* C Tonga
Haapsalu *106 D2 Ger.* Hapsal. Läänemaa, W Estonia
Ha'Arava *see* 'Arabah, Wādī al
Haarlem *86 C3 prev.* Harlem. Noord-Holland, W Netherlands
Haast *151 B6* West Coast, South Island, New Zealand
Hachijo-jima *131 D6 island* Izu-shotō, SE Japan
Hachinohe *130 D3* Aomori, Honshū, C Japan
Hacıqabal *117 H3 prev.* Qazimämmäd. SE Azerbaijan
Haḑabat al Jilf al Kabīr *72 A2 var.* Gilf Kebir Plateau. *plateau* SW Egypt
Hadama *see* Nazrēt
Hadejia *75 G4* Jigawa, N Nigeria
Hadejia *75 G3 river* N Nigeria
Hadera *119 A6 var.* Khadera; *prev.* Ḩadera. Haifa, N Israel
Ḩadera *see* Hadera
Hadhdhunmathi Atoll *132 A5 atoll* S Maldives
Ha Đông *136 D3 var.* Hadong. Ha Tây, N Vietnam
Hadong *see* Ha Đông
Hadramaut *121 C6 Eng.* Hadramaut. *mountain range* S Yemen
Hadramaut *see* Ḩaḑramawt
Hadrianopolis *see* Edirne
Haerbin/Haerhpin/Ha-erh-pin *see* Harbin
Hafnia *see* Denmark
Hafnia *see* København
Hafren *see* Severn
Hafun, Ras *see* Xaafuun, Raas
Hagåtña *144 B1 , var.* Agaña. *dependent territory capital* (Guam) NW Guam
Hagerstown *41 E4* Maryland, NE USA
Ha Giang *136 D3* Ha Giang, N Vietnam
Hagios Evstrátios *see* Ágios Efstrátios
HaGolan *see* Golan Heights
Hagondange *90 D3* Moselle, NE France
Haguenau *90 E3* Bas-Rhin, NE France
Haibowan *see* Wuhai
Haicheng *128 D3* Liaoning, NE China
Haidarabad *see* Hyderābād
Haifa *see* Hefa
Haifa, Bay of *see* Mifrats Hefa
Haifong *see* Hai Phong
Haikou *128 C7 var.* Hai-k'ou, Hoihow, *Fr.* Hoï-Hao. *province capital* Hainan, S China
Hai-k'ou *see* Haikou
Ḩā'il *120 B4* Ḩā'il, NW Saudi Arabia
Hailuoto *84 D4 Swe.* Karlö. *island* W Finland
Hainan *128 B7 var.* Hainan Sheng, Qiong. *province* S China
Hainan Dao *128 C7 island* S China
Hainan Sheng *see* Hainan
Hainasch *see* Ainaži
Haines *36 D4* Alaska, USA
Hainichen *94 D4* Sachsen, E Germany
Hai Phong *136 D3 var.* Haifong, Haiphong. N Vietnam
Haiphong *see* Hai Phong
Haiti *54 D3 off.* Republic of Haiti. *country* C West Indies

HAITI
West Indies

Official name Republic of Haiti
Formation 1804 / 1844
Capital Port-au-Prince
Population 10.3 million / 968 people per sq mile (374 people per sq km)
Total area 10,714 sq. miles (27,750 sq. km)
Languages French Creole*, French*
Religions Roman Catholic 55%, Protestant 28%, Other (including Voodoo) 16%, Nonreligious 1%
Ethnic mix Black African 95%, Mulatto (mixed race) and European 5%
Government Presidential system
Currency Gourde = 100 centimes
Literacy rate 49%
Calorie consumption 2105 kilocalories

Haiti, Republic of *see* Haiti
Haiya *72 C3* Red Sea, NE Sudan
Hajdúhadház *99 D6* Hajdú-Bihar, E Hungary
Hajine *see* Abū Ḩardān
Hajnówka *98 E3 Ger.* Hermhausen. Podlaskie, NE Poland
Hakodate *130 D3* Hokkaidō, NE Japan
Hal *see* Halle
Ḩalab *118 B2 Eng.* Aleppo, *Fr.* Alep; *anc.* Beroea. Ḩalab, NW Syria
Hala'ib Triangle *72 C3 region* Egypt/Sudan
Ḩalāniyāt, Juzur al *121 D6 var.* Jazā'ir Bin Ghalfān, *Eng.* Kuria Muria Islands. *island group* S Oman
Halberstadt *94 C4* Sachsen-Anhalt, C Germany
Halden *85 B6 prev.* Fredrikshald. Østfold, S Norway
Halfmoon Bay *151 A8 var.* Oban. Stewart Island, Southland, New Zealand
Haliacmon *see* Aliákmonas
Halifax *39 F4 province capital* Nova Scotia, SE Canada
Halkida *see* Chalkída
Halle *87 B6 Fr.* Hal. Vlaams Brabant, C Belgium
Halle *94 C4 var.* Halle an der Saale. Sachsen-Anhalt, C Germany
Halle an der Saale *see* Halle
Halle-Neustadt *94 C4* Sachsen-Anhalt, C Germany
Halley *154 B2 UK research station* Antarctica
Hall Islands *142 B2 island group* C Micronesia
Halls Creek *146 C3* Western Australia
Halmahera, Laut *139 F4 Eng.* Halmahera Sea. *sea* E Indonesia
Halmahera, Pulau *139 F3 prev.* Djailolo, Gilolo, Jailolo. *island* E Indonesia
Halmahera Sea *see* Halmahera, Laut
Halmstad *85 B7* Halland, S Sweden
Ha Long *136 E3 prev.* Hông Gai, *var.* Hon Gai, Hongay. Quang Ninh, N Vietnam
Hälsingborg *see* Helsingborg
Hamada *131 B6* Shimane, Honshū, SW Japan
Hamadān *120 C3 anc.* Ecbatana. Hamadān, W Iran
Ḩamāh *118 B3 var.* Hama; *anc.* Epiphania, *Bibl.* Hamath. Ḩamāh, W Syria
Hamamatsu *131 D6 var.* Hamamatu. Shizuoka, Honshū, S Japan
Hamamatu *see* Hamamatsu
Hamar *85 B5 prev.* Storhammer. Hedmark, S Norway
Hamath *see* Ḩamāh
Hamburg *94 B3* Hamburg, N Germany
Hamd, Wadi al *120 A4 dry watercourse* W Saudi Arabia
Hämeenlinna *85 D5 Swe.* Tavastehus. Etelä-Suomi, S Finland
HaMela h, Yam *see* Dead Sea
Hamersley Range *146 A4 mountain range* Western Australia
Hamhŭng *129 E3* C North Korea
Hami *126 C3 var.* Ha-mi, *Uigh.* Kumul, Qomul. Xinjiang Uygur Zizhiqu, NW China
Ha-mi *see* Hami
Hamilton *42 A5 dependent territory capital* (Bermuda) C Bermuda
Hamilton *38 D5* Ontario, S Canada
Hamilton *150 D3* Waikato, North Island, New Zealand
Hamilton *88 C4* S Scotland, United Kingdom
Hamilton *42 C2* Alabama, S USA
Hamim, Wadi al *71 G2 river* NE Libya
Hamīs Musait *see* Khamīs Mushayț
Hamm *94 B4 var.* Hamm in Westfalen. Nordrhein-Westfalen, W Germany
Ḩammāmāt, Khalīj al *see* Hammamet, Golfe de
Hammamet, Golfe de *102 D3 Ar.* Khalīj al Ḩammāmāt. *gulf* NE Tunisia
Ḩammār, Hawr al *120 C3 lake* SE Iraq
Hamm in Westfalen *see* Hamm
Hampden *151 B7* Otago, South Island, New Zealand
Hampstead *89 A7* Maryland, USA
Ħamrun *102 B5* C Malta
Hāmūn, Daryācheh-ye *see* Şāberī, Hāmūn-e/Sīstān, Daryācheh-ye
Hamwih *see* Southampton
Hâncești *see* Hîncești
Hancewicze *see* Hantsavichy
Handan *128 C4 var.* Han-tan. Hebei, E China
Haneda *130 A2* (Tōkyō) Tōkyō, Honshū, S Japan
Hanford *47 C6* California, W USA
Hangayn Nuruu *126 D2 mountain range* C Mongolia
Hang-chou/Hangchow *see* Hangzhou
Hangö *see* Hanko
Hangzhou *128 D5 var.* Hang-chou, Hangchow. *province capital* Zhejiang, SE China
Hania *see* Chaniá
Hanka, Lake *see* Khanka, Lake
Hanko *85 D6 Swe.* Hangö. Etelä-Suomi, SW Finland
Han-kou/Han-k'ou/Hankow *see* Wuhan
Hanmer Springs *151 C5* Canterbury, South Island, New Zealand
Hannibal *45 G4* Missouri, C USA
Hannover *94 B3 Eng.* Hanover. Niedersachsen, NW Germany
Hanöbukten *85 B7 bay* S Sweden

Ha Nôi *136 D3 Eng.* Hanoi, *Fr.* Hanoï. *country capital* (Vietnam) N Vietnam
Hanover *see* Hannover
Han Shui *127 E4 river* C China
Han-tan *see* Handan
Hantsavichy *107 B6 Pol.* Hancewicze, *Rus.* Gantsevichi. Brestskaya Voblasts', SW Belarus
Hanyang *see* Wuhan
Hanzhong *128 B5* Shaanxi, C China
Hãora *135 F4 prev.* Howrah. West Bengal, NE India
Haparanda *84 D4* Norrbotten, N Sweden
Hapsal *see* Haapsalu
Haradok *107 E5 Rus.* Gorodok. Vitsyebskaya Voblasts', N Belarus
Haradzyets *107 B6 Rus.* Gorodets. Brestskaya Voblasts', SW Belarus
Haramachi *130 D4* Fukushima, Honshū, E Japan
Harany *107 D5 Rus.* Gorany. Vitsyebskaya Voblasts', N Belarus
Harare *78 D3 prev.* Salisbury. *country capital* (Zimbabwe) Mashonaland East, NE Zimbabwe
Harbavichy *107 E6 Rus.* Gorbovichi. Mahilyowskaya Voblasts', E Belarus
Harbel *74 C5* W Liberia
Harbin *129 E2 var.* Haerbin, Haerh-pin, Kharbin; *prev.* Haerhpin, Pingkiang, Pinkiang. *province capital* Heilongjiang, NE China
Hardangerfjorden *85 A6 fjord* S Norway
Hardangervidda *85 A6 plateau* S Norway
Hardenberg *86 E3* Overijssel, E Netherlands
Harelbeke *87 A6 var.* Harlebeke. West-Vlaanderen, W Belgium
Harem *see* Ḩārim
Haren *86 E2* Groningen, NE Netherlands
Hārer *73 D5* E Ethiopia
Hargeisa *see* Hargeysa
Hargeysa *73 D5 var.* Hargeisa. Woqooyi Galbeed, NW Somalia
Hariana *see* Haryāna
Hari, Batang *138 B4 prev.* Djambi. *river* Sumatera, W Indonesia
Ḩārim *118 B2 var.* Harem. Idlib, W Syria
Harima-nada *131 B6 sea* S Japan
Harirud *123 E4 var.* Tedzhen, *Turkm.* Tejen. *river* Afghanistan/Iran
Harlan *45 F3* Iowa, C USA
Harlebeke *see* Harelbeke
Harlem *see* Haarlem
Harlingen *86 D2 Fris.* Harns. Fryslân, N Netherlands
Harlingen *49 G5* Texas, SW USA
Harlow *89 E6* E England, United Kingdom
Harney Basin *46 B4 basin* Oregon, NW USA
Härnösand *85 C5 var.* Hernösand. Västernorrland, C Sweden
Harns *see* Harlingen
Harper *74 D5 var.* Cape Palmas. NE Liberia
Harricana *38 D3 river* Québec, SE Canada
Harris *88 B3 physical region* NW Scotland, United Kingdom
Harrisburg *41 E4 state capital* Pennsylvania, NE USA
Harrisonburg *41 E4* Virginia, NE USA
Harrison, Cape *39 F2 headland* Newfoundland and Labrador, E Canada
Harris Ridge *see* Lomonosov Ridge
Harrogate *89 D5* N England, United Kingdom
Hârşova *108 D5 prev.* Hîrşova. Constanţa, SE Romania
Harstad *84 C2* Troms, N Norway
Hartford *41 G3 state capital* Connecticut, NE USA
Hartlepool *89 D5* N England, United Kingdom
Harunabad *see* Eslāmābād-e Gharb
Har Us Gol *126 C2 lake* Hovd, W Mongolia
Har Us Nuur *126 C2 lake* NW Mongolia
Harwich *89 E6* E England, United Kingdom
Haryāna *134 D2 var.* Hariana. *cultural region* N India
Hashemite Kingdom of Jordan *see* Jordan
Hasselt *87 C6* Limburg, NE Belgium
Hassetché *see* Al Ḩasakah
Hasta Colonia/Hasta Pompeia *see* Asti
Hastings *150 E4* Hawke's Bay, North Island, New Zealand
Hastings *89 E7* SE England, United Kingdom
Hastings *45 E4* Nebraska, C USA
Haţeg *108 B4 Ger.* Wallenthal, *Hung.* Hátszeg; *prev.* Hatzeg, Hötzing. Hunedoara, SW Romania
Hátszeg *see* Haţeg
Hattem *86 D3* Gelderland, E Netherlands
Hatteras, Cape *43 G1 headland* North Carolina, SE USA
Hatteras Plain *35 D6 abyssal plain* W Atlantic Ocean
Hattiesburg *42 C3* Mississippi, S USA
Hatton Bank *see* Hatton Ridge
Hatton Ridge *80 B2 var.* Hatton Bank. *undersea ridge* N Atlantic Ocean
Hat Yai *137 C7 var.* Ban Hat Yai. Songkhla, SW Thailand
Hatzeg *see* Haţeg
Hatzfeld *see* Jimbolia
Haugesund *85 A6* Rogaland, S Norway
Haukeligrend *85 A6* Telemark, S Norway
Haukivesi *85 E5 lake* SE Finland
Hauraki Gulf *150 D2 gulf* North Island, N New Zealand
Hauroko, Lake *151 A7 lake* South Island, New Zealand
Hautes Fagnes *87 D6 Ger.* Hohes Venn. *mountain range* E Belgium
Hauts Plateaux *70 D2 plateau* Algeria/Morocco
Hauzenberg *95 D6* Bayern, SE Germany
Havana *35 D6* Illinois, N USA
Havana *see* La Habana
Havant *89 D7* S England, United Kingdom
Havelock *43 F1* North Carolina, SE USA
Havelock North *150 E4* Hawke's Bay, North Island, New Zealand
Haverfordwest *89 C6* SW Wales, United Kingdom
Havířov *99 C5* Moravskoslezský Kraj, E Czech Republic
Havre *44 C1* Montana, NW USA
Havre *see* le Havre
Havre-St-Pierre *39 F3* Québec, E Canada
Hawaii *47 A8 off.* State of Hawaii, *also known as* Aloha State, Paradise of the Pacific, *var.* Hawai'i. *state* USA, C Pacific Ocean
Hawai'i *47 B8 var.* Hawaii. *island* Hawai'ian Islands, USA, C Pacific Ocean
Hawai'ian Islands *152 D2 prev.* Sandwich Islands. *island group* Hawaii, USA
Hawaiian Ridge *152 H4 undersea ridge* N Pacific Ocean
Hawea, Lake *151 B6 lake* South Island, New Zealand
Hawera *150 D4* Taranaki, North Island, New Zealand
Hawick *88 C4* SE Scotland, United Kingdom
Hawke Bay *150 E4 bay* North Island, New Zealand
Hawkeye State *see* Iowa
Hawlēr *see* Arbīl
Hawthorne *47 C6* Nevada, W USA
Hay *149 C6* New South Wales, SE Australia
HaYarden *see* Jordan
Hayastani Hanrapetut'yun *see* Armenia
Hayes *38 B2 river* Manitoba, C Canada
Hay River *37 E4* Northwest Territories, W Canada
Hays *45 E5* Kansas, C USA
Haysyn *108 D3 Rus.* Gaysin. Vinnyts'ka Oblast', C Ukraine
Hazar *122 B2 prev. Rus.* Cheleken. Balkan Welaýaty, W Turkmenistan
Heard and McDonald Islands *141 B7 Australian external territory* S Indian Ocean
Hearst *38 C4* Ontario, S Canada
Heart of Dixie *see* Alabama
Heathrow *89 A8* (London) SE England, United Kingdom
Hebei *128 C4 var.* Hebei Sheng, Hopeh, Hopei, Ji; *prev.* Chihli. *province* E China
Hebei Sheng *see* Hebei
Hebron *119 A6 var.* Al Khalīl, El Khalil, *Heb.* Hevron; *anc.* Kiriath-Arba. S West Bank
Heemskerk *86 C3* Noord-Holland, W Netherlands
Heerde *86 D3* Gelderland, E Netherlands
Heerenveen *86 D2 Fris.* It Hearrenfean. Fryslân, N Netherlands
Heerhugowaard *86 C2* Noord-Holland, NW Netherlands
Heerlen *87 D6* Limburg, SE Netherlands
Heerwegen *see* Polkowice
Hefa *119 A5 var.* Haifa, *hist.* Caiffa, Caiphas; *anc.* Sycaminum. Haifa, N Israel
Hefa, Mifraz *see* Mifrats Hefa
Hefei *128 D5 var.* Hofei, *hist.* Luchow. *province capital* Anhui, E China
Hegang *129 E2* Heilongjiang, NE China
Hei *see* Heilongjiang
Heide *94 B2* Schleswig-Holstein, N Germany
Heidelberg *95 B5* Baden-Württemberg, SW Germany
Heidenheim *see* Heidenheim an der Brenz
Heidenheim an der Brenz *95 B6 var.* Heidenheim. Baden-Württemberg, S Germany
Hei-ho *see* Nagqu
Heilbronn *95 B6* Baden-Württemberg, SW Germany
Heiligenbeil *see* Mamonovo
Heilongjiang *128 D2 var.* Hei, Heilongjiang Sheng, Hei-lung-chiang, Heilungkiang. *province* NE China
Heilong Jiang *see* Amur
Heilongjiang Sheng *see* Heilongjiang
Heiloo *86 C3* Noord-Holland, NW Netherlands
Heilsberg *see* Lidzbark Warmiński
Hei-lung-chiang/Heilungkiang *see* Heilongjiang
Heimdal *85 B5* Sør-Trøndelag, S Norway
Heinaste *see* Ainaži
Hekimhan *116 D3* Malatya, C Turkey
Helena *44 B2 state capital* Montana, NW USA
Helensville *150 D2* Auckland, North Island, New Zealand
Helgoland Bay *see* Helgoländer Bucht
Helgoländer Bucht *94 A2 var.* Helgoland Bay, Heligoland Bight. *bay* NW Germany
Heligoland Bight *see* Helgoländer Bucht
Heliopolis *see* Baalbek
Hellas *see* Greece
Hellenic Republic *see* Greece
Hellevoetsluis *86 B4* Zuid-Holland, SW Netherlands
Hellín *93 E4* Castilla-La Mancha, C Spain
Darya-ye Helmand *122 D5 var.* Rūd-e Hīrmand. *river* Afghanistan/Iran
Helmantica *see* Salamanca
Helmond *87 D5* Noord-Brabant, S Netherlands
Helsingborg *85 B7 prev.* Hälsingborg. Skåne, S Sweden
Helsingfors *see* Helsinki
Helsinki *85 D6 Swe.* Helsingfors. *country capital* (Finland) Etelä-Suomi, S Finland
Heltau *see* Cisnădie
Helvetia *see* Switzerland
Henan *128 C5 var.* Henan Sheng, Honan, Yu. *province* C China
Henderson *40 B5* Kentucky, S USA
Henderson *47 D7* Nevada, W USA
Henderson *49 H3* Texas, SW USA
Hendū Kosh *see* Hindu Kush
Hengchow *see* Hengyang
Hengduan Shan *128 A5 mountain range* SW China
Hengelo *86 E3* Overijssel, E Netherlands
Hengnan *see* Hengyang
Hengyang *128 C6 var.* Hengnan, Heng-yang; *prev.* Hengchow. Hunan, S China
Heng-yang *see* Hengyang
Heniches'k *109 F4 Rus.* Genichesk. Khersons'ka Oblast', S Ukraine
Hennebont *90 A3* Morbihan, NW France
Henrique de Carvalho *see* Saurimo
Henzada *see* Hinthada
Herakleion *see* Irákleio
Herāt *122 D4 var.* Herat; *anc.* Aria. Herāt, W Afghanistan
Heredia *53 E4* Heredia, C Costa Rica
Hereford *49 E2* Texas, SW USA
Herford *94 B4* Nordrhein-Westfalen, NW Germany
Héristal *see* Herstal
Herk-de-Stad *87 C6* Limburg, NE Belgium
Herlen Gol/Herlen He *see* Kerulen
Hermannstadt *see* Sibiu
Hermansverk *85 A5* Sogn Og Fjordane, S Norway
Hermhausen *see* Hajnówka
Hermiston *46 C2* Oregon, NW USA
Hermon, Mount *119 B5 Ar.* Jabal ash Shaykh. *mountain* S Syria
Hermosillo *50 B2* Sonora, NW Mexico
Hermoupolis *see* Ermoúpoli
Hernösand *see* Härnösand
Herrera del Duque *92 D3* Extremadura, W Spain
Herselt *87 C5* Antwerpen, C Belgium
Herstal *87 D6 Fr.* Héristal. Liège, E Belgium
Herzogenbusch *see* 's-Hertogenbosch
Hesse *see* Hessen
Hessen *95 B5 Eng./Fr.* Hesse. *state* C Germany
Hevron *see* Hebron
Heydebrech *see* Kędzierzyn-Kozle
Heydekrug *see* Šilutė
Heywood Islands *146 C3 island group* Western Australia
Hibbing *45 F1* Minnesota, N USA
Hibernia *see* Ireland
Hidalgo del Parral *50 C2 var.* Parral. Chihuahua, N Mexico
Hida-sanmyaku *131 C5 mountain rang* Honshū, S Japan
Hierosolyma *see* Jerusalem
Hierro *70 A3 var.* Ferro. *island* Islas Canarias, Spain, NE Atlantic Ocean
High Atlas *70 C2 Eng.* High Atlas. *mountain range* C Morocco
High Atlas *see* Haut Atlas
High Plains *see* Great Plains
High Point *43 E1* North Carolina, SE USA
Hiiumaa *106 C2 Ger.* Dagden, *Swe.* Dagö. *island* W Estonia
Hikurangi *150 D2* Northland, North Island, New Zealand
Hildesheim *94 B4* Niedersachsen, N Germany
Hilla *see* Al Ḩillah
Hillaby, Mount *55 G1 mountain* N Barbados
Hill Bank *52 C1* Orange Walk, N Belize
Hillegom *86 C3* Zuid-Holland, W Netherlands
Hilo *47 B8* Hawaii, USA, C Pacific Ocear
Hilton Head Island *43 E2* South Carolina, SE USA
Hilversum *86 C3* Noord-Holland, C Netherlands
Himalaya/Himalaya Shan *see* Himalaya
Himalayas *135 E2 var.* Himalaya, *Chin.* Himalaya Shan. *mountain range* S Asi
Himeji *131 C6 var.* Himezi. Hyōgo, Honshū, SW Japan
Himezi *see* Himeji
Ḩimş *118 B4 var.* Homs; *anc.* Emesa. Ḩimş, C Syria
Hînceşti *108 D4 var.* Hânceşti; *prev.* Kotovsk. C Moldova
Hinchinbrook Island *148 D3 island* Queensland, NE Australia
Hinds *151 C6* Canterbury, South Island, New Zealand
Hindu Kush *123 F4 Per.* Hendū Kosh. *mountain range* Afghanistan/Pakistan
Hinesville *43 E3* Georgia, SE USA
Hinnøya *84 C3 Lapp.* Iinnasuolu. *islan* C Norway
Hinson Bay *42 A5 bay* W Bermuda W Atlantic Ocean
Hinthada *136 B4 var.* Henzada. Ayeyarwady, SW Myanmar (Burma)
Hios *see* Chíos
Hirfanlı Barajı *116 C3 reservoir* C Turkey
Hīrmand, Rūd-e *see* Helmand, Daryā-y
Hirosaki *130 D3* Aomori, Honshū, C Japan
Hiroshima *131 B6 var.* Hirosima. Hiroshima, Honshū, SW Japan
Hirschberg/Hirschberg im Riesengebirge/Hirschberg in Schlesien *see* Jelenia Góra
Hirson *90 D3* Aisne, N France
Hîrşova *see* Hârşova
Hispalis *see* Sevilla

spana/Hispania *see* Spain
spaniola *56 B1 island* Dominion Republic/Haiti
tachi *131 D5 var.* Hitati. Ibaraki, Honshū, S Japan
tati *see* Hitachi
tra *84 A4 prev.* Hitteren. *island* S Norway
tteren *see* Hitra
jälmaren *85 C6 Eng.* Lake Hjalmar. *lake* C Sweden
jalmar, Lake *see* Hjälmaren
jørring *85 B7* Nordjylland, N Denmark
kakabo Razi *136 B1 mountain* Myanmar (Burma)/China
lobyne *109 F2 Rus.* Globino. Poltavs'ka Oblast', NE Ukraine
ukhiv *109 F1 Rus.* Glukhov. Sums'ka Oblast', NE Ukraine
lybokaye *107 D5 Rus.* Glubokoye. Vitsyebskaya Voblasts', N Belarus
oa Binh *136 D3* Hoa Binh, N Vietnam
oang Lien Son *136 D3 mountain range* N Vietnam
obart *149 C8 prev.* Hobarton, Hobart Town. *state capital* Tasmania, SE Australia
obarton/Hobart Town *see* Hobart
obbs *49 E3* New Mexico, SW USA
obro *85 A7* Nordjylland, N Denmark
ô Chi Minh *137 E6 var.* Ho Chi Minh City; *prev.* Saigon. S Vietnam
o Chi Minh City *see* Hô Chi Minh
odeida *see* Al Ḩudaydah
ódmezővásárhely *99 D7* Csongrád, SE Hungary
odna, Chott El *102 C4 var.* Chott el-Hodna, *Ar.* Shatt al-Hodna. *salt lake* N Algeria
odna, Chott el-/Hodna, Shatt al- *see* Hodna, Chott El
odonín *99 C5 Ger.* Göding. Jihomoravský Kraj, SE Czech Republic
oei *see* Huy
oey *see* Huy
of *95 C5* Bayern, SE Germany
ofei *see* Hefei
ōfu *131 B7* Yamaguchi, Honshū, SW Japan
ofuf *see* Al Hufūf
ogoley Islands *see* Chuuk Islands
ohensalza *see* Inowrocław
ohenstadt *see* Zábřeh
ohes Venn *see* Hautes Fagnes
ohe Tauern *95 C7 mountain range* W Austria
ohhot *127 F3 var.* Huhehot, Huhohaote, *Mong.* Kukukhoto; *prev.* Kweisui, Kwesui. Nei Mongol Zizhiqu, N China
ôi An *137 E5 prev.* Faifo. Quang Nam-Đa Năng, C Vietnam
oï-Hao/Hoihow *see* Haikou
okianga Harbour *150 C2 inlet* SE Tasman Sea
okitika *151 B5* West Coast, South Island, New Zealand
okkaido *130 C2 prev.* Ezo, Yeso, Yezo. *island* NE Japan
ola Prystan' *109 E4 Rus.* Golaya Pristan. Khersons'ka Oblast', S Ukraine
olbrook *48 B2* Arizona, SW USA
oletown *55 G1 prev.* Jamestown. W Barbados
olguín *54 C2* Holguín, SE Cuba
olin Gol *127 G2 prev.* Hulingol. Nei Mongol Zizhiqu, N China
ollabrunn *95 E6* Niederösterreich, NE Austria
olland *see* Netherlands
ollandia *see* Jayapura
olly Springs *42 C1* Mississippi, S USA
olman *37 E3* Victoria Island, Northwest Territories, N Canada
olmsund *84 D4* Västerbotten, N Sweden
olon *119 A6 var.* Kholon; *prev.* Holon. Tel Aviv, C Israel
olon *see* Holon
olovanivs'k *109 E3 Rus.* Golovanevsk. Kirovohrads'ka Oblast', C Ukraine
olstebro *85 A7* Midtjylland, W Denmark
olsteinborg/Holsteinsborg/ Holstenborg/Holstensborg *see* Sisimiut
olyhead *89 C5 Wel.* Caer Gybi. NW Wales, United Kingdom
ombori *75 E3* Mopti, S Mali
Homs *see* Al Khums, Libya
Homs *see* Ḩimş
Homyel' *107 D7 Rus.* Gomel'. Homyel'skaya Voblasts', SE Belarus
Honan *see* Henan, China
Honan *see* Luoyang, China
Hondo *49 F4* Texas, SW USA
Hondo *see* Honshū
Honduras *52 C2 off.* Republic of Honduras. *country* Central America

HONDURAS
Central America

Official name Republic of Honduras
Formation 1838 / 1838
Capital Tegucigalpa
Population 8.1 million / 187 people per sq mile (72 people per sq km)
Total area 43,278 sq. miles (112,090 sq. km)
Languages Spanish*, Garífuna (Carib), English Creole
Religions Roman Catholic 97%, Protestant 3%
Ethnic mix Mestizo 90%, Black 5%, Amerindian 4%, White 1%
Government Presidential system
Currency Lempira = 100 centavos
Literacy rate 85%
Calorie consumption 2651 kilocalories

Honduras, Golfo de *see* Honduras, Gulf of
Honduras, Gulf of *52 C2 Sp.* Golfo de Honduras. *gulf* W Caribbean Sea
Honduras, Republic of *see* Honduras
Hønefoss *85 B6* Buskerud, S Norway
Honey Lake *47 B5 lake* California, W USA
Hon Gai *see* Ha Long
Hongay *see* Ha Long
Hông Gai *see* Ha Long
Hông Hà, Sông *see* Red River
Hong Kong *128 A1* Hong Kong, S China
Hong Kong Island *128 B2 island* S China Asia
Honiara *144 C3 country capital* (Solomon Islands) Guadalcanal, C Solomon Islands
Honjō *130 D4 var.* Honzyô, Yurihonjō. Akita, Honshū, C Japan
Honolulu *47 A8 state capital* O'ahu, Hawaii, USA, C Pacific Ocean
Honshu *131 E5 var.* Hondo, Honsyû. *island* SW Japan
Honsyû *see* Honshū
Honte *see* Westerschelde
Honzyô *see* Honjō
Hoogeveen *86 E2* Drenthe, NE Netherlands
Hoogezand-Sappemeer *86 E2* Groningen, NE Netherlands
Hoorn *86 C2* Noord-Holland, NW Netherlands
Hoosier State *see* Indiana
Hopa *117 E2* Artvin, NE Turkey
Hope *36 C3* British Columbia, SW Canada
Hopedale *39 F2* Newfoundland and Labrador, NE Canada
Hopeh/Hopei *see* Hebei
Hopkinsville *40 B5* Kentucky, S USA
Horasan *117 F3* Erzurum, NE Turkey
Horizon Deep *152 D4 trench* W Pacific Ocean
Horki *107 E6 Rus.* Gorki. Mahilyowskaya Voblasts', E Belarus
Horlivka *109 G3 Rom.* Adâncata, *Rus.* Gorlovka. Donets'ka Oblast', E Ukraine
Hormoz, Tangeh-ye *see* Hormuz, Strait of
Hormuz, Strait of *120 D4 var.* Strait of Ormuz, *Per.* Tangeh-ye Hormoz. *strait* Iran/Oman
Cape Horn *65 C8 Eng.* Cape Horn. *headland* S Chile
Horn, Cape *see* Hornos, Cabo de
Hornsby *148 E1* New South Wales, SE Australia
Horodnya *109 E1 Rus.* Gorodnya. Chernihivs'ka Oblast', NE Ukraine
Horodok *108 B2 Pol.* Gródek Jagielloński, *Rus.* Gorodok, Gorodok Yagellonski. L'vivs'ka Oblast', NW Ukraine
Horodyshche *109 E2 Rus.* Gorodishche. Cherkas'ka Oblast', C Ukraine
Horoshiri-dake *130 D2 var.* Horosiri Dake. *mountain* Hokkaidō, N Japan
Horosiri Dake *see* Horoshiri-dake
Horsburgh Atoll *132 A4 var.* Goidhoo Atoll. *atoll* N Maldives
Horseshoe Bay *42 A5 bay* W Bermuda W Atlantic Ocean
Horseshoe Seamounts *80 A4 seamount range* E Atlantic Ocean
Horsham *149 B7* Victoria, SE Australia
Horst *87 D5* Limburg, SE Netherlands
Horten *85 B6* Vestfold, S Norway
Horyn' *107 B7 Rus.* Goryn. *river* NW Ukraine
Hosingen *87 D7* Diekirch, NE Luxembourg
Hospitalet *see* L'Hospitalet de Llobregat
Hotan *126 B4 var.* Khotan, *Chin.* Ho-t'ien. Xinjiang Uygur Zizhiqu, NW China
Ho-t'ien *see* Hotan
Hoting *84 C4* Jämtland, C Sweden
Hot Springs *42 B1* Arkansas, C USA
Hötzing *see* Haţeg
Houayxay *136 C3 var.* Ban Houayxay. Bokèo, N Laos
Houghton *40 B1* Michigan, N USA
Houilles *91 B5* Yvelines, Île-de-France, N France Europe
Houlton *41 H1* Maine, NE USA
Houma *42 B3* Louisiana, S USA
Houston *49 H4* Texas, SW USA
Hovd *126 C2 var.* Khovd, Kobdo; *prev.* Jirgalanta. Hovd, W Mongolia
Hove *89 E7* SE England, United Kingdom
Hoverla, Hora *108 C3 Rus.* Gora Goverla. *mountain* W Ukraine
Hovsgol, Lake *see* Hövsgöl Nuur
Hövsgöl Nuur *126 D1 var.* Lake Hovsgol. *lake* N Mongolia
Howa, Ouadi *see* Howar, Wādi
Howar, Wadi *72 A3 var.* Ouadi Howa. *river* Chad/Sudan
Howrah *see* Hāora
Hoy *88 C2 island* N Scotland, United Kingdom
Hoyerswerda *94 D4 Lus.* Wojerecy. Sachsen, E Germany
Hpa-an *136 B4 var.* Pa-an. Kayin State, S Myanmar (Burma)
Hpyu *see* Phyu
Hradec Králové *99 B5 Ger.* Königgrätz. Královéhradecký Kraj, N Czech Republic
Hrandzichy *107 B5 Rus.* Grandichi. Hrodzyenskaya Voblasts', W Belarus
Hranice *99 C5 Ger.* Mährisch-Weisskirchen. Olomoucký Kraj, E Czech Republic
Hrebinka *109 E2 Rus.* Grebenka. Poltavs'ka Oblast', NE Ukraine
Hrodna *107 B5 Pol.* Grodno. Hrodzyenskaya Voblasts', W Belarus
Hrvatska *see* Croatia
Hsia-men *see* Xiamen
Hsiang-t'an *see* Xiangtan
Hsi Chiang *see* Xi Jiang
Hsing-K'ai Hu *see* Khanka, Lake
Hsi-ning/Hsining *see* Xining
Hsinking *see* Changchun
Hsin-yang *see* Xinyang
Hsu-chou *see* Xuzhou
Htawei *see* Dawei
Huacho *60 C4* Lima, W Peru
Hua Hin *see* Ban Hua Hin
Huaihua *128 C5* Hunan, S China
Huailai *128 C3 var.* Shacheng. Hebei, E China
Huainan *128 D5 var.* Huai-nan, Hwainan. Anhui, E China
Huai-nan *see* Huainan
Huajuapan *51 F5 var.* Huajuapan de León. Oaxaca, SE Mexico
Huajuapan de León *see* Huajuapan
Hualapai Peak *48 A2 mountain* Arizona, SW USA
Huallaga, Río *60 C3 river* N Peru
Huambo *78 B2 Port.* Nova Lisboa. Huambo, C Angola
Huancavelica *60 D4* Huancavelica, SW Peru
Huancayo *60 D3* Junín, C Peru
Huang Hai *see* Yellow Sea
Huangshi *128 C5 var.* Huang-shih, Hwangshih. Hubei, C China
Huang-shih *see* Huangshi
Huanta *60 D4* Ayacucho, C Peru
Huánuco *60 C3* Huánuco, C Peru
Huanuni *61 F4* Oruro, W Bolivia
Huaral *60 C4* Lima, W Peru
Huarás *see* Huaraz
Huaraz *60 C3 var.* Huarás. Ancash, W Peru
Huarmey *60 C3* Ancash, W Peru
Huatabampo *50 C2* Sonora, NW Mexico
Hubli *124 B3* Karnātaka, SW India
Huddersfield *89 D5* N England, United Kingdom
Hudiksvall *85 C5* Gävleborg, C Sweden
Hudson Bay *37 G4 bay* NE Canada
Hudson, Détroit d' *see* Hudson Strait
Hudson Strait *37 H3 Fr.* Détroit d'Hudson. *strait* Northwest Territories/ Québec, NE Canada
Hudur *see* Xuddur
Huê *136 E4* Th,a Thiên-Huê, C Vietnam
Huehuetenango *52 A2* Huehuetenango, W Guatemala
Huelva *92 C4 anc.* Onuba. Andalucía, SW Spain
Huesca *93 F2 anc.* Osca. Aragón, NE Spain
Huéscar *93 E4* Andalucía, S Spain
Hughenden *148 C3* Queensland, NE Australia
Hugo *49 G2* Oklahoma, C USA
Huhehot/Huhohaote *see* Hohhot
Huíla Plateau *78 B2 plateau* S Angola
Huixtla *51 G5* Chiapas, SE Mexico
Hulingol *see* Holin Gol
Hull *38 D4* Québec, SE Canada
Hull *see* Kingston upon Hull
Hull Island *see* Orona
Hulst *87 B5* Zeeland, SW Netherlands
Hulun *see* Hulun Buir
Hulun Buir *127 F1 var.* Hailar; *prev.* Hulun. Nei Mongol Zizhiqu, N China
Hu-lun Ch'ih *see* Hulun Nur
Hulun Nur *127 F1 var.* Hu-lun Ch'ih; *prev.* Dalai Nor. *lake* NE China
Humaitá *62 D2* Amazonas, N Brazil
Humboldt River *47 C5 river* Nevada, W USA
Humphreys Peak *48 B1 mountain* Arizona, SW USA
Humpolec *99 B5 Ger.* Gumpolds, Humpoletz. Vysočina, C Czech Republic
Humpoletz *see* Humpolec
Hunan *128 C6 var.* Hunan Sheng, Xiang. *province* S China
Hunan Sheng *see* Hunan
Hunedoara *108 B4 Ger.* Eisenmarkt, *Hung.* Vajdahunyad. Hunedoara, SW Romania
Hünfeld *95 B5* Hessen, C Germany
Hungarian People's Republic *see* Hungary
Hungary *99 C6 off.* Republic of Hungary, *Ger.* Ungarn, *Hung.* Magyarország, *Rom.* Ungaria, *SCr.* Madarska, *Ukr.* Uhorshchyna; *prev.* Hungarian People's Republic. *country* C Europe

HUNGARY
Central Europe

Official name Republic of Hungary
Formation 1918 / 1947
Capital Budapest
Population 10 million / 280 people per sq mile (108 people per sq km)
Total area 35,919 sq. miles (93,030 sq. km)
Languages Hungarian* (Magyar)
Religions Roman Catholic 52%, Calvinist 16%, Other 15%, Nonreligious 14%, Lutheran 3%
Ethnic mix Magyar 90%, Roma 4%, German 3%, Serb 2%, Other 1%
Government Parliamentary system
Currency Forint = 100 fillér
Literacy rate 99%
Calorie consumption 2968 kilocalories

Hungary, Plain of *see* Great Hungarian Plain
Hungary, Republic of *see* Hungary
Hunjiang *see* Baishan
Hunter Island *149 B8 island* Tasmania, SE Australia
Huntington *40 D4* West Virginia, NE USA
Huntington Beach *47 B8* California, W USA
Huntly *150 D3* Waikato, North Island, New Zealand
Huntsville *42 D1* Alabama, S USA

Huntsville 49 G3 Texas, SW USA
Hurghada *see* Al Ghurdaqah
Huron 45 E3 South Dakota, N USA
Huron, Lake 40 D2 *lake* Canada/USA
Hurukawa *see* Furukawa
Hurunui 151 C5 *river* South Island, New Zealand
Húsavík 83 E4 Nordhurland Eystra, NE Iceland
Husté *see* Khust
Husum 94 B2 Schleswig-Holstein, N Germany
Huszt *see* Khust
Hutchinson 45 E5 Kansas, C USA
Hutchinson Island 43 F4 *island* Florida, SE USA
Huy 87 C6 *Dut.* Hoei, Hoey. Liège, E Belgium
Huzi *see* Fuji
Hvannadalshnúkur 83 E5 *volcano* S Iceland
Hvar 100 B4 *It.* Lesina; *anc.* Pharus. *island* S Croatia
Hwainan *see* Huainan
Hwange 78 D3 *prev.* Wankie. Matabeleland North, W Zimbabwe
Hwang-Hae *see* Yellow Sea
Hwangshih *see* Huangshi
Hyargas Nuur 126 C2 *lake* NW Mongolia
Hyderābād 134 D5 *var.* Haidarabad. *state capital* Telangana, C India
Hyderābād 134 B3 *var.* Haidarabad. Sind, SE Pakistan
Hyères 91 D6 Var, SE France
Hyères, Îles d' 91 D6 *island group* S France
Hypanis *see* Kuban'
Hyrcania *see* Gorgān
Hyvinge *see* Hyvinkää
Hyvinkää 85 D5 *Swe.* Hyvinge. Etelä-Suomi, S Finland

I

Iader *see* Zadar
Ialomiţa 108 C5 *river* SE Romania
Iaşi 108 D3 *Ger.* Jassy. Iaşi, NE Romania
Ibadan 75 F5 Oyo, SW Nigeria
Ibagué 58 B3 Tolima, C Colombia
Ibar *see* Ibër
Ibarra 60 B1 *var.* San Miguel de Ibarra. Imbabura, N Ecuador
Ibër 100 D4 *Serb.* Ibar. *river* C Serbia
Iberia *see* Spain
Iberian Mountains *see* Ibérico, Sistema
Iberian Peninsula 80 B4 *physical region* Portugal/Spain
Iberian Plain 80 B4 *abyssal plain* E Atlantic Ocean
Ibérica, Cordillera *see* Ibérico, Sistema
Ibérico, Sistema 93 E2 *var.* Cordillera Ibérica, *Eng.* Iberian Mountains. *mountain range* NE Spain
Ibiza *see* Eivissa
Ibo *see* Sassandra
Ica 60 D4 Ica, SW Peru
Icaria *see* Ikaría
Içá, Rio 62 C2 *var.* Río Putumayo. *river* NW South America
Içá, Rio *see* Putumayo, Río
İçel *see* Mersin
Iceland 83 E4 *off.* Republic of Iceland, *Dan.* Island, *Icel.* Ísland. *country* N Atlantic Ocean

ICELAND
Northwest Europe

Official name Republic of Iceland
Formation 1944 / 1944
Capital Reykjavík
Population 300,000 / 8 people per sq mile (3 people per sq km)
Total area 39,768 sq. miles (103,000 sq. km)
Languages Icelandic*
Religions Evangelical Lutheran 84%, Other (mostly Christian) 10%, Roman Catholic 3%, Nonreligious 3%
Ethnic mix Icelandic 94%, Other 5%, Danish 1%
Government Parliamentary system
Currency Icelandic króna = 100 aurar
Literacy rate 99%
Calorie consumption 3339 kilocalories

Iceland Basin 80 B1 *undersea basin* N Atlantic Ocean
Icelandic Plateau *see* Iceland Plateau
Iceland Plateau 155 B6 *var.* Icelandic Plateau. *undersea plateau* S Greenland Sea
Iceland, Republic of *see* Iceland
Iconium *see* Konya
Iculisma *see* Angoulême
Idabel 49 H2 Oklahoma, C USA
Idaho 46 D3 *off.* State of Idaho, *also known as* Gem of the Mountains, Gem State. *state* NW USA
Idaho Falls 46 E3 Idaho, NW USA
Idensalmi *see* Iisalmi
Idfū 72 B2 *var.* Edfu. SE Egypt
Idi Amin, Lac *see* Edward, Lake
Idîni 74 B2 Trarza, W Mauritania
Idlib 118 B3 Idlib, NW Syria
Idre 85 B5 Dalarna, C Sweden
Iecava 106 C3 S Latvia
Ieper 87 A6 *Fr.* Ypres. West-Vlaanderen, W Belgium
Ierápetra 105 D8 Kríti, Greece, E Mediterranean Sea
Ierisós *see* Ierissós
Ierissós 104 C4 *var.* Ierisós. Kentrikí Makedonía, N Greece
Iferouâne 75 G2 Agadez, N Niger
Ifôghas, Adrar des 75 E2 *var.* Adrar des Iforas. *mountain range* NE Mali
Iforas, Adrar des *see* Ifôghas, Adrar des
Igarka 114 D3 Krasnoyarskiy Kray, N Russian Federation
Igaunija *see* Estonia
Iglau/Iglawa/Igława *see* Jihlava
Iglesias 97 A5 Sardegna, Italy, C Mediterranean Sea
Igloolik 37 G2 Nunavut, N Canada
Igoumenítsa 104 A4 Ípeiros, W Greece
Iguaçu, Rio 63 E4 *Sp.* Río Iguazú. *river* Argentina/Brazil
Iguaçu, Saltos do 63 E4 *Sp.* Cataratas del Iguazú; *prev.* Victoria Falls. *waterfall* Argentina/Brazil
Iguala 51 E4 *var.* Iguala de la Independencia. Guerrero, S Mexico
Iguala de la Independencia *see* Iguala
Iguazú, Cataratas del *see* Iguaçu, Saltos do
Iguazú, Río *see* Iguaçu, Rio
Iguid, Erg *see* Iguîdi, 'Erg
Iguîdi, 'Erg 70 C3 *var.* Erg Iguid. *desert* Algeria/Mauritania
Ihavandhippolhu Atoll 132 A3 *var.* Ihavandiffulu Atoll. *atoll* N Maldives
Ihavandiffulu Atoll *see* Ihavandhippolhu Atoll
Ihosy 79 F4 Fianarantsoa, S Madagascar
Iinnasuolu *see* Hinnøya
Iisalmi 84 E4 *var.* Idensalmi. Itä-Suomi, C Finland
IJmuiden 86 C3 Noord-Holland, W Netherlands
IJssel 86 D3 *var.* Yssel. *river* Netherlands
IJsselmeer 86 C2 *prev.* Zuider Zee. *lake* N Netherlands
IJsselmuiden 86 D3 Overijssel, E Netherlands
Ijzer 87 A6 *river* W Belgium
Ikaahuk *see* Sachs Harbour
Ikaluktutiak *see* Cambridge Bay
Ikaría 105 D6 *var.* Kariot, Nicaria, Nikaria; *anc.* Icaria. *island* Dodekánisa, Greece, Aegean Sea
Ikela 77 D6 Equateur, C Dem. Rep. Congo
Iki 131 A7 *island* SW Japan
Ilagan 139 E1 Luzon, N Philippines
Ilave 61 E4 Puno, S Peru
Iława 98 D3 *Ger.* Deutsch-Eylau. Warmińsko-Mazurskie, NE Poland
Ilebo 77 C6 *prev.* Port-Francqui. Kasai-Occidental, W Dem. Rep. Congo
Île-de-France 90 C3 *cultural region* N France
Ilerda *see* Lleida
Ilfracombe 89 C7 SW England, United Kingdom
Ílhavo 92 B2 Aveiro, N Portugal
Iliamna Lake 36 C3 *lake* Alaska, USA
Il'ichevsk *see* Illichivs'k, Ukraine
Ilici *see* Elche
Iligan 139 E2 *off.* Iligan City. Mindanao, S Philippines
Iligan City *see* Iligan
Illapel 64 B4 Coquimbo, C Chile
Illichivs'k 109 E4 *Rus.* Il'ichevsk. Odes'ka Oblast', SW Ukraine
Illicis *see* Elche
Illinois 40 A4 *off.* State of Illinois, *also known as* Prairie State, Sucker State. *state* C USA
Illinois River 40 B4 *river* Illinois, N USA
Illurco *see* Lorca
Illuro *see* Mataró
Ilo 61 E4 Moquegua, SW Peru
Iloilo 139 E2 *off.* Iloilo City. Panay Island, C Philippines
Iloilo City *see* Iloilo
Ilorin 75 F4 Kwara, W Nigeria
Ilovlya 111 B6 Volgogradskaya Oblast', SW Russian Federation
Iluh *see* Batman
Il'yaly *see* Gurbansoltan Eje
Imatra 85 E5 Etelä-Suomi, SE Finland
Imbros *see* Gökçeada
Imishli *see* İmişli
İmişli 117 H3 *Rus.* Imishli. C Azerbaijan
Imola 96 C3 Emilia-Romagna, N Italy
Imperatriz 63 F2 Maranhão, NE Brazil
Imperia 96 A3 Liguria, NW Italy
Impfondo 77 C5 Likouala, NE Congo
Imphāl 135 H3 *state capital* Manipur, NE India
Imroz Adası *see* Gökçeada
Inagua Islands *see* Little Inagua
Inagua Islands *see* Great Inagua
Inarijärvi 84 D2 *Lapp.* Aanaarjävri, *Swe.* Enareträsk. *lake* N Finland
Inău *see* Ineu
Inawashiro-ko 131 D5 *var.* Inawasiro Ko. *lake* Honshū, C Japan
Inawasiro Ko *see* Inawashiro-ko
İncesu 116 D3 Kayseri, Turkey Asia
Incheon 129 E4 *off.* Incheon Gwang-yeoksi, *prev.* Inch'ŏn, *Jap.* Jinsen; *prev.* Chemulpo. NW South Korea
Incheon-Gwang-yeoksi *see* Incheon
Inch'ŏn *see* Incheon
Incudine, Monte 91 E7 *mountain* Corse, France, C Mediterranean Sea
Indefatigable Island *see* Santa Cruz, Isla
Independence 45 F4 Missouri, C USA
Independence Fjord 83 E1 *fjord* N Greenland
Independence Island *see* Malden Island
Independence Mountains 46 C4 *mountain range* Nevada, W USA
India 124 B3 *off.* Republic of India, *var.* Indian Union, Union of India, *Hind.* Bhārat. *country* S Asia

INDIA
South Asia

Official name Republic of India
Formation 1947 / 1947
Capital New Delh
Population 1.25 billion / 1091 people per sq mile (421 people per sq km)
Total area 1,269,338 sq. miles (3,287,590 sq. km)
Languages Hindi*, English*, Urdu, Bengali, Marathi, Telugu, Tamil, Bihari, Gujarati, Kanarese
Religions Hindu 81%, Muslim 13%, Christian 2%, Sikh 2%, Buddhist 1%, Other 1%
Ethnic mix Indo-Aryan 72%, Dravidian 25%, Mongoloid and other 3%
Government Parliamentary system
Currency Indian rupee = 100 paise
Literacy rate 63%
Calorie consumption 2459 kilocalories

India *see* Inđija
Indiana 40 B4 *off.* State of Indiana, *also known as* Hoosier State. *state* N USA
Indianapolis 40 C4 *state capital* Indiana, N USA
Indian Church 52 C1 Orange Walk, N Belize
Indian Desert *see* Thar Desert
Indianola 45 F4 Iowa, C USA
Indian Union *see* India
India, Republic of *see* India
India, Union of *see* India
Indigirka 115 F2 *river* NE Russian Federation
Inđija 100 D3 *Hung.* India; *prev.* Indjija. Vojvodina, N Serbia
Indira Point 132 G3 *headland* Andaman and Nicobar Island, India, NE Indian Ocean
Indjija *see* Inđija
Indomed Fracture Zone 141 B6 *tectonic feature* SW Indian Ocean
Indonesia 138 B4 *off.* Republic of Indonesia, *Ind.* Republik Indonesia; *prev.* Dutch East Indies, Netherlands East Indies, United States of Indonesi *country* SE Asia

INDONESIA
Southeast Asia

Official name Republic of Indonesia
Formation 1949 / 1999
Capital Jakarta
Population 250 million / 360 people per sq mile (139 people per sq km)
Total area 741,096 sq. miles (1,919,440 sq. km)
Languages Javanese, Sundanese, Madurese, Bahasa Indonesian*, Dutch
Religions Sunni Muslim 86%, Christian 9%, Hindu 2%, Other 2%, Buddhist 1%
Ethnic mix Javanese 41%, Other 28%, Sundanese 15%, Coastal Malays 12%, Madurese 3%
Government Presidential system
Currency Rupiah = 100 sen
Literacy rate 93%
Calorie consumption 2713 kilocalories

Indonesian Borneo *see* Kalimantan
Indonesia, Republic of *see* Indonesia
Indonesia, Republik *see* Indonesia
Indonesia, United States of *see* Indonesia
Indore 134 D4 Madhya Pradesh, C India
Indreville *see* Châteauroux
Indus 134 C2 *Chin.* Yindu He; *prev.* Yin-tu Ho. *river* S Asia
Indus Cone *see* Indus Fan
Indus Fan 112 C5 *var.* Indus Cone. *undersea fan* N Arabian Sea
Indus, Mouths of the 134 B4 *delta* S Pakistan
İnebolu 116 C2 Kastamonu, N Turkey
Ineu 108 A4 *Hung.* Borosjenő; *prev.* Ină Arad, W Romania
Infiernillo, Presa del 51 E4 *reservoir* S Mexico
Inglewood 46 D2 California, W USA
Ingolstadt 95 C6 Bayern, S Germany
Ingulets *see* Inhulets'
Inguri *see* Enguri
Inhambane 79 E4 Inhambane, SE Mozambique
Inhulets' 109 F3 *Rus.* Ingulets. Dnipropetrovs'ka Oblast', E Ukraine
I-ning *see* Yining
Inis *see* Ennis
Inis Ceithleann *see* Enniskillen
Inn 95 C6 *river* C Europe
Innaanganeq 82 C1 *var.* Kap York. *headland* NW Greenland
Inner Hebrides 88 B4 *island group* W Scotland, United Kingdom
Inner Islands 79 H1 *var.* Central Group *island group* NE Seychelles
Innisfail 148 D3 Queensland, NE Australia
Inniskilling *see* Enniskillen
Innsbruch *see* Innsbruck
Innsbruck 95 C7 *var.* Innsbruch. Tirol, W Austria
Inoucdjouac *see* Inukjuak
Inowrazlaw *see* Inowrocław
Inowrocław 98 C3 *Ger.* Hohensalza; *prev.* Inowrazlaw. Kujawski-pomorskie, C Poland
I-n-Sakane, 'Erg 75 E2 *desert* N Mali
I-n-Salah 70 D3 *var.* In Salah. C Algeria
Insterburg *see* Chernyakhovsk
Insula *see* Lille
Inta 110 E3 Respublika Komi, NW Russian Federation
Interamna *see* Teramo
Interamna Nahars *see* Terni
International Falls 45 F1 Minnesota, N USA
Inukjuak 38 D2 *var.* Inoucdjouac; *prev.* Port Harrison. Québec, NE Canada
Inuuvik *see* Inuvik
Inuvik 36 D3 *var.* Inuuvik. Northwest Territories, NW Canada
Invercargill 151 A7 Southland, South Island, New Zealand
Inverness 88 C3 N Scotland, United Kingdom

IRAN
Southwest Asia

Official name Islamic Republic of Iran
Formation 1502 / 1990
Capital Tehran
Population 77.4 million / 123 people per sq mile (47 people per sq km)
Total area 636,293 sq. miles (1,648,000 sq. km)
Languages Farsi*, Azeri, Luri, Gilaki, Mazanderani, Kurdish, Turkmen, Arabic, Baluchi
Religions Shi'a Muslim 89%, Sunni Muslim 9%, Other 2%
Ethnic mix Persian 51%, Azari 24%, Other 10%, Lur and Bakhtiari 8%, Kurdish 7%
Government Islamic theocracy
Currency Iranian rial = 100 dinars
Literacy rate 84%
Calorie consumption 3058 kilocalories

IRAQ
Southwest Asia

Official name Republic of Iraq
Formation 1932 / 1990
Capital Baghdad
Population 33.8 million / 200 people per sq mile (77 people per sq km)
Total area 168,753 sq. miles (437,072 sq. km)
Languages Arabic*, Kurdish*, Turkic languages, Armenian, Assyrian
Religions Shi'a Muslim 60%, Sunni Muslim 35%, Other (including Christian) 5%

IRAQ
(continued)

Ethnic mix Arab 80%, Kurdish 15%, Turkmen 3%, Other 2%
Government Parliamentary system
Currency New Iraqi dinar = 1000 fils
Literacy rate 79%
Calorie consumption 2489 kilocalories

IRELAND
Northwest Europe

Official name Ireland
Formation 1922 / 1922
Capital Dublin
Population 4.5 million / 169 people per sq mile (65 people per sq km)
Total area 27,135 sq. miles (70,280 sq. km)
Languages English*, Irish*
Religions Roman Catholic 87%, Other and nonreligious 10%, Anglican 3%
Ethnic mix Irish 99%, Other 1%
Government Parliamentary system
Currency Euro = 100 cents
Literacy rate 99%
Calorie consumption 3591 kilocalories

ISRAEL
Southwest Asia

Official name State of Israel
Formation 1948 / 1994
Capital Jerusalem (not internationally recognized)
Population 7.7 million / 981 people per sq mile (379 people per sq km)
Total area 8019 sq. miles (20,770 sq. km)
Languages Hebrew*, Arabic*, Yiddish, German, Russian, Polish, Romanian, Persian
Religions Jewish 76%, Muslim (mainly Sunni) 16%, Other 4%, Druze 2%, Christian 2%
Ethnic mix Jewish 76%, Arab 20%, Other 4%
Government Parliamentary system
Currency Shekel = 100 agorot
Literacy rate 98%
Calorie consumption 3619 kilocalories

ITALY
Southern Europe

Official name Italian Republic
Formation 1861 / 1947
Capital Rome
Population 61 million / 537 people per sq mile (207 people per sq km)
Total area 116,305 sq. miles (301,230 sq. km)
Languages Italian*, German, French, Rhaeto-Romanic, Sardinian

ITALY
(continued)

Religions Roman Catholic 85%, Other and nonreligious 13%, Muslim 2%
Ethnic mix Italian 94%, Other 4%, Sardinian 2%
Government Parliamentary system
Currency Euro = 100 cents
Literacy rate 99%
Calorie consumption 3539 kilocalories

J

Jabbūl, Sabkhat al *118 B2 sabkha* NW Syria
Jablah *118 A3 var.* Jeble, *Fr.* Djéblé. Al Lādhiqīyah, W Syria
Jaca *93 F1* Aragón, NE Spain
Jacaltenango *52 A2* Huehuetenango, W Guatemala
Jackson *42 B2 state capital* Mississippi, S USA
Jackson *45 H5* Missouri, C USA
Jackson *42 C1* Tennessee, S USA
Jackson Head *151 A6 headland* South Island, New Zealand
Jacksonville *43 E3* Florida, SE USA
Jacksonville *40 B4* Illinois, N USA
Jacksonville *43 F1* North Carolina, SE USA
Jacksonville *49 G3* Texas, SW USA
Jacmel *54 D3 var.* Jaquemel. S Haiti
Jacob *see* Nkayi
Jacobābād *134 B3* Sind, SE Pakistan
Jadotville *see* Likasi
Jadransko More/Jadransko Morje *see* Adriatic Sea
Jaén *60 B2* Cajamarca, N Peru
Jaén *92 D4* Andalucía, SW Spain
Jaffna *132 D3* Northern Province, N Sri Lanka
Jagannath *see* Puri
Jagdalpur *135 E5* Chhattīsgarh, C India
Jagdaqi *127 G1* Nei Mongol Zizhiqu, N China
Jagodina *100 D4 prev.* Svetozarevo. Serbia, C Serbia
Jahra *see* Al Jahrā'
Jailolo *see* Halmahera, Pulau
Jaipur *134 D3 prev.* Jeypore. *state capital* Rājasthān, N India
Jaisalmer *134 C3* Rājasthān, NW India
Jajce *100 B3* Federacija Bosne I Hercegovine, W Bosnia and Herzegovina
Jakarta *138 C5 prev.* Djakarta, *Dut.* Batavia. *country capital* (Indonesia) Jawa, C Indonesia
Jakobstad *84 D4 Fin.* Pietarsaari. Länsi-Suomi, W Finland
Jakobstadt *see* Jēkabpils
Jalālābād *123 F4 var.* Jalalabad, Jelalabad. Nangarhār, E Afghanistan
Jalal-Abad *see* Dzhalal-Abad, Dzhalal-Abadskaya Oblast', Kyrgyzstan
Jalandhar *134 D2 prev.* Jullundur. Punjab, N India
Jalapa *52 D3* Nueva Segovia, NW Nicaragua
Jalpa *50 D4* Zacatecas, C Mexico
Jālū *71 G3 var.* Jūlā. NE Libya
Jaluit Atoll *144 D2 var.* Jālwōj. *atoll* Ralik Chain, S Marshall Islands
Jālwōj *see* Jaluit Atoll
Jamaame *73 D6 It.* Giamame; *prev.* Margherita. Jubbada Hoose, S Somalia
Jamaica *54 A4 country* W West Indies

JAMAICA
West Indies

Official name Jamaica
Formation 1962 / 1962
Capital Kingston
Population 2.8 million / 670 people per sq mile (259 people per sq km)
Total area 4243 sq. miles (10,990 sq. km)
Languages English Creole, English*
Religions Other and nonreligious 45%, Other Protestant 20%, Church of God 18%, Baptist 10%, Anglican 7%
Ethnic mix Black African 91%, Mulatto (mixed race) 7%, East Indian 1%, European and Chinese 1%
Government Parliamentary system
Currency Jamaican dollar = 100 cents
Literacy rate 88%
Calorie consumption 2789 kilocalories

Jamaica *56 A1 island* W West Indies
Jamaica Channel *54 D3 channel* Haiti/Jamaica
Jamālpur *135 F3* Bihār, NE India
Jambi *138 B4 var.* Telanaipura; *prev.* Djambi. Sumatera, W Indonesia
Jamdena *see* Yamdena, Pulau
James Bay *38 C3 bay* Ontario/Québec, E Canada
James River *45 E2 river* North Dakota/South Dakota, N USA
James River *41 E5 river* Virginia, NE USA
Jamestown *41 E3* New York, NE USA
Jamestown *45 E2* North Dakota, N USA
Jamestown *see* Holetown
Jammu *134 D2 prev.* Jummoo. *state capital* Jammu and Kashmir, NW India
Jammu and Kashmīr *134 D1 disputed region* India/Pakistan
Jāmnagar *134 C4 prev.* Navanagar. Gujarāt, W India
Jamshedpur *135 F4* Jhārkhand, NE India
Jamuna *see* Brahmaputra
Janaúba *63 F3* Minas Gerais, SE Brazil
Janesville *40 B3* Wisconsin, N USA
Janina *see* Ioánnina
Janischken *see* Joniškis
Jankovac *see* Jánoshalma
Jan Mayen *83 F4 Norwegian dependency* N Atlantic Ocean
Jánoshalma *99 C7 SCr.* Jankovac. Bács-Kiskun, S Hungary
Janów *see* Ivanava, Belarus
Janow/Janów *see* Jonava, Lithuania
Janów Poleski *see* Ivanava
Japan *130 C4 var.* Nippon, *Jap.* Nihon. *country* E Asia

JAPAN
East Asia

Official name Japan
Formation 1590 / 1972
Capital Tokyo
Population 127 million / 874 people per sq mile (338 people per sq km)
Total area 145,882 sq. miles (377,835 sq. km)
Languages Japanese*, Korean, Chinese
Religions Shinto and Buddhist 76%, Buddhist 16%, Other (including Christian) 8%
Ethnic mix Japanese 99%, Other (mainly Korean) 1%
Government Parliamentary system
Currency Yen = 100 sen
Literacy rate 99%
Calorie consumption 2719 kilocalories

Japan, Sea of *130 A4 var.* East Sea, *Rus.* Yapanskoye More. *sea* NW Pacific Ocean
Japan Trench *125 F1 trench* NW Pacific Ocean
Japen *see* Yapen, Pulau
Japiim *62 C2 var.* Máncio Lima. Acre, W Brazil
Japurá, Rio *62 C2 var.* Río Caquetá, Yapurá. *river* Brazil/Colombia
Japurá, Rio *see* Caquetá, Río
Jaqué *53 G5* Darién, SE Panama
Jaquemel *see* Jacmel
Jarablos *see* Jarābulus
Jarābulus *118 C2 var.* Jarablos, Jerablus, *Fr.* Djérablous. Ḩalab, N Syria
Jarbah, Jazīrat *see* Jerba, Île de
Jardines de la Reina, Archipiélago de los *54 B2 island group* C Cuba
Jarīd, Shaṭṭ al *see* Jerid, Chott el
Jarocin *98 C4* Wielkopolskie, C Poland
Jaroslau *see* Jarosław
Jarosław *99 E5 Ger.* Jaroslau, *Rus.* Yaroslav. Podkarpackie, SE Poland
Jarqo'rg'on *123 E3 Rus.* Dzharkurgan. Surkhondaryo Viloyati, S Uzbekistan
Jarvis Island *145 G2 US unincorporated territory* C Pacific Ocean
Jasło *99 D5* Podkarpackie, SE Poland
Jastrzębie-Zdrój *99 C5* Śląskie, S Poland
Jataí *63 E3* Goiás, C Brazil
Jativa *see* Xàtiva
Jauf *see* Al Jawf
Jaunpiebalga *106 D3* NE Latvia
Jaunpur *135 E3* Uttar Pradesh, N India
Java *152 A3* South Dakota, N USA
Javalambre *93 E3 mountain* E Spain
Java Sea *138 D4 Ind.* Laut Jawa. *sea* W Indonesia
Java Trench *124 D5 var.* Sunda Trench. *trench* E Indian Ocean
Jawa, Laut *see* Java Sea
Jawhar *73 D6 var.* Jowhar, *It.* Giohar. Shabeellaha Dhexe, S Somalia
Jaworów *see* Yavoriv
Jaya, Puncak *139 G4 prev.* Puntjak Carstensz, Puntjak Sukarno. *mountain* Papua, E Indonesia
Jayapura *139 H4 var.* Djajapura, *Dut.* Hollandia; *prev.* Kotabaru, Sukarnapura. Papua, E Indonesia
Jay Dairen *see* Dalian
Jayhawker State *see* Kansas
Jaz Murian, Hamun-e *120 E4 lake* SE Iran
Jebba *75 F4* Kwara, W Nigeria
Jebel, Bahr el *see* White Nile
Jeble *see* Jablah
Jedda *see* Jiddah
Jędrzejów *98 D4 Ger.* Endersdorf. Świętokrzyskie, C Poland
Jefferson City *45 G5 state capital* Missouri, C USA
Jega *75 F4* Kebbi, NW Nigeria
Jehol *see* Chengde
Jeju-do *129 E4 Jap.* Saishū; *prev.* Cheju-do, Quelpart. *island* S South Korea
Jeju Strait *129 E4 var.* Jeju-haehyŏp; *prev.* Cheju-Strait. *strait* S South Korea
Jeju-haehyŏp *see* Jeju Strait
Jēkabpils *106 D4 Ger.* Jakobstadt. S Latvia
Jelalabad *see* Jalālābād
Jelenia Góra *98 B4 Ger.* Hirschberg, Hirschberg im Riesengebirge, Hirschberg in Riesengebirge, Hirschberg in Schlesien. Dolnośląskie, SW Poland
Jelgava *106 C3 Ger.* Mitau. C Latvia
Jemappes *87 B6* Hainaut, S Belgium
Jember *138 D5 prev.* Djember. Jawa, C Indonesia
Jena *94 C4* Thüringen, C Germany
Jengish Chokusu *see* Tomür Feng
Jenin *119 A6* N West Bank
Jerablus *see* Jarābulus
Jerada *70 D2* NE Morocco
Jérémie *54 D3* SW Haiti
Jerez *see* Jeréz de la Frontera, Spain
Jerez de la Frontera *92 C5 var.* Jerez; *prev.* Xeres. Andalucía, SW Spain
Jerez de los Caballeros *92 C4* Extremadura, W Spain
Jericho *119 B6 Ar.* Arīḩā, *Heb.* Yeriḩo. E West Bank
Jerid, Chott el *71 E2 var.* Shaṭṭ al Jarīd. *salt lake* SW Tunisia
Jersey *89 D8 British Crown Dependency* Channel Islands, NW Europe
Jerusalem *103 H4 Ar.* Al Quds, Al Quds ash Sharīf, *Heb.* Yerushalayim; *anc.* Hierosolyma. *country capital* (Israel) Jerusalem, NE Israel
Jesenice *95 D7 Ger.* Assling. NW Slovenia
Jesselton *see* Kota Kinabalu
Jessore *135 G4* Khulna, W Bangladesh
Jesús María *64 C3* Córdoba, C Argentina
Jeypore *see* Jaipur, Rājasthān, India
Jhānsi *134 D3* Uttar Pradesh, N India
Jhārkhand *135 F4 cultural region* NE India
Jhelum *134 C2* Punjab, NE Pakistan
Ji *see* Hebei, China
Ji *see* Jilin, China
Jiangmen *128 C6* Guangdong, S China
Jiangsu *128 D4 var.* Chiang-su, Jiangsu Sheng, Kiangsu, Su. *province* E China
Jiangsu *see* Nanjing
Jiangsu Sheng *see* Jiangsu
Jiangxi *128 C6 var.* Chiang-hsi, Gan, Jiangxi Sheng, Kiangsi. *province* S China
Jiangxi Sheng *see* Jiangxi
Jiaxing *128 D5* Zhejiang, SE China
Jiayi *128 D6 prev.* Chiai; *var.* Chia-i, Chiayi, Kiayi, Jiayi, *Jap.* Kagi. C Taiwan
Jibuti *see* Djibouti
Jiddah *121 A5 Eng.* Jedda. Makkah, W Saudi Arabia
Jih-k'a-tse *see* Xigazê
Jihlava *99 B5 Ger.* Iglau, *Pol.* Igława. Vysocina, S Czech Republic
Jilib *73 D6 It.* Gelib. Jubbada Dhexe, S Somalia
Jilin *128 E3 var.* Chi-lin, Girin, Kirin; *prev.* Yungki, Yunki. Jilin, NE China
Jilin *128 E3 var.* Chi-lin, Girin, Ji, Jilin Sheng, Kirin. *province* NE China
Jilin Sheng *see* Jilin
Jilong *128 D6 prev.* Chilung; *var.* Keelung, *Jap.* Kirun, Kirun'; *prev. Sp.* Santissima Trinidad. N Taiwan
Jīma *73 C5 var.* Jimma, *It.* Gimma. Oromīya, C Ethiopia
Jimbolia *108 A4 Ger.* Hatzfeld, *Hung.* Zsombolya. Timiș, W Romania
Jiménez *50 D2* Chihuahua, N Mexico
Jimma *see* Jīma
Jimsar *126 C3* Xinjiang Uygur Zizhiqu, NW China
Jin *see* Shanxi
Jin *see* Tianjin Shi
Jinan *128 C4 var.* Chinan, Chi-nan, Tsinan. *province capital* Shandong, E China
Jingdezhen *128 C5* Jiangxi, S China
Jinghong *128 A6 var.* Yunjinghong. Yunnan, SW China
Jinhua *128 D5* Zhejiang, SE China
Jining *127 F3* Shandong, E China
Jinja *73 C6* S Uganda
Jinotega *52 D3* Jinotega, NW Nicaragua
Jinotepe *52 D3* Carazo, SW Nicaragua
Jinsen *see* Incheon
Jinzhong *128 C4 var.* Yuci. Shanxi, C China
Jinzhou *128 D3 var.* Chin-chou, Chinchow; *prev.* Chinhsien. Liaoning, NE China
Jirgalanta *see* Hovd
Jisr ash Shadadi *see* Ash Shadādah
Jiu *108 B5 Ger.* Schil, Schyl, *Hung.* Zsil, Zsily. *river* S Romania
Jiujiang *128 C5* Jiangxi, S China
Jixi *129 E2* Heilongjiang, NE China
Jīzān *121 B6 var.* Qīzān. Jīzān, SW Sau Arabia
Jizzax *123 E2 Rus.* Dzhizak. Jizzax Viloyati, C Uzbekistan
João Belo *see* Xai-Xai
João Pessoa *63 G2 prev.* Paraíba. *state capital* Paraíba, E Brazil
Joazeiro *see* Juazeiro
Job'urg *see* Johannesburg
Jo-ch'iang *see* Ruoqiang
Jodhpur *134 C3* Rājasthān, NW India
Joensuu *85 E5* Itä-Suomi, SE Finland
Jōetsu *131 C5 var.* Zyôetu. Niigata, Honshū, C Japan
Jogjakarta *see* Yogyakarta
Johannesburg *78 D4 var.* Egoli, Erautini, Gauteng, *abbrev.* Job'urg. Gauteng, NE South Africa
Johannisburg *see* Pisz
John Day River *46 C3 river* Oregon, NW USA
John o'Groats *88 C2* N Scotland, United Kingdom
Johnston Atoll *143 E1 US unincorporated territory* C Pacific Ocean
Johor Baharu *see* Johor Bahru
Johor Bahru *138 B3 var.* Johor Baharu, Johore Bahru. Johor, Peninsular Malaysia
Johore Bahru *see* Johor Bahru
Johore Strait *138 A1 strait* Johor, Peninsular Malaysia, Malaysia/Singapore Asia Andaman Sea/South China Sea
Joinvile *see* Joinville
Joinville *63 E4 var.* Joinvile. Santa Catarina, S Brazil
Jokkmokk *84 C3 Lapp.* Dálvvadis. Norrbotten, N Sweden
Jokyakarta *see* Yogyakarta
Joliet *40 B3* Illinois, N USA
Jonava *106 B4 Ger.* Janow, *Pol.* Janów. Kaunas, C Lithuania
Jonesboro *42 B1* Arkansas, C USA
Joniškis *106 C3 Ger.* Janischken. Šiauliai, N Lithuania
Jönköping *85 B7* Jönköping, S Sweden
Jonquière *39 E4* Québec, SE Canada
Joplin *45 F5* Missouri, C USA
Jordan *119 B6 off.* Hashemite Kingdom of Jordan, *Ar.* Al Mamlaka al Urdunīya al Hashemīyah, Al Urdunn; *prev.* Transjordan. *country* SW Asia

JORDAN
Southwest Asia

Official name Hashemite Kingdom of Jordan
Formation 1946 / 1967
Capital Amman
Population 7.3 million / 213 people per sq mile (82 people per sq km)
Total area 35,637 sq. miles (92,300 sq. km)
Languages Arabic*
Religions Muslim (mainly Sunni) 92%, Christian 6%, Other 2%
Ethnic mix Arab 98%, Circassian 1%, Armenian 1%
Government Monarchy

ORDAN
(continued)

Currency Jordanian dinar = 1000 fils
Literacy rate 98%
Calorie consumption 3149 kilocalories

rdan *119 B5 Ar.* Urdunn, *Heb.* HaYarden. *river* SW Asia
rhāt *135 H3* Assam, NE India
›s *75 G4* Plateau, C Nigeria
›seph Bonaparte Gulf *146 D2 gulf* N Australia
›s Plateau *75 G4 plateau* C Nigeria
›tunheimen *85 A5 mountain range* S Norway
›ûnié *118 A4 var.* Junīyah. W Lebanon
›ure *86 D2 Fris.* De Jouwer. Fryslân, N Netherlands
›utseno *85 E5* Etelä-Suomi, SE Finland
›whar *see* Jawhar
Storm Thurmond Reservoir *see* Clark Hill Lake
ıan Aldama *50 D3* Zacatecas, C Mexico
ıan de Fuca, Strait of *46 A1 strait* Canada/USA
ıan Fernández, Islas *57 A6 Eng.* Juan Fernandez Islands. *island group* W Chile
ıan Fernandez Islands *see* Juan Fernández, Islas
ıazeiro *63 G2 prev.* Joazeiro. Bahia, E Brazil
ıazeiro do Norte *63 G2* Ceará, E Brazil
ıba *73 B5 var.* Jūbā. *country capital* (South Sudan) Central Equatoria, S South Sudan
ıba *73 D6 Amh.* Genalē Wenz, *It.* Guiba, *Som.* Ganaane, Webi Jubba. *river* Ethiopia/Somalia
ıbba, Webi *see* Juba
ıbbulpore *see* Jabalpur
ícar *93 E3 var.* Jucar. *river* C Spain
ıchitán *51 F5 var.* Juchitán de Zaragosa. Oaxaca, SE Mexico
ıchitán de Zaragosa *see* Juchitán
ıdayyidat Hāmir *120 B3* Al Anbār, S Iraq
ıdenburg *95 D7* Steiermark, C Austria
ıgoslavija *see* Serbia
ıigalpa *52 D3* Chontales, S Nicaragua
ıiz de Fora *63 F4* Minas Gerais, SE Brazil
ıjuy *see* San Salvador de Jujuy
ılā *see* Jālū, Libya
ılia Beterrae *see* Béziers
ıliaca *61 E4* Puno, SE Peru
ıliana Top *59 G3 mountain* C Suriname
ılianehåb *see* Qaqortoq
ılio Briga *see* Bragança
ılióbriga *see* Logroño
ıliomagus *see* Angers
ıllundur *see* Jalandhar
ımilla *93 E4* Murcia, SE Spain
ımmoo *see* Jammu
ımna *see* Yamuna
ımporn *see* Chumphon
ınction City *45 F4* Kansas, C USA
ıneau *36 D4 state capital* Alaska, USA
ınín *64 C4* Buenos Aires, E Argentina
ınīyah *see* Joûnié
ınkseylon *see* Phuket
ır *73 B5 river* W South Sudan
ıra *90 D4 cultural region* E France
ıra *95 A7 var.* Jura Mountains. *mountain range* France/Switzerland
ura *88 B4 island* SW Scotland, United Kingdom
ura Mountains *see* Jura
urbarkas *106 B4 Ger.* Georgenburg, Jurburg. Tauragė, W Lithuania
urburg *see* Jurbarkas
ūrmala *106 C3* C Latvia
uruá, Rio *62 C2 var.* Río Yuruá. *river* Brazil/Peru
uruena, Rio *62 D3 river* V Brazil
utiapa *52 B2* Jutiapa, S Guatemala
uticalpa *52 D2* Olancho, C Honduras
utland *63 A7 Den.* Jylland. *peninsula* W Denmark
uvavum *see* Salzburg
užna Morava *101 E5 Ger.* Südliche Morava. *river* SE Serbia
waneng *78 C4* Southern, S Botswana
ylland *see* Jutland
yrgalan *see* Dzhergalan
yväskylä *85 D5* Länsi-Suomi, C Finland

K

K2 *126 A4 Chin.* Qogir Feng, *Eng.* Mount Godwin Austen. *mountain* China/Pakistan
Kaafu Atoll *see* Male' Atoll
Kaaimanston *59 G3* Sipaliwini, N Suriname
Kaakhka *see* Kaka
Kaala *see* Caála
Kaamanen *84 D2 Lapp.* Gámas. Lappi, N Finland
Kaapstad *see* Cape Town
Kaaresuvanto *84 C3 Lapp.* Gárassavon. Lappi, N Finland
Kabale *73 B6* SW Uganda
Kabinda *77 D7* Kasai-Oriental, SE Dem. Rep. Congo
Kabinda *see* Cabinda
Kābol *see* Kābul
Kabompo *78 C2 river* W Zambia
Kābul *123 E4 prev.* Kābol. *country capital* (Afghanistan) Kābul, E Afghanistan
Kabul *123 E4 var.* Daryā-ye Kābul. *river* Afghanistan/Pakistan
Kābul, Daryā-ye *see* Kabul
Kabwe *78 D2* Central, C Zambia
Kachchh, Gulf of *134 B4 var.* Gulf of Cutch, Gulf of Kutch. *gulf* W India
Kachchh, Rann of *134 B4 var.* Rann of Kachh, Rann of Kutch. *salt marsh* India/Pakistan
Kachh, Rann of *see* Kachchh, Rann of
Kadan Kyun *137 B5 prev.* King Island. *island* Myeik Archipelago, S Myanmar (Burma)
Kadavu *145 E4 prev.* Kandavu. *island* S Fiji
Kadoma *78 D3 prev.* Gatooma. Mashonaland West, C Zimbabwe
Kadugli *72 B4* Southern Kordofan, S Sudan
Kaduna *75 G4* Kaduna, C Nigeria
Kadzhi-Say *see* Bokonbayevo
Kaédi *74 C3* Gorgol, S Mauritania
Kaffa *see* Feodosiya
Kafue *78 D2* Lusaka, SE Zambia
Kafue *78 C2 river* C Zambia
Kaga Bandoro *76 C4 prev.* Fort-Crampel. Nana-Grébizi, C Central African Republic
Kagan *see* Kogon
Kâghet *74 D1 var.* Karet. *physical region* N Mauritania
Kagi *see* Jiayi
Kagoshima *131 B8 var.* Kagosima. Kagoshima, Kyūshū, SW Japan
Kagoshima-wan *131 A8 bay* SW Japan
Kagosima *see* Kagoshima
Kagul *see* Cahul
Darya-ye Kahmard *123 E4 prev.* Darya-i-surkhab. *river* NE Afghanistan
Kahramanmaraş *116 D4 var.* Kahraman Maraş, Maraş, Marash. Kahramanmaraş, S Turkey
Kaiapoi *151 C6* Canterbury, South Island, New Zealand
Kaifeng *128 C4* Henan, C China
Kai, Kepulauan *139 F4 prev.* Kei Islands. *island group* Maluku, SE Indonesia
Kaikohe *150 C2* Northland, North Island, New Zealand
Kaikoura *151 C5* Canterbury, South Island, New Zealand
Kaikoura Peninsula *151 C5 peninsula* South Island, New Zealand
Kainji Lake *see* Kainji Reservoir
Kainji Reservoir *75 F4 var.* Kainji Lake. *reservoir* W Nigeria
Kaipara Harbour *150 C2 harbour* North Island, New Zealand
Kairouan *71 E2 var.* Al Qayrawān. E Tunisia
Kaisaria *see* Kayseri
Kaiserslautern *95 A5* Rheinland-Pfalz, SW Germany
Kaišiadorys *107 B5* Kaunas, S Lithuania
Kaitaia *150 C2* Northland, North Island, New Zealand
Kajaani *84 E4 Swe.* Kajana. Oulu, C Finland
Kajan *see* Kayan, Sungai
Kajana *see* Kajaani
Kajisay *see* Bokonbayevo
Kaka *122 C2 Rus.* Kaakhka. Ahal Welaýaty, S Turkmenistan
Kake *36 D4* Kupreanof Island, Alaska, USA
Kakhovka *109 F4* Khersons'ka Oblast', S Ukraine
Kakhovs'ke Vodoskhovyshche *109 F4 Rus.* Kakhovskoye Vodokhranilishche. *reservoir* SE Ukraine
Kakhovskoye Vodokhranilishche *see* Kakhovs'ke Vodoskhovyshche
Kākināda *132 D1 prev.* Cocanada. Andhra Pradesh, E India
Kakshaal-Too, Khrebet *see* Kokshaal-Tau
Kaktovik *36 D2* Alaska, USA
Kalaallit Nunaat *see* Greenland
Kalahari Desert *78 B4 desert* Southern Africa
Kalaikhum *see* Qal'aikhum
Kalámai *see* Kalámata
Kalamariá *104 B4* Kentrikí Makedonía, N Greece
Kalamás *104 A4 var.* Thiamis; *prev.* Thýamis. *river* W Greece
Kalámata *105 B6 prev.* Kalámai. Pelopónnisos, S Greece
Kalamazoo *40 C3* Michigan, N USA
Kalambaka *see* Kalampáka
Kálamos *105 C5* Attikí, C Greece
Kalampáka *104 B4 var.* Kalambaka. Thessalía, C Greece
Kalanchak *109 F4* Khersons'ka Oblast', S Ukraine
Kalarash *see* Călăraşi
Kalasin *136 D4 var.* Muang Kalasin. Kalasin, E Thailand
Kālat *134 B2 var.* Kelat, Khelat. Baluchistān, SW Pakistan
Kalāt *see* Qalāt
Kalbarri *147 A5* Western Australia
Kalecik *116 C3* Ankara, N Turkey
Kalemie *77 E6 prev.* Albertville. Katanga, SE Dem. Rep. Congo
Kale Sultanie *see* Çanakkale
Kalgan *see* Zhangjiakou
Kalgoorlie *147 B6* Western Australia
Kalima *77 D6* Maniema, E Dem. Rep. Congo
Kalimantan *138 D4 Eng.* Indonesian Borneo. *geopolitical region* Borneo, C Indonesia
Kalinin *see* Tver'
Kaliningrad *106 A4* Kaliningradskaya Oblast', W Russian Federation
Kaliningrad *see* Kaliningradskaya Oblast'
Kaliningradskaya Oblast' *106 B4 var.* Kaliningrad. *province and enclave* W Russian Federation
Kalinkavichy *107 C7 Rus.* Kalinkovichi. Homyel'skaya Voblasts', SE Belarus
Kalinkovichi *see* Kalinkavichy
Kalisch/Kalish *see* Kalisz
Kalispell *44 B1* Montana, NW USA
Kalisz *98 C4 Ger.* Kalisch, *Rus.* Kalish; *anc.* Calisia. Wielkopolskie, C Poland
Kalix *84 D4* Norrbotten, N Sweden
Kalixälven *84 D3 river* N Sweden
Kallaste *106 E3 Ger.* Krasnogor. Tartumaa, SE Estonia
Kallavesi *85 E5 lake* SE Finland
Kalloní *105 D5* Lésvos, E Greece
Kalmar *85 C7 var.* Calmar. Kalmar, S Sweden
Kalmthout *87 C5* Antwerpen, N Belgium
Kalpáki *104 A4* Ípeiros, W Greece
Kalpeni Island *132 B3 island* Lakshadweep, India, N Indian Ocean
Kaltdorf *see* Pruszków
Kaluga *111 B5* Kaluzhskaya Oblast', W Russian Federation
Kalush *108 C2 Pol.* Kałusz. Ivano-Frankivs'ka Oblast', W Ukraine
Kałusz *see* Kalush
Kalutara *132 D4* Western Province, SW Sri Lanka
Kalvarija *107 B5 Pol.* Kalwaria. Marijampolė, S Lithuania
Kalwaria *see* Kalvarija
Kalyān *134 C5* Mahārāshtra, W India
Kálymnos *105 D6 var.* Kálimnos. *island* Dodekánisa, Greece, Aegean Sea
Kama *110 D4 river* NW Russian Federation
Kamarang *59 F3* W Guyana
Kambryk *see* Cambrai
Kamchatka *115 G3 Eng.* Kamchatka. *peninsula* E Russian Federation
Kamchatka *see* Kamchatka, Poluostrov
Kamenets-Podol'skiy *see* Kam"yanets'-Podil's'kyy
Kamenka Dneprovskaya *see* Kam"yanka-Dniprovs'ka
Kamenskoye *see* Romaniv
Kamensk-Shakhtinskiy *111 B6* Rostovskaya Oblast', SW Russian Federation
Kamina *77 D7* Katanga, S Dem. Rep. Congo
Kamishli *see* Al Qāmishlī
Kamloops *37 E5* British Columbia, SW Canada
Kammu Seamount *152 C2 guyot* N Pacific Ocean
Kampala *73 B6 country capital* (Uganda) S Uganda
Kâmpóng Cham *137 D6 prev.* Kompong Cham. Kâmpóng Cham, C Cambodia
Kâmpóng Chhnăng *137 D6 prev.* Kompong. Kâmpóng Chhnăng, C Cambodia
Kâmpóng Saôm *see* Sihanoukville
Kâmpóng Spoe *137 D6 prev.* Kompong Speu. Kâmpóng Spœ, S Cambodia
Kâmpóng Thum *137 D5 prev.* Trâpeăng Vêng. Kâmpóng Thum, C Cambodia
Kâmpóng Trâbêk *137 D5 prev.* Phumĭ Kâmpóng Trâbêk, Phum Kompong Trabek. Kâmpóng Thum, C Cambodia
Kâmpôt *137 D6* Kâmpôt, SW Cambodia
Kampuchea *see* Cambodia
Kampuchea, Democratic *see* Cambodia
Kampuchea, People's Democratic Republic of *see* Cambodia
Kam"yanets'-Podil's'kyy *108 C3 Rus.* Kamenets-Podol'skiy. Khmel'nyts'ka Oblast', W Ukraine
Kam"yanka-Dniprovs'ka *109 F3 Rus.* Kamenka Dneprovskaya. Zaporiz'ka Oblast', SE Ukraine
Kamyshin *111 B6* Volgogradskaya Oblast', SW Russian Federation
Kanaky *see* New Caledonia
Kananga *77 D6 prev.* Luluabourg. Kasai-Occidental, S Dem. Rep. Congo
Kanara *see* Karnātaka
Kanash *111 C5* Chuvashskaya Respublika, W Russian Federation
Kanazawa *131 C5* Ishikawa, Honshū, SW Japan
Kanbe *136 B4* Yangon, SW Myanmar (Burma)
Kānchīpuram *132 C2 prev.* Conjeeveram. Tamil Nādu, SE India
Kandahār *123 E5 Per.* Qandahār. Kandahār, S Afghanistan
Kandalakša *see* Kandalaksha
Kandalaksha *110 B2 var.* Kandalakša, *Fin.* Kantalahti. Murmanskaya Oblast', NW Russian Federation
Kandangan *138 D4* Borneo, C Indonesia
Kandau *see* Kandava
Kandava *106 C3 Ger.* Kandau. W Latvia
Kandavu *see* Kadavu
Kandi *75 F4* N Benin
Kandy *132 D3* Central Province, C Sri Lanka
Kane Fracture Zone *66 B4 fracture zone* NW Atlantic Ocean
Kāne'ohe *47 A8 var.* Kaneohe. O'ahu, Hawaii, USA, C Pacific Ocean
Kanestron, Akrotírio *see* Palioúri, Akrotírio
Kanëv *see* Kaniv
Kanevskoye Vodokhranilishche *see* Kanivs'ke Vodoskhovyshche
Kangān *see* Bandar-e Kangān
Kangaroo Island *149 A7 island* South Australia
Kangertittivaq *83 E4 Dan.* Scoresby Sund. *fjord* E Greenland
Kangikajik *83 E4 var.* Kap Brewster. *headland* E Greenland
Kaniv *109 E2 Rus.* Kanëv. Cherkas'ka Oblast', C Ukraine
Kanivs'ke Vodoskhovyshche *109 E2 Rus.* Kanevskoye Vodokhranilishche. *reservoir* C Ukraine
Kanjiža *100 D2 Ger.* Altkanischa, *Hung.* Magyarkanizsa, Ókanizsa; *prev.* Stara Kanjiža. Vojvodina, N Serbia
Kankaanpää *85 D5* Länsi-Suomi, SW Finland
Kankakee *40 B3* Illinois, N USA
Kankan *74 D4* E Guinea
Kannur *132 B2 var.* Cannanore. Kerala, SW India
Kano *75 G4* Kano, N Nigeria
Kānpur *135 E3 Eng.* Cawnpore. Uttar Pradesh, N India

Kansas 45 F5 off. State of Kansas, also known as Jayhawker State, Sunflower State. state C USA
Kansas City 45 F4 Kansas, C USA
Kansas City 45 F4 Missouri, C USA
Kansas River 45 F5 river Kansas, C USA
Kansk 115 E4 Krasnoyarskiy Kray, S Russian Federation
Kansu see Gansu
Kantalahti see Kandalaksha
Kántanos 105 C7 Kríti, Greece, E Mediterranean Sea
Kantemirovka 111 B6 Voronezhskaya Oblast', W Russian Federation
Kantipur see Kathmandu
Kanton 145 F3 var. Abariringa, Canton Island; prev. Mary Island. atoll Phoenix Islands, C Kiribati
Kanye 78 C4 Southern, SE Botswana
Kaohsiung see Gaoxiong
Kaolack 74 B3 var. Kaolak. W Senegal
Kaolak see Kaolack
Kaolan see Lanzhou
Kaoma 78 C2 Western, W Zambia
Kapelle 87 B5 Zeeland, SW Netherlands
Kapellen 87 C5 Antwerpen, N Belgium
Kapka, Massif du 76 C2 mountain range E Chad
Kaplangky, Plato see Gaplaňgyr Platosy
Kapoeas see Kapuas, Sungai
Kapoeta 73 C5 Eastern Equatoria, SE South Sudan
Kaposvár 99 C7 Somogy, SW Hungary
Kappeln 94 B2 Schleswig-Holstein, N Germany
Kaproncza see Koprivnica
Kapstad see Cape Town
Kapsukas see Marijampolė
Kaptsevichy 107 C7 Rus. Koptsevichi. Homyel'skaya Voblasts', SE Belarus
Kapuas, Sungai 138 C4 prev. Kapoeas. river Borneo, C Indonesia
Kapuskasing 38 C4 Ontario, S Canada
Kapyl' 107 C6 Rus. Kopyl'. Minskaya Voblasts', C Belarus
Kara-Balta 123 F2 Chuyskaya Oblast', N Kyrgyzstan
Karabil', Vozvyshennost' see Garabil Belentligi
Kara-Bogaz-Gol, Zaliv see Garabogaz Aylagy
Karabük 116 C2 Karabük, NW Turkey
Karāchi 134 B3 Sind, SE Pakistan
Karácsonkő see Piatra-Neamţ
Karadeniz see Black Sea
Karadeniz Boğazi see İstanbul Boğazı
Karaferiye see Véroia
Karaganda see Karagandy
Karagandy 114 C4 prev. Karaganda, Kaz. Qaraghandy. Karagandy, C Kazakhstan
Karaginskiy, Ostrov 115 H2 island E Russian Federation
Karagumskiy Kanal see Garagum Kanaly
Karak see Al Karak
Kara-Kala see Magtymguly
Karakax see Moyu
Karakılısse see Ağrı
Karakol 123 G2 var. Karakolka. Issyk-Kul'skaya Oblast', NE Kyrgyzstan
Karakol 123 G2 prev. Przheval'sk. Issyk-Kul'skaya Oblast', NE Kyrgyzstan
Karakolka see Karakol
Karakoram Range 134 D1 mountain range C Asia
Karaköse see Ağrı
Karakul' see Qarokŭl, Tajikistan
Kara Kum see Garagum
Kara Kum Canal/Karakumskiy Kanal see Garagum Kanaly
Karakumy, Peski see Garagum
Karamai see Karamay
Karaman 116 C4 Karaman, S Turkey
Karamay 126 B2 var. Karamai, Kelamayi; prev. Chin. K'o-la-ma-i. Xinjiang Uygur Zizhiqu, NW China
Karamea Bight 151 B5 gulf South Island, New Zealand
Karapelit 104 E1 Rom. Stejarul. Dobrich, NE Bulgaria
Kara-Say 123 G2 Issyk-Kul'skaya Oblast', NE Kyrgyzstan
Karasburg 78 B4 Karas, S Namibia
Kara Sea 114 D2 Eng. Kara Sea. sea Arctic Ocean
Kara Sea see Karskoye More
Kara Strait 110 E2 Eng. Kara Strait. strait N Russian Federation
Kara Strait see Karskiye Vorota, Proliv
Karatau 114 C5 Kaz. Qarataū. Zhambyl, S Kazakhstan
Karavás 105 B7 Kýthira, S Greece
Karbalā' 120 B3 var. Kerbala, Kerbela. Karbalā', S Iraq
Kardeljevo see Ploče
Kardhítsa see Kardítsa
Kardítsa 105 B5 var. Kardhítsa. Thessalía, C Greece
Kärdla 106 C2 Ger. Kertel. Hiiumaa, W Estonia
Karet see Kâgheţ
Kargı 116 C2 Çorum, N Turkey
Kargilik see Yecheng
Kariba 78 D2 Mashonaland West, N Zimbabwe
Kariba, Lake 78 D3 reservoir Zambia/Zimbabwe
Karibib 78 B3 Erongo, C Namibia
Karies see Karyés
Karigasniemi 84 D2 Lapp. Garegegasnjárga. Lappi, N Finland
Karimata, Selat 138 C4 strait W Indonesia
Karīmnagar 134 D5 Telangana, C India
Karin 72 D4 Woqooyi Galbeed, N Somalia
Kariot see Ikaría
Káristos see Kárystos
Karkinits'ka Zatoka 109 E4 Rus. Karkinitskiy Zaliv. gulf S Ukraine
Karkinitskiy Zaliv see Karkinits'ka Zatoka
Karkūk see Kirkūk
Karleby see Kokkola
Karl-Marx-Stadt see Chemnitz
Karlö see Hailuoto
Karlovac 100 B3 Ger. Karlstadt, Hung. Károlyváros. Karlovac, C Croatia
Karlovy Vary 99 A5 Ger. Karlsbad; prev. Eng. Carlsbad. Karlovarský Kraj, W Czech Republic
Karlsbad see Karlovy Vary
Karlsburg see Alba Iulia
Karlskrona 85 C7 Blekinge, S Sweden
Karlsruhe 95 B6 var. Carlsruhe. Baden-Württemberg, SW Germany
Karlstad 85 B6 Värmland, C Sweden
Karlstadt see Karlovac
Karnāl 134 D2 Haryāna, N India
Karnātaka 132 C1 var. Kanara; prev. Maisur, Mysore. cultural region W India
Karnobat 104 D2 Burgas, E Bulgaria
Karnul see Kurnool
Karol see Carei
Károly-Fehérvár see Alba Iulia
Károlyváros see Karlovac
Karpaten see Carpathian Mountains
Kárpathos 105 E7 Kárpathos, SE Greece
Kárpathos 105 E7 It. Scarpanto; anc. Carpathos, Carpathus. island SE Greece
Karpaty see Carpathian Mountains
Karpenísi 105 B5 prev. Karpenísion. Stereá Elláda, C Greece
Karpenísion see Karpenísi
Karpilovka see Aktsyabrski
Kars 117 F2 var. Qars. Kars, NE Turkey
Karsau see Kārsava
Kārsava 106 D4 Ger. Karsau; prev. Rus. Korsovka. E Latvia
Karshi see Qarshi, Uzbekistan
Karyés 104 C4 var. Karies. Ágion Óros, N Greece
Kárystos 105 C6 var. Káristos. Évvoia, C Greece
Kasai 77 C6 var. Cassai, Kassai. river Angola/Dem. Rep. Congo
Kasaji 77 D7 Katanga, S Dem. Rep. Congo
Kasama 78 D1 Northern, N Zambia
Kasan see Koson
Kāsaragod 132 B2 Kerala, SW India
Kaschau see Košice
Kāshān 120 C3 Eşfahān, C Iran
Kashgar see Kashi
Kashi 126 A3 Chin. Kaxgar, K'o-shih, Uigh. Kashgar. Xinjiang Uygur Zizhiqu, NW China
Kasi see Vārānasi
Kasongo 77 D6 Maniema, E Dem. Rep. Congo
Kasongo-Lunda 77 C7 Bandundu, SW Dem. Rep. Congo
Kásos 105 D7 island S Greece
Kaspīy Mangy Oypaty see Caspian Depression
Kaspiysk 111 B8 Respublika Dagestan, SW Russian Federation
Kaspiyskoye More/Kaspiy Tengizi see Caspian Sea
Kassa see Košice
Kassai see Kasai
Kassala 72 C4 Kassala, E Sudan
Kassel 94 B4 prev. Cassel. Hessen, C Germany
Kasserine 71 E2 var. Al Qaşrayn. W Tunisia
Kastamonu 116 C2 var. Castamoni, Kastamuni. Kastamonu, N Turkey
Kastamuni see Kastamonu
Kastaneá see Kastaniá
Kastaniá 104 B4 prev. Kastaneá. Kentrikí Makedonía, N Greece
Kastélli see Kíssamos
Kastoría 104 B4 Dytikí Makedonía, N Greece
Kástro 105 C6 Sífnos, Kykládes, Greece, Aegean Sea
Kastsyukovichy 107 E7 Rus. Kostyukovichi. Mahilyowskaya Voblasts', E Belarus
Kastsyukowka 107 D7 Rus. Kostyukovka. Homyel'skaya Voblasts', SE Belarus
Kasulu 73 B7 Kigoma, W Tanzania
Kasumiga-ura 131 D5 lake Honshū, S Japan
Katahdin, Mount 41 G1 mountain Maine, NE USA
Katalla 36 C3 Alaska, USA
Katana see Qaţanā
Katanning 147 B7 Western Australia
Katawaz see Zarghūn Shahr
Katchall Island 133 F3 island Nicobar Islands, India, NE Indian Ocean
Kateríni 104 B4 Kentrikí Makedonía, N Greece
Katha 136 B2 Sagaing, N Myanmar (Burma)
Katherine 148 A2 Northern Territory, N Australia
Kathmandu 124 C3 prev. Kantipur. country capital (Nepal) Central, C Nepal
Katikati 150 D3 Bay of Plenty, North Island, New Zealand
Katima Mulilo 78 C3 Caprivi, NE Namibia
Katiola 74 D4 C Côte d'Ivoire
Káto Achaïa 105 B5 var. Kato Ahaia, Káto Akhaía. Dytikí Elláda, S Greece
Kato Ahaia/Káto Akhaía see Káto Achaïa
Katoúna 105 A5 Dytikí Elláda, C Greece
Katowice 99 C5 Ger. Kattowitz. Śląskie, S Poland
Katsina 75 G3 Katsina, N Nigeria
Kattakurgan see Kattaqo'rg'on
Kattaqo'rg'on 123 E2 Rus. Kattakurgan. Samarqand Viloyati, C Uzbekistan
Kattavía 105 E7 Ródos, Dodekánisa, Greece, Aegean Sea
Kattegat 85 B7 Dan. Kattegatt. strait N Europe
Kattegatt see Kattegat
Kattowitz see Katowice
Kaua'i 47 A7 var. Kauai. island Hawai'ian Islands, Hawaii, USA, C Pacific Ocean
Kauai see Kaua'i
Kauen see Kaunas
Kaufbeuren 95 C6 Bayern, S Germany
Kaunas 106 B4 Ger. Kauen, Pol. Kowno; prev. Rus. Kovno. Kaunas, C Lithuania
Kavadar see Kavadarci
Kavadarci 101 E6 Turk. Kavadar. C Macedonia
Kavaja see Kavajë
Kavajë 101 C6 It. Cavaia, Kavaja. Tiranë, W Albania
Kavakli see Topolovgrad
Kavála 104 C3 prev. Kaválla. Anatolikí Makedonía kai Thráki, NE Greece
Kāvali 132 D2 Andhra Pradesh, E India
Kaválla see Kavála
Kavango see Cubango/Okavango
Kavaratti Island 132 A3 island Lakshadweep, Lakshadweep, SW India Asia N Indian Ocean
Kavarna 104 E2 Dobrich, NE Bulgaria
Kavengo see Cubango/Okavango
Kavir, Dasht-e 120 D3 var. Great Salt Desert. salt pan N Iran
Kavkaz see Caucasus
Kawagoe 131 D5 Saitama, Honshū, S Japan
Kawasaki 130 A2 Kanagawa, Honshū, S Japan
Kawerau 150 E3 Bay of Plenty, North Island, New Zealand
Kaxgar see Kashi
Kaya 75 E3 C Burkina Faso
Kayan 136 B4 Yangon, SW Myanmar (Burma)
Kayan, Sungai 138 D3 prev. Kajan. river Borneo, C Indonesia
Kayes 74 C3 Kayes, W Mali
Kayseri 116 D3 var. Kaisaria; anc. Caesarea Mazaca, Mazaca. Kayseri, C Turkey
Kazach'ye 115 F2 Respublika Sakha (Yakutiya), NE Russian Federation
Kazakhskaya SSR/Kazakh Soviet Socialist Republic see Kazakhstan
Kazakhstan 114 B4 off. Republic of Kazakhstan, var. Kazakstan, Kaz. Qazaqstan, Qazaqstan Respublikasy; prev. Kazakh Soviet Socialist Republic, Rus. Kazakhskaya SSR. country C Asia

KAZAKHSTAN
Central Asia

Official name Republic of Kazakhstan
Formation 1991 / 1991
Capital Astana
Population 16.4 million / 16 people per sq mile (6 people per sq km)
Total area 1,049,150 sq. miles (2,717,300 sq. km)
Languages Kazakh*, Russian, Ukrainian, German, Uzbek, Tatar, Uighur
Religions Muslim (mainly Sunni) 47%, Orthodox Christian 44%, Other 9%
Ethnic mix Kazakh 57%, Russian 27%, Other 8%, Uzbek 3%, Ukrainian 3%, German 2%
Government Presidential system
Currency Tenge = 100 tiyn
Literacy rate 99%
Calorie consumption 3107 kilocalories

Kazakhstan, Republic of see Kazakhstan
Kazakh Uplands 114 C4 Eng. Kazakh Uplands, Kirghiz Steppe. uplands C Kazakhstan
Kazakh Uplands see Saryarka
Kazakstan see Kazakhstan
Kazan' 111 C5 Respublika Tatarstan, W Russian Federation
Kazandzhik see Bereket
Kazanlik see Kazanlŭk
Kazanlŭk 104 D2 prev. Kazanlik. Stara Zagora, C Bulgaria
Kazatin see Kozyatyn
Kazbegi see Kazbek
Kazbek 117 F1 var. Kazbegi, Geor. Mqinvartsveri. mountain N Georgia
Kāzerūn 120 D4 Fārs, S Iran
Kazvin see Qazvīn
Kéa see Tziá
Kéa see Ioulís
Kea, Mauna 47 B8 mountain Hawaii, USA
Kéamu see Aneityum
Kearney 45 E4 Nebraska, C USA
Keban Barajı 117 E3 reservoir C Turkey
Kebkabiya 72 A4 Northern Darfur, W Sudan
Kebnekaise 84 C3 Lapp. Giebnegáisi. mountain N Sweden
Kecskemét 99 D7 Bács-Kiskun, C Hungary
Kediri 138 D5 Jawa, C Indonesia
Kędzierzyn-Kozle 99 C5 Ger. Heydebrech. Opolskie, S Poland
Keelung see Jilong
Keetmanshoop 78 B4 Karas, S Namibia
Kefallinía see Kefalloniá
Kefalloniá 105 A5 var. Kefallinía. island Iónia Nisiá, Greece, C Mediterranean Sea
Kefe see Feodosiya
Kegel see Keila
Kehl 95 A6 Baden-Württemberg, SW Germany
Kei Islands see Kai, Kepulauan
Keijō see Seoul
Keila 106 D2 Ger. Kegel. Harjumaa, NW Estonia
Keïta 75 F3 Tahoua, C Niger
Keith 149 B7 South Australia
Kēk-Art 123 G2 prev. Alaykel', Alay-Kuu. Oshskaya Oblast', SW Kyrgyzstan
Kékes 99 C6 mountain N Hungary

:lamayi *see* Karamay
:lang *see* Klang
:lat *see* Kālat
:lifskiy Uzboy *see* Kelif Uzboýy
:lif Uzboýy *122 D3 Rus.* Kelifskiy Uzboy. *salt marsh* E Turkmenistan
:lkit Çayı *117 E3 river* N Turkey
:lmė *106 B4* Šiaulai, C Lithuania
:lo *76 B4* Tandjilé, SW Chad
:lowna *37 E5* British Columbia, SW Canada
:lso *46 B2* Washington, NW USA
eltsy *see* Kielce
eluang *138 B3 var.* Kluang. Johor, Peninsular Malaysia
em' *110 B3* Respublika Kareliya, NW Russian Federation
:mah *117 E3* Erzincan, E Turkey
:maman *see* Cukai
:merovo *114 D4 prev.* Shcheglovsk. Kemerovskaya Oblast', C Russian Federation
:mi *84 D4* Lappi, NW Finland
:mijärvi *84 D3 Swe.* Kemiträsk. Lappi, N Finland
emijoki *84 D3 river* NW Finland
emin *123 G2 prev.* Bystrovka. Chuyskaya Oblast', N Kyrgyzstan
emins Island *see* Nikumaroro
emiträsk *see* Kemijärvi
emmuna *102 A5 var.* Comino. *island* C Malta
empele *84 D4* Oulu, C Finland
empten *95 B7* Bayern, S Germany
endal *89 D5* NW England, United Kingdom
endari *139 E4* Sulawesi, C Indonesia
enedy *49 G4* Texas, SW USA
enema *74 C4* SE Sierra Leone
ëneurgench *see* Köneürgenç
enge *77 C6* Bandundu, SW Dem. Rep. Congo
engtung *136 C3 pev.* Keng Tung. Shan State, E Myanmar (Burma)
eng Tung *see* Kengtung
énitra *70 C2 prev.* Port-Lyautey. NW Morocco
ennett *45 H5* Missouri, C USA
ennewick *46 C2* Washington, NW USA
enora *38 A3* Ontario, S Canada
enosha *40 B3* Wisconsin, N USA
entau *114 B5* Yuzhnyy Kazakhstan, S Kazakhstan
entucky *40 C5 off.* Commonwealth of Kentucky, *also known as* Bluegrass State. *state* C USA
entucky Lake *40 B5 reservoir* Kentucky/Tennessee, S USA
enya *73 C6 off.* Republic of Kenya. *country* E Africa

KENYA
East Africa

Official name Republic of Kenya
Formation 1963 / 1963
Capital Nairobi
Population 44.4 million / 203 people per sq mile (78 people per sq km)
Total area 224,961 sq. miles (582,650 sq. km)
Languages Kiswahili*, English*, Kikuyu, Luo, Kalenjin, Kamba
Religions Christian 80%, Muslim 10%, Traditional beliefs 9%, Other 1%
Ethnic mix Other 28%, Kikuyu 22%, Luhya 14%, Luo 14%, Kalenjin 11%, Kamba 11%
Government Presidential system
Currency Kenya shilling = 100 cents
Literacy rate 72%
Calorie consumption 2189 kilocalories

:enya, Mount *see* Kirinyaga
:enya, Republic of *see* Kenya
eokuk *45 G4* Iowa, C USA
éos *see* Tziá
ępno *98 C4* Wielkopolskie, C Poland
:eppel Island *see* Niuatoputapu
:erak *see* Al Karak
:erala *132 C2 cultural region* S India
:erasunt *see* Giresun
:eratéa *105 C6 var.* Keratea. Attikí, C Greece
:eratea *see* Keratéa
:erbala/Kerbela *see* Karbalā'
:erch *109 G5 Rus.* Kerch'. Avtonomna Respublika Krym, SE Ukraine
Kerch' *see* Kerch
Kerchens'ka Protska/Kerchenskiy Proliv *see* Kerch Strait
Kerch Strait *109 G4 var.* Bosporus Cimmerius, Enikale Strait, *Rus.* Kerchenskiy Proliv, *Ukr.* Kerchens'ka Protska. *strait* Black Sea/Sea of Azov
Keremitlik *see* Lyulyakovo
Kerguelen *141 C7 island* C French Southern and Antarctic Lands
Kerguelen Plateau *141 C7 undersea plateau* S Indian Ocean
Kerí *105 A6* Zákynthos, Iónia Nisiá, Greece, C Mediterranean Sea
Kerikeri *150 D2* Northland, North Island, New Zealand
Kerkenah, Îles de *102 D4 var.* Kerkenna Islands, *Ar.* Juzur Qarqannah. *island group* E Tunisia
Kerkenna Islands *see* Kerkenah, Îles de
Kerki *see* Atamyrat
Kérkira *see* Kérkyra
Kerkrade *87 D6* Limburg, SE Netherlands
Kerkuk *see* Kirkūk
Kérkyra *104 A4 var.* Kérkira, *Eng.* Corfu. Kérkyra, Iónia Nisiá, Greece, C Mediterranean Sea
Kermadec Islands *152 C4 island group* New Zealand, SW Pacific Ocean
Kermadec Trench *143 E4 trench* SW Pacific Ocean
Kermān *120 D3 var.* Kirman; *anc.* Carmana. Kermān, C Iran
Kermānshāh *120 C3 var.* Qahremānshahr; *prev.* Bākhtarān. Kermānshāhān, W Iran
Kerrville *49 F4* Texas, SW USA
Kertel *see* Kärdla
Kerulen *127 E2 Chin.* Herlen He, *Mong.* Herlen Gol. *river* China/Mongolia
Kerýneia *see* Girne
Kesennuma *130 D4* Miyagi, Honshū, C Japan
Keszthely *99 C7* Zala, SW Hungary
Ketchikan *36 D4* Revillagigedo Island, Alaska, USA
Kętrzyn *98 D2 Ger.* Rastenburg. Warmińsko-Mazurskie, NE Poland
Kettering *89 D6* C England, United Kingdom
Kettering *40 C4* Ohio, N USA
Keupriya *see* Primorsko
Keuruu *85 D5* Länsi-Suomi, C Finland
Keweenaw Peninsula *40 B1 peninsula* Michigan, N USA
Key Largo *43 F5* Key Largo, Florida, SE USA
Keystone State *see* Pennsylvania
Key West *43 E5* Florida Keys, Florida, SE USA
Kezdivásárhely *see* Târgu Secuiesc
Khabarovsk *115 G4* Khabarovskiy Kray, SE Russian Federation
Khachmas *see* Xaçmaz
Khadera *see* Hadera
Khairpur *134 B3* Sind, SE Pakistan
Khalīj as Suways *72 B2 var.* Suez, Gulf of. *gulf* NE Egypt
Khalkidhikí *see* Chalkidikí
Khalkís *see* Chalkída
Gulf of Khambhat *134 C4 Eng.* Gulf of Cambay. *gulf* W India
Khamīs Mushayṭ *121 B6 var.* Hamïs Musait. 'Asīr, SW Saudi Arabia
Khānābād *123 E3* Kunduz, NE Afghanistan
Khān al Baghdādī *see* Al Baghdādī
Khandwa *134 D4* Madhya Pradesh, C India
Khanh Hung *see* Soc Trăng
Khaniá *see* Chaniá
Khanka, Lake *129 E2 var.* Hsing-K'ai Hu, Lake Hanka, *Chin.* Xingkai Hu, *Rus.* Ozero Khanka. *lake* China/ Russian Federation
Khanka, Ozero *see* Khanka, Lake
Khankendi *see* Xankändi
Khanthabouli *see* Savannakhét
Khanty-Mansiysk *114 C3 prev.* Ostyako-Voguls'k. Khanty-Mansiyskiy Avtonomnyy Okrug-Yugra, C Russian Federation
Khān Yūnis *119 A7 var.* Khān Yūnus. S Gaza Strip
Khān Yūnus *see* Khān Yūnis
Khanzi *see* Ghanzi
Kharagpur *135 F4* West Bengal, NE India
Kharbin *see* Harbin
Kharkiv *109 G2 Rus.* Khar'kov. Kharkivs'ka Oblast', NE Ukraine
Khar'kov *see* Kharkiv
Kharmanli *104 D3* Khaskovo, S Bulgaria
Khartoum *72 B4 var.* El Khartûm, Khartum. *country capital* (Sudan) Khartoum, C Sudan
Khartum *see* Khartoum
Khasavyurt *111 B8* Respublika Dagestan, SW Russian Federation
Khash, Dasht-e *122 D5 Eng.* Khash Desert. *desert* SW Afghanistan
Khash Desert *see* Khāsh, Dasht-e
Khashim Al Qirba/Khashm al Qirbah *see* Khashm el Girba
Khashm el Girba *72 C4 var.* Khashim Al Qirba, Khashm al Qirbah. Kassala, E Sudan
Khaskovo *104 D3* Khaskovo, S Bulgaria
Khaybar, Kowtal-e *see* Khyber Pass
Khaydarkan *123 F2 var.* Khaydarken. Batkenskaya Oblast', SW Kyrgyzstan
Khaydarken *see* Khaydarkan
Khazar, Baḥr-e/Khazar, Daryā-ye *see* Caspian Sea
Khelat *see* Kālat
Kherson *109 E4* Khersons'ka Oblast', S Ukraine
Kheta *115 E2 river* N Russian Federation
Khíos *see* Chíos
Khirbet el 'Aujā et Taḥtā *119 E7* E West Bank Asia
Khiva/Khiwa *see* Xiva
Khmel'nitskiy *see* Khmel 'nyts'kyy
Khmel 'nyts'kyy *108 C2 Rus.* Khmel'nitskiy; *prev.* Proskurov. Khmel'nyts'ka Oblast', W Ukraine
Khodasy *107 E6 Rus.* Khodosy. Mahilyowskaya Voblasts', E Belarus
Khodoriv *108 C2 Pol.* Chodorów, *Rus.* Khodorov. L'vivs'ka Oblast', NW Ukraine
Khodorov *see* Khodoriv
Khodosy *see* Khodasy
Khodzhent *see* Khujand
Khoi *see* Khvoy
Khojend *see* Khujand
Khokand *see* Qo'qon
Kholm *see* Khulm
Kholm *see* Chełm
Kholon *see* Holon
Khoms *see* Al Khums
Khong Sedone *see* Muang Khôngxédôn
Khon Kaen *136 D4 var.* Muang Khon Kaen. Khon Kaen, E Thailand
Khor *115 G4* Khabarovskiy Kray, SE Russian Federation
Khorat *see* Nakhon Ratchasima
Khorog *see* Khorugh
Khorugh *123 F3 Rus.* Khorog. S Tajikistan
Khōst *123 F4 prev.* Khowst. Khōst, E Afghanistan
Khotan *see* Hotan
Khouribga *70 B2* C Morocco
Khovd *see* Hovd
Khowst *see* Khōst
Khoy *see* Khvoy
Khoyniki *107 D8* Homyel'skaya Voblasts', SE Belarus
Khudzhand *see* Khujand
Khujand *123 E2 var.* Khodzhent, Khojend, *Rus.* Khudzhand; *prev.* Leninabad, *Taj.* Leninobod. N Tajikistan
Khulm *123 E3 var.* Kholm, Tashqurghan. Balkh, N Afghanistan
Khulna *135 G4* Khulna, SW Bangladesh
Khums *see* Al Khums
Khust *108 B3 var.* Husté, *Cz.* Chust, *Hung.* Huszt. Zakarpats'ka Oblast', W Ukraine
Khvoy *120 C2 var.* Khoi, Khoy. Āžarbāyjān-e Bākhtarī, NW Iran
Khyber Pass *134 C1 var.* Kowtal-e Khaybar. *pass* Afghanistan/Pakistan
Kiangmai *see* Chiang Mai
Kiang-ning *see* Nanjing
Kiangsi *see* Jiangxi
Kiangsu *see* Jiangsu
Kiáto *105 B6 prev.* Kiáton. Pelopónnisos, S Greece
Kiáton *see* Kiáto
Kiayi *see* Jiayi
Kibangou *77 B6* Niari, SW Congo
Kibombo *77 D6* Maniema, E Dem. Rep. Congo
Kıbrıs/Kıbrıs Cumhuriyeti *see* Cyprus
Kičevo *101 D6* SW FYR Macedonia
Kidderminster *89 D6* C England, United Kingdom
Kiel *94 B2* Schleswig-Holstein, N Germany
Kielce *98 D4 Rus.* Keltsy. Świętokrzyskie, C Poland
Kieler Bucht *94 B2 bay* N Germany
Kiev *see* Kyyiv
Kiev Reservoir *109 E1 Eng.* Kiev Reservoir, *Rus.* Kiyevskoye Vodokhranilishche. *reservoir* N Ukraine
Kiev Reservoir *see* Kyyivs'ke Vodoskhovyshche
Kiffa *74 C3* Assaba, S Mauritania
Kigali *73 B6 country capital* (Rwanda) C Rwanda
Kigoma *73 B7* Kigoma, W Tanzania
Kihnu *106 C2 var.* Kihnu Saar, *Ger.* Kühnö. *island* SW Estonia
Kihnu Saar *see* Kihnu
Kii-suido *131 C7 strait* S Japan
Kikinda *100 D3 Ger.* Grosskikinda, *Hung.* Nagykikinda; *prev.* Velika Kikinda. Vojvodina, N Serbia
Kikládhes *see* Kykládes
Kikwit *77 C6* Bandundu, W Dem. Rep. Congo
Kilien Mountains *see* Qilian Shan
Kilimane *see* Quelimane
Kilimanjaro *69 E5 region* E Tanzania
Kilimanjaro *73 C7 var.* Uhuru Peak. *volcano* NE Tanzania
Kilingi-Nõmme *106 D3 Ger.* Kurkund. Pärnumaa, SW Estonia
Kilis *116 D4* Kilis, S Turkey
Kiliya *108 D4 Rom.* Chilia-Nouă. Odes'ka Oblast', SW Ukraine
Kilkenny *89 B6 Ir.* Cill Chainnigh. Kilkenny, S Ireland
Kilkís *104 B3* Kentrikí Makedonía, N Greece
Killarney *89 A6 Ir.* Cill Airne. Kerry, SW Ireland
Killeen *49 G3* Texas, SW USA
Kilmain *see* Quelimane
Kilmarnock *88 C4* W Scotland, United Kingdom
Kilwa *see* Kilwa Kivinje
Kilwa Kivinje *73 C7 var.* Kilwa. Lindi, SE Tanzania
Kimberley *78 C4* Northern Cape, C South Africa
Kimberley Plateau *146 C3 plateau* Western Australia
Kimch'aek *129 E3 prev.* Sŏngjin. E North Korea
Kími *see* Kými
Kinabalu, Gunung *138 D3 mountain* East Malaysia
Kindersley *37 F5* Saskatchewan, S Canada
Kindia *74 C4* Guinée-Maritime, SW Guinea
Kindley Field *42 A4 air base* E Bermuda
Kindu *77 D6 prev.* Kindu-Port-Empain. Maniema, C Dem. Rep. Congo
Kindu-Port-Empain *see* Kindu
Kineshma *111 C5* Ivanovskaya Oblast', W Russian Federation
King Abdullah Economic City *121 A5* Makkah, W Saudi Arabia
King Charles Islands *see* Kong Karls Land
King Christian IX Land *see* Kong Christian IX Land
King Frederik VI Coast *see* Kong Frederik VI Kyst
King Frederik VIII Land *see* Kong Frederik VIII Land
King Island *149 B8 island* Tasmania, SE Australia
King Island *see* Kadan Kyun
Kingissepp *see* Kuressaare
Kingman *48 A1* Arizona, SW USA
Kingman Reef *145 E2 US territory* C Pacific Ocean
Kingsford Smith *148 E2* (Sydney) New South Wales, SE Australia
King's Lynn *89 E6 var.* Bishop's Lynn, Kings Lynn, Lynn, Lynn Regis. E England, United Kingdom
Kings Lynn *see* King's Lynn
King Sound *146 B3 sound* Western Australia
Kingsport *43 E1* Tennessee, S USA
Kingston *54 B5 country capital* (Jamaica) E Jamaica
Kingston *38 D5* Ontario, SE Canada
Kingston *41 F3* New York, NE USA

Kingston upon Hull 89 D5 var. Hull. E England, United Kingdom
Kingston upon Thames 89 A8 SE England, United Kingdom
Kingstown 55 H4 country capital (Saint Vincent and the Grenadines) Saint Vincent, Saint Vincent and the Grenadines
Kingstown see Dún Laoghaire
Kingsville 49 G5 Texas, SW USA
King William Island 37 F3 island Nunavut, N Canada
Kinneret, Yam see Tiberias, Lake
Kinrooi 87 D5 Limburg, NE Belgium
Kinshasa 77 B6 prev. Léopoldville. country capital (Dem. Rep. Congo) Kinshasa, W Dem. Rep. Congo
Kintyre 88 B4 peninsula W Scotland, United Kingdom
Kinyeti 73 B5 mountain S South Sudan
Kiparissía see Kyparissía
Kipili 73 B7 Rukwa, W Tanzania
Kipushi 77 D8 Katanga, SE Dem. Rep. Congo
Kirdzhali see Kŭrdzhali
Kirghizia see Kyrgyzstan
Kirghiz Range 123 F2 Rus. Kirgizskiy Khrebet; prev. Alexander Range. mountain range Kazakhstan/ Kyrgyzstan
Kirghiz SSR see Kyrgyzstan
Kirghiz Steppe see Saryarka
Kirgizskaya SSR see Kyrgyzstan
Kirgizskiy Khrebet see Kirghiz Range
Kiriath-Arba see Hebron
Kiribati 145 F2 off. Republic of Kiribati. country C Pacific Ocean

KIRIBATI
Australasia & Oceania

Official name Republic of Kiribati
Formation 1979 / 1979
Capital Tarawa Atoll
Population 103,248 / 377 people per sq mile (145 people per sq km)
Total area 277 sq. miles (717 sq. km)
Languages English*, Kiribati
Religions Roman Catholic 55%, Kiribati Protestant Church 36%, Other 9%
Ethnic mix Micronesian 99%, Other 1%
Government Presidential system
Currency Australian dollar = 100 cents
Literacy rate 99%
Calorie consumption 3022 kilocalories

Kiribati, Republic of see Kiribati
Kırıkhan 116 D4 Hatay, S Turkey
Kırıkkale 116 C3 province C Turkey
Kirin see Jilin
Kirinyaga 73 C6 prev. Mount Kenya. volcano C Kenya
Kirishi 110 B4 var. Kirisi. Leningradskaya Oblast', NW Russian Federation
Kirisi see Kirishi
Kiritimati 145 G2 prev. Christmas Island. atoll Line Islands, E Kiribati
Kirkenes 84 E2 Fin. Kirkkoniemi. Finnmark, N Norway
Kirk-Kilissa see Kırklareli
Kirkkoniemi see Kirkenes
Kirkland Lake 38 D4 Ontario, S Canada
Kırklareli 116 A2 prev. Kirk-Kilissa. Kırklareli, NW Turkey
Kirkpatrick, Mount 154 B3 mountain Antarctica
Kirksville 45 G4 Missouri, C USA
Kirkūk 120 B3 var. Karkūk, Kerkuk. At Ta'mím, N Iraq
Kirkwall 88 C2 NE Scotland, United Kingdom
Kirkwood 45 G4 Missouri, C USA
Kir Moab/Kir of Moab see Al Karak
Kirov 111 C5 prev. Vyatka. Kirovskaya Oblast', NW Russian Federation
Kirovabad see Gäncä
Kirovakan see Vanadzor
Kirovo-Chepetsk 111 D5 Kirovskaya Oblast', NW Russian Federation
Kirovohrad 109 E3 Rus. Kirovograd; prev. Kirovo, Yelizavetgrad, Zinov'yevsk. Kirovohrads'ka Oblast', C Ukraine
Kirovo/Kirovograd see Kirovohrad
Kīrthar Range 134 B3 mountain range S Pakistan
Kiruna 84 C3 Lapp. Giron. Norrbotten, N Sweden
Kirun/Kirun' see Jilong
Kisalföld see Little Alföld
Kisangani 77 D5 prev. Stanleyville. Orientale, NE Dem. Rep. Congo
Kishinev see Chişinău
Kislovodsk 111 B7 Stavropol'skiy Kray, SW Russian Federation
Kismaayo 73 D6 var. Chisimayu, Kismayu, It. Chisimaio. Jubbada Hoose, S Somalia
Kismayu see Kismaayo
Kíssamos 105 C7 prev. Kastélli. Kríti, Greece, E Mediterranean Sea
Kissidougou 74 C4 Guinée-Forestière, S Guinea
Kissimmee, Lake 43 E4 lake Florida, SE USA
Kistna see Krishna
Kisumu 73 C6 prev. Port Florence. Nyanza, W Kenya
Kisvárda 99 E6 Ger. Kleinwardein. Szabolcs-Szatmár-Bereg, E Hungary
Kita 74 D3 Kayes, W Mali
Kitab see Kitob
Kitakyūshū 131 A7 var. Kitakyûsyû. Fukuoka, Kyūshū, SW Japan
Kitakyûsyû see Kitakyūshū
Kitami 130 D2 Hokkaidō, NE Japan
Kitchener 38 C5 Ontario, S Canada
Kíthnos see Kýthnos
Kitimat 36 D4 British Columbia, SW Canada
Kitinen 84 D3 river N Finland
Kitob 123 E3 Rus. Kitab. Qashqadaryo Viloyati, S Uzbekistan
Kitwe 78 D2 var. Kitwe-Nkana. Copperbelt, C Zambia
Kitwe-Nkana see Kitwe
Kitzbüheler Alpen 95 C7 mountain range W Austria
Kivalina 36 C2 Alaska, USA
Kivalo 84 D3 ridge C Finland
Kivertsi 108 C1 Pol. Kiwerce, Rus. Kivertsy. Volyns'ka Oblast', NW Ukraine
Kivertsy see Kivertsi
Kivu, Lac see Kivu, Lake
Kivu, Lake 77 E6 Fr. Lac Kivu. lake Rwanda/Dem. Rep. Congo
Kiwerce see Kivertsi
Kiyev see Kyyiv
Kiyevskoye Vodokhranilishche see Kyyivs'ke Vodoskhovyshche
Kızıl Irmak 116 C3 river C Turkey
Kizil Kum see Kyzyl Kum
Kizyl-Arvat see Serdar
Kjølen see Kölen
Kladno 99 A5 Středočeský, NW Czech Republic
Klagenfurt 95 D7 Slvn. Celovec. Kärnten, S Austria
Klaipėda 106 B3 Ger. Memel. Klaipeda, NW Lithuania
Klamath Falls 46 B4 Oregon, NW USA
Klamath Mountains 46 A4 mountain range California/Oregon, W USA
Klang 138 B3 var. Kelang; prev. Port Swettenham. Selangor, Peninsular Malaysia
Klarälven 85 B6 river Norway/Sweden
Klatovy 99 A5 Ger. Klattau. Plzeňský Kraj, W Czech Republic
Klattau see Klatovy
Klausenburg see Cluj-Napoca
Klazienaveen 86 E2 Drenthe, NE Netherlands
Kleines Ungarisches Tiefland see Little Alföld
Klein Karas 78 B4 Karas, S Namibia
Kleinwardein see Kisvárda
Kleisoúra 105 A5 Ípeiros, W Greece
Klerksdorp 78 D4 North-West, N South Africa
Klimavichy 107 E7 Rus. Klimovichi. Mahilyowskaya Voblasts', E Belarus
Klimovichi see Klimavichy
Klintsy 111 A5 Bryanskaya Oblast', W Russian Federation
Klisura 104 C2 Plovdiv, C Bulgaria
Ključ 100 B3 Federacija Bosne I Hercegovine, NW Bosnia and Herzegovina
Kłobuck 98 C4 Śląskie, S Poland
Klosters 95 B7 Graubünden, SE Switzerland
Kluang see Keluang
Kluczbork 98 C4 Ger. Kreuzburg, Kreuzburg in Oberschlesien. Opolskie, S Poland
Klyuchevskaya Sopka, Vulkan 115 H3 volcano E Russian Federation
Knin 100 B4 Šibenik-Knin, S Croatia
Knjaževac 100 E4 Serbia, E Serbia
Knokke-Heist 87 A5 West-Vlaanderen, NW Belgium
Knoxville 42 D1 Tennessee, S USA
Knud Rasmussen Land 82 D1 physical region N Greenland
Kobdo see Hovd
Kōbe 131 C6 Hyōgo, Honshū, SW Japan
København 85 B7 Eng. Copenhagen; anc. Hafnia. country capital (Denmark) Sjælland, København, E Denmark
Kobenni 74 D3 Hodh el Gharbi, S Mauritania
Koblenz 95 A5 prev. Coblenz, Fr. Coblence; anc. Confluentes. Rheinland-Pfalz, W Germany
Kobrin see Kobryn
Kobryn 107 A6 Rus. Kobrin. Brestskaya Voblasts', SW Belarus
Kobuleti 117 F2 prev. K'obulet'i. W Georgia
K'obulet'i see Kobuleti
Kočani 101 E6 NE FYR Macedonia
Kočevje 95 D8 Ger. Gottschee. S Slovenia
Koch Bihār 135 G3 West Bengal, NE India
Kochchi see Kochi
Kochi 132 C3 var. Cochin, Kochchi. Kerela SW India
Kōchi 131 B7 var. Kôti. Kōchi, Shikoku, SW Japan
Kochiu see Gejiu
Kodiak 36 C3 Kodiak Island, Alaska, USA
Kodiak Island 36 C3 island Alaska, USA
Koedoes see Kudus
Koeln see Köln
Koepang see Kupang
Ko-erh-mu see Golmud
Koetai see Mahakam, Sungai
Koetaradja see Banda Aceh
Kōfu 131 D5 var. Kôhu. Yamanashi, Honshū, S Japan
Kogarah 148 E2 New South Wales, E Australia
Kogon 122 D2 Rus. Kagan. Buxoro Viloyati, C Uzbekistan
Kőhalom see Rupea
Kohīma 135 H3 state capital Nāgāland, E India
Koh I Noh see Büyükağrı Dağı
Kohtla-Järve 106 E2 Ida-Virumaa, NE Estonia
Kôhu see Kōfu
Kokand see Qo'qon
Kokchetav see Kokshetau
Kokkola 84 D4 Swe. Karleby; prev. Swe. Gamlakarleby. Länsi-Suomi, W Finland
Koko 75 F4 Kebbi, W Nigeria
Kokomo 40 C4 Indiana, N USA
Koko Nor see Qinghai Hu, China
Koko Nor see Qinghai, China
Kokrines 36 C2 Alaska, USA
Kokshaal-Tau 123 G2 Rus. Khrebet Kakshaal-Too. mountain range China/ Kyrgyzstan
Kokshetau 114 C4 Kaz. Kökshetaū; prev. Kokchetav. Kokshetau, N Kazakhstan
Kökshetaū see Kokshetau
Koksijde 87 A5 West-Vlaanderen, W Belgium
Koksoak 38 D2 river Québec, E Canada
Kokstad 78 D5 KwaZulu/Natal, E South Africa
Kolaka 139 E4 Sulawesi, C Indonesia
K'o-la-ma-i see Karamay
Kola Peninsula 110 C2 Eng. Kola Peninsula. peninsula NW Russian Federation
Kola Peninsula see Kol'skiy Poluostrov
Kolari 84 D3 Lappi, NW Finland
Kolárovo 99 C6 Ger. Gutta; prev. Guta, Hung. Gúta. Nitriansky Kraj, SW Slovakia
Kolberg see Kołobrzeg
Kolda 74 C3 S Senegal
Kolding 85 A7 Syddanmark, C Denmark
Kölen 81 E1 Nor. Kjølen. mountain range Norway/Sweden
Kolguyev, Ostrov 110 C2 island NW Russian Federation
Kolhāpur 132 B1 Mahārāshtra, SW India
Kolhumadulu 132 A5 var. Thaa Atoll. atoll S Maldives
Kolín 99 B5 Ger. Kolin. Střední Čechy, C Czech Republic
Kolka 106 C2 NW Latvia
Kolkasrags 106 C2 prev. Eng. Cape Domesnes. headland NW Latvia
Kolkata 135 G4 prev. Calcutta. West Bengal, N India
Kollam 132 C3 var. Quilon. Kerala, SW India
Kolmar see Colmar
Köln 94 A4 var. Koeln, Eng./Fr. Cologn[e] prev. Cöln; anc. Colonia Agrippina, Oppidum Ubiorum. Nordrhein-Westfalen, W Germany
Koło 98 C3 Wielkopolskie, C Poland
Kołobrzeg 98 B2 Ger. Kolberg. Zachodnio-pomorskie, NW Poland
Kolokani 74 D3 Koulikoro, W Mali
Kolomea see Kolomyya
Kolomna 111 B5 Moskovskaya Oblast', W Russian Federation
Kolomyya 108 C3 Ger. Kolomea. Ivan[o]-Frankivs'ka Oblast', W Ukraine
Kolosjoki see Nikel'
Kolozsvár see Cluj-Napoca
Kolpa 100 A2 Ger. Kulpa, SCr. Kupa. river Croatia/Slovenia
Kolpino 110 B4 Leningradskaya Oblast', NW Russian Federation
Kólpos Mórfu see Güzelyurt Körfezi
Kolwezi 77 D7 Katanga, S Dem. Rep. Congo
Kolyma 115 G2 river NE Russian Federation
Komatsu 131 C5 var. Komatu. Ishikawa, Honshū, SW Japan
Komatu see Komatsu
Kommunizm, Qullai see Ismoili Somon[i,] Qullai
Komoé 75 E4 var. Komoé Fleuve. river E Côte d'Ivoire
Komoé Fleuve see Komoé
Komotau see Chomutov
Komotiní 104 D3 var. Gümüljina, Turk. Gümülcine. Anatolikí Makedonía kai Thráki, NE Greece
Kompong see Kâmpóng Chhnăng
Kompong Cham see Kâmpóng Cham
Kompong Som see Sihanoukville
Kompong Speu see Kâmpóng Spoe
Komrat see Comrat
Komsomolets, Ostrov 115 E1 island Severnaya Zemlya, N Russian Federation
Komsomol'sk-na-Amure 115 G4 Khabarovskiy Kray, SE Russian Federation
Kondolovo 104 E3 Burgas, E Bulgaria
Kondopoga 110 B3 Respublika Kareliya, NW Russian Federation
Kondoz see Kunduz
Köneürgenç 122 C2 var. Köneürgench, Rus. Këneurgench; prev. Kunya-Urgench. Daşoguz Welaýaty, N Turkmenistan
Kong Christian IX Land 82 D4 Eng. King Christian IX Land. physical regio[n] SE Greenland
Kong Frederik IX Land 82 C3 physical region SW Greenland
Kong Frederik VIII Land 83 E2 Eng. King Frederik VIII Land. physical region NE Greenland
Kong Frederik VI Kyst 82 C4 Eng. King Frederik VI Coast. physical region SE Greenland
Kong Karls Land 83 G2 Eng. King Charles Islands. island group SE Svalbard
Kongo see Congo (river)
Kongolo 77 D6 Katanga, E Dem. Rep. Congo
Kongor 73 B5 Jonglei, E South Sudan
Kong Oscar Fjord 83 E3 fjord E Greenland
Kongsberg 85 B6 Buskerud, S Norway
Kông, Tônlé 137 E5 var. Xê Kong. river Cambodia/Laos
Kong, Xê see Kông, Tônlé
Königgrätz see Hradec Králové
Königshütte see Chorzów
Konin 98 C3 Ger. Kuhnau. Weilkopolskie, C Poland
Koninkrijk der Nederlanden see Netherlands
Konispol 101 C7 var. Konispoli. Vlorë, S Albania
Konispoli see Konispol
Kónitsa 104 A4 Ípeiros, W Greece

nitz *see* Chojnice
onjic *100 C4* Federacija Bosne I Hercegovine, S Bosnia and Herzegovina
onosha *110 C4* Arkhangel'skaya Oblast', NW Russian Federation
onotop *109 F1* Sums'ka Oblast', NE Ukraine
onstantinovka *see* Kostyantynivka
onstanz *95 B7 var.* Constanz, *Eng.* Constance, *hist.* Kostnitz; *anc.* Constantia. Baden-Württemberg, S Germany
onstanza *see* Constanța
onya *116 C4 var.* Konieh, *prev.* Konia; *anc.* Iconium. Konya, C Turkey
opaonik *101 D5 mountain range* S Serbia
opar *see* Koper
oper *95 D8 It.* Capodistria; *prev.* Kopar. SW Slovenia
öpetdag Gershi *122 C3 mountain range* Iran/Turkmenistan
öpetdag Gershi/Kopetdag, Khrebet *see* Koppeh Dāgh
oppeh Dagh *120 D2 Rus.* Khrebet Kopetdag, *Turkm.* Köpetdag Gershi. *mountain range* Iran/Turkmenistan
opreinitz *see* Koprivnica
oprivnica *100 B2 Ger.* Kopreinitz, *Hung.* Kaproncza. Koprivnica-Križevci, N Croatia
öprülü *see* Veles
optsevichi *see* Kaptsevichy
opyl' *see* Kapyl'
orat *see* Nakhon Ratchasima
orat Plateau *136 D4 plateau* E Thailand
orba *135 E4* Chhattīsgarh, C India
orça *see* Korçë
orçë *101 D6 var.* Korça, *Gk.* Korytsa, *It.* Corriza; *prev.* Koritsa. Korçë, SE Albania
orčula *100 B4 It.* Curzola; *anc.* Corcyra Nigra. *island* S Croatia
orea Bay *127 G3 bay* China/North Korea
orea, Democratic People's Republic of *see* North Korea
orea, Republic of *see* South Korea
orea Strait *131 A7 Jap.* Chōsen-kaikyō, *Kor.* Taehan-haehyŏp. *channel* Japan/South Korea
orhogo *74 D4* N Côte d'Ivoire
órinthos *105 B6 anc.* Corinthus *Eng.* Corinth. Pelopónnisos, S Greece
oritsa *see* Korçë
ōriyama *131 D5* Fukushima, Honshū, C Japan
orla *126 C3 Chin.* K'u-erh-lo. Xinjiang Uygur Zizhiqu, NW China
örmend *99 B7* Vas, W Hungary
oróni *105 B6* Pelopónnisos, S Greece
oror *144 A2* (Palau) Oreor, N Palau
őrös *see* Križevci
orosten' *108 D1* Zhytomyrs'ka Oblast', NW Ukraine
oro Toro *76 C2* Borkou-Ennedi-Tibesti, N Chad
orsovka *see* Kārsava
ortrijk *87 A6 Fr.* Courtrai. West-Vlaanderen, W Belgium
oryak Range *115 H2 var.* Koryakskiy Khrebet, *Eng.* Koryak Range. *mountain range* NE Russian Federation
oryak Range *see* Koryakskoy e Nagor'ye
oryakskiy Khrebet *see* Koryakskoye Nagor'ye
oryazhma *110 C4* Arkhangel'skaya Oblast', NW Russian Federation
orytsa *see* Korçë
os *105 E6* Kos, Dodekánisa, Greece, Aegean Sea
os *105 E6 It.* Coo; *anc.* Cos. *island* Dodekánisa, Greece, Aegean Sea
o-saki *131 A7 headland* Nagasaki, Tsushima, SW Japan
ościan *98 B4 Ger.* Kosten. Wielkopolskie, C Poland
ościerzyna *98 C2* Pomorskie, NW Poland
osciusko, Mount *see* Kosciuszko, Mount
osciuszko, Mount *149 C7 prev.* Mount Kosciusko. *mountain* New South Wales, SE Australia
o-shih *see* Kashi
Koshikijima-retto *131 A8 var.* Kosikizima Rettô. *island group* SW Japan
Kōshū *see* Gwangju
Košice *99 D6 Ger.* Kaschau, *Hung.* Kassa. Košický Kraj, E Slovakia
Kosikizima Rettô *see* Koshikijima-rettō
Köslin *see* Koszalin
Koson *123 E3 Rus.* Kasan. Qashqadaryo Viloyati, S Uzbekistan
Kosovo *101 D5 prev.* Autonomous Province of Kosovo and Metohija. *country* SE Europe

KOSOVO (not fully recognized)
Southeast Europe

Official name Republic of Kosovo
Formation 2008 / 2008
Capital Prishtinë
Population 1.8 million / 427 people per sq mile (165 people per sq km)
Total area 4212 sq miles (10,908 sq km)
Languages Albanian*, Serbian*, Bosniak, Gorani, Roma, Turkish
Religions Muslim 92%, Roman Catholic 4%, Orthodox Christian 4%
Ethnic mix Albanian 92%, Serb 4%, Bosniak and Gorani 2%, Turkish 1%, Roma 1%
Government Parliamentary system
Currency Euro = 100 cents
Literacy rate 92%
Calorie consumption Not available

Kosovo and Metohija, Autonomous Province of *see* Kosovo
Kosovo Polje *see* Fushë Kosovë
Kosovska Mitrovica *see* Mitrovicë
Kosrae *144 C2 prev.* Kusaie. *island* Caroline Islands, E Micronesia
Kossou, Lac de *74 D5 lake* C Côte d'Ivoire
Kostanay *114 C4 var.* Kustanay, *Kaz.* Qostanay. Kostanay, N Kazakhstan
Kosten *see* Kościan
Kostenets *104 C2 prev.* Georgi Dimitrov. Sofiya, W Bulgaria
Kostnitz *see* Konstanz
Kostroma *110 B4* Kostromskaya Oblast', NW Russian Federation
Kostyantynivka *109 G3 Rus.* Konstantinovka. Donets'ka Oblast', SE Ukraine
Kostyukovichi *see* Kastsyukovichy
Kostyukovka *see* Kastsyukowka
Koszalin *98 B2 Ger.* Köslin. Zachodnio-pomorskie, NW Poland
Kota *134 D3 prev.* Kotah. Rājasthān, N India
Kota Baharu *see* Kota Bharu
Kota Bahru *see* Kota Bharu
Kotabaru *see* Jayapura
Kota Bharu *138 B3 var.* Kota Baharu, Kota Bahru. Kelantan, Peninsular Malaysia
Kotaboemi *see* Kotabumi
Kotabumi *138 B4 prev.* Kotaboemi. Sumatera, W Indonesia
Kotah *see* Kota
Kota Kinabalu *138 D3 prev.* Jesselton. Sabah, East Malaysia
Kotel'nyy, Ostrov *115 E2 island* Novosibirskiye Ostrova, N Russian Federation
Kotka *85 E5* Etelä-Suomi, S Finland
Kotlas *110 C4* Arkhangel'skaya Oblast', NW Russian Federation
Kotonu *see* Cotonou
Kotor *101 C5 It.* Cattaro. SW Montenegro
Kotovs'k *108 D3 Rus.* Kotovsk. Odes'ka Oblast', SW Ukraine
Kotovsk *see* Hîncești
Kottbus *see* Cottbus
Kotto *76 D4 river* Central African Republic/Dem. Rep. Congo
Kotuy *115 E2 river* N Russian Federation
Koudougou *75 E4* C Burkina Faso
Koulamoutou *77 B6* Ogooué-Lolo, C Gabon
Koulikoro *74 D3* Koulikoro, SW Mali
Koumra *76 C4* Moyen-Chari, S Chad
Kourou *59 H3* N French Guiana
Kousseir *see* Al Quşayr
Kousséri *76 B3 prev.* Fort-Foureau. Extrême-Nord, NE Cameroon
Koutiala *74 D4* Sikasso, S Mali
Kouvola *85 E5* Etelä-Suomi, S Finland
Kovel' *108 C1 Pol.* Kowel. Volyns'ka Oblast', NW Ukraine
Kovno *see* Kaunas
Koweit *see* Kuwait
Kowel *see* Kovel'
Kowloon *128 A2* Hong Kong, S China
Kowno *see* Kaunas
Kozáni *104 B4* Dytikí Makedonía, N Greece
Kozara *100 B3 mountain range* NW Bosnia and Herzegovina
Kozarska Dubica *see* Bosanska Dubica
Kozhikode *132 C2 var.* Calicut. Kerala, SW India
Kozu-shima *131 D6 island* E Japan
Kozyatyn *108 D2 Rus.* Kazatin. Vinnyts'ka Oblast', C Ukraine
Kpalimé *75 E5 var.* Palimé. SW Togo
Krâchéh *137 D6 prev.* Kratie. Krâchéh, E Cambodia
Kragujevac *100 D4* Serbia, C Serbia
Krainburg *see* Kranj
Kra, Isthmus of *137 B6 isthmus* Malaysia/Thailand
Krakau *see* Kraków
Kraków *99 D5 Eng.* Cracow, *Ger.* Krakau; *anc.* Cracovia. Małopolskie, S Poland
Krâlănh *137 D5* Siĕmréab, NW Cambodia
Kralendijk *55 F5 dependent territory capital* (Bonaire) Lesser Antilles, S Caribbean Sea
Kraljevo *100 D4 prev.* Rankovićevo. Serbia, C Serbia
Kramators'k *109 G3 Rus.* Kramatorsk. Donets'ka Oblast', SE Ukraine
Kramatorsk *see* Kramators'k
Kramfors *85 C5* Västernorrland, C Sweden
Kranéa *see* Kraniá
Kraniá *104 B4 var.* Kranéa. Dytikí Makedonía, N Greece
Kranj *95 D7 Ger.* Krainburg. N Slovenia
Kranz *see* Zelenogradsk
Krāslava *106 D4* SE Latvia
Krasnaye *107 C5 Rus.* Krasnoye. Minskaya Voblasts', C Belarus
Krasnoarmeysk *111 C6* Saratovskaya Oblast', W Russian Federation
Krasnodar *111 A7 prev.* Ekaterinodar, Yekaterinodar. Krasnodarskiy Kray, SW Russian Federation
Krasnodon *109 H3* Luhans'ka Oblast', E Ukraine
Krasnogor *see* Kallaste
Krasnogvardeyskoye *see* Krasnohvardiys'ke
Krasnohvardiys'ke *109 F4 Rus.* Krasnogvardeyskoye. Avtonomna Respublika Krym, S Ukraine
Krasnokamensk *115 F4* Zabaykal'skiy Kray, S Russian Federation
Krasnokamsk *111 D5* Permskiy Kray, W Russian Federation
Krasnoperekops'k *109 F4 Rus.* Krasnoperekopsk. Avtonomna Respublika Krym, S Ukraine
Krasnoperekopsk *see* Krasnoperekops'k
Krasnostav *see* Krasnystaw
Krasnovodsk *see* Türkmenbaşy
Krasnovodskiy Zaliv *see* Türkmenbasy Aylagy
Krasnowodsk Aylagy *see* Türkmenbasy Aylagy
Krasnoyarsk *114 D4* Krasnoyarskiy Kray, S Russian Federation
Krasnoye *see* Krasnaye
Krasnystaw *98 E4 Rus.* Krasnostav. Lubelskie, SE Poland
Krasnyy Kut *111 C6* Saratovskaya Oblast', W Russian Federation
Krasnyy Luch *109 H3 prev.* Krindachevka. Luhans'ka Oblast', E Ukraine
Kratie *see* Krâchéh
Krâvanh, Chuŏr Phnum *137 C6 Eng.* Cardamom Mountains, *Fr.* Chaîne des Cardamomes. *mountain range* W Cambodia
Krefeld *94 A4* Nordrhein-Westfalen, W Germany
Kreisstadt *see* Krosno Odrzańskie
Kremenchug *see* Kremenchuk
Kremenchugskoye Vodokhranilishche/Kremenchuk Reservoir *see* Kremenchuts'ke Vodoskhovyshche
Kremenchuk *109 F2 Rus.* Kremenchug. Poltavs'ka Oblast', NE Ukraine
Kremenchuk Reservoir *109 F2 Eng.* Kremenchuk Reservoir, *Rus.* Kremenchugskoye Vodokhranilishche. *reservoir* C Ukraine
Kremenets' *108 C2 Pol.* Krzemieniec, *Rus.* Kremenets. Ternopil's'ka Oblast', W Ukraine
Kremennaya *see* Kreminna
Kreminna *109 G2 Rus.* Kremennaya. Luhans'ka Oblast', E Ukraine
Kresena *see* Kresna
Kresna *104 C3 var.* Kresena. Blagoevgrad, SW Bulgaria
Kretikon Delagos *see* Kritikó Pélagos
Kretinga *106 B3 Ger.* Krottingen. Klaipėda, NW Lithuania
Kreutz *see* Cristuru Secuiesc
Kreuz *see* Križevci, Croatia
Kreuz *see* Risti, Estonia
Kreuzburg/Kreuzburg in Oberschlesien *see* Kluczbork
Krichëv *see* Krychaw
Krievija *see* Russian Federation
Krindachevka *see* Krasnyy Luch
Krishna *132 C1 prev.* Kistna. *river* C India
Krishnagiri *132 C2* Tamil Nādu, SE India
Kristiania *see* Oslo
Kristiansand *85 A6 var.* Christiansand. Vest-Agder, S Norway
Kristianstad *85 B7* Skåne, S Sweden
Kristiansund *84 A4 var.* Christiansund. Møre og Romsdal, S Norway
Krivoy Rog *see* Kryvyy Rih
Križevci *100 B2 Ger.* Kreuz, *Hung.* Kőrös. Varaždin, NE Croatia
Krk *100 A3 It.* Veglia; *anc.* Curieta. *island* NW Croatia
Kroatien *see* Croatia
Krolevets' *109 F1 Rus.* Krolevets. Sums'ka Oblast', NE Ukraine
Krolevets *see* Krolevets'
Królewska Huta *see* Chorzów
Kronach *95 C5* Bayern, E Germany
Kronstadt *see* Brașov
Kroonstad *78 D4* Free State, C South Africa
Kropotkin *111 A7* Krasnodarskiy Kray, SW Russian Federation
Krosno *99 D5 Ger.* Krossen. Podkarpackie, SE Poland
Krosno Odrzańskie *98 B3 Ger.* Crossen, Kreisstadt. Lubuskie, W Poland
Krossen *see* Krosno
Krottingen *see* Kretinga
Krško *95 E8 Ger.* Gurkfeld; *prev.* Videm-Krško. E Slovenia
Krugloye *see* Kruhlaye
Kruhlaye *107 D6 Rus.* Krugloye. Mahilyowskaya Voblasts', E Belarus
Kruja *see* Krujë
Krujë *101 C6 var.* Kruja, *It.* Croia. Durrës, C Albania
Krummau *see* Český Krumlov
Krung Thep, Ao *137 C5 var.* Bight of Bangkok. *bay* S Thailand
Krung Thep Mahanakhon *see* Ao Krung Thep
Krupki *107 D6* Minskaya Voblasts', C Belarus
Krušné Hory *see* Erzgebirge
Krychaw *107 E7 Rus.* Krichëv. Mahilyowskaya Voblasts', E Belarus
Kryms'ki Hory *109 F5 mountain range* S Ukraine
Kryms'kyy Pivostriv *109 F5 Eng.* Crimea. *peninsula* S Ukraine
Krynica *99 D5 Ger.* Tannenhof. Małopolskie, S Poland
Kryve Ozero *109 E3* Odes'ka Oblast', SW Ukraine
Kryvyy Rih *109 F3 Rus.* Krivoy Rog. Dnipropetrovs'ka Oblast', SE Ukraine
Krzemieniec *see* Kremenets'
Ksar al Kabir *see* Ksar-el-Kebir
Ksar al Soule *see* Er-Rachidia
Ksar-el-Kebir *70 C2 var.* Alcázar, Ksar al Kabir, Ksar-el-Kébir, *Ar.* Al-Kasr al-Kebir, Al-Qsar al-Kbir, *Sp.* Alcazarquivir. NW Morocco
Ksar-el-Kébir *see* Ksar-el-Kebir
Kuala Dungun *see* Dungun
Kuala Lumpur *138 B3 country capital* (Malaysia) Kuala Lumpur, Peninsular Malaysia

Kuala Terengganu *138 B3 var.* Kuala Trengganu. Terengganu, Peninsular Malaysia
Kualatungkal *138 B4* Sumatera, W Indonesia
Kuang-chou *see* Guangzhou
Kuang-hsi *see* Guangxi Zhuangzu Zizhiqu
Kuang-tung *see* Guangdong
Kuang-yuan *see* Guangyuan
Kuantan *138 B3* Pahang, Peninsular Malaysia
Kuba *see* Quba
Kuban' *109 G5 var.* Hypanis. *river* SW Russian Federation
Kubango *see* Cubango/Okavango
Kuching *138 C3 prev.* Sarawak. Sarawak, East Malaysia
Kŭchnay Darwāshān *122 D5 prev.* Kŭchnay Darweyshān. Helmand, S Afghanistan
Kŭchnay Darweyshān *see* Kŭchnay Darwāshān
Kuçova *see* Kuçovë
Kuçovë *101 C6 var.* Kuçova; *prev.* Qyteti Stalin. Berat, C Albania
Kudara *see* Ghŭdara
Kudus *138 C5 prev.* Koedoes. Jawa, C Indonesia
Kuei-lin *see* Guilin
Kuei-Yang/Kuei-yang *see* Guiyang
K'u-erh-lo *see* Korla
Kueyang *see* Guiyang
Kugaaruk *37 G3 prev.* Pelly Bay. Nunavut, N Canada
Kugluktuk *53 E3 var.* Qurlurtuuq; *prev.* Coppermine. Nunavut, NW Canada
Kuhmo *84 E4* Oulu, E Finland
Kuhnau *see* Konin
Kühnö *see* Kihnu
Kuibyshev *see* Kuybyshevskoye Vodokhranilishche
Kuito *78 B2 Port.* Silva Porto. Bié, C Angola
Kuji *130 D3 var.* Kuzi. Iwate, Honshū, C Japan
Kukës *101 D5 var.* Kukësi. Kukës, NE Albania
Kukësi *see* Kukës
Kukong *see* Shaoguan
Kukukhoto *see* Hohhot
Kula Kangri *135 G3 var.* Kulhakangri. *mountain* Bhutan/China
Kuldīga *106 B3 Ger.* Goldingen. W Latvia
Kuldja *see* Yining
Kulhakangri *see* Kula Kangri
Kullorsuaq *82 D2 var.* Kuvdlorssuak. Kitaa, C Greenland
Kulm *see* Chełmno
Kulmsee *see* Chełmża
Kŭlob *123 F3 Rus.* Kulyab. SW Tajikistan
Kulpa *see* Kolpa
Kulu *116 C3* Konya, W Turkey
Kulunda Steppe *see* Ravnina Kulyndy
Kulundinskaya Ravnina *see* Ravnina Kulyndy
Kulyab *see* Kŭlob
Kum *see* Qom
Kuma *111 B7 river* SW Russian Federation
Kumamoto *131 A7* Kumamoto, Kyūshū, SW Japan
Kumanova *see* Kumanovo
Kumanovo *101 E5 Turk.* Kumanova. N Macedonia
Kumasi *75 E5 prev.* Coomassie. C Ghana
Kumayri *see* Gyumri
Kumba *77 A5* Sud-Ouest, W Cameroon
Kumertau *111 D6* Respublika Bashkortostan, W Russian Federation
Kumillā *see* Comilla
Kumo *75 G4* Gombe, E Nigeria
Kumon Range *136 B2 mountain range* N Myanmar (Burma)
Kumul *see* Hami
Kunashiri *see* Kunashir, Ostrov
Kunashir, Ostrov *130 E1 var.* Kunashiri. *island* Kuril'skiye Ostrova, SE Russian Federation
Kunda *106 E2* Lääne-Virumaa, NE Estonia
Kunduz *123 E3 prev.* Kondoz. *province* NE Afghanistan
Kunene *69 C6 var.* Kunene. *river* Angola/Namibia
Kunene *see* Cunene
Kungsbacka *85 B7* Halland, S Sweden
Kungur *111 D5* Permskiy Kray, NW Russian Federation
Kunlun Mountains *see* Kunlun Shan
Kunlun Shan *126 B4 Eng.* Kunlun Mountains. *mountain range* NW China
Kunming *128 B6 var.* K'un-ming; *prev.* Yunnan. *province capital* Yunnan, SW China
K'un-ming *see* Kunming
Kununurra *146 D3* Western Australia
Kunya-Urgench *see* Köneürgenç
Kuopio *85 E5* Itä-Suomi, C Finland
Kupa *see* Kolpa
Kupang *139 E5 prev.* Koepang. Timor, C Indonesia
Kup"yans'k *109 G2 Rus.* Kupyansk. Kharkivs'ka Oblast', E Ukraine
Kupyansk *see* Kup"yans'k
Kür *see* Kura
Kura *117 H3 Az.* Kür, *Geor.* Mtkvari, *Turk.* Kura Nehri. *river* SW Asia
Kura Nehri *see* Kura
Kurashiki *131 B6 var.* Kurasiki. Okayama, Honshū, SW Japan
Kurasiki *see* Kurashiki
Kurdistan *117 F4 cultural region* SW Asia
Kŭrdzhali *104 D3 var.* Kirdzhali. Kŭrdzhali, S Bulgaria
Kure *131 B7* Hiroshima, Honshū, SW Japan
Küre Dağları *116 C2 mountain range* N Turkey
Kuressaare *106 C2 Ger.* Arensburg; *prev.* Kingissepp. Saaremaa, W Estonia
Kureyka *112 D2 river* N Russian Federation
Kurgan-Tyube *see* Qŭrghonteppa
Kuria Muria Islands *see* Ḩalāniyāt, Juzur al
Kuril'skiye Ostrova *115 H4 Eng.* Kuril Islands. *island group* SE Russian Federation
Kuril Islands *see* Kuril'skiye Ostrova
Kuril-Kamchatka Depression *see* Kuril Trench
Kuril Trench *113 F3 var.* Kuril-Kamchatka Depression. *trench* NW Pacific Ocean
Kuril'sk *130 E1 Jap.* Shana. Kuril'skiye Ostrova, Sakhalinskaya Oblats', SE Russian Federation
Ku-ring-gai *148 E1* New South Wales, E Australia
Kurisches Haff *see* Courland Lagoon
Kurkund *see* Kilingi-Nõmme
Kurnool *132 C1 var.* Karnul. Andhra Pradesh, S India
Kursk *111 A6* Kurskaya Oblast', W Russian Federation
Kurskiy Zaliv *see* Courland Lagoon
Kuršumlija *101 D5* Serbia, S Serbia
Kurtbunar *see* Tervel
Kurtitsch/Kürtös *see* Curtici
Kuruktag *126 C3 mountain range* NW China
Kurume *131 A7* Fukuoka, Kyūshū, SW Japan
Kurupukari *59 F3* C Guyana
Kusaie *see* Kosrae
Kushiro *130 D2 var.* Kusiro. Hokkaidō, NE Japan
Kushka *see* Serhetabat
Kusiro *see* Kushiro
Kuskokwim Mountains *36 C3 mountain range* Alaska, USA
Kustanay *see* Kostanay
Küstence/Küstendje *see* Constanţa
Kütahya *116 B3 prev.* Kutaia. Kütahya, W Turkey
Kutai *see* Mahakam, Sungai
Kutaisi *117 F2 prev.* K'ut'aisi *95 F2* W Georgia W Georgia
K'ut'aisi *see* Kutaisi
Kūt al 'Amārah *see* Al Kūt
Kut al Imara *see* Al Kūt
Kutaradja/Kutaraja *see* Banda Aceh
Kutch, Gulf of *see* Kachchh, Gulf of
Kutch, Rann of *see* Kachchh, Rann of
Kutina *100 B3* Sisak-Moslavina, NE Croatia
Kutno *98 C3* Łódzkie, C Poland
Kuujjuaq *39 E2 prev.* Fort-Chimo. Québec, E Canada
Kuusamo *84 E3* Oulu, E Finland
Kuvango *see* Cubango
Kuvdlorssuak *see* Kullorsuaq
Kuwait *120 C4 off.* State of Kuwait, *var.* Dawlat al Kuwait, Koweit, Kuweit. *country* SW Asia

KUWAIT
Southwest Asia

Official name State of Kuwait
Formation 1961 / 1961
Capital Kuwait City
Population 3.4 million / 494 people per sq mile (191 people per sq km) / 96%
Total area 6880 sq. miles (17,820 sq. km)
Languages Arabic*, English
Religions Sunni Muslim 45%, Shi'a Muslim 40%, Christian, Hindu, and other 15%
Ethnic mix Kuwaiti 45%, Other Arab 35%, South Asian 9%, Other 7%, Iranian 4%
Government Monarchy
Currency Kuwaiti dinar = 1000 fils
Literacy rate 96%
Calorie consumption 3471 kilocalories

Kuwait *see* Al Kuwayt
Kuwait City *see* Al Kuwayt
Kuwait, Dawlat al *see* Kuwait
Kuwait, State of *see* Kuwait
Kuwajleen *see* Kwajalein Atoll
Kuwayt *120 C3* Maysān, E Iraq
Kuweit *see* Kuwait
Kuybyshev *see* Samara
Kuybyshev Reservoir *111 C5 var.* Kuibyshev, *Eng.* Kuybyshev Reservoir. *reservoir* W Russian Federation
Kuybyshev Reservoir *see* Kuybyshevskoye Vodokhranilishche
Kuytun *126 B2* Xinjiang Uygur Zizhiqu, NW China
Kuzi *see* Kuji
Kuznetsk *111 B6* Penzenskaya Oblast', W Russian Federation
Kuźnica *98 E2* Białystok, NE Poland Europe
Kvaløya *84 C2 island* N Norway
Kvarnbergsvattnet *84 B4 var.* Frostviken. *lake* N Sweden
Kvarner *100 A3 var.* Carnaro, *It.* Quarnero. *gulf* W Croatia
Kvitøya *83 G1 island* NE Svalbard
Kwajalein Atoll *144 C1 var.* Kuwajleen. *atoll* Ralik Chain, C Marshall Islands
Kwando *see* Cuando
Kwangchow *see* Guangzhou
Kwangchu *see* Gwangju
Kwangju *see* Gwangju
Kwango *77 C7 Port.* Cuango. *river* Angola/Dem. Rep. Congo
Kwangsi/Kwangsi Chuang Autonomous Region *see* Guangxi Zhuangzu Zizhiqu
Kwangtung *see* Guangdong
Kwangyuan *see* Guangyuan
Kwanza *see* Cuanza
Kweichu *see* Guiyang
Kweilin *see* Guilin
Kweisui *see* Hohhot
Kweiyang *see* Guiyang
Kwekwe *78 D3 prev.* Que Que. Midlands, C Zimbabwe
Kwesui *see* Hohhot
Kwidzyń *98 C2 Ger.* Marienwerder. Pomorskie, N Poland
Kwigillingok *36 C3* Alaska, USA
Kwilu *77 C6 river* W Dem. Rep. Congo
Kwito *see* Cuito
Kyabé *76 C4* Moyen-Chari, S Chad
Kyaikkami *137 B5 prev.* Amherst. Mon State, S Myanmar (Burma)
Kyaiklat *136 B4* Ayeyarwady, SW Myanmar (Burma)
Kyaikto *136 B4* Mon State, S Myanmar (Burma)
Kyakhta *115 E5* Respublika Buryatiya, S Russian Federation
Kyaukse *136 B3* Mandalay, C Myanmar (Burma)
Kyjov *99 C5 Ger.* Gaya. Jihomoravský Kraj, SE Czech Republic
Kými *105 C5 prev.* Kími. Évvoia, C Greece
Kyŏngsŏng *see* Seoul
Kyōto *131 C6* Kyōto, Honshū, SW Japan
Kyparissía *105 B6 var.* Kiparissía. Pelopónnisos, S Greece
Kypros *see* Cyprus
Kyrá Panagía *105 C5 island* Vóreies Sporádes, Greece, Aegean Sea
Kyrenia *see* Girne
Kyrgyz Republic *see* Kyrgyzstan
Kyrgyzstan *123 F2 off.* Kyrgyz Republic *var.* Kirghizia; *prev.* Kirgizskaya SSR, Kirghiz SSR, Republic of Kyrgyzstan. *country* C Asia

KYRGYZSTAN
Central Asia

Official name Kyrgyz Republic
Formation 1991 / 1991
Capital Bishkek
Population 5.5 million / 72 people per sq mile (27 people per sq km) / 34%
Total area 76,641 sq. miles (198,500 sq. km)
Languages Kyrgyz*, Russian*, Uzbek, Tatar, Ukrainian
Religions Muslim (mainly Sunni) 70%, Orthodox Christian 30%
Ethnic mix Kyrgyz 69%, Uzbek 14%, Russian 9%, Other 6%, Dungan 1%, Uighur 1%
Government Presidential system
Currency Som = 100 tyiyn
Literacy rate 99%
Calorie consumption 2828 kilocalories

Kyrgyzstan, Republic of *see* Kyrgyzstan
Kythira *105 C7 var.* Kíthira, *It.* Cerigo, *Lat.* Cythera. *island* S Greece
Kýthnos *105 C6* Kńythnos, Kykládes, Greece, Aegean Sea
Kythnos *105 C6 var.* Kíthnos, Thermiá, *It.* Termia; *anc.* Cythnos. *island* Kykládes, Greece, Aegean Sea
Kythréa *see* Değirmenlik
Kyushu *131 B7 var.* Kyûsyû. *island* SW Japan
Kyushu-Palau Ridge *125 F3 var.* Kyusyu-Palau Ridge. *undersea ridge* W Pacific Ocean
Kyustendil *104 B2 anc.* Pautalia. Kyustendil, W Bulgaria
Kyûsyû *see* Kyūshū
Kyusyu-Palau Ridge *see* Kyushu-Palau Ridge
Kyyiv *109 E2 Eng.* Kiev, *Rus.* Kiyev. *country capital* (Ukraine) Kyyivs'ka Oblast', N Ukraine
Kyzyl *114 D4* Respublika Tyva, C Russia Federation
Kyzyl Kum *122 D2 var.* Kizil Kum, Qizil Qum, *Uzb.* Qizilqum. *desert* Kazakhstan/Uzbekistan
Kyzylorda *114 B5 var.* Kzyl-Orda, Qizil Orda, Qyzylorda; *prev.* Kzylorda, Perovsk. Kyzylorda, S Kazakhstan
Kyzylrabot *see* Qizilrabot
Kyzyl-Suu *123 G2 prev.* Pokrovka. Issyk-Kul'skaya Oblast', NE Kyrgyzstan
Kzyl-Orda *see* Kyzylorda
Kzylorda *see* Kyzylorda

L

Laaland *see* Lolland
La Algaba *92 C4* Andalucía, S Spain
Laarne *87 B5* Oost-Vlaanderen, NW Belgium
La Asunción *59 E1* Nueva Esparta, NE Venezuela
Laatokka *see* Ladozhskoye, Ozero
Laâyoune *70 B3 var.* Aaiún. *country capital* (Western Sahara) NW Western Sahara
La Banda Oriental *see* Uruguay
la Baule-Escoublac *90 A4* Loire-Atlantique, NW France
Labé *74 C4* NW Guinea
Labe *see* Elbe
Laborca *see* Laborec
Laborec *99 E5 Hung.* Laborca. *river* E Slovakia
Labrador *39 F2 cultural region* Newfoundland and Labrador, SW Canada
Labrador Basin *34 E3 var.* Labrador Sea Basin. *undersea basin* Labrador Sea
Labrador Sea *82 A4 sea* NW Atlantic Ocean
Labrador Sea Basin *see* Labrador Basin
Labudalin *see* Ergun
Labutta *137 A5* Ayeyarwady, SW Myanmar (Burma)
Laç *101 C6 var.* Laci. Lezhë, C Albania
La Calera *64 B4* Valparaíso, C Chile
La Carolina *92 D4* Andalucía, S Spain

accadive Islands *132 A3 Eng.* Laccadive Islands. *island group* India, N Indian Ocean
accadive Islands/Laccadive Minicoy and Amindivi Islands, the *see* Lakshadweep
a Ceiba *52 D2* Atlántida, N Honduras
achanás *104 B3* Kentrikí Makedonía, N Greece
a Chaux-de-Fonds *95 A7* Neuchâtel, W Switzerland
achlan River *149 C6 river* New South Wales, SE Australia
aci *see* Laç
Ciotat *91 D6 anc.* Citharista. Bouches-du-Rhône, SE France
acobriga *see* Lagos
a Concepción *53 E5 var.* Concepción. Chiriquí, W Panama
a Concepción *58 C1* Zulia, NW Venezuela
a Condamine *91 C8* W Monaco
aconia *41 G2* New Hampshire, NE USA
a Crosse *40 A2* Wisconsin, N USA
a Cruz *52 D4* Guanacaste, NW Costa Rica
ake Ladoga *110 B3 Eng.* Lake Ladoga, *Fin.* Laatokka. *lake* NW Russian Federation
adoga, Lake *see* Ladozhskoye, Ozero
adysmith *40 B2* Wisconsin, N USA
ae *144 B3* Morobe, W Papua New Guinea
a Esperanza *52 C2* Intibucá, SW Honduras
afayette *40 C4* Indiana, N USA
afayette *42 B3* Louisiana, S USA
a Fé *54 A2* Pinar del Río, W Cuba
afia *75 G4* Nassarawa, C Nigeria
a Flèche *90 B4* Sarthe, NW France
agdo, Lac de *76 B4 lake* N Cameroon
aghouat *70 D2* N Algeria
agos *75 F5* Lagos, SW Nigeria
agos *92 B5 anc.* Lacobriga. Faro, S Portugal
agos de Moreno *51 E4* Jalisco, SW Mexico
agouira *70 A4* SW Western Sahara
a Grande *46 C3* Oregon, NW USA
a Guaira *66 B4* Distrito Federal, N Venezuela
agunas *64 B1* Tarapacá, N Chile
agunillas *61 G4* Santa Cruz, SE Bolivia
a Habana *54 B2 var.* Havana. *country capital* (Cuba) Ciudad de La Habana, W Cuba
ahat *138 B4* Sumatera, W Indonesia
a Haye *see* 's-Gravenhage
aholm *85 B7* Halland, S Sweden
ahore *134 D2* Punjab, NE Pakistan
ahr *95 A6* Baden-Württemberg, S Germany
ahti *85 D5 Swe.* Lahtis. Etelä-Suomi, S Finland
ahtis *see* Lahti
aï *76 B4 prev.* Behagle, De Behagle. Tandjilé, S Chad
aibach *see* Ljubljana
ai Châu *136 D3* Lai Châu, N Vietnam
aila *see* Laylā
a Junta *44 D5* Colorado, C USA
ake Charles *42 A3* Louisiana, S USA
ake City *43 E3* Florida, SE USA
ake District *89 C5 physical region* NW England, United Kingdom
ake Havasu City *48 A2* Arizona, SW USA
ake Jackson *49 H4* Texas, SW USA
akeland *43 E4* Florida, SE USA
akeside *47 C8* California, W USA
ake State *see* Michigan
akewood *44 D4* Colorado, C USA
akhnau *see* Lucknow
akonikós Kólpos *105 B7 gulf* S Greece
akselv *84 D2 Lapp.* Leavdnja. Finnmark, N Norway
a Laon *see* Laon
alibela *72 C4* Āmara, Ethiopia
a Libertad *52 B1* Petén, N Guatemala
a Ligua *64 B4* Valparaíso, C Chile
alín *92 C1* Galicia, NW Spain
alitpur *135 F3* Central, C Nepal
a Louvière *87 B6* Hainaut, S Belgium
a Maddalena *96 A4* Sardegna, Italy, C Mediterranean Sea
a Manche *see* English Channel
amar *44 D5* Colorado, C USA
a Marmora, Punta *97 A5 mountain* Sardegna, Italy, C Mediterranean Sea
La Massana *91 A8* La Massana, W Andorra Europe
Lambaréné *77 A6* Moyen-Ogooué, W Gabon
Lamego *92 C2* Viseu, N Portugal
Lamesa *49 E3* Texas, SW USA
Lamezia Terme *97 D6* Calabria, SE Italy
Lamía *105 B5* Stereá Elláda, C Greece
Lamoni *45 F4* Iowa, C USA
Lampang *136 C4 var.* Muang Lampang. Lampang, NW Thailand
Lámpeia *105 B6* Dytikí Elláda, S Greece
Lanbi Kyun *137 B6 prev.* Sullivan Island. *island* Myeik Archipelago, S Myanmar (Burma)
Lancang Jiang *see* Mekong
Lancaster *89 D5* NW England, United Kingdom
Lancaster *47 C7* California, W USA
Lancaster *41 F4* Pennsylvania, NE USA
Lancaster Sound *37 F2 sound* Nunavut, N Canada
Lan-chou/Lan-chow/Lanchow *see* Lanzhou
Landao *see* Lantau Island
Landen *87 C6* Vlaams Brabant, C Belgium
Lander *44 C3* Wyoming, C USA
Landerneau *90 A3* Finistère, NW France
Landes *91 B5 cultural region* SW France
Land of Enchantment *see* New Mexico
The Land of Opportunity *see* Arkansas
Land of Steady Habits *see* Connecticut
Land of the Midnight Sun *see* Alaska
Landsberg *see* Gorzów Wielkopolski, Lubuskie, Poland
Landsberg an der Warthe *see* Gorzów Wielkopolski
Land's End *89 B8 headland* SW England, United Kingdom
Landshut *95 C6* Bayern, SE Germany
Langar *123 E2 Rus.* Lyangar. Navoiy Viloyati, C Uzbekistan
Langfang *128 D4* Hebei, E China
Langkawi, Pulau *137 B7 island* Peninsular Malaysia
Langres *90 D4* Haute-Marne, N France
Langsa *138 A3* Sumatera, W Indonesia
Lang Shan *127 E3 mountain range* N China
Lang Sơn *136 D3 var.* Langson. Lang Sơn, N Vietnam
Langson *see* Lang Sơn
Lang Suan *137 B6* Chumphon, SW Thailand
Languedoc *91 C6 cultural region* S France
Länkäran *117 H3 Rus.* Lenkoran'. S Azerbaijan
Lansing *40 C3 state capital* Michigan, N USA
Lanta, Ko *137 B7 island* S Thailand
Lantau Island *128 A2 Cant.* Tai Yue Shan, *Chin.* Landao. *island* Hong Kong, S China
Lan-ts'ang Chiang *see* Mekong
Lantung, Gulf of *see* Liaodong Wan
Lanzarote *70 B3 island* Islas Canarias, Spain, NE Atlantic Ocean
Lanzhou *128 B4 var.* Lan-chou, Lanchow, Lan-chow; *prev.* Kaolan. *province capital* Gansu, C China
Lao Cai *136 D3* Lao Cai, N Vietnam
Laodicea/Laodicea ad Mare *see* Al Lādhiqīyah
Laoet *see* Laut, Pulau
Laon *90 D3 var.* la Laon; *anc.* Laudunum. Aisne, N France
Lao People's Democratic Republic *see* Laos
La Orchila, Isla *58 D1 island* N Venezuela
La Oroya *60 C3* Junín, C Peru
Laos *136 D4 off.* Lao People's Democratic Republic. *country* SE Asia

LAOS
Southeast Asia

Official name Lao People's Democratic Republic
Formation 1953 / 1953
Capital Vientiane
Population 6.8 million / 76 people per sq mile (29 people per sq km)
Total area 91,428 sq. miles (236,800 sq. km)
Languages Lao*, Mon-Khmer, Yao, Vietnamese, Chinese, French

LAOS
(continued)

Religions Buddhist 65%, Other (including animist) 34%, Christian 1%
Ethnic mix Lao Loum 66%, Lao Theung 30%, Lao Soung 2%, Other 2%
Government One-party state
Currency Kip = 100 at
Literacy rate 73%
Calorie consumption 2356 kilocalories

La Palma *53 G5* Darién, SE Panama
La Palma *70 A3 island* Islas Canarias, Spain, NE Atlantic Ocean
La Paz *61 F4 var.* La Paz de Ayacucho. *country capital* (Bolivia-seat of government) La Paz, W Bolivia
La Paz *50 B3* Baja California Sur, NW Mexico
La Paz, Bahía de *50 B3 bay* NW Mexico
La Paz de Ayacucho *see* La Paz
La Pérouse Strait *130 D1 Jap.* Sōya-kaikyō, *Rus.* Proliv Laperuza. *strait* Japan/Russian Federation
Laperuza, Proliv *see* La Pérouse Strait
Lápithos *see* Lapta
Lapland *84 D3 Fin.* Lappi, *Swe.* Lappland. *cultural region* N Europe
La Plata *64 D4* Buenos Aires, E Argentina
La Plata *see* Sucre
La Pola *92 D1 var.* Pola de Lena. Asturias, N Spain
Lappeenranta *85 E5 Swe.* Villmanstrand. Etelä-Suomi, SE Finland
Lappi/Lappland *see* Lapland
Lappo *see* Lapua
Lapta *102 C5 Gk.* Lápithos. NW Cyprus
Laptev Sea *115 E2 Eng.* Laptev Sea. *sea* Arctic Ocean
Laptev Sea *see* Laptevykh, More
Lapua *85 D5 Swe.* Lappo. Länsi-Suomi, W Finland
Lapurdum *see* Bayonne
Łapy *98 E3* Podlaskie, NE Poland
La Quiaca *64 C2* Jujuy, N Argentina
L'Aquila *96 C4 var.* Aquila, Aquila degli Abruzzi. Abruzzo, C Italy
Laracha *92 B1* Galicia, NW Spain
Laramie *44 C4* Wyoming, C USA
Laramie Mountains *44 C3 mountain range* Wyoming, C USA
Laredo *93 E1* Cantabria, N Spain
Laredo *49 F5* Texas, SW USA
La Réunion *see* Réunion
Largeau *see* Faya
Largo *43 E4* Florida, SE USA
Largo, Cayo *54 B2 island* W Cuba
Lario *see* Como, Lago di
La Rioja *64 C3* La Rioja, NW Argentina
La Rioja *93 E2 autonomous community* N Spain
Lárisa *104 B4 var.* Larissa. Thessalía, C Greece
Larissa *see* Lárisa
Lārkāna *134 B3 var.* Larkhana. Sind, SE Pakistan
Larkhana *see* Lārkāna
Larnaca *see* Lárnaka
Lárnaka *102 C5 var.* Larnaca, Larnax. SE Cyprus
Larnax *see* Lárnaka
la Rochelle *90 B4 anc.* Rupella. Charente-Maritime, W France
la Roche-sur-Yon *90 B4 prev.* Bourbon Vendée, Napoléon-Vendée. Vendée, NW France
La Roda *93 E3* Castilla-La Mancha, C Spain
La Romana *55 E3* E Dominican Republic
Larvotto *91 C8* N Monaco Europe
La-sa *see* Lhasa
Las Cabezas de San Juan *92 C5* Andalucía, S Spain
Las Cruces *48 D3* New Mexico, SW USA
La See d'Urgel *see* La Seu d'Urgell
La Serena *64 B3* Coquimbo, C Chile
La Seu d'Urgell *93 G1 prev.* La See d'Urgel, Seo de Urgel. Cataluña, NE Spain
La Seu d'Urgell *see* La Seu d'Urgell
la Seyne-sur-Mer *91 D6* Var, SE France
Lashio *136 B3* Shan State, E Myanmar (Burma)
Lashkar Gāh *122 D5 var.* Lash-Kar-Gar'. Helmand, S Afghanistan
Lash-Kar-Gar' *see* Lashkar Gāh
La Sila *97 D6 mountain range* SW Italy
La Sirena *52 D3* Región Autónoma Atlántico Sur, E Nicaragua
Łask *98 C4* Łódzkie, C Poland
Las Lomitas *64 D2* Formosa, N Argentina
La Solana *93 E4* Castilla-La Mancha, C Spain
Las Palmas *70 A3 var.* Las Palmas de Gran Canaria. Gran Canaria, Islas Canarias, Spain, NE Atlantic Ocean
Las Palmas de Gran Canaria *see* Las Palmas
La Spezia *96 B3* Liguria, NW Italy
Lassa *see* Lhasa
Las Tablas *53 F5* Los Santos, S Panama
Last Frontier, The *see* Alaska
Las Tunas *54 C2 var.* Victoria de las Tunas. Las Tunas, E Cuba
La Suisse *see* Switzerland
Las Vegas *47 D7* Nevada, W USA
Latacunga *60 B1* Cotopaxi, C Ecuador
Latakia *see* Al Lādhiqīyah
la Teste *91 B5* Gironde, SW France
Latina *97 C5 prev.* Littoria. Lazio, C Italy
La Tortuga, Isla *59 E1 var.* Isla Tortuga. *island* N Venezuela
La Tuque *39 E4* Québec, SE Canada
Latvia *106 C3 off.* Republic of Latvia, *Ger.* Lettland, *Latv.* Latvija, Latvijas Republika; *prev.* Latvian SSR, *Rus.* Latviyskaya SSR. *country* NE Europe

LATVIA
Northeast Europe

Official name Republic of Latvia
Formation 1991 / 1991
Capital Riga
Population 2.1 million / 84 people per sq mile (33 people per sq km)
Total area 24,938 sq. miles (64,589 sq. km)
Languages Latvian*, Russian
Religions Other 43%, Lutheran 24%, Roman Catholic 18%, Orthodox Christian 15%
Ethnic mix Latvian 62%, Russian 27%, Other 4%, Belarussian 3%, Ukrainian 2%, Polish 2%
Government Parliamentary system
Currency Euro = 100 cents
Literacy rate 99%
Calorie consumption 3293 kilocalories

Latvian SSR/Latvija/Latvijas Republika/Latviyskaya SSR *see* Latvia
Latvia, Republic of *see* Latvia
Laudunum *see* Laon
Laudus *see* St-Lô
Lauenburg/Lauenburg in Pommern *see* Lębork
Lau Group *145 E4 island group* E Fiji
Lauis *see* Lugano
Launceston *149 C8* Tasmania, SE Australia
La Unión *52 C2* Olancho, C Honduras
La Unión *93 F4* Murcia, SE Spain
Laurel *42 C3* Mississippi, S USA
Laurel *44 C2* Montana, NW USA
Laurentian Highlands *see* Laurentian Mountains
Laurentian Mountains *39 E3 var.* Laurentian Highlands, *Fr.* Les Laurentides. *plateau* Newfoundland and Labrador/Québec, Canada
Laurentides, Les *see* Laurentian Mountains
Lauria *97 D6* Basilicata, S Italy
Laurinburg *43 F1* North Carolina, SE USA
Lauru *see* Choiseul
Lausanne *95 A7 It.* Losanna. Vaud, SW Switzerland
Laut, Pulau *138 D4 prev.* Laoet. *island* Borneo, C Indonesia
Laval *38 D4* Québec, SE Canada
Laval *90 B3* Mayenne, NW France
La Vall d'Uixó *93 F3 var.* Vall D'Uxó. Valenciana, E Spain
La Vega *55 E3 var.* Concepción de la Vega. C Dominican Republic
La Vila Joiosa *see* Villajoyosa
Lávrio *105 C6 prev.* Lávrion. Attikí, C Greece
Lávrion *see* Lávrio
Lawrence *41 G3* Massachusetts, NE USA
Lawrenceburg *42 C1* Tennessee, S USA
Lawton *49 F2* Oklahoma, C USA
La Yarada *61 E4* Tacna, SW Peru

Laylā *121 C5 var.* Laila. Ar Riyāḑ, C Saudi Arabia
Lazarev Sea *154 B1 sea* Antarctica
Lázaro Cárdenas *51 E5* Michoacán, SW Mexico
Leal *see* Lihula
Leamhcán *see* Lucan
Leamington *38 C5* Ontario, S Canada
Leavdnja *see* Lakselv
Lebak *139 E3* Mindanao, S Philippines
Lebanese Republic *see* Lebanon
Lebanon *45 G5* Missouri, C USA
Lebanon *41 G2* New Hampshire, NE USA
Lebanon *46 B3* Oregon, NW USA
Lebanon *118 A4 off.* Lebanese Republic, *Ar.* Al Lubnān, *Fr.* Liban. *country* SW Asia

LEBANON
Southwest Asia

Official name Republic of Lebanon
Formation 1941 / 1941
Capital Beirut
Population 4.8 million / 1215 people per sq mile (469 people per sq km)
Total area 4015 sq. miles (10,400 sq. km)
Languages Arabic*, French, Armenian, Assyrian
Religions Muslim 60%, Christian 39%, Other 1%
Ethnic mix Arab 95%, Armenian 4%, Other 1%
Government Parliamentary system
Currency Lebanese pound = 100 piastres
Literacy rate 90%
Calorie consumption 3181 kilocalories

Lebanon, Mount *see* Liban, Jebel
Lebap *122 D2* Lebapskiy Velayat, NE Turkmenistan
Lebedin *see* Lebedyn
Lebedyn *109 F2 Rus.* Lebedin. Sums'ka Oblast', NE Ukraine
Lębork *98 C2 var.* Lębórk, *Ger.* Lauenburg, Lauenburg in Pommern. Pomorskie, N Poland
Lebrija *92 C5* Andalucía, S Spain
Lebu *65 A5* Bío Bío, C Chile
le Cannet *91 D6* Alpes-Maritimes, SE France
Le Cap *see* Cap-Haïtien
Lecce *97 E6* Puglia, SE Italy
Lechainá *105 B6 var.* Lehena, Lekhainá. Dytikí Elláda, S Greece
Ledo Salinarius *see* Lons-le-Saunier
Leduc *37 E5* Alberta, SW Canada
Leech Lake *45 F2 lake* Minnesota, N USA
Leeds *89 D5* N England, United Kingdom
Leek *86 E2* Groningen, NE Netherlands
Leer *94 A3* Niedersachsen, NW Germany
Leeuwarden *86 D1 Fris.* Ljouwert. Fryslân, N Netherlands
Leeuwin, Cape *142 A5 headland* Western Australia
Leeward Islands *55 G3 island group* E West Indies
Leeward Islands *see* Sotavento, Ilhas de
Lefkáda *105 A5 prev.* Levkás. Lefkáda, Iónia Nisiá, Greece, C Mediterranean Sea
Lefkáda *105 A5 It.* Santa Maura, *prev.* Levkás; *anc.* Leucas. *island* Iónia Nisiá, Greece, C Mediterranean Sea
Lefká Óri *105 C7 mountain range* Kríti, Greece, E Mediterranean Sea
Lefkímmi *105 A5 var.* Levkímmi. Kérkyra, Iónia Nisiá, Greece, C Mediterranean Sea
Lefkosía/Lefkoşa *see* Nicosia
Legaceaster *see* Chester
Legaspi *see* Legazpi City
Legazpi City *139 E2 var.* Legaspi. C Philippines
Leghorn *see* Livorno
Legnica *98 B4 Ger.* Liegnitz. Dolnośląskie, SW Poland
le Havre *90 B3 Eng.* Havre; *prev.* le Havre-de-Grâce. Seine-Maritime, N France
le Havre-de-Grâce *see* le Havre
Lehena *see* Lechainá
Leicester *89 D6 Lat.* Batae Coritanorum. C England, United Kingdom
Leiden *86 B3 prev.* Leyden; *anc.* Lugdunum Batavorum. Zuid-Holland, W Netherlands
Leie *90 D2 Fr.* Lys. *river* Belgium/France
Leinster *89 B6 Ir.* Cúige Laighean. *cultural region* E Ireland
Leipsic *see* Leipzig
Leipsoí *105 E6 island* Dodekánisa, Greece, Aegean Sea
Leipzig *94 C4 Pol.* Lipsk, *hist.* Leipsic; *anc.* Lipsia. Sachsen, E Germany
Leiria *92 B3 anc.* Collipo. Leiria, C Portugal
Leirvik *85 A6* Hordaland, S Norway
Lek *86 C4 river* SW Netherlands
Lekhainá *see* Lechainá
Lekhchevo *see* Boychinovtsi
Leksand *85 C5* Dalarna, C Sweden
Lel'chitsy *see* Lyel'chytsy
le Léman *see* Geneva, Lake
Lelystad *86 D3* Flevoland, C Netherlands
Léman, Lac *see* Geneva, Lake
le Mans *90 B3* Sarthe, NW France
Lemberg *see* L'viv
Lemesós *102 C5 var.* Limassol. SW Cyprus
Lemhi Range *46 D3 mountain range* Idaho, C USA North America
Lemnos *see* Límnos
Lemovices *see* Limoges
Lena *115 F3 river* NE Russian Federation
Lena Tablemount *141 B7 seamount* S Indian Ocean
Len Dao *128 C8 island* S Spratly Islands
Leninabad *see* Khujand
Leninakan *see* Gyumri
Lenine *109 G5 Rus.* Lenino. Avtonomna Respublika Krym, S Ukraine
Lenīngor *see* Leninogorsk
Leningrad *see* Sankt-Peterburg
Leningradskaya *154 B4 Russian research station* Antarctica
Lenino *see* Lenine, Ukraine
Leninobod *see* Khujand
Leninogorsk *see* Ridder
Leninpol' *123 F2* Talasskaya Oblast', NW Kyrgyzstan
Lenin-Turkmenski *see* Türkmenabat
Lenkoran' *see* Länkäran
Lenti *99 B7* Zala, SW Hungary
Lentia *see* Linz
Leoben *95 E7* Steiermark, C Austria
León *51 E4 var.* León de los Aldamas. Guanajuato, C Mexico
León *52 C3* León, NW Nicaragua
León *92 D1* Castilla y León, NW Spain
León de los Aldamas *see* León
Leonídi *see* Leonídio
Leonídio *105 B6 var.* Leonídi. Pelopónnisos, S Greece
Léopold II, Lac *see* Mai-Ndombe, Lac
Léopoldville *see* Kinshasa
Lepe *92 C4* Andalucía, S Spain
Lepel' *see* Lyepyel'
le Portel *90 C2* Pas-de-Calais, N France
Le Puglie *see* Puglia
le Puy *91 C5 prev.* le Puy-en-Velay, *hist.* Anicium, Podium Anicensis. Haute-Loire, C France
le Puy-en-Velay *see* le Puy
Léré *76 B4* Mayo-Kébbi, SW Chad
Lérida *see* Lleida
Lerma *92 D2* Castilla y León, N Spain
Leros *105 D6 island* Dodekánisa, Greece, Aegean Sea
Lerrnayin Gharabakh *see* Nagorno-Karabakh
Lerwick *88 D1* NE Scotland, United Kingdom
Lesbos *116 A3 anc.* Lesbos. *island* E Greece
Lesbos *see* Lésvos
Les Cayes *see* Cayes
Les Gonaïves *see* Gonaïves
Leshan *128 B5* Sichuan, C China
les Herbiers *90 B4* Vendée, NW France
Lesh/Leshi *see* Lezhë
Lesina *see* Hvar
Leskovac *101 E5* Serbia, SE Serbia
Lesnoy *114 C3* Sverdlovskaya Oblast', C Russian Federation
Lesotho *78 D4 off.* Kingdom of Lesotho; *prev.* Basutoland. *country* S Africa

LESOTHO
Southern Africa

Official name Kingdom of Lesotho
Formation 1966 / 1966
Capital Maseru
Population 2.2 million / 188 people per sq mile (72 people per sq km)
Total area 11,720 sq. miles (30,355 sq. km)

LESOTHO
(continued)

Languages English*, Sesotho*, isiZulu
Religions Christian 90%, Traditional beliefs 10%
Ethnic mix Sotho 99%, European and Asian 1%
Government Parliamentary system
Currency Loti = 100 lisente; South African rand = 100 cents
Literacy rate 76%
Calorie consumption 2595 kilocalories

Lesotho, Kingdom of *see* Lesotho
les Sables-d'Olonne *90 B4* Vendée, NW France
Lesser Antarctica *see* West Antarctica
Lesser Antilles *55 G4 island group* E West Indies
Lesser Caucasus *117 F2 Rus.* Malyy Kavkaz. *mountain range* SW Asia
Lesser Khingan Range *see* Xiao Hinggan Ling
Lesser Sunda Islands *139 E5 Eng.* Lesser Sunda Islands. *island group* C Indonesia
Lesser Sunda Islands *see* Nusa Tenggara
Leszno *98 B4 Ger.* Lissa. Wielkopolskie, C Poland
Lethbridge *37 E5* Alberta, SW Canada
Lethem *59 F3* S Guyana
Leti, Kepulauan *139 F5 island group* E Indonesia
Letpadan *136 B4* Bago, SW Myanmar (Burma)
Letsôk-aw Kyun *137 B6 var.* Letsutan Island; *prev.* Domel Island. *island* Myeik Archipelago, S Myanmar (Burma)
Letsutan Island *see* Letsôk-aw Kyun
Lettland *see* Latvia
Lëtzebuerg *see* Luxembourg
Leucas *see* Lefkáda
Leuven *87 C6 Fr.* Louvain, *Ger.* Löwen. Vlaams Brabant, C Belgium
Leuze *see* Leuze-en-Hainaut
Leuze-en-Hainaut *87 B6 var.* Leuze. Hainaut, SW Belgium
Léva *see* Levice
Levanger *84 B4* Nord-Trøndelag, C Norway
Levelland *49 E2* Texas, SW USA
Leverkusen *94 A4* Nordrhein-Westfalen, W Germany
Levice *99 C6 Ger.* Lewentz, *Hung.* Léva, Lewenz. Nitriansky Kraj, SW Slovakia
Levin *150 D4* Manawatu-Wanganui, North Island, New Zealand
Levkás *see* Lefkáda
Levkímmi *see* Lefkímmi
Lewentz/Lewenz *see* Levice
Lewis, Isle of *88 B2 island* NW Scotland, United Kingdom
Lewis Range *44 B1 mountain range* Montana, NW USA
Lewiston *46 C2* Idaho, NW USA
Lewiston *41 G2* Maine, NE USA
Lewistown *44 C1* Montana, NW USA
Lexington *40 C5* Kentucky, S USA
Lexington *45 E4* Nebraska, C USA
Leyden *see* Leiden
Leyte *139 F2 island* C Philippines
Leżajsk *99 E5* Podkarpackie, SE Poland
Lezha *see* Lezhë
Lezhë *101 C6 var.* Lezha; *prev.* Lesh, Leshi. Lezhë, NW Albania
Lhasa *126 C5 var.* La-sa, Lassa. Xizang Zizhiqu, W China
Lhaviyani Atoll *see* Faadhippolhu Atoll
Lhazê *126 C5 var.* Quxar. Xizang Zizhiqu, China E Asia
L'Hospitalet de Llobregat *93 G2 var.* Hospitalet. Cataluña, NE Spain
Liancourt Rocks *131 A5 Jap.* Takeshima, *Kor.* Dokdo. *island group* Japan/South Korea
Lianyungang *128 D4 var.* Xinpu. Jiangsu, E China
Liao *see* Liaoning
Liaodong Wan *127 G3 Eng.* Gulf of Lantung, Gulf of Liaotung. *gulf* NE China
Liao He *125 E1 river* NE China
Liaoning *128 D3 var.* Liao, Liaoning Sheng, Shengking, *hist.* Fengtien, Shenking. *province* NE China
Liaoning Sheng *see* Liaoning
Liaoyuan *129 E3 var.* Dongliao, Shuan liao, *Jap.* Chengchiatun. Jilin, NE Chi
Liard *see* Fort Liard
Liban *see* Lebanon
Liban, Jebel *118 B4 Ar.* Jabal al Gharbt, Jabal Lubnān, *Eng.* Mount Lebanon. *mountain range* C Lebanon
Libau *see* Liepāja
Libby *44 A1* Montana, NW USA
Liberal *45 E5* Kansas, C USA
Liberalitas Julia *see* Évora
Liberec *98 B4 Ger.* Reichenberg. Liberecký Kraj, N Czech Republic
Liberia *52 D4* Guanacaste, NW Costa Rica
Liberia *74 C5 off.* Republic of Liberia. *country* W Africa

LIBERIA
West Africa

Official name Republic of Liberia
Formation 1847 / 1847
Capital Monrovia
Population 4.3 million / 116 people per sq mile (45 people per sq km)
Total area 43,000 sq. miles (111,370 sq. km)
Languages Kpelle, Vai, Bassa, Kru, Grebo, Kissi, Gola, Loma, English*
Religions Christian 40%, Traditional beliefs 40%, Muslim 20%
Ethnic mix Indigenous tribes (12 groups) 49%, Kpellé 20%, Bassa 16%, Gio 8%, Krou 7%
Government Presidential system
Currency Liberian dollar = 100 cents
Literacy rate 43%
Calorie consumption 2251 kilocalories

Liberia, Republic of *see* Liberia
Libian Desert *see* Libyan Desert
Lībīyah, Aş Şahrā' al *see* Libyan Desert
Libourne *91 B5* Gironde, SW France
Libreville *77 A5 country capital* (Gabon) Estuaire, NW Gabon
Libya *71 F3 prev.* Great Socialist People' Libyan Arab Jamahiriya, Al Jamāhīrīya al 'Arabīyah al Lībīyah ash Sha'bīyah al Ishtirākīy, Libyan Arab Republic. *country* N Africa

LIBYA
North Africa

Official name State of Libya
Formation 1951 / 1951
Capital Tripoli
Population 6.2 million / 9 people per sq mile (4 people per sq km)
Total area 679,358 sq. miles (1,759,540 sq. km)
Languages Arabic*, Tuareg
Religions Muslim (mainly Sunni) 97%, Other 3%
Ethnic mix Arab and Berber 97%, Other 3%
Government Transitional regime
Currency Libyan dinar = 1000 dirhams
Literacy rate 90%
Calorie consumption 3211 kilocalories

Libyan Arab Republic *see* Libya
Libyan Desert *71 H4 var.* Libian Desert, *Ar.* Aş Şahrā' al Lībīyah. *desert* N Afric
Libyan Plateau *103 F4 var.* Aḑ Diffah. *plateau* Egypt/Libya
Lichtenfels *95 C5* Bayern, SE Germany
Lichtenvoorde *86 E4* Gelderland, E Netherlands
Lichuan *128 C5* Hubei, C China
Lida *107 B5* Hrodzyenskaya Voblasts', W Belarus
Lidhorikíon *see* Lidoríki
Lidköping *85 B6* Västra Götaland, S Sweden
Lidokhorikion *see* Lidoríki
Lidoríki *105 B5 prev.* Lidhorikíon, Lidokhorikion. Stereá Elláda, C Greec
Lidzbark Warmiński *98 D2 Ger.* Heilsberg. Olsztyn, N Poland
Liechtenstein *94 D1 off.* Principality of Liechtenstein. *country* C Europe

LIECHTENSTEIN
Central Europe

Official name Principality of Liechtenstein

.IECHTENSTEIN
(continued)

ormation 1719 / 1719
:apital Vaduz
opulation 37,000 / 597 people
er sq mile (231 people per sq km)
'otal area 62 sq. miles (160 sq. km)
anguages German*, Alemannish
ialect, Italian
.eligions Roman Catholic 79%,
)ther 13%, Protestant 8%
thnic mix Liechtensteiner 66%,
)ther 12%, Swiss 10%, Austrian 6%,
ierman 3%, Italian 3%
iovernment Parliamentary system
:urrency Swiss franc = 100 rappen/
entimes
.iteracy rate 99%
:alorie consumption Not available

echtenstein, Principality of *see* Liechtenstein
ège *87 D6 Dut.* Luik, *Ger.* Lüttich. Liège, E Belgium
egnitz *see* Legnica
enz *95 D7* Tirol, W Austria
epāja *106 B3 Ger.* Libau. W Latvia
etuva *see* Lithuania
evenhof *see* Līvāni
ezen *95 D7* Steiermark, C Austria
ffey *89 B6 river* Ireland
fou *144 D5 island* Îles Loyauté, E New Caledonia
ger *see* Loire
gure, Appennino *96 A2 Eng.* Ligurian Mountains. *mountain range* NW Italy
gure, Mar *see* Ligurian Sea
gurian Mountains *see* Ligure, Appennino
gurian Sea *96 A3 Fr.* Mer Ligurienne, *It.* Mar Ligure. *sea* N Mediterranean Sea
gurienne, Mer *see* Ligurian Sea
hu'e *47 A7 var.* Lihue. Kaua'i, Hawaii, USA
hue *see* Līhu'e
hula *106 D2 Ger.* Leal. Läänemaa, W Estonia
ivi Laht *see* Riga, Gulf of
kasi *77 D7 prev.* Jadotville. Shaba, SE Dem. Rep. Congo
knes *85 A6* Vest-Agder, S Norway
lle *90 C2 var.* l'Isle, *Dut.* Rijssel, *Flem.* Ryssel, *prev.* Lisle; *anc.* Insula. Nord, N France
llehammer *85 B5* Oppland, S Norway
llestrøm *85 B6* Akershus, S Norway
longwe *79 E2 country capital* (Malawi) Central, W Malawi
lybaeum *see* Marsala
ma *60 C4 country capital* (Peru) Lima, W Peru
manowa *99 D5* Małopolskie, S Poland
massol *see* Lemesós
merick *89 A6 Ir.* Luimneach. Limerick, SW Ireland
mín Vathéos *see* Sámos
mnos *103 F3 anc.* Lemnos. *island* E Greece
moges *91 C5 anc.* Augustoritum Lemovicensium, Lemovices. Haute-Vienne, C France
món *53 E4 var.* Puerto Limón. Limón, E Costa Rica
món *52 D2* Colón, NE Honduras
monum *see* Poitiers
mousin *91 C5 cultural region* C France
moux *91 C6* Aude, S France
mpopo *78 D3 var.* Crocodile. *river* S Africa
nares *64 B4* Maule, C Chile
nares *51 E3* Nuevo León, NE Mexico
nares *92 D4* Andalucía, S Spain
ncoln *89 D5 anc.* Lindum, Lindum Colonia. E England, United Kingdom
ncoln *41 H2* Maine, NE USA
ncoln *45 F4 state capital* Nebraska, C USA
ncoln Sea *34 D2 sea* Arctic Ocean
nden *59 F3* E Guyana
ndhos *see* Líndos
ndi *73 D8* Lindi, SE Tanzania
ndos *105 E7 var.* Líndhos. Ródos, Dodekánisa, Greece, Aegean Sea
ndum/Lindum Colonia *see* Lincoln
ne Islands *145 G3 island group* E Kiribati
Lingeh *see* Bandar-e Lengeh
Lingen *94 A3 var.* Lingen an der Ems. Niedersachsen, NW Germany
Lingen an der Ems *see* Lingen
Lingga, Kepulauan *138 B4 island group* W Indonesia
Lingling *129 C6 prev.* Yongzhou, Zhishan. Hunan, S China
Linköping *85 C6* Östergötland, S Sweden
Linz *95 D6 anc.* Lentia. Oberösterreich, N Austria
Lion, Gulf of *91 C7 Eng.* Gulf of Lion, Gulf of Lions; *anc.* Sinus Gallicus. *gulf* S France
Lion, Gulf of/Lions, Gulf of *see* Lion, Golfe du
Liozno *see* Lyozna
Lipari *97 D6 island* Isole Eolie, S Italy
Lipari Islands/Lipari, Isole *see* Eolie, Isole
Lipetsk *111 B5* Lipetskaya Oblast', W Russian Federation
Lipno *98 C3* Kujawsko-pomorskie, C Poland
Lipova *108 A4 Hung.* Lippa. Arad, W Romania
Lipovets *see* Lypovets'
Lippa *see* Lipova
Lipsia/Lipsk *see* Leipzig
Lira *73 B6* N Uganda
Lisala *77 C5* Equateur, N Dem. Rep. Congo
Lisboa *92 B4 Eng.* Lisbon; *anc.* Felicitas Julia, Olisipo. *country capital* (Portugal) Lisboa, W Portugal
Lisbon *see* Lisboa
Lisichansk *see* Lysychans'k
Lisieux *90 B3 anc.* Noviomagus. Calvados, N France
Liski *111 B6 prev.* Georgiu-Dezh. Voronezhskaya Oblast', W Russian Federation
Lisle/l'Isle *see* Lille
Lismore *149 E5* New South Wales, SE Australia
Lissa *see* Vis, Croatia
Lissa *see* Leszno, Poland
Lisse *86 C3* Zuid-Holland, W Netherlands
Litang *128 A5 var.* Gaocheng. Sichuan, C China
Lītani, Nahr el *119 B5 var.* Nahr al Litant. *river* C Lebanon
Litant, Nahr al *see* Lītani, Nahr el
Litauen *see* Lithuania
Lithgow *149 D6* New South Wales, SE Australia
Lithuania *106 B4 off.* Republic of Lithuania, *Ger.* Litauen, *Lith.* Lietuva, *Pol.* Litwa, *Rus.* Litva; *prev.* Lithuanian SSR, *Rus.* Litovskaya SSR. *country* NE Europe

LITHUANIA
Northeast Europe

Official name Republic of Lithuania
Formation 1991 / 1991
Capital Vilnius
Population 3 million / 119 people per sq mile (46 people per sq km)
Total area 25,174 sq. miles (65,200 sq. km)
Languages Lithuanian*, Russian
Religions Roman Catholic 77%, Other 17%, Russian Orthodox 4%, Protestant 1%, Old Believers 1%
Ethnic mix Lithuanian 85%, Polish 7%, Russian 6%, Belarussian 1%, Other 1%
Government Parliamentary system
Currency Litas = 100 centu
Literacy rate 99%
Calorie consumption 3463 kilocalories

Lithuanian SSR *see* Lithuania
Lithuania, Republic of *see* Lithuania
Litóchoro *104 B4 var.* Litohoro, Litókhoron. Kentrikí Makedonía, N Greece
Litohoro/Litókhoron *see* Litóchoro
Litovskaya SSR *see* Lithuania
Little Alföld *99 C6 Ger.* Kleines Ungarisches Tiefland, *Hung.* Kisalföld, *Slvk.* Podunajská Rovina. *plain* Hungary/Slovakia
Little Andaman *133 F2 island* Andaman Islands, India, NE Indian Ocean
Little Barrier Island *150 D2 island* N New Zealand
Little Bay *93 H5 bay* Alboran Sea, Mediterranean Sea
Little Cayman *54 B3 island* E Cayman Islands
Little Falls *45 F2* Minnesota, N USA
Littlefield *49 E2* Texas, SW USA
Little Inagua *54 D2 var.* Inagua Islands. *island* S Bahamas
Little Minch, The *88 B3 strait* NW Scotland, United Kingdom
Little Missouri River *44 D2 river* NW USA
Little Nicobar *133 G3 island* Nicobar Islands, India, NE Indian Ocean
Little Rhody *see* Rhode Island
Little Rock *42 B1 state capital* Arkansas, C USA
Little Saint Bernard Pass *91 D5 Fr.* Col du Petit St-Bernard, *It.* Colle del Piccolo San Bernardo. *pass* France/Italy
Little Sound *42 A5 bay* Bermuda, NW Atlantic Ocean
Littleton *44 D4* Colorado, C USA
Littoria *see* Latina
Litva/Litwa *see* Lithuania
Liu-chou/Liuchow *see* Liuzhou
Liuzhou *128 C6 var.* Liu-chou, Liuchow. Guangxi Zhuangzu Zizhiqu, S China
Livanátai *see* Livanátes
Livanátes *105 B5 prev.* Livanátai. Stereá Elláda, C Greece
Līvāni *106 D4 Ger.* Lievenhof. SE Latvia
Liverpool *39 F5* Nova Scotia, SE Canada
Liverpool *89 C5* NW England, United Kingdom
Livingston *44 B2* Montana, NW USA
Livingston *49 H3* Texas, SW USA
Livingstone *49 H3 var.* Maramba. Southern, S Zambia
Livingstone *78 C3 var.* Maramba. Southern, S Zambia
Livingstone Mountains *151 A7 mountain range* South Island, New Zealand
Livno *100 B4* Federacija Bosne I Hercegovine, SW Bosnia and Herzegovina
Livojoki *84 D4 river* C Finland
Livonia *40 D3* Michigan, N USA
Livorno *96 B3 Eng.* Leghorn. Toscana, C Italy
Lixian Jiang *see* Black River
Lixoúri *105 A5 prev.* Lixoúrion. Kefallinía, Iónia Nisiá, Greece, C Mediterranean Sea
Lixoúrion *see* Lixoúri
Lizarra *see* Estella
Ljouwert *see* Leeuwarden
Ljubelj *see* Loibl Pass
Ljubljana *95 D7 Ger.* Laibach, *It.* Lubiana; *anc.* Aemona, Emona. *country capital* (Slovenia) C Slovenia
Ljungby *85 B7* Kronoberg, S Sweden
Ljusdal *85 C5* Gävleborg, C Sweden
Ljusnan *85 C5 river* C Sweden
Llanelli *89 C6 prev.* Llanelly. SW Wales, United Kingdom
Llanelly *see* Llanelli
Llanes *92 D1* Asturias, N Spain
Llanos *58 D2 physical region* Colombia/Venezuela
Lleida *93 F2 Cast.* Lérida; *anc.* Ilerda. Cataluña, NE Spain
Llucmajor *93 G3* Mallorca, Spain, W Mediterranean Sea
Loaita Island *128 C8 island* W Spratly Islands
Loanda *see* Luanda
Lobatse *78 C4 var.* Lobatsi. Kgatleng, SE Botswana
Lobatsi *see* Lobatse
Löbau *94 D4* Sachsen, E Germany
Lobito *78 B2* Benguela, W Angola
Lob Nor *see* Lop Nur
Lobositz *see* Lovosice
Loburi *see* Lop Buri
Locarno *95 B8 Ger.* Luggarus. Ticino, S Switzerland
Lochem *86 E3* Gelderland, E Netherlands
Lockport *41 E3* New York, NE USA
Lodja *77 D6* Kasai-Oriental, C Dem. Rep. Congo
Lodwar *73 C6* Rift Valley, NW Kenya
Łódź *98 D4 Rus.* Lodz. Łódź, C Poland
Loei *136 C4 var.* Loey, Muang Loei. Loei, C Thailand
Loey *see* Loei
Lofoten *84 B3 var.* Lofoten Islands. *island group* C Norway
Lofoten Islands *see* Lofoten
Logan *44 B3* Utah, W USA
Logan, Mount *36 D3 mountain* Yukon, W Canada
Logroño *93 E1 anc.* Vareia, *Lat.* Juliobriga. La Rioja, N Spain
Loibl Pass *95 D7 Ger.* Loiblpass, *Slvn.* Ljubelj. *pass* Austria/Slovenia
Loiblpass *see* Loibl Pass
Loikaw *136 B4* Kayah State, C Myanmar (Burma)
Loire *90 B4 var.* Liger. *river* C France
Loja *60 B2* Loja, S Ecuador
Lokitaung *73 C5* Rift Valley, NW Kenya
Lokoja *75 G4* Kogi, C Nigeria
Loksa *106 E2 Ger.* Loxa. Harjumaa, NW Estonia
Lolland *85 B8 prev.* Laaland. *island* S Denmark
Lom *104 C1 prev.* Lom-Palanka. Montana, NW Bulgaria
Lomami *77 D6 river* C Dem. Rep. Congo
Lomas *60 D4* Arequipa, SW Peru
Lomas de Zamora *64 D4* Buenos Aires, E Argentina
Lombardia *96 B2 Eng.* Lombardy. *region* N Italy
Lombardy *see* Lombardia
Lombok, Pulau *138 D5 island* Nusa Tenggara, C Indonesia
Lomé *75 F5 country capital* (Togo) S Togo
Lomela *77 D6* Kasai-Oriental, C Dem. Rep. Congo
Lommel *87 C5* Limburg, N Belgium
Lomond, Loch *88 B4 lake* C Scotland, United Kingdom
Lomonosov Ridge *155 B3 var.* Harris Ridge, *Rus.* Khrebet Homonsova. *undersea ridge* Arctic Ocean
Lomonsova, Khrebet *see* Lomonosov Ridge
Lom-Palanka *see* Lom
Lompoc *47 B7* California, W USA
Lom Sak *136 C4 var.* Muang Lom Sak. Phetchabun, C Thailand
Łomża *98 D3 Rus.* Lomzha. Podlaskie, NE Poland
Lomzha *see* Łomża
Loncoche *65 B5* Araucanía, C Chile
Londinium *see* London
London *89 A7 anc.* Augusta, *Lat.* Londinium. *country capital* (United Kingdom) SE England, United Kingdom
London *38 C5* Ontario, S Canada
London *40 C5* Kentucky, S USA
Londonderry *88 B4 var.* Derry, *Ir.* Doire. NW Northern Ireland, United Kingdom
Londonderry, Cape *146 C2 cape* Western Australia
Londrina *63 E4* Paraná, S Brazil
Lone Star State *see* Texas
Long Bay *43 F2 bay* W Jamaica
Long Beach *47 C7* California, W USA
Longford *89 B5 Ir.* An Longfort. Longford, C Ireland
Long Island *54 D2 island* C Bahamas
Long Island *41 G4 island* New York, NE USA
Longlac *38 C3* Ontario, S Canada
Longmont *44 D4* Colorado, C USA
Longreach *148 C4* Queensland, E Australia
Long Strait *115 G1 Eng.* Long Strait. *strait* NE Russian Federation
Long Strait *see* Longa, Proliv
Longview *49 H3* Texas, SW USA
Longview *46 B2* Washington, NW USA
Long Xuyên *137 D6 var.* Longxuyen. An Giang, S Vietnam
Longxuyen *see* Long Xuyên
Longyan *128 D6* Fujian, SE China
Longyearbyen *83 G2 dependent territory capital* (Svalbard) Spitsbergen, W Svalbard
Lons-le-Saunier *90 D4 anc.* Ledo Salinarius. Jura, E France
Lop Buri *137 C5 var.* Loburi. Lop Buri, C Thailand
Lop Nor *see* Lop Nur
Lop Nur *126 C3 var.* Lob Nor, Lop Nor, Lo-pu Po. *seasonal lake* NW China
Loppersum *86 E1* Groningen, NE Netherlands
Lo-pu Po *see* Lop Nur
Lorca *93 E4 Ar.* Lurka; *anc.* Eliocroca, *Lat.* Illurco. Murcia, S Spain

Lord Howe Island *142 C4 island* E Australia
Lord Howe Rise *142 C4 undersea rise* SW Pacific Ocean
Loreto *50 B3* Baja California Sur, NW Mexico
Lorient *90 A3 prev.* l'Orient. Morbihan, NW France
l'Orient *see* Lorient
Lorn, Firth of *88 B4 inlet* W Scotland, United Kingdom
Loro Sae *see* East Timor
Lörrach *95 A7* Baden-Württemberg, S Germany
Lorraine *90 D3 cultural region* N France
Los Alamos *48 C1* New Mexico, SW USA
Los Amates *52 B2* Izabal, E Guatemala
Los Ángeles *65 B5* Bío Bío, C Chile
Los Angeles *47 C7* California, W USA
Losanna *see* Lausanne
Lošinj *100 A3 Ger.* Lussin, *It.* Lussino. *island* W Croatia
Loslau *see* Wodzisław Śląski
Los Mochis *50 C3* Sinaloa, C Mexico
Losonc/Losontz *see* Lučenec
Los Roques, Islas *58 D1 island group* N Venezuela
Lot *91 B5 cultural region* S France
Lot *91 B5 river* S France
Lotagipi Swamp *73 C5 wetland* Kenya/Sudan
Lötzen *see* Giżycko
Loualaba *see* Lualaba
Louangnamtha *136 C3 var.* Luong Nam Tha. Louang Namtha, N Laos
Louangphabang *124 D3 var.* Louangphrabang, Luang Prabang. Louangphabang, N Laos
Louangphrabang *see* Louangphabang
Loubomo *see* Dolisie
Loudéac *90 A3* Côtes d'Armor, NW France
Loudi *128 C5* Hunan, S China
Louga *74 B3* NW Senegal
Louisiade Archipelago *144 B4 island group* SE Papua New Guinea
Louisiana *42 A2 off.* State of Louisiana, *also known as* Creole State, Pelican State. *state* S USA
Louisville *40 C5* Kentucky, S USA
Louisville Ridge *143 E4 undersea ridge* S Pacific Ocean
Loup River *45 E4 river* Nebraska, C USA
Lourdes *91 B6* Hautes-Pyrénées, S France
Lourenço Marques *see* Maputo
Louth *89 E5* E England, United Kingdom
Loutrá *104 C4* Kentrikí Makedonía, N Greece
Louvain *see* Leuven
Louvain-la Neuve *87 C6* Walloon Brabant, C Belgium
Louviers *90 C3* Eure, N France
Lovech *104 C2* Lovech, N Bulgaria
Loveland *44 D4* Colorado, C USA
Lovosice *98 A4 Ger.* Lobositz. Ústecký Kraj, NW Czech Republic
Lóvua *78 C1* Moxico, E Angola
Lowell *41 G3* Massachusetts, NE USA
Löwen *see* Leuven
Lower California *48 A4 Eng.* Lower California. *peninsula* NW Mexico
Lower California *see* Baja California
Lower Hutt *151 D5* Wellington, North Island, New Zealand
Lower Lough Erne *89 A5 lake* SW Northern Ireland, United Kingdom
Lower Red Lake *45 F1 lake* Minnesota, N USA
Lower Rhine *see* Neder Rijn
Lower Tunguska *115 E3 Eng.* Lower Tunguska. *river* N Russian Federation
Lower Tunguska *see* Nizhnyaya Tunguska
Lowestoft *89 E6* E England, United Kingdom
Loxa *see* Loksa
Lo-yang *see* Luoyang
Loyauté, Îles *144 D5 island group* S New Caledonia
Loyev *see* Loyew
Loyew *107 D8 Rus.* Loyev. Homyel'skaya Voblasts', SE Belarus
Loznica *100 C3* Serbia, W Serbia
Lu *see* Shandong, China
Lualaba *77 D6 Fr.* Loualaba. *river* SE Dem. Rep. Congo
Luanda *78 A1 var.* Loanda, *Port.* São Paulo de Loanda. *country capital* (Angola) Luanda, NW Angola
Luang Prabang *see* Louangphabang
Luang, Thale *137 C7 lagoon* S Thailand
Luangua, Rio *see* Luangwa
Luangwa *73 B8 var.* Aruângua, Rio Luangua. *river* Mozambique/Zambia
Luanshya *78 D2* Copperbelt, C Zambia
Luarca *92 C1* Asturias, N Spain
Lubaczów *99 E5 var.* Lúbaczów. Podkarpackie, SE Poland
L'uban' *98 B4* Leningradskaya Oblast', Russian Federation
Lubānas Ezers *see* Lubāns
Lubango *78 B2 Port.* Sá da Bandeira. Huíla, SW Angola
Lubāns *106 D4 var.* Lubānas Ezers. *lake* E Latvia
Lubao *77 D6* Kasai-Oriental, C Dem. Rep. Congo
Lübben *94 D4* Brandenburg, E Germany
Lübbenau *94 D4* Brandenburg, E Germany
Lubbock *49 E2* Texas, SW USA
Lübeck *94 C2* Schleswig-Holstein, N Germany
Lubelska, Wyżyna *98 E4 plateau* SE Poland
Lüben *see* Lubin
Lubiana *see* Ljubljana
Lubin *98 B4 Ger.* Lüben. Dolnośląskie, SW Poland
Lublin *98 E4 Rus.* Lyublin. Lubelskie, E Poland
Lubliniec *98 C4* Śląskie, S Poland
Lubnān, Jabal *see* Liban, Jebel
Lubny *109 F2* Poltavs'ka Oblast', NE Ukraine
Lubsko *98 B4 Ger.* Sommerfeld. Lubuskie, W Poland
Lubumbashi *77 E8 prev.* Élisabethville. Shaba, SE Dem. Rep. Congo
Lubutu *77 D6* Maniema, E Dem. Rep. Congo
Luca *see* Lucca
Lucan *89 B5 Ir.* Leamhcán. Dublin, E Ireland
Lucanian Mountains *see* Lucano, Appennino
Lucano, Appennino *97 D5 Eng.* Lucanian Mountains. *mountain range* S Italy
Lucapa *78 C1 var.* Lukapa. Lunda Norte, NE Angola
Lucca *96 B3 anc.* Luca. Toscana, C Italy
Lucea *54 A4* W Jamaica
Lucena *139 E1 off.* Lucena City. Luzon, N Philippines
Lucena *92 D4* Andalucía, S Spain
Lucena City *see* Lucena
Lučenec *99 D6 Ger.* Losontz, *Hung.* Losonc. Banskobystrický Kraj, C Slovakia
Lucentum *see* Alicante
Lucerna/Lucerne *see* Luzern
Luchow *see* Hefei
Łuck *see* Luts'k
Lucknow *135 E3 var.* Lakhnau. *state capital* Uttar Pradesh, N India
Lüda *see* Dalian
Luda Kamchiya *104 D2 river* E Bulgaria
Ludasch *see* Luduş
Lüderitz *78 B4 prev.* Angra Pequena. Karas, SW Namibia
Ludhiāna *134 D2* Punjab, N India
Ludington *40 C2* Michigan, N USA
Ludsan *see* Ludza
Luduş *108 B4 Ger.* Ludasch, *Hung.* Marosludas. Mureş, C Romania
Ludvika *85 C6* Dalarna, C Sweden
Ludwigsburg *95 B6* Baden-Württemberg, SW Germany
Ludwigsfelde *94 D3* Brandenburg, NE Germany
Ludwigshafen *95 B5 var.* Ludwigshafen am Rhein. Rheinland-Pfalz, W Germany
Ludwigshafen am Rhein *see* Ludwigshafen
Ludwigslust *94 C3* Mecklenburg-Vorpommern, N Germany
Ludza *106 D4 Ger.* Ludsan. E Latvia
Luebo *77 C6* Kasai-Occidental, SW Dem. Rep. Congo
Luena *78 C2 var.* Lwena, *Port.* Luso. Moxico, E Angola
Lufira *77 E7 river* SE Dem. Rep. Congo
Lufkin *49 H3* Texas, SW USA
Luga *110 A4* Leningradskaya Oblast', NW Russian Federation
Lugano *95 B8 Ger.* Lauis. Ticino, S Switzerland
Lugansk *see* Luhans'k
Lugdunum *see* Lyon
Lugdunum Batavorum *see* Leiden
Lugenda, Rio *79 E2 river* N Mozambique
Luggarus *see* Locarno
Lugh Ganana *see* Luuq
Lugo *92 C1 anc.* Lugus Augusti. Galicia, NW Spain
Lugoj *108 A4 Ger.* Lugosch, *Hung.* Lugos. Timiş, W Romania
Lugos/Lugosch *see* Lugoj
Lugus Augusti *see* Lugo
Luguvallium/Luguvallum *see* Carlisle
Luhans'k *109 H3 Rus.* Lugansk; *prev.* Voroshilovgrad. Luhans'ka Oblast', E Ukraine
Luimneach *see* Limerick
Lukapa *see* Lucapa
Lukenie *77 C6 river* C Dem. Rep. Congo
Lukovit *104 C2* Lovech, N Bulgaria
Łuków *98 E4 Ger.* Bogendorf. Lubelskie, E Poland
Lukuga *77 D7 river* SE Dem. Rep. Congo
Luleå *84 D4* Norrbotten, N Sweden
Luleälven *84 C3 river* N Sweden
Lulonga *77 C5 river* NW Dem. Rep. Congo
Lulua *77 D7 river* S Dem. Rep. Congo
Luluabourg *see* Kananga
Lumber State *see* Maine
Lumbo *79 F2* Nampula, NE Mozambique
Lumsden *151 A7* Southland, South Island, New Zealand
Lund *85 B7* Skåne, S Sweden
Lüneburg *94 C3* Niedersachsen, N Germany
Lunga, Isola *see* Dugi Otok
Lungkiang *see* Qiqihar
Lungué-Bungo *78 C2 var.* Lungwebungu. *river* Angola/Zambia
Lungwebungu *see* Lungué-Bungo
Luninets *see* Luninyets
Łuniniec *see* Luninyets
Luninyets *107 B7 Pol.* Łuniniec, *Rus.* Luninets. Brestskaya Voblasts', SW Belarus
Lunteren *86 D4* Gelderland, C Netherlands
Luong Nam Tha *see* Louangnamtha
Luoyang *128 C4 var.* Honan, Lo-yang. Henan, C China
Lupatia *see* Altamura
Lúrio *79 F2* Nampula, NE Mozambique
Lúrio, Rio *79 E2 river* NE Mozambique
Lurka *see* Lorca
Lusaka *78 D2 country capital* (Zambia) Lusaka, SE Zambia
Lushnja *see* Lushnjë
Lushnjë *101 C6 var.* Lushnja. Fier, C Albania
Luso *see* Luena
Lussin/Lussino *see* Lošinj
Lūt, Baḩrat/Lut, Bahret *see* Dead Sea
Lut, Dasht-e *120 D3 var.* Kavīr-e Lūt. *desert* E Iran
Lutetia/Lutetia Parisiorum *see* Paris
Lūt, Kavīr-e *see* Lūt, Dasht-e
Luton *89 D6* E England, United Kingdom
Łutselk'e *37 F4 prev.* Snowdrift. Northwest Territories, W Canada
Luts'k *108 C1 Pol.* Łuck, *Rus.* Lutsk. Volyns'ka Oblast', NW Ukraine
Lutsk *see* Luts'k
Lüttich *see* Liège
Lutzow-Holm Bay *154 C2 var.* Lutzow-Holm Bay. *bay* Antarctica
Lutzow-Holm Bay *see* Lützow Holmbukta
Luuq *73 D6 It.* Lugh Ganana. Gedo, SW Somalia
Luvua *77 D7 river* SE Dem. Rep. Congo
Luwego *73 C8 river* S Tanzania
Luxembourg *87 D8 country capital* (Luxembourg) Luxembourg, S Luxembourg
Luxembourg *87 D8 off.* Grand Duchy of Luxembourg, *var.* Lëtzebuerg, Luxemburg. *country* NW Europe

LUXEMBOURG
Northwest Europe

Official name Grand Duchy of Luxembourg
Formation 1867 / 1867
Capital Luxembourg-Ville

LUXEMBOURG
Northwest Europe

Population 500,000 / 501 people per sq mile (193 people per sq km)
Total area 998 sq. miles (2586 sq. km)
Languages Luxembourgish*, German*, French*
Religions Roman Catholic 97%, Protestant, Orthodox Christian, and Jewish 3%
Ethnic mix Luxembourger 62%, Foreign residents 38%
Government Parliamentary system
Currency Euro = 100 cents
Literacy rate 99%
Calorie consumption 3568 kilocalories

Luxemburg *see* Luxembourg
Luxor *72 B2 Ar.* Al Uqşur. E Egypt
Luza *110 C4* Kirovskaya Oblast', NW Russian Federation
Luz, Costa de la *92 C5 coastal region* SW Spain
Luzern *95 B7 Fr.* Lucerne, *It.* Lucerna. Luzern, C Switzerland
Luzon *139 E1 island* N Philippines
Luzon Strait *125 E3 strait* Philippines/Taiwan
L'viv *108 B2 Ger.* Lemberg, *Pol.* Lwów, *Rus.* L'vov. L'vivs'ka Oblast', W Ukraine
L'vov *see* L'viv
Lwena *see* Luena
Lwów *see* L'viv
Lyakhavichy *107 B6 Rus.* Lyakhovichi. Brestskaya Voblasts', SW Belarus
Lyakhovichi *see* Lyakhavichy
Lyallpur *see* Faisalābād
Lyangar *see* Langar
Lyck *see* Ełk
Lycksele *84 C4* Västerbotten, N Sweden
Lycopolis *see* Asyūţ
Lyel'chytsy *107 C7 Rus.* Lel'chitsy. Homyel'skaya Voblasts', SE Belarus
Lyepyel' *107 D5 Rus.* Lepel'. Vitsyebskaya Voblasts', N Belarus
Lyme Bay *89 C7 bay* S England, United Kingdom
Lynchburg *41 E5* Virginia, NE USA
Lynn *see* King's Lynn
Lynn Lake *37 F4* Manitoba, C Canada
Lynn Regis *see* King's Lynn
Lyon *91 D5 Eng.* Lyons; *anc.* Lugdunum. Rhône, E France
Lyons *see* Lyon
Lyozna *107 E6 Rus.* Liozno. Vitsyebskaya Voblasts', NE Belarus
Lypovets' *108 D2 Rus.* Lipovets. Vinnyts'ka Oblast', C Ukraine
Lys *see* Leie
Lysychans'k *109 H3 Rus.* Lisichansk. Luhans'ka Oblast', E Ukraine
Lyttelton *151 C6* South Island, New Zealand
Lyublin *see* Lublin
Lyubotin *see* Lyubotyn
Lyubotyn *109 G2 Rus.* Lyubotin. Kharkivs'ka Oblast', E Ukraine
Lyulyakovo *104 E2 prev.* Keremitlik. Burgas, E Bulgaria
Lyusina *107 B6 Rus.* Lyusino. Brestskaya Voblasts', SW Belarus
Lyusino *see* Lyusina

M

Maale *see* Male'
Ma'ān *119 B7* Ma'ān, SW Jordan
Maardu *106 D2 Ger.* Maart. Harjumaa, NW Estonia
Ma'aret-en-Nu'man *see* Ma'arrat an Nu'mān
Ma'arrat an Nu'mān *118 B3 var.* Ma'aret-en-Nu'man, *Fr.* Maarret enn Naamâne. Idlib, NW Syria
Maarret enn Naamâne *see* Ma'arrat an Nu'mān
Maart *see* Maardu
Maas *see* Meuse
Maaseik *87 D5 prev.* Maeseyck. Limburg, NE Belgium
Maastricht *87 D6 var.* Maestricht; *anc.* Traiectum ad Mosam, Traiectum Tungorum. Limburg, SE Netherlands
Macao *129 C6 Port.* Macau. Guangdong, SE China

Macapá *63 E1 state capital* Amapá, N Brazil
Macarsca *see* Makarska
Macassar *see* Makassar
Macău *see* Makó, Hungary
Macau *see* Macao
MacCluer Gulf *see* Berau, Teluk
Macdonnell Ranges *146 D4 mountain range* Northern Territory, C Australia
Macedonia *see* Macedonia, FYR
Macedonia, FYR *101 D6 off.* the Former Yugoslav Republic of Macedonia, *var.* Macedonia, *Mac.* Makedonija, *abbrev.* FYR Macedonia, FYROM. *country* SE Europe

MACEDONIA
Southeast Europe

Official name Republic of Macedonia
Formation 1991 / 1991
Capital Skopje
Population 2.1 million / 212 people per sq mile (82 people per sq km)
Total area 9781 sq. miles (25,333 sq. km)
Languages Macedonian*, Albanian*, Turkish, Romani, Serbian
Religions Orthodox Christian 65%, Muslim 29%, Roman Catholic 4%, Other 2%
Ethnic mix Macedonian 64%, Albanian 25%, Turkish 4%, Roma 3%, Serb 2%, Other 2%
Government Presidential / parliamentary system
Currency Macedonian denar = 100 deni
Literacy rate 98%
Calorie consumption 2923 kilocalories

Macedonia, the Former Yugoslav Republic of *see* Macedonia, FYR
Maceió *63 G3 state capital* Alagoas, E Brazil
Machachi *60 B1* Pichincha, C Ecuador
Machala *60 B2* El Oro, SW Ecuador
Machanga *79 E3* Sofala, E Mozambique
Machilīpatnam *132 D1 var.* Bandar Masulipatnam. Andhra Pradesh, E India
Machiques *58 C2* Zulia, NW Venezuela
Macías Nguema Biyogo *see* Bioco, Isla de
Măcin *108 D5* Tulcea, SE Romania
Mackay *148 D4* Queensland, NE Australia
Mackay, Lake *146 C4 salt lake* Northern Territory/Western Australia
Mackenzie *37 E3 river* Northwest Territories, NW Canada
Mackenzie Bay *154 D3 bay* Antarctica
Mackenzie Mountains *36 D3 mountain range* Northwest Territories, NW Canada
Macleod, Lake *146 A4 lake* Western Australia
Macomb *40 A4* Illinois, N USA
Macomer *97 A5* Sardegna, Italy, C Mediterranean Sea
Mâcon *91 D5 anc.* Matisco, Matisco Ædourum. Saône-et-Loire, C France
Macon *42 D2* Georgia, SE USA
Macon *45 G4* Missouri, C USA
Macquarie Ridge *154 C5 undersea ridge* SW Pacific Ocean
Macuspana *51 G4* Tabasco, SE Mexico
Ma'dabā *119 B6 var.* Mādabā, Madeba; *anc.* Medeba. Ma'dabā, NW Jordan
Mādabā *see* Ma'dabā
Madagascar *79 F3 off.* Democratic Republic of Madagascar, *Malg.* Madagasikara; *prev.* Malagasy Republic. *country* W Indian Ocean

MADAGASCAR
Indian Ocean

Official name Republic of Madagascar
Formation 1960 / 1960
Capital Antananarivo
Population 22.9 million / 102 people per sq mile (39 people per sq km)
Total area 226,656 sq. miles (587,040 sq. km)
Languages Malagasy*, French*, English*
Religions Traditional beliefs 52%, Christian (mainly Roman Catholic) 41%, Muslim 7%
Ethnic mix Other Malay 46%, Merina 26%, Betsimisaraka 15%, Betsileo 12%, Other 1%

MADAGASCAR
(continued)

Government Presidential / parliamentary system
Currency Ariary = 5 iraimbilanja
Literacy rate 64%
Calorie consumption 2092 kilocalories

Madagascar *79 F3 island* W Indian Ocean
Madagascar Basin *69 E7 undersea basin* W Indian Ocean
Madagascar, Democratic Republic of *see* Madagascar
Madagascar Plateau *69 E7 var.* Madagascar Ridge, Madagascar Rise, *Rus.* Madagaskarskiy Khrebet. *undersea plateau* W Indian Ocean
Madagascar Rise/Madagascar Ridge *see* Madagascar Plateau
Madagasikara *see* Madagascar
Madagaskarskiy Khrebet *see* Madagascar Plateau
Madang *144 B3* Madang, N Papua New Guinea
Madanīyīn *see* Médenine
Mađarska *see* Hungary
Made *86 C4* Noord-Brabant, S Netherlands
Madeba *see* Ma'dabā
Madeira *70 A2 var.* Ilha de Madeira. *island* Madeira, Portugal, NE Atlantic Ocean
Madeira, Ilha de *see* Madeira
Madeira Plain *66 C3 abyssal plain* E Atlantic Ocean
Madeira, Rio *62 D2 var.* Río Madera. *river* Bolivia/Brazil
Madeleine, Îles de la *39 F4 Eng.* Magdalen Islands. *island group* Québec, E Canada
Madera *47 B6* California, W USA
Madera, Río *see* Madeira, Rio
Madhya Pradesh *135 E4 prev.* Central Provinces and Berar. *cultural region* C India
Madīnat ath Thawrah *118 C2 var.* Ath Thawrah. Ar Raqqah, N Syria
Madioen *see* Madiun
Madison *45 F3* South Dakota, N USA
Madison *40 B3 state capital* Wisconsin, N USA
Madiun *138 D5 prev.* Madioen. Jawa, C Indonesia
Madoera *see* Madura, Pulau
Madona *106 D4 Ger.* Modohn. E Latvia
Madras *see* Tamil Nādu
Madras *see* Chennai
Madre de Dios, Río *61 E3 river* Bolivia/Peru
Madre del Sur, Sierra *51 E5 mountain range* S Mexico
Madre, Laguna *51 F3 lagoon* NE Mexico
Madre, Laguna *49 G5 lagoon* Texas, SW USA
Madre Occidental, Sierra *50 C3 var.* Western Sierra Madre. *mountain range* C Mexico
Madre Oriental, Sierra *51 E3 var.* Eastern Sierra Madre. *mountain range* C Mexico
Madre, Sierra *52 B2 var.* Sierra de Soconusco. *mountain range* Guatemala/Mexico
Madrid *92 D3 country capital* (Spain) Madrid, C Spain
Madura *see* Madurai
Madurai *132 C3 prev.* Madura, Mathurai. Tamil Nādu, S India
Madura, Pulau *138 D5 prev.* Madoera. *island* C Indonesia
Maebashi *131 D5 var.* Maebasi, Mayebashi. Gunma, Honshū, S Japan
Maebasi *see* Maebashi
Mae Nam Khong *see* Mekong
Mae Nam Nan *136 C4 river* NW Thailand
Mae Nam Yom *136 C4 river* W Thailand
Maeseyck *see* Maaseik
Maestricht *see* Maastricht
Maéwo *144 D4 prev.* Aurora. *island* C Vanuatu
Mafia *73 D7 island* E Tanzania
Mafraq/Muḩāfaẓat al Mafraq *see* Al Mafraq
Magadan *115 G3* Magadanskaya Oblast', E Russian Federation
Magallanes *see* Punta Arenas
Magallanes, Estrecho de *see* Magellan, Strait of
Magangué *58 B2* Bolívar, N Colombia
Magdalena *61 F3* El Beni, N Bolivia
Magdalena *50 B1* Sonora, NW Mexico
Magdalena, Isla *50 B3 island* NW Mexico
Magdalena, Río *58 B2 river* C Colombia
Magdalen Islands *see* Madeleine, Îles de la
Magdeburg *94 C4* Sachsen-Anhalt, C Germany
Magelang *138 C5* Jawa, C Indonesia
Magellan, Strait of *65 B8 Sp.* Estrecho de Magallanes. *strait* Argentina/Chile
Magerøy *see* Magerøya
Magerøya *84 D1 var.* Magerøy, *Lapp.* Máhkarávju. *island* N Norway
Maggiore, Lago *see* Maggiore, Lake
Maggiore, Lake *96 B1 It.* Lago Maggiore. *lake* Italy/Switzerland
Maglaj *100 C3* Federacija Bosne I Hercegovine, N Bosnia and Herzegovina
Maglie *97 E6* Puglia, SE Italy
Magna *44 B4* Utah, W USA
Magnesia *see* Manisa
Magnitogorsk *114 B4* Chelyabinskaya Oblast', C Russian Federation
Magnolia State *see* Mississippi
Magta' Lahjar *74 C3 var.* Magta Lahjar, Magta' Lahjar, Magtá Lahjar. Brakna, SW Mauritania
Magtymguly *122 C3 prev.* Garrygala; *Rus.* Kara-gala. W Turkmenistan
Magway *136 A3 var.* Magwe. Magway, W Myanmar (Burma)
Magyar-Becse *see* Bečej
Magyarkanizsa *see* Kanjiža
Magyarország *see* Hungary
Mahajanga *79 F2 var.* Majunga. Mahajanga, NW Madagascar
Mahakam, Sungai *138 D4 var.* Koetai, Kutai. *river* Borneo, C Indonesia
Mahalapye *78 D3 var.* Mahalatswe. Central, SE Botswana
Mahalatswe *see* Mahalapye
Māhān *120 D3* Kermān, E Iran
Mahanādi *135 F4 river* E India
Mahārāshtra *134 D5 cultural region* W India
Mahbés *see* El Mahbas
Mahbūbnagar *134 D5* Telangana, C India
Mahdia *71 F2 var.* Al Mahdīyah, Mehdia. NE Tunisia
Mahé *79 H1 island* Inner Islands, NE Seychelles
Mahia Peninsula *150 E4 peninsula* North Island, New Zealand
Mahilyow *107 D6 Rus.* Mogilëv. Mahilyowskaya Voblasts', E Belarus
Máhkarávju *see* Magerøya
Mahmūd-e 'Erāqī *see* Maḩmūd-e Rāqī
Maḩmūd-e Rāqī *123 E4 var.* Mahmūd-e 'Erāqī. Kāpīsā, NE Afghanistan
Mahón *see* Maó
Mähren *see* Moravia
Mährisch-Weisskirchen *see* Hranice
Maicao *58 C1* La Guajira, N Colombia
Mai Ceu/Mai Chio *see* Maych'ew
Maīdān Shahr *123 E4 prev.* Meydān Shahr. Vardak, E Afghanistan
Maidstone *89 E7* SE England, United Kingdom
Maiduguri *75 H4* Borno, NE Nigeria
Mailand *see* Milano
Maimāna *see* Maīmanah
Maīmanah *122 D3 var.* Meymaneh, Maymana. Fāryāb, NW Afghanistan
Main *95 B5 river* C Germany
Mai-Ndombe, Lac *77 C6 prev.* Lac Léopold II. *lake* W Dem. Rep. Congo
Maine *41 G2 off.* State of Maine, *also known as* Lumber State, Pine Tree State. *state* NE USA
Maine *90 B3 cultural region* NW France
Maine, Gulf of *41 H2 gulf* NE USA
Mainland *88 C2 island* N Scotland, United Kingdom
Mainland *88 D1 island* NE Scotland, United Kingdom
Mainz *95 B5 Fr.* Mayence. Rheinland-Pfalz, SW Germany
Maio *74 A3 var.* Mayo. *island* Ilhas de Sotavento, SE Cape Verde
Maisur *see* Mysore, India
Maisur *see* Karnātaka, India
Maizhokunggar *126 C5* Xizang Zizhiqu, W China
Majorca *93 G3 Eng.* Majorca; *anc.* Baleares Major. *island* Islas Baleares, Spain, W Mediterranean Sea
Majorca *see* Mallorca
Mājro *see* Majuro Atoll
Majunga *see* Mahajanga
Majuro Atoll *144 D2 var.* Mājro. *atoll* Ratak Chain, SE Marshall Islands
Makale *see* Mek'elē
Makarov Basin *155 B3 undersea basin* Arctic Ocean
Makarska *100 B4 It.* Macarsca. Split-Dalmacija, SE Croatia
Makasar *see* Makassar
Makasar, Selat *see* Makassar Straits
Makassar *139 E4 var.* Macassar, Makasar; *prev.* Ujungpandang. Sulawesi, C Indonesia
Makassar Straits *138 D4 Ind.* Makasar Selat. *strait* C Indonesia
Makay *79 F3 var.* Massif du Makay. *mountain range* SW Madagascar
Makay, Massif du *see* Makay
Makedonija *see* Macedonia, FYR
Makeni *74 C4* C Sierra Leone
Makeyevka *see* Makiyivka
Makhachkala *114 A4 prev.* Petrovsk-Port. Respublika Dagestan, SW Russian Federation
Makin *144 D2 prev.* Pitt Island. *atoll* Tungaru, W Kiribati
Makira *see* San Cristobal
Makiyivka *109 G3 Rus.* Makeyevka; *prev.* Dmitriyevsk. Donets'ka Oblast', E Ukraine
Makkah *121 A5 Eng.* Mecca. Makkah, W Saudi Arabia
Makkovik *39 F2* Newfoundland and Labrador, NE Canada
Makó *99 D7 Rom.* Macău. Csongrád, SE Hungary
Makoua *77 B5* Cuvette, C Congo
Makran Coast *120 E4 coastal region* SE Iran
Makrany *107 A6 Rus.* Mokrany. Brestskaya Voblasts', SW Belarus
Mākū *120 B2* Āżarbāyjān-e Gharbī, NW Iran
Makurdi *75 G4* Benue, C Nigeria
Mala *see* Malaita, Solomon Islands
Malabār Coast *132 B3 coast* SW India
Malabo *77 A5 prev.* Santa Isabel. *country capital* (Equatorial Guinea) Isla de Bioco, NW Equatorial Guinea
Malaca *see* Málaga
Malacca, Strait of *138 B3 Ind.* Selat Malaka. *strait* Indonesia/Malaysia
Malacka *see* Malacky
Malacky *99 C6 Hung.* Malacka. Bratislavský Kraj, W Slovakia
Maladzyechna *107 C5 Pol.* Molodeczno, *Rus.* Molodechno. Minskaya Voblasts', C Belarus
Málaga *92 D5 anc.* Malaca. Andalucía, S Spain
Malagarasi River *73 B7 river* W Tanzania Africa
Malagasy Republic *see* Madagascar
Malaita *144 C3 var.* Mala. *island* N Solomon Islands
Malakal *73 B5* Upper Nile, NE South Sudan
Malakula *see* Malekula
Malang *138 D5* Jawa, C Indonesia
Malange *see* Malanje
Malanje *78 B1 var.* Malange. Malanje, NW Angola
Mälaren *85 C6 lake* C Sweden
Malatya *117 E4 anc.* Melitene. Malatya, SE Turkey
Mala Vyska *109 E3 Rus.* Malaya Viska. Kirovohrads'ka Oblast', S Ukraine
Malawi *79 E1 off.* Republic of Malaŵi; *prev.* Nyasaland, Nyasaland Protectorate. *country* S Africa

MALAWI
Southern Africa

Official name Republic of Malawi
Formation 1964 / 1964
Capital Lilongwe
Population 16.4 million / 451 people per sq mile (174 people per sq km)
Total area 45,745 sq. miles (118,480 sq. km)

MALAWI
(continued)

Languages Chewa, Lomwe, Yao, Ngoni, English*
Religions Protestant 55%, Roman Catholic 20%, Muslim 20%, Traditional beliefs 5%
Ethnic mix Bantu 99%, Other 1%
Government Presidential system
Currency Malawi kwacha = 100 tambala
Literacy rate 61%
Calorie consumption 2334 kilocalories

Malawi, Lake *see* Nyasa, Lake
Malaŵi, Republic of *see* Malawi
Malaya Viska *see* Mala Vyska
Malay Peninsula *124 D4 peninsula* Malaysia/Thailand
Malaysia *138 B3 off.* Malaysia, *var.* Federation of Malaysia; *prev.* the separate territories of Federation of Malaya, Sarawak and Sabah (North Borneo) and Singapore. *country* SE Asia

MALAYSIA
Southeast Asia

Official name Federation of Malaysia
Formation 1963 / 1965
Capital Kuala Lumpur; Putrajaya (administrative)
Population 29.7 million / 234 people per sq mile (90 people per sq km)
Total area 127,316 sq. miles (329,750 sq. km)
Languages Bahasa Malaysia*, Malay, Chinese, Tamil, English
Religions Muslim (mainly Sunni) 61%, Buddhist 19%, Christian 9%, Hindu 6%, Other 5%
Ethnic mix Malay 53%, Chinese 26%, Indigenous tribes 12%, Indian 8%, Other 1%
Government Parliamentary system
Currency Ringgit = 100 sen
Literacy rate 93%
Calorie consumption 2855 kilocalories

Malaysia, Federation of *see* Malaysia
Malbork *98 C2 Ger.* Marienburg, Marienburg in Westpreussen. Pomorskie, N Poland
Malchin *94 C3* Mecklenburg-Vorpommern, N Germany
Malden *45 H5* Missouri, C USA
Malden Island *145 G3 prev.* Independence Island. *atoll* E Kiribati
Maldives *132 A4 off.* Maldivian Divehi, Republic of Maldives. *country* N Indian Ocean

MALDIVES
Indian Ocean

Official name Republic of Maldives
Formation 1965 / 1965
Capital Male'
Population 394,491 / 3400 people per sq mile (1315 people per sq km)
Total area 116 sq. miles (300 sq. km)
Languages Dhivehi* (Maldivian), Sinhala, Tamil, Arabic
Religions Sunni Muslim 100%
Ethnic mix Arab–Sinhalese–Malay 100%
Government Presidential system
Currency Rufiyaa = 100 laari
Literacy rate 98%
Calorie consumption 2722 kilocalories

Maldives, Republic of *see* Maldives
Maldivian Divehi *see* Maldives
Male' *132 B4 Div.* Maale. *country capital* (Maldives) Male' Atoll, C Maldives
Male' Atoll *132 B4 var.* Kaafu Atoll. *atoll* C Maldives
Malekula *144 D4 var.* Malakula; *prev.* Mallicolo. *island* W Vanuatu
Malesína *105 C5* Stereá Elláda, E Greece
Malheur Lake *46 C3 lake* Oregon, NW USA
Mali *75 E3 off.* Republic of Mali, *Fr.* République du Mali; *prev.* French Sudan, Sudanese Republic. *country* W Africa

MALI
West Africa

Official name Republic of Mali
Formation 1960 / 1960
Capital Bamako
Population 15.3 million / 32 people per sq mile (13 people per sq km)
Total area 478,764 sq. miles (1,240,000 sq. km)
Languages Bambara, Fulani, Senufo, Soninke, French*
Religions Muslim (mainly Sunni) 90%, Traditional beliefs 6%, Christian 4%
Ethnic mix Bambara 52%, Other 14%, Fulani 11%, Saracolé 7%, Soninka 7%, Tuareg 5%, Mianka 4%
Government Transitional regime
Currency CFA franc = 100 centimes
Literacy rate 34%
Calorie consumption 2833 kilocalories

Malik, Wadi al *see* Milk, Wadi el
Mali Kyun *137 B5 var.* Tavoy Island. *island* Myeik Archipelago, S Myanmar (Burma)
Malin *see* Malyn
Malindi *73 D7* Coast, SE Kenya
Malines *see* Mechelen
Mali, Republic of *see* Mali
Mali, République du *see* Mali
Malkiye *see* Al Mālikīyah
Malko Tŭrnovo *104 E3* Burgas, E Bulgaria
Mallaig *88 B3* N Scotland, United Kingdom
Mallawī *72 B2 var.* Mallawi. C Egypt
Mallawi *see* Mallawī
Mallicolo *see* Malekula
Malmberget *84 C3 Lapp.* Malmivaara. Norrbotten, N Sweden
Malmédy *87 D6* Liège, E Belgium
Malmivaara *see* Malmberget
Malmö *85 B7* Skåne, S Sweden
Maloelap *see* Maloelap Atoll
Maloelap Atoll *144 D1 var.* Maloelap. *atoll* E Marshall Islands
Małopolska, Wyżyna *98 D4 plateau* S Poland
Malozemel'skaya Tundra *110 D3 physical region* NW Russian Federation
Malta *106 D4* SE Latvia
Malta *44 C1* Montana, NW USA
Malta *97 C8 off.* Republic of Malta. *country* C Mediterranean Sea

MALTA
Southern Europe

Official name Republic of Malta
Formation 1964 / 1964
Capital Valletta
Population 400,000 / 3226 people per sq mile (1250 people per sq km)
Total area 122 sq. miles (316 sq. km)
Languages Maltese*, English*
Religions Roman Catholic 98%, Other and nonreligious 2%
Ethnic mix Maltese 96%, Other 4%
Government Parliamentary system
Currency Euro = 100 cents
Literacy rate 92%
Calorie consumption 3389 kilocalories

Malta *97 C8 island* Malta, C Mediterranean Sea
Malta, Canale di *see* Malta Channel
Malta Channel *97 C8 It.* Canale di Malta. *strait* Italy/Malta
Malta, Republic of *see* Malta
Maluku, Laut *see* Molucca Sea
Malung *85 B6* Dalarna, C Sweden
Malventum *see* Benevento
Malvina, Isla Gran *see* West Falkland
Malvinas, Islas *see* Falkland Islands
Malyn *108 D2 Rus.* Malin. Zhytomyrs'ka Oblast', N Ukraine
Malyy Kavkaz *see* Lesser Caucasus
Mamberamo, Sungai *139 H4 river* Papua, E Indonesia
Mambij *see* Manbij
Mamonovo *106 A4 Ger.* Heiligenbeil. Kaliningradskaya Oblast', W Russian Federation
Mamoré, Rio *61 F3 river* Bolivia/Brazil
Mamou *74 C4* W Guinea
Mamoudzou *79 F2 dependent territory capital* (Mayotte) C Mayotte
Mamuno *78 C3* Ghanzi, W Botswana
Manacor *93 G3* Mallorca, Spain, W Mediterranean Sea
Manado *139 F3 prev.* Menado. Sulawesi, C Indonesia
Managua *52 D3 country capital* (Nicaragua) Managua, W Nicaragua
Managua, Lake *52 C3 var.* Xolotlán. *lake* W Nicaragua
Manakara *79 G4* Fianarantsoa, SE Madagascar
Manama *see* Al Manāmah
Mananjary *79 G3* Fianarantsoa, SE Madagascar
Manáos *see* Manaus
Manapouri, Lake *151 A7 lake* South Island, New Zealand
Manar *see* Mannar
Manas, Gora *123 E2 mountain* Kyrgyzstan/Uzbekistan
Manaus *62 D2 prev.* Manáos. *state capital* Amazonas, NW Brazil
Manavgat *116 B4* Antalya, SW Turkey
Manbij *118 C2 var.* Mambij, *Fr.* Membidj. Ḥalab, N Syria
Manchester *89 D5 Lat.* Mancunium. NW England, United Kingdom
Manchester *41 G3* New Hampshire, NE USA
Man-chou-li *see* Manzhouli
Manchurian Plain *125 E1 plain* NE China
Máncio Lima *see* Japiim
Mancunium *see* Manchester
Mand *see* Mand, Rūd-e
Mandalay *136 B3* Mandalay, C Myanmar (Burma)
Mandan *45 E2* North Dakota, N USA
Mandeville *54 B5* C Jamaica
Mándra *105 C6* Attikí, C Greece
Rud-e Mand *120 D4 var.* Mand. *river* S Iran
Mandurah *147 A6* Western Australia
Manduria *97 E5* Puglia, SE Italy
Mandya *132 C2* Karnātaka, C India
Manfredonia *97 D5* Puglia, SE Italy
Mangai *77 C6* Bandundu, W Dem. Rep. Congo
Mangaia *145 G5 island group* S Cook Islands
Mangalia *108 D5 anc.* Callatis. Constanța, SE Romania
Mangalmé *76 C3* Guéra, SE Chad
Mangalore *132 B2* Karnātaka, W India
Mangaung *see* Bloemfontein
Mango *see* Sansanné-Mango, Togo
Mangoky *79 F3 river* W Madagascar
Manhattan *45 F4* Kansas, C USA
Manicouagan, Réservoir *38 D3 lake* Québec, E Canada
Manihiki *145 G4 atoll* N Cook Islands
Manihiki Plateau *143 E3 undersea plateau* C Pacific Ocean
Maniitsoq *82 C3 var.* Manîtsoq, *Dan.* Sukkertoppen. Kitaa, S Greenland
Manila *139 E1 off.* City of Manila. *country capital* (Philippines) Luzon, N Philippines
Manila, City of *see* Manila
Manisa *116 A3 var.* Manissa, *prev.* Saruhan; *anc.* Magnesia. Manisa, W Turkey
Manissa *see* Manisa
Manitoba *37 F5 province* S Canada
Manitoba, Lake *37 F5 lake* Manitoba, S Canada
Manitoulin Island *38 C4 island* Ontario, S Canada
Manîtsoq *see* Maniitsoq
Manizales *58 B3* Caldas, W Colombia
Manjimup *147 A7* Western Australia
Mankato *45 F3* Minnesota, N USA
Manlleu *93 G2* Cataluña, NE Spain
Manly *148 E1* Iowa, C USA
Manmād *134 C5* Mahārāshtra, W India
Mannar *132 C3 var.* Manar. Northern Province, NW Sri Lanka
Mannar, Gulf of *132 C3 gulf* India/Sri Lanka
Mannheim *95 B5* Baden-Württemberg, SW Germany
Manokwari *139 G4* New Guinea, E Indonesia
Manono *77 E7* Shaba, SE Dem. Rep. Congo
Manosque *91 D6* Alpes-de-Haute-Provence, SE France
Manra *145 F3 prev.* Sydney Island. *atoll* Phoenix Islands, C Kiribati
Mansa *78 D2 prev.* Fort Rosebery. Luapula, N Zambia
Mansel Island *37 G3 island* Nunavut, NE Canada
Mansfield *40 D4* Ohio, N USA
Manta *60 A2* Manabí, W Ecuador
Manteca *47 B6* California, W USA
Mantoue *see* Mantova
Mantova *96 B2 Eng.* Mantua, *Fr.* Mantoue. Lombardia, NW Italy
Mantua *see* Mantova
Manuae *145 G4 island* S Cook Islands
Manukau *see* Manurewa
Manurewa *150 D3 var.* Manukau. Auckland, North Island, New Zealand
Manzanares *93 E3* Castilla-La Mancha, C Spain
Manzanillo *54 C3* Granma, E Cuba
Manzanillo *50 D4* Colima, SW Mexico
Manzhouli *127 F1 var.* Man-chou-li. N Mongol Zizhiqu, N China
Mao *76 B3* Kanem, W Chad
Maó *93 H3 Cast.* Mahón, *Eng.* Port Mahon; *anc.* Portus Magonis. Menorc Spain, W Mediterranean Sea
Maoke, Pegunungan *139 H4 Dut.* Sneeuw-gebergte, *Eng.* Snow Mountains. *mountain range* Papua, E Indonesia
Maoming *128 C6* Guangdong, S China
Mapmaker Seamounts *125 H2 seamount range* N Pacific Ocean
Maputo *78 D4 prev.* Lourenço Marques *country capital* (Mozambique) Maput S Mozambique
Marabá *63 F2* Pará, NE Brazil
Maracaibo *58 C1* Zulia, NW Venezuela
Maracaibo, Gulf of *see* Venezuela, Golfo de
Maracaibo, Lake *58 C2 var.* Lake Maracaibo. *inlet* NW Venezuela
Maracaibo, Lake *see* Maracaibo, Lago de
Maracay *58 D2* Aragua, N Venezuela
Marada *see* Marādah
Marādah *71 G3 var.* Marada. N Libya
Maradi *75 G3* Maradi, S Niger
Maragha *see* Marāgheh
Marāgheh *120 C2 var.* Maragha. Āžarbāyjān-e Khāvarī, NW Iran
Marajó, Baía de *63 F1 bay* N Brazil
Marajó, Ilha de *63 E1 island* N Brazil
Marakesh *see* Marrakech
Maramba *see* Livingstone
Maramba *see* Livingstone
Maranhão *63 F2 off.* Estado do Maranhão. *state* E Brazil
Maranhão *63 F2 off.* Estado do Maranhão. *region* E Brazil
Maranhão, Estado do *see* Maranhão
Marañón, Río *60 B2 river* N Peru
Marathon *38 C4* Ontario, S Canada
Marathón *see* Marathónas
Marathónas *105 C5 prev.* Marathón. Attikí, C Greece
Märäzä *see* Qobustan
Marbella *92 D5* Andalucía, S Spain
Marble Bar *146 B4* Western Australia
Marburg *see* Marburg an der Lahn, Germany
Marburg *see* Maribor, Slovenia
Marburg an der Lahn *94 B4 hist.* Marburg. Hessen, W Germany
March *see* Morava
Marche *96 C3 Eng.* Marches. *region* C Italy
Marche *91 C5 cultural region* C France
Marche-en-Famenne *87 C7* Luxembourg, SE Belgium
Marchena, Isla *60 B5 var.* Bindloe Island. *island* Galápagos Islands, Ecuador, E Pacific Ocean
Marches *see* Marche
Mar Chiquita, Laguna *64 C3 lake* C Argentina
Marcounda *see* Markounda
Mardān *134 C1* Khyber Pakhtunkhwa, N Pakistan
Mar del Plata *65 D5* Buenos Aires, E Argentina
Mardin *117 E4* Mardin, SE Turkey
Maré *144 D5 island* Îles Loyauté, E New Caledonia
Marea Neagră *see* Black Sea
Mareeba *148 D3* Queensland, NE Australia
Marek *see* Dupnitsa
Marganets *see* Marhanets'
Margarita, Isla de *59 E1 island* N Venezuela

Margate *89 E7 prev.* Mergate. SE England, United Kingdom
Margherita *see* Jamaame
Margherita, Lake *73 C5 Eng.* Lake Margherita, *It.* Abbaia. *lake* SW Ethiopia
Margherita, Lake *see* Ābaya Hāyk'
Marghita *108 B3 Hung.* Margitta. Bihor, NW Romania
Margitta *see* Marghita
Marhanets' *109 F3 Rus.* Marganets. Dnipropetrovs'ka Oblast', E Ukraine
María Cleofas, Isla *50 C4 island* C Mexico
Maria Island *149 C8 island* Tasmania, SE Australia
María Madre, Isla *50 C4 island* C Mexico
María Magdalena, Isla *50 C4 island* C Mexico
Mariana Trench *125 G4 var.* Challenger Deep. *trench* W Pacific Ocean
Mariánské Lázně *99 A5 Ger.* Marienbad. Karlovarský Kraj, W Czech Republic
Marías, Islas *50 C4 island group* C Mexico
Maria-Theresiopel *see* Subotica
Maribor *95 E7 Ger.* Marburg. NE Slovenia
Marica *see* Maritsa
Maridi *73 B5* Western Equatoria, SW South Sudan
Marie Byrd Land *154 A3 physical region* Antarctica
Marie-Galante *55 G4 var.* Ceyre to the Caribs. *island* SE Guadeloupe
Marienbad *see* Mariánské Lázně
Marienburg *see* Alūksne, Latvia
Marienburg *see* Malbork, Poland
Marienburg in Westpreussen *see* Malbork
Marienhausen *see* Viļaka
Mariental *78 B4* Hardap, SW Namibia
Marienwerder *see* Kwidzyń
Mariestad *85 B6* Västra Götaland, S Sweden
Marietta *42 D2* Georgia, SE USA
Marijampolė *106 B4 prev.* Kapsukas. Marijampolė, S Lithuania
Marília *63 E4* São Paulo, S Brazil
Marín *92 B1* Galicia, NW Spain
Mar'ina Gorka *see* Mar"ina Horka
Mar"ina Horka *107 C6 Rus.* Mar'ina Gorka. Minskaya Voblasts', C Belarus
Maringá *63 E4* Paraná, S Brazil
Marion *45 G3* Iowa, C USA
Marion *40 D4* Ohio, N USA
Marion, Lake *43 E2 reservoir* South Carolina, SE USA
Mariscal Estigarribia *64 D2* Boquerón, NW Paraguay
Maritsa *104 D3 var.* Marica, *Gk.* Évros, *Turk.* Meriç; *anc.* Hebrus. *river* SW Europe
Maritzburg *see* Pietermaritzburg
Mariupol' *109 G4 prev.* Zhdanov. Donets'ka Oblast', SE Ukraine
Marka *73 D6 var.* Merca. Shabeellaha Hoose, S Somalia
Markham, Mount *154 B4 mountain* Antarctica
Markounda *76 C4 var.* Marcounda. Ouham, NW Central African Republic
Marktredwitz *95 C5* Bayern, E Germany
Marlborough *148 D4* Queensland, E Australia
Marmanda *see* Marmande
Marmande *91 B5 anc.* Marmanda. Lot-et-Garonne, SW France
Sea of Marmara *116 A2 Eng.* Sea of Marmara. *sea* NW Turkey
Marmara, Sea of *see* Marmara Denizi
Marmaris *116 A4* Muğla, SW Turkey
Marne *90 C3 cultural region* N France
Marne *90 D3 river* N France
Maro *76 C4* Moyen-Chari, S Chad
Maroantsetra *79 G2* Toamasina, NE Madagascar
Maromokotro *79 G2 mountain* N Madagascar
Maroni *59 G3 Dut.* Marowijne. *river* French Guiana/Suriname
Marosheviz *see* Toplița
Marosludas *see* Luduș
Marosvásárhely *see* Târgu Mureș
Marotiri *143 F4 var.* Îlots de Bass, Morotiri. *island group* Îles Australes, SW French Polynesia
Maroua *76 B3* Extrême-Nord, N Cameroon
Marowijne *see* Maroni
Marquesas Fracture Zone *153 E3 fracture zone* E Pacific Ocean
Marquette *40 B1* Michigan, N USA
Marrakech *70 C2 var.* Marakesh, *Eng.* Marrakesh; *prev.* Morocco. W Morocco
Marrakesh *see* Marrakech
Marrawah *149 C8* Tasmania, SE Australia
Marree *149 B5* South Australia
Marsá al Burayqah *71 G3 var.* Al Burayqah. N Libya
Marsabit *73 C6* Eastern, N Kenya
Marsala *97 B7 anc.* Lilybaeum. Sicilia, Italy, C Mediterranean Sea
Marsberg *94 B4* Nordrhein-Westfalen, W Germany
Marseille *91 D6 Eng.* Marseilles; *anc.* Massilia. Bouches-du-Rhône, SE France
Marseilles *see* Marseille
Marshall *45 F2* Minnesota, N USA
Marshall *49 H2* Texas, SW USA
Marshall Islands *144 C1 off.* Republic of the Marshall Islands. *country* W Pacific Ocean

MARSHALL ISLANDS
Australasia & Oceania

Official name Republic of the Marshall Islands
Formation 1986 / 1986
Capital Majuro
Population 69,747 / 996 people per sq mile (385 people per sq km)
Total area 70 sq. miles (181 sq. km)
Languages Marshallese*, English*, Japanese, German
Religions Protestant 90%, Roman Catholic 8%, Other 2%
Ethnic mix Micronesian 90%, Other 10%
Government Presidential system
Currency US dollar = 100 cents
Literacy rate 91%
Calorie consumption Not available

Marshall Islands, Republic of the *see* Marshall Islands
Marshall Seamounts *125 H3 seamount range* SW Pacific Ocean
Marsh Harbour *54 C1* Great Abaco, W Bahamas
Martaban *see* Mottama
Martha's Vineyard *41 G3 island* Massachusetts, NE USA
Martigues *91 D6* Bouches-du-Rhône, SE France
Martin *99 C5 Ger.* Sankt Martin, *Hung.* Turócszentmárton; *prev.* Turčiansky Svätý Martin. Zilinský Kraj, N Slovakia
Martinique *55 G4 French overseas department* E West Indies
Martinique Channel *see* Martinique Passage
Martinique Passage *55 G4 var.* Dominica Channel, Martinique Channel. *channel* Dominica/ Martinique
Marton *150 D4* Manawatu-Wanganui, North Island, New Zealand
Martos *92 D4* Andalucía, S Spain
Marungu *77 E7 mountain range* SE Dem. Rep. Congo
Mary *122 D3 prev.* Merv. Mary Welaýaty, S Turkmenistan
Maryborough *149 D4* Queensland, E Australia
Maryborough *see* Port Laoise
Mary Island *see* Kanton
Maryland *41 E5 off.* State of Maryland, *also known as* America in Miniature, Cockade State, Free State, Old Line State. *state* NE USA
Maryland, State of *see* Maryland
Maryville *45 F4* Missouri, C USA
Maryville *42 D1* Tennessee, S USA
Masai Steppe *73 C7 grassland* NW Tanzania
Masaka *73 B6* SW Uganda
Masallı *117 H3 Rus.* Masally. S Azerbaijan
Masally *see* Masallı
Masasi *73 C8* Mtwara, SE Tanzania
Masawa/Massawa *see* Mits'iwa
Masaya *52 D3* Masaya, W Nicaragua
Mascarene Basin *141 B5 undersea basin* W Indian Ocean
Mascarene Islands *79 H4 island group* W Indian Ocean
Mascarene Plain *141 B5 abyssal plain* W Indian Ocean
Mascarene Plateau *141 B5 undersea plateau* W Indian Ocean
Maseru *78 D4 country capital* (Lesotho) W Lesotho
Mas-ha *119 D7* W West Bank Asia
Mashhad *120 E2 var.* Meshed. Khorāsān-Razavī, NE Iran
Masindi *73 B6* W Uganda
Masīra *see* Maşīrah, Jazīrat
Masira, Gulf of *121 E5 var.* Gulf of Masira. *bay* E Oman
Masira, Gulf of *see* Maşīrah, Khalīj
Maşīrah, Jazīrat *121 E5 var.* Masīra. *island* E Oman
Masis *see* Büyükağrı Dağı
Maskat *see* Masqaţ
Mason City *45 F3* Iowa, C USA
Masqaţ *121 E5 var.* Maskat, *Eng.* Muscat. *country capital* (Oman) NE Oman
Massa *96 B3* Toscana, C Italy
Massachusetts *41 G3 off.* Commonwealth of Massachusetts, *also known as* Bay State, Old Bay State, Old Colony State. *state* NE USA
Massenya *76 B3* Chari-Baguirmi, SW Chad
Massif Central *91 C5 plateau* C France
Massilia *see* Marseille
Massoukou *see* Franceville
Mastanli *see* Momchilgrad
Masterton *151 D5* Wellington, North Island, New Zealand
Masty *107 B5 Rus.* Mosty. Hrodzyenskaya Voblasts', W Belarus
Masuda *131 B6* Shimane, Honshū, SW Japan
Masuku *see* Franceville
Masvingo *78 D3 prev.* Fort Victoria, Nyanda, Victoria. Masvingo, SE Zimbabwe
Maşyāf *118 B3 Fr.* Misiaf. Ḩamāh, C Syria
Matadi *77 B6* Bas-Congo, W Dem. Rep. Congo
Matagalpa *52 D3* Matagalpa, C Nicaragua
Matale *132 D3* Central Province, C Sri Lanka
Matam *74 C3* NE Senegal
Matamata *150 D3* Waikato, North Island, New Zealand
Matamoros *50 D3* Coahuila, NE Mexico
Matamoros *51 E2* Tamaulipas, C Mexico
Matane *39 E4* Québec, SE Canada
Matanzas *54 B2* Matanzas, NW Cuba
Matara *132 D4* Southern Province, S Sri Lanka
Mataram *138 D5* Pulau Lombok, C Indonesia
Mataró *93 G2 anc.* Illuro. Cataluña, E Spain
Mataura *151 B7* Southland, South Island, New Zealand
Mataura *151 B7 river* South Island, New Zealand
Mata Uta *see* Matā'utu
Matā'utu *145 E4 var.* Mata Uta. *dependent territory capital* (Wallis and Futuna) Île Uvea, Wallis and Futuna
Matera *97 E5* Basilicata, S Italy
Mathurai *see* Madurai
Matianus *see* Orūmīyeh, Daryācheh-ye
Matías Romero *51 F5* Oaxaca, SE Mexico
Matisco/Matisco Ædourum *see* Mâcon
Mato Grosso *63 E3 off.* Estado de Mato Grosso; *prev.* Matto Grosso. *state* W Brazil
Mato Grosso *63 E3 off.* Estado de Mato Grosso; *prev.* Matto Grosso. *region* W Brazil
Mato Grosso do Sul *63 E4 off.* Estado de Mato Grosso do Sul. *state* S Brazil
Mato Grosso do Sul *63 E4 off.* Estado de Mato Grosso do Sul. *region* S Brazil
Mato Grosso do Sul, Estado de *see* Mato Grosso do Sul
Mato Grosso, Estado de *see* Mato Grosso
Mato Grosso, Planalto de *56 C4 plateau* C Brazil
Matosinhos *92 B2 prev.* Matozinhos. Porto, NW Portugal
Matozinhos *see* Matosinhos
Matsue *131 B6 var.* Matsuye, Matue. Shimane, Honshū, SW Japan
Matsumoto *131 C5 var.* Matumoto. Nagano, Honshū, S Japan
Matsuyama *131 B7 var.* Matuyama. Ehime, Shikoku, SW Japan
Matsuye *see* Matsue
Matterhorn *95 A8 It.* Monte Cervino. *mountain* Italy/Switzerland
Matthews Ridge *59 F2* N Guyana
Matthew Town *54 D2* Great Inagua, S Bahamas
Matto Grosso *see* Mato Grosso
Matucana *60 C4* Lima, W Peru
Matue *see* Matsue
Matumoto *see* Matsumoto
Maturín *59 E2* Monagas, NE Venezuela
Matuyama *see* Matsuyama
Mau *135 E3 var.* Maunāth Bhanjan. Uttar Pradesh, N India
Maui *47 B8 island* Hawaii, USA, C Pacific Ocean
Maun *78 C3* North-West, C Botswana
Maunāth Bhanjan *see* Mau
Mauren *94 E1* NE Liechtenstein Europe
Maurice *see* Mauritius
Mauritania *74 C2 off.* Islamic Republic of Mauritania, *Ar.* Mūrītānīyah. *country* W Africa

MAURITANIA
West Africa

Official name Islamic Republic of Mauritania
Formation 1960 / 1960
Capital Nouakchott
Population 3.9 million / 10 people per sq mile (4 people per sq km)
Total area 397,953 sq. miles (1,030,700 sq. km)
Languages Arabic*, Hassaniyah Arabic, Wolof, French
Religions Sunni Muslim 100%
Ethnic mix Maure 81%, Wolof 7%, Tukolor 5%, Other 4%, Soninka 3%
Government Presidential system
Currency Ouguiya = 5 khoums
Literacy rate 46%
Calorie consumption 2791 kilocalories

Mauritania, Islamic Republic of *see* Mauritania
Mauritius *79 H3 off.* Republic of Mauritius, *Fr.* Maurice. *country* W Indian Ocean

MAURITIUS
Indian Ocean

Official name Republic of Mauritius
Formation 1968 / 1968
Capital Port Louis
Population 1.2 million / 1671 people per sq mile (645 people per sq km)
Total area 718 sq. miles (1860 sq. km)
Languages French Creole, Hindi, Urdu, Tamil, Chinese, English*, French
Religions Hindu 48%, Roman Catholic 24%, Muslim 17%, Protestant 9%, Other 2%
Ethnic mix Indo-Mauritian 68%, Creole 27%, Sino-Mauritian 3%, Franco-Mauritian 2%
Government Parliamentary system
Currency Mauritian rupee = 100 cents
Literacy rate 89%
Calorie consumption 3055 kilocalories

Mauritius *141 B5 island* W Indian Ocean
Mauritius, Republic of *see* Mauritius
Mawlamyaing *see* Mawlamyine
Mawlamyine *136 B4 var.* Mawlamyaing, Moulmein. Mon State, S Myanmar (Burma)
Mawson *154 D2 Australian research station* Antarctica
Mayadin *see* Al Mayādīn
Mayaguana *54 D2 island* SE Bahamas
Mayaguana Passage *54 D2 passage* SE Bahamas
Mayagüez *55 F3* W Puerto Rico
Mayamey *120 D2* Semnān, N Iran
Maya Mountains *52 B2 Sp.* Montañas Mayas. *mountain range* Belize/ Guatemala
Mayas, Montañas *see* Maya Mountains

Maych'ew *72 C4 var.* Mai Chio, *It.* Mai Ceu. Tigray, N Ethiopia
Mayebashi *see* Maebashi
Mayence *see* Mainz
Mayfield *151 B6* Canterbury, South Island, New Zealand
Maykop *111 A7* Respublika Adygeya, SW Russian Federation
Maymana *see* Maīmanah
Maymyo *see* Pyin-Oo-Lwin
Mayo *see* Maio
Mayor Island *150 D3 island* NE New Zealand
Mayor Pablo Lagerenza *see* Capitán Pablo Lagerenza
Mayotte *79 F2 French territorial collectivity* E Africa
May Pen *54 B5* C Jamaica
Mayyit, Al Baḩr al *see* Dead Sea
Mazabuka *78 D2* Southern, S Zambia
Mazaca *see* Kayseri
Mazagan *see* El-Jadida
Mazār-e Sharīf *123 E3 var.* Mazār-i Sharif. Balkh, N Afghanistan
Mazār-i Sharif *see* Mazār-e Sharīf
Mazatlán *50 C3* Sinaloa, C Mexico
Mažeikiai *106 B3* Telšiai, NW Lithuania
Mazirbe *106 C2* NW Latvia
Mazra'a *see* Al Mazra'ah
Mazury *98 D3 physical region* NE Poland
Mazyr *107 C7 Rus.* Mozyr'. Homyel'skaya Voblasts', SE Belarus
Mbabane *78 D4 country capital* (Swaziland) NW Swaziland
Mbacké *see* Mbaké
Mbaïki *77 C5 var.* M'Baiki. Lobaye, SW Central African Republic
M'Baiki *see* Mbaïki
Mbaké *74 B3 var.* Mbacké. W Senegal
Mbala *78 D1 prev.* Abercorn. Northern, NE Zambia
Mbale *73 C6* E Uganda
Mbandaka *77 C5 prev.* Coquilhatville. Equateur, NW Dem. Rep. Congo
M'Banza Congo *78 B1 var.* Mbanza Congo; *prev.* São Salvador, São Salvador do Congo. Dem. Rep. Congo, NW Angola
Mbanza-Ngungu *77 B6* Bas-Congo, W Dem. Rep. Congo
Mbarara *73 B6* SW Uganda
Mbé *76 B4* Nord, N Cameroon
Mbeya *73 C7* Mbeya, SW Tanzania
Mbomou/M'Bomu/Mbomu *see* Bomu
Mbour *74 B3* W Senegal
Mbuji-Mayi *77 D7 prev.* Bakwanga. Kasai-Oriental, S Dem. Rep. Congo
McAlester *49 G2* Oklahoma, C USA
McAllen *49 G5* Texas, SW USA
McCamey *49 E3* Texas, SW USA
McComb *42 B3* Mississippi, S USA
McCook *45 E4* Nebraska, C USA
McKean Island *145 E3 island* Phoenix Islands, C Kiribati
Mount McKinley *36 C3 var.* Denali. *mountain* Alaska, USA
McKinley Park *36 C3* Alaska, USA
M'Clintock Channel *37 F2 channel* Nunavut, N Canada
McMinnville *46 B3* Oregon, NW USA
McMurdo *154 B4 US research station* Antarctica
McPherson *45 E5* Kansas, C USA
McPherson *see* Fort McPherson
Mdantsane *78 D5* Eastern Cape, SE South Africa
Mead, Lake *47 D6 reservoir* Arizona/Nevada, W USA
Mecca *see* Makkah
Mechelen *87 C5 Eng.* Mechlin, *Fr.* Malines. Antwerpen, C Belgium
Mechlin *see* Mechelen
Mecklenburger Bucht *94 C2 bay* N Germany
Mecsek *99 C7 mountain range* SW Hungary
Medan *138 B3* Sumatera, E Indonesia
Medeba *see* Ma'dabā
Medellín *58 B3* Antioquia, NW Colombia
Médenine *71 F2 var.* Madanīyīn. SE Tunisia
Medeshamstede *see* Peterborough
Medford *46 B4* Oregon, NW USA
Medgidia *108 D5* Constanța, SE Romania
Medgyes *see* Mediaș
Mediaș *108 B4 Ger.* Mediasch, *Hung.* Medgyes. Sibiu, C Romania
Mediasch *see* Mediaș
Medicine Hat *37 F5* Alberta, SW Canada
Medina *see* Al Madīnah
Medinaceli *93 E2* Castilla y León, N Spain
Medina del Campo *92 D2* Castilla y León, N Spain
Medinat Israel *see* Israel
Mediolanum *see* Saintes, France
Mediolanum *see* Milano, Italy
Mediomatrica *see* Metz
Mediterranean Sea *102 D3 Fr.* Mer Méditerranée. *sea* Africa/Asia/Europe
Méditerranée, Mer *see* Mediterranean Sea
Médoc *91 B5 cultural region* SW France
Medvezh'yegorsk *110 B3* Respublika Kareliya, NW Russian Federation
Meekatharra *147 B5* Western Australia
Meemu Atoll *see* Mulakatholhu
Meerssen *87 D6 var.* Mersen. Limburg, SE Netherlands
Meerut *134 D2* Uttar Pradesh, N India
Megáli Préspa, Límni *see* Prespa, Lake
Meghālaya *113 G3 cultural region* NE India
Mehdia *see* Mahdia
Meheso *see* Mī'ēso
Me Hka *see* Nmai Hka
Mehrīz *120 D3* Yazd, C Iran
Mehtar Lām *123 F4 var.* Mehtarlām, Meterlam, Methariam, Metharlam. Laghmān, E Afghanistan
Mehtarlām *see* Mehtar Lām
Meiktila *136 B3* Mandalay, C Myanmar (Burma)
Méjico *see* Mexico
Mejillones *64 B2* Antofagasta, N Chile
Mek'elē *72 C4 var.* Makale. Tigray, N Ethiopia
Mékhé *74 B3* NW Senegal
Mekong *124 D3 var.* Lan-ts'ang Chiang, *Cam.* Mékôngk, *Chin.* Lancang Jiang, *Lao.* Mènam Khong, Nam Khong, *Th.* Mae Nam Khong, *Tib.* Dza Chu, *Vtn.* Sông Tiên Giang. *river* SE Asia
Mékôngk *see* Mekong
Mekong, Mouths of the *137 E6 delta* S Vietnam
Melaka *138 B3 var.* Malacca. Melaka, Peninsular Malaysia
Melaka, Selat *see* Malacca, Strait of
Melanesia *144 D3 island group* W Pacific Ocean
Melanesian Basin *142 C2 undersea basin* W Pacific Ocean
Melbourne *149 C7 state capital* Victoria, SE Australia
Melbourne *43 E4* Florida, SE USA
Meleda *see* Mljet
Melekeok *144 A2 country capital* (Palau) NW Pacific Ocean
Melghir, Chott *71 E2 var.* Chott Melrhir. *salt lake* E Algeria
Melilla *80 B5 anc.* Rusaddir, Russadir. Melilla, Spain, N Africa
Melilla *70 D2 enclave* Spain, N Africa
Melita *37 F5* Manitoba, S Canada
Melita *see* Mljet
Melitene *see* Malatya
Melitopol' *109 F4* Zaporiz'ka Oblast', SE Ukraine
Melle *87 B5* Oost-Vlaanderen, NW Belgium
Mellerud *85 B6* Västra Götaland, S Sweden
Mellieħa *102 B5* E Malta
Mellizo Sur, Cerro *65 A7 mountain* S Chile
Melo *64 E4* Cerro Largo, NE Uruguay
Melodunum *see* Melun
Melrhir, Chott *see* Melghir, Chott
Melsungen *94 B4* Hessen, C Germany
Melun *90 C3 anc.* Melodunum. Seine-et-Marne, N France
Melville Bay/Melville Bugt *see* Qimusseriarsuaq
Melville Island *146 D2 island* Northern Territory, N Australia
Melville Island *37 E2 island* Parry Islands, Northwest Territories, NW Canada
Melville, Lake *39 F2 lake* Newfoundland and Labrador, E Canada
Melville Peninsula *37 G3 peninsula* Nunavut, NE Canada
Melville Sound *see* Viscount Melville Sound
Membidj *see* Manbij
Memel *see* Neman, NE Europe
Memel *see* Klaipeda, Lithuania
Memmingen *95 B6* Bayern, S Germany
Memphis *42 C1* Tennessee, S USA
Menaam *see* Menaldum
Menado *see* Manado
Ménaka *75 F3* Goa, E Mali
Menaldum *86 D1 Fris.* Menaam. Fryslân, N Netherlands
Mènam Khong *see* Mekong
Mendaña Fracture Zone *153 F4 fracture zone* E Pacific Ocean
Mende *91 C5 anc.* Mimatum. Lozère, S France
Mendeleyev Ridge *155 B2 undersea ridge* Arctic Ocean
Mendocino Fracture Zone *152 D2 fracture zone* NE Pacific Ocean
Mendoza *64 B4* Mendoza, W Argentina
Menemen *116 A3* İzmir, W Turkey
Menengiyn Tal *127 F2 plain* E Mongolia
Menongue *78 B2 var.* Vila Serpa Pinto, *Port.* Serpa Pinto. Cuando Cubango, C Angola
Mentawai, Kepulauan *138 A4 island group* W Indonesia
Meppel *86 D2* Drenthe, NE Netherlands
Meran *see* Merano
Merano *96 C1 Ger.* Meran. Trentino-Alto Adige, N Italy
Merca *see* Marka
Mercedes *64 D3* Corrientes, NE Argentina
Mercedes *64 D4* Soriano, SW Uruguay
Meredith, Lake *49 E1 reservoir* Texas, SW USA
Merefa *109 G2* Kharkivs'ka Oblast', E Ukraine
Mergate *see* Margate
Mergui *see* Myeik
Mergui Archipelago *see* Myeik Archipelago
Mérida *51 H3* Yucatán, SW Mexico
Mérida *92 C4 anc.* Augusta Emerita. Extremadura, W Spain
Mérida *58 C2* Mérida, W Venezuela
Meridian *42 C2* Mississippi, S USA
Mérignac *91 B5* Gironde, SW France
Merín, Laguna *see* Mirim Lagoon
Merkulovichi *see* Myerkulavichy
Merowe *72 B3* Northern, N Sudan
Merredin *147 B6* Western Australia
Mersen *see* Meerssen
Mersey *89 D5 river* NW England, United Kingdom
Mersin *116 C4 var.* İçel. İçel, S Turkey
Mērsrags *106 C3* NW Latvia
Meru *73 C6* Eastern, C Kenya
Merv *see* Mary
Merzifon *116 D2* Amasya, N Turkey
Merzig *95 A5* Saarland, SW Germany
Mesa *48 B2* Arizona, SW USA
Meseritz *see* Międzyrzecz
Meshed *see* Mashhad
Mesopotamia *57 C5 var.* Mesopotamia Argentina. *physical region* NE Argentina
Mesopotamia Argentina *see* Mesopotamia
Messalo, Rio *79 E2 var.* Mualo. *river* NE Mozambique
Messana/Messene *see* Messina
Messina *97 D7 var.* Messana, Messene; *anc.* Zancle. Sicilia, Italy, C Mediterranean Sea
Messina *see* Musina
Messina, Strait of *97 D7 Eng.* Strait of Messina. *strait* SW Italy
Messina, Strait of *see* Messina, Stretto di
Messíni *105 B6* Pelopónnisos, S Greece
Mesta *see* Néstos
Mestghanem *see* Mostaganem
Mest'ia *117 F1 prev.* Mestia, *var.* Mestiya. N Georgia
Mestia *see* Mest'ia
Mestiya *see* Mest'ia
Mestre *96 C2* Veneto, NE Italy
Metairie *42 B3* Louisiana, S USA
Metán *64 C2* Salta, N Argentina
Metapán *52 B2* Santa Ana, NW El Salvador
Meta, Río *58 D3 river* Colombia/Venezuela
Meterlam *see* Mehtar Lām
Methariam/Metharlam *see* Mehtar Lām
Metis *see* Metz
Metković *100 B4* Dubrovnik-Neretva, SE Croatia
Métsovo *104 B4 prev.* Métsovon. Ípeiros, C Greece
Métsovon *see* Métsovo
Metz *90 D3 anc.* Divodurum Mediomatricum, Mediomatrica, Met Moselle, NE France
Meulaboh *138 A3* Sumatera, W Indonesia
Meuse *87 C6 Dut.* Maas. *river* W Europ
Mexcala, Río *see* Balsas, Río
Mexicali *50 A1* Baja California Norte, NW Mexico
Mexicanos, Estados Unidos *see* Mexico
México *51 E4 var.* Ciudad de México, *Eng.* Mexico City. *country capital* (Mexico) México, C Mexico
Mexico *45 G4* Missouri, C USA
Mexico *50 C3 off.* United Mexican State *var.* Méjico, México, *Sp.* Estados Unidos Mexicanos. *country* N Central America

MEXICO
North America

Official name United Mexican States
Formation 1836 / 1848
Capital Mexico City
Population 122 million / 166 people per sq mile (64 people per sq km)
Total area 761,602 sq. miles (1,972,550 sq. km)
Languages Spanish*, Nahuatl, Mayan, Zapotec, Mixtec, Otomi, Totonac, Tzotzil, Tzeltal
Religions Roman Catholic 77%, Other 14%, Protestant 6%, Nonreligious 3%
Ethnic mix Mestizo 60%, Amerindian 30%, European 9%, Other 1%
Government Presidential system
Currency Mexican peso = 100 centavos
Literacy rate 94%
Calorie consumption 3024 kilocalories

México *see* Mexico
Mexico City *see* México
México, Golfo de *see* Mexico, Gulf of
Mexico, Gulf of *51 F2 Sp.* Golfo de México. *gulf* W Atlantic Ocean
Meyadine *see* Al Mayādīn
Meydān Shahr *see* Maīdān Shahr
Meymaneh *see* Maīmanah
Mezen' *110 D3 river* NW Russian Federation
Mezőtúr *99 D7* Jász-Nagykun-Szolnok, E Hungary
Mġarr *102 A5* Gozo, N Malta
Miadzioł Nowy *see* Myadzyel
Miahuatlán *51 F5 var.* Miahuatlán de Porfirio Díaz. Oaxaca, SE Mexico
Miahuatlán de Porfirio Díaz *see* Miahuatlán
Miami *43 F5* Florida, SE USA
Miami *49 G1* Oklahoma, C USA
Miami Beach *43 F5* Florida, SE USA
Mīāneh *120 C2 var.* Miyāneh. Āžarbāyjān-e Sharqī, NW Iran
Mianyang *128 B5* Sichuan, C China
Miastko *98 C2 Ger.* Rummelsburg in Pommern. Pomorskie, N Poland
Mi Chai *see* Nong Khai
Michalovce *99 E5 Ger.* Grossmichel, *Hung.* Nagymihály. Košický Kraj, E Slovakia
Michigan *40 C1 off.* State of Michigan, *also known as* Great Lakes State, Lake State, Wolverine State. *state* N USA
Michigan, Lake *40 C2 lake* N USA
Michurin *see* Tsarevo
Michurinsk *111 B5* Tambovskaya Oblast', W Russian Federation
Micoud *55 F2* SE Saint Lucia
Micronesia *144 B1 off.* Federated States of Micronesia. *country* W Pacific Ocea

MICRONESIA
Australasia & Oceania

Official name Federated States of Micronesia
Formation 1986 / 1986
Capital Palikir (Pohnpei Island)
Population 106,104 / 392 people per sq mile (151 people per sq km)
Total area 271 sq. miles (702 sq. km)
Languages Trukese, Pohnpeian, Kosraean, Yapese, English*
Religions Roman Catholic 50%, Protestant 47%, Other 3%

MICRONESIA
(continued)

Ethnic mix Chuukese 49%, Pohnpeian 24%, Other 14%, Kosraean 6%, Yapese 5%, Asian 2%
Government Nonparty system
Currency US dollar = 100 cents
Literacy rate 81%
Calorie consumption Not available

Micronesia *144 C1 island group* W Pacific Ocean
Micronesia, Federated States of *see* Micronesia
Mid-Atlantic Cordillera *see* Mid-Atlantic Ridge
Mid-Atlantic Ridge *66 C3 var.* Mid-Atlantic Cordillera, Mid-Atlantic Rise, Mid-Atlantic Swell. *undersea ridge* Atlantic Ocean
Mid-Atlantic Rise/Mid-Atlantic Swell *see* Mid-Atlantic Ridge
Middelburg *87 B5* Zeeland, SW Netherlands
Middelharnis *86 B4* Zuid-Holland, SW Netherlands
Middelkerke *87 A5* West-Vlaanderen, W Belgium
Middle America Trench *35 B7 trench* E Pacific Ocean
Middle Andaman *133 F2 island* Andaman Islands, India, NE Indian Ocean
Middle Atlas *70 C2 Eng.* Middle Atlas. *mountain range* N Morocco
Middle Atlas *see* Moyen Atlas
Middleburg Island *see* 'Eua
Middle Congo *see* Congo (Republic of)
Middlesboro *40 C5* Kentucky, S USA
Middlesbrough *89 D5* N England, United Kingdom
Middletown *41 F4* New Jersey, NE USA
Middletown *41 F3* New York, NE USA
Mid-Indian Basin *141 C5 undersea basin* N Indian Ocean
Mid-Indian Ridge *141 C5 var.* Central Indian Ridge. *undersea ridge* C Indian Ocean
Midland *38 D5* Ontario, S Canada
Midland *40 C3* Michigan, N USA
Midland *49 E3* Texas, SW USA
Mid-Pacific Mountains *152 C2 var.* Mid-Pacific Seamounts. *seamount range* NW Pacific Ocean
Mid-Pacific Seamounts *see* Mid-Pacific Mountains
Midway Islands *152 D2 US territory* C Pacific Ocean
Miechów *99 D5* Małopolskie, S Poland
Międzyrzec Podlaski *98 E3* Lubelskie, E Poland
Międzyrzecz *98 B3 Ger.* Meseritz. Lubuskie, W Poland
Mielec *99 D5* Podkarpackie, SE Poland
Miercurea-Ciuc *108 C4 Ger.* Szeklerburg, *Hung.* Csíkszereda. Harghita, C Romania
Mieres del Camín *92 D1 var.* Mieres del Camino. Asturias, NW Spain
Mieres del Camino *see* Mieres del Camín
Mī'ēso *73 D5 var.* Meheso, Miesso. Oromīya, C Ethiopia
Miesso *see* Mī'ēso
Mifrats Hefa *119 A5 Eng.* Bay of Haifa; *prev.* MifrazHefa. *bay* N Israel
Miguel Asua *50 D3 var.* Miguel Auza. Zacatecas, C Mexico
Miguel Auza *see* Miguel Asua
Mijdrecht *86 C3* Utrecht, C Netherlands
Mikashevichi *see* Mikashevichy
Mikashevichy *107 C7 Pol.* Mikaszewicze, *Rus.* Mikashevichi. Brestskaya Voblasts', SW Belarus
Mikaszewicze *see* Mikashevichy
Mikhaylovgrad *see* Montana
Mikhaylovka *111 B6* Volgogradskaya Oblast', SW Russian Federation
Míkonos *see* Mýkonos
Mikre *104 C2* Lovech, N Bulgaria
Mikun' *110 D4* Respublika Komi, NW Russian Federation
Mikuni-sanmyaku *131 D5 mountain range* Honshū, N Japan Asia
Mikura-jima *131 D6 island* E Japan
Milagro *60 B2* Guayas, SW Ecuador
Milan *see* Milano
Milange *79 E2* Zambézia, NE Mozambique
Milano *96 B2 Eng.* Milan, *Ger.* Mailand; *anc.* Mediolanum. Lombardia, N Italy
Milas *116 A4* Muğla, SW Turkey
Milashavichy *107 C7 Rus.* Milashevichi. Homyel'skaya Voblasts', SE Belarus
Milashevichi *see* Milashavichy
Mildura *149 C6* Victoria, SE Australia
Mile *see* Mili Atoll
Miles *149 D5* Queensland, E Australia
Miles City *44 C2* Montana, NW USA
Milford *see* Milford Haven
Milford Haven *89 C6 prev.* Milford. SW Wales, United Kingdom
Milford Sound *151 A6* Southland, South Island, New Zealand
Milford Sound *151 A6 inlet* South Island, New Zealand
Milh, Bahr al *see* Razāzah, Buḩayrat ar
Mili Atoll *144 D2 var.* Mile. *atoll* Ratak Chain, SE Marshall Islands
Mil'kovo *115 H3* Kamchatskiy Kray, E Russian Federation
Milk River *37 E5* Alberta, SW Canada
Milk River *44 C1 river* Montana, NW USA
Milk, Wadi el *88 B4 var.* Wadi al Malik. *river* C Sudan
Milledgeville *43 E2* Georgia, SE USA
Mille Lacs Lake *45 F2 lake* Minnesota, N USA
Millennium Island *143 F3 prev.* Caroline Island, Thornton Island. *atoll* Line Islands, E Kiribati
Millerovo *111 B6* Rostovskaya Oblast', SW Russian Federation
Mílos *105 C6 island* Kykládes, Greece, Aegean Sea
Mílos *105 C6 island* Kykládes, Greece, Aegean Sea
Mílos *105 C7 island* Kykládes, Greece, Aegean Sea
Milton *151 B7* Otago, South Island, New Zealand
Milton Keynes *89 D6* SE England, United Kingdom
Milwaukee *40 B3* Wisconsin, N USA
Mimatum *see* Mende
Min *see* Fujian
Mīnā' Qābūs *140 B3* NE Oman
Minas Gerais *63 F3 off.* Estado de Minas Gerais. *state* E Brazil
Minas Gerais *63 F3 off.* Estado de Minas Gerais. *region* E Brazil
Minas Gerais, Estado de *see* Minas Gerais
Minatitlán *51 F4* Veracruz-Llave, E Mexico
Minbu *136 A3* Magway, W Myanmar (Burma)
Minch, The *88 B3 var.* North Minch. *strait* NW Scotland, United Kingdom
Mindanao *139 F2 island* S Philippines
Mindanao Sea *see* Bohol Sea
Mindelheim *95 C6* Bayern, S Germany
Mindello *see* Mindelo
Mindelo *74 A2 var.* Mindello; *prev.* Porto Grande. São Vicente, N Cape Verde
Minden *94 B4 anc.* Minthun. Nordrhein-Westfalen, NW Germany
Mindoro *139 E2 island* N Philippines
Mindoro Strait *139 E2 strait* W Philippines
Mineral Wells *49 F2* Texas, SW USA
Mingäçevir *117 G2 Rus.* Mingechaur, Mingechevir. C Azerbaijan
Mingāora *see* Saīdu
Mingechaur/Mingechevir *see* Mingäçevir
Mingora *see* Saīdu
Minho *92 B2 former province* N Portugal
Minho *92 B2 Sp.* Miño. *river* Portugal/Spain
Minho, Rio *see* Miño
Minicoy Island *132 B3 island* SW India
Minius *see* Miño
Minna *75 G4* Niger, C Nigeria
Minneapolis *45 F2* Minnesota, N USA
Minnesota *45 F2 off.* State of Minnesota, *also known as* Gopher State, New England of the West, North Star State. *state* N USA
Miño *92 B2 var.* Mino, Minius, *Port.* Rio Minho. *river* Portugal/Spain
Miño *see* Minho, Rio
Minorca *93 H3 Eng.* Minorca; *anc.* Balearis Minor. *island* Islas Baleares, Spain, W Mediterranean Sea
Minorca *see* Menorca
Minot *45 E1* North Dakota, N USA
Minsk *107 C6 country capital* (Belarus) Minskaya Voblasts', C Belarus
Minskaya Wzvyshsha *107 C6 mountain range* C Belarus
Mińsk Mazowiecki *98 D3 var.* Nowo-Minsk. Mazowieckie, C Poland
Minthun *see* Minden
Minto, Lac *38 D2 lake* Québec, C Canada
Minya *see* Al Minyā
Miraflores *50 C3* Baja California Sur, NW Mexico
Miranda de Ebro *93 E1* La Rioja, N Spain
Mirgorod *see* Myrhorod
Miri *138 D3* Sarawak, East Malaysia
Mirim Lagoon *63 E5 var.* Lake Mirim, *Sp.* Laguna Merín. *lagoon* Brazil/Uruguay
Mirim, Lake *see* Mirim Lagoon
Mírina *see* Mýrina
Mīrjāveh *120 E4* Sīstān va Balūchestān, SE Iran
Mirny *154 C3 Russian research station* Antarctica
Mirnyy *115 F3* Respublika Sakha (Yakutiya), NE Russian Federation
Mīrpur Khās *134 B3* Sind, SE Pakistan
Mirtoan Sea *105 C6 Eng.* Mirtoan Sea; *anc.* Myrtoum Mare. *sea* S Greece
Mirtoan Sea *see* Mirtóo Pélagos
Misiaf *see* Maşyāf
Miskito Coast *see* La Mosquitia
Miskitos, Cayos *53 E2 island group* NE Nicaragua
Miskolc *99 D6* Borsod-Abaúj-Zemplén, NE Hungary
Misool, Pulau *139 F4 island* Maluku, E Indonesia
Mişrātah *71 F2 var.* Misurata. NW Libya
Mission *49 G5* Texas, SW USA
Mississippi *42 B2 off.* State of Mississippi, *also known as* Bayou State, Magnolia State. *state* SE USA
Mississippi Delta *42 B4 delta* Louisiana, S USA
Mississippi River *35 C6 river* C USA
Missoula *44 B1* Montana, NW USA
Missouri *45 F5 off.* State of Missouri, *also known as* Bullion State, Show Me State. *state* C USA
Missouri River *45 E3 river* C USA
Mistassini, Lac *38 D3 lake* Québec, SE Canada
Mistelbach an der Zaya *95 E6* Niederösterreich, NE Austria
Misti, Volcán *61 E4 volcano* S Peru
Misurata *see* Mişrātah
Mitau *see* Jelgava
Mitchell *149 D5* Queensland, E Australia
Mitchell *45 E3* South Dakota, N USA
Mitchell, Mount *43 E1 mountain* North Carolina, SE USA
Mitchell River *148 C2 river* Queensland, NE Australia
Mi Tho *see* My Tho
Mitilíni *see* Mytilíni
Mito *131 D5* Ibaraki, Honshū, S Japan
Mitrovica *see* Mitrovicë
Mitrovica/Mitrowitz *see* Sremska Mitrovica, Serbia
Mitrovicë *101 D5 Serb.* Mitrovica, *prev.* Kosovska Mitrovica, Titova Mitrovica. N Kosovo
Mits'iwa *72 C4 var.* Masawa, Massawa. E Eritrea
Mitspe Ramon *119 A7 prev.* Mizpe Ramon. Southern, S Israel
Mittelstadt *see* Baia Sprie
Mitú *58 C4* Vaupés, SE Colombia
Mitumba, Chaîne des/Mitumba Range *see* Mitumba, Monts
Mitumba Range *77 E7 var.* Chaîne des Mitumba, Mitumba Range. *mountain range* E Dem. Rep. Congo
Miueru Wantipa, Lake *77 E7 lake* N Zambia
Miyake-jima *131 D6 island* Sakishima-shotō, SW Japan
Miyako *130 D4* Iwate, Honshū, C Japan
Miyakonojō *131 B8 var.* Miyakonzyô. Miyazaki, Kyūshū, SW Japan
Miyakonzyô *see* Miyakonojō
Miyāneh *see* Mīāneh
Miyazaki *131 B8* Miyazaki, Kyūshū, SW Japan
Mizil *108 C5* Prahova, SE Romania
Miziya *104 C1* Vratsa, NW Bulgaria
Mizpe Ramon *see* Mitspe Ramon
Mjøsa *85 B6 var.* Mjøsen. *lake* S Norway
Mjøsen *see* Mjøsa
Mladenovac *100 D4* Serbia, C Serbia
Mława *98 D3* Mazowieckie, C Poland
Mljet *101 B5 It.* Meleda; *anc.* Melita. *island* S Croatia
Mmabatho *78 C4* North-West, N South Africa
Moab *44 B5* Utah, W USA
Moa Island *148 C1 island* Queensland, NE Australia
Moanda *77 B6 var.* Mouanda. Haut-Ogooué, SE Gabon
Moba *77 E7* Katanga, E Dem. Rep. Congo
Mobay *see* Montego Bay
Mobaye *77 C5* Basse-Kotto, S Central African Republic
Moberly *45 G4* Missouri, C USA
Mobile *42 C3* Alabama, S USA
Mobutu Sese Seko, Lac *see* Albert, Lake
Moçâmedes *see* Namibe
Mochudi *78 C4* Kgatleng, SE Botswana
Mocímboa da Praia *79 F2 var.* Vila de Mocímboa da Praia. Cabo Delgado, N Mozambique
Môco *78 B2 var.* Morro de Môco. *mountain* W Angola
Mocoa *58 A4* Putumayo, SW Colombia
Môco, Morro de *see* Môco
Mocuba *79 E3* Zambézia, NE Mozambique
Modena *96 B3 anc.* Mutina. Emilia-Romagna, N Italy
Modesto *47 B6* California, W USA
Modica *97 C7 anc.* Motyca. Sicilia, Italy, C Mediterranean Sea
Modimolle *78 D4 prev.* Nylstroom. Limpopo, NE South Africa
Modohn *see* Madona
Modriča *100 C3* Republika Srpska, N Bosnia and Herzegovina
Moe *149 C7* Victoria, SE Australia
Möen *see* Møn, Denmark
Moero, Lac *see* Mweru, Lake
Moeskroen *see* Mouscron
Mogadiscio/Mogadishu *see* Muqdisho
Mogador *see* Essaouira
Mogilëv *see* Mahilyow
Mogilev-Podol'skiy *see* Mohyliv-Podil's'kyy
Mogilno *98 C3* Kujawsko-pomorskie, C Poland
Moḩammadābād-e Rīgān *120 E4* Kermān, SE Iran
Mohammedia *70 C2 prev.* Fédala. NW Morocco
Mohave, Lake *47 D7 reservoir* Arizona/Nevada, W USA
Mohawk River *41 F3 river* New York, NE USA
Mohéli *see* Mwali
Mohns Ridge *83 F3 undersea ridge* Greenland Sea/Norwegian Sea
Moho *61 E4* Puno, SE Peru
Mohoro *73 C7* Pwani, E Tanzania
Mohyliv-Podil's'kyy *108 D3 Rus.* Mogilev-Podol'skiy. Vinnyts'ka Oblast', C Ukraine
Moi *85 A6* Rogaland, S Norway
Moili *see* Mwali
Mo i Rana *84 C3* Nordland, C Norway
Mõisaküla *106 D3 Ger.* Moiseküll. Viljandimaa, S Estonia
Moiseküll *see* Mõisaküla
Moissac *91 B6* Tarn-et-Garonne, S France
Mojácar *93 E5* Andalucía, S Spain
Mojave Desert *47 D7 plain* California, W USA
Mokrany *see* Makrany
Moktama *see* Mottama
Mol *87 C5 prev.* Moll. Antwerpen, N Belgium
Moldavia *see* Moldova
Moldavian SSR/Moldavskaya SSR *see* Moldova
Molde *85 A5* Møre og Romsdal, S Norway
Moldotau, Khrebet *see* Moldo-Too, Khrebet
Moldo-Too, Khrebet *123 G2 prev.* Khrebet Moldotau. *mountain range* C Kyrgyzstan

Moldova *108 D3 off.* Republic of Moldova, *var.* Moldavia; *prev.* Moldavian SSR, *Rus.* Moldavskaya SSR. *country* SE Europe

MOLDOVA
Southeast Europe

Official name Republic of Moldova
Formation 1991 / 1991
Capital Chisinau
Population 3.5 million / 269 people per sq mile (104 people per sq km)
Total area 13,067 sq. miles (33,843 sq. km)
Languages Moldovan*, Ukrainian, Russian
Religions Orthodox Christian 93%, Other 6%, Baptist 1%
Ethnic mix Moldovan 84%, Ukrainian 7%, Gagauz 5%, Russian 2%, Bulgarian 1%, Other 1%
Government Parliamentary system
Currency Moldovan leu = 100 bani
Literacy rate 99%
Calorie consumption 2837 kilocalories

Moldova Nouă *108 A4 Ger.* Neumoldowa, *Hung.* Újmoldova. Caraş-Severin, SW Romania
Moldova, Republic of *see* Moldova
Moldoveanul *see* Vârful Moldoveanu
Molfetta *97 E5* Puglia, SE Italy
Moll *see* Mol
Mollendo *61 E4* Arequipa, SW Peru
Mölndal *85 B7* Västra Götaland, S Sweden
Molochans'k *109 G4 Rus.* Molochansk. Zaporiz'ka Oblast', SE Ukraine
Molodechno/Molodeczno *see* Maladzyechna
Molodezhnaya *154 C2 Russian research station* Antarctica
Moloka'i *47 B8 var.* Molokai. *island* Hawai'ian Islands, Hawaii, USA
Molokai Fracture Zone *153 E2 tectonic feature* NE Pacific Ocean
Molopo *78 C4 seasonal river* Botswana/ South Africa
Mólos *105 B5* Stereá Elláda, C Greece
Molotov *see* Severodvinsk, Arkhangel'skaya Oblast', Russian Federation
Molotov *see* Perm', Permskaya Oblast', Russian Federation
Moluccas *139 F4 Dut.* Molukken, *Eng.* Moluccas; *prev.* Spice Islands. *island group* E Indonesia
Moluccas *see* Maluku
Molucca Sea *139 F4 Ind.* Laut Maluku. *sea* E Indonesia
Molukken *see* Maluku
Mombasa *73 D7* Coast, SE Kenya
Mombetsu *see* Monbetsu
Momchilgrad *104 D3 prev.* Mastanli. Kŭrdzhali, S Bulgaria
Møn *85 B8 prev.* Möen. *island* SE Denmark
Mona, Canal de la *see* Mona Passage
Monaco *91 C7 var.* Monaco-Ville; *anc.* Monoecus. *country capital* (Monaco) S Monaco
Monaco *91 E6 off.* Principality of Monaco. *country* W Europe

MONACO
Southern Europe

Official name Principality of Monaco
Formation 1861 / 1861
Capital Monaco-Ville
Population 36,136 / 48,181 people per sq mile (18,531 people per sq km)
Total area 0.75 sq. miles (1.95 sq. km)
Languages French*, Italian, Monégasque, English
Religions Roman Catholic 89%, Protestant 6%, Other 5%
Ethnic mix French 47%, Other 21%, Italian 16%, Monégasque 16%
Government Monarchical / parliamentary system
Currency Euro = 100 cents
Literacy rate 99%
Calorie consumption Not available

Monaco *see* München
Monaco, Port de *91 C8 bay* S Monaco W Mediterranean Sea
Monaco, Principality of *see* Monaco
Monaco-Ville *see* Monaco
Monahans *49 E3* Texas, SW USA
Mona, Isla *55 E3 island* W Puerto Rico
Mona Passage *55 E3 Sp.* Canal de la Mona. *channel* Dominican Republic/ Puerto Rico
Monastir *see* Bitola
Monbetsu *130 D2 var.* Mombetsu, Monbetu. Hokkaidō, NE Japan
Monbetu *see* Monbetsu
Moncalieri *96 A2* Piemonte, NW Italy
Monchegorsk *110 C2* Murmanskaya Oblast', NW Russian Federation
Monclova *50 D2* Coahuila, NE Mexico
Moncton *39 F4* New Brunswick, SE Canada
Mondovì *96 A2* Piemonte, NW Italy
Monfalcone *96 D2* Friuli-Venezia Giulia, NE Italy
Monforte de Lemos *92 C1* Galicia, NW Spain
Mongo *76 C3* Guéra, C Chad
Mongolia *126 C2 Mong.* Mongol Uls. *country* E Asia

MONGOLIA
East Asia

Official name Mongolia
Formation 1924 / 1924
Capital Ulan Bator
Population 2.8 million / 5 people per sq mile (2 people per sq km)
Total area 604,247 sq. miles (1,565,000 sq. km)
Languages Khalkha Mongolian*, Kazakh, Chinese, Russian
Religions Tibetan Buddhist 50%, Nonreligious 40%, Shamanist and Christian 6%, Muslim 4%
Ethnic mix Khalkh 95%, Kazakh 4%, Other 1%
Government Presidential / parliamentary system
Currency Tugrik (tögrög) = 100 möngö
Literacy rate 98%
Calorie consumption 2463 kilocalories

Mongolia, Plateau of *124 D1 plateau* E Mongolia
Mongol Uls *see* Mongolia
Mongora *see* Saïdu
Mongos, Chaîne des *see* Bongo, Massif des
Mongu *78 C2* Western, W Zambia
Monkchester *see* Newcastle upon Tyne
Monkey Bay *79 E2* Southern, SE Malawi
Monkey River *see* Monkey River Town
Monkey River Town *52 C2 var.* Monkey River. Toledo, SE Belize
Monoecus *see* Monaco
Mono Lake *47 C6 lake* California, W USA
Monostor *see* Beli Manastir
Monóvar *93 F4 Cat.* Monòver. Valenciana, E Spain
Monòver *see* Monóvar
Monroe *42 B2* Louisiana, S USA
Monrovia *74 C5 country capital* (Liberia) W Liberia
Mons *87 B6 Dut.* Bergen. Hainaut, S Belgium
Monselice *96 C2* Veneto, NE Italy
Montana *104 C2 prev.* Ferdinand, Mikhaylovgrad. Montana, NW Bulgaria
Montana *44 B1 off.* State of Montana, *also known as* Mountain State, Treasure State. *state* NW USA
Montargis *90 C4* Loiret, C France
Montauban *91 B6* Tarn-et-Garonne, S France
Montbéliard *90 D4* Doubs, E France
Mont Cenis, Col du *91 D5 pass* E France
Mont-de-Marsan *91 B6* Landes, SW France
Monteagudo *61 G4* Chuquisaca, S Bolivia
Montecarlo *91 C8* Misiones, NE Argentina
Monte Caseros *64 D3* Corrientes, NE Argentina
Monte Cristi *54 D3 var.* San Fernando de Monte Cristi. NW Dominican Republic
Monte Croce Carnico, Passo di *see* Plöcken Pass
Montegiardino *96 E2* SE San Marino
Montego Bay *54 A4 var.* Mobay. W Jamaica
Montélimar *91 D5 anc.* Acunum Acusio, Montilium Adhemari. Drôme, E France
Montemorelos *51 E3* Nuevo León, NE Mexico
Montenegro *101 C5 Serb.* Crna Gora. *country* SW Europe

MONTENEGRO
Southeast Europe

Official name Montenegro
Formation 2006 / 2006
Capital Podgorica
Population 600,000 / 113 people per sq mile (43 people per sq km)
Total area 5332 sq. miles (13,812 sq. km)
Languages Montenegrin*, Serbian, Albanian, Bosniak, Croatian
Religions Orthodox Christian 74%, Muslim 18%, Roman Catholic 4%, Other 4%
Ethnic mix Montenegrin 43%, Serb 32%, Other 12%, Bosniak 8%, Albanian 5%
Government Parliamentary system
Currency Euro = 100 cents
Literacy rate 98%
Calorie consumption 3568 kilocalories

Monte Patria *64 B3* Coquimbo, N Chile
Monterey *47 B6* California, W USA
Monterey *see* Monterrey
Monterey Bay *47 A6 bay* California, W USA
Montería *58 B2* Córdoba, NW Colombia
Montero *61 G4* Santa Cruz, C Bolivia
Monterrey *51 E3 var.* Monterey. Nuevo León, NE Mexico
Montes Claros *63 F3* Minas Gerais, SE Brazil
Montevideo *64 D4 country capital* (Uruguay) Montevideo, S Uruguay
Montevideo *45 F2* Minnesota, N USA
Montgenèvre, Col de *91 D5 pass* France/Italy
Montgomery *42 D2 state capital* Alabama, S USA
Montgomery *see* Sāhīwāl
Monthey *95 A7* Valais, SW Switzerland
Montilium Adhemari *see* Montélimar
Montluçon *90 C4* Allier, C France
Montoro *92 D4* Andalucía, S Spain
Montpelier *41 G2 state capital* Vermont, NE USA
Montpellier *91 C6* Hérault, S France
Montréal *39 E4 Eng.* Montreal. Québec, SE Canada
Montrose *88 D3* E Scotland, United Kingdom
Montrose *44 C5* Colorado, C USA
Montserrat *55 G3 var.* Emerald Isle. *UK dependent territory* E West Indies
Monywa *136 B3* Sagaing, C Myanmar (Burma)
Monza *96 B2* Lombardia, N Italy
Monze *78 D2* Southern, S Zambia
Monzón *93 F2* Aragón, NE Spain
Moonie *149 D5* Queensland, E Australia
Moon-Sund *see* Väinameri
Moora *147 A6* Western Australia
Moore *49 G1* Oklahoma, C USA
Moore, Lake *147 B6 lake* Western Australia
Moorhead *45 F2* Minnesota, N USA
Moose *38 C3 river* Ontario, S Canada
Moosehead Lake *41 G1 lake* Maine, NE USA
Moosonee *38 C3* Ontario, SE Canada
Mopti *75 E3* Mopti, C Mali
Moquegua *61 E4* Moquegua, SE Peru
Mora *85 C5* Dalarna, C Sweden
Morales *52 C2* Izabal, E Guatemala
Morant Bay *54 B5* E Jamaica
Moratalla *93 E4* Murcia, SE Spain
Morava *99 C5 var.* March. *river* C Europe
Morava *see* Moravia, Czech Republic
Morava *see* Velika Morava, Serbia
Moravia *99 B5 Cz.* Morava, *Ger.* Mähren. *cultural region* E Czech Republic
Moray Firth *88 C3 inlet* N Scotland, United Kingdom
Morea *see* Pelopónnisos
Moreau River *44 D2 river* South Dakota, N USA
Moree *149 D5* New South Wales, SE Australia
Morelia *51 E4* Michoacán, S Mexico
Morena, Sierra *92 C4 mountain range* S Spain
Moreni *108 C5* Dâmboviţa, S Romania
Morgan City *42 B3* Louisiana, S USA
Murghāb, Daryā-ye *see* Murgap
Morioka *130 D4* Iwate, Honshū, C Japa
Morlaix *90 A3* Finistère, NW France
Mormon State *see* Utah
Mornington Abyssal Plain *67 A7 abyssal plain* SE Pacific Ocean
Mornington Island *148 B2 island* Wellesley Islands, Queensland, N Australia
Morocco *70 B3 off.* Kingdom of Morocco, *Ar.* Al Mamlakah. *country* N Africa

MOROCCO
North Africa

Official name Kingdom of Morocco
Formation 1956 / 1969
Capital Rabat
Population 33 million / 192 people per sq mile (74 people per sq km)
Total area 172,316 sq. miles (446,300 sq. km)
Languages Arabic*, Tamazight (Berber), French, Spanish
Religions Muslim (mainly Sunni) 99%, Other (mostly Christian) 1%
Ethnic mix Arab 70%, Berber 29%, European 1%
Government Monarchical / parliamentary system
Currency Moroccan dirham = 100 centimes
Literacy rate 67%
Calorie consumption 3334 kilocalories

Morocco *see* Marrakech
Morocco, Kingdom of *see* Morocco
Morogoro *73 C7* Morogoro, E Tanzania
Moro Gulf *139 E3 gulf* S Philippines
Morón *54 C2* Ciego de Ávila, C Cuba
Mörön *126 D2* Hövsgöl, N Mongolia
Morondava *79 F3* Toliara, W Madagascar
Moroni *79 F2 country capital* (Comoros) Grande Comore, NW Comoros
Morotai, Pulau *139 F3 island* Maluku, E Indonesia
Morotiri *see* Marotiri
Morphou *see* Güzelyurt
Morrinsville *150 D3* Waikato, North Island, New Zealand
Morris *45 F2* Minnesota, N USA
Morris Jesup, Kap *83 E1 headland* N Greenland
Morvan *90 D4 physical region* C France
Moscow *46 C2* Idaho, NW USA
Moscow *see* Moskva
Mosel *95 A5 Fr.* Moselle. *river* W Europe
Mosel *see* Moselle
Moselle *87 E8 Ger.* Mosel. *river* W Europe
Moselle *see* Mosel
Mosgiel *151 B7* Otago, South Island, New Zealand
Moshi *73 C7* Kilimanjaro, NE Tanzania
Mosjøen *84 B4* Nordland, C Norway
Moskovskiy *see* Moskva
Moskva *111 B5 Eng.* Moscow. *country capital* (Russian Federation) Gorod Moskva, W Russian Federation
Moskva *123 E3 Rus.* Moskovskiy; *prev.* Chubek. SW Tajikistan
Moson and Magyaróvár *see* Mosonmagyaróvár
Mosonmagyaróvár *99 C6 Ger.* Wieselburg-Ungarisch-Altenburg; *prev.* Moson and Magyaróvár, *Ger.* Wieselburg and Ungarisch-Altenburg. Győr-Moson-Sopron, NW Hungary
Mosquito Coast *53 E3 var.* Miskito Coast, *Eng.* Mosquito Coast. *coastal region* E Nicaragua
Mosquito Coast *see* La Mosquitia
Mosquito Gulf *53 F4 Eng.* Mosquito Gulf. *gulf* N Panama
Mosquito Gulf *see* Mosquitos, Golfo de los
Moss *85 B6* Østfold, S Norway
Mossâmedes *see* Namibe
Mosselbaai *78 C5 var.* Mosselbai, *Eng.* Mossel Bay. Western Cape, SW South Africa

osselbai/Mossel Bay *see* Mosselbaai

ossendjo *77 B6* Niari, SW Congo

ossoró *63 G2* Rio Grande do Norte, NE Brazil

ost *98 A4 Ger.* Brüx. Ústecký Kraj, NW Czech Republic

osta *102 B5 var.* Musta. C Malta

ostaganem *70 D2 var.* Mestghanem. NW Algeria

ostar *100 C4* Federacija Bosne I Hercegovine, S Bosnia and Herzegovina

osty *see* Masty

osul *see* Al Mawṣil

ota del Cuervo *93 E3* Castilla-La Mancha, C Spain

otagua, Río *52 B2 river* Guatemala/Honduras

other of Presidents/Mother of States *see* Virginia

otril *92 D5* Andalucía, S Spain

otru *108 B4* Gorj, SW Romania

ottama *136 B4 prev.* Martaban; *var.* Moktama. Mon State, S Myanmar (Burma)

otueka *151 C5* Tasman, South Island, New Zealand

otul *51 H3 var.* Motul de Felipe Carrillo Puerto. Yucatán, SE Mexico

otul de Felipe Carrillo Puerto *see* Motul

otyca *see* Modica

ouanda *see* Moanda

ouhoun *see* Black Volta

ouila *77 A6* Ngounié, C Gabon

oukden *see* Shenyang

ould Bay *37 E2* Prince Patrick Island, Northwest Territories, N Canada

oulins *90 C4* Allier, C France

oulmein *see* Mawlamyine

oundou *76 B4* Logone-Occidental, SW Chad

oûng Roessei *137 D5* Bătdâmbâng, W Cambodia

oun Hou *see* Black Volta

ountain Home *42 B1* Arkansas, C USA

ountain State *see* Montana

ountain State *see* West Virginia

ount Cook *151 B6* Canterbury, South Island, New Zealand

ount Desert Island *41 H2 island* Maine, NE USA

ount Gambier *149 B7* South Australia

ount Isa *148 B3* Queensland, C Australia

ount Magnet *147 B5* Western Australia

ount Pleasant *45 G4* Iowa, C USA

ount Pleasant *40 C3* Michigan, N USA

ount Vernon *40 B5* Illinois, N USA

ount Vernon *46 B1* Washington, NW USA

ourdi, Dépression du *76 C2 desert lowland* Chad/Sudan

ouscron *87 A6 Dut.* Moeskroen. Hainaut, W Belgium

ouse River *see* Souris River

oussoro *76 B3* Kanem, W Chad

oyen-Congo *see* Congo (Republic of)

o'ynoq *122 C1 Rus.* Muynak. Qoraqalpog'iston Respublikasi, NW Uzbekistan

oyobamba *60 B2* San Martín, NW Peru

oyu *126 B3 var.* Karakax. Xinjiang Uygur Zizhiqu, NW China

oyynkum, Peski *123 F1 Kaz.* Moyynqum. *desert* S Kazakhstan

oyynqum *see* Moyynkum, Peski

ozambika, Lakandranon' i *see* Mozambique Channel

ozambique *79 E3 off.* Republic of Mozambique; *prev.* People's Republic of Mozambique, Portuguese East Africa. *country* S Africa

MOZAMBIQUE
Southern Africa

Official name Republic of Mozambique
Formation 1975 / 1975
Capital Maputo
Population 25.8 million / 85 people per sq mile (33 people per sq km)
Total area 309,494 sq. miles (801,590 sq. km)
Languages Makua, Xitsonga, Sena, Lomwe, Portuguese*
Religions Traditional beliefs 56%, Christian 30%, Muslim 14%

MOZAMBIQUE
(continued)

Ethnic mix Makua Lomwe 47%, Tsonga 23%, Malawi 12%, Shona 11%, Yao 4%, Other 3%
Government Presidential system
Currency New metical = 100 centavos
Literacy rate 51%
Calorie consumption 2267 kilocalories

Mozambique Basin *see* Natal Basin

Mozambique, Canal de *see* Mozambique Channel

Mozambique Channel *79 E3 Fr.* Canal de Mozambique, *Mal.* Lakandranon' i Mozambika. *strait* W Indian Ocean

Mozambique, People's Republic of *see* Mozambique

Mozambique Plateau *69 D7 var.* Mozambique Rise. *undersea plateau* SW Indian Ocean

Mozambique, Republic of *see* Mozambique

Mozambique Rise *see* Mozambique Plateau

Mozyr' *see* Mazyr

Mpama *77 B6 river* C Congo

Mpika *78 D2* Northern, NE Zambia

Mqinvartsveri *see* Kazbek

Mrągowo *98 D2 Ger.* Sensburg. Warmińsko-Mazurskie, NE Poland

Mthatha *78 D5 prev.* Umtata. Eastern Cape, SE South Africa

Mtkvari *see* Kura

Mtwara *73 D8* Mtwara, SE Tanzania

Mualo *see* Messalo, Rio

Muang Chiang Rai *see* Chiang Rai

Muang Kalasin *see* Kalasin

Muang Khammouan *see* Thakhèk

Muang Khôg *137 D5* Champasak, S Laos

Muang Khôngxédôn *137 D5 var.* Khong Sedone. Salavan, S Laos

Muang Khon Kaen *see* Khon Kaen

Muang Lampang *see* Lampang

Muang Loei *see* Loei

Muang Lom Sak *see* Lom Sak

Muang Nakhon Sawan *see* Nakhon Sawan

Muang Namo *136 C3* Oudômxai, N Laos

Muang Nan *see* Nan

Muang Phalan *136 D4 var.* Muang Phalane. Savannakhét, S Laos

Muang Phalane *see* Muang Phalan

Muang Phayao *see* Phayao

Muang Phitsanulok *see* Phitsanulok

Muang Phrae *see* Phrae

Muang Roi Et *see* Roi Et

Muang Sakon Nakhon *see* Sakon Nakhon

Muang Samut Prakan *see* Samut Prakan

Muang Sing *136 C3* Louang Namtha, N Laos

Muang Ubon *see* Ubon Ratchathani

Muang Xaignabouri *see* Xaignabouli

Muar *138 B3 var.* Bandar Maharani. Johor, Peninsular Malaysia

Mucojo *79 F2* Cabo Delgado, N Mozambique

Mudanjiang *129 E3 var.* Mu-tan-chiang. Heilongjiang, NE China

Mudon *137 B5* Mon State, S Myanmar (Burma)

Muenchen *see* München

Muenster *see* Münster

Mufulira *78 D2* Copperbelt, C Zambia

Mughla *see* Muğla

Muğla *116 A4 var.* Mughla. Muğla, SW Turkey

Mūḩ, Sabkhat al *118 C3 lake* C Syria

Muhu Väin *see* Väinameri

Muisne *60 A1* Esmeraldas, NW Ecuador

Mukacheve *108 B3 Hung.* Munkács, *Rus.* Mukachevo. Zakarpats'ka Oblast', W Ukraine

Mukachevo *see* Mukacheve

Mukalla *see* Al Mukallā

Mukden *see* Shenyang

Mula *93 E4* Murcia, SE Spain

Mulakatholhu *132 B4 var.* Meemu Atoll, Mulaku Atoll. *atoll* C Maldives

Mulaku Atoll *see* Mulakatholhu

Muleshoe *49 E2* Texas, SW USA

Mulhacén *93 E5 var.* Cerro de Mulhacén. *mountain* S Spain

Mulhacén, Cerro de *see* Mulhacén

Mülhausen *see* Mulhouse

Mülheim *95 A6 var.* Mulheim an der Ruhr. Nordrhein-Westfalen, W Germany

Mulheim an der Ruhr *see* Mülheim

Mulhouse *90 E4 Ger.* Mülhausen. Haut-Rhin, NE France

Müller-gerbergte *see* Muller, Pegunungan

Muller, Pegunungan *138 D4 Dut.* Müller-gerbergte. *mountain range* Borneo, C Indonesia

Mull, Isle of *88 B4 island* W Scotland, United Kingdom

Mulongo *77 D7* Katanga, SE Dem. Rep. Congo

Multān *134 C2* Punjab, E Pakistan

Mumbai *134 C5 prev.* Bombay. *state capital* Mahārāshtra, W India

Munamägi *see* Suur Munamägi

Münchberg *95 C5* Bayern, E Germany

München *95 C6 var.* Muenchen, *Eng.* Munich, *It.* Monaco. Bayern, SE Germany

Muncie *40 C4* Indiana, N USA

Mungbere *77 E5* Orientale, NE Dem. Rep. Congo

Mu Nggava *see* Rennell

Munich *see* München

Munkács *see* Mukacheve

Münster *94 A4 var.* Muenster, Münster in Westfalen. Nordrhein-Westfalen, W Germany

Munster *89 A6 Ir.* Cúige Mumhan. *cultural region* S Ireland

Münster in Westfalen *see* Münster

Muong Xiang Ngeun *136 C4 var.* Xieng Ngeun. Louangphabang, N Laos

Muonio *84 D3* Lappi, N Finland

Muonioälv/Muoniojoki *see* Muonionjoki

Muonionjoki *84 D3 var.* Muoniojoki, *Swe.* Muonioälv. *river* Finland/Sweden

Muqāṭ *119 C5* Al Mafraq, E Jordan

Muqdisho *73 D6 Eng.* Mogadishu, *It.* Mogadiscio. *country capital* (Somalia) Banaadir, S Somalia

Mur *95 E7 SCr.* Mura. *river* C Europe

Mura *see* Mur

Muradiye *117 F3* Van, E Turkey

Murapara *see* Murupara

Murata *96 E2* S San Marino

Murchison River *147 A5 river* Western Australia

Murcia *93 F4* Murcia, SE Spain

Murcia *93 E4 autonomous community* SE Spain

Mureș *108 A4 river* Hungary/Romania

Murfreesboro *42 D1* Tennessee, S USA

Murgab *see* Murghob

Murgap *122 D3* Mary Welaýaty, S Turkmenistan

Murgap *122 D3 var.* Deryasy Murgap, Murghab, *Pash.* Daryā-ye Murghāb, *Rus.* Murgab. *river* Afghanistan/Turkmenistan

Murghob *123 F3 Rus.* Murgab. SE Tajikistan

Murgon *149 E5* Queensland, E Australia

Mūrītānīyah *see* Mauritania

Müritz *94 C3 var.* Müritzee. *lake* NE Germany

Müritzee *see* Müritz

Murmansk *110 C2* Murmanskaya Oblast', NW Russian Federation

Murmashi *110 C2* Murmanskaya Oblast', NW Russian Federation

Murom *111 B5* Vladimirskaya Oblast', W Russian Federation

Muroran *130 D3* Hokkaidō, NE Japan

Muros *92 B1* Galicia, NW Spain

Murray Fracture Zone *153 E2 fracture zone* NE Pacific Ocean

Murray Range *see* Murray Ridge

Murray Ridge *112 C5 var.* Murray Range. *undersea ridge* N Arabian Sea

Murray River *149 B6 river* SE Australia

Murrumbidgee River *149 C6 river* New South Wales, SE Australia

Murska Sobota *95 E7 Ger.* Olsnitz. NE Slovenia

Murupara *150 E3 var.* Murapara. Bay of Plenty, North Island, New Zealand

Murviedro *see* Sagunto

Murwāra *135 E4* Madhya Pradesh, N India

Murwillumbah *149 E5* New South Wales, SE Australia

Murzuq, Edeyin *see* Murzuq, Idhān

Murzuq, Idhan *71 F4 var.* Edeyin Murzuq. *desert* SW Libya

Mürzzuschlag *95 E7* Steiermark, E Austria

Muş *117 F3 var.* Mush. Muş, E Turkey

Musa, Gebel *72 C2 var.* Gebel Mûsa. *mountain* NE Egypt

Mûsa, Gebel *see* Mūsá, Jabal

Musala *104 B3 mountain* W Bulgaria

Muscat *see* Masqaṭ

Muscat and Oman *see* Oman

Muscatine *45 G3* Iowa, C USA

Musgrave Ranges *147 D5 mountain range* South Australia

Musina *78 D3 prev.* Messina. Limpopo, NE South Africa

Muskegon *40 C3* Michigan, N USA

Muskogean *see* Tallahassee

Muskogee *49 G1* Oklahoma, C USA

Musoma *73 C6* Mara, N Tanzania

Musta *see* Mosta

Mustafa-Pasha *see* Svilengrad

Musters, Lago *65 B6 lake* S Argentina

Muswellbrook *149 D6* New South Wales, SE Australia

Mut *116 C4* İçel, S Turkey

Mu-tan-chiang *see* Mudanjiang

Mutare *78 D3 var.* Mutari; *prev.* Umtali. Manicaland, E Zimbabwe

Mutari *see* Mutare

Mutina *see* Modena

Mutsu-wan *130 D3 bay* N Japan

Muttonbird Islands *151 A8 island group* SW New Zealand

Mu Us Shadi *127 E3 var.* Ordos Desert; *prev.* Mu Us Shamo. *desert* N China

Mu Us Shamo *see* Mu Us Shadi

Muy Muy *52 D3* Matagalpa, C Nicaragua

Muynak *see* Mo'ynoq

Mužlja *100 D3 Hung.* Felsőmuzslya; *prev.* Gornja Mužlja. Vojvodina, N Serbia

Mwali *79 F2 var.* Moili, *Fr.* Mohéli. *island* S Comoros

Mwanza *73 B6* Mwanza, NW Tanzania

Mweka *77 C6* Kasai-Occidental, C Dem. Rep. Congo

Mwene-Ditu *77 D7* Kasai-Oriental, S Dem. Rep. Congo

Mweru, Lake *77 D7 var.* Lac Moero. *lake* Dem. Rep. Congo/Zambia

Myadel' *see* Myadzyel

Myadzyel *107 C5 Pol.* Miadzioł Nowy, *Rus.* Myadel'. Minskaya Voblasts', N Belarus

Myanaung *136 B4* Ayeyarwady, SW Myanmar (Burma)

Myanmar *136 A3 off.* Union of Myanmar. *country* SE Asia. *See also* Burma

MYANMAR (BURMA)
Southeast Asia

Official name Republic of the Union of Myanmar
Formation 1948 / 1948
Capital Nay Pyi Taw
Population 53.3 million / 210 people per sq mile (81 people per sq km)
Total area 261,969 sq. miles (678,500 sq. km)
Languages Burmese* (Myanmar), Shan, Karen, Rakhine, Chin, Yangbye, Kachin, Mon
Religions Buddhist 89%, Christian 4%, Muslim 4%, Other 2%, Animist 1%
Ethnic mix Burman (Bamah) 68%, Other 12%, Shan 9%, Karen 7%, Rakhine 4%
Government Presidential system
Currency Kyat = 100 pyas
Literacy rate 93%
Calorie consumption 2528 kilocalories

Myaungmya *136 A4* Ayeyarwady, SW Myanmar (Burma)

Myaydo *see* Aunglan

Myeik *137 B6 var.* Mergui. Tanintharyi, S Myanmar (Burma)

Myeik Archipelago *137 B6 prev.* Mergui Archipelago. *island group* S Myanmar (Burma)

Myerkulavichy *107 D7 Rus.* Merkulovichi. Homyel'skaya Voblasts', SE Belarus

Myingyan *136 B3* Mandalay, C Myanmar (Burma)

Myitkyina *136 B2* Kachin State, N Myanmar (Burma)

Mykolayiv *109 E4 Rus.* Nikolayev. Mykolayivs'ka Oblast', S Ukraine
Mykonos *105 D6 var.* Míkonos. *island* Kykládes, Greece, Aegean Sea
Myrhorod *109 F2 Rus.* Mirgorod. Poltavs'ka Oblast', NE Ukraine
Mýrina *104 D4 var.* Mírina. Límnos, SE Greece
Myrtle Beach *43 F2* South Carolina, SE USA
Mýrtos *105 D8* Kríti, Greece, E Mediterranean Sea
Myrtoum Mare *see* Mirtóo Pélagos
Myślibórz *98 B3* Zachodnio-pomorskie, NW Poland
Mysore *132 C2 var.* Maisur. Karnātaka, W India
Mysore *see* Karnātaka
My Tho *137 E6 var.* Mi Tho. Tiền Giang, S Vietnam
Mytilene *see* Mytilíni
Mytilíni *105 D5 var.* Mitilíni; *anc.* Mytilene. Lésvos, E Greece
Mzuzu *79 E2* Northern, N Malawi

N

Naberezhnyye Chelny *111 D5 prev.* Brezhnev. Respublika Tatarstan, W Russian Federation
Nablus *119 A6 var.* Nābulus, *Heb.* Shekhem; *anc.* Neapolis, *Bibl.* Shechem. N West Bank
Nābulus *see* Nablus
Nacala *79 F2* Nampula, NE Mozambique
Na-Ch'ii *see* Nagqu
Nada *see* Danzhou
Nadi *145 E4 prev.* Nandi. Viti Levu, W Fiji
Nadur *102 A5* Gozo, N Malta
Nadvirna *108 C3 Pol.* Nadwórna, *Rus.* Nadvornaya. Ivano-Frankivs'ka Oblast', W Ukraine
Nadvoitsy *110 B3* Respublika Kareliya, NW Russian Federation
Nadvornaya/Nadwórna *see* Nadvirna
Nadym *114 C3* Yamalo-Nenetskiy Avtonomnyy Okrug, N Russian Federation
Náfpaktos *105 B5 var.* Návpaktos. Dytikí Elláda, C Greece
Náfplio *105 B6 prev.* Návplion. Pelopónnisos, S Greece
Naga *139 E2 off.* Naga City; *prev.* Nueva Caceres. Luzon, N Philippines
Naga City *see* Naga
Nagano *131 C5* Nagano, Honshū, S Japan
Nagaoka *131 D5* Niigata, Honshū, C Japan
Nagara Pathom *see* Nakhon Pathom
Nagara Sridharmaraj *see* Nakhon Si Thammarat
Nagara Svarga *see* Nakhon Sawan
Nagasaki *131 A7* Nagasaki, Kyūshū, SW Japan
Nagato *131 A7* Yamaguchi, Honshū, SW Japan
Nāgercoil *132 C3* Tamil Nādu, SE India
Nagorno-Karabakh *117 G3 var.* Nagorno- Karabakhskaya Avtonomnaya Oblast, *Arm.* Lerrnayin Gharabakh, *Az.* Dağliq Quarabağ, *Rus.* Nagornyy Karabakh. *former autonomous region* SW Azerbaijan
Nagorno- Karabakhskaya Avtonomnaya Oblast *see* Nagorno-Karabakh
Nagornyy Karabakh *see* Nagorno-Karabakh
Nagoya *131 C6* Aichi, Honshū, SW Japan
Nāgpur *134 D4* Mahārāshtra, C India
Nagqu *126 C5 Chin.* Na-Ch'ii; *prev.* Hei-ho. Xizang Zizhiqu, W China
Nagybánya *see* Baia Mare
Nagybecskerek *see* Zrenjanin
Nagydisznód *see* Cisnădie
Nagyenyed *see* Aiud
Nagykálló *99 E6* Szabolcs-Szatmár-Bereg, E Hungary
Nagykanizsa *99 C7 Ger.* Grosskanizsa. Zala, SW Hungary
Nagykároly *see* Carei
Nagykikinda *see* Kikinda
Nagykőrös *99 D7* Pest, C Hungary
Nagymihály *see* Michalovce
Nagysurány *see* Šurany
Nagyszalonta *see* Salonta
Nagyszeben *see* Sibiu
Nagyszentmiklós *see* Sânnicolau Mare
Nagyszöllös *see* Vynohradiv
Nagyszombat *see* Trnava
Nagytapolcsány *see* Topoľčany
Nagyvárad *see* Oradea
Naha *130 A3* Okinawa, Okinawa, SW Japan
Nahariya *119 A5 prev.* Nahariyya. Northern, N Israel
Nahariyya *see* Nahariya
Nahuel Huapí, Lago *65 B5 lake* W Argentina
Nain *39 F2* Newfoundland and Labrador, NE Canada
Nā'īn *120 D3* Eşfahān, C Iran
Nairobi *69 E5 country capital* (Kenya) Nairobi Area, S Kenya
Nairobi *73 C6* Nairobi Area, S Kenya
Naissus *see* Niš
Najaf *see* An Najaf
Najima *see* Fukuoka
Najin *129 E3* NE North Korea
Najrān *121 B6 var.* Abā as Su'ūd. Najrān, S Saudi Arabia
Nakambé *see* White Volta
Nakamura *131 B7 var.* Shimanto. Kōchi, Shikoku, SW Japan
Nakatsugawa *131 C6 var.* Nakatugawa. Gifu, Honshū, SW Japan
Nakatugawa *see* Nakatsugawa
Nakhichevan' *see* Naxçıvan
Nakhodka *115 G5* Primorskiy Kray, SE Russian Federation
Nakhon Pathom *137 C5 var.* Nagara Pathom, Nakorn Pathom. Nakhon Pathom, W Thailand
Nakhon Ratchasima *137 C5 var.* Khorat, Korat. Nakhon Ratchasima, E Thailand
Nakhon Sawan *137 C5 var.* Muang Nakhon Sawan, Nagara Svarga. Nakhon Sawan, W Thailand
Nakhon Si Thammarat *137 C7 var.* Nagara Sridharmaraj, Nakhon Sithamnaraj. Nakhon Si Thammarat, SW Thailand
Nakhon Sithamnaraj *see* Nakhon Si Thammarat
Nakorn Pathom *see* Nakhon Pathom
Nakuru *73 C6* Rift Valley, SW Kenya
Nal'chik *111 B8* Kabardino-Balkarskaya Respublika, SW Russian Federation
Nālūt *71 F2* NW Libya
Namakan Lake *40 A1 lake* Canada/USA
Namangan *123 F2* Namangan Viloyati, E Uzbekistan
Nambala *78 D2* Central, C Zambia
Nam Co *126 C5 lake* W China
Nam Định *136 D3* Nam Ha, N Vietnam
Namib Desert *78 B3 desert* W Namibia
Namibe *78 A2 Port.* Moçâmedes, Mossâmedes. Namibe, SW Angola
Namibia *78 B3 off.* Republic of Namibia, *var.* South West Africa, *Afr.* Suidwes-Afrika, *Ger.* Deutsch-Südwestafrika; *prev.* German Southwest Africa, South-West Africa. *country* S Africa

NAMIBIA
Southern Africa

Official name Republic of Namibia
Formation 1990 / 1994
Capital Windhoek
Population 2.3 million / 7 people per sq mile (3 people per sq km)
Total area 318,694 sq. miles (825,418 sq. km)
Languages Ovambo, Kavango, English*, Bergdama, German, Afrikaans
Religions Christian 90%, Traditional beliefs 10%
Ethnic mix Ovambo 50%, Other tribes 22%, Kavango 9%, Damara 7%, Herero 7%, Other 5%
Government Presidential system
Currency Namibian dollar = 100 cents; South African rand = 100 cents
Literacy rate 76%
Calorie consumption 2086 kilocalories

Namibia, Republic of *see* Namibia
Nam Khong *see* Mekong
Namnetes *see* Nantes
Namo *see* Namu Atoll
Nam Ou *136 C3 river* N Laos
Nampa *46 D3* Idaho, NW USA
Nampula *79 E2* Nampula, NE Mozambique
Namsos *84 B4* Nord-Trøndelag, C Norway
Nam Tha *136 C4 river* N Laos
Namu Atoll *144 D2 var.* Namo. *atoll* Ralik Chain, C Marshall Islands
Namur *87 C6 Dut.* Namen. Namur, SE Belgium
Namyit Island *128 C8 island* S Spratly Islands
Nan *136 C4 var.* Muang Nan. Nan, NW Thailand
Nanaimo *36 D5* Vancouver Island, British Columbia, SW Canada
Nanchang *128 C5 var.* Nan-ch'ang, Nanch'ang-hsien. *province capital* Jiangxi, S China
Nan-ch'ang *see* Nanchang
Nanch'ang-hsien *see* Nanchang
Nan-ching *see* Nanjing
Nancy *90 D3* Meurthe-et-Moselle, NE France
Nandaime *52 D3* Granada, SW Nicaragua
Nānded *134 D5* Mahārāshtra, C India
Nandi *see* Nadi
Nándorhgy *see* Oţelu Roşu
Nandyāl *132 C1* Andhra Pradesh, E India
Nan Hai *see* South China Sea
Naniwa *see* Ōsaka
Nanjing *128 D5 var.* Nan-ching, Nanking; *prev.* Chianning, Chian-ning, Kiang-ning, Jiangsu. *province capital* Jiangsu, E China
Nanking *see* Nanjing
Nanning *128 B6 var.* Nan-ning; *prev.* Yung-ning. Guangxi Zhuangzu Zizhiqu, S China
Nan-ning *see* Nanning
Nanortalik *82 C5* Kitaa, S Greenland
Nanpan Jiang *136 D2 river* S China
Nanping *128 D6 var.* Nan-p'ing; *prev.* Yenping. Fujian, SE China
Nan-p'ing *see* Nanping
Nansei Syotō Trench *see* Ryukyu Trench
Nansen Basin *155 C4 undersea basin* Arctic Ocean
Nansen Cordillera *see* Gakkel Ridge
Nansha Qundao *see* Spratly Islands
Nanterre *90 D1* Hauts-de-Seine, N France
Nantes *90 B4 Bret.* Naoned; *anc.* Condivincum, Namnetes. Loire-Atlantique, NW France
Nantucket Island *41 G3 island* Massachusetts, NE USA
Nanumaga *145 E3 var.* Nanumanga. *atoll* NW Tuvalu
Nanumanga *see* Nanumaga
Nanumea Atoll *145 E3 atoll* NW Tuvalu
Nanyang *128 C5 var.* Nan-yang. Henan, C China
Nan-yang *see* Nanyang
Naoned *see* Nantes
Napa *47 B6* California, W USA
Napier *150 E4* Hawke's Bay, North Island, New Zealand
Naples *43 E5* Florida, SE USA
Naples *see* Napoli
Napo *56 A3 province* NE Ecuador
Napoléon-Vendée *see* la Roche-sur-Yon
Napoli *97 C5 Eng.* Naples, *Ger.* Neapel; *anc.* Neapolis. Campania, S Italy
Napo, Río *60 C1 river* Ecuador/Peru
Naracoorte *149 B7* South Australia
Naradhivas *see* Narathiwat
Narathiwat *137 C7 var.* Naradhivas. Narathiwat, SW Thailand
Narbada *see* Narmada
Narbo Martius *see* Narbonne
Narbonne *91 C6 anc.* Narbo Martius. Aude, S France
Narborough Island *see* Fernandina, Isla
Nares Abyssal Plain *see* Nares Plain
Nares Plain *35 E6 var.* Nares Abyssal Plain. *abyssal plain* NW Atlantic Ocean
Nares Stræde *see* Nares Strait
Nares Strait *82 D1 Dan.* Nares Stræde. *strait* Canada/Greenland
Narew *98 E3 river* E Poland
Narmada *124 B3 var.* Narbada. *river* C India
Narova *see* Narva
Narovlya *see* Narowlya
Narowlya *107 C8 Rus.* Narovlya. Homyel'skaya Voblasts', SE Belarus
Närpes *85 D5 Fin.* Närpiö. Länsi-Suom W Finland
Närpiö *see* Närpes
Narrabri *149 D6* New South Wales, SE Australia
Narrogin *147 B6* Western Australia
Narva *106 E2* Ida-Virumaa, NE Estonia
Narva *106 E2 prev.* Narova. *river* Estonia/Russian Federation
Narva Bay *106 E2 Est.* Narva Laht, *Ger.* Narwa-Bucht, *Rus.* Narvskiy Zaliv. *ba* Estonia/Russian Federation
Narva Laht *see* Narva Bay
Narva Reservoir *106 E2 Est.* Narva Veehoidla, *Rus.* Narvskoye Vodokhranilishche. *reservoir* Estonia/Russian Federation
Narva Veehoidla *see* Narva Reservoir
Narvik *84 C3* Nordland, C Norway
Narvskiy Zaliv *see* Narva Bay
Narvskoye Vodokhranilishche *see* Narva Reservoir
Narwa-Bucht *see* Narva Bay
Nar'yan-Mar *110 D3 prev.* Beloshchel'y Dzerzhinskiy. Nenetskiy Avtonomnyy Okrug, NW Russian Federation
Naryn *123 G2* Narynskaya Oblast', C Kyrgyzstan
Nassau *54 C1 country capital* (The Bahamas) New Providence, N Bahamas
Năsăud *108 B3 Ger.* Nussdorf, *Hung.* Naszód. Bistriţa-Năsăud, N Romania
Nase *see* Naze
Nāshik *134 C5 prev.* Nāsik. Mahārāshtr W India
Nashua *41 G3* New Hampshire, NE USA
Nashville *42 C1 state capital* Tennessee, S USA
Näsijärvi *85 D5 lake* SW Finland
Nāsik *see* Nāshik
Nasir, Buhayrat/ Nâşir, Buḩayrat/ Nâşir,Buḩeiret *see* Nasser, Lake
Nāsiri *see* Ahvāz
Nasiriya *see* An Nāşirīyah
Nasser, Lake *72 B3 var.* Buhayrat Nasir, Buḩayrat Nāşir, Buḩeiret Nâşir. *lake* Egypt/Sudan
Naszód *see* Năsăud
Nata *78 C3* Central, NE Botswana
Natal *63 G2 state capital* Rio Grande do Norte, E Brazil
Natal Basin *141 A6 var.* Mozambique Basin. *undersea basin* W Indian Ocear
Natanya *see* Netanya
Natchez *42 B3* Mississippi, S USA
Natchitoches *42 A2* Louisiana, S USA
Nathanya *see* Netanya
Natitingou *75 F4* NW Benin
Natsrat *see* Natzrat
Natuna Islands *see* Natuna, Kepulauan
Natuna, Kepulauan *124 D4 var.* Natun Islands. *island group* W Indonesia
Naturaliste Plateau *141 E6 undersea plateau* E Indian Ocean
Natzrat *119 A5 var.* Natsrat, *Ar.* En Nazira, *Eng.* Nazareth; *prev.* Nazerat. Northern, N Israel
Naugard *see* Nowogard
Naujamiestis *106 C4* Panevėžys, C Lithuania
Nauru *144 D2 off.* Republic of Nauru; *prev.* Pleasant Island. *country* W Pacific Ocean

NAURU
Australasia & Oceania

Official name Republic of Nauru
Formation 1968 / 1968
Capital Yaren District
Population 9434 / 1165 people per sq mile (449 people per sq km)
Total area 8.1 sq. miles (21 sq. km)
Languages Nauruan*, Kiribati, Chinese, Tuvaluan, English
Religions Nauruan Congregational Church 60%, Roman Catholic 35%, Other 5%
Ethnic mix Nauruan 93%, Chinese 5%, European 1%, Other Pacific islanders 1%
Government Nonparty system
Currency Australian dollar = 100 cents
Literacy rate 95%
Calorie consumption Not available

Nauru, Republic of *see* Nauru
Nauta *60 C2* Loreto, N Peru

avahrudak *107 C6 Pol.* Nowogródek, *Rus.* Novogrudok. Hrodzyenskaya Voblasts', W Belarus
avanagar *see* Jāmnagar
avapolatsk *107 D5 Rus.* Novopolotsk. Vitsyebskaya Voblasts', N Belarus
avarra *93 E2 Eng./Fr.* Navarre. *autonomous community* N Spain
avarre *see* Navarra
avassa Island *54 C3 US unincorporated territory* C West Indies
avoi *see* Navoiy
avoiy *123 E2 Rus.* Navoi. Navoiy Viloyati, C Uzbekistan
avojoa *50 C2* Sonora, NW Mexico
avolat *see* Navolato
avolato *50 C3 var.* Navolat. Sinaloa, C Mexico
ávpaktos *see* Náfpaktos
ávplion *see* Náfplio
awabashah *see* Nawābshāh
awābshāh *134 B3 var.* Nawabashah. Sind, S Pakistan
axçıvan *117 G3 Rus.* Nakhichevan'. SW Azerbaijan
áxos *105 D6 var.* Naxos. Náxos, Kykládes, Greece, Aegean Sea
áxos *105 D6 island* Kykládes, Greece, Aegean Sea
ayoro *130 D2* Hokkaidō, NE Japan
ay Pyi Taw *136 B4 country capital* (Myanmar (Burma)) Mandalay, C Myanmar (Burma)
azareth *see* Natzrat
azca *60 D4* Ica, S Peru
azca Ridge *57 A5 undersea ridge* E Pacific Ocean
aze *130 B3 var.* Nase. Kagoshima, Amami-ōshima, SW Japan
azerat *see* Natzrat
azilli *116 A4* Aydın, SW Turkey
azrēt *73 C5 var.* Adama, Hadama. Oromīya, C Ethiopia
'Dalatando *78 B1 Port.* Salazar, Vila Salazar. Cuanza Norte, NW Angola
Ndélé *76 C4* Bamingui-Bangoran, N Central African Republic
Ndendé *77 B6* Ngounié, S Gabon
Ndindi *77 A6* Nyanga, S Gabon
N'djaména *76 B3 var.* Ndjamena; *prev.* Fort-Lamy. *country capital* (Chad) Chari-Baguirmi, W Chad
Ndjamena *see* N'Djaména
Ndjolé *77 A5* Moyen-Ogooué, W Gabon
Ndola *78 D2* Copperbelt, C Zambia
Ndzouani *see* Nzwani
Neagh, Lough *89 B5 lake* E Northern Ireland, United Kingdom
Néa Moudanía *104 C4 var.* Néa Moudhaniá. Kentrikí Makedonía, N Greece
Néa Moudhaniá *see* Néa Moudanía
Neapel *see* Napoli
Neápoli *104 B4 prev.* Neápolis. Dytikí Makedonía, N Greece
Neápoli *105 D8* Kríti, Greece, E Mediterranean Sea
Neápoli *105 C7* Pelopónnisos, S Greece
Neápolis *see* Neápoli, Greece
Neapolis *see* Napoli, Italy
Neapolis *see* Nablus, West Bank
Near Islands *36 A2 island group* Aleutian Islands, Alaska, USA
Néa Zíchni *104 C3 var.* Néa Zíkhni; *prev.* Néa Zíkhna. Kentrikí Makedonía, NE Greece
Néa Zíkhna/Néa Zíkhni *see* Néa Zíchni
Nebaj *52 B2* Quiché, W Guatemala
Nebitdag *see* Balkanabat
Neblina, Pico da *62 C1 mountain* NW Brazil
Nebraska *44 D4 off.* State of Nebraska, *also known as* Blackwater State, Cornhusker State, Tree Planters State. *state* C USA
Nebraska City *45 F4* Nebraska, C USA
Neches River *49 H3 river* Texas, SW USA
Neckar *95 B6 river* SW Germany
Necochea *65 D5* Buenos Aires, E Argentina
Nederland *see* Netherlands
Neder Rijn *86 D4 Eng.* Lower Rhine. *river* C Netherlands
Nederweert *87 D5* Limburg, SE Netherlands
Neede *86 E3* Gelderland, E Netherlands
Neerpelt *87 D5* Limburg, NE Belgium
Neftekamsk *111 D5* Respublika Bashkortostan, W Russian Federation
Neftezavodsk *see* Seýdi
Negara Brunei Darussalam *see* Brunei
Negēlē *73 D5 var.* Negelli, *It.* Neghelli. Oromīya, C Ethiopia
Negelli *see* Negēlē
Negev *119 A7 Eng.* Negev. *desert* S Israel
Negev *see* HaNegev
Neghelli *see* Negēlē
Negomane *79 E2 var.* Negomano. Cabo Delgado, N Mozambique
Negomano *see* Negomane
Negombo *132 C3* Western Province, SW Sri Lanka
Negotin *100 E4* Serbia, E Serbia
Negra, Punto *60 A3 headland* NW Peru
Negreşti *see* Negreşti-Oaş
Negreşti-Oaş *108 B3 Hung.* Avasfelsőfalu; *prev.* Negreşti. Satu Mare, NE Romania
Negro, Río *65 C5 river* E Argentina
Negro, Rio *62 D1 river* N South America
Negro, Río *64 D4 river* Brazil/Uruguay
Negros *139 E2 island* C Philippines
Nehbandān *120 E3* Khorāsān, E Iran
Neijiang *128 B5* Sichuan, C China
Neiva *58 B3* Huila, S Colombia
Nellore *132 D2* Andhra Pradesh, E India
Nelson *151 C5* Nelson, South Island, New Zealand
Nelson *37 G4 river* Manitoba, C Canada
Néma *74 D3* Hodh ech Chargui, SE Mauritania
Neman *106 B4 Ger.* Ragnit. Kaliningradskaya Oblast', W Russian Federation
Neman *106 A4 Bel.* Nyoman, *Ger.* Memel, *Lith.* Nemunas, *Pol.* Niemen. *river* NE Europe
Nemausus *see* Nîmes
Neméa *105 B6* Pelopónnisos, S Greece
Nemetocenna *see* Arras
Nemours *90 C3* Seine-et-Marne, N France
Nemunas *see* Neman
Nemuro *130 E2* Hokkaidō, NE Japan
Neochóri *105 B5* Dytikí Elláda, C Greece
Nepal *135 E3 off.* Nepal. *country* S Asia

NEPAL
South Asia

Official name Nepal
Formation 1769 / 1769
Capital Kathmandu
Population 27.8 million / 526 people per sq mile (203 people per sq km)
Total area 54,363 sq. miles (140,800 sq. km)
Languages Nepali*, Maithili, Bhojpuri
Religions Hindu 81%, Buddhist 11%, Muslim 4%, Other (including Christian) 4%
Ethnic mix Other 52%, Chhetri 16%, Hill Brahman 13%, Tharu 7%, Magar 7%, Tamang 5%
Government Transitional regime
Currency Nepalese rupee = 100 paisa
Literacy rate 57%
Calorie consumption 2580 kilocalories

Nereta *106 C4* S Latvia
Neretva *100 C4 river* Bosnia and Herzegovina/Croatia
Neris *107 C5 Bel.* Viliya, *Pol.* Wilia; *prev. Pol.* Wilja. *river* Belarus/Lithuania
Neris *see* Viliya
Nerva *92 C4* Andalucía, S Spain
Neryungri *115 F4* Respublika Sakha (Yakutiya), NE Russian Federation
Neskaupstaður *83 E5* Austurland, E Iceland
Ness, Loch *88 C3 lake* N Scotland, United Kingdom
Nesterov *see* Zhovkva
Néstos *104 C3 Bul.* Mesta, *Turk.* Kara Su. *river* Bulgaria/Greece
Nesvizh *see* Nyasvizh
Netanya *119 A6 var.* Natanya, Nathanya. Central, C Israel
Netherlands *86 C3 off.* Kingdom of the Netherlands, *var.* Holland, *Dut.* Koninkrijk der Nederlanden, Nederland. *country* NW Europe

NETHERLANDS
Northwest Europe

Official name Kingdom of the Netherlands
Formation 1648 / 1839

NETHERLANDS
(continued)

Capital Amsterdam; The Hague (administrative)
Population 16.8 million / 1283 people per sq mile (495 people per sq km)
Total area 16,033 sq. miles (41,526 sq. km)
Languages Dutch*, Frisian
Religions Roman Catholic 36%, Other 34%, Protestant 27%, Muslim 3%
Ethnic mix Dutch 82%, Other 12%, Surinamese 2%, Turkish 2%, Moroccan 2%
Government Parliamentary system
Currency Euro = 100 cents
Literacy rate 99%
Calorie consumption 3147 kilocalories

Netherlands East Indies *see* Indonesia
Netherlands Guiana *see* Suriname
Netherlands, Kingdom of the *see* Netherlands
Netherlands New Guinea *see* Papua
Nettilling Lake *37 G3 lake* Baffin Island, Nunavut, N Canada
Netze *see* Noteć
Neu Amerika *see* Puławy
Neubrandenburg *94 D3* Mecklenburg-Vorpommern, NE Germany
Neuchâtel *95 A7 Ger.* Neuenburg. Neuchâtel, W Switzerland
Neuchâtel, Lac de *95 A7 Ger.* Neuenburger See. *lake* W Switzerland
Neuenburger See *see* Neuchâtel, Lac de
Neufchâteau *87 D8* Luxembourg, SE Belgium
Neugradisk *see* Nova Gradiška
Neuhof *see* Zgierz
Neukuhren *see* Pionerskiy
Neumarkt *see* Târgu Secuiesc, Covasna, Romania
Neumarkt *see* Târgu Mureş
Neumoldowa *see* Moldova Nouă
Neumünster *94 B2* Schleswig-Holstein, N Germany
Neunkirchen *95 A5* Saarland, SW Germany
Neuquén *65 B5* Neuquén, SE Argentina
Neuruppin *94 C3* Brandenburg, NE Germany
Neusalz an der Oder *see* Nowa Sól
Neu Sandec *see* Nowy Sącz
Neusatz *see* Novi Sad
Neusiedler See *95 E6 Hung.* Fertő. *lake* Austria/Hungary
Neusohl *see* Banská Bystrica
Neustadt *see* Baia Mare, Maramureş, Romania
Neustadt an der Haardt *see* Neustadt an der Weinstrasse
Neustadt an der Weinstrasse *95 B5 prev.* Neustadt an der Haardt, *hist.* Niewenstat; *anc.* Nova Civitas. Rheinland-Pfalz, SW Germany
Neustadtl *see* Novo mesto
Neustettin *see* Szczecinek
Neustrelitz *94 D3* Mecklenburg-Vorpommern, NE Germany
Neutra *see* Nitra
Neu-Ulm *95 B6* Bayern, S Germany
Neuwied *95 A5* Rheinland-Pfalz, W Germany
Neuzen *see* Terneuzen
Nevada *47 C5 off.* State of Nevada, *also known as* Battle Born State, Sagebrush State, Silver State. *state* W USA
NevadaSierra *92 D5 mountain range* S Spain
Nevada, Sierra *47 C6 mountain range* W USA
Nevers *90 C4 anc.* Noviodunum. Nièvre, C France
Neves *76 E2* São Tomé, S Sao Tome and Principe, Africa
Nevinnomyssk *111 B7* Stavropol'skiy Kray, SW Russian Federation
Nevşehir *116 C3 var.* Nevshehr. Nevşehir, C Turkey
Newala *73 C8* Mtwara, SE Tanzania
New Albany *40 C5* Indiana, N USA
New Amsterdam *59 G3* E Guyana
Newark *41 F4* New Jersey, NE USA
New Bedford *41 G3* Massachusetts, NE USA
Newberg *46 B3* Oregon, NW USA
New Bern *43 F1* North Carolina, SE USA
New Braunfels *49 G4* Texas, SW USA
Newbridge *89 B6 Ir.* An Droichead Nua. Kildare, C Ireland
New Britain *144 B3 island* E Papua New Guinea
New Brunswick *39 E4 Fr.* Nouveau-Brunswick. *province* SE Canada
New Caledonia *144 D4 var.* Kanaky, *Fr.* Nouvelle-Calédonie. *French overseas territory* SW Pacific Ocean
New Caledonia *144 C5 island* SW Pacific Ocean
New Caledonia Basin *142 C4 undersea basin* W Pacific Ocean
Newcastle *149 D6* New South Wales, SE Australia
Newcastle *see* Newcastle upon Tyne
Newcastle upon Tyne *88 D4 var.* Newcastle, *hist.* Monkchester, *Lat.* Pons Aelii. NE England, United Kingdom
New Delhi *134 D3 country capital* (India) Delhi, N India
New England of the West *see* Minnesota
Newfoundland *39 G3 Fr.* Terre-Neuve. *island* Newfoundland and Labrador, SE Canada
Newfoundland and Labrador *39 F2 Fr.* Terre Neuve. *province* E Canada
Newfoundland Basin *66 B3 undersea feature* NW Atlantic Ocean
New Georgia Islands *144 C3 island group* NW Solomon Islands
New Glasgow *39 F4* Nova Scotia, SE Canada
New Goa *see* Panaji
New Guinea *144 A3 Dut.* Nieuw Guinea, *Ind.* Irian. *island* Indonesia/Papua New Guinea
New Hampshire *41 F2 off.* State of New Hampshire, *also known as* Granite State. *state* NE USA
New Haven *41 G3* Connecticut, NE USA
New Hebrides *see* Vanuatu
New Iberia *42 B3* Louisiana, S USA
New Ireland *144 C3 island* NE Papua New Guinea
New Jersey *41 F4 off.* State of New Jersey, *also known as* The Garden State. *state* NE USA
Newman *146 B4* Western Australia
Newmarket *89 E6* E England, United Kingdom
New Mexico *48 C2 off.* State of New Mexico, *also known as* Land of Enchantment, Sunshine State. *state* SW USA
New Orleans *42 B3* Louisiana, S USA
New Plymouth *150 C4* Taranaki, North Island, New Zealand
Newport *89 D7* S England, United Kingdom
Newport *89 C7* SE Wales, United Kingdom
Newport *40 C4* Kentucky, S USA
Newport *41 G2* Vermont, NE USA
Newport News *41 F5* Virginia, NE USA
New Providence *54 C1 island* Bahamas
Newquay *89 C7* SW England, United Kingdom
Newry *89 B5 Ir.* An tIúr. SE Northern Ireland, United Kingdom
New Sarum *see* Salisbury
New Siberian Islands *115 F1 Eng.* New Siberian Islands. *island group* N Russian Federation
New Siberian Islands *see* Novosibirskiye Ostrova
New South Wales *149 C6 state* SE Australia
Newton *45 G3* Iowa, C USA
Newton *45 F5* Kansas, C USA
Newtownabbey *89 B5 Ir.* Baile na Mainistreach. E Northern Ireland, United Kingdom
New Ulm *45 F2* Minnesota, N USA
New York *41 F4* New York, NE USA
New York *41 F3 state* NE USA
New Zealand *150 A4 country* SW Pacific Ocean

NEW ZEALAND
Australasia & Oceania

Official name New Zealand
Formation 1947 / 1947
Capital Wellington
Population 4.5 million / 43 people per sq mile (17 people per sq km)
Total area 103,737 sq. miles (268,680 sq. km)

NEW ZEALAND
(continued)

Languages English*, Maori*
Religions Anglican 24%, Other 22%, Presbyterian 18%, Nonreligious 16%, Roman Catholic 15%, Methodist 5%
Ethnic mix European 75%, Maori 15%, Other 7%, Samoan 3%
Government Parliamentary system
Currency New Zealand dollar = 100 cents
Literacy rate 99%
Calorie consumption 3170 kilocalories

Neyveli *132 C2* Tamil Nādu, SE India
Nezhin *see* Nizhyn
Ngangze Co *126 B5 lake* W China
Ngaoundéré *76 B4 var.* N'Gaoundéré. Adamaoua, N Cameroon
N'Gaoundéré *see* Ngaoundéré
Ngazidja *79 F2 Fr.* Grande Comore, *var.* Njazidja. *island* NW Comoros
N'Giva *78 B3 var.* Ondjiva, *Port.* Vila Pereira de Eça. Cunene, S Angola
Ngo *77 B6* Plateaux, SE Congo
Ngoko *77 B5 river* Cameroon/Congo
Ngourti *75 H3* Diffa, E Niger
Nguigmi *75 H3 var.* N'Guigmi. Diffa, SE Niger
N'Guigmi *see* Nguigmi
N'Gunza *see* Sumbe
Nguru *75 G3* Yobe, NE Nigeria
Nha Trang *137 E6* Khanh Hoa, S Vietnam
Niagara Falls *38 D5* Ontario, S Canada
Niagara Falls *41 E3* New York, NE USA
Niagara Falls *40 D3 waterfall* Canada/USA
Niamey *75 F3 country capital* (Niger) Niamey, SW Niger
Niangay, Lac *75 E3 lake* E Mali
Nia-Nia *77 E5* Orientale, NE Dem. Rep. Congo
Nias, Pulau *138 A3 island* W Indonesia
Nicaea *see* Nice
Nicaragua *52 D3 off.* Republic of Nicaragua. *country* Central America

NICARAGUA
Central America

Official name Republic of Nicaragua
Formation 1838 / 1838
Capital Managua
Population 6.1 million / 133 people per sq mile (51 people per sq km)
Total area 49,998 sq. miles (129,494 sq. km)
Languages Spanish*, English Creole, Miskito
Religions Roman Catholic 80%, Protestant Evangelical 17%, Other 3%
Ethnic mix Mestizo 69%, White 17%, Black 9%, Amerindian 5%
Government Presidential system
Currency Córdoba oro = 100 centavos
Literacy rate 78%
Calorie consumption 2564 kilocalories

Lake Nicaragua *52 D4 var.* Cocibolca, Gran Lago, *Eng.* Lake Nicaragua. *lake* S Nicaragua
Nicaragua, Lake *see* Nicaragua, Lago de
Nicaragua, Republic of *see* Nicaragua
Nicaria *see* Ikaría
Nice *91 D6 It.* Nizza; *anc.* Nicaea. Alpes-Maritimes, SE France
Nicephorium *see* Ar Raqqah
Nicholas II Land *see* Severnaya Zemlya
Nicholls Town *54 C1* Andros Island, NW Bahamas
Nicobar Islands *124 B4 island group* India, E Indian Ocean
Nicosia *102 C5 Gk.* Lefkosía, *Turk.* Lefkoşa. *country capital* (Cyprus) C Cyprus
Nicoya *52 D4* Guanacaste, W Costa Rica
Nicoya, Golfo de *52 D5 gulf* W Costa Rica
Nicoya, Península de *52 D4 peninsula* NW Costa Rica
Nida *106 A3 Ger.* Nidden. Klaipėda, SW Lithuania
Nidaros *see* Trondheim
Nidden *see* Nida
Nidzica *98 D3 Ger.* Niedenburg. Warmińsko-Mazurskie, NE Poland
Niedenburg *see* Nidzica
Niedere Tauern *99 A6 mountain range* C Austria
Niemen *see* Neman
Nieśwież *see* Nyasvizh
Nieuw Amsterdam *59 G3* Commewijne, NE Suriname
Nieuw-Bergen *86 D4* Limburg, SE Netherlands
Nieuwegein *86 C4* Utrecht, C Netherlands
Nieuw Guinea *see* New Guinea
Nieuw Nickerie *59 G3* Nickerie, NW Suriname
Niewenstat *see* Neustadt an der Weinstrasse
Niğde *116 C4* Niğde, C Turkey
Niger *75 F3 off.* Republic of Niger. *country* W Africa

NIGER
West Africa

Official name Republic of Niger
Formation 1960 / 1960
Capital Niamey
Population 17.8 million / 36 people per sq mile (14 people per sq km)
Total area 489,188 sq. miles (1,267,000 sq. km)
Languages Hausa, Djerma, Fulani, Tuareg, Teda, French*
Religions Muslim 99%, Other (including Christian) 1%
Ethnic mix Hausa 53%, Djerma and Songhai 21%, Tuareg 11%, Fulani 7%, Kanuri 6%, Other 2%
Government Presidential system
Currency CFA franc = 100 centimes
Literacy rate 16%
Calorie consumption 2546 kilocalories

Niger *75 F4 river* W Africa
Nigeria *75 F4 off.* Federal Republic of Nigeria. *country* W Africa

NIGERIA
West Africa

Official name Federal Republic of Nigeria
Formation 1960 / 1961
Capital Abuja
Population 174 million / 494 people per sq mile (191 people per sq km)
Total area 356,667 sq. miles (923,768 sq. km)
Languages Hausa, English*, Yoruba, Ibo
Religions Muslim 50%, Christian 40%, Traditional beliefs 10%
Ethnic mix Other 29%, Hausa 21%, Yoruba 21%, Ibo 18%, Fulani 11%
Government Presidential system
Currency Naira = 100 kobo
Literacy rate 51%
Calorie consumption 2724 kilocalories

Nigeria, Federal Republic of *see* Nigeria
Niger, Mouths of the *75 F5 delta* S Nigeria
Niger, Republic of *see* Niger
Nihon *see* Japan
Niigata *131 D5* Niigata, Honshū, C Japan
Niihama *131 B7* Ehime, Shikoku, SW Japan
Ni'ihau *47 A7 var.* Niihau. *island* Hawaii, USA, C Pacific Ocean
Nii-jima *131 D6 island* E Japan
Nijkerk *86 D3* Gelderland, C Netherlands
Nijlen *87 C5* Antwerpen, N Belgium
Nijmegen *86 D4 Ger.* Nimwegen; *anc.* Noviomagus. Gelderland, SE Netherlands
Nikaria *see* Ikaría
Nikel' *110 C2 Finn.* Kolosjoki. Murmanskaya Oblast', NW Russian Federation
Nikiniki *139 E5* Timor, S Indonesia
Niklasmarkt *see* Gheorgheni
Nikolainkaupunki *see* Vaasa
Nikolayev *see* Mykolayiv
Nikol'sk *see* Ussuriysk
Nikol'sk-Ussuriyskiy *see* Ussuriysk
Nikopol' *109 F3* Dnipropetrovs'ka Oblast', SE Ukraine
Nikšić *101 C5* C Montenegro
Nikumaroro *145 E3*; *prev.* Gardner Island. *atoll* Phoenix Islands, C Kiribati
Nikunau *145 E3 var.* Nukunau; *prev.* Byron Island. *atoll* Tungaru, W Kiribati
Nile *72 B2 former province* NW Uganda
Nile *68 D3 Ar.* Nahr an Nīl. *river* N Africa
Nile Delta *72 B1 delta* N Egypt
Nīl, Nahr an *see* Nile
Nîmes *91 C6 anc.* Nemausus, Nismes. Gard, S France
Nimwegen *see* Nijmegen
Nine Degree Channel *132 B3 channel* India/Maldives
Ninetyeast Ridge *141 D5 undersea feature* E Indian Ocean
Ninety Mile Beach *150 C1 beach* North Island, New Zealand
Ningbo *128 D5 var.* Ning-po, Yin-hsien; *prev.* Ninghsien. Zhejiang, SE China
Ning-hsia *see* Ningxia
Ninghsien *see* Ningbo
Ning-po *see* Ningbo
Ningsia/Ningsia Hui/Ningsia Hui Autonomous Region *see* Ningxia
Ningxia *128 B4 off.* Ningxia Huizu Zizhiqu, *var.* Ning-hsia, Ningsia, *Eng.* Ningsia Hui, Ningsia Hui Autonomous Region. *autonomous region* N China
Ningxia Huizu Zizhiqu *see* Ningxia
Nio *see* Íos
Niobrara River *45 E3 river* Nebraska/Wyoming, C USA
Nioro *74 D3 var.* Nioro du Sahel. Kayes, W Mali
Nioro du Sahel *see* Nioro
Niort *90 B4* Deux-Sèvres, W France
Nipigon *38 B4* Ontario, S Canada
Nipigon, Lake *38 B3 lake* Ontario, S Canada
Nippon *see* Japan
Niš *101 E5 Eng.* Nish, *Ger.* Nisch; *anc.* Naissus. Serbia, SE Serbia
Nişab *120 B4* Al Ḩudūd ash Shamālīyah, N Saudi Arabia
Nisch/Nish *see* Niš
Nisibin *see* Nusaybin
Nisiros *see* Nísyros
Nisko *98 E4* Podkrapackie, SE Poland
Nismes *see* Nîmes
Nistru *see* Dniester
Nísyros *105 E7 var.* Nisiros. *island* Dodekánisa, Greece, Aegean Sea
Nitra *99 C6 Ger.* Neutra, *Hung.* Nyitra. Nitriansky Kraj, SW Slovakia
Nitra *99 C6 Ger.* Neutra, *Hung.* Nyitra. *river* W Slovakia
Niuatobutabu *see* Niuatoputapu
Niuatoputapu *145 E4 var.* Niuatobutabu; *prev.* Keppel Island. *island* N Tonga
Niue *145 F4 self-governing territory in free association with New Zealand* S Pacific Ocean
Niulakita *145 E3 var.* Nurakita. *atoll* S Tuvalu
Niutao *145 E3 atoll* NW Tuvalu
Nivernais *90 C4 cultural region* C France
Nizāmābād *134 D5* Telangana, C India
Nizhnegorskiy *see* Nyzhn'ohirs'kyy
Nizhnekamsk *111 C5* Respublika Tatarstan, W Russian Federation
Nizhnevartovsk *114 D3* Khanty-Mansiyskiy Avtonomnyy Okrug-Yugra, C Russian Federation
Nizhniy Novgorod *111 C5 prev.* Gor'kiy. Nizhegorodskaya Oblast', W Russian Federation
Nizhniy Odes *110 D4* Respublika Komi, NW Russian Federation
Nizhyn *109 E1 Rus.* Nezhin. Chernihivs'ka Oblast', NE Ukraine
Nizza *see* Nice
Njazidja *see* Ngazidja
Njombe *73 C8* Iringa, S Tanzania
Nkayi *77 B6 prev.* Jacob. Bouenza, S Congo
Nkongsamba *76 A4 var.* N'Kongsamba. Littoral, W Cameroon
N'Kongsamba *see* Nkongsamba
Nmai Hka *136 B2 var.* Me Hka. *river* N Myanmar (Burma)
Nobeoka *131 B7* Miyazaki, Kyūshū, SW Japan
Noboribetsu *130 D3 var.* Noboribetu. Hokkaidō, NE Japan
Noboribetu *see* Noboribetsu
Nogales *50 B1* Sonora, NW Mexico
Nogales *48 B3* Arizona, SW USA
Nogal Valley *see* Dooxo Nugaaleed
Noire, Rivi`ere *see* Black River
Nokia *85 D5* Länsi-Suomi, W Finland
Nokou *76 B3* Kanem, W Chad
Nola *77 B5* Sangha-Mbaéré, SW Central African Republic
Nolinsk *111 C5* Kirovskaya Oblast', NW Russian Federation
Nongkaya *see* Nong Khai
Nong Khai *136 C4 var.* Mi Chai, Nongkaya. Nong Khai, E Thailand
Nonouti *144 D2 prev.* Sydenham Island. *atoll* Tungaru, W Kiribati
Noord-Beveland *86 B4 var.* North Beveland. *island* SW Netherlands
Noordwijk aan Zee *86 C3* Zuid-Holland, W Netherlands
Noordzee *see* North Sea
Nora *85 C6* Örebro, C Sweden
Norak *123 E3 Rus.* Nurek. W Tajikistan
Nord *83 F1* Avannaarsua, N Greenland
Nordaustlandet *83 G1 island* NE Svalbard
Norden *94 A3* Niedersachsen, NW Germany
Norderstedt *94 B3* Schleswig-Holstein, N Germany
Nordfriesische Inseln *see* North Frisian Islands
Nordhausen *94 C4* Thüringen, C Germany
Nordhorn *94 A3* Niedersachsen, NW Germany
Nord, Mer du *see* North Sea
Nord-Ouest, Territoires du *see* Northwest Territories
Nordsee/Nordsjøen/Nordsøen *see* North Sea
Norfolk *45 E3* Nebraska, C USA
Norfolk *41 F5* Virginia, NE USA
Norfolk Island *142 D4 Australian external territory* SW Pacific Ocean
Norfolk Ridge *142 D4 undersea feature* W Pacific Ocean
Norge *see* Norway
Norias *49 G5* Texas, SW USA
Noril'sk *114 D3* Krasnoyarskiy Kray, N Russian Federation
Norman *49 G1* Oklahoma, C USA
Normandes, Îles *see* Channel Islands
Normandie *90 B3 Eng.* Normandy. *cultural region* N France
Normandy *see* Normandie
Normanton *148 C3* Queensland, NE Australia
Norrköping *85 C6* Östergötland, S Sweden
Norrtälje *85 C6* Stockholm, C Sweden
Norseman *147 B6* Western Australia
Norske Havet *see* Norwegian Sea
North Albanian Alps *101 C5 Alb.* Bjeshkët e Namuna, *SCr.* Prokletije. *mountain range* SE Europe
Northallerton *89 D5* N England, United Kingdom
Northam *147 A6* Western Australia
North America *34 continent*
Northampton *89 D6* C England, United Kingdom
North Andaman *133 F2 island* Andaman Islands, India, NE Indian Ocean
North Australian Basin *141 E5 Fr.* Bassin Nord de l' Australie. *undersea feature* E Indian Ocean
North Bay *38 D4* Ontario, S Canada
North Beveland *see* Noord-Beveland
North Borneo *see* Sabah
North Cape *150 C1 headland* North Island, New Zealand
North Cape *84 D1 Eng.* North Cape. *headland* N Norway
North Cape *see* Nordkapp
North Carolina *43 E1 off.* State of North Carolina, *also known as* Old North State, Tar Heel State, Turpentine State. *state* SE USA
North Channel *40 D2 lake channel* Canada/USA
North Charleston *43 F2* South Carolina, SE USA
North Dakota *44 D2 off.* State of North Dakota, *also known as* Flickertail State, Peace Garden State, Sioux State. *state* N USA
North Devon Island *see* Devon Island
North East Frontier Agency/North East Frontier Agency of Assam *see* Arunāchal Pradesh

ortheast Providence Channel *54 C1 channel* N Bahamas
ortheim *94 B4* Niedersachsen, C Germany
orthern Cook Islands *145 F4 island group* N Cook Islands
orthern Dvina *110 C4 var.* Northern Dvina. *river* NW Russian Federation
orthern Dvina *see* Severnaya Dvina
orthern Ireland *88 B4 var.* The Six Counties. *cultural region* Northern Ireland, United Kingdom
orthern Mariana Islands *142 B1 US commonwealth territory* W Pacific Ocean
orthern Rhodesia *see* Zambia
orthern Sporades *105 C5 var.* Vóreioi Sporádes, Vórioi Sporádhes, *Eng.* Northern Sporades. *island group* E Greece
orthern Sporades *see* Vóreies Sporádes
orthern Territory *144 A5 territory* N Australia
orth European Plain *81 E3 plain* N Europe
orthfield *45 F2* Minnesota, N USA
orth Fiji Basin *142 D3 undersea feature* N Coral Sea
orth Frisian Islands *94 B2 var.* Nordfriesische Inseln. *island group* N Germany
orth Huvadhu Atoll *132 B5 var.* Gaafu Alifu Atoll. *atoll* S Maldives
orth Island *150 B2 island* N New Zealand
orth Korea *129 E3 off.* Democratic People's Republic of Korea, *Kor.* Chosŏn-minjujuŭi-inmin-kanghwaguk. *country* E Asia

NORTH KOREA
East Asia

Official name Democratic People's Republic of Korea
Formation 1948 / 1953
Capital Pyongyang
Population 24.9 million / 536 people per sq mile (207 people per sq km)
Total area 46,540 sq. miles (120,540 sq. km)
Languages Korean*
Religions Atheist 100%
Ethnic mix Korean 100%
Government One-party state
Currency North Korean won = 100 chon
Literacy rate 99%
Calorie consumption 2103 kilocalories

orth Little Rock *42 B1* Arkansas, C USA
orth Minch *see* Minch, The
orth Mole *93 G4 harbour wall* NW Gibraltar Europe
orth Platte *45 E4* Nebraska, C USA
orth Platte River *44 D4 river* C USA
orth Pole *155 B3 pole* Arctic Ocean
orth Saskatchewan *37 F5 river* Alberta/Saskatchewan, S Canada
orth Sea *80 D3 Dan.* Nordsøen, *Dut.* Noordzee, *Fr.* Mer du Nord, *Ger.* Nordsee, *Nor.* Nordsjøen; *prev.* German Ocean, *Lat.* Mare Germanicum. *sea* NW Europe
orth Siberian Lowland *115 E2 var.* North Siberian Plain, *Eng.* North Siberian Lowland. *lowlands* N Russian Federation
orth Siberian Lowland/North Siberian Plain *see* Severo-Sibirskaya Nizmennost'
orth Star State *see* Minnesota
orth Taranaki Bight *150 C3 gulf* North Island, New Zealand
orth Uist *88 B3 island* NW Scotland, United Kingdom
orthwest Atlantic Mid-Ocean Canyon *34 E4 undersea feature* N Atlantic Ocean
orth West Highlands *88 C3 mountain range* N Scotland, United Kingdom
orthwest Pacific Basin *113 G4 undersea feature* NW Pacific Ocean
orthwest Territories *37 E3 Fr.* Territoires du Nord-Ouest. *territory* NW Canada
orthwind Plain *155 B2 undersea feature* Arctic Ocean
orton Sound *36 C2 inlet* Alaska, USA
Norway *85 A5 off.* Kingdom of Norway, *Nor.* Norge. *country* N Europe

NORWAY
Northern Europe

Official name Kingdom of Norway
Formation 1905 / 1905
Capital Oslo
Population 5 million / 42 people per sq mile (16 people per sq km)
Total area 125,181 sq. miles (324,220 sq. km)
Languages Norwegian* (Bokmål "book language" and Nynorsk "new Norsk"), Sámi
Religions Evangelical Lutheran 88%, Other and nonreligious 8%, Muslim 2%, Pentecostal 1%, Roman Catholic 1%
Ethnic mix Norwegian 93%, Other 6%, Sámi 1%
Government Parliamentary system
Currency Norwegian krone = 100 øre
Literacy rate 99%
Calorie consumption 3484 kilocalories

Norway, Kingdom of *see* Norway
Norwegian Basin *83 F4 undersea feature* NW Norwegian Sea
Norwegian Sea *83 F4 var.* Norske Havet. *sea* NE Atlantic Ocean
Norwich *89 E6* E England, United Kingdom
Nösen *see* Bistrița
Noshiro *130 D4 var.* Nosiro; *prev.* Noshirominato. Akita, Honshū, C Japan
Noshirominato/Nosiro *see* Noshiro
Nosivka *109 E1 Rus.* Nosovka. Chernihivs'ka Oblast', NE Ukraine
Nosop *78 C4 river* E Namibia
Nosovka *see* Nosivka
Noṣratābād *120 E3* Sīstān va Balūchestān, E Iran
Noteć *98 C3 Ger.* Netze. *river* NW Poland
Nóties Sporádes *see* Dodekánisa
Nottingham *89 D6* C England, United Kingdom
Nouâdhibou *74 B2 prev.* Port-Étienne. Dakhlet Nouâdhibou, W Mauritania
Nouakchott *74 B2 country capital* (Mauritania) Nouakchott District, SW Mauritania
Nouméa *144 C5 dependent territory capital* (New Caledonia) Province Sud, S New Caledonia
Nouveau-Brunswick *see* New Brunswick
Nouvelle-Calédonie *see* New Caledonia
Nouvelle Écosse *see* Nova Scotia
Nova Civitas *see* Neustadt an der Weinstrasse
Nova Gorica *95 D8* W Slovenia
Nova Gradiška *100 C3 Ger.* Neugradisk, *Hung.* Újgradiska. Brod-Posavina, NE Croatia
Nova Iguaçu *63 F4* Rio de Janeiro, SE Brazil
Nova Lisboa *see* Huambo
Novara *96 B2 anc.* Novaria. Piemonte, NW Italy
Novaria *see* Novara
Nova Scotia *39 F4 Fr.* Nouvelle Écosse. *province* SE Canada
Nova Scotia *35 E5 physical region* SE Canada
Novaya Sibir', Ostrov *115 F1 island* Novosibirskiye Ostrova, NE Russian Federation
Novaya Zemlya *110 D1 island group* N Russian Federation
Novaya Zemlya Trough *see* East Novaya Zemlya Trough
Novgorod *see* Velikiy Novgorod
Novi Grad *see* Bosanski Novi
Novi Iskŭr *104 C2* Sofiya-Grad, W Bulgaria
Noviodunum *see* Nevers, Nièvre, France
Noviomagus *see* Lisieux, Calvados, France
Noviomagus *see* Nijmegen, Netherlands
Novi Pazar *101 D5 Turk.* Yenipazar. Serbia, S Serbia
Novi Sad *100 D3 Ger.* Neusatz, *Hung.* Újvidék. Vojvodina, N Serbia
Novoazovs'k *109 G4 Rus.* Novoazovsk. Donets'ka Oblast', E Ukraine
Novocheboksarsk *111 C5* Chuvashskaya Respublika, W Russian Federation
Novocherkassk *111 B7* Rostovskaya Oblast', SW Russian Federation
Novodvinsk *110 C3* Arkhangel'skaya Oblast', NW Russian Federation
Novograd-Volynskiy *see* Novohrad-Volyns'kyy
Novogrudok *see* Navahrudak
Novohrad-Volyns'kyy *108 D2 Rus.* Novograd-Volynskiy. Zhytomyrs'ka Oblast', N Ukraine
Novokazalinsk *see* Ayteke Bi
Novokuznetsk *114 D4 prev.* Stalinsk. Kemerovskaya Oblast', S Russian Federation
Novolazarevskaya *154 C2 Russian research station* Antarctica
Novo mesto *95 E8 Ger.* Rudolfswert; *prev. Ger.* Neustadtl. SE Slovenia
Novomoskovsk *111 B5* Tul'skaya Oblast', W Russian Federation
Novomoskovs'k *109 F3 Rus.* Novomoskovsk. Dnipropetrovs'ka Oblast', E Ukraine
Novopolotsk *see* Navapolatsk
Novoradomsk *see* Radomsko
Novo Redondo *see* Sumbe
Novorossiysk *111 A7* Krasnodarskiy Kray, SW Russian Federation
Novoshakhtinsk *111 B6* Rostovskaya Oblast', SW Russian Federation
Novosibirsk *114 D4* Novosibirskaya Oblast', C Russian Federation
Novotroitsk *111 D6* Orenburgskaya Oblast', W Russian Federation
Novotroitskoye *see* Novotroyits'ke, Ukraine
Novotroyits'ke *109 F4 Rus.* Novotroitskoye. Khersons'ka Oblast', S Ukraine
Novo-Urgench *see* Urganch
Novovolyns'k *108 C1 Rus.* Novovolynsk. Volyns'ka Oblast', NW Ukraine
Novy Dvor *107 B6 Rus.* Novyy Dvor. Hrodzyenskaya Voblasts', W Belarus
Novyy Bug *see* Novyy Buh
Novyy Buh *109 E3 Rus.* Novyy Bug. Mykolayivs'ka Oblast', S Ukraine
Novyy Dvor *see* Novy Dvor
Novyy Margilan *see* Farg'ona
Novyy Uzen' *see* Zhanaozen
Nowa Sól *98 B4 var.* Nowasól, *Ger.* Neusalz an der Oder. Lubuskie, W Poland
Nowasól *see* Nowa Sól
Nowogard *98 B2 var.* Nowógard, *Ger.* Naugard. Zachodnio-pomorskie, NW Poland
Nowogródek *see* Navahrudak
Nowo-Minsk *see* Mińsk Mazowiecki
Nowy Dwór Mazowiecki *98 D3* Mazowieckie, C Poland
Nowy Sącz *99 D5 Ger.* Neu Sandec. Małopolskie, S Poland
Nowy Tomyśl *98 B3 var.* Nowy Tomysl. Wielkopolskie, C Poland
Nowy Tomysl *see* Nowy Tomyśl
Noyon *90 C3* Oise, N France
Nsanje *79 E3* Southern, S Malawi
Nsawam *75 E5* SE Ghana
Ntomba, Lac *77 C6 var.* Lac Tumba. *lake* NW Dem. Rep. Congo
Nubian Desert *72 B3 desert* NE Sudan
Nu Chiang *see* Salween
Nu'eima *119 E7* E West Bank Asia
Nueva Caceres *see* Naga
Nueva Gerona *54 B2* Isla de la Juventud, S Cuba
Nueva Rosita *50 D2* Coahuila, NE Mexico
Nuevitas *54 C2* Camagüey, E Cuba
Nuevo, Bajo *53 G1 island* NW Colombia South America
Nuevo Casas Grandes *50 C1* Chihuahua, N Mexico
Nuevo, Golfo *65 C6 gulf* S Argentina
Nuevo Laredo *51 E2* Tamaulipas, NE Mexico
Nui Atoll *145 E3 atoll* W Tuvalu
Nu Jiang *see* Salween
Nûk *see* Nuuk
Nukha *see* Şäki
Nuku'alofa *145 E5 country capital* (Tonga) Tongatapu, S Tonga
Nukufetau Atoll *145 E3 atoll* C Tuvalu
Nukulaelae Atoll *145 E3 var.* Nukulailai. *atoll* E Tuvalu
Nukulailai *see* Nukulaelae Atoll
Nukunau *see* Nikunau
Nukunonu Atoll *145 E3 island* C Tokelau
Nukus *122 C2* Qoraqalpog'iston Respublikasi, W Uzbekistan
Nullarbor Plain *147 C6 plateau* South Australia/Western Australia
Nunap Isua *82 C5 var.* Uummannarsuaq, *Dan.* Kap Farvel, *Eng.* Cape Farewell. *cape* S Greenland
Nunavut *37 F3 territory* N Canada
Nuneaton *89 D6* C England, United Kingdom
Nunivak Island *36 B2 island* Alaska, USA
Nunspeet *86 D3* Gelderland, E Netherlands
Nuoro *97 A5* Sardegna, Italy, C Mediterranean Sea
Nuquí *58 A3* Chocó, W Colombia
Nurakita *see* Niulakita
Nurata *see* Nurota
Nurek *see* Norak
Nuremberg *see* Nürnberg
Nurmes *84 E4* Itä-Suomi, E Finland
Nürnberg *95 C5 Eng.* Nuremberg. Bayern, S Germany
Nurota *123 E2 Rus.* Nurata. Navoiy Viloyati, C Uzbekistan
Nusaybin *117 F4 var.* Nisibin. Manisa, SE Turkey
Nussdorf *see* Năsăud
Nutmeg State *see* Connecticut
Nuuk *82 C4 var.* Nûk, *Dan.* Godthaab, Godthåb. *dependent territory capital* (Greenland) Kitaa, SW Greenland
Nyagan' *114 C3* Khanty-Mansiyskiy Avtonomnyy Okrug-Yugra, N Russian Federation
Nyainqentanglha Shan *126 C5 mountain range* W China
Nyala *72 A4* Southern Darfur, W Sudan
Nyamapanda *78 D3* Mashonaland East, NE Zimbabwe
Nyamtumbo *73 C8* Ruvuma, S Tanzania
Nyanda *see* Masvingo
Nyandoma *110 C4* Arkhangel'skaya Oblast', NW Russian Federation
Nyantakara *73 B7* Kagera, NW Tanzania
Nyasa, Lake *79 E2 var.* Lake Malawi; *prev.* Lago Nyassa. *lake* E Africa
Nyasaland/Nyasaland Protectorate *see* Malawi
Nyassa, Lago *see* Nyasa, Lake
Nyasvizh *107 C6 Pol.* Nieśwież, *Rus.* Nesvizh. Minskaya Voblasts', C Belarus
Nyaunglebin *136 B4* Bago, SW Myanmar (Burma)
Nyeri *73 C6* Central, C Kenya
Nyíregyháza *99 D6* Szabolcs-Szatmár-Bereg, NE Hungary
Nyitra *see* Nitra
Nykøbing *85 B8* Sjælland, SE Denmark
Nyköping *85 C6* Södermanland, S Sweden
Nylstroom *see* Modimolle
Nyngan *149 D6* New South Wales, SE Australia
Nyoman *see* Neman
Nyurba *115 F3* Respublika Sakha (Yakutiya), NE Russian Federation
Nyzhn'ohirs'kyy *109 F4 Rus.* Nizhnegorskiy. Avtonomna Respublika Krym, S Ukraine
NZ *see* New Zealand
Nzega *73 C7* Tabora, C Tanzania
Nzérékoré *74 D4* SE Guinea
Nzwani *79 F2 Fr.* Anjouan, *var.* Ndzouani. *island* SE Comoros

Oa'hu *47 A7 var.* Oahu. *island* Hawai'ian Islands, Hawaii, USA
Oak Harbor *46 B1* Washington, NW USA
Oakland *47 B6* California, W USA
Oamaru *151 B7* Otago, South Island, New Zealand
Oaxaca *51 F5 var.* Oaxaca de Juárez; *prev.* Antequera. Oaxaca, SE Mexico
Oaxaca de Juárez *see* Oaxaca
Ob' *112 C2 river* C Russian Federation
Obal' *107 D5 Rus.* Obol'. Vitsyebskaya Voblasts', N Belarus
Oban *88 C4* W Scotland, United Kingdom
Oban *see* Halfmoon Bay
Obando *see* Puerto Inírida

Obdorsk *see* Salekhard
Óbecse *see* Bečej
Obeliai 106 C4 Panevėžys, NE Lithuania
Oberhollabrunn *see* Tulln
Ob', Gulf of 114 D3 *Eng.* Gulf of Ob. *gulf* N Russian Federation
Ob', Gulf of *see* Obskaya Guba
Obidovichi *see* Abidavichy
Obihiro 130 D2 Hokkaidō, NE Japan
Obo 76 D4 Haut-Mbomou, E Central African Republic
Obock 72 D4 E Djibouti
Obol' *see* Obal'
Oborniki 98 C3 Wielkolpolskie, W Poland
Obrovo *see* Abrova
Ob' Tablemount 141 B7 *undersea feature* S Indian Ocean
Ocala 43 E4 Florida, SE USA
Ocaña 58 B2 Norte de Santander, N Colombia
Ocaña 92 D3 Castilla-La Mancha, C Spain
O Carballiño 92 C1 *Cast.* Carballiño. Galicia, NW Spain
Occidental, Cordillera 58 B2 *mountain range* W South America
Occidental, Cordillera 61 E4 *mountain range* Bolivia/Chile
Ocean Falls 36 D5 British Columbia, SW Canada
Ocean Island *see* Banaba
Oceanside 47 C8 California, W USA
Ocean State *see* Rhode Island
Ochakiv 109 E4 *Rus.* Ochakov. Mykolayivs'ka Oblast', S Ukraine
Ochakov *see* Ochakiv
Ochamchira *see* Ochamchire
Ochamchire 117 E2 *prev.* Och'amch'ire. W Georgia
Och'amch'ire *see* Ochamchire
Ocho Rios 54 B4 C Jamaica
Ochrida *see* Ohrid
Ochrida, Lake *see* Ohrid, Lake
Ocotal 52 D3 Nueva Segovia, NW Nicaragua
Ocozocuautla 51 G5 Chiapas, SE Mexico
October Revolution Island 115 E2 *Eng.* October Revolution Island. *island* Severnaya Zemlya, N Russian Federation
October Revolution Island *see* Oktyabr'skoy Revolyutsii, Ostrov
Ocú 53 F5 Herrera, S Panama
Ōdate 130 D3 Akita, Honshū, C Japan
Oddur *see* Xuddur
Ödemiş 116 A4 İzmir, SW Turkey
Ödenburg *see* Sopron
Odenpäh *see* Otepää
Odense 85 B7 Syddtjylland, C Denmark
Oder 98 B3 *Cz./Pol.* Odra. *river* C Europe
Oderhaff *see* Szczeciński, Zalew
Odesa 109 E4 *Rus.* Odessa. Odes'ka Oblast', SW Ukraine
Odessa 49 E3 Texas, SW USA
Odessa *see* Odesa
Odessus *see* Varna
Odienné 74 D4 NW Côte d'Ivoire
Odisha 135 F4 *prev.* Orissa. *cultural region* NE India
Ôdôngk 137 D6 Kâmpóng Spoe, S Cambodia
Odoorn 86 E2 Drenthe, NE Netherlands
Odra *see* Oder
Oesel *see* Saaremaa
Of 117 E2 Trabzon, NE Turkey
Ofanto 97 D5 *river* S Italy
Offenbach 95 B5 *var.* Offenbach am Main. Hessen, W Germany
Offenbach am Main *see* Offenbach
Offenburg 95 B6 Baden-Württemberg, SW Germany
Ogaadeen *see* Ogaden
Ogaden 73 D5 *Som.* Ogaadeen. *plateau* Ethiopia/Somalia
Ōgaki 131 C6 Gifu, Honshū, SW Japan
Ogallala 44 D4 Nebraska, C USA
Ogbomosho 75 F4 *var.* Ogmoboso. Oyo, W Nigeria
Ogden 44 B4 Utah, W USA
Ogdensburg 41 F2 New York, NE USA
Ogmoboso *see* Ogbomosho
Ogulin 100 A3 Karlovac, NW Croatia
Ohio 40 C4 *off.* State of Ohio, *also known as* Buckeye State. *state* N USA
Ohio River 40 C4 *river* N USA
Ohlau *see* Oława
Ohri *see* Ohrid
Ohrid 101 D6 *Turk.* Ochrida, Ohri. SW FYR Macedonia
Ohrid, Lake 101 D6 *var.* Lake Ochrida, *Alb.* Liqeni i Ohrit, *Mac.* Ohridsko Ezero. *lake* Albania/FYR Macedonia
Ohridsko Ezero/Ohrit, Liqeni i *see* Ohrid, Lake
Ohura 150 D3 Manawatu-Wanganui, North Island, New Zealand
Oirschot 87 C5 Noord-Brabant, S Netherlands
Oise 90 C3 *river* N France
Oistins 55 G2 S Barbados
Ōita 131 B7 Ōita, Kyūshū, SW Japan
Ojinaga 50 D2 Chihuahua, N Mexico
Ojos del Salado, Cerro 64 B3 *mountain* W Argentina
Okaihau 150 C2 Northland, North Island, New Zealand
Ókanizsa *see* Kanjiža
Okāra 134 C2 Punjab, E Pakistan
Okavanggo *see* Cubango/Okavango
Okavango *see* Cubango
Okavango Delta 78 C3 *wetland* N Botswana
Okayama 131 B6 Okayama, Honshū, SW Japan
Okazaki 131 C6 Aichi, Honshū, C Japan
Okeechobee, Lake 43 E4 *lake* Florida, SE USA
Okefenokee Swamp 43 E3 *wetland* Georgia, SE USA
Okhotsk 115 G3 Khabarovskiy Kray, E Russian Federation
Okhotsk, Sea of 113 F3 *sea* NW Pacific Ocean
Okhtyrka 109 F2 *Rus.* Akhtyrka. Sums'ka Oblast', NE Ukraine
Oki-guntō *see* Oki-shotō
Okinawa 130 A3 *island* SW Japan
Okinawa-shoto 130 A3 *island group* Nansei-shotō, SW Japan Asia
Oki-shotō 131 B6 *var.* Oki-guntō. *island group* SW Japan
Oklahoma 49 F2 *off.* State of Oklahoma, *also known as* The Sooner State. *state* C USA
Oklahoma City 49 G1 *state capital* Oklahoma, C USA
Okmulgee 49 G1 Oklahoma, C USA
Oko, Wadi 72 C3 *river* NE Sudan
Oktyabr'skiy 111 D6 Volgogradskaya Oblast', SW Russian Federation
Oktyabr'skiy *see* Aktsyabrski
Okulovka 110 B4 *var.* Okulovka. Novgorodskaya Oblast', W Russian Federation
Okulovka *see* Okulovka
Okushiri-to 130 C3 *var.* Okusiri Tô. *island* NE Japan
Okusiri Tô *see* Okushiri-tō
Oláh-Toplicza *see* Toplița
Öland 85 C7 *island* S Sweden
Olavarría 65 D5 Buenos Aires, E Argentina
Oława 98 C4 *Ger.* Ohlau. Dolnośląskie, SW Poland
Olbia 97 A5 *prev.* Terranova Pausania. Sardegna, Italy, C Mediterranean Sea
Old Bay State/Old Colony State *see* Massachusetts
Old Dominion *see* Virginia
Oldebroek 86 D3 Gelderland, E Netherlands
Oldenburg 94 B3 Niedersachsen, NW Germany
Oldenburg 94 C2 *var.* Oldenburg in Holstein. Schleswig-Holstein, N Germany
Oldenburg in Holstein *see* Oldenburg
Oldenzaal 86 E3 Overijssel, E Netherlands
Old Harbour 54 B5 C Jamaica
Old Line State *see* Maryland
Old North State *see* North Carolina
Olëkma 115 F4 *river* C Russian Federation
Olëkminsk 115 F3 Respublika Sakha (Yakutiya), NE Russian Federation
Oleksandrivka 109 E3 *Rus.* Aleksandrovka. Kirovohrads'ka Oblast', C Ukraine
Oleksandriya 109 F3 *Rus.* Aleksandriya. Kirovohrads'ka Oblast', C Ukraine
Olenegorsk 110 C2 Murmanskaya Oblast', NW Russian Federation
Olenëk 115 E3 Respublika Sakha (Yakutiya), NE Russian Federation
Olenëk 115 E3 *river* NE Russian Federation
Oléron, Île d' 91 A5 *island* W France
Olevs'k 108 D1 *Rus.* Olevsk. Zhytomyrs'ka Oblast', N Ukraine
Olevsk *see* Olevs'k
Ölgiy 126 C2 Bayan-Ölgiy, W Mongolia
Olhão 92 B5 Faro, S Portugal
Olifa 78 B3 Kunene, NW Namibia
Ólimbos *see* Ólympos
Olimpo *see* Fuerte Olimpo
Olisipo *see* Lisboa
Olita *see* Alytus
Oliva 93 F4 Valenciana, E Spain
Olivet 90 C4 Loiret, C France
Olmaliq 123 E2 *Rus.* Almalyk. Toshkent Viloyati, E Uzbekistan
Olmütz *see* Olomouc
Olomouc 99 C5 *Ger.* Olmütz, *Pol.* Ołomuniec. Olomoucký Kraj, E Czech Republic
Ołomuniec *see* Olomouc
Olonets 110 B3 Respublika Kareliya, NW Russian Federation
Olovyannaya 115 F4 Zabaykal'skiy Kray, S Russian Federation
Olpe 94 B4 Nordrhein-Westfalen, W Germany
Olshanka *see* Vil'shanka
Olsnitz *see* Murska Sobota
Olsztyn 98 D2 *Ger.* Allenstein. Warmińsko-Mazurskie, N Poland
Olt 108 B5 *var.* Oltul, *Ger.* Alt. *river* S Romania
Oltenița 108 C5 *prev. Eng.* Oltenitsa; *anc.* Constantiola. Călărași, SE Romania
Oltenitsa *see* Oltenița
Oltul *see* Olt
Olvera 92 D5 Andalucía, S Spain
Ol'viopol' *see* Pervomays'k
Olympia 46 B2 *state capital* Washington, NW USA
Olympic Mountains 46 A2 *mountain range* Washington, NW USA
Olympus, Mount 104 B4 *var.* Ólimbos, *Eng.* Mount Olympus. *mountain* N Greece
Omagh 89 B5 *Ir.* An Ómaigh. W Northern Ireland, United Kingdom
Omaha 45 F4 Nebraska, C USA
Oman 121 D6 *off.* Sultanate of Oman, *Ar.* Salṭanat 'Umān; *prev.* Muscat and Oman. *country* SW Asia

OMAN
Southwest Asia

Official name Sultanate of Oman
Formation 1951 / 1951
Capital Muscat
Population 3.6 million / 44 people per sq mile (17 people per sq km)
Total area 82,031 sq. miles (212,460 sq. km)
Languages Arabic*, Baluchi, Farsi, Hindi, Punjabi
Religions Ibadi Muslim 75%, Other Muslim and Hindu 25%
Ethnic mix Arab 88%, Baluchi 4%, Persian 3%, Indian and Pakistani 3%, African 2%
Government Monarchy
Currency Omani rial = 1000 baisa
Literacy rate 87%
Calorie consumption Not available

Oman, Gulf of 120 E4 *Ar.* Khalīj 'Umān. *gulf* N Arabian Sea
Oman, Sultanate of *see* Oman
Omboué 77 A6 Ogooué-Maritime, W Gabon
Omdurman 72 B4 *var.* Umm Durmān. Khartoum, C Sudan
Ometepe, Isla de 52 D4 *island* S Nicaragua
Ommen 86 E3 Overijssel, E Netherlands
Omsk 114 C4 Omskaya Oblast', C Russian Federation
Ōmuta 131 A7 Fukuoka, Kyūshū, SW Japan
Onda 93 F3 Valenciana, E Spain
Ondjiva *see* N'Giva
Öndörhaan 127 E2 *var.* Undur Khan; *prev.* Tsetsen Khan. Hentiy, E Mongolia
Onega 110 C3 Arkhangel'skaya Oblast', NW Russian Federation
Onega 110 B4 *river* NW Russian Federation
Lake Onega 110 B4 *Eng.* Lake Onega. *lake* NW Russian Federation
Onega, Lake *see* Onezhskoye Ozero
Onex 95 A7 Genève, SW Switzerland
Ongole 132 D1 Andhra Pradesh, E India
Onitsha 75 G5 Anambra, S Nigeria
Onon Gol 127 E2 *river* N Mongolia
Onslow 146 A4 Western Australia
Onslow Bay 43 F1 *bay* North Carolina, E USA
Ontario 38 B3 *province* S Canada
Ontario, Lake 41 E3 *lake* Canada/USA
Onteniente *see* Ontinyent
Ontinyent 93 F4 *var.* Onteniente. Valenciana, E Spain
Ontong Java Rise 125 H4 *undersea feature* W Pacific Ocean
Onuba *see* Huelva
Oodeypore *see* Udaipur
Oos-Londen *see* East London
Oostakker 87 B5 Oost-Vlaanderen, NW Belgium
Oostburg 87 B5 Zeeland, SW Netherlands
Oostende 87 A5 *Eng.* Ostend, *Fr.* Ostende. West-Vlaanderen, NW Belgium
Oosterbeek 86 D4 Gelderland, SE Netherlands
Oosterhout 86 C4 Noord-Brabant, S Netherlands
Opatija 100 A2 *It.* Abbazia. Primorje-Gorski Kotar, NW Croatia
Opava 99 C5 *Ger.* Troppau. Moravskoslezský Kraj, E Czech Republic
Ópazova *see* Stara Pazova
Opelika 42 D2 Alabama, S USA
Opelousas 42 B3 Louisiana, S USA
Ophiusa *see* Formentera
Opmeer 86 C2 Noord-Holland, NW Netherlands
Opochka 110 A4 Pskovskaya Oblast', W Russian Federation
Opole 98 C4 *Ger.* Oppeln. Opolskie, S Poland
Oporto *see* Porto
Opotiki 150 E3 Bay of Plenty, North Island, New Zealand
Oppeln *see* Opole
Oppidum Ubiorum *see* Köln
Oqtosh 123 E2 *Rus.* Aktash. Samarqand Viloyati, C Uzbekistan
Oradea 108 B3 *prev.* Oradea Mare, *Ger.* Grosswardein, *Hung.* Nagyvárad. Bihor, NW Romania
Oradea Mare *see* Oradea
Orahovac *see* Rahovec
Oral *see* Ural'sk
Oran 70 D2 *var.* Ouahran, Wahran. NW Algeria
Orange 149 D6 New South Wales, SE Australia
Orange 91 D6 *anc.* Arausio. Vaucluse, SE France
Orangeburg 43 E2 South Carolina, SE USA
Orange Cone *see* Orange Fan
Orange Fan 69 C7 *var.* Orange Cone. *undersea feature* SW Indian Ocean
Orange Mouth/Orangemund *see* Oranjemund
Orange River 78 B4 *Afr.* Oranjerivier. *river* S Africa
Orange Walk 52 C1 Orange Walk, N Belize
Oranienburg 94 D3 Brandenburg, NE Germany
Oranjemund 78 B4 *var.* Orangemund; *prev.* Orange Mouth. Karas, SW Namibia
Oranjerivier *see* Orange River
Oranjestad 55 E5 *dependent territory capital* (Aruba) Lesser Antilles, S Caribbean Sea
Orany *see* Varėna
Orașul Stalin *see* Brașov
Oravicabánya *see* Oravița
Oravița 108 A4 *Ger.* Orawitza, *Hung.* Oravicabánya. Caraș-Severin, SW Romania
Orawitza *see* Oravița
Orbetello 96 B4 Toscana, C Italy
Orcadas 154 A1 *Argentinian research station* South Orkney Islands, Antarctica
Orchard Homes 44 B1 Montana, NW USA
Ordino 91 A8 Ordino, NW Andorra Europe
Ordos Desert *see* Mu Us Shadi

rdu *116 D2 anc.* Cotyora. Ordu, N Turkey
rdzhonikidze *109 F3* Dnipropetrovs'ka Oblast', E Ukraine
rdzhonikidze *see* Vladikavkaz, Russian Federation
rdzhonikidze *see* Yenakiyeve, Ukraine
realla *59 G3* E Guyana
rebro *85 C6* Örebro, C Sweden
regon *46 B3 off.* State of Oregon, *also known as* Beaver State, Sunset State, Valentine State, Webfoot State. *state* NW USA
regon City *46 B3* Oregon, NW USA
regon, State of *see* Oregon
rekhov *see* Orikhiv
rël *111 B5* Orlovskaya Oblast', W Russian Federation
rem *44 B4* Utah, W USA
re Mountains *95 C5 Cz.* Krušné Hory, *Eng.* Ore Mountains. *mountain range* Czech Republic/Germany
re Mountains *see* Erzgebirge/Krušné Hory
renburg *111 D6 prev.* Chkalov. Orenburgskaya Oblast', W Russian Federation
rense *see* Ourense
restiáda *104 D3 prev.* Orestiás. Anatolikí Makedonía kai Thráki, NE Greece
restiás *see* Orestiáda
rgan Peak *48 D3 mountain* New Mexico, SW USA
rgeyev *see* Orhei
rhei *108 D3 var.* Orheiu, *Rus.* Orgeyev. N Moldova
rheiu *see* Orhei
riental, Cordillera *60 D3 mountain range* Bolivia/Peru
riental, Cordillera *58 B3 mountain range* C Colombia
rihuela *93 F4* Valenciana, E Spain
rikhiv *109 G3 Rus.* Orekhov. Zaporiz'ka Oblast', SE Ukraine
rinoco, Río *59 E2 river* Colombia/ Venezuela
rissa *see* Odisha
rissaar *see* Orissaare
rissaare *106 C2 Ger.* Orissaar. Saaremaa, W Estonia
ristano *97 A5* Sardegna, Italy, C Mediterranean Sea
rito *58 A4* Putumayo, SW Colombia
rizaba, Volcán Pico de *35 C7 var.* Citlaltépetl. *mountain* S Mexico
rkney *see* Orkney Islands
rkney Islands *88 C2 var.* Orkney, Orkneys. *island group* N Scotland, United Kingdom
rkneys *see* Orkney Islands
rlando *43 E4* Florida, SE USA
rléanais *90 C4 cultural region* C France
rléans *90 C4 anc.* Aurelianum. Loiret, C France
rléansville *see* Chlef
rly *90 E2* (Paris) Essonne, N France
rlya *107 B6* Hrodzyenskaya Voblasts', W Belarus
rmsö *see* Vormsi
rmuz, Strait of *see* Hormuz, Strait of
rnsköldsvik *85 C5* Västernorrland, C Sweden
rolaunum *see* Arlon
rol Dengizi *see* Aral Sea
romocto *39 F4* New Brunswick, SE Canada
rona *145 F3 prev.* Hull Island. *atoll* Phoenix Islands, C Kiribati
ropeza *see* Cochabamba
rosirá Rodhópis *see* Rhodope Mountains
rpington *89 B8* United Kingdom
rschowa *see* Orşova
rsha *107 E6* Vitsyebskaya Voblasts', NE Belarus
rsk *114 B4* Orenburgskaya Oblast', W Russian Federation
rşova *108 A4 Ger.* Orschowa, *Hung.* Orsova. Mehedinţi, SW Romania
rtelsburg *see* Szczytno
rthez *91 B6* Pyrénées-Atlantiques, SW France
rtona *96 D4* Abruzzo, C Italy
ruba *see* Aruba
ruro *61 F4* Oruro, W Bolivia
ryokko *see* Yalu
ss *86 D4* Noord-Brabant, S Netherlands
Ōsaka *131 C6 hist.* Naniwa. Ōsaka, Honshū, SW Japan
Ōsaki *see* Furukawa
Osa, Península de *53 E5 peninsula* S Costa Rica
Osborn Plateau *141 D5 undersea feature* E Indian Ocean
Osca *see* Huesca
Ösel *see* Saaremaa
Osh *123 F2* Oshskaya Oblast', SW Kyrgyzstan
Oshawa *38 D5* Ontario, SE Canada
Oshikango *78 B3* Ohangwena, N Namibia
O-shima *131 D6 island* S Japan
Oshkosh *40 B2* Wisconsin, N USA
Oshmyany *see* Ashmyany
Osiek *see* Osijek
Osijek *100 C3 prev.* Osiek, Osjek, *Ger.* Esseg, *Hung.* Eszék. Osijek-Baranja, E Croatia
Osipenko *see* Berdyans'k
Osipovichi *see* Asipovichy
Osjek *see* Osijek
Oskaloosa *45 G4* Iowa, C USA
Oskarshamn *85 C7* Kalmar, S Sweden
Öskemen *see* Ust'-Kamenogorsk
Oskil *see* Oskol
Oskol *109 G2 Rus.* Oskil. *river* Russian Federation/Ukraine
Oslo *85 B6 prev.* Christiania, Kristiania. *country capital* (Norway) Oslo, S Norway
Osmaniye *116 D4* Osmaniye, S Turkey
Osnabrück *94 A3* Niedersachsen, NW Germany
Osogov Mountains *104 B3 var.* Osogovske Planine, Osogovski Planina, *Mac.* Osogovski Planini. *mountain range* Bulgaria/FYR Macedonia
Osogovske Planine/Osogovski Planina/ Osogovski Planini *see* Osogov Mountains
Oşorhei *see* Târgu Mureş
Osorno *65 B5* Los Lagos, C Chile
Ossa, Serra d' *92 C4 mountain range* SE Portugal
Ossora *115 H2* Krasnoyarskiy Kray, E Russian Federation
Ostee *see* Baltic Sea
Ostend/Ostende *see* Oostende
Oster *109 E1* Chernihivs'ka Oblast', N Ukraine
Östermyra *see* Seinäjoki
Osterode/Osterode in Ostpreussen *see* Ostróda
Österreich *see* Austria
Östersund *85 C5* Jämtland, C Sweden
Ostia Aterni *see* Pescara
Ostiglia *96 C2* Lombardia, N Italy
Ostrava *99 C5* Moravskoslezský Kraj, E Czech Republic
Ostróda *98 D3 Ger.* Osterode, Osterode in Ostpreussen. Warmińsko-Mazurskie, NE Poland
Ostrołęka *98 D3 Ger.* Wiesenhof, *Rus.* Ostrolenka. Mazowieckie, C Poland
Ostrolenka *see* Ostrołęka
Ostrov *110 A4 Latv.* Austrava. Pskovskaya Oblast', W Russian Federation
Ostrovets *see* Ostrowiec Świętokrzyski
Ostrovnoy *110 C2* Murmanskaya Oblast', NW Russian Federation
Ostrów *see* Ostrów Wielkopolski
Ostrowiec *see* Ostrowiec Świętokrzyski
Ostrowiec Świętokrzyski *98 D4 var.* Ostrowiec, *Rus.* Ostrovets. Świętokrzyskie, C Poland
Ostrów Mazowiecka *98 D3 var.* Ostrów Mazowiecki. Mazowieckie, NE Poland
Ostrów Mazowiecki *see* Ostrów Mazowiecka
Ostrowo *see* Ostrów Wielkopolski
Ostrów Wielkopolski *98 C4 var.* Ostrów, *Ger.* Ostrowo. Wielkopolskie, C Poland
Ostyako-Voguls'k *see* Khanty-Mansiysk
Osum *see* Osumit, Lumi i
Osumi-shoto *131 A8 island group* Kagoshima, Nansei-shotō, SW Japan Asia East China Sea Pacific Ocean
Osumit, Lumi i *101 D7 var.* Osum. *river* SE Albania
Osuna *92 D4* Andalucía, S Spain
Oswego *41 F2* New York, NE USA
Otago Peninsula *151 B7 peninsula* South Island, New Zealand
Otaki *150 D4* Wellington, North Island, New Zealand
Otaru *130 C2* Hokkaidō, NE Japan
Otavalo *60 B1* Imbabura, N Ecuador
Otavi *78 B3* Otjozondjupa, N Namibia
Oţelu Roşu *108 B4 Ger.* Ferdinandsberg, *Hung.* Nándorhgy. Caras-Severin, SW Romania
Otepää *106 D3 Ger.* Odenpäh. Valgamaa, SE Estonia
Oti *75 E4 river* N Togo
Otira *151 C6* West Coast, South Island, New Zealand
Otjiwarongo *78 B3* Otjozondjupa, N Namibia
Otorohanga *150 D3* Waikato, North Island, New Zealand
Otranto, Canale d' *see* Otranto, Strait of
Otranto, Strait of *101 C6 It.* Canale d'Otranto. *strait* Albania/Italy
Otrokovice *99 C5 Ger.* Otrokowitz. Zlínský Kraj, E Czech Republic
Otrokowitz *see* Otrokovice
Ōtsu *131 C6 var.* Ôtu. Shiga, Honshū, SW Japan
Ottawa *38 D5 country capital* (Canada) Ontario, SE Canada
Ottawa *40 B3* Illinois, N USA
Ottawa *45 F5* Kansas, C USA
Ottawa *41 E2 Fr.* Outaouais. *river* Ontario/Québec, SE Canada
Ottawa Islands *38 C1 island group* Nunavut, C Canada
Ottignies *87 C6* Wallon Brabant, C Belgium
Ottumwa *45 G4* Iowa, C USA
Ôtu *see* Ōtsu
Ouachita Mountains *42 A1 mountain range* Arkansas/Oklahoma, C USA
Ouachita River *42 B2 river* Arkansas/ Louisiana, C USA
Ouagadougou *75 E4 var.* Wagadugu. *country capital* (Burkina Faso) C Burkina Faso
Ouahigouya *75 E3* NW Burkina Faso
Ouahran *see* Oran
Oualâta *74 D3 var.* Oualata. Hodh ech Chargui, SE Mauritania
Ouanary *59 H3* E French Guiana
Ouanda Djallé *76 D4* Vakaga, NE Central African Republic
Ouarâne *74 D2 desert* C Mauritania
Ouargla *71 E2 var.* Wargla. NE Algeria
Ouarzazate *70 C3* S Morocco
Oubangui *77 C5 Fr.* Oubangui. *river* C Africa
Oubangui *see* Ubangi
Oubangui-Chari *see* Central African Republic
Oubangui-Chari, Territoire de l' *see* Central African Republic
Oudjda *see* Oujda
Ouessant, Île d' *90 A3 Eng.* Ushant. *island* NW France
Ouésso *77 B5* Sangha, NW Congo
Oujda *70 D2 Ar.* Oudjda, Ujda. NE Morocco
Oujeft *74 C2* Adrar, C Mauritania
Oulu *84 D4 Swe.* Uleåborg. Oulu, Finland
Oulujärvi *84 D4 Swe.* Uleträsk. *lake* C Finland
Oulujoki *84 D4 Swe.* Uleälv. *river* C Finland
Ounasjoki *84 D3 river* N Finland
Ounianga Kébir *76 C2* Borkou-Ennedi-Tibesti, N Chad
Oup *see* Auob
Oupeye *87 D6* Liège, E Belgium
Our *87 D6 river* NW Europe
Ourense *92 C1 Cast.* Orense, *Lat.* Aurium. Galicia, NW Spain
Ourique *92 B4* Beja, S Portugal
Ours, Grand Lac de l' *see* Great Bear Lake
Ourthe *87 D7 river* E Belgium
Ouse *89 D5 river* N England, United Kingdom
Outaouais *see* Ottawa
Outer Hebrides *88 B3 var.* Western Isles. *island group* NW Scotland, United Kingdom
Outer Islands *79 G1 island group* SW Seychelles Africa W Indian Ocean
Ouvéa *144 D5 island* Îles Loyauté, NE New Caledonia
Ouyen *149 C6* Victoria, SE Australia
Ovalle *64 B3* Coquimbo, N Chile
Ovar *92 B2* Aveiro, N Portugal
Overflakkee *86 B4 island* SW Netherlands
Overijse *87 C6* Vlaams Brabant, C Belgium
Oviedo *92 C1 anc.* Asturias. Asturias, NW Spain
Ovilava *see* Wels
Ovruch *108 D1* Zhytomyrs'ka Oblast', N Ukraine
Owando *77 B5 prev.* Fort Rousset. Cuvette, C Congo
Owase *131 C6* Mie, Honshū, SW Japan
Owatonna *45 F3* Minnesota, N USA
Owen Fracture Zone *140 B4 tectonic feature* W Arabian Sea
Owen, Mount *151 C5 mountain* South Island, New Zealand
Owensboro *40 B5* Kentucky, S USA
Owen Stanley Range *144 B3 mountain range* S Papua New Guinea
Owerri *75 G5* Imo, S Nigeria
Owo *75 F5* Ondo, SW Nigeria
Owyhee River *46 C4 river* Idaho/Oregon, NW USA
Oxford *151 C6* Canterbury, South Island, New Zealand
Oxford *89 D6 Lat.* Oxonia. S England, United Kingdom
Oxkutzcab *51 H4* Yucatán, SE Mexico
Oxnard *47 B7* California, W USA
Oxonia *see* Oxford
Oxus *see* Amu Darya
Oyama *131 D5* Tochigi, Honshū, S Japan
Oyem *77 B5* Woleu-Ntem, N Gabon
Oyo *77 B6* Cuvette, C Congo
Oyo *75 F4* Oyo, W Nigeria
Ozark *42 D3* Alabama, S USA
Ozark Plateau *45 G5 plain* Arkansas/ Missouri, C USA
Ozarks, Lake of the *45 F5 reservoir* Missouri, C USA
Ozbourn Seamount *152 D4 undersea feature* W Pacific Ocean
Ózd *99 D6* Borsod-Abaúj-Zemplén, NE Hungary
Ozieri *97 A5* Sardegna, Italy, C Mediterranean Sea

Paamiut *82 B4 var.* Pâmiut, *Dan.* Frederikshåb. S Greenland
Pa-an *see* Hpa-an
Pabianice *98 C4* Łódzski, Poland
Pabna *135 G4* Rajshahi, W Bangladesh
Pacaraima, Sierra/Pacaraim, Serra *see* Pakaraima Mountains
Pachuca *51 E4 var.* Pachuca de Soto. Hidalgo, C Mexico
Pachuca de Soto *see* Pachuca
Pacific-Antarctic Ridge *154 B5 undersea feature* S Pacific Ocean
Pacific Ocean *152 D3 ocean*
Padalung *see* Phatthalung
Padang *138 B4* Sumatera, W Indonesia
Paderborn *94 B4* Nordrhein-Westfalen, NW Germany
Padma *see* Brahmaputra
Padma *see* Ganges
Padova *96 C2 Eng.* Padua; *anc.* Patavium. Veneto, NE Italy
Padre Island *49 G5 island* Texas, SW USA
Padua *see* Padova
Paducah *40 B5* Kentucky, S USA
Paeroa *150 D3* Waikato, North Island, New Zealand
Páfos *102 C5 var.* Paphos. W Cyprus
Pag *100 A3 It.* Pago. *island* Zadar, C Croatia
Page *48 B1* Arizona, SW USA
Pago *see* Pag
Pago Pago *145 F4 dependent territory capital* (American Samoa) Tutuila, W American Samoa
Pahiatua *150 D4* Manawatu-Wanganui, North Island, New Zealand
Pahsien *see* Chongqing
Paide *106 D2 Ger.* Weissenstein. Järvamaa, N Estonia
Paihia *150 D2* Northland, North Island, New Zealand
Päijänne *85 D5 lake* S Finland
Paine, Cerro *65 A7 mountain* S Chile
Painted Desert *48 B1 desert* Arizona, SW USA
Paisance *see* Piacenza
Paisley *88 C4* W Scotland, United Kingdom
País Vasco *93 E1 cultural region* N Spain

Paita *60 B3* Piura, NW Peru
Pakanbaru *see* Pekanbaru
Pakaraima Mountains *59 E3 var.* Serra Pacaraim, Sierra Pacaraima. *mountain range* N South America
Pakistan *134 A2 off.* Islamic Republic of Pakistan, *var.* Islami Jamhuriya e Pakistan. *country* S Asia

PAKISTAN
South Asia

Official name Islamic Republic of Pakistan
Formation 1947 / 1971
Capital Islamabad
Population 182 million / 612 people per sq mile (236 people per sq km)
Total area 310,401 sq. miles (803,940 sq. km)
Languages Punjabi, Sindhi, Pashtu, Urdu*, Baluchi, Brahui
Religions Sunni Muslim 77%, Shi'a Muslim 20%, Hindu 2%, Christian 1%
Ethnic mix Punjabi 56%, Pathan (Pashtun) 15%, Sindhi 14%, Mohajir 7%, Baluchi 4%, Other 4%
Government Parliamentary system
Currency Pakistani rupee = 100 paisa
Literacy rate 55%
Calorie consumption 2428 kilocalories

Pakistan, Islamic Republic of *see* Pakistan
Pakistan, Islami Jamhuriya e *see* Pakistan
Paknam *see* Samut Prakan
Pakokku *136 A3* Magway, C Myanmar (Burma)
Pak Phanang *137 C7 var.* Ban Pak Phanang. Nakhon Si Thammarat, SW Thailand
Pakruojis *106 C4* Šiaulai, N Lithuania
Paks *99 C7* Tolna, S Hungary
Paksé *see* Pakxé
Pakxé *137 D5 var.* Paksé. Champasak, S Laos
Palafrugell *93 G2* Cataluña, NE Spain
Palagruža *101 B5 It.* Pelagosa. *island* SW Croatia
Palaiá Epídavros *105 C6* Pelopónnisos, S Greece
Palaiseau *90 D2* Essonne, N France
Palamós *93 G2* Cataluña, NE Spain
Palamuse *106 E2 Ger.* Sankt-Bartholomäi. Jõgevamaa, E Estonia
Palanka *see* Bačka Palanka
Pālanpur *134 C4* Gujarāt, W India
Palantia *see* Palencia
Palapye *78 D3* Central, SE Botswana
Palau *144 A2 var.* Belau. *country* W Pacific Ocean

PALAU
Australasia & Oceania

Official name Republic of Palau
Formation 1994 / 1994
Capital Melekeok
Population 21,108 / 108 people per sq mile (42 people per sq km)
Total area 177 sq. miles (458 sq. km)
Languages Palauan*, English*, Japanese, Angaur, Tobi, Sonsorolese
Religions Christian 66%, Modekngei 34%
Ethnic mix Palauan 74%, Filipino 16%, Other 6%, Chinese and other Asian 4%
Government Nonparty system
Currency US dollar = 100 cents
Literacy rate 99%
Calorie consumption Not available

Palawan *139 E2 island* W Philippines
Palawan Passage *138 D2 passage* W Philippines
Paldiski *106 D2 prev.* Baltiski, *Eng.* Baltic Port, *Ger.* Baltischport. Harjumaa, NW Estonia
Palembang *138 B4* Sumatera, W Indonesia
Palencia *92 D2 anc.* Palantia, Pallantia. Castilla y León, NW Spain
Palerme *see* Palermo
Palermo *97 C7 Fr.* Palerme; *anc.* Panhormus, Panormus. Sicilia, Italy, C Mediterranean Sea
Pāli *134 C3* Rājasthān, N India
Palikir *144 C2 country capital* (Micronesia) Pohnpei, E Micronesia
Palimé *see* Kpalimé
Palioúri, Akrotírio *104 C4 var.* Akrotírio Kanestron. *headland* N Greece
Palk Strait *132 C3 strait* India/Sri Lanka
Pallantia *see* Palencia
Palliser, Cape *151 D5 headland* North Island, New Zealand
Palma *93 G3 var.* Palma de Mallorca. Mallorca, Spain, W Mediterranean Sea
Palma del Río *92 D4* Andalucía, S Spain
Palma de Mallorca *see* Palma
Palmar Sur *53 E5* Puntarenas, SE Costa Rica
Palma Soriano *54 C3* Santiago de Cuba, E Cuba
Palm Beach *148 E1* New South Wales, E Australia
Palmer *154 A2 US research station* Antarctica
Palmer Land *154 A3 physical region* Antarctica
Palmerston *145 F4 island* S Cook Islands
Palmerston *see* Darwin
Palmerston North *150 D4* Manawatu-Wanganui, North Island, New Zealand
The Palmetto State *see* South Carolina
Palmi *97 D7* Calabria, SW Italy
Palmira *58 B3* Valle del Cauca, W Colombia
Palm Springs *47 D7* California, W USA
Palmyra *see* Tudmur
Palmyra Atoll *145 G2 US privately owned unincorporated territory* C Pacific Ocean
Palo Alto *47 B6* California, W USA
Paloe *see* Denpasar, Bali, C Indonesia
Paloe *see* Palu
Palu *139 E4 prev.* Paloe. Sulawesi, C Indonesia
Pamiers *91 B6* Ariège, S France
Pamir *123 F3 var.* Daryā-ye Pāmīr, *Taj.* Dar"yoi Pomir. *river* Afghanistan/ Tajikistan
Pāmīr, Daryā-ye *see* Pamir
Pamir/Pāmīr, Daryā-ye *see* Pamirs
Pamirs *123 F3 Pash.* Daryā-ye Pāmīr, *Rus.* Pamir. *mountain range* C Asia
Pâmiut *see* Paamiut
Pamlico Sound *43 G1 sound* North Carolina, SE USA
Pampa *49 E1* Texas, SW USA
Pampa Aullagas, Lago *see* Poopó, Lago
Pampas *64 C4 plain* C Argentina
Pampeluna *see* Pamplona
Pamplona *58 C2* Norte de Santander, N Colombia
Pamplona *93 E1 Basq.* Iruña, *prev.* Pampeluna; *anc.* Pompaelo. Navarra, N Spain
Panaji *132 B1 var.* Pangim, Panjim, New Goa. *state capital* Goa, W India
Panamá *53 G4 var.* Ciudad de Panama, *Eng.* Panama City. *country capital* (Panama) Panamá, C Panama
Panama *53 G5 off.* Republic of Panama. *country* Central America

PANAMA
Central America

Official name Republic of Panama
Formation 1903 / 1903
Capital Panama City
Population 3.9 million / 133 people per sq mile (51 people per sq km)
Total area 30,193 sq. miles (78,200 sq. km)
Languages English Creole, Spanish*, Amerindian languages, Chibchan languages
Religions Roman Catholic 84%, Protestant 15%, Other 1%
Ethnic mix Mestizo 70%, Black 14%, White 10%, Amerindian 6%
Government Presidential system
Currency Balboa = 100 centésimos; US dollar
Literacy rate 94%
Calorie consumption 2644 kilocalories

Panama Basin *35 C8 undersea feature* E Pacific Ocean
Panama Canal *53 F4 canal* E Panama
Panama City *42 D3* Florida, SE USA
Panama City *see* Panamá
Gulf of Panama *53 G5 var.* Gulf of Panama. *gulf* S Panama
Panama, Gulf of *see* Panamá, Golfo de
Isthmus of Panama *53 G4 Eng.* Isthmus of Panama; *prev.* Isthmus of Darien. *isthmus* E Panama
Panama, Isthmus of *see* Panama, Istmo de
Panama, Republic of *see* Panama
Panay Island *139 E2 island* C Philippines
Pančevo *100 D3 Ger.* Pantschowa, *Hung.* Pancsova. Vojvodina, N Serbia
Pancsova *see* Pančevo
Paneas *see* Bāniyās
Panevėžys *106 C4* Panevėžys, C Lithuania
Pangim *see* Panaji
Pangkalpinang *138 C4* Pulau Bangka, W Indonesia
Pang-Nga *see* Phang-Nga
Panhormus *see* Palermo
Panjim *see* Panaji
Panopolis *see* Akhmīm
Pánormos *105 C7* Kríti, Greece, E Mediterranean Sea
Panormus *see* Palermo
Pantanal *63 E3 var.* Pantanalmato-Grossense. *swamp* SW Brazil
Pantanalmato-Grossense *see* Pantanal
Pantelleria, Isola di *97 B7 island* SW Italy
Pantschowa *see* Pančevo
Pánuco *51 E3* Veracruz-Llave, E Mexico
Pao-chi/Paoki *see* Baoji
Paola *102 B5* E Malta
Pao-shan *see* Baoshan
Pao-t'ou/Paotow *see* Baotou
Papagayo, Golfo de *52 C4 gulf* NW Costa Rica
Papakura *150 D3* Auckland, North Island, New Zealand
Papantla *51 F4 var.* Papantla de Olarte. Veracruz-Llave, E Mexico
Papantla de Olarte *see* Papantla
Papeete *145 H4 dependent territory capital* (French Polynesia) Tahiti, W French Polynesia
Paphos *see* Páfos
Papilė *106 B3* Šiaulai, NW Lithuania
Papillion *45 F4* Nebraska, C USA
Papua *139 H4 var.* Irian Barat, West Irian, West New Guinea, West Papua; *prev.* Dutch New Guinea, Irian Jaya, Netherlands New Guinea. *province* E Indonesia
Papua and New Guinea, Territory of *see* Papua New Guinea
Papua, Gulf of *144 B3 gulf* S Papua New Guinea
Papua New Guinea *144 B3 off.* Independent State of Papua New Guinea; *prev.* Territory of Papua and New Guinea. *country* NW Melanesia

PAPUA NEW GUINEA
Australasia & Oceania

Official name Independent State of Papua New Guinea
Formation 1975 / 1975
Capital Port Moresby
Population 7.3 million / 42 people per sq mile (16 people per sq km)
Total area 178,703 sq. miles (462,840 sq. km)
Languages Pidgin English, Papuan, English*, Motu, 800 (est.) native languages
Religions Protestant 60%, Roman Catholic 37%, Other 3%
Ethnic mix Melanesian and mixed race 100%
Government Parliamentary system
Currency Kina = 100 toea
Literacy rate 60%
Calorie consumption 2193 kilocalories

Papua New Guinea, Independent State of *see* Papua New Guinea
Papuk *100 C3 mountain range* NE Croatia
Pará *63 E2 off.* Estado do Pará. *state* NE Brazil
Pará *63 E2 off.* Estado do Pará. *region* NE Brazil
Pará *see* Belém
Paracel Islands *125 E3 disputed territory* SE Asia
Paraćin *100 D4* Serbia, C Serbia
Paradise of the Pacific *see* Hawaii
Pará, Estado do *see* Pará
Paragua, Río *59 E3 river* SE Venezuela
Paraguay *64 C2 country* C South America

PARAGUAY
South America

Official name Republic of Paraguay
Formation 1811 / 1938
Capital Asunción
Population 6.8 million / 44 people per sq mile (17 people per sq km)
Total area 157,046 sq. miles (406,750 sq. km)
Languages Guaraní, Spanish*, German
Religions Roman Catholic 90%, Protestant (including Mennonite) 10%
Ethnic mix Mestizo 91%, Other 7%, Amerindian 2%
Government Presidential system
Currency Guaraní = 100 céntimos
Literacy rate 94%
Calorie consumption 2698 kilocalories

Paraguay *64 D2 var.* Río Paraguay. *river* C South America
Paraguay, Río *see* Paraguay
Parahiba/Parahyba *see* Paraíba
Paraíba *63 G2 off.* Estado da Paraíba; *prev.* Parahiba, Parahyba. *state* E Brazil
Paraíba *63 G2 off.* Estado da Paraíba; *prev.* Parahiba, Parahyba. *region* E Brazil
Paraíba *see* João Pessoa
Paraíba, Estado da *see* Paraíba
Parakou *75 F4* C Benin
Paramaribo *59 G3 country capital* (Suriname) Paramaribo, N Suriname
Paramushir, Ostrov *115 H3 island* SE Russian Federation
Paraná *63 E4* Entre Ríos, E Argentina
Paraná *63 E5 off.* Estado do Paraná. *state* S Brazil
Paraná *63 E5 off.* Estado do Paraná. *region* S Brazil
Paraná *57 C5 var.* Alto Paraná. *river* C South America
Paraná, Estado do *see* Paraná
Paranésti *104 C3 var.* Paranéstio. Anatolikí Makedonía kai Thráki, NE Greece
Paranéstio *see* Paranésti
Paraparaumu *151 D5* Wellington, North Island, New Zealand
Parchim *94 C3* Mecklenburg-Vorpommern, N Germany
Parczew *98 E4* Lubelskie, E Poland
Pardubice *99 B5 Ger.* Pardubitz. Pardubický Kraj, C Czech Republic
Pardubitz *see* Pardubice
Parechcha *107 B5 Pol.* Porzecze, *Rus.* Porech'ye. Hrodzyenskaya Voblasts', W Belarus
Parecis, Chapada dos *62 D3 var.* Serra dos Parecis. *mountain range* W Brazil
Parecis, Serra dos *see* Parecis, Chapada dos
Parenzo *see* Poreč
Parepare *139 E4* Sulawesi, C Indonesia
Párga *105 A5* Ípeiros, W Greece
Paria, Golfo de *see* Paria, Gulf of
Paria, Gulf of *59 E1 var.* Golfo de Paria. *gulf* Trinidad and Tobago/Venezuela
Parika *59 F2* NE Guyana
Parikiá *105 D6* Kykládes, Greece, Aegean Sea
Paris *90 D1 anc.* Lutetia, Lutetia Parisiorum, Parisii. *country capital* (France) Paris, N France
Paris *49 G2* Texas, SW USA
Parisii *see* Paris
Parkersburg *40 D4* West Virginia, NE USA
Parkes *149 D6* New South Wales, SE Australia
Parkhar *see* Farkhor
Parma *96 B2* Emilia-Romagna, N Italy
Parnahyba *see* Parnaíba
Parnaíba *63 F2 var.* Parnahyba. Piauí, E Brazil
Pärnu *106 D2 Ger.* Pernau, *Latv.* Pērnava; *prev. Rus.* Pernov. Pärnumaa, SW Estonia
Pärnu *106 D2 var.* Parnu Jõgi, *Ger.* Pernau. *river* SW Estonia
Pärnu-Jaagupi *106 D2 Ger.* Sankt-Jakobi. Pärnumaa, SW Estonia
Parnu Jõgi *see* Pärnu
Pärnu Laht *106 D2 Ger.* Pernauer Bucht *bay* SW Estonia

aropamisus Range see Sefid Kūh, Selseleh-ye
áros 105 C6 island Kykládes, Greece, Aegean Sea
arral 64 B4 Maule, C Chile
arral see Hidalgo del Parral
'arramatta 148 D1 New South Wales, SE Australia
arras 50 D3 var. Parras de la Fuente. Coahuila, NE Mexico
arras de la Fuente see Parras
arsons 45 F5 Kansas, C USA
asadena 47 C7 California, W USA
asadena 49 H4 Texas, SW USA
aşcani 108 C3 Hung. Páskán. Iaşi, NE Romania
asco 46 C2 Washington, NW USA
asewalk 94 D3 Mecklenburg-Vorpommern, NE Germany
ashkeni see Bolyarovo
asinler 117 F3 Erzurum, NE Turkey
áskán see Paşcani
asłęk 98 D2 Ger. Preußisch Holland. Warmińsko-Mazurskie, NE Poland
'asni 134 A3 Baluchistān, SW Pakistan
aso de Indios 65 B6 Chubut, S Argentina
assarowitz see Požarevac
assau 95 D6 Bayern, SE Germany
'asso Fundo 63 E5 Rio Grande do Sul, S Brazil
'astavy 107 C5 Pol. Postawy, Rus. Postavy. Vitsyebskaya Voblasts', NW Belarus
'astaza, Río 60 B2 river Ecuador/Peru
'asto 58 A4 Nariño, SW Colombia
'asvalys 106 C4 Panevėžys, N Lithuania
'atagonia 57 B7 physical region Argentina/Chile
'atalung see Phatthalung
'atani see Pattani
'atavium see Padova
'atea 150 D4 Taranaki, North Island, New Zealand
'aterson 41 F3 New Jersey, NE USA
'athein 136 A4 var. Bassein. Ayeyarwady, SW Myanmar (Burma)
'átmos 105 D6 island Dodekánisa, Greece, Aegean Sea
'atna 135 F3 var. Azimabad. state capital Bihār, N India
'atnos 117 F3 Ağrı, E Turkey
'atos, Lagoa dos 63 E5 lagoon S Brazil
'átra 105 B5 Eng. Patras; prev. Pátrai. Dytikí Elláda, S Greece
'átrai/Patras see Pátra
'attani 137 C7 var. Patani. Pattani, SW Thailand
'attaya 137 C5 Chon Buri, S Thailand
'atuca, Río 52 D2 river E Honduras
'au 91 B6 Pyrénées-Atlantiques, SW France
'aulatuk 37 E3 Northwest Territories, NW Canada
'aungde 136 B4 Bago, C Myanmar (Burma)
'autalia see Kyustendil
'avia 96 B2 anc. Ticinum. Lombardia, N Italy
'āvilosta 106 B3 W Latvia
'avlikeni 104 D2 Veliko Tŭrnovo, N Bulgaria
'avlodar 114 C4 Pavlodar, NE Kazakhstan
'avlograd see Pavlohrad
'avlohrad 109 G3 Rus. Pavlograd. Dnipropetrovs'ka Oblast', E Ukraine
'awai, Pulau 138 A2 island SW Singapore Asia
'awn, Nam 136 B3 river C Myanmar (Burma)
Pax Augusta see Badajoz
Pax Julia see Beja
Paxoí 105 A5 island Iónia Nisiá, Greece, C Mediterranean Sea
Payo Obispo see Chetumal
Paysandú 64 D4 Paysandú, W Uruguay
Pazar 117 E2 Rize, NE Turkey
Pazardzhik 104 C3 prev. Tatar Pazardzhik. Pazardzhik, SW Bulgaria
'eace Garden State see North Dakota
Peach State see Georgia
Pearl Islands 53 G5 Eng. Pearl Islands. island group SE Panama
Pearl Islands see Perlas, Archipiélago de las
Pearl Lagoon 53 E3 Eng. Pearl Lagoon. lagoon E Nicaragua
Pearl Lagoon see Perlas, Laguna de
Pearl River 42 B3 river Louisiana/Mississippi, S USA
Pearsall 49 F4 Texas, SW USA
Peawanuk 38 C2 Ontario, S Canada
Peć see Pejë
Pechora 110 D3 Respublika Komi, NW Russian Federation
Pechora 110 D3 river NW Russian Federation
Pechora Sea 110 D2 Eng. Pechora Sea. sea NW Russian Federation
Pechora Sea see Pechorskoye More
Pecos 49 E3 Texas, SW USA
Pecos River 49 E3 river New Mexico/Texas, SW USA
Pécs 99 C7 Ger. Fünfkirchen, Lat. Sopianae. Baranya, SW Hungary
Pedra Lume 74 A3 Sal, NE Cape Verde
Pedro Cays 54 C3 island group Greater Antilles, S Jamaica North America N Caribbean Sea W Atlantic Ocean
Pedro Juan Caballero 64 D2 Amambay, E Paraguay
Peer 87 D5 Limburg, NE Belgium
Pegasus Bay 151 C6 bay South Island, New Zealand
Pegu see Bago
Pehuajó 64 C4 Buenos Aires, E Argentina
Pei-ching see Beijing/Beijing Shi
Peine 94 B3 Niedersachsen, C Germany
Pei-p'ing see Beijing/Beijing Shi
Peipsi Järv/Peipus-See see Peipus, Lake
Peipus, Lake 106 E3 Est. Peipsi Järv, Ger. Peipus-See, Rus. Chudskoye Ozero. lake Estonia/Russian Federation
Peiraías 105 C6 prev. Piraiévs, Eng. Piraeus. Attikí, C Greece
Pejë 101 D5 Serb. Peć. W Kosovo
Pèk see Phônsaven
Pekalongan 138 C4 Jawa, C Indonesia
Pekanbaru 138 B3 var. Pakanbaru. Sumatera, W Indonesia
Pekin 40 B4 Illinois, N USA
Peking see Beijing/Beijing Shi
Pelagie 97 B8 island group SW Italy
Pelagosa see Palagruža
Pelican State see Louisiana
Pelly Bay see Kugaaruk
Pélmonostor see Beli Manastir
Peloponnese 105 B6 var. Morea, Eng. Peloponnese; anc. Peloponnesus. peninsula S Greece
Peloponnese/Peloponnesus see Pelopónnisos
Pematangsiantar 138 B3 Sumatera, W Indonesia
Pemba 79 F2 prev. Port Amelia, Porto Amélia. Cabo Delgado, NE Mozambique
Pemba 73 D7 island E Tanzania
Pembroke 38 D4 Ontario, SE Canada
Penang see Pinang, Pulau, Peninsular Malaysia
Penang see George Town
Penas, Golfo de 65 A7 gulf S Chile
Penderma see Bandırma
Pendleton 46 C3 Oregon, NW USA
Pend Oreille, Lake 46 D2 lake Idaho, NW USA
Peneius see Pineiós
Peng-pu see Bengbu
Penibético, Sistema see Béticos, Sistemas
Peniche 92 B3 Leiria, W Portugal
Peninsular State see Florida
Penninae, Alpes/Pennine, Alpi see Pennine Alps
Pennine Alps 95 A8 Fr. Alpes Pennines, It. Alpi Pennine, Lat. Alpes Penninae. mountain range Italy/Switzerland
Pennine Chain see Pennines
Pennines 89 D5 var. Pennine Chain. mountain range N England, United Kingdom
Pennines, Alpes see Pennine Alps
Pennsylvania 41 E4 off. Commonwealth of Pennsylvania, also known as Keystone State. state NE USA
Penobscot River 41 G2 river Maine, NE USA
Penong 149 A6 South Australia
Penonomé 53 F5 Coclé, C Panama
Penrhyn 145 G3 atoll N Cook Islands
Penrhyn Basin 143 F3 undersea feature C Pacific Ocean
Penrith 148 D1 New South Wales, SE Australia
Penrith 89 D5 NW England, United Kingdom
Pensacola 42 C3 Florida, SE USA
Pentecost 144 D4 Fr. Pentecôte. island C Vanuatu
Pentecôte see Pentecost
Penza 111 C6 Penzenskaya Oblast', W Russian Federation
Penzance 89 C7 SW England, United Kingdom
Peoria 40 B4 Illinois, N USA
Perchtoldsdorf 95 E6 Niederösterreich, NE Austria
Percival Lakes 146 C4 lakes Western Australia
Perdido, Monte 93 F1 mountain NE Spain
Perece Vela Basin see West Mariana Basin
Pereira 58 B3 Risaralda, W Colombia
Peremyshl see Przemyśl
Pergamino 64 C4 Buenos Aires, E Argentina
Périgueux 91 C5 anc. Vesuna. Dordogne, SW France
Perito Moreno 65 B6 Santa Cruz, S Argentina
Perleberg 94 C3 Brandenburg, N Germany
Perlepe see Prilep
Perm' 114 C3 prev. Molotov. Permskiy Kray, NW Russian Federation
Pernambuco 63 G2 off. Estado de Pernambuco. region E Brazil
Pernambuco 63 G2 off. Estado de Pernambuco. state E Brazil
Pernambuco see Recife
Pernambuco Abyssal Plain see Pernambuco Plain
Pernambuco, Estado de see Pernambuco
Pernambuco Plain 67 C5 var. Pernambuco Abyssal Plain. undersea feature E Atlantic Ocean
Pernau see Pärnu
Pernauer Bucht see Pärnu Laht
Pērnava see Pärnu
Pernik 104 B2 prev. Dimitrovo. Pernik, W Bulgaria
Pernov see Pärnu
Perote 51 F4 Veracruz-Llave, E Mexico
Pérouse see Perugia
Perovsk see Kyzylorda
Perpignan 91 C6 Pyrénées-Orientales, S France
Perryton 49 F1 Texas, SW USA
Perryville 45 H5 Missouri, C USA
Persia see Iran
Persian Gulf 120 C4 var. Gulf, The, Ar. Khalīj al 'Arabī, Per. Khalīj-e Fars. gulf SW Asia
Perth 147 A6 state capital Western Australia
Perth 88 C4 C Scotland, United Kingdom
Perth Basin 141 E6 undersea feature SE Indian Ocean
Peru 60 C3 off. Republic of Peru. country W South America

PERU
South America

Official name Republic of Peru
Formation 1824 / 1941
Capital Lima
Population 30.4 million / 62 people per sq mile (24 people per sq km)
Total area 496,223 sq. miles (1,285,200 sq. km)
Languages Spanish*, Quechua*, Aymara
Religions Roman Catholic 81%, Other 19%
Ethnic mix Amerindian 45%, Mestizo 37%, White 15%, Other 3%
Government Presidential system
Currency New sol = 100 céntimos
Literacy rate 94%
Calorie consumption 2624 kilocalories

Peru see Beru
Peru Basin 67 A5 undersea feature E Pacific Ocean
Peru-Chile Trench 56 A4 undersea feature E Pacific Ocean
Perugia 96 C4 Fr. Pérouse; anc. Perusia. Umbria, C Italy
Perugia, Lake of see Trasimeno, Lago
Peru, Republic of see Peru
Perusia see Perugia
Péruwelz 87 B6 Hainaut, SW Belgium
Pervomays'k 109 E3 prev. Ol'viopol'. Mykolayivs'ka Oblast', S Ukraine
Pervyy Kuril'skiy Proliv 115 H3 strait E Russian Federation
Pesaro 96 C3 anc. Pisaurum. Marche, C Italy
Pescara 96 D4 anc. Aternum, Ostia Aterni. Abruzzo, C Italy
Peshāwar 134 C1 Khyber Pakhtunkhwa, N Pakistan
Peshkopi 101 C6 var. Peshkopia, Peshkopija. Dibër, NE Albania
Peshkopia/Peshkopija see Peshkopi
Pessac 91 B5 Gironde, SW France
Petach-Tikva see Petah Tikva
Petah Tikva 119 A6 var. Petach-Tikva, Petah Tiqva, Petakh Tikva; prev. Petah Tiqwa. Tel Aviv, C Israel
Petah Tiqwa see Petah Tikva
Petakh Tikva/Petah Tiqva see Petah Tikva
Pétange 87 D8 Luxembourg, SW Luxembourg
Petchaburi see Phetchaburi
Peterborough 149 B6 South Australia
Peterborough 38 D5 Ontario, SE Canada
Peterborough 89 E6 prev. Medeshamstede. E England, United Kingdom
Peterhead 88 D3 NE Scotland, United Kingdom
Peter I Øy 154 A3 Norwegian dependency Antarctica
Petermann Bjerg 83 E3 mountain C Greenland
Petersburg 41 E5 Virginia, NE USA
Peters Mine 59 F3 var. Peter's Mine. N Guyana
Petit St-Bernard, Col du see Little Saint Bernard Pass
Peto 51 H4 Yucatán, SE Mexico
Petoskey 40 C2 Michigan, N USA
Petra see Wādī Mūsā
Petrich 104 C3 Blagoevgrad, SW Bulgaria
Petrikau see Piotrków Trybunalski
Petrikov see Pyetrykaw
Petrinja 100 B3 Sisak-Moslavina, C Croatia
Petroaleksandrovsk see To'rtkok'l
Petrodvorets 110 A4 Fin. Pietarhovi. Leningradskaya Oblast', NW Russian Federation
Petrograd see Sankt-Peterburg
Petrokov see Piotrków Trybunalski
Petropavl see Petropavlovsk
Petropavlovsk 114 C4 Kaz. Petropavl. Severnyy Kazakhstan, N Kazakhstan
Petropavlovsk-Kamchatskiy 115 H3 Kamchatskiy Kray, E Russian Federation
Petroşani 108 B4 var. Petroşeni, Ger. Petroschen, Hung. Petrozsény. Hunedoara, W Romania
Petroschen/Petroşeni see Petroşani
Petroskoi see Petrozavodsk
Petrovgrad see Zrenjanin
Petrovsk-Port see Makhachkala
Petrozavodsk 114 B2 Fin. Petroskoi. Respublika Kareliya, NW Russian Federation
Petrozsény see Petroşani
Pettau see Ptuj
Pevek 115 G1 Chukotskiy Avtonomnyy Okrug, NE Russian Federation
Pezinok 99 C6 Ger. Bösing, Hung. Bazin. Bratislavský Kraj, W Slovakia
Pforzheim 95 B6 Baden-Württemberg, SW Germany
Pfungstadt 95 B5 Hessen, W Germany
Phangan, Ko 137 C6 island SW Thailand
Phang-Nga 137 B7 var. Pang-Nga, Phangnga. Phangnga, SW Thailand
Phangnga see Phang-Nga
Phan Rang/Phanrang see Phan Rang-Thap Cham
Phan Rang-Thap Cham 137 E6 var. Phanrang, Phan Rang, Phan Rang Thap Cham. Ninh Thuận, S Vietnam
Phan Thiêt 137 E6 Bình Thuận, S Vietnam
Pharnacia see Giresun
Pharus see Hvar
Phatthalung 137 C7 var. Padalung, Patalung. Phatthalung, SW Thailand
Phayao 136 C4 var. Muang Phayao. Phayao, NW Thailand
Phenix City 42 D2 Alabama, S USA
Phet Buri see Phetchaburi
Phetchaburi 137 C5 var. Bejraburi, Petchaburi, Phet Buri. Phetchaburi, SW Thailand

Philadelphia *41 F4* Pennsylvania, NE USA
Philadelphia *see* 'Amman
Philippine Basin *125 F3 undersea feature* W Pacific Ocean
Philippine Islands *139 E1 island group* W Pacific Ocean
Philippines *139 E1 off.* Republic of the Philippines. *country* SE Asia

PHILIPPINES
Southeast Asia

Official name Republic of the Philippines
Formation 1946 / 1946
Capital Manila
Population 98.4 million / 855 people per sq mile (330 people per sq km)
Total area 115,830 sq. miles (300,000 sq. km)
Languages Filipino*, English*, Tagalog, Cebuano, Ilocano, Hiligaynon, many other local languages
Religions Roman Catholic 81%, Protestant 9%, Muslim 5%, Other (including Buddhist) 5%
Ethnic mix Other 34%, Tagalog 28%, Cebuano 13%, Ilocano 9%, Hiligaynon 8%, Bisaya 8%
Government Presidential system
Currency Philippine peso = 100 centavos
Literacy rate 95%
Calorie consumption 2608 kilocalories

Philippine Sea *125 F3 sea* W Pacific Ocean
Philippines, Republic of the *see* Philippines
Philippine Trench *142 A1 undersea feature* W Philippine Sea
Philippopolis *see* Plovdiv
Phitsanulok *136 C4 var.* Bisnulok, Muang Phitsanulok, Pitsanulok. Phitsanulok, C Thailand
Phlórina *see* Flórina
Phnom Penh *see* Phnum Penh
Phnum Penh *137 D6 var.* Phnom Penh. *country capital* (Cambodia) Phnum Penh, S Cambodia
Phoenix *48 B2 state capital* Arizona, SW USA
Phoenix Islands *145 E3 island group* C Kiribati
Phôngsali *136 C3 var.* Phong Saly. Phôngsali, N Laos
Phong Saly *see* Phôngsali
Phônsaven *136 D4 var.* Xieng Khouang; *prev.* Pèk, Xiangkhoang. Xiangkhoang, N Laos
Phou Louang *see* Annamite Mountains
Phrae *136 C4 var.* Muang Phrae, Prae. Phrae, NW Thailand
Phra Nakhon Si Ayutthaya *see* Ayutthaya
Phra Thong, Ko *137 B6 island* SW Thailand
Phuket *137 B7 var.* Bhuket, Puket, *Mal.* Ujung Salang; *prev.* Junkseylon, Salang. Phuket, SW Thailand
Phuket, Ko *137 B7 island* SW Thailand
Phumĭ Kâmpóng Trâbêk *see* Kâmpóng Trâbêk
Phumĭ Sâmraông *see* Sâmraông
Phum Kompong Trabek *see* Kâmpóng Trâbêk
Phum Samrong *see* Sâmraông
Phu Vinh *see* Tra Vinh
Phyu *136 B4 var.* Hpyu, Pyu. Bago, C Myanmar (Burma)
Piacenza *96 B2 Fr.* Paisance; *anc.* Placentia. Emilia-Romagna, N Italy
Piatra-Neamț *108 C4 Hung.* Karácsonkő. Neamț, NE Romania
Piauhy *see* Piauí
Piauí *63 F2 off.* Estado do Piauí; *prev.* Piauhy. *state* E Brazil
Piauí *63 F2 off.* Estado do Piauí; *prev.* Piauhy. *region* E Brazil
Piauí, Estado do *see* Piauí
Picardie *90 C3 Eng.* Picardy. *cultural region* N France
Picardy *see* Picardie
Piccolo San Bernardo, Colle di *see* Little Saint Bernard Pass
Pichilemu *64 B4* Libertador, C Chile
Pico *92 A5 var.* Ilha do Pico. *island* Azores, Portugal, NE Atlantic Ocean
Pico, Ilha do *see* Pico
Picos *63 F2* Piauí, E Brazil
Picton *151 C5* Marlborough, South Island, New Zealand
Piedmont *see* Piemonte
Piedras Negras *51 E2 var.* Ciudad Porfirio Díaz. Coahuila, NE Mexico
Pielavesi *84 D4 lake* C Finland
Pielinen *84 E4 var.* Pielisjärvi. *lake* E Finland
Pielisjärvi *see* Pielinen
Piemonte *96 A2 Eng.* Piedmont. *region* NW Italy
Pierre *45 E3 state capital* South Dakota, N USA
Piešťany *99 C6 Ger.* Pistyan, *Hung.* Pöstyén. Tranavský Kraj, W Slovakia
Pietarhovi *see* Petrodvorets
Pietari *see* Sankt-Peterburg
Pietarsaari *see* Jakobstad
Pietermaritzburg *78 C5 var.* Maritzburg. KwaZulu/Natal, E South Africa
Pietersburg *see* Polokwane
Bay of Pigs *54 B2 Eng.* Bay of Pigs. *bay* SE Cuba
Pigs, Bay of *see* Cochinos, Bahía de
Pihkva Järv *see* Pskov, Lake
Pijijiapán *51 G5* Chiapas, SE Mexico
Pikes Peak *44 C5 mountain* Colorado, C USA
Pikeville *40 D5* Kentucky, S USA
Pikinni *see* Bikini Atoll
Piła *98 B3 Ger.* Schneidemühl. Wielkopolskie, C Poland
Pilar *64 D3 var.* Villa del Pilar. Ñeembucú, S Paraguay
Pilcomayo, Rio *57 C5 river* C South America
Pilos *see* Pýlos
Pilsen *see* Plzeň
Pilzno *see* Plzeň
Pinang *see* Pinang, Pulau, Peninsular Malaysia
Pinang *see* George Town
Pinang, Pulau *138 B3 var.* Penang, Pinang; *prev.* Prince of Wales Island. *island* Peninsular Malaysia
Pinar del Río *54 A2* Pinar del Río, W Cuba
Píndhos/Píndhos Óros *see* Píndos
Píndos *104 A4 var.* Píndhos Óros, *Eng.* Pindus Mountains; *prev.* Píndhos. *mountain range* C Greece
Pindus Mountains *see* Píndos
Pine Bluff *42 B2* Arkansas, C USA
Pine Creek *146 D2* Northern Territory, N Australia
Pinega *110 C3 river* NW Russian Federation
Pineiós *104 B4 var.* Piniós; *anc.* Peneius. *river* C Greece
Pineland *49 H3* Texas, SW USA
Pínes, Akrotírio *104 C4 var.* Akrotírio Pínnes. *headland* N Greece
Pines, The Isle of the *see* Juventud, Isla de la
Pine Tree State *see* Maine
Pingdingshan *128 C4* Henan, C China
Pingkiang *see* Harbin
Ping, Mae Nam *136 B4 river* W Thailand
Piniós *see* Pineiós
Pinkiang *see* Harbin
Pínnes, Akrotírio *see* Pínes, Akrotírio
Pinos, Isla de *see* Juventud, Isla de la
Pinotepa Nacional *51 F5 var.* Santiago Pinotepa Nacional. Oaxaca, SE Mexico
Pinsk *107 B7 Pol.* Pińsk. Brestskaya Voblasts', SW Belarus
Pinta, Isla *60 A5 var.* Abingdon. *island* Galápagos Islands, Ecuador, E Pacific Ocean
Piombino *96 B3* Toscana, C Italy
Pioneer Mountains *46 D3 mountain range* Montana, N USA North America
Pionerskiy *106 A4 Ger.* Neukuhren. Kaliningradskaya Oblast', W Russian Federation
Piotrków Trybunalski *98 D4 Ger.* Petrikau, *Rus.* Petrokov. Łodzkie, C Poland
Piraeus/Piraiévs *see* Peiraías
Pírgos *see* Pýrgos
Pirineos *see* Pyrenees
Piripiri *63 F2* Piauí, E Brazil
Pirna *94 D4* Sachsen, E Germany
Pirot *101 E5* Serbia, SE Serbia
Piryatin *see* Pyryatyn
Pisa *96 B3 var.* Pisae. Toscana, C Italy
Pisae *see* Pisa
Pisaurum *see* Pesaro
Pisco *60 D4* Ica, SW Peru
Písek *99 A5* Budějovický Kraj, S Czech Republic
Pishan *126 A3 var.* Guma. Xinjiang Uygur Zizhiqu, NW China
Pishpek *see* Bishkek
Pistoia *96 B3 anc.* Pistoria, Pistoriæ. Toscana, C Italy
Pistoria/Pistoriæ *see* Pistoia
Pistyan *see* Piešťany
Pisz *98 D3 Ger.* Johannisburg. Warmińsko-Mazurskie, NE Poland
Pita *74 C4* NW Guinea
Pitalito *58 B4* Huila, S Colombia
Pitcairn Group of Islands *see* Pitcairn, Henderson, Ducie & Oeno Islands
Pitcairn Island *143 G4 island* S Pitcairn Group of Islands
Pitcairn, Henderson, Ducie & Oeno Islands *143 G4 var.* Pitcairn Group of Islands. *UK dependent territory* C Pacific Ocean
Piteå *84 D4* Norrbotten, N Sweden
Pitești *108 B5* Argeș, S Romania
Pitsanulok *see* Phitsanulok
Pitt Island *see* Makin
Pittsburg *45 F5* Kansas, C USA
Pittsburgh *41 E4* Pennsylvania, NE USA
Pittsfield *41 F3* Massachusetts, NE USA
Piura *60 B2* Piura, NW Peru
Pivdennyy Buh *109 E3 Rus.* Yuzhnyy Bug. *river* S Ukraine
Placentia *see* Piacenza
Placetas *54 B2* Villa Clara, C Cuba
Plainview *49 E2* Texas, SW USA
Pláka *105 C7* Kykládes, Greece, Aegean Sea
Planeta Rica *58 B2* Córdoba, NW Colombia
Planken *94 E1* C Liechtenstein Europe
Plano *49 G2* Texas, SW USA
Plasencia *92 C3* Extremadura, W Spain
Plate, River *64 D4 var.* River Plate. *estuary* Argentina/Uruguay
Plate, River *see* Plata, Río de la
Platinum *36 C3* Alaska, USA
Plattensee *see* Balaton
Platte River *45 E4 river* Nebraska, C USA
Plattsburgh *41 F2* New York, NE USA
Plauen *95 C5 var.* Plauen im Vogtland. Sachsen, E Germany
Plauen im Vogtland *see* Plauen
Pļaviņas *106 D4 Ger.* Stockmannshof. S Latvia
Plây Cu *see* Plei Ku
Pleasant Island *see* Nauru
Plei Ku *137 E5 prev.* Plây Cu. Gia Lai, C Vietnam
Plenty, Bay of *150 E3 bay* North Island, New Zealand
Plérin *90 A3* Côtes d'Armor, NW France
Plesetsk *110 C3* Arkhangel'skaya Oblast', NW Russian Federation
Pleshchenitsy *see* Plyeshchanitsy
Pleskau *see* Pskov
Pleskauer See *see* Pskov, Lake
Pleskava *see* Pskov
Pleszew *98 C4* Wielkopolskie, C Poland
Pleven *104 C2 prev.* Plevna. Pleven, N Bulgaria
Plevlja/Plevlje *see* Pljevlja
Plevna *see* Pleven
Pljevlja *100 C4 prev.* Plevlja, Plevlje. N Montenegro
Plocce *see* Ploče
Ploče *100 B4 It.* Plocce; *prev.* Kardeljevo. Dubrovnik-Neretva, SE Croatia
Płock *98 D3 Ger.* Plozk. Mazowieckie, C Poland
Plöcken Pass *95 C7 Ger.* Plöckenpass, *It.* Passo di Monte Croce Carnico. *pass* SW Austria
Plöckenpass *see* Plöcken Pass
Ploești *see* Ploiești
Ploiești *108 C5 prev.* Ploești. Prahova, SE Romania
Plomári *105 D5 prev.* Plomárion. Lésvos, E Greece
Plomárion *see* Plomári
Płońsk *98 D3* Mazowieckie, C Poland
Plovdiv *104 C3 prev.* Eumolpias; *anc.* Evmolpia, Philippopolis, *Lat.* Trimontium. Plovdiv, C Bulgaria
Plozk *see* Płock
Plungė *106 B3* Telšiai, W Lithuania
Plyeshchanitsy *107 D5 Rus.* Pleshchenitsy. Minskaya Voblasts', N Belarus
Plymouth *89 C7* SW England, United Kingdom
Plzeň *99 A5 Ger.* Pilsen, *Pol.* Pilzno. Plzeňský Kraj, W Czech Republic
Po *80 D4 river* N Italy
Pobedy, Pik *see* Tomür Feng
Po, Bocche del *see* Po, Foci del
Pocahontas *42 B1* Arkansas, C USA
Pocatello *46 E4* Idaho, NW USA
Pochinok *111 A5* Smolenskaya Oblast', W Russian Federation
Pocking *95 D6* Bayern, SE Germany
Poděbrady *99 B5 Ger.* Podiebrad. Středočeský Kraj, C Czech Republic
Podgorica *101 C5 prev.* Titograd. *country capital* (Montenegro) S Montenegro
Podiebrad *see* Poděbrady
Podil's'ka Vysochina *108 D3 plateau* W Ukraine
Podium Anicensis *see* le Puy
Podol'sk *111 B5* Moskovskaya Oblast', W Russian Federation
Podravska Slatina *see* Slatina
Podujevë *101 D5 Serb.* Podujevo. N Kosovo
Podujevo *see* Podujevë
Podunajská Rovina *see* Little Alföld
Poetovio *see* Ptuj
Pogradec *101 D6 var.* Pogradeci. Korçë, SE Albania
Pogradeci *see* Pogradec
Pohjanlahti *see* Bothnia, Gulf of
Pohnpei *144 C2 prev.* Ponape Ascension Island. *island* E Micronesia
Poictiers *see* Poitiers
Poinsett, Cape *154 D4 headland* Antarctica
Point de Galle *see* Galle
Pointe-à-Pitre *55 G3* Grande Terre, C Guadeloupe
Pointe-Noire *77 B6* Kouilou, S Congo
Point Lay *36 C2* Alaska, USA
Poitiers *90 B4 prev.* Poictiers; *anc.* Limonum. Vienne, W France
Poitou *90 B4 cultural region* W France
Pokharā *135 E3* Western, C Nepal
Pokrovka *see* Kyzyl-Suu
Pokrovs'ke *109 G3 Rus.* Pokrovskoye. Dnipropetrovs'ka Oblast', E Ukraine
Pokrovskoye *see* Pokrovs'ke
Pola *see* Pula
Pola de Lena *see* La Pola
Poland *98 B4 off.* Republic of Poland, *var.* Polish Republic, *Pol.* Polska, Rzeczpospolita Polska; *prev. Pol.* Polska Rzeczpospolita Ludowa, The Polish People's Republic. *country* C Europe

POLAND
Northern Europe

Official name Republic of Poland
Formation 1918 / 1945
Capital Warsaw
Population 38.2 million / 325 people per sq mile (126 people per sq km)
Total area 120,728 sq. miles (312,685 sq. km)
Languages Polish*
Religions Roman Catholic 93%, Other and nonreligious 5%, Orthodox Christian 2%
Ethnic mix Polish 98%, Other 2%
Government Parliamentary system
Currency Zloty = 100 groszy
Literacy rate 99%
Calorie consumption 3485 kilocalories

Poland, Republic of *see* Poland
Polatlı *116 C3* Ankara, C Turkey
Polatsk *107 D5 Rus.* Polotsk. Vitsyebskaya Voblasts', N Belarus
Pol-e Khomrī *see* Pul-e Khumrī
Poli *see* Pólis
Polikastro/Políkastron *see* Polýkastro
Polikrayshte *see* Dolna Oryakhovitsa
Pólis *102 C5 var.* Poli. W Cyprus
Polish People's Republic, The *see* Poland
Polish Republic *see* Poland
Polkowice *98 B4 Ger.* Heerwegen. Dolnośląskie, W Poland
Pollença *93 G3* Mallorca, Spain, W Mediterranean Sea
Pologi *see* Polohy
Polohy *109 G3 Rus.* Pologi. Zaporiz'ka Oblast', SE Ukraine
Polokwane *78 D4 prev.* Pietersburg. Limpopo, NE South Africa

Polonne *108 D2 Rus.* Polonnoye. Khmel'nyts'ka Oblast', NW Ukraine
Polonnoye *see* Polonne
Polotsk *see* Polatsk
Polska/Polska, Rzeczpospolita/Polska Rzeczpospolita Ludowa *see* Poland
Polski Trŭmbesh *104 D2 prev.* Polsko Kosovo. Ruse, N Bulgaria
Polsko Kosovo *see* Polski Trŭmbesh
Poltava *109 F2* Poltavs'ka Oblast', NE Ukraine
Poltoratsk *see* Aşgabat
Põlva *106 E3 Ger.* Pölwe. Põlvamaa, SE Estonia
Pölwe *see* Põlva
Polyarnyy *110 C2* Murmanskaya Oblast', NW Russian Federation
Polýkastro *104 B3 var.* Polikastro; *prev.* Políkastron. Kentrikí Makedonía, N Greece
Polynesia *143 F4 island group* C Pacific Ocean
Pomeranian Bay *94 D2 Ger.* Pommersche Bucht, *Pol.* Zatoka Pomorska. *bay* Germany/Poland
Pomir, Dar"yoi *see* Pamir/Pāmīr, Daryā-ye
Pommersche Bucht *see* Pomeranian Bay
Pomorska, Zatoka *see* Pomeranian Bay
Pomorskiy Proliv *110 D2 strait* NW Russian Federation
Po, Mouth of the *96 C2 var.* Bocche del Po. *river* NE Italy
Pompaelo *see* Pamplona
Pompano Beach *43 F5* Florida, SE USA
Ponape Ascension Island *see* Pohnpei
Ponca City *49 G1* Oklahoma, C USA
Ponce *55 F3* C Puerto Rico
Pondicherry *132 C2 var.* Puduchcheri, *Fr.* Pondichéry. Pondicherry, SE India
Ponferrada *92 C1* Castilla y León, NW Spain
Poniatowa *98 E4* Lubelskie, E Poland
Pons Aelii *see* Newcastle upon Tyne
Pons Vetus *see* Pontevedra
Ponta Delgada *92 B5* São Miguel, Azores, Portugal, NE Atlantic Ocean
Ponta Grossa *63 E4* Paraná, S Brazil
Pontarlier *90 D4* Doubs, E France
Ponteareas *92 B2* Galicia, NW Spain
Ponte da Barca *92 B2* Viana do Castelo, N Portugal
Pontevedra *92 B1 anc.* Pons Vetus. Galicia, NW Spain
Pontiac *40 D3* Michigan, N USA
Pontianak *138 C4* Borneo, C Indonesia
Pontisarae *see* Pontoise
Pontivy *90 A3* Morbihan, NW France
Pontoise *90 C3 anc.* Briva Isarae, Cergy-Pontoise, Pontisarae. Val-d'Oise, N France
Ponziane Island *97 C5 island* C Italy
Poole *89 D7* S England, United Kingdom
Poona *see* Pune
Poopó, Lago *61 F4 var.* Lago Pampa Aullagas. *lake* W Bolivia
Popayán *58 B4* Cauca, SW Colombia
Poperinge *87 A6* West-Vlaanderen, W Belgium
Poplar Bluff *45 G5* Missouri, C USA
Popocatépetl *51 E4 volcano* S Mexico
Popper *see* Poprad
Poprad *99 D5 Ger.* Deutschendorf, *Hung.* Poprád. Prešovský Kraj, E Slovakia
Poprád *99 D5 Ger.* Popper, *Hung.* Poprád. *river* Poland/Slovakia
Porbandar *134 B4* Gujarāt, W India
Porcupine Plain *80 B3 undersea feature* E Atlantic Ocean
Pordenone *96 C2 anc.* Portenau. Friuli-Venezia Giulia, NE Italy
Poreč *100 A2 It.* Parenzo. Istra, NW Croatia
Porech'ye *see* Parechcha
Pori *85 D5 Swe.* Björneborg. Länsi-Suomi, SW Finland
Porirua *151 D5* Wellington, North Island, New Zealand
Porkhov *110 A4* Pskovskaya Oblast', W Russian Federation
Porlamar *59 E1* Nueva Esparta, NE Venezuela
Póros *105 C6* Póros, S Greece
Póros *105 A5* Kefallinía, Iónia Nisiá, Greece, C Mediterranean Sea
Porsangenfjorden *84 D2 Lapp.* Porsáŋgguvuotna. *fjord* N Norway
Porsáŋgguvuotna *see* Porsangenfjorden
Porsgrunn *85 B6* Telemark, S Norway
Portachuelo *61 G4* Santa Cruz, C Bolivia
Portadown *89 B5 Ir.* Port An Dúnáin. S Northern Ireland, United Kingdom
Portalegre *92 C3 anc.* Ammaia, Amoea. Portalegre, E Portugal
Port Alexander *36 D4* Baranof Island, Alaska, USA
Port Alfred *78 D5* Eastern Cape, S South Africa
Port Amelia *see* Pemba
Port An Dúnáin *see* Portadown
Port Angeles *46 B1* Washington, NW USA
Port Antonio *54 B5* NE Jamaica
Port Arthur *49 H4* Texas, SW USA
Port Augusta *149 B6* South Australia
Port-au-Prince *54 D3 country capital* (Haiti) C Haiti
Port Blair *133 F2* Andaman and Nicobar Islands, SE India
Port Charlotte *43 E4* Florida, SE USA
Port Darwin *see* Darwin
Port d'Envalira *91 B8* E Andorra Europe
Port Douglas *148 D3* Queensland, NE Australia
Port Elizabeth *78 C5* Eastern Cape, S South Africa
Portenau *see* Pordenone
Porterville *47 C7* California, W USA
Port-Étienne *see* Nouâdhibou
Port Florence *see* Kisumu
Port-Francqui *see* Ilebo
Port-Gentil *77 A6* Ogooué-Maritime, W Gabon
Port Harcourt *75 G5* Rivers, S Nigeria
Port Hardy *36 D5* Vancouver Island, British Columbia, SW Canada
Port Harrison *see* Inukjuak
Port Hedland *146 B4* Western Australia
Port Huron *40 D3* Michigan, N USA
Portimão *92 B4 var.* Vila Nova de Portimão. Faro, S Portugal
Port Jackson *148 E1 harbour* New South Wales, E Australia
Portland *149 B7* Victoria, SE Australia
Portland *41 G2* Maine, NE USA
Portland *46 B3* Oregon, NW USA
Portland *49 G4* Texas, SW USA
Portland Bight *54 B5 bay* S Jamaica
Portlaoighise *see* Port Laoise
Port Laoise *89 B6 var.* Portlaoise, *Ir.* Portlaoighise; *prev.* Maryborough. C Ireland
Portlaoise *see* Port Laoise
Port Lavaca *49 G4* Texas, SW USA
Port Lincoln *149 A6* South Australia
Port Louis *79 H3 country capital* (Mauritius) NW Mauritius
Port-Lyautey *see* Kénitra
Port Macquarie *149 E6* New South Wales, SE Australia
Port Mahon *see* Maó
Portmore *54 B5* C Jamaica
Port Moresby *144 B3 country capital* (Papua New Guinea) Central/National Capital District, SW Papua New Guinea
Port Natal *see* Durban
Porto *92 B2 Eng.* Oporto; *anc.* Portus Cale. Porto, NW Portugal
Porto Alegre *63 E5 var.* Pôrto Alegre. *state capital* Rio Grande do Sul, S Brazil
Porto Alegre *76 E2* São Tomé, S Sao Tome and Principe, Africa
Porto Alegre *76 E2* São Tomé, S Sao Tome and Principe, Africa
Porto Alexandre *see* Tombua
Porto Amélia *see* Pemba
Porto Bello *see* Portobelo
Portobelo *53 G4 var.* Porto Bello, Puerto Bello. Colón, N Panama
Port O'Connor *49 G4* Texas, SW USA
Porto Edda *see* Sarandë
Portoferraio *96 B4* Toscana, C Italy
Port-of-Spain *55 H5 country capital* (Trinidad and Tobago) Trinidad, Trinidad and Tobago
Porto Grande *see* Mindelo
Portogruaro *96 C2* Veneto, NE Italy
Porto-Novo *75 F5 country capital* (Benin) S Benin
Porto Rico *see* Puerto Rico
Porto Santo *70 A2 var.* Ilha do Porto Santo. *island* Madeira, Portugal, NE Atlantic Ocean
Porto Santo, Ilha do *see* Porto Santo
Porto Torres *97 A5* Sardegna, Italy, C Mediterranean Sea
Porto Velho *62 D2 var.* Velho. *state capital* Rondônia, W Brazil
Portoviejo *60 A2 var.* Puertoviejo. Manabí, W Ecuador
Port Pirie *149 B6* South Australia
Port Rex *see* East London
Port Said *see* Būr Sa'īd
Portsmouth *89 D7* S England, United Kingdom
Portsmouth *41 G3* New Hampshire, NE USA
Portsmouth *40 D4* Ohio, N USA
Portsmouth *41 F5* Virginia, NE USA
Port Stanley *see* Stanley
Port Sudan *72 C3* Red Sea, NE Sudan
Port Swettenham *see* Klang/Pelabuhan Klang
Port Talbot *89 C7* S Wales, United Kingdom
Portugal *92 B3 off.* Portuguese Republic. *country* SW Europe

PORTUGAL
Southwest Europe

Official name The Portuguese Republic
Formation 1139 / 1640
Capital Lisbon
Population 10.6 million / 299 people per sq mile (115 people per sq km)
Total area 35,672 sq. miles (92,391 sq. km)
Languages Portuguese*
Religions Roman Catholic 92%, Protestant 4%, Nonreligious 3%, Other 1%
Ethnic mix Portuguese 98%, African and other 2%
Government Parliamentary system
Currency Euro = 100 cents
Literacy rate 94%
Calorie consumption 3456 kilocalories

Portuguese East Africa *see* Mozambique
Portuguese Guinea *see* Guinea-Bissau
Portuguese Republic *see* Portugal
Portuguese Timor *see* East Timor
Portuguese West Africa *see* Angola
Portus Cale *see* Porto
Portus Magnus *see* Almería
Portus Magonis *see* Maó
Port-Vila *144 D4 var.* Vila. *country capital* (Vanuatu) Éfaté, C Vanuatu
Porvenir *61 E3* Pando, NW Bolivia
Porvenir *65 B8* Magallanes, S Chile
Porvoo *85 E6 Swe.* Borgå. Etelä-Suomi, S Finland
Porzecze *see* Parechcha
Posadas *64 D3* Misiones, NE Argentina
Poschega *see* Požega
Posen *see* Poznań
Posnania *see* Poznań
Postavy/Postawy *see* Pastavy
Posterholt *87 D5* Limburg, SE Netherlands
Postojna *95 D8 Ger.* Adelsberg, *It.* Postumia. SW Slovenia
Postumia *see* Postojna
Pöstyén *see* Piešt'any
Potamós *105 C7* Antikýthira, S Greece
Potentia *see* Potenza
Potenza *97 D5 anc.* Potentia. Basilicata, S Italy
Poti *117 F2 prev.* P'ot'i. W Georgia
P'ot'i *see* Poti
Potiskum *75 G4* Yobe, NE Nigeria
Potomac River *41 E5 river* NE USA
Potosí *61 F4* Potosí, S Bolivia
Potsdam *94 D3* Brandenburg, NE Germany
Potwar Plateau *134 C2 plateau* NE Pakistan
Poŭthĭsăt *137 D6 prev.* Pursat. Poŭthĭsăt, W Cambodia
Po, Valle del *see* Po Valley
Po Valley *96 C2 It.* Valle del Po. *valley* N Italy
Považská Bystrica *99 C5 Ger.* Waagbistritz, *Hung.* Vágbeszterce. Trenčiansky Kraj, W Slovakia
Poverty Bay *150 E4 inlet* North Island, New Zealand
Póvoa de Varzim *92 B2* Porto, NW Portugal
Powder River *44 D2 river* Montana/Wyoming, NW USA
Powell *44 C2* Wyoming, C USA
Powell, Lake *44 B5 lake* Utah, W USA
Požarevac *100 D4 Ger.* Passarowitz. Serbia, NE Serbia
Poza Rica *51 F4 var.* Poza Rica de Hidalgo. Veracruz-Llave, E Mexico
Poza Rica de Hidalgo *see* Poza Rica
Požega *100 D4 prev.* Slavonska Požega, *Ger.* Poschega, *Hung.* Pozsega. Požega-Slavonija, NE Croatia
Požega *100 D4* Serbia
Poznań *98 C3 Ger.* Posen, Posnania. Wielkolpolskie, C Poland
Pozoblanco *92 D4* Andalucía, S Spain
Pozsega *see* Požega
Pozsony *see* Bratislava
Pozzallo *97 C8* Sicilia, Italy, C Mediterranean Sea
Prachatice *99 A5 Ger.* Prachatitz. Jihočeský Kraj, S Czech Republic
Prachatitz *see* Prachatice
Prado del Ganso *see* Goose Green
Prae *see* Phrae
Prag/Praga/Prague *see* Praha
Praha *99 A5 Eng.* Prague, *Ger.* Prag, *Pol.* Praga. *country capital* (Czech Republic) Středočeský Kraj, NW Czech Republic
Praia *74 A3 country capital* (Cape Verde) Santiago, S Cape Verde
Prairie State *see* Illinois
Prathet Thai *see* Thailand
Prato *96 B3* Toscana, C Italy
Pratt *45 E5* Kansas, C USA
Prattville *42 D2* Alabama, S USA
Pravda *see* Glavinitsa
Pravia *92 C1* Asturias, N Spain
Preny *see* Prienai
Prenzlau *94 D3* Brandenburg, NE Germany
Prerau *see* Přerov
Přerov *99 C5 Ger.* Prerau. Olomoucký Kraj, E Czech Republic
Preschau *see* Prešov
Prescott *48 B2* Arizona, SW USA
Preševo *101 D5* Serbia, SE Serbia
Presidente Epitácio *63 E4* São Paulo, S Brazil
Presidente Stroessner *see* Ciudad del Este
Prešov *99 D5 var.* Preschau, *Ger.* Eperies, *Hung.* Eperjes. Prešovský Kraj, E Slovakia
Prespa, Lake *101 D6 Alb.* Liqen i Prespës, *Gk.* Límni Megáli Préspa, Limni Prespa, *Mac.* Prespansko Ezero, *Serb.* Prespansko Jezero. *lake* SE Europe
Prespa, Limni/Prespansko Ezero/Prespansko Jezero/Prespës, Liqen i *see* Prespa, Lake
Presque Isle *41 H1* Maine, NE USA
Pressburg *see* Bratislava
Preston *89 D5* NW England, United Kingdom
Prestwick *88 C4* W Scotland, United Kingdom
Pretoria *78 D4 country capital* (South Africa) (admin. capital) NE South Africa
Preussisch Eylau *see* Bagrationovsk
Preußisch Holland *see* Pasłęk
Preussisch-Stargard *see* Starogard Gdański
Préveza *105 A5* Ípeiros, W Greece
Pribilof Islands *36 A3 island group* Alaska, USA
Priboj *100 C4* Serbia, W Serbia
Price *44 B4* Utah, W USA
Prichard *42 C3* Alabama, S USA
Priekulė *106 B3 Ger.* Prökuls. Klaipėda, W Lithuania
Prienai *107 B5 Pol.* Preny. Kaunas, S Lithuania
Prieska *78 C4* Northern Cape, C South Africa
Prijedor *100 B3* Republika Srpska, NW Bosnia and Herzegovina
Prijepolje *100 D4* Serbia, W Serbia
Prikaspiyskaya Nizmennost' *see* Caspian Depression
Prilep *101 D6 Turk.* Perlepe. S FYR Macedonia
Priluki *see* Pryluky
Primorsk *106 A4 Ger.* Fischhausen. Kaliningradskaya Oblast', W Russian Federation
Primorsko *104 E2 prev.* Keupriya. Burgas, E Bulgaria
Primorsk/Primorskoye *see* Prymors'k
Prince Albert *37 F5* Saskatchewan, S Canada
Prince Edward Island *39 F4 Fr.* Île-du Prince-Édouard. *province* SE Canada

Prince Edward Islands *69 E8 island group* S South Africa
Prince George *37 E5* British Columbia, SW Canada
Prince of Wales Island *148 B1 island* Queensland, E Australia
Prince of Wales Island *37 F2 island* Queen Elizabeth Islands, Nunavut, NW Canada
Prince of Wales Island *see* Pinang, Pulau
Prince Patrick Island *37 E2 island* Parry Islands, Northwest Territories, NW Canada
Prince Rupert *36 D4* British Columbia, SW Canada
Prince's Island *see* Príncipe
Princess Charlotte Bay *148 C2 bay* Queensland, NE Australia
Princess Elizabeth Land *154 C3 physical region* Antarctica
Príncipe *77 A5 var.* Príncipe Island, *Eng.* Prince's Island. *island* N Sao Tome and Principe
Príncipe Island *see* Príncipe
Prinzapolka *53 E3* Región Autónoma Atlántico Norte, NE Nicaragua
Pripet *107 C7 Bel.* Prypyats', *Ukr.* Pryp"yat'. *river* Belarus/Ukraine
Pripet Marshes *107 B7 wetland* Belarus/Ukraine
Prishtinë *101 D5 var. Pristina, Serb.* Priština. C Kosovo
Priština/Pristina *see* Prishtinë
Privas *91 D5* Ardèche, E France
Prizren *101 D5* S Kosovo
Probolinggo *138 D5* Jawa, C Indonesia
Probstberg *see* Wyszków
Progreso *51 H3* Yucatán, SE Mexico
Prokhladnyy *111 B8* Kabardino-Balkarskaya Respublika, SW Russian Federation
Prokletije *see* North Albanian Alps
Prökuls *see* Priekulė
Prokuplje *101 D5* Serbia, SE Serbia
Prome *see* Pyay
Promyshlennyy *110 E3* Respublika Komi, NW Russian Federation
Prościejów *see* Prostějov
Proskurov *see* Khmel'nyts'kyy
Prossnitz *see* Prostějov
Prostějov *99 C5 Ger.* Prossnitz, *Pol.* Prościejów. Olomoucký Kraj, E Czech Republic
Provence *91 D6 cultural region* SE France
Providence *41 G3 state capital* Rhode Island, NE USA
Providence *see* Fort Providence
Providencia, Isla de *53 F3 island* NW Colombia, Caribbean Sea
Provideniya *155 B1* Chukotskiy Avtonomnyy Okrug, NE Russian Federation
Provo *44 B4* Utah, W USA
Prudhoe Bay *36 D2* Alaska, USA
Prusa *see* Bursa
Pruszków *98 D3 Ger.* Kaltdorf. Mazowieckie, C Poland
Prut *108 D4 Ger.* Pruth. *river* E Europe
Pruth *see* Prut
Pružana *see* Pruzhany
Pruzhany *107 B6 Pol.* Prużana. Brestskaya Voblasts', SW Belarus
Prychornomor'ska Nyzovyna *see* Black Sea Lowland
Prydniprovs'ka Nyzovyna/ Prydnyaprowskaya Nizina *see* Dnieper Lowland
Prydz Bay *154 D3 bay* Antarctica
Pryluky *109 E2 Rus.* Priluki. Chernihivs'ka Oblast', NE Ukraine
Prymors'k *109 G4 Rus.* Primorsk; *prev.* Primorskoye. Zaporiz'ka Oblast', SE Ukraine
Pryp"yat'/Prypyats' *see* Pripet
Przemyśl *99 E5 Rus.* Peremyshl. Podkarpackie, C Poland
Przheval'sk *see* Karakol
Psará *105 D5 island* E Greece
Psel *109 F2 Rus.* Psël. *river* Russian Federation/Ukraine
Psël *see* Psel
Pskov *114 B2 Ger.* Pleskau, *Latv.* Pleskava. Pskovskaya Oblast', W Russian Federation
Pskov, Lake *106 E3 Est.* Pihkva Järv, *Ger.* Pleskauer See, *Rus.* Pskovskoye Ozero. *lake* Estonia/Russian Federation
Pskovskoye Ozero *see* Pskov, Lake
Ptich' *see* Ptsich
Ptsich *107 C7 Rus.* Ptich'. Homyel'skaya Voblasts', SE Belarus
Ptsich *107 C7 Rus.* Ptich'. *river* SE Belarus
Ptuj *95 E7 Ger.* Pettau; *anc.* Poetovio. NE Slovenia
Pucallpa *60 C3* Ucayali, C Peru
Puck *98 C2* Pomorskie, N Poland
Pudasjärvi *84 D4* Oulu, C Finland
Puebla *51 F4 var.* Puebla de Zaragoza. Puebla, S Mexico
Puebla de Zaragoza *see* Puebla
Pueblo *44 D5* Colorado, C USA
Puerto Acosta *61 E4* La Paz, W Bolivia
Puerto Aisén *65 B6* Aisén, S Chile
Puerto Ángel *51 F5* Oaxaca, SE Mexico
Puerto Argentino *see* Stanley
Puerto Ayacucho *58 D3* Amazonas, SW Venezuela
Puerto Baquerizo Moreno *60 B5 var.* Baquerizo Moreno. Galápagos Islands, Ecuador, E Pacific Ocean
Puerto Barrios *52 C2* Izabal, E Guatemala
Puerto Bello *see* Portobelo
Puerto Berrío *58 B2* Antioquia, C Colombia
Puerto Cabello *58 D1* Carabobo, N Venezuela
Puerto Cabezas *53 E2 var.* Bilwi. Región Autónoma Atlántico Norte, NE Nicaragua
Puerto Carreño *58 D3* Vichada, E Colombia
Puerto Cortés *52 C2* Cortés, NW Honduras
Puerto Cumarebo *58 C1* Falcón, N Venezuela
Puerto Deseado *65 C7* Santa Cruz, SE Argentina
Puerto Escondido *51 F5* Oaxaca, SE Mexico
Puerto Francisco de Orellana *60 B1 var.* Coca. NE Ecuador
Puerto Gallegos *see* Río Gallegos
Puerto Inírida *58 D3 var.* Obando. Guainía, E Colombia
Puerto La Cruz *59 E1* Anzoátegui, NE Venezuela
Puerto Lempira *53 E2* Gracias a Dios, E Honduras
Puerto Limón *see* Limón
Puertollano *92 D4* Castilla-La Mancha, C Spain
Puerto López *58 C1* La Guajira, N Colombia
Puerto Maldonado *61 E3* Madre de Dios, E Peru
Puerto México *see* Coatzacoalcos
Puerto Montt *65 B5* Los Lagos, C Chile
Puerto Natales *65 B7* Magallanes, S Chile
Puerto Obaldía *53 H5* Kuna Yala, NE Panama
Puerto Plata *55 E3 var.* San Felipe de Puerto Plata. N Dominican Republic
Puerto Presidente Stroessner *see* Ciudad del Este
Puerto Princesa *139 E2 off.* Puerto Princesa City. Palawan, W Philippines
Puerto Princesa City *see* Puerto Princesa
Puerto Príncipe *see* Camagüey
Puerto Rico *55 F3 off.* Commonwealth of Puerto Rico; *prev.* Porto Rico. *US commonwealth territory* C West Indies
Puerto Rico *56 B1 island* C West Indies
Puerto Rico, Commonwealth of *see* Puerto Rico
Puerto Rico Trench *56 B1 trench* NE Caribbean Sea
Puerto San José *see* San José
Puerto San Julián *65 B7 var.* San Julián. Santa Cruz, SE Argentina
Puerto Suárez *61 H4* Santa Cruz, E Bolivia
Puerto Vallarta *50 D4* Jalisco, SW Mexico
Puerto Varas *65 B5* Los Lagos, C Chile
Puerto Viejo *53 E4* Heredia, NE Costa Rica
Puertoviejo *see* Portoviejo
Puget Sound *46 B1 sound* Washington, NW USA
Puglia *97 E5 var.* Le Puglie, *Eng.* Apulia. *region* SE Italy
Pukaki, Lake *151 B6 lake* South Island, New Zealand
Pukekohe *150 D3* Auckland, North Island, New Zealand
Puket *see* Phuket
Pukhavichy *107 C6 Rus.* Pukhovichi. Minskaya Voblasts', C Belarus
Pukhovichi *see* Pukhavichy
Pula *100 A3 It.* Pola; *prev.* Pulj. Istra, NW Croatia
Pulaski *40 D5* Virginia, NE USA
Puławy *98 D4 Ger.* Neu Amerika. Lubelskie, E Poland
Pul-e Khumrī *123 E4 prev.* Pol-e Khomrī, *var.* Pul-i-Khumri. Baghlān, NE Afghanistan
Pul-i-Khumri *see* Pul-e Khumrī
Pulj *see* Pula
Pullman *46 C2* Washington, NW USA
Pułtusk *98 D3* Mazowieckie, C Poland
Puná, Isla *60 A2 island* SW Ecuador
Pune *134 C5 prev.* Poona. Mahārāshtra, W India
Punjab *134 C2 prev.* West Punjab, Western Punjab. *province* E Pakistan
Puno *61 E4* Puno, SE Peru
Punta Alta *65 C5* Buenos Aires, E Argentina
Punta Arenas *65 B8 prev.* Magallanes. Magallanes, S Chile
Punta Gorda *52 C2* Toledo, SE Belize
Punta Gorda *53 E4* Región Autónoma Atlántico Sur, SE Nicaragua
Puntarenas *52 D4* Puntarenas, W Costa Rica
Punto Fijo *58 C1* Falcón, N Venezuela
Pupuya, Nevado *61 E4 mountain* W Bolivia
Puri *135 F5 var.* Jagannath. Odisha, E India
Puriramya *see* Buriram
Purmerend *86 C3* Noord-Holland, C Netherlands
Pursat *see* Poŭthĭsăt, Poŭthĭsăt, W Cambodia
Purus, Rio *62 C2 var.* Río Purús. *river* Brazil/Peru
Pusan *see* Busan
Pushkino *see* Biläsuvar
Püspökladány *99 D6* Hajdú-Bihar, E Hungary
Putorana, Gory/Putorana Mountains *see* Putorana, Plato
Putorana Mountains *115 E3 var.* Gory Putorana, *Eng.* Putorana Mountains. *mountain range* N Russian Federation
Putrajaya *138 B3 administrative capital* (Malaysia) Kuala Lumpur, Peninsular Malaysia
Puttalam *132 C3* North Western Province, W Sri Lanka
Puttgarden *94 C2* Schleswig-Holstein, N Germany
Putumayo, Río *58 B5 var.* Içá, Rio. *river* NW South America
Putumayo, Río *see* Içá, Rio
Puurmani *106 D2 Ger.* Talkhof. Jõgevamaa, E Estonia
Pyatigorsk *111 B7* Stavropol'skiy Kray, SW Russian Federation
Pyatikhatki *see* P"yatykhatky
P"yatykhatky *109 F3 Rus.* Pyatikhatki. Dnipropetrovs'ka Oblast', E Ukraine
Pyay *136 B4 var.* Prome, Pye. Bago, C Myanmar (Burma)
Pye *see* Pyay
Pyetrykaw *107 C7 Rus.* Petrikov. Homyel'skaya Voblasts', SE Belarus
Pyin-Oo-Lwin *136 B3 var.* Maymyo. Mandalay, C Myanmar (Burma)
Pýlos *105 B6 var.* Pilos. Pelopónnisos, S Greece
P'yŏngyang *129 E3 var.* P'yŏngyang-si, *Eng.* Pyongyang. *country capital* (North Korea) SW North Korea
P'yŏngyang-si *see* P'yŏngyang
Pyramid Lake *47 C5 lake* Nevada, W USA
Pyrenaei Montes *see* Pyrenees
Pyrenees *102 B2 Fr.* Pyrénées, *Sp.* Pirineos; *anc.* Pyrenaei Montes. *mountain range* SW Europe
Pýrgos *105 B6 var.* Pírgos. Dytikí Elláda, S Greece
Pyritz *see* Pyrzyce
Pyryatyn *109 E2 Rus.* Piryatin. Poltavs'ka Oblast', NE Ukraine
Pyrzyce *98 B3 Ger.* Pyritz. Zachodnio-pomorskie, NW Poland
Pyu *see* Phyu
Pyuntaza *136 B4* Bago, SW Myanmar (Burma)

Q

Qā' al Jafr *119 C7 lake* S Jordan
Qaanaaq *82 D1 var.* Qânâq, *Dan.* Thule Avannaarsua, N Greenland
Qabātiya *119 E6* N West Bank Asia
Qābis *see* Gabès
Qābis, Khalīj *see* Gabès, Golfe de
Qacentina *see* Constantine
Qafṣah *see* Gafsa
Qagan Us *see* Dulan
Qahremānshahr *see* Kermānshāh
Qaidam Pendi *126 C4 basin* C China
Qal'aikhum *123 F3 Rus.* Kalaikhum. S Tajikistan
Qalāt *123 E5 Per.* Kalāt. Zābul, S Afghanistan
Qal'at Bīshah *121 B5* 'Asīr, SW Saudi Arabia
Qalqiliya *see* Qalqīlya
Qalqīlya *119 D6 var.* Qalqiliya. Central, W West Bank Asia
Qamanittuaq *see* Baker Lake
Qamdo *126 D5* Xizang Zizhiqu, W China
Qamishly *see* Al Qāmishlī
Qânâq *see* Qaanaaq
Qaqortoq *82 C4 Dan.* Julianehåb. Kitaa, S Greenland
Qaraghandy/Qaraghandy Oblysy *see* Karagandy
Qara Qum *see* Garagum
Qarataū *see* Karatau, Zhambyl, Kazakhstan
Qarkilik *see* Ruoqiang
Qarokŭl *123 F3 Rus.* Karakul'. E Tajikistan
Qarqannah, Juzur *see* Kerkenah, Îles de
Qars *see* Kars
Qarshi *123 E3 Rus.* Karshi; *prev.* Bek-Budi. Qashqadaryo Viloyati, S Uzbekistan
Qasigianguit *see* Qasigiannguit
Qasigiannguit *82 C3 var.* Qasigianguit, *Dan.* Christianshåb. Kitaa, C Greenland
Qaṣr al Farāfirah *72 B2 var.* Qasr Farâfra. W Egypt
Qasr Farâfra *see* Qaṣr al Farāfirah
Qaṭanā *119 B5 var.* Katana. Rīf Dimashq, S Syria
Qatar *120 C4 off.* State of Qatar, *Ar.*

QATAR
Southwest Asia

Official name State of Qatar
Formation 1971 / 1971
Capital Doha
Population 2.2 million / 518 people per sq mile (200 people per sq km)
Total area 4416 sq. miles (11,437 sq. km)
Languages Arabic*
Religions Muslim (mainly Sunni) 95%, Other 5%
Ethnic mix Qatari 20%, Indian 20%, Other Arab 20%, Nepalese 13%, Filipino 10%, Other 10%, Pakistani 7%
Government Monarchy
Currency Qatar riyal = 100 dirhams
Literacy rate 97%
Calorie consumption Not available

Dawlat Qaṭar. *country* SW Asia
Qatar, State of *see* Qatar
Qattara Depression *72 A1 var.* Munkhafaḍ al Qaṭṭārah *var.* Monkhafad el Qaṭṭâra, *Eng.* Qattara Depression. *desert* NW Egypt
Qaṭṭārah, Munkhafaḍ al *see* Qattara Depression
Qaṭṭâra, Monkhafad el *see* Qattara Depression
Qausuittuq *see* Resolute
Qazaqstan/Qazaqstan Respublikasy *see* Kazakhstan
Qazimämmäd *see* Hacıqabal
Qazris *see* Cáceres
Qazvīn *120 C2 var.* Kazvin. Qazvīn, N Iran
Qena *see* Qinā
Qeqertarssuaq *see* Qeqertarsuaq

Qeqertarsuaq *82 C3 var.* Qeqertarssuaq, *Dan.* Godhavn. Kitaa, S Greenland
Qeqertarsuaq *82 C3 island* W Greenland
Qeqertarsuup Tunua *82 C3 Dan.* Disko Bugt. *inlet* W Greenland
Qerveh *see* Qorveh
Qeshm *120 D4 var.* Jazīreh-ye Qeshm, Qeshm Island. *island* S Iran
Qeshm Island/Qeshm, Jazīreh-ye *see* Qeshm
Qilian Shan *126 D3 var.* Kilien Mountains. *mountain range* N China
Qimusseriarsuaq *82 C2 Dan.* Melville Bugt, *Eng.* Melville Bay. *bay* NW Greenland
Qinā *72 B2 var.* Qena; *anc.* Caene, Caenepolis. E Egypt
Qing *see* Qinghai
Qingdao *128 D4 var.* Ching-Tao, Ch'ing-tao, Tsingtao, Tsintao, *Ger.* Tsingtau. Shandong, E China
Qinghai *126 C4 var.* Chinghai, Koko Nor, Qing, Qinghai Sheng, Tsinghai. *province* C China
Qinghai Hu *126 D4 var.* Ch'ing Hai, Tsing Hai, *Mong.* Koko Nor. *lake* C China
Qinghai Sheng *see* Qinghai
Qinhuangdao *128 D3* Hebei, E China
Qinzhou *128 B6* Guangxi Zhuangzu Zizhiqu, S China
Qiong *see* Hainan
Qiqihar *128 D2 var.* Ch'i-ch'i-ha-erh, Tsitsihar; *prev.* Lungkiang. Heilongjiang, NE China
Qira *126 B4* Xinjiang Uygur Zizhiqu, NW China
Qita Ghazzah *see* Gaza Strip
Qitai *126 C3* Xinjiang Uygur Zizhiqu, NW China
Qīzān *see* Jīzān
Qizil Orda *see* Kyzylorda
Qizil Qum/Qizilqum *see* Kyzyl Kum
Qizilrabot *123 G3 Rus.* Kyzylrabot. SE Tajikistan
Qobustan *117 H2 prev.* Märäzä. E Azerbaijan
Qogir Feng *see* K2
Qom *120 C3 var.* Kum, Qum. Qom, N Iran
Qomolangma Feng *see* Everest, Mount
Qomul *see* Hami
Qo'qon *123 F2 var.* Khokand, *Rus.* Kokand. Farg'ona Viloyati, E Uzbekistan
Qorveh *120 C3 var.* Qerveh, Qurveh. Kordestān, W Iran
Qostanay/Qostanay Oblysy *see* Kostanay
Qoubaïyât *118 B4 var.* Al Qubayyāt. N Lebanon
Qoussantîna *see* Constantine
Quang Ngai *137 E5 var.* Quangngai, Quang Nghia. Quang Ngai, C Vietnam
Quangngai *see* Quang Ngai
Quang Nghia *see* Quang Ngai
Quan Long *see* Ca Mau
Quanzhou *128 D6 var.* Ch'uan-chou, Tsinkiang; *prev.* Chin-chiang. Fujian, SE China
Quanzhou *128 C6* Guangxi Zhuangzu Zizhiqu, S China
Qu'Appelle *37 F5 river* Saskatchewan, S Canada
Quarles, Pegunungan *139 E4 mountain range* Sulawesi, C Indonesia
Quarnero *see* Kvarner
Quartu Sant' Elena *97 A6* Sardegna, Italy, C Mediterranean Sea
Quba *117 H2 Rus.* Kuba. N Azerbaijan
Qubba *see* Ba'qūbah
Québec *39 E4 var.* Quebec. *province capital* Québec, SE Canada
Québec *38 D3 var.* Quebec. *province* SE Canada
Queen Charlotte Islands *36 C5 Fr.* Îles de la Reine-Charlotte. *island group* British Columbia, SW Canada
Queen Charlotte Sound *36 C5 sea area* British Columbia, W Canada
Queen Elizabeth Islands *37 E1 Fr.* Îles de la Reine-Élisabeth. *island group* Nunavut, N Canada
Queensland *148 B4 state* N Australia
Queenstown *151 B7* Otago, South Island, New Zealand
Queenstown *78 D5* Eastern Cape, S South Africa
Quelimane *79 E3 var.* Kilimane, Kilmain, Quilimane. Zambézia, NE Mozambique
Quelpart *see* Jeju-do
Quepos *53 E4* Puntarenas, S Costa Rica
Que Que *see* Kwekwe
Quera *see* Chur
Querétaro *51 E4* Querétaro de Arteaga, C Mexico
Quesada *53 E4 var.* Ciudad Quesada, San Carlos. Alajuela, N Costa Rica
Quetta *134 B2* Baluchistān, SW Pakistan
Quetzalcoalco *see* Coatzacoalcos
Quezaltenango *52 A2 var.* Quetzaltenango. Quezaltenango, W Guatemala
Quibdó *58 A3* Chocó, W Colombia
Quilimane *see* Quelimane
Quillabamba *60 D3* Cusco, C Peru
Quilon *see* Kollam
Quimper *90 A3 anc.* Quimper Corentin. Finistère, NW France
Quimper Corentin *see* Quimper
Quimperlé *90 A3* Finistère, NW France
Quincy *40 A4* Illinois, N USA
Qui Nhon/Quinhon *see* Quy Nhơn
Quissico *79 E4* Inhambane, S Mozambique
Quito *60 B1 country capital* (Ecuador) Pichincha, N Ecuador
Qulyndy Zhazyghy *see* Ravnina Kulyndy
Qum *see* Qom
Qurein *see* Al Kuwayt
Qŭrghonteppa *123 E3 Rus.* Kurgan-Tyube. SW Tajikistan
Qurlurtuuq *see* Kugluktuk
Qurveh *see* Qorveh
Quṣayr *see* Al Quṣayr
Quxar *see* Lhazê
Quy Nhơn *137 E5 var.* Quinhon, Qui Nhon. Binh Đinh, C Vietnam
Qyteti Stalin *see* Kuçovë
Qyzylorda *see* Kyzylorda

R

Raab *100 B1 Hung.* Rába. *river* Austria/Hungary
Raab *see* Rába
Raab *see* Győr
Raahe *84 D4 Swe.* Brahestad. Oulu, W Finland
Raalte *86 D3* Overijssel, E Netherlands
Raamsdonksveer *86 C4* Noord-Brabant, S Netherlands
Raasiku *106 D2 Ger.* Rasik. Harjumaa, NW Estonia
Rába *99 B7 Ger.* Raab. *river* Austria/Hungary
Rába *see* Raab
Rabat *70 C2 var.* al Dar al Baida. *country capital* (Morocco) NW Morocco
Rabat *102 B5* W Malta
Rabat *see* Victoria
Rabbah Ammon/Rabbath Ammon *see* 'Amman
Rabinal *52 B2* Baja Verapaz, C Guatemala
Rabka *99 D5* Małopolskie, S Poland
Râbniţa *see* Rîbniţa
Rabyānah Ramlat *71 G4 var.* Rebiana Sand Sea, Ṣaḥrā' Rabyānah. *desert* SE Libya
Rabyānah, Ṣaḥrā' *see* Rabyānah, Ramlat
Răcari *see* Durankulak
Race, Cape *39 H3 headland* Newfoundland, Newfoundland and Labrador, E Canada
Rach Gia *137 D6* Kiên Giang, S Vietnam
Rach Gia, Vinh *137 D6 bay* S Vietnam
Racine *40 B3* Wisconsin, N USA
Rácz-Becse *see* Bečej
Rădăuţi *108 C3 Ger.* Radautz, *Hung.* Rádóc. Suceava, N Romania
Radautz *see* Rădăuţi
Rádeyilikóé *see* Fort Good Hope
Rádóc *see* Rădăuţi
Radom *98 D4* Mazowieckie, C Poland
Radomsko *98 D4 Rus.* Novoradomsk. Łódzkie, C Poland
Radomyshl' *108 D2* Zhytomyrs'ka Oblast', N Ukraine
Radoviš *101 E6 prev.* Radovište. E Macedonia
Radovište *see* Radoviš
Radviliškis *106 B4* Šiaulai, N Lithuania
Radzyń Podlaski *98 E4* Lubelskie, E Poland
Rae-Edzo *see* Edzo
Raetihi *150 D4* Manawatu-Wanganui, North Island, New Zealand
Rafa *see* Rafah
Rafaela *64 C3* Santa Fe, E Argentina
Rafah *119 A7 var.* Rafa, Rafaḩ, *Heb.* Rafiah, Raphiah. SW Gaza Strip
Rafḩah *120 B4* Al Ḩudūd ash Shamālīyah, N Saudi Arabia
Rafiah *see* Rafah
Raga *73 A5* Western Bahr el Ghazal, W South Sudan
Ragged Island Range *54 C2 island group* S Bahamas
Ragnit *see* Neman
Ragusa *97 C7* Sicilia, Italy, C Mediterranean Sea
Ragusa *see* Dubrovnik
Rahachow *107 D7 Rus.* Rogachëv. Homyel'skaya Voblasts', SE Belarus
Rahaeng *see* Tak
Rahaţ, Ḩarrat *121 B5 lava flow* W Saudi Arabia
Rahīmyār Khān *134 C3* Punjab, SE Pakistan
Rahovec *101 D5 Serb.* Orahovac. W Kosovo
Raiatea *145 G4 island* Îles Sous le Vent, W French Polynesia
Rāichūr *132 C1* Karnātaka, C India
Raidestos *see* Tekirdağ
Rainier, Mount *34 A4 volcano* Washington, NW USA
Rainy Lake *38 A4 lake* Canada/USA
Raipur *135 E4* Chhattīsgarh, C India
Rājahmundry *135 E5* Andhra Pradesh, E India
Rajang *see* Rajang, Batang
Rajang, Batang *138 D3 var.* Rajang. *river* East Malaysia
Rājapālaiyam *132 C3* Tamil Nādu, SE India
Rājasthān *134 C3 cultural region* NW India
Rājkot *134 C4* Gujarāt, W India
Rāj Nāndgaon *135 E4* Chhattīsgarh, C India
Rajshahi *135 G3 prev.* Rampur Boalia. Rajshahi, W Bangladesh
Rakahanga *145 F3 atoll* N Cook Islands
Rakaia *151 B6 river* South Island, New Zealand
Rakka *see* Ar Raqqah
Rakke *106 E2* Lääne-Virumaa, NE Estonia
Rakvere *106 E2 Ger.* Wesenberg. Lääne-Virumaa, N Estonia
Raleigh *43 F1 state capital* North Carolina, SE USA
Ralik Chain *144 D1 island group* Ralik Chain, W Marshall Islands
Ramadi *see* Ar Ramādī
Râmnicul-Sărat *see* Râmnicu Sărat
Râmnicu Sărat *108 C4 prev.* Râmnicul-Sărat, Rîmnicu-Sărat. Buzău, E Romania
Râmnicu Vâlcea *108 B4 prev.* Rîmnicu Vîlcea. Vâlcea, C Romania
Rampur Boalia *see* Rajshahi
Ramree Island *136 A4 island* W Myanmar (Burma)
Ramtha *see* Ar Ramthā
Rancagua *64 B4* Libertador, C Chile
Rānchi *135 F4* Jhārkhand, N India
Randers *85 B7* Midtjylland, C Denmark
Ráneš *see* Ringvassøya
Rangiora *151 C6* Canterbury, South Island, New Zealand
Rangitikei *150 D4 river* North Island, New Zealand
Rangoon *see* Yangon
Rangpur *135 G3* Rajshahi, N Bangladesh
Rankin Inlet *37 G3* Nunavut, C Canada
Rankovićevo *see* Kraljevo
Ranong *137 B6* Ranong, SW Thailand
Rapa Nui *see* Pascua, Isla de
Raphiah *see* Rafah
Rapid City *44 D3* South Dakota, N USA
Räpina *106 E3 Ger.* Rappin. Põlvamaa, SE Estonia
Rapla *106 D2 Ger.* Rappel. Raplamaa, NW Estonia
Rappel *see* Rapla
Rappin *see* Räpina
Rarotonga *145 G5 island* S Cook Islands, C Pacific Ocean
Ras al'Ain *see* Ra's al 'Ayn
Ra's al 'Ayn *118 D1 var.* Ras al'Ain. Al Ḩasakah, N Syria
Ra's an Naqb *119 B7* Ma'ān, S Jordan
Raseiniai *106 B4* Kaunas, C Lithuania
Rasht *120 C2 var.* Resht. Gīlān, NW Iran
Rasik *see* Raasiku
Râşnov *108 C4 prev.* Rîşno, Rozsnyó, *Hung.* Barcarozsnyó. Braşov, C Romania
Rastenburg *see* Kętrzyn
Ratak Chain *144 D1 island group* Ratak Chain, E Marshall Islands
Ratān *85 C5* Jämtland, C Sweden
Rat Buri *see* Ratchaburi
Ratchaburi *137 C5 var.* Rat Buri. Ratchaburi, W Thailand
Ratisbon/Ratisbona/Ratisbonne *see* Regensburg
Rat Islands *36 A2 island group* Aleutian Islands, Alaska, USA
Ratlām *134 D4 prev.* Rutlam. Madhya Pradesh, C India
Ratnapura *132 D4* Sabaragamuwa Province, S Sri Lanka
Raton *48 D1* New Mexico, SW USA
Rättvik *85 C5* Dalarna, C Sweden
Raudhatain *see* Ar Rawḑatayn
Raufarhöfn *83 E4* Nordhurland Eystra, NE Iceland
Raukawa *see* Cook Strait
Raukumara Range *150 E3 mountain range* North Island, New Zealand
Rāulakela *see* Rāurkela
Rauma *85 D5 Swe.* Raumo. Länsi-Suomi, SW Finland
Raumo *see* Rauma
Rāurkela *135 F4 var.* Rāulakela, Rourkela. Odisha, E India
Ravenna *96 C3* Emilia-Romagna, N Italy
Ravi *134 C2 river* India/Pakistan
Ravnina Kulyndy *114 C4 prev.* Kulunda Steppe, *Kaz.* Qulyndy Zhazyghy, *Rus.* Kulundinskaya Ravnina. *grassland* Kazakhstan/Russian Federation
Rāwalpindi *134 C1* Punjab, NE Pakistan
Rawa Mazowiecka *98 D4* Łódzkie, C Poland
Rawicz *98 C4 Ger.* Rawitsch. Wielkopolskie, C Poland
Rawitsch *see* Rawicz
Rawlins *44 C3* Wyoming, C USA
Rawson *65 C6* Chubut, SE Argentina
Rayak *118 B4 var.* Rayaq, Riyāq. E Lebanon
Rayaq *see* Rayak
Rayong *137 C5* Rayong, S Thailand
Razazah, Buhayrat ar *120 B3 var.* Baḩr al Milḩ. *lake* C Iraq
Razdolnoye *see* Rozdol'ne
Razelm, Lacul *see* Razim, Lacul
Razgrad *104 D2* Razgrad, N Bulgaria
Razim, Lacul *108 D5 prev.* Lacul Razelm. *lagoon* NW Black Sea
Reading *89 D7* S England, United Kingdom
Reading *41 F4* Pennsylvania, NE USA
Realicó *64 C4* La Pampa, C Argentina
Reăng Kesei *137 D5* Bătdâmbâng, W Cambodia
Greater Antarctica *see* East Antarctica
Rebecca, Lake *147 C6 lake* Western Australia
Rebiana Sand Sea *see* Rabyānah, Ramlat
Rebun-to *130 C2 island* NE Japan
Rechitsa *see* Rechytsa
Rechytsa *107 D7 Rus.* Rechitsa. Brestskaya Voblasts', SW Belarus
Recife *63 G2 prev.* Pernambuco. *state capital* Pernambuco, E Brazil
Recklinghausen *94 A4* Nordrhein-Westfalen, W Germany
Recogne *87 C7* Luxembourg, SE Belgium
Reconquista *64 D3* Santa Fe, C Argentina
Red Deer *37 E5* Alberta, SW Canada
Redding *47 B5* California, W USA
Redon *90 B4* Ille-et-Vilaine, NW France
Red River *45 E1 river* Canada/USA
Red River *136 C2 var.* Yuan, *Chin.* Yuan Jiang, *Vtn.* Sông Hông Hà. *river* China/Vietnam
Red River *35 C6 river* S USA
Red River *42 B3 river* Louisiana, S USA
Red Sea *72 C3 var.* Sinus Arabicus. *sea* Africa/Asia
Red Wing *45 G2* Minnesota, N USA
Reefton *151 C5* West Coast, South Island, New Zealand

Reese River *47 C5 river* Nevada, W USA
Refahiye *117 E3* Erzincan, C Turkey
Regensburg *95 C6 Eng.* Ratisbon, *Fr.* Ratisbonne, *hist.* Ratisbona; *anc.* Castra Regina, Reginum. Bayern, SE Germany
Regenstauf *95 C6* Bayern, SE Germany
Rēgestān *122 D5 prev.* Rīgestān, *var.* Registan. *desert region* S Afghanistan
Reggane *70 D3* C Algeria
Reggio *see* Reggio nell'Emilia
Reggio Calabria *see* Reggio di Calabria
Reggio di Calabria *97 D7 var.* Reggio Calabria, *Gk.* Rhegion; *anc.* Regium, Rhegium. Calabria, SW Italy
Reggio Emilia *see* Reggio nell'Emilia
Reggio nell'Emilia *96 B2 var.* Reggio Emilia, *abbrev.* Reggio; *anc.* Regium Lepidum. Emilia-Romagna, N Italy
Reghin *108 C4 Ger.* Sächsisch-Reen, *Hung.* Szászrégen; *prev.* Reghinul Săsesc, *Ger.* Sächsisch-Regen. Mureş, C Romania
Reghinul Săsesc *see* Reghin
Regina *37 F5 province capital* Saskatchewan, S Canada
Reginum *see* Regensburg
Registan *see* Rēgestān
Regium *see* Reggio di Calabria
Regium Lepidum *see* Reggio nell'Emilia
Rehoboth *78 B3* Hardap, C Namibia
Rehovot *119 A6 ; prev.* Reḥovot. Central, C Israel
Reḥovot *see* Rehovot
Reichenau *see* Bogatynia, Poland
Reichenberg *see* Liberec
Reid *147 D6* Western Australia
Reikjavik *see* Reykjavík
Ré, Île de *90 A4 island* W France
Reims *90 D3 Eng.* Rheims; *anc.* Durocortorum, Remi. Marne, N France
Reindeer Lake *37 F4 lake* Manitoba/Saskatchewan, C Canada
Reine-Charlotte, Îles de la *see* Queen Charlotte Islands
Reine-Élisabeth, Îles de la *see* Queen Elizabeth Islands
Reinga, Cape *150 C1 headland* North Island, New Zealand
Reinosa *92 D1* Cantabria, N Spain
Reka *see* Rijeka
Rekhovot *see* Rehovot
Reliance *37 F4* Northwest Territories, C Canada
Remi *see* Reims
Rendina *see* Rentína
Rendsburg *94 B2* Schleswig-Holstein, N Germany
Rengat *138 B4* Sumatera, W Indonesia
Reni *108 D4* Odes'ka Oblast', SW Ukraine
Rennell *144 C4 var.* Mu Nggava. *island* S Solomon Islands
Rennes *90 B3 Bret.* Roazon; *anc.* Condate. Ille-et-Vilaine, NW France
Reno *47 C5* Nevada, W USA
Renqiu *128 C4* Hebei, E China
Rentína *105 B5 var.* Rendina. Thessalía, C Greece
Reps *see* Rupea
Repulse Bay *37 G3* Northwest Territories, N Canada
Reschitza *see* Reşiţa
Resht *see* Rasht
Resicabánya *see* Reşiţa
Resistencia *64 D3* Chaco, NE Argentina
Reşiţa *108 A4 Ger.* Reschitza, *Hung.* Resicabánya. Caraş-Severin, W Romania
Resolute *37 F2 Inuit* Qausuittuq. Cornwallis Island, Nunavut, N Canada
Resolution Island *39 E1 island* Nunavut, NE Canada
Resolution Island *151 A7 island* SW New Zealand
Réunion *79 H4 off.* La Réunion. *French overseas department* W Indian Ocean
Réunion *141 B5 island* W Indian Ocean
Reus *93 F2* Cataluña, E Spain
Reutlingen *95 B6* Baden-Württemberg, S Germany
Reuver *87 D5* Limburg, SE Netherlands
Reval/Revel *see* Tallinn
Revillagigedo Island *50 B5 island* Alexander Archipelago, Alaska, USA
Rexburg *46 E3* Idaho, NW USA
Reyes *61 F3* El Beni, NW Bolivia
Rey, Isla del *53 G5 island* Archipiélago de las Perlas, SE Panama
Reykjanes Basin *82 C5 var.* Irminger Basin. *undersea basin* N Atlantic Ocean
Reykjanes Ridge *80 A1 undersea ridge* N Atlantic Ocean
Reykjavík *83 E5 var.* Reikjavik. *country capital* (Iceland) Höfudhborgarsvaedhi, W Iceland
Reynosa *51 E2* Tamaulipas, C Mexico
Reẕā'īyeh, Daryācheh-ye *see* Orūmīyeh, Daryācheh-ye
Rezé *90 A4* Loire-Atlantique, NW France
Rēzekne *106 D4 Ger.* Rositten; *prev. Rus.* Rezhitsa. SE Latvia
Rezhitsa *see* Rēzekne
Rezovo *104 E3 Turk.* Rezve. Burgas, E Bulgaria
Rezve *see* Rezovo
Rhaedestus *see* Tekirdağ
Rhegion/Rhegium *see* Reggio di Calabria
Rheims *see* Reims
Rhein *see* Rhine
Rheine *94 A3 var.* Rheine in Westfalen. Nordrhein-Westfalen, NW Germany
Rheine in Westfalen *see* Rheine
Rheinisches Schiefergebirge *95 A5 var.* Rhine State Uplands, *Eng.* Rhenish Slate Mountains. *mountain range* W Germany
Rhenish Slate Mountains *see* Rheinisches Schiefergebirge
Rhin *see* Rhine
Rhine *80 D4 Dut.* Rijn, *Fr.* Rhin, *Ger.* Rhein. *river* W Europe
Rhinelander *40 B2* Wisconsin, N USA
Rhine State Uplands *see* Rheinisches Schiefergebirge
Rho *96 B2* Lombardia, N Italy
Rhode Island *41 G3 off.* State of Rhode Island and Providence Plantations, *also known as* Little Rhody, Ocean State. *state* NE USA
Rhodes *105 E7 var.* Ródhos, *Eng.* Rhodes, *It.* Rodi; *anc.* Rhodos. *island* Dodekánisa, Greece, Aegean Sea
Rhodes *see* Ródos
Rhodesia *see* Zimbabwe
Rhodope Mountains *104 C3 var.* Rodhópi Óri, *Bul.* Rhodope Planina, Rodopi, *Gk.* Orosirá Rodhópis, *Turk.* Dospad Dagh. *mountain range* Bulgaria/Greece
Rhodope Planina *see* Rhodope Mountains
Rhône *80 C4 river* France/Switzerland
Rhum *88 B3 var.* Rum. *island* W Scotland, United Kingdom
Ribble *89 D5 river* NW England, United Kingdom
Ribeira *see* Sanata Uxía de Ribeira
Ribeirão Preto *63 F4* São Paulo, S Brazil
Riberalta *61 F2* El Beni, N Bolivia
Rîbniţa *108 D3 var.* Râbniţa, *Rus.* Rybnitsa. NE Moldova
Rice Lake *40 A2* Wisconsin, N USA
Richard Toll *74 B3* N Senegal
Richfield *44 B4* Utah, W USA
Richland *46 C2* Washington, NW USA
Richmond *151 C5* Tasman, South Island, New Zealand
Richmond *40 C5* Kentucky, S USA
Richmond *41 E5 state capital* Virginia, NE USA
Richmond Range *151 C5 mountain range* South Island, New Zealand
Ricobayo, Embalse de *92 C2 reservoir* NW Spain
Ricomagus *see* Riom
Ridder *114 D4 Kaz.* Leningor, *prev.* Leninogorsk. Vostochnyy Kazakhstan, E Kazakhstan
Ridgecrest *47 C7* California, W USA
Ried *see* Ried im Innkreis
Ried im Innkreis *95 D6 var.* Ried. Oberösterreich, NW Austria
Riemst *87 D6* Limburg, NE Belgium
Riesa *94 D4* Sachsen, E Germany
Rift Valley *see* Great Rift Valley
Rīga *106 C3 Eng.* Riga. *country capital* (Latvia) C Latvia
Rigaer Bucht *see* Riga, Gulf of
Riga, Gulf of *106 C3 Est.* Liivi Laht, *Ger.* Rigaer Bucht, *Latv.* Rīgas Jūras Līcis, *Rus.* Rizhskiy Zaliv; *prev. Est.* Riia Laht. *gulf* Estonia/Latvia
Rīgas Jūras Līcis *see* Riga, Gulf of
Rīgestān *see* Rēgestān
Riia Laht *see* Riga, Gulf of
Riihimäki *85 D5* Etelä-Suomi, S Finland
Rijeka *100 A2 Ger.* Sankt Veit am Flaum, *It.* Fiume, *Slvn.* Reka; *anc.* Tarsatica. Primorje-Gorski Kotar, NW Croatia
Rijn *see* Rhine
Rijssel *see* Lille
Rijssen *86 E3* Overijssel, E Netherlands
Rimah, Wadi ar *120 B4 var.* Wādī ar Rummah. *dry watercourse* C Saudi Arabia
Rimini *96 C3 anc.* Ariminum. Emilia-Romagna, N Italy
Rîmnicu-Sărat *see* Râmnicu Sărat
Rîmnicu Vîlcea *see* Râmnicu Vâlcea
Rimouski *39 E4* Québec, SE Canada
Ringebu *85 B5* Oppland, S Norway
Ringen *see* Rõngu
Ringkøbing Fjord *85 A7 fjord* W Denmark
Ringvassøya *84 C2 Lapp.* Ráneš. *island* N Norway
Rio *see* Rio de Janeiro
Riobamba *60 B1* Chimborazo, C Ecuador
Rio Branco *56 B3 state capital* Acre, W Brazil
Rio Branco, Território de *see* Roraima
Río Bravo *51 E2* Tamaulipas, C Mexico
Río Cuarto *64 C4* Córdoba, C Argentina
Rio de Janeiro *63 F4 var.* Rio. *state capital* Rio de Janeiro, SE Brazil
Río Gallegos *65 B7 var.* Gallegos, Puerto Gallegos. Santa Cruz, S Argentina
Rio Grande *63 E5 var.* São Pedro do Rio Grande do Sul. Rio Grande do Sul, S Brazil
Río Grande *50 D3* Zacatecas, C Mexico
Rio Grande do Norte *63 G2 off.* Estado do Rio Grande do Norte. *state* E Brazil
Rio Grande do Norte *63 G2 off.* Estado do Rio Grande do Norte. *region* E Brazil
Rio Grande do Norte, Estado do *see* Rio Grande do Norte
Rio Grande do Sul *63 E5 off.* Estado do Rio Grande do Sul. *state* S Brazil
Rio Grande do Sul *63 E5 off.* Estado do Rio Grande do Sul. *region* S Brazil
Rio Grande do Sul, Estado do *see* Rio Grande do Sul
Rio Grande Plateau *see* Rio Grande Rise
Rio Grande Rise *57 E6 var.* Rio Grande Plateau. *undersea plateau* SW Atlantic Ocean
Ríohacha *58 B1* La Guajira, N Colombia
Río Lagartos *51 H3* Yucatán, SE Mexico
Riom *91 C5 anc.* Ricomagus. Puy-de-Dôme, C France
Río Verde *51 E4 var.* Rioverde. San Luis Potosí, C Mexico
Rioverde *see* Río Verde
Ripoll *93 G2* Cataluña, NE Spain
Rishiri-to *130 C2 var.* Risiri Tô. *island* NE Japan
Risiri Tô *see* Rishiri-tō
Rişno *see* Râşnov
Risti *106 D2 Ger.* Kreuz. Läänemaa, W Estonia
Rivas *52 D4* Rivas, SW Nicaragua
Rivera *64 D3* Rivera, NE Uruguay
River Falls *40 A2* Wisconsin, N USA
Riverside *47 C7* California, W USA
Riverton *151 A7* Southland, South Island, New Zealand
Riverton *44 C3* Wyoming, C USA
Rivière-du-Loup *39 E4* Québec, SE Canada
Rivne *108 C2 Pol.* Równe, *Rus.* Rovno. Rivnens'ka Oblast', NW Ukraine
Rivoli *96 A2* Piemonte, NW Italy
Riyadh/Riyāḍ, Minṭaqat ar *see* Ar Riyāḍ
Riyāq *see* Rayak
Rize *117 E2* Rize, NE Turkey
Rizhao *128 D4* Shandong, E China
Rizhskiy Zaliv *see* Riga, Gulf of
Rkîz *74 C3* Trarza, W Mauritania
Road Town *55 F3 dependent territory capital* (British Virgin Islands) Tortola, C British Virgin Islands
Roanne *91 C5 anc.* Rodunma. Loire, E France
Roanoke *41 E5* Virginia, NE USA
Roanoke River *43 F1 river* North Carolina/Virginia, SE USA
Roatán *52 C2 var.* Coxen Hole, Coxin Hole. Islas de la Bahía, N Honduras
Roat Kampuchea *see* Cambodia
Roazon *see* Rennes
Robbie Ridge *143 E3 undersea ridge* W Pacific Ocean
Robert Williams *see* Caála
Robinson Range *147 B5 mountain range* Western Australia
Robson, Mount *37 E5 mountain* British Columbia, SW Canada
Robstown *49 G4* Texas, SW USA
Roca Partida, Isla *50 B5 island* W Mexico
Rocas, Atol das *63 G2 island* E Brazil
Rochefort *87 C7* Namur, SE Belgium
Rochefort *90 B4 var.* Rochefort sur Mer. Charente-Maritime, W France
Rochefort sur Mer *see* Rochefort
Rochester *45 G3* Minnesota, N USA
Rochester *41 G2* New Hampshire, NE USA
Rocheuses, Montagnes/Rockies *see* Rocky Mountains
Rockall Bank *80 B2 undersea bank* N Atlantic Ocean
Rockall Trough *80 B2 trough* N Atlantic Ocean
Rockdale *148 E2* Texas, SW USA
Rockford *40 B3* Illinois, N USA
Rockhampton *148 D4* Queensland, E Australia
Rock Hill *43 E1* South Carolina, SE USA
Rockingham *147 A6* Western Australia
Rock Island *40 B3* Illinois, N USA
Rock Sound *54 C1* Eleuthera Island, C Bahamas
Rock Springs *44 C3* Wyoming, C USA
Rockstone *59 F3* C Guyana
Rocky Mount *43 F1* North Carolina, SE USA
Rocky Mountains *34 B4 var.* Rockies, *Fr.* Montagnes Rocheuses. *mountain range* Canada/USA
Roden *86 E2* Drenthe, NE Netherlands
Rodez *91 C5 anc.* Segodunum. Aveyron, S France
Rodhópi Óri *see* Rhodope Mountains
Ródhos/Rodi *see* Ródos
Rodopi *see* Rhodope Mountains
Rodosto *see* Tekirdağ
Rodunma *see* Roanne
Roermond *87 D5* Limburg, SE Netherlands
Roeselare *87 A6 Fr.* Roulers; *prev.* Rousselaere. West-Vlaanderen, W Belgium
Rogachëv *see* Rahachow
Rogatica *100 C4* Republika Srpska, SE Bosnia and Herzegovina
Rogers *42 A1* Arkansas, C USA
Roger Simpson Island *see* Abemama
Roi Ed *see* Roi Et
Roi Et *137 D5 var.* Muang Roi Et, Roi Ed. Roi Et, E Thailand
Roja *106 C2* NW Latvia
Rokiškis *106 C4* Panevėžys, NE Lithuania
Rokycany *99 A5 Ger.* Rokytzan. Plzeňský Kraj, W Czech Republic
Rokytzan *see* Rokycany
Rôlas, Ilha das *76 E2 island* S Sao Tome and Principe, Africa, E Atlantic Ocean
Rolla *45 G5* Missouri, C USA
Röm *see* Rømø
Roma *96 C4 Eng.* Rome. *country capital* (Italy) Lazio, C Italy
Roma *149 D5* Queensland, E Australia
Roman *104 C2* Vratsa, NW Bulgaria
Roman *108 C4 Hung.* Románvásár. Neamţ, NE Romania
Romania *108 B4 Bul.* Rumŭniya, *Ger.* Rumänien, *Hung.* Románia, *Rom.* România, *SCr.* Rumunjska, *Ukr.* Rumuniya, *prev.* Republica Socialistă România, Roumania, Rumania, Socialist Republic of Romania, *prev. Rom.* Romînia. *country* SE Europe

ROMANIA
Southeast Europe

Official name Romania
Formation 1878 / 1947
Capital Bucharest
Population 21.7 million / 244 people per sq mile (94 people per sq km)
Total area 91,699 sq. miles (237,500 sq. km)
Languages Romanian*, Hungarian (Magyar), Romani, German
Religions Romanian Orthodox 87%, Protestant 5%, Roman Catholic 5%, Greek Orthodox 1%, Greek Catholic (Uniate) 1%, Other 1%

ROMANIA
(continued)

Ethnic mix Romanian 89%, Magyar 7%, Roma 2%, Other 2%
Government Presidential system
Currency New Romanian leu = 100 bani
Literacy rate 99%
Calorie consumption 3363 kilocalories

România, Republica Socialistă *see* Romania
Romania, Socialist Republic of *see* Romania
Romaniv *109 F3 Rus.* Dneprodzerzhinsk, *prev.* Dniprodzerzhyns'k, *prev.* Kamenskoye. Dnipropetrovs'ka Oblast', E Ukraine
Románvásár *see* Roman
Rome *42 D2* Georgia, SE USA
Rome *see* Roma
Romînia *see* Romania
Romny *109 F2* Sums'ka Oblast', NE Ukraine
Rømø *85 A7 Ger.* Röm. *island* SW Denmark
Roncador, Serra do *56 D4 mountain range* C Brazil
Ronda *92 D5* Andalucía, S Spain
Rondônia *62 D3 off.* Estado de Rondônia; *prev.* Território de Rondônia. *state* W Brazil
Rondônia *62 D3 off.* Estado de Rondônia; *prev.* Território de Rondônia. *region* W Brazil
Rondônia, Estado de *see* Rondônia
Rondônia, Território de *see* Rondônia
Rondonópolis *63 E3* Mato Grosso, W Brazil
Rongelap Atoll *144 D1 var.* Rōnlap. *atoll* Ralik Chain, NW Marshall Islands
Rõngu *106 D3 Ger.* Ringen. Tartumaa, SE Estonia
Rōnlap *see* Rongelap Atoll
Rønne *85 B8* Bornholm, E Denmark
Ronne Ice Shelf *154 A3 ice shelf* Antarctica
Roosendaal *87 C5* Noord-Brabant, S Netherlands
Roosevelt Island *154 B4 island* Antarctica
Roraima *62 D1 off.* Estado de Roraima; *prev.* Território de Rio Branco, Território de Roraima. *state* N Brazil
Roraima *62 D1 off.* Estado de Roraima; *prev.* Território de Rio Branco, Território de Roraima. *region* N Brazil
Roraima, Estado de *see* Roraima
Roraima, Mount *59 E3 mountain* N South America
Roraima, Território de *see* Roraima
Røros *85 B5* Sør-Trøndelag, S Norway
Ross *151 B6* West Coast, South Island, New Zealand
Rosa, Lake *54 D2 lake* Great Inagua, S Bahamas
Rosario *64 D4* Santa Fe, C Argentina
Rosario *64 D2* San Pedro, C Paraguay
Rosario *see* Rosarito
Rosarito *50 A1 var.* Rosario. Baja California Norte, NW Mexico
Roscianum *see* Rossano
Roscommon *40 C2* Michigan, N USA
Roseau *55 G4 prev.* Charlotte Town. *country capital* (Dominica) SW Dominica
Roseburg *46 B4* Oregon, NW USA
Rosenau *see* Rožňava
Rosenberg *49 G4* Texas, SW USA
Rosenberg *see* Ružomberok, Slovakia
Rosengarten *94 B3* Niedersachsen, N Germany
Rosenheim *95 C6* Bayern, S Germany
Rosia *93 H5* W Gibraltar Europe
Rosia Bay *93 H5 bay* SW Gibraltar Europe W Mediterranean Sea Atlantic Ocean
Roșiori de Vede *108 B5* Teleorman, S Romania
Rositten *see* Rēzekne
Roslavl' *111 A5* Smolenskaya Oblast', W Russian Federation
Rosmalen *86 C4* Noord-Brabant, S Netherlands
Rossano *97 E6 anc.* Roscianum. Calabria, SW Italy
Ross Ice Shelf *154 B4 ice shelf* Antarctica
Rossiyskaya Federatsiya *see* Russian Federation
Rosso *74 B3* Trarza, SW Mauritania
Rossosh' *111 B6* Voronezhskaya Oblast', W Russian Federation
Ross Sea *154 B4 sea* Antarctica
Rostak *see* Ar Rustāq
Rostock *94 C2* Mecklenburg-Vorpommern, NE Germany
Rostov *see* Rostov-na-Donu
Rostov-na-Donu *111 B7 var.* Rostov, *Eng.* Rostov-on-Don. Rostovskaya Oblast', SW Russian Federation
Rostov-on-Don *see* Rostov-na-Donu
Roswell *48 D2* New Mexico, SW USA
Rota *144 B1 island* S Northern Mariana Islands
Rotcher Island *see* Tamana
Rothera *154 A2 UK research station* Antarctica
Rotomagus *see* Rouen
Rotorua *150 D3* Bay of Plenty, North Island, New Zealand
Rotorua, Lake *150 D3 lake* North Island, New Zealand
Rotterdam *86 C4* Zuid-Holland, SW Netherlands
Rottweil *95 B6* Baden-Württemberg, S Germany
Rotuma *145 E4 island* NW Fiji Oceania S Pacific Ocean
Roubaix *90 C2* Nord, N France
Rouen *90 C3 anc.* Rotomagus. Seine-Maritime, N France
Roulers *see* Roeselare
Roumania *see* Romania
Round Rock *49 G3* Texas, SW USA
Rourkela *see* Räurkela
Rousselaere *see* Roeselare
Roussillon *91 C6 cultural region* S France
Rouyn-Noranda *38 D4* Québec, SE Canada
Rovaniemi *84 D3* Lappi, N Finland
Rovigno *see* Rovinj
Rovigo *96 C2* Veneto, NE Italy
Rovinj *100 A3 It.* Rovigno. Istra, NW Croatia
Rovno *see* Rivne
Rovuma, Rio *79 F2 var.* Ruvuma. *river* Mozambique/Tanzania
Rovuma, Rio *see* Ruvuma
Równe *see* Rivne
Roxas City *139 E2* Panay Island, C Philippines
Royale, Isle *40 B1 island* Michigan, N USA
Royan *91 B5* Charente-Maritime, W France
Rozdol'ne *109 F4 Rus.* Razdolnoye. Avtonomna Respublika Krym, S Ukraine
Rožňava *99 D6 Ger.* Rosenau, *Hung.* Rozsnyó. Košický Kraj, E Slovakia
Rózsahegy *see* Ružomberok
Rozsnyó *see* Râșnov, Romania
Rozsnyó *see* Rožňava, Slovakia
Ruanda *see* Rwanda
Ruapehu, Mount *150 D4 volcano* North Island, New Zealand
Ruapuke Island *151 B8 island* SW New Zealand
Ruatoria *150 E3* Gisborne, North Island, New Zealand
Ruawai *150 D2* Northland, North Island, New Zealand
Rubezhnoye *see* Rubizhne
Rubizhne *109 H3 Rus.* Rubezhnoye. Luhans'ka Oblast', E Ukraine
Ruby Mountains *47 D5 mountain range* Nevada, W USA
Rucava *106 B3* SW Latvia
Rudensk *see* Rudzyensk
Rūdiškės *107 B5* Vilnius, S Lithuania
Rudnik *see* Dolni Chiflik
Rudny *see* Rudnyy
Rudnyy *114 C4 var.* Rudny. Kostanay, N Kazakhstan
Rudolf, Lake *see* Turkana, Lake
Rudolfswert *see* Novo mesto
Rudzyensk *107 C6 Rus.* Rudensk. Minskaya Voblasts', C Belarus
Rufiji *73 C7 river* E Tanzania
Rufino *64 C4* Santa Fe, C Argentina
Rugāji *106 D4* E Latvia
Rügen *94 D2 headland* NE Germany
Ruggell *94 E1* N Liechtenstein Europe
Ruhja *see* Rūjiena
Ruhnu *106 C2 var.* Ruhnu Saar, *Swe.* Runö. *island* SW Estonia
Ruhnu Saar *see* Ruhnu
Rujen *see* Rūjiena
Rūjiena *106 D3 Est.* Ruhja, *Ger.* Rujen. N Latvia
Rukwa, Lake *73 B7 lake* SE Tanzania
Rum *see* Rhum
Ruma *100 D3* Vojvodina, N Serbia
Rumadiya *see* Ar Ramādī
Rumania/Rumänien *see* Romania
Rumbek *73 B5* El Buhayrat, C South Sudan
Rum Cay *54 D2 island* C Bahamas
Rumia *98 C2* Pomorskie, N Poland
Rummah, Wādī ar *see* Rimah, Wādī ar
Rummelsburg in Pommern *see* Miastko
Rumuniya/Rumŭniya/Rumunjska *see* Romania
Runanga *151 B5* West Coast, South Island, New Zealand
Rundu *78 C3 var.* Runtu. Okavango, NE Namibia
Runö *see* Ruhnu
Runtu *see* Rundu
Ruoqiang *126 C3 var.* Jo-ch'iang, *Uigh.* Charkhlik, Charkhliq, Qarkilik. Xinjiang Uygur Zizhiqu, NW China
Rupea *108 C4 Ger.* Reps, *Hung.* Kőhalom; *prev.* Cohalm. Brașov, C Romania
Rupel *87 B5 river* N Belgium
Rupella *see* la Rochelle
Rupert, Rivière de *38 D3 river* Québec, C Canada
Rusaddir *see* Melilla
Ruschuk/Rusçuk *see* Ruse
Ruse *104 D1 var.* Ruschuk, Rustchuk, *Turk.* Rusçuk. Ruse, N Bulgaria
Russadir *see* Melilla
Russellville *42 A1* Arkansas, C USA
Russia *see* Russian Federation
Russian America *see* Alaska
Russian Federation *112 D2 off.* Russian Federation, *var.* Russia, *Latv.* Krievija, *Rus.* Rossiyskaya Federatsiya. *country* Asia/Europe

RUSSIAN FEDERATION
Europe / Asia

Official name Russian Federation
Formation 1480 / 1991
Capital Moscow
Population 143 million / 22 people per sq mile (8 people per sq km)
Total area 6,592,735 sq. miles (17,075,200 sq. km)
Languages Russian*, Tatar, Ukrainian, Chavash, various other national languages
Religions Orthodox Christian 75%, Muslim 14%, Other 11%
Ethnic mix Russian 80%, Other 12%, Tatar 4%, Ukrainian 2%, Bashkir 1%, Chavash 1%
Government Presidential / parliamentary system
Currency Russian rouble = 100 kopeks
Literacy rate 99%
Calorie consumption 3358 kilocalories

Russian Federation *see* Russian Federation
Rustaq *see* Ar Rustāq
Rustavi *117 G2 prev.* Rust'avi. SE Georgia
Rust'avi *see* Rustavi
Rustchuk *see* Ruse
Ruston *42 B2* Louisiana, S USA
Rutanzige, Lake *see* Edward, Lake
Rutba *see* Ar Ruṭbah
Rutlam *see* Ratlām
Rutland *41 F2* Vermont, NE USA
Rutog *126 A4 var.* Rutög, Rutok. Xizang Zizhiqu, W China
Rutok *see* Rutog
Ruvuma *69 E5 var.* Rio Rovuma. *river* Mozambique/Tanzania
Ruvuma *see* Rovuma, Rio
Ruwenzori *77 E5 mountain range* Dem. Rep. Congo/Uganda
Ruzhany *107 B6* Brestskaya Voblasts', SW Belarus
Ružomberok *99 C5 Ger.* Rosenberg, *Hung.* Rózsahegy. Žilinský Kraj, N Slovakia
Rwanda *73 B6 off.* Rwandese Republic; *prev.* Ruanda. *country* C Africa

RWANDA
Central Africa

Official name Republic of Rwanda
Formation 1962 / 1962
Capital Kigali
Population 11.8 million / 1225 people per sq mile (473 people per sq km)
Total area 10,169 sq. miles (26,338 sq. km)
Languages Kinyarwanda*, French*, Kiswahili, English*
Religions Christian 94%, Muslim 5%, Traditional beliefs 1%
Ethnic mix Hutu 85%, Tutsi 14%, Other (including Twa) 1%
Government Presidential system
Currency Rwanda franc = 100 centimes
Literacy rate 66%
Calorie consumption 2148 kilocalories

Rwandese Republic *see* Rwanda
Ryazan' *111 B5* Ryazanskaya Oblast', W Russian Federation
Rybach'ye *see* Balykchy
Rybinsk *110 B4 prev.* Andropov. Yaroslavskaya Oblast', W Russian Federation
Rybnik *99 C5* Śląskie, S Poland
Rybnitsa *see* Rîbnița
Ryde *148 E1* United Kingdom
Ryki *98 D4* Lubelskie, E Poland
Rykovo *see* Yenakiyeve
Rypin *98 C3* Kujawsko-pomorskie, C Poland
Ryssel *see* Lille
Rysy *99 C5 mountain* S Poland
Ryukyu Islands *130 A2 Eng.* Ryukyu Islands. *island group* SW Japan
Ryukyu Islands *125 E3 Eng.* Ryukyu Islands. *island group* SW Japan
Ryukyu Islands *see* Nansei-shotō
Ryukyu Islands *see* Nansei-shotō
Ryukyu Trench *125 F3 var.* Nansei Syotō Trench. *trench* S East China Sea
Rzeszów *99 E5* Podkarpackie, SE Poland
Rzhev *110 B4* Tverskaya Oblast', W Russian Federation

S

Saale *94 C4 river* C Germany
Saalfeld *95 C5 var.* Saalfeld an der Saale. Thüringen, C Germany
Saalfeld an der Saale *see* Saalfeld
Saarbrücken *95 A6 Fr.* Sarrebruck. Saarland, SW Germany
Sääre *106 C2 var.* Sjar. Saaremaa, W Estonia
Saare *see* Saaremaa
Saaremaa *106 C2 Ger.* Oesel, Ösel; *prev.* Saare. *island* W Estonia
Saariselkä *84 D2 Lapp.* Suoločielgi. Lappi, N Finland
Sab' Ābār *118 C4 var.* Sab'a Biyar, Sa'b Bi'ār. Ḥimṣ, C Syria
Sab'a Biyar *see* Sab' Ābār
Šabac *100 D3* Serbia, W Serbia
Sabadell *93 G2* Cataluña, E Spain
Sabah *138 D3 prev.* British North Borneo, North Borneo. *state* East Malaysia
Sabanalarga *58 B1* Atlántico, N Colombia
Sabaneta *58 C1* Falcón, N Venezuela
Sabaria *see* Szombathely
Sab'atayn, Ramlat as *121 C6 desert* C Yemen
Sabaya *61 F4* Oruro, S Bolivia
Sa'b Bi'ār *see* Sab' Ābār
Saberi, Hamun-e *122 C5 var.* Daryācheh-ye Hāmun, Daryācheh-ye Sīstān. *lake* Afghanistan/Iran
Sabhā *71 F3* C Libya
Sabi *see* Save
Sabinas *51 E2* Coahuila, NE Mexico
Sabinas Hidalgo *51 E2* Nuevo León, NE Mexico
Sabine River *49 H3 river* Louisiana/Texas, SW USA
Sabkha *see* As Sabkhah
Sable, Cape *43 E5 headland* Florida, SE USA
Sable Island *39 G4 island* Nova Scotia, SE Canada
Şabyā *121 B6* Jīzān, SW Saudi Arabia
Sabzawar *see* Sabzevār

Sabzevār *120 D2 var.* Sabzawar. Khorāsān-Razavī, NE Iran
Sachsen *94 D4 Eng.* Saxony, *Fr.* Saxe. *state* E Germany
Sachs Harbour *37 E2 var.* Ikaahuk. Banks Island, Northwest Territories, N Canada
Sächsisch-Reen/Sächsisch-Regen *see* Reghin
Sacramento *47 B5 state capital* California, W USA
Sacramento Mountains *48 D2 mountain range* New Mexico, SW USA
Sacramento River *47 B5 river* California, W USA
Sacramento Valley *47 B5 valley* California, W USA
Sá da Bandeira *see* Lubango
Ṣa'dah *121 B6* NW Yemen
Sado *see* Sadoga-shima
Sadoga-shima *131 C5 var.* Sado. *island* C Japan
Saena Julia *see* Siena
Safad *see* Tsefat
Ṣafāqis *see* Sfax
Ṣafāshahr *120 D3 var.* Deh Bīd. Fārs, C Iran
Safed *see* Tsefat
Säffle *85 B6* Värmland, C Sweden
Safford *48 C3* Arizona, SW USA
Safi *70 B2* W Morocco
Sagaing *136 B3* Sagaing, C Myanmar (Burma)
Sagami-nada *131 D6 inlet* SW Japan
Sagan *see* Żagań
Sāgar *134 D4 prev.* Saugor. Madhya Pradesh, C India
Sagarmāthā *see* Everest, Mount
Sagebrush State *see* Nevada
Saghez *see* Saqqez
Saginaw *40 C3* Michigan, N USA
Saginaw Bay *40 D2 lake bay* Michigan, N USA
Sagua la Grande *54 B2* Villa Clara, C Cuba
Sagunto *93 F3 Cat.* Sagunt, *Ar.* Murviedro; *anc.* Saguntum. Valenciana, E Spain
Sagunt/Saguntum *see* Sagunto
Sahara *68 B3 desert* Libya/Algeria
Ṣaḥrā al Gharbīya *72 B2 Eng.* Western Desert, *desert* Egypt
Saharan Atlas *70 D2 var.* Saharan Atlas. *mountain range* Algeria/Morocco
Saharan Atlas *see* Atlas Saharien
Sahel *74 D3 physical region* C Africa
Sāḥilīyah, Jibāl as *118 B3 mountain range* NW Syria
Sāhīwāl *134 C2 prev.* Montgomery. Punjab, E Pakistan
Saïda *119 A5 var.* Ṣaydā, Sayida; *anc.* Sidon. W Lebanon
Sa'īdābād *see* Sīrjān
Saidpur *135 G3 var.* Syedpur. Rajshahi, NW Bangladesh
Saīdu *134 C1 var.* Mingora, Mongora; *prev.* Mingāora. Khyber Pakhtunkhwa, N Pakistan
Saigon *see* Hô Chi Minh
Saimaa *85 E5 lake* SE Finland
St Albans *89 E6 anc.* Verulamium. E England, United Kingdom
Saint Albans *40 D5* West Virginia, NE USA
St Andrews *88 C4* E Scotland, United Kingdom
Saint Anna Trough *see* Svyataya Anna Trough
St. Ann's Bay *54 B4* C Jamaica
St. Anthony *39 G3* Newfoundland and Labrador, SE Canada
Saint Augustine *43 E3* Florida, SE USA
St Austell *89 C7* SW England, United Kingdom
St.Botolph's Town *see* Boston
St-Brieuc *90 A3* Côtes d'Armor, NW France
St. Catharines *38 D5* Ontario, S Canada
St-Chamond *91 D5* Loire, E France
Saint Christopher and Nevis, Federation of *see* Saint Kitts and Nevis
Saint Christopher-Nevis *see* Saint Kitts and Nevis
Saint Clair, Lake *40 D3 var.* Lac à L'Eau Claire. *lake* Canada/USA
St-Claude *91 D5 anc.* Condate. Jura, E France
Saint Cloud *45 F2* Minnesota, N USA
Saint Croix *55 F3 island* S Virgin Islands (US)
Saint Croix River *40 A2 river* Minnesota/Wisconsin, N USA
St David's Island *42 B5 island* E Bermuda
St-Denis *79 G4 dependent territory capital* (Réunion) NW Réunion
St-Dié *90 E4* Vosges, NE France
St-Egrève *91 D5* Isère, E France
Sainte Marie, Cap *see* Vohimena, Tanjona
Saintes *91 B5 anc.* Mediolanum. Charente-Maritime, W France
St-Étienne *91 D5* Loire, E France
St-Flour *91 C5* Cantal, C France
St-Gall/Saint Gall/St. Gallen *see* Sankt Gallen
St-Gaudens *91 B6* Haute-Garonne, S France
Saint George *149 D5* Queensland, E Australia
St George *42 B4* N Bermuda
Saint George *44 A5* Utah, W USA
St. George's *55 G5 country capital* (Grenada) SW Grenada
St-Georges *39 E4* Québec, SE Canada
St-Georges *59 H3* E French Guiana
Saint George's Channel *89 B6 channel* Ireland/Wales, United Kingdom
St George's Island *42 B4 island* E Bermuda
Saint Helena *69 B6 UK dependent territory* C Atlantic Ocean
St Helier *89 D8 British Crown Dependency capital* (Jersey) S Jersey, Channel Islands
St.Iago de la Vega *see* Spanish Town
Saint Ignace *40 C2* Michigan, N USA
St-Jean, Lac *39 E4 lake* Québec, SE Canada
Saint Joe River *46 D2 river* Idaho, NW USA North America
St. John *39 F4* New Brunswick, SE Canada
Saint-John *see* Saint John
Saint John *41 H1 Fr.* Saint-John. *river* Canada/USA
St John's *55 G3 country capital* (Antigua and Barbuda) Antigua, Antigua and Barbuda
St. John's *39 H3 province capital* Newfoundland and Labrador, E Canada
Saint Joseph *45 F4* Missouri, C USA
St Julian's *see* San Ġiljan
St Kilda *88 A3 island* NW Scotland, United Kingdom
Saint Kitts and Nevis *55 F3 off.* Federation of Saint Christopher and Nevis, *var.* Saint Christopher-Nevis. *country* E West Indies

SAINT KITTS & NEVIS
West Indies

Official name Federation of Saint Christopher and Nevis
Formation 1983 / 1983
Capital Basseterre
Population 51,134 / 368 people per sq mile (142 people per sq km)
Total area 101 sq. miles (261 sq. km)
Languages English*, English Creole
Religions Anglican 33%, Methodist 29%, Other 22%, Moravian 9%, Roman Catholic 7%
Ethnic mix Black 95%, Mixed race 3%, White 1%, Other and Amerindian 1%
Government Parliamentary system
Currency Eastern Caribbean dollar = 100 cents
Literacy rate 98%
Calorie consumption 2507 kilocalories

St-Laurent *see* St-Laurent-du-Maroni
St-Laurent-du-Maroni *59 H3 var.* St-Laurent. NW French Guiana
St-Laurent, Fleuve *see* St. Lawrence
St. Lawrence *39 E4 Fr.* Fleuve St-Laurent. *river* Canada/USA
St. Lawrence, Gulf of *39 F3 gulf* NW Atlantic Ocean
Saint Lawrence Island *36 B2 island* Alaska, USA
St-Lô *90 B3 anc.* Briovera, Laudus. Manche, N France
St-Louis *90 E4* Haut-Rhin, NE France
Saint Louis *74 B3* NW Senegal
Saint Louis *45 G4* Missouri, C USA
Saint Lucia *55 E1 country* SE West Indies

SAINT LUCIA
West Indies

Official name Saint Lucia
Formation 1979 / 1979
Capital Castries
Population 162,781 / 690 people per sq mile (267 people per sq km)
Total area 239 sq. miles (620 sq. km)
Languages English*, French Creole
Religions Roman Catholic 90%, Other 10%
Ethnic mix Black 83%, Mulatto (mixed race) 13%, Asian 3%, Other 1%
Government Parliamentary system
Currency Eastern Caribbean dollar = 100 cents
Literacy rate 95%
Calorie consumption 2629 kilocalories

Saint Lucia Channel *55 H4 channel* Martinique/Saint Lucia
St-Malo *90 B3* Ille-et-Vilaine, NW France
St-Malo, Golfe de *90 A3 gulf* NW France
Saint Martin *see* Sint Maarten
St.Matthew's Island *see* Zadetkyi Kyun
St.Matthias Group *144 B3 island group* NE Papua New Guinea
St. Moritz *95 B7 Ger.* Sankt Moritz, *Rmsch.* San Murezzan. Graubünden, SE Switzerland
St-Nazaire *90 A4* Loire-Atlantique, NW France
Saint Nicholas *see* São Nicolau
Saint-Nicolas *see* Sint-Niklaas
St-Omer *90 C2* Pas-de-Calais, N France
Saint Paul *45 F2 state capital* Minnesota, N USA
St-Paul, Île *141 C6 var.* St.Paul Island. *island* Île St-Paul, NE French Southern and Antarctic Lands, Antarctica, Indian Ocean
St.Paul Island *see* St-Paul, Île
St Peter Port *89 D8 British Crown Dependency capital* (Guernsey) C Guernsey, Channel Islands
Saint Petersburg *43 E4* Florida, SE USA
Saint Petersburg *see* Sankt-Peterburg
St-Pierre and Miquelon *39 G4 Fr.* Îles St-Pierre et Miquelon. *French territorial collectivity* NE North America
St-Quentin *90 C3* Aisne, N France
Saint Thomas *see* São Tomé, Sao Tome and Principe
Saint Thomas *see* Charlotte Amalie, Virgin Islands (US)
Saint Ubes *see* Setúbal
Saint Vincent *55 G4 island* N Saint Vincent and the Grenadines
Saint Vincent *see* São Vicente
Saint Vincent and the Grenadines *55 H4 country* SE West Indies

SAINT VINCENT & THE GRENADINES
West Indies

Official name Saint Vincent and the Grenadines
Formation 1979 / 1979
Capital Kingstown
Population 103,220 / 788 people per sq mile (304 people per sq km)
Total area 150 sq. miles (389 sq. km)
Languages English*, English Creole
Religions Anglican 47%, Methodist 28%, Roman Catholic 13%, Other 12%
Ethnic mix Black 66%, Mulatto (mixed race) 19%, Other 12%, Carib 2%, Asian 1%
Government Parliamentary system
Currency Eastern Caribbean dollar = 100 cents
Literacy rate 88%
Calorie consumption 2960 kilocalories

Saint Vincent, Cape *see* São Vicente, Cabo de
Saint Vincent Passage *55 H4 passage* Saint Lucia/Saint Vincent and the Grenadines
Saint Yves *see* Setúbal
Saipan *142 B1 island/country capital* (Northern Mariana Islands) S Northern Mariana Islands
Saishū *see* Jeju-do
Sajama, Nevado *61 F4 mountain* W Bolivia
Sajószentpéter *99 D6* Borsod-Abaúj-Zemplén, NE Hungary
Sakākah *120 B4* Al Jawf, NW Saudi Arabia
Sakakawea, Lake *44 D1 reservoir* North Dakota, N USA
Sak'art'velo *see* Georgia
Sakata *130 D4* Yamagata, Honshū, C Japan
Sakhalin *115 G4 var.* Sakhalin. *island* SE Russian Federation
Sakhalin *see* Sakhalin, Ostrov
Sakhon Nakhon *see* Sakon Nakhon
Şäki *117 G2 Rus.* Sheki; *prev.* Nukha. NW Azerbaijan
Saki *see* Saky
Sakishima-shoto *130 A3 var.* Sakisima Syotô. *island group* SW Japan
Sakisima Syotô *see* Sakishima-shotō
Sakiz *see* Saqqez
Sakiz-Adasi *see* Chíos
Sakon Nakhon *136 D4 var.* Muang Sakon Nakhon, Sakhon Nakhon. Sakon Nakhon, E Thailand
Saky *109 F5 Rus.* Saki. Avtonomna Respublika Krym, S Ukraine
Sal *74 A3 island* Ilhas de Barlavento, NE Cape Verde
Sala *85 C6* Västmanland, C Sweden
Salacgrīva *106 C3 Est.* Salatsi. N Latvia
Sala Consilina *97 D5* Campania, S Italy
Salado, Río *62 D5 river* E Argentina
Salado, Río *64 C3 river* C Argentina
Ṣalālah *121 D6* SW Oman
Salamá *52 B2* Baja Verapaz, C Guatemala
Salamanca *64 B4* Coquimbo, C Chile
Salamanca *92 D2 anc.* Helmantica, Salmantica. Castilla y León, NW Spain
Salamīyah *118 B3 var.* As Salamīyah. Ḥamāh, W Syria
Salang *see* Phuket
Salantai *106 B3* Klaipėda, NW Lithuania
Salatsi *see* Salacgrīva
Salavan *137 D5 var.* Saravan, Saravane. Salavan, S Laos
Salavat *111 D6* Respublika Bashkortostan, W Russian Federation
Sala y Gomez *153 F4 island* Chile, E Pacific Ocean
Sala y Gomez Fracture Zone *see* Sala y Gomez Ridge
Sala y Gomez Ridge *153 G4 var.* Sala y Gomez Fracture Zone. *fracture zone* SE Pacific Ocean
Salazar *see* N'Dalatando
Šalčininkai *107 C5* Vilnius, SE Lithuania
Salduba *see* Zaragoza
Saldus *106 B3 Ger.* Frauenburg. W Latvia
Sale *149 C7* Victoria, SE Australia
Salé *70 C2* NW Morocco
Salekhard *114 D3 prev.* Obdorsk. Yamalo-Nenetskiy Avtonomnyy Okrug, N Russian Federation
Salem *132 C2* Tamil Nādu, SE India
Salem *46 B3 state capital* Oregon, NW USA
Salerno *97 D5 anc.* Salernum. Campania, S Italy
Salerno, Gulf of *97 C5 Eng.* Gulf of Salerno. *gulf* S Italy
Salerno, Gulf of *see* Salerno, Golfo di
Salernum *see* Salerno
Salihorsk *107 C7 Rus.* Soligorsk. Minskaya Voblasts', S Belarus
Salima *79 E2* Central, C Malawi
Salina *45 E5* Kansas, C USA
Salina Cruz *51 F5* Oaxaca, SE Mexico
Salinas *60 A2* Guayas, W Ecuador
Salinas *47 B6* California, W USA
Salisbury *89 D7 var.* New Sarum. S England, United Kingdom
Salisbury *see* Harare
Sállan *see* Sørøya
Salliq *see* Coral Harbour
Sallyana *see* Şalyān
Salmantica *see* Salamanca
Salmon River *46 D3 river* Idaho, NW USA

Salmon River Mountains *46 D3 mountain range* Idaho, NW USA
Salo *85 D6* Länsi-Suomi, SW Finland
Salon-de-Provence *91 D6* Bouches-du-Rhône, SE France
Salonica/Salonika *see* Thessaloníki
Salonta *108 A3 Hung.* Nagyszalonta. Bihor, W Romania
Sal'sk *111 B7* Rostovskaya Oblast', SW Russian Federation
Salt *see* As Salṭ
Salta *64 C2* Salta, NW Argentina
Saltash *89 C7* SW England, United Kingdom
Saltillo *51 E3* Coahuila, NE Mexico
Salt Lake City *44 B4 state capital* Utah, W USA
Salto *64 D4* Salto, N Uruguay
Salton Sea *47 D8 lake* California, W USA
Salvador *63 G3 prev.* São Salvador. *state capital* Bahia, E Brazil
Salween *124 C2 Bur.* Thanlwin, *Chin.* Nu Chiang, Nu Jiang. *river* SE Asia
Şalyān *135 E3 var.* Sallyana. Mid Western, W Nepal
Salzburg *95 D6 anc.* Juvavum. Salzburg, N Austria
Salzgitter *94 C4 prev.* Watenstedt-Salzgitter. Niedersachsen, C Germany
Salzwedel *94 C3* Sachsen-Anhalt, N Germany
Šamac *see* Bosanski Šamac
Samakhixai *see* Attapu
Samalayuca *50 C1* Chihuahua, N Mexico
Samar *139 F2 island* C Philippines
Samara *114 B3 prev.* Kuybyshev. Samarskaya Oblast', W Russian Federation
Samarang *see* Semarang
Samarinda *138 D4* Borneo, C Indonesia
Samarkand *see* Samarqand
Samarkandski/Samarkandskoye *see* Temirtau
Samarobriva *see* Amiens
Samarqand *123 E2 Rus.* Samarkand. Samarqand Viloyati, C Uzbekistan
Samawa *see* As Samāwah
Sambalpur *135 F4* Odisha, E India
Sambava *79 G2* Antsiranana, NE Madagascar
Sambir *108 B2 Rus.* Sambor. L'vivs'ka Oblast', NW Ukraine
Sambor *see* Sambir
Sambre *90 D2 river* Belgium/France
Samfya *78 D2* Luapula, N Zambia
Saminatal *94 E2 valley* Austria/ Liechtenstein Europe
Samnān *see* Semnān
Sam Neua *see* Xam Nua
Samoa *145 E4 off.* Independent State of Samoa, *var.* Sāmoa; *prev.* Western Samoa. *country* W Polynesia

SAMOA
Australasia & Oceania

Official name Independent State of Samoa
Formation 1962 / 1962
Capital Apia
Population 200,000 / 183 people per sq mile (71 people per sq km)
Total area 1104 sq. miles (2860 sq. km)
Languages Samoan*, English*
Religions Christian 99%, Other 1%
Ethnic mix Polynesian 91%, Euronesian 7%, Other 2%
Government Parliamentary system
Currency Tala = 100 sene
Literacy rate 99%
Calorie consumption 2872 kilocalories

Sāmoa *see* Samoa
Samoa Basin *143 E3 undersea basin* W Pacific Ocean
Samoa, Independent State of *see* Samoa
Samobor *100 A2* Zagreb, N Croatia
Sámos *105 E6 prev.* Limín Vathéos. Sámos, Dodekánisa, Greece, Aegean Sea
Sámos *105 D6 island* Dodekánisa, Greece, Aegean Sea
Samothrace *see* Samothráki
Samothráki *104 D4* Samothráki, NE Greece
Samothraki *104 C4 anc.* Samothrace. *island* NE Greece
Sampit *138 C4* Borneo, C Indonesia
Sâmraông *137 D5 prev.* Phumĭ Sâmraông, Phum Samrong. Siĕmréab, NW Cambodia
Samsun *116 D2 anc.* Amisus. Samsun, N Turkey
Samt'redia *117 F2 prev.* Samtredia. W Georgia
Samtredia *see* Samt'redia
Samui, Ko *137 C6 island* SW Thailand
Samut Prakan *137 C5 var.* Muang Samut Prakan, Paknam. Samut Prakan, C Thailand
San *74 D3* Ségou, C Mali
San *99 E5 river* SE Poland
Şan'ā' *121 B6 Eng.* Sana. *country capital* (Yemen) W Yemen
Sana *100 B3 river* NW Bosnia and Herzegovina
Sanae *154 B2 South African research station* Antarctica
Sanaga *77 B5 river* C Cameroon
San Ambrosio, Isla *57 A5 Eng.* San Ambrosio Island. *island* W Chile
San Ambrosio Island *see* San Ambrosio, Isla
Sanandaj *120 C3 prev.* Sinneh. Kordestān, W Iran
San Andrés, Isla de *53 F3 island* NW Colombia, Caribbean Sea
San Andrés Tuxtla *51 F4 var.* Tuxtla. Veracruz-Llave, E Mexico
San Angelo *49 F3* Texas, SW USA
San Antonio *52 B2* Toledo, S Belize
San Antonio *64 B4* Valparaíso, C Chile
San Antonio *49 F4* Texas, SW USA
San Antonio Oeste *65 C5* Río Negro, E Argentina
San Antonio River *49 G4 river* Texas, SW USA
Sanata Uxía de Ribeira *92 B1 var.* Ribeira. Galicia, NW Spain
Sanāw *121 C6 var.* Sanaw. NE Yemen
San Benedicto, Isla *50 B4 island* W Mexico
San Benito *52 B1* Petén, N Guatemala
San Benito *49 G5* Texas, SW USA
San Bernardino *47 C7* California, W USA
San Blas *50 C3* Sinaloa, C Mexico
San Blas, Cape *42 D3 headland* Florida, SE USA
San Blas, Cordillera de *53 G4 mountain range* NE Panama
San Carlos *52 D4* Río San Juan, S Nicaragua
San Carlos *48 B2* Arizona, SW USA
San Carlos *see* Quesada, Costa Rica
San Carlos de Ancud *see* Ancud
San Carlos de Bariloche *65 B5* Río Negro, SW Argentina
San Carlos del Zulia *58 C2* Zulia, W Venezuela
San Clemente Island *47 B8 island* Channel Islands, California, W USA
San Cristóbal *58 C2* Táchira, W Venezuela
San Cristobal *144 C4 var.* Makira. *island* SE Solomon Islands
San Cristóbal *see* San Cristóbal de Las Casas
San Cristóbal de Las Casas *51 G5 var.* San Cristóbal. Chiapas, SE Mexico
San Cristóbal, Isla *60 B5 var.* Chatham Island. *island* Galápagos Islands, Ecuador, E Pacific Ocean
Sancti Spíritus *54 B2* Sancti Spíritus, C Cuba
Sandakan *138 D3* Sabah, East Malaysia
Sandalwood Island *see* Sumba, Pulau
Sandanski *104 C3 prev.* Sveti Vrach. Blagoevgrad, SW Bulgaria
Sanday *88 D2 island* NE Scotland, United Kingdom
Sanders *48 C2* Arizona, SW USA
Sand Hills *44 D3 mountain range* Nebraska, C USA
San Diego *47 C8* California, W USA
Sandnes *85 A6* Rogaland, S Norway
Sandomierz *98 D4 Rus.* Sandomir. Świętokrzyskie, C Poland
Sandomir *see* Sandomierz
Sandoway *see* Thandwe
Sandpoint *46 C1* Idaho, NW USA
Sand Springs *49 G1* Oklahoma, C USA
Sandusky *40 D3* Ohio, N USA
Sandvika *85 A6* Akershus, S Norway
Sandviken *85 C6* Gävleborg, C Sweden
Sandwich Island *see* Efate
Sandwich Islands *see* Hawai'ian Islands
Sandy Bay *93 H5* Saskatchewan, C Canada
Sandy City *44 B4* Utah, W USA
Sandy Lake *38 B3 lake* Ontario, C Canada
San Esteban *52 D2* Olancho, C Honduras
San Eugenio/San Eugenio del Cuareim *see* Artigas
San Felipe *58 D1* Yaracuy, NW Venezuela
San Felipe de Puerto Plata *see* Puerto Plata
San Félix, Isla *57 A5 Eng.* San Felix Island. *island* W Chile
San Felix Island *see* San Félix, Isla
San Fernando *92 C5 prev.* Isla de León. Andalucía, S Spain
San Fernando *55 H5* Trinidad, Trinidad and Tobago
San Fernando *46 D1* California, W USA
San Fernando *58 D2 var.* San Fernando de Apure. Apure, C Venezuela
San Fernando de Apure *see* San Fernando
San Fernando del Valle de Catamarca *64 C3 var.* Catamarca. Catamarca, NW Argentina
San Fernando de Monte Cristi *see* Monte Cristi
San Francisco *47 B6* California, W USA
San Francisco del Oro *50 C2* Chihuahua, N Mexico
San Francisco de Macorís *55 E3* C Dominican Republic
San Fructuoso *see* Tacuarembó
San Gabriel *60 B1* Carchi, N Ecuador
San Gabriel Mountains *46 E1 mountain range* California, USA
Sangihe, Kepulauan *see* Sangir, Kepulauan
San Ġiljan *102 B5 var.* St Julian's. N Malta
Sangir, Kepulauan *139 F3 var.* Kepulauan Sangihe. *island group* N Indonesia
Sāngli *132 B1* Mahārāshtra, W India
Sangmélima *77 B5* Sud, S Cameroon
Sangre de Cristo Mountains *48 D1 mountain range* Colorado/New Mexico, C USA
San Ignacio *52 B1 prev.* Cayo, El Cayo. Cayo, W Belize
San Ignacio *61 F3* El Beni, N Bolivia
San Ignacio *50 B2* Baja California Sur, NW Mexico
San Joaquin Valley *47 B7 valley* California, W USA
San Jorge, Gulf of *65 C6 var.* Gulf of San Jorge. *gulf* S Argentina
San Jorge, Gulf of *see* San Jorge, Golfo
San José *53 E4 country capital* (Costa Rica) San José, C Costa Rica
San José *61 G3 var.* San José de Chiquitos. Santa Cruz, E Bolivia
San José *52 B3 var.* Puerto San José. Escuintla, S Guatemala
San Jose *47 B6* California, W USA
San José *see* San José del Guaviare, Colombia
San José de Chiquitos *see* San José
San José de Cúcuta *see* Cúcuta
San José del Guaviare *58 C4 var.* San José. Guaviare, S Colombia
San Juan *64 B4* San Juan, W Argentina
San Juan *55 F3 dependent territory capital* (Puerto Rico) NE Puerto Rico
San Juan *see* San Juan de los Morros
San Juan Bautista *64 D3* Misiones, S Paraguay
San Juan Bautista *see* Villahermosa
San Juan Bautista Tuxtepec *see* Tuxtepec
San Juan de Alicante *see* Sant Joan d'Alacant
San Juan del Norte *53 E4 var.* Greytown. Río San Juan, SE Nicaragua
San Juan de los Morros *58 D2 var.* San Juan. Guárico, N Venezuela
San Juanito, Isla *50 C4 island* C Mexico
San Juan Mountains *48 D1 mountain range* Colorado, C USA
San Juan, Río *53 E4 river* Costa Rica/ Nicaragua
San Juan River *48 C1 river* Colorado/ Utah, W USA
San Julián *see* Puerto San Julián
Sankt-Bartholomäi *see* Palamuse
Sankt Gallen *95 B7 var.* St. Gallen, *Eng.* Saint Gall, *Fr.* St-Gall. Sankt Gallen, NE Switzerland
Sankt-Georgen *see* Sfântu Gheorghe
Sankt-Jakobi *see* Pärnu-Jaagupi, Pärnumaa, Estonia
Sankt Martin *see* Martin
Sankt Moritz *see* St. Moritz
Sankt-Peterburg *110 B4 prev.* Leningrad, Petrograd, *Eng.* Saint Petersburg, *Fin.* Pietari. Leningradskaya Oblast', NW Russian Federation
Sankt Pölten *95 E6* Niederösterreich, N Austria
Sankt Veit am Flaum *see* Rijeka
Sankuru *77 D6 river* C Dem. Rep. Congo
Şanlıurfa *117 E4 prev.* Sanli Urfa, Urfa; *anc.* Edessa. şanlıurfa, S Turkey
Sanli Urfa *see* Şanlıurfa
San Lorenzo *61 G5* Tarija, S Bolivia
San Lorenzo *60 A1* Esmeraldas, N Ecuador
San Lorenzo, Isla *60 C4 island* W Peru
Sanlúcar de Barrameda *92 C5* Andalucía, S Spain
San Luis *64 C4* San Luis, C Argentina
San Luis *52 B2* Petén, NE Guatemala
San Luis *see* San Luis Río Colorado
San Luis Obispo *47 B7* California, W USA
San Luis Potosí *51 E3* San Luis Potosí, C Mexico
San Luis Río Colorado *50 A1 var.* San Luis Río Colorado. Sonora, NW Mexico
San Luis Río Colorado *see* San Luis Río Colorado
San Marcos *52 A2* San Marcos, W Guatemala
San Marcos *49 G4* Texas, SW USA
San Marcos de Arica *see* Arica
San Marino *96 E1 country capital* (San Marino) C San Marino
San Marino *96 D1 off.* Republic of San Marino. *country* S Europe

SAN MARINO
Southern Europe

Official name Republic of San Marino
Formation 1631 / 1631
Capital San Marino
Population 32,448 / 1352 people per sq mile (532 people per sq km)
Total area 23.6 sq. miles (61 sq. km)
Languages Italian*
Religions Roman Catholic 93%, Other and nonreligious 7%
Ethnic mix Sammarinese 88%, Italian 10%, Other 2%
Government Parliamentary system
Currency Euro = 100 cents
Literacy rate 99%
Calorie consumption Not available

San Marino, Republic of *see* San Marino
San Martín *154 A2 Argentinian research station* Antarctica
San Mateo *59 E2* Anzoátegui, NE Venezuela
San Matías *61 H3* Santa Cruz, E Bolivia
San Matías, Gulf of *65 C5 var.* Gulf of San Matías. *gulf* E Argentina
San Matías, Gulf of *see* San Matías, Golfo
Sanmenxia *128 C4 var.* Shan Xian. Henan, C China
Sânmiclăuş Mare *see* Sânnicolau Mare
San Miguel *52 C3* San Miguel, SE El Salvador
San Miguel *50 D2* Coahuila, N Mexico
San Miguel de Ibarra *see* Ibarra
San Miguel de Tucumán *64 C3 var.* Tucumán. Tucumán, N Argentina
San Miguelito *53 G4* Panamá, C Panama
San Miguel, Río *61 G3 river* E Bolivia
San Murezzan *see* St. Moritz
Sannār *see* Sennar
Sânnicolaul-Mare *see* Sânnicolau Mare
Sânnicolau Mare *108 A4 var.* Sânnicolaul-Mare, *Hung.* Nagyszentmiklós; *prev.* Sânmiclăuş Mare, Sînnicolau Mare. Timiş, W Romania

Sanok *99 E5* Podkarpackie, SE Poland
San Pablo *61 F5* Potosí, S Bolivia
San Pedro *52 C1* Corozal, NE Belize
San-Pédro *74 D5* S Côte d'Ivoire
San Pedro *50 D3 var.* San Pedro de las Colonias. Coahuila, NE Mexico
San Pedro de la Cueva *50 C2* Sonora, NW Mexico
San Pedro de las Colonias *see* San Pedro
San Pedro de Lloc *60 B3* La Libertad, NW Peru
San Pedro Mártir, Sierra *50 A1 mountain range* NW Mexico
San Pedro Sula *52 C2* Cortés, NW Honduras
San Rafael *64 B4* Mendoza, W Argentina
San Rafael Mountains *47 C7 mountain range* California, W USA
San Ramón de la Nueva Orán *64 C2* Salta, N Argentina
San Remo *96 A3* Liguria, NW Italy
San Salvador *52 B3 country capital* (El Salvador) San Salvador, SW El Salvador
San Salvador *54 D2 prev.* Watlings Island. *island* E Bahamas
San Salvador de Jujuy *64 C2 var.* Jujuy. Jujuy, N Argentina
San Salvador, Isla *60 A4 island* Ecuador
Sansanné-Mango *75 E4 var.* Mango. N Togo
San Sebastián *93 E1* País Vasco, N Spain *see also* Donostia
Sansepolcro *96 C3* Toscana, C Italy
San Severo *97 D5* Puglia, SE Italy
Santa Ana *61 F3* El Beni, N Bolivia
Santa Ana *52 B3* Santa Ana, NW El Salvador
Santa Ana *46 D2* California, W USA
Santa Ana de Coro *see* Coro
Santa Ana Mountains *46 E2 mountain range* California, W USA
Santa Barbara *50 C2* Chihuahua, N Mexico
Santa Barbara *47 C7* California, W USA
Santa Cataliña de Armada *92 B1 var.* Santa Comba. Galicia, NW Spain
Santa Catalina Island *47 B8 island* Channel Islands, California, W USA
Santa Catarina *63 E5 off.* Estado de Santa Catarina. *region* S Brazil
Santa Catarina *63 E5 off.* Estado de Santa Catarina. *state* S Brazil
Santa Catarina, Estado de *see* Santa Catarina
Santa Clara *54 B2* Villa Clara, C Cuba
Santa Clarita *46 D1* California, USA
Santa Comba *see* Santa Cataliña de Armada
Santa Cruz *76 E2* São Tomé, S Sao Tome and Principe, Africa
Santa Cruz *47 B6* California, W USA
Santa Cruz *61 G4 department* E Bolivia
Santa Cruz Barillas *see* Barillas
Santa Cruz del Quiché *52 B2* Quiché, W Guatemala
Santa Cruz de Tenerife *70 A3* Tenerife, Islas Canarias, Spain, NE Atlantic Ocean
Santa Cruz, Isla *60 B5 var.* Indefatigable Island, Isla Chávez. *island* Galápagos Islands, Ecuador, E Pacific Ocean
Santa Cruz Islands *144 D3 island group* E Solomon Islands
Santa Cruz, Río *65 B7 river* S Argentina
Santa Elena *52 B1* Cayo, W Belize
Santa Fe *64 C4* Santa Fe, C Argentina
Santa Fe *48 D1 state capital* New Mexico, SW USA
Santa Fe *see* Bogotá
Santa Fe de Bogotá *see* Bogotá
Santa Genoveva *50 B3 mountain* NW Mexico
Santa Isabel *144 C3 var.* Bughotu. *island* N Solomon Islands
Santa Isabel *see* Malabo
Santa Lucia Range *47 B7 mountain range* California, W USA
Santa Margarita, Isla *50 B3 island* NW Mexico
Santa Maria *63 E5* Rio Grande do Sul, S Brazil
Santa Maria *47 B7* California, USA
Santa Maria *92 A5 island* Azores, Portugal, NE Atlantic Ocean
Santa Maria del Buen Aire *see* Buenos Aires
Santa María, Isla *60 A5 var.* Isla Floreana, Charles Island. *island* Galápagos Islands, Ecuador, E Pacific Ocean
Santa Marta *58 B1* Magdalena, N Colombia
Santa Maura *see* Lefkáda
Santa Monica *46 D1* California, W USA
Santana *76 E2* São Tomé, C Sao Tome and Principe, Africa
Santander *92 D1* Cantabria, N Spain
Santarém *63 E2* Pará, N Brazil
Santarém *92 B3 anc.* Scalabis. Santarém, W Portugal
Santa Rosa *64 C4* La Pampa, C Argentina
Santa Rosa *see* Santa Rosa de Copán
Santa Rosa de Copán *52 C2 var.* Santa Rosa. Copán, W Honduras
Santa Rosa Island *47 B8 island* California, W USA
Santa Uxía de Ribeira *92 B1 var.* Ribeira. NW Spain
Sant Carles de la Rápida *see* Sant Carles de la Ràpita
Sant Carles de la Ràpita *93 F3 var.* Sant Carles de la Rápida. Cataluña, NE Spain
Santiago *64 B4 var.* Gran Santiago. *country capital* (Chile) Santiago, C Chile
Santiago *55 E3 var.* Santiago de los Caballeros. N Dominican Republic
Santiago *53 F5* Veraguas, S Panama
Santiago *74 A3 var.* São Tiago. *island* Ilhas de Sotavento, S Cape Verde
Santiago *see* Santiago de Compostela
Santiago *see* Santiago de Cuba, Cuba
Santiago de Compostela *92 B1 var.* Santiago, *Eng.* Compostella; *anc.* Campus Stellae. Galicia, NW Spain
Santiago de Cuba *54 C3 var.* Santiago. Santiago de Cuba, E Cuba
Santiago de Guayaquil *see* Guayaquil
Santiago del Estero *64 C3* Santiago del Estero, C Argentina
Santiago de los Caballeros *see* Santiago, Dominican Republic
Santiago de los Caballeros *see* Ciudad de Guatemala, Guatemala
Santiago Pinotepa Nacional *see* Pinotepa Nacional
Santiago, Río *60 B2 river* N Peru
Santi Quaranta *see* Sarandë
Santissima Trinidad *see* Jilong
Sant Joan d'Alacant *93 F4 Cast.* San Juan de Alicante. País Valenciano, E Spain
Sant Julià de Lòria *91 A8* Sant Julià de Lòria, SW Andorra Europe
Santo *see* Espiritu Santo
Santo Antão *74 A2 island* Ilhas de Barlavento, N Cape Verde
Santo António *76 E1* Príncipe, N Sao Tome and Principe, Africa
Santo Domingo *55 D3 prev.* Ciudad Trujillo. *country capital* (Dominican Republic) SE Dominican Republic
Santo Domingo de los Colorados *60 B1* Pichincha, NW Ecuador
Santo Domingo Tehuantepec *see* Tehuantepec
Santorini *see* Thíra
Santorini *105 D7 island* Kykládes, Greece, Aegean Sea
San Tomé de Guayana *see* Ciudad Guayana
Santos *63 F4* São Paulo, S Brazil
Santos Plateau *57 D5 undersea plateau* SW Atlantic Ocean
Santo Tomé *64 D3* Corrientes, NE Argentina
Santo Tomé de Guayana *see* Ciudad Guayana
San Valentín, Cerro *65 A6 mountain* S Chile
San Vicente *52 C3* San Vicente, C El Salvador
São Francisco, Rio *63 F3 river* E Brazil
Sao Hill *73 C7* Iringa, S Tanzania
São João da Madeira *92 B2* Aveiro, N Portugal
São Jorge *92 A5 island* Azores, Portugal, NE Atlantic Ocean
São Luís *63 F2 state capital* Maranhão, NE Brazil
São Mandol *see* São Manuel, Rio
São Manuel, Rio *63 E3 var.* São Mandol, Teles Pirés. *river* C Brazil
São Marcos, Baía de *63 F1 bay* N Brazil
São Miguel *92 A5 island* Azores, Portugal, NE Atlantic Ocean
Saona, Isla *55 E3 island* SE Dominican Republic
Saône *91 D5 river* E France
São Nicolau *74 A3 Eng.* Saint Nicholas. *island* Ilhas de Barlavento, N Cape Verde
São Paulo *63 E4 state capital* São Paulo, S Brazil
São Paulo *63 E4 off.* Estado de São Paulo. *region* S Brazil
São Paulo *63 E4 off.* Estado de São Paulo. *state* S Brazil
São Paulo de Loanda *see* Luanda
São Paulo, Estado de *see* São Paulo
São Pedro do Rio Grande do Sul *see* Rio Grande
São Roque, Cabo de *63 G2 headland* E Brazil
São Salvador *see* Salvador, Brazil
São Salvador/São Salvador do Congo *see* M'Banza Congo, Angola
São Tiago *see* Santiago
São Tomé *77 A5 country capital* (Sao Tome and Principe) São Tomé, S Sao Tome and Principe
São Tomé *76 E2 Eng.* Saint Thomas. *island* S Sao Tome and Principe
Sao Tome and Principe *76 D1 off.* Democratic Republic of Sao Tome and Principe. *country* E Atlantic Ocean

SÃO TOMÉ & PRÍNCIPE
West Africa

Official name The Democratic Republic of São Tomé and Príncipe
Formation 1975 / 1975
Capital São Tomé
Population 200,000 / 539 people per sq mile (208 people per sq km)
Total area 386 sq. miles (1001 sq. km)
Languages Portuguese Creole, Portuguese*
Religions Roman Catholic 84%, Other 16%
Ethnic mix Black 90%, Portuguese and Creole 10%
Government Presidential system
Currency Dobra = 100 céntimos
Literacy rate 70%
Calorie consumption 2676 kilocalories

Sao Tome and Principe, Democratic Republic of *see* Sao Tome and Principe
São Tomé, Pico de *76 D2 mountain* São Tomé, C Sao Tome and Principe, Africa
São Vicente *74 A3 Eng.* Saint Vincent. *island* Ilhas de Barlavento, N Cape Verde
São Vicente, Cabo de *92 B5 Eng.* Cape Saint Vincent, *Port.* Cabode São Vicente. *cape* S Portugal
São Vicente, Cabo de *see* São Vicente, Cabo de
Sápai *see* Sápes
Sapele *75 F5* Delta, S Nigeria
Sápes *104 D3 var.* Sápai. Anatolikí Makedonía kai Thráki, NE Greece
Sapir *119 B7 prev.* Sappir. Southern, S Israel
Sa Pobla *93 G3* Mallorca, Spain, W Mediterranean Sea
Sappir *see* Sapir
Sapporo *130 D2* Hokkaidō, NE Japan
Sapri *97 D6* Campania, S Italy
Sapulpa *49 G1* Oklahoma, C USA
Saqqez *120 C2 var.* Saghez, Sakiz, Saqqiz. Kordestān, NW Iran
Saqqiz *see* Saqqez
Sara Buri *137 C5 var.* Saraburi. Saraburi, C Thailand
Saraburi *see* Sara Buri
Saragossa *see* Zaragoza
Saragt *see* Sarahs
Saraguro *60 B2* Loja, S Ecuador
Sarahs *122 D3 var.* Saragt, *Rus.* Serakhs. Ahal Welaýaty, S Turkmenistan
Sarajevo *100 C4 country capital* (Bosnia and Herzegovina) Federacija Bosne I Hercegovine, SE Bosnia and Herzegovina
Sarakhs *120 E2* Khorāsān-Razavī, E Irar
Saraktash *111 D6* Orenburgskaya Oblast', W Russian Federation
Saran' *114 C4 Kaz.* Saran. Karagandy, C Kazakhstan
Saranda *see* Sarandë
Sarandë *101 C7 var.* Saranda, *It.* Porto Edda; *prev.* Santi Quaranta. Vlorë, S Albania
Saransk *111 C5* Respublika Mordoviya, W Russian Federation
Sarasota *43 E4* Florida, SE USA
Saratov *114 B3* Saratovskaya Oblast', W Russian Federation
Saravan/Saravane *see* Salavan
Sarawak *138 D3 state* East Malaysia
Sarawak *see* Kuching
Sarcelles *90 D1* Val-d'Oise, Île-de-France, N France Europe
Sardinia *97 A5 Eng.* Sardinia. *island* Italy, C Mediterranean Sea
Sardinia *see* Sardegna
Sarera, Teluk *see* Cenderawasih, Teluk
Sargasso Sea *66 B4 sea* W Atlantic Ocea
Sargodha *134 C2* Punjab, NE Pakistan
Sarh *76 C4 prev.* Fort-Archambault. Moyen-Chari, S Chad
Sārī *120 D2 var.* Sari, Sāri. Māzandarān N Iran
Saría *105 E7 island* SE Greece
Sarıkamış *117 F3* Kars, NE Turkey
Sarikol Range *123 G3 Rus.* Sarykol'skiy Khrebet. *mountain range* China/ Tajikistan
Sark *89 D8 Fr.* Sercq. *island* Channel Islands
Şarkışla *116 D3* Sivas, C Turkey
Sarmiento *65 B6* Chubut, S Argentina
Sarnia *38 C5* Ontario, S Canada
Sarny *108 C1* Rivnens'ka Oblast', NW Ukraine
Sarochyna *107 D5 Rus.* Sorochino. Vitsyebskaya Voblasts', N Belarus
Sarov *111 C5 prev.* Sarova. Respublika Mordoviya, SW Russian Federation
Sarova *see* Sarov
Sarpsborg *85 B6* Østfold, S Norway
Sarrebruck *see* Saarbrücken
Sartène *91 E7* Corse, France, C Mediterranean Sea
Sarthe *90 B4 river* N France
Sárti *104 C4* Kentrikí Makedonía, N Greece
Saruhan *see* Manisa
Sarykol'skiy Khrebet *see* Sarikol Range
Sary-Tash *123 F2* Oshskaya Oblast', SW Kyrgyzstan
Saryyesik-Atyrau, Peski *123 G1 desert* E Kazakhstan
Sasebo *131 A7* Nagasaki, Kyūshū, SW Japan
Saskatchewan *37 F5 province* SW Canada
Saskatchewan *37 F5 river* Manitoba/ Saskatchewan, C Canada
Saskatoon *37 F5* Saskatchewan, S Canad
Sasovo *111 B5* Ryazanskaya Oblast', W Russian Federation
Sassandra *74 D5* S Côte d'Ivoire
Sassandra *74 D5 var.* Ibo, Sassandra Fleuve. *river* S Côte d'Ivoire
Sassandra Fleuve *see* Sassandra
Sassari *97 A5* Sardegna, Italy, C Mediterranean Sea
Sassenheim *86 C3* Zuid-Holland, W Netherlands
Sassnitz *94 D2* Mecklenburg-Vorpommern, NE Germany
Sathmar *see* Satu Mare
Sátoraljaújhely *99 D6* Borsod-Abaúj-Zemplén, NE Hungary
Satpura Range *134 D4 mountain range* C India
Satsuma-Sendai *131 A8* Kagoshima, Kyūshū, SW Japan
Satsunan-shoto *130 A3 island group* Nansei-shotō, SW Japan Asia
Sattanen *84 D3* Lappi, NE Finland
Satu Mare *108 B3 Ger.* Sathmar, *Hung.* Szatmárrnémeti. Satu Mare, NW Romania
Sau *see* Sava
Saudi Arabia *121 B5 off.* Kingdom of Saudi Arabia, Al 'Arabīyah as Su'ūdīyah, *Ar.* Al Mamlakah al 'Arabīyah as Su'ūdīyah. *country* SW Asia

SAUDI ARABIA
Southwest Asia

Official name Kingdom of Saudi Arabia
Formation 1932 / 1932
Capital Riyadh
Population 28.8 million / 35 people per sq mile (14 people per sq km)
Total area 756,981 sq. miles (1,960,582 sq. km)
Languages Arabic*
Religions Sunni Muslim 85%, Shi'a Muslim 15%
Ethnic mix Arab 72%, Foreign residents (mostly south and southeast Asian) 20%, Afro-Asian 8%
Government Monarchy
Currency Saudi riyal = 100 halalat
Literacy rate 94%
Calorie consumption 3122 kilocalories

audi Arabia, Kingdom of *see* Saudi Arabia
auer *see* Sûre
augor *see* Sāgar
aulkrasti *106 C3* C Latvia
ault Sainte Marie *38 C4* Michigan, N USA
ault Sainte Marie *40 C1* Michigan, N USA
ault Ste. Marie *38 C4* Ontario, S Canada
aumur *90 B4* Maine-et-Loire, NW France
aurimo *78 C1* *Port.* Henrique de Carvalho, Vila Henrique de Carvalho. Lunda Sul, NE Angola
ava *107 E6* Mahilyowskaya Voblasts', E Belarus
avá *52 D2* Colón, N Honduras
avai'i *145 E4* *island* NW Samoa
avannah *43 E2* Georgia, SE USA
avannah River *43 E2* *river* Georgia/ South Carolina, SE USA
avannakhét *136 D4* *var.* Khanthabouli. Savannakhét, S Laos
avanna-La-Mar *54 A5* W Jamaica
avaria *see* Szombathely
ave *100 B3* *Eng.* Save, *Ger.* Sau, *Hung.* Száva. *river* SE Europe
ave *see* Sava
ave, Rio *79 E3* *var.* Sabi. *river* Mozambique/Zimbabwe
averne *90 E3* *var.* Zabern; *anc.* Tres Tabernae. Bas-Rhin, NE France
avigliano *96 A2* Piemonte, NW Italy
avigsivik *see* Savissivik
avinski *see* Savinskiy
avinskiy *110 C3* *var.* Savinski. Arkhangel'skaya Oblast', NW Russian Federation
avissivik *82 D1* *var.* Savigsivik. Avannaarsua, N Greenland
avoie *91 D5* *cultural region* E France
avona *96 A2* Liguria, NW Italy
avu Sea *139 E5* *Ind.* Laut Sawu. *sea* S Indonesia
awakin *see* Suakin
awdirī *see* Sodiri
awhāj *72 B2* *var.* Sawhāj, *var.* Sohâg, Suliag. C Egypt
awhāj *see* Sawhāj
awqirah *121 D6* *var.* Suqrah. S Oman
awu, Laut *see* Savu Sea
axe *see* Sachsen
axony *see* Sachsen
ayaboury *see* Xaignabouli
ayanskiy Khrebet *112 D3* *mountain range* S Russian Federation
ayat *122 D3* *Rus.* Sayat. Lebap Welaýaty, E Turkmenistan
ayaxché *52 B2* Petén, N Guatemala
aydā/Sayida *see* Saïda
ayḥūt *121 D6* E Yemen
aynshand *127 E2* Dornogovĭ, SE Mongolia
ayre *41 E3* Pennsylvania, NE USA
ay'ūn *121 C6* *var.* Saywūn. C Yemen
aywūn *see* Say'ūn
calabis *see* Santarém
candinavia *66 D2* *geophysical region* NW Europe
carborough *89 D5* N England, United Kingdom
carpanto *see* Kárpathos
cebeli *see* Shebeli
chaan *94 E1* W Liechtenstein Europe
Schaerbeek *87 C6* Brussels, C Belgium
Schaffhausen *95 B7* *Fr.* Schaffhouse. Schaffhausen, N Switzerland
Schaffhouse *see* Schaffhausen
Schagen *86 C2* Noord-Holland, NW Netherlands
Schaulen *see* Šiauliai
Schebschi Mountains *see* Shebshi Mountains
Scheessel *94 B3* Niedersachsen, NW Germany
Schefferville *39 E2* Québec, E Canada
Schelde *see* Scheldt
Scheldt *87 B5* *Dut.* Schelde, *Fr.* Escaut. *river* W Europe
Schell Creek Range *47 D5* *mountain range* Nevada, W USA
Schenectady *41 F3* New York, NE USA
Schertz *49 G4* Texas, SW USA
Schiermonnikoog *86 D1* *Fris.* Skiermûntseach. *island* Waddeneilanden, N Netherlands
Schijndel *86 D4* Noord-Brabant, S Netherlands
Schil *see* Jiu
Schiltigheim *90 E3* Bas-Rhin, NE France
Schivelbein *see* Świdwin
Schleswig *94 B2* Schleswig-Holstein, N Germany
Schleswig-Holstein *94 B2* *state* N Germany
Schlettstadt *see* Sélestat
Schlochau *see* Człuchów
Schneekoppe *see* Sněžka
Schneidemühl *see* Piła
Schoden *see* Skuodas
Schönebeck *94 C4* Sachsen-Anhalt, C Germany
Schönlanke *see* Trzcianka
Schooten *see* Schoten
Schoten *87 C5* *var.* Schooten. Antwerpen, N Belgium
Schouwen *86 B4* *island* SW Netherlands
Schwabenalb *see* Schwäbische Alb
Schwäbische Alb *95 B6* *var.* Schwabenalb, *Eng.* Swabian Jura. *mountain range* S Germany
Schwandorf *95 C5* Bayern, SE Germany
Schwaz *95 C7* Tirol, W Austria
Schweidnitz *see* Świdnica
Schweinfurt *95 B5* Bayern, SE Germany
Schweiz *see* Switzerland
Schwerin *94 C3* Mecklenburg-Vorpommern, N Germany
Schwertberg *see* Świecie
Schwiebus *see* Świebodzin
Schwyz *95 B7* *var.* Schwiz. Schwyz, C Switzerland
Schyl *see* Jiu
Scio *see* Chíos
Scoresby Sound/Scoresbysund *see* Ittoqqortoormiit
Scoresby Sund *see* Kangertittivaq
Scotia Sea *57 C8* *sea* SW Atlantic Ocean
Scotland *88 C3* *cultural region* Scotland, U K
Scott Base *154 B4* *NZ research station* Antarctica
Scott Island *154 B5* *island* Antarctica
Scottsbluff *44 D3* Nebraska, C USA
Scottsboro *42 D1* Alabama, S USA
Scottsdale *48 B2* Arizona, SW USA
Scranton *41 F3* Pennsylvania, NE USA
Scrobesbyrig' *see* Shrewsbury
Scupi *see* Skopje
Scutari *see* Shkodër
Scutari, Lake *101 C5* *Alb.* Liqeni i Shkodrës, *SCr.* Skadarsko Jezero. *lake* Albania/Montenegro
Scyros *see* Skýros
Searcy *42 B1* Arkansas, C USA
Seattle *46 B2* Washington, NW USA
Sébaco *52 D3* Matagalpa, W Nicaragua
Sebaste/Sebastia *see* Sivas
Sebastían Vizcaíno, Bahía *50 A2* *bay* NW Mexico
Sebastopol *see* Sevastopol'
Sebenico *see* Šibenik
Sechura, Bahía de *60 A3* *bay* NW Peru
Secunderābād *134 D5* *var.* Sikandarabad. Telangana, C India
Sedan *90 D3* Ardennes, N France
Seddon *151 D5* Marlborough, South Island, New Zealand
Seddonville *151 C5* West Coast, South Island, New Zealand
Sédhiou *74 B3* SW Senegal
Sedlez *see* Siedlce
Sedona *48 B2* Arizona, SW USA
Sedunum *see* Sion
Seeland *see* Sjælland
Seenu Atoll *see* Addu Atoll
Seesen *94 B4* Niedersachsen, C Germany
Segestica *see* Sisak
Segezha *110 B3* Respublika Kareliya, NW Russian Federation
Seghedin *see* Szeged
Segna *see* Senj
Segodunum *see* Rodez
Ségou *74 D3* *var.* Segu. Ségou, C Mali
Segovia *92 D2* Castilla y León, C Spain
Segoviao Wangkí *see* Coco, Río
Segu *see* Ségou
Séguédine *75 H2* Agadez, NE Niger
Seguin *49 G4* Texas, SW USA
Segura *93 E4* *river* S Spain
Seinäjoki *85 D5* *Swe.* Östermyra. Länsi-Suomi, W Finland
Seine *90 D1* *river* N France
Seine, Baie de la *90 B3* *bay* N France
Sejong City *128 E4* *administrative capital* (South Korea) C South Korea
Sekondi *see* Sekondi-Takoradi
Sekondi-Takoradi *75 E5* *var.* Sekondi. S Ghana
Selânik *see* Thessaloníki
Selenga *127 E1* *Mong.* Selenge Mörön. *river* Mongolia/Russian Federation
Selenge Mörön *see* Selenga
Sélestat *90 E4* *Ger.* Schlettstadt. Bas-Rhin, NE France
Seleucia *see* Silifke
Selfoss *83 E5* Sudhurland, SW Iceland
Sélibabi *74 C3* *var.* Sélibaby. Guidimaka, S Mauritania
Sélibaby *see* Sélibabi
Selma *47 C6* California, W USA
Selseleh-ye Sefid Kuh *122 D4* *Eng.* Paropamisus Range. *mountain range* W Afghanistan
Selway River *46 D2* *river* Idaho, NW USA North America
Selwyn Range *148 B3* *mountain range* Queensland, C Australia
Selzaete *see* Zelzate
Semarang *138 C5* *var.* Samarang. Jawa, C Indonesia
Sembé *77 B5* Sangha, NW Congo
Semendria *see* Smederevo
Semey *114 D4* *prev.* Semipalatinsk. Vostochnyy Kazakhstan, E Kazakhstan
Semezhevo *see* Syemyezhava
Seminole *49 E3* Texas, SW USA
Seminole, Lake *42 D3* *reservoir* Florida/ Georgia, SE USA
Semipalatinsk *see* Semey
Semnān *120 D3* *var.* Samnān. Semnān, N Iran
Semois *87 C8* *river* SE Belgium
Sendai *130 D4* Miyagi, Honshū, C Japan
Sendai-wan *130 D4* *bay* E Japan
Senec *99 C6* *Ger.* Wartberg, *Hung.* Szenc; *prev.* Szempcz. Bratislavský Kraj, W Slovakia
Senegal *74 B3* *off.* Republic of Senegal, *Fr.* Sénégal. *country* W Africa

SENEGAL
West Africa

Official name Republic of Senegal
Formation 1960 / 1960
Capital Dakar
Population 14.1 million / 190 people per sq mile (73 people per sq km)
Total area 75,749 sq. miles (196,190 sq. km)
Languages Wolof, Pulaar, Serer, Diola, Mandinka, Malinké, Soninké, French*
Religions Sunni Muslim 95%, Christian (mainly Roman Catholic) 4%, Traditional beliefs 1%
Ethnic mix Wolof 43%, Serer 15%, Peul 14%, Other 14%, Toucouleur 9%, Diola 5%
Government Presidential system
Currency CFA franc = 100 centimes
Literacy rate 52%
Calorie consumption 2426 kilocalories

Senegal *74 C3* *Fr.* Sénégal. *river* W Africa
Senegal, Republic of *see* Senegal
Senftenberg *94 D4* Brandenburg, E Germany
Senia *see* Senj
Senica *99 C6* *Ger.* Senitz, *Hung.* Szenice. Trnavský Kraj, W Slovakia
Seniça *see* Sjenica
Senitz *see* Senica
Senj *100 A3* *Ger.* Zengg, *It.* Segna; *anc.* Senia. Lika-Senj, NW Croatia
Senja *84 C2* *prev.* Senjen. *island* N Norway
Senjen *see* Senja
Sejong City *128 E4* *country capital* (South Korea) (administrative) C South Korea
Senkaku-shoto *130 A3* *island group* SW Japan
Senlis *90 C3* Oise, N France
Sennar *72 C4* *var.* Sannār. Sinnar, C Sudan
Senones *see* Sens
Sens *90 C3* *anc.* Agendicum, Senones. Yonne, C France
Sensburg *see* Mrągowo
Sên, Stœng *137 D5* *river* C Cambodia
Senta *100 D3* *Hung.* Zenta. Vojvodina, N Serbia
Seo de Urgel *see* La Seu d'Urgell
Seoul *129 E4* *off.* Seoul Teukbyeolsi, *prev.* Sŏul, *Jap.* Keijō; *prev.* Kyŏngsŏng. *country capital* (South Korea) NW South Korea
Seoul Teukbyeolsi *see* Seoul
Şepşi-Sângeorz/Sepsiszentgyőrgy *see* Sfântu Gheorghe
Sept-Îles *39 E3* Québec, SE Canada
Seraing *87 D6* Liège, E Belgium
Serakhs *see* Sarahs
Seram, Laut *139 F4* *Eng.* Ceram Sea. *sea* E Indonesia
Pulau Seram *139 F4* *var.* Serang, *Eng.* Ceram. *island* Maluku, E Indonesia
Serang *138 C5* Jawa, C Indonesia
Serang *see* Seram, Pulau
Serasan, Selat *138 C3* *strait* Indonesia/ Malaysia
Serbia *100 D4* *off.* Federal Republic of Serbia; *prev.* Yugoslavia, *SCr.* Jugoslavija. *country* SE Europe

SERBIA
Southeast Europe

Official name Republic of Serbia
Formation 2006 / 2008
Capital Belgrade
Population 9.5 million / 318 people per sq mile (128 people per sq km)
Total area 29,905 sq miles (77,453 sq km)
Languages Serbian*, Hungarian (Magyar)
Religions Orthodox Christian 85%, Roman Catholic 6%, Other 6%, Muslim 3%
Ethnic mix Serb 83%, Other 10%, Magyar 4%, Bosniak 2%, Roma 1%
Government Parliamentary system
Currency Dinar = 100 para
Literacy rate 98%
Calorie consumption 2823 kilocalories

Serbia, Federal Republic of *see* Serbia
Sercq *see* Sark
Serdar *122 C2* *prev. Rus.* Gyzyrlabat, Kizyl-Arvat. Balkan Welaýaty, W Turkmenistan
Serdica *see* Sofiya
Serdobol' *see* Sortavala
Serenje *78 D2* Central, E Zambia
Seres *see* Sérres
Seret/Sereth *see* Siret
Serhetabat *122 D4* *prev. Rus.* Gushgy, Kushka. Mary Welaýaty, S Turkmenistan
Sérifos *105 C6* *anc.* Seriphos. *island* Kykládes, Greece, Aegean Sea
Seriphos *see* Sérifos
Serov *114 C3* Sverdlovskaya Oblast', C Russian Federation
Serowe *78 D3* Central, SE Botswana
Serpa Pinto *see* Menongue
Serpent's Mouth, The *59 F2* *Sp.* Boca de la Serpiente. *strait* Trinidad and Tobago/Venezuela
Serpiente, Boca de la *see* Serpent's Mouth, The
Serpukhov *111 B5* Moskovskaya Oblast', W Russian Federation

Sérrai see Sérres
Serrana, Cayo de 53 F2 island group NW Colombia South America
Serranilla, Cayo de 53 F2 island group NW Colombia South America Caribbean Sea
Serravalle 96 E1 N San Marino
Sérres 104 C3 var. Seres; prev. Sérrai. Kentrikí Makedonía, NE Greece
Sesdlets see Siedlce
Sesto San Giovanni 96 B2 Lombardia, N Italy
Sesvete 100 B2 Zagreb, N Croatia
Setabis see Xàtiva
Sète 91 C6 prev. Cette. Hérault, S France
Setesdal 85 A6 valley S Norway
Sétif 71 E2 var. Stif. N Algeria
Setté Cama 77 A6 Ogooué-Maritime, SW Gabon
Setúbal 92 B4 Eng. Saint Ubes, Saint Yves. Setúbal, W Portugal
Setúbal, Baía de 92 B4 bay W Portugal
Seul, Lac 38 B3 lake Ontario, S Canada
Sevan 117 G2 C Armenia
Sevan, Lake 117 G3 Eng. Lake Sevan, Rus. Ozero Sevan. lake E Armenia
Sevan, Lake/Sevan, Ozero see Sevana Lich
Sevastopol' 109 F5 Eng. Sebastopol. Avtonomna Respublika Krym, Ukraine
Severn 38 B2 river Ontario, S Canada
Severn 89 D6 Wel. Hafren. river England/Wales, United Kingdom
Severnaya Zemlya 115 E2 var. Nicholas II Land. island group N Russian Federation
Severnyy 110 E3 Respublika Komi, NW Russian Federation
Severodonetsk see Syeverodonets'k
Severodvinsk 110 C3 prev. Molotov, Sudostroy. Arkhangel'skaya Oblast', NW Russian Federation
Severomorsk 110 C2 Murmanskaya Oblast', NW Russian Federation
Seversk 114 D4 Tomskaya Oblast', C Russian Federation
Sevier Lake 44 A4 lake Utah, W USA
Sevilla 92 C4 Eng. Seville; anc. Hispalis. Andalucía, SW Spain
Seville see Sevilla
Sevlievo 104 D2 Gabrovo, N Bulgaria
Sevluš/Sevlyush see Vynohradiv
Seward's Folly see Alaska
Seychelles 79 G1 off. Republic of Seychelles. country W Indian Ocean

SEYCHELLES
Indian Ocean

Official name Republic of Seychelles
Formation 1976 / 1976
Capital Victoria
Population 90,846 / 874 people per sq mile (336 people per sq km)
Total area 176 sq. miles (455 sq. km)
Languages French Creole*, English*, French*
Religions Roman Catholic 82%, Anglican 6%, Other (including Muslim) 6%, Other Christian 3%, Hindu 2%, Seventh-day Adventist 1%
Ethnic mix Creole 89%, Indian 5%, Other 4%, Chinese 2%
Government Presidential system
Currency Seychelles rupee = 100 cents
Literacy rate 92%
Calorie consumption 2426 kilocalories

Seychelles, Republic of see Seychelles
Seyðisfjörður 83 E5 Austurland, E Iceland
Seýdi 122 D2 Rus. Seydi; prev. Neftezavodsk. Lebap Welaýaty, E Turkmenistan
Seyhan see Adana
Sfákia see Chóra Sfakíon
Sfântu Gheorghe 108 C4 Ger. Sankt-Georgen, Hung. Sepsiszentgyőrgy; prev. Şepşi-Sângeorz, Sfintu Gheorghe. Covasna, C Romania
Sfax 71 F2 Ar. Şafāqis. E Tunisia
Sfintu Gheorghe see Sfântu Gheorghe
's-Gravenhage 86 B4 var. Den Haag, Eng. The Hague, Fr. La Haye. country capital (Netherlands) (seat of government) Zuid-Holland, W Netherlands
's-Gravenzande 86 B4 Zuid-Holland, W Netherlands
Shaan/Shaanxi Sheng see Shaanxi
Shaanxi 128 B5 var. Shaan, Shaanxi Sheng, Shan-hsi, Shenshi, Shensi. province C China
Shabani see Zvishavane
Shabeelle, Webi see Shebeli
Shache 126 A3 var. Yarkant. Xinjiang Uygur Zizhiqu, NW China
Shacheng see Huailai
Shackleton Ice Shelf 154 D3 ice shelf Antarctica
Shaddādī see Ash Shadādah
Shāhābād see Eslāmābād-e Gharb
Sha Hi see Orūmīyeh, Daryācheh-ye
Shahjahanabad see Delhi
Shahr-e Kord 120 C3 var. Shahr Kord. Chahār MaḤall va Bakhtīārī, C Iran
Shahr Kord see Shahr-e Kord
Shāhrūd 120 D2 prev. Emāmrūd, Emāmshahr. Semnān, N Iran
Shalkar 114 B4 var. Chelkar. Aktyubinsk, W Kazakhstan
Shām, Bādiyat ash see Syrian Desert
Shana see Kuril'sk
Shandī see Shendi
Shandong 128 D4 var. Lu, Shandong Sheng, Shantung. province E China
Shandong Sheng see Shandong
Shanghai 128 D5 var. Shang-hai. Shanghai Shi, E China
Shangrao 128 D5 Jiangxi, S China
Shan-hsi see Shaanxi, China
Shan-hsi see Shanxi, China
Shannon 89 A6 Ir. An tSionainn. river W Ireland
Shan Plateau 136 B3 plateau E Myanmar (Burma)
Shansi see Shanxi
Shantar Islands see Shantarskiye Ostrova
Shantarskiye Ostrova 115 G3 Eng. Shantar Islands. island group E Russian Federation
Shantou 128 D6 var. Shan-t'ou, Swatow. Guangdong, S China
Shan-t'ou see Shantou
Shantung see Shandong
Shanxi 128 C4 var. Jin, Shan-hsi, Shansi, Shanxi Sheng. province C China
Shan Xian see Sanmenxia
Shanxi Sheng see Shanxi
Shaoguan 128 C6 var. Shao-kuan, Cant. Kukong; prev. Ch'u-chiang. Guangdong, S China
Shao-kuan see Shaoguan
Shaqrā' 120 B4 Ar Riyāḑ, C Saudi Arabia
Shaqrā see Shuqrah
Shar 114 D5 var. Charsk. Vostochnyy Kazakhstan, E Kazakhstan
Shari 130 D2 Hokkaidō, NE Japan
Shari see Chari
Sharjah see Ash Shāriqah
Shark Bay 147 A5 bay Western Australia
Sharqī, Al Jabal ash/Sharqi, Jebel esh see Anti-Lebanon
Shashe 78 D3 var. Shashi. river Botswana/Zimbabwe
Shashi see Shashe
Shatskiy Rise 125 G1 undersea rise N Pacific Ocean
Shawnee 49 G1 Oklahoma, C USA
Shaykh, Jabal ash see Hermon, Mount
Shchadryn 107 D7 Rus. Shchedrin. Homyel'skaya Voblasts', SE Belarus
Shchedrin see Shchadryn
Shcheglovsk see Kemerovo
Shchëkino 111 B5 Tul'skaya Oblast', W Russian Federation
Shchors 109 E1 Chernihivs'ka Oblast', N Ukraine
Shchuchin see Shchuchyn
Shchuchinsk 114 C4 prev. Shchuchye. Akmola, N Kazakhstan
Shchuchye see Shchuchinsk
Shchuchyn 107 B5 Pol. Szczuczyn Nowogródzki, Rus. Shchuchin. Hrodzyenskaya Voblasts', W Belarus
Shebekino 111 A6 Belgorodskaya Oblast', W Russian Federation
Shebelē Wenz, Wabē see Shebeli
Shebeli 73 D5 Amh. Wabē Shebelē Wenz, It. Scebeli, Som. Webi Shabeelle. river Ethiopia/Somalia
Sheberghān see Shibirghān
Sheboygan 40 B2 Wisconsin, N USA
Shebshi Mountains 76 A4 var. Schebschi Mountains. mountain range E Nigeria
Shechem see Nablus
Shedadi see Ash Shadādah
Sheffield 89 D5 N England, United Kingdom
Shekhem see Nablus
Sheki see Şäki
Shelby 44 B1 Montana, NW USA
Sheldon 45 F3 Iowa, C USA
Shelekhov Gulf 115 G2 Eng. Shelekhov Gulf. gulf E Russian Federation
Shelekhov Gulf see Shelikhova, Zaliv
Shendi 72 C4 var. Shandī. River Nile, NE Sudan
Shengking see Liaoning
Shenking see Liaoning
Shenshi/Shensi see Shaanxi
Shenyang 128 D3 Chin. Shen-yang, Eng. Moukden, Mukden; prev. Fengtien. province capital Liaoning, NE China
Shen-yang see Shenyang
Shepetivka 108 D2 Rus. Shepetovka. Khmel'nyts'ka Oblast', NW Ukraine
Shepetovka see Shepetivka
Shepparton 149 C7 Victoria, SE Australia
Sherbrooke 39 E4 Québec, SE Canada
Shereik 72 C3 River Nile, N Sudan
Sheridan 44 C2 Wyoming, C USA
Sherman 49 G2 Texas, SW USA
's-Hertogenbosch 86 C4 Fr. Bois-le-Duc, Ger. Herzogenbusch. Noord-Brabant, S Netherlands
Shetland Islands 88 D1 island group NE Scotland, United Kingdom
Shevchenko see Aktau
Shibarghān see Shibirghān
Shiberghan/Shiberghān see Shibirghān
Shibirghān 123 E3 var. Sheberghān, Shiberghan, Shiberghān. Jowzjān, N Afghanistan
Shibetsu 130 D2 var. Sibetu. Hokkaidō, NE Japan
Shibh Jazirat Sīnā' see Sinai
Shibirghān 123 E3 var. Shibarghān, Shiberghan, Shiberghān; prev. Sheberghān. Jowzjān, N Afghanistan
Shibushi-wan 131 B8 bay SW Japan
Shigatse see Xigazê
Shih-chia-chuang/Shihmen see Shijiazhuang
Shihezi 126 C2 Xinjiang Uygur Zizhiqu, NW China
Shiichi see Shyichy
Shijiazhuang 128 C4 var. Shih-chia-chuang; prev. Shihmen. province capital Hebei, E China
Shikārpur 134 B3 Sind, S Pakistan
Shikoku 131 C7 var. Sikoku. island SW Japan
Shikoku Basin 125 F2 var. Sikoku Basin. undersea basin N Philippine Sea
Shikotan, Ostrov 130 E2 Jap. Shikotan-tō. island NE Russian Federation
Shikotan-tō see Shikotan, Ostrov
Shilabo 73 D5 Sumalē, E Ethiopia
Shiliguri 135 F3 prev. Siliguri. West Bengal, NE India
Shilka 115 F4 river S Russian Federation
Shillong 135 G3 state capital Meghālaya, NE India
Shimanto see Nakamura
Shimbir Berris see Shimbiris
Shimbiris 72 E4 var. Shimbir Berris. mountain N Somalia
Shimoga 132 C2 Karnātaka, W India
Shimonoseki 131 A7 var. Simonoseki, hist. Akamagaseki, Bakan. Yamaguchi, Honshū, SW Japan
Shinano-gawa 131 C5 var. Sinano Gawa. river Honshū, C Japan
Shīndand 122 D4 prev. Shīndand. Herāt, W Afghanistan
Shīndand see Shīndand
Shingū 131 C6 var. Singû. Wakayama, Honshū, SW Japan
Shinjō 130 D4 var. Sinzyô. Yamagata, Honshū, C Japan
Shinyanga 73 C7 Shinyanga, NW Tanzania
Shiprock 48 C1 New Mexico, SW USA
Shirāz 120 D4 var. Shīrāz. Fārs, S Iran
Shishchitsy see Shyshchytsy
Shivpuri 134 D3 Madhya Pradesh, C India
Shizugawa 130 D4 Miyagi, Honshū, NE Japan
Shizuoka 131 D6 var. Sizuoka. Shizuoka, Honshū, S Japan
Shklov see Shklow
Shklow 107 D6 Rus. Shklov. Mahilyowskaya Voblasts', E Belarus
Shkodër 101 C5 var. Shkodra, It. Scutari, SCr. Skadar. Shkodër, NW Albania
Shkodra see Shkodër
Shkodrës, Liqeni i see Scutari, Lake
Shkumbinit, Lumi i 101 C6 var. Shkumbî, Shkumbin. river C Albania
Shkumbî/Shkumbin see Shkumbinit, Lumi i
Sholāpur see Solāpur
Shostka 109 F1 Sums'ka Oblast', NE Ukraine
Show Low 48 B2 Arizona, SW USA
Show Me State see Missouri
Shpola 109 E3 Cherkas'ka Oblast', N Ukraine
Shqipëria/Shqipërisë, Republika e see Albania
Shreveport 42 A2 Louisiana, S USA
Shrewsbury 89 D6 hist. Scrobesbyrig'. W England, United Kingdom
Shu 114 C5 Kaz. Shū. Zhambyl, SE Kazakhstan
Shuang-liao see Liaoyuan
Shū, Kazakhstan see Shu
Shumagin Islands 36 B3 island group Alaska, USA
Shumen 104 D2 Shumen, NE Bulgaria
Shumilina 107 E5 Rus. Shumilino. Vitsyebskaya Voblasts', NE Belarus
Shumilino see Shumilina
Shunsen see Chuncheon
Shuqrah 121 B7 var. Shaqrā. SW Yemen
Shwebo 136 B3 Sagaing, C Myanmar (Burma)
Shyichy 107 C7 Rus. Shiichi. Homyel'skaya Voblasts', SE Belarus
Shymkent 114 B5 prev. Chimkent. Yuzhnyy Kazakhstan, S Kazakhstan
Shyshchytsy 107 C6 Rus. Shishchitsy. Minskaya Voblasts', C Belarus
Siam see Thailand
Siam, Gulf of see Thailand, Gulf of
Sian see Xi'an
Siang see Brahmaputra
Siangtan see Xiangtan
Šiauliai 106 B4 Ger. Schaulen. Šiauliai, N Lithuania
Siazan' see Siyäzän
Sibay 111 D6 Respublika Bashkortostan, W Russian Federation
Šibenik 100 B4 It. Sebenico. Šibenik-Knin, S Croatia
Siberia 115 E3 var. Siberia. physical region NE Russian Federation
Siberia see Sibir'
Siberoet see Siberut, Pulau
Siberut, Pulau 138 A4 prev. Siberoet. island Kepulauan Mentawai, W Indonesia
Sibi 134 B2 Baluchistān, SW Pakistan
Sibir' 115 E3 var. Siberia. physical region NE Russian Federation
Sibiti 77 B6 Lékoumou, S Congo
Sibiu 108 B4 Ger. Hermannstadt, Hung. Nagyszeben. Sibiu, C Romania
Sibolga 138 B3 Sumatera, W Indonesia
Sibu 138 D3 Sarawak, East Malaysia
Sibut 76 C4 prev. Fort-Sibut. Kémo, S Central African Republic
Sibuyan Sea 139 E2 sea W Pacific Ocean
Sichon 137 C6 var. Ban Sichon, Si Chon. Nakhon Si Thammarat, SW Thailand
Si Chon see Sichon
Sichuan 128 B5 var. Chuan, Sichuan Sheng, Ssu-ch'uan, Szechuan, Szechwan. province C China
Sichuan Pendi 128 B5 basin C China
Sichuan Sheng see Sichuan
Sicilian Channel see Sicily, Strait of
Sicily 97 C7 Eng. Sicily; anc. Trinacria. island Italy, C Mediterranean Sea
Sicily, Strait of 97 B7 var. Sicilian Channel. strait C Mediterranean Sea
Sicuani 61 E4 Cusco, S Peru
Sidári 104 A4 Kérkyra, Iónia Nisiá, Greece, C Mediterranean Sea
Sidas 138 C4 Borneo, C Indonesia

Siderno *97 D7* Calabria, SW Italy
Sidhirókastron *see* Sidirókastro
Sīdī Barrānī *72 A1* NW Egypt
Sidi Bel Abbès *70 D2 var.* Sidi bel Abbès, Sidi-Bel-Abbès. NW Algeria
Sidirókastro *104 C3 prev.* Sidhirókastron. Kentrikí Makedonía, NE Greece
Sidley, Mount *154 B4 mountain* Antarctica
Sidney *44 D1* Montana, NW USA
Sidney *44 D4* Nebraska, C USA
Sidney *40 C4* Ohio, N USA
Sidon *see* Saïda
Sidra *see* Surt
Sidra/Sidra, Gulf of *see* Surt, Khalīj, N Libya
Siebenbürgen *see* Transylvania
Siedlce *98 E3 Ger.* Sedlez, *Rus.* Sesdlets. Mazowieckie, C Poland
Siegen *94 B4* Nordrhein-Westfalen, W Germany
Siemiatycze *98 E3* Podlaskie, NE Poland
Siena *96 B3 Fr.* Sienne; *anc.* Saena Julia. Toscana, C Italy
Sienne *see* Siena
Sieradz *98 C4* Sieradz, C Poland
Sierpc *98 D3* Mazowieckie, C Poland
Sierra Leone *74 C4 off.* Republic of Sierra Leone. *country* W Africa

SIERRA LEONE
West Africa

Official name Republic of Sierra Leone
Formation 1961 / 1961
Capital Freetown
Population 6.1 million / 221 people per sq mile (85 people per sq km)
Total area 27,698 sq. miles (71,740 sq. km)
Languages Mende, Temne, Krio, English*
Religions Muslim 60%, Christian 30%, Traditional beliefs 10%
Ethnic mix Mende 35%, Temne 32%, Other 21%, Limba 8%, Kuranko 4%
Government Presidential system
Currency Leone = 100 cents
Literacy rate 44%
Calorie consumption 2333 kilocalories

Sierra Leone Basin *66 C4 undersea basin* E Atlantic Ocean
Sierra Leone, Republic of *see* Sierra Leone
Sierra Leone Ridge *see* Sierra Leone Rise
Sierra Leone Rise *66 C4 var.* Sierra Leone Ridge, Sierra Leone Schwelle. *undersea rise* E Atlantic Ocean
Sierra Leone Schwelle *see* Sierra Leone Rise
Sierra Vista *48 B3* Arizona, SW USA
Sífnos *105 C6 anc.* Siphnos. *island* Kykládes, Greece, Aegean Sea
Sigli *138 A3* Sumatera, W Indonesia
Siglufjörður *83 E4* Nordhurland Vestra, N Iceland
Signal Peak *48 A2 mountain* Arizona, SW USA
Signan *see* Xi'an
Signy *154 A2 UK research station* South Orkney Islands, Antarctica
Siguatepeque *52 C2* Comayagua, W Honduras
Siguiri *74 D4* NE Guinea
Sihanoukville *137 D6 var.* Kâmpóng Saôm; *prev.* Kompong Som. Kâmpóng Saôm, SW Cambodia
Siilinjärvi *84 E4* Itä-Suomi, C Finland
Siirt *117 F4 var.* Sert; *anc.* Tigranocerta. Siirt, SE Turkey
Sikandarabad *see* Secunderābād
Sikasso *74 D4* Sikasso, S Mali
Sikeston *45 H5* Missouri, C USA
Sikhote-Alin', Khrebet *115 G4 mountain range* SE Russian Federation
Siking *see* Xi'an
Siklós *99 C7* Baranya, SW Hungary
Sikoku *see* Shikoku
Sikoku Basin *see* Shikoku Basin
Šilalė *106 B4* Tauragė, W Lithuania
Silchar *135 G3* Assam, NE India
Silesia *98 B4 physical region* SW Poland
Silifke *116 C4 anc.* Seleucia. İçel, S Turkey
Siliguri *see* Shiliguri
Siling Co *126 C5 lake* W China
Silinhot *see* Xilinhot
Silistra *104 E1 var.* Silistria; *anc.* Durostorum. Silistra, NE Bulgaria
Silistria *see* Silistra
Sillamäe *106 E2 Ger.* Sillamäggi. Ida-Virumaa, NE Estonia
Sillamäggi *see* Sillamäe
Sillein *see* Žilina
Šilutė *106 B4 Ger.* Heydekrug. Klaipėda, W Lithuania
Silvan *117 E4* Dıyarbakır, SE Turkey
Silva Porto *see* Kuito
Silver State *see* Colorado
Silver State *see* Nevada
Simanichy *107 C7 Rus.* Simonichi. Homyel'skaya Voblasts', SE Belarus
Simav *116 B3* Kütahya, W Turkey
Simav Çayı *116 A3 river* NW Turkey
Simbirsk *see* Ul'yanovsk
Simeto *97 C7 river* Sicilia, Italy, C Mediterranean Sea
Simeulue, Pulau *138 A3 island* NW Indonesia
Simferopol' *109 F5* Avtonomna Respublika Krym, S Ukraine
Simitla *104 C3* Blagoevgrad, SW Bulgaria
Şimlăul Silvaniei/Şimleul Silvaniei *see* Şimleu Silvaniei
Şimleu Silvaniei *108 B3 Hung.* Szilágysomlyó; *prev.* Şimlăul Silvaniei, Şimleul Silvaniei. Sălaj, NW Romania
Simonichi *see* Simanichy
Simonoseki *see* Shimonoseki
Simpelveld *87 D6* Limburg, SE Netherlands
Simplon Pass *95 B8 pass* S Switzerland
Simpson *see* Fort Simpson
Simpson Desert *148 B4 desert* Northern Territory/South Australia
Sinai *72 C2 var.* Sinai Peninsula, *Ar.* Shibh Jazirat Sīnā', Sīnā. *physical region* NE Egypt
Sinaia *108 C4* Prahova, SE Romania
Sinano Gawa *see* Shinano-gawa
Sīnā/Sinai Peninsula *see* Sinai
Sincelejo *58 B2* Sucre, NW Colombia
Sind *see* Sindh
Sindelfingen *95 B6* Baden-Württemberg, SW Germany
Sindh *134 B3 prev.* Sind. *province* SE Pakistan
Sindi *106 D2 Ger.* Zintenhof. Pärnumaa, SW Estonia
Sines *92 B4* Setúbal, S Portugal
Singan *see* Xi'an
Singapore *138 B3 country capital* (Singapore) (Singapore) S Singapore
Singapore *138 A1 off.* Republic of Singapore. *country* SE Asia

SINGAPORE
Southeast Asia

Official name Republic of Singapore
Formation 1965 / 1965
Capital Singapore
Population 5.4 million / 22,881 people per sq mile (8852 people per sq km)
Total area 250 sq. miles (648 sq. km)
Languages Mandarin*, Malay*, Tamil*, English*
Religions Buddhist 55%, Taoist 22%, Muslim 16%, Hindu, Christian, and Sikh 7%
Ethnic mix Chinese 74%, Malay 14%, Indian 9%, Other 3%
Government Parliamentary system
Currency Singapore dollar = 100 cents
Literacy rate 96%
Calorie consumption Not available

Singapore, Republic of *see* Singapore
Singen *95 B6* Baden-Württemberg, S Germany
Singida *73 C7* Singida, C Tanzania
Singkang *139 E4* Sulawesi, C Indonesia
Singkawang *138 C3* Borneo, C Indonesia
Singora *see* Songkhla
Singû *see* Shingū
Sining *see* Xining
Siniscola *97 A5* Sardegna, Italy, C Mediterranean Sea
Sinj *100 B4* Split-Dalmacija, SE Croatia
Sinkiang/Sinkiang Uighur Autonomous Region *see* Xinjiang Uygur Zizhiqu
Sinnamarie *see* Sinnamary
Sinnamary *59 H3 var.* Sinnamarie. N French Guiana
Sinneh *see* Sanandaj
Sînnicolau Mare *see* Sânnicolau Mare
Sinoe, Lacul *see* Sinoie, Lacul
Sinoie, Lacul *108 D5 prev.* Lacul Sinoe. *lagoon* SE Romania
Sinop *116 D2 anc.* Sinope. Sinop, Turkey
Sinope *see* Sinop
Sinsheim *95 B6* Baden-Württemberg, SW Germany
Sint Maarten *55 G3 Eng.* Saint Martin. *island* Lesser Antilles
Sint-Michielsgestel *86 C4* Noord-Brabant, S Netherlands
Sîn-Miclăuş *see* Gheorgheni
Sint-Niklaas *87 B5 Fr.* Saint-Nicolas. Oost-Vlaanderen, N Belgium
Sint-Pieters-Leeuw *87 B6* Vlaams Brabant, C Belgium
Sintra *92 B3 prev.* Cintra. Lisboa, W Portugal
Sinujiif *73 E5* Nugaal, NE Somalia
Sinus Aelaniticus *see* Aqaba, Gulf of
Sinus Gallicus *see* Lion, Golfe du
Sinyang *see* Xinyang
Sinzyô *see* Shinjō
Sion *95 A7 Ger.* Sitten; *anc.* Sedunum. Valais, SW Switzerland
Sioux City *45 F3* Iowa, C USA
Sioux Falls *45 F3* South Dakota, N USA
Sioux State *see* North Dakota
Siphnos *see* Sífnos
Siping *128 D3 var.* Ssu-p'ing, Szeping; *prev.* Ssu-p'ing-chieh. Jilin, NE China
Siple, Mount *154 A4 mountain* Siple Island, Antarctica
Siquirres *53 E4* Limón, E Costa Rica
Siracusa *97 D7 Eng.* Syracuse. Sicilia, Italy, C Mediterranean Sea
Sir Edward Pellew Group *148 B2 island group* Northern Territory, NE Australia
Siret *108 C3 var.* Siretul, *Ger.* Sereth, *Rus.* Seret. *river* Romania/Ukraine
Siretul *see* Siret
Siria *see* Syria
Sirikit Reservoir *136 C4 lake* N Thailand
Sīrjān *120 D4 prev.* Sa'īdābād. Kermān, S Iran
Sirna *see* Sýrna
Şırnak *117 F4* Şırnak, SE Turkey
Síros *see* Sýros
Sirte *see* Surt
Sirte, Gulf of *71 F2 Eng.* Gulf of Sidra, Gulf of Sirti, Sidra. *gulf* N Libya
Sirti, Gulf of *see* Surt, Khalīj
Sisak *100 B3 var.* Siscia, *Ger.* Sissek, *Hung.* Sziszek; *anc.* Segestica. Sisak-Moslavina, C Croatia
Siscia *see* Sisak
Sisimiut *82 C3 var.* Holsteinborg, Holsteinsborg, Holstenborg, Holstensborg. Kitaa, S Greenland
Sissek *see* Sisak
Sīstān, Daryācheh-ye *see* Şāberī, Hāmūn-e
Sitaş Cristuru *see* Cristuru Secuiesc
Siteía *105 D8 var.* Sitía. Kríti, Greece, E Mediterranean Sea
Sitges *93 G2* Cataluña, NE Spain
Sitía *see* Siteía
Sittang *see* Sittoung
Sittard *87 D5* Limburg, SE Netherlands
Sitten *see* Sion
Sittoung *136 B4 var.* Sittang. *river* S Myanmar (Burma)
Sittwe *136 A3 var.* Akyab. Rakhine State, W Myanmar (Burma)
Siuna *52 D3* Región Autónoma Atlántico Norte, NE Nicaragua
Siut *see* Asyūt
Sivas *116 D3 anc.* Sebastia, Sebaste. Sivas, C Turkey
Siverek *117 E4* Şanlıurfa, S Turkey
Siwa *see* Sīwah
Sīwah *72 A2 var.* Siwa. NW Egypt
Six Counties, The *see* Northern Ireland
Six-Fours-les-Plages *91 D6* Var, SE France
Siyäzän *117 H2 Rus.* Siazan'. NE Azerbaijan
Sjar *see* Sääre
Sjenica *101 D5 Turk.* Seniça. Serbia, SW Serbia
Skadar *see* Shkodër
Skadarsko Jezero *see* Scutari, Lake
Skagerak *see* Skagerrak
Skagerrak *85 A6 var.* Skagerak. *channel* N Europe
Skagit River *46 B1 river* Washington, NW USA
Skalka *84 C3 Lapp.* Skalkká. *lake* N Sweden
Skalkká *see* Skalka
Skarżysko-Kamienna *98 D4* Świętokrzyskie, C Poland
Skaudvilė *106 B4* Tauragė, SW Lithuania
Skegness *89 E6* E England, United Kingdom
Skellefteå *84 D4* Västerbotten, N Sweden
Skellefteälven *84 C4 river* N Sweden
Ski *85 B6* Akershus, S Norway
Skíathos *105 C5* Skíathos, Vóreies Sporádes, Greece, Aegean Sea
Skidal' *107 B5 Rus.* Skidel'. Hrodzyenskaya Voblasts', W Belarus
Skidel' *see* Skidal'
Skiermûntseach *see* Schiermonnikoog
Skierniewice *98 D3* Łódzkie, C Poland
Skiftet *106 C1 strait* Finland Atlantic Ocean Baltic Sea Gulf of Bothnia/Gulf of Finland
Skíros *see* Skýros
Skópelos *105 C5* Skópelos, Vóreies Sporádes, Greece, Aegean Sea
Skopje *101 D6 var.* Üsküb, *Turk.* Üsküp, *prev.* Skoplje; *anc.* Scupi. *country capital* (Macedonia) N FYR Macedonia
Skoplje *see* Skopje
Skovorodino *115 F4* Amurskaya Oblast', SE Russian Federation
Skudnesfjorden *85 A6 fjord* S Norway
Skuodas *106 B3 Ger.* Schoden, *Pol.* Szkudy. Klaipėda, NW Lithuania
Skye, Isle of *88 B3 island* NW Scotland, United Kingdom
Skylge *see* Terschelling
Skýros *105 C5 var.* Skíros. Skńyros, Vóreies Sporádes, Greece, Aegean Sea
Skýros *105 C5 var.* Skíros; *anc.* Scyros. *island* Vóreies Sporádes, Greece, Aegean Sea
Slagelse *85 B7* Sjælland, E Denmark
Slatina *100 C3 Hung.* Szlatina; *prev.* Podravska Slatina. Virovitica-Podravina, NE Croatia
Slatina *108 B5* Olt, S Romania
Slavgorod *see* Slawharad
Slavonski Brod *100 C3 Ger.* Brod, *Hung.* Bród; *prev.* Brod, Brod na Savi. Brod-Posavina, NE Croatia
Slavuta *108 C2* Khmel'nyts'ka Oblast', NW Ukraine
Slavyansk *see* Slov"yans'k
Slawharad *107 E7 Rus.* Slavgorod. Mahilyowskaya Voblasts', E Belarus
Sławno *98 C2* Zachodnio-pomorskie, NW Poland
Slēmānī *see* As Sulaymānīyah
Sliema *102 B5* N Malta
Sligo *89 A5 Ir.* Sligeach. Sligo, NW Ireland
Sliven *104 D2 var.* Slivno. Sliven, C Bulgaria
Slivnitsa *104 B2* Sofiya, W Bulgaria
Slivno *see* Sliven
Slobozia *108 C5* Ialomiţa, SE Romania
Slonim *107 B6 Pol.* Słonim. Hrodzyenskaya Voblasts', W Belarus
Słonim *see* Slonim
Slovakia *99 C6 off.* Slovenská Republika, *Ger.* Slowakei, *Hung.* Szlovákia, *Slvk.* Slovensko. *country* C Europe

SLOVAKIA
Central Europe

Official name Slovak Republic
Formation 1993 / 1993
Capital Bratislava
Population 5.5 million / 290 people per sq mile (112 people per sq km)
Total area 18,859 sq. miles (48,845 sq. km)
Languages Slovak*, Hungarian (Magyar), Czech
Religions Roman Catholic 69%, Nonreligious 13%, Other 13%, Greek Catholic (Uniate) 4%, Orthodox Christian 1%
Ethnic mix Slovak 86%, Magyar 10%, Roma 2%, Czech 1%, Other 1%
Government Parliamentary system
Currency Euro = 100 cents
Literacy rate 99%
Calorie consumption 2902 kilocalories

Slovak Ore Mountains *see* Slovenské rudohorie
Slovenia *95 D8 off.* Republic of Slovenia, *Ger.* Slowenien, *Slvn.* Slovenija. *country* SE Europe

SLOVENIA
Central Europe

Official name Republic of Slovenia
Formation 1991 / 1991
Capital Ljubljana
Population 2.1 million / 269 people per sq mile (104 people per sq km)
Total area 7820 sq. miles (20,253 sq. km)
Languages Slovenian*
Religions Roman Catholic 58%, Other 28%, Atheist 10%, Orthodox Christian 2%, Muslim 2%
Ethnic mix Slovene 83%, Other 12%, Serb 2%, Croat 2%, Bosniak 1%
Government Parliamentary system
Currency Euro = 100 cents
Literacy rate 99%
Calorie consumption 3173 kilocalories

Slovenia, Republic of *see* Slovenia
Slovenija *see* Slovenia
Slovenská Republika *see* Slovakia
Slovenské rudohorie *99 D6 Eng.* Slovak Ore Mountains, *Ger.* Slowakisches Erzgebirge, Ungarisches Erzgebirge. *mountain range* C Slovakia
Slovensko *see* Slovakia
Slov"yans'k *109 G3 Rus.* Slavyansk. Donets'ka Oblast', E Ukraine
Slowakei *see* Slovakia
Slowakisches Erzgebirge *see* Slovenské rudohorie
Slowenien *see* Slovenia
Słubice *98 B3 Ger.* Frankfurt. Lubuskie, W Poland
Sluch *108 D1 river* NW Ukraine
Słupsk *98 C2 Ger.* Stolp. Pomorskie, N Poland
Slutsk *107 C6* Minskaya Voblasts', S Belarus
Smallwood Reservoir *39 F2 lake* Newfoundland and Labrador, S Canada
Smara *70 B3 var.* Es Semara. N Western Sahara
Smarhon' *107 C5 Pol.* Smorgonie, *Rus.* Smorgon'. Hrodzyenskaya Voblasts', W Belarus
Smederevo *100 D4 Ger.* Semendria. Serbia, N Serbia
Smederevska Palanka *100 D4* Serbia, C Serbia
Smela *see* Smila
Smila *109 E2 Rus.* Smela. Cherkas'ka Oblast', C Ukraine
Smilten *see* Smiltene
Smiltene *106 D3 Ger.* Smilten. N Latvia
Smøla *84 A4 island* W Norway
Smolensk *111 A5* Smolenskaya Oblast', W Russian Federation
Smorgon'/Smorgonie *see* Smarhon'
Smyrna *see* İzmir
Snake *34 B4 river* Yukon, NW Canada
Snake River *46 C3 river* NW USA
Snake River Plain *46 D4 plain* Idaho, NW USA
Sneek *86 D2 Fris.* Snits. Fryslân, N Netherlands
Sneeuw-gebergte *see* Maoke, Pegunungan
Sněžka *98 B4 Ger.* Schneekoppe, *Pol.* Śnieżka. *mountain* N Czech Republic/ Poland
Śniardwy, Jezioro *98 D2 Ger.* Spirdingsee. *lake* NE Poland
Sniečkus *see* Visaginas
Śnieżka *see* Sněžka
Snina *99 E5 Hung.* Szinna. Prešovský Kraj, E Slovakia
Snits *see* Sneek
Snowdonia *89 C6 mountain range* NW Wales, United Kingdom
Snowdrift *see* Łutselk'e
Snow Mountains *see* Maoke, Pegunungan
Snyder *49 F3* Texas, SW USA
Sobradinho, Barragem de *see* Sobradinho, Represa de
Sobradinho, Represa de *63 F2 var.* Barragem de Sobradinho. *reservoir* E Brazil
Sochi *111 A7* Krasnodarskiy Kray, SW Russian Federation
Société, Îles de la/Society Islands *see* Société, Archipel de la
Society Islands *145 G4 var.* Archipel de Tahiti, Îles de la Société, *Eng.* Society Islands. *island group* W French Polynesia
Soconusco, Sierra de *see* Madre, Sierra
Socorro *48 D2* New Mexico, SW USA
Socorro, Isla *50 B5 island* W Mexico
Socotra *121 C7 var.* Sokotra, *Eng.* Socotra. *island* SE Yemen
Socotra *see* Suquṭrā
Soc Trăng *137 D6 var.* Khanh Hung. Soc Trăng, S Vietnam
Socuéllamos *93 E3* Castilla-La Mancha, C Spain
Sodankylä *84 D3* Lappi, N Finland
Sodari *see* Sodiri
Söderhamn *85 C5* Gävleborg, C Sweden
Södertälje *85 C6* Stockholm, C Sweden
Sodiri *72 B4 var.* Sawdirī, Sodari. Northern Kordofan, C Sudan
Soekaboemi *see* Sukabumi
Soemba *see* Sumba, Pulau
Soengaipenoeh *see* Sungaipenuh
Soerabaja *see* Surabaya
Soerakarta *see* Surakarta
Sofia *see* Sofiya
Sofiya *104 C2 var.* Sophia, *Eng.* Sofia, *Lat.* Serdica. *country capital* (Bulgaria) Sofiya-Grad, W Bulgaria
Sogamoso *58 B3* Boyacá, C Colombia
Sognefjorden *85 A5 fjord* NE North Sea
Sohâg *see* Sawhāj
Sohar *see* Ṣuḥār
Sohm Plain *66 B3 abyssal plain* NW Atlantic Ocean
Sohrau *see* Żory
Sokal' *108 C2 Rus.* Sokal. L'vivs'ka Oblast', NW Ukraine
Söke *116 A4* Aydın, SW Turkey
Sokhumi *117 E1 Rus.* Sukhumi. NW Georgia
Sokodé *75 F4* C Togo
Sokol *110 C4* Vologodskaya Oblast', NW Russian Federation
Sokółka *98 E3* Podlaskie, NE Poland
Sokolov *99 A5 Ger.* Falkenau an der Eger; *prev.* Falknov nad Ohří. Karlovarský Kraj, W Czech Republic
Sokone *74 B3* W Senegal
Sokoto *75 F3* Sokoto, NW Nigeria
Sokoto *75 F4 river* NW Nigeria
Sokotra *see* Suquṭrā
Solāpur *124 B3 var.* Sholāpur. Mahārāshtra, W India
Solca *108 C3 Ger.* Solka. Suceava, N Romania
Sol, Costa del *92 D5 coastal region* S Spain
Soldeu *91 B7* NE Andorra Europe
Solec Kujawski *98 C3* Kujawsko-pomorskie, C Poland
Soledad *58 B1* Atlántico, N Colombia
Isla Soledad *see* East Falkland
Soligorsk *see* Salihorsk
Solikamsk *114 C3* Permskiy Kray, NW Russian Federation
Sol'-Iletsk *111 D6* Orenburgskaya Oblast', W Russian Federation
Solingen *94 A4* Nordrhein-Westfalen, W Germany
Solka *see* Solca
Sollentuna *85 C6* Stockholm, C Sweden
Solo *see* Surakarta
Solok *138 B4* Sumatera, W Indonesia
Solomon Islands *144 C3 prev.* British Solomon Islands Protectorate. *country* W Solomon Islands N Melanesia W Pacific Ocean

SOLOMON ISLANDS
Australasia & Oceania

Official name Solomon Islands
Formation 1978 / 1978
Capital Honiara
Population 600,000 / 56 people per sq mile (21 people per sq km)
Total area 10,985 sq. miles (28,450 sq. km)
Languages English*, Pidgin English, Melanesian Pidgin, around 120 native languages
Religions Church of Melanesia34%, Roman Catholic 19%, South Seas Evangelical Church 17%, Methodist 11%, Seventh-day Adventist 10%, Other 9%
Ethnic mix Melanesian 93%, Polynesian 4%, Micronesian 2%, Other 1%
Government Parliamentary system
Currency Solomon Islands dollar = 100 cents
Literacy rate 77%
Calorie consumption 2473 kilocalories

Solomon Islands *144 C3 island group* Papua New Guinea/Solomon Islands
Solomon Sea *144 B3 sea* W Pacific Ocean
Soltau *94 B3* Niedersachsen, NW Germany
Sol'tsy *110 A4* Novgorodskaya Oblast', W Russian Federation
Solun *see* Thessaloníki
Solwezi *78 D2* North Western, NW Zambia
Sōma *130 D4* Fukushima, Honshū, C Japan
Somalia *73 D5 off.* Somali Democratic Republic, *Som.* Jamuuriyada Demuqraadiga Soomaaliyeed, Soomaaliya; *prev.* Italian Somaliland, Somaliland Protectorate. *country* E Africa

SOMALIA
East Africa

Official name Federal Republic of Somalia
Formation 1960 / 1960
Capital Mogadishu
Population 10.5 million / 43 people per sq mile (17 people per sq km)
Total area 246,199 sq. miles (637,657 sq. km)
Languages Somali*, Arabic*, English, Italian
Religions Sunni Muslim 99%, Christian 1%
Ethnic mix Somali 85%, Other 15%
Government Nonparty system
Currency Somali shilin = 100 senti
Literacy rate 24%
Calorie consumption 1696 kilocalories

Somali Basin *69 E5 undersea basin* W Indian Ocean
Somali Democratic Republic *see* Somalia
Somaliland *73 D5 disputed territory* N Somalia
Somaliland Protectorate *see* Somalia
Sombor *100 C3 Hung.* Zombor. Vojvodina, NW Serbia
Someren *87 D5* Noord-Brabant, SE Netherlands
Somerset *42 A5 var.* Somerset Village. W Bermuda
Somerset *40 C5* Kentucky, S USA
Somerset Island *42 A5 island* W Bermuda
Somerset Island *37 F2 island* Queen Elizabeth Islands, Nunavut, NW Canada
Somerset Village *see* Somerset
Somers Islands *see* Bermuda
Somerton *48 A2* Arizona, SW USA
Someș *108 B3 river* Hungary/Romania Europe
Somme *90 C2 river* N France
Sommerfeld *see* Lubsko
Somotillo *52 C3* Chinandega, NW Nicaragua
Somoto *52 D3* Madriz, NW Nicaragua
Songea *73 C8* Ruvuma, S Tanzania
Sŏngjin *see* Kimch'aek
Songkhla *137 C7 var.* Songkla, *Mal.* Singora. Songkhla, SW Thailand
Songkla *see* Songkhla
Sonoran Desert *48 A3 var.* Desierto de Altar. *desert* Mexico/USA
Sonsonate *52 B3* Sonsonate, W El Salvador
Soochow *see* Suzhou
Soomaaliya/Soomaaliyeed, Jamuuriyada Demuqraadiga *see* Somalia
Soome Laht *see* Finland, Gulf of
Sop Hao *136 D3* Houaphan, N Laos
Sophia *see* Sofiya
Sopianae *see* Pécs
Sopot *98 C2 Ger.* Zoppot. Pomorskie, N Poland
Sopron *99 B6 Ger.* Ödenburg. Győr-Moson-Sopron, NW Hungary
Sorau/Sorau in der Niederlausitz *see* Żary
Sorgues *91 D6* Vaucluse, SE France
Sorgun *116 D3* Yozgat, C Turkey
Soria *93 E2* Castilla y León, N Spain
Soroca *108 D3 Rus.* Soroki. N Moldova
Sorochino *see* Sarochyna
Soroki *see* Soroca
Sorong *139 F4* Papua, E Indonesia
Sørøy *see* Sørøya
Sørøya *84 C2 var.* Sørøy, *Lapp.* Sállan. *island* N Norway
Sortavala *110 B3 prev.* Serdobol'. Respublika Kareliya, NW Russian Federation
Sotavento, Ilhas de *74 A3 var.* Leeward Islands. *island group* S Cape Verde
Sotkamo *84 E4* Oulu, C Finland
Souanké *77 B5* Sangha, NW Congo
Soueida *see* As Suwaydā'
Souflí *104 D3 prev.* Souflíon. Anatolikí Makedonía kai Thráki, NE Greece
Souflíon *see* Souflí
Soufrière *55 F2* W Saint Lucia
Soukhné *see* As Sukhnah
Sŏul *see* Seoul
Soûr *119 A5 var.* Ṣūr; *anc.* Tyre. SW Lebanon
Souris River *45 E1 var.* Mouse River. *river* Canada/USA
Soúrpi *105 B5* Thessalía, C Greece
Sousse *71 F2 var.* Sūsah. NE Tunisia
South Africa *78 C4 off.* Republic of South Africa, *Afr.* Suid-Afrika. *country* S Africa

SOUTH AFRICA
Southern Africa

Official name Republic of South Africa
Formation 1934 / 1994
Capital Pretoria; Cape Town; Bloemfontein
Population 52.8 million / 112 people per sq mile (43 people per sq km)
Total area 471,008 sq. miles (1,219,912 sq. km)
Languages English*, isiZulu*, isiXhosa*, Afrikaans*, Sepedi*, Setswana*, Sesotho*, Xitsonga*, siSwati*, Tshivenda*, isiNdebele*
Religions Christian 68%, Traditional beliefs and animist 29%, Muslim 2%, Hindu 1%
Ethnic mix Black 89%, White 9%, Asian 2%
Government Presidential system
Currency Rand = 100 cents
Literacy rate 94%
Calorie consumption 3007 kilocalories

South Africa, Republic of *see* South Africa
South America *56 continent*
Southampton *89 D7 hist.* Hamwih, *Lat.* Clausentum. S England, United Kingdom
Southampton Island *37 G3 island* Nunavut, NE Canada
South Andaman *133 F2 island* Andaman Islands, India, NE Indian Ocean
South Australia *149 A5 state* S Australia
South Australian Basin *142 B5 undersea basin* SW Indian Ocean
South Bend *40 C3* Indiana, N USA
South Beveland *see* Zuid-Beveland
South Bruny Island *149 C8 island* Tasmania, SE Australia
South Carolina *43 E2 off.* State of South Carolina, *also known as* The Palmetto State. *state* SE USA
South Carpathians *see* Carpații Meridionalii
South China Basin *125 E4 undersea basin* SE South China Sea
South China Sea *125 E4 Chin.* Nan Hai, *Ind.* Laut Cina Selatan, *Vtn.* Biển Đông. *sea* SE Asia
South Dakota *44 D2 off.* State of South Dakota, *also known as* The Coyote State, Sunshine State. *state* N USA

Southeast Indian Ridge *141 D7 undersea ridge* Indian Ocean/Pacific Ocean
Southeast Pacific Basin *153 E5 var.* Belling Hausen Mulde. *undersea basin* SE Pacific Ocean
South East Point *149 C7 headland* Victoria, S Australia
Southend-on-Sea *89 E6* E England, United Kingdom
Southern Alps *151 B6 mountain range* South Island, New Zealand
Southern Cook Islands *145 F4 island group* S Cook Islands
Southern Cross *147 B6* Western Australia
Southern Indian Lake *37 F4 lake* Manitoba, C Canada
Southern Ocean *67 B7 ocean* Atlantic Ocean/Indian Ocean/Pacific Ocean
Southern Uplands *88 C4 mountain range* S Scotland, United Kingdom
South Fiji Basin *142 D4 undersea basin* S Pacific Ocean
South Geomagnetic Pole *154 B3 pole* Antarctica
South Georgia *57 D8 island* South Georgia and the South Sandwich Islands, SW Atlantic Ocean
South Goulburn Island *146 E2 island* Northern Territory, N Australia
South Huvadhu Atoll *132 A5 atoll* S Maldives
South Indian Basin *141 D7 undersea basin* Indian Ocean/Pacific Ocean
South Island *151 C6 island* S New Zealand
South Korea *129 E4 off.* Republic of Korea, *Kor.* Taehan Min'guk. *country* E Asia

SOUTH KOREA
East Asia

Official name Republic of Korea
Formation 1948 / 1953
Capital Seoul; Sejong City
Population 49.3 million / 1293 people per sq mile (499 people per sq km)
Total area 38,023 sq. miles (98,480 sq. km)
Languages Korean*
Religions Mahayana Buddhist 47%, Protestant 38%, Roman Catholic 11%, Confucianist 3%, Other 1%
Ethnic mix Korean 100%
Government Presidential system
Currency South Korean won = 100 chon
Literacy rate 99%
Calorie consumption 3329 kilocalories

South Lake Tahoe *47 C5* California, W USA
South Orkney Islands *154 A2 island group* Antarctica
South Ossetia *117 F2 former autonomous region* SW Georgia
South Pacific Basin *see* Southwest Pacific Basin
South Platte River *44 D4 river* Colorado/Nebraska, C USA
South Pole *154 B3 pole* Antarctica
South Sandwich Islands *57 D8 island group* SW Atlantic Ocean
South Sandwich Trench *57 E8 trench* SW Atlantic Ocean
South Shetland Islands *154 A2 island group* Antarctica
South Shields *88 D4* NE England, United Kingdom
South Sioux City *45 F3* Nebraska, C USA
South Sudan *73 B5 off.* Republic of South Sudan. *country* E Africa

SOUTH SUDAN
East Africa

Official name Republic of South Sudan
Formation 2011 / 2011
Capital Juba
Population 11.3 million / 45 people per sq mile (18 people per sq km)
Total area 248,777 sq. miles (644,329 sq. km)
Languages Arabic, Dinka, Nuer, Zande, Bari, Shilluk, Lotuko, English*

SOUTH SUDAN
(continued)

Religions Over 50% Christian beliefs
Ethnic mix Dinka 40%, Nuer 15%, Bari 10%, Shilluk/Anwak 10%, Azande 10%, Arab 10%, Other 5%
Government Transitional regime
Currency South Sudan pound = 100 piastres
Literacy rate 37%
Calorie consumption Not available

South Taranaki Bight *150 C4 bight* SE Tasman Sea
South Tasmania Plateau *see* Tasman Plateau
South Uist *88 B3 island* NW Scotland, United Kingdom
South-West Africa/South West Africa *see* Namibia
South West Cape *151 A8 headland* Stewart Island, New Zealand
Southwest Indian Ocean Ridge *see* Southwest Indian Ridge
Southwest Indian Ridge *141 B6 var.* Southwest Indian Ocean Ridge. *undersea ridge* SW Indian Ocean
Southwest Pacific Basin *143 E4 var.* South Pacific Basin. *undersea basin* SE Pacific Ocean
Sovereign Base Area *102 C5 uk military installation* S Cyprus
Soweto *78 D4* Gauteng, NE South Africa
Sōya-kaikyō *see* La Pérouse Strait
Spain *92 D3 off.* Kingdom of Spain, *Sp.* España; *anc.* Hispania, Iberia, *Lat.* Hispana. *country* SW Europe

SPAIN
Southwest Europe

Official name Kingdom of Spain
Formation 1492 / 1713
Capital Madrid
Population 46.9 million / 243 people per sq mile (94 people per sq km)
Total area 194,896 sq. miles (2504,782 sq. km)
Languages Spanish*, Catalan*, Galician*, Basque*
Religions Roman Catholic 96%, Other 4%
Ethnic mix Castilian Spanish 72%, Catalan 17%, Galician 6%, Basque 2%, Other 2%, Roma 1%
Government Parliamentary system
Currency Euro = 100 cents
Literacy rate 98%
Calorie consumption 3183 kilocalories

Spain, Kingdom of *see* Spain
Spalato *see* Split
Spanish Town *54 B5 hist.* St.Iago de la Vega. C Jamaica
Sparks *47 C5* Nevada, W USA
Sparta *see* Spárti
Spartanburg *43 E1* South Carolina, SE USA
Spárti *105 B6 Eng.* Sparta. Pelopónnisos, S Greece
Spearfish *44 D2* South Dakota, N USA
Speightstown *55 G1* NW Barbados
Spencer *45 F3* Iowa, C USA
Spencer Gulf *149 B6 gulf* South Australia
Spey *88 C3 river* NE Scotland, United Kingdom
Spice Islands *see* Maluku
Spiess Seamount *67 C7 seamount* S Atlantic Ocean
Spijkenisse *86 B4* Zuid-Holland, SW Netherlands
Spíli *105 C8* Kríti, Greece, E Mediterranean Sea
Spīn Bōldak *123 E5 prev.* Spīn Būldak. Kandahār, S Afghanistan
Spīn Būldak *see* Spīn Bōldak
Spirdingsee *see* Śniardwy, Jezioro
Spitsbergen *83 F2 island* NW Svalbard
Split *100 B4 It.* Spalato. Split-Dalmacija, S Croatia
Špoģi *106 D4* SE Latvia
Spokane *46 C2* Washington, NW USA
Spratly Islands *138 B2 Chin.* Nansha Qundao. *disputed territory* SE Asia
Spree *94 D4 river* E Germany
Springfield *40 B4 state capital* Illinois, N USA
Springfield *41 G3* Massachusetts, NE USA
Springfield *45 G5* Missouri, C USA
Springfield *40 C4* Ohio, N USA
Springfield *46 B3* Oregon, NW USA
Spring Garden *59 F2* NE Guyana
Spring Hill *43 E4* Florida, SE USA
Springs Junction *151 C5* West Coast, South Island, New Zealand
Springsure *148 D4* Queensland, E Australia
Sprottau *see* Szprotawa
Spruce Knob *41 E4 mountain* West Virginia, NE USA
Srbinje *see* Foča
Srbobran *100 D3 var.* Bácsszenttamás, *Hung.* Szenttamás. Vojvodina, N Serbia
Srebrenica *100 C4* Republika Srpska, E Bosnia and Herzegovina
Sredets *104 D2 prev.* Syulemeshlii. Stara Zagora, C Bulgaria
Sredets *104 E2 prev.* Grudovo. Burgas, E Bulgaria
Sremska Mitrovica *100 C3 prev.* Mitrovica, *Ger.* Mitrowitz. Vojvodina, NW Serbia
Srepok, Sông *see* Srêpôk, Tônle
Srêpôk, Tônle *137 E5 var.* Sông Srepok. *river* Cambodia/Vietnam
Sri Aman *138 C3* Sarawak, East Malaysia
Sri Jayewardenapura Kotte *132 D3 administrative capital* (Sri Lanka) *var.* Sri Jayawardanapura. Western Province, W Sri Lanka
Srīkākulam *135 F5* Andhra Pradesh, E India
Sri Lanka *132 D3 off.* Democratic Socialist Republic of Sri Lanka; *prev.* Ceylon. *country* S Asia

SRI LANKA
South Asia

Official name Democratic Socialist Republic of Sri Lanka
Formation 1948 / 1948
Capital Colombo; Sri Jayewardenapura Kotte
Population 21.3 million / 852 people per sq mile (329 people per sq km)
Total area 25,332 sq. miles (65,610 sq. km)
Languages Sinhala*, Tamil*, Sinhala-Tamil, English
Religions Buddhist 69%, Hindu 15%, Muslim 8%, Christian 8%
Ethnic mix Sinhalese 74%, Tamil 18%, Moor 7%, Other 1%
Government Presidential / parliamentary system
Currency Sri Lanka rupee = 100 cents
Literacy rate 91%
Calorie consumption 2488 kilocalories

Sri Lanka, Democratic Socialist Republic of *see* Sri Lanka
Srinagarind Reservoir *137 C5 lake* W Thailand
Srpska, Republika *100 B3 republic* Bosnia and Herzegovina
Ssu-ch'uan *see* Sichuan
Ssu-p'ing/Ssu-p'ing-chieh *see* Siping
Stabroek *87 B5* Antwerpen, N Belgium
Stade *94 B3* Niedersachsen, NW Germany
Stadskanaal *86 E2* Groningen, NE Netherlands
Stafford *89 D6* C England, United Kingdom
Staicele *106 D3* N Latvia
Ştaierdorf-Anina *see* Anina
Stájerlakanina *see* Anina
Stakhanov *109 H3* Luhans'ka Oblast', E Ukraine
Stalin *see* Varna
Stalinabad *see* Dushanbe
Stalingrad *see* Volgograd
Stalino *see* Donets'k
Stalinobod *see* Dushanbe
Stalinsk *see* Novokuznetsk
Stalinski Zaliv *see* Varnenski Zaliv
Stalin, Yazovir *see* Iskŭr, Yazovir
Stalowa Wola *98 E4* Podkarpackie, SE Poland
Stamford *41 F3* Connecticut, NE USA
Stampalia *see* Astypálaia
Stanislau *see* Ivano-Frankivs'k
Stanislav *see* Ivano-Frankivs'k
Stanisławów *see* Ivano-Frankivs'k
Stanke Dimitrov *see* Dupnitsa
Stanley *65 D7 var.* Port Stanley, Puerto Argentino. *dependent territory capital* (Falkland Islands) East Falkland, Falkland Islands
Stanleyville *see* Kisangani
Stann Creek *see* Dangriga
Stanovoy Khrebet *113 E3 mountain range* SE Russian Federation
Stanthorpe *149 D5* Queensland, E Australia
Staphorst *86 D2* Overijssel, E Netherlands
Starachowice *98 D4* Świętokrzyskie, C Poland
Stara Kanjiža *see* Kanjiža
Stara Pazova *100 D3 Ger.* Altpasua, *Hung.* Ópazova. Vojvodina, N Serbia
Stara Planina *see* Balkan Mountains
Stara Zagora *104 D2 Lat.* Augusta Trajana. Stara Zagora, C Bulgaria
Starbuck Island *145 G3 prev.* Volunteer Island. *island* E Kiribati
Stargard in Pommern *see* Stargard Szczeciński
Stargard Szczeciński *98 B3 Ger.* Stargard in Pommern. Zachodnio-pomorskie, NW Poland
Stari Bečej *see* Bečej
Starobel'sk *see* Starobil's'k
Starobil's'k *109 H2 Rus.* Starobel'sk. Luhans'ka Oblast', E Ukraine
Starobin *107 C7 var.* Starobyn. Minskaya Voblasts', S Belarus
Starobyn *see* Starobin
Starogard Gdański *98 C2 Ger.* Preussisch-Stargard. Pomorskie, N Poland
Starokonstantinov *see* Starokostyantyniv
Starokostyantyniv *108 D2 Rus.* Starokonstantinov. Khmel'nyts'ka Oblast', NW Ukraine
Starominskaya *111 A7* Krasnodarskiy Kray, SW Russian Federation
Staryya Darohi *107 C6 Rus.* Staryye Dorogi. Minskaya Voblasts', S Belarus
Staryye Dorogi *see* Staryya Darohi
Staryy Oskol *111 B6* Belgorodskaya Oblast', W Russian Federation
State College *41 E4* Pennsylvania, NE USA
Staten Island *see* Estados, Isla de los
Statesboro *43 E2* Georgia, SE USA
States, The *see* United States of America
Staunton *41 E5* Virginia, NE USA
Stavanger *85 A6* Rogaland, S Norway
Stavers Island *see* Vostok Island
Stavropol' *111 B7 prev.* Voroshilovsk. Stavropol'skiy Kray, SW Russian Federation
Stavropol' *see* Tol'yatti
Steamboat Springs *44 C4* Colorado, C USA
Steenwijk *86 D2* Overijssel, N Netherlands
Steier *see* Steyr
Steierdorf/Steierdorf-Anina *see* Anina
Steinamanger *see* Szombathely
Steinkjer *84 B4* Nord-Trøndelag, C Norway
Stejarul *see* Karapelit
Stendal *94 C3* Sachsen-Anhalt, C Germany
Stepanakert *see* Xankändi
Stephenville *49 F3* Texas, SW USA
Sterling *44 D4* Colorado, C USA
Sterling *40 B3* Illinois, N USA
Sterlitamak *114 B3* Respublika Bashkortostan, W Russian Federation
Stettin *see* Szczecin
Stettiner Haff *see* Szczeciński, Zalew
Stevenage *89 E6* E England, United Kingdom
Stevens Point *40 B2* Wisconsin, N USA
Stewart Island *151 A8 island* S New Zealand
Steyerlak-Anina *see* Anina
Steyr *95 D6 var.* Steier. Oberösterreich, N Austria
St. Helena Bay *78 B5 bay* SW South Africa
Stif *see* Sétif

Stillwater *49 G1* Oklahoma, C USA
Štip *101 E6* E FYR Macedonia
Stirling *88 C4* C Scotland, United Kingdom
Stjørdalshalsen *84 B4* Nord-Trøndelag, C Norway
St-Maur-des-Fossés *90 E2* Val-de-Marne, Île-de-France, N France Europe
Stockach *95 B6* Baden-Württemberg, S Germany
Stockholm *85 C6 country capital* (Sweden) Stockholm, C Sweden
Stockmannshof *see* Pļaviņas
Stockton *47 B6* California, W USA
Stockton Plateau *49 E4 plain* Texas, SW USA
Stœng Trĕng *137 D5 prev.* Stung Treng. Stœng Trêng, NE Cambodia
Stoke *see* Stoke-on-Trent
Stoke-on-Trent *89 D6 var.* Stoke. C England, United Kingdom
Stolbce *see* Stowbtsy
Stolbtsy *see* Stowbtsy
Stolp *see* Słupsk
Stolpmünde *see* Ustka
Stómio *104 B4* Thessalía, C Greece
Store Bælt *see* Storebælt
Storebelt *see* Storebælt
Støren *85 B5* Sør-Trøndelag, S Norway
Storfjorden *83 G2 fjord* S Norway
Storhammer *see* Hamar
Stornoway *88 B2* NW Scotland, United Kingdom
Storsjön *85 B5 lake* C Sweden
Storuman *84 C4* Västerbotten, N Sweden
Storuman *84 C4 lake* N Sweden
Stowbtsy *107 C6 Pol.* Stolbce, *Rus.* Stolbtsy. Minskaya Voblasts', C Belarus
Strabane *89 B5 Ir.* An Srath Bán. W Northern Ireland, United Kingdom
Strakonice *99 A5 Ger.* Strakonitz. Jihočeský Kraj, S Czech Republic
Strakonitz *see* Strakonice
Stralsund *94 D2* Mecklenburg-Vorpommern, NE Germany
Stranraer *89 C5* S Scotland, United Kingdom
Strasbourg *90 E3 Ger.* Strassburg; *anc.* Argentoratum. Bas-Rhin, NE France
Strășeni *108 D3 var.* Strasheny. C Moldova
Strasheny *see* Strășeni
Strassburg *see* Strasbourg, France
Strassburg *see* Aiud, Romania
Stratford *150 D4* Taranaki, North Island, New Zealand
Strathfield *148 E2* New South Wales, E Australia
Straubing *95 C6* Bayern, SE Germany
Strehaia *108 B5* Mehedinți, SW Romania
Strelka *114 D4* Krasnoyarskiy Kray, C Russian Federation
Strigonium *see* Esztergom
Strofilia *see* Strofyliá
Strofyliá *105 C5 var.* Strofilia. Évvoia, C Greece
Stromboli *97 D6 island* Isole Eolie, S Italy
Stromeferry *88 C3* N Scotland, United Kingdom
Strömstad *85 B6* Västra Götaland, S Sweden
Strömsund *84 C4* Jämtland, C Sweden
Struga *101 D6* SW FYR Macedonia
Struma *see* Strymónas
Strumica *101 E6* E FYR Macedonia
Strumyani *104 C3* Blagoevgrad, SW Bulgaria
Strymónas *104 C3 Bul.* Struma. *river* Bulgaria/Greece
Stryy *108 B2* L'vivs'ka Oblast', NW Ukraine
Studholme *151 B6* Canterbury, South Island, New Zealand
Stuhlweissenberg *see* Székesfehérvár
Stung Treng *see* Stœng Trĕng
Sturgis *44 D3* South Dakota, N USA
Stuttgart *95 B6* Baden-Württemberg, SW Germany
Stykkishólmur *83 E4* Vesturland, W Iceland
Styr *108 C1 Rus.* Styr'. *river* Belarus/Ukraine
Su *see* Jiangsu
Suakin *72 C3 var.* Sawakin. Red Sea, NE Sudan
Subačius *106 C4* Panevėžys, NE Lithuania
Subaykhān *118 E3* Dayr az Zawr, E Syria
Subotica *100 D2 Ger.* Maria-Theresiopel, *Hung.* Szabadka. Vojvodina, N Serbia
Suceava *108 C3 Ger.* Suczawa, *Hung.* Szucsava. Suceava, NE Romania
Su-chou *see* Suzhou
Suchow *see* Xuzhou, Jiangsu, China
Suchow *see* Suzhou, Jiangsu, China
Sucker State *see* Illinois
Sucre *61 F4 hist.* Chuquisaca, La Plata. *country capital* (Bolivia-legal capital) Chuquisaca, S Bolivia
Suczawa *see* Suceava
Sudan *72 A4 off.* Republic of Sudan, *Ar.* Jumhuriyat as-Sudan; *prev.* Anglo-Egyptian Sudan. *country* N Africa

SUDAN
East Africa

Official name Republic of the Sudan
Formation 1956 / 2011
Capital Khartoum
Population 38 million / 53 people per sq mile (20 people per sq km)
Total area 718,722 sq. miles (1,861,481 sq. km)
Languages Arabic*, Nubian, Beja, Fur
Religions Nearly the whole population is Muslim (mainly Sunni)
Ethnic mix Arab 60%, Other 18%, Nubian 10%, Beja 8%, Fur 3%, Zaghawa 1%
Government Presidential system
Currency New Sudanese pound = 100 piastres
Literacy rate 73%
Calorie consumption 2346 kilocalories

Sudanese Republic *see* Mali
Sudan, Jumhuriyat as- *see* Sudan
Sudan, Republic of *see* Sudan
Sudbury *38 C4* Ontario, S Canada
Sudd *73 B5 swamp region* C South Sudan
Sudeten *98 B4 var.* Sudetes, Sudetic Mountains, *Cz./Pol.* Sudety. *mountain range* Czech Republic/Poland
Sudetes/Sudetic Mountains/Sudety *see* Sudeten
Südkarpaten *see* Carpații Meridionalii
Südliche Morava *see* Južna Morava
Sudong, Pulau *138 A2 island* SW Singapore Asia
Sudostroy *see* Severodvinsk
Sue *73 B5 river* W South Sudan
Sueca *93 F3* Valenciana, E Spain
Sue Wood Bay *42 B5 bay* W Bermuda North America W Atlantic Ocean
Suez *72 B1 Ar.* As Suways, El Suweis. NE Egypt
Suez Canal *72 B1 Ar.* Qanāt as Suways. *canal* NE Egypt
Suez, Gulf of *see* Khalīj as Suways
Suğla Gölü *116 C4 lake* SW Turkey
Şuḩār *121 D5 var.* Sohar. N Oman
Sühbaatar *127 E1* Selenge, N Mongolia
Suhl *95 C5* Thüringen, C Germany
Suicheng *see* Suixi
Suid-Afrika *see* South Africa
Suidwes-Afrika *see* Namibia
Suixi *128 C6 var.* Suicheng. Guangdong, S China
Sujāwal *134 B3* Sind, SE Pakistan
Sukabumi *138 C5 prev.* Soekaboemi. Jawa, C Indonesia
Sukagawa *131 D5* Fukushima, Honshū, C Japan
Sukarnapura *see* Jayapura
Sukarno, Puntjak *see* Jaya, Puncak
Sukhne *see* As Sukhnah
Sukhona *110 C4 var.* Tot'ma. *river* NW Russian Federation
Sukhumi *see* Sokhumi
Sukkertoppen *see* Maniitsoq
Sukkur *134 B3* Sind, SE Pakistan
Sukumo *131 B7* Kōchi, Shikoku, SW Japan
Sulaimaniya *see* As Sulaymānīyah
Sulaiman Range *134 C2 mountain range* C Pakistan
Sula, Kepulauan *139 E4 island group* C Indonesia
Sulawesi, Laut *see* Celebes Sea
Sulechów *98 B3 Ger.* Züllichau. Lubuskie, W Poland
Suliag *see* Sawhāj
Sullana *60 B2* Piura, NW Peru
Sullivan Island *see* Lanbi Kyun
Sulphur Springs *49 G2* Texas, SW USA
Sultānābād *see* Arāk
Sulu Archipelago *139 E3 island group* SW Philippines
Sülüktü *see* Sulyukta
Sulu, Laut *see* Sulu Sea
Sulu Sea *139 E2 var.* Laut Sulu. *sea* SW Philippines
Sulyukta *123 E2 Kir.* Sülüktü. Batkenskaya Oblast', SW Kyrgyzstan
Sumatra *137 B8 Eng.* Sumatra. *island* W Indonesia
Sumatra *see* Sumatera
Šumava *see* Bohemian Forest
Sumba, Pulau *139 E5 Eng.* Sandalwood Island; *prev.* Soemba. *island* Nusa Tenggara, C Indonesia
Sumba, Selat *139 E5 strait* Nusa Tenggara, S Indonesia
Sumbawanga *73 B7* Rukwa, W Tanzania
Sumbe *78 B2 var.* N'Gunza, *Port.* Novo Redondo. Cuanza Sul, W Angola
Sumeih *73 B5* Southern Darfur, S Sudan
Sumgait *see* Sumqayıt, Azerbaijan
Summer Lake *46 B4 lake* Oregon, NW USA
Summit *93 H5* Alaska, USA
Sumqayıt *117 H2 Rus.* Sumgait. E Azerbaijan
Sumy *109 F2* Sums'ka Oblast', NE Ukraine
Sunbury *149 C7* Victoria, SE Australia
Sunda Islands *see* Greater Sunda Islands
Sunda, Selat *138 B5 strait* Jawa/Sumatera, SW Indonesia
Sunda Trench *see* Java Trench
Sunderland *88 D4 var.* Wearmouth. NE England, United Kingdom
Sundsvall *85 C5* Västernorrland, C Sweden
Sunflower State *see* Kansas
Sungaipenuh *138 B4 prev.* Soengaipenoeh. Sumatera, W Indonesia
Sunnyvale *47 A6* California, W USA
Sunset State *see* Oregon
Sunshine State *see* Florida
Sunshine State *see* New Mexico
Sunshine State *see* South Dakota
Suntar *115 F3* Respublika Sakha (Yakutiya), NE Russian Federation
Sunyani *75 E5* W Ghana
Suoločielgi *see* Saariselkä
Suomenlahti *see* Finland, Gulf of
Suomen Tasavalta/Suomi *see* Finland
Suomussalmi *84 E4* Oulu, E Finland
Suŏng *137 D6* Kâmpóng Cham, C Cambodia
Suoyarvi *110 B3* Respublika Kareliya, NW Russian Federation
Supe *60 C3* Lima, W Peru
Supérieur, Lac *see* Superior, Lake
Superior *40 A1* Wisconsin, N USA
Superior, Lake *40 B1 Fr.* Lac Supérieur. *lake* Canada/USA
Suqrah *see* Şawqirah
Şūr *121 E5* NE Oman
Şūr *see* Soûr
Surabaja *see* Surabaya
Surabaya *138 D5 prev.* Surabaja, Soerabaja. Jawa, C Indonesia
Surakarta *138 C5 Eng.* Solo; *prev.* Soerakarta. Jawa, S Indonesia
Šurany *99 C6 Hung.* Nagysurány. Nitriansky Kraj, SW Slovakia
Sūrat *134 C4* Gujarāt, W India
Suratdhani *see* Surat Thani
Surat Thani *137 C6 var.* Suratdhani. Surat Thani, SW Thailand
Surazh *107 E5* Vitsyebskaya Voblasts', NE Belarus
Surdulica *101 E5* Serbia, SE Serbia
Sûre *87 D7 var.* Sauer. *river* W Europe
Surendranagar *134 C4* Gujarāt, W India
Surfers Paradise *149 E5* Queensland, E Australia
Surgut *114 D3* Khanty-Mansiyskiy Avtonomnyy Okrug-Yugra, C Russian Federation
Surin *137 D5* Surin, E Thailand
Surinam *see* Suriname
Suriname *59 G3 off.* Republic of Suriname, *var.* Surinam; *prev.* Dutch Guiana, Netherlands Guiana. *country* N South America

SURINAME
South America

Official name Republic of Suriname
Formation 1975 / 1975
Capital Paramaribo
Population 500,000 / 8 people per sq mile (3 people per sq km)
Total area 63,039 sq. miles (163,270 sq. km)
Languages Sranan (Creole), Dutch*, Javanese, Sarnami Hindi, Saramaccan, Chinese, Carib
Religions Hindu 27%, Protestant 25%, Roman Catholic 23%, Muslim 20%, Traditional beliefs 5%
Ethnic mix East Indian 27%, Creole 18%, Black 15%, Javanese 15%, Mixed race 13%, Other 6%, Amerindian 4%, Chinese 2%
Government Presidential / parliamentary system
Currency Surinamese dollar = 100 cents
Literacy rate 95%
Calorie consumption 2727 kilocalories

Suriname, Republic of *see* Suriname
Sūrīya/Sūrīyah, Al-Jumhūrīyah al-'Arabīyah as- *see* Syria
Surkhab, Darya-i- *see* Kahmard, Daryā-ye
Surkhob *123 F3 river* C Tajikistan
Surt *71 G2 var.* Sidra, Sirte. N Libya
Surtsey *83 E5 island* S Iceland
Suruga-wan *131 D6 bay* SE Japan
Susa *96 A2* Piemonte, NE Italy
Sūsah *see* Sousse
Susanville *47 B5* California, W USA
Susitna *36 C3* Alaska, USA
Susteren *87 D5* Limburg, SE Netherlands
Susuman *115 G3* Magadanskaya Oblast', E Russian Federation
Sutlej *134 C2 river* India/Pakistan
Suur Munamägi *106 D3 var.* Munamägi, *Ger.* Eier-Berg. *mountain* SE Estonia
Suur Väin *106 C2 Ger.* Grosser Sund. *strait* W Estonia
Suva *145 E4 country capital* (Fiji) Viti Levu, W Fiji
Suvalkai/Suvalki *see* Suwałki
Suvorovo *104 E2 prev.* Vetrino. Varna, E Bulgaria
Suwałki *98 E2 Lith.* Suvalkai, *Rus.* Suvalki. Podlaskie, NE Poland
Şuwār *see* Aş Şuwār
Suways, Qanāt as *see* Suez Canal
Suweida *see* As Suwaydā'
Suzhou *128 D5 var.* Soochow, Su-chou, Suchow; *prev.* Wuhsien. Jiangsu, E China
Svalbard *83 E1 Norwegian dependency* Arctic Ocean
Svartisen *84 C3 glacier* C Norway
Svay Riĕng *137 D6* Svay Riĕng, S Cambodia
Sveg *85 B5* Jämtland, C Sweden
Svenstavik *85 C5* Jämtland, C Sweden
Sverdlovsk *see* Yekaterinburg
Sverige *see* Sweden
Sveti Vrach *see* Sandanski
Svetlogorsk *see* Svyetlahorsk
Svetlograd *111 B7* Stavropol'skiy Kray, SW Russian Federation
Svetlovodsk *see* Svitlovods'k
Svetozarevo *see* Jagodina
Svilengrad *104 D3 prev.* Mustafa-Pasha. Khaskovo, S Bulgaria
Svitlovods'k *109 F3 Rus.* Svetlovodsk. Kirovohrads'ka Oblast', C Ukraine
Svizzera *see* Switzerland
Svobodnyy *115 G4* Amurskaya Oblast', SE Russian Federation
Svyataya Anna Trough *155 C4 var.* Saint Anna Trough. *trough* N Kara Sea
Svyetlahorsk *107 D7 Rus.* Svetlogorsk. Homyel'skaya Voblasts', SE Belarus
Swabian Jura *see* Schwäbische Alb
Swakopmund *78 B3* Erongo, W Namibia
Swan Islands *53 E1 island group* NE Honduras North America
Swansea *89 C7 Wel.* Abertawe. S Wales, United Kingdom
Swarzędz *98 C3* Poznań, W Poland

Swatow *see* Shantou
Swaziland *78 D4 off.* Kingdom of Swaziland. *country* S Africa

SWAZILAND
Southern Africa

Official name Kingdom of Swaziland
Formation 1968 / 1968
Capital Mbabane
Population 1.2 million / 181 people per sq mile (70 people per sq km)
Total area 6704 sq. miles (17,363 sq. km)
Languages English*, siSwati*, isiZulu, Xitsonga
Religions Traditional beliefs 40%, Other 30%, Roman Catholic 20%, Muslim 10%
Ethnic mix Swazi 97%, Other 3%
Government Monarchy
Currency Lilangeni = 100 cents
Literacy rate 83%
Calorie consumption 2275 kilocalories

Swaziland, Kingdom of *see* Swaziland
Sweden *84 B4 off.* Kingdom of Sweden, *Swe.* Sverige. *country* N Europe

SWEDEN
Northern Europe

Official name Kingdom of Sweden
Formation 1523 / 1921
Capital Stockholm
Population 9.6 million / 60 people per sq mile (23 people per sq km)
Total area 173,731 sq. miles (449,964 sq. km)
Languages Swedish*, Finnish, Sámi
Religions Evangelical Lutheran 75%, Other 13%, Muslim 5%, Other Protestant 5%, Roman Catholic 2%
Ethnic mix Swedish 86%, Foreign-born or first-generation immigrant 12%, Finnish and Sámi 2%
Government Parliamentary system
Currency Swedish krona = 100 öre
Literacy rate 99%
Calorie consumption 3160 kilocalories

Sweden, Kingdom of *see* Sweden
Sweetwater *49 F3* Texas, SW USA
Świdnica *98 B4 Ger.* Schweidnitz. Wałbrzych, SW Poland
Świdwin *98 B2 Ger.* Schivelbein. Zachodnio-pomorskie, NW Poland
Świebodzice *98 B4 Ger.* Freiburg in Schlesien, Swiebodzice. Walbrzych, SW Poland
Świebodzin *98 B3 Ger.* Schwiebus. Lubuskie, W Poland
Świecie *98 C3 Ger.* Schwertberg. Kujawsko-pomorskie, C Poland
Swindon *89 D7* S England, United Kingdom
Swinemünde *see* Świnoujście
Świnoujście *98 B2 Ger.* Swinemünde. Zachodnio-pomorskie, NW Poland
Swiss Confederation *see* Switzerland
Switzerland *95 A7 off.* Swiss Confederation, *Fr.* La Suisse, *Ger.* Schweiz, *It.* Svizzera; *anc.* Helvetia. *country* C Europe

SWITZERLAND
Central Europe

Official name Swiss Confederation
Formation 1291 / 1857
Capital Bern
Population 8.1 million / 528 people per sq mile (204 people per sq km)
Total area 15,942 sq. miles (41,290 sq. km)
Languages German*, Swiss-German, French*, Italian*, Romansch
Religions Roman Catholic 42%, Protestant 35%, Other and nonreligious 19%, Muslim 4%
Ethnic mix German 64%, French 20%, Other 9.5%, Italian 6%, Romansch 0.5%**Government** Parliamentary system
Currency Swiss franc = 100 rappen/centimes
Literacy rate 99%
Calorie consumption 3487 kilocalories

ycaminum *see* Hefa
ydenham Island *see* Nonouti
Sydney *148 D1 state capital* New South Wales, SE Australia
Sydney *39 G4* Cape Breton Island, Nova Scotia, SE Canada
Sydney Island *see* Manra
Syedpur *see* Saidpur
Syemyezhava *107 C6 Rus.* Semezhevo. Minskaya Voblasts', C Belarus
Syene *see* Aswān
Syeverodonets'k *109 H3 Rus.* Severodonetsk. Luhans'ka Oblast', E Ukraine
Syktyvkar *110 D4 prev.* Ust'-Sysol'sk. Respublika Komi, NW Russian Federation
Sylhet *135 G3* Sylhet, NE Bangladesh
Synel'nykove *109 G3* Dnipropetrovs'ka Oblast', E Ukraine
Syowa *154 C2 Japanese research station* Antarctica
Syracuse *41 E3* New York, NE USA
Syracuse *see* Siracusa
Syrdar'ya *114 B4* Sirdaryo Viloyati, E Uzbekistan
Syria *118 B3 off.* Syrian Arab Republic, *var.* Siria, Syrie, *Ar.* Al-Jumhūrīyah al-'Arabīyah as-Sūrīyah, Sūrīya. *country* SW Asia

SYRIA
Southwest Asia

Official name Syrian Arab Republic
Formation 1941 / 1967
Capital Damascus
Population 21.9 million / 308 people per sq mile (119 people per sq km)
Total area 71,498 sq. miles (184,180 sq. km)
Languages Arabic*, French, Kurdish, Armenian, Circassian, Turkic languages, Assyrian, Aramaic
Religions Sunni Muslim 74%, Alawi 12%, Christian 10%, Druze 3%, Other 1%
Ethnic mix Arab 90%, Kurdish 9%, Armenian, Turkmen, and Circassian 1%
Government Presidential system
Currency Syrian pound = 100 piastres
Literacy rate 85%
Calorie consumption 3106 kilocalories

Syrian Arab Republic *see* Syria
Syrian Desert *119 D5 Ar.* Al Hamad, Bādiyat ash Shām. *desert* SW Asia
Syrie *see* Syria
Sýrna *105 E7 var.* Sirna. *island* Kykládes, Greece, Aegean Sea
Sýros *105 C6 var.* Síros. *island* Kykládes, Greece, Aegean Sea
Syulemeshlii *see* Sredets
Syvash, Zaliv *see* Syvash, Zatoka
Syvash, Zatoka *109 F4 Rus.* Zaliv Syvash. *inlet* S Ukraine
Syzran' *111 C6* Samarskaya Oblast', W Russian Federation
Szabadka *see* Subotica
Szamotuły *98 B3* Poznań, W Poland
Szászrégen *see* Reghin
Szatmárnémeti *see* Satu Mare
Száva *see* Sava
Szczecin *98 B3 Eng./Ger.* Stettin. Zachodnio-pomorskie, NW Poland
Szczecinek *98 B2 Ger.* Neustettin. Zachodnio-pomorskie, NW Poland
Szczeciński, Zalew *98 A2 var.* Stettiner Haff, *Ger.* Oderhaff. *bay* Germany/ Poland
Szczuczyn Nowogródzki *see* Shchuchyn
Szczytno *98 D3 Ger.* Ortelsburg. Warmińsko-Mazurskie, NE Poland
Szechuan/Szechwan *see* Sichuan
Szeged *99 D7 Ger.* Szegedin, *Rom.* Seghedin. Csongrád, SE Hungary
Szegedin *see* Szeged
Székelykeresztúr *see* Cristuru Secuiesc
Székesfehérvár *99 C6 Ger.* Stuhlweissenberg; *anc.* Alba Regia. Fejér, W Hungary
Szeklerburg *see* Miercurea-Ciuc
Szekler Neumarkt *see* Târgu Secuiesc
Szekszárd *99 C7* Tolna, S Hungary
Szempcz/Szenc *see* Senec
Szenice *see* Senica
Szenttamás *see* Srbobran
Szeping *see* Siping
Szilágysomlyó *see* Şimleu Silvaniei
Szinna *see* Snina
Sziszek *see* Sisak
Szitás-Keresztúr *see* Cristuru Secuiesc
Szkudy *see* Skuodas
Szlatina *see* Slatina
Szlovákia *see* Slovakia
Szolnok *99 D6* Jász-Nagykun-Szolnok, C Hungary
Szombathely *99 B6 Ger.* Steinamanger; *anc.* Sabaria, Savaria. Vas, W Hungary
Szprotawa *98 B4 Ger.* Sprottau. Lubuskie, W Poland
Sztálinváros *see* Dunaújváros
Szucsava *see* Suceava

T

Tabariya, Bahrat *see* Tiberias, Lake
Table Rock Lake *49 G1 reservoir* Arkansas/Missouri, C USA
Tábor *99 B5* Jihočeský Kraj, S Czech Republic
Tabora *73 B7* Tabora, W Tanzania
Tabrīz *120 C2 var.* Tebriz; *anc.* Tauris. Āzarbāyjān-e Sharqi, NW Iran
Tabuaeran *145 G2 prev.* Fanning Island. *atoll* Line Islands, E Kiribati
Tabūk *120 A4* Tabūk, NW Saudi Arabia
Täby *85 C6* Stockholm, C Sweden
Tachau *see* Tachov
Tachov *99 A5 Ger.* Tachau. Plveňský Kraj, W Czech Republic
Tacloban *139 F2 off.* Tacloban City. Leyte, C Philippines
Tacloban City *see* Tacloban
Tacna *61 E4* Tacna, SE Peru
Tacoma *46 B2* Washington, NW USA
Tacuarembó *64 D4 prev.* San Fructuoso. Tacuarembó, C Uruguay
Tademait, Plateau du *70 D3 plateau* C Algeria
Tadmor/Tadmur *see* Tudmur
Tādpatri *132 C2* Andhra Pradesh, E India
Tadzhikistan *see* Tajikistan
Taegu *see* Daegu
Taehan-haehyŏp *see* Korea Strait
Taehan Min'guk *see* South Korea
Taejŏn *see* Daejeon
Tafassâsset, Ténéré du *75 G2 desert* N Niger
Tafila/Ṭafīlah, Muḥāfaẓat aṭ *see* Aṭ Ṭafīlah
Taganrog *111 A7* Rostovskaya Oblast', SW Russian Federation
Taganrog, Gulf of *109 G4 Rus.* Taganrogskiy Zaliv, *Ukr.* Tahanroz'ka Zatoka. *gulf* Russian Federation/ Ukraine
Taganrogskiy Zaliv *see* Taganrog, Gulf of
Taguatinga *63 F3* Tocantins, C Brazil
Tagus *92 C3 Port.* Rio Tejo, *Sp.* Río Tajo. *river* Portugal/Spain
Tagus Plain *80 A4 abyssal plain* E Atlantic Ocean
Tahanroz'ka Zatoka *see* Taganrog, Gulf of
Tahat *71 E4 mountain* SE Algeria
Tahiti *145 H4 island* Îles du Vent, W French Polynesia
Tahiti, Archipel de *see* Société, Archipel de la
Tahlequah *49 G1* Oklahoma, C USA
Tahoe, Lake *47 B5 lake* California/ Nevada, W USA
Tahoua *75 F3* Tahoua, W Niger
Taibei *128 D6 var.* T'aipei; *Jap.* Taihoku; *prev.* Daihoku. *country capital* (Taiwan) N Taiwan
Taichū *see* Taizhong
T'aichung *see* Taizhong
Taiden *see* Daejeon
Taieri *151 B7 river* South Island, New Zealand
Taihape *150 D4* Manawatu-Wanganui, North Island, New Zealand
Taihoku *see* Taibei
Taikyū *see* Daegu
Tailem Bend *149 B7* South Australia
T'ainan *see* Tainan
Tainan *128 D6 prev.* Dainan, T'ainan. S Taiwan
Taipei *see* Taibei
Taiping *138 B3* Perak, Peninsular Malaysia
Taiwan *128 D6 off.* Republic of China, *var.* Formosa, Formo'sa. *country* E Asia

TAIWAN
East Asia

Official name Republic of China (ROC)
Formation 1949 / 1949
Capital Taipei
Population 23.3 million / 1871 people per sq mile (722 people per sq km)
Total area 13,892 sq. miles (35,980 sq. km)
Languages Amoy Chinese, Mandarin Chinese*, Hakka Chinese
Religions Buddhist, Confucianist, and Taoist 93%, Christian 5%, Other 2%
Ethnic mix Han (pre-20th-century migration) 84%, Han (20th-century migration) 14%, Aboriginal 2%
Government Presidential system
Currency Taiwan dollar = 100 cents
Literacy rate 98%
Calorie consumption 2959 kilocalories

Taiwan *see* Taizhong
T'aiwan Haihsia/Taiwan Haixia *see* Taiwan Strait
Taiwan Strait *128 D6 var.* Formosa Strait, *Chin.* T'aiwan Haihsia, Taiwan Haixia. *strait* China/Taiwan
Taiyuan *128 C4 var.* T'ai-yuan, T'ai-yüan; *prev.* Yangku. *province capital* Shanxi, C China
T'ai-yuan/T'ai-yüan *see* Taiyuan
Taizhong *128 D6 Jap.* Taichū; *prev.* T'aichung, Taiwan. C Taiwan
Ta'izz *121 B7* SW Yemen
Tajikistan *123 E3 off.* Republic of Tajikistan, *Rus.* Tadzhikistan, *Taj.* Jumhurii Tojikiston; *prev.* Tajik S.S.R. *country* C Asia

TAJIKISTAN
Central Asia

Official name Republic of Tajikistan
Formation 1991 / 1991
Capital Dushanbe
Population 8.2 million / 148 people per sq mile (57 people per sq km)
Total area 55,251 sq. miles (143,100 sq. km)
Languages Tajik*, Uzbek, Russian
Religions Sunni Muslim 95%, Shi'a Muslim 3%, Other 2%
Ethnic mix Tajik 80%, Uzbek 15%, Other 3%, Russian 1%, Kyrgyz 1%
Government Presidential system
Currency Somoni = 100 diram
Literacy rate 99%
Calorie consumption 2101 kilocalories

Tajikistan, Republic of *see* Tajikistan
Tajik S.S.R *see* Tajikistan
Tajo, Río *see* Tagus
Tak *136 C4 var.* Rahaeng. Tak, W Thailand
Takao *see* Gaoxiong
Takaoka *131 C5* Toyama, Honshū, SW Japan
Takapuna *150 D2* Auckland, North Island, New Zealand
Takeshima *see* Liancourt Rocks
Takhiatash *see* Taxiatosh
Takhtakupyr *see* Taxtako'pir
Takikawa *130 D2* Hokkaidō, NE Japan
Takla Makan Desert *126 B3 Eng.* Takla Makan Desert. *desert* NW China
Takla Makan Desert *see* Taklimakan Shamo
Takow *see* Gaoxiong
Takutea *145 G4 island* S Cook Islands
Talabriga *see* Aveiro, Portugal
Talabriga *see* Talavera de la Reina, Spain
Talachyn *107 D6 Rus.* Tolochin. Vitsyebskaya Voblasts', NE Belarus
Talamanca, Cordillera de *53 E5 mountain range* S Costa Rica
Talara *60 B2* Piura, NW Peru
Talas *123 F2* Talasskaya Oblast', NW Kyrgyzstan
Talaud, Kepulauan *139 F3 island group* E Indonesia

Talavera de la Reina *92 D3 anc.* Caesarobriga, Talabriga. Castilla-La Mancha, C Spain
Talca *64 B4* Maule, C Chile
Talcahuano *65 B5* Bío Bío, C Chile
Taldykorgan *114 C5 Kaz.* Taldyqorghan; *prev.* Taldy-Kurgan. Taldykorgan, SE Kazakhstan
Taldy-Kurgan/Taldyqorghan *see* Taldykorgan
Ta-lien *see* Dalian
Taliq-an *see* Tāloqān
Tal'ka *107 C6* Minskaya Voblasts', C Belarus
Talkhof *see* Puurmani
Tallahassee *42 D3 prev.* Muskogean. *state capital* Florida, SE USA
Tall al Abyaḍ *see* At Tall al Abyaḍ
Tallin *see* Tallinn
Tallinn *106 D2 Ger.* Reval, *Rus.* Tallin; *prev.* Revel. *country capital* (Estonia) Harjumaa, NW Estonia
Tall Kalakh *118 B4 var.* Tell Kalakh. Ḥimṣ, C Syria
Tallulah *42 B2* Louisiana, S USA
Talnakh *114 D3* Krasnoyarskiy Kray, N Russian Federation
Tal'ne *109 E3 Rus.* Tal'noye. Cherkas'ka Oblast', C Ukraine
Tal'noye *see* Tal'ne
Taloga *49 F1* Oklahoma, C USA
Tāloqān *123 E3 var.* Taliq-an. Takhār, NE Afghanistan
Talsen *see* Talsi
Talsi *106 C3 Ger.* Talsen. NW Latvia
Taltal *64 B2* Antofagasta, N Chile
Talvik *84 D2* Finnmark, N Norway
Tamabo, Banjaran *138 D3 mountain range* East Malaysia
Tamale *75 E4* C Ghana
Tamana *145 E3 prev.* Rotcher Island. *atoll* Tungaru, W Kiribati
Tamanrasset *71 E4 var.* Tamenghest. S Algeria
Tamar *89 C7 river* SW England, United Kingdom
Tamar *see* Tudmur
Tamatave *see* Toamasina
Tamazunchale *51 E4* San Luis Potosí, C Mexico
Tambacounda *74 C3* SE Senegal
Tambov *111 B6* Tambovskaya Oblast', W Russian Federation
Tambura *73 B5* Western Equatoria, SW South Sudan
Tamchaket *see* Tâmchekkeṭ
Tâmchekkeṭ *74 C3 var.* Tamchaket. Hodh el Gharbi, S Mauritania
Tamenghest *see* Tamanrasset
Tamil Nādu *132 C3 prev.* Madras. *cultural region* SE India
Tam Ky *137 E5* Quang Nam-ƒa Năng, C Vietnam
Tammerfors *see* Tampere
Tampa *43 E4* Florida, SE USA
Tampa Bay *43 E4 bay* Florida, SE USA
Tampere *85 D5 Swe.* Tammerfors. Länsi-Suomi, W Finland
Tampico *51 E3* Tamaulipas, C Mexico
Tamworth *149 D6* New South Wales, SE Australia
Tanabe *131 C7* Wakayama, Honshū, SW Japan
Tana Bru *84 D2* Finnmark, N Norway
Tanais *see* Don
Lake Tana *72 C4 var.* Lake Tana. *lake* NW Ethiopia
Tana, Lake *see* T'ana Hāyk'
Tanami Desert *146 D3 desert* Northern Territory, N Australia
Tananarive *see* Antananarivo
Ţăndărei *108 D5* Ialomiţa, SE Romania
Tandil *65 D5* Buenos Aires, E Argentina
Tandjoengkarang *see* Bandar Lampung
Tanega-shima *131 B8 island* Nansei-shotō, SW Japan
Tanen Taunggyi *see* Tane Range
Tane Range *136 B4 Bur.* Tanen Taunggyi. *mountain range* W Thailand
Tanezrouft *70 D4 desert* Algeria/Mali
Ţanf, Jabal aţ *118 D4 mountain* SE Syria
Tanga *73 C7* Tanga, E Tanzania
Tanganyika and Zanzibar *see* Tanzania
Tanganyika, Lake *73 B7 lake* E Africa
Tanger *70 C2 var.* Tangiers, Tangier, *Fr./Ger.* Tangerk, *Sp.* Tánger; *anc.* Tingis. NW Morocco
Tangerk *see* Tanger
Tanggula Shan *126 C4 mountain* W China
Tangier *see* Tanger
Tangiers *see* Tanger
Tangra Yumco *126 B5 var.* Tangro Tso. *lake* W China
Tangro Tso *see* Tangra Yumco
Tangshan *128 D3 var.* T'ang-shan. Hebei, E China
T'ang-shan *see* Tangshan
Tanimbar, Kepulauan *139 F5 island group* Maluku, E Indonesia
Tanintharyi *137 B6 prev.* Tenasserim. S Myanmar (Burma)
Tanjungkarang/Tanjungkarang-Telukbetung *see* Bandar Lampung
Tanna *144 D4 island* S Vanuatu
Tannenhof *see* Krynica
Tan-Tan *70 B3* SW Morocco
Tan-tung *see* Dandong
Tanzania *73 C7 off.* United Republic of Tanzania, *Swa.* Jamhuri ya Muungano wa Tanzania; *prev.* German East Africa, Tanganyika and Zanzibar. *country* E Africa

TANZANIA
East Africa

Official name United Republic of Tanzania
Formation 1964 / 1964
Capital Dodoma
Population 49.3 million / 144 people per sq mile (56 people per sq km)
Total area 364,898 sq. miles (945,087 sq. km)
Languages Kiswahili*, Sukuma, Chagga, Nyamwezi, Hehe, Makonde, Yao, Sandawe, English*
Religions Christian 63%, Muslim 35%, Other 2%
Ethnic mix Native African (over 120 tribes) 99%, European, Asian, and Arab 1%
Government Presidential system
Currency Tanzanian shilling = 100 cents
Literacy rate 68%
Calorie consumption 2167 kilocalories

Tanzania, Jamhuri ya Muungano wa *see* Tanzania
Tanzania, United Republic of *see* Tanzania
Taoudenit *see* Taoudenni
Taoudenni *75 E2 var.* Taoudenit. Tombouctou, N Mali
Tapa *106 E2 Ger.* Taps. Lääne-Virumaa, NE Estonia
Tapachula *51 G5* Chiapas, SE Mexico
Tapaiu *see* Gvardeysk
Tapajós, Rio *63 E2 var.* Tapajóz. *river* NW Brazil
Tapajóz *see* Tapajós, Rio
Taps *see* Tapa
Ţarābulus *71 F2 var.* Ţarābulus al Gharb, *Eng.* Tripoli. *country capital* (Libya) NW Libya
Ţarābulus al Gharb *see* Ţarābulus
Tarābulus/Ţarābulus ash Shām *see* Tripoli
Taraclia *108 D4 Rus.* Tarakilya. S Moldova
Tarakilya *see* Taraclia
Mount Taranaki *150 C4 var.* Egmont. *volcano* North Island, New Zealand
Tarancón *93 E3* Castilla-La Mancha, C Spain
Taranto *97 E5 var.* Tarentum. Puglia, SE Italy
Taranto, Gulf of *97 E6 Eng.* Gulf of Taranto. *gulf* S Italy
Taranto, Gulf of *see* Taranto, Golfo di
Tarapoto *60 C2* San Martín, N Peru
Tarare *91 D5* Rhône, E France
Tarascon *91 D6* Bouches-du-Rhône, SE France
Tarawa *144 D2 atoll* Tungaru, W Kiribati
Taraz *114 C5 prev.* Aulie Ata, Auliye-Ata, Dzhambul, Zhambyl. Zhambyl, S Kazakhstan
Tarazona *93 E2* Aragón, NE Spain
Tarbes *91 B6 anc.* Bigorra. Hautes-Pyrénées, S France
Tarcoola *149 A6* South Australia
Taree *149 D6* New South Wales, SE Australia
Tarentum *see* Taranto
Târgovişte *108 C5 prev.* Tîrgovişte. Dâmboviţa, S Romania
Targu Jiu *108 B4 prev.* Tîrgu Jiu. Gorj, W Romania
Târgul-Neamţ *see* Târgu-Neamţ
Târgul-Săcuiesc *see* Târgu Secuiesc
Târgu Mureş *108 B4 prev.* Oşorhei, Tîrgu Mures, *Ger.* Neumarkt, *Hung.* Marosvásárhely. Mureş, C Romania
Târgu-Neamţ *108 C3 var.* Târgul-Neamţ; *prev.* Tîrgu-Neamţ. Neamţ, NE Romania
Târgu Ocna *108 C4 Hung.* Aknavásár; *prev.* Tîrgu Ocna. Bacău, E Romania
Târgu Secuiesc *108 C4 Ger.* Neumarkt, Szekler Neumarkt, *Hung.* Kezdivásárhely; *prev.* Chezdi-Oşorheiu, Târgul-Săcuiesc, Tîrgu Secuiesc. Covasna, E Romania
Tar Heel State *see* North Carolina
Tarija *61 G5* Tarija, S Bolivia
Tarīm *121 C6* C Yemen
Tarim Basin *124 C2 Eng.* Tarim Basin. *basin* NW China
Tarim Basin *see* Tarim Pendi
Tarim He *126 B3 river* NW China
Tarma *60 C3* Junín, C Peru
Tarn *91 C6 cultural region* S France
Tarn *91 C6 river* S France
Tarnobrzeg *98 D4* Podkarpackie, SE Poland
Tarnopol *see* Ternopil'
Tarnów *99 D5* Małopolskie, S Poland
Tarraco *see* Tarragona
Tarragona *93 G2 anc.* Tarraco. Cataluña, E Spain
Tarrasa *see* Terrassa
Tàrrega *93 F2 var.* Tarrega. Cataluña, NE Spain
Tarsatica *see* Rijeka
Tarsus *116 C4* İçel, S Turkey
Tartous/Tartouss *see* Ţarţūs
Tartu *106 D3 Ger.* Dorpat; *prev. Rus.* Yurev, Yury'ev. Tartumaa, SE Estonia
Ţarţūs *118 A3 off.* Muḥāfaẓat Ţarţūs, *var.* Tartous, Tartus. *governorate* W Syria
Ţarţūs, Muḥāfaẓat *see* Ţarţūs
Ta Ru Tao, Ko *137 B7 island* S Thailand Asia
Tarvisio *96 D2* Friuli-Venezia Giulia, NE Italy
Tarvisium *see* Treviso
Tashauz *see* Daşoguz
Tashi Chho Dzong *see* Thimphu
Tashkent *see* Toshkent
Tash-Kömür *see* Tash-Kumyr
Tash-Kumyr *123 F2 Kir.* Tash-Kömür. Dzhalal-Abadskaya Oblast', W Kyrgyzstan
Tashqurghan *see* Khulm
Tasikmalaja *see* Tasikmalaya
Tasikmalaya *138 C5 prev.* Tasikmalaja. Jawa, C Indonesia
Tasman Basin *142 C5 var.* East Australian Basin. *undersea basin* S Tasman Sea
Tasman Bay *151 C5 inlet* South Island, New Zealand
Tasmania *149 B8 prev.* Van Diemen's Land. *state* SE Australia
Tasmania *152 B4 island* SE Australia
Tasman Plateau *142 C5 var.* South Tasmania Plateau. *undersea plateau* SW Tasman Sea
Tasman Sea *142 C5 sea* SW Pacific Ocean
Tassili-n-Ajjer *71 E4 plateau* E Algeria
Tatabánya *99 C6* Komárom-Esztergom, NW Hungary
Tatar Pazardzhik *see* Pazardzhik
Tathlīth *121 B5* 'Asīr, S Saudi Arabia
Tatra Mountains *99 D5 Ger.* Tatra, *Hung.* Tátra, *Pol./Slvk.* Tatry. *mountain range* Poland/Slovakia
Tatra/Tátra *see* Tatra Mountains
Tatry *see* Tatra Mountains
Ta-t'ung/Tatung *see* Datong
Tatvan *117 F3* Bitlis, SE Turkey
Ta'ū *145 F4 var.* Tau. *island* Manua Islands, E American Samoa
Taukum, Peski *123 G1 desert* SE Kazakhstan
Taumarunui *150 D4* Manawatu-Wanganui, North Island, New Zealand
Taungdwingyi *136 B3* Magway, C Myanmar (Burma)
Taunggyi *136 B3* Shan State, C Myanmar (Burma)
Taungoo *136 B4* Bago, C Myanmar (Burma)
Taunton *89 C7* SW England, United Kingdom
Taupo *150 D3* Waikato, North Island, New Zealand
Taupo, Lake *150 D3 lake* North Island, New Zealand
Tauragė *106 B4 Ger.* Tauroggen. Tauragė, SW Lithuania
Tauranga *150 D3* Bay of Plenty, North Island, New Zealand
Tauris *see* Tabrīz
Tauroggen *see* Tauragė
Taurus Mountains *116 C4 Eng.* Taurus Mountains. *mountain range* S Turkey
Taurus Mountains *see* Toros Dağları
Tavas *116 B4* Denizli, SW Turkey
Tavastehus *see* Hämeenlinna
Tavira *92 C5* Faro, S Portugal
Tavoy *see* Dawei
Tavoy Island *see* Mali Kyun
Ta Waewae Bay *151 A7 bay* South Island, New Zealand
Tawakoni, Lake *49 G2 reservoir* Texas, SW USA
Tawau *138 D3* Sabah, East Malaysia
Ţawkar *see* Tokar
Tawzar *see* Tozeur
Taxco *51 E4 var.* Taxco de Alarcón. Guerrero, S Mexico
Taxco de Alarcón *see* Taxco
Taxiatosh *122 C2 Rus.* Takhiatash. Qoraqalpog'iston Respublikasi, W Uzbekistan
Taxtako'pir *122 D1 Rus.* Takhtakupyr. Qoraqalpog'iston Respublikasi, NW Uzbekistan
Tay *88 C3 river* C Scotland, United Kingdom
Taylor *49 G3* Texas, SW USA
Taymā' *120 A4* Tabūk, NW Saudi Arabia
Taymyr, Ozero *115 E2 lake* N Russian Federation
Taymyr, Poluostrov *115 E2 peninsula* N Russian Federation
Taz *114 D3 river* N Russian Federation
Tbilisi *117 G2 var.* T'bilisi, *Eng.* Tiflis. *country capital* (Georgia) SE Georgia
T'bilisi *see* **Tbilisi**
Tchad *see* Chad
Tchad, Lac *see* Chad, Lake
Tchien *see* Zwedru
Tchongking *see* Chongqing
Tczew *98 C2 Ger.* Dirschau. Pomorskie, N Poland
Te Anau *151 A7* Southland, South Island, New Zealand
Te Anau, Lake *151 A7 lake* South Island, New Zealand
Teapa *51 G4* Tabasco, SE Mexico
Teate *see* Chieti
Tebingtinggi *138 B3* Sumatera, N Indonesia
Tebriz *see* Tabrīz
Techirghiol *108 D5* Constanţa, SE Romania
Tecomán *50 D4* Colima, SW Mexico
Tecpan *51 E5 var.* Tecpan de Galeana. Guerrero, S Mexico
Tecpan de Galeana *see* Tecpan
Tecuci *108 C4* Galaţi, E Romania
Tedzhen *see* Harīrūd/Tejen
Tedzhen *see* Tejen
Tees *89 D5 river* N England, United Kingdom
Tefé *62 D2* Amazonas, N Brazil
Tegal *138 C4* Jawa, C Indonesia
Tegelen *87 D5* Limburg, SE Netherlands
Tegucigalpa *52 C3 country capital* (Honduras) Francisco Morazán, SW Honduras
Teheran *see* Tehrān
Tehrān *120 C3 var.* Teheran. *country capital* (Iran) Tehrān, N Iran

Tehuacán *51 F4* Puebla, S Mexico
Tehuantepec *51 F5 var.* Santo Domingo Tehuantepec. Oaxaca, SE Mexico
Gulf of Tehuantepec *51 F5 var.* Gulf of Tehuantepec. *gulf* S Mexico
Tehuantepec, Gulf of *see* Tehuantepec, Golfo de
Isthmus of Tehuantepec *51 F5 var.* Isthmus of Tehuantepec. *isthmus* SE Mexico
Tehuantepec, Isthmus of *see* Tehuantepec, Istmo de
Tejen *122 C3 Rus.* Tedzhen. Ahal Welaýaty, S Turkmenistan
Tejen *see* Harīrūd
Tejo, Rio *see* Tagus
Te Kao *150 C1* Northland, North Island, New Zealand
Tekax *51 H4 var.* Tekax de Álvaro Obregón. Yucatán, SE Mexico
Tekax de Álvaro Obregón *see* Tekax
Tekeli *114 C5* Almaty, SE Kazakhstan
Tekirdağ *116 A2 It.* Rodosto; *anc.* Bisanthe, Raidestos, Rhaedestus. Tekirdağ, NW Turkey
Te Kuiti *150 D3* Waikato, North Island, New Zealand
Tela *52 C2* Atlántida, NW Honduras
Telanaipura *see* Jambi
Telangana *134 D5 cultural region* SE India
Tel Aviv-Jaffa *see* Tel Aviv-Yafo
Tel Aviv-Yafo *119 A6 var.* Tel Aviv-Jaffa. Tel Aviv, C Israel
Teles Pirés *see* São Manuel, Rio
Telish *104 C2 prev.* Azizie. Pleven, N Bulgaria
Tell Abiad/Tell Abyad *see* At Tall al Abyaḍ
Tell Kalakh *see* Tall Kalakh
Tell Shedadi *see* Ash Shadādah
Tel'man/Tel'mansk *see* Gubadag
Teloekbetoeng *see* Bandar Lampung
Telo Martius *see* Toulon
Telschen *see* Telšiai
Telšiai *106 B3 Ger.* Telschen. Telšiai, NW Lithuania
Telukbetung *see* Bandar Lampung
Temerin *100 D3* Vojvodina, N Serbia
Temeschburg/Temeschwar *see* Timişoara
Temesvár/Temeswar *see* Timişoara
Temirtau *114 C4 prev.* Samarkandski, Samarkandskoye. Karagandy, C Kazakhstan
Tempio Pausania *97 A5* Sardegna, Italy, C Mediterranean Sea
Temple *49 G3* Texas, SW USA
Temuco *65 B5* Araucanía, C Chile
Temuka *151 B6* Canterbury, South Island, New Zealand
Tenasserim *see* Tanintharyi
Ténenkou *74 D3* Mopti, C Mali
Ténéré *75 G3 physical region* C Niger
Tenerife *70 A3 island* Islas Canarias, Spain, NE Atlantic Ocean
Tengger Shamo *127 E3 desert* N China
Tengréla *74 D4 var.* Tingréla. N Côte d'Ivoire
Tenkodogo *75 E4* S Burkina Faso
Tennant Creek *148 A3* Northern Territory, C Australia
Tennessee *42 C1 off.* State of Tennessee, *also known as* The Volunteer State. *state* SE USA
Tennessee River *42 C1 river* S USA
Tenos *see* Tínos
Tepelena *see* Tepelenë
Tepelenë *101 C7 var.* Tepelena, *It.* Tepeleni. Gjirokastër, S Albania
Tepeleni *see* Tepelenë
Tepic *50 D4* Nayarit, C Mexico
Teplice *98 A4 Ger.* Teplitz; *prev.* Teplice-Šanov, Teplitz-Schönau. Ústecký Kraj, NW Czech Republic
Teplice-Šanov/Teplitz/Teplitz-Schönau *see* Teplice
Tequila *50 D4* Jalisco, SW Mexico
Teraina *145 G2 prev.* Washington Island. *atoll* Line Islands, E Kiribati
Teramo *96 C4 anc.* Interamna. Abruzzi, C Italy
Tercan *117 E3* Erzincan, NE Turkey
Terceira *92 A5 var.* Ilha Terceira. *island* Azores, Portugal, NE Atlantic Ocean
Terceira, Ilha *see* Terceira
Terekhovka *see* Tsyerakhowka
Teresina *63 F2 var.* Therezina. *state capital* Piauí, NE Brazil
Termez *see* Termiz
Termia *see* Kýthnos
Términos, Laguna de *51 G4 lagoon* SE Mexico
Termiz *123 E3 Rus.* Termez. Surkhondaryo Viloyati, S Uzbekistan
Termoli *96 D4* Molise, C Italy
Terneuzen *87 B5 var.* Neuzen. Zeeland, SW Netherlands
Terni *96 C4 anc.* Interamna Nahars. Umbria, C Italy
Ternopil' *108 C2 Pol.* Tarnopol, *Rus.* Ternopol'. Ternopil's'ka Oblast', W Ukraine
Ternopol' *see* Ternopil'
Terracina *97 C5* Lazio, C Italy
Terranova di Sicilia *see* Gela
Terranova Pausania *see* Olbia
Terrassa *93 G2 Cast.* Tarrasa. Cataluña, E Spain
Terre Adélie *154 C4 physical region* Antarctica
Terre Haute *40 B4* Indiana, N USA
Terre Neuve *see* Newfoundland and Labrador
Terschelling *86 C1 Fris.* Skylge. *island* Waddeneilanden, N Netherlands
Teruel *93 F3 anc.* Turba. Aragón, E Spain
Tervel *104 E1 prev.* Kurtbunar, *Rom.* Curtbunar. Dobrich, NE Bulgaria
Tervueren *see* Tervuren
Tervuren *87 C6 var.* Tervueren. Vlaams Brabant, C Belgium
Teseney *72 C4 var.* Tessenei. W Eritrea
Tessalit *75 E2* Kidal, NE Mali
Tessaoua *75 G3* Maradi, S Niger
Tessenderlo *87 C5* Limburg, NE Belgium
Tessenei *see* Teseney
Testigos, Islas los *59 E1 island group* N Venezuela
Tete *79 E2* Tete, NW Mozambique
Teterow *94 C3* Mecklenburg-Vorpommern, NE Germany
Tétouan *70 C2 var.* Tetouan, Tetuán. N Morocco
Tetovo *101 D5* Razgrad, N Bulgaria
Tetschen *see* Děčín
Tetuán *see* Tétouan
Teverya *see* Tverya
Te Waewae Bay *151 A7 bay* South Island, New Zealand
Texarkana *42 A2* Arkansas, C USA
Texarkana *49 H2* Texas, SW USA
Texas *49 F3 off.* State of Texas, *also known as* Lone Star State. *state* S USA
Texas City *49 H4* Texas, SW USA
Texel *86 C2 island* Waddeneilanden, NW Netherlands
Texoma, Lake *49 G2 reservoir* Oklahoma/Texas, C USA
Teziutlán *51 F4* Puebla, S Mexico
Thaa Atoll *see* Kolhumadulu
Thai, Ao *see* Thailand, Gulf of
Thai Binh *136 D3* Thai Binh, N Vietnam
Thailand *137 C5 off.* Kingdom of Thailand, *Th.* Prathet Thai; *prev.* Siam. *country* SE Asia

THAILAND
Southeast Asia

Official name Kingdom of Thailand
Formation 1238 / 1907
Capital Bangkok
Population 67 million / 340 people per sq mile (131 people per sq km)
Total area 198,455 sq. miles (514,000 sq. km)
Languages Thai*, Chinese, Malay, Khmer, Mon, Karen, Miao
Religions Buddhist 95%, Muslim 4%, Other (including Christian) 1%
Ethnic mix Thai 83%, Chinese 12%, Malay 3%, Khmer and Other 2%
Government Transitional regime
Currency Baht = 100 satang
Literacy rate 96%
Calorie consumption 2757 kilocalories

Thailand, Gulf of *137 C6 var.* Gulf of Siam, *Th.* Ao Thai, *Vtn.* Vinh Thai Lan. *gulf* SE Asia
Thailand, Kingdom of *see* Thailand
Thai Lan, Vinh *see* Thailand, Gulf of
Thai Nguyên *136 D3* Băc Thai, N Vietnam
Thakhèk *136 D4 var.* Muang Khammouan. Khammouan, C Laos
Thamarīd *see* Thamarīt
Thamarīt *121 D6 var.* Thamarīd, Thumrayt. SW Oman
Thames *150 D3* Waikato, North Island, New Zealand
Thames *89 B8 river* S England, United Kingdom
Thandwe *136 A4 var.* Sandoway. Rakhine State, W Myanmar (Burma)
Thanh Hoa *136 D3* Thanh Hoa, N Vietnam
Thanintari Taungdan *see* Bilauktaung Range
Thanlwin *see* Salween
Thar Desert *134 C3 var.* Great Indian Desert, Indian Desert. *desert* India/Pakistan
Tharthar, Buhayrat ath *120 B3 lake* C Iraq
Thásos *104 C4* Thásos, E Greece
Thásos *104 C4 island* E Greece
Thaton *136 B4* Mon State, S Myanmar (Burma)
Thayetmyo *136 A4* Magway, C Myanmar (Burma)
The Crane *55 H2 var.* Crane. S Barbados
The Dalles *46 B3* Oregon, NW USA
The Flatts Village *see* Flatts Village
The Hague *see* 's-Gravenhage
Theodosia *see* Feodosiya
The Pas *37 F5* Manitoba, C Canada
Therezina *see* Teresina
Thérma *105 D6* Ikaría, Dodekánisa, Greece, Aegean Sea
Thermaic Gulf *104 B4 Eng.* Thermaic Gulf; *anc.* Thermaicus Sinus. *gulf* N Greece
Thermaic Gulf/Thermaicus Sinus *see* Thermaïkós Kólpos
Thermiá *see* Kýthnos
Thérmo *105 B5* Dytikí Elláda, C Greece
The Rock *93 H4* New South Wales, SE Australia
The Sooner State *see* Oklahoma
Thessaloníki *104 C3 Eng.* Salonica, Salonika, *SCr.* Solun, *Turk.* Selânik. Kentrikí Makedonía, N Greece
The Valley *55 G3 dependent territory capital* (Anguilla) E Anguilla
The Village *49 G1* Oklahoma, C USA
The Volunteer State *see* Tennessee
Thiamis *see* Kalamás
Thian Shan *see* Tien Shan
Thibet *see* Xizang Zizhiqu
Thief River Falls *45 F1* Minnesota, N USA
Thienen *see* Tienen
Thiers *91 C5* Puy-de-Dôme, C France
Thiès *74 B3* W Senegal
Thikombia *see* Cikobia
Thimbu *see* Thimphu
Thimphu *135 G3 var.* Thimbu; *prev.* Tashi Chho Dzong. *country capital* (Bhutan) W Bhutan
Thionville *90 D3 Ger.* Diedenhofen. Moselle, NE France
Thíra *105 D7 var.* Santorini. Kykládes, Greece, Aegean Sea
Thiruvananthapuram *132 C3 var.* Trivandrum, Tiruvantapuram. *state capital* Kerala, SW India
Thitu Island *128 C8 island* NW Spratly Islands
Tholen *86 B4 island* SW Netherlands
Thomasville *42 D3* Georgia, SE USA
Thompson *37 F4* Manitoba, C Canada
Thonon-les-Bains *91 D5* Haute-Savoie, E France
Thorenburg *see* Turda
Thorlákshöfn *83 E5* Sudhurland, SW Iceland
Thorn *see* Toruń
Thornton Island *see* Millennium Island
Thorshavn *see* Tórshavn
Thospitis *see* Van Gölü
Thouars *90 B4* Deux-Sèvres, W France
Thoune *see* Thun
Thracian Sea *104 D4 Gk.* Thrakikó Pélagos; *anc.* Thracium Mare. *sea* Greece/Turkey
Thracium Mare/Thrakikó Pélagos *see* Thracian Sea
Three Gorges Reservoir *129 C5 reservoir* C China
Three Kings Islands *150 C1 island group* N New Zealand
Thrissur *132 C3 var.* Trichūr. Kerala, SW India
Thuin *87 B7* Hainaut, S Belgium
Thule *see* Qaanaaq
Thumrayt *see* Thamarīt
Thun *95 A7 Fr.* Thoune. Bern, W Switzerland
Thunder Bay *38 B4* Ontario, S Canada
Thuner See *95 A7 lake* C Switzerland
Thung Song *137 C7 var.* Cha Mai. Nakhon Si Thammarat, SW Thailand
Thurso *88 C2* N Scotland, United Kingdom
Thýamis *see* Kalamás
Tianjin *128 D4 var.* Tientsin. Tianjin Shi, E China
Tianjin *see* Tianjin Shi
Tianjin Shi *128 D4 var.* Jin, Tianjin, T'ien-ching, Tientsin. *municipality* E China
Tian Shan *see* Tien Shan
Tianshui *128 B4* Gansu, C China
Tiba *see* Chiba
Tiber *96 C4 Eng.* Tiber. *river* C Italy
Tiber *see* Tevere, Italy
Tiber *see* Tivoli, Italy
Tiberias *see* Tverya
Tiberias, Lake *119 B5 var.* Chinnereth, Sea of Bahr Tabariya, Sea of Galilee, *Ar.* Bahrat Tabariya, *Heb.* Yam Kinneret. *lake* N Israel
Tibesti *76 C2 var.* Tibesti Massif, *Ar.* Tībistī. *mountain range* N Africa
Tibesti Massif *see* Tibesti
Tibet *see* Xizang Zizhiqu
Tibetan Autonomous Region *see* Xizang Zizhiqu
Tibet, Plateau of *126 B4 var.* Xizang Gaoyuan, *Eng.* Plateau of Tibet. *plateau* W China
Tibet, Plateau of *see* Qingzang Gaoyuan
Tībistī *see* Tibesti
Tibnī *see* At Tibnī
Tiburón, Isla *50 B2 var.* Isla del Tiburón. *island* NW Mexico
Tiburón, Isla del *see* Tiburón, Isla
Tichau *see* Tychy
Tîchît *74 D2 var.* Tichitt. Tagant, C Mauritania
Tichitt *see* Tîchît
Ticinum *see* Pavia
Ticul *51 H3* Yucatán, SE Mexico
Tidjikdja *see* Tidjikja
Tidjikja *74 C2 var.* Tidjikdja; *prev.* Fort-Cappolani. Tagant, C Mauritania
T'ien-ching *see* Tianjin Shi
Tienen *87 C6 var.* Thienen, *Fr.* Tirlemont. Vlaams Brabant, C Belgium
Tiên Giang, Sông *see* Mekong
Tien Shan *126 B3 Chin.* Thian Shan, Tian Shan, T'ien Shan, *Rus.* Tyan'-Shan'. *mountain range* C Asia
Tientsin *see* Tianjin
Tierp *85 C6* Uppsala, C Sweden
Tierra del Fuego *65 B8 island* Argentina/Chile
Tiflis *see* Tbilisi
Tifton *42 D3* Georgia, SE USA
Tifu *139 F4* Pulau Buru, E Indonesia
Tighina *108 D4 Rus.* Bendery; *prev.* Bender. E Moldova
Tigranocerta *see* Siirt
Tigris *120 B2 Ar.* Dijlah, *Turk.* Dicle. *river* Iraq/Turkey
Tiguentourine *71 E3* E Algeria
Ti-hua/Tihwa *see* Ürümqi
Tijuana *50 A1* Baja California Norte, NW Mexico
Tikhoretsk *111 A7* Krasnodarskiy Kray, SW Russian Federation
Tikhvin *110 B4* Leningradskaya Oblast', NW Russian Federation
Tiki Basin *143 G3 undersea basin* S Pacific Ocean
Tikinsso *52 C4 river* C Guinea
Tikirarjuaq *see* Whale Cove

Tiksi *115 F2* Respublika Sakha (Yakutiya), NE Russian Federation
Tilburg *86 C4* Noord-Brabant, S Netherlands
Tilimsen *see* Tlemcen
Tilio Martius *see* Toulon
Tillabéri *75 F3 var.* Tillabéry. Tillabéri, W Niger
Tillabéry *see* Tillabéri
Tílos *105 E7 island* Dodekánisa, Greece, Aegean Sea
Timan Ridge *110 D3 Eng.* Timan Ridge. *ridge* NW Russian Federation
Timan Ridge *see* Timanskiy Kryazh
Timaru *151 B6* Canterbury, South Island, New Zealand
Timbaki/Timbákion *see* Tympáki
Timbedgha *74 D3 var.* Timbédra. Hodh ech Chargui, SE Mauritania
Timbédra *see* Timbedgha
Timbuktu *see* Tombouctou
Timiş *108 A4 county* SW Romania
Timişoara *108 A4 Ger.* Temeschwar, Temeswar, *Hung.* Temesvár; *prev.* Temeschburg. Timiş, W Romania
Timmins *38 C4* Ontario, S Canada
Timor *125 F5 island* Nusa Tenggara, C Indonesia
Timor Sea *125 F5 sea* E Indian Ocean
Timor Timur *see* East Timor
Timor Trench *see* Timor Trough
Timor Trough *125 F5 var.* Timor Trench. *trough* NE Timor Sea
Timrå *85 C5* Västernorrland, C Sweden
Tindouf *70 C3* W Algeria
Tineo *92 C1* Asturias, N Spain
Tingis *see* Tanger
Tingo María *60 C3* Huánuco, C Peru
Tingréla *see* Tengréla
Tinhosa Grande *76 E2 island* N Sao Tome and Principe, Africa, E Atlantic Ocean
Tinhosa Pequena *76 E1 island* N Sao Tome and Principe, Africa, E Atlantic Ocean
Tinian *144 B1 island* S Northern Mariana Islands
Tínos *105 D6* Tínos, Kykládes, Greece, Aegean Sea
Tínos *105 D6 anc.* Tenos. *island* Kykládes, Greece, Aegean Sea
Tip *101 E6* Papua, E Indonesia
Tipitapa *52 D3* Managua, W Nicaragua
Tip Top Mountain *38 C4 mountain* Ontario, S Canada
Tirana *see* Tiranë
Tiranë *101 C6 var.* Tirana. *country capital* (Albania) Tiranë, C Albania
Tiraspol *108 D4 Rus.* Tiraspol'. E Moldova
Tiraspol' *see* Tiraspol
Tiree *88 B3 island* W Scotland, United Kingdom
Tîrgovişte *see* Târgovişte
Tîrgu Jiu *see* Targu Jiu
Tîrgu Mures *see* Târgu Mureş
Tîrgu-Neamţ *see* Târgu-Neamţ
Tîrgu Ocna *see* Târgu Ocna
Tîrgu Secuiesc *see* Târgu Secuiesc
Tirlemont *see* Tienen
Tírnavos *see* Týrnavos
Tirnovo *see* Veliko Tŭrnovo
Tirol *95 C7 off.* Land Tirol, *var.* Tyrol, *It.* Tirolo. *state* W Austria
Tirol, Land *see* Tirol
Tirolo *see* Tirol
Tirreno, Mare *see* Tyrrhenian Sea
Tiruchchirāppalli *132 C3 prev.* Trichinopoly. Tamil Nādu, SE India
Tiruppattūr *132 C2* Tamil Nādu, SE India
Tiruvantapuram *see* Thiruvanathapuram
Tisa *103 F1 Ger.* Theiss, *Rom./Slvn./SCr.* Tisa, *Rus.* Tissa, *Ukr.* Tysa. *river* SE Europe
Tisa *see* Tisza
Tiszakécske *99 D7* Bács-Kiskun, C Hungary
Titano, Monte *96 E1 mountain* C San Marino
Titicaca, Lake *61 E4 lake* Bolivia/Peru
Titograd *see* Podgorica
Titose *see* Chitose
Titova Mitrovica *see* Mitrovicë
Titovo Užice *see* Užice
Titu *108 C5* Dâmboviţa, S Romania
Titule *77 D5* Orientale, N Dem. Rep. Congo
Tiverton *89 C7* SW England, United Kingdom
Tivoli *96 C4 anc.* Tiber. Lazio, C Italy
Tizimín *51 H3* Yucatán, SE Mexico
Tizi Ouzou *71 E1 var.* Tizi-Ouzou. N Algeria
Tizi-Ouzou *see* Tizi Ouzou
Tiznit *70 B3* SW Morocco
Tjilatjap *see* Cilacap
Tjirebon *see* Cirebon
Tlaquepaque *50 D4* Jalisco, C Mexico
Tlascala *see* Tlaxcala
Tlaxcala *51 F4 var.* Tlascala, Tlaxcala de Xicohténcatl. Tlaxcala, C Mexico
Tlaxcala de Xicohténcatl *see* Tlaxcala
Tlemcen *70 D2 var.* Tilimsen, Tlemsen. NW Algeria
Tlemsen *see* Tlemcen
Toamasina *79 G3 prev./Fr.* Tamatave. Toamasina, E Madagascar
Toba, Danau *138 B3 lake* Sumatera, W Indonesia
Tobago *55 H5 island* NE Trinidad and Tobago
Toba Kakar Range *134 B2 mountain range* NW Pakistan
Tobol *see* Tobyl
Tobol'sk *114 C3* Tyumenskaya Oblast', C Russian Federation
Tobruch/Tobruk *see* Ţubruq
Tobyl *114 C4 prev.* Tobol. *river* Kazakhstan/Russian Federation
Tocantins *63 E3 off.* Estado do Tocantins. *state* C Brazil
Tocantins *63 E3 off.* Estado do Tocantins. *region* C Brazil
Tocantins, Estado do *see* Tocantins
Tocantins, Rio *63 F2 river* N Brazil
Tocoa *52 D2* Colón, N Honduras
Tocopilla *64 B2* Antofagasta, N Chile
Todi *96 C4* Umbria, C Italy
Todos os Santos, Baía de *63 G3 bay* E Brazil
Toetoes Bay *151 B8 bay* South Island, New Zealand
Tofua *145 E4 island* Ha'apai Group, C Tonga
Togo *75 E4 off.* Togolese Republic; *prev.* French Togoland. *country* W Africa

TOGO
West Africa

Official name The Togolese Republic
Formation 1960 / 1960
Capital Lomé
Population 6.2 million / 295 people per sq mile (114 people per sq km)
Total area 21,924 sq. miles (56,785 sq. km)
Languages Ewe, Kabye, Gurma, French*
Religions Christian 47%, Traditional beliefs 33%, Muslim 14%, Other 6%
Ethnic mix Ewe 46%, Other African 41%, Kabye 12%, European 1%
Government Presidential system
Currency CFA franc = 100 centimes
Literacy rate 60%
Calorie consumption 2366 kilocalories

Togolese Republic *see* Togo
Tojikiston, Jumhurii *see* Tajikistan
Tokanui *151 B7* Southland, South Island, New Zealand
Tokar *72 C3 var.* Ţawkar. Red Sea, NE Sudan
Tokat *116 D3* Tokat, N Turkey
Tokelau *145 E3 NZ overseas territory* W Polynesia
Tőketerebes *see* Trebišov
Tokio *see* Tōkyō
Tokmak *109 G4 var.* Velykyy Tokmak. Zaporiz'ka Oblast', SE Ukraine
Tokmak *see* Tomok
Tokoroa *150 D3* Waikato, North Island, New Zealand
Tokounou *74 C4* C Guinea
Tokushima *131 C6 var.* Tokusima. Tokushima, Shikoku, SW Japan
Tōkyō *130 A1 var.* Tokio. *country capital* (Japan) Tōkyō, Honshū, S Japan
Tōkyō-wan *130 A2 bay* S Japan
Tolbukhin *see* Dobrich
Toledo *92 D3 anc.* Toletum. Castilla-La Mancha, C Spain
Toledo *40 D3* Ohio, N USA
Toledo Bend Reservoir *49 G3 reservoir* Louisiana/Texas, SW USA
Toletum *see* Toledo
Toliara *79 F4 var.* Toliary; *prev.* Tuléar. Toliara, SW Madagascar
Toliary *see* Toliara
Tolmein *see* Tolmin
Tolmin *95 D7 Ger.* Tolmein, *It.* Tolmino. W Slovenia
Tolmino *see* Tolmin
Tolna *99 C7 Ger.* Tolnau. Tolna, S Hungary
Tolnau *see* Tolna
Tolochin *see* Talachyn
Tolosa *93 E1* País Vasco, N Spain
Tolosa *see* Toulouse
Toluca *51 E4 var.* Toluca de Lerdo. México, S Mexico
Toluca de Lerdo *see* Toluca
Tol'yatti *111 C6 prev.* Stavropol'. Samarskaya Oblast', W Russian Federation
Tomah *40 B2* Wisconsin, N USA
Tomakomai *130 D2* Hokkaidō, NE Japan
Tomar *92 B3* Santarém, W Portugal
Tomaschow *see* Tomaszów Mazowiecki
Tomaschow *see* Tomaszów Lubelski
Tomaszów *see* Tomaszów Mazowiecki
Tomaszów Lubelski *98 E4 Ger.* Tomaschow. Lubelskie, E Poland
Tomaszów Mazowiecka *see* Tomaszów Mazowiecki
Tomaszów Mazowiecki *98 D4 var.* Tomaszów Mazowiecka; *prev.* Tomaszów, *Ger.* Tomaschow. Łódzkie, C Poland
Tombigbee River *42 C3 river* Alabama/Mississippi, S USA
Tombouctou *75 E3 Eng.* Timbuktu. Tombouctou, N Mali
Tombua *78 A2 Port.* Porto Alexandre. Namibe, SW Angola
Tomelloso *93 E3* Castilla-La Mancha, C Spain
Tomini, Gulf of *see* Teluk Tomini
Tomini, Teluk *139 E4 Eng.* Gulf of Tomini; *prev.* Teluk Gorontalo. *bay* Sulawesi, C Indonesia
Tomok *123 G2 prev.* Tokmak. Chuyskaya Oblast', N Kyrgyzstan
Tomsk *114 D4* Tomskaya Oblast', C Russian Federation
Tomür Feng *126 B3 pre. Pik Pobedy; Kyrg.* Jengish Chokusu. *mountain* China/Kyrgyzstan
Toncontín *52 C3 prev.* Tegucigalpa. *country capital* (Honduras) Francisco Morazán, SW Honduras
Tonezh *see* Tonyezh
Tonga *145 E4 off.* Kingdom of Tonga, *var.* Friendly Islands. *country* SW Pacific Ocean

TONGA
Australasia & Oceania

Official name Kingdom of Tonga
Formation 1970 / 1970
Capital Nuku'alofa
Population 106,322 / 382 people per sq mile (148 people per sq km)
Total area 289 sq. miles (748 sq. km)
Languages English*, Tongan*
Religions Free Wesleyan 41%, Other 17%, Roman Catholic 16%, Church of Jesus Christ of Latter-day Saints 14%, Free Church of Tonga 12%
Ethnic mix Tongan 98%, Other 2%
Government Monarchy
Currency Pa'anga (Tongan dollar) = 100 seniti
Literacy rate 99%
Calorie consumption Not available

Tonga, Kingdom of *see* Tonga
Tongatapu *145 E5 island* Tongatapu Group, S Tonga
Tongatapu Group *145 E5 island group* S Tonga
Tonga Trench *143 E3 trench* S Pacific Ocean
Tongchuan *128 C4* Shaanxi, C China
Tongeren *87 D6 Fr.* Tongres. Limburg, NE Belgium
Tongking, Gulf of *see* Tonkin, Gulf of
Tongliao *127 G2* Nei Mongol Zizhiqu, N China
Tongres *see* Tongeren
Tongshan *see* Xuzhou, Jiangsu, China
Tongtian He *126 C4 var.* Zhi Qu. *river* C China
Tonj *73 B5* Warap, W South Sudan
Tonkin, Gulf of *128 B7 var.* *Tongking, Gulf of, Chin.* Beibu Wan, *Vtn.* Vinh Bắc Bô. *gulf* China/Vietnam
Tônlé Sap *137 D5 Eng.* Great Lake. *lake* W Cambodia
Tonopah *47 C6* Nevada, W USA
Tonyezh *107 C7 Rus.* Tonezh. Homyel'skaya Voblasts', SE Belarus
Tooele *44 B4* Utah, W USA
Toowoomba *149 E5* Queensland, E Australia
Topeka *45 F4 state capital* Kansas, C USA
Toplicza *see* Topliţa
Topliţa *108 C3 Ger.* Töplitz, *Hung.* Maroshevíz; *prev.* Topliţa Română, *Hung.* Oláh-Toplicza, Toplicza. Harghita, C Romania
Topliţa Română/Töplitz *see* Topliţa
Topoľčany *99 C6 Hung.* Nagytapolcsány. Nitriansky Kraj, W Slovakia
Topolovgrad *104 D3 prev.* Kavakli. Khaskovo, S Bulgaria
Topolya *see* Bačka Topola
Top Springs Roadhouse *146 E3* Northern Territory, N Australia
Torda *see* Turda
Torez *109 H3* Donets'ka Oblast', SE Ukraine
Torgau *94 D4* Sachsen, E Germany
Torhout *87 A5* West-Vlaanderen, W Belgium
Torino *96 A2 Eng.* Turin. Piemonte, NW Italy
Tornacum *see* Tournai
Torneå *see* Tornio
Torneträsk *84 C3 lake* N Sweden
Tornio *84 D4 Swe.* Torneå. Lappi, NW Finland
Tornionjoki *84 D3 river* Finland/Sweden
Tornionjoki *84 D3 river* Finland/Sweden
Toro *92 D2* Castilla y León, N Spain
Toronto *38 D5 province capital* Ontario, S Canada
Torquay *89 C7* SW England, United Kingdom
Torrance *46 D2* California, W USA
Torre, Alto da *92 B3 mountain* C Portugal
Torre del Greco *97 D5* Campania, S Italy
Torrejón de Ardoz *93 E3* Madrid, C Spain
Torrelavega *92 D1* Cantabria, N Spain
Torrens, Lake *149 A6 salt lake* South Australia
Torrent *93 F3 Cas.* Torrente, *var.* Torrent de l'Horta. Valenciana, E Spain
Torrent de l'Horta/Torrente *see* Torrent
Torreón *50 D3* Coahuila, NE Mexico
Torres Strait *148 C1 strait* Australia/Papua New Guinea
Torres Vedras *92 B3* Lisboa, C Portugal
Torrington *44 D3* Wyoming, C USA
Tórshavn *83 F5 Dan.* Thorshavn. *Dependent territory capital* Faroe Islands
To'rtkok'l *122 D2 var.* Türtkül, *Rus.* Turtkul'; *prev.* Petroaleksandrovsk. Qoraqalpog'iston Respublikasi, W Uzbekistan
Tortoise Islands *see* Galápagos Islands
Tortosa *93 F2 anc.* Dertosa. Cataluña, E Spain
Tortue, Montagne *59 H3 mountain range* C French Guiana
Tortuga, Isla *see* La Tortuga, Isla

Toruń *98 C3 Ger.* Thorn. Toruń, Kujawsko-pomorskie, C Poland
Tõrva *106 D3 Ger.* Törwa. Valgamaa, S Estonia
Törwa *see* Tõrva
Torzhok *110 B4* Tverskaya Oblast', W Russian Federation
Tosa-wan *131 B7 bay* SW Japan
Toscana *96 B3 Eng.* Tuscany. *region* C Italy
Toscano, Archipelago *96 B4 Eng.* Tuscan Archipelago. *island group* C Italy
Toshkent *123 E2 Eng./Rus.* Tashkent. *country capital* (Uzbekistan) Toshkent Viloyati, E Uzbekistan
Totana *93 E4* Murcia, SE Spain
Tot'ma *see* Sukhona
Totness *59 G3* Coronie, N Suriname
Tottori *131 B6* Tottori, Honshū, SW Japan
Touâjîl *74 C2* Tiris Zemmour, N Mauritania
Touggourt *71 E2* NE Algeria
Toukoto *74 C3* Kayes, W Mali
Toul *90 D3* Meurthe-et-Moselle, NE France
Toulon *91 D6 anc.* Telo Martius, Tilio Martius. Var, SE France
Toulouse *91 B6 anc.* Tolosa. Haute-Garonne, S France
Toungoo *see* Taungoo
Touraine *90 B4 cultural region* C France
Tourane *see* Đa Nẵng
Tourcoing *90 C2* Nord, N France
Tournai *87 A6 var.* Tournay, *Dut.* Doornik; *anc.* Tornacum. Hainaut, SW Belgium
Tournay *see* Tournai
Tours *90 B4 anc.* Caesarodunum, Turoni. Indre-et-Loire, C France
Tovarkovskiy *111 B5* Tul'skaya Oblast', W Russian Federation
Tower Island *see* Genovesa, Isla
Townsville *148 D3* Queensland, NE Australia
Towoeti Meer *see* Towuti, Danau
Towraghoudī *122 D4* Herāt, NW Afghanistan
Towson *41 F4* Maryland, NE USA
Towuti, Danau *139 E4 Dut.* Towoeti Meer. *lake* Sulawesi, C Indonesia
Toyama *131 C5* Toyama, Honshū, SW Japan
Toyama-wan *131 B5 bay* W Japan
Toyohara *see* Yuzhno-Sakhalinsk
Toyota *131 C6* Aichi, Honshū, SW Japan
Tozeur *71 E2 var.* Tawzar. W Tunisia
Trâblous *see* Tripoli
Trabzon *117 E2 Eng.* Trebizond; *anc.* Trapezus. Trabzon, NE Turkey
Traiectum ad Mosam/Traiectum Tungorum *see* Maastricht
Traiskirchen *95 E6* Niederösterreich, NE Austria
Trajani Portus *see* Civitavecchia
Trajectum ad Rhenum *see* Utrecht
Trakai *107 C5 Ger.* Traken, *Pol.* Troki. Vilnius, SE Lithuania
Traken *see* Trakai
Tralee *89 A6 Ir.* Trá Lí. SW Ireland
Trá Lí *see* Tralee
Tralles Aydin *see* Aydın
Trang *137 C7* Trang, S Thailand
Transantarctic Mountains *154 B3 mountain range* Antarctica
Transilvania *see* Transylvania
Transilvaniei, Alpi *see* Carpații Meridionalii
Transjordan *see* Jordan
Transnistria *108 D3 cultural region* NE Moldova
Transsylvanische Alpen/ Transylvanian Alps *see* Carpații Meridionalii
Transylvania *108 B4 Eng.* Ardeal, Transilvania, *Ger.* Siebenbürgen, *Hung.* Erdély. *cultural region* NW Romania
Transylvanian Alps *108 B4 var.* Alpi Transilvaniei, Carpații Sudici, *Eng.* South Carpathians, Transylvanian Alps, *Ger.* Südkarpaten, Transsylvanische Alpen, *Hung.* Déli-Kárpátok, Erdélyi-Havasok. *mountain range* C Romania
Trapani *97 B7 anc.* Drepanum. Sicilia, Italy, C Mediterranean Sea
Trâpeăng Vêng *see* Kâmpóng Thum
Trapezus *see* Trabzon
Traralgon *149 C7* Victoria, SE Australia
Trasimenischersee *see* Trasimeno, Lago
Trasimeno, Lago *96 C4 Eng.* Lake of Perugia, *Ger.* Trasimenischersee. *lake* C Italy
Traù *see* Trogir
Traverse City *40 C2* Michigan, N USA
Tra Vinh *137 D6 var.* Phu Vinh. Tra Vinh, S Vietnam
Travis, Lake *49 F3 reservoir* Texas, SW USA
Travnik *100 C4* Federacija Bosne I Hercegovine, C Bosnia and Herzegovina
Trbovlje *95 E7 Ger.* Trifail. C Slovenia
Treasure State *see* Montana
Třebíč *99 B5 Ger.* Trebitsch. Vysočina, C Czech Republic
Trebinje *101 C5* Republika Srpska, S Bosnia and Herzegovina
Trebišov *99 D6 Hung.* Tőketerebes. Košický Kraj, E Slovakia
Trebitsch *see* Třebíč
Trebnitz *see* Trzebnica
Tree Planters State *see* Nebraska
Trélazé *90 B4* Maine-et-Loire, NW France
Trelew *65 C6* Chubut, SE Argentina
Tremelo *87 C5* Vlaams Brabant, C Belgium
Trenčín *99 C5 Ger.* Trentschin, *Hung.* Trencsén. Trenčiansky Kraj, W Slovakia
Trencsén *see* Trenčín
Trengganu, Kuala *see* Kuala Terengganu
Trenque Lauquen *64 C4* Buenos Aires, E Argentina
Trent *see* Trento
Trento *96 C2 Eng.* Trent, *Ger.* Trient; *anc.* Tridentum. Trentino-Alto Adige, N Italy
Trenton *41 F4 state capital* New Jersey, NE USA
Trentschin *see* Trenčín
Tres Arroyos *65 D5* Buenos Aires, E Argentina
Treskavica *100 C4 mountain range* SE Bosnia and Herzegovina
Tres Tabernae *see* Saverne
Treves/Trèves *see* Trier
Treviso *96 C2 anc.* Tarvisium. Veneto, NE Italy
Trichinopoly *see* Tiruchchirāppalli
Trichūr *see* Thrissur
Tridentum/Trient *see* Trento
Trier *95 A5 Eng.* Treves, *Fr.* Trèves; *anc.* Augusta Treverorum. Rheinland-Pfalz, SW Germany
Triesen *94 E2* SW Liechtenstein Europe
Triesenberg *94 E2* SW Liechtenstein
Trieste *96 D2 Slvn.* Trst. Friuli-Venezia Giulia, NE Italy
Trifail *see* Trbovlje
Tríkala *104 B4 prev.* Trikkala. Thessalía, C Greece
Trikkala *see* Tríkala
Trimontium *see* Plovdiv
Trinacria *see* Sicilia
Trincomalee *132 D3 var.* Trinkomali. Eastern Province, NE Sri Lanka
Trindade, Ilha da *67 C5 island* Brazil, W Atlantic Ocean
Trinidad *61 F3* El Beni, N Bolivia
Trinidad *64 D4* Flores, S Uruguay
Trinidad *44 D5* Colorado, C USA
Trinidad *55 H5 island* C Trinidad and Tobago
Trinidad and Tobago *55 H5 off.* Republic of Trinidad and Tobago. *country* SE West Indies

TRINIDAD & TOBAGO
West Indies

Official name Republic of Trinidad and Tobago
Formation 1962 / 1962
Capital Port-of-Spain
Population 1.3 million / 656 people per sq mile (253 people per sq km)
Total area 1980 sq. miles (5128 sq. km)
Languages English Creole, English*, Hindi, French, Spanish

TRINIDAD & TOBAGO
(continued)

Religions Roman Catholic 26%, Hindu 23%, Other and nonreligious 23%, Anglican 8%, Baptist 7%, Pentecostal 7%, Muslim 6%
Ethnic mix East Indian 40%, Black 38%, Mixed race 20%, White and Chinese 1% Other 1%
Government Parliamentary system
Currency Trinidad and Tobago dollar = 100 cents
Literacy rate 99%
Calorie consumption 2889 kilocalories

Trinidad and Tobago, Republic of *see* Trinidad and Tobago
Trinité, Montagnes de la *59 H3 mountain range* C French Guiana
Trinity River *49 G3 river* Texas, SW USA
Trinkomali *see* Trincomalee
Trípoli *105 B6 prev.* Trípolis. Pelopónnisos, S Greece
Tripoli *118 B4 var.* Tarābulus, Ţarābulus ash Shām, Trâblous; *anc.* Tripolis. N Lebanon
Tripoli *see* Ţarābulus
Trípolis *see* Trípoli, Greece
Tripolis *see* Tripoli, Lebanon
Tristan da Cunha *69 B7 UK dependent territory* SE Atlantic Ocean
Triton Island *128 B7 island* S Paracel Islands
Trivandrum *see* Thiruvanathapuram
Trnava *99 C6 Ger.* Tyrnau, *Hung.* Nagyszombat. Trnavský Kraj, W Slovakia
Trnovo *see* Veliko Tŭrnovo
Trogir *100 B4 It.* Traù. Split-Dalmacija, S Croatia
Troglav *100 B4 mountain* Bosnia and Herzegovina/Croatia
Trois-Rivières *39 E4* Québec, SE Canada
Troki *see* Trakai
Trollhättan *85 B6* Västra Götaland, S Sweden
Tromsø *84 C2 Fin.* Tromssa. Troms, N Norway
Tromssa *see* Tromsø
Trondheim *84 B4 Ger.* Drontheim; *prev.* Nidaros, Trondhjem. Sør-Trøndelag, S Norway
Trondheimsfjorden *84 B4 fjord* S Norway
Trondhjem *see* Trondheim
Troódos *102 C5 var.* Troodos Mountains. *mountain range* C Cyprus
Troodos Mountains *see* Troódos
Troppau *see* Opava
Troy *42 D3* Alabama, S USA
Troy *41 F3* New York, NE USA
Troyan *104 C2* Lovech, N Bulgaria
Troyes *90 D3 anc.* Augustobona Tricassium. Aube, N France
Trst *see* Trieste
Trstenik *100 E4* Serbia, C Serbia
Trucial States *see* United Arab Emirates
Trujillo *52 D2* Colón, NE Honduras
Trujillo *60 B3* La Libertad, NW Peru
Trujillo *92 C3* Extremadura, W Spain
Truk Islands *see* Chuuk Islands
Trŭn *104 B2* Pernik, W Bulgaria
Truro *39 F4* Nova Scotia, SE Canada
Truro *89 C7* SW England, United Kingdom
Trzcianka *98 B3 Ger.* Schönlanke. Pila, Wielkopolskie, C Poland
Trzebnica *98 C4 Ger.* Trebnitz. Dolnośląskie, SW Poland
Tsalka *117 F2* S Georgia Asia
Tsamkong *see* Zhanjiang
Tsangpo *see* Brahmaputra
Tsarevo *104 E2 prev.* Michurin. Burgas, E Bulgaria
Tsarigrad *see* İstanbul
Tsaritsyn *see* Volgograd
Tschakathurn *see* Čakovec
Tschaslau *see* Čáslav
Tschenstochau *see* Częstochowa
Tsefat *119 B5 var.* Safed, *Ar.* Safad; *prev.* Ẕefat. Northern, N Israel
Tselinograd *see* Astana
Tsetsen Khan *see* Öndörhaan
Tsetserleg *126 D2* Arhangay, C Mongolia
Tshela *77 B6* Bas-Congo, W Dem. Rep. Congo
Tshikapa *77 C7* Kasai-Occidental, SW Dem. Rep. Congo
Tshuapa *77 D6 river* C Dem. Rep. Congo
Tsinan *see* Jinan
Tsing Hai *see* Qinghai Hu, China
Tsinghai *see* Qinghai, China
Tsingtao/Tsingtau *see* Qingdao
Tsinkiang *see* Quanzhou
Tsintao *see* Qingdao
Tsitsihar *see* Qiqihar
Tsu *131 C6 var.* Tu. Mie, Honshū, SW Japan
Tsugaru-kaikyo *130 C3 strait* N Japan
Tsumeb *78 B3* Oshikoto, N Namibia
Tsuruga *131 C6 var.* Turuga. Fukui, Honshū, SW Japan
Tsuruoka *130 D4 var.* Turuoka. Yamagata, Honshū, C Japan
Tsushima *131 A7 var.* Tsushima-tō, Tusima. *island group* SW Japan
Tsushima-tō *see* Tsushima
Tsyerakhowka *107 D8 Rus.* Terekhovka. Homyel'skaya Voblasts', SE Belarus
Tsyurupinsk *see* Tsyurupyns'k
Tsyurupyns'k *109 E4 Rus.* Tsyurupinsk. Khersons'ka Oblast', S Ukraine
Tu *see* Tsu
Tuamotu, Archipel des *see* Tuamotu, Îles
Tuamotu Fracture Zone *143 H3 fracture zone* E Pacific Ocean
Tuamotu Islands *145 H4 var.* Archipel des Tuamotu, Dangerous Archipelago, Tuamotu Islands. *island group* N French Polynesia
Tuamotu Islands *see* Tuamotu, Îles
Tuapi *53 E2* Región Autónoma Atlántico Norte, NE Nicaragua
Tuapse *111 A7* Krasnodarskiy Kray, SW Russian Federation
Tuba City *48 B1* Arizona, SW USA
Tubbergen *86 E3* Overijssel, E Netherlands
Tubeke *see* Tubize
Tubize *87 B6 Dut.* Tubeke. Walloon Brabant, C Belgium
Tubmanburg *74 C5* NW Liberia
Ţubruq *71 H2 Eng.* Tobruk, *It.* Tobruch. NE Libya
Tubuai, Îles/Tubuai Islands *see* Australes, Îles
Tucker's Town *42 B5* E Bermuda
Tuckum *see* Tukums
Tucson *48 B3* Arizona, SW USA
Tucumán *see* San Miguel de Tucumán
Tucumcari *49 E2* New Mexico, S W USA
Tucupita *59 E2* Delta Amacuro, NE Venezuela
Tucuruí, Represa de *63 F2 reservoir* NE Brazil
Tudela *93 E2 Basq.* Tutera; *anc.* Tutela. Navarra, N Spain
Tudmur *118 C3 var.* Tadmur, Tamar, *Gk.* Palmyra, *Bibl.* Tadmor. Ḩimş, C Syria
Tuguegarao *139 E1* Luzon, N Philippines
Tuktoyaktuk *37 E3* Northwest Territories, NW Canada
Tukums *106 C3 Ger.* Tuckum. W Latvia
Tula *111 B5* Tul'skaya Oblast', W Russian Federation
Tulancingo *51 E4* Hidalgo, C Mexico
Tulare Lake Bed *47 C7 salt flat* California, W USA
Tulcán *60 B1* Carchi, N Ecuador
Tulcea *108 D5* Tulcea, E Romania
Tul'chin *see* Tul'chyn
Tul'chyn *108 D3 Rus.* Tul'chin. Vinnyts'ka Oblast', C Ukraine
Tuléar *see* Toliara
Tulia *49 E2* Texas, SW USA
Ţūlkarm *119 D7* West Bank, Israel
Tulle *91 C5 anc.* Tutela. Corrèze, C France
Tulln *95 E6 var.* Oberhollabrunn. Niederösterreich, NE Austria
Tully *148 D3* Queensland, NE Australia
Tulsa *49 G1* Oklahoma, C USA
Tuluá *58 B3* Valle del Cauca, W Colombia

Tulun *115 E4* Irkutskaya Oblast', S Russian Federation
Tumaco *58 A4* Nariño, SW Colombia
Tumba, Lac *see* Ntomba, Lac
Tumbes *60 A2* Tumbes, NW Peru
Tumkūr *132 C2* Karnātaka, W India
Tumuc-Humac Mountains *63 E1 var.* Serra Tumucumaque. *mountain range* N South America
Tumucumaque, Serra *see* Tumuc-Humac Mountains
Tunca Nehri *see* Tundzha
Tunduru *73 C8* Ruvuma, S Tanzania
Tundzha *104 D3 Turk.* Tunca Nehri. *river* Bulgaria/Turkey
Tungabhadra Reservoir *132 C2 lake* S India
Tungaru *145 E2 prev.* Gilbert Islands. *island group* W Kiribati
T'ung-shan *see* Xuzhou
Tungsten *36 D4* Northwest Territories, W Canada
Tung-t'ing Hu *see* Dongting Hu
Tunis *71 E1 var.* Tūnis. *country capital* (Tunisia) NE Tunisia
Tunis, Golfe de *102 D3 Ar.* Khalīj Tūnis. *gulf* NE Tunisia
Tunisia *71 F2 off.* Tunisian Republic, *Ar.* Al Jumhūrīyah at Tūnisīyah, *Fr.* République Tunisienne. *country* N Africa

TUNISIA
North Africa

Official name The Tunisian Republic
Formation 1956 / 1956
Capital Tunis
Population 11 million / 183 people per sq mile (71 people per sq km)
Total area 63,169 sq. miles (163,610 sq. km)
Languages Arabic*, French
Religions Muslim (mainly Sunni) 98%, Christian 1%, Jewish 1%
Ethnic mix Arab and Berber 98%, Jewish 1%, European 1%
Government Transitional regime
Currency Tunisian dinar = 1000 millimes
Literacy rate 80%
Calorie consumption 3362 kilocalories

Tunisian Republic *see* Tunisia
Tunisienne, République *see* Tunisia
Tūnisīyah, Al Jumhūrīyah at *see* Tunisia
Tūnis, Khalīj *see* Tunis, Golfe de
Tunja *58 B3* Boyacá, C Colombia
Tuong Buong *see* Tương Đương
Tương Đương *136 D4 var.* Tuong Buong. Nghê An, N Vietnam
Tüp *see* Tyup
Tupelo *42 C2* Mississippi, S USA
Tupiza *61 G5* Potosí, S Bolivia
Turabah *121 B5* Makkah, W Saudi Arabia
Turangi *150 D4* Waikato, North Island, New Zealand
Turan Lowland *122 C2 var.* Turan Plain, *Kaz.* Turan Oypaty, *Rus.* Turanskaya Nizmennost', *Turk.* Turan Pesligi, *Uzb.* Turan Pasttekisligi. *plain* C Asia
Turan Oypaty/Turan Pesligi/Turan Plain/Turanskaya Nizmennost' *see* Turan Lowland
Turan Pasttekisligi *see* Turan Lowland
Ţurayf *120 A3* Al Ḩudūd ash Shamālīyah, NW Saudi Arabia
Turba *see* Teruel
Turbat *134 A3* Baluchistān, SW Pakistan
Turčianský Svätý Martin *see* Martin
Turda *108 B4 Ger.* Thorenburg, *Hung.* Torda. Cluj, NW Romania
Turek *98 C3* Wielkopolskie, C Poland
Turfan *see* Turpan
Turin *see* Torino
Turkana, Lake *73 C6 var.* Lake Rudolf. *lake* N Kenya
Turkestan *see* Turkistan
Turkey *116 B3 off.* Republic of Turkey, *Turk.* Türkiye Cumhuriyeti. *country* SW Asia

TURKEY
Asia / Europe

Official name Republic of Turkey
Formation 1923 / 1939

TURKEY
(continued)

Capital Ankara
Population 74.9 million / 252 people per sq mile (97 people per sq km)
Total area 301,382 sq. miles (780,580 sq. km)
Languages Turkish*, Kurdish, Arabic, Circassian, Armenian, Greek, Georgian, Ladino
Religions Muslim (mainly Sunni) 99%, Other 1%
Ethnic mix Turkish 70%, Kurdish 20%, Other 8%, Arab 2%
Government Parliamentary system
Currency new Turkish lira = 100 kurus
Literacy rate 95%
Calorie consumption 3680 kilocalories

Turkey, Republic of *see* Turkey
Turkish Republic of Northern Cyprus *102 D5 disputed territory* Cyprus
Turkistan *114 B5 prev.* Turkestan. Yuzhnyy Kazakhstan, S Kazakhstan
Türkiye Cumhuriyeti *see* Turkey
Türkmenabat *122 D3 prev. Rus.* Chardzhev, Chardzhou, Chardzhui, Lenin-Turkmenski, *Turkm.* Chärjew. Lebap Welaýaty, E Turkmenistan
Türkmen Aylagy *122 B2 Rus.* Turkmenskiy Zaliv. *lake gulf* W Turkmenistan
Turkmenbashi *see* Türkmenbaşy
Türkmenbaşy *122 B2 Rus.* Turkmenbashi; *prev.* Krasnovodsk. Balkan Welaýaty, W Turkmenistan
Türkmenbasy Aylagy *122 A2 prev. Rus.* Krasnovodskiy Zaliv, *Turkm.* Krasnowodsk Aylagy. *lake Gulf* W Turkmenistan
Turkmenistan *122 B2 ; prev.* Turkmenskaya Soviet Socialist Republic. *country* C Asia

TURKMENISTAN
Central Asia

Official name Turkmenistan
Formation 1991 / 1991
Capital Ashgabat
Population 5.1 million / 27 people per sq mile (10 people per sq km)
Total area 188,455 sq. miles (488,100 sq. km)
Languages Turkmen*, Uzbek, Russian, Kazakh, Tatar
Religions Sunni Muslim 89%, Orthodox Christian 9%, Other 2%
Ethnic mix Turkmen 85%, Other 6%, Uzbek 5%, Russian 4%
Government Presidential system
Currency Manat = 100 tenge
Literacy rate 99%
Calorie consumption 2883 kilocalories

Turkmenskaya Soviet Socialist Republic *see* Turkmenistan
Turkmenskiy Zaliv *see* Türkmen Aylagy
Turks and Caicos Islands *55 E2 UK dependent territory* N West Indies
Turku *85 D6 Swe.* Åbo. Länsi-Suomi, SW Finland
Turlock *47 B6* California, W USA
Turnagain, Cape *150 D4 headland* North Island, New Zealand
Turnau *see* Turnov
Turnhout *87 C5* Antwerpen, N Belgium
Turnov *98 B4 Ger.* Turnau. Liberecký Kraj, N Czech Republic
Tŭrnovo *see* Veliko Tŭrnovo
Turnu Măgurele *108 B5 var.* Turnu-Măgurele. Teleorman, S Romania
Turnu Severin *see* Drobeta-Turnu Severin
Turócszentmárton *see* Martin
Turoni *see* Tours
Turpan *126 C3 var.* Turfan. Xinjiang Uygur Zizhiqu, NW China
Turpan Depression *see* Turpan Pendi
Turpan Pendi *126 C3 Eng.* Turpan Depression. *depression* NW China
Turpentine State *see* North Carolina
Tŭrtkŭl/Turtkul' *see* To'rtkok'l
Turuga *see* Tsuruga
Turuoka *see* Tsuruoka
Tuscaloosa *42 C2* Alabama, S USA
Tuscan Archipelago *see* Toscano, Archipelago
Tuscany *see* Toscana
Tusima *see* Tsushima
Tutela *see* Tulle, France
Tutela *see* Tudela, Spain
Tutera *see* Tudela
Tuticorin *132 C3* Tamil Nādu, SE India
Tutrakan *104 D1* Silistra, NE Bulgaria
Tutuila *145 F4 island* W American Samoa
Tuvalu *145 E3 prev.* Ellice Islands. *country* SW Pacific Ocean

TUVALU
Australasia & Oceania

Official name Tuvalu
Formation 1978 / 1978
Capital Funafuti Atoll
Population 10,698 / 1070 people per sq mile (411 people per sq km)
Total area 10 sq. miles (26 sq. km)
Languages Tuvaluan, Kiribati, English*
Religions Church of Tuvalu 97%, Baha'i 1%, Seventh-day Adventist 1%, Other 1%
Ethnic mix Polynesian 96%, Micronesian 4%
Government Nonparty system
Currency = 100 cents; Tuvaluan dollar = 100 cents
Literacy rate 98%
Calorie consumption Not available

Tuwayq, Jabal *121 C5 mountain range* C Saudi Arabia
Tuxpan *50 D4* Jalisco, C Mexico
Tuxpan *50 D4* Nayarit, C Mexico
Tuxpán *51 F4 var.* Tuxpán de Rodríguez Cano. Veracruz-Llave, E Mexico
Tuxpán de Rodríguez Cano *see* Tuxpán
Tuxtepec *51 F4 var.* San Juan Bautista Tuxtepec. Oaxaca, S Mexico
Tuxtla *51 G5 var.* Tuxtla Gutiérrez. Chiapas, SE Mexico
Tuxtla *see* San Andrés Tuxtla
Tuxtla Gutiérrez *see* Tuxtla
Tuy Hoa *137 E5* Phu Yên, S Vietnam
Tuz, Lake *116 C3 lake* C Turkey
Tver' *110 B4 prev.* Kalinin. Tverskaya Oblast', W Russian Federation
Tverya *119 B5 var.* Tiberias; *prev.* Teverya. Northern, N Israel
Twin Falls *46 D4* Idaho, NW USA
Tyan'-Shan' *see* Tien Shan
Tychy *99 D5 Ger.* Tichau. Śląskie, S Poland
Tyler *49 G3* Texas, SW USA
Tylos *see* Bahrain
Tympáki *105 C8 var.* Timbaki; *prev.* Timbákion. Kríti, Greece, E Mediterranean Sea
Tynda *115 F4* Amurskaya Oblast', SE Russian Federation
Tyne *88 D4 river* N England, United Kingdom
Tyôsi *see* Chōshi
Tyras *see* Dniester
Tyre *see* Soûr
Tyrnau *see* Trnava
Týrnavos *104 B4 var.* Tírnavos. Thessalía, C Greece
Tyrol *see* Tirol
Tyros *see* Bahrain
Tyrrhenian Sea *97 B6 It.* Mare Tirreno. *sea* N Mediterranean Sea
Tyumen' *114 C3* Tyumenskaya Oblast', C Russian Federation
Tyup *123 G2 Kir.* Tüp. Issyk-Kul'skaya Oblast', NE Kyrgyzstan
Tywyn *89 C6* W Wales, United Kingdom
Tzekung *see* Zigong
Tziá *105 C6 prev.* Kéa, Kéos; *anc.* Ceos. *island* Kykládes, Greece, Aegean Sea

U

Uaco Cungo *78 B1* C Angola
UAE *see* United Arab Emirates
Uanle Uen *see* Wanlaweyn
Uaupés, Rio *see* Vaupés, Río
Ubangi-Shari *see* Central African Republic
Ube *131 B7* Yamaguchi, Honshū, SW Japan
Ubeda *93 E4* Andalucía, S Spain
Uberaba *63 F4* Minas Gerais, SE Brazil
Uberlândia *63 F4* Minas Gerais, S E Brazil
Ubol Rajadhani/Ubol Ratchathani *see* Ubon Ratchathani
Ubon Ratchathani *137 D5 var.* Muang Ubon, Ubol Rajadhani, Ubol Ratchathani, Udon Ratchathani. Ubon Ratchathani, E Thailand
Ubrique *92 D5* Andalucía, S Spain
Ubsu-Nur, Ozero *see* Uvs Nuur
Ucayali, Río *60 D3 river* C Peru
Uchiura-wan *130 D3 bay* NW Pacific Ocean
Uchkuduk *see* Uchquduq
Uchquduq *122 D2 Rus.* Uchkuduk. Navoiy Viloyati, N Uzbekistan
Uchtagan Gumy/Uchtagan, Peski *see* Uçtagan Gumy
Uçtagan Gumy *122 C2 var.* Uchtagan Gumy, *Rus.* Peski Uchtagan. *desert* NW Turkmenistan
Udaipur *134 C3 prev.* Oodeypore. Rājasthān, N India
Uddevalla *85 B6* Västra Götaland, S Sweden
Udine *96 D2 anc.* Utina. Friuli-Venezia Giulia, NE Italy
Udintsev Fracture Zone *154 A5 tectonic feature* S Pacific Ocean
Udipi *see* Udupi
Udon Ratchathani *see* Ubon Ratchathani
Udon Thani *136 C4 var.* Ban Mak Khaeng, Udorndhani. Udon Thani, N Thailand
Udorndhani *see* Udon Thani
Udupi *132 B2 var.* Udipi. Karnātaka, SW India
Uele *77 D5 var.* Welle. *river* NE Dem. Rep. Congo
Uelzen *94 C3* Niedersachsen, N Germany
Ufa *111 D6* Respublika Bashkortostan, W Russian Federation
Ugāle *106 C2* NW Latvia
Uganda *73 B6 off.* Republic of Uganda. *country* E Africa

UGANDA
East Africa

Official name Republic of Uganda
Formation 1962 / 1962
Capital Kampala
Population 37.6 million / 488 people per sq mile (188 people per sq km)
Total area 91,135 sq. miles (236,040 sq. km)
Languages Luganda, Nkole, Chiga, Lango, Acholi, Teso, Lugbara, English*
Religions Christian 85%, Muslim (mainly Sunni) 12%, Other 3%
Ethnic mix Other 50%, Baganda 17%, Banyakole 10%, Basoga 9%, Iteso 7%, Bakiga 7%
Government Presidential system
Currency Uganda shilling = 100 cents
Literacy rate 73%
Calorie consumption 2279 kilocalories

Uganda, Republic of *see* Uganda
Uhorshchyna *see* Hungary
Uhuru Peak *see* Kilimanjaro
Uíge *78 B1 Port.* Carmona, Vila Marechal Carmona. Uíge, NW Angola
Uinta Mountains *44 B4 mountain range* Utah, W USA
Uitenhage *78 C5* Eastern Cape, S South Africa
Uithoorn *86 C3* Noord-Holland, C Netherlands
Ujda *see* Oujda
Ujelang Atoll *144 C1 var.* Wujlān. *atoll* Ralik Chain, W Marshall Islands
Újgradiska *see* Nova Gradiška
Újmoldova *see* Moldova Nouă
Ujungpandang *see* Makassar
Ujung Salang *see* Phuket
Újvidék *see* Novi Sad
UK *see* United Kingdom

Ukhta *114 C3* Respublika Komi, NW Russian Federation
Ukiah *47 B5* California, W USA
Ukmergė *106 C4 Pol.* Wiłkomierz. Vilnius, C Lithuania
Ukraina *see* Ukraine
Ukraine *108 C2 off.* Ukraine, *Rus.* Ukraina, *Ukr.* Ukrayina; *prev.* Ukrainian Soviet Socialist Republic, Ukrainskay S.S.R. *country* SE Europe

UKRAINE
Eastern Europe

Official name Ukraine
Formation 1991 / 1991
Capital Kiev
Population 45.2 million / 194 people per sq mile (75 people per sq km)
Total area 233,089 sq. miles (603,700 sq. km)
Languages Ukrainian*, Russian, Tatar
Religions Christian (mainly Orthodox) 95%, Other 5%
Ethnic mix Ukrainian 78%, Russian 17%, Other 5%
Government Presidential system
Currency Hryvna = 100 kopiykas
Literacy rate 99%
Calorie consumption 3142 kilocalories

Ukraine *see* Ukraine
Ukrainian Soviet Socialist Republic *see* Ukraine
Ukrainskay S.S.R/Ukrayina *see* Ukraine
Ulaanbaatar *127 E2 Eng.* Ulan Bator; *prev.* Urga. *country capital* (Mongolia) Töv, C Mongolia
Ulaangom *126 C2* Uvs, NW Mongolia
Ulan Bator *see* Ulaanbaatar
Ulanhad *see* Chifeng
Ulan-Ude *115 E4 prev.* Verkhneudinsk. Respublika Buryatiya, S Russian Federation
Uleälv *see* Oulujoki
Uleträsk *see* Oulujärvi
Ulft *86 E4* Gelderland, E Netherlands
Ullapool *88 C3* N Scotland, United Kingdom
Ulm *95 B6* Baden-Württemberg, S Germany
Ulsan *129 E4 Jap.* Urusan. SE South Korea
Ulster *89 B5 province* Northern Ireland, United Kingdom/Ireland
Ulungur Hu *126 B2 lake* NW China
Uluṟu *147 D5 var.* Ayers Rock. *monolith* Northern Territory, C Australia
Ul'yanovka *109 E3* Kirovohrads'ka Oblast', C Ukraine
Ul'yanovsk *111 C5 prev.* Simbirsk. Ul'yanovskaya Oblast', W Russian Federation
Umán *51 H3* Yucatán, SE Mexico
Uman' *109 E3 Rus.* Uman. Cherkas'ka Oblast', C Ukraine
Uman *see* Uman'
Umanak/Umanaq *see* Uummannaq
'Umān, Khalīj *see* Oman, Gulf of
'Umān, Salṭanat *see* Oman
Umbrian-Machigian Mountains *see* Umbro-Marchigiano, Appennino
Umbro-Marchigiano, Appennino *96 C3 Eng.* Umbrian-Machigian Mountains. *mountain range* C Italy
Umeå *84 C4* Västerbotten, N Sweden
Umeälven *84 C4 river* N Sweden
Umiat *36 D2* Alaska, USA
Umm Buru *72 A4* Western Darfur, W Sudan
Umm Durmān *see* Omdurman
Umm Ruwaba *72 C4 var.* Umm Ruwābah, Um Ruwāba. Northern Kordofan, C Sudan
Umm Ruwābah *see* Umm Ruwaba
Umnak Island *36 A3 island* Aleutian Islands, Alaska, USA
Um Ruwāba *see* Umm Ruwaba
Umtali *see* Mutare
Umtata *see* Mthatha
Una *100 B3 river* Bosnia and Herzegovina/Croatia
Unac *100 B3 river* W Bosnia and Herzegovina
Unalaska Island *36 A3 island* Aleutian Islands, Alaska, USA
'Unayzah *120 B4 var.* Anaiza. Al Qaṣīm, C Saudi Arabia
Unci *see* Almería
Uncía *61 F4* Potosí, C Bolivia
Uncompahgre Peak *44 B5 mountain* Colorado, C USA
Undur Khan *see* Öndörhaan
Ungaria *see* Hungary
Ungarisches Erzgebirge *see* Slovenské rudohorie
Ungarn *see* Hungary
Ungava Bay *39 E1 bay* Québec, E Canada
Ungava Peninsula *see* Ungava, Péninsule d'
Ungava, Péninsule d' *38 D1 Eng.* Ungava Peninsula. *peninsula* Québec, SE Canada
Ungeny *see* Ungheni
Ungheni *108 D3 Rus.* Ungeny. W Moldova
Unguja *see* Zanzibar
Üngüz Angyrsyndaky Garagum *122 C2 Rus.* Zaunguzskiye Garagumy. *desert* N Turkmenistan
Ungvár *see* Uzhhorod
Unimak Island *36 B3 island* Aleutian Islands, Alaska, USA
Union *43 E1* South Carolina, SE USA
Union City *42 C1* Tennessee, S USA
Union of Myanmar *see* Burma
United Arab Emirates *121 C5 Ar.* Al Imārāt al 'Arabīyah al Muttaḥidah, *abbrev.* UAE; *prev.* Trucial States. *country* SW Asia

UNITED ARAB EMIRATES
Southwest Asia

Official name United Arab Emirates
Formation 1971 / 1972
Capital Abu Dhabi
Population 9.3 million / 288 people per sq mile (111 people per sq km)
Total area 32,000 sq. miles (82,880 sq. km)
Languages Arabic*, Farsi, Indian and Pakistani languages, English
Religions Muslim (mainly Sunni) 96%, Christian, Hindu, and other 4%
Ethnic mix Asian 60%, Emirian 25%, Other Arab 12%, European 3%
Government Monarchy
Currency UAE dirham = 100 fils
Literacy rate 90%
Calorie consumption 3215 kilocalories

United Arab Republic *see* Egypt
United Kingdom *89 B5 off.* United Kingdom of Great Britain and Northern Ireland, *abbrev.* UK. *country* NW Europe

UNITED KINGDOM
Northwest Europe

Official name United Kingdom of Great Britain and Northern Ireland
Formation 1707 / 1922
Capital London
Population 63.1 million / 676 people per sq mile (261 people per sq km)
Total area 94,525 sq. miles (244,820 sq. km)
Languages English*, Welsh* *(in Wales)*, Scottish Gaelic, Irish Gaelic
Religions Anglican 45%, Other and nonreligious 36%, Roman Catholic 9%, Presbyterian 4%, Muslim 3%, Methodist 2%, Hindu 1%
Ethnic mix English 80%, Scottish 9%, West Indian, Asian, and other 5%, Northern Irish 3%, Welsh 3%
Government Parliamentary system
Currency Pound sterling = 100 pence
Literacy rate 99%
Calorie consumption 3414 kilocalories

United Kingdom of Great Britain and Northern Ireland *see* United Kingdom
United Mexican States *see* Mexico
United Provinces *see* Uttar Pradesh
United States of America *35 B5 off.* United States of America, *var.* America, The States, *abbrev.* U.S., USA. *country* North America

UNITED STATES
North America

Official name United States of America
Formation 1776 / 1959
Capital Washington D.C.
Population 320 million / 88 people per sq mile (34 people per sq km)
Total area 3,717,792 sq. miles (9,626,091 sq. km)
Languages English, Spanish, Chinese, French, German, Tagalog, Vietnamese, Italian, Korean, Russian, Polish
Religions Protestant 52%, Roman Catholic 25%, Other and nonreligious 20%, Jewish 2%, Muslim 1%
Ethnic mix White 60%, Hispanic 17%, Black American/African 14%, Asian 6%, Other 3%
Government Presidential system
Currency US dollar = 100 cents
Literacy rate 99%
Calorie consumption 3639 kilocalories

United States of America *see* United States of America
Unst *88 D1 island* NE Scotland, United Kingdom
Ünye *116 D2* Ordu, W Turkey
Upala *52 D4* Alajuela, NW Costa Rica
Upata *59 E2* Bolívar, E Venezuela
Upemba, Lac *77 D7 lake* SE Dem. Rep. Congo
Upernavik *82 C2 var.* Upernivik. Kitaa, C Greenland
Upernivik *see* Upernavik
Upington *78 C4* Northern Cape, W South Africa
'Upolu *145 F4 island* SE Samoa
Upper Klamath Lake *46 A4 lake* Oregon, NW USA
Upper Lough Erne *89 A5 lake* SW Northern Ireland, United Kingdom
Upper Red Lake *45 F1 lake* Minnesota, N USA
Upper Volta *see* Burkina Faso
Uppsala *85 C6* Uppsala, C Sweden
Uqsuqtuuq *see* Gjoa Haven
Ural *114 B4 Kaz.* Zayyq. *river* Kazakhstan/Russian Federation
Ural Mountains *114 C3 var.* Ural'skiy Khrebet, *Eng.* Ural Mountains. *mountain range* Kazakhstan/Russian Federation
Ural Mountains *see* Ural'skiye Gory
Ural'sk *114 B3 Kaz.* Oral. Zapadnyy Kazakhstan, NW Kazakhstan
Ural'skiy Khrebet *see* Ural'skiye Gory
Uraricoera *62 D1* Roraima, N Brazil
Ura-Tyube *see* Üroteppa
Urbandale *45 F3* Iowa, C USA
Urdunn *see* Jordan
Uren' *111 C5* Nizhegorodskaya Oblast', W Russian Federation
Urga *see* Ulaanbaatar
Urganch *122 D2 Rus.* Urgench; *prev.* Novo-Urgench. Xorazm Viloyati, W Uzbekistan
Urgench *see* Urganch
Urgut *123 E3* Samarqand Viloyati, C Uzbekistan
Urmia, Lake *121 C2 var.* Matianus, Sha Hi, Urumi Yeh, *Eng.* Lake Urmia; *prev.* Daryācheh-ye Reẕā'īyeh. *lake* NW Iran
Urmia, Lake *see* Orūmīyeh, Daryācheh-ye
Uroševac *see* Ferizaj
Üroteppa *123 E2 Rus.* Ura-Tyube. NW Tajikistan
Uruapan *51 E4 var.* Uruapan del Progreso. Michoacán, SW Mexico
Uruapan del Progreso *see* Uruapan
Uruguai, Rio *see* Uruguay
Uruguay *64 D4 off.* Oriental Republic of Uruguay; *prev.* La Banda Oriental. *country* E South America

URUGUAY
South America

Official name Eastern Republic of Uruguay
Formation 1828 / 1828
Capital Montevideo
Population 3.4 million / 50 people per sq mile (19 people per sq km)

URUGUAY
(continued)

Total area 68,039 sq. miles (176,220 sq. km)
Languages Spanish*
Religions Roman Catholic 66%, Other and nonreligious 30%, Jewish 2%, Protestant 2%
Ethnic mix White 90%, Mestizo 6%, Black 4%
Government Presidential system
Currency Uruguayan peso = 100 centésimos
Literacy rate 98%
Calorie consumption 2939 kilocalories

Uruguay *64 D3 var.* Rio Uruguai, Río Uruguay. *river* E South America
Uruguay, Oriental Republic of *see* Uruguay
Uruguay, Río *see* Uruguay
Urumchi *see* Ürümqi
Urumi Yeh *see* Orūmīyeh, Daryācheh-ye
Ürümqi *126 C3 var.* Tihwa, Urumchi, Urumqi, Urumtsi, Wu-lu-k'o-mu-shi, Wu-lu-mu-ch'i; *prev.* Ti-hua. Xinjiang Uygur Zizhiqu, NW China
Urumtsi *see* Ürümqi
Urundi *see* Burundi
Urup, Ostrov *115 H4 island* Kuril'skiye Ostrova, SE Russian Federation
Urusan *see* Ulsan
Urziceni *108 C5* Ialomiţa, SE Romania
Usa *110 E3 river* NW Russian Federation
Uşak *116 B3 prev.* Ushak. Uşak, W Turkey
Ushak *see* Uşak
Ushant *see* Ouessant, Île d'
Ushuaia *65 B8* Tierra del Fuego, S Argentina
Usinsk *110 E3* Respublika Komi, NW Russian Federation
Üsküb/Üsküp *see* Skopje
Usmas Ezers *106 B3 lake* NW Latvia
Usol'ye-Sibirskoye *115 E4* Irkutskaya Oblast', C Russian Federation
Ussel *91 C5* Corrèze, C France
Ussuriysk *115 G5 prev.* Nikol'sk, Nikol'sk-Ussuriyskiy, Voroshilov. Primorskiy Kray, SE Russian Federation
Ustica *97 B6 island* S Italy
Ust'-Ilimsk *115 E4* Irkutskaya Oblast', C Russian Federation
Ústí nad Labem *98 A4 Ger.* Aussig. Ústecký Kraj, NW Czech Republic
Ustinov *see* Izhevsk
Ustka *98 C2 Ger.* Stolpmünde. Pomorskie, N Poland
Ust'-Kamchatsk *115 H2* Kamchatskiy Kray, E Russian Federation
Ust'-Kamenogorsk *114 D5 Kaz.* Öskemen. Vostochnyy Kazakhstan, E Kazakhstan
Ust'-Kut *115 E4* Irkutskaya Oblast', C Russian Federation
Ust'-Olenëk *115 E3* Respublika Sakha (Yakutiya), NE Russian Federation
Ustrzyki Dolne *99 E5* Podkarpackie, SE Poland
Ust'-Sysol'sk *see* Syktyvkar
Ust Urt *see* Ustyurt Plateau
Ustyurt Plateau *122 B1 var.* Ust Urt, *Uzb.* Ustyurt Platosi. *plateau* Kazakhstan/Uzbekistan
Ustyurt Platosi *see* Ustyurt Plateau
Usulután *52 C3* Usulután, SE El Salvador
Usumacinta, Río *52 B1 river* Guatemala/Mexico
Usumbura *see* Bujumbura
U.S./USA *see* United States of America
Utah *44 B4 off.* State of Utah, *also known as* Beehive State, Mormon State. *state* W USA
Utah Lake *44 B4 lake* Utah, W USA
Utena *106 C4* Utena, E Lithuania
Utica *41 F3* New York, NE USA
Utina *see* Udine
Utrecht *86 C4 Lat.* Trajectum ad Rhenum. Utrecht, C Netherlands
Utsunomiya *131 D5 var.* Utunomiya. Tochigi, Honshū, S Japan
Uttarakhand *135 E2 cultural region* N India

Uttar Pradesh *135 E3 prev.* United Provinces, United Provinces of Agra and Oudh. *cultural region* N India
Utunomiya *see* Utsunomiya
Uulu *106 D2* Pärnumaa, SW Estonia
Uummannaq *82 C3 var.* Umanak, Umanaq. Kitaa, C Greenland
Uummannarsuaq *see* Nunap Isua
Uvalde *49 F4* Texas, SW USA
Uvaravichy *107 D7 Rus.* Uvarovichi. Homyel'skaya Voblasts', SE Belarus
Uvarovichi *see* Uvaravichy
Uvea, Île *145 E4 island* N Wallis and Futuna
Uvs Nuur *126 C1 var.* Ozero Ubsu-Nur. *lake* Mongolia/Russian Federation
'Uwaynāt, Jabal al *88 A3 var.* Jebel Uweinat. *mountain* Libya/Sudan
Uweinat, Jebel *see* 'Uwaynāt, Jabal al
Uyo *75 G5* Akwa Ibom, S Nigeria
Uyuni *61 F5* Potosí, W Bolivia
Uzbekistan *122 D2 off.* Republic of Uzbekistan. *country* C Asia

UZBEKISTAN
Central Asia

Official name Republic of Uzbekistan
Formation 1991 / 1991
Capital Tashkent
Population 28.9 million / 167 people per sq mile (65 people per sq km)
Total area 172,741 sq. miles (447,400 sq. km)
Languages Uzbek*, Russian, Tajik, Kazakh
Religions Sunni Muslim 88%, Orthodox Christian 9%, Other 3%
Ethnic mix Uzbek 80%, Russian 6%, Other 6%, Tajik 5%, Kazakh 3%
Government Presidential system
Currency Som = 100 tiyin
Literacy rate 99%
Calorie consumption 2675 kilocalories

Uzbekistan, Republic of *see* Uzbekistan
Uzhgorod *see* Uzhhorod
Uzhhorod *108 B2 Rus.* Uzhgorod; *prev.* Ungvár. Zakarpats'ka Oblast', W Ukraine
Užice *100 D4 prev.* Titovo Užice. Serbia, W Serbia

V

Vaal *78 D4 river* C South Africa
Vaals *87 D6* Limburg, SE Netherlands
Vaasa *85 D5 Swe.* Vasa; *prev.* Nikolainkaupunki. Länsi-Suomi, W Finland
Vaassen *86 D3* Gelderland, E Netherlands
Vác *99 C6 Ger.* Waitzen. Pest, N Hungary
Vadodara *134 C4 prev.* Baroda. Gujarāt, W India
Vaduz *94 E2 country capital* (Liechtenstein) W Liechtenstein
Vág *see* Váh
Vágbeszterce *see* Považská Bystrica
Váh *99 C5 Ger.* Waag, *Hung.* Vág. *river* W Slovakia
Váhtjer *see* Gällivare
Väinameri *106 C2 prev.* Muhu Väin, *Ger.* Moon-Sund. *sea* E Baltic Sea
Vajdahunyad *see* Hunedoara
Valachia *see* Wallachia
Valday *110 B4* Novgorodskaya Oblast', W Russian Federation
Valdecañas, Embalse de *92 D3 reservoir* W Spain
Valdepeñas *93 E4* Castilla-La Mancha, C Spain
Valdez *36 C3* Alaska, USA
Valdia *see* Weldiya
Valdivia *65 B5* Los Ríos, C Chile
Val-d'Or *38 D4* Québec, SE Canada
Valdosta *43 E3* Georgia, SE USA
Valence *91 D5 anc.* Valentia, Valentia Julia, Ventia. Drôme, E France
Valencia *93 F3* Valenciana, E Spain
Valencia *46 D1* California, USA
Valencia *58 D1* Carabobo, N Venezuela
Valencia, Gulf of *93 F3 var.* Gulf of Valencia. *gulf* E Spain
Valencia, Gulf of *see* Valencia, Golfo de
Valenciana *93 F3 var.* Valencia, *Cat.* València; *anc.* Valentia. *autonomous community* NE Spain
Valencia/València *see* Valenciana
Valenciennes *90 D2* Nord, N France
Valentia *see* Valence, France
Valentia *see* Valenciana
Valentia Julia *see* Valence
Valentine State *see* Oregon
Valera *58 C2* Trujillo, NW Venezuela
Valetta *see* Valletta
Valga *106 D3 Ger.* Walk, *Latv.* Valka. Valgamaa, S Estonia
Valira *91 A8 river* Andorra/Spain
Valjevo *100 C4* Serbia, W Serbia
Valjok *see* Válljohka
Valka *106 D3 Ger.* Walk. N Latvia
Valka *see* Valga
Valkenswaard *87 D5* Noord-Brabant, S Netherlands
Valladolid *51 H3* Yucatán, SE Mexico
Valladolid *92 D2* Castilla y León, NW Spain
Vall D'Uxó *see* La Vall d'Uixó
Valle de La Pascua *58 D2* Guárico, N Venezuela
Valledupar *58 B1* Cesar, N Colombia
Vallejo *47 B6* California, W USA
Vallenar *64 B3* Atacama, N Chile
Valletta *97 C8 prev.* Valetta. *country capital* (Malta) E Malta
Valley City *45 E2* North Dakota, N USA
Válljohka *84 D2 var.* Valjok. Finnmark, N Norway
Valls *93 G2* Cataluña, NE Spain
Valmiera *106 D3 Est.* Volmari, *Ger.* Wolmar. N Latvia
Valona *see* Vlorë
Valozhyn *107 C5 Pol.* Wołożyn, *Rus.* Volozhin. Minskaya Voblasts', C Belarus
Valparaíso *64 B4* Valparaíso, C Chile
Valparaiso *40 C3* Indiana, N USA
Valverde del Camino *92 C4* Andalucía, S Spain
Van *117 F3* Van, E Turkey
Vanadzor *117 F2 prev.* Kirovakan. N Armenia
Vancouver *36 D5* British Columbia, SW Canada
Vancouver *46 B3* Washington, NW USA
Vancouver Island *36 D5 island* British Columbia, SW Canada
Vanda *see* Vantaa
Van Diemen Gulf *146 D2 gulf* Northern Territory, N Australia
Van Diemen's Land *see* Tasmania
Vaner, Lake *see* Vänern
Vänern *85 B6 Eng.* Lake Vaner; *prev.* Lake Vener. *lake* S Sweden
Vangaindrano *79 G4* Fianarantsoa, SE Madagascar
Van Horn *48 D3* Texas, SW USA
Lake Van *117 F3 Eng.* Lake Van; *anc.* Thospitis. *salt lake* E Turkey
Van, Lake *see* Van Gölü
Vannes *90 A3 anc.* Dariorigum. Morbihan, NW France
Vantaa *85 D6 Swe.* Vanda. Etelä-Suomi, S Finland
Vanua Levu *145 E4 island* N Fiji
Vanuatu *144 C4 off.* Republic of Vanuatu; *prev.* New Hebrides. *country* SW Pacific Ocean

VANUATU
Australasia & Oceania

Official name Republic of Vanuatu
Formation 1980 / 1980
Capital Port Vila
Population 300,000 / 64 people per sq mile (25 people per sq km)
Total area 4710 sq. miles (12,200 sq. km)
Languages Bislama* (Melanesian pidgin), English*, French*, other indigenous languages
Religions Presbyterian 37%, Other 19%, Anglican 15%, Roman Catholic 15%, Traditional beliefs 8%, Seventh-day Adventist 6%
Ethnic mix ni-Vanuatu 94%, European 4%, Other 2%
Government Parliamentary system
Currency Vatu = 100 centimes
Literacy rate 83%
Calorie consumption 2820 kilocalories

Vanuatu, Republic of *see* Vanuatu
Van Wert *40 C4* Ohio, N USA
Vapincum *see* Gap
Varakļāni *106 D4* C Latvia
Vārānasi *135 E3 prev.* Banaras, Benares, *hist.* Kasi. Uttar Pradesh, N India
Varangerfjorden *84 E2 Lapp.* Várjjatvuotna. *fjord* N Norway
Varangerhalvøya *84 D2 Lapp.* Várnjárga. *peninsula* N Norway
Varannó *see* Vranov nad Topl'ou
Varasd *see* Varaždin
Varaždin *100 B2 Ger.* Warasdin, *Hung.* Varasd. Varaždin, N Croatia
Varberg *85 B7* Halland, S Sweden
Vardar *101 E6 Gk.* Axiós. *river* FYR Macedonia/Greece
Varde *85 A7* Syddtjylland, W Denmark
Vareia *see* Logroño
Varėna *107 B5 Pol.* Orany. Alytus, S Lithuania
Varese *96 B2* Lombardia, N Italy
Vârful Moldoveanu *108 B4 var.* Moldoveanul; *prev.* Vîrful Moldoveanu. *mountain* C Romania
Várjjatvuotna *see* Varangerfjorden
Varkaus *85 E5* Itä-Suomi, C Finland
Varna *104 E2 prev.* Stalin; *anc.* Odessus. Varna, E Bulgaria
Varnenski Zaliv *104 E2 prev.* Stalinski Zaliv. *bay* E Bulgaria
Várnjárga *see* Varangerhalvøya
Varshava *see* Warszawa
Vasa *see* Vaasa
Vasilikí *105 A5* Lefkáda, Iónia Nisiá, Greece, C Mediterranean Sea
Vasilishki *107 B5 Pol.* Wasiliszki. Hrodzyenskaya Voblasts', W Belarus
Vasil'kov *see* Vasyl'kiv
Vaslui *108 D4* Vaslui, C Romania
Västerås *85 C6* Västmanland, C Sweden
Vasyl'kiv *109 E2 var.* Vasil'kov. Kyyivs'ka Oblast', N Ukraine
Vaté *see* Efate
Vatican City *97 A7 off.* Vatican City. *country* S Europe

VATICAN CITY
Southern Europe

Official name State of the Vatican City
Formation 1929 / 1929
Capital Vatican City
Population 839 / 4935 people per sq mile (1907 people per sq km)
Total area 0.17 sq. miles (0.44 sq. km)
Languages Italian*, Latin*
Religions Roman Catholic 100%
Ethnic mix Most resident lay persons are Italian
Government Papal state
Currency Euro = 100 cents
Literacy rate 99%
Calorie consumption Not available

Vatican City *see* Vatican City
Vatnajökull *83 E5 glacier* SE Iceland
Vatter, Lake *see* Vättern
Vättern *85 B6 Eng.* Lake Vatter; *prev.* Lake Vetter. *lake* S Sweden
Vaughn *48 D2* New Mexico, SW USA
Vaupés, Río *58 C4 var.* Rio Uaupés. *river* Brazil/Colombia
Vava'u Group *145 E4 island group* N Tonga
Vavuniya *132 D3* Northern Province, N Sri Lanka
Vawkavysk *107 B6 Pol.* Wołkowysk, *Rus.* Volkovysk. Hrodzyenskaya Voblasts', W Belarus
Växjö *85 C7 var.* Vexiö. Kronoberg, S Sweden
Vaygach, Ostrov *110 E2 island* NW Russian Federation
Veendam *86 E2* Groningen, NE Netherlands
Veenendaal *86 D4* Utrecht, C Netherlands
Vega *84 B4 island* C Norway
Veglia *see* Krk
Veisiejai *107 B5* Alytus, S Lithuania
Vejer de la Frontera *92 C5* Andalucía, S Spain
Veldhoven *87 D5* Noord-Brabant, S Netherlands
Velebit *100 A3 mountain range* C Croatia
Velenje *95 E7 Ger.* Wöllan. N Slovenia
Veles *101 E6 Turk.* Köprülü. C FYR Macedonia
Velho *see* Porto Velho
Velika Kikinda *see* Kikinda
Velika Morava *100 D4 var.* Glavn'a Morava, Morava, *Ger.* Grosse Morava. *river* C Serbia
Velikaya *113 G2 river* NE Russian Federation
Veliki Bečkerek *see* Zrenjanin
Velikiye Luki *110 A4* Pskovskaya Oblast', W Russian Federation
Velikiy Novgorod *110 B4 prev.* Novgorod. Novgorodskaya Oblast', W Russian Federation
Veliko Tŭrnovo *104 D2 prev.* Tirnovo, Trnovo, Tŭrnovo. Veliko Tŭrnovo, N Bulgaria
Velingrad *104 C3* Pazardzhik, C Bulgaria
Vel'ký Krtíš *99 D6* Banskobystrický Kraj, C Slovakia
Vellore *132 C2* Tamil Nādu, SE India
Velobriga *see* Viana do Castelo
Velsen *see* Velsen-Noord
Velsen-Noord *86 C3 var.* Velsen. Noord-Holland, W Netherlands
Vel'sk *110 C4 var.* Velsk. Arkhangel'skaya Oblast', NW Russian Federation
Velvendós *see* Velvéntos
Velvéntos *104 B4 var.* Velvendós. C Greece
Velykyy Tokmak *see* Tokmak
Vendôme *90 C4* Loir-et-Cher, C France
Venedig *see* Venezia
Vener, Lake *see* Vänern
Venetia *see* Venezia
Venezia *96 C2 Eng.* Venice, *Fr.* Venise, *Ger.* Venedig; *anc.* Venetia. Veneto, NE Italy
Venezia, Golfo di *see* Venice, Gulf of
Venezuela *58 D2 off.* Republic of Venezuela; *prev.* Estados Unidos de Venezuela, United States of Venezuela. *country* N South America

VENEZUELA
South America

Official name Bolivarian Republic of Venezuela
Formation 1830 / 1830
Capital Caracas
Population 30.4 million / 89 people per sq mile (34 people per sq km)
Total area 352,143 sq. miles (912,050 sq. km)
Languages Spanish*, Amerindian languages
Religions Roman Catholic 96%, Protestant 2%, Other 2%
Ethnic mix Mestizo 69%, White 20%, Black 9%, Amerindian 2%
Government Presidential system
Currency Bolívar fuerte = 100 céntimos
Literacy rate 96%
Calorie consumption 2880 kilocalories

Venezuela, Estados Unidos de *see* Venezuela
Venezuela, Gulf of *58 C1 Eng.* Gulf of Maracaibo, Gulf of Venezuela. *gulf* NW Venezuela
Venezuela, Gulf of *see* Venezuela, Golfo de
Venezuelan Basin *56 B1 undersea basin* E Caribbean Sea
Venezuela, Republic of *see* Venezuela
Venezuela, United States of *see* Venezuela
Venice *42 C4* Louisiana, S USA
Venice *see* Venezia
Venice, Gulf of *96 C2 It.* Golfo di Venezia, *Slvn.* Beneški Zaliv. *gulf* N Adriatic Sea
Venise *see* Venezia
Venlo *87 D5 prev.* Venloo. Limburg, SE Netherlands

Venloo *see* Venlo
Venta *106 B3 Ger.* Windau. *river* Latvia/ Lithuania
Venta Belgarum *see* Winchester
Ventia *see* Valence
Ventimiglia *96 A3* Liguria, NW Italy
Ventspils *106 B2 Ger.* Windau. NW Latvia
Vera *64 D3* Santa Fe, C Argentina
Veracruz *51 F4 var.* Veracruz Llave. Veracruz-Llave, E Mexico
Veracruz Llave *see* Veracruz
Vercellae *see* Vercelli
Vercelli *96 A2 anc.* Vercellae. Piemonte, NW Italy
Verdal *see* Verdalsøra
Verdalsøra *84 B4 var.* Verdal. Nord-Trøndelag, C Norway
Verde, Cabo *see* Cape Verde
Verde, Costa *92 D1 coastal region* N Spain
Verden *94 B3* Niedersachsen, NW Germany
Veria *see* Véroia
Verkhnedvinsk *see* Vyerkhnyadzvinsk
Verkhneudinsk *see* Ulan-Ude
Verkhoyanskiy Khrebet *115 F3 mountain range* NE Russian Federation
Vermillion *45 F3* South Dakota, N USA
Vermont *41 F2 off.* State of Vermont, *also known as* Green Mountain State. *state* NE USA
Vernal *44 B4* Utah, W USA
Vernon *49 F2* Texas, SW USA
Verőcze *see* Virovitica
Véroia *104 B4 var.* Veria, Vérroia, *Turk.* Karaferiye. Kentrikí Makedonía, N Greece
Verona *96 C2* Veneto, NE Italy
Vérroia *see* Véroia
Versailles *90 D1* Yvelines, N France
Versecz *see* Vršac
Verulamium *see* St Albans
Verviers *87 D6* Liège, E Belgium
Vesdre *87 D6 river* E Belgium
Veselinovo *104 D2* Shumen, NE Bulgaria
Vesontio *see* Besançon
Vesoul *90 D4 anc.* Vesulium, Vesulum. Haute-Saône, E France
Vesterålen *84 B2 island group* N Norway
Vestfjorden *84 C3 fjord* C Norway
Vestmannaeyjar *83 E5* Sudhurland, S Iceland
Vesulium/Vesulum *see* Vesoul
Vesuna *see* Périgueux
Vesuvius *97 D5 Eng.* Vesuvius. *volcano* S Italy
Vesuvius *see* Vesuvio
Veszprém *99 C7 Ger.* Veszprim. Veszprém, W Hungary
Veszprim *see* Veszprém
Vetrino *see* Suvorovo
Vetrino *see* Vyetryna
Vetter, Lake *see* Vättern
Veurne *87 A5 var.* Furnes. West-Vlaanderen, W Belgium
Vexiö *see* Växjö
Viacha *61 F4* La Paz, W Bolivia
Viana de Castelo *see* Viana do Castelo
Viana do Castelo *92 B2 var.* Viana de Castelo; *anc.* Velobriga. Viana do Castelo, NW Portugal
Vianen *86 C4* Utrecht, C Netherlands
Viangchan *136 C4 Eng./Fr.* Vientiane. *country capital* (Laos) C Laos
Viangphoukha *136 C3 var.* Vieng Pou Kha. Louang Namtha, N Laos
Viareggio *96 B3* Toscana, C Italy
Viborg *85 A7* Midtjylland, NW Denmark
Vic *93 G2 var.* Vich; *anc.* Ausa, Vicus Ausonensis. Cataluña, NE Spain
Vicentia *see* Vicenza
Vicenza *96 C2 anc.* Vicentia. Veneto, NE Italy
Vich *see* Vic
Vichy *91 C5* Allier, C France
Vicksburg *42 B2* Mississippi, S USA
Victoria *79 H1 country capital* (Seychelles) Mahé, SW Seychelles
Victoria *36 D5 province capital* Vancouver Island, British Columbia, SW Canada
Victoria *102 A5 var.* Rabat. Gozo, NW Malta
Victoria *49 G4* Texas, SW USA
Victoria *149 C7 state* SE Australia
Victoria *see* Masvingo, Zimbabwe
Victoria Bank *see* Vitória Seamount
Victoria de Durango *see* Durango
Victoria de las Tunas *see* Las Tunas
Victoria Falls *78 C3* Matabeleland North, W Zimbabwe
Victoria Falls *78 C2 waterfall* Zambia/ Zimbabwe
Victoria Falls *see* Iguaçu, Saltos do
Victoria Island *37 F3 island* Northwest Territories/Nunavut, NW Canada
Victoria, Lake *73 B6 var.* Victoria Nyanza. *lake* E Africa
Victoria Land *154 C4 physical region* Antarctica
Victoria Nyanza *see* Victoria, Lake
Victoria River *146 D3 river* Northern Territory, N Australia
Victorville *47 C7* California, W USA
Vicus Ausonensis *see* Vic
Vicus Elbii *see* Viterbo
Vidalia *43 E2* Georgia, SE USA
Videm-Krško *see* Krško
Vídeň *see* Wien
Vidin *104 B1 anc.* Bononia. Vidin, NW Bulgaria
Vidzy *107 C5* Vitsyebskaya Voblasts', NW Belarus
Viedma *65 C5* Río Negro, E Argentina
Vieja, Sierra *48 D3 mountain range* Texas, SW USA
Vieng Pou Kha *see* Viangphoukha
Vienna *see* Wien, Austria
Vienna *see* Vienne, France
Vienne *91 D5 anc.* Vienna. Isère, E France
Vienne *90 B4 river* W France
Vientiane *see* Viangchan
Vientos, Paso de los *see* Windward Passage
Vierzon *90 C4* Cher, C France
Viesīte *106 C4 Ger.* Eckengraf. S Latvia
Vietnam *136 D4 off.* Socialist Republic of Vietnam, *Vtn.* Công Hoa Xa Hôi Chu Nghia Viêt Nam. *country* SE Asia

VIETNAM
Southeast Asia

Official name Socialist Republic of Vietnam
Formation 1976 / 1976
Capital Hanoi
Population 91.7 million / 730 people per sq mile (282 people per sq km)
Total area 127,243 sq. miles (329,560 sq. km)
Languages Vietnamese*, Chinese, Thai, Khmer, Muong, Nung, Miao, Yao, Jarai
Religions Other 74%, Buddhist 14%, Roman Catholic 7%, Cao Dai 3%, Protestant 2%
Ethnic mix Vietnamese 86%, Other 8%, Muong 2%, Tay 2%, Thai 2%
Government One-party state
Currency Dông = 10 hao = 100 xu
Literacy rate 94%
Calorie consumption 2703 kilocalories

Vietnam, Socialist Republic of *see* Vietnam
Vietri *see* Viêt Tri
Viêt Tri *136 D3 var.* Vietri. Vinh Phu, N Vietnam
Vieux Fort *55 F2* S Saint Lucia
Vigo *92 B2* Galicia, NW Spain
Viipuri *see* Vyborg
Vijayawāda *132 D1 prev.* Bezwada. Andhra Pradesh, SE India
Vila *see* Port-Vila
Vila Artur de Paiva *see* Cubango
Vila da Ponte *see* Cubango
Vila de João Belo *see* Xai-Xai
Vila de Mocímboa da Praia *see* Mocímboa da Praia
Vila do Conde *92 B2* Porto, NW Portugal
Vila do Zumbo *78 D2 prev.* Vila do Zumbu, Zumbo. Tete, NW Mozambique
Vila do Zumbu *see* Vila do Zumbo
Vilafranca del Penedès *93 G2 var.* Villafranca del Panadés. Cataluña, NE Spain
Vila General Machado *see* Camacupa
Vila Henrique de Carvalho *see* Saurimo
Viļaka *106 D4 Ger.* Marienhausen. NE Latvia
Vilalba *92 C1* Galicia, NW Spain
Vila Marechal Carmona *see* Uíge
Vila Nova de Gaia *92 B2* Porto, NW Portugal
Vila Nova de Portimão *see* Portimão
Vila Pereira de Eça *see* N'Giva
Vila Real *92 C2 var.* Vila Rial. Vila Real, N Portugal
Vila Rial *see* Vila Real
Vila Robert Williams *see* Caála
Vila Salazar *see* N'Dalatando
Vila Serpa Pinto *see* Menongue
Vileyka *see* Vilyeyka
Vilhelmina *84 C4* Västerbotten, N Sweden
Vilhena *62 D3* Rondônia, W Brazil
Vília *105 C5* Attikí, C Greece
Viliya *107 C5 Lith.* Neris. *river* W Belarus
Viliya *see* Neris
Viljandi *106 D2 Ger.* Fellin. Viljandimaa, S Estonia
Vilkaviškis *106 B4 Pol.* Wyłkowyszki. Marijampolė, SW Lithuania
Villa Acuña *50 D2 var.* Ciudad Acuña. Coahuila, NE Mexico
Villa Bella *61 F2* El Beni, N Bolivia
Villacarrillo *93 E4* Andalucía, S Spain
Villa Cecilia *see* Ciudad Madero
Villach *95 D7 Slvn.* Beljak. Kärnten, S Austria
Villacidro *97 A5* Sardegna, Italy, C Mediterranean Sea
Villa Concepción *see* Concepción
Villa del Pilar *see* Pilar
Villafranca de los Barros *92 C4* Extremadura, W Spain
Villafranca del Panadés *see* Vilafranca del Penedès
Villahermosa *51 G4 prev.* San Juan Bautista. Tabasco, SE Mexico
Villajoyosa *93 F4 Cat.* La Vila Joíosa. Valenciana, E Spain
Villa María *64 C4* Córdoba, C Argentina
Villa Martín *61 F5* Potosí, SW Bolivia
Villa Mercedes *64 C4* San Juan, Argentina
Villanueva *50 D3* Zacatecas, C Mexico
Villanueva de la Serena *92 C3* Extremadura, W Spain
Villanueva de los Infantes *93 E4* Castilla-La Mancha, C Spain
Villarrica *64 D2* Guairá, SE Paraguay
Villavicencio *58 B3* Meta, C Colombia
Villaviciosa *92 D1* Asturias, N Spain
Villazón *61 G5* Potosí, S Bolivia
Villena *93 F4* Valenciana, E Spain
Villeurbanne *91 D5* Rhône, E France
Villingen-Schwenningen *95 B6* Baden-Württemberg, S Germany
Villmanstrand *see* Lappeenranta
Vilna *see* Vilnius
Vilnius *107 C5 Pol.* Wilno, *Ger.* Wilna; *prev. Rus.* Vilna. *country capital* (Lithuania) Vilnius, SE Lithuania
Vil'shanka *109 E3 Rus.* Olshanka. Kirovohrads'ka Oblast', C Ukraine
Vilvoorde *87 C6 Fr.* Vilvorde. Vlaams Brabant, C Belgium
Vilvorde *see* Vilvoorde
Vilyeyka *107 C5 Pol.* Wilejka, *Rus.* Vileyka. Minskaya Voblasts', NW Belarus
Vilyuy *115 F3 river* NE Russian Federation
Viña del Mar *64 B4* Valparaíso, C Chile
Vinaròs *93 F3* Valenciana, E Spain
Vincennes *40 B4* Indiana, N USA
Vindhya Mountains *see* Vindhya Range
Vindhya Range *134 D4 var.* Vindhya Mountains. *mountain range* N India
Vindobona *see* Wien
Vineland *41 F4* New Jersey, NE USA
Vinh *136 D4* Nghê An, N Vietnam
Vinh Loi *see* Bac Liêu
Vinishte *104 C2* Montana, NW Bulgaria
Vinita *49 G1* Oklahoma, C USA
Vinkovci *100 C3 Ger.* Winkowitz, *Hung.* Vinkovcze. Vukovar-Srijem, E Croatia
Vinkovcze *see* Vinkovci
Vinnitsa *see* Vinnytsya
Vinnytsya *108 D2 Rus.* Vinnitsa. Vinnyts'ka Oblast', C Ukraine
Vinogradov *see* Vynohradiv
Vinson Massif *154 A3 mountain* Antarctica
Viranşehir *117 E4* Şanlıurfa, SE Turkey
Vîrful Moldoveanu *see* Vârful Moldoveanu
Virginia *45 G1* Minnesota, N USA
Virginia *41 E5 off.* Commonwealth of Virginia, *also known as* Mother of Presidents, Mother of States, Old Dominion. *state* NE USA
Virginia Beach *41 F5* Virginia, NE USA
Virgin Islands *see* British Virgin Islands
Virgin Islands (US) *55 F3 var.* Virgin Islands of the United States; *prev.* Danish West Indies. *US unincorporated territory* E West Indies
Virgin Islands of the United States *see* Virgin Islands (US)
Virôchey *137 E5* Rôtânôkiri, NE Cambodia
Virovitica *100 C2 Ger.* Virovititz, *Hung.* Verőcze; *prev. Ger.* Werowitz. Virovitica-Podravina, NE Croatia
Virovititz *see* Virovitica
Virton *87 D8* Luxembourg, SE Belgium
Virtsu *106 D2 Ger.* Werder. Läänemaa, W Estonia
Vis *100 B4 It.* Lissa; *anc.* Issa. *island* S Croatia
Vis *see* Fish
Visaginas *106 C4 prev.* Sniečkus. Utena, E Lithuania
Visākhapatnam *135 E5 var.* Vishakhapatnam. Andhra Pradesh, SE India
Visalia *47 C6* California, W USA
Visby *85 C7 Ger.* Wisby. Gotland, SE Sweden
Viscount Melville Sound *37 F2 prev.* Melville Sound. *sound* Northwest Territories, N Canada
Visé *87 D6* Liège, E Belgium
Viseu *92 C2 prev.* Vizeu. Viseu, N Portugal
Vishakhapatnam *see* Visākhapatnam
Vislinskiy Zaliv *see* Vistula Lagoon
Visoko *100 C4* Federacija Bosne I Hercegovine, C Bosnia and Herzegovina
Visttasjohka *84 D3 river* N Sweden
Vistula *98 C2 Eng.* Vistula, *Ger.* Weichsel. *river* C Poland
Vistula *see* Wisła
Vistula Lagoon *98 C2 Ger.* Frisches Haff, *Pol.* Zalew Wiślany, *Rus.* Vislinskiy Zaliv. *lagoon* Poland/Russian Federation
Vitebsk *see* Vitsyebsk
Viterbo *96 C4 anc.* Vicus Elbii. Lazio, C Italy
Viti *see* Fiji
Viti Levu *145 E4 island* W Fiji
Vitim *115 F4 river* C Russian Federation
Vitória *63 F4 state capital* Espírito Santo, SE Brazil
Vitoria *see* Vitoria-Gasteiz
Vitoria Bank *see* Vitória Seamount
Vitória da Conquista *63 F3* Bahia, E Brazil
Vitoria-Gasteiz *93 E1 var.* Vitoria, *Eng.* Vittoria. País Vasco, N Spain
Vitória Seamount *67 B5 var.* Victoria Bank, Vitoria Bank. *seamount* C Atlantic Ocean
Vitré *90 B3* Ille-et-Vilaine, NW France
Vitsyebsk *107 E5 Rus.* Vitebsk. Vitsyebskaya Voblasts', NE Belarus
Vittoria *97 C7* Sicilia, Italy, C Mediterranean Sea
Vittoria *see* Vitoria-Gasteiz
Vizcaya, Golfo de *see* Biscay, Bay of
Vizianagaram *135 E5 var.* Vizianagram. Andhra Pradesh, E India
Vizianagram *see* Vizianagaram
Vjosës, Lumi i *101 C7 var.* Vijosa, Vijosë, *Gk.* Aóos. *river* Albania/Greece

Vlaanderen *87 A6 Eng.* Flanders, *Fr.* Flandre. *cultural region* Belgium/ France
Vlaardingen *86 B4* Zuid-Holland, SW Netherlands
Vladikavkaz *111 B8 prev.* Dzaudzhikau, Ordzhonikidze. Respublika Severnaya Osetiya, SW Russian Federation
Vladimir *111 B5* Vladimirskaya Oblast', W Russian Federation
Vladimirovka *see* Yuzhno-Sakhalinsk
Vladimir-Volynskiy *see* Volodymyr-Volyns'kyy
Vladivostok *115 G5* Primorskiy Kray, SE Russian Federation
Vlagtwedde *86 E2* Groningen, NE Netherlands
Vlasotince *101 E5* Serbia, SE Serbia
Vlieland *86 C1 Fris.* Flylân. *island* Waddeneilanden, N Netherlands
Vlijmen *86 C4* Noord-Brabant, S Netherlands
Vlissingen *87 B5 Eng.* Flushing, *Fr.* Flessingue. Zeeland, SW Netherlands
Vlodava *see* Włodawa
Vlonë/Vlora *see* Vlorë
Vlorë *101 C7 prev.* Vlonë, *It.* Valona, Vlora. Vlorë, SW Albania
Vlotslavsk *see* Włocławek
Vöcklabruck *95 D6* Oberösterreich, NW Austria
Vogelkop *see* Doberai, Jazirah
Vohimena, Tanjona *79 F4 Fr.* Cap Sainte Marie. *headland* S Madagascar
Voiron *91 D5* Isère, E France
Vojvodina *100 D3 Ger.* Wojwodina. Vojvodina, N Serbia
Volga *111 B7 river* NW Russian Federation
Volga Uplands *81 G3 var.* Volga Uplands. *mountain range* W Russian Federation
Volga Uplands *see* Privolzhskaya Vozvyshennost'
Volgodonsk *111 B7* Rostovskaya Oblast', SW Russian Federation
Volgograd *111 B7 prev.* Stalingrad, Tsaritsyn. Volgogradskaya Oblast', SW Russian Federation
Volkhov *110 B4* Leningradskaya Oblast', NW Russian Federation
Volkovysk *see* Vawkavysk
Volmari *see* Valmiera
Volnovakha *109 G3* Donets'ka Oblast', SE Ukraine
Volodymyr-Volyns'kyy *108 C1 Pol.* Włodzimierz, *Rus.* Vladimir-Volynskiy. Volyns'ka Oblast', NW Ukraine
Vologda *110 B4* Vologodskaya Oblast', W Russian Federation
Vólos *105 B5* Thessalía, C Greece
Volozhin *see* Valozhyn
Vol'sk *111 C6* Saratovskaya Oblast', W Russian Federation
Volta *75 E5 river* SE Ghana
Volta Blanche *see* White Volta
Volta, Lake *75 E5 reservoir* SE Ghana
Volta Noire *see* Black Volta
Volturno *97 D5 river* S Italy
Volunteer Island *see* Starbuck Island
Volzhskiy *111 B6* Volgogradskaya Oblast', SW Russian Federation
Võnnu *106 E3 Ger.* Wendau. Tartumaa, SE Estonia
Voorst *86 D3* Gelderland, E Netherlands
Voranava *107 C5 Pol.* Werenów, *Rus.* Voronovo. Hrodzyenskaya Voblasts', W Belarus
Vorderrhein *95 B7 river* SE Switzerland
Vóreioi Sporádes *see* Vóreies Sporádes
Vórioi Sporádhes *see* Vóreies Sporádes
Vorkuta *114 C2* Respublika Komi, NW Russian Federation
Vormsi *106 C2 var.* Vormsi Saar, *Ger.* Worms, *Swed.* Ormsö. *island* W Estonia
Vormsi Saar *see* Vormsi
Voronezh *111 B6* Voronezhskaya Oblast', W Russian Federation
Voronovo *see* Voranava
Voroshilov *see* Ussuriysk
Voroshilovgrad *see* Luhans'k, Ukraine
Voroshilovsk *see* Stavropol', Russian Federation
Võru *106 D3 Ger.* Werro. Võrumaa, SE Estonia
Vosges *90 E4 mountain range* NE France
Vostochnyy Sayan *115 E4 Mong.* Dzüün Soyonï Nuruu, *Eng.* Eastern Sayans. *mountain range* Mongolia/Russian Federation
Vostock Island *see* Vostok Island
Vostok *154 C3 Russian research station* Antarctica
Vostok Island *145 G3 var.* Vostock Island; *prev.* Stavers Island. *island* Line Islands, SE Kiribati
Voznesens'k *109 E3 Rus.* Voznesensk. Mykolayivs'ka Oblast', S Ukraine
Vranje *101 E5* Serbia, SE Serbia
Vranov *see* Vranov nad Topl'ou
Vranov nad Topl'ou *99 D5 var.* Vranov, *Hung.* Varannó. Prešovský Kraj, E Slovakia
Vratsa *104 C2* Vratsa, NW Bulgaria
Vrbas *100 C3* Vojvodina, NW Serbia
Vrbas *100 C3 river* N Bosnia and Herzegovina
Vršac *100 E3 Ger.* Werschetz, *Hung.* Versecz. Vojvodina, NE Serbia
Vsetín *99 C5 Ger.* Wsetin. Zlínský Kraj, E Czech Republic
Vučitrn *see* Vushtrri
Vukovar *100 C3 Hung.* Vukovár. Vukovar-Srijem, E Croatia
Vulcano, Isola *97 C7 island* Isole Eolie, S Italy
Vung Tau *137 E6 prev. Fr.* Cape Saint Jacques, Cap Saint-Jacques. Ba Ria-Vung Tau, S Vietnam
Vusan *see* Busan
Vushtrri *101 D5 Serb.* Vučitrn. N Kosovo
Vyatka *111 C5 river* NW Russian Federation
Vyatka *see* Kirov
Vyborg *110 B3 Fin.* Viipuri. Leningradskaya Oblast', NW Russian Federation
Vyerkhnyadzvinsk *107 D5 Rus.* Verkhnedvinsk. Vitsyebskaya Voblasts', N Belarus
Vyetryna *107 D5 Rus.* Vetrino. Vitsyebskaya Voblasts', N Belarus
Vynohradiv *108 B3 Cz.* Sevluš, *Hung.* Nagyszöllös, *Rus.* Vinogradov; *prev.* Sevlyush. Zakarpats'ka Oblast', W Ukraine

W

Wa *75 E4* NW Ghana
Waag *see* Váh
Waagbistritz *see* Považská Bystrica
Waal *86 C4 river* S Netherlands
Wabash *40 C4* Indiana, N USA
Wabash River *40 B5 river* N USA
Waco *49 G3* Texas, SW USA
Wad Al-Hajarah *see* Guadalajara
Waddān *71 F3* NW Libya
Waddenzee *86 C1 var.* Wadden Zee. *sea* SE North Sea
Wadden Zee *see* Waddenzee
Waddington, Mount *36 D5 mountain* British Columbia, SW Canada
Wādī as Sīr *119 B6 var.* Wadi es Sir. 'Ammān, NW Jordan
Wadi es Sir *see* Wādī as Sīr
Wadi Halfa *72 B3 var.* Wādī Ḥalfā'. Northern, N Sudan
Wādī Mūsā *119 B7 var.* Petra. Ma'ān, S Jordan
Wad Madanī *see* Wad Medani
Wad Medani *72 C4 var.* Wad Madanī. Gezira, C Sudan
Waflia *139 F4* Pulau Buru, E Indonesia
Wagadugu *see* Ouagadougou
Wagga Wagga *149 C7* New South Wales, SE Australia
Wagin *147 B7* Western Australia
Wāh *134 C1* Punjab, NE Pakistan
Wahai *139 F4* Pulau Seram, E Indonesia
Wahaybah, Ramlat Al *see* Wahībah, Ramlat Āl
Wahiawā *47 A8 var.* Wahiawa. O'ahu, Hawaii, USA, C Pacific Ocean
Wahībah, Ramlat Ahl *see* Wahībah, Ramlat Āl
Wahibah Sands *121 E5 var.* Ramlat Ahl Wahībah, Ramlat Al Wahaybah, *Eng.* Wahībah Sands. *desert* N Oman
Wahībah Sands *see* Wahībah, Ramlat Āl
Wahpeton *45 F2* North Dakota, N USA
Wahran *see* Oran
Waiau *151 A7 river* South Island, New Zealand
Waigeo, Pulau *139 G4 island* Maluku, E Indonesia
Waikaremoana, Lake *150 E4 lake* North Island, New Zealand
Wailuku *47 B8* Maui, Hawaii, USA, C Pacific Ocean
Waimate *151 B6* Canterbury, South Island, New Zealand
Waiouru *150 D4* Manawatu-Wanganui, North Island, New Zealand
Waipara *151 C6* Canterbury, South Island, New Zealand
Waipawa *150 E4* Hawke's Bay, North Island, New Zealand
Waipukurau *150 D4* Hawke's Bay, North Island, New Zealand
Wairau *151 C5 river* South Island, New Zealand
Wairoa *150 E4* Hawke's Bay, North Island, New Zealand
Wairoa *150 D2 river* North Island, New Zealand
Waitaki *151 B6 river* South Island, New Zealand
Waitara *150 D4* Taranaki, North Island, New Zealand
Waitzen *see* Vác
Waiuku *150 D3* Auckland, North Island, New Zealand
Wakasa-wan *131 C6 bay* C Japan
Wakatipu, Lake *151 A7 lake* South Island, New Zealand
Wakayama *131 C6* Wakayama, Honshū, SW Japan
Wake Island *152 C2 US unincorporated territory* NW Pacific Ocean
Wake Island *142 D1 atoll* NW Pacific Ocean
Wakkanai *130 C1* Hokkaidō, NE Japan
Walachei/Walachia *see* Wallachia
Wałbrzych *98 B4 Ger.* Waldenburg, Waldenburg in Schlesien. Dolnośląskie, SW Poland
Walcourt *87 C7* Namur, S Belgium
Wałcz *98 B3 Ger.* Deutsch Krone. Zachodnio-pomorskie, NW Poland
Waldenburg/Waldenburg in Schlesien *see* Wałbrzych
Waldia *see* Weldiya
Wales *36 C2* Alaska, USA
Wales *89 C6 Wel.* Cymru. *cultural region* Wales, United Kingdom
Walgett *149 D5* New South Wales, SE Australia
Walk *see* Valga, Estonia
Walk *see* Valka, Latvia
Walker Lake *47 C5 lake* Nevada, W USA
Wallachia *108 B5 var.* Walachia, *Ger.* Walachei, *Rom.* Valachia. *cultural region* S Romania
Walla Walla *46 C2* Washington, NW USA
Wallenthal *see* Haţeg
Wallis and Futuna *145 E4 Fr.* Territoire de Wallis et Futuna. *French overseas territory* C Pacific Ocean
Wallis et Futuna, Territoire de *see* Wallis and Futuna
Walnut Ridge *42 B1* Arkansas, C USA
Waltenberg *see* Zalău
Walthamstow *89 B7* Waltham Forest, SE England, United Kingdom
Walvisbaai *see* Walvis Bay
Walvis Bay *78 A4 Afr.* Walvisbaai. Erongo, NW Namibia
Walvish Ridge *see* Walvis Ridge
Walvis Ridge *69 B7 var.* Walvish Ridge. *undersea ridge* E Atlantic Ocean
Wan *see* Anhui
Wanaka *151 B6* Otago, South Island, New Zealand
Wanaka, Lake *151 A6 lake* South Island, New Zealand
Wanchuan *see* Zhangjiakou
Wandel Sea *83 E1 sea* Arctic Ocean
Wandsworth *89 A8* Wandsworth, SE England, United Kingdom
Wanganui *150 D4* Manawatu-Wanganui, North Island, New Zealand
Wangaratta *149 C7* Victoria, SE Australia
Wankie *see* Hwange
Wanki, Río *see* Coco, Río
Wanlaweyn *73 D6 var.* Wanle Weyn, *It.* Uanle Uen. Shabeellaha Hoose, SW Somalia
Wanle Weyn *see* Wanlaweyn
Wanxian *see* Wanzhou
Wanzhou *128 B5 var.* Wanxian. Chongqing Shi, C China
Warangal *135 E5* Telangana, C India
Warasdin *see* Varaždin
Warburg *94 B4* Nordrhein-Westfalen, W Germany
Ware *37 E4* British Columbia, W Canada
Waremme *87 C6* Liège, E Belgium
Waren *94 C3* Mecklenburg-Vorpommern, NE Germany
Wargla *see* Ouargla
Warkworth *150 D2* Auckland, North Island, New Zealand
Warnemünde *94 C2* Mecklenburg-Vorpommern, NE Germany
Warner *49 G1* Oklahoma, C USA
Warnes *61 G4* Santa Cruz, C Bolivia
Warrego River *149 C5 seasonal river* New South Wales/Queensland, E Australia
Warren *40 D3* Michigan, N USA
Warren *40 D3* Ohio, N USA
Warren *41 E3* Pennsylvania, NE USA
Warri *75 F5* Delta, S Nigeria
Warrnambool *149 B7* Victoria, SE Australia
Warsaw/Warschau *see* Warszawa
Warszawa *98 D3 Eng.* Warsaw, *Ger.* Warschau, *Rus.* Varshava. *country capital* (Poland) Mazowieckie, C Poland
Warta *98 B3 Ger.* Warthe. *river* W Poland
Wartberg *see* Senec
Warthe *see* Warta
Warwick *149 E5* Queensland, E Australia
Washington *44 A2* NE England, United Kingdom
Washington D.C. *41 E4 country capital* (USA) District of Columbia, NE USA
Washington Island *see* Teraina
Washington, Mount *41 G2 mountain* New Hampshire, NE USA
Wash, The *89 E6 inlet* E England, United Kingdom
Wasiliszki *see* Vasilishki
Waspam *53 E2 var.* Waspán. Región Autónoma Atlántico Norte, NE Nicaragua
Waspán *see* Waspam
Watampone *139 E4 var.* Bone. Sulawesi, C Indonesia
Watenstedt-Salzgitter *see* Salzgitter
Waterbury *41 F3* Connecticut, NE USA
Waterford *89 B6 Ir.* Port Láirge. Waterford, S Ireland
Waterloo *45 G3* Iowa, C USA
Watertown *41 F2* New York, NE USA
Watertown *45 F2* South Dakota, N USA
Waterville *41 G2* Maine, NE USA
Watford *89 A7* E England, United Kingdom
Watlings Island *see* San Salvador
Watsa *77 E5* Orientale, NE Dem. Rep. Congo
Watts Bar Lake *42 D1 reservoir* Tennessee, S USA
Wau *73 B5 var.* Wāw. Western Bahr el Ghazal, W South Sudan
Waukegan *40 B3* Illinois, N USA
Waukesha *40 B3* Wisconsin, N USA
Wausau *40 B2* Wisconsin, N USA
Waverly *45 G3* Iowa, C USA
Wavre *87 C6* Walloon Brabant, C Belgium
Wāw *see* Wau
Wawa *38 C4* Ontario, S Canada
Waycross *43 E3* Georgia, SE USA
Wearmouth *see* Sunderland
Webfoot State *see* Oregon
Webster City *45 F3* Iowa, C USA
Weddell Plain *154 A2 abyssal plain* SW Atlantic Ocean

Weddell Sea *154 A2* *sea* SW Atlantic Ocean
Weener *94 A3* Niedersachsen, NW Germany
Weert *87 D5* Limburg, SE Netherlands
Weesp *86 C3* Noord-Holland, C Netherlands
Węgorzewo *98 D2* *Ger.* Angerburg. Warmińsko-Mazurskie, NE Poland
Weichsel *see* Wisła
Weimar *94 C4* Thüringen, C Germany
Weissenburg *see* Alba Iulia, Romania
Weissenburg in Bayern *95 C6* Bayern, SE Germany
Weissenstein *see* Paide
Weisskirchen *see* Bela Crkva
Weiswampach *87 D7* Diekirch, N Luxembourg
Wejherowo *98 C2* Pomorskie, NW Poland
Welchman Hall *55 G1* C Barbados
Weldiya *72 C4* *var.* Waldia, *It.* Valdia. Āmara, N Ethiopia
Welkom *78 D4* Free State, C South Africa
Welle *see* Uele
Wellesley Islands *148 B2* *island group* Queensland, N Australia
Wellington *151 D5* *country capital* (New Zealand) Wellington, North Island, New Zealand
Wellington *45 F5* Kansas, C USA
Wellington *see* Wellington, Isla
Wellington, Isla *65 A7* *var.* Wellington. *island* S Chile
Wells *46 D4* Nevada, W USA
Wellsford *150 D2* Auckland, North Island, New Zealand
Wells, Lake *147 C5* *lake* Western Australia
Wels *95 D6* *anc.* Ovilava. Oberösterreich, N Austria
Wembley *89 A8* Alberta, W Canada
Wemmel *87 B6* Vlaams Brabant, C Belgium
Wenatchee *46 B2* Washington, NW USA
Wenchi *75 E4* W Ghana
Wen-chou/Wenchow *see* Wenzhou
Wendau *see* Võnnu
Wenden *see* Cēsis
Wenzhou *128 D5* *var.* Wen-chou, Wenchow. Zhejiang, SE China
Werda *78 C4* Kgalagadi, S Botswana
Werder *see* Virtsu
Werenów *see* Voranava
Werkendam *86 C4* Noord-Brabant, S Netherlands
Werowitz *see* Virovitica
Werro *see* Võru
Werschetz *see* Vršac
Wesenberg *see* Rakvere
Weser *94 B3* *river* NW Germany
Wessel Islands *148 B1* *island group* Northern Territory, N Australia
West Antarctica *154 A3* *prev.* Lesser Antarctica. *physical region* Antarctica
West Australian Basin *see* Wharton Basin
West Bank *119 A6* *disputed region* SW Asia
West Bend *40 B3* Wisconsin, N USA
West Bengal *135 F4* *cultural region* NE India
West Cape *151 A7* *headland* South Island, New Zealand
West Des Moines *45 F3* Iowa, C USA
Westerland *94 B2* Schleswig-Holstein, N Germany
Western Australia *146 B4* *state* W Australia
Western Bug *see* Bug
Western Carpathians *99 E7* *mountain range* W Romania Europe
Western Desert *72 B2* *var.* Sahara el Gharbîya, *Eng.* Western Desert. *desert* C Egypt
Western Desert *see* Şaḩrā' al Gharbīya
Western Dvina *85 E7* *Bel.* Dzvina, *Ger.* Düna, *Latv.* Daugava, *Rus.* Zapadnaya Dvina. *river* W Europe
Western Ghats *134 C5* *mountain range* SW India
Western Isles *see* Outer Hebrides
Western Punjab *see* Punjab
Western Sahara *70 B3* *disputed territory* N Africa
Western Samoa *see* Samoa
Western Sayans *114 D4* *Eng.* Western Sayans. *mountain range* S Russian Federation
Western Sayans *see* Zapadnyy Sayan
Western Scheldt *87 B5* *Eng.* Western Scheldt; *prev.* Honte. *inlet* S North Sea
Western Scheldt *see* Westerschelde
Western Sierra Madre *see* Madre Occidental, Sierra
West Falkland *65 C7* *var.* Gran Malvina, Isla Gran Malvina. *island* W Falkland Islands
West Fargo *45 F2* North Dakota, N USA
West Frisian Islands *86 C1* *Eng.* West Frisian Islands. *island group* N Netherlands
West Frisian Islands *see* Waddeneilanden
West Irian *see* Papua
Westliche Morava *see* Zapadna Morava
West Mariana Basin *142 B1* *var.* Perece Vela Basin. *undersea feature* W Pacific Ocean
West Memphis *42 B1* Arkansas, C USA
West New Guinea *see* Papua
Weston-super-Mare *89 D7* SW England, United Kingdom
West Palm Beach *43 F4* Florida, SE USA
West Papua *see* Papua
Westport *151 C5* West Coast, South Island, New Zealand
West Punjab *see* Punjab
West River *see* Xi Jiang
West Siberian Plain *114 C3* *Eng.* West Siberian Plain. *plain* C Russian Federation
West Siberian Plain *see* Zapadno-Sibirskaya Ravnina
West Virginia *40 D4* *off.* State of West Virginia, *also known as* Mountain State. *state* NE USA
Wetar, Pulau *139 F5* *island* Kepulauan Damar, E Indonesia
Wetzlar *95 B5* Hessen, W Germany
Wevok *36 C2* *var.* Wewuk. Alaska, USA
Wewuk *see* Wevok
Wexford *89 B6* *Ir.* Loch Garman. SE Ireland
Weyburn *37 F5* Saskatchewan, S Canada
Weymouth *89 D7* S England, United Kingdom
Wezep *86 D3* Gelderland, E Netherlands
Whakatane *150 E3* Bay of Plenty, North Island, New Zealand
Whale Cove *37 G3* *var.* Tikirarjuaq. Nunavut, C Canada
Whangarei *150 D2* Northland, North Island, New Zealand
Wharton Basin *141 D5* *var.* West Australian Basin. *undersea feature* E Indian Ocean
Whataroa *151 B6* West Coast, South Island, New Zealand
Wheatland *44 D3* Wyoming, C USA
Wheeler Peak *48 D1* *mountain* New Mexico, SW USA
Wheeling *40 D4* West Virginia, NE USA
Whitby *89 D5* N England, United Kingdom
Whitefish *44 B1* Montana, NW USA
Whitehaven *89 C5* NW England, United Kingdom
Whitehorse *36 D4* *territory capital* Yukon, W Canada
White Nile *72 B4* *Ar.* Al Baḩr al Abyaḑ, An Nīl al Abyaḑ, Bahr el Jebel. *river* NE South Sudan
White Nile *72 B4* *var.* Bahr el Jebel. *river* S Sudan
White River *44 D3* *river* South Dakota, N USA
White Sea *110 C3* *Eng.* White Sea. *sea* NW Russian Federation
White Sea *see* Beloye More
White Volta *75 E4* *var.* Nakambé, *Fr.* Volta Blanche. *river* Burkina Faso/Ghana
Whitianga *150 D2* Waikato, North Island, New Zealand
Whitney, Mount *47 C6* *mountain* California, W USA
Whitsunday Group *148 D3* *island group* Queensland, E Australia
Whyalla *149 B6* South Australia
Wichita *45 F5* Kansas, C USA
Wichita Falls *49 F2* Texas, SW USA
Wichita River *49 F2* *river* Texas, SW USA
Wickenburg *48 B2* Arizona, SW USA
Wicklow *89 B6* *Ir.* Cill Mhantáin. *county* E Ireland
Wicklow Mountains *89 B6* *Ir.* Sléibhte Chill Mhantáin. *mountain range* E Ireland
Wieliczka *99 D5* Małopolskie, S Poland
Wieluń *98 C4* Sieradz, C Poland
Wien *95 E6* *Eng.* Vienna, *Hung.* Bécs, *Slvk.* Vídeň, *Slvn.* Dunaj; *anc.* Vindobona. *country capital* (Austria) Wien, NE Austria
Wiener Neustadt *95 E6* Niederösterreich, E Austria
Wierden *86 E3* Overijssel, E Netherlands
Wiesbaden *95 B5* Hessen, W Germany
Wieselburg and Ungarisch-Altenburg/ Wieselburg-Ungarisch-Altenburg *see* Mosonmagyaróvár
Wiesenhof *see* Ostrołęka
Wight, Isle of *89 D7* *island* United Kingdom
Wigorna Ceaster *see* Worcester
Wijchen *86 D4* Gelderland, SE Netherlands
Wijk bij Duurstede *86 D4* Utrecht, C Netherlands
Wilcannia *149 C6* New South Wales, SE Australia
Wilejka *see* Vilyeyka
Wilhelm, Mount *144 B3* *mountain* C Papua New Guinea
Wilhelm-Pieck-Stadt *see* Guben
Wilhelmshaven *94 B3* Niedersachsen, NW Germany
Wilia/Wilja *see* Neris
Wilkes Barre *41 F3* Pennsylvania, NE USA
Wilkes Land *154 C4* *physical region* Antarctica
Wiłkomierz *see* Ukmergė
Willard *48 D2* New Mexico, SW USA
Willcox *48 C3* Arizona, SW USA
Willebroek *87 B5* Antwerpen, C Belgium
Willemstad *55 E5* *dependent territory capital* (Curaçao) Lesser Antilles, S Caribbean Sea
Williston *44 D1* North Dakota, N USA
Wilmington *41 F4* Delaware, NE USA
Wilmington *43 F2* North Carolina, SE USA
Wilmington *40 C4* Ohio, N USA
Wilna/Wilno *see* Vilnius
Wilrijk *87 C5* Antwerpen, N Belgium
Winchester *89 D7* *hist.* Wintanceaster, *Lat.* Venta Belgarum. S England, United Kingdom
Winchester *41 E4* Virginia, NE USA
Windau *see* Ventspils, Latvia
Windau *see* Venta, Latvia/Lithuania
Windhoek *78 B3* *Ger.* Windhuk. *country capital* (Namibia) Khomas, C Namibia
Windhuk *see* Windhoek
Windorah *148 C4* Queensland, C Australia
Windsor *38 C5* Ontario, S Canada
Windsor *89 D7* S England, United Kingdom
Windsor *41 G3* Connecticut, NE USA
Windward Islands *55 H4* *island group* E West Indies
Windward Islands *see* Barlavento, Ilhas de, Cape Verde
Windward Passage *54 D3* *Sp.* Paso de los Vientos. *channel* Cuba/Haiti
Winisk *38 C2* *river* Ontario, C Canada
Winkowitz *see* Vinkovci
Winnebago, Lake *40 B2* *lake* Wisconsin, N USA
Winnemucca *47 C5* Nevada, W USA
Winnipeg *37 G5* *province capital* Manitoba, S Canada
Winnipeg, Lake *37 G5* *lake* Manitoba, C Canada
Winnipegosis, Lake *38 A3* *lake* Manitoba, C Canada
Winona *45 G3* Minnesota, N USA
Winschoten *86 E2* Groningen, NE Netherlands
Winsen *94 B3* Niedersachsen, N Germany
Winston Salem *43 E1* North Carolina, SE USA
Winsum *86 D1* Groningen, NE Netherlands
Wintanceaster *see* Winchester
Winterswijk *86 E4* Gelderland, E Netherlands
Winterthur *95 B7* Zürich, NE Switzerland
Winton *148 C4* Queensland, E Australia
Winton *151 A7* Southland, South Island, New Zealand
Wisby *see* Visby
Wisconsin *40 A2* *off.* State of Wisconsin, *also known as* Badger State. *state* N USA
Wisconsin Rapids *40 B2* Wisconsin, N USA
Wisconsin River *40 B3* *river* Wisconsin, N USA
Wiślany, Zalew *see* Vistula Lagoon
Wismar *94 C2* Mecklenburg-Vorpommern, N Germany
Wittenberge *94 C3* Brandenburg, N Germany
Wittlich *95 A5* Rheinland-Pfalz, SW Germany
Wittstock *94 C3* Brandenburg, NE Germany
W. J. van Blommesteinmeer *59 G3* *reservoir* E Suriname
Władysławowo *98 C2* Pomorskie, N Poland
Włocławek *98 C3* *Ger./Rus.* Vlotslavsk. Kujawsko-pomorskie, C Poland
Włodawa *98 E4* *Rus.* Vlodava. Lubelskie, SE Poland
Włodzimierz *see* Volodymyr-Volyns'kyy
Wlotzkasbaken *78 B3* Erongo, W Namibia
Wodonga *149 C7* Victoria, SE Australia
Wodzisław Śląski *99 C5* *Ger.* Loslau. Śląskie, S Poland
Wojerecy *see* Hoyerswerda
Wōjjā *see* Wotje Atoll
Wojwodina *see* Vojvodina
Woking *89 D7* SE England, United Kingdom
Wolf, Isla *60 A4* *island* Galápagos Islands, W Ecuador, South America
Wolfsberg *95 D7* Kärnten, SE Austria
Wolfsburg *94 C3* Niedersachsen, N Germany
Wolgast *94 D2* Mecklenburg-Vorpommern, NE Germany
Wołkowysk *see* Vawkavysk
Wöllan *see* Velenje
Wollaston Lake *37 F4* Saskatchewan, C Canada
Wollongong *149 D6* New South Wales, SE Australia
Wolmar *see* Valmiera
Wołożyn *see* Valozhyn
Wolvega *86 D2* *Fris.* Wolvegea. Fryslân, N Netherlands
Wolvegea *see* Wolvega
Wolverhampton *89 D6* C England, United Kingdom
Wolverine State *see* Michigan
Wŏnsan *129 E3* SE North Korea
Woodburn *46 B3* Oregon, NW USA
Woodland *47 B5* California, W USA
Woodruff *40 B2* Wisconsin, N USA
Woods, Lake of the *38 A3* *Fr.* Lac des Bois. *lake* Canada/USA
Woodville *150 D4* Manawatu-Wanganui, North Island, New Zealand
Woodward *49 F1* Oklahoma, C USA
Worcester *78 C5* Western Cape, SW South Africa

Worcester *89 D6 hist.* Wigorna Ceaster. W England, United Kingdom
Worcester *41 G3* Massachusetts, NE USA
Workington *89 C5* NW England, United Kingdom
Worland *44 C3* Wyoming, C USA
Wormatia *see* Worms
Worms *95 B5 anc.* Augusta Vangionum, Borbetomagus, Wormatia. Rheinland-Pfalz, SW Germany
Worms *see* Vormsi
Worthington *45 F3* Minnesota, N USA
Wotje Atoll *144 D1 var.* Wōjjā. *atoll* Ratak Chain, E Marshall Islands
Woudrichem *86 C4* Noord-Brabant, S Netherlands
Wrangel Island *115 F1 Eng.* Wrangel Island. *island* NE Russian Federation
Wrangel Island *see* Vrangelya, Ostrov
Wrangel Plain *155 B2 undersea feature* Arctic Ocean
Wrocław *98 C4 Eng./Ger.* Breslau. Dolnośląskie, SW Poland
Września *98 C3* Wielkopolskie, C Poland
Wsetin *see* Vsetín
Wuchang *see* Wuhan
Wuday'ah *121 C6 spring/well* S Saudi Arabia
Wuhai *127 E3 var.* Haibowan. Nei Mongol Zizhiqu, N China
Wuhan *128 C5 var.* Han-kou, Han-k'ou, Hanyang, Wuchang, Wu-han; *prev.* Hankow. *province capital* Hubei, C China
Wu-han *see* Wuhan
Wuhsien *see* Suzhou
Wuhsi/Wu-his *see* Wuxi
Wuhu *128 D5 var.* Wu-na-mu. Anhui, E China
Wujlān *see* Ujelang Atoll
Wukari *75 G4* Taraba, E Nigeria
Wuliang Shan *128 A6 mountain range* SW China
Wu-lu-k'o-mu-shi/Wu-lu-mu-ch'i *see* Ürümqi
Wu-na-mu *see* Wuhu
Wuppertal *94 A4 prev.* Barmen-Elberfeld. Nordrhein-Westfalen, W Germany
Würzburg *95 B5* Bayern, SW Germany
Wusih *see* Wuxi
Wuxi *128 D5 var.* Wuhsi, Wu-hsi, Wusih. Jiangsu, E China
Wuyi Shan *125 E3 mountain range* SE China
Wye *89 C6 Wel.* Gwy. *river* England/Wales, United Kingdom
Wyłkowyszki *see* Vilkaviškis
Wyndham *146 D3* Western Australia
Wyoming *40 C3* Michigan, N USA
Wyoming *44 B3 off.* State of Wyoming, *also known as* Equality State. *state* C USA
Wyszków *98 D3 Ger.* Probstberg. Mazowieckie, NE Poland

X

Xaafuun, Raas *72 E4 var.* Ras Hafun. *cape* NE Somalia
Xaçmaz *117 H2 Rus.* Khachmas. N Azerbaijan
Xaignabouli *136 C4 prev.* Muang Xaignabouri, *Fr.* Sayaboury. Xaignabouli, N Laos
Xai-Xai *79 E4 prev.* João Belo, Vila de João Belo. Gaza, S Mozambique
Xalapa *51 F4* Veracruz-Llave, Mexico
Xam Nua *136 D3 var.* Sam Neua. Houaphan, N Laos
Xankändi *117 G3 Rus.* Khankendi; *prev.* Stepanakert. SW Azerbaijan
Xánthi *104 C3* Anatolikí Makedonía kai Thráki, NE Greece
Xàtiva *93 F3 Cas.* Xátiva; *anc.* Setabis, *var.* Jativa. Valenciana, E Spain
Xauen *see* Chefchaouen
Xäzär Dänizi *see* Caspian Sea
Xeres *see* Jerez de la Frontera
Xiaguan *see* Dali
Xiamen *128 D6 var.* Hsia-men; *prev.* Amoy. Fujian, SE China
Xi'an *128 C4 var.* Changan, Sian, Signan, Siking, Singan, Xian. *province capital* Shaanxi, C China
Xiang *see* Hunan
Xiangkhoang *see* Phônsaven
Xiangtan *128 C5 var.* Hsiang-t'an, Siangtan. Hunan, S China
Xiao Hinggan Ling *128 D2 Eng.* Lesser Khingan Range. *mountain range* NE China
Xichang *128 B5* Sichuan, C China
Xieng Khouang *see* Phônsaven
Xieng Ngeun *see* Muong Xiang Ngeun
Xigazê *126 C5 var.* Jih-k'a-tse, Shigatse, Xigaze. Xizang Zizhiqu, W China
Xi Jiang *124 D3 var.* Hsi Chiang, *Eng.* West River. *river* S China
Xilinhot *127 F2 var.* Silinhot. Nei Mongol Zizhiqu, N China
Xilokastro *see* Xylókastro
Xin *see* Xinjiang Uygur Zizhiqu
Xingkai Hu *see* Khanka, Lake
Xingu, Rio *63 E2 river* C Brazil
Xingxingxia *126 D3* Xinjiang Uygur Zizhiqu, NW China
Xining *127 E4 var.* Hsining, Hsi-ning, Sining. *province capital* Qinghai, C China
Xinjiang *see* Xinjiang Uygur Zizhiqu
Xinjiang Uygur Zizhiqu *126 B3 var.* Sinkiang, Sinkiang Uighur Autonomous Region, Xin, Xinjiang. *autonomous region* NW China
Xinpu *see* Lianyungang
Xinxiang *128 C4* Henan, C China
Xinyang *128 C5 var.* Hsin-yang, Sinyang. Henan, C China
Xinzo de Limia *92 C2* Galicia, NW Spain
Xiqing Shan *124 D2 mountain range* C China
Xiva *122 D2 Rus.* Khiva, Khiwa. Xorazm Viloyati, W Uzbekistan
Xixón *see* Gijón
Xizang *see* Xizang Zizhiqu
Xizang Gaoyuan *see* Qingzang Gaoyuan
Xizang Zizhiqu *126 B4 var.* Thibet, Tibetan Autonomous Region, Xizang, *Eng.* Tibet. *autonomous region* W China
Xolotlán *see* Managua, Lago de
Xucheng *see* Xuwen
Xuddur *73 D5 var.* Hudur, *It.* Oddur. Bakool, SW Somalia
Xuwen *128 C7 var.* Xucheng. Guangdong, S China
Xuzhou *128 D4 var.* Hsu-chou, Suchow, Tongshan; *prev.* T'ung-shan. Jiangsu, E China
Xylókastro *105 B5 var.* Xilokastro. Pelopónnisos, S Greece

Y

Ya'an *128 B5 var.* Yaan. Sichuan, C China
Yabēlo *73 C5* Oromīya, C Ethiopia
Yablis *53 E2* Región Autónoma Atlántico Norte, NE Nicaragua
Yablonovyy Khrebet *115 F4 mountain range* S Russian Federation
Yabrai Shan *127 E3 mountain range* NE China
Yafran *71 F2* NW Libya
Yaghan Basin *67 B7 undersea feature* SE Pacific Ocean
Yagotin *see* Yahotyn
Yahotyn *109 E2 Rus.* Yagotin. Kyyivs'ka Oblast', N Ukraine
Yahualica *50 D4* Jalisco, SW Mexico
Yakima *46 B2* Washington, NW USA
Yakima River *46 B2 river* Washington, NW USA
Yakoruda *104 C3* Blagoevgrad, SW Bulgaria
Yaku-shima *131 B8 island* Nansei-shotō, SW Japan
Yakutat *36 D4* Alaska, USA
Yakutsk *115 F3* Respublika Sakha (Yakutiya), NE Russian Federation
Yala *137 C7* Yala, SW Thailand
Yalizava *107 D6 Rus.* Yelizovo. Mahilyowskaya Voblasts', E Belarus
Yalong Jiang *128 A5 river* C China
Yalova *116 B3* Yalova, NW Turkey
Yalpug, Ozero *see* Yalpuh, Ozero
Yalpuh, Ozero *108 D4 Rus.* Ozero Yalpug. *lake* SW Ukraine
Yalta *109 F5* Avtonomna Respublika Krym, S Ukraine
Yalu *125 E2 Chin.* Yalu Jiang, *Jap.* Oryokko, *Kor.* Amnok-kang. *river* China/North Korea
Yalu Jiang *see* Yalu
Yamaguchi *131 B7 var.* Yamaguti. Yamaguchi, Honshū, SW Japan
Yamal, Poluostrov *114 D2 peninsula* N Russian Federation
Yamanīyah, Al Jumhūrīyah al *see* Yemen
Yambio *73 B5 var.* Yambiyo. Western Equatoria, S South Sudan
Yambiyo *see* Yambio
Yambol *104 D2 Turk.* Yanboli. Yambol, E Bulgaria
Yamdena, Pulau *139 G5 prev.* Jamdena. *island* Kepulauan Tanimbar, E Indonesia
Yamoussoukro *74 D5 country capital* (Côte d'Ivoire) C Côte d'Ivoire
Yamuna *134 D3 prev.* Jumna. *river* N India
Yana *115 F2 river* NE Russian Federation
Yanboli *see* Yambol
Yanbu' al Baḥr *121 A5* Al Madīnah, W Saudi Arabia
Yangambi *77 D5* Orientale, N Dem. Rep. Congo
Yangchow *see* Yangzhou
Yangiyo'l *123 E2 Rus.* Yangiyul'. Toshkent Viloyati, E Uzbekistan
Yangiyul' *see* Yangiyo'l
Yangku *see* Taiyuan
Yangon *136 B4 Eng.* Rangoon. Yangon, S Myan mar (Burma)
Yangtze *128 B5 var.* Yangtze Kiang, *Eng.* Yangtze. *river* C China
Yangtze *see* Chang Jiang
Yangtze Kiang *see* Chang Jiang
Yangzhou *128 D5 var.* Yangchow. Jiangsu, E China
Yankton *45 E3* South Dakota, N USA
Yannina *see* Ioánnina
Yanskiy Zaliv *113 F2 bay* N Russian Federation
Yantai *128 D4 var.* Yan-t'ai; *prev.* Chefoo, Chih-fu. Shandong, E China
Yaoundé *77 B5 var.* Yaunde. *country capital* (Cameroon) Centre, S Cameroon
Yap *144 A1 island* Caroline Islands, W Micronesia
Yapanskoye More East Sea/ Japan, Sea of
Yapen, Pulau *139 G4 prev.* Japen. *island* E Indonesia
Yap Trench *142 B2 var.* Yap Trough. *undersea feature* SE Philippine Sea
Yap Trough *see* Yap Trench
Yapurá *see* Caquetá, Río, Brazil/ Colombia
Yapurá *see* Japurá, Rio, Brazil/ Colombia
Yaqui, Río *50 C2 river* NW Mexico
Yaransk *111 C5* Kirovskaya Oblast', NW Russian Federation
Yarega *110 D4* Respublika Komi, NW Russian Federation
Yarkant *see* Shache
Yarlung Zangbo Jiang *see* Brahmaputra
Yarmouth *39 F5* Nova Scotia, SE Canada
Yarmouth *see* Great Yarmouth
Yaroslav *see* Jarosław
Yaroslavl' *110 B4* Yaroslavskaya Oblast', W Russian Federation
Yarumal *58 B2* Antioquia, NW Colombia
Yasyel'da *107 B7 river* Brestskaya Voblasts', SW Belarus Europe
Yatsushiro *131 A7 var.* Yatusiro. Kumamoto, Kyūshū, SW Japan
Yatusiro *see* Yatsushiro
Yaunde *see* Yaoundé
Yavarí *see* Javari, Rio
Rio Yavari *62 C2 var.* Yavarí. *river* Brazil/Peru
Yaviza *53 H5* Darién, SE Panama
Yavoriv *108 B2 Pol.* Jaworów, *Rus.* Yavorov. L'vivs'ka Oblast', NW Ukraine
Yavorov *see* Yavoriv
Yazd *120 D3 var.* Yezd. Yazd, C Iran
Yazoo City *42 B2* Mississippi, S USA
Yding Skovhøj *85 A7 hill* C Denmark
Ýdra *105 C6 var.* Ídhra. *island* Ýdra, S Greece
Ye *137 B5* Mon State, S Myanmar (Burma)
Yecheng *126 A3 var.* Kargilik. Xinjiang Uygur Zizhiqu, NW China
Yefremov *111 B5* Tul'skaya Oblast', W Russian Federation
Yekaterinburg *114 C3 prev.* Sverdlovsk. Sverdlovskaya Oblast', C Russian Federation
Yekaterinodar *see* Krasnodar
Yekaterinoslav *see* Dnipropetrovs'k
Yelets *111 B5* Lipetskaya Oblast', W Russian Federation
Yelisavetpol *see* Gäncä
Yelizavetgrad *see* Kirovohrad
Yelizovo *see* Yalizava
Yell *88 D1 island* NE Scotland, United Kingdom
Yellowhammer State *see* Alabama
Yellowknife *37 E4 territory capital* Northwest Territories, W Canada
Yellow River *128 C4 var.* Yellow River. *river* C China
Yellow River *see* Huang He
Yellow Sea *128 D4 Chin.* Huang Hai, *Kor.* Hwang-Hae. *sea* E Asia
Yellowstone River *44 C2 river* Montana/ Wyoming, NW USA
Yel'sk *107 C7* Homyel'skaya Voblasts', SE Belarus
Yelwa *75 F4* Kebbi, W Nigeria
Yemen *121 C7 off.* Republic of Yemen, *Ar.* Al Jumhuriyah al Yamaniyah, Al Yaman. *country* SW Asia

YEMEN
Southwest Asia

Official name Republic of Yemen
Formation 1990 / 1990
Capital Sana
Population 24.4 million / 114 people per sq mile (44 people per sq km)
Total area 203,849 sq. miles (527,970 sq. km)
Languages Arabic*
Religions Sunni Muslim 55%, Shi'a Muslim 42%, Christian, Hindu, and Jewish 3%
Ethnic mix Arab 99%, Afro-Arab, Indian, Somali, and European 1%
Government Transitional regime
Currency Yemeni rial = 100 fils
Literacy rate 66%
Calorie consumption 2185 kilocalories

Yemen, Republic of *see* Yemen
Yemva *110 D4 prev.* Zheleznodorozhnyy. Respublika Komi, NW Russian Federation
Yenakiyeve *109 G3 Rus.* Yenakiyevo; *prev.* Ordzhonikidze, Rykovo. Donets'ka Oblast', E Ukraine
Yenakiyevo *see* Yenakiyeve
Yenangyaung *136 A3* Magway, W Myanmar (Burma)
Yendi *75 E4* NE Ghana
Yengisar *126 A3* Xinjiang Uygur Zizhiqu, NW China
Yenierenköy *102 D4 var.* Yialousa, *Gk.* Agialoúsa. NE Cyprus
Yenipazar *see* Novi Pazar
Yenisey *114 D3 river* Mongolia/Russian Federation
Yenping *see* Nanping
Yeovil *89 D7* SW England, United Kingdom
Yeppoon *148 D4* Queensland, E Australia
Yerevan *117 F3 Eng.* Erivan. *country capital* (Armenia) C Armenia
Yeriho *see* Jericho
Yertis *114 C4 var.* Irtish, *Kaz.* Ertis; *prev.* Irtysh. *river* C Asia
Yerushalayim *see* Jerusalem
Yesil' *114 C4 Kaz.* Esil. *river* Kazakhstan/Russian Federation
Yeso *see* Hokkaidō
Yeu, Île d' *90 A4 island* NW France
Yevlakh *see* Yevlax
Yevlax *117 G2 Rus.* Yevlakh. C Azerbaijan

Yevpatoriya *109 F5* Avtonomna Respublika Krym, S Ukraine
Yeya *109 H4 river* SW Russian Federation
Yezerishche *see* Yezyaryshcha
Yezo *see* Hokkaidō
Yezyaryshcha *107 E5 Rus.* Yezerishche. Vitsyebskaya Voblasts', NE Belarus
Yialousa *see* Yenierenköy
Yiannitsá *see* Giannitsá
Yichang *128 C5* Hubei, C China
Yıldızeli *116 D3* Sivas, N Turkey
Yinchuan *128 B4 var.* Yinch'uan, Yin-ch'uan, Yinchwan. *province capital* Ningxia, N China
Yinchwan *see* Yinchuan
Yindu He *see* Indus
Yin-hsien *see* Ningbo
Yining *126 B2 var.* I-ning, *Uigh.* Gulja, Kuldja. Xinjiang Uygur Zizhiqu, NW China
Yin-tu Ho *see* Indus
Yisrael/Yisra'el *see* Israel
Yíthion *see* Gýtheio
Yogyakarta *138 C5 prev.* Djokjakarta, Jogjakarta, Jokyakarta. Jawa, C Indonesia
Yokohama *131 D5* Aomori, Honshū, C Japan
Yokohama *130 A2* Kanagawa, Honshū, S Japan
Yokote *130 D4* Akita, Honshū, C Japan
Yola *75 H4* Adamawa, E Nigeria
Yonago *131 B6* Tottori, Honshū, SW Japan
Yong'an *128 D6 var.* Yongan. Fujian, SE China
Yongzhou *see* Lingling
Yonkers *41 F3* New York, NE USA
Yonne *90 C4 river* C France
Yopal *58 C3 var.* El Yopal. Casanare, C Colombia
York *89 D5 anc.* Eboracum, Eburacum. N England, United Kingdom
York *45 E4* Nebraska, C USA
York, Cape *148 C1 headland* Queensland, NE Australia
York, Kap *see* Innaanganeq
Yorkton *37 F5* Saskatchewan, S Canada
Yoro *52 C2* Yoro, C Honduras
Yoshkar-Ola *111 C5* Respublika Mariy El, W Russian Federation
Yösönbulag *see* Altay
Youngstown *40 D4* Ohio, N USA
Youth, Isle of *54 A2 var.* Isla de Pinos, *Eng.* Isle of Youth; *prev.* The Isle of the Pines. *island* W Cuba
Youth, Isle of *see* Juventud, Isla de la
Ypres *see* Ieper
Yreka *46 B4* California, W USA
Yrendagüé *see* General Eugenio A. Garay
Yssel *see* IJssel
Ysyk-Köl *see* Issyk-Kul', Ozero
Ysyk-Köl *see* Balykchy
Yu *see* Henan
Yuan *see* Red River
Yuan Jiang *see* Red River
Yuba City *47 B5* California, W USA
Yucatán, Canal de *see* Yucatan Channel
Yucatan Channel *51 H3 Sp.* Canal de Yucatán. *channel* Cuba/Mexico
Yucatan Peninsula *35 C7 Eng.* Yucatan Peninsula. *peninsula* Guatemala/ Mexico
Yucatan Peninsula *see* Yucatán, Península de
Yuci *see* Jinzhong
Yue *see* Guangdong
Yue Shan, Tai *see* Lantau Island
Yueyang *128 C5* Hunan, S China
Yugoslavia *see* Serbia
Yukhavichy *107 D5 Rus.* Yukhovichi. Vitsyebskaya Voblasts', N Belarus
Yukhovichi *see* Yukhavichy
Yukon *36 D3 prev.* Yukon Territory, *Fr.* Territoire du Yukon. *territory* NW Canada
Yukon River *36 C2 river* Canada/USA
Yukon, Territoire du *see* Yukon
Yukon Territory *see* Yukon
Yulin *128 C6* Guangxi Zhuangzu Zizhiqu, S China
Yuma *48 A2* Arizona, SW USA
Yumendong *128 A3 prev.* Laojunmiao. Gansu, N China
Yun *see* Yunnan
Yungki *see* Jilin
Yung-ning *see* Nanning
Yunjinghong *see* Jinghong
Yunki *see* Jilin
Yunnan *128 A6 var.* Yun, Yunnan Sheng, Yünnan, Yun-nan. *province* SW China
Yunnan *see* Kunming
Yunnan Sheng *see* Yunnan
Yünnan/Yun-nan *see* Yunnan
Yurev *see* Tartu
Yurihonjō *see* Honjō
Yuruá, Río *see* Juruá, Rio
Yury'ev *see* Tartu
Yushu *126 D4 var.* Gyêgu. Qinghai, C China
Yuty *64 D3* Caazapá, S Paraguay
Yuzhno-Sakhalinsk *115 H4 Jap.* Toyohara; *prev.* Vladimirovka. Ostrov Sakhalin, Sakhalinskaya Oblast', SE Russian Federation
Yuzhnyy Bug *see* Pivdennyy Buh
Yuzhou *see* Chongqing
Ýylanly *see* Gurbansoltan Eje

Z

Zaandam *see* Zaanstad
Zaanstad *86 C3 prev.* Zaandam. Noord-Holland, C Netherlands
Zabaykal'sk *115 F5* Zabaykal'skiy Kray, S Russian Federation
Zabern *see* Saverne
Zabīd *121 B7* W Yemen
Żabinka *see* Zhabinka
Ząbkowice *see* Ząbkowice Śląskie
Ząbkowice Śląskie *98 B4 var.* Ząbkowice, *Ger.* Frankenstein, Frankenstein in Schlesien. Dolnośląskie, SW Poland
Zábřeh *99 C5 Ger.* Hohenstadt. Olomoucký Kraj, E Czech Republic
Zacapa *52 B2* Zacapa, E Guatemala
Zacatecas *50 D3* Zacatecas, C Mexico
Zacatepec *51 E4* Morelos, S Mexico
Zacháro *105 B6 var.* Zaharo, Zakháro. Dytikí Elláda, S Greece
Zadar *100 A3 It.* Zara; *anc.* Iader. Zadar, SW Croatia
Zadetkyi Kyun *137 B6 var.* St.Matthew's Island. *island* Myeik Archipelago, S Myanmar (Burma)
Zafra *92 C4* Extremadura, W Spain
Żagań *98 B4 var.* Zagań, Żegań, *Ger.* Sagan. Lubuskie, W Poland
Zagazig *see* Az Zaqāzīq
Zágráb *see* Zagreb
Zagreb *100 B2 Ger.* Agram, *Hung.* Zágráb. *country capital* (Croatia) Zagreb, N Croatia
Zagros Mountains *120 C3 Eng.* Zagros Mountains. *mountain range* W Iran
Zagros Mountains *see* Zāgros, Kūhhā-ye
Zaharo *see* Zacháro
Zāhedān *120 E4 var.* Zahidan; *prev.* Duzdab. Sīstān va Balūchestān, SE Iran
Zahidan *see* Zāhedān
Zaḩlah *see* Zahlé
Zahlé *118 B4 var.* Zaḩlah. C Lebanon
Záhony *99 E6* Szabolcs-Szatmár-Bereg, NE Hungary
Zaire *see* Congo (river)
Zaire *see* Congo (Democratic Republic of)
Zaječar *100 E4* Serbia, E Serbia
Zakataly *see* Zaqatala
Zakháro *see* Zacháro
Zakhidnyy Buh/Zakhodni Buh *see* Bug
Zākhō *see* Zaxo
Zākhū *see* Zaxo
Zakopane *99 D5* Małopolskie, S Poland
Zákynthos *105 A6 var.* Zákinthos, *It.* Zante. *island* Iónia Nísoi, Greece, C Mediterranean Sea
Zalaegerszeg *99 B7* Zala, W Hungary
Zalău *108 B3 Ger.* Waltenberg, *Hung.* Zilah; *prev. Ger.* Zillenmarkt. Sălaj, NW Romania
Ẓalim *121 B5* Makkah, W Saudi Arabia
Zambesi/Zambeze *see* Zambezi
Zambezi *78 C2* North Western, W Zambia
Zambezi *78 D2 var.* Zambesi, *Port.* Zambeze. *river* S Africa
Zambia *78 C2 off.* Republic of Zambia; *prev.* Northern Rhodesia. *country* S Africa

ZAMBIA
Southern Africa

Official name Republic of Zambia
Formation 1964 / 1964
Capital Lusaka
Population 14.5 million / 51 people per sq mile (20 people per sq km)
Total area 290,584 sq. miles (752,614 sq. km)
Languages Bemba, Tonga, Nyanja, Lozi, Lala-Bisa, Nsenga, English*
Religions Christian 63%, Traditionalbeliefs 36%, Muslim and Hindu 1%
Ethnic mix Bemba 34%, Other African 26%, Tonga 16%, Nyanja 14%, Lozi 9%, European 1%
Government Presidential system
Currency New Zambian kwacha = 100 ngwee
Literacy rate 61%
Calorie consumption 1937 kilocalories

Zambia, Republic of *see* Zambia
Zamboanga *139 E3 off.* Zamboanga City. Mindanao, S Philippines
Zamboanga City *see* Zamboanga
Zambrów *98 E3* Łomża, E Poland
Zamora *92 D2* Castilla y León, NW Spain
Zamora de Hidalgo *50 D4* Michoacán, SW Mexico
Zamość *98 E4 Rus.* Zamoste. Lubelskie, E Poland
Zamoste *see* Zamość
Zancle *see* Messina
Zanda *126 A4* Xizang Zizhiqu, W China
Zanesville *40 D4* Ohio, N USA
Zanjān *120 C2 var.* Zenjan, Zinjan. Zanjān, NW Iran
Zante *see* Zákynthos
Zanthus *147 C6* Western Australia, S Australia Oceania
Zanzibar *73 D7* Zanzibar, E Tanzania
Zanzibar *73 C7 Swa.* Unguja. *island* E Tanzania
Zaozhuang *128 D4* Shandong, E China
Zapadna Morava *100 D4 Ger.* Westliche Morava. *river* C Serbia
Zapadnaya Dvina *110 A4* Tverskaya Oblast', W Russian Federation
Zapadnaya Dvina *see* Western Dvina
Zapadnyy Bug *see* Bug
Zapala *65 B5* Neuquén, W Argentina
Zapiola Ridge *67 B6 undersea feature* SW Atlantic Ocean
Zapolyarnyy *110 C2* Murmanskaya Oblast', NW Russian Federation
Zaporizhzhya *109 F3 Rus.* Zaporozh'ye; *prev.* Aleksandrovsk. Zaporiz'ka Oblast', SE Ukraine
Zaporozh'ye *see* Zaporizhzhya
Zapotiltic *50 D4* Jalisco, SW Mexico
Zaqatala *117 G2 Rus.* Zakataly. NW Azerbaijan
Zara *116 D3* Sivas, C Turkey
Zara *see* Zadar
Zarafshan *see* Zarafshon
Zarafshon *122 D2 Rus.* Zarafshan. Navoiy Viloyati, N Uzbekistan
Zarafshon *see* Zeravshan
Zaragoza *93 F2 Eng.* Saragossa; *anc.* Caesaraugusta, Salduba. Aragón, NE Spain
Zarand *120 D3* Kermān, C Iran
Zaranj *122 D5* Nīmrōz, SW Afghanistan
Zarasai *106 C4* Utena, E Lithuania
Zárate *64 D4 prev.* General José F.Uriburu. Buenos Aires, E Argentina
Zarautz *93 E1 var.* Zarauz. País Vasco, N Spain
Zarauz *see* Zarautz
Zaraza *59 E2* Guárico, N Venezuela
Zarghūn Shahr *123 E4 var.* Katawaz. Paktīkā, SE Afghanistan
Zaria *75 G4* Kaduna, C Nigeria
Zarós *105 D8* Kríti, Greece, E Mediterranean Sea
Zarqa *see* Az Zarqā'
Żary *98 B4 Ger.* Sorau, Sorau in der Niederlausitz. Lubuskie, W Poland
Zaunguzskiye Garagumy *see* Üngüz Angyrsyndaky Garagum
Zavertse *see* Zawiercie
Zavet *104 D1* Razgrad, NE Bulgaria
Zavidovići *100 C3* Federacija Bosne I Hercegovine, N Bosnia and Herzegovina
Zawia *see* Az Zāwiyah
Zawiercie *98 D4 Rus.* Zavertse. Śląskie, S Poland
Zawīlah *71 F3 var.* Zuwaylah, *It.* Zueila. C Libya
Zaxo *120 B2 Ar.* Zākhū, *var.* Zākhō. Dahūk, N Iraq
Zaysan Köl *see* Zaysan, Ozero
Zaysan, Ozero *114 D5 Kaz.* Zaysan Köl. *lake* E Kazakhstan
Zayyq *see* Zhayyk
Zbarazh *108 C2* Ternopil's'ka Oblast', W Ukraine
Zduńska Wola *98 C4* Sieradz, C Poland
Zealand *85 B8 Eng.* Zealand, *Ger.* Seeland. *island* E Denmark
Zealand *see* Sjælland
Zeebrugge *87 A5* West-Vlaanderen, NW Belgium
Zeewolde *86 D3* Flevoland, C Netherlands
Ẓefat *see* Tsefat
Żegań *see* Żagań
Zeiden *see* Codlea
Zeist *86 C4* Utrecht, C Netherlands
Zele *87 B5* Oost-Vlaanderen, NW Belgium
Zelenoborskiy *110 B2* Murmanskaya Oblast', NW Russian Federation
Zelenograd *111 B5* Moskovskaya Oblast', W Russian Federation
Zelenogradsk *106 A4 Ger.* Cranz, Kranz. Kaliningradskaya Oblast', W Russian Federation
Zelle *see* Celle
Zel'va *107 B6 Pol.* Zelwa. Hrodzyenskaya Voblasts', W Belarus
Zelwa *see* Zel'va
Zelzate *87 B5 var.* Selzaete. Oost-Vlaanderen, NW Belgium
Žemaičių Aukštumas *106 B4 physical region* W Lithuania
Zemst *87 C5* Vlaams Brabant, C Belgium
Zemun *100 D3* Serbia, N Serbia
Zengg *see* Senj
Zenica *100 C4* Federacija Bosne I Hercegovine, C Bosnia and Herzegovina
Zenta *see* Senta
Zeravshan *123 E3 Taj./Uzb.* Zarafshon. *river* Tajikistan/Uzbekistan
Zevenaar *86 D4* Gelderland, SE Netherlands
Zevenbergen *86 C4* Noord-Brabant, S Netherlands
Zeya *113 E3 river* SE Russian Federation
Zgerzh *see* Zgierz
Zgierz *98 C4 Ger.* Neuhof, *Rus.* Zgerzh. Łódź, C Poland
Zgorzelec *98 B4 Ger.* Görlitz. Dolnośląskie, SW Poland
Zhabinka *107 A6 Pol.* Żabinka. Brestskaya Voblasts', SW Belarus
Zhambyl *see* Taraz
Zhanaozen *114 A4 Kaz.* Zhangaözen; *prev.* Novyy Uzen'. Mangistau, W Kazakhstan
Zhangaözen *see* Zhanaozen
Zhangaqazaly *see* Ayteke Bi
Zhang-chia-k'ou *see* Zhangjiakou
Zhangdian *see* Zibo
Zhangjiakou *128 C3 var.* Changkiakow, Zhang-chia-k'ou, *Eng.* Kalgan; *prev.* Wanchuan. Hebei, E China
Zhangzhou *128 D6* Fujian, SE China
Zhanjiang *128 C7 var.* Chanchiang, Chan-chiang, *Cant.* Tsamkong, *Fr.* Fort-Bayard. Guangdong, S China
Zhaoqing *128 C6* Guangdong, S China
Zhayyk *see* Ural
Zhdanov *see* Mariupol'
Zhe *see* Zhejiang
Zhejiang *12 8 D5 var.* Che-chiang, Chekiang, Zhe, Zhejiang Sheng. *province* SE China
Zhejiang Sheng *see* Zhejiang

Zheleznodorozhnyy *106 A4* Kaliningradskaya Oblast', W Russian Federation
Zheleznodorozhnyy *see* Yemva
Zheleznogorsk *111 A5* Kurskaya Oblast', W Russian Federation
Zhëltyye Vody *see* Zhovti Vody
Zhengzhou *128 C4 var.* Ch'eng-chou, Chengchow; *prev.* Chenghsien. *province capital* Henan, C China
Zhezkazgan *114 C4 Kaz.* Zhezqazghan; *prev.* Dzhezkazgan. Karagandy, C Kazakhstan
Zhezqazghan *see* Zhezkazgan
Zhidachov *see* Zhydachiv
Zhishan *see* Lingling
Zhitkovichi *see* Zhytkavichy
Zhitomir *see* Zhytomyr
Zhlobin *107 D7* Homyel'skaya Voblasts', SE Belarus
Zhmerinka *see* Zhmerynka
Zhmerynka *108 D2 Rus.* Zhmerinka. Vinnyts'ka Oblast', C Ukraine
Zhodino *see* Zhodzina
Zhodzina *107 D6 Rus.* Zhodino. Minskaya Voblasts', C Belarus
Zholkev/Zholkva *see* Zhovkva
Zhonghua Renmin Gongheguo *see* China
Zhosaly *114 B4 prev.* Dzhusaly. Kzylorda, SW Kazakhstan
Zhovkva *108 B2 Pol.* Zółkiew, *Rus.* Zholkev, Zholkva; *prev.* Nesterov. L'vivs'ka Oblast', NW Ukraine
Zhovti Vody *109 F3 Rus.* Zhëltyye Vody. Dnipropetrovs'ka Oblast', E Ukraine
Zhovtneve *109 E4 Rus.* Zhovtnevoye. Mykolayivs'ka Oblast', S Ukraine
Zhovtnevoye *see* Zhovtneve
Zhi Qu *see* Tongtian He
Zhydachiv *108 B2 Pol.* Żydaczów, *Rus.* Zhidachov. L'vivs'ka Oblast', NW Ukraine
Zhytkavichy *107 C7 Rus.* Zhitkovichi. Homyel'skaya Voblasts', SE Belarus
Zhytomyr *108 D2 Rus.* Zhitomir. Zhytomyrs'ka Oblast', NW Ukraine
Zibo *128 D4 var.* Zhangdian. Shandong, E China
Zichenau *see* Ciechanów
Zielona Góra *98 B4 Ger.* Grünberg, Grünberg in Schlesien, Grüneberg. Lubuskie, W Poland
Zierikzee *86 B4* Zeeland, SW Netherlands
Zigong *128 B5 var.* Tzekung. Sichuan, C China
Ziguinchor *74 B3* SW Senegal
Zilah *see* Zalău
Žilina *99 C5 Ger.* Sillein, *Hung.* Zsolna. Zlínský Kraj, N Slovakia
Zillenmarkt *see* Zalău
Zimbabwe *78 D3 off.* Republic of Zimbabwe; *prev.* Rhodesia. *country* S Africa

ZIMBABWE
Southern Africa

Official name Republic of Zimbabwe
Formation 1980 / 1980
Capital Harare
Population 14.1 million / 94 people per sq mile (36 people per sq km)
Total area 150,803 sq. miles (390,580 sq. km)
Languages Shona, isiNdebele, English*
Religions Syncretic 50%, Christian 25%, Traditional beliefs 24%, Other (including Muslim) 1%
Ethnic mix Shona 71%, Ndebele 16%, Other African 11%, White 1%, Asian 1%
Government Presidential system
Currency Zimbabwe dollar suspended in 2009; nine other currencies are legal tender
Literacy rate 84%
Calorie consumption 2210 kilocalories

Zimbabwe, Republic of *see* Zimbabwe
Zimnicea *108 C5* Teleorman, S Romania
Zimovniki *111 B7* Rostovskaya Oblast', SW Russian Federation
Zinder *75 G3* Zinder, S Niger
Zinov'yevsk *see* Kirovohrad
Zintenhof *see* Sindi
Zipaquirá *58 B3* Cundinamarca, C Colombia
Zittau *94 D4* Sachsen, E Germany
Zlatni Pyasŭtsi *104 E2* Dobrich, NE Bulgaria
Zlín *99 C5 prev.* Gottwaldov. Zlínský Kraj, E Czech Republic
Złoczów *see* Zolochiv
Złotów *98 C3* Wielkopolskie, C Poland
Znamenka *see* Znam"yanka
Znam"yanka *109 F3 Rus.* Znamenka. Kirovohrads'ka Oblast', C Ukraine
Żnin *98 C3* Kujawsko-pomorskie, C Poland
Zoetermeer *86 C4* Zuid-Holland, W Netherlands
Zółkiew *see* Zhovkva
Zolochev *see* Zolochiv
Zolochiv *109 G2 Rus.* Zolochev. Kharkivs'ka Oblast', E Ukraine
Zolochiv *108 C2 Pol.* Złoczów, *var.* Zolochev. L'vivs'ka Oblast', W Ukraine
Zolote *109 H3 Rus.* Zolotoye. Luhans'ka Oblast', E Ukraine
Zolotonosha *109 E2* Cherkas'ka Oblast', C Ukraine
Zolotoye *see* Zolote
Zólyom *see* Zvolen
Zomba *79 E2* Southern, S Malawi
Zombor *see* Sombor
Zongo *77 C5* Equateur, N Dem. Rep. Congo
Zonguldak *116 C2* Zonguldak, NW Turkey
Zonhoven *87 D6* Limburg, NE Belgium
Zoppot *see* Sopot
Żory *99 C5 var.* Zory, *Ger.* Sohrau. Śląskie, S Poland
Zouar *76 C2* Borkou-Ennedi-Tibesti, N Chad
Zouérat *74 C2 var.* Zouérate, Zouîrât. Tiris Zemmour, N Mauritania
Zouérate *see* Zouérat
Zouîrât *see* Zouérat
Zrenjanin *100 D3 prev.* Petrovgrad, Veliki Bečkerek, *Ger.* Grossbetschkerek, *Hung.* Nagybecskerek. Vojvodina, N Serbia
Zsil/Zsily *see* Jiu
Zsolna *see* Žilina
Zsombolya *see* Jimbolia
Zsupanya *see* Županja
Zubov Seamount *67 D5 undersea feature* E Atlantic Ocean
Zueila *see* Zawīlah
Zug *95 B7 Fr.* Zoug. Zug, C Switzerland
Zugspitze *95 C7 mountain* S Germany
Zuid-Beveland *87 B5 var.* South Beveland. *island* SW Netherlands
Zuider Zee *see* IJsselmeer
Zuidhorn *86 E1* Groningen, NE Netherlands
Zuidlaren *86 E2* Drenthe, NE Netherlands
Zula *72 C4* E Eritrea
Züllichau *see* Sulechów
Zumbo *see* Vila do Zumbo
Zundert *87 C5* Noord-Brabant, S Netherlands
Zunyi *128 B5* Guizhou, S China
Županja *100 C3 Hung.* Zsupanya. Vukovar-Srijem, E Croatia
Zürich *95 B7 Eng./Fr.* Zurich, *It.* Zurigo. Zürich, N Switzerland
Zurich, Lake *95 B7 Eng.* Lake Zurich. *lake* NE Switzerland
Zurich, Lake *see* Zürichsee
Zurigo *see* Zürich
Zutphen *86 D3* Gelderland, E Netherlands
Zuwārah *71 F2* NW Libya
Zuwaylah *see* Zawīlah
Zuyevka *111 D5* Kirovskaya Oblast', NW Russian Federation
Zvenigorodka *see* Zvenyhorodka
Zvenyhorodka *109 E2 Rus.* Zvenigorodka. Cherkas'ka Oblast', C Ukraine
Zvishavane *78 D3 prev.* Shabani. Matabeleland South, S Zimbabwe
Zvolen *99 C6 Ger.* Altsohl, *Hung.* Zólyom. Banskobystrický Kraj, C Slovakia
Zvornik *100 C4* E Bosnia and Herzegovina
Zwedru *74 D5 var.* Tchien. E Liberia
Zwettl *95 E6* Wien, NE Austria
Zwevegem *87 A6* West-Vlaanderen, W Belgium
Zwickau *95 C5* Sachsen, E Germany
Zwolle *86 D3* Overijssel, E Netherlands
Żydaczów *see* Zhydachiv
Zyôetu *see* Jōetsu
Żyrardów *98 D3* Mazowieckie, C Poland
Zyryanovsk *114 D5* Vostochnyy Kazakhstan, E Kazakhstan

Key to map pages

North & West Asia 112-113

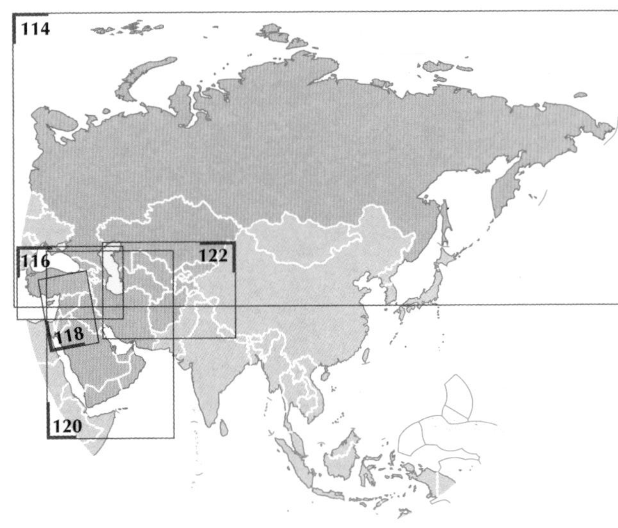

South & East Asia 124-125

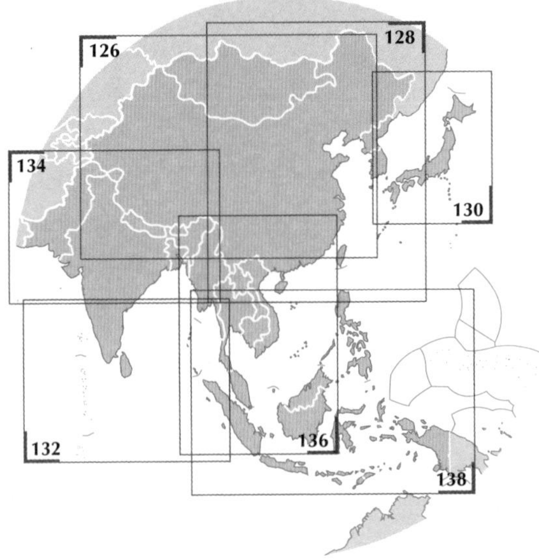